THE 35TH REGIMENT OF FOOT
THE ROYAL SUSSEX REGIMENT
MILITARY HONOURS AND AWARDS
1701-1966

RICHARD BUCKMAN

Published by

The Naval & Military Press Ltd
Unit 5 Riverside, Brambleside
Bellbrook Industrial Estate
Uckfield, East Sussex
TN22 1QQ England

Tel: +44 (0)1825 749494

www.naval-military-press.com
www.nmarchive.com

Copyright © Richard Buckman (2022)

All rights reserved. No part of this publication may be reproduced, stored in or introduced into a retrieval system, or transmitted, in any form, or by means (electronic, mechanical, photocopying, recording or otherwise) without the prior written permission of the author/publisher. Any person who does any unauthorised act in relation to this publication may be liable to criminal prosecution and civil claim for damages.

This book is subject to the condition that it shall not, by way of trade or otherwise be lent, sold, hired out or otherwise circulated without the author/publisher's prior consent in any form and without a similar condition, including this condition, being imposed.

Contents

Acknowledgements & Forewords

Period 1701-1859

The founding of the regiment 1701 its titles and its colonels from 1701-1861
Battle Honours of the 35th of Foot 1704-1806
Spanish War of Succession, French & Indian War, European, Turkish, Greek Islands and Waterloo, Burma and the Indian Mutiny from 1702-1859
Honours and Awards 1806-1859
Medal Index
Alphabetical Index

Period 1860-1920

Dedication, Poem, Acknowledgements and Foreword
Battle Honours of The Royal Sussex Regiment 1704-1919
Colonels 1861-1926 and Marches of the regiment and Motto
Honours & Awards 1861-1914
1881-1914 Battles in Egypt & Sudan, the Boer War
Allocation of Brigades and Divisions 1914-1918 including the Sussex Yeomanry (16th Bn. R.S.R.)
Two Royal Sussex military songs
Honours and Awards Oct 1914-Oct 1920
Poem
Medal Index
Alphabetical Index

Period 1921-1966

Dedication and Epitaph
Acknowledgements, Bibliography and Forewords
Battle Honours 1704-1945
Colonels of the regiment 1914-1966
Dispositions of the regiment 1939-1945
Honours and Awards 1921-1966
Supplement to the London Gazette 1967 and laying up of the Colours
Poem
Medal Index
Alphabetical Index

Supplements

List of Prisoners of War 1940-1945
Roll of Honour 1939-1953

Acknowledgements

With grateful thanks to The Royal Sussex regimental archives (Matthew Jones, Asst. County Archivist, County Hall, Chichester) the British Library Newspapers (Colindale),the London Gazette for all confirmations on awards and dates, the Royal Sussex Regimental Society (Living History), the book, "An Historical Memoir of the 35th Royal Sussex Regiment" by Richard Trimen (1873) and an extract from the book "The Campaign in Holland 1799" by A Subaltern (1861), and "Peninsular Roll Call" by Lionel S. Challis (1949), The British Army Against Napoleon: Facts, Lists and Trivia, 1805-1815 by Bob Burnham and Ron McGuigan, Kevin Asplin for the Indian Mutiny List and the College of Arms for Lt-Col. Berkeley's K.T.S. conformation, these acknowledgements cover the period 1701 to 1859.

Foreword

This book is about 35th Regiment of Foot, The Royal Sussex Regiment and their exploits and awards from 1701 to 1966 in their various military actions, it has taken 21 years to complete.
The Royal Hanoverian Guelphic Order was instituted on 28th April 1815 by the Prince Regent (later King George IV.) The awards of the Royal Hanoverian Guelphic Order are not *"Gazetted"* so the actual date of the award is unknown, but they can be found in the Officers' List a year after they were awarded.

Arthur Chichester, 3rd Earl of Donegall
(1666 – 10 April 1706)

Lord Donegall founded the regiment in Belfast on the 28th June 1701, becoming its first Colonel. In 1704 he accompanied the regiment to fight in the War of the Spanish Succession in Spain, he was appointed Major-General of the Spanish forces. He was killed in action in 1706 at the fort of Montjuich near Barcelona, and is buried in the City.

Titles held by the Regiment:-

The Belfast Regiment (1701)
Earl of Donegall's Regiment of Foot (1701)
Gorges' Regiment of Foot (1706)
Otway's Regiment of Foot (1717)
35th Regiment of Foot (the Prince of Orange's Own Regiment) (July 1st 1751)
35th (Dorsetshire) Regiment of Foot (August 1st 1782)
35th (Sussex) Regiment of Foot (July 4th 1805)
35th (Royal Sussex) Regiment of Foot (June 15th 1832)
1st Battalion The Royal Sussex Regiment (July 1st 1881)

Nickname:- The Orange Lilies (the Prince of Orange's Own Regiment).

1748 – 2nd Battalion of 35th Foot raised, disbanded 1749
1799 – 2nd Battalion of 35th Foot raised, disbanded 1803
1805 – 2nd Battalion of 35th Foot raised, disbanded 1817

The Regiment's seniority number was 35 in 1747, but it was first known as The Belfast Regiment or, as was common with other regiments at the time it was known by the name of its Colonel.

Colonels of the Regiment were:-

1701-1706 Maj-Gen. Arthur Chichester, 3rd Earl of Donegall (June 28th)
1706-1717 Lt-Gen. Richard Gorges (April 15th)
1717-1764 Gen. Charles Otway (July 26th)
1764-1803 Gen. Henry Fletcher (August 10th)
1803-1819 Gen. Charles Lennox, 4th Duke of Richmond, K.G. (March 17th)
1819-1840 Gen. Sir John Oswald, G.C.B., G.C.M.G.,K.C.B. (October 9th)
1840-1845 Lt-Gen. Sir Richard Downes Jackson, K.C.B. (June 15th)
1845-1857 Gen. Sir George Henry Berkeley, K.C.B. (July 11th)
1857-1861 Lt-Gen. John Leslie, K.H. (September 26th)

March of the Regiment

Roussillon (after Quebec 1759)

Battle Honours

The 35th Regiment of Foot

"Gibraltar, 1704-5," "Louisbourg, 1758," "Quebec, 1759," "Martinique," "Havannah, 1762," "St. Lucia, 1778," "Maida, 1806"

(These are borne on the colours)

War of the Spanish Succession 1701-14

Battles and Sieges at which the 35th Regiment of Foot took part

Battle of Cadiz, August 15th to September 30th 1702
Siege of Gibraltar, September 1704 to May 3rd 1705
Siege of Barcelona, April 3rd to April 27th 1706
Battle of Almansa, April 25th 1707

Battle of Cadiz
August 15th to September 30th 1702

The landing was on August 15th in a fresh wind causing 25 landing craft to capsize with the loss of 20 men. A Spanish 4 gun battery opened fire on them, 4 Dutch troops lost their legs, and they were met with a charge of 50 Spanish cavalry. The foremost 1200 troops were the grenadiers led by Brigadier Pallant and Lord Donegall who were able to disperse the cavalry. They marched on to the deserted town of Rota, then took Fort St. Catherine and then entered the town of Port St. Mary. Unfortunately later the troops plundered the town whose warehouses belonged to English and Dutch merchants. Prince George sent a report back home disparaging the officers in charge. The British troops lost interest in fighting due to their share of the loot and momentum was lost, after an abortive attempt to take Port Royal, and due to poor weather, the troops re-embarked and sailed off. The attempt to seize Cadiz had finished in utter failure.

The Daily Courant of Thursday September 17th 1702 gives an account of the landings and the taking of the towns. The Post Boy of September 19th 1702 also gives an account of the taking of the towns, also the English Post September 21st 1702.

Siege of Gibralta
September 1704-May 3rd 1705

Earl Donegall and his regiment arrived as part of the reinforcements on December 20th 1704 with much needed supplies. On January 16-18 1705, further reinforcements arrived. The Bourbon Spanish and French land force continued to bombard Gibraltar, inflicting further damage on the town's weak fortifications but were unable to make any progress against the reinforced garrison. They were being vigorously opposed with counter-bombardments, which killed many of their number, and by sallies, two of which were carried out successfully by the confederates on 23 and 31 December. Relations steadily went downhill between the Spanish and French besieging forces, due to the lack of progress they were making, the appalling conditions they were enduring in the open and the steady stream of casualties being caused by the counter-bombardment and outbreaks of epidemic disease, with storms and heavy rain making life a misery. By the New Year of 1705, the besieging force was disintegrating and had dropped in numbers from around 7,000 men to only 4,000, the remainder having either become casualties or simply deserting. King Louis the XIV sent 4,500 French and Irish reinforcements on the 7th February to seize the Round Tower, this they accomplished but a counter-attack drove them out with the attacking force losing around 200 men. On March 31st Admiral Leake further reinforced the garrison with British and Portuguese troops. The French abandoned the siege on April 12th, the Spanish withdrew to form a blockade and the garrison destroyed the Spanish batteries losing some men, but on the 3rd May the siege was over.

Siege of Barcelona
April 3rd to April 27th 1706

The Siege of Barcelona took place between 3 and 27 April 1706 when a Franco- Spanish army led by King Phillip V laid siege to Barcelona in an attempt to recapture it following its fall to the British the year before. The siege was abandoned, following the appearance of a large English fleet under the command of Admiral John Leake carrying reinforcements. The Franco-Spanish army was forced to abandon its supplies and artillery in its hasty retreat. Phillip was cut off from returning to Madrid, and so he crossed into France. Barcelona remained in Allied hands until 1714.

Battle of Almansa 1707
April 25th

The Battle of Almansa, fought on 25th April 1707, was one of the most decisive engagements of the War of the Spanish Succession. At Almansa, the Franco–Spanish army under Berwick soundly defeated the allied forces of Portugal, England, and the United Provinces led by the Earl of Galway, reclaiming most of eastern Spain for the Bourbons.

Captain Nathaniell Lane, Captain John Withchells, Captain Emy were killed.

Taken prisoner

Lieutenant-Colonel William Hamilton, Captain Henry Deel, Captain Dunbar, Captain Cudmore, Captain Michael Bowmer, Captain Eager, Lieutenant Waring all wounded, Lieutenant Gardner, Lieutenant Daly, Lieutenant Devall, Lieutenant Christian, Ensign Richard Willoughby, Ensign Oliver Arthur, Ensign O'Brien, Ensign Dunbar, Ensign Jones, Ensign Seers.

French & Indian War 1754-63 in America

August 3rd to August 9th 1757

Siege of Fort William Henry (Lake George, province of New York)

Colonel George Monro was commanding the 35th of Foot, 60th of Foot and the New Jersey Militia, but due to General Webb's supineness and inactivity in not coming to raise the siege, he capitulated to General Montcalm, and was allowed to leave the fort under arms (unloaded), but the Huron allies of the French attacked the column, killing about 30 and taking many, including women and children prisoner and many were mistreated. The French stood by and let it happen, this the regiment remembered when they met Montcalm and his army at the Battle of Quebec on the 13th September 1759. The garrison lost about 300 during the siege. Later all the refugees and released prisoners were afterwards led to an entrenched camp where food and shelter were provided for them and a strong guard set for their protection. On August 15th the British in the camp were finally sent under escort to Fort Edward, but there is no preserved record held by the any of the regiments of who were there or of those murdered afterwards.

Colonel Monro died six weeks (24th September) after this massacre, he never recovered from the loss of the people murdered by the French and her allies. It is possible that Ensigns Frederick Phillips, William Mason, Embule Ormby and William Brown died there, going by the amendments in the Army Lists of 1757 and 1758.

James Fenimore Cooper's book:- The Last of the Mohicans was based on this incident.

Leedes Intelligencer

Tuesday August 30th 1757

Extract of a letter from an Officer now with Lord Loundon, dated at sea, June 28th

"A packet, I am just now informed, is to be dispatched in a few Minutes. We have with us six Regiments, viz. 22d, 42d, 48th, and the 2d & 4th Battalions of Royal Americans. Lord Loudon and General Abercrombie are here. General Webb commands on the Frontiers of New York, and has with him 35th Regiment and the 1st Battalion of the Royal Americans, 4500 Provincial Troops, and two Ranging Companies. Col. Stanwix commands on the Frontiers of Pennsylvania, and has under him half his own Battalion and 200 Provincials, Lieutenant-Colonel Bouquet, with the other Half of that Battalion, has gone to South Carolina to assist that Colony's Forces in Case of Need.

"You see how extensive the Scene of War will be. If we find Mr. Holbourne at Halifax, with the Regiments promised from England, I hope to be able by next Packet to send you an Account of the Fallsome French Fort; and as is in this Case the Enemy's chief Force will be drawn to us, Mr. Webb will not only be safe, but able to make Conquests; but if Mr. Holbourne does not arrive, the Enemy's whole Force may be directed against Mr. Webb, which he may find difficult to resist, though covered by the Forts William and Edward, and within Reach of being supported by all the Militia of New York, which are good and numerous."

Against the French in Canada

Siege of Louisbourg (Cape Breton Island) 1758
June 2nd to July 27th

On 16th May an Order stated that such of the regiment 35th regiment are under articles of capitulation, are to hold themselves in readiness to relieve the outposts of Fort Sackville, Dartmouth, the Eastern Battery etc., but under an order subsequently issued in consequence of the treatment received by the garrison of Fort Henry the year before, the capitulation there entered into by Colonel Monro should be considered null and void, that is, all the officers and soldiers should serve as usual, instead of not bearing arms for eighteen months. The regiment was posted to the 2nd Brigade commanded by Colonel Murray. It was composed of the 15th, 35th, 40th and 78th Regiments of Foot. Among the orders of the 4th June, Lieutenant-Colonel Fletcher, 35th Regiment was appointed to command the four oldest companies of grenadiers among which ranked the grenadier company of the regiment.

The troops commanded by General Wolfe landed on the 8th, they landed under heavy fire through a dangerous surf but drove the French from their entrenchments into Louisbourg taking 70 prisoners. By the 11th the whole army had landed despite bad weather and were camped before Louisbourg. On the 13th General Wolfe with the light infantry with the Highlanders attacked and took the batteries on one side of the harbour and turned the guns to fire on the harbour and the town.

The siege was at once started and with much success until the 21st July when three French ships were set on fire and a tremendous bombardment of the town, that the Governor could not hold out beyond the 26th, when he was obliged to surrender, himself and his troops becoming prisoners of war. Over 5000 troops were taken prisoner, the regiment was engaged in all actions.

Lt. Richard Allen, Lt. Thomas Brown, Adj. James Cockburne, Ens. Thomas Armstrong wounded.

See *London Gazette* Publication date: 15th August 1758 Issue: 9818 for a full account of the battle.

Battle of Quebec 1759
September 13th

The New-York Gazette Monday 31st December 1759

Extract

The 12th, we received orders to embark on the transports again, and to hold ourselves in readiness to land the next morning at daylight, under the heights of Abraham: accordingly we landed at the break of day, and immediately attacked and routed a considerable body of the enemy and took possession of their battery of four 24 pounders, and one 13inch mortar with but a inconsiderable loss on our side. We then took post on the plains of Abraham, wither M. Montcalm, (on hearing we were landed, for he did not at all expect us) hasted with his whole army, consisting of cavalry as well as infantry, to give us battle; about 9 o'clock, we observed the enemy marching down towards us in three columns, at ten they formed their line of battle, which was a least six deep, having their flanks covered by a thick wood on each side, into which they threw above 1000 Canadians and Indians who galled us much. We got two six pounders to fire against the enemy very soon, six more besides to Royal Howitzers, came up two by two, and fell into service occasionally; whilst the enemy were making haste to attack before our artillery should be got up, as they dreaded our quick firing; accordingly their regulars marched briskly up to us, and gave us their first fire at about 50 yards distant, which we did not return, as it was Gen. Wolfe's express orders not to fire until they were close up to us, and then the action became general: our artillery fired so briskly, seconded by the small arms of the regiments, who behaved with great intrepidity, order, and regularity, with a cheerfulness that foretold victory on our side, and in about 15 minutes they gave way, so that we fairly beat them in open field, drove them before us, part into Quebec, the rest ran precariously cross St. Charles's river over a bridge of boats, and some through the water.

The enemy lost in the engagement Lieut. Gen. Montcalm, who had three wounds from our six-pounder grape, of which he died the next day; one colonel, two Lieut. Colonels, and at least 1500 officers and men killed and wounded, and 200 taken prisoner at their very sally ports, of which many were officers: We lost the brave Gen. Wolfe, who received three wounds, but had the satisfaction before his death to see his own plan, so well executed, as to beat the enemy totally: He then said "I thank God, now I shall die contented." Were his last words. Brigadier General Monckton; Colonel Carlton, quarter master general; Major Barry, adjutant-general and several other officers wounded.

At four in the afternoon, M. Boucanville appeared, in our rear with about 1500 foot and 200 horse, upon which Brigadier Gen. Burton with the 35th and 48th regiments marched to the left to receive him, but he no sooner perceived our dispositions made to engage him, than he faced to the right about, and made a most precipitate retreat.

At ten o'clock at night we surprised their guard and took possession of their grand hospital, wherein we found between 12 and 1500 sick and wounded. We remained that night on the field of battle, and on the 14th in the morning we secured the bridge of boats they had over Charles river, and possessed ourselves of all the posts and avenues that were or might have been of any consequence leading to the town, and began to prepare for attacking the garrison in form, and got up for that purpose, 12 heavy 24 pounders; six heavy 12 pounders, some large mortars, and the 4 inch howitzers, to play upon the town, and had been employed three days, intending to make a breach, and storm the city sword in hand, but were prevented by their beating a parley; and sent out a flag of truce with articles of capitulation, and the next day, being the 18th of September, the articles were signed, and we took possession of the city, where we found 180 pieces of cannon, from 2 to 36 pounders; a number of mortars from 9 inch to 15 inches, field pieces, howitzers, Royals, &c. with a large quantity of artillery stores, &c. &c.

The day after the engagement the enemy abandoned Beauport, leaving behind about 50 pieces of cannon, and 4 mortars, having first set fire to all their floating batteries, and blown up their magazines of powder.

M. Vaudreuill, the governor-general of New-France stole out of the city before the capitulation; leaving about 600 men, under the command of Mons. Ramsay, by whom the capitulation was signed. The poor remains of the French regulars, with about 10,000 Canadians, retired to Jaques Quartiers, under the command of M. Levy, but the Canadians deserted him in great numbers, and came in and surrendered themselves.

Sept. 19th, the French garrison were embarked on board transports; such of the inhabitants as would come in and take the oaths of allegiance were permitted to enjoy their estates.

Brigadier General Murray is governor of the town, and the whole left to garrison it.

During the whole siege from first to last 535 houses were burned down, amongst which is the whole eastern part of the lower town (save 6 or 8 Houses) which makes a very dismal appearance.

Casualty List

Lieutenant-General Charles Otway's, (35th)

Capt. John Maunsell, Capt. Luke Gardiner wounded, Capt. George Fletcher, Lt. William Hamilton (Q/M) Lt. William Mason killed. Lt. Charles Gore, Lt. Richard Allen, Lt. Gabriel Maturin, Lt. James Cockburne wounded. 6 rank and file killed. 1 Serjeant, 28 rank and file wounded.

Battle of Sainte-Foy (Quebec) 1760
April 28th

Capt. Charles Ince died of wounds
Lt. Thomas Brown, Ens. Cornelius Lysaght wounded
3 Serjeants and 43 rank and file wounded
12 rank and file killed.

"London Gazette" Saturday June 14th to Tuesday June 17th 1760

Whitehall June 17th

AN Officer arrived this Day, from Halifax in Nova Scotia, with an Account, That, on the 28th of April, Brigadier General Murray, with 3000 Men of the Garrison of Quebec, attacked, near that Place, the French Army supposed to consist of the greatest Part of the Force of Canada, as they were on their March to make an Attempt against the said Place; and, after a warm and obstinate Engagement, with a considerable Loss of Men, as well as of some Field Pieces, which could not be brought away, was obliged, by the Superiority of the Enemy's Numbers to retire back into Quebec. Brigadier Murray was making all possible Dispositions for the most vigorous Defence of that Place, until the Arrival of His Majesty's Ships, under the Command of Lord Colville, which sailed from Halifax, for the River St. Lawrence, on the 22nd of April; as well as of those, under the Command of Captain Swanton, who had been met, the 20th of April, off the Coasts of Newfoundland.

Against the French in the Caribbean

Battle of Martinique 1762
January 5th to February 12th

The troops disembarked on the 16th January near Fort Royal. The grenadiers of the army commanded by Lieutenant-Colonel Fletcher of the regiment, and Lieutenant-Colonels Massey and Vaughan landed first, they were followed by the light companies under command of Lieutenant-Colonel Scott and Major Leland, and the brigades of infantry followed. On the 24th the British advanced at daybreak against the enemy, Grant's grenadiers including the regiment's attacked the French outposts and drove them back, the light companies turned them left and forced them to abandon their works and retreat to the fort. The British batteries opened fire on the 30th and by the 4th of February the French Governor capitulated having lost 1000 men. The following day 800 men of the garrison surrendered and marched out. Shortly afterwards the whole island surrendered.

January 24th

Lt. Charles Gore wounded, grenadier company
Capt. Andrew Simpson, 1 Serjeant and 14 rank and file wounded, light company

Battle of Havanna 1762
June 7th to August 14th

The troops landed on the 7th June between the two forts, and the Earl of Ablemarle with the grenadiers and light infantry of the army advanced to Coxemar. Moro Fort was invested by the light infantry, one of the redoubts was taken but the fort was too strong so it was besieged from the 13th. On the 14th the light infantry was sent to Chorera, the Spaniards made many sorties to no effect, and the 1st July the British batteries opened fire, this continued throughout July. On the 30th Fort Moro was stormed with two companies of the regiment in assistance of the 90th Foot, the enemy lost 370 men and the rest taken prisoner. With the capture of the fort and British batteries opening fire on the Land Gate on the 11th August, the Spanish governor surrendered on the 14th, Fort La-Punta and other places followed suit.

Capt. William Widdrington killed in action
1 Drummer and 19 rank and file killed
Lt. James Fitzgerald, Ensign Chandler, 1 Serjeant and 25 rank and file wounded
11 Missing
17 died

American War of Independence 1775-1783

Battles at which the 35th Regiment of Foot took part

Battle of Bunker Hill 17th June 1775
Battle of Long Island 27th June 1776
Battle of Harlem Heights 15th September 1776
Battle of Pelham Manor 18th October 1776
Battle of White Plains 28th October 1776

Battle of Bunker Hill June 17th 1775
(The Heights of Charles-Town)

Pennsylvania Journal and Weekly Advertiser
Wednesday October 4th 1775

A letter from the Honourable Lieutenant-General Gage June 23rd 1775 to the Earl Dartmouth.

My Lord,
I am to acquaint your Lordship of an action that happened on the 17th instant, between His Majesty's troops and a large body of the rebel forces.
An alarm was given at break of day on the 17th instant, by a firing from the Lively ship of war, and advice was soon received, that the rebels had broken ground, and were raising a battery, on the heights of the Peninsular of Charles-Town, against the town of Bolton. They were plainly seen at work, and, in a few hours, a battery of six guns played upon their works. Preparations were instantly made for landing a body of men to drive them off, and ten companies of the grenadiers, ten of light infantry, with the 5th, 38th, 43rd and 52nd with a proportion of field artillery, under the command of Major General Howe and Brigadier General Pigot, were embarked with great expedition, and landed on the Peninsular without opposition, under protection of some ships of war, armed vessels and boats, by whose fire the rebels were kept within their works.
The troops formed soon as landed; the light infantry posted on the right, and the grenadiers upon their left. The 5th and 38th battalions drew up in the rear of those corps, and the 43rd and 52nd battalions made a third line. The rebels upon the heights were perceived to be in great force, and strongly posted. A redoubt thrown up on the 16th at night, with other works, full of men, defended with cannon, and a large body posted in the houses in Charlestown, covered their right flank, and their centre and left were covered by a breastwork, part of it cannon proof, which reached from the left of the redoubt to the Mystick or Medford river.
This appearance of the rebels strength, and the large column seen pouring in to their assistance, occasioned an application for the troops to be reinforced with four companies of light infantry and grenadiers, the 47th battalion, and the 1st battalion of marines; the whole when in conjunction, making a body of something above 2000 men. These troops advanced, formed in two lines, and the attack began by a sharp cannonade from our field pieces and howitzers, the lines advanced slowly, and frequently halting to give time for the artillery to fire. The light infantry was directed to force the left point of the breastwork, to take the rebel in flank, and the grenadiers to attack in front, supported by the 5th and 52nd battalions. These orders were executed with perseverance, under heavy fire from the vast numbers of rebels; and not withstanding various impediments before the troops could reach the works, and though the left, under Brigadier General Pigot, was engaged also with the rebels at Charlestown which at a critical moment was set on fire, the Brigadier pursued his point, and carried the redoubt.
The rebels were then forced from other strongholds, and pursued till they were drove clear of the Peninsular, leaving five pieces of cannon behind them. The loss the rebels sustained must have been very considerable from the great numbers they carried off during the time of action, and buried in holes, since discovered, exclusive of what they suffered by the shipping and boats; near hundred were buried the day after, and thirty found wounded in the field, three of which are since dead.
I enclose your Lordship a return of the killed and wounded of His Majesty's troops.

Return of the officers, non-commissioned officers and privates, killed and wounded of His Majesty's troops, at the attack of the redoubts and entrenchments on the Heights of Charlestown, 17th June 1775.

Fletcher's (35th)

Lieutenant William Baird killed, Captain James Lyon, died of wounds, Captain Edward Drew, Lieutenant Hugh Massey, Lieutenant Colin Campbell, Ensign John Madden wounded.
18 rank and file killed. 3 Serjeants, 2 Drummers, 41 rank and file wounded.

Battle of Harlem Heights September 15th 1776

The Scots Magazine Sunday December 1st 1776

America: Operations of the army under General Howe

Lt-Gen. Heister with his corps, having orders to join on the march, the army moved in two columns on the 25th, and took a position with the Bronx in the front, the right of the line being at the distance of four miles from the White-plains; upon which the rebels immediately quitted their detached camps between Knights-bridge and White-plains, assembling their whole force at the latter place, behind entrenchments that had been thrown up by the advanced corps.

The army marched by the right in two columns towards White-plains early on the 28th, Lt-Gen. Clinton leading the right, and Lt-Gen. Heister the left column.

Before noon, all the enemy's advanced parties were drove back to their works by the light infantry and chasseurs, and the army formed, with the right upon the road from Mamaroneck to the White-plains, about a mile from the centre of their lines, and the left to the Bronx, near the same distance from the right flank of their entrenchments.

A corps of the enemy was formed on a commanding ground, separated from the right flank of their entrenchments by the Bronx, which also, by changing its course at right angles, separated this corps in front from the left of the King's army.

Col. Raille, who commanded a brigade of Hessians on the left, observing this position of the enemy, and seeing a height on the other side of the Bronx unoccupied by them, from whence their flank might be galled, took possession of it with great alacrity, to the approbation of Lt-Gen. Heister, who was acquainted with this movement by Sir William Erskine.

Upon viewing the situation, orders were given for a battalion of Hessians to pass the Bronx, and attack this detached corps, supported by the 2d brigade of the British, under the command of Brig. Leslie, and the Hessian grenadiers sent from the right, commanded by Col. Donop; giving directions at the same time for Col. Raille to charge the enemy's flank as the Hessian battalion advanced to them in front; but their being some difficulty in passing the Bronx, the 28th and 35th regiments, who were the first to support, passed it in a place most practicable, and formed on the opposite side, though under the enemy's fire, with the greatest steadiness; ascended the steep hill, in defiance to all opposition; and, rushing on the enemy, routed, and drove them back from their works.

These two battalions were closely supported by the 5th and 49th regiments, who showed the same zeal to distinguish themselves; the Hessian grenadiers also coming up, and passing the Bronx, ascended the height with the greatest alacrity, and in the best order.

This material post being gained, the Hessian grenadiers were ordered forward upon the heights, within the cannon-shot of the entrenchments; the Bronx, from its winding course, being still between them and the enemy's right flank: The 2d brigade of the British formed in the rear of the Hessian grenadiers, and the two brigades of Hessians on the left of the 2d brigade, with their left upon the road leading from Terry town to White-plains.

The right and centre of the army did not remove from their ground. In this position the troops lay upon their arms that night, and with very little alteration encamped next day.

The officers and men of the British and Hessian artillery deserve much commendation for their active services on this occasion.

The killed, wounded, and prisoners taken from the enemy, during the course of this day, is said to be not less than 250.

The loss of his Majesty's troops and allies was small, as your Lordship will observe by the general return, considering the strength of the ground from whence the enemy was forced; though the loss of Lt-Col. Robert Carr of the 35th regiment, who died the next day of his wounds, is much to be lamented.

The enemy drew back drew back their encampment on the night of the 28th, and, observing their lines next morning much strengthened by additional works, the designed attack upon them was deferred, and the 4th brigade, left with Lord Percy, with two battalions of the 6th brigade, were ordered to join the army.

Battle of Pelham Manor October 18th 1776
&
Battle of White Plains October 28th 1776

"London Gazette" Tuesday December 17th to Saturday December 21st 1776

Whitehall, December 1st, 1776.

HIS Majesty's Ships Active and Fowey are arrived from New York, but bring no Letters from General Sir William Howe, the General being, at the Time of their failing on the 13th ult. With the Army in the Country, at a considerable Distance from New York. The Accounts which have been received of the late Operations of His Majesty's Forces are to the following Effect: That on the 12th of October the Guards, Light Infantry, and Reserve, together with Colonel Donop's Corps of Hessian Grenadiers and Chasseurs, marched from the advanced Posts on New York Island, and embarking in Boats at Turtle Bay, passed up the East River through Hell-Gates, and landed on Frogs-Neck. That having crossed the Neck, they found the Bridge, which joined it to the Main, had been broken down by the Rebels, who had thrown up some Works on the opposite Side. That being joined by the First, Second, and Sixth Brigades from Long Island, the Troops embarked again in Boats, and landed in Pelham's Manor the 18th without Opposition; and marching on, through a random Fire of the Rebels from behind Stone Walls, gained the Road which leads from Connecticut to King's Bridge. The Rebels, apprehending their Communication to the Eastward would be cut off, moved from their Camp at King's Bridge, and extended their Left to the White Plains, a Chain of stony Hills so called. On the 21st His Majesty's Light Troops took Possession of the Heights of New Rochelle. Colonel Rogers, with his New York Companies, having taken Post at Maramack, was attacked by a Party of the Rebels, which he drove back with considerable Loss.

On the 25th the advanced Corps moved forward to the Road which leads to die White Plains, where the Rebels appeared determined to make a Stand; but, on the 27th, the Party that was posted there, struck their Tents in the Night, and moved off to the Entrances of the White Plains, where the Main Body of the Rebels was entrenched, having the Bronx's River in their Front, the Banks of which are swampy, and the River deep, except at the Ford, where the Banks are steep and rocky. On the 28th in the Morning, our Army marched in Columns to attack the Rebels, who, seeing the Troops in Motion, a Body of about 8,000 came out of their Lines, and posted themselves on the Top of a very steep Hill above the Ford. The Second Brigade, consisting of the 5th, 28th, 35th, and 49th Regiments, with a Battalion of Hessians, and a Party of the Light Dragoons, marched down, and crossing the Ford, though much annoyed by the Rebels Grapeshot, ascended the Hill with the greatest Intrepidity, attacked and routed the Body of Rebels that were posted there, driving them to their Entrenchments in the- Entrances to the White Plains, where General Howe was preparing to attack them on the Morning of the 1st of November; but, being prevented by a very heavy Rain, the Rebels quitted their Entrenchments in the Night following, and retired towards Connecticut and the Highlands, abandoning their Camp at King's Bridge, after setting Fire to their Huts and Barracks they had built for their Winter Quarters, which was immediately taken Possession of by a Detachment of the King's Troops, where they found between Sixty and Seventy Piece of Cannon, large Quantities of Provisions, which the Rebels had spoiled, and a great Number of Hogs heads of Rum, which the General ordered to be destroyed. There is no exact Return of our Loss in the different Attacks, but it is supposed to have been between 190 and 200 killed and wounded.

Extra of a Letter from General Sir William Howe to Lord George Germain,
Dated, New York, January 5, 1777

IN Consequence of the Advantage gained by the Enemy at Trenton, on the 26th of last Month, and the Necessity of an Alteration in the Cantonments, Lord Cornwallis deferring his going to England by this

Opportunity, went from hence to Jersey on the 1st Instant, and reached Prince Town that Night, to which Place General Grant had advanced, with a Body of Troops from Brunswick and Hillsborough, upon gaining Intelligence that the Enemy, on receiving Reinforcements from Virginia, Maryland, and from the Militia of Pennsylvania, had re-passed the Delaware into Jersey. On the 2d Lord Cornwallis having received Accounts of the Rebel Army being posted at Trenton, advanced thither, leaving the 4th Brigade under the Command of Lieutenant Colonel Mawhood, at Prince-Town, and the 2d Brigade with Brigadier General Leslie at Maidenhead. On the Approach of the British Troops the Enemy's forward Posts were driven back upon their Army, which was formed In a strong Position, behind a Creek running through Trenton. During the Night of the 2d the Enemy quitted this Situation, and marching by Allen's Town, and from thence to Prince-Town, fell in on the Morning of the 3d with the 17th and 55th Regiments, on their March to join Brigadier General Leslie at Maidenhead. Lieutenant Colonel Mawhood, not being apprehensive of the Enemy's Strength, attacked and beat back the Troops that first presented themselves to him, but finding them at Length very superior to him in Numbers, he pushed forward with the 17th Regiment, and joined Brigadier General Leslie. The 55th Regiment retired, by the Way of Hillsborough to Brunswick, and the Enemy proceeding immediately to Prince-Town, the 40th Regiment also retired to Brunswick. The Loss upon this Occasion to His Majesty's Troops is 17 Killed, and nearly 200 Wounded and Missing Captain Leslie of the 17th is among the few Killed, and for further Particulars I beg Leave so refer your Lordship to the enclosed Return. Captain Phillips, of the 35th Grenadiers, returning from hence to join his Company, was on this Day beset between Brunswick and Prince Town by some lurking Villains, who murdered him in a most barbarous Manner; which is a Mode if War the Enemy seem from several late Instances to have adopted, with a Degree of Barbarity that Savages could not Exceed. It has not yet come to my Knowledge how much the Enemy has suffered, but it is certain there were many Killed and Wounded, and among the former a General Mercer from Virginia. The Bravery and Conduct of Lieutenant-Colonel Mawhood, and the. Behaviour of the Regiments under his Command, particularly the 17th, are highly commended by Lord Cornwallis. His Lordship finding the Enemy had made this Movement, and having heard the Fire occasioned by Colonel Mawhood's Attack, returned immediately, from Trenton; but the Enemy being some Hours March in Front, and keeping the Advantage by an immediate Departure from Prince Town, retreated by King's Town, breaking down the Bridge behind them, and crossed the Millstone River at a Bridge under Rocky Hill to throw themselves into a strong Country. Lord Cornwallis seeing it could not answer any Purpose to continue his Pursuit, returned with his whole Force to Brunswick, and the Troops upon the Right being assembled at Elisabeth Town, Major-General Vaughan has that Command.

Captain Erasmus John Phillips murdered January 3rd.

Battle of Monmouth 1778
June 26th

Part of General Sir William Howe's Philadelphia Campaign.

The British attacked the Continental left wing with their light infantry and the 42nd Regiment in the van. They were met by a storm of fire from the Continentals. The battle raged back and forth for an hour until three American regiments were sent though woods to enfilade the attacking British right flank. The attack was successful and sent the British back to reform.
Foiled on the left, Cornwallis personally led a heavy attack against their right wing, with a force comprising British and Hessian grenadiers, light infantry, and two Guards battalions, and the 37th and 44th Regiments. The attack was met by enfilading fire from four 6-pound cannons on Combs Hill, as well as accurate volleys from the Continental regiments. The British persisted up the ravine slope but within minutes five high-ranking officers and many men were down from heavy fire. The attackers recoiled down the slope.
During Cornwallis' abortive attack on the right wing, another British force made up of grenadiers, light infantry and light dragoons hit the Continental's forward force, who were protected behind a long hedge.

Three times the British were driven back by grapeshot and bullets: but an overwhelming fourth attack overlapped the position and forced these units to fall back to the main American line.

The British made no further attempts on the main American line, although cannonading from both sides continued until 6 p.m. At this point, the British fell back to a strong position east of the Ravine. Darkness brought an end to the battle, and the British were able to withdraw during the night to resume their march to New York. This engagement ended in a draw with losses on both sides mainly due to the heat (100F), the Americans held the field but the British were able to get their army and supplies safely to New York.

35th of Foot Grenadier Company (lead by Captain Hugh Massey)

West Indies 1778

Battle of the Vigie peninsula (St. Lucia)
December 13th to December 19th

On the 13th December the troops landed on St. Lucia, the reserve under Brigadier-General Medows Consisting of the 5th Foot, the grenadiers and light infantry in which were two flank companies of the regiment were landed at Grand Cul-de-Sac where they forced the heights and captured a gun. Brigadier-General Prescott with five battalions including the 35th landed soon after and kept up communications with the reserve whilst guarding the bay. On the 14th the reserve supported by Prescott, took the town of Morne Fortune and other places, the French retiring from their posts and batteries. The reserve then occupied the post of Vigie which commandeered the north side of Careenage harbour. On the 15th a French and American fleet landed 5000 French troops which attacked the post of Vigie three times but were repulsed each time leaving 400 dead and 1100 wounded. The fleet withdrew and tried to land at Grand Cul-de-Sac, the British troops under Brigadier-General Calder including elements of the 35th then held the heights around Grand-Cul-de-Sac causing the French Fleet to withdraw. The French remained on the island until the garrison surrendered on 28th December and the French left the island that evening for Martinique.

Grenadier Company

Lt. Thomas Williams killed

Capture and Loss of Guadeloupe 1794
February 11th to December 10th

35th of Foot Flank Company Light Infantry

"London Gazette" Wednesday 21st May 1794

A Letter (of which the following is an Extract) from Sir Charles Grey, K.B. dated Basseterre, Guadeloupe, April 22, 1794, was Yesterday received by the Right Honourable Henry Dundas, His Majesty's Principal Secretary of State for the Home Department.
SIR,
IN my Dispatch of the 12th Instant, by the Sea Flower, I had the Honour to acquaint you with the Capture of that Part of the Island of Guadeloupe denominated Grand Terre. The 43d Regiment being landed to garrison Fort Prince of Wales, (late Fort Fleur d'Epee) the Town of Pointe. a Pitre, &c. and the other Troops re-embarked, at Twelve o'Clock the 14th, the Quebec, with several other Frigates and some Transports, dropped down opposite to Petit Bourg, with Grenadiers and Light Infantry,

commanded by Prince Edward, and began landing at Five o'Clock in the Afternoon, at which Time I joined them, and was received with great Demonstrations of Joy by the French People on Marquis de Bouillie's Estate ; and I returned on Board the Boyne at Ten o'Clock the fame Evening.

At Day-Break in the Morning of the 15th I went to St. Mary's, where I found Lieutenant-Colonel Coote, with the . First Light Infantry, having got there before Day, from Petit Bourg; and the Second Battalion of Grenadiers joined at Ten o'Clock. The Troops advancing (April the 16th) reached Trou Chien, which the Enemy had abandoned, although very strong, and before Dark we halted on the high Ground over Trois Rivierre, from whence we saw the Enemy's Two Redoubts and their strong Post of Palmiste. I intended to have attacked the Enemy that Night, but the Troops were too much fatigued, from the difficult March they had just finished. Major-General Dundas landed at Vieux Habitant at eleven o'Clock in the Night of the 17th, with the Third Battalion of Grenadiers, and the Second and Third Battalions of Light Infantry, with Hub Opposition and no Loss, (having sailed from Pointe a Pitre the 15th preceding) taking Possession of Morne Magdaline, and destroying Two Batteries: Then detaching Lieutenant-Colonel Blundell, with the Second Battalion of Light Infantry, he forced several very difficult Posts of the Enemy during the Night. I made a Disposition for the Attack of the Enemy's Redoubt d'Arbaud, at Grande Ance, and their Battery d'Anet, to be executed during that Night; but at Eight o'Clock in the Evening they evacuated the former, setting Fire to every Thing in and about it, and I ordered the Attack of the latter to proceed, which was well executed by Lieutenant-Colonel Coote and the First Light Infantry, who were in Possession of it by Day-Break of the 18th, having killed, wounded, or taken every one of those who were defending it, without any Loss.

At Twelve o'Clock on the Night of the 19th I moved forward, with the First and Second Battalions of Grenadiers and the First Light Infantry, from Trois Rivierre and Grande Ance, and took their famous Post of Palmiste, with all their Batteries, at Day-Break of the 20th, commanding Fort St. Charles and Basseterre; and communicating with Major-General Dundas's Division on the Morning of the 21st, who had made his Approach by Morne Howel; after which General Collot capitulated, surrendering Guadeloupe and all its Dependencies, comprehending the Islands of Marie-Galante, Desirada, the Saints, &c. on the same Terms that were allowed to Rochambeau at Martinique, and Ricard at St. Lucia, to match out with that the Honours of War, and lay down their Arms, to be sent to France/and not to serve against the British Forces or their Allies during the War. Accordingly at Eight o'Clock this Morning the French Garrison of Fort St. Charles marched out, consisting of 55 Regulars of the Regiments of Guadeloupe, and the 14th of France, and 818 National Guards and others. Prince Edward, with the Grenadiers and Light Infantry, taking Possession, immediately hoisting the British Colours, and changing the Name of it to Fort Matilda. The Terms of Capitulation are transmitted herewith, but the Forts and Batteries are so numerous, and some of them at such Distance, that a Return of the Ordnance, Stores, &c. cannot be obtained in Time for the failing of this Vessel, as I am unwilling to detain her so long as would be necessary for that Purpose. From a Return found amongst General Collot's Papers, it appears that the Number of Men able to carry Arms in Guadeloupe, is 5877, and the Number of Fire Arms actually delivered out to them is 4044.

In former Dispatches I have mentioned that Lieutenant-General Prescott was left to command at Martinique, and Colonel Sir Charles Gordon at St. Lucia; and the Conquest of Guadeloupe and its Dependencies being now also completely accomplished, I have placed Major-General Dundas in the Command of this Island, with a proper Garrison; and HIS Majesty may place the firmest Reliance on the Ability, Experience and Zeal for the good of his Service and their Country, of those excellent Officers. Although I have not been wanting in my several Dispatches to you, Sir, to bestow just Praise on the Forces I have the Honour to command, yet I conceive it a Duty, which I embrace with infinite Pleasure, to repeat, that, to the Unanimity and extraordinary Exertions of the Navy and Army on this Service, under Fatigues and Difficulties never exceeded, His Majesty and their Country are indebted for the rapid Success which, in so short a Space of Time, has extended the British Empire, by adding to it the valuable Islands of Martinique, St. Lucia, Guadeloupe, the Saints, Marie-Galante, and Desirada. Captain Thomas Grey, one of my. Aides de Camp, will have the Honour to deliver this Dispatch, and can communicate any other Particulars or Information you may desire.

P.S. Since closing this Letter Returns are received, and transmitted herewith, of the Killed, Wounded, and Miffing, and of the Batteries and Ordnance taken; but that of the Stores could not be obtained.

ARTICLES of CAPITULATION between their Excellencies Sir Charles Grey, K. B. General and Commander in Chief of His Britannic Majesty's Troops in the West Indies, &c. &c. &c. and Vice-Admiral Sir John Jervis, K.B., Commander in Chief of His Majesty's Naval Forces &c. &c. &c.. and George Henry Victor Collet, Major-General and Governor of Guadeloupe, Marie Galante, Desiada and Dependencies.

T'HE Commanders in Chief of His Britannic Majesty's Forces are induced to grant to the long Humanity with which he has treated the Prisoners under his Care, the Honour of marching out of Fort St. Charles, at the Head of the Garrison, which shall in every Respect be subject to and treated in the same Manner as that of Fort Bourbon, to wit, to lay down their Arms as Prisoners, and not to serve against His Britannic Majesty during the present War, nor against His Allies.

The Post of Houelmcut to be immediately withdrawn, and the Troops there to retire into Fort St. Charles. The said Post is to be delivered up to the British Troops, exactly in the State in which it is, as well as Fort St. Charles, and all other Military Posts in the Island.

The Garrison of Fort St. Charles to march out of that Fortress the 22d of this Month at Eight o'Clock in the Morning. The British Troops are to take Possession of the Gates of Fort St. Charles. To-night Marie-Galante, Desirada, and all the Dependencies of this Government, are to be included in the present Capitulation.

Given at Guadalupe, April 20, 1794

Par leurs Excellences,
V. Collot. G. Fisher. Charles Grey. Geo. Purvis. J. Jervis.

Return of Killed, Wounded and Missing in the Army commanded by His Excellency General Sir Charles Grey, K.B. in the Attack and Capture of Fort St. Charles, the Batteries, and Town of Basseterre.

1st Battalion of Grenadiers. 3 Rank and File missing.
1st Battalion of Light Infantry. 2 Rank and. File killed ; 2 Rank and File wounded.
2d Ditto. I Rank and File wounded.
3d Ditto. 1 Rank and File wounded; 2 Rank. and File missing.
Total. 2 Rank and File killed; 4 Rank and File wounded; 5 Rank and File missing
(Signed)
F.R.A. DUNDAS, Adj. General

During the Battle and the Occupation of the island by yellow fever 10th February to 10th December

Capt. Charles Grove, killed Point à Pitre 26/02/1794
Capt./Lt. James Johnstone died yellow fever
Lt. Irvine died yellow fever
Lt. Frederick Mukins died yellow fever
Lt. Aldworth Phaire died yellow fever
Lt. William Henry Seagrave died yellow fever
Ens. Christopher George Barry died yellow fever
Ens. Michael Nash died yellow fever
Ens. Philip Sanders died yellow fever

List of prisoners living at Point à Pitre Guadeloupe
January 1st 1795

Capt. George Eiston died February 1795
Lt. Charles Strickland

Ens. William Thomas Holmes

Captain James Fitzgerald died 1795

Siege of Malta
September 2nd 1798 to September 4th 1800

Major-General Pigot took companies of the 1/35th to Malta in the middle of June 1800, the battalion joining them later. The French had held out for two years suffering great privations, with the arrival of Pigot and his reinforcements the French commander in Valetta surrendered on the 4th September and the garrison marched out on the 7th. The British then took control of Valetta and the forts of Manoel and Tigue. The first British standard to be flown over Valetta was the King's Colour of the 35th Regiment of Foot.

Battle of Bergen (Netherlands)
September 19th 1799

1/35th of Foot

"London Gazette" Tuesday September 24th 1799

Head-Quarters Schagen Brug, Sept. 20, 1799
SIR, IN my Dispatch of the 16th Instant I acquainted you with my Intention of making an Attack upon the Whole of the Enemy's Position, the Moment that the Reinforcements joined. Upon the 19th, every necessary Arrangement being made, the Army moved forward in Four principal Columns in the following Order: The Left Column, under the Command of Lieutenant-General Sir Ralph Abercromby, consisting of Two Squadrons of the 18th Light Dragoons, Major-General the Earl of Chatham's Brigade, Major-General Moore's Brigade, Major-General the Earl of Cavan's Brigade, First Battalion of British Grenadiers of the Line, First Battalion of Light Infantry of the Line; The 23d and 55th Regiments under Colonel Macdonald, destined to turn the Enemy's Right on the Zuyder Zee, marched at Six o'clock on the Evening of the 18th. The Columns upon the Right, the First commanded by Lieutenant-General D'Hermann, consisting of The 7th Light Dragoon Twelve Battalions of Ruffians, and Major-General Manners' Brigade; the Second, commanded by Lieutenant-General Dundas, consisting of Two Squadrons of the 11th Light Dragoons,
Two Brigades of Foot Guards, and Major-General His Highness Prince William's Brigade; the Third Column, commanded by Lieutenant-General Sir James Pulteney, consisting of Two Squadrons of the 11th Light Dragoons, Major-General Don's Brigade, Major-General Coote's Brigade; marched from the Positions they occupied at Daybreak the Morning of the 19th. The Object of the First Column was, to drive the Enemy from the Heights of Camper Duyne, the Villages under these Heights, and finally to take Possession of Bergen: the Second was to force the Enemy's Position at Walmenhuysen and Schoreldam, and to co-operate with the Column under Lieutenant-General D'Hermann: and the Third, to take Possession of Ouds Carspel at the Head of the Lange Dyke, a great Road leading to Alkmaer. It is necessary to observe, that the Country in. which we had to act, presented in every Direction the most formidable Obstacles. The Enemy upon their Left occupied to great Advantage the High Sand-Hills which extend from the Sea in front of Petten to the Town of Bergen, and were entrenched in Three intermediate Villages. The Country over which the Columns under Lieutenant-Generals Dundas and Sir James Pulteney had to move for the Attack of the fortified Posts of Walmenhuysen, Schoreldam, and the Lange Dyke, is a Plain intersected every Three or Four Hundred Yards by broad deep wet

Ditches and Canals. The Bridges across the only Two or Three Roads which led to these Places were destroyed, and Abbatis were laid at different Distances: Lieutenant-General D'Hermann's Column commenced its Attack, which was conducted with the greatest Spirit and Gallantry, at Half past Three o'clock in the Morning, and by Eight had succeeded in so great a Degree as to be in Possession of Bergen. In the wooded Country which surrounds this Village the principal Force of the Enemy was placed, and the Russian Troops, advancing with an Intrepidity which overlooked the formidable Resistance with which they were to meet, had not retained that Order which was necessary to preserve the Advantages they had gained; and they were, in consequence, after a most vigorous Resistance, obliged to retire from Bergen, (where, I am much concerned to state, Lieutenants-General D'Hermann and Tchertchekoff were made Prisoners, the latter dangerously wounded, and fell back upon Schorel, which Village they were also forced to abandon, but which was immediately retaken by Major-General Manners' Brigade, notwithstanding the very heavy Fire of the Enemy. Here this Brigade was immediately reinforced by Two Battalions of Russians, which had co-operated with Lieutenant-General Dundas in the Attack of Walmenhuysen, by Major-General D'Oyley's Brigade of Guards, and by the 35th Regiment under the Command of his Highness Prince William. The Action was renewed by these Troops for a considerable Time with Success; but the entire Want of Ammunition on the Part of the Russians, and the exhausted State of the whole Corps engaged in that particular Situation, obliged them to retire, which they did in good Order, upon Petten and the Zyper Sluys.

As soon as it was sufficiently light, the Attack upon the Village of Walmenhuysen, where the Enemy was strongly posted with Cannon, was made by Lieutenant-General Dundas. Three Battalions of Ruffians, who formed a separate Corps, destined to co-operate from Krabbendam in this Attack, commanded by Major-General Sedmoratzky, very gallantly stormed the Village on its Left Flank, while at the same Time it was entered on the Right by the 1st Regiment of Guards. The Grenadier Battalion of the Guards had been previously detached to march upon Schoreldam, on the Left of Lieutenant-General D'Hermann's Column, as was the 3d Regiment of Guards and the 2d Battalion of the 5th Regiment, to keep up the Communication with that under Lieutenant-General Sir James Pulteney. The Remainder of Lieutenant-General Dundas's Column, which, after taking Possession of Walmenhuysen, had been joined by the First Battalion of the Fifth Regiment, marched against Schoreldam, which Place they maintained, under a very heavy and galling Fire, until the Troops engaged on their Right had retired at the Conclusion of the Action. The Column under Lieutenant-General Sir James Pulteney proceeded to its Object of Attack at the Time appointed, and after overcoming the greatest Difficulties and the most determined Opposition, carried by Storm the principal Post of Ouds Carspel at the Head of the Lange Dyke; upon which Occasion the 40th Regiment, under the Command of Colonel Spencer, embraced a favourable Opportunity which presented itself of highly distinguishing themselves.

This Point was defended by the chief Force of the Batavian Army under the Command of General Daendels. The Circumstances, however, which occurred on the Right rendered it impossible to profit by this brilliant Exploit, which will ever reflect the highest Credit on the General Officers and Troops engaged in it and made it necessary to withdraw Lieutenant-General Sir James. Pulteney's Column from the Position which he had taken within a short Distance of Alkmaer. The same circumstances led to the Necessity of recalling the Corps under Lieutenant-General Sir Ralph Abercromby, who had proceeded without Interruption to Hoorne, of which City he had taken Possession, together with its Garrison.

The Whole of the Army has therefore re-occupied its former Position.

The well-grounded Hopes I had entertained of complete Success in this Operation, and which were fully justified by the Result of the Three, and by the First Successes of the Fourth Attack upon the Right, add to the great Disappointment I must naturally feel on this Occasion; but the Circumstances which have occurred should have considered of very little general Importance, had I not to lament the Loss of many brave Officers and Soldiers, both of His Majesty's and the Russian Troops, who have fallen.

The Gallantry displayed by the Troops engaged, the Spirit with which they overcame every Obstacle which Nature and Art opposed to them, add the Cheerfulness with which they maintained the Fatigues of an Action which tasted without Intermission from Half past Three o'clock in the Morning until Five in the Afternoon, are beyond my Powers to describe or to extol. Their exertions fully entitle them to the Admiration and Gratitude of their King and Country. Having thus faithfully detailed the Events of this First Attack, and paid the Tribute of Regret due to the distinguished Merit of those who fell, I have much Consolation in being enabled to state that the Efforts which have been made, although not crowned with immediate Success, so far from militating against the general Object of the Campaign,

promise to be highly useful to our future Operations. The Capture of Sixty Officers and upwards of Three Thousand Men, and the Destruction of Sixteen Pieces of Cannon, with large Supplies of Ammunition, which the intersected Nature of the Country did not admit of being withdrawn, are convincing Proofs that the Loss of the Enemy in the Field has been far superior to our own ; and in addition to this it is material to state that nearly Fifteen Thousand of the Allied Troops had unavoidably no Share in this Action. In viewing the several Circumstances which occurred during this arduous Day, I cannot avoid expressing the Obligations I owe to Lieutenant-Generals Dundas and Sir James Pulteney for their able Assistance, and also to mention my great Satisfaction at the Conduct of Major-Generals His Highness Prince William, D'Oyley, Manners, Burrard, and Don, to whose spirited Exertions the Credit gained by the Brigades they commanded is greatly to be imputed. Captain Sir Home Popham and the several Officers of my Staff exerted themselves to the utmost, and rendered me most essential Service. I feel also much indebted to the spirited Conduct of a Detachment of Seamen, under the Direction of Sir Home Popham and Captain Godfrey of the Navy, in the Conduct of Three Gun Boats, each carrying One 12 Pound Carronade, which acted with considerable Effect on the Alkmaer Canal; nor must I omit expressing my Acknowledgments to the Russian Major-Generals Essen, Sedmoratzky, and Schutorss. I transmit herewith Returns of the Killed, Wounded, and Missing. I am, Sir, yours,
FREDERICK

Ensign John Renton distinguished himself by rescuing the Colours of the 1st Battalion from capture in the hand-to-hand fighting.
Lieutenant-Colonel John Oswald and Major Adam Hay, wounded; Major Peter Hayes Petit, wounded and taken Prisoner; Captain James Bennett Manoury, Ensign George Wilkinson, Ensign Matthew Deane, and Ensign John Jones, wounded. 2 Sergeants and 1 Drummer missing.
350 men unaccounted for, 100 presumed dead the rest wounded or missing.

Extract from the book: The campaign in Holland 1799

8th Brigade, under Major-General His Royal Highness Prince William of Gloucester: The 1st battalion 5th regiment, 686 strong ; 2nd battalion 5th, 666; 1st battalion 35th regiment 607, and 2nd battalion 35th, 614.

Meanwhile, Lieutenant-General Dundas, after detaching the grenadier battalion of the Guards to observe Schoreldam, and placing the 8th Brigade, under Major-General Prince William of Gloucester, in reserve between St Maarten's and Ennigenbrug, had, with the remainder of the second or right column, attacked at daylight the village of Warmanhuysen. At this juncture, the body of fugitive Russians from Bergen appeared outside of Schorel, the French following close behind them; and after one last effort to make a stand, the former were driven pell-mell into and out of the village. The enemy were then checked, however, by the 9th brigade, consisting of the 1st and 2nd battalions 9th regiment and the 56th regiment, under Mayor-General Manners, which advanced by the road from Schoreldam, in the teeth of a heavy fire, and retook the village. This brigade was in its turn forced to retreat, closely pursued by the enemy, until they were joined by the 1st battalion 35th regiment, about 600 strong, under Prince William of Gloucester, this single battalion being the only one in his brigade which had not been detached. Finding that the command in this quarter had devolved upon himself, by the capture of the Russian lieutenant-generals, Prince William determined to attempt the re-capture of Schorel. By staying the onward progress of the enemy with the 35th for a few moments, he gave time for Major-General Manners' brigade to form up in his rear, and then, pushing forward with this support, he succeeded in carrying the village, and the wood skirting it. Directly afterwards, the Duke of York brought up the 1st brigade of Guards, under Major-General D'Oyley, and two Russian battalions of Major-General Sedmoratzky's brigade, from Warmanhuysen; and the whole then pursued the enemy up the sand-hills, and forced them to retire on Bergen.

Battle of Beverwyk and Wyck-op-Zee October 8th 1799

In the centre, the village of Heyloo, lying between Alkmaar and Limmen, was occupied by a detachment from the division under Lieutenant-General Dundas, while, on the left, the 8th brigade, under Prince William of Gloucester, had been detached by Lieutenant-General Sir James Pulteney to re-occupy the town of Hoorn. On the 8th of October, accordingly, its left and centre divisions entered Alkmaar, and again took up the positions they had occupied before the action of the 2nd, and in the evening their light troops appeared in front of Petten and Erabbendam. Next day General Brune re-established his headquarters at Alkmaar, and occupied Warmanhuysen and Drixhoorn with detachments, while his cavalry scoured the country to within cannon-shot of the British advanced posts. On his right, the Dutch troops, under General Daendels, entered Hoom, from which the 8th brigade, under Prince William of Gloucester, forming the rear-guard of the British left wing, had retreated to the village of Winckel, and there taken post behind the canal called the Verlaat. Next day General Daendels advanced from Hoom, and, on being joined by General Dumonceau's brigade, he resolved to commence offensive operations by attacking Prince William at Winckel.

Accordingly, the whole Dutch force, amounting to about 6,000 men, with 15 pieces of artillery, was put in motion at about 11 o'clock, in order to force the passage of the Verlaat, to defend which Prince William had only about 1,050 effective bayonets, with two six-pounders and one howitzer. Nevertheless the assailants met with a gallant resistance. On their left. General Bonhomme, who advanced at the head of four battalions supported by General Dumonceau, was repulsed in an attempt to carry a bridge across the canal, with the loss of 100 men killed and wounded and 13 made prisoners, by six companies of the 2nd battalion 35th regiment, under Lieutenant-Colonel Massey, directed by Prince William himself, who were drawn up in some fields to the right of the bridge, and were supported at about one o'clock, when the action was nearly over, by a single field-piece detached from Wirickel.

Meanwhile, Daendels himself, with not less than 5,000 men, had advanced against the British left, consisting of the 1st and 2nd battalions 5th regiment, together scarcely 600 strong, which were posted in front of the village, under cover of a small redoubt erected upon the dyke of the Verlaat. To cover the exposed flank of the brigade, this dyke had been cut across to a depth of nine feet. Owing to their great numerical superiority, the Dutch troops shortly succeeded in forcing a passage across the canal, but then Lieutenant-Colonel Bligh, in command of the 1st battalion 5th, who had promptly perceived that were the enemy allowed to advance further the retreat of the brigade would be cut off, planted the colours, as a rallying point for his regiment, on the top of the dyke, and maintained his ground there until he had secured and covered the retreat of the remainder of the British force. The 2nd battalions 5th and 35th had also maintained their positions, until ordered to retreat by Prince William, in consequence of orders received from the commander-in-chief, when the whole brigade were brought out with their guns, ammunition, and baggage, with the loss of only 3 killed and 12 wounded. No attempt was made to harass it in its retreat, and by nightfall it arrived at Oude Sluys.

The grenadier and light infantry battalions took part

Lt. Joseph Phillott grenadier company killed
5 officers killed,
Wounded Captain George Duncan Robertson of the 1/35th, Lt. James Nicholson of the 2/35th
9 rank and file killed
84 rank and file wounded and 17 rank and file missing

Siege of Malta
August 1st 1798 to September 4th 1800

"London Gazette" Tuesday October 7th to Saturday October 11th 1800

Malta September 5, 1800

Sir,

I Have great Satisfaction in acquainting you with the Surrender of the Fortress of La Valletta, with all its Dependencies, after sustaining a Blockade of Two Years. The Capitulation has been signed this Day. I had every Reason to suppose that this most formidable Fortress was likely soon to fall, from the Circumstance of the Two French Frigates, La Justice and La Diane, going out of the Harbour a few Nights ago; One of which, La Diane, by the Vigi, lance of the blockading Squadron, was soon captured, and there are still some Hopes that the other may have shared the same Fate. Judging of how much. Consequence it maybe that you should have the earliest Intimation of this importance. Capture, I have delayed, till another Opportunity sending Returns of the Stores, &c. found in the Place, which could not yet be made up. During the short Time you were here, you must have been sensible of the great Exertions which Brigadier-General Graham must have made with the limited Force he had, previous to my Arrival with a Reinforcement, he has ever since continued these Exertions; and I consider that the Surrender of the Place has been accelerated by the Decision of his Conduct, 'in preventing any more Inhabitants from coming out of the Fortress a short Time before I came here. He was sent to negotiate the Terms of Capitulation with General Vaubois, and I am much indebted to him for his Assistance in that Business; I am happy to say, that I have experienced every Support from Brigadier-General Moncrieff, and the Officers of the British and Allied Troops whose Conduct in every Respect has been most exemplary.

The Service of the Engineer Department, under Captain Gordon, has been carried on with great Zeal and Perseverance. I think it right to mention to you, that Lieutenant Vivion of the Royal Artillery, the Assistant Quarter-Master-General, has been of considerable Service. He was landed here with his Party from the Stromboli Bomb at the Commencement of the Blockade; and for a long. Time did Duty with these few Men without any other British or Regular Troops of any Description. I have great Pleasure in acknowledging the constant and ready Assistance and Co-operation I have received from Captain Ball of His Majesty's Ship the Alexander, who has been employed on Shore during the greater Part of the Blockade. His Name and Services are already well known to His Majesty's Ministers; and I am sure I need not say more than that those he has performed here do Credit to his former Character I herewith transmit you the Terms of the Capitulation, I have derived great Assistance from my Aide-de-Camp Captain Dalrymple, who has for some Time been doing Duty as Assistant-Adjutant-General.

I have the Honour to be, &c..,
(Signed)
H. PIGOT, Major-General

Battle of Maida (Italy)
July 4th 1806

Excerpt from *"London Gazette"* **Friday September 5th 1806 Extraordinary**

General Regnier was encamped on the Side of a woody Hill, below the Village of Maida, sloping into the Plain of St. Euphemia; his Flanks were strengthened by a thick impervious Underwood. The Amato, a River perfectly fordable, but of which the Sides are extremely marshy, ran along his Front; my Approach to him from the Sea Side (along the Borders of which, I directed my March, until I had. nearly turned his Left) was across a spacious Plain; which gave him every Opportunity of minutely observing my Movements. After some loose firing of the Flankers to cover the Deployments of the Two Armies, by Nine o' Clock in the Morning the opposing Fronts were warmly engaged, when the Prowess of the Riyal Nations seemed now fairly to be at Trial before the World, and the Superiority was greatly and gloriously decided to be our own. The Corps which formed the Right of the advanced Line, was the Battalion of Light Infantry commanded by Lieutenant Colonel Kempt, consisting of the Light Companies of the 20th, 27th, 35th, 58th, 61st, 81st, and Watteville's, together with One Hundred and Fifty chosen Battalion Men of the 35th Regiment, under Major Robinson. Directly opposed to them, was the favourite French Regiment the 1st Legere. The Two Corps at the distance of about One Hundred Yards fired reciprocally a few Rounds, when, as if by mutual Agreement, the Firing was suspended, and in close compact Order and awful Silence, they advanced towards each other, until their Bayonets began to cross at this momentous Crisis the Enemy became appalled. They broke, and endeavoured to fly, but it was too late; they were overtaken with the most dreadful Slaughter.

Brigadier-General Ackland, whose Brigade was immediately on the Left of the Light Infantry, with great Spirit availed himself of this favourable Moment to press instantly forward upon the Corps in his Front; the brave 78th Regiment, commanded by Lieutenant-Colonel Macleod, and the 81st Regiment, under Major Plenderleath, both distinguished themselves on this Occasion.

The Enemy fled with Dismay and Disorder before them, leaving the Plain covered with their dead and wounded. The Enemy being thus completely discomfited on their Left, began to make a new Effort, with their Right, in the Hopes of recovering the Day. They were resisted most gallantly by the Brigade under Brigadier-General Cole. Nothing could shake the undaunted Firmness of the Grenadiers under Lieutenant-Colonel O'Callaghan, and of the 27th Regiment under Lieutenant-Colonel Smith. The Cavalry, successively repelled from before their Front, made an Effort to turn their Left, when Lieutenant Colonel Ross, who had that Morning landed from Messina with the 20th Regiment, and was coming up to the Army during the Action, having observed their Movement, threw his Regiment opportunely into a small Cover upon their Flank, and by a heavy and well directed Fire, entirely disconcerted this Attempt.

This was the last feeble Struggle of the Enemy, who now, astonished and dismayed by the Intrepidity with which they were assailed, began precipitately to retire, leaving the Field covered with Carnage. Above Seven Hundred Bodies of their Dead have been buried upon the Ground. The Wounded and Prisoners already in our Hands (among which are General Compere, and an Aid-de Camp, the Lieutenant Colonel of the Swiss Regiment, and a long List of Officers of different Ranks) amount to above One Thousand. There are also above One Thousand Men lest in Monteleone and the different Posts between this and Reggio, who have mostly notified their Readiness to surrender, whenever a British Force shall be sent to receive their Submission, and to protect them from the Fury of the People. The Peasantry are hourly bringing in Fugitives, who dispersed in the Woods and Mountains after the Battle. In short, never has the Pride of our presumptuous Enemy been more severely humbled, nor the Superiority of the British Troops more gloriously proved, than in the Events of this memorable Day.

His Majesty may, perhaps, still deign to appreciate more highly the Achievements of this little Army, where it is known that the Second Division which the Enemy were said to be expecting had all joined them the Night before the Action; no Statement that I have heard of their Numbers places them at a less Calculation than Seven Thousand Men.

Our victorious Infantry continued the Pursuit of the routed Enemy so long as they were able; but as the latter dispersed in every Direction, and we were under the Necessity of preserving our Order, the Trial of speed became unequal:

The total Loss occasioned to the Enemy by this Conflict cannot be less than Four Thousand Men. When I oppose to the above our own small comparative Loss, as underneath detailed, His Majesty will, I hope, discern in the Fact, the happy Effects of that established Discipline to which we owe the Triumphs by which our Army has been latterly so highly distinguished.

I have the Honour to be, &c.

J. STUART, Maj. Gen.

Causalities

1/35th Grenadier Company lost 4 killed and 27 wounded
1/35th Light Company 1 officer, 7 rank and file killed
1 officer, 1 Drummer and 41 rank and file wounded

(For Major Robinson read Robertson, no Robinson on Army List 35th of Foot 1806)

Gold Medal

Major George Duncan Robertson

Anglo-Turkish War 1807-1809 (Egypt)
Alexandria Expedition March 18th to September 25th 1807

1807

18th March

1st & 2nd Battalions

Killed in action

Capt. Thomas Joddrell, Capt. Robert Westerman, Pte. Busby and Pte. John Dyke.
Lt. Robert Cameron wounded, 1 Serjeant and 4 rank and file wounded

April 10-17

Lt. Richard Cust (Brigade Major) 3 Serjeants and 26 rank and file wounded
1 rank and file killed

19th April

Lt. Theophilius Daly, Lt. John M. Philpott killed
14 rank and file wounded

21st April

Capt. Henry Tarleton, Capt. Andrew Peck, Lt. George Wilkinson killed.
Capt. Charles Archibald Macalister, Lt. William Walker wounded and taken prisoner, the rest of the men killed or taken prisoner.

The retreat from Rosetta the 1/35th covered this under command of Capt. Crosby Joseph Riddell, 2/35th under Major Jeremiah O'Keefe.
Captain John Henry Slessor, 4 Serjeants and 58 rank and file wounded.

"London Gazette" Tuesday July 14th to Saturday July 18th 1807

"Extract from despatch"

Rosetta Lines, April 17, 1807.

I HAVE the Honour of Stating, that on the 3d Instant 1 marched with the Division of infantry under my Command from the Eastern Heights of Alexandria to the Wells of Aboukir; the Cavalry, Artillery, and Engineers' Stores had been previously forwarded to the Caravanserai. This Post had been retained with much Spirit by a Detachment of the Marines after the Retreat of the Army under Lieutenant-Colonel Bruce, and was of essential Value to our present Operations.

The greatest Part of the 4th Instant was employed in passing the Infantry and Camels to the Caravanserai, in landing Guns and Ammunition, and in substituting the latter and entrenching Tools for Camp Equipage.

A Body of Two Hundred Seamen, under Lieutenant Robinson, were added to the Army. Captain Hallowell kindly offered to accompany me; he has since continued with the Army, and I cannot sufficiently express how infinitely obliged every Department has been by his active Co-operation. The Village of Edko was understood to be favourable to us. A more certain Supply of Water, and a less precarious Communication with our Fleet, offered themselves by the Lake than by the Northern Shore. To advance upon Rosetta by the Route of Edko was preferred to that of Marabaut. Lieutenant-Colonel McLeod, to whom I entrusted the Advance of the Army, consisting of the Light Infantry Battalion, Three Companies of the 78th Regiment, Two Six-Pounders, and a Detachment of Dragoons, moved forwards towards Edko on the Evening of the 4th ; he took a strong Position behind that Village early next Morning On the 5th the Army advanced to the same Position; Captain Nicholls, of the Marines, was left in Command at the Caravanserai with a Detachment of Forty Rank and File.

In consequence of Information of the Enemy being established in Force at the Village of Harriet, it was advisable to occupy that post on our Advance to Aboumandour; our Rear would by this Measure be secured dining Operations against Rosetta, and au uninterrupted Communication be established with the Depot on the Lake Edko. Lieutenant-Colonel McLeod accordingly advanced Upon Hamet on the 6th instant; he met with some of the Enemy's Cavalry about a League from that Village, whom he caused to retire after a slight Skirmish: being reinforced by the Grenadiers of the 35th Regiment and De Kbit's; he pushed forward and occupied the Post without Opposition.

Return of Killed, Wounded, and Missing of the Army serving against Rosetta, from the 6th to the 18th of April, inclusive, 1807.

35th Reg.- I Rank and File, killed ; 1 Captain, 3 Serjeants, 2 Rank and File, wounded

Names of Officers wounded

Captain Thomas Joddrell, of the 2nd Battalion, 35th Regiment, since dead

Camp, Eastern Heights, Alexandria,

April 25, 1807

SIR, I HAVE the Honour of reporting to you, that I Yesterday returned to this Position with the Remains of the Army lately under my Command. The Events which have attended the Service on which that Army has been engaged, have been of a peculiar Nature, and the Result has been as peculiarly unfortunate. I feel it therefore to be incumbent upon me, in justification of my own Conduct, and in justice to those brave Men who have been my Companions in Arms, to intrude upon your Attention a more than ordinary Detail of our Proceedings.

I had the Honour of stating in my last, that the Expectation of the Junction of the Mamelukes had chiefly induced me to persevere in the Attack of Rosetta: Every Exertion was continued to be made by such Artillery as we could command, in reducing the Enemy to surrender, but without Effect: The mistaken Ground upon which we were acting respecting the Mamelukes, and the genial Deception of our Informers, were now about to become manifest.

On the 19th the Enemy left his Position opposite Hamet, and crossing the River near Elsine, established himself there. He advanced from Dibet against Hamet on the same Day, and attacking Major Vogelsang's Position on the Left, as repulsed with Loss; a Division was made at the same Time at Rosetta, in a Sortie against the Left of our Lines, by about Eighty Cavalry and Two Hundred Infantry; the 35th Regiment and the Dragoons, were engaged; they repulsed the Enemy with much Spirit, and drove him as usual to his Walls. The 35th had in this Affair Two killed and Fourteen wounded. I this Evening detached the Light Companies of the 35th and of De Rolle's to the Post of El Hamet under the Command of Captain Tarleton of the former. His Orders were to drive the Enemy across the Nile, either during that Night, or early next Morning. On attempting to effect this Service on the 20th, the Enemy was found to be powerful in Cavalry, and Captain Tarleton retired. I must here state the Nature of the Position of Hamet: From Lake Edko to the Nile is an Isthmus about Two Miles and a Half in extent, varying according to the Depth of Water in the Lake. The Remains of a deep Canal with high Banks extend from the River nearly Two-thirds across this Isthmus; the Banks command the Plain on either Side. The Village of Hamet is on the southern Side of the Canal, about half way across; its Inhabitants were friendly to us. On the Banks of the Nile and at Hamet and the only Two regular Passes through the Banks of the Canal. At each of these was posted a Gun, and a Proportion of Major Vogelsang's Detachment. From the Termination of the Canal to the Lake is a Plain, passable by Cavalry. A Picquet guarded this Flank.

As Captain Tarleton retreated, he divided his Detachment; he directed the March of his own Company to the left Position, and sent the De Rolle's, reinforced to One Hundred Rank and File, to Hamet Village. While crossing the Plain, the latter Detachment, under Captain Reinack's Orders, was suddenly attacked by 200 Cavalry, and as it should appear, was with little Opposition routed; Two Thirds were cut in Pieces. Report of this reaching me by Eleven o'Clock in the Forenoon, I detached Lieutenant Colonel MacLeod with Two Companies of the 78th Regiment, One of the Thirty fifth] a Picquet of Dragoons under Captain Delancy, and a Six-Pounder, to reinforce the Post, and take the Command. Two more Companies followed in the Afternoon, with a Day's Provision for his whole Force, Ammunition, &c. all which arrived safely. On the Arrival of the Reinforcement, the Enemy retired towards Dileg, and I received Assurance from the Lieutenant-Colonel before Sunset, of the perfect Security of his Post; he had detached Three Companies, the Dragoons, and a Three Pounder, under Captain Tarleton's Orders, to the Plains on the Right, and had reinforced the Centre Post by a Company of the 35th Regiment; the average Strength of these Companies were Sixty Rank and File.

During this Day, the Enemy made no Movement against our Lines at Rosetta, but sent Reinforcements to Hamet from the Town by the right Bank of the Nile. 1 visited the Post of Hamet during the Night of the 20th, But had the good Fortune to escape the Enemy's Cavalry, who had turned Captain Tarleton's Position at Sunset, to the Number of One Hundred and Fifty. Having reconnoitred the line of Defence, which I found to be weak in many Parts and very extensive, 1 confirmed my former Instruction, to Lieutenant-Colonel MacLeod, vis, that he should defend the Post to the utmost, bill if likely to be forced or turned that he should concentrate and appuyer himself upon the Lake; that if this was not feasible, he should fall back on the main Army. I at the same Time Concerted Measures for a general Retreat on the succeeding Night, unless certain Intelligence of the Mamelukes should arrive on the 21st.

Although he hid One Third of my Force under his Orders, I gave him Reason to expect a Reinforcement of Eighty Men more, with Ammunition, on the ensuing Morning.

About Seven o'Clock on the Morning of the 21st, I received the following Express from him: The Cavalry to be were not to been seen this Morning but, to my utter Astonishment, from Sixty to Seventy large Germs, and large Brig, are now coming down the Nile upon us. I do not know what to say of this; it appears, undoubted, a Reinforcement to the Enemy, and one of considerable Magnitude. I take it for granted they have Gun-Boats among them. I must make Preparation, and be ready to retire upon you; Let me know as soon as possible My Answer, immediately dispatched, was not received, the Dragoon being unable to penetrate to the Post. The Reinforcement also, which had marched under the Orders of your Aide de-Camp, Captain A'Court, was obliged to return. Not a Moment was to be lost in breaking up from the Position before Rosetta and in supporting the Hamet Detachment. The Advance upon us of a strong Body of Cavalry in that Direction, prevented my detaching single Corps to their Relief, and it was necessary that the whole Army should move together. The Field Guns were first withdrawn from the Batteries; all Camels were laden with Ammunition and indispensable Stores, the Carronades and Mortars kept up their Fire on the Town to the last Moment that could be spared, and were then deployed and buried; all spare Ammunition and Stores were set Fire to and blown up The Picquets remained in their Flecches until the Field Train, the Wounded, and the Stores were assembled in the Plains, under the Charge of the 78th and De Roll's Regiment, which formed a Square round them The brave 35th then retreated, followed by the Picquets The enemy sallying from the Town in all Directions, surrounded our Square; but the bold Front Which the 35th kept, under the Command of Captain Riddle, and the flanking Position of the Light Infantry Battalion, under Major O'Keefe, on the Heights of Aboumandour, prevailed him from making any Impression.

Nothing could surpass the Steadiness of the Troops you had entrusted to my Command. The 35th Regiment fired by its Wings and Platoons retiring and the 78th with its Front Rank kneeling, as during the Movements of a Field Day.

Under the Direction of Colonel Oswald, who regulated Proceedings in the Rear, I felt confident of the good Conduct of the Whole. About Ten o'Clock, our little Army advanced across the sandy Plain, in a Direction of the Lake Edko, and the Right of the Hamet Position. We arrived there about One o'Clock, under continual Fire, and after a sultry March; our Loss was not, however, considerable, the greater Body of the Enemy being kept at a Distance by the Fire of our Artillery from the Flanks of the Square. To my Surprise not an Individual of the Hamet Detachment joined us on this March, nor could Firing be heard in that Direction; our last Account of their Proceedings left them warmly engaged near to the Village of Hamet on the Rosetta Side. Failing to meet them on this shore of the Lake, it was necessary, in some Measure, to retrace our Steps, and to look for them nearer to El Hamet. This could be effected by gaining some Sand Hills, which were about a Mile on our Left. Our March was accordingly directed towards them, the Light Infantry now leading the Front of the Square, advanced with Activity, and the Enemy who occupied them, dispersed in all Directions. From those Hills, which completely commanded a View of the Plain and Hamet Position, the Enemy were seen to be in Possession of the latter, and not any Appearance of our Detachment in the former. It was a. parent they had either effected a separate Retreat to Edko, or been completely defeated, in either Case it was advisable under all Circumstances, that the Army should continue its original Retreat; this was resumed in the same good Order as before; the Left being Banked by the Lake, the Enemy ceased to pursue us Our Casualties during this Retreat did not exceed Fifty killed and wounded, and none were captured.

The loss of our Enemy was considerable, but we made no Prisoners By Sunset we arrived at the Depot. Lieutenant Tilly, with his usual Activity, had, in consequence of my Express to him in the Morning, safely embarked all Provisions and Stores. Having left our Wounded and our Twelve-Pounder on board Germs here, and refreshed the Army, we advanced to Edko, and took up our former Position about Two in the Morning.

On the 22nd the Whole of the Stores, which were at Edko, were safely embarked tor the Caravanserai, when the Army marched to that Post, and arrived in the Afternoon without Opposition. On the succeeding Day the Troops embarked for Aboukir's Wells the Caravanserai was blown up under the Direction of Captain Hallowell. No certain Intelligence has reached me respecting the Fate of the Detachment under Lieutenant-Colonel MacLeod. General Report confirms their Defeat in the Forenoon of the 21st, and states many of them to be Prisoners. On this I will make no Comment. Every Step which a Sense of Duty could dictate was taken in older to secure the Post of Hamet; and it will, I sincerely trust, appear to you that none which Prudence could fugged were omitted, in order that a Junction should be formed with the Detachment. That our unfortunate Comrades did their Duty must not be doubted; that all was lost, save Honour, when they surrendered, must also not be doubted. In closing this Letter I am bound to state, that I have been ably supported by those who were under my Orders. To Colonel Oswald I owe every Thing that a Commander can owe to his Second in command. To Lieutenant Tilly for his Exertions on the Lake, and Captain Nicholls for his Services at the Caravanserai our Army was indebted for its uninterrupted Supply. Wherever Naval Assistance has been required, it has been given, under the able Superintendence of Captain Hallowell, with a Zeal so peculiar to our Naval Operations. In every Department and to each commanding Officer, our Country is under much Obligation, for they exerted themselves to the utmost. They all deserve that better Fortune should have attended their zealous Endeavours.

1 have the Honour to enclose a Return of the Killed, Wounded, and Missing, since the 19th Instant. The Missing imply the Detachment at Hamet alone, none being missing from the main army.

I have the Honour to be, &c.

(Signed) W. STEWART, Brig. Gen.

Return of Killed, Wounded, and Missing of the Army serving against Rosetta, from the 19th to the 21st April, inclusive, 1807

35th Reg. 1 Rank and File, killed; 1 Lieutenants, 4 Serjeants, 58 Rank and File, wounded ; 2 Captains, 2 Lieutenants, 7 Serjeants, 2 Drummers, 134 Rank and File, missing.

Names of Officers wounded

Light Infantry Batt. Lieutenant Arthur, of the 35th
35th Reg. Lieutenants Daly and Phillott

Names of officers missing

Light Infantry Batt. Captains Tarleton (of the 35th), Lieutenant Westerman (of the 35th),
1st Batt. 35th Reg. Captains Macalister and Pike, Lieutenants Wilkinson and Walker.

Return of Prisoners taken by the Enemy, transmitted by Major-General Fraser, the 20th of May, 1807.
Alexandria, May 20, 1807.

Prisoners of War

1st Batt. 35th Reg. 1 Captain, 6 Serjeants, 2 Drummers, and 84 Rank and File

Prisoners of War not at Cairo

1st Batt. 35th Reg. I Lieutenant,

RECAPITULATION

1st Batt 35th Reg. 1 Captain, 1 Lieutenant, 6 Serjeants, 2 Drummers, 84 Rank and File

Officers, Prisoners of War

Captain Macalister of the 35th

Officers Prisoners, but not at Cairo

Lieutenant Walker, of the 35th Regiment

This is the most correct Return we have been able to procure, but we cannot expect it to be very accurate.

(Signed) GEORGE AIREY,
Acting Deputy Adjutant-General

"London Gazette" Tuesday February 16th to Saturday February 20th 1808

Horse-Guards, February 10,1808
HIS MAJESTY has been pleased to grant His most gracious Permission to the Flank Companies of the 1st Battalions of the 35th and 61st Regiments, and such other Officers and Men of those Corps as were serving with the Army in Calabria, to assume and wear on their Appointments the Word "MAIDA" as an honourable and lasting Testimony, of the distinguished Gallantry displayed by those Detachments, in common with the other Regiments, which were engaged in the Action which was fought, between the British: and French Armies on the 4th July 1806, on the Plains of Maida.
By Order of His Royal Highness the Commander in Chief,
HARRY CALVERT, Adj.-Gen.

Walcheren Expedition 1809 (Holland)
July 30th to December 9th

Left Wing

1st Division under Lieutenant-General Sir John Craddock

Major-General Graham's Brigade

3/1st, 2/35th, 2/81st

Middelburg, 2nd August, 1809

Return of the Rank and Names of Officers, and of the Number of Non-Commissioned Officers and Rank and File, killed, wounded, and missing, in the Island of Walcheren, from the Time of landing on the Evening of the 30th July to the 1st of August inclusive.

2nd Batt. 35th Foot 4 Rank and File killed ; 2 Captains, 14 Rank and File, wounded; 11 Rank and File missing.

Siege of Flushing
August 1st to August 16th

Lt.-Colonel Peter Hayes Petit severely wounded, 3 Serjeants and 51 rank and file wounded.
1 Serjeant killed.

Head-Quarters, Middelburg, 7th August 1809

2/35th Foot

Captain Charles Frederick, wounded as per date Return, since died
Captain Thomas Tisdall slightly wounded

From the 8th Instant to the Surrender of Flushing, on the Morning of the 15th inclusive, Head-Quarters, Middelburg 16th August 1809

2/35th Foot 1 Serjeant killed

"London Gazette" Tuesday August 8th to Saturday August 12th 1809

Middelburg 8th August 1809

MY Lord,
SINCE closing my Dispatch of Yesterday's Date, the Enemy, towards Five o' Clock in the Evening; in considerable Force, made a vigorous Sortie upon the Right of our Line occupied by Major-General Graham's Division. The Attack was principally directed upon our advanced Piquets, which were supported by the 3rd Battalion of the Royals, the 5th and 35th Regiment under Colonel Hay. These Corps, together with Detachments of the Royal Artillery, the 95th and light Battalions of the King's German Legion, received the Enemy with their accustomed Intrepidity; and after a sharp Contest of some Duration forced him to retire with very considerable Loss killed, Wounded and Prisoners. In this Affair the Enemy has had another Opportunity of witnessing the superior Gallantry of British Troops; in no Instance has he succeeded in making the least Impression on throughout our Line, and on this Occasion, so far from profiting by his Attempts he has been obliged to relinquish some very advantageous Ground where our advanced Posts are now established. I cannot too strongly express my Sense of the unremitting Vigilance and Ability manifested by Major-General Graham, in securing and maintaining his Post against the repeated Attempts of the Enemy to dislodge him; and I have great Satisfaction in acquainting your Lordship, that the Major-General mentions, in Terms of the warmest Approbation, the distinguished Conduct and Gallantry of the Officers and Troops engaged on this Occasion. I am now enabled to transmit, for your Lordship's Information, an Abstract Return of the Ordnance, Ammunition, and Stores that have fallen into our Hands since our arrival in this Island.
I have the Honour to be, &c
CHATHAM.

Friday August 31st 1809

Letters from the army in Walcheren state a most gallant achievement performed by our townsman, Captain George Arthur, of the 35th Regiment of Foot, with his light company, consisting of 81 rank and file. He was ordered to protect the retreat of our out-lying piquets, who were driven in. With the upmost gallantry Captain A. dashed forward, and found himself opposed by 300 of the enemy, which he immediately attacked with great spirit and resolution. They did not stand the charge long, but, after a severe conflict, 81 of the enemy fell killed and wounded. Captain A. took 73 prisoners, the rest of the enemy effectively dispersed, and he returned with his prisoners to the main body of the army. Captain A. lost in this affair 3 serjeants, 3 corporals, and 23 ranks and file killed or wounded. General Sir. E. Coote, in his consequence of Captain G. Arthur's skill and gallantry in this business, has promoted him, we are happy to hear to the rank of Deputy-Assistant-Adjutant-General to the division of the army under Lieut.-General Sir J. Hope, Bart.

September 2nd 1809

Lt.-Colonel Peter Hayes Petit dies in Deal of wounds he received at the battle of Flushing

Ionian Island Campaigns
Capture of Zante (Zakynthos)
October 2nd 1809

Troops landed on the 1st October about three miles from the town, and invested the castle which, with its garrison 400 men, capitulated on the following day, Major Charles William Clarke, with a detachment of the regiment, having previously established himself in the town of Zante, the gates were then taken passion of by the grenadiers.

Capture of Cephalonia
October 3rd 1809

Bay of Zante October 3rd 1809

SIR,
IN consequence of your Excellency's Communication to Rear-Admiral Sir Alexander Ball at Malta, we were fortunate enough to find the Spartan Frigate off the Islands, having on board Mr. Foresti, His Majesty's Minister to the Septinsular Republic Considerations arising from the Advance in the Season, and the precarious State of the Weather, induced Captain Spranger to point out Zante at the primary Object of Attack. Having from Mr. Foresti obtained the most ample and correct Information respecting that Island, the Expedition stood in and came to an Anchor in its Road led towards the Close of the Day on the 1st of October. Captain Spranger and myself were equally desirous to avoid involving the Inhabitants in the Misfortunes which a direct Attack upon the Town must have occasioned. It was therefore determined, that early on the. Day following the Troops should be landed at a convenient Bay Three Miles distant, protected by the Frigates and Gun Boats. The first Division of the. Troops (as per Margin), under the immediate Orders of Lieutenant-Colonel Lowe, effected a most regular Debarkation at the Point proposed, and in Two Columns proceeded immediately towards a Position turning the Defence of the Town, and cutting off its Communication with the Castle. Lieutenant-Colonel Lowe led his Column to the, Left, clearing an Eminence upon which the Enemy was said to be posted, and by this Movement a detached Battery was turned, some Prisoners made and a more direct Intercourse with the Shipping, established. The Corps which I accompanied marched by a Valley, till it ascended the Height contiguous to the Castle, which the light Troops pushed forward to invest.
Royal Artillery, a Four-Pounder, mounting Guns.
Light Infantry, 35th Regiment.
2 Companies Royal Corsican Rangers (Grenadiers) and 2 Companies 35th Regiment.
3 Companies 44th Regiment.
Amounting to 600 Men.
2 Rank and file of the regiment wounded.

Capture of Ithaca
October 8th 1809

Vathy, Capital of the island of Ithaca 8th October 1809
SIR,
I HAVE the Honour to inform you that the Island of Ithaca was this Day surrendered to the Detachment of British Troops under my Command, in Concert with His Majesty's Ship Philomel. Finding the Enemy's Batteries commanded the Harbour in such a Manner as to render ineffectual the Fire from the Ships, I immediately landed the Troops and Marines, accompanied by a Division of Seamen under the Direction of Captain Crawley, I marched without Loss of Time to the Enemy's principal Fort, situated on an Eminence, with the Determination to take it by Assault: Our Intention was however frustrated by the unconditional Surrender of the French Commandant and his Garrison. During our March the Enemy was held in Check by the Fire of a Gun-Boat detached by Captain Crawley for that Purpose. The Garrison, consisting of near Eighty Men have been made Prisoners of War, with the Exception of a few Albanians, who escaped to the Mountains, but who must inevitably fall into our Hands. It is impossible that I can express the Obligation I am under to Captain Crawley for the very handsome Manner in which he gave every Assistance his Power to ensure the Success of the Enterprise. To Mr. Foresti, His Majesty's Minister to the Sevens Isles, I beg also to offer my sincere Acknowledgments for the great Service he rendered to me on this Occasion, and I feel it my Duty to report the, uniform

good Conduct of the Officers and Men of the 35th Regiment, Royal Corsican Rangers, and Royal Marines composing the Detachment I had the Honour to command. I have only to add the extreme Joy of the Inhabitants in being rescued from the Slavery under which they had hitherto groaned.
I have the Honour to be, &c.
(Signed) R. CHURCH, Captain,
Assistant Quarter-Master-General,
To Brig. Gen. Oswald, &c. &c. &c.

His Majesty's Ship Warrior, Cephalonia, 12th October 1809

SIR,
I HAVE the Honour to transmit to your Excellency the accompanying Report upon the Capture of the Island as Ithaca. The Enterprise was entrusted to Captain Crawley, of His Majesty's Ship Philomel, and to Captain Church, with Detachments from the 35th and Royal Corsican Rangers. The Manner in which it has been effected, will, I have no doubt, appear to your Excellency creditable to those Officers, and to the Forces under their Orders.
I have the Honour to be, &c.
(Signed) J. OSWALD,
Commanding Troops in the Ionian Isles.
To Lieut. Gen. Sir John Stuart, K. B. &V. &c. &c.

Capture of Cerigo (Kythira)
October 12th

Spartan, off the Island of Cerigo, 13th October 1809

Sir,
IN my last from Zante I expressed a Hope that we might be able to reduce the Island of Cerigo without any farther Reinforcement. This Idea was strengthened by Papers and Plans found upon the late Governor of the Island, made Prisoner at Zante. Major Clarke and myself decided upon making our first Attack upon the Forts in the Harbour of Avlemmeno, in order to prevent the Escape of any Vessels which might be there. The Forts are those of St. Nicholas and St. Joaquin. The first is a Stone Building mounting Nine Guns; the latter an Embrasure Battery of Four Guns. At Four P. M. on the 9th Instant we ran into the Bay. The Forts opened upon us, but were both silenced in a few Minutes by the Ship and Schooner, whilst the Troops under Major Clarke landing made several Prisoners. The Enemy had One killed and One wounded upon this Occasion. Only One Man of the Thirty-fifth was wounded on our Side.
At Daylight on the 10th we weighed with the Intention of immediately attacking the Castle of Capsel in the Bay of Cerigo, but variable Winds prevented our getting round At Two P. M. the Troops and Marines were landed in a small Cove in the Bay of St Nicholas, and marched forwards towards the Castle, one Watch of the Spartan following with Three small Field Pieces. I landed with the Troop that I might be enabled by Signal to command the Resources of the Ship without the Delay of sending Messages, foreseeing that fire could not be brought to act against the Castle whilst the Wind continued Southerly. The Nature of the Country rendered our Approach to the Castle extremely difficult, particularly for the Guns, which did not arrive till Ten o'clock on the 11th Instant at the Position the Troop occupied, a Height on a Level with the Castle, within Four Hundred Yards of it. A Fire commenced on both Sides with Gun and Musketry, which continued the greatest Part of the Day. In the Evening fuse Rockets were landed from the Ship, and in the Course of the Night some of them thrown at the Citadel. At Daylight I ordered Two Twelve Pounders to be landed from the Ship, but before they could he disembarked a Flag of Truce came out with an Offer of surrendering, provided the Garrison was allowed to return to Corfu. This we refused; and after some Deliberation it surrendered on the same Terms as those of Zante and Cephalonia. At Ten o'clock our Troops took Possession of the Castle.

It is to the Zeal and Ability of Major Clarke, and the judicious Arrangements which he made of the Forces under his Command, that the speedy Reduction of this strong Post may be attributed. The Enemy were cut off from any Prospect of Escape or Relief, and were convinced that our Means of Offence were hourly increasing.

I cannot speak too highly of the Conduct of the Officers and Men of both Services, as well in respect to the cheerful Perseverance under Fatigue, as to their Gallantry when opposed to the Enemy. I am happy to say our Loss has been much less than might have been expected One Bombardier of the Royal Artillery killed, Two Privates of the 35th Regiment wounded. I cannot in Justice to Lieutenant Willes, first of the Spartan, close this Letter without saying, that Fort St. Joaquin of Two Eighteen and Two Nitre Pounders was completely silenced by the gallant Manner in which he attacked it in the Prize Schooner under his Orders with a Party of the 35th Regiment on board. The Inhabitants of the Island received us with every Demonstration of Joy. I have sent Lieutenant Willes in the Schooner with the Dispatches, and shall remain off this Place till I receive your further Directions. I enclose for your Information the Articles of Capitulation, together with a List of Artillery, &c. found on the Island.

I have, &c.
(Signed) J. BRENTON.
Captain Spranger, His Majesty's Ship Warrior.

Onboard His Majesty's Ship Warrior
Zante Bay, October 16th 1809

SIR,
THE Spartan Frigate, having on board a Detachment of Royal Artillery, with light Guns, and Two Companies of the 35th Regiment, under the Orders of Major Clarke of that Corps, sailed from Cephalonia on the 6th Instant, instructed to proceed off Cerigo, block up its Port, and, if Circumstances warranted to make an immediate Attack upon the Island. It was Captain Spranger's I mention and my own to have followed with considerable Reinforcements but a Continuance of adverse Gales prevented our getting farther than this Bay, where a Tender from Captain Brenton has just reached us, conveying Dispatches, of which the accompanying are Copies, announcing the Surrender of Cerigo to the previously detached Force. Major Clarke goes fully into the Details of the Military Operations. They characterize an ardent Spirit of Enterprize; and he seems to have been perfectly seconded by the Officers and Men under his Orders, surmounting Difficulties greater than I apprehended he had the Means of overcoming. The Enterprize which your Excellency confided to me being thus happily accomplished, it only remains for me to testify my fullest Approbation of the Conduct of the Troops. A Discipline has been maintained that did Honour to the Soldier, and reflected the utmost Credit upon the commanding and subordinate Officers. I am under the greatest Obligations to the Officers of the Staff of my Command; they have been most assiduous in the Discharge of their respective Duties. I must recur in the warmest Terms of Acknowledgment to the never ceasing Aid received from Captain Spranger; it was my good Fortune to act with an Officer who, while our Views and Objects were the fame, cordially united in the Means of attending them. A similar Harmony, and good Correspondence has reigned through every Branch of the two Services. Our Success was accelerated, and our subsequent political Arrangements facilitated, by the personal Exertions and judicious Councils of Mr. Foresti, His Majesty's Minister to the Septinsular Republic, and we greatly profited in being accompanied by a Gentleman so loved and esteemed by the Inhabitants of these Isles. Mr. Foresti's distinguished Merits have received the Commendations of the most illustrious of our Countrymen ; to add my humble Tribute would be presumptuous, were it not called for by Feelings of Gratitude and Respect towards so worthy a Servant of our Sovereign. I will now proceed to place the Islands is a Posture of Defence, sufficient to afford probable Security; and I am led to believe it may be accomplished without causing any Expense to His Majesty's Government.

I have the Honour to be, &c.
(Signed) J. OSWALD,
Commanding Troops in the Ionian Isles

"London Gazette" Saturday December 2nd to Tuesday December 5th 1809

His Majesty's Ship Warrior, Bay of Zante, October 3, 1809

Sir, I HAVE the Honour to acquaint you, for the Information of the Commander in Chief, that, in pursuance of His Lordship's Orders, 1 sailed from Messina on the 23d ultimo, in Company with the Sloop Philomel, two large Gun Boats, and the Transports, with Troops under the Command of Brigadier-General Oswald, and proceeded off Cephalonia, where we arrived on the 28th, and continued in Sight of the Island until the 1st of October, during which Days we were joined, as had been previously arranged, by the Spartan from Malta, and the Magnificent, Belle Poole, and Kingfisher, from Corfu, and anchored that Night in the Bay of Zante, just without Reach of the nearest Battery. At Daylight on the following Morning, the Troops assembled alongside the Warrior, and under Cover of the Spartan, Belle Poole, and Gun Boats, who soon silenced the Batteries, landed a Division of the Army in the most perfect Order, about Three Miles from the Town, and whilst General Oswald was advancing, Captains Brenton and Brisbane, and the Gun Boats, conducted by Mr. Cole, my First Lieutenant, were actively employed in keeping the Enemy, who had re-manned their Batteries, in Check, and covering the second Disembarkation, when the whole Army moved forward and closely invested the Castle, to which the French had retired from every Direction. A Proclamation, herewith annexed, was in the Meantime distributed to the Inhabitants, explanatory of our Views, and finding, as was expected, that they rejoiced in the Expulsion of these common Disturbers of Mankind, I forbore attacking with the Ships a strong Battery on the Mole Head, which could not be taken without destroying a great Part of the Town; and have the Satisfaction of adding, that in the Course of the Day, the Enemy though advantageously situated in a most important and commanding Position, thought proper to capitulate on the Terms which I have the Honour to enclose.

I am,. &c.
(Signed.)
J.W. SPRANGER.
Rear Admiral Martin, &c. &c, &c.

"London Gazette" Tuesday December 5th to Saturday December 9th 1809

MY LORD,

A DISPATCH, which I had the Honour to address to your Lordship on the 26th Ultimo, apprized you of the Representations that had been made to Vice-Admiral Lord Collingwood, and to myself, of the Solicitude of the Inhabitants of Zante, Cephalonia, and other Dependencies of the Ionian Government, to receive the Assistance of a British Force to liberate them from French Oppression.

The consequent Equipment of an Expedition under Brigadier-General Oswald, to act cooperatively with a Squadron under Captain Spranger, of His Majesty's Ship Warrior, was at the same time detailed to your Lordship, and stated to have sailed in the Prosecution of this Object on the 23d of last Month from Medina.

The Reports with which Captain Oswald, of the 35th Regiment, Yesterday arrived from Zante, and which I have now the Satisfaction of transmitting to your Lordship, will mark the able Manner in which this Service has been carried into Effect by the Officers by whom it was conducted; and I hope His Majesty will graciously deign to approve the Adoption of a Project, the Success of which opens such Means of opposing future Obstacles to the probable views of the enemy as well as disappointing them in the hoped Utility of their present Usurpations in that Quarter.

I have the Honour to be, &c.
J. STUART, Count of Maida,
Lieutenant-General.

Capture of Santa Maura (Lefkada)
March 21st to April 16th 1810

Brigadier-General John Oswald with his regiment 1/35th, Greek light Infantry, Royal Corsican Rangers etc. Arrived the 21st and landed south of the town on the 22nd. The French and his troops abandoned the town and retired to the fort and some strong field works. The troops took the town, a force was left behind to protect the town. Lieutenant-Colonel Francis John Wilder of the regiment with two battalions, the seamen and marines, the Greek light infantry stormed the first redoubt driving the enemy to another redoubt. To support the attack on this second redoubt Major Clarke of the regiment who commanded two companies of the regiment was sent for from the town. The Greek infantry tried storming the redoubt but could not effect an opening, so that Major Charles William Clarke and his battalion with two companies of the Calabrian Free Corps. Commanded by Brevet-Major Robert Oswald (35th), was brought to the front, stormed, and drove out the enemy to the gates of the fort.
On the next day the batteries were commenced up and on the 8th the batteries opened fire and a siege began. On the 15th, Captain Lorenzo Moore of the 35th grenadier company led a charge with other troops who stormed forward through grape and shot and carried the works with their bayonets, on the following day the enemy capitulated, 74 French surrendering themselves.

Return of Killed, Wounded, and Missing of the Troops under the Command of Brigadier-General Oswald, in Storming Three of the Enemy's entrenched Batteries. St. Maura, 22nd March 1810.

Camp, St. Maura, 24th March 1810

22nd March

35th Regiment 2 Rank and File, wounded

Calabrian Free Corps Major Robert Oswald, severely wounded
Return of Killed and Wounded of the Troops under the Command of Brigadier-General Oswald, before the Fortress of St. Maura, from the 23rd of March to the 16th of April 1810.

6th April

35th Regiment 1 Rank and File, wounded

7th April

35th Regiment Major Charles William Clarke killed

8th April

35th Regiment 1 Rank and File, killed

15th April

35th Regiment 1 Serjeant, 1 Rank and File, killed ; 2 Rank and File, wounded

(Signed)   R. CUST,
 Acting Assist. Adj. Gen.

"London Gazette" From Tuesday June 19th to Saturday June 23rd 1810

Messina, April 26, 1810

MY LORD,
SINCE my Dispatch to your Lordship of the 24th Instant, I have received from Brigadier-General Oswald the satisfactory Account which I have the Honour to transmit herewith, of the complete Reduction of the Island and Fortress of St Maura, and of the Surrender of the French Force by which they were garrisoned to His Majesty's Arms. On the Service so successfully accomplished by Brigadier-General Oswald, it only remains with me to express the sanguine Hope, that the Consequences will be as beneficial as the Achievement has been brilliant; and that himself and the gallant Troops who have been the Companions of his Enterprise, will receive their best Recompense in their Sovereign's most gracious Approbation.
I have the Honour to be, &c.
J. STUART,
    Count of Maida, Lieut-Gen

Extract from dispatch

Upon the Evening of the 15th, Captain Thackeray desiring to reconnoitre the Approach and Ground for the breaching Battery, then in Agitation, it became necessary to drive the Enemy from an Entrenchment he held within Three Hundred Paces of his Rampart. The Service was entrusted to Lieutenant-Colonel Moore, of the 35th Regiment, who led the Grenadiers of that Regiment, Light Company of Roll's, and Subaltern Detachments of the Corsican Rifles, and Royal Marines. This Corp was pushing undauntedly through a heavy Fire of Grape and Musketry, carried the Enemy's Line at the Point of the Bayonet. Upon the Lieutenant-Colonel and Captain Thackeray reporting to me, that it was practicable to establish our Troops there, the Detachment was directed to stand fast, and by incessant and judicious Labour during the Night, the Entrenchment was converted into a second Parallel, from whence the Fire of the Enemy, however severe, could not dislodge it.

Our Sharpshooters and Infantry fpm thence greatly distressed the opposing Artillery; and I am convinced hastened the Enemy's Decision to surrender.

In the course of these Operations, it has afforded me infinite Satisfaction to observe, that the Skill of our Officers, and the Courage of our men, have uniformly, converted the Labours of the Enemy into Works of Security for ourselves. I am happy to say, that upon the whole our Loss has been inconsiderable; remarkably so, when the Circumstances of the Siege are taken into Consideration. The Skill and Attention of Mr. Gunning, Surgeon to the Forces, (of whom I cannot speak top highly, or too strongly recommend to your Excellency,) and that of the other Medical Officers, will 1 trust be the means of preserving the valuable Lives of our wounded Officers and Men. I am deeply concerned to say, that since my last Report, a chance Cannon Shot has deprived the Army of Major Clarke; an Officer whose early Exploits and distinguished Qualities promised to render him one of its brightest Ornaments. This Dispatch will be presented by Lieutenant Hartzenbuhler, my Aide-de-Camp, whom I again recommend to your Excellency's Notice and Projection.
I have the Honour to be, &c.
 (Signed) J. OSWALD,
Brig. Gen. Commanding Troops in the Ionian Isles.

Siege of Badajoz (16 March – 6 April 1812)

Gold Medal

Lt-Col. George Henry Berkeley, Assistant-Adjutant-General (35th of Foot)

**Capture of Cape Ceste
July 20th 1812**

"London Gazette" From Saturday October 3rd to October 6th 1812

Admiralty Office, October 6, 1812
Extract from a Dispatch from Vice Admiral Sir Edward Pellew.

And also a letter from Captain Rowley, of the Eagle, reporting the capture by storm, on the 20th July, and subsequent destruction of the battery of Cape Ceste, in the Adriatic, by a detachment from the 35th regiment and a party of marines, under Captain Rutherford, of the 35th, embarked in the boats of the Eagle, under Lieutenant Cannon and the capture by the latter of an enemy's gun-boat on the 22d.

1813

**With Austrian Army at Trieste and Apennines Campaign 1813-1814
Capture of Lagosta and Curzola February 21st 1813**

"London Gazette" Saturday June 5th 1813

Lissa, February 23, 1813

My Lord,
I HAVE the honour to inform your Lordship, that in consequence of information having been received here, that several merchant vessels bound to this island, had been captured by a French privateer, and carried into the island of Lagosta, Admiral Fremantle and myself judged it expedient to lose no time in putting an end to a system, which was likely to become very detrimental to the prosperity of this island, and to our commercial interests in general. For this purpose I embarked on board His Majesty's frigate Apollo, commanded by Captain Taylor, on the 19th ultimo, with detachments from this garrison amounting to about three hundred men, including artillery, with two six-pounders, two howitzers, and two mountain guns. The troops, together with a detachment of seamen and marines, landed on the island of Lagosta on the 21st, and marched towards the principal work, constructed by the enemy for the defence of the island, from whence the garrison, opened a well-directed fire of shot and shells. As the work in question is situated on the summit of a high conical hill, commanding the town, I found it necessary to take up a favourable position, from whence I was enabled to forward the preparations necessary for the reduction of the fort. During this interval, Captains May, 35th, and Ronea, Calabries Free Corps, together with Mr. G. Bowen, First Lieutenant of His Majesty's ship Apollo, with a party of forty men, succeeded in spiking the guns of one of the enemy's lower batteries, and in destroying a magazine of provisions, both of which were within musket shot of the fort. On this occasion a French serjeant of artillery and two soldiers were taken prisoners. Mr. Ullark, purser of His Majesty's ship

Apollo, volunteered his services on both these occasions. Having received certain intelligence that a detachment of three hundred men, commanded by a Lieutenant-Colonel, had marched from Ragusa to reinforce the garrison of Lagosta, and being aware of the great difficulty which would have attended the attempt to get battering artillery on the only hill which commanded the fort, Captain Taylor and myself were induced to offer favourable conditions to the French commandant, who, after some hesitation,, agreed to surrender (together with the garrison, consisting of one hundred and thirty-nine men), on the terms, a copy of which I have the honour to enclose your Lordship. I have also the honour to enclose your Lordship a return of the enemy's ordnance, ammunition, and stores, which fell into our hands. It is particularly gratifying to me to be able to inform your Lordship, that during the whole of our operation, the inhabitants gave us the most unequivocal proofs of their attachment, and rendered us the most efficacious assistance. Finding that the French privateer, together with the prizes, had taken refuge in the island of Curzola, Captain Taylor and myself immediately proceeded thither. We landed (without delay) the troops under my command, with one hundred and twenty seamen and marines, together with a howitzer and field-piece. Major Slessor, 35th, advanced at daybreak with the flankers, and got possession of a fortified building on the height, which commands the town within musket shot. In this operation he was supported by a second party, under the command of my Military Secretary, Captain Ball, 81st regiment. The enemy opened a sharp fire of musketry from their lines, as also from the windows and doors of the houses, and endeavoured: to bring an eighteen-pounder in one of the towers of the town wall to bear on our position, which we presented by a well-directed fire from the howitzer, six-pounder, and musketry.

Captain Taylor, in order to accelerate the surrender of the town, undertook to silence the sea batteries, which he accomplished in the most brilliant and effectual manner, after a continued firing of three hours, during which, the Apollo was always, within range of grapeshot from the batteries. This point being effected, Captain Taylor and myself judged it expedient to send Major Slessor with a flag of truce into the town, proposing that the women and children should be allowed to quit it before we erected our mortar batteries; the enemy availed himself of this opportunity to offer to capitulate on terms which, with certain modifications, we agreed to, in consequence of which the garrison, consisting of a lieutenant-colonel and about one hundred men, marched out of the town, which we immediately occupied.

We found on taking possession of the town that the French had packed up the church plate and bells of Lagosta and Curzola, for the purpose of sending them to the Continent, and Captain Taylor and myself experienced the most heartfelt satisfaction in restoring them to the oppressed inhabitants. I have the honour to transmit your Lordship returns of the ordnance, stores, and ammunition which we got possession of at Curzola. I have also the honour to enclose your Lordship a copy of the terms of capitulation, which were signed at the moment that the expected French corps intended to reinforce the menaced Islands appeared on the Peninsula of Sabioncello only a mile distant from the town of Curzola. To express my approbation of the conduct of Captain Taylor throughout the whole of the expedition, I fulfil-a duty which, is peculiarly grateful to my feelings. He unremittingly aided me with his advice, and promoted very considerably the success of the expedition by his personal exertions on shore with the troops. I have the fullest reason to be satisfied with the support which I experienced from Major Slessor, of the 35th, and the whole of the officers. Lieutenant Rains, who had the direction of the artillery, performed the service allotted him with the greatest zeal. The services of Lieutenant McDonald, of the 35th, who had the direction of the gunboats which accompanied the expedition, were found of great utility. I feel great satisfaction in communicating to your Lordship, that during the whole of this service, which was rather severe, owing to the unusual coldness of the weather, the conduct of the troops was highly praiseworthy, and they were ably supported by the seamen and marines who acted with us on shore.

I have the honour to be, &c.
(Signed)
G. D. ROBERTSON, Lieut. Col.
To His Excellency Lieutenant-General Lord William Bentinck, &c. &c. &c.

"London Gazette" From Saturday July 3rd to Tuesday July 6th 1813

Extract

Admiralty-Office, July 6, 1813. Copy of a Letter from Captain Taylor, of his Majesty's Ship Apollo, addressed to Rear-Admiral Fremantle, and transmitted by Vice-Admiral Sir Edward Pellew to John Wilson Croker, Esq.

His Majesty's Ship Apollo, Curzola, SIR, February 4, 1813. IN compliance with your orders of the 18th January, we proceeded, with two hundred and fifty men under Lieutenant-Colonel Robertson, on board the Apollo, Esperanza privateer, and four gunboats, to the attack of the island of Augusta, and I have the honour to acquaint you that it surrendered on the 29th. During this service, which was attended with excessive fatigue, by the nature of the mountains over which we had to pass, a distinguished share fell to Captain Rorica, who with fifteen Calabrese, Mr. Thomas Ullock, Purser of the Apollo, an artilleryman, and our guide, Antonio Langaletta, spiked the guns of the lower battery, under musketry of the fort, likewise to Captain May (35th regiment), Lieutenant George Bowen, and Mr. Ullock, of the Apollo, with forty men and the assistance of the inhabitants, who destroyed a store of provisions, took a Serjeant of artillery, and two soldiers in the town, also under the musketry of the fort. I do not mean, by mentioning these in particular, to take from the merits of others, who were all equally zealous. I cannot either avoid mentioning the great exertions of the gun boats under Lieutenant McDonald, (35th regiment) the barge, launch, and yawl, under Messrs. William Henry Brand, William Hutchinson, and William David Fowkes, midshipmen of the Apollo; they drew a continual fire of the fort and battery upon them, and captured a boat attempting to get out with dispatches. The fort stands upon the pinnacle of a mountain, which position is so strong, that fifty English soldiers, with the good disposition of the inhabitants, are likely to resist any force the enemy may send against it. Its garrison consisted of one hundred and thirty-nine men. It has one mortar, one eighteen, and two eight-pounders, three eighteen pounders in the lower battery, and there are several musketry out-works. We have only to lament the loss of one man on our side, an inhabitant, killed; the enemy had one wounded. Colonel Robertson having left a garrison in Augusta, we sailed on the 1st with the Imogene, and gun-boat No. 43, to attack this island. Although it blew excessive hard in squalls, we succeeded in landing one hundred and sixty soldiers, seventy seamen, and fifty marines, with a howitzer, and1 six-pounder field gun, the same night, at Port Bufalo, which enabled Major Slessor (35th regiment), with the flankers, to surprise the hill, with a musketry work upon it, that commands the town. Hearing that three hundred enemy's troops to relieve Augusta, were arrived on the opposite shore (Sabionalla), I directed Lieutenant Charles Taylor, acting commander of the Imogene, to bring away or destroy their boats", and if fired at from Curzola, not to return it to the town, which instructions he obeyed-with the utmost forbearance, as he fired over all, when their fire was directed at him. Mr. Antonio Parbo, commander of the gun-boats, likewise behaved gallantly; his vessel was hulled three or four times. Finding that the enemy appeared determined to hold out (although our field-guns were upon the hill, and our advance in the suburbs within pistol shot), and that the civic guard were collecting in the country I took off the Apollo's seamen to attack the sea batteries, which, in the morning of the 3d, after about three hours firing, were silenced, they then agreed to capitulate; and I am happy to add, that we thereby have captured the privateer which molested the trade of the Adriatic so much, also two of her prizes. In this I lament the loss of two seamen, Charles McGregor, killed by grape : and Edward Williams, drowned, by the sinking of the yawl in securing the ship; William Ward, slightly wounded. I have also to regret that the ship's mainmast is very badly wounded, as well as a quantity of rigging cut. Upon the walls of the town, and in its towers, were three eighteen-pounders and eight small guns. It would be presumption in me to speak of my co-adjustor Lieutenant-Colonel Robertson's conduct, throughout our little expedition, in a military point of view but I may say, no service could have been performed with greater cordiality between all under his command, and our officers, seamen, and marines. The day the island surrendered we captured seven vessels in the Channel, bound to Ragusa and Cattaro, principally with grain, for which places are in great distress.

Against the French in Portugal and Spain

"London Gazette" Tuesday September 14th 1813
Siege and capture of St. Sebastian

Extract from a dispatch

Oyarzim, Sept. 1, 1813

It was impossible to restrain the impetuosity of the troops, and in an hour more the enemy were driven from all the complication of defences prepared in the streets, suffering a severe loss on their retreat to the castle, and leaving the whole town in our possession. Though it must be evident to your Lordship, that the troops were all animated with the most enthusiastic and devoted gallantry, and that all are en titled to the highest commendation yet, I am sure; your Lordship Will wish to be informed more particularly concerning those, who, from their situations; had opportunities of gaining peculiar distinction; and as the distance I was at myself, does not enable me to perform this act of justice from personal observation, I have taken every pains to collect information from the superior officers. Lieutenant-General Sir James Leith justified, in the fullest manner, the confidence reposed in his tried judgment and distinguished gallantry, conducting, and directing the attack, till obliged to be reluctantly' carried off, after receiving a most severe contusion on the breast, and having his left arm broken. Major-General Hay succeeded to the command, and ably conducted the attack to the last. Lieutenant-General Sir J. Leith expresses his great obligations to Major-Generals Hay and Robinson, (the latter was obliged to leave the field from a severe wound in the face), and to Lieutenant-Colonels Berkeley and Gomm, Assistant-Adjutant-General,, and Assistant-Quarter-Master-General of the 5th division, for their zealous services, during this arduous contest. He warmly recommends to your Lordship's notice, his Aid-de-Camp, Captain Belches, of the 59th foot; and, in conjunction with Major-General Hay, he bears testimony to the highly-meritorious conduct of Captain James Stewart, of the 3d battalion Royal Scots, Aid-de-Camp to Major-General Kay; and he recommends to your Lordship's notice, Major-General Robinson's Aid-de-Camp, Captain Wood, 4th foot, as also Captains Williamson and Jones of that regiment; the former was severely wounded in the command of the 4th, following the forlorn hope in the best style, and remaining long after his wound Captain Jones succeeded to, the command of the brigade, and conducted it with great ability.

I have the honour, &c. (Signed) T. GRAHAM.

"London Gazette" Tuesday October 5th 1813

The Prince Regent Is therefore graciously pleased to command, in the name and on the behalf of his Majesty, that, in commemoration of the brilliant victories obtained by His Majesty's arms in the battles of Roleia and Vimiera, Corunna, Talavera de la Reyna, Busaco, Barrossa, Fuertes de Onor, Albuera, and Salamanca, and in the assaults and captures of Cuidad Rodrigo and Badajos, the undermentioned Officers of the Army, present on those occasions, shall enjoy the privilege of wearing badges of distinction; and His Royal Highness having approved of the crosses, medals and clasps, which have been prepared, is pleased to command that they shall be worn by General officers and suspended by a ribbon of the colour of the colour of the slash, with a blue edge, round the neck and by the Commanding Officers of Battalions, or corps equivalent thereto, and Officers who may have succeeded to the actual command during the engagement; the Chiefs of Military Departments, and their Deputies and Assistants (having the rank of Field Officers), and such other Officers as may be specially recommended, attached by a ribbon of the same description to the buttonhole o£ their uniform.

Gold Medal (Salamanca)

Lieutenant-Colonel George H.F. Berkeley, Assistant-Adjutant-General (35th of Foot)

Officers entitled to wear a Medal and, one Clasp

Talavera de la Reyna

Military General Service Medal & Clasp (also known as Silver Medal)

Lieutenant-Colonel George H.F. Berkeley, Assistant-Adjutant-General (35th of Foot)

With Austrian Army at Trieste and Apennines Campaign 1813-1814

Capture of Lesina & Brazza
(Hvar & Brac)
Between August & September 1813

Captain William Hoste R.N. with troops of the 1/35th Foot.

1/35th (2 Companies) under Colonel Robertson and some foreign troops join the Austrians under Major-General Count Nugent on 12th October who was besieging Trieste. Enabling them to oust the French from northern Italy from Fiume to Genoa.

Split
October 14th 1813

Captain William Hoste R.N. in the next month helped to take Split with troops of the 1/35th of Foot.

Siege of Castle San Giusto, Trieste
October 16th to October 29th

"London Gazette" Saturday December 11th 1813

Trieste, November, 1813

My Lord,
AS the troops under my command have been augmented by a body of British troops, which joined me, under the orders of Colonel Robertson, I think it right to inform your Lordship of their further operations. By my former letter, your Lordship has been informed of my proceedings, as far as the taking of Fiume, and the first operations in that neighbourhood. Eugene Beauharnois had his principal force at Laybach, and my position annoying his rear and communication, he sent a force, six times superior to mine, composed of sixteen battalions with twenty guns, to attack me. After a very well fought action, on the 14th of September, and many movements which had been pre-concerted with Admiral Freemantle, the enemy's object entirely failed, and we got possession of the whole of Istria, guarding the ridge of mountains which run from Trieste to Fiume, On the 21st I met Admiral Freemantle, with part of the British squadron, at Capo d'Istria which post we strongly fortified. Our position stretching still more in the enemy's flank than before, forced him to keep a large force against me; General Radavojavich made very able use of this circumstance, and pushed the enemy on all sides towards Laybach. On the 23d a general movement took place: I marched to Basovizza, near Trieste, and covering my left against that place, I moved towards Prevald and Adelsberg.

The enemy was now forced to a precipitate retreat, and Eugene Beauharnois, after losing in different actions about ten thousand men, mostly prisoners, arrived the 2d of October with about twenty thousand men at Prevald, taking up a line between that place and Optshina, in communication with Trieste. At midnight, between the 3d and 4th of October, I attacked his right at Optshina, and forced it to retreat towards Gorizia. On the 5th the brigades of Stahremberg and Csirick, forced the enemy's position at Santo Croce, at the same time that I took the bridge of Morna, near Gorizia. In the night the enemy passed the Isonzo, and we took possession of Gorizia. The Isonzo offering us now a strong position, I marched back upon Trieste with part of my troops. Admiral Freemantle had already landed marines, and made preparations for the siege. The rapidity of our movements had prevented the transport of a battering train: there were, consequently, no other guns but those of the fleet, which Admiral Freemantle landed with great activity, at the same time the batteries were begun. On the 12th, the town of Trieste was taken by Baron D'Aspre, and we pushed our posts, on that side, close to the ramparts. Colonel Robertson landed from Lissa, with detachments of the 35th, De Roll's, the Corsicans, Calabrese, and the Italian Levy, with six pieces of field artillery and two mortars.

The 16th our fire commenced, and in the evening the windmill, a strong round tower, was occupied. Our works were approached on different points, and the posts the enemy occupied in advance were taken, except the Schanza. A company of Croats got possession of a wood, three hundred yards from the ramparts, from whence, during the rest of the siege, they very much annoyed the enemy at his guns. On the 23d the Schanza was taken, greatly owing to the courage and exertions of Captain Bowley. Three batteries, for eighteen and thirty-two pounders, were immediately begun, and Captain Berenstil opened a trench, which formed a first parallel, at the distance of four hundred yards. A mortar battery was built near the Schanza, and one for howitzers, in the prolongation of the attack in front. Captain Rains occupied, with two mortars, a battery in the rear, which threw with great effect. As soon as these batteries were ready, the enemy capitulated.

The labour of all these works was incredible, owing to the soft ground, occasioned by the continual rains, and the fire of the enemy; and nothing but the extraordinary exertions of the men, and the perfect harmony winch prevailed, could have overcome the difficulties. The officers, seamen, and marines, of the British squadron, particularly exerted themselves, and were animated by the presence of the Admiral, who himself superintended the works and directed the batteries.

Of the British land troops, the Calabrese had the most opportunity to distinguish themselves. Captain Ronca, a brave officer, was wounded; after which the command devolved upon Lieutenant Butler, who showed bravery and activity. Colonel Robertson was destined for the right of the attack if it had been continued. Lieutenant Rains, of the Royal Artillery, directed the fire of the mortars, with great effect and intelligence. Captain Angelo, of the 21st regiment, who was with me during the operations that preceded the siege, has rendered very essential service.

Captain Berenstil, of the Italian Levy, acted as engineer, and deserves to be most particularly recommended he was continually in the trenches, without being relieved. The fall of the castle of Trieste closes one most important part of our operations, and gives us the possession of the coast from Dalmatia to the top of the Adriatic, with all the roads that lead from thence. The whole of these operations prove how, by the mutual assistance of the army and navy, a yet superior force will be at length overcome, I always found Admiral Freemantle in readiness to support me; and, by the confidence, which that he gave me, I was enabled to undertake operations, which otherwise would have been destructive. It was this that allowed me to act in rear of the enemy, and give up frequently my land communication, convinced that it would soon be opened again.

As to the siege of the castle of Trieste, your Lordship will perceive, by the above, that the greatest part of the credit must heaven to Admiral Freemantle and the navy, and it is my duty to ac knowledge it. The result of this first part of the campaign, it, that besides the killed and wounded in the different actions, the enemy has sustained a loss in prisoners, which is greater than the number of troops. I command.

I have the honour to be, &c.
(Signed)

NUGENT, Major-General

Battle of the Nive
(December 9th to 13th 1813)

Gold Medal

Lieutenant-Colonel George H.F. Berkeley, Assistant-Adjutant-General (35th of Foot)

Friday January 28th 1814

K.T.S.

From the records of the College of Arms

The records include an Earl Marshal's Warrant of 24th March 1814 following a Royal Warrant of 28th January 1814 relating to George Henry Frederick Berkeley, Lieutenant Colonel of the 35th (or Sussex) Regiment of Foot and Assistant Adjutant General to the Forces. In view of his great courage and intrepidity in several actions with the enemy in the Peninsular he was given permission to accept and wear the Insignia of the third class of a Knight of the Portuguese Military Order of the Tower and Sword.

Knight of the Order of the Tower and Sword *(missing from London Gazette)*

His Majesty's royal licence and permission, that he may accept and wear the insignia of a Knight of the Royal Portuguese Military Order of the Tower and Sword, with which His Royal Highness the Prince Regent of Portugal hath been pleased to honour him, as a testimony of the high sense which that Prince entertains of the great courage and intrepidity displayed by the said Lieutenant-Colonel George H.F. Berkeley in several actions with the enemy in the Peninsula; provided nevertheless, that His Majesty's said licence, and permission doth not authorise, and shall not be deemed or construed to authorise, the assumption of any style, appellation, rank, precedence, or privilege appertaining unto a Knight Bachelor of these realms: And His Royal Highness hath been further pleased to command, that the said royal concession and declaration be registered, together with the relative documents, in His Majesty's College of Arms.

Lieutenant-Colonel George H.F. Berkeley, Assistant-Adjutant-General (35th of Foot)

British expedition to the Netherlands 1814
Merxem (Netherlands)
January 13th & February 2nd 1814

2/35th part of Major General Mackenzie's Brigade

"London Gazette" Sunday February 13th 1814

Downing Street, February 13, 1814

A DISPATCH, of which the following is a copy, was last night received at Earl Bathurst's Office, addressed to his Lordship by General Sir Thomas Graham, dated Merxem, February 6, 1814.

Head-Quarters, Merxem February 6, 1814

My Lord,

1 SHOULD have been happy to have had to announce to your Lordships that the movement on Antwerp, fixed by General Bulow, for the 2d instant bas produced a greater effect but the want of time, and of the greater means, will account to your Lordship for the disappointment of our hopes of a more satisfactory result; for General Bulow received (after we had got the better of all the great obstacles in the way of taking a position near the town,) orders to proceed to the southward to act in concert with the grand army 5 and the state of the weather, for some time back, not only prevented my receiving the supplies of ordnance and ordnance stores from England, but made it impossible to land much of what was on board the transports near Williamstadt, the ice cutting off all communications with them.

I have, however, sincere pleasure in assuring your Lordship that every part of the service was conducted by the officers at the Head of the different departments, with all the zeal and intelligence possible.

To make up for the want of our own artillery, all the serviceable Dutch mortars, with all the ammunition that could be collected, were prepared at Williamstadt, and on the evening of the 1st, the troops of the first and second divisions, that could be spared from other services, were collected at Braeschat, and next morning this village (fortified with much labour ever since our first attack) was carried in the most gallant style in a which shorter time, and with much less loss than I could have believed possible.

Major-General Gibbs, commanding the 2d Division (in the absence of Major-General McKenzie, confined by a dangerous fall from his horse), ably seconded by Major-General Taylor, and by Lieutenant-Colonel Henries, commanding Major-General Gibbs's brigade, conducted this attack, in which all the troops engaged behaved with the usual spirit and intrepidity of British soldiers.

I feel particularly indebted to the officers already named, and also to Lieutenant-Colonel Cameron, commanding the detachments of the three battalions of the 95th; to Lieutenant-Colonel Hompesch with the 25th regiment to Major A. Kelly; with the 54th to Lieutenant-Colonel Brown with the 56th and Major Kelly with the 73d; for the distinguished manner in which those corps attacked the left and centre of the village, forcing the enemy from every strong hold, and storming the mill-battery on Ferdinand's-Dyke while Major-General Taylor with the 52d, under Lieutenant-Colonel Gibbs, the 35th, under Major Macalister, and the 78th, under Lieutenant-Colonel Lindsay, marching to the right, and directly on the mill of Ferdinand's-Dyke, threatened the enemy's communication from Merxem towards Antwerp.

Two pieces of camion and a considerable number of prisoners fell into our hands. No time was lost in marking out the batteries, which by the very great exertions of. the artillery, under Lieutenant-Colonel Sir G. Wood, and the engineers, under Lieutenant-Colonel Carmichael Smyth, and the good-will of the working parties, were completed by half-past three, P.M. of the 3d. The batteries, as per margin opened at that hour. During the short trial of the fire that evening, the defective, state of the Williamstadt mortars and ammunition was too visible. Our means were thus diminished, and much time was lost, as it was not till twelve, at noon, the following day (the 4th) that the fire could be opened again.

That day's fire disabled five of the six 24 pounders. Yesterday the fire was kept up all day as per margin. The practice was admirable, but there was not a sufficient number of shells falling to prevent the enemy from extinguishing fire whenever it broke out among the ships, and our fire ceased, entirely at sunset yesterday. It is impossible for me to speak too highly of the Indefatigable exertions of the two branches of the Ordnance Department.

I have much reason to be satisfied with the steadiness of the troops, and the attention of the Officers of all ranks, during the continuance of this service. Detachments of the rifle corps did the most advanced duty, under the able direction of Lieut-Col. Cameron, in a way that gave security to the batteries on Ferdinand's Dyke, and though this line was enfiladed, and every part of the village under the range of shot and shells from the enemy, I am happy to say the casualties, on the whole have not been numerous. As soon as everything is cleared away, we shall move back into such cantonments as I have concerted with General Bulow. I cannot conclude this dispatch without expressing my admiration of the manner in which General Bulow formed the disposition of the movement and supported this attack. The enemy were in great force on the Deurne and Berchem Roads, but were everywhere driven by the gallant Prussians, though not without considerable loss.

I have, &c.
(Signed) THOMAS GRAHAM

Abstract Return of Killed, Wounded, and Missing of the Army under the Command of His Excellency General Sir Thomas Graham, K.B. in the Attack upon the Village of Merxem, on the Morning of the 2nd February 1814.

2nd Batt. 35th Foot Lieutenant Thomas Austin, severely (lost left leg below the knee).
He saved William (later William IV) Duke of Clarence from being captured.

Capture of Paxos 14th February

A detachment of 1/35th onboard H.M.S. Apollo assist at the capture of Paxos.

"London Gazette" Tuesday April 19th 1814

Admiralty-Office, April 19, 1814.
Copy of a Letter from the late Captain Taylor, of His Majesty's Ship Apollo, addressed to Rear-Admiral Fremantle and transmitted by, Rear-Admiral Sir Jehu Gore to John Wilson Croker, Esq.

His Majesty's Ship Apollo, Channel of Corfu, February 16, 1814.
Sir, IT blowing very hard from the northward on the 6th, I took the opportunity of running to Xante to propose measures for commencing hostilities against Corfu, and as a preliminary, to take the island of Paxo. His Excellency Lieutenant-General Campbell readily came into my views, and gave me a carte blanche for all the troops which could be spared from St. Maura, with a few of the 2d Greek light infantry from Cephalonia, and placed these forces under Lieutenant-Colonel Church, of the latter corps. On the I3th we landed under the lee of the island, in a hard southerly gale, and rain, with the above Greeks, a party of seamen, and marines, of the Apollo, a detachment of the 35th regiment, and of the Royal Corsican Rangers, making the whole one hundred and sixty men. The movements of the troops, under Lieutenant-Colonel Church, through the length of this rugged island, were so rapid, that we gave the enemy barely tune to prepare for resistance, and in consequence of their confusion, succeeded without filing even one musket. The force of the enemy were one hundred and twenty-two men (without the militia), and an enclosed fort of three guns, well calculated for a defence against a surprise, being upon an elevated island, which forms the harbour.
I have the honour to be, &c.
(Signed) R. VF. TAYLOR,
To Thomas Fremantle, Esq. Admiral of the White

Siege of Bergen-op-Zoom
March 8th

British attempt to take Bergen-Op-Zoom, but it is a disaster, 2/35th covers the British retreat.

With the Austrian Campaign in Trieste and Apennines

Capture of Parga in Greece
March 22nd

At the siege of Ragusa, the 1/35th were part of the unused reinforcements. Hoste's "Bacannte" sailed with a detachment of the 1/35th of Foot to Trieste then on to Parga, where upon her arrival the French garrison surrendered and Hoste took possession of the town.

"London Gazette" Tuesday April 19th 1814

Horse-Guards, March 28, 1814

The Prince Regent has been graciously pleased, in the name and on the behalf of His Majesty, to command, that, in commemoration of the brilliant victory obtained over the enemy by the army under the orders of the Marquess of Wellington in the battle of Vittoria on the 21st of June 1813, the undermentioned Officers, present upon that memorable occasion, shall enjoy the privilege of bearing Badges of distinction, In conformity to the regulations published on the 7th of October last, viz:

Battle of Vittoria

Gold Medal

Lieutenant-Colonel George F. H. Berkeley, Assistant-Adjutant-General (35th of Foot)

"London Gazette" Tuesday September 13th 1814

Horse-Guards, June 1, 1814.

The Prince Regent has been graciously pleased, in the name and on the behalf of His Majesty, to command, that, in consideration of the distinguished services of the troops engaged in the battles in the Pyrenees, from the 28th July to the 2d of August 1813; of the Nivelle, on the 10th of November 1813; and at the siege and capture of St Sebastian, in August and September 1813, the undermentioned Officers present upon those memorable occasions, shall enjoy the privilege of bearing badges of distinction, in conformity to the regulation published on the 7th of October last, viz:

Siege and capture of St. Sebastian

Gold Medal

Lieutenant-Colonel George H.F. Berkeley, Assistant-Adjutant-General (35th of Foot)

The Prince Regent has also been pleased to command, in the name and on the behalf of His Majesty, that the following Officers who were present in the former battles and sieges in the Peninsula, shall receive appropriate badges in commemoration of their services upon those occasions, viz.

Battle of Busaco

Gold Medal

Lieutenant-Colonel George H.F. Berkeley, Assistant-Adjutant-General (35th of Foot)

Battle of Fuentes de Onor

Gold Medal

Lieutenant-Colonel George H.F. Berkeley, Assistant-Adjutant-General (35th of Foot)
Captain Thomas Weare, A.D.C. to Sir John Oswald, was awarded three clasps to his Military General Service Medal (Silver Medal). (Vittoria, St. Sebastian and Nivelle.)

1814-1815

Gold Medal

From the Emperor of Austria for his service with Austrian Army 1813/14 in the Adriatic.

Maj. John Henry Slessor, 1/35th Regiment of Foot

"London Gazette" Wednesday January 4th 1815

Whitehall, January 2, 1815

His Royal Highness the Prince Regent, acting in the name and on the behalf of His Majesty, has been graciously pleased to appoint and nominate the undermentioned Officers of His Majesty's Naval and Military Forces, to be Knights Commanders of the Most Honourable Military Order of the Bath, viz.

K.C.B.

Lieutenant-Colonel George Henry Frederick Berkeley, 35th Regiment of Foot

"London Gazette" Tuesday February 24th 1815

Whitehall, February 23, 1815

Fourth Class St. Wladimir

His Royal Highness the Prince Regent has been pleased, in the name and on the behalf of His Majesty, to give and grant unto Captain Henry George Macleod, of the 35th Regiment of Foot (late a Lieutenant in the Royal Regiment of Artillery), His Majesty's royal licence and permission, that he may accept and wear the insignia of. the Imperial Russian Order of St. Wladimir, of the fourth class, with which, the Emperor of Russia hath been pleased to honour him, in testimony of His Imperial Majesty's approbation, of the distinguished services rendered by the said Captain Macleod during the siege of Danzig provided nevertheless, that His Majesty's said licence and permission doth not authorise, and shall not be deemed or construed to authorise, the assumption or any style, appellation, rank, precedence, or privilege appertaining unto a Knight Bachelor these realms: And His Royal Highness hath been further pleased to command, that the said royal concession and declaration be registered, together with the relative documents, in His Majesty's College of Arms.

Battle of Waterloo (United Kingdom of the Netherlands)
Sunday June 18th 1815

2/35th in reserve brigade on the road between Brainc-le-Comte and Hal.

"London Gazette" Tuesday June 22nd 1815

General Staff

Lieutenant-Colonel Sir G.H.F. Berkeley, K.C.B. 35th Foot, A. A. G. (severely wounded)

Assault and taking of Cambray
June 24th 1815

"London Gazette" Saturday July 8th 1815

June 6, 1815

My Lord,

LIEUTENANT-COLONEL Sir N. Campbell (Major of 54th regiment) having asked my leave to go to head-quarters to request your Grace's permission to return to England, I beg leave to take the opportunity of mentioning, that I feel much obliged to him for his conduct in closing, in the town of Cambray with, the light companies of M. General Johnson's brigade, and, in leading one of the columns of attack. The one which he commanded escaladed, at the angle formed (on our right side) by the Valenciennes gateway, and the curtine of the body of the place.

A second, commanded by Colonel Sir William. Douglas, of the 91st regiment, and directed by Lieutenant Gilbert, Royal Engineers, took advantage of the reduced height in that part of the escarpe (which, on an average, is on that side about fifty-five feet) by placing their ladders on a covered communication from this place, to a large ravelin near the Amiens road.

The Valenciennes gate was broken open by Sir N. Campbell, and draw bridges let down in about half an hour, when on entering the town, I found that the attack made by Colonel Mitchell's brigade,, on the side of the Paris gate had also succeeded the one directed by Captain Sharpe, Royal Engineers, forced the outer gates of the Corre Port in the Horn work and passed both ditches, by means of the rails of the draw bridges, which they scrambled over by the side, not being able to force the main gate they escaladed by the breach (the state of which your Grace had observed) in the morning, and before which, although the ditch was said to have twelve feet water, a footing on dry ground was found, by wading through a narrow port in the angle of the gate, within the rampart. I have every reason to be satisfied with the light infantry of the division, who, by their fire, covered the attacks of the parties, of sixty men each, which preceded the column.

The three brigades of artillery of Lieutenant Colonel Webber Smith, and Majors Knott and Browne, under the direction of Lieutenant-Colonel Hawker, made particularly good practice, and immediately silenced the fire of the enemy's artillery, except from two guns on each flank of the citadel, which could not be got at, and two field pieces on the ramparts of the town, above the Valenciennes gate, and which played upon the troops as they debouched from the cover they had been posted in. Twenty prisoners were made at the horn work of the Paris gate, and about an hundred and thirty altogether in the town. Their fire was very slack, and even that, I foresaw, they were forced to, by the garrison of the citadel. I left the 23rd and 91st regiments in town, with two guns and a troop of Ensdorff hussars, and am much indebted to Sir William Douglas and Colonel Dalmer for their assistance in preserving order. Some depredations were committed, but of no consequence, when the circumstances we entered by are considered. From the division as well as my personal staff, I received every assistance in the course of the three days operations.

I am., &c.
(Signed)
CHARLES COLVILLE

Return of Killed, Wounded, and Missing of the Allied Army, under the Command of Field-Marshal His Grace the Duke of Wellington, K.G. and G.C.B. in the Assault and Taking of Cambray, on the 24th June 1815.

35th Foot, 2nd Batt.—1 rank and file killed.

"London Gazette" Saturday September 16th 1815

Whitehall, June 4,
HIS Royal Highness the Prince Regent, acting in the name and on behalf of His Majesty, has been graciously pleased to nominate and appoint the undermentioned Officers, belonging to His Majesty's Naval and Military Forces, to be Companions of the Most Honourable Military Order of the Bath, in conformity with the ordinance relating to the third class of the said Order, as published in the London Gazette of the 2d of January 1815.

C.B.

Lieutenant-Colonel Lorenzo Moore, 35th Regiment of Foot

"London Gazette" Monday September 18th 1815

Basseterre, Guadeloupe August 12th

Extract from dispatch

During the absence of Major-General Douglass, with the line Lieutenant-Colonel Berkeley, Deputy-Adjutant-General, has conducted that department with zeal and ability and has rendered me essential assistance.

I Have the honour to be, &c.
James Leith, Commander of the Forces

"London Gazette" Saturday September 23rd 1815

Paris, August 21, 1815

MY LORD,
I HAVE the honour to enclose a list of Officers upon whom His Imperial Majesty the Emperor of Russia has conferred decorations of different classes of the Orders of St. George, Anne, and Wladimir respectively, in testimony of His Imperial Majesty's approbation of their services and conduct, particularly in the late battles fought in the Netherlands, which I beg your Lordship to lay before His Royal Highness the Prince Regent, and request His Royal Highness's permission for them to accept the same.

I have, &c.
WELLINGTON.

Order of St. Wladimir Fourth Class

Lieutenant-Colonel Sir George H.F. Berkeley, K.C.B. (35th Foot) Assistant Quarter-Master-General

"London Gazette" Tuesday October 31st 1815

Head-Quarters, Paris, October 8, 1815

MY LORD,

I HAVE the honour to enclose a list of Officers upon whom His Majesty the King of the LOW Countries has conferred decorations of different classes of the Wilhelm's Order, in testimony of His Majesty's approbation of their services and conduct, particularly in the late battles fought in the Netherlands, which I beg your Lordship to lay before His Royal Highness the Prince Regent, and request His Royal Highness's permission for them to wear the same.

I have, &c.

WELLINGTON.

Knight Fourth Class Wilhelm's Order (M.W.O.)

Lieutenant-Colonel Sir George H.F. Berkeley, K.C.B. (35th Foot)

"London Gazette" Tuesday April 23rd 1816

Horse- Guards, March 10, 1816.

MEMORANDUM.

The Prince Regent, has been graciously pleased; in the name and on the behalf of His Majesty, to command, that, in commemoration of the brilliant and decisive victory of Waterloo; a medal shall be conferred upon every Officer, Non-Commissioned Officer, and Soldier of the British Army present upon that memorable occasion.
His Royal Highness has further been pleased to command, that the ribband issued with the medal shall never be worn, but with the medal suspended to it.
By command of His Royal Highness the Prince Regent,
FREDERICK, Commander in Chief.

H. Torrens
Maj. Gen. and Mil. Sec.

Waterloo Medal

Berkeley George Henry Frederick Lt-Col. K.C.B.	Assistant-Adjutant-General
Slessor John Maj.	Staff & General Officer Service
MacLeod Henry George Capt.	Deputy-Assistant-Quartermaster-General

2nd Battalion

Lieutenant-Colonel

Macalister Charles

Major

Green William, Wall Charles William.

Captain

Dromgoole Nicholas Fleming, McNeill Thomas, Rawson William, Rutherford Henry.

Lieutenant

Amos J.W., Barnwell Aylmer, Breary Christopher Spencer, Farrant William Broome, Hay John, Heilderbrand John, McDonough Thomas, Middleton H., Murdock Peter, Scarfe Samuel S., Shewell Edward, Stenton Francis, Thoburn Robert, Tomkins Newland Richard, Wilder James, Wilkins George.

Ensign

Hamilton Alexander *Duke*, Hedding William Levitt, Hewetson John, Hilebrand John, Macalister William, Macdonnell Antony Joseph, Potenger Herbert, Rainsforth William, Thomas John, Wyatt John Barwis.

Surgeon

Doyle Charles Simon, M.D.

Assistant Surgeon

Keoghoe William, Purcell James

Quarter Master

Foote Robert

Paymaster

Bury William

Sergeant-Major

Hickman Benjamin

Quarter Master Sergeant

Howe William, Price Jns.

Armoury Sergeant

Burgin William

Sergeant

Bennett George, Benwell William, Brown James William, Burnell Robert, Burt Richard, Castle Thomas, Cooper John, Dann Jns., Hodges William, Kirby John, McLaughlin Farrell, McNally William, Monaghan Peter, Moore Thomas, Phillips William, Smeeton John, Steel Samuel, Summers Frederick, Stockwell Robert, Terrell John, Tully Alexander, Watkins James, Willis Rowland.

Corporal

Baxter James, Brice William, Critchley Thomas, Davis William, Edmunds Charles, Harris Thomas, Hart Connor, Head George, Hoar James, Holder Daniel, Ketchley Joseph, King Merrick, Lamb Richard, Law James, Penny Thomas, Rice Joseph, Sanson Thomas, Smith Robert, Smith Robert, Taylor William, Virge William, Wilson Thomas.

Drummer

Anderson William, Cass Joshua, Clissold Edmund, Davis James, Deammer Thomas, Dix Jns., Down Aaron, Duich Joshua, Edwards John, Graham Nathaniel, Latty John, McDonald Thomas, Osmon John, Shuter John, Smith Samuel, Smith Thomas, Wymark John.

Private

Alder John, Aldridge George, Alexander Jns., Alloway Thomas, Anderson John, Apps Charles Pte., Arnold Jns., Attwood James, Arthur Evan, Austin William, Ayling James, Ayres George, Baglin Charles, Bailey William, Baker William, Ballam Samuel, Barnes Joshua, Barnes Samuel, Barnwell Robert, Barry George, Bartlett Robert, Bassell Charles, Basset Tomas, Bassett Michael, Bastin Jns., Bates John, Bawn Daniel, Bayliss William, Bell John, Bell John, Bennett Jns., Bennion George, Berry George, Berry Joshua, Berry Thomas, Bexall Iram, Birch Stephen, Bird Lawrence, Bith James, Bond Samuel, Bonner Richard, Boulter William, Briant Job, Broadley Jns., Broom George, Broom James, Brown Jns., Brown Luc, Brown Thomas, Brown William, Browning Richard, Bruton Mark, Buckwell James, Bulbeck William, Bull Henry, Burridge Jns., Burrows Thomas, Burt Robert, Bushrod John, Bussey George, Bussey Isaac, Byrnes Patrick, Cadman Jns., Cadman William, Calcutt William, Cannon Matthew, Cardial James, Carmichael Joshua, Cass Henry, Challan Robert, Churcher William, Clarke Jns., Clarke Thomas, Clayton James, Clayton John, Clinch William, Coggin Thomas, Collins Hugh, Collins James, Colurn Joshua, Conner James, Conway Maurice, Cook William, Cooper Robert, Cooper William, Coote Edward, Costello Thomas, Cranfield John, Crawford John, Creaton Patrick, Croom Thomas, Cutchley Peter, Daley Patrick, Damon Samuel, Daniels Henry, Daughty George, Davis Charles, Davis James, Davis James, Davis Jns., Davis Richard, Davis Robert, Davis William, Day James, De France John, De Putron John, Deevey Charles, Denning John, Dewell Humphrey, Dickinson William, Dillon Patrick, Dobson Thomas, Donough George, Dowling Charles, Dowling Jns., Doyle Patrick, Drum Patrick, Dunford Francis, Dunston William, Edmunds John, Eade James, Edwards David, Egan William, Ellford James, Elliott George, Elloway David, Enwright John, Essex Edward, Evan Arthur, Everrett William, Fallon Patrick, Farley James, Farrell Loughlin, Farrell Thomas, Farrell William, Feltham William, Flinn Charles, Fogden William, Ford Francis, Ford George, Frandell Thomas, Frankham Thomas, Fry John, Galline Abraham, Gallop John, Garaythy Bartholomew, Gardner Joshua, Gay James, Geer Joshua, Geer Thomas, Gibbons Thomas, Gifford William, Gillard Richard, Ginn Owen, Glannen Denis, Glannon James, Glover Thomas, Gosling Thomas, Gough James, Grant James, Griffin Henry, Grogan John, Grounsell John, Groves James, Gullick James, Gurney John, Hackett Thomas, Hansford Solomon, Harding John, Harding William, Harris Francis, Harris Richard, Harris Stephen, Hartley William, Harwood Samuel, Hawkins John, Hawthron James, Hayes Cornelius, Hayles John, Heath Robert, Heathcot Robert, Henderson James, Henderson William, Hendon William, Heron John, Hewett John, Hide James, Hill George, Hill Samuel, Hill William, Hills Bascom, Hiscock Anthony, Hiscock John, Hobbs John, Hodges Charles, Hogg John, Holder James, Holder Richard, Holland Samuel, Holloway William, Holt John, Hooley Francis, Huggins Samuel, Hughes James, Hull Jeremiah, Humphries Thomas, Hunt James, Hunt Stephen, Hutchings Henry, Hurry George, Ide

William, Irwin Christopher, Issac William, Ives Henry, Jackson Henry, Jackson Robert, James John, Johnstone James, Jones Charles, Jones Edward, Jones James, Jones Thomas, Jones William, Jones William, Jupp Frederick, Keenan James, Keineham Hugh, Kelly Michael, Kendrick John, Keneway James, Kennedy Barnard, Kennedy Owen, Kennedy Patrick, Kenny Michael, Ketchley Richard, Kinchington Ambrose, King John, Kingston James, Kinsman William, Kitely Thomas, Knowlson Frederick, Knowlton Jasper, Lane Charles, Laneway William, Lawler James, Lawrance Robert, Leavey Hugh, Leavey William, Leech William, Lester James, Lines William, Lloyd William, Long William, Lovedore George, Lovell George, Lower Henry, Lucas Joshua, Lucas Thomas, Maggs Francis, Mallen James, Mangen John, Manning Richard, Mapham Edward, Martin Edmund, Martin Francis, Mason Thomas, Maylerd Matthew, Mayo Thomas, McClean Jacob, McClean John, McCombs John, McCormick Andrew, McCue Timothy, McFadden Edward, McGee Bernard, Meade William, Mealey Francis, Merrett William, Mines James, Mingle Judd, Mitchell Andrew, Mitchell Thomas, Modry William, Molloy Charles, Monaghan Patrick, Monck Joshua, Monck William, Moore William, Moran Thomas, Morgan Joshua, Morgan Stephen, Mulvey William, Murphy Daniel, Murphy John, Murphy Michael, Murphy Patrick, New William, Newbold John, Newman James, Newman John, Nixon George, Nixon James, Oates James, Okey Charles, Oland George, O'Neal James, Orchard Richard, Orham Thomas, Osbourne John, Oxenbridge Edward, Padon John, Page George, Palmer James, Palmer Thomas, Parfitt John, Parson Henry, Patching Thomas, Payne James, Payne John, Payne William, Pearce John, Pegler John, Pelly Thomas, Pennycott Charles, Perkins Arthur, Perkiss Joshua, Phillips Henry, Phillips James, Phillips James, Pittman James, Pollard John, Poole George, Postons James, Poulton Joshua, Powell John, Pratten Isaac, Preston Jacob, Price John, Price William, Prideaux John, Prignell Abraham, Pritchard John, Pritchard William, Pritchard William, Punchon Robert, Quinn Henry, Quinn James, Quinn William, Renfield Henry, Rhodes David, Ridler George, Ripley George, Ritchings William, Roach John, Roberts Peter, Rogers Timothy, Ronde Joshua, Rosser Robert, Rumble John, Rumery William, Russell Thomas, Samways John, Sandell Thomas, Sandle Steven, Scott Alexander, Seabright John, Seary Brian, Sertin John, Sheevin Patrick, Sheppard William, Sherwood Thomas, Short Solomon, Sibley Daniel, Simes Charles, Simpson John, Smith Samuel, Smith William, Smith William, Sparrow William, Spence Thomas, Spittle Amos, Squires William, Stagg William, Staples Joshua, Steer John, Stevens Daniel, Stevens Joshua, Stocker Richard, Stockwell Samuel, Straw John, Sturt Thomas, Summers Thomas, Swift John, Sworn Samuel, Talbut Stephen, Tasker Daniel, Thomas Benjamin, Thomas Charles, Thomas Joshua, Thomas Nathaniel, Thomas William, Thompson John, Tick William, Tindall John, Tippen Edward, Travers John, Trim John, Trimm Thomas, Trower James, Tune John, Turner John, Turner John, Turner William, Turner William, Tyrrell Patrick, Underwood Thomas, Veale Henry, Vetch Charles, Waldridge Thomas, Walters John, Walton Henry, Ward George, Warner Thomas, Warton Solomon, Watkins William, Weare Samuel, Webb George, Webb John, Webley Robert, Wellbeloved George, Wells John, West John, West Peter, Westrip Thomas, White Matthew, Whitear James, Wickham George, Wicks James, Williams John, Willis Charles, Willoughby George, Wills John, Wilson James, Wilson John, Winders George, Wood William, Woods Charles, Woods John, Workman John, Worrall William, Wrenn William, Wyatt Charles.

"London Gazette" Saturday June 14th 1817

Kt.

Carlton-House, May 29, 1817

His Royal Highness the. Prince Regent was this day pleased, in the name and on the behalf of His Majesty, to confer the honour of Knighthood on Major-General Francis John Wilder.

"London Gazette" Friday June 15th 1832

His Majesty has been graciously pleased to direct that the 35th Regiment of Foot, shall be permitted to bear the appellation of Royal, and be in future styled the 35th or Royal Sussex Regiment; and that the facings be accordingly changed from orange to blue.

1834

K.C.H.

Military Knight Commander of the Royal Hanoverian Guelphic Order

Major-General Lorenzo Moore

"London Gazette" Friday March 21st 1834

St. James' Palace, March 19, 1834

Kt.

The King was this day pleased to confer the honour of Knighthood upon Major-General Lorenzo Moore, Companion of the Most Honourable Military Order of the Bath, and Military Knight Commander of the Royal Hanoverian Guelphic Order.

Londonderry Sentinel Monday 21st July 1834

The 35th (Royal Sussex) Regiment on Monday 21st July the highly interesting ceremony of presenting colours to this highly distinguished corps took place in the quadrangle of the Royal Hibernian Military School. Shortly after four, the gallant Colonel of the 35th, Lieutenant-General Sir John Oswald G.C.B. appeared in front of the line – the troops formed into hollow squares, and the ceremony was proceeded with. The Lieutenant-General commanding and Lady Vivian; and the Commandant of the garrison and Lady Blakeney, with several other personages of distinction, occupied the centre of the square. The honour of presenting the new colours was committed to the fair hands of Lady Vivian. The new colours were now brought out, and a trophy of arms formed with the drums, &c. Of the regiment – the colours resting upon them. After a suitable prayer by the Chaplain of the garrison, the Ensign advanced to where

Lady Vivian stood: they were taken by the Majors, Semple and Buller, and her Ladyship pronounced a handsome address in delivering the colours to the regiment. Sir John Oswald addressed the officers and men of the regiment at great length, and with all the fervour and eloquence of a veteran who had passed through most of the trying dangers to which the regiment had been subjected in the performance of their duty to their King and Country. In your name (said Sir John) I cannot but express the gratitude we feel for the honour conferred upon us by our most gracious Monarch in giving us the denomination we now bear – "The Royal Sussex Regiment" and changing the colour of our facings (lately altered from orange to blue) and that of one of our standards. I trust the blue flag, which William the Fourth has bestowed upon us, will be followed by you with the same zeal the same credit and honour, as the orange one bestowed on us by William the Third. It is customary (said the gallant Colonel) upon such an occasion as this to recite some portion of the history of the corps upon which such an honour is conferred. The formation of the 35th regiment dates from an epoch in the history of this country. Lord Donegall (the third Earl of that name I believe) served at a time which I hope Ireland is destined never more to see, when this lovely island was desolated with civil war, and its fertile plains deluged with blood, - Lord Donegall, an ardent and brave officer served in the time of William the Third, and he brought this, as the Belfast Regiment over to Britain, fully equipped and ready for the field, without obtaining a single penny from the public purse. The regiment is early found embarked in the expedition under the Duke of Ormond, to co-operate with a naval force under Admiral Rooke, for the reduction of Cadiz. The regiment was then for a while under the gallant Earl of Peterborough, and was the foremost at the storming of Barcelona. At this successful attack the brave Donegall saved the regiment at the expense of his own life. Charles the Seventh, who was at that time King of Spain, was so sensible of the virtues and valour of the ill-fated Earl, that he wrote to Queen Anne, recommending this regiment in the strongest terms to her warmest protection, as well as the family of so worthy a gentleman as the brave Donegall, and that she place all the marks of favour and acknowledgement which her Majesty might bestow on the family and the regiment to his own account. Sir John continued to give an animated history of the regiment in more modern times, down to the field of Waterloo, in which the second battalion took a part. Upwards of 400 of the nobility and gentry afterwards partook of a splendid banquet, prepared for them on this splendid occasion.

A copy of King Charles' letter was printed in the Belfast News-Letter August 13th 1831. A copy of the page is held at West Sussex Record Office.

1836

K.H.

Knight of the Royal Hanoverian Guelphic Order

Lieutenant-Colonel Henry George Macleod

Lieutenant-Colonel George Weare

1837

K.H.

Knight of the Royal Hanoverian Guelphic Order

Major James Jocelyn Anderson
Major William Green
Lieutenant-Colonel John Leslie

1857

Burma

Shoay-Gyeen

Whilst skirmishing with the rebel Kerens during the month of January.

22nd Serjeant H. McAusland and 1 private killed and 3 wounded

25th Lt. Mars Mourier Pohle and 5 privates wounded and 2 privates killed

Indian Mutiny
10 May 1857 – 1 November 1858

"London Gazette" Wednesday May 19th 1858

Nominal Return of Staff Officers of Her Majesty's Service, Killed and Wounded in action during the operations before Lucknow, from 2nd to 21st March 1858, inclusive.

Head-Quarters, Camp, before Lucknow, March 28, 1858.

2nd Infantry Division

Captain Robert Crosse Stewart, 35th Foot, Deputy Assistant Adjutant-General, severely wounded.

"London Gazette" Tuesday August 3rd 1858

NOMINAL LIST of Casualties in Action at Jugderpore, on the 23rd April 1858
Head-Quarters, Camp, Futtyghur, June 1, 1858

35th Regiment of Foot

Rank and Names killed

Captain Arthur John Le Grand
Lieutenant William Glynne Massey

Assistant-Surgeon William George Clarke
1527 Colour-Serjeant Richard Bush
360 Colour-Serjeant William Russell
287 Serjeant William Britton,
2490 Serjeant William Johnson,
2352 Serjeant Thomas Morton,
2228 Corporal George Barnes,
1956 Corporal William Barrett,
2007 Corporal David Heard,
303 Private Charles Ancell, 1781 Private Henry Atkins, 1 Private Joseph Banks, 149 Private Henry Bew, 2985 Private William Boxall, 138 Private James Bowker, 217 Private William Breakle, 2335 Private William Burbridge, 2929 Private James Carey, 275 Private Frederick Carter, 280 Private Peter Cassidy, 80 Private Robert Cassidy, 294 Private Abraham Clegg, 170 Private Thomas Connor, 362 Private Daniel Connor, 1496 Private William Cook, 2047 Private Patrick Cronan, 2807 Private James Cross, 349 Private William Dighan, 109 Private James Dooley, 392 Private Patrick Eigo, 2931 Private William Ekid, 332 Private Richard Fields, 227 Private John Francis, 2627 Private Samuel Frost, 169 Private Peter Gallagher, 131 Private Joseph King George, 357 Private James Gibbons, 391 Private Andrew Gilmore, 186 Private Henry Godfrey, 2806 Private John Goodall, 156 Private John Gouldthorpe, 120 Private Thomas Griffiths, 2988 Private James Gumbrell, 229 Private Samuel Hannah,136 Private William Hardman, 97 Private James Hargreaves, 317 Private Daniel Hayes, 402 Private John Hayes, 119 Private William Hill, 2782 Private John Hills, 17 Private Arthur Horsley, 315 Private Thomas Howe, 230 Private Robert Hughes, 263 Private William Humphrey, 300 Private William Hutchins, 215 Private William Iddon, 2989 Private William Irvine, 2614 Private George Johnston, 232 Private James Johnston, 341 Private William Johnston, 222 Private John Jones, 337 Private Benjamin Jubb, 182 Private Peter Kelly, 155 Private John Kinchella, 100 Private James Lake, 144 Private William Lomax, 210 Private John Malady, 345 Private Archibald McLean, 377 Private John McNeill, 241 Private John McNolty, 98 Private Samuel McQuade, 2905 Private James McTagert, 4 Private Andrew Miller, 236 Private Patrick Monaghan, 381 Private John Mooney, 2686 Private William Moynihan, 147 Private Thomas Mudge, 2154 Private Patrick Murphy, 1908 Private William Murphy, 257 Private Thomas Murray, 31 Private James Nolan, 742 Private John Pattinson, 353 Private William Penny, 1836 Private George Poole, 255 Private Samuel Potter, 2608 Private Henry Pratt, 304 Private Philip Reilly, 312 Private George Rippon, 285 Private Thomas Roberts, 336 Private Charles Scruby, 2884 Private Ambrose Serjeant, 351 Private Robert Skinner, 2764 Private John Smith, 348 Private George Spence, ?2041 Private George Spicer, 2056 Private John Taylor, 347 Private William Taylor, 302 Private John Underwood, 142 Private John Vaughey, 2994 Private Thomas Watson, 184 Private William Wilson, 87 Private John Wooding.

"London Gazette" Tuesday August 10th 1858

Brigadier-General Sir Edward Lugard, K.C.B., Commanding Azimghur Field Force, to the Chief of the Staff.
Camp, Judgespore, May 10th 1858.

Extract
On the 7th I moved from Arrah by the railroad to Beheea, with the force as per margin, leaving my heavy baggage, sick, &c., behind, with eight Infantry and 145 dismounted Sikh Cavalry for their protection, in addition to the party of the 35th Foot and Naval Brigade already holding the entrenched position, and taking nothing but provisions and tents, which in this season are absolutely necessary for the protection of the lives of Europeans, many having already fallen a sacrifice to coup-de-soleil.

From 10 May 1857 to 1 November 1858

Indian Mutiny Medal

Lt.-Colonel

Hutchinson Edward Hely

Captain

Blythe Samuel Fritche
Harris John
Lee Ranulph Charles
Le Grand Arthur J.
Morton M. Villiers Sankey
Stewart Robert Crosse
Tisdall Archibald

Lieutenant & Adjutant

Ross Robert Hill

Lieutenant

Davis John
Ford Alfred John
Massey William Glynne
Parsons Richard
Payne William Henry Bayly
Revell Albert John
Ross Richard
Triman Richard
Troup Robert Henry Williamson

Ensign

Dillon Timothy John

Surgeon

Chambers John Walker

Assistant Surgeon

Clark William George
Patterson Leslie Ogilby
Thisleton Edward

Sergeant-Major

1657 Bolger Patrick

Quartermaster Sergeant

2627 Palmer William

Colour Sergeant

1527 Bush Richard
1427 Hadden George
2305 Ham William
1859 Hemons Joseph
2458 Hoey Michael
1311 Moody Thomas
2133 Murphy Jeremiah
1360 Russell William

Hospital Sergeant

1220 Ryan Thomas S.

Sergeant

287 Britton William
2841 Dillon Arthur C.
2578 Drake Thomas
2187 Fulcher Arthur
Fulter Thomas
1929 Hart Richard
1626 Hutchinson James
2490 Johnston William
355 McArthur William
2352 Morton Thomas
1766 Parker George
2300 Rowley James
2447 Ruxton George
394 Sandwell William
2367 Sharpe William
1854 Simpson Richard
2389 Trill Jesse
2809 Yarrow Thomas

Corporal

492 Barnes George
1956 Barrett William
1634 Boyle James
1723 Burgess Charles
2128 Butler Matthew
2683 Butler Thomas
86 Derham John
Dewhurst Edmond
307 Ford George
2388 Foster Arthur
2007 Heard David
2572 Heffernan John
240 Higgins Alfred
2117 Martyn Henry
2207 Monaghan James
2208 Moynihan Jeremiah
292 Pittaway Charles

1659 Powell William
2477 Regan Daniel
2732 Simms John
2961 Walton Henry
114 West Francis
1529 West Thomas

Drummer

2529 Bromley George
1577 Bridger Edward
2488 Campbell John
Fitzgerald Patrick
2000 Matson John
91 Twohey Thomas

Private

368 Adams William John, 303 Ancell Charles, 2515 Ansley John, 2416 Askins Edward, 1781 Atkins Henry, 2820 Baker James, 1 Banks Joseph, 1754 Baylis Charles, 2768 Beasley James, 2980 Beatty John, 1542 Beddell Henry, 356 Bell Robert, 374 Berry Henry, 2897 Berry William, 2895 Best William, 149 Bew Henry, 2040 Bowden Edmond, 138 Bowker James, 2826 Boxall Job, 2985 Boxall William, 2498 Bradley Henry, 99 Brady John, 2789 Braidon William, 207 Bratton John, 217 Breakle William, 663 Brooks Henry, 1926 Broomwich Charles, 1608 Brown Charles, 2890 Brown Charles, 2714 Brownlee David, 451 Bryce Robert, 2335 Burbridge William, 2845 Burfoot Richard, 367 Burns Thomas, 3006 Burrage Peter, 2030 Burt Charles, 40 Byrne John, 2825 Byrne Patrick, 473 Cain David, 502 Campbell David, 2762 Carey John, 275 Carter Frederick, 280 Cassidy Peter, 80 Cassidy Robert, Chambers Samuel, 479 Chapman David, 2001 China William, 335 Clark James, 288 Clarke James, 294 Clegg Abraham, 2414 Clelland James, 2830 Cocks Charles, Cocker James, 106 Coe James, 258 Coleman John, 2445 Collier Bernard, 164 Collier Joseph, 271 Collins Eli, 360 Collum John, 2931 Comely George, 2126 Condon David, 2182 Connell Jeremiah, 2794 Connolly Robert, 2973 Connolly Thomas, 2155 Connor Thady, 362 Connor Daniel, 170 Connor Thomas, 1496 Cook William, 209 Corny Bartholomew, 2904 Corrigan Richard, 411 Craig James, 2047 Cronan Patrick, 2807 Cross James, 2692 Crossman Reuben, 295 Crotty John, 2689 Crum James, 2892 Crum William, 60 Cummings John, 68 Cummisky James, 2738 Cutmore William, 1974 Dadds John, 2907 Daniel Richard, 1418 Darcey Thomas, 2511 Dart William, 1645 Davenport Thomas, 140 Dawes James, 950 Dawson Robert, 48 Dayes Alfred, 2996 Deall Frederick, 2137 Dennehy Bartholomew, 3010 Diamond John, 2035 Dibbin John, 349 Dighan William, 220 Dillon Patrick, 494 Dival Frederick, 2722 Dobbin Charles, 2559 Donaghy Thomas, 8 Donovan Timothy, 109 Dooley James, 207 Doran Patrick, Dougherty Edward, 482 Elphick Levi, 376 Doyle Bartholomew, 276 Duffy James, 112 Dyer Henry, 1789 Dyer William, 267 Eatough John, 428 Eatough Miles, 2984 Edwards Charles, 392 Eigo Patrick, 2931 Ekid William, 2847 Elcom James, 2797 Emmens Charles, 2967 Evans William, 330 Eyton William, 2799 Farley George, 29 Farrell Patrick, 159 Farrell Patrick, 2475 Fawcett William, 458 Featherstone Thomas, 332 Fields Richard, 487 Findlay John, 2894 Finlayson Thomas, 41 Fitzgerald John, 456 Fitzsimmons John, 2507 Fleming Patrick, 1935 Flynn Richard, 2705 Ford Timothy, 2850 Foster John, 227 Francis John, 2481 Franklin John, 2839 French George, 2627 Frost Samuel, 2885 Fry Thomas, 1661 Gallagher Patrick, Garrett James, 2723 Garrity Patrick, 3000 Garvey James, 131 George Joseph King, 357 Gibbons James, 391 Gilmore Andrew, 2232 Goddard Arthur, 186 Godfrey Henry, 2781 Godwin Henry, 2806 Goodhall John, 156 Gouldthorpe John, 2987 Gower William, 282 Graeme James, 437 Graham James, 69 Graham John, 2868 Green Cornelius, 120 Griffiths Thomas, 1443 Guile George, 2988 Gumbrell James, 2708 Haber James, 266 Hamilton James, 229 Hannah Samuel, 136 Hardman William, 433 Hardy David, 97 Hargreaves James, 124 Harling John, Harman John, Harmer John, 2210 Harrington Andrew, 2046 Harrington George, 2046 Harris George, 2952 Harris William, 498 Harrison William, 501 Harrison William, 317 Hayes Daniel, 402 Hayes John, 262 Hembrow John, 2378 Henderson David, 2753 Henderson James, 28 Herne Peter, 2685 Herriott Henry, 67 Hill James, 298

Hill James, 119 Hill William, 2782 Hills John, 473 Hitchcock Henry, 416 Hogg John, 338 Holden George, 2772 Holder Frederick, 141 Hool Thomas, 176 Horan James, 17 Hosley Arthur, 2032 Hosely William, 2824 Houghton James, 315 Howe Thomas, 1424 Hubbard James, 230 Hughes Robert, 439 Hughes William, 3001 Humphries James, 263 Humphrey William, 2351 Hunter Charles, 255 Huntley George, 2177 Hurley Daniel, 300 Hutchins William, 215 Iddon William, Iliff John, 2989 Irvine William, 1687 Jamieson William, Johns William, 2614 Johnston George, 2974 Johnston George, 232 Johnston James, 341 Johnston William, 2864 Jones George, 222 Jones John, 1130 Jones John, 1674 Jones William, 2954 Jordan Daniel, 337 Jubb Benjamin, 174 Kavanagh Matthew, 358 Kelly Isaac, 2720 Kelly John, 182 Kelly Peter, 737 Kemp Joseph, 2875 Ketchell Richard, 2452 Kilbride Denis, 2941 Killchrist James, 155 Kinchella John, 175 King George, 319 Knight Edward, 100 Lake James, 1365 Lavender Thomas, 2108 Leary Daniel, 496 Ledward Charles, 265 Lee Hugh, 386 Leeman Simon, 3003 Leonard William, 1345 Lewis Joseph, 2946 Lloyd Owen, 2124 Locker William, 144 Lomax William, 436 Long John, 20 Loughlin Patrick, 2700 Luff William, 2659 Lyons John, 2740 Madden John, 24 Madden Matthew, 2101 Mahoney Michael, 326 Mahoney William, 210 Malady John, 1849 Manning Thomas, 333 Mantle Nathan, 2746 Marshall John, 440 Martin George, 2000 Matson John, 49 Matthews George, 290 McAlston Robert, 2337 McAndrews John, 2639 McArthur Duncan, 167 McBlane Robert, 443 McBride Michael, 193 McCall Peter, 272 McClelland James, 467 McDermott John, 2925 McDermott Owen, 111 McDonald George, 168 McDonnough Michael, 442 McEvoy John, 22 McEvoy Thomas, 468 McGonigle William, 2439 McGovern Robert S., 2993 McIntyre John, 421 McKay George, 395 McKean Miles, 2387 McKenna John, 2374 McKnight John, 345 McLean Alexander, 345 McLean Archibald, 409 McLeod James, 364 McLoughlin John, 2223 McManaman James, 2631 McManaman John, 2981 McMullen Thomas, 3211 McNamara James, 377 McNeill John, 241 McNolty John, 2798 McPherson Alexander, 235 McPhillips Thomas, 98 McQuade Samuel, 2631 McQuain Michael, 2905 McTagert James, 2842 McWilliams James, Meehan Arthur, 3004 Meehan Thomas, 3065 Meehan William, 4 Miller Andrew, 361 Minnock John, 1735 Misem John, 462 Mitchell Allen, 2963 Molyneaux James, 190 Monaghan Patrick, 236 Monaghan Patrick, 770 Monaghan Peter, 2408 Moodie Alexander, 381 Mooney John, 42 Moore Edward, 189 Moore Michael, 43 Moran Thomas, 2686 Moynihan William, 2176 Moyston George, 147 Mudge Thomas, 2195 Murdock Richard, 2514 Murphy Patrick, 44 Murphy William, 1908 Murphy William, 257 Murray Thomas, 2455 Murray Thomas, 1961 Myles John, 76 Niblett Charles, Nicholl Jabeth, 385 Nichols John, 31 Nolan James, 396 Oaten Edwin, 2667 O'Brien William, 238 O'Keefe Patrick, Osborne James, 1715 Palmer James, 2671 Parish John, Parker Charles, 293 Parker John, 1095 Parker William, 81 Parkhouse Samuel, 226 Pate Henry, 742 Pattison John, 1719 Penn Joseph, 353 Penny William,1836 Poole George, 255 Potter Samuel, 2608 Pratt Henry, 2606 Presley William, 480 Prince Robert, 122 Prince William, 2927 Properjohn Charles J., 2139 Purtell Simon, 205 Quinn Arthur, 1844 Quinn Edward, 393 Quinn John R., 2933 Radway Joseph, 2582 Ramsay Joseph, 2728 Rawlings Thomas, 2667 Rayner Henry, 248 Reeves Richard, 2595 Reid James, 304 Reilly Philip, 500 Rhodes William, 484 Richards Edward, 2425 Richards Edward, Rider Richard, Rielly Thomas, 2649 Ring Michael, 312 Rippon George, 1955 Rivers John, 19 Roach John, 285 Roberts Thomas, 299 Robertson Thomas, 286 Robinson Hugh, 102 Robinson Thomas, Rocheford Patrick, 2643 Rodde Henry C., 2663 Ross John B., 1220 Ryan John, 243 Ryan Patrick, 2418 Saul Jeremiah, 154 Scott Edward, 336 Scruby Charles, 160 Seddon Samuel, 2884 Serjeant Ambrose, 620 Sharrock Thomas, 2924 Shea Michael, 2136 Shoebridge Samuel, 2732 Simms John, 2758 Simms William, 243 Simpson Thomas, 351 Skinner Robert, 2764 Smith John, 180 Smith Thomas, 283 Smith Thomas, 204 Smith William, 348 Spence George, 429 Spencer William, 2041 Spicer Edward, 1560 Spratt Samuel, 2058 Stack James, 508 Standing Thomas, 2715 Steere Alfred, 465 Stone George, 60 Stowe Richard, 9 Strawbridge John, 2779 Sullivan John, 1709 Sullivan William, 2698 Sully George, 171 Suthers Israel, 2325 Sutton Joseph, 2068 Sweeny Bernard, 2056 Taylor John, Taylor Joseph, 2859 Taylor Joseph, 444 Taylor Peter, 113 Taylor Richard, 347 Taylor William, 414 Teather Charles George, 2969 Tester James, 2410 Thompson William, 2812 Thumbwood James, Timmins John, 2912 Torney Peter, 2537 Traut Richard, 2755 Trood Edward, 3009 Tunney Henry, 2778 Turner James, 302 Underwood John, 142 Vaughey John, 115 Waite John, 46 Waldie George, 53 Walsh John, 2811 Watson Charles, 2994 Watson Thomas, 183 Webb Richard, 417 Webb William, 2508 Weily Michael, 1139 Weller William, 239 West Charles, 2374 Williams John, 495 Williams Reuben, 2487 Wilson David, 153 Wilson George, 184 Wilson William, 87 Wooding John, 116 Woolfe Benjamin, 2713 Wren William, 72 Wright Charles.

"London Gazette" **Tuesday May 17th 1859**

War-Office, May 16, 1859

THE Queen has been graciously pleased to make and ordain a Special Statute of the Most Honourable Order of the Bath, authorising the following appointments to the said Order :
To be Extra Members of the Military Division of the Third Class, or Companions ; viz.:

C.B.

Lieutenant-Colonel John McNeill Walter, 35th Regiment of Foot

K.C.B.

Berkeley G.H.F. Lt-Col., K.T.S.

Kt.

Moore L. Maj-Gen., K.C.H.
Wilder F.J. Maj-Gen.

C.B.

McNeill J.C. Col., V.C.,C.M.G.
Moore L. Lt-Col.
Walter J.McN. Lt-Col.

K.C.H.

Moore L. Maj-Gen.

K.H.

Anderson J.J. Maj.
Green W. Maj.
Leslie J. Lt-Col.
Macleod H.G. Lt-Col.
Weare T. Lt-Col.

K.T.S.

Berkeley G.H.F. Lt-Col., K.C.B.

M.W.O. (Knight Fourth Class Wilhelm's Order, Netherlands)

Berkeley G.H.F. Lt-Col., K.C.B.,K.T.S.

Order of St. Wladimir Fourth Class (Russia)

Berkeley G.H.F. Lt-Col., K.C.B.,K.T.S.
Macleod H.G. Capt., K.H.

GOLD CROSS

Berkeley G.H.F. Lt-Col.

Gold Medal (Maida)

Robertson G.D. Maj.

Gold Medal (Busaco)

Berkeley G.H.F. Lt-Col.

Gold Medal (Fuentes de Onor)

Berkeley G.H.F. Lt-Col.

Gold Medal (Badajoz)

Berkeley G.H.F. Lt-Col.

Gold Medal (Salamanca)

Berkeley G.H.F. Lt-Col.

Gold Medal (Vittoria)

Berkeley G.H.F. Lt-Col.

Gold Medal (St. Sebastian)

Berkeley G.H.F. Lt-Col.

Gold Medal (Nive)

Berkeley G.H.F. Lt-Col.

Gold Clasps

Berkeley G.H.F. Lt-Col. (3)

Gold Medal (Austria)

Slessor J.H. Maj.

Military General Service Medal (Silver Medal)

Berkeley G.H.F. Lt-Col.
Weare T. Capt.

Clasp

Berkeley G.H.F. Lt-Col.
Weare T. Capt. (3)

M.I.D.

Berkeley G.H.F. Lt-Col., K.C.B.
McDonald W. Lt.
Slessor J.H. Maj.

Waterloo Medal

See List of 23rd April 1816

Indian Mutiny Medal

See List of 10 May 1857 – 1 November 1858

The Gold Cross replaced the first four Gold Medals, each arm of the Cross showed the action for which the Gold Medal was awarded. Further Gold Medals became Gold Clasps each showed the action for which the medal was awarded and worn on the Ribbon.

Alphabetical Index

Adams W.J. Pte.	10/05/1857-01/11/58
Alder J. Pte.	23/04/1816
Aldridge G. Pte.	23/04/1816
Alexander Jns. Pte.	23/04/1816
Allen R. Lt.	02/06-27/07/1758,31/12/1759
Alloway T. Pte.	23/04/1816
Amos J.W. Lt.	23/04/1816
Anderson J.J. Maj., K.H.	1837
Ancell C. Pte.	10/05/1857-03/08/58
Ansley J. Pte.	10/05/1857-01/11/58
Apps C. Pte.	23/04/1816
Arnold Jns. Pte.	23/04/1816
Arthur G. Capt.	14/18/07/1807,31/08/09
Arthur O. Ens.	27/04/1707
Armstrong T. Ens.	02/06-27/07/1758
Askins E. Pte.	10/05/1857-01/11/58
Atkins H. Pte.	10/05/1857-03/08/58
Arthur E. Pte.	23/04/1816
Austin T. Lt.	13/02/1814
Austin W. Pte.	23/04/1816
Ayling J. Pte.	23/04/1816
Ayres G. Pte.	23/04/1816
Baglin C. Pte.	23/04/1816
Bailey W. Pte.	23/04/1816
Baird W. Capt.	17/06/1775
Baker J. Pte.	10/05/1857-01/11/58
Baker W. Pte.	23/04/1816
Ballam S. Pte.	23/04/1816
Banks J. Lt.	01/12/1776
Banks J. Pte.	10/05/1857-03/08/58
Barnes G. Cpl.	10/05/1857-03/08/58
Barnes J. Pte.	23/04/1816
Barnes S. Pte.	23/04/1816
Barnwell A. Lt.	23/04/1816
Barrett W. Cpl.	10/05/1857-03/08/1858
Barry C.G. Ens.	10/02-10/12/1794
Barry G. Pte.	23/04/1816
Bartlett R. Pte.	23/04/1816
Bassell C. Pte.	23/04/1816
Basset T. Pte.	23/04/1816
Bassett M. Pte.	23/04/1816
Bastin Jns. Pte.	23/04/1816
Bates J. Pte.	23/04/1816
Bawn D. Pte.	23/04/1816
Baxter J. Cpl.	23/04/1816
Bayliss C. Pte.	10/05/1857-01/11/58
Bayliss W. Pte.	23/04/1816
Beasley J. Pte,	10/05/1857-01/11/58
Beatty J. Pte.	10/05/1857-01/11/58
Beddell H. Pte.	10/05/1857-01/11/58
Bell J. Pte.	23/04/1816

Bell J. Pte.	23/04/1816
Bell R. Pte.	10/05/1857-01/11/58
Bennett G. Pte.	23/04/1816
Bennett Jns. Pte.	23/04/1816
Bennion G. Pte.	23/04/1816
Benwell W. Sgt.	23/04/1816
Berkeley G.H.F. Lt-Col. K.C.B.,K.T.S., G/Cross., Gold Medal (7) Clasps (3)., General Service Medal & Clasp., M.W.O.IV Cl., St. W. IV Cl., M.I.D.	16/03-12/04/1812,14/09/13,05/01/13, 19/04/14,28/01/14,13/09/14,14/01/15, 22/06/15,18/09/15,23/09/15,31/10/15, 23/04/16
Berry G. Pte.	23/04/1816
Berry H. Pte.	10/05/1857-01/11/58
Berry J. Pte.	23/04.1816
Berry W. Pte.	10/05/1857-01/11/58
Best W. Pte.	10/05/1857-01/11/58
Bew H. Pte.	10/05/1857-03/08/58
Bexall I. Pte.	23/04/1816
Birch S. Pte.	23/04/1816
Bird L. Pte.	23/04/1816
Bith J. Pte.	23/04/1816
Bliss J.M. Lt.	23/04/1816
Blyth S.F. Capt.	10/05/1857-01/11/58
Bolger P. Sgt./Mjr.	10/05/1857-01/11/58
Bond S. Pte.	23/04/1816
Bonner R. Pte.	23/04/1816
Boulter W. Pte.	23/04/1816
Bowden E. Pte.	10/05/1857-01/11/58
Bowmer M. Capt.	27/04/1707
Bowker J. Pte.	10/05/1857-03/08/58
Boxall J. Pte.	10/05/1857-01/11/58
Boxall W. Pte.	10/05/1857-03/08/58
Boyle J. Cpl.	10/05/1857-01/11/58
Bradley H. Pte.	10/05/1857-01/11/58
Brady J. Pte.	10/05/1857-01/11/58
Braidon W. Pte.	10/05/1857-01/11/58
Bratton J. Pte.	10/05/1857-01/11/58
Breakle W. Pte.	10/05/1857-03/08/58
Breary C.S. Lt.	23/04/1816
Briant J. Pte.	23/04/1816
Brice W. Cpl.	23/04/1816
Bridger E. Pte.	10/05/1857-01/11/58
Britton W. Sgt.	10/05/1857-03/08/58
Bromley G. Drmr.	10/05/1857-01/11/58
Brooks H. Pte.	10/05/1857-01/11/58
Brooks R. Pte.	10/05/1857-01/11/58
Broomwich C. Pte.	10/05/1857-01/11/58
Brown C. Pte.	10/05/1857-01/11/58
Brown C. Pte.	10/05/1857-01/11/58
Brown T. Lt.	02/06-27/07/1758,28/04/1760
Brownlee D. Pte.	10/05/1857-01/11/58
Broadley Jns. Pte.	23/04/1816
Broom G. Pte.	23/04/1816
Broom J. Pte.	23/04/1816
Brown Jns. Pte.	23/04/1816

Brown J.W. Sgt.	23/04/1816
Brown L. Pte.	23/04/1816
Brown T. Pte.	23/04/1816
Brown W. Ens.	09/08/1757
Brown W. Pte.	23/04/1816
Browning R. Pte.	23/04/1816
Bruton M. Pte.	23/04/1816
Bryce R. Pte.	10/05/1857-01/11/58
Buckwell J. Pte.	23/04/1816
Bulbeck W. Pte.	23/04/1816
Bull H. Pte.	23/04/1816
Burbridge W. Pte.	10/05/1857-03/08/1858
Burgin W. Armoury Sgt.	23/04/1816
Burfoot R. Pte.	10/05/1857-01/11/58
Burgess C. Cpl.	10/05/1857-01/11/58
Burnell R. Sgt.	23/04/1816
Burns T. Pte.	10/05/1857-01/11/58
Burrage P. Pte.	10/05/1857-01/11/58
Burridge Jns. Pte.	23/04/1816
Burrows T. Pte.	23/04/1816
Burt C. Pte.	10/05/1857-01/11/58
Burt R. Sgt.	23/04/1816
Burt R. Pte.	23/04/1816
Bury W. Paymaster	23/04/1816
Busby Pte.	18/03/1807
Bush R. C/Sgt.	10/05/1857-03/08/58
Bushrod J. Pte.	23/04/1816
Bussey G. Pte.	23/04/1816
Bussey I. Pte.	23/04/1816
Butler M. Cpl.	10/05/1857-01/11/58
Butler T. Pte.	10/05/1857-01/11/58
Byrne J. Pte.	10/05/1857-01/11/58
Byrne P. Pte.	10/05/1857-01/11/58
Byrnes P. Pte.	23/04/1816
Cadman Jns. Pte.	23/04/1816
Cadman W. Pte.	23/04/1816
Cain D. Pte.	10/05/1857-01/11/58
Calcutt W. Pte.	23/04/1816
Cameron R. Lt.	18/03/1807
Campbell C. Lt.	17/06/1775
Campbell D. Pte.	10/05/1857-01/11/58
Campbell J. Drmr.	10/05/1857-01/11/58
Cannon M. Pte.	23/04/1816
Cantello W. Drmr.	10/05/1857-01/11/58
Cardial J. Pte.	23/04/1816
Carey J. Pte.	10/05/1857-03/08/58
Carmichael J. Pte.	23/04/1816
Carr R. Lt-Col.	01/12/1776
Carter F. Pte.	10/05/1857-03/08/58
Cass H. Pte.	23/04/1816
Cass J. Drmr.	23/04/1816
Cassidy P. Pte.	10/05/1857-03/08/58
Cassidy R. Pte.	10/05/1857-03/08/58
Castle T. Sgt.	23/04/1816
Challan R. Pte.	23/04/1816

Chambers J.W. Surgeon	10/05/1857-01/11/58
Chambers S. Pte.	10/05/1857-01/11/58
Chapman D. Pte.	10/05/1857-01/11/58
China W. Pte.	10/05/1857-01/11/58
Christian Lt.	27/04/1707
Churcher W. Pte.	23/04/1816
Clarke J. Pte.	10/05/1857-01/11/58
Clarke C.W. Maj.	07/04/1809,02/10/09,13/10/09,16/10/09, 07/04/1015/04/10,19/06/10
Clarke J. Pte.	10/05/1857-01/11/58
Clarke Jns. Pte.	23/04/1816
Clarke T. Pte.	23/04/1816
Clarke W.G. Asst/Surgeon	10/05/1857-03/08/58
Clayton J. Pte.	23/04/1816
Clayton J. Pte.	23/04/1816
Clegg A. Pte.	10/05/1857-03/08/58
Clelland J. Pte.	10/05/1857-01/11/58
Clinch W. Pte.	23/04/1816
Clissold T. Drmr.	23/04/1816
Cockburne J. Lt.	2/06-27/07/1758,31/12/1759
Cocker J. Pte.	10/05/1857-01/11/58
Cocks C. Pte.	10/05/1857-01/11/58
Coe J. Pte.	10/05/1857-01/11/58
Coggin T. Pte.	23/04/1816
Coleman J. Pte.	10/05/1857-01/11/58
Collier B. Pte.	10/05/1857-01/11/58
Collier J. Pte.	10/05/1857-01/11/58
Collins E. Pte.	10/05/1857-01/11/58
Collins H. Pte.	23/04/1816
Collins J. Pte.	23/04/1816
Collum J. Pte.	10/05/1857-01/11/58
Colurn J. Pte.	23/04/1816
Comely G. Pte.	10/05/1857-01/11/58
Condon D. Pte.	10/05/1857-01/11/58
Connell J. Pte.	10/05/1857-01/11/58
Conner J. Pte.	23/04/1816
Connolly R.	10/05/1857-01/11/58
Connolly T. Pte.	10/05/1857-01/11/58
Connor D. Pte.	10/05/1857-03/08/58
Connor Thady Pte.	10/05/1857-01/11/58
Connor Thomas Pte.	10/05/1857-03/08/58
Conway M. Pte.	23/04/1816
Cook W. Pte.	23/04/1816
Cook W. Pte.	10/05/1857-03/08/58
Cooper J. Sgt.	23/04/1816
Cooper R. Pte.	23.04/1816
Cooper W. Pte.	23/04/1816
Coote E. Pte.	23/04/1816
Corny B. Pte.	10/05/1857-01/11/58
Corrigan R. Pte.	10/05/1857-01/11/58
Costello T. Pte.	23/04/1816
Craig J. Pte.	10/05/1857-01/11/58
Cranfield J. Pte.	23/04/1816
Crawford J. Pte.	23/04/1816
Creaton P. Pte.	23/04/1816

Name	Date
Critchley T. Pte.	23/04/1816
Cronan P. Pte.	10/05/1857-03/08/58
Croom T. Pte.	23/04/1816
Cross J. Pte.	10/05/1857-03/08/58
Crossman R. Pte.	10/05/1857-01/11/58
Crotty J. Pte.	10/05/1857-01/11/58
Crum J. Pte.	10/05/1857-01/11/58
Crum W. Pte.	10/05/1857-01/11/58
Cudmore Capt.	27/04/1707
Cummings J. Pte.	10/05/1857-01/11/58
Cummisky W. Pte.	10/05/1857-01/11/58
Cust R. Lt.	10-17/04/1807,15/04/10
Cutchley G. Pte.	23/04/1816
Cutmore W. Pte.	10/05/1857-01/11/58
Dadds J. Pte.	10/05/1857-01/11/58
Daley P. Pte.	23/04/1816
Daly Ens.	27/04/1707
Daly T. Lt.	19/04/1807,14-18/07/07
Damon S. Pte.	23/04/1816
Daniel H. Pte.	23/04/1816
Daniel R. Pte.	10/05/1857-01/11/58
Dann Jns. Sgt.	23/04/1816
Darcey T. Pte.	10/05/1857-01/11/58
Dart W. Pte.	10/05/1857-01/11/58
Daughty G. Pte.	23/04/1816
Davenport T. Pte.	10/05/1857-01/11/58
Davis C. Pte.	23/04/1816
Davis J. Pte.	23/04/1816
Davis J. Drmr.	23/04/1816
Davis J. Pte.	23/04/1816
Davis Jns.	23/04/1816
Davis J. Lt.	10/05/1857-01/11/58
Davis R. Pte.	23/04/1816
Davis R. Pte.	23/04/1816
Davis W. Pte.	23/04/1816
Davis W. Cpl.	23/04/1816
Dawes J. Pte.	10/05/1857-01/11/58
Dawson R. Pte.	10/05/1857-01/11/58
Day J. Pte.	23/04/1816
Dayes A. Pte.	10/05/1857-01/11/58
Deall F. Pte.	10/05/1857-01/11/58
Deel H. Capt.	27/04/1707
Deammer T. Drmr.	23/04/1816
Deane M. Ens.	20/09/1799
De France J. Pte.	23/04/1816
Deevey C. Pte.	23/04/1816
De France J. Pte.	23/04/1816
Dennehy B. Pte.	10/05/1857-01/11/58
Denning J. Pte.	23/04/1816
De Putron J. Pte.	23/04/1816
Derham J. Cpl.	10/05/1857-01/11/58
Devall Lt.	27/04/1707
Dewell H. Pte.	23/04/1816
Dewhurst E. Cpl.	10/05/1857-01/11/58
Diamond J. Pte.	10/05/1857-01/11/58

Dibbin J. Pte.	10/05/1857-01/11/58
Dickinson W. Pte.	23/04/1816
Dighan W. Pte.	10/05/1857-03/08/58
Dillon P. Pte.	23/04/1816
Dillon P. Pte.	10/05/1857-01/11/58
Dillon T.J. Pte.	10/05/1857-01/11/58
Dival F. Pte.	10/05/1857-01/11/58
Dix Jns. Drmr.	23/04/1816
Dobbin C. Pte.	10/05/1857-01/11/58
Dobson T. Pte.	23/04/1816
Donaghy T. Pte.	10/05/1857-01/11/58
Donegall A. *Earl of*	15/08/1702,20/12/04,21/07/1834
Donough G. Pte.	23/04/1816
Donovan T. Pte.	10/05/1857-01/11/58
Dooley J. Pte.	10/05/1857-03/08/58
Doran P. Pte.	10/05/1857-01/11/58
Dowling Charles, Pte.	23/04/1816
Dowling Jns. Pte.	23/04/1816
Down A. Drmr.	23/04/1816
Doyle B. Pte.	10/05/1857-01/11/58
Doyle C.S. Surgeon	23/04/1816
Drake T. Sgt.	10/05/1857-01/11/58
Doyle P. Pte.	23/04/1816
Drew E. Capt.	17/06/1775
Dromgoole N.F. Capt.	23/04/1816
Drum P. Pte.	23/04/1816
Duffy J. Pte.	10/05/1857-01/11/58
Duich J. Pte.	23/04/1816
Dunbar Capt.	27/04/1707
Dunford F. Pte.	23/04/1816
Dunstan W. Pte.	23/04/1816
Dyer H. Pte.	10/05/1857-01/11/58
Dyer W. Pte.	10/05/1857-01/11/58
Dyke J. Pte.	18/03/1807
Eade James Pte.	23/04/1816
Eager Capt.	27/04/1707
Eatough J. Pte.	10/05/1857-01/11/58
Eatough M. Pte.	10/05/1857-01/11/58
Edmund C. Cpl.	23/04/1816
Edmunds J. Pte.	23/04/1816
Edwards C. Pte.	10/05/1857-01/11/58
Edwards D. Pte.	23/04/1816
Edwards J. Drmr.	23/04/1816
Egan W. Pte.	23/04/1816
Eigo P. Pte.	10/05/1857-03/08/58
Eiston G. Capt.	01/01/1795
Ekid W. Pte.	10/05/1857-03/08/58
Elcom J. Pte.	10/05/1857-01/11/58
Ellford J. Pte.	23/04/1816
Elliott G. Pte.	23/04/1816
Elloway D. Pte.	23/04/1816
Elphick L. Pte.	10/05/1857-01/11/58
Emmens C. Pte.	10/05/1857-01/11/58
Enwright J. Pte.	23/04/1816
Essex E. Pte.	23/04/1816

Evan A.	Pte.	23/04/1816
Evans W.	Pte.	10/05/1857-01/11/58
Everrett W.	Pte.	23/04/1816
Eyton W.	Pte.	10/05/1857-01/11/58
Fallon P.	Pte.	23/04/1816
Farley G.	Pte.	10/05/1857-01/11/58
Farley J.	Pte.	23/04/1816
Farrant W.B.	Lt.	23/04/1816
Farrell L.	Pte.	23/04/1816
Farrell P.	Pte.	10/05/1857-01/11/58
Farrell P.	Pte.	10/05/1857-01/11/58
Farrell T.	Pte.	23/04/1816
Farrell W.	Pte.	23/04/1816
Fawcett W.	Pte.	10/05/1857-01/11/58
Featherstone T.	Pte.	10/05/1857-01/11/58
Feltham W.	Pte.	23/04/1816
Fields R.	Pte.	10/05/1857-03/08/58
Findlay J.	Pte.	10/05/1857-01/11/58
Finlayson T.	Pte.	10/05/1857-01/11/58
Fitzgerald P.	Drmr.	10/05/1857-01/11/58
Fitzgerald J.	Capt.	01/01/1795
Fitzgerald J.	Pte.	10/05/1857-01/11/58
Fitzsimmons J.	Pte.	10/05/1857-01/11/58
Fleming P.	Pte.	10/05/1857-01/11/58
Fletcher G.	Capt.	31/12/1759
Fletcher H.	Lt-Col.	02/06/1758,16/01/1762
Flinn C.	Pte.	23/04/1816
Flynn R.	Pte.	10/05/1857-01/11/58
Fogden W.	Pte.	23/04/1816
Foote R.	Q/Master	23/04/1816
Ford A.J.	Lt.	10/05/1857-01/11/58
Ford F.	Pte.	23/04/1816
Ford G.	Pte.	23/04/1816
Ford G.	Cpl.	10/05/1857-01/11/58
Ford T.	Pte.	10/05/1857-01/11/58
Foster J.	Pte.	10/05/1857-01/11/58
Foster A.	Cpl.	10/05/1857-01/11/58
Francis J.	Pte.	10/05/1857-03/08/58
Frandell T.	Pte.	23/04/1816
Frankham T.	Pte.	23/04/1816
Franklin J.	Pte.	10/05/1857-01/11/58
Frederick C.	Capt.	07/08/1809
French G.	Pte.	10/05/1857-01/11/58
Frost S.	Pte.	10/05/1857-03/08/58
Fry J.	Pte.	23/04/1816
Fry T.	Pte.	10/05/1857-01/11/58
Fulcher A.	Sgt.	10/05/1857-01/11/58
Fulter T.	Sgt.	10/05/1857-01/11/58
Gallagher P.	Pte.	10/05/1857-03/08/58
Galline A.	Pte.	23/04/1816
Gallop J.	Pte.	23/04/1816
Garaythy B.	Pte.	23/04/1816
Gardiner L.	Capt.	31/12/1759
Gardner	Capt.	27/04/1707
Gardner J.	Pte.	23/04/1816

Garrett J. Pte.	10/05/1857-01/11/58
Garrity P. Pte.	10/05/1857-01/11/58
Garvey J. Pte.	10/05/1857-01/11/58
Gay J. Pte.	23/04/1816
Geer J. Pte.	23/04/1816
Geer T. Pte.	23/04/1816
George J.K. Pte.	10/05/1857-03/08/58
Gibbons J. Pte.	10/05/1857-03/08/58
Gibbons T. Pte.	23/04/1816
Gifford W. Pte.	23/04/1816
Gilmore A. Pte.	10/05/1857-03/08/58
Gillard R. Pte.	23/04/1816
Ginn O. Pte.	23/04/1816
Glannen D. Pte.	23/04/1816
Glannon J. Pte.	23/04/1816
Glover T. Pte.	23/04/1816
Goddard A. Pte.	10/05/1857-01/11/58
Godfrey H. Pte.	10/05/1857-03/08/58
Godwin H. Pte.	10/05/1857-01/11/58
Goodall J. Pte.	10/05/1857-03/08/58
Gore C. Lt.	31/12/1759,24/01/1762
Gosling T. Pte.	23/04/1816
Gough J. Pte.	23/04/1816
Gouldthorpe J. Pte.	10/05/1857-01/11/58
Gower W. Pte.	10/05/1857-01/11/58
Graeme J. Pte.	10/05/1857-01/11/58
Graham J. Pte.	10/05/1857-01/11/58
Graham J. Pte.	10/05/1857-01/11/58
Graham N. Drmr.	23/04/1816
Grant J. Pte.	23/04/1816
Green C. Pte.	10/05/1857-01/11/58
Green W. Maj., K.H.	23/04/1816,1837
Griffin H. Pte.	23/04/1816
Griffiths T. Pte.	10/05/1857-03/08/58
Grogan J. Pte.	23/04/1816
Grounsell J. Pte.	23/04/1816
Grove C. Capt.	21/05/1794
Groves J. Pte.	23/04/1816
Guile G. Pte.	10/05/1857-01/11/58
Gullick J. Pte.	23/04/1816
Gumbrell J. Pte.	10/05/1857-03/08/58
Gurney J. Pte.	23/04/1816
Haber J. Pte.	10/05/1857-01/11/58
Hackett T. Pte.	23/04/1816
Hadden G. C/Sgt.	10/05/1857-01/11/58
Ham W. C/Sgt.	10/05/1857-01/11/58
Hamilton A.D. Ens.	23/04/1816
Hamilton J. Pte.	10/05/1857-01/11/58
Hamilton W. Lt.-Col.	27/04/1707
Hamilton W. Lt.	31/12/1759
Hannah S. Pte.	10/05/1857-03/08/58
Hansford S. Pte.	23/04/1816
Harding J. Pte.	23/04/1816
Harding W. Pte.	23/04/1816
Hardman W. Pte.	10/05/1857-03/08/58

Hardy D. Pte.	10/05/1857-01/11/58
Hargreaves J. Pte.	10/05/1857-03/08/58
Harling J. Pte.	10/05/1857-01/11/58
Harman J. Pte.	10/05/1857-01/11/58
Harmer G. Pte.	10/05/1857-01/11/58
Harrington A. Pte.	10/05/1857-01/11/58
Harrington G. Pte.	10/05/1857-01/11/58
Harris F. Pte.	23/04/1816
Harris G. Pte.	10/05/1857-01/11/58
Harris J. Capt.	10/05/1857-01/11/58
Harris R. Pte.	23/04/1816
Harris S. Pte.	23/04/1816
Harris T. Pte.	23/04/1816
Harris W. Pte.	10/05/1857-01/11/58
Harrison W. Pte.	10/05/1857-01/11/58
Harrison W. Pte.	10/05/1857-01/11/58
Hart C. Cpl.	23/04/1816
Hart R. Sgt.	10/05/1857-01/11/58
Hartley W. Pte.	23/04/1816
Harwood S. Pte.	23/04/1816
Hawkins J. Pte.	23/04/1816
Hawthron J. Pte.	23/04/1816
Hay A. Maj.	20/09/1799
Hay J. Lt.	23/04/1816
Hayes C. Pte.	23/04/1816
Hayes D. Pte.	10/05/1857-03/08/58
Hayes J. Pte.	10/05/1857-03/08/58
Hayes J. Pte.	10/05/1857-01/11/58
Hayles J. Pte.	23/04/1816
Head G. Cpl.	23/04/1816
Head J. Cpl.	23/04/1816
Heard D. Cpl.	10/05/1857-03/08/58
Heath R. Pte.	23/04/1816
Heathcot R. Pte.	23/04/1816
Hedding W.L. Ens.	23/04/1816
Heffernan J. Cpl.	10/05/1857-01/11/58
Heilderbrand J. Lt.	23/04/1816
Hembrow J. Pte.	10/05/1857-01/11/58
Hemons J. C/Sgt.	10/05/1857-01/11/58
Henderson D. Pte.	10/05/1857-01/11/58
Henderson J. Pte.	10/05/1857-01/11/58
Henderson J. Pte.	23/04/1816
Henderson W. Pte.	23/04/1816
Hendon W. Pte.	23/04/1816
Herd D. Cpl.	10/05/1857-01/11/58
Herne P. Pte.	10/05/1857-01/11/58
Heron J. Pte.	23/04/1816
Herriott H. Pte.	10/05/1857-01/11/58
Hewett J. Pte.	23/04/1816
Hewetson J. Ens.	23/04/1816
Hickman B. Sgt/Maj.	23/04/1816
Hide J. Pte.	23/04/1816
Higgins A. Cpl.	10/05/1857-01/11/58
Hilebrand J. Ens.	23/04/1816
Hill G. Pte.	23/04/1816

Hill J. Pte.	10/05/1857-01/11/58
Hill J. Pte.	10/05/1857-01/11/58
Hill S. Pte.	23/04/1816
Hill W. Pte.	23/04/1816
Hill W. Pte.	10/05/1857-03/08/58
Hills B. Pte.	23/04/1816
Hills J. Pte.	10/05/1857-03/08/58
Hiscock A. Pte.	23/04/1816
Hiscock J. Pte.	23/04/1816
Hoar J. Cpl.	23/04/1816
Hobbs J. Pte.	23/04/1816
Hodges C. Pte.	23/04/1816
Hodges W. Sgt.	23/04/1816
Hoey M. C/Sgt.	10/05/1857-01/11/58
Hogg J. Pte.	23/04/1816
Hogg J. Pte.	10/05/1857-01/11/58
Holden G. Pte.	10/05/1857-01/11/58
Holder D. Cpl.	23/04/1816
Holder J. Pte.	23/04/1816
Holder F. Pte.	10/05/1857-01/11/58
Holder R. Pte.	23/04/1816
Holland S. Pte.	23/04/1816
Holloway W. Pte.	23/04/1816
Holmes T. Ens.	01/01/1795
Holt J. Pte.	23/04/1816
Hool T. Pte.	10/05/1857-01/11/58
Hooley F. Pte.	23/04/1816
Horan J. Pte.	10/05/1857-01/11/58
Hosley A. Pte.	10/05/1857-0308/58
Hosely W. Pte.	10/05/1857-01/11/58
Houghton E. Pte.	10/05/1857-01/11/58
Houghton J. Pte.	10/05/1857-01/11/58
Howe T. Pte.	10/05/1857-03/08/58
Howe W. Q/M/Sgt.	23/04/1816
Huggins S. Pte.	23/04/1816
Hughes J. Pte.	23/04/1816
Hughes R. Pte.	10/05/1857-03/08/58
Hughes W. Pte.	10/05/1857-01/11/58
Hull J. Pte.	23/04/1816
Humphrey W. Pte.	10/05/1857-03/08/58
Humphries J. Pte.	10/05/1867-01/11/58
Humphries T. Pte.	23/04/1816
Hunt J. Pte.	23/04/1816
Hunt S. Pte.	23/04/1816
Hunter C. Pte.	10/05/1857-01/11/58
Huntley G. Pte.	10/05/1857-01/11/58
Hurry G. Pte.	23/04/1816
Hutchings H. Pte.	23/04/1816
Hutchins W. Pte.	10/05/1857-03/08/58
Hutchinson E.H. Lt-Col.	10/05/1857-01/11/58
Hutchinson J. Sgt.	10/05/1857-01/11/58
Iddon W. Pte.	10/05/1857-03/08/58
Iliff J. Pte.	10/05/1857-01/11/58
Ince C. Captain	28/04/1760
Ide W. Pte.	23/04/1816

Irvine C. Pte.	23/04/1816
Issac W. Pte.	23/04/1816
Ives H. Pte.	23/04/1816
Irvine J. Lt.	10/02-10/12/1794
Irvine W. Pte.	10/05/1857-03/08/58
Jackson H. Pte.	23/04/1816
Jackson R. Pte.	23/04/1816
James J. Pte.	23/04/1816
Jamieson W. Pte.	10/05/1857-01/11/58
Joddrell T. Capt.	18/03/1807,17/04/07
Johns W. Pte.	10/05/1857-01/11/58
Johnson J. Pte.	10/05/1857-03/08/58
Johnson W. Sgt.	10/05/1857-03/08/58
Johnson W. Pte.	10/05/1857-03/08/58
Johnston G. Pte.	10/05/1857-03/08/58
Johnston G. Pte.	10/05/1857-01/11/58
Johnston J. Pte.	10/05/1857-01/11/58
Johnston W. Pte.	10/05/1857-01/11/58
Johnston W. Sgt.	10/05/1857-01/11/58
Johnstone J. Capt./Lt.	10/02-10/12/1794
Johnstone J. Pte.	23/04/1816
Jones Ens.	27/04/1707
Jones C. Pte.	23/04/1816
Jones E. Pte.	23/04/1816
Jones J. Ens.	20/09/1799
Jones J. Pte.	23/04/1816
Jones J. Pte.	10/05/1857-03/08/58
Jones T. Pte.	23/04/1816
Jones W. Pte.	23/04/1816
Jones W. Pte.	23/04/1816
Jordan D. Pte.	10/05/1857-01/11/58
Jubb B. Pte.	10/05/1857-03/08/58
Jupp F. Pte.	23/04/1816
Kavanagh M. Pte.	10/05/1857-01/11/58
Keenan H. Pte.	23/04/1816
Keineham H. Pte.	23/04/1816
Kelly I. Pte.	10/05/1857-01/11/58
Kelly J. Pte.	10/05/1857-01/11/58
Kelly P. Pte.	10/05/1857-03/08/58
Kemp J. Pte.	10/05/1857-01/11/58
Kendrick J. Pte.	23/04/1816
Keneway J. Pte.	23/04/1816
Kennedy B. Pte.	23/04/1816
Kennedy O. Pte.	23/04/1816
Kennedy P. Pte.	23/04/1816
Kenny M. Pte.	23/04/1816
Keoghoe W. Asst/Surgeon	23/04/1816
Ketchell R. Pte.	10/05/1857-01/11/58
Ketchley J. Cpl.	23/04/1816
Ketchley R. Pte.	23/04/1816
Kilbride D. Pte.	10/05/1857-01/11/58
Killchrist J. Pte.	10/05/1857-01/11/58
Kinchella J. Pte.	10/05/1857-03/08/58
Kinchington A. Pte.	23/04/1816
King G. Pte.	10/05/1857-01/11/58

King J. Pte.	23/04/1816
King M. Cpl.	23/04/1816
Kingston J. Pte.	23/04 1816
Kinsman W. Pte.	23/04/1816
Kirby J. Sgt.	23/04/1816
Kitely T. Pte.	23/04/1816
Knight E. Cpl.	10/05/1857-01/11/58
Knowlson F. Pte.	23/04/1816
Knowlton J. Pte.	23/04/1816
Lake J. Pte.	10/05/1857-03/08/58
Lamb R. Cpl.	23/04/1816
Lane C. Pte.	23/04/1816
Laneway W. Pte.	23/04/1816
Latty J. Drmr.	23/04/1816
Lavender T. Pte.	10/05/1857-01/11/58
Law J. Cpl.	23/04/1816
Lawler J. Pte.	23/04/1816
Lawrence R. Pte.	23/04/1816
Leary D. Pte.	10/05/1857-01/11/58
Leavey H. Pte.	23/04/1816
Leavey W. Pte.	23/04/1816
Ledward C. Pte.	10/05/1857-01/11/58
Lee H. Pte.	10/05/1857-01/11/58
Lee R.C. Capt.	10/05/1857-01/11/58
Leech W. Pte.	23/04/1816
Leeman S. Pte.	10/05/1857-01/11/58
Le Grand A.J. Capt.	10/05/1857-03/08/58
Leonard W. Pte.	10/05/1857-01/11/58
Leslie J. Lt-Col., K.H.	1837
Lester J. Pte.	23/04/1816
Lewis J. Pte.	10/05/1857-01/11/58
Lines W. Pte.	23/04/1816
Lloyd O. Pte.	10/05/1857-01/11/58
Lloyd W. Pte.	23/04/1816
Locker W. Pte.	10/05/1857-01/11/58
Lomax W. Pte.	10/05/1857-01/11/58
Long J. Pte.	10/05/1857-01/11/58
Long W. Pte.	23/04/1816
Loughlin P. Pte.	10/05/1857-01/11/58
Lovedore G. Pte.	23/04/1816
Lovell G. Pte.	23/04/1816
Lower H. Pte.	23/04/1816
Lucas J. Pte.	23/04/1816
Lucas T. Pte.	23/04/1816
Luff W. Pte.	10/05/1857-01/11/58
Lyon J. Capt.	17/06/1775
Lyons J. Pte.	10/05/1857-01/11/58
Lysaght C. Ens.	27/04/1760
Macalister C. Lt-Col.	21/04/1807,14/18/07/07,13/02/14,23/04/16
Macalister W. Ens.	23/04/1816
Macdonnell A.J. Ens.	23/04/1816
MacLean A. Pte.	03/08/1858
Macleod H.G. Lt-Col., K.H.,M.W.O.	24/02/1815,23/04/16,1836
Malady J, Pte.	03/08/1858
Madden J. Ens.	17/06/1775

Madden J. Pte.	10/05/1857-01/11/58
Madden M. Pte.	10/05/1857-01/11/58
Maggs F. Pte.	23/04/1816
Mahoney M. Pte.	10/05/1857-01/11/58
Mahoney W. Pte.	10/05/1857-01/11/58
Malady J. Pte.	10/05/1857-01/11/58
Mallen J. Pte.	23/04/1816
Manary J.B. Capt.	0/09/1799
Mangen J. Pte.	23/04/1816
Manning R. Pte.	23/04/1816
Manning T. Pte.	10/05/1857-01/11/58
Mantle N. Pte.	10/05/1857-01/11/58
Mapham E. Pte.	23/04/11816
Marshall J. Pte.	10/05/1857-01/11/58
Martin E. Pte.	23/04/1816
Martin F. Pte.	23/04/1816
Martin G. Pte.	10/05/1857-01/11/58
Martyn H. Cpl.	10/05/1857-01/11/58
Mason T. Pte.	23/04/1816
Mason W. Lt.	31/12/1759
Mason W. Ens.	09/08/1757
Massey H. Capt.	17/06/1775,28/06/78,08/10/1799
Massey W.G. Lt.	10/05/1857-03/08/58
Matson J. Drmr.	10/05/1857-01/11/58
Matthews G. Pte.	10/05/1857-01/11/58
Maturin G. Lt.	31/12/1759
Maunsell J. Capt.	31/12/1759
May T. Capt.	23/02/1813,03-06/07/13
Maylerd M. Pte.	23/04/1816
Mayo T. Pte.	23/04/1816
McAlston R. Pte.	10/05/1857-01/11/58
McAndrews J. Pte.	10/05/1857-01/11/58
McArthur D. Pte.	10/05/1857-01/11/58
McArthur W. Pte.	10/05/1857-01/11/58
McAusland H. Sgt.	22/01/1857
McBlane R. Pte.	10/05/1857-01/11/58
McBride M. Pte.	10/05/1857-01/11/58
McCall P. Pte.	10/05/1857-01/11/58
McClean J. Pte.	23/04/1816
McClean J. Pte.	23/04/1816
McClelland J. Drmr.	10/05/1857-01/11/58
McCombs J. Pte.	23/04/1816
McCormick A. Pte.	23/04/1816
McCue T. Pte.	23/04/1816
McDermott J. Pte.	10/05/1857-01/11/58
McDermott O. Pte.	10/05/1857-01/11/58
McDonald G. Pte.	10/05/1857-01/11/58
McDonald T. Drmr.	23/04/1816
McDonald W. Lt.	23/02/1813,03/06/07/13
McDonnough M. Pte.	10/05/1857-01/11/58
McDonough T. Lt.	23/04/1816
McEvoy J. Pte.	10/05/1857-01/11/58
McEvoy T. Pte.	10/05/1857-01/11/58
McFadden E. Pte.	23/04/1816

McGee B. Pte.	23/04/1816
McGonigle W. Pte.	10/05/1857-01/11/58
McGovern R.S. Pte.	10/05/1857-01/11/58
McIntyre J. Pte.	10/05/1857-01/11/58
McKay G. Pte.	10/05/1857-01/11/58
McKean M. Pte.	10/05/1857-01/11/58
McKenna J. Pte.	10/05/1857-01/11/58
McKnight J. Pte.	10/05/1857-01/11/58
McLaughlin F. Sgt.	23/04/1816
McLean A. Pte.	10/05/1857-01/11/58
McLean A. Pte.	10/05/1857-01/11/58
McLeod J. Pte.	10/05/1857-01/11/58
McLoughlin J. Pte.	10/05/1857-01/11/58
McManaman J. Pte.	10/05/1857-01/11/58
McManaman J. Pte.	10/05/1857-01/11/58
McMullen T. Pte.	10/05/1857-01/11/58
McNally W. Sgt.	23/04/1816
McNamara J. Pte.	10/05/1857-01/11/58
McNeill J. Pte.	10/05/1857-03/08/58
McNeill J.C. Lt-Col.	16/08/1864,23/12/70,31/03/74,17/08/80
McNeill T. Capt.	23/04/1816
McNolty J. Pte.	10/05/1857-01/11/58
McPherson A. Pte.	10/05/1857-01/11/58
McPhillips T. Pte.	10/05/1857-01/11/58
McQuade S. Pte.	10/05/1857-03/08/58
McQuain M. Pte.	10/05/1857-01/11/58
McTagert J. Pte.	10/05/1857-03/08/58
McWilliams J.	10/05/1857-01/11/58
Mead W. Pte.	23/04/1816
Mealey F. Pte.	23/04/1816
Meehan A. Pte.	10/05/1857-01/11/58
Meehan T. Pte.	10/05/1857-01/11/58
Meehan W. Pte.	10/05/1857-01/11/58
Merrett W. Pte.	23/04/1816
Miller A. Pte.	10/05/1857-03/08/58
Middleton H. Lt.	23/04/1816
Mines J. Pte.	23/04/1816
Mingle J. Pte.	23/04/1816
Minnock J. Pte.	10/05/1857-01/11/58
Misem J. Pte.	10/05/1857-01/11/58
Mitchell A. Pte.	23/04/1816
Mitchell A. Pte.	10/05/1857-01/11/58
Mitchell T. Pte.	23/04/1816
Modry W. Pte.	23/04/1816
Molloy C. Pte.	23/04/1816
Molyneaux J. Pte.	10/05/1857-01/11/58
Monaghan J. Cpl.	10/05/1857-01/11/58
Monaghan P. Pte.	23/04/1816
Monaghan Patrick Pte.	10/05/1857-01/11/58
Monaghan P. Sgt.	23/04/1816
Monaghan P. Pte.	10/05/1857-03/08/58
Monaghan P. Pte.	10/05/1857-01/11/58
Monck J. Pte.	23/04/1816

Name	Date
Monck W. Pte.	23/04/1816
Monro G. Lt-Col.	03/08/1757, 02/06/1758
Moodie A. Pte.	10/05/1857-01/11/58
Moody T. C/Sgt.	10/05/1857-01/11/58
Mooney J. Pte.	10/05/1857-01/11/58
Moore E. Pte.	10/05/1857-01/11/58
Moore L. Lt-Col., C.B., K.C.H.	15/04/1809, 19/06/10, 16/09/15, 1834
Moore M. Pte.	10/05/1857-01/11/58
Moore T. Sgt.	23/04/1816
Moore W. Pte.	23/04/1816
Moran T. Pte.	23/04/1816
Moran T. Pte.	10/05/1857-01/11/58
Morgan J. Pte.	23/04/1816
Morgan S. Pte.	23/04/1816
Morton M.V.S. Capt.	10/05/1857-01/11/58
Morton T. Sgt.	10/05/1857-03/08/58
Moynihan J. Cpl.	10/05/1857-01/11/58
Moynihan W. Pte.	10/05/1857-03/08/58
Moyston G. Pte.	10/05/1857-01/11/58
Mudge T. Pte	10/05/1857-03/08/58
Mukins F. Lt.	10/02-10/12/1794
Mulvey W. Pte.	23/04/1816
Murdock P. Lt.	23/04/1816
Murdock R. Pte.	10/05/1857-01/11/58
Murphy D. Pte.	23/04/1816
Murphy J. Pte.	23/04/1816
Murphy M. Pte.	23/04/1816
Murphy J. Sgt.	10/05/1857-01/11/58
Murphy P. Pte.	23/04/1816
Murphy P. Pte.	10/05/1857-03/08/58
Murphy W. Pte.	10/05/1857-03/08/58
Murphy W. Pte.	10/05/1857-01/11/58
Murray T. Pte.	10/05/1857-03/08/58
Murray T. Pte.	10/05/1857-01/11/58
Myles J. Pte.	10/05/1857-01/11/58
Nash M. Ens.	10/02-10/12/1794
New W. Pte.	23/04/1816
Newbold J. Pte.	23/04/1816
Newman J. Pte.	23/04/1816
Newman J. Pte.	23/04/1816
Niblett C. Pte.	10/05/1857-01/11/58
Nicholl J. Pte.	10/05/1857-01/11/58
Nichols J. Pte.	10/05/1857-01/11/58
Nicholson T. Lt.	08/10/1799
Nixon G. Pte.	23/04/1816
Nixon J. Pte.	23/04/1816
Nolan J. Pte.	10/05/1857-03/08/58
O'Brien Ens.	27/04/1707
Oaten E. Pte.	10/05/1857-01/11/58
Oates J. Pte.	23/04/1816
O'Keefe J. Maj.	21/05/1807
O'Brien W. Pte.	10/05/1857-01/11/58
O'Keefe P. Pte.	10/05/1857-01/11/58
Okey C. Pte.	23/04/1816

Oland G. Pte.	23/04/1816
O'Neal J. Pte.	23/04/1816
O'Neil P. Pte.	10/05/1857-01/11/58
Orchard R. Pte.	23/04/1816
Orham T. Pte.	23/04/1816
Ormby E. Ens.	09/07/1757
Osborne J. Pte.	10/05/1857-01/11/58
Osbourne J. Pte.	23/04/1816
Oswald J. Lt-Col.	20/09/1799,14/18/07/1807
Oswald R. Brevet-Mjr.	22/03/1809,05/09/12/09,22/03/10
Oxenbridge E. Pte.	23/04/1816
Padon J. Pte.	23/04/1816
Page G. Pte.	23/04/1816
Palmer J. Pte.	23/04/1816
Palmer J. Pte.	10/05/1857-01/11/58
Palmer T. Pte.	23/04/1816
Palmer W. Q/M/Sgt.	10/05/1857-01/11/58
Parfitt J. Pte.	23/04/1816
Parish J. Pte.	10/05/1857-01/11/58
Parker C. Pte.	10/05/1857-01/11/58
Parker G. Sgt.	10/05/1857-01/11/58
Parker J. Pte.	10/05/1857-01/11/58
Parker W. Pte.	10/05/1857-01/11/58
Parkhouse S. Pte.	10/05/1857-01/11/58
Parson H. Pte.	23/04/1816
Parsons R. Lt.	10/05/1857-01/11/58
Patching T. Pte.	23/04/1816
Pate H. Pte.	10/05/1857-01/11/58
Patterson L.G. Asst/Surgeon	10/05/1857-01/11/58
Pattinson J. Pte.	10/05/1857-03/08/58
Payne J. Pte.	23/04/1816
Payne J. Pte.	23/04/1816
Payne W. Pte.	23/04/1816
Payne W.H.B. Lt.	10/05/1857-01/11/58
Pearce J. Pte.	23/04/1816
Peck A. Capt.	21/04/1807
Pegler J. Pte.	23/04/1816
Pelly T. Pte.	23/04/1816
Penn J. Pte.	10/05/1857-01/11/58
Penny T. Cpl.	23/04/1816
Penny W. Pte.	10/05/1857-03/08/58
Pennycott C. Pte.	23/04/1816
Perkins A. Pte.	23/04/1816
Perkiss J. Pte.	23/04/1816
Petit P.H. Maj.	20/09/1799
Phaire A. Lt.	10/02-10/12/1794
Phillips E.J. Capt.	03/01/1777
Phillips H. Pte.	23/04/1816
Phillips J. Pte.	23/04/1816
Phillips J. Pte.	23/04/1816
Phillips w. Sgt.	23/04/1816
Phillott J. Lt.	08/10/1799
Phillips F. Ens.	09/7/1757
Philpott J.M. Lt.	19/04/1807

Name	Date
Pike Capt.	14-18/07/1807
Pittaway C. Cpl.	10/05/1857-01/11/58
Pittman J. Pte.	23/04/1816
Pohle M.M. Lt.	25/01/1857
Pollard J. Pte.	23/04/1816
Poole G. Pte.	23/04/1816
Poole G. Pte.	10/05/1857-03/08/58
Postons J. Pte.	23/04/1816
Potenger H. Ens.	23/04/1816
Potter S. Pte.	10/05/1857-03/08/58
Poulton J. Pte.	23/04/1816
Powell J. Pte.	23/04/1816
Powell W Cpl.	10/05/1857-01/11/58
Pratt H. Pte.	10/05/1857-03/08/58
Pratten I. Pte.	23/04/1816
Presley W. Pte.	10/05/1857-01/11/58
Preston J. Pte.	23/04/1816
Price Jns. Q/M/Sgt.	23/04/1816
Price J. Pte.	23/04/1816
Price W. Pte.	23/04/1816
Prideaux J. Pte.	23/04/1816
Prignell A. Pte.	23/04/1816
Prince R. Pte.	10/05/1857-01/11/58
Prince W. Pte.	10/05/1857-01/11/58
Pritchard J. Pte.	23/04/1816
Pritchard W. Pte.	23/04/1816
Pritchard W. Pte.	23/04/1816
Properjohn C.J. Pte.	10/05/1857-01/11/58
Punchon R. Pte.	23/04/1816
Purcell J. Asst/Surgeon	23/04/1816
Quinn E. Pte.	10/05/1857-01/11/58
Purtell S. Pte.	10/05/1857-01/11/58
Quinn H. Pte.	23/04/1816
Quinn J. Pte.	23/04/1816
Quinn J.R. Pte.	10/05/1857-01/11/58
Quinn W. Pte.	23/04/1816
Radway J. Pte.	10/05/1857-01/11/58
Rainsforth W. Ens.	23/04/1816
Ramsay J. Pte.	10/05/1857-01/11/58
Rawlings T. Pte.	10/05/1857-01/11/58
Rawson W. Capt.	23/04/1816
Rayner H. Pte.	10/05/1857-01/11/58
Reeves R. Pte.	10/05/1857-01/11/58
Regan D. Cpl.	10/05/1857-01/11/58
Reid J. Pte.	10/05/1857-01/11/58
Reilly P. Pte.	10/05/1857-03/08/58
Renfield H. Pte.	23/04/1816
Renton J. Ens.	20/09/1799
Revell A.J. Lt.	10/05/1857-01/11/58
Rhodes D. Pte.	23/04/1816
Rhodes W. Pte.	10/05/1857-01/11/58
Rice J. Cpl.	23/04/1816
Richards E. Pte.	10/05/1857-01/11/58
Richards E. Pte.	10/05/1857-01/11/58
Riddell C.J. Capt.	21/05/1807

Rider R. Pte.	10/05/1857-01/11/58
Ridler G. Pte.	23/04/1816
Rielly T. Pte.	10/05/1857-01/11/58
Ring M. Pte.	10/05/1857-01/11/58
Ripley G. Pte.	23/04/1816
Rippon G. Pte.	10/05/1857-03/08/58
Ritchings W. Pte.	23/04/1816
Rivers J. Pte.	10/05/1857-01/11/58
Roach J. Pte.	23/04/1816
Roach J. Pte.	10/05/1857-01/11/58
Roberts P. Pte.	23/04/1816
Roberts T. Pte.	10/05/1857-03/08/58
Robertson G.D. Maj., Gold Medal	08/10/1799, 04/07/1806, 05/06/13, 03-07/13, 12/10/13, 11/12/13
Robertson T. Pte.	10/05/1857-01/11/58
Robinson H. Pte.	10/05/1857-01/11/58
Robinson T. Pte.	10/05/1857-01/11/58
Rocheford P. Pte.	10/05/1857-01/11/58
Rodde H.C. Pte.	10/05/1857-01/11/58
Rogers T. Pte.	23/04/1816
Ronde J. Pte.	23/04/1816
Ross J.B. Pte.	10/05/1857-01/11/58
Ross R.H. Lt. & Adj.	10/05/1857-01/11/58
Rosser R. Pte.	23/04/1816
Rowley J. Sgt.	10/05/1857-01/11/58
Rumble J. Pte.	23/04/1816
Rumery W. Pte.	23/04/1816
Russell T. Pte.	23/04/1816
Russell W. C/Sgt.	10/05/1857-03/08/58
Rutherford H. Capt.	06/10/1812
Ruxton G. Sgt.	10/05/1857-01/11/58
Ryan J. Pte.	10/05/1857-01/11/58
Ryan P. Pte.	10/05/1857-01/11/58
Ryan T.S. Hospital Sgt.	10/05/1857-01/11/58
Samways J. Pte.	23/04/1816
Sandell T. Pte.	23/04/1816
Sanders P. Ens.	10/02-10/12/1794
Sanders R. Pte.	23/04/1816
Sandle S. Pte.	23/04/1816
Sandwell W. Sgt.	10/05/1857-01/11/58
Sansom T. Cpl.	23/04/1816
Saul J. Pte.	10/05/1857-01/11/58
Scarfe S.S. Lt.	23/04/1816
Scott A. Pte.	23/04/1816
Scott E. Pte.	10/05/1857-01/11/58
Scruby C. Pte.	10/05/1857-03/08/58
Seabright J. Pte.	23/04/1816
Seagrave W.H. Lt.	10/02-10/12/1794
Seary B. Pte.	23/04/1816
Seddon S. Pte.	10/05/1857-01/11/58
Serjeant A. Pte.	10/05/1857-03/08/58
Sertin J. Pte.	23/04/1816
Sharpe W. Sgt.	10/05/1857-01/11/58
Sharrock T. Pte.	10/05/1857-01/11/58

Shea M.	Pte.	10/05/1857-01/11/58
Sheevin P.	Pte.	23/04/1816
Sheppard W.	Pte.	23/04/1816
Sherwood T.	Pte.	23/04/1816
Shewell E.	Lt.	23/04/1816
Shoebridge S.	Pte.	10/05/1857-01/11/58
Short S.	Pte.	23/04/1816
Shuter J.	Drmr.	23/04/1816
Sibley D.	Pte.	23/04/1816
Simes C.	Pte.	23/04/1816
Simms J.	Pte.	10/05/1857-01/11/58
Simms J.	Cpl.	10/05/1857-01/11/58
Simms W.	Pte.	10/05/1857-01/11/58
Simpson A.	Capt.	24/01/1762
Simpson J.	Pte.	23/04/1816
Simpson R.	Sgt.	10/05/1857-01/11/58
Simpson T.	Pte.	10/05/1857-01/11/58
Skinner R.	Pte.	10/05/1857-03/08/58
Slessor J.H.	Maj.	18/05/1807,23/02/13,1815,23/04/16
Smeeton J.	Sgt.	23/04/1816
Smith J.	Pte.	03/08/1858
Smith R.	Cpl.	23/04/1816
Smith S.	Drmr.	23/04/1816
Smith S.	Pte.	23/04/1816
Smith T.	Drmr.	23/04/1816
Smith T.	Pte.	10/05/1857-01/11/58
Smith T.	Pte.	10/05/1857-01/11/58
Smith W.	Pte.	23/04/1816
Smith W.	Pte.	23/04/1816
Smith W.	Pte.	10/05/1857-01/11/58
Sparrow W.	Pte.	23/04/1816
Spence G.	Pte.	10/05/1857-03/08/58
Spence T.	Pte.	23/04/1816
Spencer W.	Pte.	10/05/1857-01/11/58
Spicer E.	Pte.	10/05/1857-03/08/58
Spittle A.	Pte.	23/04/1816
Spratt S.	Pte.	10/05/1857-01/11/58
Squires W.	Pte.	23/04/1816
Stack J.	Pte.	10/05/1857-01/11/58
Stagg J.	Pte.	23/04/1816
Standing T.	Pte.	10/05/1857-01/11/58
Staples S.	Pte.	23/04/1816
Steel S.	Sgt.	23/04/1816
Steer J.	Pte.	23/04/1816
Steere A.	Pte.	10/05/1857-01/11/58
Stenton F.	Lt.	23/04/1816
Stevens D.	Pte.	23/04/1816
Stevens J.	Pte.	23/04/1816
Stewart R.C.	Capt.	19/05/1858
Stickland C.	Lt.	01/01/1795
Stocker R.	Pte.	23/04/1816
Stockwell R.	Sgt.	23/04/1816
Stockwell S.	Pte.	23/04/1816
Stone G.	Pte.	10/05/1857-01/11/58
Stowe R.	Pte.	10/05/1857-01/11/58

Straw J. Pte.	23/04/1816
Strawbridge J. Pte.	10/05/1857-01/11/58
Sturt T. Pte.	23/04/1816
Summers F. Sgt.	23/04/1816
Sullivan J. Pte.	10/05/1857-01/11/58
Sullivan W. Pte.	10/05/1857-01/11/58
Summers T. Pte.	23/04/1816
Suthers I. Pte.	10/05/1857-01/11/58
Sutton J. Pte.	10/05/1857-01/11/58
Sweeny B. Pte.	10/05/1857-01/11/58
Sworn S. Pte.	23/04/1816
Swift J. Pte.	23/04/1816
Tarleton H. Capt.	21/04/1807,14-18/07/07
Talbut S. Pte.	23/04/1816
Tasker D. Pte.	23/04/1816
Taylor J. Pte.	10/05/1857-03/08/58
Taylor J. Pte.	10/05/1857-01/11/58
Taylor J. Pte.	10/05/1857-01/11/58
Taylor P. Pte.	10/05/1857-01/11/58
Taylor R. Pte.	10/05/1857-01/11/58
Taylor W. Pte.	10/05/1857-03/08/58
Teather C.G. Pte.	10/05/1857-01/11/58
Terrell J. Sgt.	23/05/1816
Tester J. Pte.	10/05/1857-01/11/58
Taylor W. Cpl.	23/04/1816
Thisleton E. Asst/ Surgeon	10/05/1857-01/11/58
Thomas B. Pte.	23/04/1816
Thomas C. Pte.	23/04/1816
Thomas J. Pte.	23/04/1816
Thomas J. Ens.	23/04/1816
Thomas N. Pte.	23/04/1816
Thomas W. Pte.	23/04/1816
Thompson J. Pte.	23/04/1816
Thompson W. Pte.	10/05/1857-01/11/58
Thumbwood J. Pte.	10/05/1857-01/11/58
Tick W. Pte.	23/04/1816
Timmins J. Pte.	10/05/1857-01/11/58
Tindal J. Pte.	23/04/1816
Tippen E. Pte.	23/04/1816
Tisdall T. Capt.	07/08/1807
Tisdall A. Capt.	10/05/1857-01/11/58
Tomkins N.R. Lt.	23/04/1816
Torney P. Pte.	10/05/1857-01/11/58
Traut R. Pte.	10/05/1857-01/11/58
Travers J. Pte.	23/04/1816
Trill J. Sgt.	10/05/1857-01/11/58
Trim J. Pte.	23/04/1816
Triman R. Lt.	10/05/1857-01/11/58
Trimm T. Pte.	23/04/1816
Trood E. Pte.	10/05/1857-01/11/58
Troup R.H.W. Lt.	10/05/1857-01/11/58
Trower J. Pte.	23/04/1816
Tully A. Sgt.	23/04/1816
Tune J. Pte.	23/04/1816
Tunney H. Pte.	10/05/1857-01/11/58

Name	Date
Turner J. Pte.	23/04/1816
Turner J. Pte.	23/04/1816
Turner J. Pte.	10/05/1857-01/11/58
Turner W. Pte.	23/04/1816
Turner W. Pte.	23/04/1816
Twohey T. Drmr.	10/05/1857-01/11/58
Tyrrell P. Pte.	23/04/1816
Underwood J. Pte.	10/05/1857-03/08/58
Underwood T. Pte.	23/04/1816
Veale H. Pte.	23/04/1816
Vaughey J. Pte.	10/05/1857-03/08/58
Vetch C. Pte.	23/04/1816
Virge W. Cpl.	23/04/1816
Waldridge T. Pte.	23/04/1816
Waite J. Pte.	10/05/1857-01/11/58
Waldie G. Pte.	10/05/1857-01/11/58
Walker W. Lt.	21/04/1807,14-18/07/07
Wall C.W. Maj.	23/04/1816
Walsh J. Pte.	10/05/1857-01/11/58
Walter J.McN. Lt-Col., C.B.	17/05/1859
Walters J. Pte.	23/04/1816
Walton H. Pte.	23/04/1816
Walton H. Cpl.	10/05/1857-01/11/58
Ward G. Pte.	23/04/1816
Waring Capt.	25/04/1707
Warner T. Pte.	23/04/1816
Warton S. Pte.	23/04/1816
Watkins J. Sgt.	23/04/1816
Watkins W. Pte.	23/04/1816
Watson C. Pte.	10/05/1857-01/11/58
Watson T. Pte.	10/05/1857-03/08/58
Weare S. Pte.	23/04/1816
Weare T. Lt-Col., K.H., General Service Medal & 3 Clasps	05/10/1813,19/04/14,13/09/14,23/04/16, 1836
Webb G. Pte.	23/04/1816
Webb R. Pte.	10/05/1857-01/11/58
Webb W. Pte.	10/05/1857-01/11/58
Webley R. Pte.	23/04/1816
Weily M. Pte.	10/05/1857-01/11/58
Wellbeloved G. Pte.	23/04/1816
Weller W. Pte.	10/05/1857-01/11/58
Wells John Pte.	23/04/1816
West C. Pte.	10/05/1857-01/11/58
West F. Cpl.	10/05/1857-01/11/58
West J. Pte.	23/04/1816
West P. Pte.	23/04/1816
West T. Cpl.	10/05/1857-01/11/58
Westrip T. Pte.	23/04/1816
Westerman R. Capt.	18/03/1807,14-18/07/07
White M. Pte.	23/04/1816
Whitear J. Pte.	23/04/1816
Wickham G. Pte.	23/04/1816
Wicks J. Pte.	23/04/1816
Widdrington W. Capt.	13/07-30/08/1762

Wilder F.J. *Sir* Maj-Gen.	22/03/1809,14/06/17
Wilder J. Pte.	23/04/1816
Wilkins G. Lt.	23/04/1816
Wilkinson G. Lt.	20/09/1799,21/04/1807,14-18/07/07
Willoughby R. Ens.	27/04/1707
Williams J. Pte.	23/04/1816
Williams J. Pte.	10/05/1857-01/11/58
Williams R. Pte.	10/05/1857-01/11/58
Williams T Lt.	31/12/1778
Willis C. Pte.	23/04/1816
Willis R. Sgt.	23/04/1816
Willoughby G. Pte.	23/04/1816
Wills J. Pte.	23/04/1816
Wilson D. Pte.	10/05/1857-01/11/58
Wilson G. Pte.	10/05/1857-01/11/58
Wilson J. Pte.	23/04/1816
Wilson T. Cpl.	23/04/1816
Wilson W. Pte.	10/05/1857-03/08/58
Wood W. Pte.	23/04/1816
Wooding J. Pte.	10/05/1857-03/08/58
Woods C. Pte.	23/04/1816
Woods J. Pte.	23/04/1816
Woolfe B. Pte.	10/05/1857-01/11/58
Workman T. Pte.	23/04/1816
Worrall W. Pte.	23/04/1816
Wren W. Pte.	10/05/1857-01/11/58
Wrenn W. Pte.	23/04/1816
Wright C. Pte.	10/05/1857-01/11/58
Wyatt C. Pte.	23/04/1816
Wyatt J.B. Ens.	23/04/1816
Wymark J. Drmr.	23/04/1816
Yarrow. T. Sgt.	10/05/1857-01/11/58

In memory of my late grandfather C.S.M. George Andrew Charman who served 21 years with the Colours from 1899 to 1920. He kept a diary of the time he spent in Palestine 1917 to 1918, and he was Mentioned in Dispatches in 1919.

It was writing a book about his Army Service that led me to write this book on all the Honours and Awards bestowed upon the Officers, N.C.O.'s and Men of The Royal Sussex Regiment, and The Sussex Yeomanry who fought with them as the 16th Battalion.

This book is dedicated to the Officers and Men who fought and died under the Colours of the Royal Sussex Regiment, in defence of their Country and their Allies, in the Great War of 1914 to 1919. Heroes all, the mentioned and rewarded and to the unsung whose deeds went unnoticed and unrewarded.

It is a book which describes in the words of the newspapers of the time, how the heroes were awarded honours for their acts of gallantry and devotion to duty in the field and in some instances the sacrifice of their lives, and where available, the Citation for their act of gallantry.

For the Fallen

"They went with songs to the battle, they were young,
Straight of limb, true of eye, steady and aglow;
They were staunch to the end against odds uncounted,
They fell with their faces to the foe.

They shall grow not old, as we that are left to grow old ;
Age shall not weary them, nor the years condemn.
At the going down of the sun and in the morning
We will remember them."

Acknowledgements

With grateful acknowledgement to the British Library Newspapers (Colindale), the National Archives (Kew), the Royal Sussex Regimental Archives (Alan Readman Asst. County Archivist, County Hall, Chichester), Colin Wood (Crawley Down) medal knowledge, David Lester (Eastbourne) for all the citations and photographs of the Southdown Battalions, Nick Deacon (Harrow) for various photographs, the Commonwealth War Graves Commission site and the Battle of Britain Archives, (Hendon), without whose assistance this book could not have been compiled. Excerpt is from the poem "For the Fallen" by Laurence Binyon (1869-1943). The poem "The Soldier" is by Rupert Brooke (1887-1915). These acknowledgements cover the period 1860-1920

Foreword

This book is in chronological order as to when the honours and awards were first announced in the newspapers or the London Gazette. Some of the recipients are mentioned more than once at different times, all the reports are from various local papers of the time, mainly the *Sussex Daily News* and the *Sussex Express,* all Citations shown are taken from the *London Gazette* and Battalion War Diaries.

Some of the awards have no citations, such as those given for New Year's Honours and the King's Birthday, unless it states in the *London Gazette* that citations will follow at a later date. Usually these awards are given not for one specific action, but for several minor ones over a period of time. This also occurred at other times during the year, as it is often stated on a Citation. Some of the M.M.'s that are published in the *"Peace Gazettes"*, may refer to an action in 1914/15, and the first six months of 1916, before the Military Medal was first instigated and have been back-awarded.

This was also the case with some M.I.D's , for example :-

The following are mentioned by Sir Douglas Haig as deserving of special mention for distinguished and gallant services and devotion to duty during the period 16th September 1918, to 15th March, 1919.

No written Citation or Oak Leaf accompanied this M.I.D., but it was written into the officer's/soldier's records.

As with the Foreign Awards, not all were *"Gazetted"* , again some were given as to the Commander's discretion, as to whom he thought should receive an award. These can be usually found mentioned in the Regimental/Battalion War Diaries.

Any omission in this book of any of the awards and decorations are purely my own mistake during research and is unintentional.

Battle Honours

The Royal Sussex Regiment

"Gibraltar, 1704-5," "Louisbourg, 1758," "Quebec, 1759," "Martinique," "Havannah, 1762," "St. Lucia, 1778," "Maida, 1806""Egypt, 1882," "Abu Klea," "Nile, 1884-85," "South Africa, 1900-02," "Mons," **"Retreat from Mons," Marne, 1914, 1918,"** "Aisne, 1914," "Armentieres, 1914," **"Ypres, 1914, 1917, 1918,"** "Gheluvelt," "Nonne Bosschen," "Givenchy, 1914," "Aubers," "Loos," **"Somme, 1916, 1918,"** "Albert, 1916, 1918," "Bazentin," "Delville Wood," "Pozieres," "Flers-Courcelette," "Morval," "Theipval," "Le Transloy," "Ancre Heights," Ancre, 1916,1918," "Arras, 1917,1918," "Vimy, 1917," "Scarpe, 1917," "Arleux," "Messines, 1917," **"Pilckem,"** "Langemarck, 1917," "Menin Road," "Polygon Wood," "Broodseinde," "Poelcapplle," "Passchendaele," "Cambrai, 1917,1918," "St. Quentin, "Bapaume, 1918," "Rosieres," "Avre," "Lys," "Kemmel." "Scherpenberg," "Soissonnais-Ourcq," "Amiens," "Drocourt-Queant," **"Hindenburg Line,"** "Epehy," "St. Quentin Canal," "Beaurevoir," "Courtrai," "Selle," "Sambre," "France and Flanders, 1914-1918," "Piave," "Vittorio, Vento," **"Italy, 1917-18,"** "Sulva," "Landing at Sulva," "Scimitar Hill," **"Gallipoli, 1915,"** "Rumani," "Egypt, 1915-17," "Gaza, "El Mughar," "Jerusalem," "Jericho," "Tell 'Asur," "Palestine, 1917-18," **"N.W. Frontier India, 1915,1916-17,"** "Murman, 1918-19," **"Afghanistan, 1919."**

SUSSEX YEOMANRY (DRAGOONS) (16th Battalion)

"Somme, 1918," "Bapaume, 1918," "Hindenburg Line," "Epehy," "Pursuit to Mons," France and Flanders, 1918," **"Gallipoli, 1915," "Egypt, 1916-17,"** "Gaza," "Jerusalem," "Tell 'Asur," "Palestine, 1917-1918.

Motto

Honi soit qui mal y pense

Nothing succeeds like Sussex

Colonels of the Regiment

1861-1863   Gen. Sir George Leigh Goldie, K.C.B.,C.B. (February 13th)
1863–1875   Gen. Arthur Simcoe Baynes (March 27th)
1875-1879   Gen. Henry Renny, C.S.I. (September 14th)
1879-1885   Gen. Sir Richard Thomas Farren, G.C.B. (June 9th)
1885-1888   Lt-Gen. William Lenox Ingall, C.B. (September 14th)
1888-1895   Lt-Gen. Robert Julian Baumgartner, C.B. (January 12th)
1895-1898   Lt-Gen. John McNeill Walter, C.B. (September 25th)
1898-1900   Lt-Gen. Sir George Samuel Young, C.B. (October 6th)
1900-1901   Gen. Sir John Davis, K.C.B. (April 12th)
1901-1903   Lt-Gen. Sir Henry Francis Williams, K.C.B. (October 6th)
1903-1914   Lt-Gen. Sir William Freeman Kelly, K.C.B. (July 29th)

2nd Battalion

1881-1883 Gen. Hon. Arthur Upton (July 1st)
(was Colonel of 107th Regiment of Foot, December 6th 1873)

Nicknames of the regiment:-

The Orange Lilies, The Haddocks and The Iron Regiment.

Marches of the Regiment

1st Bn. Quick March :- The Royal Sussex
2nd Bn. Quick March :- The Lass of Richmond Hill
5th Bn. (Cinque Ports) :- Let the Hills Resound
4th/5th Bn. (Cinque Ports) :- Let the Hills Resound
Regimental Slow March :- Roussillon

"London Gazette" Friday June 28th 1861

War-Office, June 28, 1861

THE Queen has been graciously pleased to give orders for the following appointments to the Most Honourable Order of the Bath :

To be Ordinary Members of the Military Division of the Second Class, or Knights Commanders, of the said Most Honourable Order; viz:-

K.C.B.

Lieutenant-General George Leigh Goldie, C.B.

"London Gazette" Tuesday August 16th 1864

New Zealand (Waikato Maori War)

The Queen has been graciously pleased to signify Her intention to confer the decoration of the Victoria Cross on the under-mentioned Officer, whose claim to the same has been submitted for Her Majesty's approval, for his gallant conduct in New Zealand, as recorded against his name ; viz :

V.C.

Lieutenant-Colonel John Carstairs McNeill, 107th Regiment of Foot, (later 2nd Battalion)

For the valour and presence of mind which he displayed in New Zealand, on the 30th of March, 1864, which is thus described by Private Vesper, of the Colonial Defence Force. Private Vosper states that he was sent on that day with Private Gibson, of the same Force, as an escort to Major (now Lieutenant-Colonel) McNeill, Aide-de-Camp to Lieutenant-General Sir Duncan Cameron. Lieutenant-Colonel McNeill was proceeding to Te Awamutu on duty at the time. On returning from that place, and about a mile on this side of Ohanpu, this Officer, having seen a body of the enemy in front, sent Private Gibson back to bring up Infantry from Ohanpu, and he and Private Vosper proceeded leisurely to the top of a rise to watch the enemy. Suddenly they were attacked by about 50 natives, who were concealed in the fern close at hand. Their only chance of escape was by riding for their lives, and as they turned to gallop, Private Vesper's horse fell and threw him. The natives thereupon rushed forward to seize .him, but Lieutenant-Colonel McNeill, on perceiving that Private Vosper was not following him, returned, caught his horse, and helped him to mount. the natives were firing sharply at them, and were so near that, according to Private Vesper's statement, it was only by galloping as hard as they could that they escaped. He says that he owes his life entirely to Lieutenant-Colonel McNeill's assistance, for he could not have caught his horse alone, and in a few minutes must have been killed.

Date of Act of Bravery, March 30th, 1864.

"London Gazette" Friday December 23rd 1870

THE Queen has been graciously pleased to make the following appointments to the Most Distinguished Order of Saint Michael and Saint George:-

To be Ordinary Members of the Second Class, or Knights Commanders of the said Order:-

C.M.G.

Lieutenant-Colonel John Carstairs McNeill, V.C., Military Secretary to the Governor-General of Canada.

"London Gazette" Tuesday March 31st 1874

THE Queen has been graciously pleased to give orders for the following promotions in, and appointments to, the Most Honourable Order of the Bath:-

To be Ordinary Members of the Division of the Third Class, or Companions of the said Most Honourable Order:-

C.B.

Colonel John Carstairs McNeill, V.C.,C.M.G., late 48th Regiment

"London Gazette" Tuesday August 17th 1880

THE Queen has been graciously pleased to make the following promotion in the Most Distinguished Order of Saint Michael and Saint George:-

To be an Ordinary Member of the Second Class, or Knights Commanders of the said Most Distinguished Order:-

K.C.M.G.

Colonel John Carstairs McNeill, V.C.,C.B.,C.M.G.

"London Gazette" Friday July 1st 1881

War Office, Pall Mall, 1st July, 1881
THE Queen has been pleased to approve of the following changes in the designation of Regiments of Infantry of the Line which will take effect on and after the 1st July, 1881.

Present Title	Future Title
35th (Royal Sussex)	1st Bn. of The Royal Sussex Regiment
107th (Bengal Infantry)	2nd Bn. of The Royal Sussex Regiment

(The Maltese cross of the 107th formed part of the Regiment's insignia with the Roussillion Plume commemorating the 35th's part at Quebec.)

"London Gazette" Friday 8th December 1882

Egypt and Sudan 1882-1889

THE Queen has been pleased to give orders for the following promotion in the Most Honourable Order of the Bath:-

To be an Extra Member, of the Military Division of the Second Class or Knights Commanders of the said Most Honourable Order, viz.:-

K.C.B.

Major-General Sir John Carstairs McNeill, V.C.,K.C.M.G., C.B.

"London Gazette" Tuesday May 6th 1884

Head-Quarters, Army of Occupation,
Cairo, April 14, 1884.

Sir

I HAVE the honour to forward herewith, by Captain Baynes, 1st Battalion Cameron Highlanders, who acted as Assistant Military Secretary to Major-General Sir Gerald Graham, V.C., K.C.B., during the late Expedition, a Despatch mentioning Officers, non-commissioned officers, and men who have distinguished themselves during the late campaign in the Soudan.
I have, &c.,
FREDK. STEPHENSON,
Lieutenant-General, Commanding in Egypt.

From Major-General Sir G. Graham, V.C.,.C.B, Commanding Expeditionary Force, to Lieutenant-General Stephenson, C.B., Commanding Troops in Egypt.

1st Infantry Brigade.—The 1st Infantry Brigade was commanded by Brigadier-General Sir Redvers Buller, V.C., K.C.M.G , C.B., A.D.C., who, by his coolness in action his knowledge of soldiers, and experience in the field, combined with his great personal ascendancy over Officers and men, has been most valuable. Besides the ordinary command of his brigade, Brigadier-General Buller was in charge, as Senior Military Officer, of the re-embarkation at Trinkitat, a laborious and responsible duty, which he performed to my entire satisfaction.
Brigadier-General Buller reports that he has received every assistance from his Staff: Captain Kelly, Sussex Regiment, Brigade-Major; and Lieutenant St. Aubyn, Grenadier Guards, Aide- de-Camp. Captain Kelly was severely contused by a spent case-shot at El-Teb, but remained at his duties.

Captain Williams-Freeman, Sussex Regiment did service as Provost-Marshal to my satisfaction.

Mounted Infantry.—The Mounted Infantry was most efficiently handled on all occasions by Lieutenant and Local Captain Humphreys, the Welsh Regiment. Brigadier - General Stewart reports of this Officer that he cannot speak of him too highly. He was ably assisted by Lieutenant C. H. Payne, of the 1st Gordon Highlanders. All ranks of the Mounted Infantry displayed great coolness and readiness under fire.
In a letter marked "B" attached, Brigadier-General Stewart mentions the gallant conduct of Lieutenant Marling, 3rd King's Royal Rifles, of the Mounted Infantry, whom he recommends for the distinction of the Victoria Cross. Privates George Hunter, 3rd King's Royal Rifles, and Joseph Clift, Sussex Regiment, are mentioned for gallantly and devotion at Tamai on 13th March, 1884.

D.C.M.

1166 Pte. Joseph Clift,   1st Bn. SQ 23/05/84 Tamaai 13/03/84

Statement of Lieutenant Todd Thornton. At the battle of Tamai, on 13th instant, I was sent by Captain Humphreys to support Lieutenant Marling on the right of the position which we had taken up. On my arrival at the place where Lieutenant Marling's division was engaged, I found the fire of the enemy was very hot both on our left flank and in front, and as it gradually became hotter, and the square was by this time close up, within about 200 yards, Lieutenant Marling gave the order to the men " to your horses." Just as this occurred, Private Morley of my division was shot on ray right; he was then lifted up by Privates Hunter of the Rifles and Clift of the Sussex, and placed in front of Lieutenant Marling on his horse; he, however, fell off almost immediately ; Lieutenant Marling then dismounted and gave his horse up for the purpose of carrying off Private Morley, the enemy pressing close on to them, and they succeeded in carrying him about 80 yards towards the square, by which time the fire had slackened ,and we were all in comparative safety.

F. TODD THORNTON, Lieutenant,
1st Battalion Royal Sussex Regiment,
Mounted Infantry.

1166, Private Joseph Clift, 1st Battalion Royal Sussex Regiment, states :—
I was present with my division at the battle of "Tamai " on 13th March, 1884. Just before the enemy made their attack on the squares, Private Morley, of my division, was shot and fell. The order had just been given to us to retire, and the men were running to their horses. I remained to assist Private Morley, and Lieutenant Marling, and Private Hunter, of No. I Division (3rd Battalion King's Royal Rifles), immediately came up. Private Hunter dismounted, and we put Morley on the horse, in front of Lieutenant Marling, but he slipped off almost directly. Seeing this, Lieutenant Marling dismounted, and we put him (Morley) across Lieutenant Mailing's saddle. Lieutenant Marling and myself held him on, and Private Hunter led the horse. We succeeded in bringing him away towards the square, which was then coming up. We placed him near a bush, and I remained with him for a short time, until a stretcher was brought, and he was taken into the square.

JOSEPH CLIFT, Private,
1st Battalion Royal Sussex Regiment.

Made before me at Handuk, 19-3-84

H. HUMPHREYS, Captain.

True copy
KENNETH S. BAYNES, Captain.
Assistant Military Secretary.

No. 3356, Private George Hunter, 3rd King's Royal Rifles, states : —
I was present at the battle of " Tamai," on 13th March, 1884, with my division. No. 4 Division (1st Royal Sussex) was also with us. We were under a very hot fire just before the attack on the square by the rebels, and were just on the point of retiring to get out of the way of the square, when I saw Private Morley, of the Sussex Division, fall wounded. The order—"To your horses," had been given, and we were all going to our horses. I went back to his (Private Morley's) assistance, and Lieutenant Marling also went and got off his horse, and we put Morley across the horse to bring him away. After a few yards he slipped off, and we picked him up and put him on again. Private Clift, 1st Battalion Royal Sussex, also remained with his comrade and assisted us. We succeeded in carrying him to a place of safety near the square. While we were doing this, the rebels made their attack on the square, and were close upon us. The fire from the square, and the Abyssinians, who were acting with us and behaved very well, alone saved us from being cut off.

G. HUNTER, Private,
3rd Battalion King's Royal Rifles.

Made before me at Handuk, 19.3.84
H, HUMPHREYS,- Captain,
Commanding Mounted Infantry.

True copy,
KENNETH S. BAYNES, Captain,

Assistant Military Secretary,
11th April, 1884.

"London Gazette" Friday February 20th 1885

Inclosure No. 1.
From Brigadier-General Sir H. Stewart to the Chief of the Staff.
Abu Klea Wells, January 18, 1885

Sir,

IN continuation of my Report of the 14th instant, I have the honour to inform you that the force under my command has made the following movements in carrying out your orders.
On the 14th instant the force left Gakdul at 2 P.M., and marching until dark bivouacked for the night some 10 miles on the road to Matammeh. On the 15th instant a distance of 24 miles was accomplished, and a bivouac formed among the hills marked Gebel Es Sergain on the map. On the 16th instant the force left camp at 5 A.M., and halted for breakfast at 11.30 A.M. at the spot marked in the map by the 840th kilometre.
Whilst halted a report was received from Lieut.-Colonel Barrow, 19th Hussars, who had been sent forward with his squadron to reconnoitre the neighbourhood of the Abu Klea Wells, informing me that he had seen about 50 of the enemy standing in groups on the hills about four miles north-east of Abu Klea.
Shortly afterwards the whole force was advanced—the Guards Camel Regiment, Heavy Camel Regiment, and Mounted Infantry Camel Regiment, moving on a broad front in line of columns at half-distance, the ground being favourable.
It soon became manifest that the enemy was in force, and looking to the hour (2 P.M.) it did not seem desirable to attempt to attack until the following morning. Another bivouac was therefore selected, protected from the enemy's fire so far as the ground would permit, and various small works were constructed.
During the night a continuous light fire at long ranges was kept up by the enemy, doing little damage.
Upon the 17th instant it was plain that the enemy was in force. During the night they had constructed works on our right flank, from which a distant but well aimed fire was maintained. In our front the manoeuvring of their troops in line and in column was apparent, and everything pointed to the probability of an attack upon our position being made. Under these circumstances no particular hurry to advance was made in the hope that our apparent dilatoriness might induce the enemy to push home. The camp having been suitably strengthened to admit of its being held by a comparatively small garrison—viz., 40 Mounted Infantry, 125 Sussex and details; and the enemy still hesitating to attack, an advance was made to seize the Abu Klea Well.
The force moved on foot in a square, which was formed as follows:—Left front face, two companies Mounted Infantry; right front face, two companies Guards, with the three guns Royal Artillery in the centre. Left face, two companies Mounted Infantry, one company Heavy Camel Regiment. Right face, two companies Guards, detachment Royal Sussex. Rear face, four companies Heavy Camel Regiment, with Naval Brigade and one Gardner gun in the centre.
The advance at once attracted a fairly aimed fire from the enemy in front on both flanks which, in order to enable the square to continue moving, it was absolutely necessary to hold in check by the fire of skirmishers.
The enemy's main position was soon apparent, and by passing that position well clear of its left flank, it was manifest that he must attack or be enfiladed. As the square was nearly abreast of the position the enemy delivered his attack in the shape of a singularly well organised charge commencing with a wheel to the left.
A withering fire was at once brought to bear upon the enemy, especially from the more advanced portion of the left front face of the square. The rear portion of this face taking a moment or two to close up, was not in such a favourable position to receive the enemy's attack, and I regret to say that the square was penetrated at this point by the sheer weight of the enemy's numbers.

The steadiness of the troops enabled the hand to hand conflict to be maintained, whilst severe punishment was still being meted out to those of the enemy continuing to advance, with the result that a general retreat of the enemy under a heavy artillery and rifle fire soon took place.

After reforming the square, the 19th Hussars, who had been acting in difficult ground supporting our left flank, were pushed on to seize the Abu Klea Wells, and at 5 P.M. those wells were completely in our possession.

Detachments of the corps then returned to the bivouac of the 16th instant to bring up the camel and impedimenta left there, thus completing the force here this morning at 8 A.M.

The strength of the enemy is variously estimated from 8,000 to 14,000 men. My opinion is that not less than 2,000 of the enemy operated on our right flank, 3,000 in the main attack, and 5,000 in various other positions; but it is difficult to estimate their numbers with any exactness.

Their losses have been very heavy, not less than 800 lay dead on the open ground flanking our square, and their wounded during the entire day's fighting are reported by themselves as quite exceptional. Many are submitting.

I deeply regret that the necessity of obtaining water delays my immediate advance on Matammeh, but I trust this may be overcome in a few hours.

I cannot too deeply lament the loss of the many gallant officers and men that the force has suffered; but looking to the numbers of the enemy, their bravery, their discipline and the accuracy of fire of those possessing rifles, I trust that this loss, sad as it is, may be considered as in some measure inevitable.

In conclusion, I would add that it has been my duty to command a force from which exceptional work, exceptional hardships, and it may be added, exceptional fighting has been asked. It would be impossible for me adequately to describe the admirable support that has been given to me by every officer and man of the force. A return of casualties is attached. Every possible care is being taken of the wounded. Tents have been pitched, and a strong post established over the Well, garrisoned by a detachment of the Sussex Regiment.

I have, &c.,
HERBERT STEWART,
Brigadier- General.

Enclosure No. 3. Approximate State of Troops, &c., under command of Brigadier-General Sir H. Stewart, at Abu Klea, 17th January, 1885

Including

1st Battalion Royal Sussex Regiment—Major M. S. J. Sunderland, 8 officers, 250 non-commissioned officers and men, 4 Native drivers and interpreters, 2 horses.

"London Gazette" Tuesday March 10th 1885

Enclosure No. 3 Report on Proceedings from January 24th to February 1st.
January 24th.—Left Matammeh at eight A.M. in steamers.
The "Bordein," with Colonel Sir Charles Wilson, Captain Gascoigne (late Royal Horse Guards), Khasm-el-Mous Bey, 10 non-commissioned officers and privates, Royal Sussex Regiment, and 110 Soudanese troops. The " Tall Howeiya," with Captain Trafford and 10 men Royal Sussex Regiment, Abdul Hamid Bey, 80 Soudanese troops, and Lieutenant Stuart-Wortley, King's Royal Rifles, 11 A.M. stopped for wood at the village of Gandatu on east bank. Sheikh Hussein of the Shagiya tribe sent a messenger on board to say that his tribe was ready to join the English as soon as their power was established. Our victories at Abu Klea and near Matammeh had great effect, the enemy estimating their total loss at 3,000. They had heard that another English Army was advancing by the Nile, Stopped for the night near Derrera. The natives believed that Abdul-Kadir Pasha was at Gakdul.

"London Gazette" Friday April 10th 1885

From Colonel Sir C. W. Wilson to Chief of Staff

Korti, March 14, 1885

SIR,

AS a supplement.. to my report of the 22nd January last, I have the honour to furnish the following additional particulars respecting the movements of the force which left Jakdul on the 14th January, from 10.15 A.M. on the 19th when, Brigadier-General Sir Herbert Stewart having been severely wounded, I assumed command as senior officer. After consultation with Sir H. Stewart and Lieutenant-Colonel the Honourable E. T. Boscawen, the next senior officer, I determined to strengthen the zeribah, and, after leaving a garrison in it, to march for the Nile. The hospital within the zeribah was protected by a strong wall of commissariat and ordnance stores in which openings were left for the guns and Gardner. The zeribah round the camels was strengthened, and a small redoubt was built on a knoll occupied by our skirmishers, which commanded the zeribah at a distance of 80 yards. These works were thrown up under fire, and the boxes for the wall of the redoubt were carried across from the zeribah by the officers and men of the Heavy and Guards Camel Regiments, assisted by a detachment of Royal Engineers. Mr. Burleigh, correspondent of the Daily Telegraph, volunteered his services and took an active part in this arduous duty.

Two companies, one from the Guards and one from the Mounted Infantry Camel Regiment, were thrown out as skirmishers to keep down the enemy's fire whilst the zeribah was being strengthened and reparations were being made for the march to the Nile. The fighting force was formed up in square on the least exposed side of the zeribah, and about 3 P.M. marched towards a gravel ridge on which a large force of the enemy, with several banners; was collected. As the square moved round the zeribah a warm fire was opened upon it, and several men fell and were carried back to the hospital. The enemy's riflemen, who were well concealed in the lush grass, kept up a continuous fire upon the force until it arrived within 600 yards of the gravel ridge; at this moment the fire became much heavier, and there were several casualties, but it suddenly ceased as the spearmen, led by several men on horseback, came running down the hill. The appearance of the spearmen, which indicated an approaching crisis in the fight, was greeted by a loud cheer from the men, who were at once halted to receive the charge. The enemy left from 250 to 300 dead on the ground over which they charged, but it was ascertained afterwards that many more were killed in the long grass and in rear of the ridge, and that a number of wounded were carried off to Matammeh; amongst the killed were five sheikhs or emirs of the Baggarah Arabs. On the defeat of the spearmen, a strong force of the enemy, which had taken up a position to the left front of the square, and been kept in check by a well-directed artillery fire from the zeribah, dispersed in the direction of Matammeh, the square then marched without further opposition to the Nile, and bivouacked on its bank shortly after dark, The fighting force in the square was composed of half the Heavy Camel Regiment, Lieutenant-Colonel the Honourable R. A. Talbot, 1st Life Guards ; the Guards Camel Regiment. Lieutenant-Colonel Willson, Scots Guards; the Mounted Infantry Camel Regiment, Major Barrow; a detachment Royal Sussex Regiment, Major Sunderland; a detachment 19th Hussars, dismounted men, Lieutenant Craven; and a detachment Royal Engineers, Lieutenant Lawson acted as a reserve within the square.

"London Gazette" Tuesday August 25th 1885

The Secretary of State for War has received the following Despatches from General Lord Wolseley, G.C.B., G.C.M.G., commanding Her Majesty's Forces in Egypt, relative to the recent operations on the Upper Nile and near Suakin :—

37. The 2nd Brigade was commanded by Major-General Sir John McNeill, V.C. This officer led the troops who crowned the Dihilbat Hill at Hasheen on the 20th March, and on the 22nd had command at the action of the zereba, of which he held until the final advance on Tamai. Sir J. McNeill afterwards

commanded the force covering the advance of the railway to my entire satisfaction. He was ably assisted by Brevet Lieut.-Colonel Kelly, Royal Sussex Regiment, Brigade-Major. Colonel W. H. Ralston, 2nd Battalion East Surrey Regiment; Lieutenant-Colonel A. G. Huyshe, 1st Battalion Berkshire Regiment; Lieutenant.-Colonel R. H. Truell, 1st Battalion Shropshire Light Infantry; and Lieutenant-Colonel N. F. Way, Royal Marine Light Infantry, commanded their respective battalions with energy and efficiency.

The 2nd Brigade was composed of three remarkably fine battalions, and of the Royal Marines. Throughout the campaign this brigade displayed all the qualities of the best troops. The battalion of Royal Marines did excellent service and bore their share in gallantly repulsing the formidable attack on the zereba on the 22nd March, and in the subsequent hard work. This battalion did arduous duty during the summer of 1884, when it held Suakin against the attacks of the Arabs, and had to bear up against the trying climate.

List of Officers, Non-Commissioned Officers and Men whose services are deserving of Special Mention.

Colonel John Ormsby Vandeleur, Royal Sussex Regiment,
Major Marsden Samuel James Sunderland, Royal Sussex Regiment,
Captain Lionel James Trafford, Royal Sussex Regiment,

THE Queen has been graciously pleased to give orders for the following promotions in, and appointments to, the Most Honourable Order of the Bath :—

To be Ordinary Members of the Military Division of the Third Class, or Companions of the said Most Honourable Order, viz. :—

C.B.

Colonel John Ormsby Vandeleur, Commanding 1st Bn. Royal Sussex Regiment,

THE Queen has been graciously pleased to approve of the following Promotions being conferred upon the undermentioned Officers in recognition of their services during the recent operations in the Soudan. Dated 15th June, 1885 :—

To be Lieutenant-Colonels

Major Marsden Samuel James Sunderland, 1st Bn. Royal Sussex Regiment,

To be Majors

Captain Lionel James Trafford, the Royal Sussex Regiment,

D.C.M.

Cowstick S.E. Pte. 1440　　　1st Bn. SQ 25/08/85
Recent operations in the Sudan
Dale E. Pte. 688　　　1st Bn. SQ 25/08/85
Recent operations in the Sudan
Paine C. Pte. 1434　　　1st Bn. SQ 25/08/85
Recent operations in the Sudan
Othen W. L/Sgt. 318　　　1st Bn. SQ 25/08/85
Recent operations in the Sudan

Special General Order

"Sir Charles Wilson has brought to notice the steadiness and courage displayed by Lance-Corporal Othen and Privates Dale, Cowstick, and Paine, 1st Battalion Royal Sussex Regiment, on the afternoon and night of February 3rd. The first three were employed under Captain Gascoign in bringing down a large nuggar, on which were sick and wounded from the wrecked steamer "Bordein". This nuggar grounded and for the whole night the party on board were exposed to the fire of the enemy on the bank, until the nuggar was got off at 9a.m. on the morning of the 4th. Throughout this trying time Lance-Corporal Othen and Privates Dale and Cowstick were conspicuous by their steadiness and coolness. Private Paine was sent by Captain Gascoign from the nuggar to Sir Charles Wilson's camp to ask for assistance. He made his way there alone at night and afterwards returned to join Captain Gascoign again."

Major Sunderland who commanded the half Battalion at Abu Klea, and Captain Trafford, who commanded the party which went through to Khartoum were promoted to Brevet rank.

"London Gazette" **Thursday 6th October 1885**

THE Queen has been pleased to give and grant unto the undermentioned Officers in Her Majesty's Service Her Majesty's Royal licence and permission that they may accept and wear the Insignia of the several Classes of the Orders of the Osmanieh and the Medjidieh attached to their respective names, which His Highness the Khedive of Egypt, authorized by His Imperial Majesty the Sultan, has been pleased to confer upon them in approbation of their distinguished services before the enemy during the operations in the Soudan of last year:—

Fourth Class Medjidieh

Captain George Charles Peere Williams-Freeman, the Royal Sussex Regiment,
Major and Brevet Lieutenant-Colonel William Freeman Kelly, the Royal Sussex Regiment,

"London Gazette" **Friday October 23rd 1885**

THE Queen has been pleased to give and grant unto the undermentioned Officers in Her Majesty's Service Her Royal licence and permission that they may accept and wear the Insignia of the Fourth Classes of the Orders of the Osmanieh and of the Medjidieh, which His Highness the Khedive of Egypt, authorized by His Imperial Majesty the Sultan, has been pleased to confer upon them, in recognition of their services whilst actually and entirely employed beyond Her Majesty's Dominions in the Egyptian Army ; —

Fourth Class Medjidieh

Captain Benjamin Doniethorpe Alsop Donne, The Royal Sussex Regiment,

1886

By General Order No. 10 of 1886 the Regiment was permitted to bear the words "The Nile 1884,5" and "Abu Klea" on the colours.

"London Gazette" **Tuesday August 30th 1887**

THE Queen has been pleased to give and grant unto the undermentioned Officers of Her Majesty's Army Her Royal licence and authority that they may accept and wear the Insignia of the Order of the Medjidieh of the Fourth Class, which His Highness the Khedive of Egypt, authorized by His Imperial

Majesty the Sultan, has been pleased to confer upon them, in recognition of their services whilst actually and entirely employed beyond Her Majesty's Dominions : —

Fourth Class Medjidieh

Lieutenant Frederick St. Duthus Skinner, the Royal Sussex Regiment,

Hazara 1889

"London Gazette" **Friday April 12th 1889**

D.S.O.

Lieutenant-Colonel Marsden Samuel James Sunderland, 2nd Bn. Royal Sussex Regiment

"For services during the operation in Hazara".

Egypt

"London Gazette" **Friday September 6th 1889**

From Major-General Sir F. Grenfell, K.C.B., A.D.C., Commanding the Nile Field Force, to Major-General the Hon. Sir J. C. Dormer, K.C.B., Commanding in Egypt.
Toski, August 4, 1889.
Sir,
I HAVE the honour to forward a report on the action which was fought near Toski on August 3rd.

The following Officers commanded Infantry Battalions, and I have already reported their good service in the body of my despatch :—

Brevet Major Benjamin Doniethorpe Alsop Donne, Royal Sussex Regiment.

The centre was stormed with great steadiness by the 10th Soudanese Battalion, under Brevet Major Donne, Sussex Regiment (E.A.), who drove the Dervishes from the heights, inflicting great loss on them, as they retreated from their cover behind the hill, and capturing a large number of standards.

"London Gazette" **Friday January 17th 1890**

THE Queen has been pleased to give and grant unto the undermentioned Officers in Her Majesty's Army Her Royal Licence and permission that they may accept and wear the insignia of certain classes of the Orders of the Osmanieh and the Medjidieh, as signified against their respective names, which His Highness the Khedive of Egypt, authorized by His Imperial Majesty the Sultan, has been pleased to confer upon them in recognition of their services in the actions at Toski and Gemaizah whilst actually and entirely employed beyond Her Majesty's Dominions with the Egyptian Army :-

DECORATIONS for action at TOSKI on the NILE.

Third Class Medjidieh

Captain and Brevet Major Benjamin Doniethorpe Alsop Donne,   Royal Sussex Regiment,

"London Gazette" Tuesday November 29th 1892

Her Majesty the Queen has been graciously pleased to confer the Volunteer Officers' Decoration upon the undermentioned Officers of the Volunteer Force, who have been duly recommended for the same under the terms of the Royal Warrant, dated 25th July, 1892 :—

1st Volunteer Battalion, the Royal Sussex Regiment

Honorary Colonel Henry Verrall
Lieutenant-Colonel and Honorary Colonel William Cloves Tamplin,
Major and Honorary Lieutenant-Colonel Hugh John Verrall,
Captain and Honorary Major George Thomas Shaft,
Captain and Honorary Major Henry John Richard Livesay,
Captain and Honorary Major Henry Charles Malden, retired
Captain Edmund Evan Scott, retired
Captain John Colbatch Clark, retired

2nd Volunteer Battalion the Royal Sussex Regiment

Honorary Colonel the Right Honourable Sir Walter Barrtelot-Bartlelot, Bart., C.B.
Lieutenant-Colonel and Honorary Colonel Sir Henry Fletcher, Bart.
Major and Honorary Lieutenant-Colonel William Henry Campion
Major and Honorary Lieutenant-Colonel Henry , Duke of Norfolk, K.G.
Captain and Honorary Major Arthur Henty
Captain and Honorary Major Edwin Henty
Quartermaster and Honorary Captain Alfred Cortis
Brigade - Surgeon – Lieutenant- Colonel Charles Francis Lewis
Lieutenant and Honorary Captain James Richardson Pearless, retired.

1st Cinque Ports Rifle Volunteer Corp

Major Francis William Aitkens,
Quartermaster and Honorary Major Stanley Thomas Weston,
Acting Chaplain the Reverend Arthur Eden

"London Gazette" Tuesday January 24th 1893

Her Majesty the Queen has been graciously pleased to confer the Volunteer Officers' Decoration upon the undermentioned Officers of the Volunteer Force, who have been duly recommended for the same under the terms of the Royal Warrant, dated 25th July, 1892 :—

SOUTH-EASTERN DISTRICT

RIFLE.

1st Volunteer Battalion, The Royal Sussex Regiment

Honorary Major and Adjutant James Arthur Bloomfield, retired,

Honorary Chaplain the Reverend Henry Herbert Wyatt, M.A., retired,

1st Cinque Ports Rifle Volunteer Corp

Honorary Major and Adjutant Spence D. Turner, retired,

"London Gazette" **Friday July 21st 1893**

Her Majesty the Queen has been graciously pleased to confer the Volunteer Officers' Decoration upon the undermentioned Officers of the Volunteer Force, who have been duly recommended for the same under the terms of the Royal Warrant, dated 25th July, 1892 :—

SOUTH-EASTERN DISTRICT

RIFLE

1st Volunteer Battalion, The Royal Sussex Regiment

Captain Wilson Stuckey,

"London Gazette" **Friday August 15th 1893**

THE Queen has been pleased to give and grant unto Major Benjamin Doniethorpe Alsop Donne, of the Royal Sussex Regiment, Her Majesty's Royal licence and authority that he may accept and wear the Insignia of the Third Class of the Order of the Osmanieh, which His Highness the Khedive of Egypt, authorized by His Imperial Majesty the Sultan, has been pleased to confer upon him in recognition of his services while actually and entirely employed beyond Her Majesty's Dominions as an officer of the Egyptian Army.

Order of Osmanieh (3rd Class)

Major Benjamin Doniethorpe Alsop Donne, Royal Sussex Regiment

"London Gazette" **Tuesday February 16th 1897**

THE Queen has been graciously pleased to confer the Volunteer Officers' Decoration upon the undermentioned Officers of the volunteer Force, who have been duly recommended for the same under the terms of the Royal Warrant, dated 25th July, 1892 :—

SOUTH-EASTERN DISTRICT

RIFLE

1st Volunteer Battalion, The Royal Sussex

Captain and Honorary Major Frederick Cecil Parsons,

2nd Volunteer Battalion, The Royal Sussex Regiment.

Captain and Honorary Major John James Lister,

"London Gazette" Friday May 14th 1897

THE Queen has been graciously pleased to confer the Volunteer Officers' Decoration upon the undermentioned Officers of the volunteer Force, who have been duly recommended for the same under the terms of the Royal Warrant, dated 25th July, 1892 :—

SOUTH-EASTERN DISTRICT

RIFLE

2nd Volunteer Battalion, The Royal Sussex Regiment.

Surgeon-Lieutenant Giles Lockwood Lang Hawken, retired,

"London Gazette" Tuesday November 9th 1897

THE Queen has been graciously pleased to confer the Volunteer Officers' Decoration upon the undermentioned Officers of the volunteer Force, who have been duly recommended for the same under the terms of the Royal Warrant, dated 25th July, 1892 :—

SOUTH-EASTERN –DISTRICT

RIFLE

1st Volunteer Battalion, The Royal Sussex Regiment.

Major and Honorary Lieutenant-Colonel Alfred Freeman Gell,
2nd Volunteer Battalion, The Royal Sussex Regiment.

Captain and Honorary Major Edward Henry Joseph David Mostyn,

India and Burma 1898

Tirah

"London Gazette" Tuesday April 5th 1898

From General Sir W. S. A. Lockhart, K.C.B., K.C.S.I., Commanding Tirah Expeditionary Force, to the Adjutant-General in India.— No. 812-T.C. Head Quarters, Tirah Expeditionary Force, Camp Rawalpindi, dated the 26th January, 1898. IN continuation of my letter No. 524-T.C., dated 9th December, 1897, I have the honour to submit, for the information of His Excellency the Commander-in-Chief in India, the following account of the operations of the force under my command from the 1st November, 1897, up to the present date.

8. On December 15th and 16th, the Peshawar Column under Brigadier-General Hammond, left Swaikot for Jamrud, which was reached on the 17th. There it was joined on the 19th by the troops of the 1st Division, together with the Ghurkha Scouts and the head-quarter wing of the 1st Battalion, Royal Scots Fusiliers. The Peshawar Column and the 1st Division, Main Column, were halted at Jamrud from December 19th to 22nd, the troops which had returned from Tirah needing rest after their fatiguing march. At this time three British corps in the Main Column, which had been much weakened by losses in action or by sickness, were relieved by battalions from India, the 1st Battalion, Devonshire Regiment, being replaced by the 2nd Battalion, Royal Sussex Regiment, from Peshawar, the 1st Battalion, Dorsetshire Regiment, by the 1st Battalion, Duke of Cornwall's Light Infantry, from Rawalpindi, and the 1st Battalion, Northamptonshire Regiment by the 2nd Battalion, King's Own Yorkshire Light Infantry, also from Rawalpindi. Shortly after wards the same reason obliged me to dispense with the services of the head-quarter wing of the 1st Battalion, Royal Scots Fusiliers.

"London Gazette" Wednesday June 7th 1898

The following General Order, dated 6th May, 1898, publishing a Despatch from General Sir W. S. A. Lockhart, G.C.B., K.C.S.I. regarding the operations of the Tirah Expeditionary Force from the 27th January to the 5th April, 1898, has been received from the Government of India:—

13. Since the publication of my previous despatches, the undermentioned officers, whose names were omitted in the first instance, have been specially recommended for their good services by the General Officers concerned :

M.I.D.

Lieutenant-Colonel Charles Haydon Wilkinson Cafe, 2nd Battalion, Royal Sussex Regiment.

15. I have the honour to forward, for favourable consideration, lists of the British non-commissioned officers and men and of the native ranks who have shown conspicuous gallantry in the field-during the operations subsequent to the 26th January, 1898, and whom I recommend for the Distinguished Conduct Medal and the Order of Merit. The necessary documents are appended.

D.C.M.

Day J. Pte.	4633	2nd Bn.	SQ 9-7-98	NWF 97/98
Finucane A. Sgt.	3762	2nd Bn.	SQ 9-7-98	NWF 97/98
Maudling F. Pte.	4591	2nd Bn.	SQ 9-7-98	NWF 97/98

On the night of 7th February, No. 16 Piquet was attacked with great determination in the rear by the enemy, who fired from ranges of 10 to 20 yards and threw big stones into the sangar, but Lance-Sergeant Arthur Finucane, and Privates No.3659 George Upton, No.4971 Charles Phillpot, No.3110 Charles Overton, No.3929 William Terry, No.4768 Frederick Wells and No.5011 William Newbury, 2nd Royal Sussex Regiment, defended the picquet for one and a quarter hours, with still greater determination. Private Newbury was wounded in two places, but is doing well.
With a full knowledge of the circumstances Brigadier-General Hart has recommended Lance-Sergeant Finucane for the "Distinguished Conduct Medal."

"London Gazette" Tuesday August 9th 1898

THE Queen has been graciously pleased to confer the Volunteer Officers' Decoration upon the undermentioned Officers of the Volunteer Force, who have been duly recommended for the same under the terms of the Royal Warrant, dated 25th July, 1892 :—

SOUTH-EASTERN DISTRICT

RIFLE

2nd Volunteer Battalion, The Royal Sussex Regiment

Surgeon-Lieutenant Adolphus William Wisden Caudle, retired,

"London Gazette" Tuesday October 31st 1899

The Queen has been graciously pleased to confer the Volunteer Officers' Decoration upon the undermentioned Officers of the Volunteer Force, who have been duly recommended for the same under the terms of the Royal Warrant, dated 25th July, 1892;—

SOUTH-EASTERN DISTRICT

RIFLE

2nd Volunteer Battalion, The Royal Sussex Regiment.
Captain and Honorary Major Robert Masterman Helme,

South Africa 1899-1902

Special Number of *"The Illustrated London News"*

The Transvaal War 1899-1900

SUSSEX

The Royal Sussex Regiment :- The 1st Battalion, under Colonel B.D.A. Donne, was first in action at Sand River, where on May 9 it led General Bruce Hamilton's Brigade in the charge on the kopjes, and carried the position with the bayonet with insignificant loss. It fought at Doornkop on May 29, sustaining about twenty causalities, and at the Diamond Hill engagement, fifteen miles east of Pretoria, on June 12, when the Volunteer Company won high praise for its conduct under fire. It made a bold attack on the Boer position at Retief's Nek, near Bethlehem, July 23. The failure was in no way due to the men, who behaved splendidly, going into action after marching all through a cold and rough night in order to join General Hunter. The battalion, with the Black Watch, made a direct attack across open country on the Boer position, and drove the enemy from the outlying hills. In this engagement five officers and thirty-four men were killed or wounded, Captain Sir W.G. Barttelot, of the Volunteer Company, being among those killed. A large number of 1st Volunteer Battalion and the whole of the 2nd Battalion offered for active service. The county raised a company for the Imperial Yeomanry.

"London Gazette" Tuesday October 2nd 1900

D.C.M.

No. 5292 Corporal P. Hoad, 1st Bn.
(SQ 26/09/00 Brandwater Basin 26/08/00)

No. 4634 Lance-Corporal C.C. Neville, 1st Bn.
(SQ 26/09/00 Brandwater Basin 26/08/00)

The D.C.M.'s for Cpl. Hoad and Pte. Neville were awarded for rescuing Captain Mackenzie who had been shot in the ankle and had fallen out in the open and under a hail of fire, with Lieutenant Hopkins leading them they were able to carry Captain Mackenzie to safety.

"London Gazette" Tuesday October 16th 1900

THE Queen has been graciously pleased to give orders for the following promotion in, and appointments to, the Most Honourable Order of the Bath :

To be an Ordinary Member of the Civil Division of the Second Class, or Knights Commander, of the said Most Honourable Order, viz.:-

K.C.B.

Colonel Sir Henry Fletcher, Bart., commanding the Sussex Volunteer Infantry Brigade, and formerly commanding the 2nd Volunteer Battalion, the Royal Sussex Regiment.

"London Gazette" Friday February 8th 1901

From Lieutenant-General Sir A. Hunter, K.C.B., D.S.O., Commanding Operations in the Eastern Districts of the Orange River Colony, to the Chief of the Staff, South Africa. Fouriesburg, 4th August, 1900.

14. At 3 P.M. on 16th of July, the wires being cut, on receiving news of this outbreak of the enemy, I dispatched Brigadier-General Ridley with 800 Mounted Infantry to reinforce General Broadwood, and sent Lieutenant-Colonel Donne with the 1st Battalion Royal Sussex Regiment and 81st Battery, Royal Field Artillery, to occupy Meyer's Kop. I also directed Major-General Clements to relieve Sir Leslie Rundle's troops at Witnek with a portion of his force. I failed, therefore, in giving effect to the first part of the Commander-in-Chief's instructions.

18. On 22nd July, having ordered a concentration of the troops of Major-Generals Clements and Paget, with a view to a simultaneous assault on 23rd July upon Slabbert's Nek, and a demonstration by Sir Leslie Rundle's forces along their whole front, I left Bethlehem at 11 A.M. with the intention of attacking Retief's Nek, taking with me the Highland Brigade under Major-General MacDonald, two 5-in. guns, the 5th and 76th Batteries, Royal Field Artillery, Lavat's Scouts, and Rimington's Guides. At the same time 1 directed Lieutenant-Colonel Donne to join me the next morning from Meyer's Kop with the 1st Battalion Royal Sussex Regiment and 81st Battery, Royal Field Artillery. With the idea of deceiving the enemy, my force started, in the first instance, as if going to Naauwport Nek, but changing direction, it moved to Boshof's Farm under Vaal Kranz, about 3 miles to the north of Retief's Nek, where it bivouacked. My mounted troops were engaged towards the close of the day with some 200 Boers who retired into the nek as dusk fell.

20. The following morning, 23rd July, soon after daybreak my force moved out of its bivouacs, the 2nd Battalion Seaforth Highlanders being left to furnish an outpost line round Boshof's Farm to protect the convoy. At 8 A.M. my artillery opened fire shelling the nek and the kopjes on either side of it, and at 9 A.M., the 2nd Battalion Black Watch (under Lieutenant-Colonel Carthew-Yorstoun) moved forward to occupy a prominent hill to our left front which seemed to be a starting point from which the enemy's position might be turned. My direct advance, however, upon the nek was delayed until 1.40 P.M., awaiting the arrival of Colonel Donne's troops from Meyer's Kop, but at that hour the 81st Battery, Royal Field Artillery, opened fire to the west of the road leading up into the nek, the Sussex Regiment advanced towards a high conical hill overlooking the right side of the nek, whilst the Highland Light Infantry moved forward to try and gain the precipitous height commanding the nek to our left These hills, and an intervening shelter trench connecting the two within the nek itself, were heavily bombarded

by my field batteries and the two 5-inch guns. At dusk the Sussex Regiment, unable to gain ground, was compelled to fall back on the 81st Field Battery, Royal Field Artillery, the Highland Light Infantry had gained a footing, albeit not a very firm one, on the lower spurs and kloofs of the rocky height to our left of the nek, whilst the Black Watch, who had been heavily fired at throughout the day, and whom I supported with two guns of the 5th. Battery, Royal Field Artillery, had not only obtained possession of the conical hill already alluded to, but a further crest which practically turned the enemy's position in the nek, and gave access to the wide valley lying beyond and within the mountains.

21. My casualties during the day were 1 Officer and 11 men killed ; 6 Officers and 68 men wounded.

22. During the night a portion of the Highland Light Infantry, guided by several men of Lovat's Scouts, succeeded in gaining possession of the highest peak of the hill on the east of the pass, a point of vantage whence a successful occupation of the whole height was made the next day.

23. At daybreak on the 24th July, I pressed the success already achieved overnight. Bringing the Sussex Regiment and 81st Battery, Royal Field Artillery, back to Boshof's Farm to act as escort to the convoy, ordered Major-General MacDonald to bring up the Seaforth Highlanders in a wide-turning movement to my left, and beyond the Black Watch, who had come at daybreak under fire of a Boer gun at the foot I of the hills beyond Baniboehoek Farm. This turning movement was completely successful, the Seaforth Highlanders, supported by the 76th Battery, Royal Field Artillery, advancing with quiet gallantry and seizing the edge of the kloof which runs down by Bamboehoek, whence a heavy fire was poured upon the retiring Boers. The seizure of this point at 11.40 A.M. enabled the Black Watch and Seaforth Highlanders to descend into the valley beyond, thus completely turning the enemy's position already compromised by the footing gained by the Highland Light Infantry on the height overlooking the nek. I then, at 1.10 P.M., directed the whole of my artillery and baggage to move upon the now evacuated nek. and. by 3 P.M., bivouacked at Reliefs Nek Farm, about a mile beyond the position previously held by the enemy.

24. There I learnt the complete success of the simultaneous attack which I had ordered upon Slabbert's Nek by the force under Major-General Clements, whose troops also bivouacked in the valley, four miles beyond my own head-quarters.

25. Major-General Clements having marched himself from Bester's Kop, had effected a junction between his own troops and those of Major- General Paget, about two and a half miles north of Slabbert's Nek at 10 A.M. on 23rd July. He at once proceeded to secure a position for his artillery, whence the enemy's trenches within the nek were bombarded and his guns silenced. Then, whilst lie held the enemy in front with the Royal Munster Fusiliers, he directed Lieutenant-Colonel Grenfell with Brabant's Horse (2nd Regiment) to seize a ridge which ran down from the high ground to his right of the nek. Lieutenant- Colonel Grenfell was unable to make much progress, but wider turning movements still more to the right by portions of the 2nd Battalion Wiltshire Regiment (Lieutenant-Colonel Carter) and the Royal Irish Regiment (under Lieutenant-Colonel Guinness) gave a footing on the high ground which paved the way for success next day.

26. Major-General Clements directed his troops to bivouac on the night of the 23rd in the positions they had gained, and at 4.30 A.M. on the 24th, Lieutenant-Colonel Guinness with four companies Royal Irish Regiment and two companies 2nd Battalion Wiltshire Regiment, favoured by some clouds which obscured the crest, was able to gain a ridge to the west of, and overlooking the enemy's position. This ridge had previously been reconnoitred and occupied by a portion of 2nd Regiment, Brabant's Horse, under Captain Cholmondeley, who found it unoccupied by the enemy. Having gained this commanding ground, Lieutenant-Colonel Guinness was directed by Major-General Clements to clear the intervening space between it and the nek, which was evacuated by the enemy when he saw that his position was turned.

27. At 11 A.M., Major-General Clements ordered a general advance into the now vacated nek, sending the mounted troops and artillery of Major-General Paget's force, under Lieutenant-Colonel Burn, in pursuit of the retiring Boers.

28. Major-General Clements reports that the position occupied by the Boers, who brought several guns and pompoms into action, was one of great strength, and the fact that his turning movement was directed over ground from 1,500 to 3,000 feet high is sufficient to explain the arduous nature of the operation. His casualties during the two days' fighting amounted to one Officer and seven men killed, and three officers and 39 rank and file wounded.

29. On the evening of 24th July, having apprised Lieutenant-General Sir Leslie Rundle of the success of these operations and directed him to push on and effect a junction with me towards Fouriesburg, and having detailed Lieutenant-Colonel Donne with the 1st Battalion Royal Sussex Regiment and 2nd Battalion Bedfordshire Regiment and six guns to remain in occupation of the captured neks, I ordered Major-General MacDonald to start at daybreak next morning, with the Highland Brigade, two 5-inch guns, Lovat's Scouts, and the 5th Battery Royal Field Artillery, and join Major-General Bruce Hamilton now at Heilbron Farm, assigning to him the important task of occupying or blocking the enemy's possible exits at Naauwport Nek and Golden Gate. Major-General MacDonald bivouacked on the night of the 25th at Middelvlei. I also ordered Colonel Hacket Pain with the garrison of Witnek to Slabbert's and Relief's Neks.

30. At 7 A.M. on the 25th July, taking with me the 81st Battery Royal Field Artillery and Rimington's Guides, and effecting a junction with the troops under Major-Generals Clements and Paget beyond Slabbert's Nek, I pushed on with them for 9 miles in the direction of Fouriesburg, upon which place the Boers had retired on the previous day, executing a reconnaissance with my mounted troops to within 3 miles of the town. I was not anxious to press too closely on the enemy's rear, so as not to drive him out towards Naauwport Nek and Golden Gate till General MacDonald had blocked those exits.

31. The following day, the 26th, I entered Fouriesburg with my mounted troops and found that the town had already been occupied by a portion of Sir Leslie Rundle's Division, headed by Driscoll's Scouts, after a forced march from Commando Nek of 25 miles. The enemy had retired from the town in the direction of Naauwport Nek and Golden Gate, where I trusted that they would be anticipated by Major-Generals MacDonald and Bruce Hamilton, whose casualties on this day in an action fought outside the former pass amounted to one man killed, two officers and ten men wounded. To strengthen the force at his disposal, I now ordered Lieutenant-Colonel Donne, on being relieved by Lieutenant-Colonel Pain's troops (the Worcestershire Regiment, half Battalion Wiltshire Regiment, four guns), now set free from Witnek by our occupation of Fouriesburg, to push on with his two battalions and guns from Retief's Nek, and effect a junction with the Highland Brigade towards Naauwport Nek ; I also strengthened Donne by two squadrons Scottish Yeomanry under Lieutenant-Colonel Burn from Fouriesburg. This he did, and on the 27th Major-General MacDonald informed me that having left Lieutenant-Colonel Hughes Hallett with the Seaforth Highlanders, 2nd Battalion Bedfordshire Regiment, and one 5-inch gun opposite to Naauwport, he was moving on with the remainder of his force to establish Major-General Bruce Hamilton, towards Golden Gate.

"London Gazette" Tuesday March 5th 1901

THE King has been graciously pleased to confer the Volunteer Officers' Decoration upon the undermentioned Officers of the Volunteer Force, who have been duly recommended for the same under the terms of the Royal Warrant, dated 25th July, 1892 :—

SOUTH-EASTERN DISTRICT

RIFLE

2nd Volunteer Battalion, The Royal Sussex Regiment

 Capt. & Hon. Major Barnard Thornton Hodgson,

"London Gazette" Tuesday April 16th 1901

A DESPATCH from Earl Roberts, KG.,G.C.B. to the Right Honourable the Secretary of State for War, War Office, London S.W.

IN continuation of my despatch. No. 9, dated Johannesburg, 15th Nov., 1900, I have the honour to bring to your notice the excellent work done during the campaign up to the 29th November, 1900, by the various Departments of the Army which have contributed so much to the success of the operations in the field.

Finally, I wish to bring the names of the following officers to notice for meritorious services performed. It has been found impossible at this date to make the list complete, and junior officers especially will be brought to notice later.

M.I.D.

Lt-Colonel Benjamin Doniethorpe Alsop Donne, 1st Bn. Royal Sussex Regiment,
Colonel Robert A. Finlayson, Kimberley Regiment,
(Later Lt-Col. In The Royal Sussex Regiment)

"London Gazette" Friday April 19th 1901

King has been graciously pleased to give orders for the following promotions in, and appointments to, the Most Honourable Order of the Bath and the Most Distinguished Order of Saint Michael and Saint George ; for the following appointments to the Distinguished Service Order; award for the following promotions in the Army; in recognition of the services of the undermentioned Officers during the operations in South Africa.
The rewards given below are for services in South Africa up to the 29th November, 1900 the day on which Field-Marshal Lord Roberts handed over the command, and which date (except where otherwise stated) they bear. Owing to the multitude of recommendations forwarded to the Commander-in-Chief, it has not yet been possible to fully examine those for regimental service, or those relating to the Militia, Yeomanry, volunteers, and certain other services. Further distinctions will . be notified later. These will bear the same date as those now given, viz.. the, 29th November, 1900, except where otherwise stated.

To be Ordinary Members of the Military Division of the Third Class, or Companions of the said Most Honourable Order, viz. :—

C.B.

Lieutenant - Colonel Benjamin Doniethorpe Alsop Donne,
1st Bn. Royal Sussex Regiment

To be Ordinary Members of the Third Class or Companions of the said Most Distinguished Order:—

C.M.G.

Colonel Robert A. Finlayson, Kimberley Regiment,
(Later Lt-Col. In The Royal Sussex Regiment)

D.C.M.

Gill J. Pte. 3697   1st Bn.   19/04/01
(SK 18/04/01 Brandwater Basin 26/08/00)

"London Gazette" Friday May 7th 1901

The following Despatch has been received from Lord Kitchener, G.C.B., &c., Commander-in-Chief, South Africa: -

From Lord Kitchener to the Secretary of State for War.
Army Head-Quarters, Pretoria,
8th March, 1901

17. In addition to the good leading and able command exercised by the various Officers mentioned in the body of this despatch, I desire to bring to your notice the valuable services rendered in connection with these operations by the Officers, non-commissioned officers, and men, named in the two lists submitted herewith.

I have, &c.

KITCHENER OF KARTOUM General;
Commanding-in-Chief, South Africa.

List of Non-commissioned Officers and men.

551 Lance-Sergeant A. Ockelford, 1st Battalion Royal Sussex Regiment,

"London Gazette" Tuesday July 9th 1901

17: I forward herewith lists (A) of Officers, (B) of non-commissioned officers and men, whom I wish to bring to your notice for consideration. I would ask that the promotions made by me amongst the latter (List B) may not prejudice the grant of any further rewards you may consider desirable.

I have, &c.,
KITCHENER, General,
Commanding-in-Chief, South Africa.

Royal Sussex Regiment

Major Lewis Eugene Du Moulin;

I desire to bring to your notice the very good work done by him in command of convoys, though almost constantly harassed by the enemy, no captures have been made from him, and his casualties have been very small – a proof that his men have been well trained and handled.

General Lyttelton's despatch on operations against De Wet in February, 1901.

"London Gazette" Tuesday July 30th 1901

THE King has been graciously pleased to confer the Volunteer Officers' Decoration upon the undermentioned Officers of the Volunteer Force, who have been duly recommended for the same under the terms of the Royal Warrant, dated 25th July, 1892:—

SOUTH-EASTERN DISTRICT
RIFLE

1st Volunteer Battalion Royal Sussex Regiment

Lt-Col. & Hon. Colonel Cecil Somers Clarke,

"London Gazette" Tuesday September 10th 1901

A DESPATCH from Earl Roberts, K.G.,G.C.B., &c., to the Right Honourable the Secretary of State for War, War Office, London, W.:—
London, September 4, 1901.

Sir, In continuation of my Despatch, dated London, 2nd April, 1901, in which I reported on the various departments of the Army in South Africa, and brought to notice the names of certain Staff and other Officers together with a number of Colonial Officers and men who have distinguished themselves, I now have the honour to farther bring to your notice the names of the following regimental Officers, Non-commissioned Officers, and men of the Regulars, Militia, Yeomanry, and Volunteers, together with a few Irregulars and Civilians, who, with their various units, have rendered special and meritorious service. The names are arranged regimentally, by precedence of corps, for the purpose of more ready reference: —

Royal Sussex Regiment 1st Battalion

Major L.E. du Moulin,
Major J.G. Panton,
Captain A.R. Gilbert,

Captain F.W.T. Robinson,
　　　　　Captain Charles Powlett Aldridge,

Captain E.W.B. Green,
Captain E.L. Mackenzie,
Lieutenant R. Bellamy,
Lieutenant E.F. Villiers,
Lieutenant C.E. Bond,
Quartermaster and Honorary Lieutenant R. Pearce,
Sergeant-Major S. Thwaits,
3871 Colour-Sergeant Thomas Albert Jones,
2697 Colour-Sergeant A.E. Weston,
3238 Colour-Sergeant A. Nye,
3443 Colour-Sergeant W. Ticehurst,
2676 Colour-Sergeant R.C. Wayman,
2055 Sergeant A. Snaith,
3029 Sergeant W.H. Kemp,
7042 Sergeant F. Ross, (Volunteer Company)
5118 Lance-Sergeant A. Ockleford,
2382 Corporal G. Weston,
3378 Corporal P. Penfold,
7009 Lance-Corporal H. Rowe, (Honorary Captain Cadet Corps. 2nd Volunteer Battalion)
5792 Private T.H. Say,
3582 Private J. Stripp,
7076 Private F.H. Symes, (Volunteer Company)

The Royal Sussex Regiment 3rd Battalion

Captain Fiennes W. E. Blake (attached 1st Battalion).
14th Battalion Imperial Yeomanry

Lieutenant Edward John D'Almeida Cory, 1st Cinque Ports Volunteer Rifle Corps.

"London Gazette" Friday September 27th 1901

D.S.O.

Lieutenant and Adjutant R. Bellamy, 1st Bn.

"Robert Bellamy, Lieut., Royal Sussex Regiment.
In recognition of services during the operations in South Africa."

Captain F.W.T. Robinson, 1st Bn.

"Frederick William Templeton Robinson, Royal Sussex Regiment.
In recognition for services during the operations in South Africa."

Mentioned in Despatches *"London Gazette"* 10th September, 1901

Captain E.L. Mackenzie, 1st Bn.

"Edward Leslie Mackenzie, Royal Sussex Regiment.
In recognition for services during the operations in South Africa."

Mentioned in Despatches *"London Gazette"* 10th September, 1901

Lieutenant E.F. Villiers, 1st Bn.

"Evelyn Fontaine Villiers, Royal Sussex Regiment.
In recognition for services during the operations in South Africa."

Mentioned in Despatches *"London Gazette"* 10th September, 1901

Lieutenant A.R. Hopkins was specially promoted for services in the field to a Captaincy in the Manchester Regiment.

Brevet Lt.-Colonel

Major Lewis Eugene du Moulin, 1st Bn.

Brevet Major

Captain Arthur Robert Gilbert, 1st Bn.

D.C.M.

Thwaits S.	Sgt-Major	1st Bn.	
Jones T.A.	Clr-Sgt. 3871	1st Bn.	
Nye A.	Clr-Sgt. 3238	1st Bn.	
Weston A.E.	Clr-Sgt. 2697	1st Bn.	(k.i.a. Jan. 28th 1902)
Weston G.	Sgt. 2382	1st Bn.	
Snaith H.	Sgt. 2055	1st Bn.	
Ockleford A.	L/Sgt. 5118	1st Bn.	
Say T.H.	Pte. 5792	1st Bn.	(Brandwater Basin 26/08/00)

Ross P.T. Tpr. 16484   14th Bn. Imp.Yeo. 69th Coy. Sussex Yeomanry,

The D.C.M. awarded to Private Say was for bandaging Lieutenant Anderson who had been shot in the throat, this first aid he had to do whilst under a storm of bullets from the Boer positions.

D.S.O.

7th Imperial Yeomanry
1st Cinque Ports Volunteer Rifle Corps.

Lieutenant (Captain) Edward John D'Almeida Cory ,

"London Gazette" November 19th 1901

THE King has been graciously pleased to confer the Volunteer Officers' Decoration upon the undermentioned Officers of the Volunteer Force, who have been duly recommended for the same under the terms of the Royal Warrant, dated 25th July, 1892 :—

SOUTH-EASTERN DISTRICT

RIFLE

1st Cinque Ports Volunteer Rifle Corps.

Lieutenant-Colonel and Honorary Colonel Alan Richardson,
Lord Kitchener's Mentions 1st June, 1902

No. 3603 Corporal A. Baldwin, (promoted Sergeant) 1st Bn.
"For several instances of marked gallantry in action."

No. 8187 Private A. Blease, Vol. Coy. 1st Bn.

No. 8225 Drummer R. Robertson, Vol. Coy. 1st Bn.

No. 8355 Private J. Lockhart, Vol. Coy. 1st Bn.

"For gallantry and initiative in repulse of a Boer raiding party at Balmoral on 5th April, 1902"

(Promoted Corporals by C-in-C)

("London Gazette" 18th July, 1902)

No. 3772 Sergeant-Drummer T. Gates, 1st Bn.

No. 1807 Q.M.S. C. Pittman, 1st Bn.

No. 4927 Lance-Corporal T. Scrase, 1st Bn.

(*London Gazette*" 29th July, 1902)

"*London Gazette*" Thursday June 26th 1902

The KING has been graciously pleased to give orders for the following Promotions and Appointments in the Army, and the following Promotions in, and Appointments to the Most Honourable Order of the Bath, viz.:—
To be Ordinary Members of the Civil Division of the Third Class, or Companions of the said Most Honourable Order:—

C.B.

2nd Volunteer Battalion, The Royal Sussex Regiment

Lt-Colonel and Hon. Colonel William Henry Campion,

"*London Gazette*" Friday July 18th 1902

The following Despatch has been received from Lord Kitchener,. G.C.B &c., Commanding-in-Chief, South Africa :—

LIST OF NON-COMMISSIONED OFFICERS AND MEN MENTIONED

1st Battalion Royal Sussex Regiment

No. 3606 Corporal A. Baldwin ,

For several instances of marked gallantry in action.

Promoted Sergeant by Commander-in-Chief

"*London Gazette*" Tuesday July 29th 1902

The following Despatch has been received from Lord Kitchener, G.C.B., &c., Commanding-in-Chief, South Africa :—

M.I.D.

1st Bn.

Brevet Major Arthur Robert Gilbert,

Captain Ernest Henry Montresor,

Lieutenant Charles Earbery Bond,
Lieutenant George Charles Morphett,
2nd Lt. Gerrard Evelyn Leachman,

Quartermaster & Hon. Lieutenant Robert Pearce,

No. 2676 Colour-Sergeant R.C. Wayman,
No. 3963 Sergeant W. Saxby,

3rd Bn.

Colonel the Earl of March, A.D.C.

Major Stephenson Robert Clarke,

Captain Pelham Rawston Papillon,

No. G/4657 Sgt./Major C. Amos,

No. 7133 L/Sgt. L. Pemberton,

"London Gazette" **Friday October 31st 1902**

The KING has been graciously pleased to give orders for the following appointments to the Most Honourable Order of the Bath (additional), and the Distinguished Service Order; for the following promotions in the Army; and for the grant of the Medal for Distinguished Conduct in the Field to the undermentioned Officers and soldiers; in recognition of their services during the operations in South Africa, the whole to bear date 22nd August, 1902, except where otherwise stated.

To be Ordinary Members of the Military Division of the Third Class, or Companions of the said Most Honourable Order:—

C.B.

Colonel Charles Henry, Earl of March, Aide-de-Camp to the King.

D.S.O.

Major A.R. Gilbert, 1st Bn.
"Arthur Robert Gilbert, Royal Sussex Regiment.
In recognition of services during the operations in South Africa."
Mentioned in Despatches *"London Gazette"* 10th September, 1901, 29th July, 1902

Lieutenant C.E. Bond, 1st Bn.
"Charles Earbery Bond, Royal Sussex Regiment.
In recognition of services during the operations in South Africa."

Mentioned in Despatches *"London Gazette"* 10th September, 1901, 29th July, 1902

D.C.M.

G/4657 Sgt-Major C. Amos   3rd Bn.

1807 QM/Sgt. C. Pittman   1st Bn.
3772 Sgt/Drmr. T. Gates   1st Bn.
3603 Cpl. A. Baldwin   1st Bn.
4297 L/Cpl. T. Scrase   1st Bn.

Wednesday November 5th 1902

Military Intelligence

It is generally conceded that the War Office has not erred on the side of lavishness in distributing awards among the Royal Sussex Regiment - Line and Militia - for service in the late war. The 1st Battalion endured much hard fighting and harassing service, and one C.B. (Colonel Donne's), five DSO's and a brevet majority to an officer who is already a substansive major, and the D.C.M. to some fifteen of the rank and file, are by no means extravagant rewards for over two years' service. It is true that two subalterns were specially promoted captains, but even that by no means is an adequate reward to the junior ranks, and only one of them Lieutenant C.E. Bond has received a D.S.O. a C.B. to the Earl of March is the award of the 3rd Battalion.
(The reporter obviously missed the D.C.M. to Sergeant-Major C. Amos, 3rd Bn.)

"London Gazette" Tuesday April 28th 1903

The KING has been pleased to issue a Commission under His Majesty's Royal Sign Manual to the following effect:—
EDWARD, R.

EDWARD THE SEVENTH, by the Grace of God, of the United Kingdom of Great Britain and Ireland and of the British Dominions beyond the Seas King, Defender of the Faith, to—
Our right trusty and right entirely beloved Cousin and Councillor Henry, Duke of Norfolk, Knight of Our Most Noble Order of the Garter, Knight Grand Cross of the Royal Victoria Order, upon whom has been conferred the Volunteer Officers' Decoration, Colonel Commanding 2nd Volunteer Battalion of the Royal Sussex Regiment.

"London Gazette " Friday April 22nd 1904

THE King has been graciously pleased to confer the Volunteer Officers' Decoration upon the undermentioned Officers of the Volunteer Force, who have been duly recommended for the same under the terms of the Royal Warrant, dated 25th July, 1892:—

SOUTH-EASTERN DISTRICT

RIFLE

1st Volunteer Battalion, The Royal Sussex Regiment

Capt. & Hon. Major and Instructor of Musketry George Lionel King,

"London Gazette" Tuesday June 21st 1904

ORDER OF THE INDIAN EMPIRE

The KING has been graciously pleased to make the following promotions in, and appointments to, the Most Eminent Order of the Indian Empire:—

To be Companions

William Ninnis Porter, Esq., Acting Commissioner of the Irrawaddy Division.
(Later Major in The Royal Sussex Regiment)

"London Gazette" Tuesday November 15th 1904

The KING has been graciously pleased to confer the Volunteer Officers' Decoration upon the undermentioned Officers of the Volunteer Force, who have been duly recommended for the same under the terms of the Royal Warrant dated 25th July, 1892 :—

SOUTH-EASTERN DISTRICT
RIFLE

1st Cinque Ports Volunteer Rifle Corps.

Acting Chaplain the Very Reverend Edward Reid Currie, M.A.

"London Gazette" Tuesday June 19th 1906

The KING has been graciously pleased to confer the Volunteer Officers' Decoration upon the undermentioned Officers of the Volunteer Force, who have been duly recommended for the same under the terms of the Royal Warrant dated 25th July, 1892 :—

EASTERN COMMAND

RIFLE

1st Cinque Ports Volunteer Rifle Corps.

Major Frederick George Langham,

Crete 1906

"London Gazette" Wednesday June 29th 1906

The King has been graciously pleased to give directions for the following appointment to the Most Distinguished Order of Saint Michael and Saint George, to be Ordinary Member of the Third Class, or Companion of the said Most Distinguished Order :-

C.M.G.

Lieutenant-Colonel and Brevet Colonel John Gerald Panton, The Royal Sussex Regiment (2nd Bn.), in command of the British Troops in Crete.

From the Royal Sussex Regimental Archives :-

"On 1st May, 1906, 'C', 'E' and 'H' Companies under command of Brevet Lieutenant-Colonel H.R. Lloyd arrived at Crete from Malta on the "Malacca", disembarkation took place under considerable difficulties owing to the rough state of the sea at the time, and the absence of any labour, at Kandia.

The Battalion was split into many Detachments during the elections in the British Secteur in May, and underwent a considerable amount of arduous work. On 29th June, 1906, His Majesty King Edward VII conferred the appointment of the Most Distinguished Order of St. Michael and St. George, Member of the 3rd Class on Brevet Colonel J.G. Panton, in recognition of the work performed by that officer, while in command of the British Troops in Crete.

On 10th August, 1906, the Commanding officer received a letter from H.B.M's Consul General at Canea forwarding a copy of the despatch from the foreign Office expressing the satisfaction of H.M. Government at the work carried out by the Battalion in connection with the recent elections in Crete. The following extracts are taken from the Consul-General's letter :- "I should like to express, if I may be allowed to do so to the officers of your battalion my personal thanks for the untiring way in which they have ably seconded your efforts for the maintenance of order during the late elections, and to the N.C.O.'s and men under your command, my appreciation of the most creditable and satisfactory manner, in which they have performed their duties often both difficult and fatiguing."

On the 17th August, 1906, Major and Brevet Colonel H.R. Lloyd was placed on half pay, having attained the age limit on the 14th September, 1906. Lieutenant R.B. Otter-Barry was appointed adjutant, vice Lieutenant R.N. Dick, whose tenure of that appointment had expired. On 15th September, 1906 Major and Brevet Lieutenant-Colonel H.R. Lloyd was placed on retired pay.

On the 4th September, 1906 Lieutenant J. Halton was appointed assistant adjutant vice Lieutenant R.B. Otter-Barry appointed adjutant.

During September trouble was expected in the island of Crete owing to the resignation of Prince George of Greece from the position of High Commissioner of Crete. Nothing of any account occurred in the Kandia secteur, but at Canea on the day of his departure a party of insurgents fired at the International Troops, killing a Russian caosose and wounding a Russian soldier, a Detachment under Lieutenant R. Finke of the Battalion was at Canea at the time, but took but little part in the affair.

"London Gazette" Tuesday September 4th 1906

The KING has been graciously pleased to confer the Volunteer Officers' Decoration upon the undermentioned Officers of the Volunteer Force, who have been duly recommended for the same under the terms of the Royal Warrant dated 25th July, 1892:-

EASTERN COMMAND

RIFLE

2nd Volunteer Battalion, The Royal Sussex Regiment

Acting Chaplain The Reverend Henry Kemble Southwell, M.A.

"London Gazette" Friday August 30th 1907

The KING has been graciously pleased to confer the Volunteer Officers' Decoration upon the undermentioned Officers of the Volunteer Force, who have been duly recommended for the same under the terms of the Royal Warrant dated 25th July, 1892 :—

EASTERN COMMAND

INFANTRY (VOLUNTEERS)

1st Cinque Ports Volunteer Rifle Corps;

Captain and Honorary Major Charles Ashton Selmes,

"London Gazette" Tuesday 19th November 1907

The KING has been graciously pleased to confer the Volunteer Officers' Decoration upon the undermentioned Officers of the Volunteer Force, who have been duly recommended for the same under the terms of the Royal Warrant dated 25th July, 1892 :—

EASTERN COMMAND

INFANTRY (VOLUNTEERS)

2nd Volunteer Battalion, The Royal Sussex Regiment

Capt. & Hon. Major John Stewart Oxley,

"London Gazette" Tuesday September 15th 1908

The KING has been graciously pleased to confer the Volunteer Officers' Decoration upon the undermentioned Officers of the Volunteer Force, who have been duly recommended for the same under the terms of the Royal Warrant dated 25th July, 1892 :—

EASTERN COMMAND

INFANTRY (VOLUNTEERS)

1st Volunteer Battalion, The Royal Sussex Regiment

Major and Honorary Lieutenant-Colonel Augustus Charles Woolley.

"London Gazette" Friday May 14th 1909

The KING has been graciously pleased to confer the Territorial Decoration upon the undermentioned officers of the Territorial Force who have been duly recommended for the same under the terms of the Royal Warrant dated 17th August, 1908 :—

EASTERN COMMAND

5th (Cinque Ports') Battalion, The Royal Sussex Regiment

Captain (Honorary Captain in the Army) Edward John Cory, D.S.O.

"London Gazette" Friday January 11th 1910

The KING has been graciously pleased to confer the Volunteer Officers' Decoration upon the undermentioned Officers of the Volunteer Force, who have been duly recommended for the same under the terms of the Royal Warrant dated 25th July, 1892 :—

2nd Volunteer Battalion, The Royal Sussex Regiment

Captain and Honorary Major Ernest Redford Harrison (retired),

"London Gazette" Wednesday January 11th 1911

The KING has been graciously pleased to confer the Territorial Decoration upon the undermentioned Officers of the Territorial Force, who have been duly recommended for the same under the terms of the Royal Warrant dated 17th August, 1908: —

Captain and Honorary Major Ernest Gresham Moore, 4th Battalion, The Royal Sussex Regiment,

"London Gazette" Friday March 15th 1912

The KING has been graciously pleased to confer the Territorial Decoration upon the undermentioned Officers of the Territorial Force, who have been duly recommended for the same under the terms of the Royal Warrant dated 17th August, 1908: —

Capt. & Hon. Major Leonard Charles Rudolph Messel, 4th Battalion, The Royal Sussex Regiment,

"London Gazette" Tuesday September 2nd 1913

The KING has been graciously pleased to confer the Territorial Decoration upon the undermentioned Officers of the Territorial Force, who have been duly recommended for the same under the terms of the Royal Warrant dated 17th August, 1908: —

Major James William Frederick Walter Ashby,   5th Bn. Royal Sussex Regiment,

"London Gazette" Thursday May 5th 1914

The KING has been graciously pleased to confer the Territorial Decoration upon the undermentioned Officers of the Territorial Force, who have been duly recommended for the same under the terms of the Royal Warrant dated 17th August, 1908: —

Capt. & Hon. Major William Robert Campion, 4th Bn. Royal Sussex Regiment,

"London Gazette" Tuesday May 26th 1914

The KING has been graciously pleased to confer the Territorial Decoration upon the undermentioned Officers of the Territorial Force, who have been duly recommended for the same under the terms of the Royal Warrant dated 17th August, 1908: —

Major Leonard Holmes, 6th Bn. Royal Sussex Regiment,

"London Gazette" Monday June 22nd 1914

The KING has been graciously pleased to make the following promotions in and appointments to the Royal Victorian Order: —

To be Members of the Fourth Class

Major Robert Joseph Atkinson Terry,   Royal Sussex Regiment, Provost Marshal, Aldershot.

ALLOCATION OF BATTALIONS TO BRIGADES AND DIVISIONS
1914-1918

1st   4-8-14 Pershaw. Remained in India throughout the war.

2nd   4-8-14 Woking : Went out to Western Front with 2nd Brigade, 1st Division on 12th August 1914   France ; S.W. of Bohain.

3rd   Reserve Battalion,
4-8-14 Chichester. August 1914 Dover. May 1915 to Newhaven (in Newhaven Garrison) where it remained.

1/4th   4-8-14 Horsham : Army Troops attached Home Counties Division. 24-4-15 to 160th Brigade, 53rd Division at Cambridge. May 1915 to Bedford. July 1915, to Mediterranean – Mudros. 9-8-15 landed at Sulva Bay. Moved with Division to Egypt, arrived 19th December 1915. Battalion left 53rd Division 30th May 1918. Embarked Alexandria 17th June 1918, and Taranto 22nd June, arrived France 27th June 1918, joined 101st Brigade, 34th Division 29th June 1918, at Proven. Absorbed Training Cadre of 13th Battalion 14th August 1918. 11th November, 1918, 101st Brigade, 34th Division, Belgium ; west of Courtrai.

2/4th   With 2/5th Bn. T.F. Formed at Horsham and Hastings January 1915 and November 1914. September 1915 absorbed by 3rd Line Battalions which then became 2/4th and 2/5th. 8-4-16 became 4th and 5th (Reserve) Bns. At Cambridge. 1-9-16 4th (Reserve) Battalion absorbed 5th (Reserve) and 3/6th (Cyclist) Bns. At Tunbridge Wells in Home Counties Reserve Brigade. No further change.

3/4th   With 3/5th Bn. T.F. Formed at Horsham and Hastings in March and June 1915. September 1915 became 2/4th and 2/5th Bns.

1/5th   (Cinque Ports) T.F.
4-8-14 Drill Hall, Middle Street, Hastings Army Troops attached Home Counties Division. Went out to Western Front 18th February 1915, joined 2d Brigade, 1st Division on 21st February 1915, transferred to 48th Division as Pioneers, 20th August 1915, moved with Division to Italy, arrived 29th November 1917. 4-11-18, Pioneer battalion, 48th Division, Austria ; east of Trent.

2/5th   (Cinque Ports) T.F.
With 2/4th Bn. T.F. Formed at Horsham and Hastings January 1915 and November 1914. September 1915 absorbed by 3rd Line Battalions which then became 2/4th and 2/5th. 8-4-16 became 4th and 5th (Reserve) Bns. At Cambridge. 1-9-16 4th (Reserve) Battalion absorbed 5th (Reserve) and 3/6th (Cyclist) Bns. At Tunbridge Wells in Home Counties Reserve Brigade. No further change.

1/6th   (Cyclist) T.F.
4-8-14, Montpelier Place, Brighton : August 1914 to end of 1915 in Norfolk attached to 1st Mounted Division. July 1916 at St. Leonards in General Reserve and March 1917 at Folkestone. July 1917 at Wingham, Kent attached to 1st Mounted Division. Early 1918 to Ireland at Tralee attached 6th Cyclist Brigade and in August 1918 at Limerick.

2/6th   (Cyclist) T.F.
Formed at Brighton November 19143. August and September 1915 attached to 68th Division at Bedford. November 1915 to Chiseldon and converted to infantry. February 1916 to India.

3/6th   (Cyclist) T.F.

Formed at Purfleet in 1916. 1-9-16 absorbed in 4th (Reserve) Bn.

7th (Service)
Formed at Chichester 12-8-14 – K1 – to Sobaron Barracks, Colchester in 36th Brigade, 12th Division. October 1914 to Shorncliffe. December 1914 to Folkestone in billets. March 1915 to Ramillies Barracks, Aldershot. 1-6-15 landed at Boulogne. 11-11-18, Pioneer Battalion, 12th Division, France ; Landras east of Orchies.

8th (Service) (Pioneers)
Formed at Chichester, September 1914 – K2 – to Colchester in 54th Brigade, 18th Division. 4-2-15 became Pioneer Battalion, 18th Division. May 1915 to Salisbury Plain. End July 1915 landed at Boulogne. 11th November 1918, 36th Brigade, 18th Division, France ; near Le Cateau.

9th (Service)
Formed at Chichester September 1914 – K3 – to South Downs in 73rd Brigade, 24th Division. December 1914 to Portslade in billets. April 1915 Shoreham. June 1915 Woking. 1-9-15 landed at Boulogne. 11th November 1918, 73rd Brigade, 24th Division. France ; near Bavai.

10th (Reserve)
Formed at Dover October 1914 as service battalion of K4 in 97th Brigade 0f original 32nd Division. 10-4-15 became a second reserve battalion. May 1915 to Colchester. September 1915 to Shoreham in 5th Reserve Brigade. 1-9-16 became 23rd Training Reserve Battalion in 5th Reserve Brigade at Shoreham.

11th (Service) (1st South Down)
Raised at Bexhill 7-9-14 by Lieutenant-Colonel C. Lowther, M.P. and committee July 1915 to Maidstone. 1-7-15 taken over by the War Office. September 1915 Aldershot. October 1915 to Witley and 116th Brigade, 39th Division. March 1916 landed at Le Havre. 2-33-18 reduced to training cadre. 30-6-18 to 25th Division at Boulogne and to England. At Aldershot and then to Deal where the Battalion was reconstituted absorbing 13th Royal West Kents. End August back to Aldershot in 75th Brigade, 25th Division. 9-9-18 75th Brigade became 236th and left 25th Division. 17-10-18 sailed from Dundee for North Russia.

12th (Service) (2nd South Down)
Raised at Bexhill by Lieutenant-Colonel C. Lowther, M.P. and committee. Subsequent record the same as 11th Battalion to February 1918, then 8-2-18 disbanded in France.

13th (Service) (3rd South Down)
Raised at Bexhill by Lieutenant-Colonel C. Lowther, M.P. and committee. Subsequent record same as 11th Battalion to May 1918, then 23-5-18 reduced to training cadre. 17-6-18 to 118th Brigade, 39th Division. 14-8-18 disbanded and personnel to 1/4th Battalion.

14th (Reserve)
Formed at Bexhill August 1915 as a local reserve battalion from depot companies of 11th, 12th and 13th Battalions. October 1915 to Colchester in 23rd Reserve Brigade. May 1916, Aldershot. 1-19-16 absorbed in Training Reserve battalions of 23rd Reserve Brigade at Aldershot.

15th (T.F.)
On 1-1-17 70th Provisional Battalion at Burnham, Somerset in 215th Brigade, 72nd Division became 15th Battalion. The 70th Battalion was formed in 1915 from home service personnel of the T.F. battalions and joined 72nd Division in November 1916 on formation. January 1917 Bedford. May 1917 Ipswich. Early 1918 72nd Division broken up, went to Cambridge and was disbanded about March, 1918.

16th (Sussex Yeomanry)

Formed at Mersa Matruh, Egypt on 3rd January 1917, out of dismounted Sussex Yeomanry, joined 230th Brigade, 74th Division on 10th April 1917, moved with Division to France, leaving Alexandria 1st May, arriving Marseilles 7th May 1918. 11th November 1918, 230th Brigade, 74th Division, Belgium ; N.E. of Tournai.

17th (Service)

Formed in France on 17th April 1918, as 5th Provisional Garrison Guard Battalion, and joined 199th Brigade, 66th Division same day. Transferred to 176th Brigade, 59th Division on 15th May 1918. Re-designated 17th (Garrison) Battalion. 25th May 1918, title "Garrison" was dropped on 16th July 1918. 11th November 1918, 176th Brigade, 59th Division. Belgium ; N.E. of Tournai. disbanded.

51st (Graduated)

On 27-10-17 253rd (G) Battalion (formerly 99th Training Reserve Battalion from 12th Battalion Royal West Kent) in 213th Brigade, 71st Division at Colchester became 51st battalion. 26-2-18 to 191st Brigade, 64th Division at Cromer. 71st Division was broken up. April 1918 to Thetford where it remained.

52nd (Graduated)

On 27-10-17 256th (G0 battalion (formerly 100th Training reserve Division from 24th Middlesex Battalion) in 214th Brigade, 71st Division at Colchester became 52nd Battalion. Early November 1917 to 212th Brigade, 71st Division. 18-2-18 to 191st Brigade, 64th Division at Comer. 71st Division broken up. April 1918 to Thetford where it remained.

53rd (Young Soldier)

On 27-10-17, 97th (Y.S.) Battalion (formed August 1917) in 23rd Reserve Brigade at Aldershot became 53rd Battalion. No further change.

SUSSEX YEOMANRY

Gallipoli 1915
Egypt 1916-17
Palestine 1917-18
France and Flanders 1918

1/1st   Sussex Yeomanry
4-8-14 Church Street, Brighton : South Eastern Mounted Brigade. 11-8-14 to Canterbury with brigade and remained there until September 1915. September 1915 dismounted and sailed from Liverpool in "Olympic" on 25th September. 8-10-15 landed at Cape Helles and brigade attached to 42nd division. December 1915 to Mudros. February 1916 to Egypt. 1/1st South Eastern Mounted Brigade absorbed in 3rd Dismounted Brigade. On Suez Canal Defences until July and then to Western Frontier Force. 3-1-17 formed 16th (Sussex Yeomanry) Battalion, Royal Sussex Regiment in 230th Brigade, 74th Division. May 1918 to France with 74th Division landing at Marseilles on 7th May. No change.

2/1st   Sussex Yeomanry
Formed at Brighton in September 1914 and remained here till May 1915. Then to Maresfield in 2/1st South Eastern Mounted Brigade taking over horses from 2nd King Edward's Horse. October 1915 to Canterbury with brigade which joined 4th Mounted Division in March. 1916 Brigade became 14th Mounted Brigade. July 1916 4th Mounted became 2nd Cyclist Division and Regiment became a cyclist unit in 5th Cyclist Division at Great Bentley, Essex. November 1916 2nd Cyclist Division broken up and formed 8th (Surrey and Sussex) Yeomanry Cyclist Regiment at Ipswich in 3rd Cyclist Brigade. March 1917 resumed identity still in Ipswich and then to Woodbridge. May 1917 with brigade to Bromeswell Heath, Melton, near Woodbridge. October 1917 to Grundisburgh area (west of Woodbridge). April 1918 to Ireland with 3rd Cyclist Brigade arriving Dublin on 21st April then to Clandeboye, County Down. September 1918 to Boyle, County Roscommon where it remained.

3/1st   Sussex Yeomanry
Formed at Brighton in July 1915 and affiliated to 3rd Reserve Cavalry Regiment at Canterbury. Summer 1916 to 3rd Line Groups, Home Counties Division at Crowborough. January 1917 disbanded : personnel to 2nd Line Unit and 4th (Reserve) Battalion Royal Sussex Regiment at Tunbridge Wells.

SUSSEX - BY - THE - SEA

Now is the time for marching,
Now let your hearts be gay,
Hark to the merry bugles
Sounding along our way.
So let your voices ring, my boys,
And take the time from me,
And I'll sing you a song as we march along,
Of Sussex by the Sea!

Chorus
For we're the men from Sussex, Sussex by the Sea.
We plough and sow and reap and mow,
And useful men are we;
And when you go to Sussex, whoever you may be,
You may tell them all that we stand or fall
For Sussex by the Sea!

Refrain
Oh Sussex, Sussex by the Sea!
Good old Sussex by the Sea!
You may tell them all we stand or fall,
For Sussex by the Sea.

Up in the morning early,
Start at the break of day;
March till the evening shadows
Tell us it's time to stay.
We're always moving on, my boys,
So take the time from me,
And sing this song as we march along,
Of Sussex by the Sea.

Chorus
For we're the men from Sussex, Sussex by the Sea.
We plough and sow and reap and mow,
And useful men are we;
And when you go to Sussex, whoever you may be,
You may tell them all that we stand or fall
For Sussex by the Sea!

Refrain
Oh Sussex, Sussex by the Sea!
Good old Sussex by the Sea!
You may tell them all we stand or fall,
For Sussex by the Sea.

Sometimes your feet are weary,
Sometimes the way is long,
Sometimes the day is dreary,
Sometimes the world goes wrong;
But if you let your voices ring,
Your care will fly away,
So we'll sing a song as we march along,
Of Sussex by the Sea.

Chorus
For we're the men from Sussex, Sussex by the Sea.
We plough and sow and reap and mow,
And useful men are we;
And when you go to Sussex, whoever you may be,
You may tell them all that we stand or fall
For Sussex by the Sea!

Refrain
Oh Sussex, Sussex by the Sea!
Good old Sussex by the Sea!
You may tell them all we stand or fall,
For Sussex by the Sea.

Light is the love of a soldier,
That's what the ladies say –
Lightly he goes a wooing,
Lightly he rides away.
In love and war we always are
As fair as fair can be,
And a soldier boy is the ladies' joy
In Sussex by the Sea.

Chorus
For we're the men from Sussex, Sussex by the Sea.
We plough and sow and reap and mow,
And useful men are we;
And when you go to Sussex, whoever you may be,
You may tell them all that we stand or fall
For Sussex by the Sea!

Refrain
Oh Sussex, Sussex by the Sea!
Good old Sussex by the Sea!
You may tell them all we stand or fall,
For Sussex by the Sea.

Far o'er the seas we wander,
Wide thro' the world we roam;
Far from the kind hearts yonder,
Far from our dear old home;
But ne'er shall we forget, my boys,
And true we'll ever be
To the girls so kind that we left behind
In Sussex by the Sea.

Chorus
For we're the men from Sussex, Sussex by the Sea.
We plough and sow and reap and mow,
And useful men are we;
And when you go to Sussex, whoever you may be,
You may tell them all that we stand or fall
For Sussex by the Sea!

Refrain
Oh Sussex, Sussex by the Sea!
Good old Sussex by the Sea!
You may tell them all we stand or fall,
For Sussex by the Sea.

William Ward-Higgs

MARCH OF THE ROYAL SUSSEX TERRITORIALS

For Hearth and Home, Lads, Hearth and Home,

For all we prize most dear ;

The Wife and Child are trusting us,

They shall have nought to fear !

Say ye the Foeman's guns are set !

Then tell us where and when,

And we shall show you what we are,

Just all true Sussex men.

To Arms ! To Arms ! For God and King,

We know are cause is right ;

Our Island Home is calling us,

So up , my Lads, and fight !

Say ye the Foeman's guns are set !

Then tell us where and when,

And we shall show you what we are.

Just all true Sussex men.

R. P. S-J.

Monday October 12th 1914

French Honour

The President of the French Republic has bestowed the Decoration of the Legion of Honour on the under-mentioned officer with the approval of His Majesty the King, for his gallantry during Operations between 21st and 30th August, 1914.

Croix de Chevalier

Lt. The Hon. Herbert Lytleton Pelham, 2nd Battalion Royal Sussex Regiment,
(Gazetted 3rd November 1914)
(Killed in action Monday 14th September, 1914, in support of an attack on the high ground above Troyon.)

Monday October 19th 1914

Mentioned in Dispatches

Following the Dispatch is a long list of officers and men who are mentioned for distinguished service including the following belonging to the 2nd Battalion Royal Sussex Regiment :-

Major John Bartholomew Wroughton,
Major, Edgar Walter Butler Green,
Captain, Charles Earbery Bond., DSO
Lieutenant, Vere Edmunds Crofts Dashwood,
No. 9157 Lance-Sergeant, Charles Percival Parker Clay,
No. 6868 Sergeant, T. Diplock,
No. 9275 Sergeant, Frederick Charles Jermens Marillier,
No. 10035 Private, Thomas Still,

Tuesday October 20th 1914

Sussex to the Fore

Sussex was strongly represented in the list of officers and men of the Expeditionary Force specially singled out for mention by Sir John French for distinguished service.

Honour for Linfield.

Linfield claims the first private of the Royal Sussex Regiment to be mentioned in dispatches for Distinguished Services in the present campaign. No. L/10035 Private Thomas Still of "A" Company, the 2nd Battalion. He was a smart young fellow, a farm worker by occupation before enlisting. He was well-known in the Lyoth Lane district of Linfield, between Haywoods Heath and Scaynes Hill.

Friday November 6th 1914

Linfield soldier missing.

Private T. Still, 2nd Battalion Royal Sussex Regiment mentioned in dispatches for Distinguished Conduct, is now reported wounded and missing. His parents reside in Lyoth Lane.
(killed in action 14th September, 1914)

Saturday November 7th 1914

Gallant Sussex Men

Award of Distinguished Conduct Medals.

Of 23 non-commissioned officers and men in the British Expeditionary Force to whom the King has approved of the grant of the Medal for Distinguished Conduct in the field and for acts of gallantry and devotion to duty. Two it is gratifying to announce, belong to the Royal Sussex Regiment, they are :-

No. 9157 Lance-Sergeant C.P.P. Clay,
No. 9257 Sergeant (now Second-Lieutenant) F.C.J. Marillier,

Their services are thus set out in last night's issue of the *'London Gazette'*.

Lance-Sergeant C.P.P. Clay,   2nd Battalion Royal Sussex Regiment,

Acted as scout leader, sent in very good reports on the 14th September, and several times later. He has pushed well forward and reconnoitred on occasions right up to the enemy's lines.

Sergeant (now Second-Lieutenant) F.C.J. Marillier,   2nd Battalion Royal Sussex Regiment,

Led a party on the night of the 1st October and successfully filled one of the enemy's trenches.

Sergeant Clay belongs to 'C' Company and has a long and excellent reputation as a regimental scout. He is one of six officers and men of the battalion mentioned in Sir John French's dispatch published on the 18th October last. Sergeant Marillier who since his dangerous venture of the 1st October, has been promoted to a Second - Lieutenancy, was formerly assistant master at Hailsham Council School.

In that capacity he showed keen interest in the Boy Scout's Movement, and was also a sergeant in the 5th. Battalion (Cinque Ports) Royal Sussex Regiment. About four years ago he left the teaching profession and joined the Sussex Regiment at Chichester. He was a keen, intelligent soldier, and within three years had been promoted sergeant. The fact that he has been given a commission has caused much satisfaction to his many friends in Sussex.

Tuesday November 10th 1914

Reported deaths of five more Officers

Heavy losses, have, it is feared again been sustained by the 2nd Battalion Royal Sussex Regiment. Information is to hand that the battalion was in a fierce action on the 30th October, at Bodmin Close and Shrewsbury Forest, and that the war has once more claimed a heavy toll among the officers, five more of whom are stated to have been killed :-

Lieutenant-Colonel, Hugh Trevor Commanding Crispin,
Lieutenant, Edward Arthur Lousada,   (died 2nd November)

Second-Lieutenant, Leslie Robert Croft,
Second-Lieutenant, Cuthbert Frank Shaw,
Second-Lieutenant, Frederick Charles Jermens Marillier, D.C.M.

394 other ranks killed, wounded or missing.

The death of Lieutenant Marillier is especially pathetic. He was one of the two Royal Sussex non-commissioned officers out of 23 of the British Expeditionary Force to whom the King approved the grant of the Medal for Distinguished Service in the field and for acts of gallantry and devotion to duty. The *'London Gazette'* of Friday last contained the following announcement :-
Sergeant (now Second-Lieutenant) F.C.J. Marillier of the 2nd Battalion Royal Sussex Regiment led a party on the night of the 1st October and successfully filled in one of the enemy's trenches. It was after that achievement that the gallant young officer was promoted from the ranks. Formerly an assistant master at Hailsham Council School, he identified himself with the Boy Scouts Movement, and was also a sergeant in the 5th (Cinque Ports) Battalion Royal Sussex Regiment. About four years ago he relinquished his teaching profession for a military career, joining at the Chichester Depot.
His education and keen intelligence quickly won him promotion and in three years he became sergeant. Now he has crowned a brilliant career by sacrificing his life, and profound regret will be felt by his many friends in Sussex.

Thursday December 3rd 1914

How Second-Lieutenant Marillier met his death near Ypres, from an account by Private F. Edwards 'B' Company 2nd Battalion Royal Sussex Regiment.

'According to Private Edwards, the men think nothing of such heroic deeds as helping wounded to a place of safety under heavy fire, and he very casually remarked that he had assisted two wounded comrades that way. He also referred to the promotion of Second-Lieutenant Marillier (of Hailsham), and stated that that officer was, at the time of his death, in charge of the platoon (No. 5) which Edwards was attached to. "We were advancing through a wood in Belgium", said Edwards, "and were about four miles from Ypres. We had not gone more than fifty yards, when I saw Second-Lieutenant Marillier fall. When we got to him, he was dead".

Monday January 18th 1915

Gallant Sussex man expected a 'wigging' and got the D.C.M

No. 7440 Private A. Beale, 2nd Bn. Royal Sussex Regiment,
"For gallant conduct on 10th September 1914, at Courchamps, where the casualties were very heavy from shell - fire, he managed to continue attending the wounded although one of his fingers was blown away."
The young soldier who is at present recovering from injuries at Chichester Barracks, refused to speak of the incident or series of incidents which brought him his distinction, advancing as the reason that it had not been announced in the Army Orders.
His colleagues however supplied the deficiency and the story as gleaned shows that the medal was the last thing that the hero expected. It appears that on 10th September when the Royal Sussex were advance guard and sustained heavy casualties, Beale was stretcher - bearer. It was dangerous work necessitating coolness and prompt action, and as men were falling out pretty thickly it entailed no light duties. Beale, in his mission of succour, came across a badly wounded man in an exposed position. Without thinking of himself, he proceeded to bandage his fallen comrade, and was kneeling beside him when an officer came up. The latter warned him of his danger and ordered him to "clear out". Beale however was intent on his work and replied that he would go when he had finished dressing the wounded man. The officer whom he did not know, made a note of his name, rank and number, and left young Beale with the impression that he was "in for a wigging" for disobeying orders. However, he went on with his task

and, though wounded himself, managed to get the other man away to safety. After going about in expectation of punishment for some time, he began to feel that the officer had changed his mind, but he never dreamt that honours were in store for him. Imagine his surprise when he saw a newspaper conveying the intimation that he was to receive the D.C.M. Even now he would seem to be incredulous, for though he is naturally delighted with the honour, he was very definite in his attitude when approached not to talk about his doings on the memorable 10th until the official announcement was made.

Thursday February 18th 1915

Military Cross

The award of the Military Cross has been made to :

Chaplain the Reverend Arthur Hamilton Boyd, M.A., , attd. 4th Bn. Royal Sussex Regiment,

Mentioned in Dispatches

A second supplement to the *'London Gazette'* was issued last night containing the dispatch received by the Secretary of War from Field Marshall Sir John French dated 14th January 1915.

"In accordance with the last paragraph of my dispatch of the 20th November 1914, I have honour", says Sir John French, "to bring to the notice the names of those whom I recommend for gallant and distinguished service in the field".
'The following are names which have a special local interest, and it is extremely probable there are more in the long list:-

2nd Battalion Royal Sussex Regiment

Crispin, Lieutenant-Colonel Hugh Trevor C. (killed in action 30th October, 1914, Bodmin Close Sector)
Green, Lieutenant-Colonel Edgar Walter Butler
Villiers, Captain Evelyn Fontaine D.S.O
Waithman, Captain Roland Henry
Dashwood, Lieutenant Vere Edmunds Crofts
de Chair, Lieutenant George Herbert Blackett
Finch, Lieutenant Lionel H.K.
Verrall, Lieutenant Christopher F. (killed in action, 22nd December, 1914, Fleurbaix Sector)
Burgess, No. 6995 Sergeant S.
Hollingdale, No. 8861 Private F.
Tester, No. 6940 Private W.A.

2nd Battalion Royal West Surrey Regiment

Ramsay, Second-Lieutenant (T/Lieutenant) Duncan Gavin, 2nd Bn. Royal Sussex Regiment, (attd.) (killed in action 18th December, 1914)

Friday February 19th 1915

War Honours

A long list of promotions and decorations for army officers and men for service in the field was issued last night. The following are some of the rewards that take up 23 pages of the *'London Gazette'*.

Royal Sussex Regiment Awards

Distinguished Service Order

The Distinguished Service Order is awarded for :-

"For services in connection with operations in the field".

Lieutenant-Colonel, Edgar Walter Butler Green,   2nd Bn.
(Gazetted 23rd March)

Military Cross

Lieutenant, Vere Edmund Crofts Dashwood,   2nd Bn.

Lieutenant, George Herbert Blackett de Chair,   2nd Bn.

Thursday February 25th 1915

Lieutenant V.E.C Dashwood, one of the officers of the Royal Sussex Regiment mentioned in Sir John French's dispatch, and who, with Lieutenant G.H.B de Chair, has been awarded the Military Cross, has been through the whole campaign, and is one of the very few officers left who started with the Battalion from Woking in August last. He joined the Regiment in February 1906, and got his Lieutenancy in March 1910. A particularly trying experience with which he was associated last Saturday, when it was inadvertently stated at the time he went out he had not long received his commission as Second-Lieutenant.

French Award for Sussex Officer

The award of the Croix de Chevalier was bestowed upon Major James Suarez Cameron, 2nd Battalion Royal Sussex Regiment.

Friday May 28th 1915

The KING has been graciously pleased to confer the Territorial Decoration upon the undermentioned Officers of the Territorial Force who have been duly recommended for the same under the terms of the Royal Warrant dated 17th August, 1908: —

Captain George Loyd Courthope, 5th (Cinque Ports) Battalion, The Royal Sussex Regiment,

Wednesday June 23rd 1915

Gallant Service in the Field

A supplement to the *'London Gazette'* was published last night, containing a dispatch from Field Marshall Sir John French, bringing to the notice of the Secretary of State for War, the names of these whom he recommends for gallant and distinguished service in the field, in accordance with the last paragraph of his dispatch of 5th April last. The following are classified with their various units.

2nd Battalion

Wroughton, Major (T/Lieutenant-Colonel) J.B.
Terry, Major R.J.A. M.V.O.
Bond, Captain C.E. D.S.O.
Villiers, Captain E.F. D.S.O.
Preston, Lieutenant E.H.
Jones, Quartermaster & Hon. Lieutenant T.A. D.C.M.
Batt, No. 6961 Sergeant J.
Dray, No. 8427 Sergeant W.
Richardson, No. 8256 Sergeant J.
Smethurst, No. 4708 Sergeant W.R.
Busby, No. 9843 Corporal F.

Hyland, No. 8779 Corporal H.
Attree, No. 8745 Private B.

Martin, No. 8621 Private James

Minns, No. 8149 Private W.
Wedge, No. 9068 Private A.

3rd Battalion

Dibdin, Lieutenant F.J.A. (attached 2nd Battalion Welsh Regiment)

4th Battalion

Chaplain the Reverend Arthur Hamilton Boyd, M.A., , attd. 4th Bn. Royal Sussex Regiment,

5th Battalion

Langham, Lieutenant-Colonel F.G. V.D.
Courthope, Captain G.L
Grant, Captain F.N.
Hornblower, Captain T.B.
Robins, No. 298 Corporal W.G.
Hill, No. 2223 Lance-Corporal L
Tunnell, No. 1073 Lance-Corporal J.

Friday June 25th 1915

Mentioned in Dispatches a Crowborough Signal Porter

Among those mentioned in Sir John French's dispatch issued on Wednesday, was No. 2223 Lance-Corporal L. Hill of the 5th Battalion Royal Sussex Regiment. Inhabitants of Jarvis Brook, and especially employees of the London, Brighton and South Coast Railway Company engaged at Crowborough Station, read the news with particular interest, since Lance-Corporal Hill is the tenth son of Mr. John Edward Hill, of 4 Ferndale Terrace, Jarvis Brook, and before he enlisted in the Crowborough Company of the 5th (Cinque Ports) Battalion was a signal porter at the station. He joined the 5th Sussex a few months before they left for the front. Here it was not long before he distinguished himself. He carried some dispatches under heavy fire, and his conduct on that occasion resulted him being promoted Lance-Corporal. Interviewed yesterday by a representative of the *Sussex Daily News*, his father who is an ex - soldier, said he had heard from his son only the previous day - by a peculiar coincidence the day the list was published, and that he was quite well, he did not however refer or even hint in his letter as to the praise he had won or how he had distinguished himself. "But Lambert", added Mr. Hill "was always very smart and quick, and always keen about anything he undertook, that I have not been taken by surprise".

Well known at Lewes

Corporal W.G Robins, of the 5th (Cinque Ports) Battalion Royal Sussex Regiment, who was mentioned in Sir John French's dispatch, is very well known in Lewes, especially in musical circles. His home was in Dorsetshire, but it is many years ago he came to live in Lewes, and he proved to be very popular. He was for several years a Bailiff at Lewes County Court, and was also a prominent member of the Lewes Town Band. While his services with the Lewes Musical Society was also greatly appreciated, the announcement has caused great gratification among his friends in Lewes.

Honours for a Lewes soldier.

Honours have been confirmed by the Emperor of Russia for Gallantry and Distinguished Service in the field.

A former Bailiff of the Lewes County Court, and a member of the Lewes Town band, Corporal W.G Robins of the 5th (Cinque Ports) Battalion Royal Sussex Regiment, who was a very popular resident of Lewes, has secured the Cross of the Order of St. George of the 4th Class. Robins has also had the honour to be mentioned in dispatches for conspicuous bravery in attending to wounded comrades under heavy fire.

King's Birthday Honours

For officers from the Royal Sussex Regiment who are awarded honours in the King's Birthday Honours :-

C.M.G.

Lieutenant-Colonel Frederick George Langham, V.D. 5th Bn. (Gallantry)

Major (T/Lt-Col.) John Bartholomew Wroughton, 2nd Bn.

To be Hon. Captain

Qmr. & Lt. Thomas Albert Jones, D.C.M. 2nd Bn.

To be Companion of the D.S.O.

Major Robert Joseph Atkinson Terry, M.V.O. 2nd Bn.

"For distinguished service in the field"

Awarded the M.C.

Capt. George Loyd Courthope, 5th Bn. (T.F.)

Capt. Ferris Nelson Grant, 5th Bn. (T.F.)

Lt. Frederick Joseph Aglid Dibdin, 3rd Bn. attd. 2nd Bn. Welsh Regiment

Lt.-Colonel Langham congratulated

At the sitting of the Hastings Borough Magistrates, yesterday, the Mayor (Councillor E.A. Hocking), said he was sure they would all unite with him in congratulating Lt-Col. F.G. Langham. The gallant colonel has been mentioned in dispatches and he saw in the paper that morning that he had been made a Companion of the Order of St. Michael and St. George, for distinguished conduct in the field. They were all delighted that his splendid work had been appreciated.

Thursday July 1st 1915

Award of the D.C.M.

The following is from last night's *"London Gazette"*, the award of the Distinguished Conduct Medal to C.S.M. B.N. Butcher, Royal Sussex Regiment, Sergeant G. Neiderauer and Private O. Waghorn, Royal Sussex Regiment :-

No. 8881 A/C.S.M. B.N. Butcher, 2nd Bn. Royal Sussex Regiment,

"For conspicuous gallantry on the 29th January, 1915 at Cuinchy. During an attack on the Keep, he, while under a heavy machine-gun fire, bombed the enemy, and was largely instrumental in defeating the attack. He has, on many occasions throughout the campaign rendered valuable service and has invariably shown great courage, resource, and devotion to duty."

No. 8853 Sergeant G. Neiderauer, 3rd Bn. attd. 2nd Bn. Royal Sussex Regiment,

For conspicuous gallantry on 29th January, 1915, at Cuinchy. In command of a platoon, when the Germans made an attack and established themselves behind a small bank, he, with great courage, bombed them out of their position and they were shot down.

No. 2373 Private O. Waghorn, 5th Bn. Royal Sussex Regiment,

For conspicuous gallantry on the 18th to the 20th March, 1915, at Festubert, when he remained at his sniping post doing effective work, although it had been located by the enemy, and subjected to heavy and continuous fire.

Friday July 2nd 1915

Award of the D.C.M.

The following award of the Distinguished Conduct Medal is bestowed upon No. 914 Private J. Gill, Royal Sussex Regiment :-

"For conspicuous gallantry on January 27th, 1915, at Cuinchy, when he volunteered to remain, for observation purposes, in a forward position, which was being heavily shelled. Later in the day he rescued a wounded man under fire."

Thursday August 26th 1915

Emperor of Russia Awards

His Imperial Majesty the Emperor of Russia has conferred awards for gallantry and distinguished service in the field upon a number of British officers, non-commissioned officers and men :-

Cross of the Order of St. George (3rd Class)

No. 9157 Sgt. Charles Percival Parker Clay, 2nd Bn. Royal Sussex Regiment,

Cross of the Order of St. George (4th Class)

No. 298 Cpl. William George Robins, 5th (Cinque Ports) Bn. Royal Sussex Regiment,

Medal of St. George (4th Class)

No. 7440 Bandsman Arthur Beale, 2nd Bn. Royal Sussex Regiment,
No. 5335 Sergeant Herbert Burrell, 2nd Bn. Royal Sussex Regiment, (not gazetted)

Monday September 6th 1915

A 5th Bn. Sussex Hero

Presented with the D.C.M at Hastings

There was a scene of great enthusiasm in Alexandra Park, Hastings, yesterday evening when a Distinguished Conduct Medal was presented to an N.C.O of the 5th Bn. Royal Sussex Regiment. The presentation was made immediately after a drumhead service, at which several of the Territorial Units were represented. As soon as the service was completed, Captain Mansell Officer Commanding the 3/5th. Royal Sussex, stepped forward and said that Colonel Ferguson, the Officer Commanding the 3rd Line Units, No. 10 District Eastern Command, would perform an interesting, and to the men of the 5th Royal Sussex a most gratifying ceremony. He would present one of their own Lance-Corporals with the Distinguished Conduct Medal.
They of the 5th Royal Sussex were proud that one of their own men had so soon won distinction, and they were proud that Colonel Ferguson had come to Hastings to present it - Colonel Ferguson said he was very proud to have the honour of giving out a Distinguished Conduct Medal, so nobly won.
The Authorities said that the medal was awarded to Lance-Corporal O. Waghorn, then a Private for conspicuous gallantry from the 18th to the 20th of March last at Festubert, when he remained at his sniping post doing effective work, although he had been located by the enemy and subjected to a heavy and continuous fire. On his call, three hearty cheers were given to Lance-Corporal O. Waghorn.

Thursday September 23rd 1915

Royal Sussex Regiment Sergeant Decorated

An interesting function took place on the Square, Victoria Barracks, Belfast, on Tuesday when Sergeant Arthur Beale, 2nd Royal Sussex Regiment, in the presence of a large number of officers and men, was decorated by Colonel Bill with the Distinguished Conduct Medal for gallant conduct on the field in France on the 10th. September 1914, after having been seriously wounded himself, and while still under heavy shell-fire, Sergeant Beale continued to render First-Aid to his wounded comrades until he became exhausted and was assisted to the rear. Sergeant Beale is at present engaged in recruiting duties in the Irish Brigade Office.

Monday October 4th 1915

Royal Sussex Officer awarded the Military Cross

War Office 2nd October

His Majesty the King has been graciously pleased to confer the Military Cross on the under - mentioned officer in recognition of his gallantry and devotion to duty in the field :-

Temp-Lieutenant, Eric Guy Sutton, 7th Bn. Royal Sussex Regiment,

For conspicuous gallantry on the night of September 12th, 1915, near Armentiers. With another officer he entered a mine, which was in a highly dangerous state at the time owing to gas fumes following an explosion, in order to rescue a man who had been overcome. Their prompt action undoubtedly saved the man's life.

Monday October 11th 1915

D.C.M. for Sussex Sergeant

No. 10187 Sergeant J. King, 7th Bn. Royal Sussex Regiment, (Brighton)

For conspicuous gallantry during the months of July and August, 1915, in patrol work, usually alone. On the 9th September, at Hobbs farm, Sergeant King ambushed three Germans going to their listening post, and on their refusal to surrender he shot them. He has invariably shown great courage and zeal and resource in the performance of dangerous and difficult duties.

Friday October 22nd 1915

Major R.J.A. Terry, D.S.O.,M.V.O.   (Killed in action)

"London Gazette" Monday November 8th 1915

The KING has further been pleased to approve of the award of the Distinguished Service Cross to the undermentioned officers of the Royal Naval Division in recognition of their services in the Gallipoli Peninsula: -

Lieutenant John Bigelow Dodge,   R.N.V.R. (later attd. 16th Bn. Royal Sussex Regiment)

Wednesday November 17th 1915

Two Sussex Heroes D.C.M's awarded for Gallantry

Two N.C.O's of the 2nd Battalion Royal Sussex Regiment are included in the list of those whom the King has approved the award of the Distinguished Conduct Medal, for acts of gallantry and devotion to duty in the field. the names and records of the valorous Sussex men are thus set out in the Special Supplement to the *"London Gazette"* issued last night :-

No. 4708 Sergeant W.R Smethurst, 2nd Bn. Royal Sussex Regiment,

For Conspicuous Gallantry on the 25th September 1915, near Le Rutoire. During the first assault, when numbers of men in the first line were falling back suffering from gas fumes, and at a critical time when good leadership was essential, Sergeant Smethurst got his men well in hand, and, although the gas and smoke were very thick, he led them forward, and by his bravery and example materially assisted in the attack, in which he was wounded.

Sergeant Smethurst was mentioned in Sir John French's dispatch presented on the 22nd June last, being included among several other Royal Sussex men recommended for praiseworthy work in the field.

No. 1401 T/Corporal W.S. Tilling, 2nd Bn. Royal Sussex Regiment,

For Conspicuous Gallantry on the 25th September 1915, near Hullach, in the first assault on the German trenches, Corporal Tilling was wounded and lay all day close to the German wire. When the final and successful assault was made, he, although wounded, joined in it, and, most of the machine - gunners being killed, he helped to take forward one of the abandoned guns, and dug an emplacement in the German second line for it. He was ordered back to have his wounds dressed, but continued at duty and accompanied the Battalion in the advance to the Chalk Pit, not going to the rear until the following day. His gallant conduct and devotion to duty were most marked. Corporal Tilling is a son of Mr. and Mrs. Tilling of Folkington, near Polegate.

Friday November 19th 1915

2nd Sussex Battalion Sergeant awarded the Victoria Cross

Military Cross for 9th Bn. Sussex Officer

Eighteen Officers, N.C.O's and men have been awarded the Victoria Cross in recognition of their most conspicuous bravery and devotion to duty in the field. Their names appeared in a special supplement of the *'London Gazette'* issued last night, together with a description of the deeds that won for them inclusion in the select company of heroes.

Six of the valorous 18 crowned their gallantry by giving up their lives, and among them was a Sergeant of the 2nd Battalion Royal Sussex Regiment. Soldiers of the County have proved their mettle in many a fight in the present war, and now the highest battlefield reward of all has been added to the Distinctions they have gained.

The hero himself has passed beyond, but he will never be forgotten in the chronicles of the Royal Sussex Regiment, or in the annals of the County. The name and record of the gallant "non-com" are thus set out :-

No. 6086 Sergeant Harry Wells, 2nd Bn. Royal Sussex Regiment,

For the Most Conspicuous Bravery near Le Rutoire on 25th September 1915. When his platoon officer had been killed he took command and led his men forward to within fifteen yards of the German wire. Nearly half the platoon were killed or wounded, and the remainder were much shaken, but with utmost coolness and bravery, Sergeant Wells rallied them and led them forward. Finally when very few were left, he stood up and urged them forward once more, but while doing this he was killed. He gave a magnificent example of courage and determination. Sergeant Wells joined the Royal Sussex Regiment in 1904.

Sussex Officer Honoured

Sussex is also represented among those upon whom the King has been pleased to confer the Military Cross, an officer of the 9th Battalion having distinguished himself in the big advance in September, the official announcement is :-

T/Lieutenant Edgar Theodore Harold Godwin,   9th Battalion Royal Sussex Regiment,
"For Conspicuous Gallantry at "Fosse 8" on 27th September 1915. He worked his machine-guns until both of them had been put out of action, and then directed the fire of the machine-gun of another Regiment against the flank of the enemy's counter-attack."

Tuesday November 30th 1915

Award of the D.C.M.

The award of the Distinguished Conduct Medal is bestowed upon :-

No. 3192 Lance-Sergeant W.C. Dennett, 9th Bn. Royal Sussex Regiment :-

"For conspicuous gallantry and ability on September 27th, 1915, at Fosse 8. Although never trained to the use of bombs, Lance-Sergeant Dennett, managed to find some German bombs, and with great coolness and bravery effectually checked for the time a German bombing and enfilading party. Throughout the action his gallant conduct set a fine example to all ranks."

Saturday December 11th 1915

A Brighton D.C.M. Hero's brilliant single-handed exploits

As a mere lad of 16, James Keegan ran away from his home at Brighton and enlisted in the 2nd Battalion Royal Sussex Regiment in the name of King, in order that his father, who would not hear of him joining the Army so young, might not trace him. Now at the age of 20, young Keegan, or to give him his military description, Sergeant James King, 7th Battalion Royal Sussex Regiment, is home on leave from the front with his honours thick upon him. To be more explicit, he has won the D.C.M., for to quote the official announcement, "conspicuous gallantry during the months of July and August, 1915, in patrol work, usually alone. On 9th September at Hobb's farm, Sergeant King ambuscaded three Germans going to their listening post, and on their refusing to surrender, shot them. He has invariably shown great courage, zeal, and resource in the performance of dangerous and difficult duties."
Through the good offices of Councillor Martin, a Representative of the *Sussex Daily News* was introduced to the gallant young soldier, but found him very reluctant to speak about himself, or the incidents which led up to the coveted distinction he has gained. He is fresh-coloured, clean-limbed, well-set up youth, modest, and unassuming in his manner, but very positive about one thing, and that is the Royal Sussex is the finest Regiment in the British Army.
His father, who is a smallholder under the Brighton Corporation, resides at 48, Bates Road, and his "young hopeful" is an old Stanford Road schoolboy, and lived in Brighton from three years of age, down to the time he ran away and joined the Army.

"Working on his own"

When war broke out he was stationed at Woking and expected to go off with the 2nd Battalion, but was sent to the Depot at Chichester on the instructor's staff of Kitchener's Army. He was then a corporal, but was soon made a sergeant, and on the formation of the 7th Battalion was transferred to it and went to France with it early in May last. Within about a week the men were in the firing line, and it was shortly after this that King started "working on his own" as he describes it. He frequently went out to cut the German's barbed wire entanglements, a difficult and dangerous job upon which he was sometimes out all day and night. Discovery, of course meant almost certain death, but although he has had hairbreadth escapes, he has up to the present come through everything unscathed. He has done a good deal of sniping and in one case of these experiences had the satisfaction of shooting the sniper who shot Captain Russell, his own company officer. This was at Le Tourquet. While he was in this district he accounted for eight German snipers and "shifted a good deal of barbed wire", besides cutting enemy telephone wire.

On the Battalion being moved to Houplines, King secured a very good observation and sniping post on a farm, where he was able to watch the German lines and put our own artillery on to good targets. In one of his single-handed exploits he crawled to the German lines and after a good look round took down an armour-plated loophole from their parapet and returned to the British trenches with it. This was done in broad daylight, and when questioned about it King laconically said, "It was crawling all the time; it took me an hour to crawl about 600 yards."

Daylight daring

Just about this time the Germans were very fond of sticking up boards announcing victories against the Russians. One of them proclaimed, "Warsaw belongs to Germany", and King captured it by wriggling his way across to the German lines. On another occasion he brought in a German flag which the enemy had stuck up over a trench mortar to which it was attached by wires so that the mortar would explode if it was interfered with. Young King however, spotted this in the nick of time, and after cutting the connecting wires, got back to his own lines with both flag and trench mortar. This venture was the more hazardous as it was carried out in the daytime.

Shot all three

When the British had working parties out at night fixing their wire entanglements they were considerably "annoyed" by the attentions of an enemy automatic machine-gun. Young King volunteered to stop it. It took him an hour to get there, but then he bombed it successfully. His record also includes the discovery of a German listening post. Having made his preparations he lay in wait in a little bit of a trench with his rifle at the ready and pointed straight up the trench the Germans had to use to reach the post. Just as it was getting dark three of them approached. "When the front man was only six inches from my muzzle I halted him. He said something in German and I let go and shot all three. Then I got back and reported. The Battalion afterwards took up a fresh station, and although not in the first three days' fighting of the big advance, they were in the rest of it, with the 2nd and 9th Battalions. At one stage, it is on record, the 2nd Battalion reached the top of Hill 70, but the German artillery made it too hot for them to hold.

Appreciation of the Officers

Sergeant King is the proud possessor of a letter from the Brigadier-General congratulating him on his "good work in close proximity to the enemy trenches; and the Brigadier also wrote his commanding officer, stating King was to be promoted on the field for bravery. Another letter of congratulation was from Major Sleeman, who alluded to King's scouting exploits in the German lines in broad daylight as a proof that he has a type of courage which few men possess. The Major has presented the young soldier with a pair of field glasses, a periscope, a watch and a revolver, and coupled with his congratulations a word of warning to King not to risk his life too much on minor things as "such men as you are needed out there very much". Among other gifts the sergeant has received is a silver wristwatch from his Company officer. He has led bombing parties in attacks on enemy trenches, but through all his fighting appears to have a charmed life. Men have fallen around him, yet he has never been touched. On one occasion he was with a working party of 30 a shell, known as a "whizz-bang" to Tommy Atkins, struck the ground and exploded only a foot from him. He was not touched, but two other men who were further off were victims, one being killed and the other wounded. The dashing young sergeant's eight days leave has expired and he has gone to join his Regiment in France.

Officers and Men Mentioned in Dispatches

Royal Sussex Regiment

Green, Lieutenant-Colonel (T/Brig.-General) Edgar Walter Butler, D.S.O.
Bond, Major Charles Earbery, D.S.O., (attd. Cadet School, G.H.Q.)
Willett, Major Frederick William Bagnall   A/2-I-C 2nd Bn.
Cameron, Major James Saumarez, 3rd Bn. attd. 2nd Bn.
Villiers, Major Evelyn Fontaine, D.S.O. 1st Bn. Posted 2nd Bn.
Blakeney, Lieutenant (T/Captain) Henry Edward Hugh
Hobbs, Second-Lieutenant Edward James 2nd Bn.
Jarvis, No. 8382 Private Henry (killed)

Ramsbotham, Lieutenant Geoffrey Bury 3rd Bn. Special Reserve (killed)

Fazan, Captain Eric Alfred Charles (T/Capt. R.A.M.C.) att. 5th Bn.

Royal Sussex Regiment (T.F.)

Plews, Quartermaster and Hon. Lieutenant Harry 5th Bn.

Royal Sussex Regiment (Service Battalions)

Osborn, Major (T/Lt.-Col.) William Lushington   7th Bn.
Birkett, Captain (T/Mjr.) Richard Maule (22)   2-I-C 7th Bn.

Woodhams, T/Captain Geoffrey 7th Bn.

Sutton, T/Lieutenant Eric Guy 7th Bn.
Nutley, No. 254 C.S.M. A. 7th Bn.
Jones, No. 4746 Sergeant T. 7th Bn.
Glasgow, Major (T/Lt.-Col.) A.E. 8th Bn
Fitzhugh, T/Captain V.M. 8th Bn.
Meade, T/Captain Horace Warren 8th Bn.
Lott, T/Lieutenant Harry C. 8th Bn.
Godwin, T/Lieutenant Edgar Theodore Harold M.C. 9th Bn.

General Headquarters Staff & Co.

Terry, Major Robert Joseph Atkinson, D.S.O., M.V.O.   Royal Sussex Regiment, (k.i.a.)
Tufton, Major The Hon. John Sackville Richard, Royal Sussex Regiment, Special Reserve

Friday January 8th 1916

Littlehampton Officer Honoured

Sir John French's recommendation for gallantry and distinguished conduct in the field included another Littlehampton resident, Captain G. Woodhams, son of Mr. Albert Woodhams a well-known and much esteemed townsman. Captain Woodhams was just finishing his four years at Keeble College, Oxford, when the war broke out, and had taken his degree and passed for the Indian Civil Service.
He served for four years in the Officer Training Corps. and accepted a commission in the 7th Battalion Royal Sussex Regiment, he received his Company in the early part of 1915, and since the Regiment has been in France he has seen much fighting. A very promising officer, he will receive the hearty congratulations and best wishes from a large circle of friends.

Thursday January 14th 1916

Many Sussex Soldiers Decorated

From a Special Supplement of the *'London Gazette'*.

C.M.G.

Bond, Major Charles Earbery, D.S.O., 1st Bn. Royal Sussex Regiment,

D.S.O.

Cameron, Major James Saumarez, 2nd Bn. Royal Sussex Regiment,

Tufton, Major The Hon. John Sackville Richard,
3rd Bn. Royal Sussex Regiment, S.R.

Willett, Major Frederick William Bagnall, 2nd Bn. Royal Sussex Regiment,

M.C.

Blakeney, Lieutenant (T/Capt.) Henry Edward Hugh,
Royal Sussex Regiment,

Fazan, Captain Eric Alfred Charles (T/Capt. R.A.M.C.)
att. 5th Bn. Royal Sussex Regiment,

Hobbs, 2nd Lieutenant E.J. 2nd Bn. Royal Sussex Regiment,

D.C.M.

Heaseman, No.2205 Private J.   Depot (was 2nd Bn.) Royal Sussex Regiment,
Couchman, No. 9107 Sergeant W.   2nd Bn. Royal Sussex Regiment,

Roberts, No. 766 C.Q.M.S H.   5th Bn. Royal Sussex Regiment,
Startup, No. 7422 T/Sergeant F.   2nd Bn. Royal Sussex Regiment,
Weston, No. 1981 Private G.   5th Bn. Royal Sussex Regiment,

Thursday January 21st 1916

D.C.M for Ticehurst man

Among the Sussex men to whom the Distinguished Conduct Medal has been awarded is No. 1981 G. Weston of 'C' Company 5th Bn. Royal Sussex Regiment. Although no official record is to hand of his recommendation for the D.C.M as far as can be gathered from one or two of his Company who were with him during the memorable battle of 9th May 1915, in which the 2nd and 5th Sussex played so gallant a part, Private Weston was one of the very few men of 'C' Company, 5th Battalion who escaped unhurt during the first charge.

On the order being given to retire, Private Weston managed to get back to the first fire trench with safety, but finding his own particular chum lying out between "no-man's land" badly wounded, immediately rushed back to try and assist him in under a terrific fire from machine - guns and rifles from the German lines.

In this he was successful, and again went out and assisted three other badly wounded men (Corporal Fletcher of Oakover, Ticehurst, being one of them), back into comparative safety, in which act he was nobly assisted by Private now Corporal Ford and one or two others. During the time Private Weston was rescuing these comrades he himself was shot through the foot and disabled. The local 'C' Company now has two D.C.M's. Private Waghorn of Wadhurst and Private Weston of Ticehurst, while Major Courthope has been honoured with the Military Cross. Private Weston was in Chelsea Hospital with Sergeant J. Nicholls of Ticehurst, both being sent home from France together. Sergeant Nicholls is now at home awaiting the adjustment of an artificial foot, while Private Weston is at Purfleet.

C.Q.M.S Hugh Roberts a Hailsham teacher wins D.C.M

General satisfaction has been expressed in Hailsham that C.Q.M.S Hugh Roberts 5th Battalion Royal Sussex Regiment has been awarded the Distinguished Conduct Medal. Previous to going to France C.Q.M.S Roberts was assistant master at Hailsham School. He was one of the first to sign on for foreign service soon after the outbreak of war, and left with his Battalion for France in February last, so he was with the Sussex in the terrible encounters of the 8th and 9th of May last year.

Monday March 13th 1916

D.C.M's for Sussex Men

A special supplement to the *'London Gazette'* issued on Saturday, details the act of gallantry for which were given the very numerous awards of the Distinguished Conduct Medal announced on 14th January last.

No. 9107 Sergeant W. Couchman,   2nd Bn. Royal Sussex Regiment,

For Conspicuous Gallantry and Devotion to Duty throughout the campaign.

No. 2205 Private J. Heaseman,   Depot, Royal Sussex Regiment, (Was 2nd Battalion)

For Conspicuous Gallantry and Devotion to Duty. He was wounded bringing in a wounded man, but refused to be attended to till he had bound up a wounded officer. Later, he went out twice again after wounded; on the last occasion he was again wounded in the chest. All this was in broad daylight and under fire.

No. 766 C.Q.M.S   H. Roberts,   5th Bn. Royal Sussex Regiment,

For Conspicuous Gallantry and Devotion to Duty. He went out three times over the parapet, superintended the retirement when his officers were all casualties, coming last himself. He went out again to bandage wounded men, and got several back to safety. He set a fine example.

No. 4307 Sergeant   J.W. Sanderson,   7th Bn. Royal Sussex Regiment,

For Conspicuous Gallantry when he went out twice in front of the trenches under heavy fire to search for a wounded Corporal and finally succeeded in bringing back his body.

No. 7422 T/Sergeant   F. Startup,   2nd Bn. Royal Sussex Regiment,

For Conspicuous good work and good leading throughout the campaign. He has set a fine example and has distinguished himself for coolness and bravery.

No. 1981 Private   G. Weston,   5th Bn. Royal Sussex Regiment,

For Conspicuous Gallantry and Devotion to Duty while in the field. He attended to many wounded under heavy fire and brought them back to the trenches. He then carried back five wounded in succession from the advanced trench before he himself was wounded.

Friday March 24th 1916

Report that Sergeant J. King D.C.M of the 7th Battalion Royal Sussex Regiment has been killed in action. Sergeant King's real name was Keegan.

Friday March 31st 1916

Gallantry of the 9th Battalion Recognised

Award of the Victoria Cross and three Distinguished Conduct Medals

As was generally anticipated would be the case, official recognition has been made of the gallantry of the 9th Royal Sussex Regiment. Their terrible ordeal early in February last, has already been noted in the *Sussex Daily News*. A German mine was exploded in front of their trenches, causing much damage and many casualties, but the crater was at once rushed by the survivors, reinforcements brought up, and the position held against all attacks.
Special supplements of the *"London Gazette"* issued last night notify that his Majesty the King has, in connection with this engagement, conferred the Victoria Cross on Temporary-Lieutenant Eric Archibald McNair, 9th Royal Sussex Regiment, and the Distinguished Conduct Medal on three men of the battalion. The official announcements are as follows :-

V.C.

Temporary-Lieutenant Eric Archibald McNair, 9th (Service) Battalion, The Royal Sussex Regiment.

For most conspicuous bravery. When the enemy exploded a mine, Lieutenant McNair and many men of two platoons were hoisted into the air, and many men were buried. But, though much shaken, he at once organised a party with a machine-gun to man the near edge of the crater, and opened rapid fire on a large party of the enemy, who were advancing. The enemy were driven back, leaving many dead.

Lieutenant McNair then ran back for reinforcements, and sent to another unit for bombs, ammunition and tools to replace those buried.

The communications trench being blocked, he went across the open under heavy fire and led up the reinforcements the same way. His prompt and plucky action and example undoubtedly saved the situation.

D.C.M.

No. 3058 Corporal W.C. Hughes, 9th Bn. Royal Sussex Regiment,

For conspicuous gallantry. After a severe bombardment by the enemy, in which his trench was blown in, he took eight men up to the newly made crater, occupied it, and effectually checked the advancing enemy by fire.

No. 3238 Private M.G. Jupp, 9th Bn. Royal Sussex Regiment,

For conspicuous gallantry. After being blown up with a portion of his trench, he at once took a machine-gun to the newly formed crater and continued firing on the enemy till his gun was put out of action.

No. 4256 Lance-Corporal F. Moore, 9th Bn. Royal Sussex Regiment,

For conspicuous gallantry. During a bombardment by the enemy his telephone dug-out was blown in and his instrument damaged, but he at once went back under heavy fire, fetched another one, and worked it till his dug-out was again blown in and he himself wounded.

Lieutenant McNair joined the Royal Sussex Regiment four months after the outbreak of war, and did his early period of service in the 10th Battalion, being transferred to the 9th Battalion for active service.

Details of the action

The engagement which has led to these awards has been described by a Brighton member of the machine-gun section of the battalion. Writing to friends towards the end of February last, he said :-

"We took over the trenches last Thursday week, and on the two following days we suffered one of the worst bombardments of the war. Day and night, continually, our front line trenches and support trenches were shelled with high explosives. On the Monday the bombardment reached its height. The gun team I was in went on duty at 2 o'clock, and by 3 o'clock the full fury of the German bombardment commenced.

"I cannot describe what it was like in words,. At 4 o'clock only myself and another fellow were left with the gun. We both prayed and left ourselves in God's hands. The trench was one continual flash of explosives, and how we escaped being hit I don't know. We were thrown to the bottom of the trench five times. I think having a sheet of corrugated iron over our heads saved us a lot.

"It began to get dark, but the bombardment went on until about 6 o'clock, when the whole trench rocked like a boat. It first seemed to go up one end, throwing me on my chum, and then throwing us back again. It took me a few minutes to realise that the Germans had exploded a mine. I might say that, after the first shock, my pal and I were lying at the bottom of the trench, with the corrugated iron on top of us, and it took a long to get from under it, as on it was a great quantity of earth thrown up by the mine.

"When I got to my feet and was able to look round I suffered just as severe shock as when the mine went up.

"Where there had been trenches was now simply flat ground. By the time the supports had arrived, headed by our C.O., we were able to lay our gun, and then the boys charged for the crater.

"It was good to hear the cheer of our boys. I was sorry at not being able to go with them, but our gun was in a position to fire on the gap in our line 300 yards away.

"Lance-Corporal Jupp, of Hassocks, was in charge of a gun just on the left of the crater, and when our lads charged into the crater they found him already there. There is talk of him being recommended for honours. Anyway the whole of the 9th Sussex made a name for themselves, and I am jolly proud to be one of them."

Tribute from another Regiment

A tribute to the Sussex men came also from another source. Writing on 27th February, Regimental-Sergeant-Major A.C. Andrews, who belongs to a non-Sussex regiment, said ;-

"The 9th Sussex have had a pretty rough time of it, and lost a great number of men, but they have covered themselves with glory. You see ours and the Sussex had been relieving each other periodically. Well, one turn, when the Sussex relieved us we had been having the usual spell, with the usual casualties; some days two or three, and some days none, and so on; but the very night the 9th relieved us the Germans started a big "strafe", and kept it up for four days. When we went back it was 'business as usual'.

"The 9th Sussex had quite a heavy casualty list; but there is one thing I can tell you about them.

They did a grand piece of work, which made us all proud of them and proud to have them in our Brigade. One night the Germans suddenly sprang a big mine right on top of their front line trench, and they had men flung all over the place; some killed, some wounded, some buried, and others temporarily flattened out. After the mine went up, about 60 Germans rushed out of their trenches to occupy the crater, and as soon as those of the Sussex who were left spotted them they jumped up, climbed out of the trench and mud, and, with a ringing Sussex cheer, went for them.

"The Germans turned and fled for their lives without facing a shot; the Sussex got the crater, and the same night made good ; put wire up and trenched it, and made that part of the line stronger than it was before.

"What about that for a few of Kitchener's chaps?"

"I consider it one of the most marvellous feats of the war. Can you imagine it? Men taken utterly by surprise like that, and nearly blown to kingdom come, to do such a thing! I guess there will be one or two decorations going among that little lot. Tell anyone who wants to know that they have reason to be proud of the 9th Sussex."

Corporal W.C. Hughes

Corporal W.C. Hughes is a Brighton man, 24 years of age, son of Mr. and Mrs. Hughes, of 10, Upper Russell Street, Brighton. He has been home since the action for which he has been awarded the D.C.M. but had little to say about it except that he had been glad to be able to save the life of one of his officers. A young fellow of fine physique, nearly 6ft. high, Hughes is an old Middle Street scholar, and was a familiar figure in his youth as a drummer in the Royal Field Artillery Cadets at Brighton. It is a source of great pride to Lieutenant-Colonel Burchett's Cadet battalion that Corporal Hughes is the second member of the Corps. to earn the distinction of D.C.M. - the first, Bombardier Read, who, unfortunately, was killed soon afterwards. The Corporal wrote to Lieutenant-Colonel Burchett on the 9th February last as follows :-

"Just a line to let you know that I have got back to duty again. We had a good passage across. My regiment was not in the trenches when I arrived, so I had time to get used to things a bit. We are in now, and it seems quite strange after being so quiet in dear old England.
"You will be pleased to know that I have won the D.C.M. and also been presented with a Certificate from my Divisional General. I have sent the Certificate home, so if you care to see it, my mother has got it.

"I suppose you remember me telling you about a mine exploding in front of my platoon, and only leaving four of us. With these few men I went forward, and, with the aid of a machine-gun, held the crater until reinforcements came up. We then turned to the men who had been buried, and we were able to dig two out and get them back to the trench.
"We have had a lot of snow here the last two days, and it makes it very unpleasant for us."

The R.F.A.. Cadets of Brighton have a magnificent war record, no fewer than 1,062 old members in Brighton, hove and district having joined the Services. Lieutenant-Colonel Burchett who formed the first public Cadet Corps. in Sussex, represents the county on the Territorial Cadet Association Council. In a letter since received by Mr. and Mrs. Hughes, their son says he has been decorated with the medal by the Major-General in command of his Division. A younger brother of the Corporal, aged 19, left Brighton for Service this week, and is to receive his training at Dover. Another brother, married, is attested under the Derby scheme, and will take his turn when the married men's group are called up.

Lance-Corporal Jupp

Lance-Corporal M.G.C. Jupp is a brother of V.W.C. Jupp, the Sussex County cricketer, who is also in khaki. Their parents keep the well-known Friars Oak Hotel, midway between Hassocks and St. John's Common. Lance-Corporal Jupp was for a time in the office of Messrs. T. Bannister and Co., at Haywards Heath, and played for Haywards Heath Cricket Club. He also kept goal for Haywards Heath Football Club. On leaving Messrs. Bannister's office he worked for his father at Friars Oak before he joined the Army.
Recently Mr. and Mrs. Jupp received a letter from Captain and Adjutant W.C. Norton, of the 9th Sussex Regiment, announcing that their son had been awarded the D.C.M.., and he heartily congratulated him and them. Captain Norton said Lance-Corporal Jupp was wounded in a hand the same day that he won the medal, but not badly, and he (Captain Norton) did not quite know where he had gone to, and if his parents knew, he asked them to inform Lance-Corporal Jupp of the distinction he had won, and convey to him the congratulations of the Army Corps. Commander, the Divisional Commander, the Colonel, and himself.
Mr. and Mrs. Jupp subsequently received a letter from their son mentioning that he had been awarded the D.C.M., but he said nothing about his wound, or his whereabouts, it being thought the reticence was characteristic of him and that he did not wish to cause his parents any alarm or anxiety. He wrote in cheerful style, and anticipated a turn of leave soon.

Tuesday April 4th 1916

Belgian Honour for Sussex Officer

The award of the Croix de Chevalier from the King of the Belgians was bestowed upon :-

Major J.S. Cameron, D.S.O., 2nd Bn. Royal Sussex Regiment,

Friday April 14th 1916

Young Officer of Royal Sussex Regiment killed

A gallant officer of the Royal Sussex Regiment met his death in action on the 8th of April, is Eric Guy Sutton, who in September last was awarded the Military Cross for assisting in a rescue from a mine after an explosion. The second son of the Mayor of Reading, Mr. Leonard Sutton, Lieutenant E.G. Sutton obtained his commission in the Royal Sussex Regiment in September 1914, having come over from California on the outbreak of war. He was an old Rugby boy and was 21 years of age. Three brothers are still serving in the forces.

Saturday April 15th 1916

Gallant Deeds by Officers and Men of the Seventh Royal Sussex

Honours awarded by the King

D.C.M. for a Sussex Gunner

The 7th Royal Sussex, who took part in the heavy fighting of a few weeks ago and acquitted themselves in a manner that reflected lustre not only on every member of the battalion but also upon the country from which most of them are drawn, figures prominently in the new list of war honours published last night. There is also a welcome reminder of the good work of the Sussex Field Artillery, a Gunner being the recipient of a Distinguished Conduct Medal. The officers and men singled out for individual recognition, and the brief official description of the deed for which they are decorated, are as follows :-

D.S.O.

Major (Temporary Lieutenant-Colonel) William Lushington Osborn, The Royal Sussex Regiment, Commanding 7th Battalion,

For conspicuous ability in the performance of his duties. The excellent training of his Battalion and the careful attention paid to all details of organisation of defence, ensured that the captured position he took over on relief was securely held, in spite of constant counter-attacks. He showed great initiative in launching counter-attacks.

M.C.

Temporary Second-Lieutenant, Gilbert Nagle, 7th Bn. Royal Sussex Regiment,

For conspicuous courage, when, though wounded, he continued his duties, inspiring all ranks of his command with confidence. He organised a skilful defence, and repelled two attacks.

D.C.M.

No. 206 Private R. Cheesman, 7th Bn. Royal Sussex Regiment,

For conspicuous devotion to duty. He remained with Lance-Corporal Short for 27 hours at their bombing post, refusing relief, as reliable bombers were not available to take up duty.

No. 9650 Sergeant J. Langley, 7th Bn. Royal Sussex Regiment, (Warninglid)

For conspicuous courage and resource during heavy shelling. During severe grenade fighting he organised bomb-carrying and reinforcing parties, and by personal example contributed largely to the repulse of the enemy.

No.1652 Lance-Corporal H. Short, 7th Bn. Royal Sussex Regiment, (Worthing)

For conspicuous devotion to duty. He remained with Private Cheesman for 27 hours at their bombing post, refusing relief as reliable bombers were not available to take up duty.

No. 1497 Gunner L.C. Upchurch,   1/1st Sussex Battery, Royal Field Artillery, T.F.

For conspicuous gallantry in maintaining communications when with the observing officer under heavy fire.
Sergeant James Langley is a Warninglid man, and a member of a family that has several sons in the Army. Sergeant Langley was in the 2nd Bn. Royal Sussex Regiment, and has been home once wounded. He lost a brother who was drowned in the Solent while on Naval service. It is understood Lance-Corporal Short is a Worthing man.

Thursday April 20th 1916

A Sussex Sergeant's D.C.M.

Public presentation at Salford

In November last the Distinguished Conduct Medal was awarded to Sergeant W.R. Smethurst, 2nd Battalion Royal Sussex regiment, for conspicuous gallantry, the official record of the incident being as follows :-

For conspicuous gallantry on the 25th September, 1915, near Le Rotoiro (Loos). During the first assault, when numbers of men in the first line were falling back suffering from gas fumes, and at a critical time when a good leading was essential, Sergeant Smethurst got his men well in hand, and, although the gas and smoke were very thick, he led them forward, and by his bravery and example materially assisted in the attack, in which he was wounded.
At the time he was recalled to the colours as a Reservist, the Sergeant had been for several years a motorman in the service of the Salford Tramways Committee, and at the Salford Town hall on Tuesday he was publicly presented with the medal at a meeting of the Tramways Committee and many other members of the Corporation, the military also being represented. Speeches were made, and the Sergeant was presented with an illuminated copy of a resolution passed by the Committee congratulating him on the distinction he had won. It was mentioned that more than 500 employees of the Committee had joined the Army. In acknowledging the presentation, Sergeant Smethurst mentioned that, although a time-expired man, he intended returning to the Colours after a few weeks at home.

Saturday April 29th 1916

Portslade Soldier's Distinction

Lance-Corporal R. Cheesman, 7th Bn. Royal Sussex Regiment, who as previously reported in the *Sussex Daily News*, has been awarded the D.C.M. for conspicuous devotion to duty, is a nephew of Mr. J.G.P. Moon. Woodlands, Mayfield. he remained with Lance-Corporal Short for 27 hours at their bombing post, refusing relief, as reliable bombers were not available to take up duty.

Wednesday May 3rd 1916

Heathfield Sergeant Commended

Sergeant Arthur J.G. West, son of Mrs. D. Relf, of Broad Oak, Heathfield, has recently written home to his mother. The letter states :- "We expect to get out for a rest about the end of the month. I shall not be sorry either, for it is not a very pleasant place that we are in. We had a taste of the gas and tear shells the other night. Oh! they were nasty. I was bad for about two days after. I had a piece of parchment presented to me the other day.
The parchment read as follows :- 'I have read with great pleasure the report of your Regimental commander and Brigade Commander, regarding your gallant conduct and devotion to duty in the field from August, 1915, to March, 1916. F.S. Maxse, Major-General, Commanding Division.'"

Wednesday May 17th 1916

A Royal Sussex Officer and N.C.O. Decorated

The pleasant echo of a successful raid by a party of the 2nd Royal Sussex Regiment, on the enemy trenches is the announcement in a special supplement to the *'London Gazette'* last night, that two members of the party have been decorated for their gallantry. The rewards are thus set out :-

M.C.

Second-Lieutenant Robert Shirley Osmaston, 3rd Bn. (attd. 2nd Bn.)

"For conspicuous gallantry after making a close reconnaissance of the enemy positions, he led a raid, got into a sap behind an enemy post, and after two of the enemy had been bayoneted, skilfully withdrew without a casualty, he himself, with three men covering the withdrawal".

Lieutenant Robert Shirley Osmaston was gazetted 2nd Lieutenant (on probation) in the 3rd battalion of the Royal Sussex Regiment in May of last year, and joined the 2nd battalion at the front in early December when the battalion was in a very "unhealthy" section around Loos, where the shelling every day was considerable. he got his "baptism of fire" very promptly, and underwent all the hardships of trench life during the past winter. He proved himself an alert and enterprising officer.

D.C.M.

No. 5968 Lance-Corporal A. Adams, 2nd Bn. Royal Sussex Regiment,

For conspicuous gallantry during a successful raid on the enemy's trenches. He bayoneted one of the enemy, showed a fine power of leadership, and finally joined his officer in covering the withdrawal.

Saturday May 20th 1916

Two 1st Royal Sussex men mentioned in dispatches.

Two members of the 1st Royal Sussex Regiment were mentioned in the last dispatches published relating to the fighting in France, but were included under the heading "Indian Subordinate Medical Department and Army Bearer Corps. "Last night's *'London Gazette'* supplied the necessary correction. The names of the soldiers thus honoured are :-

No. 9214 Sergeant E. Clements, (Packstore),
No. 7366 Private J.T. Rowland.

A Burwash Weald Hero

Private T. Balcombe, of the Southdown Battalion, has sent the following account of an incident in which he took a prominent part : "I and two of our chaps were working in the trenches and one of them got hit. Two of us went over into "No Man's Land" and got him. The captain wrote home and told his people, and three of us have got some cigarettes from them. The colonel told us we are recommended for the Military Medal. It was a bit hot over there that night, but it is no more than mates should do; we might be in the same fix ourselves some time, but I hope to come home again safe."
Private Balcombe received the following letter from Miss Humble-Crofts, of Waldron Rectory :-
"My brother, Captain Humble-Crofts, has told me about your rescue of a comrade who was wounded. I am writing to you now, although I do not know you personally, as I should like to congratulate you on having done a very gallant thing. The bravery of our men is a thing that all Englishwomen must be particularly proud of, and I am very glad to think that some of my brother's men have been able to prove themselves heroes. I am afraid you are having a rather hot time, but you all seem to be putting up with it splendidly. At any rate you must enjoy your spells of rest when they come. I hope the poor lad, who was wounded is getting on well. I suppose he will be lucky enough to get home for a time. I just wanted you to know that as Captain Humble-Crofts's sister I feel very proud of your bravery."

Monday May 22nd 1916

Sussex V.C. Decorated by the King

Captain McNair's Heroism

The King held an investiture at Buckingham Palace on Saturday, when he personally decorated about 90 naval and military officers for gallant services. General Sir Edmund Barrow, Military Secretary to the India Office, received the C.S.I., while Lieutenant-General Sir Francis Davies received the K.C.B. and K.C.M.G. for distinguished services in Gallipoli. There were two V.C.'s - Captain Eric Archibald McNair, Royal Sussex Regiment, and Private Henry Kenny, Loyal North Lancashires.
Captain McNair's V.C. was conferred in connection with the explosion of a mine by the Germans in front of the 9th Sussex trenches in February last, and the announcement of his decoration was made on Thursday, 30th March, simultaneously with the conferment of the D.C.M.'s on Corporal Hughes, Private Jupp and Lance-Corporal Moore, of the same regiment, for gallantry on the same occasion. The official description of Captain McNair's deed was as follows :-
When the enemy exploded a mine Lieutenant McNair and many men of two platoons were hoisted into the air, and many men were buried, but, although shaken, he at once organised a party with a machine-gun to man the near edge of the crater, and opened rapid fire on a large party of the enemy who were advancing. The enemy were driven back, leaving many dead. Lieutenant McNair then ran back for reinforcements, and sent to another unit for bombs, ammunition and tools to replace those buried.

The communication trench being blocked, he went across the open under heavy fire and led up the reinforcements the same way. His prompt and plucky action and example undoubtedly saved the situation.

Saturday June 3rd 1916

Honours for Sussex Officers and Men

The long list of military honours issued on the occasion of the King's birthday includes the following :-

C.M.G.

Major (T/Lieutenant-Colonel) Evelyn Fontaine Villiers, D.S.O., Royal Sussex Regiment,

D.S.O.

Major (T/Lieutenant-Colonel) Alfred Edgar Glasgow, Royal Sussex Regiment, commanding the 8th (Service) Battalion,

M.C.

Second-Lieutenant (T/Captain) Ernest Alfred Baker, 2nd Bn.

Quartermaster and Hon. Captain Thomas Albert Jones, D.C.M., 2nd Bn.

T/Captain Walter Charles Norton, 9th Bn.

 Captain Edward Hulton Preston, 2nd Bn.

2nd Lieutenant (T/Lieutenant) Humphrey Sayer, Sussex Yeomanry,

 Lieutenant (T/Captain) Michael Wallington, 2nd Bn.

D.C.M.

No. 5474 A/S/Major L. Bonney 9th Bn.
No. 3932 R.Q.M.S. R.W. Hearn 2nd Bn.

 No. 600 A/S/Major H. Page 7th Bn.

No. 6489 S/Major W.F. Rainsford 2nd Bn.
No. 9013 C.S.M. W. Stoughton 3rd Bn. att. 2nd Bn.

M.M.

No. 1659 Lance-Corporal, A. Horcroft, 2nd Bn.
No. 5845 Private, F. Hughes, 3rd Bn. (late 2nd Bn.)
No. 9977 Corporal, G. Larby, 2nd Bn.
No. 5325 Lance-Corporal, J. Mant, 9th Bn.
No. 10147 Lance-Corporal, W.E. Martin, 9th Bn.
No. 2205 Private, J.W. Offler, 2nd Bn.
No. 1958 Sergeant, J.W. Tutt, 8th Bn.
No. 225 Sergeant, C.A. Wilmshurst, 5th Bn.
No. 1483 Acting-Sergeant, A. Young, 2nd Bn.

Friday June 16th 1916

Mentioned in Dispatches

Staff

Evans, Captain Sydney Gerald 3rd Bn. Royal Sussex Regiment (S. R.)

Green, Lt.-Col. (T/Brig-General) E.W.B., D.S.O. 2nd Bn. Royal Sussex Regiment,
[In the early part of the year Lieutenant-Colonel (Temporary Brigadier-General) Edgar Walter Butler Green, D.S.O. was mentioned in dispatches for the fourth time, and it was in March, 1915, that he became the recipient of the D.S.O. in recognition of his meritorious services during the war. He then commanded the 2nd Battalion Royal Sussex Regiment, and towards the of 1915 was put in command of a Brigade. He gained his commission in 1890, and during the South African War, was mentioned in dispatches, receiving the Queen's Medal with three and the King's with two clasps. During the present war he has been wounded, but made a good recovery.]

Wroughton, Major (Temporary-Colonel) J.B., C.M.G.
Royal Sussex Regiment,

[Lieutenant-Colonel John Bartholomew Wroughton, C.M.G., is a son of the late Edward Norris Wroughton. Born in 1874, he entered the Royal Sussex Regiment in 1893, he became Captain in 1900, and Major in 1911. He has seen considerable fighting, and has been previously mentioned in dispatches.]

Sussex Yeomanry

Caldwell, 2nd Lieutenant (T/Lieutenant) R.McK. Royal Sussex Regiment, (T.F.)
Ward, T/Capt. B.T. London Rgt. attd. Royal Sussex Regiment,
Wood, Capt. (T/Mjr.) A.H.
Davies, No. 2398 Sergeant G.T.
Lusted, No. 1647 Sergeant G.

Royal Sussex Regiment

Villiers, Major (Temp. Lt.-Colonel) Evelyn Fontaine D.S.O. 2nd Bn.

[Major (T/Lt.-Colonel) E.F. Villiers D.S.O. has twice before been mentioned in dispatches during the war, and holds the Queen's Medal with four clasps.
Major Villiers, who is a very popular officer, resides at Belmont Street, Bognor, and is also well-known at Worthing.

At the beginning of the war he held the rank of Captain and his rise to Major and then to Temporary Lieutenant-Colonel has been very rapid. He has been twice wounded, though neither time seriously, Major Villiers had the distinction of appearing in the King's last birthday honoured list as a Companion of the Order of St. Michael and St. George. Formerly this gallant officer was Adjutant of a Battalion of Indian Volunteers. A connection of the Buckinghamshire family, he is the brother of Mr. Ernest Villiers, of Hambrook Park, on the Sussex border, who formerly represented Brighton in the House of Commons.]

Owen, Lieutenant A.G.L. (Special Reserve) 2nd Bn.

[Lieutenant Alfred George Lewys Owen (Special Reserve) was formerly on probation, and in May, 1915, was confirmed to the rank of Second-Lieutenant, within two months of which he was gazetted Lieutenant.]

Kimber, No. 8166 Sergeant A.F. 2nd Bn.
Read, No. 10208 Sergeant E.B. 2nd Bn.
Young, No. 1599 Temporary Corporal G.T. 2nd Bn.
Burden, No. 7835 Private F. 2nd Bn.
Stevens, No. G/1249 Private Ernest William 2nd Bn. (died of wounds)10/10/15
Dicker, Captain Arthur Seymour Hamilton 3rd Bn. (Special Reserve) att. 2nd Bn.
King, Lieutenant R.N.R. 3rd Bn. (Special Reserve) att. 2nd Bn.

Royal Sussex Regiment (Service Battalions)

Osborn, Major (Temp. Lieutenant-Colonel) W.L. D.S.O. 7th Bn. Royal Sussex Regiment,

[Previously mentioned in dispatches, Major (Temporary Lieutenant-Colonel) William Lushington Osborn, D.S.O., joined the Regiment in 1890 and saw a great deal of active service before the recent campaign. He was awarded the D.S.O. only two months ago for his fine leadership of the 7th Battalion in action. He is an exceedingly popular Commander.]

Impey, Captain (Temp. Major) G.H. 7th Bn. Royal Sussex Regiment,

[Captain (Temporary Major) G.H. Impey has only lately assumed the command of a Service Battalion of the Royal Sussex Regiment, in which he was temporary major. He was a Captain of less than three years' service when war broke out, and was junior Major of the 7th Service Battalion for the past year. he has seen considerable fighting.]

Woodhams, Lt. (T/Captain) Geoffrey (killed)

[This is the second time that Temporary Captain G. Woodhams (Littlehampton) has been mentioned in dispatches, but unfortunately he did not live to know it.]

 Betham Lt. (T/Captain) Robert J.A. Royal Sussex Regiment (Adjutant)

 May, Temporary Captain R.T.

[Temporary Captain Richard T. May was gazetted to that rank last February.]

 Hind, T/Lieutenant R.C.D.

 Foster, T/Second-Lieutenant Percy George (died of wounds)

Clarke, Quartermaster and Hon. Lieutenant J.E.

[During November, 1915, Quartermaster and Hon. Lieutenant Joseph Edward Clarke, of the 7th Battalion, was reported wounded.]

Beale, No. 931 Lance-Sergeant A.W.

Glasgow, Major (T/Lt.-Colonel) A.E. 8th Bn. Royal Sussex Regiment,

[Major (Temporary Lieutenant-Colonel) Alfred Edgar Glasgow, D.S.O., is another officer who has had a long association with the Royal Sussex Regiment. It was in 1899 that he attained the rank of Captain, and he became Major in 1911. He has been praised for the good work done at the front by the 8th Battalion, to the command of which he was appointed on 29th April last. He has previously been acting as Assistant Provost-Marshall. He has been mentioned in dispatches before.]

Lott, Temporary Captain H.C.
[Temporary Captain H.C. Lott was mentioned in dispatches when he was temporary Lieutenant at the beginning of the year.]

Langdon, Major (T/Lt.-Colonel) J.F.P. (Reserve of Officers)
[Major (T/Lieutenant-Colonel) John F.P. Langdon (Reserve of Officers) is an officer who has seen considerable service, having joined the Royal Sussex Regiment in 1888, serving till 1910 and retiring with the rank of Major. He afterwards rejoined, and was gazetted to the command of a battalion of the regiment.]

McIvor, Temporary Captain A.R.

Tisdall, T/Second-Lieutenant Charles Henry   (killed)

Williams, No. 512 Company Sergeant-Major O.

[Company Sergeant-Major Owen Williams has a wife living at 17, Elder Street, Brighton, and is a member of "the good old 'D' Company," 9th Battalion Royal Sussex Regiment.]

Collins, No. 3071 Corporal F.

Buxted Soldier's Distinction

The Uckfield district has every reason to be proud of the part played in the war by who responded to the call to the colours. Many have made the supreme sacrifice : others are battle-scarred : while there is a number whose conduct on the battlefield has earned them emblems of devotion to duty. The latest addition to the list is Quartermaster-Sergeant C.A. Wilmshurst, a son of Mr. and Mrs. W. Wilmshurst, of Tanyard Farm, Buxted. This young soldier, who belongs to the 5th Battalion Royal Sussex Regiment, was among those who took part in the memorable engagement on 9th May, 1915, when so many brave sons of Sussex lay down their lives for their country. Sergeant Wilmshurst, as he then was, greatly distinguished himself by continuing to fetch in the wounded in the face of heavy fire.

After more than a year his gallant conduct has been recognised and he has been awarded the Military Medal. In a letter which his parents received from their son on Wednesday, he says he has been the recipient of many congratulations from officers and others, and that he would be sending home a cutting from the Battalion Orders, notifying the award. At the time of writing he had not received the ribbon, but expected it every day. Wilmshurst was born at Tanyard Farm, Buxted, and joined the Territorials when the force was formed. His promotion to the rank of Quartermaster Sergeant took place in March last.

Thursday June 22nd 1916

Valorous Royal Sussex N.C.O.'s.

Doings that won the D.C.M.

With reference to the announcement of the award of Distinguished Conduct Medals on 3rd June, 1916, the following are the acts of gallantry for which the decorations have been awarded :-

No. 5474 Acting-Sergeant-Major. L. Bonney,   9th Bn. Royal Sussex Regiment,

For consistent good work and devotion to duty, notably during three days of operations, and during a period of mining activity.

No. 3932 R.Q.M.S. R.W. Hearn,   2nd Bn. Royal Sussex Regiment,

For conspicuous good work throughout the campaign. He has shown great devotion to duty, notably when bringing up supplies at night, frequently under fire.

No. 600 Acting-Sergeant-Major. H. Page,   7th Bn. Royal Sussex Regiment,

For consistent good work throughout. Although he has 31 years' service, he is indefatigable and has set a fine example of devotion to duty. In action he has shown great coolness.

No. 6489 Sergeant-Major. W.F. Rainsford,   2nd Bn. Royal Sussex Regiment,

For conspicuous good work throughout the campaign. He has never missed a day's work, and by his fine and cheery example has done invaluable work in training N.C.O.'s and men and keeping up the spirits and discipline of the battalion.

No. 9013 C.S.M. W. Soughton,   3rd Bn. (attd 2nd Bn.) Royal Sussex Regiment,

For conspicuous gallantry and good work throughout the campaign, notably when, after all his officers had become casualties in an attack, he took command and led his company with great determination.

Friday June 23rd 1916

D.C.M. for Sussex Sergeant

Frank Startup, of the 2nd Bn. Royal Sussex Regiment, was yesterday at Snow Hill Station presented with the Distinguished Conduct Medal by Sir J.W. Nott Bower, Chief Commissioner of the City Police. The medal was awarded "for conspicuous good work and good leading throughout the campaign. He has set a fine example and has distinguished himself for coolness and bravery." While Sergeant Startup and his platoon were out in "No Man's" land digging an advanced trench, they were heavily shelled, and on his return at night he discovered two of his men were missing. He immediately returned and conveyed them to a place of comparative safety. Startup, as a Reservist, was called up in August, 1914, and took part in the retreat from Mons. He was taken prisoner at the Aisne, but succeeded in escaping during the night. He received his discharge as a time expired man and has lately been doing police duty.

Monday June 26th 1916

Decorations for Royal Sussex Officers

Three to receive Military Cross.

Several Sussex officers have joined the ranks of those whose gallantry and devotion to duty have received recognition at the hands of his Majesty the King. The following awards are announced in the latest list :-

M.C.

T/Lieutenant Henry Steadman Lewis, 11th Bn. Royal Sussex Regiment,

For conspicuous gallantry when leading a patrol. After his party had been discovered and fired at by machine-guns he coolly completed his reconnaissance under heavy fire. with two Lance-Corporals he carried back a wounded man of his party under the same heavy fire. He has shown complete contempt of danger.

T/Second-Lieutenant Leonard Leighton Moody, 12th Bn. Royal Sussex Regiment,

For conspicuous gallantry. When in charge of a wiring party he rescued, under heavy fire of machine-guns, a man who had been hit. Later he went out three times to search for another man, and eventually found him and brought him in.

T/Second-Lieutenant Noel De Putron MacRoberts, 13th Bn. Royal Sussex Regiment,

For conspicuous gallantry. When two men of a wiring party fell wounded into the wire, 2nd-Lieutenant MacRoberts immediately went out under heavy machine-gun fire to their assistance. With the aid of two men of the wiring party, he got them into our trenches. It was bright moonlight and machine-gun fire was continuous.

Wednesday July 5th 1916

Sussex Officers Mentioned in Dispatches

A lengthy dispatch from General Sir Beauchamp Duff, G.C.B., issued last night, deals with the military operations in the Indian Empire and neighbouring territory from the beginning of the war. The operations described have been reported upon at various times. Two officers and one Serjeant of the Royal Sussex Regiment are brought to notice for their services, namely:-

Mohmand, Swat and Bunker

Lieutenant-Colonel Edward Leslie Mackenzie, D.S.O., 1st Bn.

Lieutenant William Edward Pollard-Urquhart 1st Bn. (k.i.a.).

No. 6092 Sergeant H. Blackmore, 1st Bn. att. 1st Divisional Signaling Company.

Friday July 7th 1916

The KING has been graciously pleased to confer the Territorial Decoration upon the undermentioned Officers of the Territorial Force, who have been duly recommended for the same under the terms of the Royal Warrant dated 17th August, 1908: —

Major Edward Hennah Langham, 5th Bn. Royal Sussex Regiment

Friday July 14th 1916

Mentioned in Dispatches

Gallipoli and Mesopotamia

Among those mentioned in dispatches for distinguished and gallant conduct rendered during the period of Sir General Charles Monroe's command of the Mediterranean Expeditionary Force are the following:-

Sussex Yeomanry

T/ Lt. Humphrey Sayer, M.C. (Gallipoli)

The following have been mentioned in Mesopotamia under Major-General Townshend,

Major Gerrard Evelyn Leachman, (Political Department) 1st Bn. Royal Sussex Regiment,

Friday July 28th 1916

Decorations conferred on Sussex Heroes

In a lengthy list of war honours published in a supplement to the *'London Gazette'* issued last night the following with Sussex associations were recorded :-

M.C.

Temp-Captain Frederic Percy Joscelyne, R.A.M.C. (attd. 2nd Bn. Royal Sussex Regiment,)

For consistent gallantry and devotion to duty. He has shown complete disregard of personal danger on all occasions, and has frequently carried out his duties under heavy fire. On one occasion a bullet from a machine-gun passed through his coat, but he showed complete indifference.

Temp- 2nd Lt. Noel De Putron MacRoberts, 13th Bn. Royal Sussex Regiment,

For conspicuous gallantry. When two men of a wiring party fell wounded into the wire, 2nd-Lieutenant MacRoberts immediately went out under heavy machine-gun fire to their assistance. With the aid of two men of the wiring party, he got them into our trenches. It was bright moonlight and machine-gun fire was continuous.

D.C.M.

No. SD/270 Sergeant Robert M. Budd, 11th Bn. Royal Sussex Regiment,

For conspicuous gallantry and devotion to duty. Although buried and badly bruised and shaken by the explosion of an enemy mine, he took charge, repaired and reorganised the defences, and set a fine example of cool bravery.

No. SD/1022 Private Frank Dadswell, 11th Bn. Royal Sussex Regiment,

For conspicuous gallantry and devotion to duty. Although his foot was broken by the explosion of an enemy mine, he stuck to his post on the fire step till the rescue work was completed and the defences reorganised.

No. SD/345 Corporal J. Russell, 11th Bn. Royal Sussex Regiment,

For conspicuous gallantry and devotion to duty. Although his leg was broken and his body badly crushed by the explosion of an enemy mine he rallied his men, crawled along the trench giving orders and refused assistance till all his men had been attended to.

Monday August 7th 1916

Honours for Royal Sussex Men

In the course of a letter written on Sunday, 30th July, Lance-Corporal Orin, Royal Sussex Regiment (who was back with his regiment after a long absence owing to wounds), says :-

"We have had a very strenuous time this last week or more, and have got through a lot of hard work, both in and out of the trenches, with a couple of attacks thrown in. We have been among the Australians, and what fine 'sports' they are, and how they fight. Their dare-devil-may-care spirit puts confidence and spirit into all the troops who come in contact with them. We are proud to have been with them.
"This morning after church parade a very pleasing ceremony took place. A number of honours for Distinguished Service and Conspicuous Bravery in the Field were presented by the Brigadier-General to the following N.C.O.'s and men :-

R.S.M. W.F. Rainsford	D.C.M.
R.Q.M.S. R.W. Hearn	D.C.M.
A/Sgt. A. Young	Military Medal
A/Cpl. J. Tester	Military Medal
A/Cpl. A. Horcroft	Military Medal
Private J.W. Offler	Military Medal
Private J.T. Belton	Military Medal
Private P. Gardiner	Military Medal

It is very gratifying to find so many honours among the "boys of the Royal Sussex."

Thursday August 10th 1916

Bar to Military Cross

It was announced in yesterday's *"London Gazette"*, that the award of the Military Cross was bestowed for conspicuous gallantry upon :-

T/2nd Lieutenant Noel De Putron MacRoberts, M.C. 13th Bn. Royal Sussex Regiment,

For conspicuous gallantry. He reconnoitred and cut the enemy's wire, completing his work with a torpedo, under rifle and grenade fire. Later he led a successful raid into the enemy's trenches, and, though wounded, personally accounted for two of the enemy who opposed his advance. His coolness and personal gallantry were largely responsible for the success of the raid.
(M.C. gazetted 27th July, 1916)

Friday August 11th 1916

Military Medals for fourteen men of the Royal Sussex Regiment

All the friends of the Royal Sussex Regiment will be pleased to read today that official recognition has been made of the war services of a number of its men. Different Battalions of the Regiment have borne the brunt of many a hard conflict with the enemy during the past few months, but, so far, there has been little except the casualty lists to bear witness to the valour of the men of Sussex. Those in possession of the facts have known, that the fine reputation of the Regiment has been worthily upheld.

His Majesty the King has been pleased to award the Military Medal to the following men of the Royal Sussex Regiment for "bravery in the field" :-

No. SD/3730 Private Thomas Balcombe		13th Bn.

No. 10729 Private J.T. Belton   2nd Bn.

No. SD/390 Lance-Corporal William Thomas Booth   11th Bn.

No. SD/658 Lance-Corporal Guy Compton	11th Bn.
No. SD/3101 Private Alfred Samuel Ford	13th Bn.
No. 5946 Private P.J. Gardiner	2nd Bn.
No. 3322 Private H. Gardner	9th Bn.
No. SD/3600 Private Joseph Beaton Hater	13th Bn.
No. SD/2244 Private Frederick Mason	12th Bn.
No. SD/3663 Private Frederick Henry Parvin	13th Bn.
No. 6382 Private A. Pink	9th Bn.
No. SD/3225 Private Henry Charles Scott	13th Bn.
No. SD/4109 Private Wallace Thomas Taylor	13th Bn.
No. 8513 Lance-Corporal J. Tester	2nd Bn.

SPECIAL BRIGADE ROUTINE ORDER
BY BRIG. GEN. W.L. HORNBY, D.S.O. CMDG. 116TH INFANTRY BRIGADE

13-6-16

AWARDS FOR GALLANT CONDUCT

(i) The Brigadier-General Commanding has much pleasure I announcing to all ranks of the Brigade, the following Awards for gallant conduct:-

No. 3101 Pte. Alfred Samuel Ford, 13th Bn. Royal Sussex Regiment   Military Medal

No. 3730 Pte. Thomas Balcombe, 13th Bn. Royal Sussex Regiment   Military Medal

No. 4109 Pte. Wallace Thomas Taylor, 13th Bn. Royal Sussex Regiment   Military Medal

(ii) The following is a description of the action for which the above Awards have been made.

No. 4045 Pte. Maylem S.G. and No. 3101 Pte. Ford A.S. were working in front of our parapet on the night of the 23rd/24th April. Machine Gun fire was opened on them and Pte. Maylem was wounded in the right ankle. Pte. Ford shouted to the men in the trench for help and No. 3730 Pte. T. Balcombe and No. 4109 Pte. W.T. Taylor immediately went over the parapet. The Machine Gun was at the time firing bursts of 20 to 30 rounds every few seconds keeping them on the same spot.

Between them they got Pte. Maylem to the top of the parapet, when Ptes. Ford and Balcombe got down inside the trench and the three of them lowered the wound emanon to a Machine Gun emplacement on the safe side of the parapet. At this moment the Machine Gun opened again on our parapet, and Pte. Taylor, who was still on the enemy, realising that if he jumped over he might hurt the wounded man, rolled down to the bottom of the parapet and waited till the Machine Gun ceased fire, when he got over the parapet and helped to dress Maylem's wound.

I consider the act of these three men to be one of great courage and I accordingly bring their names to notice.

(sd) F.C.W. Draffen, Lt-Col.
Commanding, 13th Bn. R. Sussex Regt.

I endorse the remarks of Officer Commanding 13th Bn. R. Sussex R. and recommend the Award of the Military Medal.

(sd) M.L. Hornby,
Br-General,
Commanding, 116th Infantry Brigade.

"Lance-Corporal" G. Compton is now Sergeant Guy Compton. He is a son of Mr. G. Compton of Woodford, and grandson of the late Mr. J.C. Compton J.P., first Chairman of the Walthamstow Urban Council. His medal, it is understood, is for service while on patrol duty, and assisting in bringing in a wounded man under fire. He was himself wounded on 12th July. Sergeant Compton was educated at Bancroft's School, Woodford Wells, and joined Kitchener's Army in September, 1914, being first in the R.G.A. and afterwards in the Royal Sussex.

Private Frederick Henry Arvin's home is at Yapton, and his medal is for bravery at Givenchy on 17th April, when a party of men were working on the wire in front of the left Company of his Battalion. Heavy machine-gun was opened upon them, and three of the party were hit. One of the wounded crawled back into the trench, and the other two fell into the barbed wire.

The remainder of the men took cover in shell holes. Lieutenant MacRoberts went to their assistance, and Privates Arvin and Joseph Beaton Hater, who also receives the medal, left cover and assisted the officer to extricate the wounded men. This took some time, but the wounded were eventually carried into the trench. It was a brilliant moonlight night when the gallant action was performed, and during the whole time enemy machine-guns were traversing the front.

The Brigadier-General in an order issued on 10th June, said : "I consider these actions showed conspicuous gallantry on the part of the men concerned, and that they were an inspiring example to their comrades."

Private H.C. Scott unfortunately has not lived to receive the reward of his gallantry. He was a native of Bognor, where he was well-known and much respected. Prior to the war he was in the employ of Messrs. Reynolds. the distinction conferred upon him was for erecting wire entanglements and cutting German wire in readiness for a raid on the succeeding night, and he was engaged in this work with an officer for four hours, at great risk. As a result of the work the raid was effected with the loss of only a few wounded and none killed. It is understood that his medal will be forwarded to his widow, who resides with her two children at 45, Steinem Street, Bognor. His parents live in Bedford Street, Bognor.

Monday August 21st 1916

Thirteen new awards to Officers and Men of the County Regiment

The tale of gallant deeds that makes up the history of the Royal Sussex Regiment receives a notable addition from the special supplement to the *"London Gazette"* issued on Saturday night. Therein are recorded the names of four officers of the regiment who have awarded the Military Cross, and of nine non-commissioned officers who have had conferred on them the Distinguished Conduct Medal. It is a worthy list, and the deeds that are chronicled will increase the pride already felt in the County Regiment, whose doings have stirred the emotions of those who dwell within the Sussex borders.
Through all the little shining paragraphs there runs a hint- sometimes it is more than that--of the native characteristic of tenacity. we read : He "stuck to his command"; or "held on as long as ammunition lasted." Several showed great coolness." The Botches have learnt by this time that the "Iron Regiment" want some moving against their will. That "won't be drub" trait is of no small value in warfare.
Appended is the list of awards, together with brief descriptions of the deeds or services for which they are made :-

M.C.

Temp 2[nd]Lt. Goodman Ambler,   7th Bn. att. 12th Bn.
For conspicuous gallantry during operations. When his company commander became a casualty he took command, and led the company into the enemy's lines, and began consolidating under heavy fire. He was wounded, but stuck to his command till the company was withdrawn.

Temp Lt. Charles Osborne Bolton,   12th Bn.

For conspicuous gallantry during operations. He organised parties and kept the Battalion supplied with ammunition and bombs in the enemy's lines, and kept his C.O. informed of the progress of the fight. He showed great coolness under heavy fire.

Temp Lt. Eric Stuart Ellis,   13th Bn.

For conspicuous gallantry during operations. He led his bombing party with great dash into the enemy's support line. He was knocked down by the blast of a shell, but pushed on, and accounted for two of the enemy with his revolver.

Temp 2nd Lt. Clifford Augustus Farnham Whitely,

For conspicuous gallantry during operations. He rallied men who had pushed on into the enemy's support trench, where they were heavily bombarded, and showed great coolness and courage. When forced back, he went into the open and rescued wounded men.

D.C.M.

No. SD/3741 Corporal R. Bush, 13th Bn.

For conspicuous gallantry during operations. When his commanding officer became a casualty he took command and, under heavy machine-gun fire and shell fire, led his men into the enemy's second line trench. He acted with great coolness and judgement.

No. SD/658 Sergeant Guy Compton M.M., 11th Bn.

For conspicuous gallantry during operations. Sergeants Compton and Green pushed forward through uncut wire and heavy machine-gun fire into the enemy's trench, organised a bombing party, and cleared 100 yards of trench, accounting for many of the enemy. Then they consolidated the position won. They set a fine example.

No. SD/874 Sergeant Edward James Green, 11th Bn.

For conspicuous gallantry during operations. Sergeants Compton and Green pushed forward through uncut wire and heavy machine-gun fire into the enemy's trench, organised a bombing party, and cleared 100 yards of trench, accounting for many of the enemy. Then they consolidated the position won. They set a fine example.

No. SD/2909 Corporal Charles Fowler, 13th Bn.

For conspicuous gallantry during operations. When he became detached from his platoon he joined a party of bombers and fought his way into the enemy's second line trench. He then organised a party to resist a counter-attack and showed great personal bravery.

No. SD/421 Sergeant Frank William Hollobone, 11th Bn.

For conspicuous gallantry during operations. He penetrated the enemy's second line, rallied men of various companies and bombed the enemy as long as ammunition lasted. He then withdrew to the enemy's first line and used an enemy rifle, his own being knocked out of his hand. He was under heavy shell fire the whole time.

No. 10094 Acting Corporal R.H.S. Sloan, 2nd Bn.

For conspicuous gallantry when assisting to hold a captured enemy post against several heavy counter-attacks. He shows great coolness, and set a fine example to those around him.

No. 8396 Temporary Sergeant H. Weal, 2nd Bn.

For conspicuous gallantry. When his officer and senior sergeant had become casualties he took command of an enemy post which the party had captured, and displayed the greatest pluck and determination in repelling heavy counter-attacks.

No. SD/2003 Company-Sergeant-Major Percy White, 12th Bn.

For conspicuous gallantry during operations. When all his officers had become casualties he took command of his company and all the men near him, consolidated his position, and, though wounded, held on under heavy fire with his few remaining men as long as ammunition lasted.

No. SD/2826 Sergeant Sidney Harry Woodward, 13th Bn.

For conspicuous gallantry during operations. He led some linesmen across the open to the enemy's front line, where they accounted for four of the enemy. He established telephone communications, and did fine work till he was severely wounded.

Tuesday August 22nd 1916

Military Cross Winners

Honour For West Sussex Officer
Temporary Second-Lieutenant Goodman Ambler, Royal Sussex Regiment, who, as announced yesterday, has been awarded the Military Cross, belongs to a family widely known and much respected in West Sussex. He is the elder son of the late Mr. Walter Ambler, who for over 20 years was a schoolmaster at Ashington. His mother is now, and has been for the past four years, residing in the pretty village of Fittleworth, and it was at her residence, Norwood Cottages, that a representative of the *Sussex Daily News* called on her yesterday. She is naturally extremely proud of the honour her son has gained. The incident, as described in yesterday's issue, took place in the first stage of the offensive, and is a little amplified by the copy of what is probably an extract from the Regimental records which Mrs. Ambler has received. This states : "Second- Lieutenant Goodman Ambler was second in command of his Company. When the Company Commander had been wounded, Lieutenant Ambler led his Company into the German lines, which he then proceeded to consolidate in spite of very heavy machine-gun and shell fire.
When wounded he remained in command of his Company, and it was not until he had withdrawn the remnants of his Company to our lines that he went to the dressing station and had his wounds attended to."

Only slightly wounded.

Happily Second-Lieutenant Ambler was only slightly wounded in the face and back, and after treatment at one of the base hospitals he soon rejoined his regiment and is still in the firing line. Mrs. Ambler said her son had plenty of nerve. When the war broke out he was in the Malay States, where he held an appointment as a master in a secondary school for six years. Coming home on leave, he applied for a commission, and was gazetted in February last year to one of the service battalions of the County Regiment. Second-Lieutenant Ambler is aged 31 and is married, his wife formerly being Miss Peacock, of Rushington, where she is at present staying. He has a brother who served in the Dardanelles with the Naval Engineers and is now attached to the Naval Air Service. The hearty congratulations of numerous Sussex friends will go out to Second-Lieutenant Ambler on the distinction he has won.

Twenty Military Medals for men of the County Regiment

The following non-commissioned officers and men of the Royal Sussex Regiment have been awarded the Military Medal for bravery in the field :-

No. SD/2213 Sergt. Godfrey Alston   12th Bn.
No. SD/2219 Sergt. William George Aukett   12th Bn.

        No. SD/2854 Pte. Albert Bailey   13th Bn.

No. SD/1830 Pte. Samuel Charles Baker   12th Bn.

No. SD/3521 L/Cpl. Charles Edward Ball   13th Bn.

        No. SD/1157 Pte. Ernest James Brown   11th Bn.

No. SD/2641 L/Cpl. George T. Chambers   13th Bn.
No. SD/5095 Pte. Frederick A. Cooper   13th Bn.
No. SD/2896 Pte. Cecil Davis   13th Bn.
No. SD/1523 L/Cpl. Alfred Drury   12th Bn.
No. SD3340 Pte. Pte. Richard Emsley   13th Bn.
No. SD/1691 L/Cpl. William David Grenyer   12th Bn.
No. SD/2698 L/Sergt. Walter Philip Gordon Harrold   13th Bn.
No. SD/2947 L/Cpl. Richard Knight   13th Bn.
No. SD/1535 L/Cpl. Charles F. Lassetter   12th Bn.
No. SD/1409 Pte. Gilbert Mills   12th Bn.
No. SD/878 Cpl. Sidney Noakes   11th Bn.
No. SD/1456 Pte. George Sharp   12th Bn.

 No. SD/1559 L/Cpl. Horace Wells   12th Bn. (Peasmarsh)

No. SD/2819 Pte. Leonard West   13th Bn.

A well-known Brightonian

No. SD/1535, Lance-Corporal C.F. Lassetter is a Brightonian, son of Mr. and Mrs. Lassetter, of 30, Kingsley Road, Preston Park. This winner of the Military Medal will be well remembered as a prominent local racing cyclist. In a letter to his mother on the 29th July he said :- "You will be surprised to hear that I have been awarded the Military Medal for the part I took in our attack. really I did not do any more than anyone else, and was only too thankful to get back unhurt. We had to go to a town some distance from here, part marching and part by motor-bus.
We were there paraded in front of the bandstand, and had a guard of honour right around us. There were three out of our Company. There was a lot of Generals and Staff Officers present, and General Monro pinned the ribbons on and shook hands with each of us. We get the medals later. Then there was a speech and a march past. We were jolly tired when we got back, and then went straight into the trenches."

Worthing Winners

Of the above Military Medal winners, four belong to Worthing. Private G. Mills, whose mother resides with other relatives at Canterbury House, West Tarring, enlisted in the Royal Sussex in November, 1914, having previously been employed in a greengrocery business, he went out in February of this year.
A few weeks ago his mother was delighted to receive a letter from him stating that he had been recommended for the Military Medal for some notable bombing work; and this was followed by another letter in which he described a brilliant ceremony at a town behind the firing line, at which General Monro pinned decorations on a number of officers and men, including himself. Mrs. Mills has since heard from an official quarter that the medal was awarded her son for conspicuous bravery with a bombing squad.

Lance-Sergeant W.P.G. Harrold is one of two soldier sons of Mr. and Mrs. Harrold, of Fallowfield, Heene Road, Worthing. The record of the deed which won him his medal is not available officially, but it is understood he rallied his men and bravely led an attack after a shell had half-buried them in a trench.

Lance-Corporal W.D. Grenyer has relatives in Lyndhurst Terrace, Worthing. He was associated with another Worthing man, Private S.C. Baker (who also secures the Medal) in carrying in and attending to wounded under heavy fire. Lance-Corporal Grenyer was in charge of the Company stretcher-bearers, and they worked hard all day in collecting the wounded and carrying them down to the aid post, refusing even to stop for food. Letters since sent home show that these two men set a splendid example of Sussex courage, and greatly inspired their comrades.

Special Brigade Order

BY BRIG. GEN. M.L. HORNBY, D.S.O., COMMANDING 116TH INFANTRY BRIGADE

18-7-16

AWARDS FOR GALLANT CONDUCT

(i)

The Brigadier General Commanding has much pleasure in announcing to all ranks of the Brigade, the following Awards for gallant conduct, on the morning of the 30th June, during the attack on the "BOAR'S HEAD", in front of RICHENBOURG L'AVOUE.

THE MILITARY MEDAL

No.			
1409	Private	G. Mills	12th Bn. Royal Sussex Regiment.
1691	L/Cpl.	W.D. Grenyer	-do-
1535	"	C.F. Lassetter	-do-
1559	"	H. Wells	-do-
2213	Sergt.	G. Alston	-do-
1523	L/Cpl.	A. Drury	-do-
2219	Sergt.	W.G. Aukett	-do-
1456	Private	G. Sharp	-do-
1830	"	S.C. Baker	-do-
2896	"	C. Davis	13th Bn. Royal Sussex Regiment
3340	"	R. Emsley	-do-
2641	L/Cpl.	G. Chambers	-do-
2598	L/Sergt.	W.P.G. Harrold	-do-
2854	Private	A. Bailey	-do-
2819	"	L. West	-do-
5095	"	F.A. Cooper	-do-
3521	L/Cpl.	C.E. Ball	-do-
2947	"	R. Knight	-do-
14081	Sergt.	A.J. Gibbon	14th Bn. Hampshire Regiment,
28049	L/Cpl.	A. McLean	116th Bde. Machine Gun Coy.
878	Cpl.	S. Noakes	11th Bn. Royal Sussex Regiment,
1157	Private	E.J. Brown	attached 116th T.M.Battery,

(ii)
The following are descriptions of the actions for which the above awards have been made :-

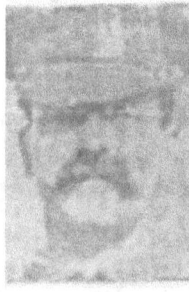

L/Cpl. Charles Edward Ball, 13th Bn. Royal Sussex Regiment,
(Brighton)

The attack became rather disorganised in the darkness and smoke. Lance-Corporal Ball got together a party of men, pushed on with them, gained a footing in the German trench, and held his ground until nearly every man was a casualty.
Ball has since been promoted to the rank of Sergeant.

Private Guy Mills,   12th Bn. Royal Sussex Regiment,

Although having no previous bombing experience, attached himself to a bombing squad and acted as bayonet man. He displayed conspicuous bravery and was personally responsible for putting an enemy Machine Gun out of action by blowing it up with a bomb, after having shot all the men in charge of the gun.

L/Corporal William D. Grenyer & Private Samuel C. Baker, 12th Bn. Royal Sussex Regiment,

L/Corporal Grenyer was in charge of the Company Stretcher Bearers among who was Pte. Baker. During the whole period of the engagement these two men attended the wounded and carried them down to the Aid Post, having on each occasion to pass through a heavy barrage which the enemy put on Copse & Hazara St. They continued working hard, collecting the wounded from No Man's land and the trenches, until 6 p.m. refusing to stop for any food. The courage and devotion to duty of these men was an inspiring example to their comrades.

L/Corporal Cecil F. Lasseter,   12th Bn. Royal Sussex Regiment,

L/Cpl. Lassetter penetrated through to the enemy's second line, where he immediately collected his men together and started the work of consolidation, after the first supply of sandbags was exhausted he came right back himself to our own lines, and carried over a fresh supply of sandbags. All this work was performed under heavy shell fire.

L/Corporal Horace Wells,   12th Bn. Royal Sussex Regiment,

This N.C.O. (a stretcher bearer) worked unceasingly for several hours, doing most excellent work among the wounded in the front Line and No Man's Land. The heavy artillery fire made it difficult to do this work, but L/Cpl. Wells would not give up although severely shaken. His bravery was an inspiring example to his comrades.

Sergeant Godfrey Alston,   12th Bn. Royal Sussex Regiment,

This N.C.O. took charge of his Company when all the Officers had either been killed or wounded. he made gigantic efforts to re-organise the remnants of the Company in front of the German wire, and was successful in carrying on the attack from a shell hole nearby. He also assisted in bringing in a number of wounded. his courage and coolness was conspicuously noticeable.

L/Corporal Alfred Drury,   12th Bn. Royal Sussex Regiment,

This N.C.O. was in charge of a carrying party. After nearly every man of his party had been killed or wounded, he went across by himself three times to the enemy's lines, carrying supplies of bombs and was preparing the position for attack. L/Cpl. Drury then helped the Company stretcher Bearers to improvise stretchers as the proper stretches were all in use. all the above was carried out under heavy shell and M.G. fire.

Sergeant William George Aukett,   12th Bn. Royal Sussex Regiment,

This N.C.O. was among the first in the assault on the enemy's line. When in their Front Line he rallied his platoon together and led them on to the second line, doing excellent work. Then, wounded, he continued to direct his men, several times crawling towards the enemy by himself to find out his position.

Private George Sharp,   12th Bn. Royal Sussex Regiment,

Private Sharp carried out most excellent work between the German front and Support Line, accounting for several of the enemy. Then, although badly wounded, he continued firing and accounted for at least 5 more of the enemy before being brought in to the Dressing Station. He showed most conspicuous bravery the whole time and was continually under heavy fire.

Private Cecil Davis,   13th Bn. Royal Sussex Regiment,

Private Davies was one of a bombing squad which had reached the enemy Second Line. The N.C.O. in command was killed and Private Davies took command, re-organised the squad, and for some considerable time held the enemy in check who were working down a communication trench. When the supply of bombs was exhausted, Private Davies used his rifle with great effect until ordered to withdraw.

Private Richard Emsley,   13th Bn. Royal Sussex Regiment,

Our trenches were subjected to a very intense and concentrated Artillery fire which caused many casualties. Regardless of danger, Pte. Emsley instead of taking cover worked up and down the trench attending to the wounded, thus showing a splendid example of courage and devotion to duty, as a stretcher bearer.

L/Sergeant Walter Philip Gordon Harrold,   13th Bn. Royal Sussex Regiment,

Whilst our troops were leaving our parapet, Sergeant Harrold was buried by the parapet being blown down by a shell in the spot where he was standing. He was extricated, and although shaken he rallied the nearest men, took them over the parapet, and led them into the German trench.

Saturday August 26th 1916

The King has graciously been pleased to bestow the Most Eminent Order of the Indian Empire Upon the following officer :-

C.I.E.

Captain Gerrard Evelyn Leachman, 1st Bn. Royal Sussex Regiment, Asst. Political Officer, Basra.

Royal Sussex Officer wins Military Cross

The King has conferred the Military Cross upon the undermentioned officer in recognition of his devotion to duty in the field :-

Second Lieutenant Karl Webber Gammon,   11th Bn. Royal Sussex Regiment,

For most conspicuous gallantry and leading when in command of a raiding party. Previous bold reconnaissance and good organisation enabled his party to get quickly to their points. Though wounded, Second-Lieutenant Gammon continued to control and direct operations fearlessly and gallantly, and he finally withdrew his party in good order.

Bognor Military Medal Winner

Private A. Bailey, whose name appeared in the *Sussex Daily News* as a winner of the Military Medal for bravery in the field, is the son of Mr. E. Bailey, of Homestead, North Bersted, Bognor. Private Bailey who is not 19 years of age, enlisted in the Royal Sussex about 20 months ago and has been at the front about six months. Prior to this, he was employed by the late Mr. John Harrison, of Aldwick, and is a well-known and popular lad. he has since been promoted to Corporal.

The following has been received by Mr. E. Bailey :-

Private Bailey formed one of the bombing squad and assisted the Corporal in charge to build a barricade in the enemy trench to block it. This was done under grenade and rifle fire and an attack by hostile bombers was repulsed. The supply of bombs ran short and Private Bailey made three journeys into "No Man's Land" to collect bombs from the fallen, these journeys being made under heavy shell fire. He returned each time with bombs and threw at least 50 with good effect.

Tuesday August 29th 1916

Brighton Military Medallist

Sergeant C.E. Ball, of the Royal Sussex Regiment, who has been awarded the Military Medal, is a Brighton man, his wife and children residing at 15, Elm grove. Immediately on the outbreak of war, Ball, then a bill inspector engaged at the Grand Theatre, Brighton, joined the Royal Sussex. The gallant act for which he was decorated, is officially described as follows :-

The attack became rather disorganised in the darkness and smoke. Lance-Corporal Ball got together a party of men, pushed on with them, gained a footing in the German trench, and held his ground until nearly every man was a casualty.
Ball has since been promoted to the rank of Sergeant.

Saturday September 2nd 1916

His Majesty the KING has been graciously pleased to award the Military Medal for bravery in the field to the undermentioned Non-commissioned Officers and Men: —

No. 999 Private Cecil E. Brown   7th Bn.

No. 184 Corporal William Butcher 7th Bn.

No. 823 Private Harry E. Cosham 7th Bn.
No. 322 Private Joseph Wilson 7th Bn.

The parents of Private Cosham live at Glass Castle Ridgeworth, Uckfield. In a letter to them Private Cosham merely mentioned that he had won the Military Medal for services performed on the 9th of July. The parents have known for some time that their son had been engaged in the dangerous mission of carrying messages from his officer. Private Cosham and his brother joined the Army at the outbreak of hostilities, and have been at the front for some time. The family is most patriotic. When the sons relinquished work in their father's market garden to go and fight for King and country, their mother and sister stepped into the breach and are carrying on the work "till the boys come home."

Corporal Noakes : Brighton

No. SD/878 Corporal S. Noakes, Royal Sussex Regiment, whose name appeared in last week's list of recipients of the Military Medal for bravery in the field, is a Brighton man, 35 years of age, his wife and two children, a boy and a girl, residing in Southover Street. By profession he is a compositor, and he served his apprenticeship at Brighton. He has for many years been associated with All Souls' Church, Brighton, and as a boy belonged to the Church Lads' Brigade, while more recently he has been lay sacristan. At the outbreak of the South African War, while still in his teens, the fighting spirit came over uppermost, and he endeavoured to enlist. For a long time, however, he was not accepted, but finally he got into the ranks, and after training left England for South Africa. He has the Queen's Medal with, two bars, for Orange Free State and Cape Colony. Returning to his trade after completion of hostilities he subsequently got married, and lived for some time at Haywards Heath, later coming to Brighton again. Corporal Noakes was employed for some two years with Mr. Gillett in Market Street. Soon after the outbreak of the present war he joined the Royal Sussex Regiment two years ago yesterday-and he went to France in March of this year. Since then he has seen much active service.

Corporal William Butcher is the second son of Mr. And Mrs. Ernest Butcher, of 7 Imberborne Lane, East Grinstead, and his parents are naturally proud that their boy should have so unflinchingly done his duty as to win this honour. They have three sons and all of them are serving their country, two in the Royal Sussex Regiment and one in the Royal Naval Air Service. Immediately on the outbreak of war their son William decided to join the Colours. He was then in the employ of Messrs. Martin, Smith & Foster, builders, and was one of the very first of the many East Grinstead lads to leave civil life and done khaki in response to the country's call. He was wounded two months ago, the most serious injury being to his right eye, caused by gun-shot wounds.

Wednesday September 6th 1916

Military Medal for Worthing man

Mr. G.C. Glenister, of 64, Ashdown Road, Worthing, has received with much satisfaction, a letter from his son, Lance-Corporal Horace Glenister, Royal Sussex Regiment, stating that he has been decorated with the Military Medal. The recipient states, "I was presented with the ribbon this morning by our Colonel, and I am wearing it." He said the Divisional General Hoped to be able to present the medal very soon. "I was recommended for the honour for some work on the 4th of August. You remember I wrote and told you I had had two narrow escapes. This morning our Company was paraded, and I was presented with a certificate from the Brigade. The Colonel shook hands with us and congratulated us, which I think was very good of him." Lance-Corporal Glenister, who is 22, joined the Army a month after the outbreak of war with three of his mates, who with him were employed by the Worthing Motor Bus Company. two of these have been killed, and one is missing. Glenister has been twice wounded, and only a week or two ago he wrote home stating that he had a narrow escape, a bullet passing through his steel helmet, while another had torn away a button and a flap on his breast pocket.

It was in this occasion that he performed the service which won for him his distinction. The Brigade certificate alluded to in the letter, which has been received by his father, records that the recipient distinguished himself on 4th August, at Pozieres, during a counter-attack by the enemy.

Saturday September 9th 1916

Death of Sergeant Hughes D.C.M.

Very many friends in Brighton will regret to read the news of the death of Sergeant Hughes, D.C.M., Royal Sussex Regiment, son of Mr. And Mrs. Hughes, of 10, Upper Street, Brighton. A letter from the officer of his platoon announces that he was killed in action on the 18th of August, and adds :-
"Your son was one of the best sergeants in the battalion, and always set a fine example by his coolness and bravery in the hour of need, and by his devotion to duty. The battalion feels his loss greatly, and in his death the Royal Sussex Regiment and the country have lost a gallant soldier, of whom we were all proud."
Sergeant Hughes (then Corporal) was one of the heroes in the terrible ordeal experienced by his battalion in February last, when the Germans exploded a mine and the Sussex men rushed the crater, and held it against all attacks till reinforcements came. This was the occasion on which Lieut. Eric McNair had the V.C. conferred on him, while three men secured the Distinguished Conduct Medal for conspicuous gallantry :- Corporal Hughes, Private Jupp, and Lance-Corporal Moore.

Of Sergeant Hughes the official record said :-

"After a severe bombardment by the enemy, in which his trench was blown in, he took eight men up to the newly made crater, occupied it, and effectually checked the advancing enemy by fire."
It was also announced that he saved the life of one of his officers. Sergeant Hughes was a young fellow of fine physique, nearly 6ft. in height. He was a scholar at Middle Street School, Brighton, and a familiar figure as a lad as a drummer in the Royal Field Artillery cadets.
He was the second of the Cadets to get the D.C.M. (the other being Bombardier Read), and the country has to mourn the loss of both these brave young fellows. Mr. and Mrs. Hughes have two other sons serving King and Country.

Monday September 11th 1916

V.C. for Hailsham Hero

In the list of heroes to whom the King has awarded the Victoria Cross is Company Sergeant-Major Nelson Victor Carter, late Royal Sussex Regiment. He gave his life for his country, and fought with a gallantry which thoroughly entitled him to the distinction which will now attach to his name. The official record of his "conspicuous bravery," as set forth in the *"London Gazette,"* is as follows :-

During an attack he was in command of the fourth wave of the assault. Under intense shell and machine-gun fire he penetrated, with a few men, into the enemy's second line and inflicted heavy casualties with bombs. When forced to retire to the enemy's first line, he captured a machine-gun and shot the gunner with his revolver. Finally, after carrying several wounded men into safety, he himself was mortally wounded and died in a few minutes. His conduct throughout the day was magnificent.

Nelson Victor Carter was born at Eastbourne on 5th April, 1883. His family moved to Hailsham when he was six years old, and have lived at Harebeating, Hailsham, ever since. He joined the Royal Field Artillery about 12 years ago, but was invalided out after several years' service at Singapore. He joined the Army at the outbreak of war and was soon promoted to be a sergeant in the Royal Sussex Regiment. He finally became Company Sergeant-Major and for a time acted as Regimental Sergeant-Major. Last February he went to France with his battalion. Sergeant-Major Carter was married and leaves a wife and one child residing at Eastbourne. He was a very clever boxer and held the championship of his battalion as a heavy-weight. Mr. and Mrs. Carter have the following other sons serving with the colours :-

Martin Luther Carter (West Kent Regiment)
Gordon Carter (A.S.C.), at the front.
Bombardier Ernest Alfred Carter (R.F.A.), who has been to the front for 14 months and has been gassed.
Jesse Carter (R.F.A.) 1st class gun-layer, has been to the front and is now in England owing to sickness.
Two other sons have been in the Army, namely Edwin Richard (R.G.A.) and Joseph Thomas (R.F.A.) Both of these have been rejected as medically unfit.

A Worthing D.C.M.

The Mayor of Worthing (Alderman J. White) has received from the War Office a Distinguished Conduct Medal which was awarded some months ago to a Worthing man, Lance-Corporal Short, of the Royal Sussex Regiment, whose home is in Park Road, with a request that he will officially present it. The mayor hopes to be able to arrange for a public ceremony, if the recipient will agree to it. Lance-Corporal Short gained the medal for 27 hours' continuous bombing, refusing offers of relief. He was severely wounded, and has undergone a serious operation, not having long ago been discharged from hospital. He was one of the first local men to enlist at Worthing at the outbreak of the war, and he proceeded straight to the depot to join the Royal Sussex Regiment.

A V.C. Hero and Eastbourne

The announcement in yesterday's issue of the honour paid to the late Company Sergeant-Major Nelson Victor Carter, Royal Sussex Regiment, has been received in a spirit of deep satisfaction by his many friends in Eastbourne. He was the first man born in Eastbourne top receive the V.C., and the greatest regret is felt that he succumbed to wounds before knowing that his consistent bravery had been officially recognised. though Sergeant-Major Carter's parents reside in the parish of Hailsham, Eastbourne must claim the hero by reason of the facts that he was born in the town, lived in Eastbourne during infancy, and spent most of his manhood at the seaside resort. His widow and child reside in Grey's Road, Old Town, Eastbourne, and prior to the outbreak of war Sergeant-Major Carter was employed as an attendant at the Old Town cinema. By a strange coincidence, the officer in command of his Company, Lieutenant (Temporary Captain) Harold C. Robinson, resides but a stone's throw from Mrs. Carter -in The Grey's.

A Lieutenant's tribute

Upon learning of the gallant soldier's death, Lieutenant Robinson, who has twice been wounded in the war, wrote to Mrs. Carter on 16th July last :-

"I should like to say how much I admired him and how I appreciated the work he did during the time I commanded his Company. When the time came for them to do their job the men rose to the occasion very finely, and I consider that it was in no small degree to the fine example always set by C.S.M. Carter. Always cheerful and working with increasing energy through the long months of training, and the trials in the trenches, he endeared himself to all, and the men would, I know, have gone anywhere with him. I personally feel that I have lost a very great friend and one of the finest men I ever knew. It was a great pleasure to me to be able to put forward his name with a recommendation for the Military Cross about a fortnight before he died, and I have no hesitation in saying that I should most certainly have recommended him for further decoration for gallantry this time had he come through. With deepest sympathy and kind regards."

Gave his life for others

It was on the morning of the beginning of the great offensive, 30th June, that C.S.M. Carter met his death. Lieutenant Robinson, who was wounded on the same day, recently stated that the deceased soldier acted with the greatest bravery in rescuing the wounded. "Men were lying wounded over the parapet," he said, "and C.S.M. Carter went over many times under heavy fire to carry them into safety. He succeeded in rescuing a number of them, but was finally mortally wounded himself while engaged in this heroic work." That the popularity of the dead V.C. hero was universal among all ranks was illustrated by the following letter written to Mrs. Carter from Drummer A. Hayward, Royal Sussex regiment, who was wounded about the same time as the Sergeant-Major met his death :- "Dear Madam,- Would you please accept my deepest sympathies for the loss of your husband.
I have always had a great respect for him. When training at Bexhill he was the favourite with the men, and they will feel his loss very much, as we all do who knew him." The many friends of the late Sergeant-Major and Mrs. Carter will hope the glory won on the field of battle by the gallant soldier will help soften the sadness of her bereavement.

Hurst Soldier's Gallantry

Sergeant Albert Nelson Peacock, of the Royal Sussex Regiment, has forwarded to his parents at Hurst Wickham, Hurst, a large card, printed in gold, and emblazoned with the badges of the four regiments composing his Brigade. It reads as follows :-

"Hohenzollern."

Presented to Lance-Sergeant A. Peacock, Royal Sussex for the great gallantry he displayed at the capture and defence of the Hohenzollern Redoubt, 2nd of March to 5th of March, 1916 by the - Brigade."

The card is signed by the Brigadier-General and is accompanied by a smaller card signed by the Divisional Commander. this states that "the Commanding Officer and Brigade Commander have informed me that you have distinguished yourself by your conduct in the field. I have read their reports with much pleasure, and have brought them to higher authorities." Lance-Sergeant A.N. Peacock, is now Sergeant he is 26 years of age, was educated at Hurst Schools, and before the war was in the employment of Mr. Greer, at Erskine Nurseries, Hurst. He is the second son of Mr. and Mrs. William Peacock, of Highfield Cottages, Hurst Wickham, who are naturally proud of these testimonies to their son's gallantry.

He was wounded in the fighting, a shrapnel wound in the hand-and was invalided to England, visiting his home after a stay at a hospital at Plymouth. He recovered and returned to the Front about Whitsuntide and was pleased to get back to his old company. Mr. and Mrs. Peacock's eldest son is serving in the Navy.

A Worthing D.C.M.

Public ceremony arranged.

The Mayor of Worthing (Alderman J. White) has arranged to present publicly at the Theatre Royal, on Monday evening next, a Distinguished Conduct Medal awarded to Lance-Corporal Short for some notable bombing work. This will be the first presentation of the kind locally since the outbreak of the war, and it should therefore prove very interesting. The D.C.M. has been won by several other Worthing soldiers, but they are still on active service, and the opportunity has not occurred to make a public presentation in their own town. Lance-Corporal Short was recently discharged from hospital, having been severely wounded. As announced previously in the Sussex Daily News, the medal as sent to the Mayor by the war Office with a request that he would arrange to hand it to the recipient.

Corporal Jupp Killed : Hassocks.

Mr. and Mrs. G.W. Jupp, of Friar's Oak, Hassocks, have received the sad intelligence that their son, Corporal M.G.C. Jupp, D.C.M. of the Machine-gun Section, Royal Sussex Regiment, has been killed in action. The news is unofficial, but the intimation comes from a chum, a sergeant, who stated that Corporal Jupp was killed on 31st August, instantaneously, while with his machine-gun, in the hottest part of the fighting on that day. Mr. and Mrs. Jupp will receive much sympathy.
 Their son, who was 22 years of age, was much respected. His gallantry in winning the D.C.M. is recent history, the honour bringing him much congratulation, including a resolution of commendation from the Clayton Parish Council. He was a well-known Mid-Sussex footballer, and at one time was on the staff of Messrs. T. Bannister and Co., of Haywards Heath. He was a brother of V.W. Jupp, the Sussex cricketer, now a dispatch rider in the R.E. Signalling Service.

Thursday September 14th 1916

Military Medal

The Military Medal has been awarded for bravery in the field to :-

No. G/22 Sgt. Ernest R. Banks, 7th Bn. Royal Sussex Regiment,
No. S/2033 Pte. James Bird, 7th Bn. Royal Sussex Regiment,
No. 601 L/Cpl. Ernest Dudman, 7th Bn. Royal Sussex Regiment,
No. G/764 Sgt. Arthur James Evans, 7th Bn. Royal Sussex Regiment,
No. 232 Pte. Sidney F. Gratwick, 7th Bn. Royal Sussex Regiment,
No. G/350 L/Cpl. William Hendry, 7th Bn. Royal Sussex Regiment,
No. 4758 Pte. Harry J. Lawrence, 7th Bn. Royal Sussex Regiment,
No. 524 L/Sgt. Albert Nelson Peacock, 7th Bn. Royal Sussex Regiment,
No. 290 Cpl. Frederick John Llewellyn Picton, 7th Bn. Royal Sussex Regiment,
No. 318 Cpl. Albert Turton, 7th Bn. Royal Sussex Regiment,
No. 322 Pte. Joseph Wilson, 7th Bn. Royal Sussex Regiment,

Saturday September 16th 1916

Yet another Hailsham soldier has distinguished himself by gallant conduct in the field, namely, Private W.T. Pattenden, Royal Sussex Regiment (Lewis Gun section), the only son of Mr. and Mrs. T. Pattenden, of Westfield, Hailsham. Private Pattenden went to the front in February, 1915, and is at

present in hospital in France. In a letter to the lad's parents his officer writes :- "Your son was slightly wounded in the arm, I think by a bullet. He will be quite all right as he was comfortable, even before going down to the dressing station.
He is a credit to the Lewis Gun Section of the battalion, for he continued to serve his gun against a German counter-attack, even after he was hit. I hope to have him back soon. I enclose a copy of the Battalion Orders, which I know you will like to have.

The copy reads as follows :-

"The Commanding Officer wishes to bring to the notice of all ranks, and express his appreciation of the conduct of the undermentioned man. Private W.T. Pattenden, who on the 22nd August, when the Gloucesters had to repel a counter-attack, got his gun into action at the top of the trench where he was covering a working party, and continued to serve it successfully after he was wounded, remaining at his post until relieved and ordered to retire."
Commenting on the incident himself Private Pattenden remarks : "I got a bit of a German bomb in my arm, but, fortunately, not enough to get me sent to 'Blighty.' Theirs are rotten bombs; if it had been one of ours I don't suppose I should have been here now. There is one satisfaction, I had the pleasure of putting a few of them out of action before they temporarily put me out. I am down at the seaside now. It was quite a treat to see the sea again after being so long away from it." In a letter from C.Q.M.S. H. Roberts, who has won the D.C.M., to Mr. Pattenden, the former states how proud the whole company is of Private Pattenden's gallant action.

Worthing D.C.M. Winner

Worthing honoured one of its gallant soldier lads yesterday evening, when Lance-Corporal H. Short, of the Royal Sussex Regiment, was officially presented by the Mayor (Alderman J. White) with the Distinguished Conduct Medal. Appropriately enough, the ceremony - at which the Corporation members were present - took place during the exhibition of the great war film, "The Battle of the Somme," at the Theatre Royal. The Mayor had been specially commissioned by the War Office to hand to Lance-Corporal Short this recognition of his valour and cool courage in the face of danger. Several other Worthing men have won the D.C.M., and quite a number the Military Medal, but the opportunity has not occurred to arrange for a ceremony in their own town, and the presentation to Lance-Corporal Short was the first of the kind made locally since the outbreak of the war, while Alderman J. White had the distinction of being one of the first of the Sussex mayors to be commissioned to decorate a fellow townsman. Lance-Corporal Short has not long been discharged from hospital. he was severely wounded during the action in which he distinguished himself, and has had a piece of bone extracted from one arm.

Thursday September 21st 1916

Military Medals for Sussex Men

Several of the Royal Sussex Regiment have recently received the Military Medal, including Lance-Corporal W.J. Bailey, who joined up soon after the outbreak of the war, and has been for a long time on the western front battle. He has been awarded the medal "For gallantry and devotion to duty between 13th and 14th July, 1916, as company runner at Bernafay Wood ." his father is still living in Hailsham and was for many years in business at the market town.

Lewes Man awarded Medal

Mrs. Short, of South Street, Lewes, has received the news in a letter from her son, Private William Short, of the Royal Sussex Regiment, that he has been awarded the Military Medal for bravery on the field, together with a parchment testimonial which was enclosed in his letter and reads as follows : "G./2605 Private W. Short, 8th Sussex Pioneers : I have read with great pleasure the report of your

Regimental Commander regarding your gallant conduct and devotion to duty on the field on 1st July, during the battle of the Somme." This is signed by the Commander of the Division.

Another of Mrs. Short's sons was killed in action some weeks ago, while a third son has been discharged from the Army through ill-health. Private W. Short has been serving for two years.

Medal for Bexhill Man

News has been received at the home of Private Winborn, Royal Sussex Regiment, that he has been awarded the Military Medal. He is the son of Mr. and Mrs. Winborn, Holliers Hill. In a letter to his mother he said it had been given to him after an engagement at the Somme.

Friday September 22nd 1916

More Military Medals for Sussex Men

The following are included in the list, issued last night, of recipients of the Military Medal for bravery in the field. All belong to the Royal Sussex Regiment except where otherwise stated :-

No. 6625 Private H. Aungier	7th Bn.
No. 2313 Private Ernest Bowers	5th Bn.
No. 1264 Private H. Glennister	7th Bn.
No. 2238 Private John H. Goddard	7th Bn.
No. 71 Sgt. (Acting C.Q.M.S.) J. Hayes	7th Bn.
No. 1312 Acting-Sergeant Arthur W. Horne	7th Bn.
No. 6092 Private Thomas Richard Burgess Kilner	Royal Warwicks (transferred from Royal Sussex)
No. 7 Acting-Sergeant Ralph Lawrence	7th Bn.
No. 333 Private (Lance-Corporal) Charles P. Mayes	7th Bn.
No. 7634 Private Harold W. J. Newport	7th Bn.
No. 124 Private Frank V. Nicholls	7th Bn.

No. 1046 Lance-Corporal Kenneth Pattenden   5th Bn.

No. 4867 C.Q.M.S. (A/C.S.M.) Alfred A. Richold 7th Bn.

No. 4199 Sergeant Leonard Rovery   7th Bn.
No. 111 Acting-Sergeant Albert Edward Selby   7th Bn.

No. G/5936 Private Joseph R. Selsby   7th Bn.
No. 725 Private Percy A.C. White   7th Bn.

No. 1677 Private Arthur R. Wilson   5th Bn.

Saturday September 23rd 1916

Decorations for Soldiers of the County Regiment
The honours list issued last night includes the following :-

M.C.

T/Second Lt. Herbert Seton Broughall   7th Bn. Royal Sussex Regiment,

For conspicuous gallantry in action. he led an assaulting party with great dash into the enemy's third trench line and did fine work there, clearing out their bombers and snipers. It was his first time under fire.

D.C.M.

No. 1849 Pte. (Actg. Cpl.) G.E. Bevan,   2nd Bn. Royal Sussex Regiment,

For conspicuous gallantry and devotion to duty. He took part in an attack, and, after being wounded in the hand, performed most devoted service in continually bringing up bombs over difficult ground exposed to very heavy fire. During one of these journeys he was able to remove a wounded officer to safety.

No. 541 Actg.-Cpl. R. Prevett,   7th Bn. Royal Sussex Regiment,

For conspicuous gallantry after an assault in organising, under very heavy shell and machine-gun fire, all requisite bombing posts. He went from post to post for 30 hours without cessation, and it was chiefly owing to his courage and activity that the hostile bombers were kept under. It is understood that Corporal Prevett is an Ardingly man.

Ardingly Man's D.C.M.

Sergeant R. Prevett, Royal Sussex Regiment, who has been awarded the Distinguished Conduct Medal for conspicuous gallantry, is an Ardingly man, his parents residing at Horncombe, on the West Hoathly Road. Sergeant Prevett is about 24 years of age, unmarried, and was one of the first Ardingly men to enlist, after the war had started.

He was well-known as a cricketer and footballer, a good all-round sportsman, one of those quiet, determined men who require a lot of beating. he has been the first soldier to bring honours to the village of Ardingly in the present war, and his achievement has caused the greatest satisfaction there. He has two brothers in the Army.

Military Medal won by Easebourne Corporal

The Military Medal has been awarded to an Easebourne soldier, Corporal Ernest Stringer, of a Service Battalion of the Royal Sussex Regiment, whose parents have been residents of Easebourne for many years. The first intimation Mr. and Mrs. Stringer received of their son's distinction was a brief and characteristically modest letter from him, dated 14th September. He wrote : "You will be pleased to hear that I have been awarded the Military Medal, also the enclosed address signed by the General of the Division. Trust this will find you all well, as it leaves me at present. Letter following in a day or so." The "address" referred to by Corporal Stringer is as follows :- "I have read with great pleasure the report of your Regimental Commander and Brigade Commander regarding your gallant conduct and devotion to duty in the field on 1st July, 1916, during the battle of the Somme." The signature is that of Major-General F.I. Maxse, Commanding the ---- Division, who resides at Little Bognor, near Petworth, and is brother-in-law to Lord Leconfield. It is since 1st July that Corporal Stringer received his promotion from Lance-Corporal. He is aged 28 and single. His mother told a Sussex Daily News Representative that he always wanted to be a soldier, and on the outbreak of the war he at once joined. He has been at the Front since July last year.

At the time he was working at Horsham for his uncle, Mr. J. Mead, but previously he had been employed in the gardens at Capron House and Cowdray House for four years. He will be heartily congratulated on the distinction he has won by numerous friends at Easebourne and Midhurst. His father has been employed on the Cowdray estate for over 17 years.

Wednesday September 27th 1916

More Honours for Sussex Soldiers

Among the awards for gallantry officially announced last night were the following :-

Awarded the Military Cross

T/ Captain Hugh Salvin Bowlby, 7th Bn. Royal Sussex Regiment,

For conspicuous gallantry in action. After launching a successful attack with two platoons, he at once re-organised his company, sent off a party with machine-guns to reinforce a captured trench, and organised a reconnoitring patrol to get in touch with the enemy. It was largely due to his coolness and courage that we were able to hold this trench against the enemy attack.

No. 8881 Coy Sergeant-Major Bernard Norris Butcher, 2nd Bn. Royal Sussex Regiment,

For conspicuous and consistent gallantry and good work. On one occasion, after all his officers had become casualties, he kept his company together, so that it rendered fine service later in the day. On another, when the battalion had suffered severely, his energy and cheery pluck were invaluable.

Awarded the D.C.M.

No. 3303 Sergeant G. Hodges, 7th Bn. Royal Sussex Regiment,

For conspicuous gallantry during operations. He led a bombing attack up a gap into the enemy's trench, and captured and consolidated 50 yards of it. Although severely wounded he continued to lead his party with greatest determination.

No. 424 Sergeant G. Ward,   7th Bn. Royal Sussex Regiment,

For conspicuous gallantry in action. He led his bombing party across the open under heavy machine-gun fire, and it was largely due to his skill and personal courage that the enemy trench was captured, and held against all attacks.

Captain Bowlby is a son of the Rev. Henry Bowlby, Headmaster of Lancing College, and he and Mrs. Bowlby will be heartily congratulated on the prowess their son has exhibited. Captain Bowlby joined the Army after the war commenced. Another son also obtained a commission, but was invalided out.

Sergeant George Hodges belongs to Haywards Heath, where he is well-known as having been Hon. Secretary of the Conservative and Unionist Club. He has been in charge of the bombers of his battalion, and it was in connection with a grenade attack that he won his medal. The wounds mentioned in the official record were a result of an enemy bomb exploding near him. The Boche's were resisting stubbornly and also using bombs. One of these fell near Sergeant Hodges Happily he heard a tinkle as it struck a stone and was able to scramble back a couple of yards before it went off. Probably this saved his life, for as it was, he was wounded in the right leg just above the ankle and in two places on the left leg, besides receiving minor cuts on the arms and back. He went on fighting, but a trip to Blighty was the result subsequently, and Sergeant Hodges has been an inmate of Bethnal Green Hospital. He had been previously wounded about a year ago, when he sustained injuries to the head.

Thursday September 28th 1916

Worthing Soldier's Distinction

A former member of the Worthing Fire Brigade, Rifleman Jones, has been awarded the French Military Medal. He was in the retreat from Mons, and has been fighting ever since.

Monday October 2nd 1916

Late 2nd Lieutenant Osmaston, M.C.

Second-Lieutenant Robert Shirley Osmaston, M.C., Royal Sussex Regiment, attached to the 23rd Squadron R.F.C. who was killed on 24th September. He was the youngest son of Mr. and Mrs. F.P. Osmaston, of Stoneshill, Limpsfield, Surrey, and was aged 21 years.

Tuesday October 10th 1916

Honour for Hove Fireman

No. 424 Sergeant G. Ward, 5th Bn. Royal Sussex Regiment, and a member of the Hove Fire Brigade, has been awarded the D.C.M. for conspicuous gallantry in action. He led his bombing party across the open under heavy machine-gun fire, and it was largely due to his skill and personal courage that the enemy trench was captured and held against all attacks.

D.C.M. for Warninglid Man

There was an interesting ceremony at Slaughham Parish church on Sunday morning. The local Company of the Sussex Volunteers attended a Church Parade, with Major J.J. Lister, J.P. in command. An appropriate sermon was preached by the Rev. W.A. Dengate. After service the Volunteers paraded outside the Church, also the Slaugham Lads' Brigade and Scouts, under Captain the Rev. W.A. Dengate. There was a numerous attendance of the residents and villagers. Major J.J. Lister presented the D.C.M. to Sergeant Langley, of the Royal Sussex Regiment. He said he was pleased to have the honour of presenting the medal to Sergeant Langley, and he read out the official narrative of the gallant conduct for which the honour had been awarded. He personally congratulated the Sergeant on his achievement, and gave him his best wishes. He pinned the medal on the Sergeant's breast and shook hands with him. The Volunteers and Scouts and the assembly generally cheered the gallant soldier. Sergeant Langley is a son of Mr. and Mrs. Langley of Warninglid. He has twice been wounded, once in the head and again in the lungs, but, now being convalescent, he is going to the Front again very shortly. He had been a member of the Scouts, who were consequently much elated that a former Scout had won the much coveted distinction. Mr. and Mrs. Langley have lost one son in the war, he being drowned off the Isle of Wight while on Naval Service.

Wednesday October 11th 1916

A Sussex War Trophy

A German machine-gun was captured by the Royal Sussex Regiment on the 9th of September, and has been given to the Battalion by the Army Commander as a trophy of war.

It was taken single-handed by Sergeant Burt, the Battalion Scout Sergeant, who was unfortunately mortally wounded the following morning when trying to rescue a wounded man. The gun, will in due course be sent to the Depot at Chichester for safe custody pending he return of the Battalion.

Tuesday October 12th 1916

Military Medal Winners

17 for the Royal Sussex

The Royal Sussex Regiment is well represented in the latest list of those upon whom the King has conferred the Military Medal for bravery in the field. Appended are the names of the members of the Regiment who have won the distinction, but the rank of the recipient may not now be that here stated :-

No. 7922 Private Ernest Brown	2nd Bn.
No. 7835 Private Frederick Burden	2nd Bn.
No. 6995 Sergeant Stanley Burgess	2nd Bn.
No. 6255 Corporal George F. Delves	2nd Bn.
No. 8618 Private Archibald E. Dunk	2nd Bn.
No. 9919 Private Harold Hemsley	2nd Bn.
No. 6014 Lance-Corporal Charles W. Kent	2nd Bn.
No. 8165 Sergeant Arthur F. Kimber	2nd Bn.
No. 8835 Corporal Alfred C. Knight	2nd Bn.
No. 10651 Private William Moore	2nd Bn.
No. 10298 Private (Actg. Sergeant) Ernest B. Read	2nd Bn.
No. 9147 Private (Lance-Corporal) George A. Scutt	2nd Bn.
No. 1657 Actg. Corporal Ernest Still	2nd Bn.
No. 9249 Private (Actg. Corporal) Edwin Tucker	2nd Bn.

 No. 7318 Sergeant (now 2nd/Lieutenant) Edward James Upton   2nd Bn.

No. 9316 Private (Lance-Corporal) Ernest W. Wade   2nd Bn.
No. 1599 Actg. Sergeant George Thomas Young   2nd Bn.

Sergeant G.T. Young, Royal Sussex Regiment, of Rustington, was one of the first to join up from that village. He is a son of Mr. Andrew Young and a brother of the gallant soldier is Mr. A.E. Young, a member of Lancing Parish Council. Two other sons have figured in the Army, one of them, Fred, losing a leg in France. Another son came from Canada to work in a munitions factory.

Saturday October 21st 1916

Battle Honours for local Officers and N.C.O.'s.

Local warriors continue to uphold the fighting fame of Sussex, and their courageous deeds on the field of battle have once more received recognition from his Majesty the King.
A special supplement to the *"London Gazette,"* issued last night, set forth the following awards among others. It will be noted with interest that a Sussex officer had a likely adventure in a "Tank" that went lame through unkind treatment by the enemy.

M.C.

2nd Lieutenant Geordie Osborn Lorne Campbell, 3rd Bn. Royal Sussex Regiment,

For conspicuous gallantry in action. When his "Tank" broke down he sent the crew back and removed all his guns to his commander's "Tank," remaining with him throughout the entire operation and personally taking charge of one of the guns.

Temporary Lieutenant Alfred David Foster, 8th Bn. Royal Sussex Regiment,

For conspicuous gallantry in action. He directed the work of his platoon in opening up communications across "No Man's Land" under heavy fire. Though wounded early in the day, he refused to leave his post till ordered back.

Temporary 2nd Lieutenant Richard Charles Hall, 8th Bn. Royal Sussex Regiment,

For conspicuous gallantry in action. Though there were only short lengths of trenches here and there in the wood, and the enemy kept up an intense barrage, he moved up and down the trenches throughout the night cheering the men and supervising their work. His cheerfulness and pluck had a great effect in steadying the men.

2nd Lieutenant Basil Charles Wright, 2nd Bn. Royal Sussex Regiment,

For conspicuous gallantry in action. After taking part in a successful assault he showed great coolness and courage in beating back a counter-attack. He has done other fine work.

D.C.M.

No. 8542 Sergeant A. Burt, 2nd Bn. Royal Sussex Regiment,

For conspicuous gallantry in carrying out repeated reconnaissance's under fire, particularly on one occasion, when he was out for over three hours, under heavy rifle and artillery fire, and brought in information of great importance.

No. G/1671 Lance-Corporal Frederick William Yeomans, 8th Bn. Royal Sussex Regiment,

For conspicuous gallantry in an attack, when, acting under orders of an officer, he organised a bombing party , and with great courage and skill, bombed his way up a communications trench, facilitating the advance, and causing the surrender of about 160 of the enemy.
Taken from 8th Bn. War Diary 15th July, 1916:-

"When the advance of the 7th Queens on 1st July was held up by a strong party of Germans in Back Trench this N.C.O. under orders of Lt. Heaton, 7th Queens organised a bombing party and with great gallantry bombed up a communication trench to Back Trench which was also bombed. The action of this bombing party was directly responsible for the surrender of about 160 Germans – The above particulars have been communicated to me by O.C. 7th Queens.-A.E. Glasgow, Lieut-Colonel, Commanding 8th Bn. Royal Sussex Pioneers,"

The Sussex Daily News states that three Royal Sussex men have been awarded the Military Medal they are as follows:-

G/ 2554 Pte. Martin Archibald Humphrey,
G/2715 Pte. Francis William Austin,
G/2774 Pte. Charles Edwards

When the advance of the 7 Queens was held up by a strong party of the enemy in BACK TRENCH these men who formed part of a platoon going out to consolidate the position when captured formed part of a bombing party under L/Cpl. Yeomans and with great gallantry bombed up a communication trench and BACK TRENCH this action being directly responsible to the capture of about 160 Germans.

This also appears in the 8th Bn. War Diaries about two weeks after the battle.
Unfortunately either through an oversight or the recommendations were lost or down-graded they do not appear in the London Gazette, so they did not receive them. It is possible they were given a Divisional Commanders certificate for gallantry as Pte. Edwards has a Vellum which states :-

Private Charles Edwards 8th Bn. Royal Sussex Pioneers Regt.

I have read with great pleasure the report of your regimental commander and brigade commander regarding your gallant conduct and devotion to duty in the field on 1st July 1916 During the Battle of the Somme.

F.J. Maxse
Major-General
Commanding 18th Division

Monday October 23rd 1916

Royal Sussex Soldiers win more Military Medals

Twelve non-commissioned officers and men of the Royal Sussex Regiment appear in the list of those soldiers to whom the King has been pleased to award the Military Medal for bravery in the field. The County regiment's proud fighting record is being finely maintained and there will be hearty congratulations to the following on the honour they have won :-

"When the advance of the 7th Queens was held up by a strong party of the enemy in back Trench these men who formed part of a platoon going out to consolidate the position when captured formed part of a bombing party under L/Corporal Yeomans and with great gallantry bombed up a communication trench and back Trench this action being directly responsible for the capture of about 160 Germans."

No. G/2776 Private William J. Bailey, 8th Bn.
"As Company Runner, Bernafay Wood 13/14th July, 1916."

No. S/384 Sergeant James Buckwell, 8th Bn.
"Showed great coolness and disregard of danger when laying out work for opening up communications across "No Man's Land" on 1st July."

No. 5420 Sergeant Alfred George Catchpole, 2nd Bn.

No. G/1955 Private Nelson Dann, 8th Bn. (Jevington)

"Displayed great courage and rendered most valuable service in putting up wire in front of a strong point in Montauban Alley under a heavy fire. He volunteered for this duty."

 No. G/2424 Private John Daughtry, 8th Bn.

No. G/2344 Lance-Corporal J. Johncox, 8th Bn.
"Bernafay Wood 13/14th July, sentry for 5 hours."

No. G/1862 Private William Perkins, 8th Bn.
No. G/22667 Private Edgar Scott, 8th Bn. (Punnetts Town)

"When their platoon was heavily shelled and forced to take cover in a trench these men remained out for half an hour in a very exposed position under a heavy fire tending a wounded comrade whom he eventually succeeded in bringing to a place of comparative safety. Private Perkins himself being wounded."

No. G/2605 Private William Short, 8th Bn.

"On 1st July did most excellent work and showed a fine disregard of personal danger during the work of consolidating captured trenches under a heavy fire."

No. 4742 Lance-Corporal (A/Cpl.) David Smith, 2nd Bn.

No. G/1834 Lance-Corporal Ernest Stringer, 8th Bn.

"On July 1st this N.C.O. did splendid work in organising working parties for consolidating captured trenches under shell fire. His coolness and disregard of personal danger after most of his senior N.C.O.'s had become casualties set a fine example to his men."

No. G/1721 Lance-Corporal Reginald Claude Victor Wimborn, 8th Bn.
"Displayed great courage and rendered most valuable service in putting up a wire in front of a strong point in Montauban Alley under a heavy fire on 1st July. He volunteered for this duty."

Wednesday October 25th 1916

Loss to Ardingley

It is deeply regretted at Ardingley that the first soldier to win a military honour has died from wounds. Sergeant R. Prevett, D.C.M., Royal Sussex Regiment, died in hospital on the 6th October, he was 24 years of age.

Saturday October 28th 1916

More Military Medals won

The King has awarded the Military Medal to the following non-commissioned officers of the Royal Sussex Regiment for bravery in the field. The list was issued on Thursday in a special supplement to the *"London Gazette"* :-

No. 7692 Corporal Henry T. Burn, 9th Bn.
No. 6814 Corporal J. Cheeseman, 9th Bn.
No. 3477 Sergeant Walter R. Chittenden, 9th Bn.
No. 6815 Lance-Corporal W. Clinch, 7th Bn.
No. 3071 Corporal Fred Collins, 9th Bn.
No. 8145 Private Louis Fuller, 9th Bn.
No. 3182 Lance-Sergeant Samuel J. Harding, 9th Bn.
No. 9992 Private Christopher J. Laming, 2nd Bn.
No. 6812 Corporal Richard Lintott, 9th Bn.

Monday October 30th 1916

Crowborough Men's Gallantry

Among those mentioned in Battalion Orders in connection with the Royal Sussex Regiment, for acts of gallantry appears :-

No. 11787 Sergeant A. Chatfield, No. 3136 Private A.W. Dray, No. 2844 Private S.H. Cozens and No. 2424 Private A. Bailey, who at 6.30 a.m. on 17th August last went out into "No Man's Land", and brought in a wounded man of another regiment (The Norfolks), who had been lying there for five days. With the exception of Private Cozens, all the above mentioned are Crowborough men. Private Cozens belongs to the neighbouring district of Jarvis Brook.

Awarded after Death

Cross-in-Hand Soldier's Gallantry

Private James Bishop, of the Royal Sussex Regiment, who was exclusively reported in the "Herald" to have died of wounds, has been posthumously awarded the Military Medal for gallantry and devotion to duty at the Front. He was the third son of Mr. Owen Bishop, of Maynard's Gate, Cross-in-Hand, and sustained the fatal wound a few hours prior to his death. He was in such a bad condition – having been wounded in both legs – that he had to have them both amputated, one just above the foot and the other higher up the leg. Deceased was twenty-eight years old, and in the September following the outbreak of the present war he answered the call of the country and enlisted in "Lowther's Own." At the time of joining up he was at Bexhill. He was a single man, one of four brothers, and was employed as a farm labourer.

Wednesday November 1st 1916

Honours for Brighton Policemen

In the list of non-commissioned officers and men of the Royal Sussex Regiment awarded the Military Medal, which appeared in Saturday's *Sussex Daily News*, the names of Corporal R. Lintott, Corporal J. Cheeseman and Lance-Corporal W. Clinch were included. It is interesting to learn that these gallant men were all in the Brighton Police Force.

Friday November 3rd 1916

Newick Men's Gallantry

Two Newick men have been personally mentioned in the Battalion Orders of the Royal Sussex Regiment, for acts of gallantry. They are :- No. 3507 Private Guy H. Brooks, who, with four others, "On the night of 14th-15th August, volunteered to go forward through a heavy barrage to bring in two wounded men and succeeded in getting them back to the dressing station," and No. 1277 Private (now L/Cpl.) Percy G. Elphick, who, with another, "On the night 9/10th August, voluntarily remained under shell-fire to dig out a man of another regiment who had been buried by a shell blowing in the communication trench, and afterwards carrying him to the dressing station." Private Brooks is the youngest son of Mr. John Brooks, Allington Road, Newick. Two of his brothers have been killed in the war, and two others are now at the front. He himself is now in hospital at Eastbourne, recovering from wounds received a little later than the date of the gallant act above mentioned. Private Elphick, is the son of the late Mr. John Elphick and Mrs. Elphick, Western Road, Newick, and has been at the front with the Royal Sussex Regiment since February 1915. Three of his brothers have served, or are still serving at the front.

Saturday November 4th 1916

Military Medal Heroes

Awards to Heathfield, Jevington and Willingdon Men

The King has sanctioned the award of the Military Medal to Lance-Corporal Nelson Dann, Royal Sussex Pioneers, son of Mr. and Mrs. J. Dann, Willingdon Lane, Jevington, for gallantry in the field. In a letter to his parents, Lance-Corporal Dann makes a brief and commonplace reference to the decoration, but the parchment letter from the Major-General Commanding the Division reads :-

"No. G/1955 Lance-Corporal Nelson Dann ; Royal Sussex Pioneers Regiment. I have read with great pleasure the report of your regimental commander and brigade commander regarding your gallant conduct and devotion to duty in the field on 1st July, 1916, during the Battle of the Somme."
Lance-Corporal Dann, who is 22 next month, was born and educated in the village, subsequently becoming gardener to the late rector – the Rev. Mr. Crake. He enlisted a month after the outbreak of the war, and went in to training at Colchester and Salisbury. Fifteen months ago he was sent to France. He enlisted with two friends, Private J. Wooler and Private W. Farrant, of Wannock, and all three have soldiered together from the very commencement.
Lance-Corporal Dann has two brothers on active service, Lance-Corporal Frederick Dann, Military Police, and Private George Dann, Suffolk Regiment (Cyclist Battalion). The latter was passed for home service.

Another Heathfield Military Medallist

News is to hand that another Heathfield man has been awarded the Military Medal. The news received by a friend at Heathfield, is that Private E. Pattenden, Royal Sussex Regiment, who was prior to his enlistment, employed by Mr. J. Mackford, Broad Oak, has won the coveted award for gallantry in the field and devotion to duty.
Private Pattenden enlisted in November, 1914, and was for some time at Abbey Wood, Woolwich. He went to France in April of this year, and although he has participated in the severe fighting of the past few months, has fortunately escaped injury.

A Willingdon Hero

The Military Medal has been awarded to Lance-Corporal W.H. Sheppard, Royal Sussex Regiment, who with Corporal Heathfield, held out an isolated position from 5.30 to 8.30 with absolute coolness in spite of heavy fire and many losses. Corporal W.H. Sheppard, who comes from Ealing, lived for two years in Willingdon, and was in the employed of Mr. Oakshott, of Westlords, Willingdon. He joined the Army on the outbreak of war.

Monday November 6th 1916

Decorated by the King

Among the recipients of the Military Cross was Lieutenant Clifford Augustus Farnham Whitely, Royal Sussex Regiment, attached to the R.F.C.

Monday November 13th 1916

More Royal Sussex Men win the Military Medal

The King has been pleased to award the Military Medal for bravery on the field to the undermentioned N.C.O.'s and men of the Royal Sussex Regiment :-

No. 2398 Sergeant George Thomas Davies, 5th Bn.
No. 2664 Private Charles H. Gaston, 5th Bn.

No. 1489 Sergeant William A. Gates, 5th Bn.

No. 2340 Lance-Corporal John Hart, 5th Bn.
No. 924 Sergeant Geoffrey Henley Hodson, 5th Bn.
No. 1891 Private Albert W. King, 5th Bn.
No. 1647 Sergeant George Lusted, 5th Bn.
No. 2595 Corporal Bernard C. Pullinger, 5th Bn.
No. 2376 Sergeant Frederick Stone, 5th Bn.
No. 1912 Lance-Corporal Thomas W. Towner, 5th Bn.

Sergeant Fred Stone is a Wadhurst man who, with many other men of the village, joined shortly after the outbreak of war. Mrs. Stone, who resides at Gloucester Road, Wadhurst, told a *Sussex Daily News* Representative that her husband's enlistment was a practical method of expressing his indignation and horror at the German treatment of the Belgian woman. Up to that time he had been in the employ of Mr. Fillery, butcher, of High Street, Wadhurst. His brother-in-law, Private Kenward, who was killed on the 9th May, 1915, enlisted on the same day in the same battalion. After a few months' home service and training, during which he gained his Corporal's stripes, he volunteered for the front and went over to France in February, 1915. On the fateful 9th May, 1915, he took part in the fighting in which so many brave Sussex lads lost their lives. For 14 hours Sergeant Stone, together with Private Skinner, a wounded Wadhurst man, remained in a shell-hole between the lines amid heavy enemy fire. One rifle bullet went through his kitbag and he was given up by his Company as lost. But he managed to return safely to the British lines the next day and was almost immediately given the rank he now holds. During the 21 months' active service the gallant sergeant has had one brief home leave, but he is remembered at Wadhurst by reason of the sympathetic letters he has written to the bereaved relatives of Wadhurst soldiers who have made the supreme sacrifice. Sergeant Stone was a keen footballer and was a popular playing member of the Wadhurst Football Club. One of his brothers is officially reported wounded and a prisoner, and another brother is in France.

Wednesday November 15th 1916

Further Honours for Officers of County Regiment

More honours have been conferred on Sussex soldiers, the chapter of whose gallant deeds shines brightly from the pages of the official records. The epitomised chronicles of their doings reveals possession of various soldierly qualities. We read of coolness and utter contempt for danger, of gallant leadership, of scouting excellence, of courage and devotion, of grim determination, of tenacity, even though wounded, and of an airman's self-sought and successful fight against the odds. They are moving little stories and Sussex people will be proud, too, of the worthy sons who have brought fresh lustre to the county's military fame. The special supplement to the *"London Gazette"* issued last night contains the following respecting members of the Royal Sussex Regiment.

Awarded the Military Cross

Temporary 2nd Lieutenant James Stewart Cassels, 11th Bn. Royal Sussex Regiment,

For conspicuous gallantry in action. He was for many hours under very shell fire, and, when the second and third waves failed to reach their objectives, he greatly assisted his company commander in re-organising the men for another attack. He displayed great coolness and utter contempt for danger.

Temporary Lieutenant Charles Samuel Mason, 2nd Bn. Royal Sussex Regiment,

For conspicuous gallantry as Scout Officer during operations. He has repeatedly carried out reconnaissances under heavy fire, and has displayed complete contempt for danger. His reports have been of the greatest use.

Temporary 2nd Lieutenant Cyril Leslie Mitchell, 11th Bn. Royal Sussex Regiment,

For conspicuous gallantry in action. When the officers in the front line had become casualties, he moved up a portion of his reserve company, and then consolidated the enemy line. He displayed great courage and devotion to duty throughout.

2nd Lieutenant (T/Captain) Francis Charles Sainton, 2nd Bn. Royal Sussex Regiment,

For conspicuous gallantry in action. Although wounded, he gallantly led his company in the attack. Later, again being wounded, he stuck to his post, displaying great courage and initiative. He set a fine example to his men.

Temp. 2nd Lieutenant Henry Harle Story, 13th Bn. Royal Sussex Regiment,

For conspicuous gallantry in action. When two companies, who were in support, he took command of both companies, re-organised them, and led them into the enemy's trenches. He displayed great coolness and bravery all day.

Awarded a Bar

Lieutenant Frederick Joseph Aglid Dibdin   M.C.   3rd Bn. Royal Sussex Regiment S.R.

For conspicuous gallantry in action. He handled his machine-guns under very heavy fire with great courage and determination. Later, he consolidated the position and rendered services of the utmost value.
(The Military Cross was awarded in *"London Gazette"* dated 23rd June, 1915).

Awarded the D.C.M.

No. SD/2922 Company Sergeant-Major E.A. Hammond, 13th Bn. Royal Sussex Regiment

For conspicuous gallantry during operations, when he rallied and re-organised his company under very heavy bombardment. Though wounded, he kept to his post, and afforded a fine example to his men of devotion to duty.

Thursday November 16th 1916

Gallant Hailsham Soldier

Private J.W. Wilmshurst for his gallant conduct on the 7th July, 1916, during the attack and capture of Ovillers, has been presented with a certificate by the Brigadier-General. Mrs. Wilmshurst who lives at Hailsham naturally feels proud of the certificate which arrived by post.

Friday November 17th 1916

More Sussex Military Medal Recipients

In the latest list of those to whom the King has awarded the Military Medal for bravery in the field appear the names of the following, who belong to Royal Sussex Regiment

No. 3628 Private Quinton W.A. Dick, 9th Bn.
No. 710 Sergeant Charles Hunt, 9th Bn.
No. 5928 Sergeant Charles H. Jarvis, 9th Bn.
No. 546 Corporal Lionel Whitcher, 9th Bn.

Monday November 20th 1916

King Decorates Heroes

The King conferred the Military Cross on the following officers and men of the Royal Sussex Regiment:-

Major George Loyd Courthope M.P., 5th Bn.
2nd Lieutenant Herbert Sefton Broughall, 7th Bn.
2nd Lieutenant Noel MacRoberts, 13th Bn.
C.S.M. Bernard Butcher, 2nd Bn.

Wednesday November 22nd 1916

Littlehampton Lad who won the Military Medal

In the trenches when 17 years old, No. 3628 Quentin William Albert Dick, Royal Sussex Regiment, who has been awarded the Military Medal for bravery in the field, is a well-known Littlehampton lad whom the inhabitants are extremely proud. Not only has he gained the honour at a very early age, but he has also to his credit over two years' service in France, during which his regiment has seen some of the severest fighting of the war. Although only 17 years of age, young Dick, joined up soon after the outbreak of war. He was keen on "having a go" at the Germans, for, as he told his widowed mother, "somebody must do the job." He anticipated a birthday, and within a months of joining the County Regiment, and when still below the legal military age, he was in the trenches. He was wounded in the shoulder, head and left hand and spent his actual eighteenth birthday in Woolwich Hospital. He returned to the front line in September last and was wounded a second time. Curiously enough, shrapnel hit him on his old wounds-the shoulder and the fingers of his left hand. A bullet passed right through him and made its exit two inches above his left hip. As the result he spent his nineteenth birthday on the 10th October, in hospital at Liverpool, where he is now convalescent.

Monday November 27th 1916

Military Crosses for Sussex Officers

The King has been pleased to confer the Military Cross on the undermentioned officers of the Royal Sussex Regiment in recognition of their gallantry and devotion to duty in the field :-

2nd Lieutenant (T/Captain) Thomas Whately Rose, 5th Bn.

For conspicuous gallantry in action. He marked out a communications trench for a distance of over 800 yards under very heavy fire. He displayed great courage and determination throughout the operation.

Lieutenant (T/Captain) George Frederick Thomas, 5th Bn.

For conspicuous gallantry in action. He organised a party of machine-gunners and bombers, and greatly assisted in repulsing an enemy attack. He displayed great courage and initiative throughout the operations.

Captain George Frederick Thomas, Royal Sussex Regiment, before going to war, was in dental practice at Tunbridge Wells, his residence being Ashington, 34, Warwick Park. As a Territorial officer he was in camp when the war cloud burst, and he has been at the front with his battalion for many months. He went out as a subaltern, but quickly gained his third star, his appointment being dated 15th September, 1915. He saw service in the Boer War.

Tuesday November 28th 1916

Another Hailsham War Hero

Mr. and Mrs. T. Pattenden, of Westfield, Hailsham, have received information that their son, Private W.T. Pattenden, Royal Sussex regiment, (Lewis Gun Section) has been awarded the Military Medal. This deed for which he receives the distinction reads in Battalion Orders as follows :- "On the 22nd, August, when the Gloucesters had to repel a counter-attack, he got his gun into action at the top of the trench, where he was covering a working party, and continued to serve it successfully after he was wounded, remaining at his post until relieved and ordered to retire. A letter from the front states he must of accounted for 100 Germans. Private Pattenden is an old scholar of Hailsham Council School, and only a few years ago obtained a scholarship at the Eastbourne Municipal School. He took an interest in the Territorials, and joined the local section which was then under the charge of Sergeant H. Roberts, who gained a D.C.M. last year. Private Pattenden went out to the front in February 1915. After his action of 22nd August he became quite a hero of his Company, and all are delighted his action has won for him a well merited distinction.

Thursday November 30th 1916

Sussex Heroes Decorated

A very interesting ceremony took place on the Recreation Ground, Newhaven, yesterday, when several men of the Royal Sussex Regiment were presented with decorations for gallantry at the front. The Battalion, under the command of Colonel Hankey, was formed up in three sides of a square. Among other officers present were Major Wood, Major Villiers, C.M.G., D.S.O., and Captain and Adjutant Nicoll. The Regimental Band was under Bandmaster Patrick. The whole of the arrangements were in the hands of Regimental Sergeant-Major Boniface. Lieutenant-General Sir J. Wolfe Murray, K.C.B., who was accompanied by his staff, was received with a general salute, and, addressing the Battalion, said he could not express in words the pleasure it gave him to be present, and for the honour conferred upon him in being asked to present these medals to the men, everyone of whom was a hero, and of whom the Royal Sussex regiment might well be proud.

After reading the official descriptions of the acts of gallantry in recognition of which the medals were conferred, the General said he was sorry the full list and records for the Military Medals had not at yet come to hand. The general then pinned the medals on the breasts of the recipients, and with a hearty shake of the hand wished each every success.

At the close of this ceremony the General again addressed the Battalion, and said he was quite sure he need not ask them to do their duty, for there was not a man among them who would under all circumstances not do this. The regiment was, and ought to be, proud of the men who had been decorated, and he saw no reason why many who were standing round should not win medals, thus proving themselves heroes, and of whom any regiment might well be proud. The recipients were as follows :-

No. 8881 C.S.M. B.N. Butcher, M.C., D.C.M. 2nd Bn.

For conspicuous gallantry on 29th January, 1915, in France. During a heavy attack on The Keep, he, while under heavy machine-gun fire, bombed the enemy and was largely instrumental in defeating the attack. He has on many occasions throughout the campaign rendered valuable service, and has invariably shown great courage, resource, and devotion to duty.

No. 5908 C.S.M. Dallaway, D.C.M. 2nd Bn.

For conspicuous gallantry on 30th October, 1914, in France, when reconnoitring in front of his company up to German lines. He has been noted for his courage, resource, and ability throughout the campaign, and in a most dangerous situation has always shown a fine example of cheerfulness and devotion to duty.

No. 9013 C.S.M. W. Soughton, D.C.M. 3rd Bn. attd. 2nd Bn.

For conspicuous gallantry and good work throughout the campaign, notably when, after all his officers had become casualties in an attack, he took command and led his company with great determination.

No. SD/658 Sergeant Guy Compton, D.C.M. M.M. 11th Bn.

For conspicuous gallantry and ability during operations. Sergeant Compton pushed forward through uncut wire and heavy machine-gun fire into the enemy's trenches, organised a bombing party, and cleared 100 yards of trench, accounting for many of the enemy. He set a fine example.

No. 2250 Private J. Heasman, D.C.M. 2nd Bn.

For conspicuous gallantry and devotion to duty. He was wounded bringing in a wounded man, but refused to be attended to till he had bound up a wounded officer. Later, he went out twice again after wounded; on the last occasion he was again wounded in the chest. All this was in broad daylight and under fire.

No. 1659 Corporal A. Horcroft, M.M. 2nd Bn.
No. SD/2641 Corporal George T. Chambers, M.M. 13th Bn.

At Buckingham Palace today Mrs. Wells, the mother of No. 8808 Sergeant Harry Wells V.C., 2nd Battalion Royal Sussex Regiment, will be presented with the Victoria Cross her son has won posthumously.

Saturday December 2nd 1916

Military Medal for Sussex Man

No. SD/503 Sergeant Richard Edward Cox 11th Bn. Royal Sussex Regiment,

The Military Medal was awarded for :-

For splendid devotion to duty and great courage displayed at Thiepval sector on 21st October, 1916. Acting as second in command of his platoon he most ably assisted his Platoon Commander by preserving a cool front. Soon after arriving in the position we had captured he went into "No Man's Land" with the first reinforcements, showing absolute contempt for the heavy shelling under which he moved. He himself brought back several wounded men, rendered such first aid as he could, and deposited them in a place of safety. During this action he was twice buried by shells bursting almost on him, but this did not deter him, and throughout by his cheerful demeanour, he helped considerably to preserve the morale of the men about him. This was a splendid example won the admiration of all ranks.

Commendations to Officers

From Sir A. Murray's dispatches :-

STAFF

Lieutenant (Temp.-Captain) Robert Egerton Loder, 1/4th Bn. Royal Sussex Regiment,
Captain (Temp.Lieutenant-Colonel) Hugh Stirling Ashworth, Cmdg. 4th Bn. Royal Sussex Regiment,

Monday December 11th 1916

Nineteen Local Military Medal Winners

The Royal Sussex Regiment is again well represented in the latest list of non-commissioned officers and men upon whom the King has conferred the Military Medal for bravery in the field. The list is as follows, but the rank shown may not be that now borne by the recipient :-

No. 5918 Private David Bell, 2nd Bn.
No. 1022 Private Reuben Bullock, 2nd Bn.

No. 3268 Private Bernard Dabson, 5th Bn.

No. SD/1189 Lance-Corporal Arthur Henry Davey, 11th Bn.

No. 7648 Private (Lance-Corporal) Albert Dunk, 2nd Bn.
No. 3062 Sergeant Jesse W.S. Foster, 2nd Bn.

No. 10190 Private F. Fuller, 2nd Bn.

No. SD/194 Lance-Corporal William Heathfield, 11th Bn.

No. 10060 Corporal James Henty, 2nd Bn.

No. 5638 Private A.E. Madgwick, 2nd Bn.

No. 1626 Private W.T. Pattenden, 5th Bn.

No. 7471 Private Alfred Rapley, 9th Bn.
No. SD/232 Private William Henry Sheppard, 11th Bn.
No. G/17761 Private William Shotter, 4th Bn.
No. 4071 Private Charles W. Turrell, 9th Bn.
No. SD/3039 Private William George Vidler, 11th Bn.

Official Citations

No. SD/194 L/Corporal William Heathfield, 11th Bn.

"Lance-Corporals Heathfield and Sheppard held out in an isolated position from 5.30 a.m. till 8 p.m. the same day. Their coolness and utter disregard to danger inspired the few men they had under them, and in spite of heavy losses, they succeeded in hanging on until ordered to withdraw by their commanding officer."

No. SD/232 L/Corporal William Henry Sheppard, 11th Bn.

"Lance-Corporals Heathfield and Sheppard held out in an isolated position from 5.30 a.m. till 8 p.m. the same day. Their coolness and utter disregard to danger inspired the few men they had under them, and in spite of heavy losses, they succeeded in hanging on until ordered to withdraw by their commanding officer."

No. 3268 Private Bernard Dabson, 5th Bn.

On several occasions Private Dabson showed great devotion to duty and bravery in rescuing wounded men from "No Man's Land", under heavy shell fire."

Tuesday December 12th 1916

A Sussex D.C.M. Winner

It is officially announced the Distinguished Conduct Medal has been conferred upon :-

No. 4040 Acting Sergeant-Major E. Haines   P.S. 5th Bn. Royal Sussex Regiment,

"For consistent gallantry and good leading in the immediate presence of the enemy. His untiring work and ability was invaluable."

Worthing Policeman Killed

News has reached the Worthing headquarters of the West Sussex Police Force, of the death of ex.-P.C. H.S. Wilkinson. He was a London man by birth and before the war belonged to the West Sussex Police Force, and was stationed at Worthing, from which he enlisted in the Royal Sussex regiment, with eight other men of the same division of the force. Three of the nine have been killed in France and the rest wounded. Wilkinson was wounded at the end of October and died from the wounds, and he has since been awarded the Military Medal, being the first Worthing Policeman to gain the distinction. On the same day on which Wilkinson was wounded, two of his old police comrades - Rowland and Upperton who were in the same Battalion of the County Regiment were killed.

Friday December 15th 1916

Three more Military Medals

The names of three non-commissioned officers of the Royal Sussex Regiment appear in the latest list of winners of the Military Medal. They are :-

No. G/1767 Lance-Corporal Charles W. Bridle, 8th Bn.
No. 2067 Lance-Corporal George F. Maskell, 8th Bn.
No. S/385 Sergeant Charles F. Moody, 8th Bn.

Worthing Men Decorated

Two more Worthing men have been decorated for devotion to duty and gallant conduct, one during operations on 21st October near the Schwaben Redoubt, and the other in the course of an attack on the Stuff Trench. They are Acting Sergeant-Major Goble, Royal Sussex Regiment, who has just received the Military Medal, is the son of Mr. and Mrs. Albert Goble, 75, Portland Road, Worthing, and Sergeant A.R. Sheppard who was formerly employed by Messrs. Heaman and Sons, and has been awarded the Military Medal.

Friday December 22nd 1916

Six Military Crosses won by Sussex Soldiers

Tributes to young officers' powers of leading are contained in the latest list of decorations for members of the Royal Sussex Regiment. A further half-dozen Military Crosses will serve to keep the County's name prominent among those gaining honours for the various soldierly qualities of gallantry, resources, skill, devotion to duty and disregard of danger. No epic story is told of any recipient; rather it is a chronicle of ordinary battlefield work-if any battlefield work can be termed "ordinary"-done with a thoroughness that of itself attracted notice. The Sussex were in the attack and successfully did what was required of them, that much becomes plain from a perusal of the records. The recipients of the Military Crosses are :-

Temp. 2nd Lieutenant Cecil Arthur Allen, 11th Bn.

For conspicuous gallantry in action. He displayed great courage and determination throughout the operations and set a splendid example to his men.

Temp. Captain John Stuart Cassy,

For conspicuous gallantry in action. He commanded his battalion with great courage and initiative throughout the operations. He has previously done fine work.

Temp. 2nd Lieutenant Emile Alfred Feuchelle,

For conspicuous gallantry in action. He assumed command and led his Company with great courage and determination, consolidating the position and establishing touch with the battalion on his right.

Temp. 2nd Lieutenant Geoffrey Salter, 11th Bn.

For conspicuous gallantry in action. He assumed command of and led his Company with great courage and skill, capturing and consolidating the position. He set a splendid example to his men.

Temp. 2nd Lieutenant Reginald Charles Young, 8th Bn.

For conspicuous gallantry in action. He carried out his work under very heavy fire with great courage and determination. He set a splendid example throughout the operations and has previously done fine work.

No. 8630 C.S.M. Joseph Joy, 7th Bn.

For conspicuous gallantry in action. He showed great coolness under shell and machine-gun fire, and organised the defences of his portion of the captured trench with great energy and skill.

Sussex Military Medal Recipients

Among the recipients of the Military Medal, a list of whom was issued last night, are the following, belong to the Royal Sussex Regiment :-

No. L/5391 Sergeant Charles Coates, 8th Bn.

"During the attack on 1st July, near Montauban this N.C.O. displayed great gallantry in repulsing a hostile bombing attack in Montauban Alley. On several other occasions during the day he rallied his platoon when under heavy fire and set a fine example of coolness and courage."
(Originally recommended for D.C.M.)
No. S/390 Private Arthur James Harris, 8th Bn.

"When acting as stretcher-bearer on 1st July, displayed great gallantry in bringing in wounded from "No Man's Land" immediately after assaulting troops had gone across. On four separate occasions he went

out and back through a heavy hostile barrage and brought in wounded from near the German front line. His gallantry and disregard of personal danger gave a fine example to the troops."
(Originally recommended for D.C.M.)

No. G/1603 Sergeant Kingsley Newman, 8th Bn.
"For great coolness and gallantry at Thiepval."

No. L/9885 Sergeant Claude Richardson, 8th Bn.
"For great coolness and gallantry at Thiepval."

No. G/17761 Private William Shotter, 13th Bn.

Saturday December 23rd 1916

Sussex Officers rewarded for services in Mesopotamia

Three Sussex officers figure among the recipients of honours conferred by the King for services rendered in connection with military operations in Mesopotamia, as follows :-

Awarded the D.S.O.

Major George Charles Morphett, 7th Bn. Royal Sussex Regiment,

To be Brevet Lieutenant-Colonels

Major Robert Nicholas Dick   1st Bn. Royal Sussex Regiment,
Major Gerrard Evelyn Leachman   1st Bn. Royal Sussex Regiment,

Monday January 1st 1917

Sussex Officers Decorated

Among the officers decorated by the King at Buckingham Palace on Saturday were :-

Quartermaster the Hon. Captain Thomas Jones, D.C.M. and 2nd Lieutenant Reginald Young of the Royal Sussex Regiment. Both received the Military Cross.

Honours for local Officers

A long list of war honours published in a supplement to the *"London Gazette"* contains the announcement that Sir Douglas Haig has been made a Field Marshall in recognition of his distinguished services in command of the British Forces in France. There are many officers having Sussex associations in the list, the following having already been noted :-

Awarded the D.S.O.

Captain (T/Lt.-Colonel) George Hastings Impey, 7th Bn. Royal Sussex Regiment,

Major (T/Lt-Col.) George Hyde Harrison, (Border Regiment) Cmdg. 11th Bn. Royal Sussex Regiment,

Awarded the M.C.

Lieutenant (T/Capt.) Albert Garnett Thomas, South Staffs. attd. 5th Bn. Royal Sussex Regiment,

To be Brevet Lieutenant-Colonel

Major (T/Brig-Gen.) William Lushington Osborn, D.S.O. Royal Sussex Regiment,
Major (T/Colonel) John Bartholomew Wroughton, C.M.G., Royal Sussex Regiment,

Granted next higher rate of pay

Quartermaster and Hon. Lieutenant Joseph Edward Clarke, Royal Sussex Regiment,

Promoted from the Ranks : Worthing

A further recognition of gallantry during the offensive on the Somme has come to Sergeant R.E. Cox, Royal Sussex Regiment, who was recently awarded the Military Medal and decorated on the field. He has now been granted a Lieutenancy and is home on short leave before resuming his duties. Lieutenant Cox was employed before the war in the Worthing branch of Messrs. Hepworth and Company. His home is at Lewes.

Tuesday January 2nd 1917

M.C. Award

The award of the Military Cross is bestowed upon :-

2nd Lieutenant Hugh Faithfull Chittenden,   Royal Sussex Regiment,
Captain Sydney Gerald Evans,   Royal Sussex Regiment,
Major Kenneth de Jong, Royal Sussex Regiment,
T/Captain Harry Chickhall Lott,   Royal Sussex Regiment,
2nd Lieutenant Henry Sadler,   Royal Sussex Regiment, Spec. Res.
T/2nd Lieutenant Harry L. Treacher, 9th Bn. Royal Sussex Regiment,
2nd Lieutenant Bernard Whiteman, 5th Bn. Royal Sussex Regiment,
No. S/327 C.S.M. Frederick Charles Leavens,   Royal Sussex Regiment,

Wednesday January 3rd 1917

Local Soldiers "Mentioned"

The first instalments of names of members of the British Forces who have been brought to notice by Sir Douglas Haig for distinguished and gallant service and devotion to duty, includes the following :-

Staff

Osborn, Major (T/Brigadier-General) W.L.   D.S.O.   Royal Sussex Regiment,
Wallington, Lieutenant (T/Captain) M.   M.C.   Royal Sussex Regiment,
Wroughton, Major (T/Colonel) J.B.   C.M.G.   Royal Sussex Regiment,

Second Lieutenant T.E. Chad M.C.

The lengthy honours list published yesterday includes the name of Temporary Second Lieutenant Thomas Ernest Chad, Royal Sussex Regiment, the only son of Mr. and Mrs. G. Chad, of the Schoolhouse, West Chiltington, who has been awarded the Military Cross. Lieutenant Chad joined the Coldstream Guards soon after the outbreak of the war, and served in that regiment for about 12 months before receiving a commission in the Sussex Regiment, which he joined in November, 1915. Altogether he has served in France for about two years, and also he has acted as Adjutant to his battalion.

Steyning Officer's Reward

Another military decoration for conspicuous service has come to Steyning. Second Lieutenant Hugh Faithful Chittenden, Royal Sussex Regiment, who is a temporary Captain while in charge of a Company, has (as already reported) won the Military Cross. He is the son of Mrs. Chittenden, of Highcroft, Goring Road, Steyning, and of the late Mr. C.H.T.F. Chittenden. The war brings its grief's and also its honours. Mrs. Chittenden has previously had the keen sorrow of losing a son in the present conflict, Lieutenant A. Chittenden, Manchester Regiment, who was killed a considerable time ago, as reported at the time of the sad event. A third son, Second Lieutenant C.C. Chittenden, A.S.C., has just gone to the front.

Chichester Officer's Medal

Second Lieutenant H. Sadler, Royal Sussex Regiment, of West Hampnett, near Chichester, has been awarded the Military Cross for gallantry during the operations on the Somme.

Thursday January 4th 1917

Mentioned in Dispatches

The second instalment of names of soldiers singled out by Sir Douglas Haig for mention in his dispatch for meritorious services include the following :-

Royal Sussex Regiment

Birkett, Captain (Temp. Lieutenant-Colonel) R.M.
Impey, Captain (Temp. Lieutenant-Colonel) G.H. D.S.O.
O'Neill, 2nd Lieutenant (Temp. Captain) F.R.
Willett, Major (Acting Lieutenant-Colonel) F.W.B.   D.S.O.
Alexander, 2nd Lieutenant J.W.R.,   Special Reserve
Atkinson, 2nd Lieutenant Lewis de Burgh   (killed)
Owen, Temp. 2nd Lieutenant (Temp. Captain) H.S.
Jones, Quartermaster. and Hon. Captain T.A.,   M.C., D.C.M.
Eve, No. 8962 Sergeant J.
Catmur, 2nd Lieutenant Harry Albert Frederick. V.   (killed)
Holdsworth, 2nd Lieutenant M.J.
Twine, 2nd Lieutenant F.P.

Blackman, No. 1164 Sergeant William

Foord, No. 451 Sergeant S.
Howard, No. 1864 Sergeant A.C.
Osborne, Lieutenant (Temp. Captain) G.F.

Hind, Temp. Lieutenant R.C.D.

Long, No. 118 Regimental Qrmr.Sergeant S.W.

Hanlon, No. 8562 Sergeant P.J.

Kemp, Temp. Lieutenant G.L.
Ireland, Temp. 2nd Lieutenant L.A.F.
Bloomfield, No. S/516 Regimental Sergt.-Major J.
Mullett No. L/5079 Co.Sergeant-Major M.R.
Moody, No. S/385 Sergeant C.F. M.M.
Langdon, Major (Temp. Lieutenant-Colonel) John Frederick Patlock R. of O.

Banham, Temp. 2nd Lieutenant J.J.

Head, No. 3359 Sergeant G.F.
Cooling, Temp. Captain J.H.

Lupton, Temp. Lieutenant R.H.

Coxhead, Temp. Captain H.J.
Cragg, Temp. 2nd Lieutenant A.B.
Cassy, Temp. Captain J.S. M.C.
Kay Robinson, Temp. Captain H.T.
Farrer, Temp. 2nd Lieutenant S.J.

Heagerty, Temp. Major William Thomas

Crowborough Man wins D.C.M.

Among the Sussex men awarded the Distinguished Conduct Medal for gallantry, and whose names appeared in the *Sussex Daily News* of Tuesday, is No. 2424 Private A. Bailey, Royal Sussex Regiment,. Private Bailey won the distinction when, assisted by several other local men, he succeeded in rescuing a wounded comrade under heavy shell fire. He is at present at home on leave, and singularly enough, first heard that he had been gazetted as a medal winner upon entering the Crowborough Liberal Club last night. His friends to set all doubts at rest, showed him of copy of the *Evening Argus*, and he was warmly congratulated upon his splendid deed and its result.

Monday January 8th 1917

SPECIAL BRIGADE ORDER

Brigadier-General H.D. Hornby, D.S.O. Commanding 116th Infantry Brigade

23rd November 1916

AWARDS FOR GALLANT CONDUCT

The Brigadier-General Commanding has much pleasure in announcing to all ranks of the Brigade, the following Awards for gallant conduct on 21st October 1916, during the attack on STUFF TRENCH. That the men of the Royal Sussex continue to uphold the splendid traditions of the county regiment, is exemplified by the fact that the names of 29 non-commissioned officers and men are included in the list issued today of those to whom the King has awarded the Military Medal for bravery in the field, while two have gained a Bar for the Military Medal already in their possession.

Military Medal

All gazetted 5th January, this list is as follows :-

No. SD/24 Private (A/Sergeant) Edward Walter Allchorn, 11th Bn.

No. G/15036 Private Alfred Bailey, 11th Bn.
No. SD/32 Corporal (A/ Sergeant) Thomas James Ball, 11th Bn.
No. SD/1655 Private Henry Scott Butler Belton, 12th Bn.
No. SD/400 Private James Bishop, 11th Bn.
No. SD/2872 Private William Thomas S. Cosstick, 13th Bn.
No. SD/503 Corporal (A/ Sergeant) Richard Edward Cox 11th Bn.
No. G/15263 Corporal Charles William Dybell 11th Bn.
No. SD/1885 Private George Waller Gibbs, attd. Light T.M.B. 12th Bn.
No. SD/1341 Lance-Sergeant Ernest George Goble 12th Bn.
No. SD/1766 Lance-Sergeant Alfred William Golden 12th Bn.
No. SD/1056 Corporal (A/Sergeant) Russell John Hopkins 11th Bn.
No. SD/320 Private Herbert Edward. Horton 11th Bn.
No. G/17862 Private Walter Gyles Jenkinson 12th Bn.
No. SD/1973 Lance-Sergeant George Henry Kibbey 12th Bn.
No. SD/879 Sergeant Frederick John Patrick 11th Bn.
No. SD/1123 Lance-Corporal Edward John Rich 11th Bn.
No. SD/1547 Private Joseph Ripley 12th Bn.
No. SD/3229 Sergeant Archibald R. Sheppard 13th Bn.
No. SD/5137 Private Alfred Sherwood 12th Bn
No. G/15756 Private Frederick E. Shirley 11th Bn.
No. SD/3463 Sergeant Charles Stanford 13th Bn.
No. G/15759 Private Herbert S. Taylor 11th Bn.
No. SD/3029 Lance-Corporal Herbert George Thompsett 13th Bn.
No. SD/3475 Private Ronald William Thorns 13th Bn.
No. SD751 Private (A/Sergeant) Henry Sydney Wilkinson 11th Bn.
No. G/16259 Private Charles Oswald Williams 12th Bn.
No. G/15655 Private Albert Windebank 13th Bn.
No. SD/1510 Private Arthur S. Woollam 12th Bn.

Citations

No. SD/24 A/Sergeant Edward Walter Allchorn, 11th Bn.

"For great gallantry and devotion to duty displayed at Thiepval Section on the 21st October 1916. This N.C.O. during the reinforcing of a newly captured trench showed great ability in placing the men in their positions. During the whole time the trench was heavily shelled but regardless of danger he worked with a most cheery manner, which won the admiration of all ranks. His section throughout was the means of the line being held at a most critical time."

No. G/15036 Private Alfred Bailey, 11th Bn.
"For conspicuous bravery and devotion to duty displayed at Thiepval (Redoubt) Section on October 21st 1916. At a time when reinforcements were urgently needed, this man in spite of terrific shelling and the fact that he was wounded, volunteered to take the message back for reinforcements-he successfully carried this mission. Throughout the whole of the engagement he worked with splendid energy and disregard to danger and by his fine example inspired the men and won him the admiration of all ranks."

No. SD/32 A/Sergeant Thomas James Ball, 11th Bn.

"For great gallantry and devotion to duty displayed at Thiepval on October 21st 1916. This N.C.O. during the reinforcing of a newly captured trench, showed great ability in placing the men in their positions. During the whole time the trench was heavily shelled but regardless of danger he worked with a most cheery manner, which won him the admiration of all ranks. His action throughout was the means of the line being held at a most critical time."

No. SD/1655 Private Henry Scott Butler Belton,   12th Bn.   attd. 116th Infantry Brigade,

"For conspicuous gallantry and devotion to duty, between 17th and 22nd October 1916 near Thiepval. Private Belton showed great devotion to duty during the operations near the Schwaben Redoubt and during the attack on Stuff Trench. Hardly an hour elapsed without the cable communication between Brigade and Battalions being broken by shellfire. This man worked day and night throughout an almost continuous bombardment, and by his great devotion to duty, succeeded in mending the cables under very great difficulty. It was generally owing to the efforts of Private Belton and his fellow signallers that touch was kept with Battalions operating in the front line."

No. SD/400 Private James Bishop,   11th Bn.

"For great gallantry and unselfish devotion to duty at THEIPVAL REDOUBT on 21st October 1916.
Throughout the action, until finally severely wounded, this man displayed unselfish devotion to duty attending the wounded. He advanced into No man's land rendered First Aid to the men lying out there, and bringing many of them to a place of safety, working the whole time under intense fire.
Further, when the remainder of the Stretcher Bearers had become casualties, he organised stretcher-bearing parties among the minor casualties and German prisoners and undoubtedly prevented absolute confusion by his splendid example.

No words can really convey his untiring energy and resource, which won him the admiration of his officers and comrades."

No. SD/2872 Private William Thomas Cosstick, 13th Bn.

"For gallant conduct and devotion to duty displayed at the Schwaben Redoubt during the operations on the 21st October 1916. Private Cosstick, who was the Company runner, repeatedly went through heavy shell fire in order to carry messages from his Company Commander in the captured German trench to Battalion Headquarters. His gallant conduct enabled close touch to be kept between the assaulting Companies and Battalion Headquarters and facilitated the success of the operations. Throughout the 21st and 22nd, his courage was most conspicuous and he was an inspiring example to his comrades."

No. SD/503 L/Sergeant Richard Edward Cox, 11th Bn.

"For splendid devotion to duty and great courage displayed at Thiepval Section on October 21st 1916. Acting as Second in Command of his platoon, he most ably assisted his Platoon Commander by preserving a cool front. Soon after arriving in the position we had captured he went into "No Man's Land" with the first reinforcements, showing absolute contempt for the heavy shelling under which he moved. He himself brought back several wounded and rendered such first aid as he could and deposited them in a place of safety. During this action he was twice buried by shells bursting almost on him, but this did not deter him and throughout, by his cheerful demeanour, he helped considerably to preserve the morale of the men about him. His splendid example won the admiration of all ranks."

No. G/15623 Corporal Charles William Dybell, 11th Bn.

"For conspicuous gallantry and devotion to duty displayed at Thiepval (Redoubt) Section on October 21st 1916. This N.C.O. was in charge of a strong point with eight men in a newly captured trench. He established his party in the strongpoint under very trying circumstances, and owing to the enemy's intense shelling, his post was blown in on three occasions, causing several casualties, but in every instance, with great coolness and disregard to danger, he collected the remaining men and succeeded in hanging on in a most precarious position for 18 hours until relieved. His cheery manner and splendid devotion to duty was a fine example to his comrades."

No. SD/1885 Private George Waller Gibbs, 12th Bn. attd. 116th T.M. Battery,

"For great coolness and gallantry to duty at Thiepval Redoubt Section on 21st October 1916. Private Gibbs was in charge of a Stokes Gun during the operation. Both before and during the attack the enemy shelled our front line heavily, and shells fell all around the gun, which was set up in the trench in the open without cover of any kind. One shell completely buried the other man on duty with this gun, and clogged the barrel up with mud. Private Gibbs remained with his gun, cleaned it out, and continued firing in spite of heavy shell fire, although the enemy were getting into our front line."

No. SD/1341 L/Sergeant Ernest George Goble, 12th Bn.

"For conspicuous devotion to duty, displayed near the Schwaben Redoubt on 21st October 1916. During the attack on Stuff Trench, L/Sergeant Goble showed great coolness and ability under very heavy shell fire. Personally directing the consolidation of the newly captured line, he succeeded in constructing a highly serviceable front line trench. His steadiness and untiring energy under heavy shell fire were a fine example to the men."

No. SD/ 1766 L/Sergeant Arthur Wilfred Golden,   12th Bn.

"For conspicuous courage, and devotion to duty, displayed near the Schwaben Redoubt on 21st October 1916. During the attack on Stuff Trench, L/Sergeant Golden showed great coolness and ability under very heavy shellfire. Personally directing the consolidation of the newly captured line, he succeeded in constructing a highly serviceable front line trench. His steadiness and untiring energy under heavy shellfire were a fine example to the men.

No. SD/1056 Sergeant Russell John Hopkins, 11th Bn.

"For great coolness and gallantry displayed at Thiepval Section on 21st October 1916. This N.C.O. did splendid work in organising and getting the men together immediately the enemy trench was occupied. His coolness and utter disregard to danger were a splendid example to the men who rallied round him and owing to his brilliant action the work of consolidation was pushed on. He also did splendid work in attending the needs of the wounded and constantly went out into "No Man's land" and brought in wounded under intense shell fire and worked throughout the day and night in such a way that his example was partly the means of the garrison holding on their precious position during most critical moments."

No. SD/320 Private Herbert Edward Horton, 11th Bn.

"For great courage and devotion to duty displayed at Thiepval Section on 21st October 1916. As Stretcher-bearer this man worked throughout the battle with utter disregard to danger in that he brought in single-handed wounded from the open, being continuously exposed to heavy shell fire. He worked with great bravery and won for him the admiration of all his comrades."

No. G/17862 Private Walter Gyles Jenkinson, 12th Bn.

"For conspicuous devotion to duty displayed near the Schwaben Redoubt on the 17th October and the night 20/21st October 1916. Private Jenkinson, a Battalion runner, frequently carried messages from Battalion Headquarters to Company Headquarters during an almost continuous bombardment. He showed complete disregard for his personal safety and was a fine example to other men."

No. SD/1975 L/Sergeant George Henry Kibbey, 12th Bn.

"For conspicuous devotion to duty displayed at the Schwaben Redoubt from 17th to 22nd October 1916. This N.C.O. for some months has been in command of the Battalion bombers, and during the time the Battalion held the line in Schwaben redoubt, he displayed great energy and initiative in repelling the various bombing attacks of the enemy. L/Sergeant Kirby has been wounded twice but remained on duty on both occasions. This N.C.O. has already on one previous occasion been recommended for gallantry, but did not receive any award."

No. SD/879 Sergeant Frederick John Patrick, 11th Bn.

"For great courage and devotion to duty, displayed at Thiepval Section on October 21st 1916. When ordered to reinforce the newly captured line, this N.C.O. advanced across the open with his platoon immediately. Under an intense barrage from the enemy he brought his men into this trench when there was a great deal of confusion and disorder owing to the very severe casualties, and to the fact that the trench had been blown in along the entire length. By his coolness and courage he quickly rallied his men and grasped the situation, and placed the line in a good state of resistance. The fine example, which he showed until relieved many hours later, kept his men in a state of coolness and preparedness and won for him the admiration of all ranks."

No. SD/1123 L/Corporal Edward John Rich, 11th Bn.

"For great courage and devotion to duty displayed at Thiepval Section on 21st October 1916. This N.C.O. and Stretcher –bearer continued throughout the operations to carry wounded back from the front line through intense shelling and continuous M.G. fire and although himself wounded he carried on with his work until the battalion was relieved. His great cheerfulness and devotion to duty was a splendid example to the men who worked with him and his utter disregard to danger whilst in a very exposed area, won the admiration of all ranks."

No. SD/1547 Private Joseph Ripley, 12th Bn.

"For conspicuous devotion to duty displayed near the Schwaben Redoubt on 17th October 1916. Private Ripley who was a Company runner, performed valuable work in guiding his Company, collecting stragglers and taking messages under very heavy fire. He crossed and re-crossed a heavy barrage four times in all. His wonderful devotion to duty was a fine example to other men."

No. SD/3229 Sergeant Archibald Richard Sheppard, 13th Bn.

"For good leading and gallant conduct displayed at the Schwaben redoubt during the operations on 21st October 1916. This N.C.O. was in charge of a platoon which he led with great determination into the enemy trenches. He displayed great courage and initiative in holding and consolidating the position, and was an inspiring example to his men under very trying circumstances."

No. SD/36 Private William Edward Shearing, 11th Bn.

"For conspicuous gallantry and devotion to duty in the operations at Menin road on the 25/27th September. Throughout the intense shelling the Battalion experienced in the operations, he many times carried stretchers, rations and messages. He also undertook, when there was a shortage of water, to find water and carry it up to the battalion. He also helped the Signallers to run out their lines under heavy shelling. All this work he did voluntarily. He showed a notable contempt of danger, and an unflagging energy, and set an inspiring example to all that were with him."

No. SD/5137 Private Alfred Sherwood, 12th Bn.

"For conspicuous courage and devotion to duty, displayed near the Schwaben Redoubt from 17th to 22nd October 1916. Private Sherwood, a Stretcher-bearer, showed great courage and entire disregard for personal danger during the almost continuous bombardment of our lines. With great energy and devotion to duty he dressed the wounds of a very large number of men under very heavy shell fire."

No. G/15756 Private Frederick E. Shirley, 11th Bn.

"For great courage and devotion to duty displayed on the 21st October 1916. This man was a runner who carried messages to and fro from all parts of the trenches under most intense shell fire. At one time his rifle was blown out of his hands, but he carried the message to its destination, going through a terrible barrage. He worked in this way for 48 hours almost without rest or food, both before and during the attack. His cheery manner to all he met was most inspiring but his great asset was his great courage. When he knew his Company Commander wanted a message got to some place through an intense barrage, he repeatedly volunteered to go and he was more than once the means of getting valuable and urgent messages through when all other means of communication was destroyed."

No. SD/3463 Sergeant Charles Stanford, 13th Bn.

"For good leading and devotion to duty displayed at Schwaben Redoubt on 21st October 1916. During the operations on October 21st, this N.C.O. was in command of a platoon. With help of 2 men he cleared a strong bombing post held by the enemy, capturing 9 prisoners. Later in the day he was wounded but continued to command his platoon until he collapsed. He showed a fine example of courage and devotion to duty to his men. This N.C.O. has been previously recommended for the Military medal."

No. G/15759 Private Herbert S. Taylor, 11th Bn.

"For unselfish devotion to duty and conspicuous bravery, displayed at Thiepval (Redoubt) Section on October 21st 1916. Under intense shell fire this man carried a wounded officer lying in the open, although himself badly wounded. He succeeded in bringing him to a place of safety and procuring aid for him, refusing to be attended to himself until the Officer had had every possible attention. His action was carried out under extreme difficulties in that the ground he had to traverse was swept by Machine-gun fire and a terrible barrage was being put up by the enemy. His great courage inspired all his comrades and won for him their admiration."

No. SD/3029 L/Corporal Herbert George Thompsett, 13th Bn.

"For gallant conduct and devotion to duty, displayed at the Schwaben Redoubt during the operations on 21/10/16. This N.C.O. was in charge of a Lewis Gun team of one of the assaulting Companies. When in the act of entering the enemy trench 4 of his team were struck down. With great coolness and gallantry, L/Corporal Thompsett seized the gun and with the aid of one man kept the gun in action until relieved on the night of 22nd/23rd. he displayed great initiative and gallantry and was an inspiring example to his comrades."

No. SD/3475 Private Ronald William Thorns, 13th Bn.

"For gallant conduct and devotion to duty, displayed at Schwaben Redoubt. During the attack on Stuff Trench on October 21st, Private Thorns, who was a Company runner, repeatedly carried messages between the captured position and Battalion Headquarters, frequently under heavy artillery fire. He displayed great courage and devotion to duty, and was an inspiring example to his comrades."

No. SD/751 A/Sergeant Henry Sydney Wilkinson, 11th Bn.

"For great coolness and gallantry displayed at Thiepval Section on October 21st 1916. This N.C.O. did splendid work in organising and getting the men together immediately the enemy trench was occupied. His coolness and utter disregard for danger was a splendid example to the men who rallied round him and owing to his brilliant action the work of consolidating pushed on. He also did splendid work in attending the needs of the wounded and constantly went into "No Man's Land" and brought in wounded under intense shell fire and worked throughout the day and night in such a manner that his example was partly the means of the garrison holding on their precious position during most critical moments."

No. G/16259 Private Charles Oswald Williams, 12th Bn.

"For devotion to duty. Private Williams acted as Headquarters runner during the occupation o Schwaben Redoubt by this Battalion, from 17th to 22nd October 1916. He showed a noticeable disregard for personal danger on many occasions and carried messages from Headquarters to the front line twice through a very heavy barrage."

No. G/15655 Private Albert Windebank, 13th Bn.

"During the attack on Stuff trench on October 21st Private Windebank was a Company runner. He carried messages repeatedly under a heavy artillery fire between the captured enemy line and battalion Headquarters in spite of the fact that he was wounded early in the day. He displayed great gallantry and devotion to duty."

No. SD/1510 Private Arthur S. Woollam, 12th Bn.

"For conspicuous courage and devotion to duty displayed near the Schwaben Redoubt from 17th to 22nd October 1916. Private Woollam, a stretcher-bearer, showed great courage and entire disregard for personal danger during the almost continuous bombardment of our lines. With great energy and devotion to duty, he dressed the wounds of a very large number of men under very heavy shell fire."

The following men of the Royal Sussex Regiment have been awarded a Bar to their Military Medal :-

No. SD/3340 Private Richard Emsley, M.M.   13th Bn.

For conspicuous gallantry and untiring devotion to duty displayed at Schwaben Redoubt during operations of 21st October, 1916. Private Emsley, who was a stretcher bearer, worked untiringly, frequently under heavy shell fire, removing wounded in the area behind the captured German line. He then went to the captured position and brought more wounded away. Seeing that the numbers were more than the regimental stretcher bearers could cope with, he personally went to the advance dressing station and brought R.A.M.C. bearers back. He showed them where the wounded were and it was largely owing to his devotion to duty that when this battalion was relieved on the night of the 22nd, all wounded had been evacuated from the captured trench. He continued to work until completely exhausted, and was a striking example of devotion to duty to his comrades.

No. 322 Private Joseph Wilson, M.M.   7th Bn.

Hove Soldier's Gallantry

The gallantry or Private R. Emsley, who has been awarded a Bar to his Military Medal, has been reported by the Town Clerk of Hove to the Park, Baths and Cemetery Committee. Private Emsley, who was one of the Cemetery workmen, joined the Army on 14th January, 1915, and the Bar has been awarded him for conspicuous gallantry and untiring devotion to duty displayed at Schwaben Redoubt during operations of 21st October, 1916. According to the Special Brigade Order, Private Emsley, who was a stretcher bearer, worked untiringly, frequently under heavy shell fire, removing wounded in the area behind the captured German line. He then went to the captured position and brought more wounded away. Seeing that the numbers were more than the regimental stretcher bearers could cope with, he personally went to the advance dressing station and brought R.A.M.C. bearers back.

He showed them where the wounded were and it was largely owing to his devotion to duty that when this battalion was relieved on the night of the 22nd, all wounded had been evacuated from the captured trench. He continued to work until completely exhausted, and was a striking example of devotion to duty to his comrades. He has been awarded the Military Medal for a similar act of gallantry.

Wednesday January 10th 1917

Presentation to Crowborough D.C.M. Winner

Stirring scenes were witnessed last night at the Crowborough Liberal Club, where a large company assembled to do honour to Private Albert Bailey (2424), Royal Sussex Regiment, who has recently been awarded the Distinguished Conduct Medal for gallantry in the field. Private Bailey was a Crowborough "boy", and won the D.C.M. in connection with the brilliant British advance between Pozieres and Thiepval, and in direct line with Ovilliers, and for subsequent good work in the field.
A wounded comrade had been lying in "No Man's Land" for five days, and when there was a call for volunteers to try and effect his rescue, Bailey and three comrades, Sergeant Chatfield (Uckfield) and Privates A. Dray and E. Cozens (Crowborough), proceeded to his assistance. Notwithstanding the heavy shelling of the position by the enemy, Private Bailey and his companions brought the stricken man of the Norfolk Regiment into safety and carried him two miles to the rear.
Bailey's name appeared in the New Year list, and the Committee of the Crowborough Liberal Club - of which the D.C.M. is a member - at once organised a testimonial.

Saturday January 13th 1917

Military Medal awarded to Heathfield and Pevensey Men

Despatch carrying under heavy fire

Another Heathfield man has been awarded the Military Medal. Private George Walter Gibbs, the elder son of the late Mr. George Walter Gibbs, and Mrs. Gibbs, of Providence Cottages, Broad Oak, Heathfield, has received the honour for bravery and devotion to duty on the field of battle. He is only 28 years of age, and is single. He enlisted in the Royal Sussex Regiment ("Lowther's Own") in November, 1914, and after a lengthy training went to France on March 4th, 1916. He was attached to a Trench Mortar Battery. He has seen some exciting times and hard fighting – he participated in the "Big Push" of July – and has had many narrow escapes. He was wounded in October, but remained in France to recuperate. Previously to enlistment he was employed as a platelayer, on the London, Brighton and South Coast Railway at Heathfield. His younger brother, Bombardier Frederick William Gibbs, who is 23 years of age, belongs to the Royal Garrison Artillery, and has been in France for 12 months. He also enlisted in October, 1914.

Private W.T. Cosstick : Pevensey Bay

Private William T. Cosstick, a sniper in the Royal Sussex Regiment, has written to his parents at Pevensey Bay to the effect that he has been awarded the Military Medal. The action which gained Private Cosstick this distinction was that after the capture of a German trench he took a message to the headquarters, in doing so he was passing through machine-gun fire all the time. He has received the ribbon. Private Cosstick is the only son of Mr. and Mrs. Samuel Cossick, and is thirty years of age. Previously to joining "Lowther's Own" two years ago he was working as a cab-driver for Mr. W.J. Bainbridge, of Pevensey Bay. He is, up to present the only volunteer from Pevensey Bay who has not been wounded since he has been in France.

Wednesday January 24th 1917

M.C. Presentation

The Military Cross was presented by His Majesty the King at Buckingham Palace among others to :-

Lieutenant (T/Capt.) M. Wallington, who was awarded the Military Cross in the King's Birthday Honours in June 1916.

Saturday January 27th 1917

Gallant Sussex Officer's reward

It was officially announced last night that the King has awarded the Military Cross to :-

Temp. 2nd Lieutenant Edmund Charles Blunden, 11th Bn. Royal Sussex Regiment,

For conspicuous gallantry in action. He displayed great courage and determination when in charge of a carrying party under heavy fire. He has previously done fine work.

Wednesday February 7th 1917

Sussex Officer Decorated

Among the officers who has the honour of being received by the King on Monday was Second Lieutenant Thomas Chad, Royal Sussex Regiment, son of Mr. and Mrs. G. Chad, of West Chiltington, who was decorated with the Military Cross. Second Lieutenant Chad has been home on a fortnight's leave.

Friday February 9th 1917

Mentioned in Dispatches

The list of these mentioned in the appendix to the dispatch from Lieutenant-General the Hon. J.C. Smuts, dealing with the operations in East Africa, contains the name of No. 9501 Sapper C. Turner, Royal Sussex Regiment, who has been engaged in the Signal Service.

Wednesday February 14th 1917

Royal Sussex Men and acts that won the D.C.M.

The following recipients of Distinguished Conduct Medals have previously been announced, but not the official records of the gallant deeds for which they were decorated. These appeared in a supplement to the *"London Gazette"* issued last night:-

No. 2424 Private A. Bailey, 5th Bn. Royal Sussex Regiment,

For conspicuous gallantry and devotion to duty. He has at all times under fire set a splendid example of courage and determination, and has always volunteered for the most dangerous work to be done.

No. 5863 C.S.M. W, Humphrey, 2nd Bn. Royal Sussex Regiment,

For conspicuous gallantry in action. He rendered invaluable services in organising parties for carrying up bombs, ammunition, etc. Later, he sent in information.
No. 9815 Corporal (A/Sergeant) F.G. Sawyer, 2nd Bn. Royal Sussex Regiment,

For conspicuous gallantry and devotion to duty. He has performed consistent good work throughout the campaign, and has at all times under fire set a splendid example.

No. 7646 Sergeant F.G.J. Spicer, 2nd Bn. Royal Sussex Regiment,
For conspicuous gallantry and devotion to duty. He has performed consistent good work throughout the campaign, and has at all times set a splendid example of courage and determination. He was wounded.

No. 3355 Drummer E.G.C. Trussler, 9th Bn. Royal Sussex Regiment, attd. M.G. Coy.

For conspicuous gallantry and devotion to duty. He has rendered most valuable services as a stretcher-bearer, and has at all times set a splendid example of courage and determination.

No. 16925 Sergeant (A/C.Q.M.S.) W. Webb, 2nd Bn. Royal Sussex Regiment, attd. M.G. Coy.

For conspicuous gallantry and devotion to duty. He has performed consistent good work throughout the campaign with the Machine Gun Section, and has at all times set a splendid example.

A Lewes Hero

A brilliant member of the Sussex Regiment in France is A/Co. Quartermaster-Sergeant W.T. Webb, youngest son of Warder S. Webb, of H.M. Prison, who resides at 2, Lancaster Street, Lewes. Q.M.S. Webb has gained rapid promotion, and has now won the Distinguished Conduct Medal.

The young non-com enlisted in the county regiment at the age of 19, and went to France with the first contingent in 1914. He had reached the rank of lance-corporal in less than six months, and upon going to France was promoted to the next rank. His promotion to sergeant rapidly followed and now he is company Q.M.S. attached to the Machine Gun Corps.

Our congratulations to the gallant soldier and to the family which has brought yet another war honour to the county town.

Friday February 16th 1917

More Honours for local men

The following are among the Officers and men upon whom decorations and medals have been awarded by Allied Powers for distinguished services rendered during the course of the campaign :-

Conferred by the Emperor of Russia

Order of St. Anne 2nd Class (With Swords)

Major (T/Colonel) John Bartholomew Wroughton, C.M.G., Royal Sussex Regiment,

Conferred by the King of Serbia

Gold Medal

No. 695 Lance-Corporal (A/Sergeant) Wilfred Arthur Budd, 4th Bn. Royal Sussex Regiment,

Silver Medal

No. 1349 Private William Knapp, 4th Bn. Royal Sussex Regiment,

Tuesday February 20th 1917

Military Medals for members of the Royal Sussex Regiment

His Majesty the King has graciously pleased to award the Military Medal for bravery in the field to the undermentioned non-commissioned Officers and men of the Royal Sussex Regiment :-

No. SD/138 Sergeant Walter Augustus Ashford, 11th Bn.
No. SD/307 Private Herbert Edward Fishenden, 11th Bn.
No. SD/141 Private William H. Hayward, 7th Bn.
No. SD/1084 Lance-Corporal John Curtis Perry, 11th Bn.

 No. SD/1171 Lance-Corporal George Alfred Sargent, 11th Bn.

No. SD/3503 Lance-Corporal William Herbert S. Waldron, 13th Bn.

 No. SD/373 Private P. Harry L. Whitton, 11th Bn.

No. 6625 Private H. Aungier, Royal Sussex Regiment, to whom the award of a Military Medal was notified in the "*London Gazette*" on the 21st September 1916, has been granted a Bar.

Tuesday February 27th 1917

"Mentioned" for Good Work

Those whose names have been brought to the notice of the Secretary of state for war for valuable services rendered in connection with the war include the following :-

Major J.R. Ashby, Royal Sussex Regiment,
Major Robert A. Finlayson, C.M.G., Royal Sussex Regiment,
Captain (T/Mjr.) H.E. Mathews, Royal Sussex Regiment,
No. L/4369 R.S.M. J.R. Boniface, Royal Sussex Regiment,
No. G/3416 Sergeant W.H. Holman, Royal Sussex Regiment,
2nd Lieutenant (T/Mjr.) A. Corbett, Sussex Yeomanry,

Honoured Sussex Officers

The list of officers whose names have been brought to the notice of the Secretary of State for War for valuable service in connection with the war includes Lieutenant-Colonel and Hon. Colonel Somers Clarke, of Brighton, whose distinction will give pleasure to many residents in the county. Colonel Somers Clarke, it may be recalled, put in a lot of hard and successful work in the training of the battalion of the Royal Sussex Regiment under his command. To his great disappointment he was not allowed, for medical reasons, to accompany his men to the front, being consequently transferred to the Territorial Force Reserve. He has a long and honourable record of service with the Volunteers and the Territorial Force.
The recognition of the valuable services rendered in connection with the war by Lieutenant-Colonel E.H.J.D. Mostyn (deceased) has given cause for much satisfaction in the Arundel district, and will also be received with feelings of pride by the officers and men who served under the deceased officer. Colonel Mostyn's work for the Territorials dated back to the inauguration of the Force, and before that

he had a prominent place in the local Volunteers. During the present war and right up to the time of his death he laboured unceasingly for the honour and efficiency of the Royal Sussex Regiment. All his sons, with the exception of the youngest, who is not of military age, are serving with the colours.

Monday March 5th 1917

Military Cross Winner

2nd Lieutenant (T/Lt.) Elmer Peter Roberts, D.C.M. Royal Sussex Regiment & No. 3. Sqdn. R.F.C.

For conspicuous gallantry in action. He three times dispersed an enemy working party with bombs and machine-gun fire from a height of 1000 ft. On another occasion he shot down an enemy machine. He has shown great determination on many occasions in taking photographs under most difficult condition. (D.C.M. gazetted 14/01/16 as No. 1689 Cpl. E.P. Roberts, R.F.C.)

Saturday March 10th 1917

Sussex Officers' Honours

Major (T/Brigadier-General) William Lushington Osborn, D.S.O., Royal Sussex Regiment is among the Officers upon whom the King of Montenegro has conferred the Order of Dunilo, 3rd Class, which decoration King George has given his officers unrestricted permission to wear.
Similar permission has been granted to Lieutenant (T/Captain) Stuart, Royal Sussex Regiment, who has had conferred on him by the Sultan of Egypt the Order of the Nile 4th Class.

Monday March 12th 1917

Awards For Gallantry

The award of the Meritorious Service Medal to two members of the Royal Sussex Regiment was announced last night, the award is for gallantry and the circumstances are described as follows :-

No. 4673 Sergeant P. Evershed 3rd Bn.

"During live grenade throwing instruction one of the class dropped his bomb. Sergeant Evershed immediately picked it up and threw it over the parapet. He had every opportunity of escaping danger himself and by his unselfish action probably saved the lives of several men who were unable to move. " Newhaven, 17th October,1916.

No. 4/3416 Sergeant W.H. Holman 4th Bn.

"During live grenade instruction a grenade failed to clear the parapet. In attempting to get to the grenade the officer in charge slipped and fell short of it. Sergeant Holman, although under cover of the traverse, immediately dashed forward, managed to pick up the grenade and threw it away, thereby averting what would have been a most serious accident." Broadwater Forest, 30th November, 1916.

Tuesday March 20th 1917

Wisborough Green Soldier wins Military Medal

For "conspicuous gallantry and leadership" during a daylight raid on the enemy's trenches near Vierstraat (Belgium) on the 24th February, the Military Medal has been conferred on Sergeant F.O. Crawford, of the Sussex Yeomanry, at present attached to the Queen's (Royal West Surrey) Regiment.

The formal presentation of this coveted distinction was made before the whole battalion, but the actual presentation will take place when the gallant young soldier returns to England, the certificate having already been received by Sergeant Crawford's parents.

The raid was made under a terrific bombardment of shot and shell. Two of the captains were killed outright as they went over the parapet, but, fearless of danger, Sergeant Crawford pushed ahead, and led his men so effectively that more than one hundred prisoners were captured, and many trophies of the incidents were secured. Sergeant Crawford was fortunate enough to escape without even so much as a scratch.

Tuesday March 27th 1917

Gallant Sussex Men

The latest list of awards for acts of gallantry and devotion to duty in the field includes the following :-

D.C.M.

No. SD/2219 C.S.M. William George Aukett, 12th Bn. Royal Sussex Regiment,

For conspicuous gallantry and devotion to duty. He was the first man to enter an enemy mine crater, and immediately collected some men to rescue the wounded. He also organised parties to consolidate and hold the far lip of the crater.

M.M.

No. G/15414 A/Corporal Alfred G.H. Garton, 12th Bn. Royal Sussex Regiment,
No. G/20779 Sergeant Alfred W. Linford, 12th Bn. Royal Sussex Regiment,

Wednesday April 4th 1917

Gallant Sussex Man

The business of the Brighton Police Court was suspended yesterday to allow the Mayor (Alderman Carden) to perform a pleasant ceremony. On behalf of the Magistrates, he presented to Private F. Burden, of, 275, Queen's Park Road, Brighton, a native of Ticehurst, the Military Medal gained as the result of his gallant conduct at the battle of Loos. The recipient of the honour was present in Court, with his wife, and he was wearing three wound stripes.

In presenting the medal to Private Burden, the Mayor said the recipient was born at Ticehurst. In 1912 he went to Canada, prior to which he had served three years in the 2nd Royal Sussex Regiment. Recalled from Canada as a Reservist when war broke out, he rejoined his old regiment at Chichester in September, 1914. Proceeding to the front, he went through all the fighting on the Aisne in the early part of the war.

During that time he was wounded three times, first at Ypres, when he was mentioned in dispatches, secondly at Givenchy, and the third time, in September, 1915, at Loos.

For his gallantry on this occasion he was awarded the Military Medal, which he was now asked to present to him. He went back to France again, but was invalided out suffering from shell shock October last. He had now, however, been discharged from the service, and only came out of hospital on the 12th March. The deed for which the medal was awarded, the Mayor added, was as follows : While advancing towards the enemy trenches at the Battle of Loos, with a bombing party, he was wounded in both feet.

When he saw his sergeant fall, he at once bound up his feet and took charge of the men, rallying them, and succeeding finally in entering the enemy trenches, which he held until reinforcements arrived. The Mayor thought everyone would agree with him that this was a record that anyone might be proud, and he congratulated Mr. Burden on possessing it. The war, he added, meant tremendous changes for the continent of Europe, and anyone who had taken part in it had done something to be proud of.

Monday April 16th 1917

Gallant Lewes Man Decorated

An interesting ceremony took place on the County Hall steps, Lewes, yesterday when Corporal W.G. Robins, a native of the county town, was decorated with the Russian Cross of the Order of St. George, 4th Class, by Lieutenant-Colonel C. Campbell, C.I.E. The Lewes Company Sussex Volunteer Regiment, under Captain Macartney, the local Cadet Company of the Sussex Yeomanry, under Captain Lintott, headed by the Royal Defence Corps. Band, and a crowd of towns people, were present to celebrate the occasion. Colonel Campbell, in the course of his address, said he was very glad to be asked to make an award to a comrade, and the finest award a soldier could receive was the reward for gallantry when on active service. He congratulated Corporal Robins on receiving this decoration granted by their Ally, Russia. Corporal Robins always intended to be a soldier, for 20 years ago he joined the Cinque Ports Volunteer Battalion of the Royal Sussex Regiment. When this great war came he was ready and went out to France to fight in the land of our firmest and warmest Ally. There he had his opportunity, and during the fighting he was able to show what he was worth. He only did his best, but it was for others to judge, and they judged his best as very good. "So I now," continued the Colonel, "pin the decoration on him, and congratulate him most heartily and wish him all good luck in the future."
Corporal Robins joined "D" Company of the Cinque Ports Battalion Royal Sussex Regiment in 1897. He spend about one year and two months in France and was discharged at the termination of the period of engagement with an exemplary character. He was recommended for the D.C.M. and was awarded the Russian Cross of St. George. He displayed great courage at the Neuve Chapelle Battle on 9th May, 1915, in stretcher work, going out under heavy fire and bringing in the wounded.

Wednesday April 18th 1917

Award of the D.S.O.

His Majesty the King has been graciously pleased to approve the appointment of the undermentioned Officer to be a Companion of the Distinguished Service Order, in recognition of his gallantry and devotion to duty in the field.

Gwynne, Roland Vaughan, T/Major, Sussex Yeomanry, attd. Royal West Surrey Regiment,

For conspicuous gallantry and judgement in commanding and carrying out a daylight raid with his battalion. His personal example of courage and coolness was of great value throughout the operation. He personally went over to the enemy lines and supervised. He was wounded.

Military Medals for Royal Sussex Men

N.C.O. receives a Bar

The King has been pleased to approve of the award of a Bar to the Military Medal to the undermentioned N.C.O.

No. 5638 Lance-Corporal A.E. Madgwick, M.M. 2nd Bn. Royal Sussex Regiment,

Awarded Military Medal

No. G/15104 Private Thomas Barfield, 12th Bn. Royal Sussex Regiment,
No. SD/1178 Lance-Corporal Paul A. Route, 11th Bn. Royal Sussex Regiment,

Thursday April 26th 1917

Military Cross for Worthing Officer

Mr. Andrew Denyer, of Worthing, received news from an official source, yesterday, that his son, Lieutenant Denyer, Royal Sussex Regiment, has been awarded the Military Cross. Lieutenant Denyer has not been long at the front. He was a very keen member and a platoon commander of the local Company of Volunteers before joining the Army, and his training there stood him in good stead, as he speedily received a commission. *(London Gazette 26th May, shows his regiment as Yorks. & Lancs.)*

T/2nd Lieutenant Augustus Andrew Denyer, Yorks. and Lancs. Regiment,

For conspicuous gallantry and devotion to duty. In spite of being subjected to the most hostile bombardment, he maintained his position, and throughout set a splendid example to his men.

Wednesday May 2nd 1917

French awards for British Soldiers

The following are among the decorations and medals awarded by the President of the French Republic at various dates to the British Forces for distinguished services rendered during the course of the campaign. The King has given unrestricted permission in all cases to wear the decorations and medals in question :-

Croix de Guerre

No. 6035 A/Sergeant James Chapman Halley, 2nd Bn. Royal Sussex Regiment,

Medaille Militaire

No. 1212 Private James Sidney Dale, 12th Bn. Royal Sussex Regiment,

For gallantry and devotion to duty. At Schwaben Redoubt on the night of 28-29th October 1916, Private Dale under heavy shellfire succeeded in repairing the telephone line between Battalion and Company headquarters.
This man has done excellent work as a linesman on numerous occasions, notably 25-26th October and 31st October, 1st November 1916, at the River Section, Thiepval.

No. 806 Sergeant Frank Gilbert Holland, 2nd Bn. Royal Sussex Regiment,

Thursday May 3rd 1917

Three dead V.C. Heroes

The King presents decorations to next of kin.

The King travelled from Windsor yesterday and held an investiture at Buckingham Palace. His Majesty presented a Victoria Cross to the next of kin of three dead heroes, one being Sergeant-Major Carter.

Sergeant-Major Carter, Royal Sussex Regiment, won the decoration by penetrating enemy trenches with a small party. He personally captured a machine-gun and shot the gunner with his revolver, and, finally, was mortally wounded after rescuing other wounded men.

Tuesday May 8th 1917

M.M. for Sussex N.C.O.

The award of the Military Medal is conferred upon :-

No. 71 Sergeant J. Hayes, 7th Bn. Royal Sussex Regiment,

For conspicuous bravery in bringing in nine wounded men and one officer under very heavy shell fire.

Wednesday May 9th 1917

Medal for Fishersgate Man

In a letter to his wife at 15, William St. Fishersgate, Corporal G. Rossetter, Royal Sussex Regiment (Pioneers), stated that he had been presented with the Military Medal Ribbon, and enclosed the parchment which was presented with the ribbon. The wording on the parchment is as follows :-

"I have read with great pleasure the Report of your Regimental Commander and Brigade Commander regarding your gallant conduct and devotion to duty in the field on 17th February 1917 to 21st February 1917 during operations against Boon Ravine." - R.P. Lee, Major-General commanding Division.

Saturday May 12th 1917

Gallant Shoreham Man

It is interesting to note that Corporal G. Rossetter, Royal Sussex Regiment, of Fishersgate, who has won the Military Medal, is a Shoreham man, being the third son of Mr. J. Rossetter, Ham Road, Shoreham. For seven years he was at the Shoreham Post Office and he played football for Shoreham. He enlisted a month after the outbreak of war and after training at Colchester and Salisbury Plain, left for France in July, 1915. He is 26 years of age. He has a brother, John, who has seen 21 years' service in the Royal Navy and has been a warrant officer during the past eight years. He is now stationed at

Gibraltar and was on H.M.S. "Majestic" when that vessel was torpedoed at the Dardenelles in May, 1915. A third brother, Charles, in now in France with the Royal Engineers.

Sussex Officer and Private Decorated

The Military Cross has been awarded to Lieutenant (T/Captain) Donald Campbell Rutter, Royal Sussex Regiment, Special Reserves, and 43rd Squadron R.F.C.,
For conspicuous gallantry and devotion to duty. He completed a valuable reconnaissance alone, at very low altitude, and in the face of heavy fire, which riddled his machine. On another occasion, he, single-handed, succeeded in driving off three hostile machines.

The Military Medal has been awarded to No. 9501 Private C. Turner, 1st Bn. Royal Sussex Regiment, attached "Z" Divisional Signalling Company.

"London Gazette" Tuesday May 15th 1917

The following despatch has been received by the Secretary of State for War from Field-Marshal Sir Douglas Haig, G.C.B., Commander-in-Chief of the British Armies in France.
General Headquarters,
9th April, 1917

Sir,—I have the honour to submit a list of names of those officers, ladies, non-commissioned officers, and men, serving, or who have served, under my command, whose distinguished and gallant services and devotion to duty I consider deserving of special mention.

I have the honour to be,
Sir,
Your obedient Servant,

D. HAIG,
Field-Marshal,
Commander-in-Chief, The British
Armies in France.

STAFF

Maj. J. S., Cameron, D.S.O., Royal Sussex Regiment,
Maj. (temp. Brig.-Gen.) A. E. Glasgow, D.S.O., Royal Sussex Regiment,
Maj. E. H. Langham T. D., Royal Sussex Regiment, (Lt. Res. of Off.)
Capt. E. H. Preston, M.C., Royal Sussex Regiment,
Bt. Lt.-Col. (temp. Col.) J. B. Wroughton, C.M.G., Royal Sussex Regiment,

Tuesday May 15th 1917

Late Captain A.D. Foster M.C.

Captain Alfred David Foster, M.C., Royal Sussex Regiment, who fell in action on 5th May, was the only child of Mrs. Foster, 1a, Nevill Park, Tunbridge Wells. He attained company rank in July last, having been given his second star in December, 1915. His Military Cross was won by directing the work of his platoon in opening up communications across "No Man's Land" under heavy fire. Wounded early in the day, he refused to leave his post till ordered back. He was 24 years of age.

Wednesday May 16th 1917

Sussex Officers Honourably Mentioned

The list of honourably mentioned soldiers submitted by Sir Douglas Haig under date 9th April and officially published last night contains the following who are in the Royal Sussex Regiment :-

Staff

Captain M.T. Turner,
Lieutenant (T/Captain) M. Wallington, M.C.,
Brevet Lieutenant-Colonel (T/Col.) J.B. Wroughton, C.M.G.,

Military Medal for Hove Man

Mrs. Bunker, Clarendon Road, Hove, has just received the gratifying news that her son, Private Jack Bunker, Royal Sussex Regiment, (Pioneers) has been presented with the Military Medal.
 The following is a copy of the wording on the parchment signed by the General Commanding his Division, which was presented to him with the ribbon:-

I have read with great pleasure the report of your Regimental Commander regarding your gallant conduct and devotion to duty in the field on 10th March, 1917, in front of Arles.
Private Bunker joined up in September, 1914, and was previously employed at Messrs. Smith and Son's Bookstall at Hove Station.

A Russian Decoration

Among the Russian Decorations awarded in July, 1916 to the British Forces for distinguished services rendered during the course of the campaign was the medal of St. George, first class, awarded to No. 10223 Sergeant Henry Rose, East Kent Regiment, (late Royal Sussex Regiment).

Thursday May 17th 1917

Glowing tribute to the Royal Sussex Regiment

BRITISH GENERAL TELLS THE STORY OF THEIR HEROISM

A striking tribute to the fighting qualities of the men of Sussex is paid by a British general holding high command on the Western front. Interviewed in Paris by a Press correspondent, he said :

The people at home do not seem to realise, as they ought to, the splendid work of the men of the New Armies, and the way in which they have stood every test imposed on them in the rough school of war. At various stages of very difficult operations I have had under my command men belonging to the Royal

Sussex Regiment, and I would not ask for better men. Their work has been beyond all praise. They have fought with the steadiness of veterans. No odds, however great, have deterred them, and they have on occasions wrested victory from what seemed certain defeat. At times they have had to hold positions at critical stages against a greatly superior foe supported by stronger gun-power.

On every occasion when I have put my trust in the men of the south they have proved worthy of it. They have won the confidence and the praise, not only of our own commanders, but of the French, and even the Germans have been forced to pay grudging tribute to their matchless valour.

I have in mind one particularly critical stage of difficult operations. Things had taken a bad turn for us, owing to the failure of a section of our line to make headway equal to that made in other directions and anticipated by headquarters. The one hope of easing the position lay in a dashing attack by our men at a point where the enemy least expected it. For this task I selected the Sussex men, who happened to be in reserve at that time. The operation I entrusted to them was in the nature of a forlorn hope-and it was the highest possible compliment we could pay to the Sussex men to select them for it.

They had had several days of hard fighting, and might well have asked to be excused the honour done them, but they responded cheerfully to the call made on them and advanced against the enemy with a steadiness that nothing could prevail against.

They fought their way in the teeth of the stoutest opposition right into the enemy's first line. From there they fought their way stubbornly inch by inch-foot by foot-into the second line. Thence they swung to the right and delivered a furious attack on fresh enemy troops massing for a new onslaught on our line at a point where the enemy counted on rolling it up and robbing us of the fruits of our hardly won victory in the centre. Before the impetuous onslaught of the Sussex the enemy gave way. Fresh troops were hurried up and every available enemy gun was concentrated on that narrow front with the object of staying the advance of the Sussex men. The latter rushed irresistibly onward bearing down on all opposition, and threatening the enemy line of retreat with such effect that he whole German line on a wide frontage was forced to give way, after withstanding for two days, attacks delivered by strong forces of ours. Our line advanced then at every point, and the victory was complete. That it was so entirely to the splendid response which the Sussex lads had made to the call sent to them.

On another occasion the enemy tried to drive a wedge into our line at a dangerous salient. They carried some trench elements by surprise, and were making headway in other directions, when they struck the Sussex men. The latter were greatly outnumbered, and might well have been pardoned had they given way-but that is not the practice of the Sussex men.

They held their ground in face of every assault, and finally dashed from their trenches, routing the foe with bayonet and driving them back to their own lines. For three days more the men of Sussex held that position against all comers : when relieved they were thanked by the Divisional Commander.

Tuesday May 22nd 1917

Sussex recipients of French Decorations

The following are among a list of decorations and medals presented by the President of the French Republic to British Forces for distinguished service during the present campaign to Officers and N.C.O.'s of the Royal Sussex Regiment :-

Croix de Guerre

Lieutenant-Colonel Hugh Stirling Ashworth,   R. P.   R.of O.

No. 320294 Lance-Corporal Willie Orme Collis, 16th Bn.

Medaille Militaire

No. 320007 R.S.M. Bernard James Webber, 16th Bn.

Wednesday May23rd 1917

Mentioned in Dispatches

Sir Douglas Haig has submitted the names of the following officers, N.C.O.'s and men of the Royal Sussex Regiment as deserving of special mention :-

Major (A/ Lt-Col.) Frederick William Bagnall Willett, D.S.O.
No. 9368 Sergeant W.T. Harris,
No. 10023 Sergeant S. Nelson,
No. 5949 Private (A/Sergeant) A. Love,
No. 828 Private (A/Sergeant) A.V. Coppard,
Lieutenant (T/Captain) (A/Lt-Col.) Alfred John Sansom,
2nd Lieutenant E.W. Williams,
Quartermaster and Hon. Lieutenant Harry Plews,
No. 1461 Corporal (L/Sgt.) A. Noakes,
No. 891 Sergeant W.H. Budgen,
No. 4017 Private P.W. Bridger,
T/ Captain Noel H. Hampton,
T/Captain Henry Edward Stewart, 8th Bn.
T/Lieutenant Walter Hubert Baddeley,
T/ 2nd Lieutenant John Marsland,
T/Quartermaster and Hon. Lieutenant Joseph Solomon,

No. 120 Sergeant A. Lee,

No. G/1379 Corporal P.R. Bussell,
No. G/2652 Sergeant J.W. Crane,
No. SR/399 Sergeant E. Rose,
No. G/2795 Corporal G.A. Stapley,
T/Captain George Meredyth Shackel,
No. 3341 Corporal (A/ L/Sgt.) S. Stillwell,
T/Major William Colsey Millward,
T/Lieutenant George Maycock,
T/2nd Lieutenant (A/Lt.) F.G. Armitage,
T/2nd Lieutenant (A/Capt.) P.F. Drew,
T/2nd Lieutenant J.C. Webber,
T/Quartermaster and Hon. Lieutenant Basil Fitzroy Swain,
T/2nd Lieutenant W.P. Ratcliff,
No. 3 Regimental Quartermaster-Sergeant A.R. Secrett,
T/Lieutenant Herbert Edward Jones,

T/2nd Lieutenant (A/Capt.) Edward Belton Wheatley,
2nd Lieutenant William Harry Ferguson,
T/Mjr. Frank Robert Leith,

Major (Acting Lieutenant-Colonel) F.W.B. Willett, D.S.O., is one of the best known officers of the Royal Sussex Regiment. He is the son of the Rev. Frederic Willett and Mrs. Willett, formerly of Scaynes Hill and Seaford, and now residing at Haywards Heath, and has a record of more than 20 years' continuous service in the Royal Sussex. He was in the South African War with the 1st Battalion, and has both medals for that campaign, the Queen's Medal having no fewer than six clasps.
Afterwards he was in India, and, being invalided home, joined the 2nd Battalion and did depot duty at Chichester. Subsequently he was in Crete and Belfast (at the time of the riots), while when war broke out he was Adjutant of the 3rd Royal Sussex. He did a wonderful amount of training work at Dover and Newhaven to fit men for the Front, and then himself joined the 2nd Battalion there, and for a time was Acting Lieutenant-Colonel in command. He won his D.S.O. "for gallant and distinguished conduct in the field" at the Battle of Loos. Major Willett married in 1904, Miss Kathleen Megaw, eldest daughter of the late Mr. Megaw, of Great Walstead, Lindfield.

Lieutenant-Colonel William Colsey Millward, Royal Sussex Regiment, is a son of Mr. Arthur Millward, the old Worcestershire cricketer. Joining the Army a Private after the outbreak of hostilities, he obtained his commission in November, 1914, and went to France, where he has received his other promotions.
He was gazetted Acting Lieutenant-Colonel a few days ago, when a reference to his remarkable military career appeared in the *Sussex Daily News*.
Captain George Meredyth Shackel is the eldest son of Dr. and Mrs. Shackel, of Enleigh, Mayfield. He was gazetted Second Lieutenant in August, 1914, and was wounded in the head at the Battle of Loos. In June, 1916, he was promoted to Captain. He was wounded a second time this month.

Second Lieutenant F.G. Armitage was gazetted Acting Lieutenant in March last while employed with a Trench Mortar Battery.
Basil Fitzroy Swain was gazetted Temporary Quartermaster with the honorary rank of Lieutenant on 2nd December, 1915.

Second Lieutenant William Harry Ferguson enlisted in the London Regiment early in the war, and in September, 1915, was gazetted to a commission in the Royal Sussex Regiment. It is a regrettable coincidence that on the same morning that his honour is made public he also figures in the casualty list among the wounded.
The name Temporary Major Frank Robert Leith, The Hermitage, Selsey, formerly of the Royal Sussex Regiment, but now in the General List, and acting as an Aide-de-Camp, is also in the list mentioned. Before the war Major Leith entered largely into the affairs of Selsey, being prominently associated with the local lifeboat organisation and the regatta. At the outset he assisted in the recruitment campaign at Chichester Barracks until he was granted a commission in the County Regiment. He served many months in the trenches before receiving his appointment on the Staff.

Saturday May 26th 1917

Mentioned in Dispatches

Quartermaster and Hon. Lieutenant Plews was at one time Colour-Sergeant Instructor of "B" Company (Rye) of the Cinque Ports Rifles, and was largely instrumental in bringing his Company to a high state of efficiency in musketry. On the death of Major Tweed, Colour-sergeant Plews was promoted to Quartermaster, and this is the second occasion on which his name has been included in dispatches.
Acting Sergeant A.V. Coppard, who is included in Sir Douglas Haig's list is the son of Mr. and Mrs. Coppard of Beaconsfield Road, Bexhill. Sergeant Coppard is well-known to be a fearless and jovial character and very popular among his comrades. In the two and a half years' active service he has been in France with a line battalion of the Royal Sussex Regiment, Coppard has been in many great battles,

starting from the retirement from Mons. He was in the advance at the Marne, the Ainse and then again at Neuve Chapelle, Loos, the Vimy Ridge and many other important actions during the war.

Monday May 28th 1917

Italian Medals for Valour

The following decorations have been awarded by the King of Italy for distinguished services rendered in the course of the campaign by members of the Royal Sussex Regiment :-

The Silver Medal for Military Valour

Second Lieutenant John Russell Willis Alexander, 3rd Bn. Royal Sussex Regiment, (S.R.)

The Bronze Medal for Military Valour

No. 3303 Sergeant George Hodges, 7th Bn. Royal Sussex Regiment,
No. G/1671 Corporal Frederick William Yeomans, 8th Bn. Royal Sussex Regiment,

Military Medal for Sussex Soldiers

The following members of the Royal Sussex Regiment have been awarded the Military Medal :-
No. G/2835 Lance-Corporal (A/Sgt.) Frank E. Bennett, 8th Bn.
No. G/1997 Private Jack Bunker, 8th Bn.
No. G/2379 Lance-Sergeant (A/Sgt.) George Caesar, 8th Bn.
No. G/1999 Lance-Corporal Joseph A. Emerson, 8th Bn.
No. G/1996 Corporal G.S. Rossetter, 8th Bn.

Meritorious Service Medal

Awarded to :-

No. 200303 (was 1836) Corporal (A/Sgt.) A.W. Yeates, Royal Sussex Regiment,

"London Gazette" Monday June 4th 1917

The KING has been graciously pleased, on the occasion of His Majesty's Birthday, to give orders for the following promotions in, and appointments to, the Most Honourable Order of the Bath, for services rendered in connection with the war: -

To be Additional Members of the Military Division of the Third Class, or Companions, of the said most Honourable Order: -

C.B.

Maj.-Gen. James Charles Young, (Colonel of the Regiment)

His Majesty the KING has been graciously pleased to approve of the undermentioned rewards for distinguished service in the field :

D.S.O.

Captain (A/Major) Hugh Thomas Kay Robinson, 13th Bn. Royal Sussex Regiment,

Brevet Lieutenant-Colonel

Major (T/Brig-General) A.E. Glasgow, D.S.O., Royal Sussex Regiment,

Royal Sussex Men Decorated

Acting Company-Sergeant-Major Lewis Bonney, who received the Distinguished Conduct Medal from the hands of the King at the investiture in Hyde Park on Saturday, was prior to enlisting, a member of the Eastbourne Police Force. From the Duke of Cornwall's Light Infantry he was transferred to a service battalion of the Royal Sussex Regiment early in 1915. The news of this honour will be received with great approval by all who have served with him. The medal was awarded for devotion to duty.

Sergeant F.G.J. Spicer, Royal Sussex Regiment, was also a recipient of the Distinguished Conduct Medal. The service for which this was conferred is thus described :-

For conspicuous gallantry and devotion to duty. He has performed consistent good work throughout the campaign, and has at all times set a splendid example of courage and determination. He was wounded.

Tuesday June 5th 1917

Military Crosses for Royal Sussex Officers

The following officers of the Royal Sussex Regiment have been awarded the Military Cross for distinguished service in the field :-

Captain John Orfeur Aglionby, Rev. M.A., attd. 2nd Bn.
T/Captain Henry Jessop Coxhead,
T/Lieutenant George Henry Gilmore, 8th Bn. (Lewisham)

Lieutenant George H. Jones,
T/Lieutenant George Maycock, 11th Bn.
Second Lieutenant (A/Cpt.) Harry Roberts, 13th Bn.
T/Captain George Francis Rothschild, 13th Bn.

Second Lieutenant (T/Lt.) Norman Winter, attd Nigerian Regiment,

Wednesday June 6th 1917

Distinguished Service Rewards

Rewards for distinguished conduct in the field have been conferred on non-commissioned officers of the Royal Sussex Regiment as follows :-

D.C.M.

No. 10145 C.S.M. F. Barnard, 9th Bn.
No. 1365 Corporal (A/Sgt.) C.S. Kenward, 2nd Bn.
No. L/5079 C.S.M. M.R. Mullett, 8th Bn.

M.S.M.

No. 118 R. Q.M.S. W. Long, 7th Bn.

Saturday June 16th 1917

A Brighton Distinction

The many friends of Mr. and Mrs. Patrick, Exeter Street, Brighton, will be glad to know that their son, Sergeant F.J. Patrick, Royal Sussex Regiment, who was awarded the Military Medal last year for bravery on the battlefield in France, is shortly leaving England to be attached to the King's West African Rifles as Second Lieutenant.

Tuesday June 19th 1917

Honours for the Royal Sussex Regiment

The following awards to members of the Royal Sussex Regiment appear in a special edition of the *"London Gazette"* issued last night :-

M.C.

Second Lieutenant (T/Lt.) Victor Richardson, (attached King's Royal Rifle Corps.)

For conspicuous gallantry and devotion to duty. Although severely wounded he continued to lead his men forward in the face of very heavy hostile fire. He was again wounded.

Bar to M.M.

No. 1312 Sergeant Arthur W. Horne, 7th Bn.
(M.M gazetted 21st Sept, 1916)

M.M.

No. 8344 Sergeant William Baker, 7th Bn.
No. 726 Private John Penticost 7th Bn.
No. 8368 Private Percy William Scott 7th Bn.
No. 10515 Private J.Y. Smith 7th Bn.

Extract from the *"London Gazette"* :-

Delete Military Medal to No. G/17761 Private William Shotter, Royal Sussex Regiment,
(M.M. gazetted 9th December, 1916)

Wednesday June 20th 1917

Shoreham Military Medal

The home of Private J.Y. Smith, Royal Sussex Regiment, whose name recently appears in the official list of those who have won the Military Medal, is at 36, New Road, Shoreham. He has had an eventful career in the Army, and on several occasions his name has been in the casualty lists. He has been wounded about four times, and once gassed. However, when home some little time ago, he was looking wonderfully fit and well, despite his experiences. It has been known for a long time now that he had earned the Military Medal, and his name makes a very belated appearance in the official list. He will be generally congratulated in the town on the honour he has worthily won, and every good wish will accompany him in his future service.

Thursday June 21st 1917

Honour won at Gaza

Arundel has learned with great pride and pleasure of the distinction gained by Captain Guy Sefton Constable, who at the outbreak of war was serving in the office of Mayor. Letters which have arrived from Egypt during the past few days show that Captain Constable has been awarded the Military Cross for gallant services rendered in the Battle of Gaza on 26th and 27th march. Members of his Company are very enthusiastic and state that the honour is very richly deserved. Captain Constable has served with the county regiment ever since the outbreak of war and also went through the Boer War.
Captain Constable, who is one of the heads of the well know Arundel brewing firm, will receive the hearty congratulations of his numerous friends in the borough and in West Sussex generally. It is also gratifying to note that Lance-Corporal A. Tester, a well-known and popular member of the Arundel Football team, has been awarded the Military Medal.

Saturday June 23rd 1917

A gallant Wick Soldier

Hearty congratulations will be extended to Private A.C.T. Richardson, 4, Boyton Place, Wick, who has been awarded the Military Medal for gallantry and devotion to duty which he displayed on the Gaza battlefield.
Tom Richardson, who is a very popular footballer, and played frequently for the Littlehampton Club, has served abroad with the "Terriers" since a month or two after the commencement of the war. In a letter to his wife he writes very modestly of the incident which won him the honour, as follows :-
"I told you a little about my luck, but I suppose, like a woman, you will want to know what I did to get the Military Medal. The boys say that I deserved it, the way I was going on. I only carried the gun with the first line for about two miles, and when I got there on the ridge I got hit in the hip. As it did not hurt me much at the time I carried on with the firing until I got another in the face, and then I found that I could not move at all, as by then my hip was giving me, too use a soldier's word, hell. I shall never forget the time we had there. We could not get out of the way and we would not retire, so we simply hung on. They have been into it again since then, and I was not there, worse luck!"

Wednesday June 27th 1917

West Sussex Soldier Wins The Military Medal

Mr. and Mrs. H. Laker, of Orchard Street, Chichester, have heard that their son, Lance-Corporal Ernest George Laker, who is a member of a Pioneer Battalion of the Royal Sussex Regiment, has won the Military Medal,
"For gallant conduct and devotion to duty in the field in the battle on 5/6th May last."
Before becoming a pioneer he was an apprentice at Messrs. J. Dunn and Son, South Street, Chichester.

Saturday June 30th 1917

Heathfield Soldier Rewarded

For gallantry on the field, it is reported that Lance-Corporal Reginald Relf, of the Royal Sussex Pioneers, has been awarded the Military Medal and a piece of parchment. His wife and two children reside at Sandy Cross, Heathfield, and he is the son of Mr. and Mrs. R. Relf, of Sandy Cross. Joining up soon after the outbreak of war, he was drafted to France in July, 1915, and twelve months later, as a private, he sustained wounds. In civilian life he was employed as a gardener to Mr. B.F. Watson, of Sedgeforth, Heathfield. As in war, so in peace, he was a good sportsman, and took an active part both in cricket and football. He belonged to the Heathfield Tower Cricket team, and played football for Heathfield United.

Tuesday July 3rd 1917

Presentation of Military Medals at Newhaven

On Sunday morning, after the usual garrison church parade, Lieutenant-Colonel C.A. Hankey (Garrison Commander), on behalf of the General Officer Commanding, presented Military Medals to the following N.C.O.'s and men of the Royal Sussex Regiment, congratulating each recipient upon his gallantry :-

No. SD/3463 Sergeant Charles Stanford, 13th Bn.

For successfully attacking a party of German bombers at Stuff Trench on 21st October, 1916, and consolidating the captured position: although wounded, he remained with the platoon until exhausted.

No. 184 Corporal William Butcher, 7th Bn.

For bravery on the field on 7th July, 1916, when he commanded a company of bombers for three days, although wounded in the right eye.

No.4742 Private David Smith, 2nd Bn.

In an attack on High Wood on 20th August, 1916, he captured an important position and retained the same against five successive counter-attacks.

No. 8145 Private Louis Fuller, 9th Bn.

For bravery on the field on 13th February, 1916, when he consolidated a German crater, digging in the front line, afterwards reconnoitred in no Man's Land, bringing in two wounded.

No.402 Private Edward A. Harman, 7th Bn.

For holding a crater for three days and nights without reinforcements, in March, 1916.

Wednesday July 4th 1917

Eastbourne Teachers Decoration

The Eastbourne Education Committee have forwarded a resolution of congratulations to Lieutenant G.H. Jones upon winning the Military Cross. Lieutenant Jones was an assistant master at Eastbourne School before joining the colours.

"London Gazette" Friday 6th July 1917

GENERAL HEADQUARTERS, 18th March, 1917.

MY LORD, In accordance with the final paragraph of my Despatch dated 1st March, 1917, I have the honour to enclose herewith a list of those officers, non-commissioned officers and men, and of other persons, whose names I desire to bring to your notice for gallant or distinguished conduct in the field, or for other valuable services.
I have the honour to be,
Your Lordship's most obedient servant,
A.J. MURRAY, General,
Commander-in-Chief, Egyptian Expeditionary Force.

M.I.D.

ROYAL SUSSEX REGIMENT

2nd Lt. (temp. Lt.) R.C.G. Middleton
No. 200276 Serjt. C.H. Hersee,
No. 200303 Corpl. (actg. Serjt.) A.W. Yeates,

Tuesday July 10th 1917

Distinguished Service Awards for Men of the County Regiment

The services for which the Distinguished Conduct Medal was conferred upon the following non-commissioned officers of the Royal Sussex Regiment were as follows :-

No. 10145 C.S.M. F. Barnard, 9th Bn.

For conspicuous gallantry and devotion to duty. He performed most valuable service in guiding reinforcements through heavy fire when most urgently needed. He has set a fine example to all.

No. 1366 Corporal (A/Sgt.) C.S. Kenward, 2nd Bn. (Nutley)
For conspicuous gallantry and devotion to duty. He has consistently performed good work throughout, and has at all times set a fine example of gallantry and leadership.

No. L/5079 C.S.M. M.R. Mullett, 8th Bn.

For conspicuous gallantry and devotion to duty. He has consistently performed good work, especially under fire, and has set a fine example to all those under him.

No. L/9905 C.S.M. W.J. Walls, M.M. 13th Bn.

For conspicuous gallantry and devotion to duty. He has set a fine example of courage and coolness when under fire, and has performed consistent good work throughout.

M.M.

The Military Medal has been awarded to the following non-commissioned officers and men of the Royal Sussex Regiment for bravery in the field :-

No. 13042 Private William T. Ball, 9th Bn.
No. G/648 Private Thomas Herman Beall, 7th Bn.
No. 8522 Private Joseph Beeney, 9th Bn.
No. 6278 Private (L/Cpl.) R.D. Billing, 9th Bn.
No. 4017 Private Percy William Bridger, 7th Bn.
No. 240396 Sergeant William Dale, 5th Bn.
No. 3410 Private Charles Thomas Emery, 7th Bn.
No. 3788 Private Samuel Isted, 7th Bn.
No. 1393 Sergeant Walter Laughton, 9th Bn.

No. 722 Private (L/Cpl.) John Todman, 9th Bn.

Thursday July 12th 1917

Captain G. Nagle M.C.

Captain G. Nagle, M.C., Royal Sussex Regiment, killed in action, was the younger son of Mr. Garret Nagle, Resident Magistrate, Belfast. He joined the battalion, of which he was the Adjutant when he fell, shortly after its formation, and was appointed Adjutant last August. He had seen a great deal of hard work in the trenches, and had been mentioned in dispatches and awarded the Military Cross in recognition of his very fine work in action on several occasions.

Friday July 13th 1917

Steyning Man's Distinction

The name of Sergeant F. Wood, Royal Sussex Regiment, of Coxham, Steyning, has only recently been officially published in the casualty lists, but he has just rejoined his regiment, having recovered from two shoulder wounds sustained at the front. It now transpires that Sergeant Wood has been recommended for and will receive the Military Medal in due course for special service at the front, and he will be heartily congratulated on the distinction. He joined up two years ago, being then employed on an Edburton farm.

Monday July 16th 1917

French Honours

The Legion of Honour, Croix de Chevalier was awarded by the President of the French Republic to :-

T/Captain Henry Edward Stewart, 8th Bn. Royal Sussex Regiment, (k.i.a. 1st June, 1917.)

The award of the Medal Militaire was made to :-

No. 15104 Private Thomas Barfield, 2nd Bn. Royal Sussex Regiment,
No. 381 Sergeant James Chillman, 2nd Bn. Royal Sussex Regiment,

Wednesday July 18th 1917

A Petworth Military Medallist

Private Frank Barham, of a Pioneer Battalion, Royal Sussex Regiment, has written home to his sister, who lives in Grove Street, Petworth, stating that he has been awarded the Military medal. In the course of his letter, Private Barham states :-

"When I got back from the rest camp I was told that I had been awarded the Military Medal, but I have not got it up as I was not back in time to have it put up with the others." Private Barham is one of three brothers serving in the Army.

He is 23 and single, and joining up at the commencement of the war was sent to France about two years ago. His brothers, Frederick and William, are in the Lancers and Dragoon Guards respectively.

Thursday July 19th 1917

Sussex Officers Honoured

The following awards to officers in the Royal Sussex Regiment were gazetted last night :-

M.C.

T/Lieutenant Charles Willard Ballard, 7th Bn. Royal Sussex Regiment,

For conspicuous gallantry and devotion to duty. He repeatedly went out on patrol under very heavy fire to gain touch with the enemy. he attacked six of the enemy single-handed and dispersed them, though they resisted with bombs and rifle fire, and though badly wounded and gassed he remained in command of his company for two days, affording a splendid example of pluck and determination.
T/Second Lieutenant Norman McCracken, 7th Bn. Royal Sussex Regiment,

For conspicuous gallantry and devotion to duty. He has performed valuable work when on patrol. He twice took out patrols under very heavy fire and came in contact with the enemy each time. He also organised the cutting of our own wire, which was carried out under heavy shell fire.

Friday July 20th 1917

Two more Sussex Officers win the Military Cross

The King has been pleased to award the Military cross to the undermentioned officers :

Second Lieutenant (T/Lt.) Godwyn Woolnough Prince, 7th Bn. Royal Sussex Regiment,

For conspicuous gallantry and devotion to duty. He volunteered and led a successful raiding party. The party reached enemy lines, despite machine-gun and rifle fire. Valuable information was obtained and the party successfully withdrawn, despite a heavy hostile barrage.
Second Lieutenant (T/Capt.) Humphrey Francis Taylor, 7th Bn. Royal Sussex Regiment,

For conspicuous gallantry and devotion to duty in leading his company to their objective during an attack with total disregard of personal safety. He later on led a bombing party against the enemy, inflicting heavy loss and capturing prisoners and machine-guns. His conduct throughout was magnificent.
Second Lieutenant Godwyn Woolnough Prince of the Royal Sussex Regiment, was transferred from a Service Battalion to a Regular Battalion in January last.

Saturday July 21st 1917

Military Medals for members of the Royal Sussex Regiment

Among the non-commissioned officers and men to whom the King has awarded the Military Medal for bravery in the field are the following members of the Royal Sussex Regiment :-

No. 5321 Private George E. Bartholomew, 7th Bn.
No. S/358 Sergeant E.V. Buckwell, 8th Bn.
"On 1st July, 1916 digging communication trench across "No Man's Land."
No. 874 Private William A. Carr, 7th Bn.
No. 5197 Private Horace R. Clayton, 7th Bn.
No. G/1792 Lance-Corporal H.W. Drewery, 8th Bn.
No. 200140 Sergeant E.F. Grimstead, 4th Bn.
No. G/3833 Private Edwin Highgate, 7th Bn.
No. G/849 Private Ernest G. Laker, 8th Bn.
No. 266 Private Henry Maughan, 7th Bn.
No. 684 Sergeant George William Preston, 7th Bn.
No. G/2159 Lance-Corporal Arthur Raynard, 8th Bn.

 No. G/2321 Lance-Corporal Reginald Relf, 8th Bn.

No. 200627 Private Alfred C.T. Richardson, 4th Bn.
No. SD/2119 Sergeant Sydney Rowland Rose, 12th Bn.

 No. G/2091 Private Walter Henry Stemp, 8th Bn.

No. 200784 Lance-Corporal Archibald Edmund Tester, 4th Bn.
No. 200673 Private John Walker, 4th Bn.

Military Cross Winner

Second Lieutenant (T/Lieutenant.) Godwyn Woolnough Prince, of the Royal Sussex Regiment, whose name appeared in yesterday's military honours list, is the son of Mr. J.W.G. Prince, of Hartfield, and is well known and much respected in the village and district. He joined the Royal Sussex Regiment in March, 1915, and went to France in July of the following year. He was shortly afterwards wounded, and returned to England. On recovery he went out again in October last. His many friends will heartily congratulate him on winning the Military Cross.

Tuesday July 24th 1917

Good Services Mentioned

Added to the list of officers, ladies, the non-commissioned officers and men recommended for distinguished and gallant services and devotion to duty in the dispatch from Sir Douglas Haigh are the following :-

Hon. Major His Highness Jam Shri Ranjitsinhji Vibhanji, Jam of Nawanagar, K.C.S.I. T/Capt. (A/Major.) H.T. Kay Robinson, D.S.O., 13th Bn. Royal Sussex Regiment,

Wednesday July 25th 1917

Captain Taylor, Burgess Hill

Temporary Captain H.F. Taylor, Royal Sussex Regiment, S.R., whose award of the Military Cross was notified in the *Sussex Daily News last week,* is the son of Mr. H.B. Taylor J.P. Chairman of the Burgess Hill Urban Council.

Friday July 27th 1917

Among the recipients of decorations awarded by the King of the Belgians for distinguished services rendered during the course of the campaign is Brevet Lieutenant-Colonel J.B. Wroughton, C.M.G., 2nd Bn. Royal Sussex Regiment, who is appointed an Officer of the Ordre of Leopold II (4th Class).

Bar to M.C.

 T/Captain George Henry Gilmore, 8th Bn. Royal Sussex Regiment, (Lewisham)

During digging operations, when his company suddenly came under an intense hostile barrage, suffering heavily, he showed complete disregard to personal safety, walking up and down in the open in order to encourage his men, thereby keeping them at work and greatly improving their protection and sustaining their morale.

(M.C. gazetted 4th June, 1917)

M.C.

T/Captain Charles Eustace Goad, 9th Bn. Royal Sussex Regiment,

He led his company in the attack in which he gained his furthest objectives and consolidated them. His fine example enabled the men to consolidate in spite of consistent shelling.

 T/Captain George Meredyth Shackel, Royal Sussex Regiment,

For conspicuous gallantry and devotion to duty. He led his company with great courage and determination. By his fine example under heavy fire, and his training of the company, he was greatly responsible for the success of the attack.

T/Captain Harold Saxon, Royal Sussex Regiment, 3rd Bn. Royal Sussex Regiment,

For conspicuous gallantry and devotion to duty. He showed great coolness and determination when in charge of mopping-up parties, consolidating the position and supervising every post under heavy shell fire on a front of 300 yards.

Tuesday July 31st 1917

Military Medals for Royal Sussex Men

The following non-commissioned officers and men of the Royal Sussex Regiment have been awarded the Military Medal for bravery in the field :-

No. G/2691 Private Frank Barham, 8th Bn.
No. 5786 Sergeant Charles Fuller, 9th Bn.
No. 16763 Private Edward Isard, 9th Bn.
No. 2200 Private Frederick J. Mann, 8th Bn.
No. S/2 Sergeant Henry Albert Shonfield, 8th Bn.
No. 2946 Corporal Herbert G. Sivyer, 9th Bn.

No. G/2376 Private James Stannard, 7th Bn.
No. 3125 Sergeant George William Tickner, 9th Bn.

Lieutenant J. Marsland M.C.

Lieutenant John Marsland, M.C., Royal Sussex Regiment, who was killed by a shell instantaneously on 23rd July, four days after his return to the front and on the second anniversary of his first landing there, was the eldest son of Mr. John and Pattie Marsland, of Walworth, and late of New Malden. He was 21 years of age.

Monday August 6th 1917

At Buckingham Palace on Saturday amongst others, Lieutenant T.W. Rose, Royal Sussex Regiment, was invested with the Military Cross by His Majesty the King.

Tuesday August 7th 1917

2nd Lt. Guy Compton, D.C.M. M.M.

2nd Lt. Guy Compton, who was killed in action on 26th July, was educated at Bancroft's School, Woodford, and afterwards spent some years learning farming. He joined the R.G.A. in August, 1914, and soon volunteered for service with the Royal Sussex Regiment. He served at the Front for some months, obtaining promotion to sergeant and winning the Military Medal and Distinguished Conduct Medal. He was wounded in July, 1916, and returned to England, but went out again at the end of June, having meanwhile obtained his commission. According to the *'London Gazette'* he was awarded the D.C.M. with Sergeant E.J. Green.

For conspicuous gallantry during operations, Sergeants Compton and Green pushed forwards through uncut wire and heavy machine-gun fire into the enemy's trench, organised a bombing party, and cleared 100 yards of trench, accounting for many of the enemy. They consolidated the position won. They set a fine example.

Thursday August 16th 1917

Sussex Officers in the Casualty List

Captain Cecil Arthur Allen (wounded) attained acting Company rank on 13th November, 1916. He was awarded the Military Cross in December, 1916, "For conspicuous gallantry in action. He displayed great courage and determination throughout the operations and set a splendid example to his men."
Second Lieutenant R.E. Cox (wounded) belongs to Lewes, being one of six sons of Mrs. Cox. Of High Street, who have donned the King's uniform. He was awarded the Military Medal when holding the rank of Sergeant, "For splendid devotion to duty and great courage displayed at Theipval sector on 21st October, 1916. Acting as second in command of his platoon he most ably assisted his Platoon Commander by preserving a cool front. Soon after arriving in the position we had captured he went into "No Man's Land" with the first reinforcements, showing absolute contempt for the heavy shelling under which he moved. He himself brought back several wounded men, rendered such first aid as he could, and deposited them in a place of safety. During his action he was twice buried by shells bursting almost on him, and throughout, by his cheerful demeanour, he helped considerably to preserve the morale of the men about him. This splendid example won the admiration of all ranks."
It was not surprising that after his heroic bearing on this occasion he was given a commission in the same unit. He rejoined his comrades as a Second lieutenant some six weeks ago.

Friday August 17th 1917

Nine Sussex Officers win Military Crosses

The Honours officially announced last night include the award of the Military Cross to the following officers of the Royal Sussex Regiment, whose deeds of gallantry are briefly described. Initiative, coolness, valour, efficiency, resource and determination - all these qualities have been recognised, and it is clear that the men of the Sussex have been skilful and devoted leaders :-

T/Lieutenant Walter Hubert Baddeley,

For conspicuous gallantry and devotion to duty. While engaged in digging operations his company suddenly came under intense hostile barrage. His company commander and many others were killed. He at once took command, showing the utmost coolness and disregard for personal safety, and it was due to his example that a most difficult and urgent piece of work was completed.

Captain Guy Sefton Constable,   4th Bn.

For conspicuous gallantry and devotion to duty. When our advance was held up by the enemy's fire he took an advanced position with a small party, and held out for the remainder of the day within a few yards of the enemy's trench under heavy fire, and after being himself wounded. his initiative and gallantry were most marked.

2nd, Lieutenant William Archibald Foy,   4th Bn.

For conspicuous gallantry and devotion to duty. He performed excellent work in digging the Lewis guns of his own and other companies, moving from gun to gun continually under heavy fire until wounded. He then made his way to another gun and gave orders for its better employment before his wound was dressed.

T/Lieutenant John Marsland,   8th Bn.

For conspicuous gallantry and devotion to duty. During digging operations in very exposed ground he showed the great coolness and disregard of his personal safety in walking up and down and encouraging his men under an enemy barrage of great intensity, it was due to his fine work , which was urgently needed, was completed without loss of time.

2nd Lieutenant George Burleigh Mountford, attd. K.R.R.C.

He was blown up by a shell and badly bruised. He alone set to work to tie up the wounded and get them down to the M.O. Previously he twice carried messages to the front line, going through heavy machine-gun fire the entire way.

Lt. (Acting Captain) Clement Vaughan Newton, 9th Bn.

For conspicuous gallantry and devotion to duty. After leading his company with great determination and courage to its objective, he showed skill and fearlessness in consolidating, personally leading out his covering parties and fearlessly exposing himself to machine-gun and rifle fire, in order to supervise and encourage the work. He held his line for four days, setting a fine example to his men.

T/Lieutenant Jack Chalmers Peskett,

For conspicuous gallantry and devotion to duty. He led his platoon with great coolness and courage, afterwards successfully withdrawing them from a difficult position and finding his way, with all the men under his command, to another part of the firing line.

Captain Stuart Keppel Reid, 4th Bn.

For conspicuous gallantry and devotion to duty. He led his company with great judgement and coolness under heavy fire. By skilful use of his Lewis gun he prevented a counter-attack on his exposed flank, having appreciated the danger at the right moment.

T/2nd Lieutenant Richard William Rumsby, 9th Bn.

For conspicuous gallantry and devotion to duty. When in charge of a mopping-out party, he did valuable work in support of the leading company, afterwards displaying great skill and initiative in making reconnaissances and collecting men who had gone astray. He has done similar excellent work on previous occasions.

2nd Lieutenant Harry George Welham, 9th Bn.

For conspicuous gallantry and devotion to duty. During an attack he showed the greatest courage and skilled leadership, personally supervising the whole line of advance until he fainted from exhaustion. Later, he took a platoon forward into shell holes during heavy bombardment, thereby saving many casualties.

The King has been graciously pleased to bestow the award the Companion of St. Michael and St. George, (Third Class) Military Division to :-

C.M.G.

Lieutenant-Colonel William Lushington Osborn, D.S.O. Royal Sussex Regiment,

Saturday August 18th 1917

D.C.M. Awards

Three Royal Sussex men have been awarded the Distinguished Conduct Medal for gallantry and devotion to duty in the field :-

No. L/10537 Lance-Corporal Alfred James Dell, 9th Bn.

For conspicuous gallantry and devotion to duty during an attack in most skilfully and fearlessly guiding his platoon close up to an intense artillery barrage, thereby saving much confusion and many casualties. His action in showing them the best route was of a most difficult nature, and had an immense tactical value, helping in a marked degree the success of the operation.

No. 200353 Corporal P. Bryant, 4th Bn.

For conspicuous gallantry and devotion to duty. After his platoon commander had been killed, he took command of the platoon and led them to the assault with great skill and courage.

No. G/10228 Corporal F.C. Fairhall, 13th Bn.

For conspicuous gallantry and devotion to duty when in charge of a bombing sap on the flank of his battalion. He held it against a determined flame attack by the enemy, shooting all the team before they could bring their projector into action. When eventually forced to retire he did so with great skill, getting all his wounded away. Throughout the whole operation he displayed remarkable personal courage, and by his fine example greatly encouraged all who were with him.

Military Medallist

The award of the Military Medal for gallantry in the field :-

No. G/415 Sgt. Walter Jesse Osborne, 7th Bn. Royal Sussex Regiment,
(Gazetted 16th August, 1917)

Wednesday August 22nd 1917

For bravery in the field

The Military Medal has been conferred upon the following members of the Royal Sussex Regiment for bravery in the field :-

No. G/6339 L/Sergeant William Bridger Bailey 9th Bn.
No. SD/5594 Private Harry Tomlinson 9th Bn.

Tuesday August 27th 1917

D.S.O. for Royal Sussex Officer

Captain (T/Lt.-Col.) Murray Victor Burrow Hill M.C. 9th Bn. Royal Sussex Regiment, has been appointed a Companion of the Distinguished Service Order.

For conspicuous gallantry and devotion to duty. At a time when our advance was delayed by a "pocket" of the enemy, he skilfully enveloped them with his support company, thereby enabling the leading line to advance and reach their objective with only slight loss. His personal reconnaissance's under fire and his arrangements for consolidation and protection have set a very fine example of coolness and ability, and thoroughly gained the confidence of all under his command.

Rewards for Sussex Officers

In a list of rewards for distinguished service in the field in Mesopotamia, published in the *"London Gazette"* appear the names of Major G. Gem and Major G.C. Morphett, D.S.O., Royal Sussex Regiment, who have been promoted Brevet Lieutenant-Colonels, and Major and Brevet Lieutenant-Colonel (Temporary Lieutenant-Colonel) Cecil Robert Gaunt, Reserve of Officers, late Dragoon Guards, who has been granted the D.S.O. the appointments are dated from 3rd June.

Saturday September 1st 1917

Local Officers Honoured

Decorations from the King of Italy and the French President

The following are among the decorations and medals awarded by the King of Italy at various dates to the British Forces for distinguished services during the course of the campaign :-

Officer of the Order of the Crown of Italy

Lt-Colonel George Sullivan Whitfield, Sussex Yeomanry (16th Bn.)

Cavalier of the Order of St. Maurice and St. Lazarus

Brevet Lt-Colonel Robert Nicholas Dick, Royal Sussex Regiment,

Lieutenant-Colonel R.N. Dick obtained his commission in the Royal Sussex Regiment on 11th February, 1899, and in the December following obtained his second star. as a Captain he took part in the East Africa (Somalialand) operations of 1908-10, being mentioned in dispatches, and subsequently receiving the medal with clasp. About two years ago he was appointed a General Staff Officer, 2nd grade, on the Indian Establishment, and in October, 1916, he was promoted to 1st grade with the temporary rank of Lieutenant-Colonel.

French Honour

The President of the French Republic has conferred the distinction of Chevalier of the Legion of Honour on Major George Charles Morphett, D.S.O., Royal Sussex Regiment.

Major George Charles Morphett, D.S.O., was adjutant of the 1st Battalion, when the great campaign was entered upon, and his association with the County Regiment extends over 18 years. He served with the Sussex in the Boer War, and before joining the line was with the Militia at Chichester. Two years ago he was selected for service on the Staff, and a short while time later came the announcement of his promotion to field rank.

Friday September 7th 1917

Another Military Medallist : Rotherfield

A few days ago the announcement was made that Private Ernest Henry Tester, Middlesex Regiment, whose home is at 3, New Road, Rotherfield had been awarded the Military Medal for gallantry in the field. News came to hand yesterday that another Rotherfield soldier had won the same distinction. He is Sergeant Clarence Packham, Royal Sussex Regiment, son of Mr. George Packham, of Railway Cottages, Town Row.
Sergeant Packham, is only 20 years of age, and the medal has, it is thought, been awarded for bravery in the severe fighting connected with the capture of the French village of St. Julien at the end of July. His father is head porter at the Rotherfield railway station, and has lost his elder son in the war.

Saturday September 15th 1917

Gallant Hove Sergeant's Death

Mr. Alfred Diplock, of 8, Connaught Road, Hove, and who for a number of years carried on a draper's business at the top of George Street, Hove, has received the news that his youngest son, Sergeant H.R. Diplock, Royal Sussex Regiment, was killed in France on 8th September. Twenty-four years of age, he won the Military Medal for gallant conduct and devotion to duty on the 20th/21st, July last. He had been in the army since April, 1911, and was promoted to the rank of Sergeant about three months ago. He was educated at the Connaught Road Higher Grade School, Hove. Writing to Sergeant Diplock's mother acquainting her of the sad news, his commanding officer says :-

B.E.F., Sept., 1917

Dear Mrs. Diplock,- Please accept my deepest sympathy at the death of your son. His death was instantaneous being killed by a shell yesterday morning about 11 o'clock. He is buried in a small cemetery well behind the front line, and his grave will be marked by a cross. His death is a very great loss to the battalion, in which he was held in great respect, always displaying a fine example of courage and cheerfulness.

It is only a very short time ago that I had the pleasure of announcing to him that he had been awarded the Military Medal for assisting a wounded man under heavy shelling. I am afraid the only comfort I can offer is that you have the knowledge that your boy died the death of a hero, fighting a hard fight for his country and civilisation. With my deepest sympathy, yours sincerely, Bertram J. Walker, Lieut.-Colonel.

Another officer writes :-

Dear Mrs. Diplock,- It is with intense regret I have to tell you of the death of your son, No. L/9685 Sergeant H.R. Diplock. He died with two of his comrades under his command, a shell dropping right into the midst of a small party. Diplock was killed instantaneously and in the performance of his duty. We shall miss this fine sergeant, so well rewarded with the Military Medal. He was loved by all, and respected by every man under him. I cannot speak to highly of his devotion to duty and his splendid loyalty.

As for you, his mother, I can only try and comfort you by telling you that your son died at his post and in the fulfilment of the grandest service of all, that for God, King and Country. We buried him this afternoon with his comrades, with a large number of sad mourners around, with a splendid rendering of the "Last Post", and a neat, conspicuous cross will soon mark his noble resting place. With all my sincere sympathy and regards, I am yours, Sydney T. Buck, Captain.

Mr. and Mrs. Diplock have two other sons serving their King and Country, Bertram Gerald Diplock, leading mechanic in the R.N.A.S., and Sydney Diplock, Q.M.S. in the Royal Sussex Regiment on home service.

Military Medals

The award of the Military Medal for gallantry and devotion to duty in the field has been won by :-
No. 931 A/Sergeant Alfred William Beale, 7th Bn. Royal Sussex Regiment,
No. 325 L/Sergeant John G. Peacock, 7th Bn. Royal Sussex Regiment,

Tuesday September 18th 1917

Royal Sussex Officer wins Military Cross

The Military Cross has been awarded to :-

2nd Lieutenant Hugh Cyril Barnes, 2nd Bn. Royal Sussex Regiment,
For conspicuous gallantry and devotion to duty as Brigade Intelligence Officer. At a time when most of the communications had been severed he remained at his post., under heavy fire of shells of all calibre, rendering clear and precise reports which were of the greatest value to our artillery. He showed the utmost gallantry and coolness in an extremely trying situation.

Thursday September 20th 1917

Local War Hero Honoured

D.C.M. and Military Medal Winners

Sussex men continue worthily to uphold the fighting traditions of the County. The latest list of winners of the Distinguished Conduct Medal issued yesterday, includes the following, and it will be agreed by anyone who reads the glowing record of their doings that the decorations in each case is richly deserved :-

No. G/10228 Corporal F.C. Fairhall, (Brighton) 13th Bn. Royal Sussex Regiment,

For conspicuous gallantry and devotion to duty when in charge of a bombing sap on the flank of his battalion. He held it against a determined flame attack by the enemy, shooting all the team before they could bring their projector into action. When eventually forced to retire he did so with great skill, getting all his wounded away. Throughout the whole operation he displayed remarkable personal courage, and by his fine example greatly encouraged all who were with him.
Corporal Fairhall, whose home is at 6, Arnold Street, Brighton, is 22 years of age and has served in the Army for four years, having been in the 2nd Battalion of the Royal Sussex Regiment before the outbreak of war. He went to France in January, 1915, and was wounded in the Battle of Loos the same year. He went out again and was wounded at the Battle of Arras. He subsequently returned to the front and took part in the recent battles.

Military Medallists

Last night's list also numbers the following among the recipients of the Military Medal :-

No. L/9685 Sergeant Horace Reginald Diplock, 8th Bn. Royal Sussex Regiment, (Hove)
No. G/4481 Private Cecil Foster, 9th Bn. Royal Sussex Regiment, (Lewisham)
No. G/2219 Sergeant George Charles Hammond, 8th Bn. Royal Sussex Regiment, (Bexhill)
No. G/3833 Private Edwin Highgate, 7th Bn. Royal Sussex Regiment, (Manning's Heath)
No. G/1787 Private Leonard S. Price, 8th Bn. Royal Sussex Regiment, (Canterbury)

Friday September 21st 1917

Military Medal for Newick Man

News has been received that the Military Medal has been won by Private John E. Mitchell, 12th Bn. Royal Sussex Regiment. The official account of the act for which the distinction was awarded is as follows -

"For most conspicuous gallantry and devotion to duty in the Battle of Ypres on 31st July and 1st and 2nd August. This man was a battalion runner, and worked untiringly for three days and nights. He had frequently to pass through heavily shelled areas, and in addition to his duties as runner, acted as guide to carrying parties by night. He showed great determination and devotion to duty throughout, and earned the admiration of all his comrades."

Private J.E. Mitchell is the son of Mr. and Mrs. James Mitchell, of Sunnyside, Newick. He enlisted in November, 1914, in the Royal Sussex Regiment, with which he went to France in March, 1916. He was wounded in the following September, but recovered, and returned to France last February.

Tuesday September 25th 1917

Honour for Sussex Officer

Among the recipients of decorations awarded by the King of the Belgians for distinguished services rendered during the course of the campaign is 2nd Lieutenant Alexander John Stevenson Grant, Royal Sussex Regiment, who is appointed a Chevalier of the Ordre de la Couronne.

Thursday September 27th 1917

Awards for Sussex Officers

A list of new recipients of the Distinguished Service Order appearing in the *"London Gazette"* contains the name of T/Lt. (A/Capt.) Noel de Putron MacRoberts, M.C., Royal Sussex Regiment.

The following Sussex officers have been awarded a Bar to the Military Cross previously received by them for gallantry :-

T/Lt. (A/Capt.) Cecil Arthur Allen, M.C., 11th Bn. Royal Sussex Regiment,
T/Lt. Richard Charles Hall, M.C., 8th Bn. Royal Sussex Regiment,
T/Capt. Henry Steedman Lewis, M.C., 11th Bn. Royal Sussex Regiment,

A list of new recipients of the Military Cross includes the name of Second Lieutenant St. Cyprian Churchill Tayler, Royal Sussex Regiment and 80th Squadron R.F.C.

Tuesday October 2nd 1917

Worthing Military Medallist

Private C.A. Lisher, Royal Sussex Regiment, who belongs to Worthing, has recently gained the Military Medal, the following being the official record :-
For most conspicuous gallantry and devotion to duty in the battle of Ypres on July 31st and August 1st and 2nd. This private was a linesman, and was on duty night and day repairing breakages caused by shell fire. The line between Brigade and Battalion Headquarters ran along the derelict German Reserve line and although the line was shelled continuously and heavily, Private Lisher went out repeatedly by day and night, often under heavy shell fire, thus enabling communication between Battalion and Brigade Headquarters to be kept up.
He is the son of Frederick George and Amelia Lisher, of 48 Orme Road, Worthing.

Monday October 8th 1917

Plumpton Man's Distinction

Lance-Corporal David Cheeseman, of the Royal Sussex Regiment, and son of Mrs. Cheeseman, North Barns Cottage, Plumpton, has written home to say he has won the Military Medal for gallant conduct around Ypres. Lance-Corporal D. Cheeseman is well known in Plumpton, where he has lived all his life. He has a brother in France, Private George Cheeseman.

Wednesday October 10th 1917

Military Medal Winners

Corporal S. Hughes : Hove

Mrs. Hughes, of Glenside, Wish Road, Hove, has been informed that her son, Corporal Sydney Hughes, of the Royal Sussex Regiment, has been awarded the Military Medal. It will be remembered that some seven years ago Mrs. Hughes was presented with the Albert Medal by the King for gallantly rescuing a child from a fire. Mrs. Hughes has also a daughter who has been decorated for services with the French Red Cross at the time of the German occupation of Douai. Mrs. Hughes' husband is also serving in France in the Royal Engineers.

("L/G" shows no Cpl. S. Hughes, R.S.R., [author])

Lance-Corporal L. Barker : Southwick

Mr. and Mrs. Barker, of Croft Cottage, Southwick, have received intimation that their second son, Lance-Corporal L. Barker, of the Royal Sussex Regiment, has been awarded the Military Medal for gallantry in action and devotion to duty. The information states that while his Lewis gun team were all gone he kept the gun in action for three days till more men were able to be sent.

Death of Hove Military Medallist

No. 9685 Sergeant H.R. Diplock, M.M., 8th Bn. Royal Sussex Regiment, (killed in action)

Friday October 12th 1917

Rotherfield N.C.O.'s Gallantry

As already announced in these columns, No. 458 Sergeant Clarence Packham, Royal Sussex Regiment, been son of Mr. George Packham, an employee at Rotherfield railway station, has awarded the Military Medal. The official record of the award is as follows :-
"For most conspicuous gallantry and good leading in the battle of Ypres on July 31st and August 1st, 2nd, and 3rd This N.C.O., in the capacity of Acting Company Sergeant-Major worked with untiring zeal under heavy shell fire in the re-organisation and consolidation under most adverse weather conditions. He displayed great courage when going round keeping up the spirits of the men, and was of great assistance to his Company Commander. His cheerfulness throughout was a magnificent incentive to all ranks."

Sergeant Clarence Packham, before enlisting in the Army, was a booking clerk at Crowborough Station.

Tuesday October 16th 1917

A Brighton Military Medallist

Mrs. Heise, 18, Bentham Road, Brighton, has just received notification that her husband, Corporal A.W. Heise, Royal Sussex regiment, has been awarded the Military Medal, "for most conspicuous gallantry, and good leading in the Battle of Ypres on 31st July, and 1st and 2nd August." The notice goes on to say :- "He led his platoon into action with great dash and vigour, himself inflicting many casualties to the enemy. Later on in the day he took over the position of Company Sergeant-Major, and by his example and cheerfulness under heavy shell fire, kept the men cheerful and prepared for the counter-attack. His courage and devotion to duty contributed largely to the success of his Company.

Corporal Heise joined up at the commencement of the war, and was wounded about two years ago. Previous to joining the colours he was employed at Messrs. Sainsburys, Western Road, Brighton.

Friday October 19th 1917

Rewards for Sussex Warriors

The following awards are officially gazetted. Except where stated all the men named belong to the Royal Sussex Regiment :-

M.C.

 T/2nd Lieutenant Horace Amon, 11th Bn.

T/2nd Lieutenant Stephen Arthur Andrews, 12th Bn.

 T/Lieutenant Cyril Bartlett, 13th Bn.

T/2nd Lieutenant Leonard George Cornes,
T/Lieutenant Herbert Edward Jones, 13th Bn.
T/Lieutenant Warren Pye Ratcliffe,
2nd lieutenant Henry Arthur Somerville, 11th Bn. & 82nd Squadron R.F.C.

 T/2nd Lieutenant (A/Capt.) Arnold George Alexander Vidler, 11th Bn.

T/2nd Lieutenant (A/Capt.) Edward Lancelot Weale,
T/2nd Lieutenant Horace John White, 13th Bn.
No. 382 C.S.M. (A/R.S.M.) Herbert James Ball, 11th Bn.

Bar to M.M.

No. SD/3029 Lance-Sergeant Herbert George Thompsett, 13th Bn.   (Brighton)

M.M.

No. SD/5966 Private Horace Atkinson, 11th Bn. (Lee)
No. SD/5743 Lance-Corporal Lawrence Barker, 11th Bn. (Broadwater)
No. SD/573 Private Arthur Beeney, 11th Bn. (Hailsham)

No. G/17790 Lance-Corporal Alfred C. Billings, 12th Bn. (East Grinstead)

No. SD/1220 Sergeant William Boreham, 12th Bn. (Rye)

No. G/16117 Private Henry C. Clarke, 12th Bn. (Brighton)

No. SD/1017 Private Horace Edward Cockett, 11th Bn. (Battle)

No. 145 Corporal (L/Sgt.) James Henry Guy Duke, (Battle)

"After his commanding officer had been wounded, Lance-Corporal Duke dressed his injuries and took charge. He collected the men and led them on to such good purpose that they won their objective, and mainly through his exertion and example."

Saturday October 20th 1917

Further Local Winners of the Military Medal

The list issued on Thursday night in the *"London Gazette"* of N.C.O.'s and men to whom the King has awarded the Military Medal includes the following who all belong to the Royal Sussex Regiment :-

No. SD/2904 L/Cpl. Edwin Edwards, 13th Bn. (Jumpers Town)
No. G/16124 Pte. A.J. Field, 12th Bn. (Burgess Hill)
No. SD/3341 Cpl. Herbert Firth, 13th Bn. (Barnsley)
No. G/15408 Pte. P. Foster, 12th Bn. (Doncaster)

 No. SD/1039 Sgt. James Charles Giles, 11th Bn. (Icklesham)

No. G/14952 Pte. Robert Green, 12th Bn. (Haddenham)
No. G/17829 Pte. Herbert J. Guiel, 12th Bn. (Worthing)
No. 3186 Cpl. Albert William Heise, 11th Bn. (Brighton)

 No. G/16429 Pte. Edward Hermitage, 13th Bn. (Ore)

No. G/15449 Cpl. Harry Jordan, 12th Bn. (Englefield Green)
No. SD/2137 Pte. Charles Alfred Lisher, 12th Bn. (Worthing)
No. G/15459 L/Cpl. William Edward Littlewood, 12th Bn. (Gainsborough)
No. SD/1070 L/Cpl. John Lloyd, 11th Bn. (Uckfield)
No. G/16046 Cpl. Thomas Lucas, 13th Bn. (Holmwood)
No. SD/2183 Cpl. William Alfred Milbourne, 12th Bn. (Wandsworth)
No. SD/3905 Cpl. (A/Sgt.) Thomas Mills, 11th Bn. (Walsall)
No. G/15594 Pte. William J. Milton, 12th Bn. (Watton-at-Stone)
No. SD/1641 Pte. John Edward Mitchell, 12th Bn. (Newick)
No. G/16722 Pte. Charles S. Norman, 11th Bn. (South Norwood)

 No. G/6356 Pte. George Francis Oliver, 12th Bn. (Eastbourne)

 No. SD/458 Sgt. Clarence Packham, 11th Bn. (Rotherfield)

No. SD/338 Sgt. Harry Pell, 11th Bn. (Louth)
No. G/9418 Pte. Jack Percival, 13th Bn. (Widnes)
No. G14161 Pte. Herbert S. Read, 12th Bn. (Upper Parkstone)
No. G/20417 Pte. Charles Bernard William Redman, 11th Bn. (East Grinstead)
No. G/15777 Cpl. Herbert Henry Renshaw, 11th Bn. (Colchester)
No. G/16744 Pte. Lawrence S. Rowlands, 11th Bn. (Purley Oaks)
No. SD/363 Pte. George Sloane, 11th Bn. (Seaford)
No. G/19872 Pte. James Smith, 12th Bn. (Cooling)
No. 1332 Sgt. S.C. Stockbridge, 13th Bn. (Harefield)

 No. SD/472 L/Sgt. William John Stone, 11th Bn. (Abingdon)

No. G/16080 Pte. William H. Taylor, 13th Bn. (Worthing)
No. SD/5649 Pte. (L/Cpl.) Sidney Toogood, 13th Bn. (Mitcham)
No. 3409 Pte. Jack S. Waters, 12th Bn. (Hove)
No. SD/1740 Sgt. Harry West, 12th Bn. (Hove)
No. SD/5772 Pte. William Hartley White, 13th Bn. (Portslade-by-Sea)

Citation for No. G/17829 Pte. Herbert J. Guiel, 12th Bn. (Worthing)

For most conspicuous gallantry and devotion to duty in the Battle of Ypres on July 31st and August 1st and 2nd. This man was a Battalion runner. He worked unceasingly during the operations without resting, and often delivered ,messages throughout heavy shellfire. He frequently, traversed ground that was a maze of battered enemy trenches and shell holes full of water; but in spite of being wet throughout and without rest he carried out most dangerous duties with courage and cheerfulness. By his conduct under most trying conditions he set a fine example to his comrades.

Tuesday October 23rd 1917

More Sussex D.C.M. Winners

The Distinguished Conduct Medal has been awarded to the undermentioned N.C.O.'s and men for acts of gallantry which have not yet been specified in the *"London Gazette"* :-

No. G/15256 Private G.W. Mallett, 11th Bn. Royal Sussex Regiment, (Norwich)
No. SD/537 A/C.S.M. B.J. Oatley, 11th Bn. Royal Sussex Regiment, (Marylebone)
No. SD/4159 Lance-Sergeant A. Sippetts, 13th Bn. Royal Sussex Regiment, (East Grinstead)
No. G/15007 Lance-Corporal E.A. Smith, 12th Bn. Royal Sussex Regiment, (Ipswich)
No. G/15987 Corporal George Welch, 13th Bn. Royal Sussex Regiment, (Chichester)

Wednesday October 24th 1917

Chichester Man's Gallantry

Of the three Chichester recipients of the D.C.M. recorded in yesterday's official list, it will be remembered that an intimation concerning the award to Sergeant George Welch, Royal Sussex Regiment, whose home is at 102, Victoria Road, Portfield, Chichester, appeared in these columns nearly a fortnight ago. The sergeant, who is not yet 21, and had been at the Front over a year before being wounded, was congratulated by his Lieutenant-Colonel in a letter written to him on 5th September upon winning the distinction for his excellent work during the fight on 31st July and subsequent days.

He adds : "I only found out afterwards that it was you who helped me on to the battalion headquarters after I collapsed from exhaustion on the third night of the battle. I want to take this opportunity of thanking you."

Monday October 29th 1917

Lieutenant-Colonel W.C. Millward D.S.O.

The official intimation of the award of the D.S.O. to Acting Lieutenant-Colonel W.C. Millward will remind many people of the young officer's wonderful career since he enlisted in the Royal Sussex Regiment in the early days of the war. From Private to Lieutenant-Colonel in just over two and a half years is a record very few soldiers have achieved. It is one of the war's romances. Lieutenant-Colonel Millward is the son of Mr. Arthur Millward, the former Worcestershire cricketer, who was for some time coach to the young players in the Sussex Nursery. He and his son live at Eastbourne subsequently.

Thursday November 1st 1917

Worthing Medallist's Death

Sergeant Jones, a former member of the Worthing Fire Brigade, and a winner of the Military Medal, has died in hospital at Huddersfield from the effects of the wounds received in action. The body is to be brought to Worthing and interred at Broadwater Cemetery on Saturday with military honours. The Worthing Fire Brigade will also attend.

Saturday November 3rd 1917
Sergeant Thompsett : Keymer

Sergeant Thompsett, Royal Sussex Regiment, of Keymer, arrived at his home yesterday from the front on leave preparatory to a period of training for a commission. He has been in the Army three years, and has been awarded the Military Medal. Mr. G. Stevens, headmaster of the Hassocks Council Schools, claims three of the "old boys" of the Hassocks Schools as winners of this distinction, all of the Royal Sussex Regiment, viz., Sergeant Thompsett, Private Taylor (a well-known Hassocks footballer before the war), and Private P. Winter.

Monday November 5th 1917

Latest Sussex winners of the Military medal

War decorations continue to be conferred upon the sons of Sussex who are so courageously upholding the country's good name on the various battle fronts. In the latest list of the awards the following are mentioned :-

Bar to M.M.

No. SD/1017 Private Horace Edward Cockett, 11th Bn. Royal Sussex Regiment, (Battle)

(M.M. gazetted 18th October 1917)

M.M.

No. G/240130 Private George Arnold, 5th Bn. Royal Sussex Regiment, (Crowborough)
No. G/240665 Corporal Robert H.W. Bryant, Royal Sussex Regiment, (St. Leonards)

No. G/2235 Private (L/Cpl.) David Cheeseman, 8th Bn. Royal Sussex Regiment, (East Chiltington)

No. G/18184 Private Albert R. Cramp, 13th Bn. Royal Sussex Regiment, (Rye)
No. G/202406 Private George Frederick Gardner, 12th Bn. Royal Sussex Regiment, (Northampton)
No. SD/5509 Lance-Corporal Arthur Gibson, 13th Bn. Royal Sussex Regiment, (Willesden)
No. G/3878 Private Thomas R. Jeffery, 8th Bn. Royal Sussex Regiment, (Newhaven)
No. G/10803 Lance-Corporal (A/Cpl.) Harold Henry Knight, 8th Bn. Royal Sussex Regiment, (Taunton)

Heathfield Hero

Corporal I.H. Farmer wins Military Medal

Since returning to France a month ago after having ten days' leave, Corporal Isaac H. Farmer, husband of Mrs. Farmer of 10, The Bungalows, Broad Oak, Heathfield, has been awarded the Military Medal for gallantry and devotion to duty. He enlisted in "Lowther's Own" Battalion of the Royal Sussex Regiment in November, 1914 and was drafted to France in March, 1916. He was exceedingly well known in the district, where he was born. Before joining the Army he was employed by Miss Emerson, of Hollians Farm. Two of his brothers are serving with the Army and one is one Government work. A sister is also doing her duty as postwoman at Broad Oak.

Tuesday November 6th 1917

More Military Medals

A special supplement to the *"London Gazette"* announces the award of the Military Medal to the following N.C.O.'s and men associated with Sussex :-

No. G/260092 Private (now Corporal) Benjamin T. Link, 9th Bn. Royal Sussex Regiment, (Tenterden)
No. G/18218 Lance-Corporal William John Martin, 13th Bn. Royal Sussex Regiment, (Etchington)
No. G/10322 Private Charles McCormick, 13th Bn. Royal Sussex Regiment, (Crawley)
No. G/14845 Lance-Sergeant John Mole, 13th Bn. Royal Sussex Regiment, (Carlton)

No. G/6435 Private Leonard Percival Newham, 13th Bn. Royal Sussex Regiment, (Eastbourne)

No. G/2244 Corporal (A/Sgt.) T.F. Relfwest, 8th Bn. Royal Sussex Regiment, (Ferner Green)
No. G/2795 Sergeant George Aubrey Stapley, 8th Bn. Royal Sussex Regiment, (Buckstrad)

No. G/2117 Sergeant Archibald Stunt, 8th Bn. Royal Sussex Regiment, (St. Leonards)

No. G/2371 Private William I. Swallow, 8th Bn. Royal Sussex Regiment, (Lower Edmonton)
No. G/201699 Private William J. Theobald, 13th Bn. Royal Sussex Regiment, (Rochester)
No. G/18000 Corporal E.E. Weeks-Pearson, 13th Bn. Royal Sussex Regiment, (Hastings)
No. G/1664 Private Thomas Wilmshurst, 8th Bn. Royal Sussex Regiment, (Hurstwood)
No. G/14899 Private Cyril Woollard, 13th Bn. Royal Sussex Regiment, (Cambridge)
No. SD/5345 Lance-Corporal Ernest Worcester, 13th Bn. Royal Sussex Regiment, (Horsham)

The Citation for Corporal E.E. Weeks-Pearson reads as follows :-

"For most conspicuous gallantry and good leading in the Battle of Ypres on July 31st and August 1st and 2nd. He rendered valuable assistance in organising ammunition, water and ration parties, and bringing them up a road heavily sniped by the enemy. He made five journeys for this purpose, and succeeded in getting rations, etc. to his company."
He has since been promoted to the rank of sergeant.

Friday November 15th 1917

Shoreham Soldier Decorated For Gallantry

The award of the Military Medal has been made to Private B.C. Bingham, (of Shoreham) Royal Sussex Regiment, "for most conspicuous gallantry and devotion to duty in the operation at Menin Road on the 25th, 26th and 27th September, 1917. This man was with his platoon in an advanced position, and in the absence of N.C.O.'s, who had become casualties, he rendered valuable assistance to his platoon commander in organising the position and in keeping up the spirits of the men. On more than one occasion he carried messages under heavy shell fire. He set a fine example of devotion to duty and disregard of personal danger.

Mentioned in Dispatches

2nd Lieutenant S.A. Andrews, M.C., 12th Bn. Royal Sussex Regiment, has been mentioned in dispatches for good work in the field.

Tuesday 20th November 1917

Rewards for Gallantry

The King has conferred on the following rewards for gallantry on local men :-

M.C.

T/2nd Lieutenant Thomas Clarke, 7th Bn. Royal Sussex Regiment,
T/2nd Lieutenant Charles Henry Lawrence, Royal Sussex Regiment,

Hove Corporal wins a Medal

Mrs. Waters, of 90, Rutland Road, Hove, has received news that her son, 3409 Corporal Jack S. Waters, 9th Bn. Royal Sussex Regiment, has been awarded the Military Medal,

"For most conspicuous gallantry and good leading in the Battle of Ypres, on July 31st, August 1st and 2nd. While crossing No Man's Land, the N.C.O. in charge of the Lewis gun team was wounded. This man at once took charge of the team, and led them to their objective. During the whole period of the operations his gun was always in action, and his cheerfulness at a very critical period was of the utmost value in keeping up the spirits of the men of his section.."
Corporal Waters, who has been in France for the last 14 months, is expected home on leave shortly.

Wednesday November 21st 1917

Rewards for Gallantry

The King has approved of the following decorations for gallantry and distinguished service in the field :-

M.M.

No. L/6430 Sergeant Edwin C. Attree, 8th Bn. Royal Sussex Regiment, (Tottenham)
No. G/2726 Lance-Corporal Frederick M. Emsley, 8th Bn. Royal Sussex Regiment, (Hove)

Thursday November 22nd 1917

Lewes Man wins D.C.M.

In recognition of his gallant conduct in the field, Sergeant Herbert Woollard, a Lewes man, has been awarded the D.C.M. Sergeant Woollard is a son of Mr. and Mrs. Woollard, of Brook Street, Lewes, and joined the Royal Sussex Regiment soon after the war broke out, relinquishing a remuneration post to do so. He has been at the front for nearly two years, and has been in all the big battles. Luckily he has escaped being wounded, although in connection with the incident for which he was awarded the Medal a German revolver bullet, fired at close range, just grazed his cheek and ear. He had his revenge by killing the German and securing his revolver. His officers, in a letter, spoke highly of his conduct on all occasions. Another son of Mr. and Mrs. Woollard - Gunner Albert Gurney Woollard - is in the R.G.A.

Walderton Military Medallist

Honour has come to Walderton in the shape of the Military Medal awarded to Private C. Blunden, Royal Sussex Regiment. The official announcement states that the medal was awarded "For most conspicuous bravery and devotion to duty in the operations at Menin Road on 25th, 26th, and 27th September.
This man was a stretcher-bearer. Regardless of all personal danger, he continuously rescued wounded men under very heavy shell fire and machine-gun fire, and assisted to carry them to the regimental aid post. This work he continued until too exhausted to carry on further. Throughout, his courage, coolness, and devotion to duty were a magnificent example to the remaining men."

Private Blunden formerly worked for Mr. Thirwell, but just previous to joining up he was employed by Mr. Warren Smith, of Emsworth. Naturally the award has caused much enthusiasm and elation in the village, being the first honour conferred on one of its men in this war.

Friday November 23rd 1917

Bar to Military Medal : Newick

Private J.E. Mitchell, Royal Sussex Regiment, who was recently awarded the Military Medal for conspicuous gallantry and devotion to duty, has now gained a further distinction in the form of a Bar to the medal for "Devotion as a runner on 25th, 26th and 27th September, 1917, east of Ypres, during very heavy shelling."
He is the son of Mr. John Mitchell, Sunnyside, Newick. He enlisted in the Royal Sussex Regiment three years ago, and proceeded to France with his battalion in March, 1916. Six months later he was wounded in an arm and brought to England, but having recovered, he returned to France in February last.

Wednesday November 28th 1917

M.C. Award for Sussex Officer

The award of the Military Cross was bestowed upon Lieutenant B.W. Skipworth, Royal Sussex Regiment, attached to 9th Bn. M.G.C.

Saturday December 1st 1917

Warnham Medallist

Corporal W.J. Cox, of the Machine-Gun Company of Sussex Territorials, has been awarded the Military Medal for gallantry stepping into the breach and taking charge of the men after his officer had been hit. Joe Cox, as he is familiarly known at his home in Warnham, is one of the most modest of individuals, and characteristically looks upon this little incident as merely a matter of course. But evidently there was more in it than he personally will disclose, and the award will afford great satisfaction to his many friends. Joe Cox will be remembered at Brighton County Cricket Club. He joined the Territorial Force when a company was formed for Warnham, he went through the Gallipoli venture with his battalion, then moved on to Egypt, and is now doing service with the machine-gun section in Palestine.

Brevet Colonelcy

Awarded to Bt. Lt-Colonel J.B. Wroughton, C.M.G. 2nd Bn. Royal Sussex Regiment,

Tuesday December 11th 1917

Military Medal for Hove Man

The many friends of Mr. and Mrs. George Taylor, 99, Montgomery Street, Hove, will be pleased to hear that their son, 8114, Private Harry Taylor, Stretcher Bearer, who went out with the First Expeditionary Force, and who has come unharmed through many of the big battles, including Mons, has been awarded the Military Medal for gallantry on the field.

Wednesday December 12th 1917

Mentioned in Dispatches

The *"London Gazette"* contains a dispatch from Sir Douglas Haig conveying a list of names of officers whose distinguished and gallant services and devotion to duty he considers deserving of special mention. The list includes the names of :-

Bt. Lt.-Colonel (T/Brig.-Gen.) A.E. Glasgow, D.S.O., Royal Sussex Regiment,
Major (T/Brig.-Gen.) C.E. Bond, C.M.G., D.S.O., Royal Sussex Regiment,
Major J.S. Cameron, D.S.O., Royal Sussex Regiment,
Captain G.H.B. de Chair, M.C., Royal Sussex Regiment,

Thursday December 13th 1917

Further Local Honours

A list published in the *"London Gazette"* of officers mentioned by Sir Douglas Haig for distinguished and gallant services and devotion to duty includes the names of :-

Captain E.H. Preston, M.C., Royal Sussex Regiment,
Lt. (T/Capt.) M. Wallington, M.C., Royal Sussex Regiment,

A list of those whom the King has honoured for bravery in the field includes the following :-

M.M.

No. G/2489 Sergeant Ernest C.A. Bunce, 8th Bn. Royal Sussex Regiment, (Victoria)
No. G/12419 Private Robert Coates, 7th Bn. Royal Sussex Regiment, (Sth. Wimbledon)
No. G/545 Lance-Corporal Richard Holman, 8th Bn. Royal Sussex Regiment, (Ardingly)

 No. G/18247 Corporal A.G. Weller, 13th Bn. Royal Sussex Regiment, (Rye)

(All gazetted 12th December, 1917)

Friday December 15th 1917

A SCOUT'S DEVOTION

Military Medal for brave Walthamstow lad.

We hear that another of Walthamstow's heroic lads has given his life for his country. Private Frederick Edward Shirley, the second son of Mr. and Mrs. Richard Shirley, of 333 Higham Hill road, was killed upon October 30th.
But 19 years of age, and a winning disposition, he left for France with a cyclist battalion in August last, and was there attached to the royal Sussex Regiment. With the gallant men of this regiment he saw very heavy fighting, and his conduct was such that, in the words of a chum, "he was loved by the C.O. downwards."

His devotion to duty was such that his recommendation for a decoration is spoken of as somewhat official. We trust that even now the award may be made and his parents receive a token of a nation's gratitude, some solace to them perhaps; at least, something to tell them of the way in which their boy, a true scout, did his duty.

The Colonel's respect

We have since received the gratifying news that Private Shirley has been awarded the Military Medal. His colonel, writing to the parents, says; "I knew your son well, and had learnt to respect him for his gallantry and fearlessness. He was a true soldier . . . brave and fearless to the last, and always cheerful and happy."

In Divisional Orders, in which the award of the decoration is announced, the colonel says; "This man was a runner-up who carried messages to and from all parts of the trenches under most heavy shell fire. At one time his rifle was blown out of his hands, but he carried the message to its destination, going through a heavy barrage." He worked in this way for 48 hours almost without rest or food, both before and during the attack. His cheery manner to all he met was most inspiring, but his great asset was his courage. When he knew his company commander wanted a message got to some place through an intense barrage, he repeatedly volunteered to go, and he was more than once the means of getting valuable and urgent messages through when all other communication were destroyed."

It is a touching circumstance that the brave lad himself had heard that he was to be recommended "for something or other," as he expressed it in a letter, written but two days before his death, to Councillor Chas. Howard.

Tuesday December 18th 1917

Sussex Officers Honoured

The King has been pleased to confer the undermentioned rewards to officers of the Royal Sussex Regiment for gallantry and distinguished service in the field :-

Bar to D.S.O.

T/Major (A/Lt.-Col.) Hugh Thomas Kay Robinson, D.S.O. 13th Bn.
(D.S.O. gazetted 4th June, 1917)

D.S.O.

T/2nd Lieutenant (A/Capt.) Philip Lindsay Clark,

M.C.

T/2nd Lieutenant William Henry Pope Bennett, 13th Bn.

T/Lieutenant Villiers Heatly Couldrey, 13th Bn.
T/2nd Lieutenant John Newton Dyke, 11th Bn.
T/2nd Lieutenant (A/Capt.) Eric John Harden, 13th Bn.
T/2nd Lieutenant Arthur Blachford Woodrow, 2nd Bn.

Wednesday December 19th 1917

Medals for Sussex Men

The most recent list of honours contains the following names of Sussex winners :-

M.M.

No. G/17894 Private John E. Potiphar, 12th Bn. Royal Sussex Regiment, (Brighton)

No. G/12966 L/Corporal Cyril Joseph Wilcock, 12th Bn. Royal Sussex Regiment, (Willesden Green)

Partridge Green Military Medallist

Private E. Hoad, of the Royal Sussex Regiment, has had a letter from his Divisional Commander congratulating him on his well-earned honour of the Military Medal. He joined at the commencement of the war, served in the Sulva Bay operations, and has been in the recent fighting. He has been wounded. His father, joined the National Reserve in November, 1914, and is still serving.

Thursday December 20th 1917

Royal Sussex Officers and Men Mentioned in Dispatches

The following officers, non-commissioned officers, and men of the Royal Sussex Regiment are among those named in Sir Douglas Haig's dispatch as deserving special mention, and now published in the *"London Gazette"* :-

Bt. Colonel J.B. Wroughton, C.M.G.
Captain (A/Mjr.) W.H.W. Apperley,
T/Captain W.H. Baddeley, M.C.,
T/Captain C. Bartlett, M.C.,
Major (T/Lt.-Col.) H.F. Bidder,
T/Captain G.O.L. Campbell, M.C.,
Major (A/Lt.-Col.) William R. Campion, T.D., M.P.,
T/Major F. Cassels,
Major (T/Lt.-Col.) W. Coote-Brown,
2nd Lieutenant (A/Capt.) E. Dolleymore,
T/2nd Lieutenant R.V.H. Ellis,
T/Major T. Foster,
T/2nd Lieutenant E.B. Glenny,
T/2nd Lieutenant (A/Capt.) E.J. Harden,
Captain (T/Lt.-Col.) M.V.B. Hill, D.S.O.,M.C.
Lieutenant (A/Capt.) J.E.C. Langham,
T/2nd Lieutenant C. Lapworth,
T/Lieutenant (A/Capt.) N. de Putron MacRoberts, D.S.O.,M.C.,
Major (A/Lt.-Col.) W.C. Millward, D.S.O.,
2nd Lieutenant O.D. Pearce,
T/Q.M. and Hon. Lt. J. Solomon,
Major (A/Lt.-Col.) R.H. Waithman,
T/2nd Lieutenant J.A. Wright,
No. 142 R.Q.M.S. F.R. Aldridge, W.O., Class 11.,
No. 1512 Sergeant P. Andrews,
No. 653 Corporal F. Bennett,
No. G/2381 R.Q.M.S. J.W. Boyce, W.O., Class 11.,
No. G/2316 Private C.E. Brown, (killed)
No. 891 Sergeant W.H. Budgen,
No. 560 Sergeant E.W. Cutting,
No. L/8712 Sergeant W. Farrell,
No. L/7688 C.S.M. W. Herridge, W.O., Class 11.,
No. 240017 Sergeant R.J. Hyland,
No. 9 Sergeant D. McArthur,
No. 3590 Sergeant A.J. Newnham,
No. 5391 C.S.M. (A/R.S.M.) C.W. Paine, W.O., Class 11.,

 No. 77888 R.Q.M.S. W. Raby, W.O., Class 11., 7th Bn.

No. 241 R.Q.M.S. N. Stevenson, W.O., Class 11.,
No. 1701 Private A. Tapner,
No. 240007 Colour-Sergeant (A/C.Q.M.S.) T.H. Tremaine,

Saturday December 22nd 1917

A Waldron Military Medallist

The youngest son of Mr. and Mrs. G. Evenden, of Crossways, Waldron, Private Frank Briton Evenden, of the Royal Sussex Regiment, has been awarded the Military Medal for an act of bravery. He is the first man of the village who has won this distinction. Private Evenden was home on leave from France a short time ago, and on his return the news of the recognition of his gallantry awaited him. He joined the Army soon after the commencement of the war.

"London Gazette" Tuesday January 1st 1918

The KING has been graciously pleased, to give directions for the following promotions in and appointments to the Most Distinguished Order of Saint Michael and Saint George, in recognition of valuable services in connection with the war. Dated 1st Jan. 1918.

To be Additional Members of the Third or Companions, of the said Most Distinguished Order: —

C.M.G.

 Lt-Col. John Arthur Coghill Somerville, Late Royal Sussex Regiment,

Wednesday January 2nd 1918

Local D.S.O. Awards

The following awards of the Distinguished Service Order have been made to the officers mentioned below :-

Major (T/Lt-Col) Harold Francis Bidder, 3rd Bn. Royal Sussex Regiment, S.R. att. M.G.C.

Major (A/Lt-Col) William Robert Campion M.P., 4th Bn. Royal Sussex Regiment,

T/Major Frank Cassels, Royal Sussex Regiment,

T/Lt-Col William Coote-Brown, Royal Sussex Regiment,

Major (A/Lt-Col) Roland Henry Waithman, 2nd Bn. Royal Sussex Regiment,

Military Cross Award to Chichester Officer

Second Lieutenant Walter F. Howard, 16th Bn. Royal Sussex Regiment, son of Mr. C.W. Howard, of East Street, Chichester, is among the recent recipients of the Military Cross, having won it for gallantry on 6th November 1917, which he describes as "a great day for the Sussex Yeomanry in Palestine."

M.C.

Captain (A/Lt.-Col.) Dudley Graham Johnson, D.S.O. South Wales Borderers, attached to the 2nd Battalion Royal Sussex Regiment,

Reverend T.J. Williams, Chaplain to the Forces 4th Class, attached to the 7th Battalion Royal Sussex Regiment,

T /Capt. Richard John Penfold Wyatt, 4th Bn.

Thursday January 3rd 1918

Military Cross Awards

Awards for whom the King has awarded the Military Cross for distinguished war service :-

No. S/516 R.S.M. Josiah Bloomfield, 8th Bn. Royal Sussex Regiment,
T/Capt. Sydney Thacker Buck, 8th Bn. Royal Sussex Regiment,
T/Capt. Frederick Pepys Cockrell, Royal Sussex Regiment, S.R.
Lt. (A/Capt.) Herbert Cecil Coleman, 9th Bn. Royal Sussex Regiment,
Capt. Walter Douglas Downes, Royal Sussex Regiment and Nigeria Regiment,

T/Lt. (A/Capt.) Percy Fredrick Drew, Royal Sussex Regiment,

T/Capt. Noel Hector Hampton, 8th Bn. Royal Sussex Regiment,

T/Capt. Richard Copeland Denton Hind, 7th Bn. Royal Sussex Regiment,

T /Capt. Harold Drummond Hillier, Gloucester Regiment, attd. Royal Sussex Regiment,
T/Lt. Leonard Archibald Frederick Ireland, 8th Bn. Royal Sussex Regiment,

T/Capt. Alexander Campbell White Knox R.A.M.C. att. 2nd Bn. Royal Sussex Regiment,

Lt (A /Capt.) Leslie Phillips Marshall, W. York R , Spec. Res. attd. Royal Sussex Regiment,

Friday January 4th 1918

More Military Crosses

The following further winners of the Military Cross are among those officially announced :-

Lieutenant Rupert Charles Godfrey Middleton, 4th Bn. Royal Sussex Regiment,

Captain Morres Nickalls, Sussex Yeomanry, (16th Bn.)
Lieutenant James Vernon Lee, Sussex Yeomanry,
No. 3461 C.S.M. William Arthur Stace, Royal Sussex Regiment,
Captain Montagu Trevor Turner, 2nd Bn. Royal Sussex Regiment,
2nd Lieutenant Frank Percival Twine, 5th Bn. Royal Sussex Regiment,
No. 6404 C.S.M. (A/R.S.M.) Percy White, 12th Bn. Royal Sussex Regiment,

Saturday January 5th 1918

More local medal winners

The list of winners of the Distinguished Conduct Medal and the Military Medal, issued last night, includes the following :-

D.C.M.

No. G/3811 A/C.S.M. J. Bartlett, 9th Bn. Royal Sussex Regiment, (Eastbourne)
No. G/9117 C.S.M. C.J. Deeprose, 2nd Bn. Royal Sussex Regiment, (Rye)
No. G/240048 Sergeant P.G. Elphick, 5th Bn. Royal Sussex Regiment, (Newick)

M.M.

No. G/20332 L/Cpl. Herbert J. Back, 8th Bn. Royal Sussex Regiment, (Faversham)
No. G/15802 Pte. Frederick Chandler, 11th Bn. Royal Sussex Regiment, (Lodsworth)
No. G/2499 L/Cpl. (A/Cpl.) Henry Hawkett, 8th Bn. Royal Sussex Regiment, (Westbourne Park)
No. G/233460 Cpl. Albert Allan Tribe, 16th Bn. Royal Sussex Regiment, attd. 74th Div. Sig. Coy. R.E. (Bognor)

Monday January 7th 1918

The Rewards of Gallantry : Brighton

An interesting ceremony took place at Preston Barracks, Brighton, on Saturday, when Colonel R.M. Rodwell, the Officer Commanding the troops at Brighton, distributed eleven Military Medals awarded for acts of gallantry in the field. Mr. A. Diplock, of 8, Connaught Road, Hove, was handed the medal gained by his son, Sergeant H.R. Diplock, Royal Sussex Regiment, who has died, the other recipients being ;-

Mr. R. Emsley, 68, Grange Road, Hove, late Private in the Royal Sussex Regiment,
(who received a medal with bar) ;
Mr. G. Scutt, Hollingdean Road, Brighton, late Private, Royal Sussex Regiment, Mr. R. Knight, 45, Arnold Street,, late Lance-Corporal, Royal Sussex Regiment.
The Colonel, who was accompanied by Adjutant Carnaghan, congratulated each recipient as he pinned the medal on his breast, and warmly shook hands with him.

The valorous deeds which gained the distinctions were recited to the troops on parade by Colonel Rodwell (who referred sympathetically to the death of Sergeant Diplock) as follows :-

Mr. R. Emsley (late No. 3340, Private, Royal Sussex Regiment).

For conspicuous gallantry and untiring devotion to duty displayed at the Schwaben Redoubt during the operations of 21st October, 1916. Private Emsley, who was a stretcher-bearer, worked untiringly frequently under heavy shell fire, removing wounded in the area behind the captured German line. He then went to the captured position and brought more wounded away. Seeing that the numbers were more than the Regimental stretcher-bearers could cope with, he personally went to the advanced dressing station and brought R.A.M.C. bearers back. He showed them where the wounded were, and it as largely owing to his devotion to duty that when his Battalion was relieved on the night of the 22nd all wounded had been evacuated from the captured trench.
He continued to work until completely exhausted, and was a striking example of devotion to duty to his comrades. He has been awarded the Bar to the Military Medal for a similar act of gallantry.

Mr. G. Scutt (late No. 9447, Lance-Corporal, Royal Sussex Regiment).

During an intense bombardment by the Germans in the Loos sector on 8th and 9th March, 1915, he established communications between the front line companies and Headquarters, by laying and repairing telephone wires, under very trying conditions, in the face of the enemy. He has been continually with the Regiment (2nd Royal Sussex) from 12th August, 1914, to 27th November, 1916, when he as wounded. He has on numerous occasions rendered valuable service in laying and repairing telephone lines, under very trying conditions.

Mr. R. Knight (late No. 2947 Lance-Corporal, Royal Sussex Regiment).

On 30th June, 1916, Lance-Corporal Knight, with a comrade, made a bombing attack on the enemy trenches, cutting barbed wire. He fell back wounded, but hearing the cries of our own wounded, he went out, and brought several in, being again wounded while doing so.

No. 9685 Sergeant H.R. Diplock, Royal Sussex Regiment, (killed in action)

For conspicuous gallantry in assisting wounded, under very heavy shell fire.

Tuesday January 8th 1918

Gallant Hove Ex-Constable

The gallant conduct of a member of the Hove Police Force now on active service abroad is referred to in the proceedings of the Watch Committee, which will be brought before the Town Council on Thursday. The Chief Constable (Mr. W. Cocks) reports to the Committee, that Henry James Baker, who joined the Royal Sussex Regiment on the 11th April, 1915, from the Police Force, has been awarded the Military Medal for gallantry, &c., during a battle from the 25th to 28th September, 1917, the following particulars of which have been sent to him :-
During a battle, 25th to 28th September, 1917, out of 4 Lewis gun teams, each of 6 men and a N.C.O. (28 men in all), three complete teams were lost going into action, I was N.C.O. in charge of remaining team. During the night of the 26th and early morning of the 27th a very heavy barrage was set up by the enemy. Three times my gun was buried. With difficulty I, with the aid of another man, recovered, re-cleaned, and got the gun into action again. Just at this time the enemy very fiercely counter-attacked. From that time we kept the gun in action until relieved, and brought it out safely.
The Committee resolved that the Report be entered on the minutes and the Town Clerk instructed to communicate to the soldier the Committee's appreciation of his gallantry.

Captain M.T. Turner, M.C., Cuckfield

Captain M.T. Turner, of the Royal Sussex Regiment, who has been awarded the Military Cross, is the eldest son of the late Mr. Montague Turner, and of Mrs. Montague Turner, of Cuckfield. He has had a long spell of service with the Royal Sussex Regiment during the war. Captain Turner was well known as a cricketer and a footballer at Cuckfield, and the honour conferred upon him is keenly appreciated by his many friends and associates in both fields of sport in days gone by.

Thursday January 10th 1918

Gallant deeds that brought rewards

The announcement of the award of decorations to the officers named below was made some time back, and the deeds for which they were singled out are now officially described :-

D.S.O.

T/Lieutenant (A/Capt.) Noel de Putron MacRoberts, M.C., 13th Bn.

For conspicuous gallantry and devotion to duty. Although wounded early in the day, he gallantly led his company under heavy shell and machine-gun fire to its objective - a village - which he captured, together with over 200 prisoners, four field guns and two machine-guns. He then remained at duty in spite of his wounds, until he reorganised his company and consolidated his position, greatly inspiring all ranks by his magnificent courage and gallantry.

Bar to M.C.

T/Lieutenant (A/Captain) Cecil Arthur Allen, M.C., 11th Bn.

For conspicuous gallantry and devotion to duty. He led his company with great dash and gallantry in the attack, and captured and consolidated his objective under heavy shell fire. Though wounded, he refused to leave his men until ordered by his commanding officer to do so. His courage and devotion to duty were a splendid example to all ranks.
(M.C. gazetted 21st December, 1916)

T/Lieutenant Richard Charles Hall, M.C., 8th Bn.

For conspicuous gallantry and devotion to duty. He was exposed to continuous shell and machine-gun fire throughout the day while marking out a track in the rear of the advancing infantry. He not only completed his task, but also attended to the wounded of his own and other units, being under fire the whole time. His determination and fearlessness were a very fine example to all.
(M.C. gazetted 20th October, 1916)

T/Captain Henry Steedman Lewis, M.C.   11th Bn.

For conspicuous gallantry and devotion to duty, when Adjutant of his Battalion. Throughout the operations he rendered his Battalion Commander most excellent service. When the Battalion was counter-attacked he passed along the line encouraging and directing his men by his cheerfulness and contempt for danger. Though rendered unconscious by a shell he remained at duty on regaining consciousness. He set a magnificent example to all.
(M.C. gazetted 24th June, 1916)

Monday January 14th 1918

A Sussex Airman's Successes

Second Lieutenant St. Cyprian Churchill Tayler, Royal Sussex Regiment and Royal Flying Corps., who recently received the Military Cross, earned this decoration :-
"For conspicuous gallantry and devotion to duty in leading offensive patrols against enemy aircraft. On five occasions at least he and his patrol have attacked and brought down hostile machines. These successes were almost entirely due to his very skilful piloting."

Palestine fighting

In the dispatch of General Sir Archibald Murray, K.C.B., lately Commander-in Chief of the Egyptian Expeditionary Force, the following names were brought to the notice "for gallant or distinguished conduct in the field" or for valuable services :-

Staff

Major J.M. Hulton, Royal Sussex Regiment,
Lieutenant (T/Cpt.) R.E. Loder, Royal Sussex Regiment, (D of W)

Yeomanry

Captain (A/Mjr.) E. The Earl Winterton,

Royal Sussex Regiment

T/Lieutenant-Colonel H.S. Ashworth, (Capt. ret. pay, R.of O.) (killed)
Major S.W.P. Beale,
Captain C.A. Field,
Lieutenant R.C.G. Middleton, M.C.
Captain (T/Mjr.) A.C. Sayer, 16th Bn.
No. 320001 C.S.M. J.C.S. Balcombe, 16th Bn.
No. 200131 C.S.M. H. Catt,
No. 320002 R.Q.M.S. S. Fennell, 16th Bn.
No. 200105 Lance-Sergeant W. Knight,
No. 200449 Sergeant H.C.C. Simmonds, 4th Bn. (killed)
No. 200087 C.S.M. J. Simmons, 4th Bn.

Wednesday January 16th 1918

Military Medal Winner

A further Royal Sussex winner of the Military Medal was announced last night :-

No. G/20296 Corporal (A/Sgt.) J.F. Turner, 12th Bn.

Thursday January 17th 1918

Mentioned in Despatches

In General Allenby's despatch from Palestine, there are mentions for the Royal Sussex Regiment :-

Quartermaster & Hon. Lieutenant C.A. Bolton,

Captain A.N.H. Weekes,

Saturday January 19th 1918

More Awards for Gallantry

The following awards for gallantry and distinguished conduct in the field are announced in a supplement to the *"London Gazette"* issued last night :-

D.S.O.

Major (T/Lt.-Col.) Richard Maul Birkett, (22) Royal Sussex Regiment, attd. Royal West Surrey Regiment,

M.C.

Captain William Herbert Wynne Apperley, 2nd Bn. Royal Sussex Regiment,
T/2nd Lieutenant Arthur Hubert Cole, Royal Sussex Regiment,

Worthing Man's Military Medal

Mr. and Mrs. J.M. Munday, of 31, Market Street, Worthing, have reason to be proud of their family, for their seven sons have served with the fighting forces. Drill Sergeant William Munday, the eldest living has been awarded the Military Medal. A member of the Royal Sussex Reserve, he was mobilised at the commencement of hostilities, and has participated in many engagements on the Western Front. Being severely wounded in an arm at Mons he is acting Drill Sergeant at a base camp. Four other sons are serving with the colours on various fronts, and two sons have already made the supreme sacrifice. (Listed in *London Gazette* in Middlesex Regiment as P/S 3549).

Tuesday January 22nd 1918

Keymer Military Medallist

Sergeant (A/C.S.M.) R.S. Whiting, Royal Sussex Regiment, eldest son of Mrs. Whiting of Milton House, Keymer, has been awarded the Military Medal for gallantry and devotion to duty on the 6th November last.

Monday January 28th 1918

The award of the Military Medal is bestowed upon the men of the Royal Sussex Regiment, listed below for gallantry in the field :-

No. SD/2365 L/Cpl. Henry James Baker, 11th Bn. (Goring-by-Sea)
No. G/16586 Pte. Britton C. Bingham, 11th Bn. (Brighton)
No. G/15882 Pte. Charles Henry Blunden, 11th Bn. (Walderton)
No. G/15888 Cpl. Walter Boniface, 13th Bn. (Seaford)
No. G/15802 Pte. Frederick Chandler, 11th Bn. (Lodsworth)
No. G/241483 Pte. George Herbert Clarke, 13th Bn. (Petsworth)
No. G/202330 Pte. Charles J. Dawes, 13th Bn. (Hertford)
No. G/12300 L/Cpl. Victor Edwin Thomas Deeprose, 11th Bn. (Westham)
No. G/9705 L/Cpl. (A/Cpl.) Maurice S.S. Dennett, 8th Bn. (Eastbourne)
No. G/5979 Pte. John Dunningham, 11th Bn. (West Bergholt)
No. SD/990 L/Cpl. William Elphick, 11th Bn. (Herstmonceux)
No. SD/1883 Cpl. Isaac Henry Farmer, 12th Bn. (Heathfield)
No. G/15224 Pte. Benjamin Faulkner, 11th Bn. (Upton)
No. SD/2909 Cpl. Charles Fowler, D.C.M., 13th Bn. (Brighton)
No. G/6271 S/Sgt. John William Key, 11th Bn. (Long Eaton)

Wednesday January 30th 1918

Five more Sussex Winners of the D.C.M.

Distinguished Conduct Medals have been awarded to the following for services described :-
No. G/15256 Private G.W. Mallett, 11th Bn. Royal Sussex Regiment,

For conspicuous gallantry and devotion to duty as stretcher-bearer. He displayed the greatest coolness and disregard of danger in attending to the wounded under very heavy fire, and very sodden and muddy ground. He further volunteered twice to carry messages in daylight under rifle fire and shell fire to the advanced posts. He continued to attend to the wounded until he fell exhausted, having set one of the finest examples of devotion to duty under the most trying circumstances.

No. SD/537 A/C.S.M. Bernard James Oatley, 11th Bn. Royal Sussex Regiment, (Marylebone)

For conspicuous gallantry and devotion to duty. Before the attack he organised and superintended carrying parties to the front line, and it was largely owing to his efforts that arrangements for the supply of ammunition, bombs, and water were successfully carried out. He showed great a dash and ability in the attack, and later went out and brought in wounded men. His good spirits, courage and devotion to duty were the admiration of all.

No. SD/4159 Lance-Corporal Arthur Sippetts, 13th Bn. Royal Sussex Regiment,

For conspicuous gallantry and devotion to duty at a critical moment, when the attacking troops were checked by machine-gun fire. He at once got a Lewis gun into action, and compelled the enemy machine-gun team to retire, shooting the gunners as they did so. By his initiative and courage he greatly facilitated the advance of the assaulting troops.

No. G/15007 Lance-Corporal E.A. Smith, 12th Bn. Royal Sussex Regiment,

For conspicuous gallantry and devotion to duty. He led his section in to action with tremendous spirit and resolution, and was always in the forefront of the fight. He bombed eleven enemy dug-outs, inflicting many casualties, and taking a number of prisoners. His great courage was a splendid example to all who came in contact with him.

No. G/15987 Corporal G. Welch, 13th Bn. Royal Sussex Regiment, (Chichester)

For conspicuous gallantry and devotion to duty in establishing and holding advance posts in a village and afterwards in rendering assistance under very fire to a number of badly wounded men. During the seventy hours in which his battalion was in the line his splendid courage and fearlessness greatly inspired the men of his company.

Military Medal Winners

To the list of winners of the Military Medal, the following Sussex names are proudly added :-

No. G/260026 Lance-Corporal Harry Bassett 13th Bn. Royal Sussex Regiment, (Balsall)
No. G/12613 Lance-Corporal J.E. Bilham 12th Bn. Royal Sussex Regiment, (Norwich)
No. SD/185 Lance-Corporal George H. Guildford, 11th Bn. Royal Sussex Regiment, (Brighton)
No. SD/2691 Lance-Corporal Richard Guttridge, 13th Bn. Royal Sussex Regiment, (Hastings)
No. G/16137 Private James Hutchings, 12th Bn. Royal Sussex Regiment, (Midhurst)
No. G/20450 Private Charles Mason, 11th Bn. Royal Sussex Regiment, (Clare, Suffolk)
No. SD/3745 Sergeant Frederick Masters, 13th Bn. Royal Sussex Regiment, (Battle)
No. G/19621 Private Sidney Newman, 12th Bn. Royal Sussex Regiment, (Wimbledon)
No. SD/2979 Private Percy Albert Nicholl, 13th Bn. Royal Sussex Regiment, (Brighton)
No. G/16245 Private Arthur W. Pascoe, 12th Bn. Royal Sussex Regiment, (Paignton)
No. G/2184 Private William Poile, 8th Bn. Royal Sussex Regiment, (Rye)
No. G/15534 Lance-Corporal William Salmon, 11th Bn. Royal Sussex Regiment, (Bishop's Stortford)
No. SD/736 Private William Edward Shearing, 11th Bn. Royal Sussex Regiment, (Cranbourne)
No. G/15312 Private William Storey, 13th Bn. Royal Sussex Regiment, (Holbeach)
No. G/15647 Private Harold T. Stubbings, 13th Bn. Royal Sussex Regiment, (Bishop's Stortford)
No. G/10327 Sergeant George E. Vicary, Royal Sussex Regiment, 13th Bn. Royal Sussex Regiment,(Lewes)
No. G/16390 Lance-Corporal (A/Cpl.) George C.F. Waters, 13th Bn. Royal Sussex Regiment, (Wadhurst)

No. SD/1916 Corporal (A/Sgt.) John E. Watson, 12th Bn. Royal Sussex Regiment, (Hastings)

No. G/20293 Sgt. Arthur G. Whiteman, 12th Bn. Royal Sussex Regiment, (Sandy, Beds.)
No. G/19825 Sergeant Arthur Harold Wileman, 11th Bn. Royal Sussex Regiment, (Luton, Beds.)

SPECIAL BRIGADE ORDER

Brigadier-General H.D. Hornby C.M.G.,D.S.O.
Commanding 116th Infantry Brigade

22nd November 1917

AWARDS FOR GALLANT CONDUCT

The Brigadier-General commanding has much pleasure in announcing to all ranks of the Brigade the following Awards for gallant conduct during the operations at Ypres.

Military Medal

No. G/16213 L/Corporal J.E. Bilham   12th Bn. Royal Sussex Regiment,

"For most conspicuous gallantry and devotion to duty in the operation at TOWER HAMLETS on 27th September 1917.
The only Company runner remaining, this man was continuously in demand to carry messages. In the course of his duties he had to pass through the enemy barrage no less than six times. His contempt of danger while guiding parties resulted in the parties always arriving at their destination without loss of morale and in good order.
The work that this man did cannot be to highly praised. It is strongly recommended that this man be awarded some distinction

No. SD/990 L/Cpl. William Elphick, 11th Bn. (Herstmonceux)

"For conspicuous gallantry, good leading and devotion to duty devotion to duty on the morning of 26th September 1917 during the operation at TOWER HAMLETS.

This N.C.O. was in charge of a pack train conveying water to the support positions. He made four journeys under the most intensive fire, and not only got his battalion water supply up but that of another battalion which had been left a long way back. He deserves the highest praise for the gallant way he stuck to his duties, and his courage and disregard for danger were undoubtedly the means of keeping the men in the front line supplied with water."

No. SD/1883 Corporal Isaac Henry Farmer 12th Bn. Royal Sussex Regiment

"For conspicuous gallantry, good leading and devotion to duty on the morning of 26th September 1917 during the operation at TOWER HAMLETS.
This N.C.O. was in charge of a Mule Pack Train carrying water, ammunition etc., to Battalion Headquarters at the forward end of the Mule Track. He worked throughout with the greatest energy, and in spite of very heavy enemy shelling succeeded in delivering to the forward point all the loads that he had been directed to take forward.
    In carrying out this work, the management of his pack mules and drivers under heavy shelling, was a difficult task. That he successfully carried out what he was directed do was due

to his devotion to duty, determination, and contempt of enemy shelling. His example was an incentive to all his comrades.

No. G/16137 Private James Hutchings		12th Bn. Royal Sussex Regiment

"For most conspicuous gallantry and devotion to duty during the operation at TOWER HAMLETS on the 24th – 28th September 1917.
During the whole of the above period this man worked strenuously and cheerfully, particularly on the night 26th/27th September, when he led a carrying party to the front line with considerable skill and courage. Again on the morning of the 27th September after 50 hours practically without rest, he was the first to volunteer for another carrying party to front line battalion Headquarters. His wonderful devotion to duty, and contempt of danger when being shelled the whole way put great confidence into his comrades, and his action was a splendid example to them all. It was mainly due to his example that the work was successfully carried out.

No. G/16245 Private Arthur W. Pascoe		12th Bn. Royal Sussex Regiment

"For most conspicuous gallantry and devotion to duty during the operations at TOWER HAMLETS on 25th and 26th of September 1917. This runner was employed on the Brigade Forward Station, and the cheerfulness and alacrity with which he obeyed all orders is much to be commended. He carried several messages under heavy shellfire and never failed to deliver them.
 On the night of the 26th September, when returning from a run and bringing up rations of the Brigade Forward party from the relay post near the wood south of Stirling castle under a heavy barrage, he and his companion were both wounded, the later mortally.

No. G/20293 Sergeant Arthur G. Whiteman		12th Bn. Royal Sussex Regiment

"For most conspicuous gallantry and devotion to duty during the operation at TOWER HAMLETS on September 27th 1917.
This Company to which sergeant Whiteman belonged was caught in a heavy enemy barrage, and two men were buried by a shell. This N.C.O. regardless of personal danger, proceeded to dig the men out, thereby exposing himself completely to the shelling of the enemy.
While he was digging these two men out, three more men were buried, and Sergeant Whiteman proceeded to dig them out also. In thus aiding his comrades he exposed himself to enemy shelling for 40 minutes continuously. His courage and gallantry was a splendid example to his men.

Bar to the Military Medal

No. G/17862 L/Corporal Walter Gyles Jenkinson		12th Bn. Royal Sussex Regiment

"For most conspicuous gallantry and devotion to duty during the operations at TOWER HAMLETS on 25th – 27th September 1917. This N.C.O. was acting as runner for 48 hours continuously. He was constantly moving from Battalion Headquarters to the front line Battalion under heavy barrage fire. He never failed to deliver his messages, and his work was beyond praise. (Military Medal gazetted 6th January 1917)

No. SD/1641 Private John Edward Mitchell   12th Bn. Royal Sussex Regiment, (Newick)

"For most conspicuous gallantry and devotion to duty at TOWER HAMLETS on the 25th, 26th and 27th September 1917. This runners' good conduct and devotion to duty under the most difficult circumstances were most noteworthy. He carried messages continuously, having frequently to cross that very heavy shelled area Dumbarton road.
He performed all his duties promptly and cheerfully, and successfully delivered all messages. He was

awarded the Military medal for his work during the operation of 31st July and subsequent days at St. Julien. (M.M. gazetted 16th October 1917)

H.E. Jones Lt.
A/Staff Captain
116th Infantry Brigade

Tuesday February 5th 1918

Military Cross Winners

The following awards for gallantry and distinguished conduct in the field are officially announced :-

Bar to M.C.

Captain Eric Alfred Charles Fazan, M.C., R.A.M.C. attd. 5th Bn. Royal Sussex Regiment,
(M.C. gazetted 14th January, 1916)

Captain Fazan, who is the eldest son of Dr. and Mrs. C.H.. Fazan, Belmont, Wadhurst, was connected with the 5th Battalion, Royal Sussex Regiment, for 10 years. He went to France with a battalion of the County Regiment in 1915, and was mentioned in dispatches for his gallantry in tending wounded during the severe fighting on 9th May of that year.

M.C.

Lieutenant Frank Henry Dear, 4th Bn. Royal Sussex Regiment, and R.F.C.

T/2nd Lt. Frederick Charles Peel, 4th Bn. Royal Sussex Regiment,
For services rendered at the Battle of Beersheba, Palestine on the 31st October, 1917.

Captain William Gerald Howell Powell-Edwards, 16th Bn. (Sussex Yeomanry)

Captain Alfred Carlisle Sayer, 16th Bn. Royal Sussex Regiment,

Lieutenant Harold Ernest Blunt, 16th Bn. Royal Sussex Regiment,

M.M.

The Military Medal for gallantry in the field was awarded to :-

No. 233460 L/Cpl. Albert Allan W. Tribe, 16th Bn. Royal Sussex Regiment, attached to the 74th Divisional Signal Company R.E. in Egypt.

Wednesday February 6th 1918

More Military Medals for Sussex

Sussex men again figure with their usual prominence in the list of Military Medal winners published yesterday evening. The following have been noted :-

No. G/2192 Lance-Corporal Albert Fuller, 8th Bn. Royal Sussex Regiment, (Brede)
No. 320024 Corporal Graham Crosskey Harris, 16th Bn. Royal Sussex Regiment, (Chichester)
No. SO/3381 Private Ernest S. Kenward, 8th Bn. Royal Sussex Regiment, (Polegate)
No. G/17522 Private (L/Cpl.) Bert Lovell, 8th Bn. Royal Sussex Regiment, (Chatham)
No. G/2004 Sergeant Robert E. Skinner, 8th Bn. Royal Sussex Regiment, (Hove)

No. G/2194 Lance-Sergeant James Vigor, 8th Bn. Royal Sussex Regiment, (Burwash)

No. G/1962 Private George A. Wratten, 8th Bn. Royal Sussex Regiment, (Horeham Road)

Sussex Medallist Killed

No. 200784 L/Corporal A.E. Tester, M.M., 4th Bn. Royal Sussex Regiment, (killed in action)

Friday February 8th 1918

Lieutenant-Colonel R.N. Dick, D.S.O.

For his services in Mesopotamia Major and Bt. Lt.-Col. (T/Brig.-Gen.) Robert Nicholas Dick, 1st Bn. Royal Sussex Regiment, has been awarded the Distinguished Service Order. Lieutenant-Colonel Dick obtained his commission in the Royal Sussex Regiment as long ago as 11th February, 1899.
As a Captain he fought in Somalialand, in 1908-10, being mentioned in dispatches and afterwards receiving the medal with clasp. About two and a half years ago he was appointed a General Staff officer on the Indian Establishment. He is a Cavalier of the Order of St. Maurice and St. Lazarus, and his present distinction will be noted with pleasure by many Sussex friends. The Distinguished Service Order medal was awarded for distinguished services rendered in connection with military operations in Mesopotamia.

"London Gazette" Monday February 18th 1918

2nd Lt. (T/Lt. and A/Capt.) Percy Woodruff Batten, 5th Bn. Royal Sussex Regiment and Tank Corps.
T/Lt. Harding John Robert Farrow, Royal Sussex Regiment,
Capt. William Henry Clement Hardy, Royal Sussex Regiment, Spec. Res.
T/2nd Lt. Arnold Lucas, Gen. List. Attd. 16th Bn. Royal Sussex Regiment,

Monday February 18th 1918

Local War Honours

At Buckingham Palace on Saturday, the King conferred a Knight-Commandership of St. Michael and St. George on Major-General Sir George Gorringe, decorated Lieutenant-Colonel R.M. Birkett, Royal Sussex Regiment, with the D.S.O., and presented Major C. Allen, Royal Sussex Regiment, with a Bar for his Military Cross.

Tuesday February 19th 1918

D.C.M. award

The *"London Gazette"* announces the award of the Distinguished Conduct Medal to :-
No. 200087 C.S.M. J. Simmons, 4th Bn. Royal Sussex Regiment, (Hurstpierpoint)

For conspicuous gallantry and devotion to duty. He showed great coolness and initiative in two engagements with the enemy, and set a splendid example to his company.

Friday February 22nd 1918

The 1914 Ribbon presented at Lewes

An "Old Contemptible" was decorated with 1914 Ribbon at Lewes on Wednesday by Colonel F.C. Lloyd, C.B., Newhaven. The presentation of the ribbon took place at the headquarters of the Labour Corps. at Lewes Old Workhouse in the presence of a large number of the Corps., under the command of Second-Lieutenant P. Goldberg. The recipient was No. 158382 Private E. Turner (landed at Le Havre with 1st Division, November, 1914), 2nd Battalion Royal Sussex Regiment.

Monday February 25th 1918

Sussex Soldiers Decorated

A list of decorations just published in the *"London Gazette"* includes the following :-

Bar to M.M.

No. G/17862 Lance-Corporal Walter Gyles Jenkinson, 12th Bn. Royal Sussex Regiment, (Marylebone)

No. SD/307 Private Herbert Edward Fishenden, 11th Bn. Royal Sussex Regiment, (Goudhurst)

No. SD/1641 Private John Edward Mitchell, 12th Bn. Royal Sussex Regiment, (Newick)

No. G/16080 Private William H. Taylor, 13th Bn. Royal Sussex Regiment, (Kingston, near Worthing)

M.M.

No. 265798 (formerly 1415) Private John Barford, 6th Bn. Royal Sussex Regiment, (Bolton)
No. L/9837 Private (L/Corporal) Ernest J.F. Corbett, 2nd Bn. Royal Sussex Regiment, (Hastings)
No. G/10998 Private Frank Eaton, 2nd Bn. Royal Sussex Regiment, (Plumstead)
No. G/1406 Private Frank B. Evenden, 2nd Bn. Royal Sussex Regiment, (Waldron)
No. G/8960 Private James J.G. Finch, 2nd Bn. Royal Sussex Regiment, (Hastings)
No. G/11601 Private Joseph Guymer, 2nd Bn. Royal Sussex Regiment, (Trowse)
No. G/5742 Private George Light, 8th Bn. Royal Sussex Regiment, (Broadwater)

Royal Sussex Officers Decorated

Among the officers decorated at Buckingham Palace on Saturday by the King were Captains G. Ambler and H. Roberts, Royal Sussex Regiment who each received the Military Cross.

Tuesday February 26th 1918

More Winners of the Military Medal

The latest list of Military Medal winners includes the following :-

No. G/2519 Sergeant Ernest James Manvell, 8th Bn. Royal Sussex Regiment, (Haywards Heath)
No. G/11294 Private William T. Reyland, 13th Bn. Royal Sussex Regiment, (Tottenham)
No. G/6071 Private (L/Corporal) John W. Rudd, 2nd Bn. Royal Sussex Regiment, (Cannock)
No. L/8558 Corporal (A/Sergeant) Charles Searle, 2nd Bn. Royal Sussex Regiment, (Worthing)
No. S/2156 Private Albert Stenning, 8th Bn. Royal Sussex Regiment, (Fittleworth)
No. L/8114 Private Harry Taylor, 2nd Bn. Royal Sussex Regiment, (Hove)
No. S/2152 Private Percy L. Weeden, 2nd Bn. Royal Sussex Regiment (Arundel)

No. SD/5416 Lance-Corporal (A/Corporal) John A. Wells, 12th Bn. Royal Sussex Regiment, (Brighton)

No. L/10472 Private Charles Woolley, 2nd Bn. Royal Sussex Regiment, (Brighton)

Thursday February 28th 1918

Sussex Officer Mentioned in Dispatches

Among those recommended for distinguished and gallant services and devotion to duty, in the dispatch from Field-Marshall, Commander-in-Chief, British Army in France, dated 7th November, and published last night, was that of T/2nd Lieutenant G.R. Alexander, Royal Sussex Regiment (killed in action).

Saturday March 2nd 1918

South Heighton Medallist

Mr. James Evans, of 4, Downs Villas, South Heighton, near Newhaven, has received news that his second son, Private James Evans, of the Royal Sussex Regiment, has been awarded the Military Medal for conspicuous gallantry at Cambrai. Private Evans has been serving in France for the last two and a half years.

Tuesday March 5th 1918

Late Captain D.C. Rutter, M.C.

Lieutenant (Temporary Captain) Donald Campbell Rutter, M.C., Royal Sussex Regiment, Special Reserve, and R.F.C., who had been missing since 7th June, last, is now officially reported to have been killed in an aerial fight on that date. He was 20 years of age and was the eldest son of Mr. H.C. Rutter, of Hazelwood, Morden, Surrey. Captain Rutter was killed on an early morning strafing patrol with 43 Squadron. (SOPWITH 1 ½ Stutters) on 7th June 1917, the first day of the Battle of Messines in the Flanders offensive.

43 Squadron History states " in the first glimmers of dawn 43 Squadron sent off the first six Sopwiths. Captain Rutter, first away at 0410 hrs. With his observer 2nd Lt. Jackson was never seen again. Almost certainly their aircraft must have received a direct hit from a heavy shell as they flew towards their targets. Captain Rutter who had seen service in the front line trenches of the Royal Sussex Regiment and the back cockpits of 43 Squadron's B.E. 2s was the only surviving Flight Commander and the sole surviving pilot in fact of the original Northern contingent."

Wednesday March 6th 1918

D.C.M. Winner

Last night's list of Distinguished Conduct Medal winners contained :-

No. G/6346 Private H. Billington, 11th Bn. Royal Sussex Regiment, (Manchester)

For conspicuous gallantry and devotion to duty as a company runner carrying messages and guiding stretcher-bearers to and from the front line under intense shell fire. He went with an urgent message to the Battalion after they had been obliged to move their Headquarters, and delivered his message under the greatest difficulties imaginable.

Thursday March 7th 1918

Further D.C.M. Awards

The following D.C.M. awards were announced last night :-

No. G/15305 Sergeant S. Rawding, 13th Bn. Royal Sussex Regiment, (Lincoln)

For conspicuous gallantry and devotion to duty in command of his platoon after his officer was killed. He captured the objective and immediately reorganised and endeavoured to gain touch with both flanks. Although wounded early in the operations he remained at duty, and only went the aid post when ordered to do so.

No. SD/251 Sergeant Albert Edward Westgate, 11th Bn. Royal Sussex Regiment, (Willingdon)

For conspicuous gallantry and devotion to duty in command of his platoon. After his officer had become a casualty he consolidated the strong point which the platoon had captured. Though seriously wounded, he continued to command the platoon until he became too exhausted and had to leave.

No. G/16259 Lance-Corporal (A/Cpl.) C.O. Williams, 12th Bn. Royal Sussex Regiment, (Enfield Wash)

For conspicuous gallantry and devotion to duty as a runner between Battalion Headquarters and the three front line companies. He was constantly delivering messages through heavy shell fire during forty-eight hours. He went to the assistance of a wounded man in the open and carried him to the dressing station through a heavy barrage.

No. SD/3049 Sergeant Herbert Woollard, 13th Bn. Royal Sussex Regiment, (Lewes)

For conspicuous gallantry and devotion to duty when in command of a platoon. On nearing his objective, under covering fire from his Lewis gun, he rushed and bombed a hostile machine-gun, killing the whole crew. On gaining the objective he rallied his men and volunteered to take out a search party to look for an outpost on the left, although he had been buried and rendered unconscious by a shell burst just previously.

No. SD/555 Sergeant Frank Worley, 11th Bn. Royal Sussex Regiment, (Worthing)

For conspicuous gallantry and devotion to duty in volunteering to carry messages to the front line when most of the runners had become casualties. On one occasion he volunteered to find another Battalion Headquarters and succeeded in delivering a most important message. He carried down a wounded man on his back, and several times assisted signallers to run out their lines. In spite of the strain and though slightly wounded he continued to volunteer for every kind of duty, and would take no rest until ordered to do so.

Saturday March 9th 1918

Military Crosses for Gallant Sussex Officers

COMPANY WHO CAPTURED NEARLY TWO HUNDRED PRISONERS

The Military Cross has been awarded to the following :-

T/2nd Lieutenant Horace Amon, 11th Bn. Royal Sussex Regiment,

For conspicuous gallantry and devotion to duty. He led his company to the final objective with great courage and skill. After the final objective had been won, he re-organised his company, pushed on in front, and consolidated under heavy fire. Throughout the three days' operations his cheerfulness, courage and determination under most adverse conditions were a splendid example to all ranks.

2nd Lieutenant S.A. Andrews, 12th Bn. Royal Sussex Regiment,

"Ypres, 31st July and 1st August, 1917. He led his company with great gallantry and dash in the attack, gaining all his objectives, consolidating his position, and holding it for two days. He set a fine example to his men by his coolness under heavy fire."

T/Lieutenant Cyril Bartlett, 13th Bn. Royal Sussex Regiment,

For conspicuous gallantry and devotion to duty. When Battalion Headquarters were blown in, though wounded, he remained on duty, and assisted in dressing a large number of wounded under a heavy barrage. His courage, coolness, and cheerfulness throughout the three days' operations were an example to the whole Battalion.

T/2nd Lieutenant Leonard George Cornes,   Royal Sussex Regiment,

For conspicuous gallantry and devotion to duty when detailed, with his platoon, to capture a strong point during an attack. With eight men he attacked the place, and put all the garrison out of action. By his dash and initiative he greatly assisted in the advance.

T/Lieutenant Herbert Edward Jones,   13th Bn. Royal Sussex Regiment,

For conspicuous gallantry and devotion to duty. After organising the transport supplies from the rear he came up to the front line to look after the wants of the men of his battalion, passing through a heavy barrage to do so. His courage, coolness and devotion to duty were a splendid example to his comrades. Afterwards he returned to the transport lines and organised the bringing up of supplies of hot food, which were most urgently required.

T/Lieutenant Warren Pye Ratcliff,   Royal Sussex Regiment,

For conspicuous gallantry and devotion to duty as transport officer. He was responsible for the supply or rations, water and material for the battalion and always got his supplies through regularly, bringing his pack train close up to the front line sometimes twice a day and always under shell fire. He carried out his duties in a most able manner, inspiring confidence by his coolness and contempt of danger.

2nd Lieutenant Henry Arthur Somerville,   11th Bn. Royal Sussex Regiment & R.F.C.

For conspicuous gallantry and devotion to duty. He consolidated the captured position under heavy fire with great energy and initiative. With a small party he established a line of advanced posts and held his position under heavy fire. He spent four hours exposed to snipers' fire endeavouring to obtain touch with the unit on his left. He set a fine example to all ranks.

T/2nd Lieutenant (A/Captain) Arnold George Alexander Vidler,   11th Bn. Royal Sussex Regiment,

For conspicuous gallantry and devotion to duty. He led his company in the attack with great coolness and determination, keeping it close to the barrage that the enemy were unable to open fire on the advancing troops. He set a splendid example of gallantry and coolness under difficult conditions, and inspired all by his cheerful bearing.

2nd Lieutenant Clarence George Walter,   Royal Sussex Regiment,

For conspicuous gallantry and devotion to duty when commanding a company during an attack. he led his men forward to the capture his objective with courage and judgement. Immediately it was captured he commenced its consolidation, which was completed in spite of heavy shell fire. Throughout the operations he displayed energy, determination, and contempt of danger, which were a fine example to his company.

T/2nd Lieutenant (A/Captain) Edward Lancelot Weale, Royal Sussex Regiment,

For conspicuous gallantry and devotion to duty. He handled his company with great skill in the attack, captured all his objectives, and took nearly 200 hundred prisoners. He consolidated the position,, and during the two following days he set a splendid example to his men under heavy shell fire.

T/2nd Lieutenant Horace John White, Royal Sussex Regiment,

For conspicuous gallantry and devotion to duty. His right flank was turned and he was forced temporarily to withdraw. Nevertheless, he went forward again as soon as possible and re-occupied his former position, which he held under very heavy fire for seventy-two hours. He displayed great courage, coolness, and contempt of danger throughout, and set a splendid example to his men.

No. SD/382 C.S.M. (A/R.S.M.) Herbert James Ball, Royal Sussex Regiment,

For conspicuous gallantry and devotion to duty. Under heavy shell fire he organised parties carrying ammunition and supplies to the captured position during an action, and organised the support troops in case of a counter-attack. He carried out his duties with unfailing energy, and it was largely owing to his efforts that the troops in the front captured positions were kept supplied.

Monday March 11th 1918

Decorated for gallantry

Among the officers decorated at Buckingham Palace on Saturday, and upon whom the King conferred the Military Cross, were Captain H.D. Hillier, Gloucesters, and Captain L.P. Marshall, West Yorks., who are attached to the Royal Sussex Regiment.

Groombridge Medallist Killed

Much sympathy is extended to Mr. And Mrs. Avis, of the Old Village Post Office, Groombridge, on the death of their son, Private Gordon Avis, M.M., Royal Sussex Regiment. It was only last autumn that he distinguished himself on the field, and for his bravery was awarded the Military Medal. Singularly, in the same action, Private Herbert Fishenden, who was an under gardener at Leyswood when he joined the Royal Sussex, also distinguished himself and was awarded a Bar to his Military Medal, and in Gordon's last letter to his mother he mentioned that they had just had a good talk and chat together about Groombridge. The sad news of his death reached his parents in a letter from his friend and comrade, Sergeant H.C. Hewson, ho stated that he was killed on 17th February and it was a great blow to him, and sent most sincere sympathy. Private C.A. Smith of the Signals Section, also wrote, "It is with the deepest regret and sympathy that I am taking this opportunity of informing you that your son Gordon was killed in action yesterday (17th). All of us who knew him so well are very sorry about his sad end. He was liked and admired by all of us in the Signals, and all are anxious to tender to you their deepest sympathy."

Belgian Decorations

The following are among the decorations and medals awarded by the King of the Belgians at various dates to the British Forces for distinguished services rendered during the course of the campaign :-

Ordre de Leopold Chevalier

Major the Hon. John Sackville Richard Tufton, D.S.O., 3rd Bn. Royal Sussex Regiment,

Croix de Guerre

Lieutenant Alexander John Stevenson Grant, 4th Bn. Royal Sussex Regiment,
Major the Hon. John Sackville Richard Tufton, D.S.O., 3rd Bn. Royal Sussex Regiment,
Bt. Colonel (T/Brig-Gen.) John Bartholomew Wroughton, C.M.G., 2nd Bn. Royal Sussex Regiment,

Wednesday March 13th 1918

Mentioned in Dispatches

The late Sir Stanley Maude, in his dispatch dated 2nd November last, mentioned, among others, the following for distinguished and gallant services and devotion to duty :-

Staff and Headquarters

Lieutenant-Colonel (T/Brigadier-General) R.N. Dick, Royal Sussex Regiment,
Brevet Lieutenant-Colonel G.C. Morphett, D.S.O., Royal Sussex Regiment,
Lieutenant F.P. Musgrave, Sussex Yeomanry.

INDIAN ARMY

SAPPERS AND MINERS : SIGNAL SERVICE

No. 9182 Corporal L. Winchester, 1st Bn. Royal Sussex Regiment,

LINES OF COMMUNICATION

No. 6536 Sergeant (A/Sergeant-Major) G. Cosens, 1st Bn. Royal Sussex Regiment,

Thursday March 14th 1918

Sussex Military Medallist

The *"London Gazette"* announces the award of the Military Medal to the Following :-

No. SD/773 Private Gordon John Avis, 11th Bn. Royal Sussex Regiment, (Groombridge)

Friday March 15th 1918

Brighton Man's Gallantry

Mrs. Bough, of 1, Edburton Avenue, Brighton, has received a communication from her husband, Private Edward Bough, Royal Sussex Regiment, stating that he has won the Military Medal. The certificate which accompanied the decoration, and was forwarded to Mrs. Bough, says :-

The Major-General commanding the --- Division wishes to place on record his appreciation of your conspicuous gallantry on 7th February, 1918, at Gouzeacourt, when you volunteered to help an officer bring in some wounded which were lying in the open. Your gallantry under very heavy shell fire was a fine example to all ranks.

Private Edward Bough joined up in October 1916, and went to France in the following December. Before joining the colours he carried on the business of a cab proprietor at Preston.

Mentioned for valuable services

The names of the undermentioned have been brought to the notice of the Secretary of State for War, for valuable services rendered in connection with the war, and when applicable an entry will be made in the record of service :-
Captain A.S.H. Dicker, 2nd Bn. Royal Sussex Regiment,
Major (T/Lieutenant-Colonel) E.F. Villiers, C.M.G., D.S.O., 2nd Bn. Royal Sussex Regiment,

Saturday March 16th 1918

MENTIONED IN DISPATCHES

The following Royal Sussex soldiers have been mentioned in dispatches for Meritorious Service :-

Major A.B. Wilkie, 4th Bn.
No. 5/2198 Colour-Sergeant H.J. Kenward,
No. 202870 C.Q.M.S., H.J. Meaton,

Wednesday March 20th 1918

Lieutenant-Colonel W.C. Millward D.S.O.

The announcement of the award of the D.S.O. to T/Major (A/Lieutenant-Colonel) William Colsey Millward, 11th Bn. Royal Sussex Regiment, was made some time ago. It is now officially announced that the honour is conferred :-

For conspicuous gallantry and devotion to duty. He assembled his battalion for the attack under artillery fire with only slight losses, and showed splendid leadership and ability in launching the attack. he personally superintended the consolidation of the captured position under heavy fire. while holding the captured position during the next two days, under heavy artillery fire, he displayed great coolness, courage and determination, and, though badly shaken by the explosion of a shell, he remained in command until his battalion was relieved. His personal example was an incentive to all ranks.

Thursday March 21st 1918

Worthing Military Medallist killed in action

Lance-Corporal C.A. Lisher, 13th Bn. Royal Sussex Regiment, only son of Mr. and Mrs. F.J. Lisher, 48, Orme Road, Worthing, has been killed in action in France. Enlisting in November, 1914, he became a popular soldier in his battalion and gained prominence as the winner of two regimental cups for boxing. For two years he took part in the fighting in France, and was home on leave in January. Last year he was awarded the Military Medal for conspicuous bravery.
He had only returned to the Front seven weeks when his parents received a letter from Lieutenant H. Tucker, an officer of the regiment, breaking the news of the death. The officer added : "I always found him optimistic, even in difficult circumstances, and, above all, without fear."

Friday March 22nd 1918

More Military Medal Winners

The following awards of the Military medal were officially announced last night :-

No. 200195 Private S. William Bateman, 4th Bn. Royal Sussex Regiment, (Littlehampton)
No. 200630 Private Arthur E. Boswell, 4th Bn. Royal Sussex Regiment, (Henfield)
No. 200176 Sergeant James Brewer, 17th Bn. Royal Sussex Regiment, (East Grinstead)
No. 320124 Private Richard W. Bridger, 16th Bn. Royal Sussex Regiment, (Midhurst)
No. G/2237 Corporal Stephen A. Buckman, 2nd Bn. Royal Sussex Regiment, (East Chiltington)
No. 200344 Private Bertram Cook, 4th Bn. Royal Sussex Regiment, (Haywards Heath)
No. G/218 Corporal (Lance-Sergeant) Archibald Cooper, 7th Bn. Royal Sussex Regiment, (Chichester)
No. 315374 Private Charles Davis, 16th Bn. Royal Sussex Regiment, (Cricklewood)
No. G/50 Private (Lance-Corporal) Edward J. Dendy, 7th Bn. Royal Sussex Regiment, (Itchingfield)
No. G/938 Corporal William Dinnage, 7th Bn. Royal Sussex Regiment, (Horsham)
No. 320212 Lance-Corporal Herbert Gardner, 16th Bn. Royal Sussex Regiment, (Upper Holloway)
No. L/9958 Sergeant Walter B. Golds, 7th Bn. Royal Sussex Regiment, (Worthing)
No. 320464 Lance-Corporal Harold Guy, 16th Bn. Royal Sussex Regiment, (Brighton)
No. 200236 Corporal (A/L/Sgt.) James Harwood, 4th Bn. Royal Sussex Regiment, (Arundel)
No. 200365 Private Edward Hoad, 4th Bn. Royal Sussex Regiment, (Partridge Green)
No. 320034 Sergeant Stanley Hoad, 16th Bn. Royal Sussex Regiment, (Lewes)
No. 200269 Corporal Henry J. Horton, 4th Bn. Royal Sussex Regiment, (Selsey)
No. 320204 Private (A/L/Cpl.) Charles Ferris Lock, 16th Bn. Royal Sussex Regiment, (East Lavant)
No. G/223 Corporal Edward G.C. Porter, 7th Bn. Royal Sussex Regiment, (Hardham)
No. 200304 Lance-Corporal William H.M. Robbins, 4th Bn. Royal Sussex Regiment, (Lewes)
No. 320117 Lance-Corporal Henry Turner, 16th Bn. Royal Sussex Regiment, (Eastbourne)
No. 320387 Private Arthur L.J. Vigar, 16th Bn. Royal Sussex Regiment, (Brighton)
No. 492023 Corporal E.B. Whitehead, R.A.M.C. attd. 16th Bn. Royal Sussex Regiment,
No. 200346 Sergeant (A/C.S.M.) Robert S. Whiting, 4th Bn. Royal Sussex Regiment, (Keymer)

Military Medal Winners for actions at Beersheba & Sheria

7 out of the 9 present plus 1 R.A.M.C.

Sgt. S. Hoad, Cpl. G. Harris, Cpl. E.B. Whitehead, R.A.M.C., L/Cpl. H. Gardner, L/Cpl. A.H. Guy, L/Cpl. H. Turner, L/Cpl. C.F. Lock, Pte. R.W. Bridger, Pte. A. Vigar & Pte. C. Davis, all 16th Bn.

Saturday March 23rd 1918

Military Cross Award

It is officially announced that the undermentioned has been awarded the Military Cross :-

T/2nd Lieutenant Thomas Clarke,   7th Bn. Royal Sussex Regiment,

For conspicuous gallantry and devotion to duty. With great dash determination he led a patrol which was sent out to obtain an identification. In spite of rifle fire and wire, which held up the rest of the patrol, he reached the enemy's line alone. He killed several of the enemy before being forced to withdraw, and then helped back two of his men who had been wounded.

Monday March 25th 1918

Military Cross Award

It has officially been announced in the *"London Gazette"* that the award of the Military Cross has been made to :-
2nd Lieutenant Charles Henry Lawrence, attd. Royal Sussex Regiment,

He was in charge of a carrying party during an attack, and had to lead it across the open in full view of the enemy under a heavy barrage. The party came under machine-gun fire and suffered heavy casualties, but he got his men forward and formed a dump in the new position. Continuing this work, he had to cross the open five times. His courage and devotion to duty were a splendid example to his men, and it was largely due to his efforts that the required dumps were successfully established in the face of very great difficulties.

Thursday March 28th 1918

Sussex Airman missing

Captain St. Cyprian Churchill Tayler, M.C., Royal Sussex Regiment, attd. R.F.C., who is reported missing, won the Military Cross only a short time ago "for conspicuous gallantry and devotion to duty in leading offensive patrols against enemy aircraft. On five occasions at least he and his patrol have attacked and brought down hostile machines. These successes were almost entirely due to his very skilful piloting".
Captain Tayler was given his third star on 13th July last, and has held the rank of Flight Commander from the same date. He belongs to a line battalion of the County Regiment, his commission dating from 16th August, 1916.

Another Chichester Medallist

Lance-Sergeant A. Cooper, son of Mr. W.K. Cooper, of Oving Road, Chichester, has won the Military Medal for conspicuous bravery at Cambrai. He has withstood the hazards of the campaign in France for three years and is now a patient of a convalescent home at Newhaven.

Saturday March 30th 1918

Distinguished Conduct Medals awarded to Sussex Men

The Distinguished Conduct Medal has been awarded the following for gallantry and distinguished conduct in the field :-

No. 320001 C.S.M. J.C.S. Balcombe, 16th, Bn. (Brighton)

For conspicuous gallantry and devotion to duty in an attack. He led the attacking waves on several occasions and got them forward to well-chosen positions. he was responsible for the capture of a large number of prisoners, and contributed largely to the success of the attack. He showed the greatest coolness, daring and initiative.

No. 150 Private H. Britt, 2nd Bn. (Robertsbridge)

For conspicuous gallantry and devotion to duty. Though he had been buried by a shell he refused to withdraw. He acted first as runner, and re-joined his Lewis gun section, inflicting casualties on the enemy. When the whole of his section was knocked out by shell fire, he continued to serve the gun single-handed, and eventually brought out of the trenches.

No. 320096 Sergeant H.E. Johnston, 16th Bn. (Brighton)

For conspicuous gallantry and devotion to duty. He took charge of a Lewis gun team who had been ordered to attack a battery of guns which was holding up the advance. With the greatest courage and determination he rushed the position and captured the guns, with three officers and twenty-five other prisoners.

Monday April 1st 1918

Another Royal Sussex D.C.M. Winner

His Majesty the King has been graciously pleased to award the Distinguished Conduct Medal to the undermentioned for gallantry and distinguished service in the field :-

No. 2030 Corporal E.W. Moss, 4th Bn. (Ipswich)

For conspicuous gallantry and devotion to duty when in charge of a bombing block in a very important position. Despite the fact that it was several times badly damaged by hostile artillery fire, he as often repaired it, and was able to repel two successive enemy counter-attacks. It was mainly due to his courage and energy that the position was maintained.

Tuesday April 2nd 1918

Sad death of a D.C.M. Winner

It is reported that on the 24th March, Lance-Corporal Alfred James Dell, D.C.M., 9th Bn. Royal Sussex Regiment was killed in action.

Thursday April 4th 1918

Sussex Soldiers awarded the Military Medal

The *"London Gazette"* announces the award of the Military Medal to the undermentioned non-commissioned officers and men :-

No. G/14942 Private (L/Cpl.) Thomas W. Dickerson, 9th Bn. Royal Sussex Regiment, (Littlington, Herts.)
No. G/946 Private James Evans, 7th Bn. Royal Sussex Regiment, (Newhaven)

No. S.D./305 Corporal (L/Sgt.) A. Farrant, 9th Bn. Royal Sussex Regiment, (Uckfield)

No. G/6697 Private Frederick Griffin, 9th Bn. Royal Sussex Regiment, (Hastings)
No. G/574 Sergeant Frederick James Ransom, 7th Bn. Royal Sussex Regiment, (Bexhill)

Saturday April 6th 1918

Award of the Military Cross

The announcement made in the *Sussex Daily News* some time ago of the award of the Military Cross to Second Lieutenant (Acting Captain) Edward Lancelot Weale, Royal Sussex Regiment, has now been officially confirmed. The record of his conspicuous gallantry and devotion to duty states :-

"He handled his Company with great skill in the attack, captured all his objectives, and took nearly 200 prisoners. He consolidated the position, and during the following two days he set a splendid example to his men under heavy shell fire."

Lieutenant Weale is a son of Mr. E. Weale, manager of the Arundel branch of the Capital and Counties Bank.

Tuesday April 9th 1918

Private A.E. Boswell : Henfield

Private A.E. Boswell, 4th Bn. Royal Sussex Regiment, of Henfield, whose name has been officially announced as a winner of the Military Medal, is one of the three sons Mr. and Mrs. H.J. Boswell have serving. Mr. Boswell is a signalman on the railway. The other two sons are Driver J. Boswell, R.F.A., and Private A. Boswell, of the Canadians. Private A.E. Boswell qualified for the medal a considerable time before Christmas.

Wednesday April 10th 1918

Sussex Officer Honoured

It is officially announced that the Military Cross has been conferred upon :-

Lieutenant Bernard William Skipworth, 3rd Bn. Royal Sussex Regiment, Special Reserve attached 9th Bn. M.G. Corps.

For conspicuous gallantry and devotion to duty in an attack. He got three machine-guns into action at the second objective with the utmost speed., and engaged the retreating enemy before the attacking companies had got forward. He set a splendid example to his men throughout.

Thursday April 11th 1918

Military Medal Winners

The King has been pleased to approve the undermentioned awards for bravery in the field :-

Bar to M.M.

No. G/13042 Private (L/Cpl.) William T. Ball, 9th Bn. Royal Sussex Regiment, (Ridley, Kent)

M.M.

No. G/19554 Private Edward Bough, 11th Bn. Royal Sussex Regiment, (Brighton)
No. G/202396 L/Corporal Frederick G. Bustin, 11th Bn. Royal Sussex Regiment, (Northampton)
No. G/200869 Private Arthur E. Hollands, 4th Bn. Royal Sussex Regiment, (Crawley)

Tuesday April 16th 1918

Belgian Decoration for Sussex Soldier

The following are among the decorations and medals conferred by the King of the Belgians on the British Forces for distinguished services rendered during the course of the campaign :-

Decoration Militaire

No. 828 Private (A/Sgt.) Albert Victor Coppard, 2nd Bn. Royal Sussex Regiment, (Hurst Green)

Thursday April 18th 1918

Local D.C.M. Winners

With reference to the announcement of the award of the Distinguished Conduct Medal in the Honours Supplement of the *"London Gazette"* dated 1st January 1918, the following are the acts of gallantry for which the decorations have been awarded :-

No. 3841 A/C.S.M. J. Bartlett, 9th Bn. Royal Sussex Regiment, (Eastbourne)

For conspicuous gallantry and devotion to duty. When his officer became a casualty during an attack he led his platoon forward with great skill and captured his furthest objective. He consolidated his position and repelled an enemy bombing attack, capturing two prisoners. He set a splendid example of courage and determination.

No. 9117 C.S.M. C.J. Deeprose, 2nd Bn. Royal Sussex Regiment, (Rye)

For conspicuous gallantry and devotion to duty since the commencement of the campaign. In and out of the line his work has always been of a high order, and his courage and cheerfulness in trying circumstances has greatly inspired all ranks. He has been wounded.

No. 240048 Sergeant P.G. Elphick, 5th Bn. Royal Sussex Regiment, (Newick)

For conspicuous gallantry and devotion to duty. This N.C.O. has constantly come to notice for his fine leadership and gallantry under very trying conditions, when carrying out work under heavy fire. By his example he has inspired his men to continue working, though exposed to great danger, thereby enabling important tasks to be completed.

Wednesday April 17th 1918

Haywards Heath Man Killed

Mr. and Mrs. S.R. Manvell, of Steeple Cottage, Butler's Green, Haywards Heath, have received the sad news that their eldest son, Sergeant E.J. Manvell, was killed in France on 23rd March by a shell at Frieres Wood.
Sergeant Manvell joined the Royal Sussex Regiment early in the war, and was awarded the Military Medal for conspicuous gallantry last year. He was 24 years of age, and is stated to be the 50th boy of St. Wilfred's School to have given up his life in the great war.

Tuesday April 23rd 1918

Two more winners of the Military Cross

His Majesty has approved the award of the Military Cross to the undermentioned Royal Sussex officers:-

T/Second Lieutenant Thomas Roderick Haddon, 12th Bn.

For conspicuous gallantry and devotion to duty. While sheltering with a party of men from intense hostile shelling of a track, a runner brought him word that wounded men were lying on the track 250 yards away. He at once proceeded, with two volunteers, to the spot and found two wounded men, one of whom, while he was attending to him, was killed in his arms. The other wounded man reached a place of safety, despite the severity of the shelling. His example and utter contempt of danger were the admiration of all ranks.

T/Second Lieutenant Douglas Walter Graham May, 9th Bn.

For conspicuous gallantry and devotion to duty. When leading a fighting patrol he entered the enemy's line and secured two prisoners, thereby obtaining an identification, which was urgently needed. His able leading and coolness prevented an alarm being raised and enabled the operation to be carried out with the greatest measure of success.

Brighton Man wins D.C.M. in Palestine

No. 56087 Private F.L. Pelling, youngest son of Mr. and Mrs. R.J. Pelling, Imperial Hotel, Queen's Road, Brighton, has been awarded the Distinguished Conduct Medal for services rendered during the fighting in Palestine. He joined the Sussex Yeomanry in 1914, and has recently been wounded.

Wednesday April 24th 1918

Gallant Sussex Officers

With reference to a list of war honours announced in December, the *"London Gazette"* now publishes details of the services for which the decorations were conferred, among them being the following :-

Bar to the D.S.O.

T/Major (A/Lt-Col.) Hugh Thomas Kay Robinson, D.S.O., 13th Bn.

For conspicuous gallantry and devotion to duty when in command of his battalion during three days' operations.
In the assembly of his troops in launching them for the attack, in the attack itself, and in holding the position, he displayed high qualities of leadership and courage.

D.S.O.

T/2nd Lieutenant (A/Captain) Philip Lindsay Clark,

For conspicuous gallantry and devotion to duty. when in command of the left flank company of the battalion. When the enemy broke through on his left he organised a defensive flank. Finding a gap on his left he filled and held it with some of his own men and of the unit on his left. He personally led a charge against the advancing enemy and dispersed them, and later repelled another attack. He was wounded by a piece of shrapnel in the head, but though dazed continued in command of his company for two days until relieved.

M.C.

T/2nd Lieutenant William Henry Pope Bennett, 13th Bn.

For conspicuous gallantry and devotion to duty when in command of the company in an attack. He captured the final objective, constructed a strong point and held it for two days under heavy fire. It was due to his skill that the casualties to his men were very few.

T/Lieutenant Villiers Heatly Couldrey, 13th Bn.

For conspicuous gallantry and devotion to duty when in command of his company in an attack. Finding the enemy holding a trench in great strength on his left, he diverted a portion of his men and mopped up this trench, killing many of the enemy and capturing 30 prisoners. He established himself in front of the final objective and maintained his position under heavy fire though cut off from the rest of the unit for 36 hours, only withdrawing when consolidation of the final objective was complete.

T/2nd Lieutenant John Newton Dyke,

For conspicuous gallantry and devotion to duty during enemy attacks. He went out single-handed to a concrete house to his front and killed two of the enemy, but was then badly wounded.

T/2nd Lieutenant (A/Captain) Eric John Harden,   13th Bn.

For conspicuous gallantry and devotion to duty in successfully establishing forward battalion dumps of R.E. material, ammunition and water under heavy fire. It was due to his organising ability that the unit was kept constantly supplied with stores throughout the battle.

Thursday April 25th 1918

Award of a Bar to the D.S.O.

Lt-Colonel H.T. Kay Robinson,   13th Bn. Royal Sussex Regiment, has just been awarded a Bar to his Distinguished Service Order for conspicuous gallantry. 2nd Lt. Bennett has earned the Military Cross for conspicuous gallantry.

The *"London Gazette"* states that the award of the Military Cross to T/2nd Lieutenant Arthur Blackford Woodrow, Royal Sussex Regiment, announced at the end of last year, was for :-

"For conspicuous gallantry and devotion to duty. He led his men in the attack on a strong point, which he captured with seven prisoners. Though severely wounded, he remained at duty for several hours, and sent excellent reports back to Battalion Headquarters".

Private J.E. Potiphar : Brighton

Mrs. Potiphar, 38, Scotland Street, Brighton, has received the news from her husband that he is a prisoner of war in Germany (Limburg). An old St. John's schoolboy, Brighton, Private J.E. Potiphar, Royal Sussex Regiment, was employed by Mr. D. Burtenshaw, decorator, Sillwood Street, Brighton, for many years. He joined up in the early part of the war, and had been in France two years. He won the Military Medal in September last for gallantry in the field. He had only just rejoined his regiment after a short leave. He has been wounded once.

Friday April 26th 1918

Rewards for gallant Royal Sussex Officers

The *"London Gazette"* publishes derails of the services for which decorations announced in January were conferred, among them being the following :-

D.S.O.

Major (T/Lieutenant-Colonel) Richard Maule Birkett, (22) 7th Bn.

For conspicuous gallantry and devotion to duty. When the advance was held up by machine-gun fire, and considerable confusion arose, he went forward to the front line and re-organised units, collecting stragglers and selecting positions for defence. He was under heavy machine-gun and shell fire the whole time, and set a splendid example of contempt of danger.

M.C.

Captain William Herbert Wynne Apperley,   2nd Bn.

For conspicuous gallantry and devotion to duty. He commanded a company with great coolness under very trying circumstances, making two personal reconnaissance's under fire of a strongly held enemy position and securing valuable information.
Again, he reconnoitred a suspected enemy machine-gun post, and brought back a machine-gun. During the whole period he showed a fine example of courage to his men.
T/2nd Lieutenant Arthur Hubert Cole,

For conspicuous gallantry and devotion to duty. He saw a party of 12 of the enemy approaching his trench. Having fired on them with rifles and a Lewis gun he at once led forward four men, and succeeded in cutting off and capturing two of the enemy. His quick grasp of the situation enabled an identification to be secured.

More Sussex winners of the Military Medal

The *"London Gazette"* announces the award of the Military Medal to the following :-

No. G/1180 Private William John Eade,   7th Bn. Royal Sussex Regiment, (Felpham)
No. G/1282 Private Alfred L. Groves,   7th Bn. Royal Sussex Regiment, (Worthing)

Saturday April 27th 1918

More Sussex winners of the Military Medal

The Military Medal has been conferred upon the following for bravery in the field :-

No. G/11362 Private Alfred E. Josland, 7th Bn. Royal Sussex Regiment, (Westminster)
No. G/22923 Private Dennis Reid Porteous, 7th Bn. Royal Sussex Regiment, (Bolton)

Tuesday April 30th 1918

Sussex Military Medallist Killed

No. G/648 Private T.H. Beall, 7th Bn. Royal Sussex Regiment,   (killed in action)

Wednesday May 1st 1918

The Belgian Croix de Guerre

Another of Crowborough's sons has won distinction in France. News has been received that Company Quartermaster-Sergeant Frank Manktelow has been awarded the Croix de Guerre by the Belgian King for bravery. Mr. and Mrs. George Manktelow, of Hartington Road, first heard of it through a comrade of their son.
A little while previously, C.Q.M.S. Manktelow had been home on leave, but said nothing of the honour, and it was only as a result of a letter to their son that the father and mother obtained confirmation of the chum's report. The recipient of the award is the fourth son of Mr. and Mrs. Manktelow, and is 26 years of age. He was in the Territorials when war broke out and accompanied his battalion of the Royal Sussex Regiment to France in February, 1915.
He has seen a lot of heavy fighting, having been in France three years and three months. He was gassed and slightly wounded in early August last year.

His brother, Lance-Corporal George Manktelow, won the Military Medal in the latter part of 1917, and is in a Canadian trench mortar battery, having come over with one of the early contingents. Both brothers are former members of the Crowborough Athletic Football Club, and played many fine games, principally in the attack. They are very popular. Another son of Mr. and Mrs. Manktelow, Alfred, is in a Pioneer Battalion of the Royal Sussex Regiment; a fourth has joined the Royal Fusiliers; while a fifth is understood to have joined the American Army. He is residing in the United States.

A Hove Military Medallist

Private George Dive Taylor, second son of Mr. and Mrs. Taylor, 99, Montgomery Street, Hove, has been awarded the Military Medal. An old Ellen Street schoolboy, he has been serving at Pershaw in India with the 1st Bn. Royal Sussex Regiment. Another son won a similar decoration in France, Bandsman Harry Taylor, 2nd Bn. Royal Sussex Regiment.

Thursday May 3rd 1918

D.C.M. award for Sussex Man

The Distinguished Conduct Medal has been awarded to the following :-
No. 17832 Corporal   E.E. Toney,   7th Bn. Royal Sussex Regiment, (Worthing)
For conspicuous gallantry and devotion to duty in a raid on the enemy's trenches. He was detailed to attack an enemy "pill-box", and, though he met with strong opposition, by his pluck and determination he overcame all resistance, killed several of the enemy, and captured two prisoners. His splendid example was undoubtedly responsible for the capture of the post.

Friday May 4th 1918

Gallant Nutley Sergeant

Sergeant C.S. Kenward, the son of Mr. George Kenward, wheelwright, Nutley, has just been the recipient of the D.C.M. for conspicuous gallantry. His Divisional General says of him that he has been with the Royal Sussex since 1915, and taken part in every engagement in which his battalion participated, and during the Somme fighting he showed the greatest gallantry and fine leadership, and that at all times he set a fine example of keenness, smartness, and devotion to duty. He had previously been recommended for the reward. The gallant Sergeant is now in hospital in Oxfordshire, having been badly gassed in the recent severe fighting.

Tuesday May 7th 1918

Sussex Officer Killed

Lieutenant-Colonel H.T. Kay Robinson, D.S.O., 13th Bn. Royal Sussex Regiment, who is reported killed in action, was the youngest son of the late Rev. W. Kay Robinson, Rector of Walwyns Castle, Pembrokeshire. He went to France on 1st March, 1916, as a Second Lieutenant in a Southdown Battalion, and was awarded the D.S.O. and Bar last year.

Wednesday May 8th 1918

Honour for Shoreham Man

Private Y.J. Smith, Royal Sussex Regiment, of 36, New Road, Shoreham, has had a remarkable experience during the present war. Three times he has been wounded and once gassed. He has also, as already reported, been awarded the Military Medal. Now a further distinction has fallen to him, he being awarded a vellum for gallant conduct during operations near Cambrai.

The Major-General commanding the Division to which he is attached has conveyed to him the pleasure with which he has heard of his having distinguished himself.

Lancing Man's Distinction

In connection with the death of Private T. Trevett, son of Mrs. Harvey Trevett, a widow, of Rose Cottage, Penhill Road, Lancing, recently reported, a letter has been received by his mother from an officer of his Brigade, from which it transpires that the Brigadier has recommended him for the Distinguished Conduct Medal. At the time of his death, the house where the headquarters of the Brigade were situated was being shelled, Private Trevett was inside at the time, when a shell exploded in the garden, and he was struck by a large fragment, passing away in a short time without recovering consciousness. "The memory of your son's splendid character still lives," the writer stated.

Thursday 9th May 1918

Local Casualty

No. SD/5743 A/Sergeant Lawrence Barker, M.M., 11th Bn. Royal Sussex Regiment, (Broadwater)

Tuesday May 14th 1918

Sussex Officer wins Military Cross

The *"London Gazette"* announces the award of the Military Cross to :-

T/2nd Lieutenant Reginald Francis Clements, 7th Bn. Royal Sussex Regiment.,

For conspicuous gallantry and devotion to duty in the field. In preparation for a raid on the enemy's lines he carried several patrols, and the accurate information which he obtained contributed largely to the success of the operation. He led men in the raid with great skill and determination, and rushed an enemy post which offered strong opposition, with the result that six of the enemy were killed, and two prisoners were captured. He showed splendid initiative and coolness.

The King has been graciously pleased to approve of the award of a Bar to the Military Medal to the undermentioned Non-Commissioned Officers :-

Bar to the M.M.

No. G/22 Sergeant Ernest R. Banks, M.M., 2nd Bn. Royal Sussex Regiment, (Guestling)
(M.M. gazetted 14th September, 1916)

No. SD/1409 Sergeant Gilbert Mills, M.M., 2nd Bn. (was 12th Bn.) Royal Sussex Regiment (Worthing)
(M.M. gazetted 23rd August, 1916)

Wednesday May 15th 1918

M.C. for Royal Sussex Officer

The *"London Gazette"* announced the award of the Military Cross to :-

T/Captain Geoffrey L. Reckitt, 7th Bn. Royal Sussex Regiment,

For conspicuous gallantry and devotion to duty in the field. He carried out a raid on the enemy's trenches at very short notice at a time when identifications were urgently required. He handled his party with great skill and set them a splendid example of contempt of danger. By his keenness and initiative he contributed very largely to the success of the operation.

Monday May 20th 1918

Mahsuds Expedition (Dispatches)

Among those whose names have been brought to notice by Lieutenant-General Sir A.A. Barret, K.C.B., K.C.S.I., K.C.V.O., for valuable services rendered during the operations against the Mahsuds, March-August ,1917, are :-

Commands and Staffs

Blois-Johnson, Colonel T.G. C.M.G., Punjabis,

The Royal Sussex Regiment

Brown, 2nd Lieutenant   G.L.
Johnson, Lieutenant-Colonel   F.W.F.
Vaughan, Major   L.
Kitchen, No. 1458 Sergeant   W.S.
Barford, No. 265798 (was1415) Private   J.
Cook, No. 1814 Private   T.H.

Nepalese Contingent (attd.)

Lewry, Sergeant H.A., 1st Bn. Royal Sussex Regiment,

Medals presented at Newhaven

Newhaven people must have been reminded of pre-war days during this week-end, with the advent of Volunteers from all parts of Sussex to camp in their midst. The advance party came into town on Wednesday, and proceeded to make arrangements for the main body, which arrived on Friday night and Saturday morning. There are now about 1,400 under canvas, and the sight on the Recreation Grounds yesterday morning was a most imposing one. A special drumhead service was held, at which about 1,000 Volunteers were on parade, together with large bodies of the naval and military units of the district. Among the principal officers present were Lord Leconfield (Lord Lieutenant of the county), commanding the Sussex Volunteers, Brigadier-General F.G. Anley, C.C., C.M.G., Colonel Money, Colonel O'Donnell, and Sir Berry Cusack-Smith, K.C.M.G. (County Adjutant). The discourse, a stirring and manly one, was given by the Rev. A.W. Dawes, and the splendid band of the Royal Sussex Regiment provided the music. It seemed as if the whole population of Newhaven had turned out to witness the imposing ceremony.

Presentation of medals

At the conclusion of the service, two medals were presented by Lord Leconfield, the recipients each being congratulated for their excellent service. The men and their records were :-

Military Medal

No. G/16124 Private A.J. Field, 12th Battalion Royal Sussex Regiment,

"For conspicuous gallantry and devotion to duty in the Battle of Ypres on 31st July and 1st and 2nd August, 1917. Throughout the operations this man was constantly employed in dressing and carrying in the wounded under heavy shell fire. He showed the greatest courage and disregard for danger, and by his efforts many men were taken to the dressing station who might have otherwise died of exposure."

Territorial Force Efficiency Medal

No. 562010 Corporal V.A.W. Busby, London Electrical Engineers, for continuous service in the Royal Engineers Volunteers and Territorial Force since November, 1904. He attended the annual training each year from 1905 to 1913, and was embodied on the 5th August, 1915.

Six Battalions of the Sussex Volunteers, together with the Sussex Motor Volunteer Corps. (A.S.C., M.T.) are represented. Captain Shimmans is acting Camp Adjutant.

Lancing Man's Distinction

A Certificate for Gallant Conduct in the field during operations near Cambrai, has been presented to Private A. Matten, Royal Sussex Regiment, of 39, South Street, Lancing. He has also recently had the misfortune to be wounded, a piece of shrapnel injuring his left hand, it being understood that two or three small bones have been broken. He is making good progress, however. Formerly employed in a market garden he has been on the Western Front nearly two years.

Tuesday May 21st 1918

Presentation of Medals

At a fete at Lower Beeding yesterday, General Smith-Dorrien, in the presence of cheering crowds, made the presentation of awards as follows :-

D.C.M.

No. 200527 Sergeant H. Patterson, 1/4th Royal Scots Fusiliers,

"For conspicuous gallantry and devotion to duty at the battle of Gaza."

No. 424 Sergeant G. Ward, (Littlehampton), 7th Bn. Royal Sussex Regiment,

"For leading a bombing attack across the open at Pozieres in 1916."

M.M.

No. 45208 Sergeant Harry Leslie Mason, South Wales Borderers,

"For attacking a pill-box at Ypres with one other man and capturing five prisoners and killing the remainder of the garrison."

No. SD/2854 Sergeant Albert Bailey (Bersted), 13th Bn. Royal Sussex Regiment,

"For at Richebourg, on the 30th June, 1916, when his platoon ran short of bombs, under heavy fire running out and collecting bombs from casualties."

No. 50 Lance-Corporal Edward J. Dendy, (Muntham), 7th Bn. Royal Sussex Regiment,

"For at Cambrai, during a German attack, picking up a German bomb which had fallen into the trench and throwing it out before it had time to explode."

No. 16550 Acting Bombardier Frederick Rogers, (formerly chauffeur at South Loge, Lower Beeding), 113th Heavy Battery, R.G.A.

"For mending telephone wires under fire."
No. G/15802 Private Frederick Chandler, (Lodsworth), 11th Bn. Royal Sussex Regiment,

"For at Menin Road, November, 1917, bringing in six wounded under heavy machine-gun fire."

The widows of the two last-mentioned received the medals won by their husbands.

M.I.D.

Major & Bt. Col. (T/Brig.-Gen.) C.E. Bond, C.M.G., D.S.O., Royal Sussex Regiment,
Major (T/Lt.-Col.) J.S. Cameron, D.S.O., Royal Sussex Regiment,
Major & Bt. Lt.-Col. (T/Brig.-Gen.) A.E. Glasgow, D.S.O., Royal Sussex Regiment,

Thursday May 23rd 1918

Sergeant E. Stringer, M.M.

GALLANT EASEBOURNE SOLDIER KILLED BY A SHELL

A gallant Easebourne soldier, Sergeant Ernest Stringer, M.M., Royal Sussex Regiment, son of Mr. and Mrs. Stringer, was killed in action on 13th May. The sad information reached the parents through a letter from Lieutenant T.S. Kerr, who writes that Sergeant Stringer was killed instantaneously, adding: "I have known your son for nearly a year and have always had a wonderful opinion of his abilities. During the last great battle I had the good fortune to have him as my platoon sergeant, and I shall never have a better man. He was always the same, cheerful, calm and collected. He was loved by all his men, and by his death I feel as if I have lost a great friend." Explaining how Sergeant Stringer met his death, Lieutenant Kerr says he was away at the time, and his supernumerary officer was in charge of the platoon. He and Sergeant Stringer were inspecting the men at "strand to", when a shell pitched on the parapet, killing the officer, Sergeant Stringer, and one other man, and wounding two men. The funeral took place at a "pretty little French cemetery. "

HIS COMPANY'S SYMPATHY

On behalf of the officers, N.C.O.'s and men of "C" Company, Sergeant Stringer's Company Officer, Captain Langham, has also written to express sympathy with Mr. and Mrs. Stringer in their great loss. The writer pays a splendid tribute to the fine soldierly qualities of Sergeant Stringer, stating : "He was one of the best N.C.O.'s I have ever known . . . . Your son has rendered valuable service during the whole of his service out here, and he will be very greatly missed both as a soldier and a man.." Mr. and Mrs. Stringer, who have resided in Easebourne for many years - Mr. Stringer having been employed on the Cowdray estate for nearly 20 years - are assured of the sympathy of the whole village in their sad loss, Sergeant Stringer was aged 30, and was single. Joining the Army on the outbreak of war, he went to France in July of the following year. He was awarded the Military Medal for gallant conduct and devotion to duty during the Battle of the Somme on `1st July, 1916, and was then promoted from lance-corporal to corporal. For gallantry during the subsequent fighting in the same month he was awarded a bar to the medal and received his third stripe. At the time of joining up Sergeant Stringer was employed by his uncle, Mr. J. Mead, of Horsham, and previously to that he worked in the gardens of Cowdray House and Capron House.

Saturday May 25th 1918

Mentioned in Dispatches

The following are further names of officers, N.C.O.'s and men mentioned in Sir Douglas Haig's dispatch of 7th April for distinguished service and devotion to duty and announced last night in a supplement to the *"London Gazette"* :-

Royal Sussex Regiment

Birkett, Major (T/Lieutenant-Colonel) R.M., D.S.O.
Clark, 2nd, Lieutenant (A/Captain) P.L., D.S.O.
Farmer, T/2nd Lieutenant G.S.
Fenton, 2nd Lieutenant (A/Captain) F.H.
Garner, T/2nd Lieutenant C.C.
Hill, T/Captain E.A.
Holland, 2nd Lieutenant A.
Lissiman, T/2nd Lieutenant H.C.
Newton, T/Captain C.V., M.C.
O'Neill, Captain (A/Major) F.R.
Osborne, Lieutenant (T/Major) G.F.
Kay Robinson, T/Major (T/Lieutenant-Colonel) H.T., D.S.O.
Sparks, T/Captain H.
Thornthwaite, T/Lieutenant J.D.
Walker, T/Lieutenant-Colonel B.J.
Whitehead, 2nd Lieutenant (T/Lieutenant) H.M.
Young, T/Captain N.E.
Cheal, No. 2643 C.Q.M.S. W.H.
Hall, No. 452 Corporal H.F.
Hewson, No. 759 Sergeant H.C.
Higham, No. G/16509 Private T.L.
Hillman, No. 20752 Private E.
Hygate, No. 2105 Corporal H.P.
Johnson, No. G/14968 Private W.G.
Parkes, No. 5985 Private (Lance-Corporal) A.
Rolt, No. 20338 Sergeant A.T.
Smith, No. G/2522 C.Q.M.S. H.P.
Still, No. 8811 Lance-Corporal C.A. (now No. 74116 M.G. Corps.)
Trowbridge, No. 6948 C.Q.M.S. S.

Thursday May 30th 1918

Felpham Medallist Killed

Information has reached Mrs. W.J. Eade, St. John's, Link Avenue, Felpham, that her husband, Private William John Eade, of the Royal Sussex Regiment, was killed on 20th May, by a shell.

He was one of five brothers serving in the Army, another being in the Navy. He had previously been wounded, and returned to France in November last. He was awarded the Military Medal for services in the field on 8th March.

"London Gazette" Friday May 31st 1918

His Majesty the KING has been graciously pleased, on the occasion of His Majesty's Birthday, to approve of the undermentioned rewards for distinguished service in connection with Military Operations in Egypt. Dated 3rd June, 1918: —

D.S.O.

Major (A/Lt-Col.) John Meredith Hulton, Royal Sussex Regiment,

His Majesty the KING has been graciously pleased, on the occasion of His Majesty's Birthday, to approve of the undermentioned rewards for distinguished service in connection with Military Operations in France and Flanders. Dated 3rd June, 1918:-

D.S.O.

T/Captain (A/Major) Bertram James Walker, Royal Sussex Regiment,

Bar to M.C.

Lieutenant (A/Captain) Alexander Douglas Hume, M.C., Royal Sussex Regiment attd. Royal Fusiliers,

M.C.

T/Captain Albert Frank Best, Royal Sussex Regiment.,
T/Captain G.L. Kemp, 8th Bn. Royal Sussex Regiment,

Lieutenant (A/Captain) John Isaac Mason, 2nd Bn. Royal Sussex Regiment,

T/Captain John Otho Paget, Royal Sussex Regiment,
T/Lt. (A/Cpt.) Harold Quincey Rangecroft, attd. 1st Bn. Lancs. Fus.
Lt. Claude Horatio Wilkins, 6th Bn. Royal Sussex Regiment,
T/Lt. John Armer Wright, 7th Bn. Royal Sussex Regiment,

D.C.M.

No. L/9010 T/R.S.M. H.A. Coles, 9th Bn. Royal Sussex Regiment, (Cocking)
No. L/7688 C.S.M. W. Herridge, 8th Bn. Royal Sussex Regiment, (Brighton)
No. G/1958 C.S.M. J.W. Tutt, 8th Bn. Royal Sussex Regiment, (Eastbourne)

Friday May 31st 1918

Sussex Officers and Men in Dispatches

The list of officers men mentioned for distinguished and gallant service and devotion to duty in Sir General Herbert Plumer's dispatch referring to the operations of the British Forces in Italy includes Lieutenant (T/Captain) W.E.P. Done, Royal Sussex Regiment, who served on the Staff, and the following other officers and men of the county regiment :-

Lieutenant (A/Captain) T.W. Rose M.C.
Lieutenant F.M. Sanger-Davis
Lieutenant T.H. Thorpe
No. 240178 Sergeant D. Bliss
No. 240045 Sergeant W.A. Lawes
No. 240353 Sergeant W.W. Rodway
No. 240465 Sergeant J.W. Woodgate

Saturday June 1st 1918

Recipients of the Military Medal

Sergeant J.Y. Smith, 8th Sussex Pioneers, of Waldron, has been awarded the Military Medal for conspicuous gallantry in the field.
Lance-Corporal W. Luxford, 11th Bn. Royal Sussex Regiment, son of Mr. and Mrs. J. Luxford, New Sapperton Farm, Heathfield, has been awarded the Military Medal for gallantry.

"London Gazette" Monday June 3rd 1918

The KING has been graciously pleased, on the occasion of His Majesty's Birthday, to confer the undermentioned Rewards for Distinguished Service: —

ROYAL AIR FORCE

D.F.C.

Lieutenant John Geoffrey Sadler Candy, R,S.R. attd. R.F.C.

"London Gazette" Friday June 7th 1918

The KING has been graciously pleased, on the occasion of His Majesty's Birthday, to give orders for the following promotions in, and appointments to, the Most Excellent Order of the British Empire, for services in connection with the War:—

To be Officers of the said Most Excellent Order:—

O.B.E. (Military Division)

Major the Honourable Neville Stephen Lytton, 11th Bn. Royal Sussex Regiment,

For services with the British Expeditionary Force in France.

Saturday June 8th 1918

Sussex Men in Italy

In connection with the military operations in Italy, the following awards are included in the King's Birthday Honours list :-

M.C.

Lieutenant Maurice Joseph Holdsworth, 4th Bn. Royal Sussex Regiment,

D.C.M.

No. G/24008 Sergeant W.H. Gilbert, 13th Bn. Royal Sussex Regiment, (Rye)

M.S.M.

No. G/240112 Sergeant J. Palmer, 5th Bn. Royal Sussex Regiment, (Mayfield)
No. G/240288 Sergeant F.C. Puxty, 5th Bn. Royal Sussex Regiment, (Flimwell)

Monday June 10th 1918

Honour for Sussex Officer

The King's Birthday Honours List includes the following award to a Royal Sussex officer :-

D.S.O.

Lieutenant-Colonel Frank William Frederick Johnson, 6th Bn. Royal Sussex Regiment,

Tuesday June 11th 1918

More King's Birthday Honours

The King's birthday honours include the following appointments for service in connection with the war :-

C.M.G.

Lt-Col. Barnard Thornton Hodgson, V.D. Royal Sussex Regiment,

To be Brevet Lieutenant-Colonel

Major P.E.P. Crawfurd, R.P., R. of O. late Royal Sussex Regiment, employed A.O.D.

Wednesday June 12th 1918

Mentioned in Dispatches

Among those mentioned for gallant and distinguished services during the period from 21st September, 1917, to 23rd February, 1918, in a dispatch from Lieutenant-General Sir G.F. Milne, K.C.B., D.S.O., Commander-in-Chief, British Salonika Force, are the following :-

Lundgren, T/Major   C.W. Sussex Yeomanry (T.F.) attd. Liverpool Regiment,
Terrey, 2nd Lieutenant   G.E. Sussex Yeomanry (T.F.) attd. Devonshire Regiment,

Military Intelligence

Captain G.S. Constable, M.C., Royal Sussex Regiment, who has been promoted Major, holds his commission in the 4th (Territorial) Battalion, with which he has been long associated. He served in the South Africa War, 1901-02, including the operations in Cape Colony and Orange River Colony (Queen's Medal with two clasps and a King's Medal with two Clasps), and in the present war he has seen much service (mentioned in dispatches, Military Cross).

Friday June 14th 1918

Henfield Military Medallist

Another Henfield man has brought distinction to his parish. This is Driver T. Golds, transport section of the Royal Sussex Regiment, son of Mr. and Mrs. A. Golds, 2, Wantley Cottages, who has qualified for the Military Medal for meritorious services at the Western front. Formerly a farm carter for Mr. Buckingham, Twinenham, he joined up in October, 1915. A brother who was in the same employ in a like capacity, Corporal B. Golds, Royal Sussex Regiment, (Territorials), and who enrolled in June, 1915, has been once wounded, in the right thigh, and is now serving in Palestine.
A third brother who is married, has unhappily been missing from the Western front since May, 1917, and has now been officially presumed dead. This is Private L.H. Golds, Royal Fusiliers, whose wife and little child live at 4, Jubilee Cottages, Worthing. He was formerly employed in a nursery, and had about two years' service to his credit. Another brother, who is 17, is in the Henfield Company of the Volunteers.

Saturday 15th June 1918

Good work recognised

Among those mentioned in a dispatch by Sir E.H.H. Allenby, G.C.M.C., K.C.B., General Officer, Commander-in Chief Egyptian Expeditionary Force, are the following officers and men of the Royal Sussex Regiment :-

Hulton, Major (A/Lieutenant-Colonel)   J.M. Royal Sussex Regiment attd. Welsh Regiment,
Jebb, Lieutenant (T/Captain)   R.D.
Patching, Lieutenant   E.G.
Ridley, Lieutenant (T/Captain)   G.W.
Piggott, No. 200099 Private (A/Staff-Sergeant)   J.

Tuesday June 18th 1918

A Military Medal has been awarded for gallantry in the field to :-

M.M.

No. 18236 Private William Smith, 7th Bn. Royal Sussex Regiment, (Peasmarsh)

The *"London Gazette"* announces the award of the Meritorious Service Medal to the undermentioned in recognition of valuable services rendered with the forces in France, during the war :-

M.S.M.

Royal Sussex Regiment

No. SD/1512 Sergeant   Philip Andrews,   12th Bn. (Eastbourne)

No. G/425 Sergeant   A. Aylmore,   7th Bn.   (Chichester)

No. G/15374 Sergeant   H. Beedham, 12th Bn. (Grimsby)
No. G/2379 Sergeant   G. Caesar, M.M. 8th Bn. (Farncombe, Surrey)
No. L/5391 Sergeant   Charles Coates, M.M. 8th Bn.   (Brighton)
No. G/929 C.Q.M.S.   C. Coleman,   7th Bn. (Littlehampton)

Wednesday June 19th 1918

The following are included in a list of recipients of the Meritorious Service Medal for valuable services with the forces in France, published in the *"London Gazette"* :-

M.S.M.

Royal Sussex Regiment

No. 8926 Sergeant J. Eve 2nd Bn. (Brighton)
No. 3359 C.S.M. G.F. Head 9th Bn. (Haslemere)
No. SD/3134 Sergeant W.A. Hills 13th Bn. (Portslade)
No. SD/808 Sergeant Albert Hunter 11th Bn. (Buxted Park)

No. 120 Sergeant A. Lee 7th Bn. (Brighton)

Thursday June 20th 1918

Meritorious Service Medal Awards

The following are included in a list published in the *"London Gazette"* of awards of the Meritorious Service Medal in recognition of valuable services rendered with the forces in France :-

Royal Sussex Regiment

No. 10023 Sergeant S. Nelson, 2nd Bn. (Newcastle-on-Tyne)
No. SD/859 C.S.M. Frank Arthur Standing, 11th Bn. (Ditchling)
No. S/391 Sergeant R.A. Taylor, 8th Bn. (Finsbury Park)
No. SD/3474 Sergeant Harvey Terry, 13th Bn. (Midhurst)

Friday June 21st 1918

Worthing Magistrate's son Mentioned in Dispatches

In a dispatch from Sir Edmund H.H. Allenby, G.C.M.G., K.C.B., the General Officer Commander-in-Chief, Egyptian Expeditionary Force, occurs the name of Lieutenant E. G. Patching, younger son of Mr. E.C. Patching, J.P., and Mrs. Patching, of Belfort, Liverpool Gardens, Worthing. He joined the Royal Sussex Regiment at the outbreak of the hostilities, and has seen service in France as well as Egypt.

Tuesday June 25th 1918

M.C. for Sussex Officer

The *"London Gazette"* announces the award of the Military Cross to the following officer :-

2nd Lieutenant (T/Capt.) Alfred John Brown, 6th Bn. Royal Sussex Regiment & R.F.C.

For conspicuous gallantry and devotion to duty in the field. While on patrol work he and his patrol attacked two enemy two-seater machines, one of which was driven down out of control, the other being seriously damaged. On the following day he attacked a hostile reconnaissance machine, which he forced to land in our lines. On a later occasion he volunteered to attack a hostile aerodrome in foggy weather. He dropped four bombs from a height of 200 feet which blew in the sides of one of the hangar, and then attacked horse and motor transport on the road, finally engaging enemy troops in the main street of a village with machine-gun fire. He has shown great skill and daring as a leader of offensive patrols.

Danehill Soldiers Gallantry

Mrs. J. Newnham, of Burnt House, Danehill, has received a second intimation of her son's gallantry and devotion to duty. He has already won the Military Medal, and Mrs. Newnham has now received a card which the officer commanding her son's division has presented to her son. The card reads : "I wish to place on record my appreciation of your gallantry and devotion to duty during operations on 25th March, when you took up successive fire positions with your Lewis gun and inflicted many casualties on the enemy, thereby greatly assisting operations."

Wednesday June 26th 1918

Bognor Man's D.C.M.

Mrs. Stone, of Melrose, Gordon Avenue, Bognor, has received the D.C.M. ribbon won by her husband, Company Sergeant-Major B.A. Stone, 13th Bn. Royal Sussex Regiment, who has been reported missing since 26th April, with the following report for which the award was made :-
For conspicuous gallantry and good leadership at Bray-sur-Somme on 26th March, 1918, and during subsequent operations. This N.C.O. acted as a Platoon Commander, and displayed marked ability and coolness throughout the operations handling his platoon under very heavy shell fire, and only withdrew when ordered to do so by his Company Commander. His tenacity in holding the line with his platoon, in the face of very heavy shell fire, when other troops had withdrawn, undoubtedly delayed the advance of the enemy at a critical period and enabled our troops to effect an orderly retirement. His good leadership throughout inspired the confidence of his men, and was of the greatest assistance to his Company Commander, and his cheerfulness and courage under the most trying conditions were an example to and the admiration of all ranks.

Friday June 28th 1918

Medal for Sussex Soldier

The award of the Military Medal for gallantry to :-

No. 315248 Private Thomas Shine, 16th Bn. Royal Sussex Regiment, (Camberwell).

Friday July 5th 1918

Military Cross Awards

The award of the Military Cross is bestowed upon :-

Captain Alfred Carlisle Sayer, 16th Bn. Royal Sussex Regiment,

For conspicuous gallantry and devotion to duty. When in command of his battalion he was ordered to carry out an attack on the enemy's position. He carried out a difficult operation in the dark with complete success, which was largely due to his personal example and courage.

T/2nd Lt. Frederick Charles Peel, Gen. List, attd. T.M. By. (4th Bn.)

For conspicuous gallantry and devotion to duty. He was in command of two detachments supporting an infantry attack, and showed great skill in getting his guns into position and covering the final attack. After the capture of the objective he pushed forward under machine gun fire, opened fire on the retreating enemy, and inflicted heavy losses. He showed splendid initiative and resource. (M.C. L/G 4th Feb.1918)

Lieutenant Harold Ernest Blunt, 16th Bn. Royal Sussex Regiment,

For conspicuous gallantry and devotion to duty. He led a patrol in front of the enemy defences with great courage and determination. He obtained very valuable information under heavy fire.

Monday July 8th 1918

Rendered Valuable Service

The following officer has been brought to the notice of the Secretary of State for War for valuable services rendered in connection with the war ;-

Lieutenant-Colonel B.T. Hodgson, C.M.G;V.D. Royal Sussex Regiment, (T.F.)

Gallant Army Doctor

A Bar to his Military Cross has been awarded to Captain Eric Alfred Arthur Fazan, M.C., R.A.M.C., attd. 5th Bn. Royal Sussex Regiment,

For conspicuous gallantry and devotion to duty. During very heavy fighting his aid post twice passed into the hands of the enemy. Although all communication with him by day was cut off for two days, he remained with his wounded, 235 of whom passed through his hands. It was due to his determination that every wounded man and all the personnel of his aid post were safely removed.

Tuesday July 9th 1918

Sussex Officer's courage in a burning aeroplane

The official record of the deed for which the Military Cross was awarded to 2nd Lieutenant Frank Henry Dear, 4th Bn. Royal Sussex Regiment, is as follows :-

For conspicuous gallantry and devotion to duty. His machine caught fire while he was engaged on a reconnaissance, and while he was endeavouring to put the fire out, his machine got into a spinning nose-dive. With great difficulty he got the fire under control and righted his machine when only a few hundred feet from the ground. He then carried out his reconnaissance. He showed great coolness and skill.

Wednesday July 10th 1918

Captain W.G.H. Powell-Edwards M.C.

The services which won the Military Cross for Captain William Gerald Howell Powell-Edwards, Sussex Yeomanry, (16th Bn. Royal Sussex Regiment), are thus officially described :-

For conspicuous gallantry and devotion to duty. He commanded the directing company in an attack against strong opposition, and showed the greatest courage and contempt of danger during an enemy counter-attack which followed the capture of the objective.

Saturday July 13th 1918

The Croix de Guerre for Sussex Soldiers

The King of the Belgians has conferred the Croix de Guerre upon the following for distinguished services rendered in the course of the campaign :-

Royal Sussex Regiment

No. G/5827 Private William Henry Chegwyn, 2nd Bn. (Ealing)
No. L/8498 Sergeant Charles Griffiths, 2nd Bn. (Halton, Hastings)

Monday July 15th 1918

Croix de Guerre for Sussex Men

The following are included in a list published in the *"London Gazette"*, of officers, N.C.O.'s and men of whom the King of the Belgians has conferred the Croix de Guerre

Royal Sussex Regiment

No. 2322 Corporal Richard Charles Holmes, 5th Bn. (Shoreham-by-Sea)
No. 240012 Sergeant Frank Mackellow, 5th Bn. (Crowborough)
No. S/375 Sergeant James Rayner, 5th Bn. (East Dulwich)

Tuesday July 16th 1918

Croix de Guerre for Sussex Men

The Croix de Guerre has been conferred on the following by the King of the Belgians, for distinguished services :-

Royal Sussex Regiment

No. G/2430 Sergeant Hilling Goward, 8th Bn. (Haywoods Heath)
No. L/9249 Corporal (L/Sergeant) Edwin Tucker, M.M. 2nd Bn. (Trealaw, South Wales)
No. SD/3487 Corporal (A/Sergeant) Isaac William Butler Watt, 2nd Bn. (Henfield)

No. SD/3490 Sergeant Richard White, 2nd Bn. (Heathfield)

No. SD/558 Sergeant Charles William Wood, 2nd Bn. (Worthing)

No. G/7243 Sergeant Frank Wood, 2nd Bn. (Steyning)

Crowborough Man's Cross

Sergeant Frank Mackellow, Royal Sussex Regiment (Crowborough) whose appeared in yesterday's *Sussex Daily News* in a list of N.C.O.'s and men on whom the King of the Belgians has conferred the Croix de Guerre, is a well-known local athlete. He is one of several sons of Mr. and Mrs. George Mackellow, of Huntingdon Road, who have been serving their country since the beginning of the war. His brother, Corporal George Mackellow, was awarded the Military Medal for devotion to duty and bravery while in France, and is in the Canadian Army. Both N.C.O.'s are former members of the Crowborough Athletic Football Club, and have many fine games with the "front line." Sergeant Mackellow went out to France with the Crowborough Company, Royal Sussex Regiment, in February, 1915, and is still serving in France.

Wednesday July 17th 1918

Military Medal Winners

The following awards were officially announced last night for gallantry in the field :-

No. 5877 Private Thomas Spencer Philips,   7th Bn. Royal Sussex Regiment,
No. 4438 Private Jack Randall,   7th Bn. Royal Sussex Regiment,   (Burton Latimer)

Thursday July 18th 1918

Medals for Sussex Men

The Military Medal has been awarded the following men of the Royal Sussex Regiment :-

No. 18236 Private William Smith,   7th Bn. (Peasmarsh)
No. 1192 Corporal (L/Sergeant) Albert W. Trevor,   7th Bn. (Portslade)

Saturday July 20th 1918

M.C. Awards

The Military Cross has been awarded to the following :-

2nd Lieutenant (T/Lt. & A/Capt.) Percy Woodruff Batten,   5th Bn. Royal Sussex Regiment, & Tank Corps.

For conspicuous gallantry and devotion to duty in the field. He led his tanks in an attack on a party of the enemy who were seen advancing on his left, and when his tank was put out of action he directed operations on foot, walking about in the open under direct fire from the enemy. He showed complete disregard of danger, and set a fine example to his men.

T/Lieutenant Harding John Robert Farrow,   7th Bn. Royal Sussex Regiment,

For conspicuous gallantry and devotion to duty in the field. He organised and carried out an attack which resulted in the capture of 200 yards of enemy trench in spite of determined enemy resistance. The success of the operation was largely due to his courage and determination.

Henfield Man's Croix de Guerre

Private I.W.B. Watt, 2nd Bn. Royal Sussex Regiment, is another Henfield man to win distinction in the war. He carried on Henfield Nurseries for five years before joining up, and he has been serving since January, 1915, being stationed on the Western Front since March, 1916.
He has now obtained the Belgian decoration of the Croix de Guerre, for distinguished transport work, and will be heartily congratulated for the same.

Monday July 22nd 1918

Gallant Royal Sussex Officers

The Military Cross has been awarded to the following :-

Captain William Henry Clement Hardy,   Royal Sussex Regiment,

For conspicuous gallantry and devotion to duty in the field. Under very heavy shell and machine-gun fire, he personally supervised the wiring in of blocks in a trench, and his foresight in organising the supply of bombs, materially helped repel three determined hostile attacks with heavy losses to the enemy. His cheerfulness and courage inspired all ranks with him.

T/2nd Lieutenant Arnold Lucas, General List attd. 16th Bn. Royal Sussex Regiment,

For conspicuous gallantry and devotion to duty in the field. When his platoon was held up in an attack by a strong enemy work he conducted an attack on the position, eventually leading a bayonet charge, which resulted in the capture of several prisoners and two machine-guns. He showed splendid courage and leadership.

Private Holder : Brighton

Mr. John Holder, of 89, Coleman Street, Brighton, has received the glad news that his son, 7963 Private B. Holder, Royal Sussex Regiment, has been awarded the Military Medal for good work as a stretcher-bearer in the last great offensive. He has served 14 years in the Royal Sussex Regiment and has been wounded three times. He was employed at Smothers' and Sons' Brewery, North Street, Brighton, until called up in August, 1914.

Tuesday July 23rd 1918

Military Cross Winners

The Military Cross (the award of which has been previously recorded) has been conferred upon the undermentioned Sussex officers for the deeds described below :-

Captain Arthur Nelson Hampton Weekes,   4th Bn.

For conspicuous gallantry and devotion to duty in the field. Having captured his first objective, he held on to his position until dark, though exposed to enfilading machine-gun fire, which caused many casualties among his men. He showed the greatest coolness and determination.

Lieutenant Robert Percival Young, 4th Bn.

For conspicuous gallantry and devotion to duty in the field. Though outflanked and short of water, he held his position with the greatest courage and determination.

Wednesday July 24th 1918

Shoreham Man's Distinction

The honour of having the Croix de Guerre pinned to his breast by the King of the Belgians has fallen to the lot of Corporal R.C. Holmes, Royal Sussex Regiment, of 7, Ham Road, Shoreham. He obtained for bravery on the battlefield at the Western Front. Formerly a Hove cabman, he has been serving for three and a half years and at the Western Front for two and a half years. He is recovering from the effects of a wound and gas.

Friday July 26th 1918

Sussex Officer wins D.S.O. for the second time

A Bar to the Distinguished Service Order has been awarded to :-

Major (T/Lt-Colonel) George Hastings Impey, D.S.O., 7th Bn.

For conspicuous gallantry and devotion to duty in the field. When his battalion was attacked and cut into two, causing it to fall back, he promptly turned out his battalion headquarters and a few men who had become lost in the neighbourhood, organised them into a garrison, and held the position with great courage and skill against all attacks for several hours, thus saving a most critical situation and allowing time for the battalion to reform, counter-attacking, and re-organising their line.

Colonel Impey was added to the D.S.O. in January, 1917.

Steyning Man's Honour

Sergeant F. Wood, Royal Sussex Regiment, of Coxham, Steyning, has achieved considerable success during the present war. It is now a considerable time since he obtained the Military Medal, and now he has been awarded the Croix de Guerre.
He is at present acting as Sergeant-Instructor, and he will be deservedly congratulated upon his achievements.

Monday July 29th 1918

Sergeant I.W.B. Watt : Henfield

It is Sergeant I.W.B. Watt, Royal Sussex Regiment (not Private) of Henfield who has been awarded the Croix de Guerre by the King of the Belgians for distinguished transport work.

Bar to Military Cross

A Bar to his Military Cross has been awarded to :-

T/Capt. Richard John Penfold Wyatt, M.C., 4th Bn. Royal Sussex Regiment,

For conspicuous gallantry and devotion to duty during long operations as brigade major, when he carried out his duties with the greatest courage and energy. On many occasions he helped by his splendid example, to keep men in their places under heavy machine-gun fire, particularly in the latter stages, when units were necessarily disorganised.

(M.C. gazetted 28/12/17)

Thursday July 30th 1918

Sussex Officer Killed

Captain Hugh Cyril Barnes, M.C., Royal Sussex Regiment, killed on the 21st July, was the youngest son of Mr. and Mrs. J. Howard Barnes, F.I.A., Muswell Avenue, London, N. He was in the H.A.C. before the war, and volunteered for foreign service on mobilisation. The end of 1914 found him at the front, and he saw a good deal of heavy fighting up to the following May, when he commenced to train for a commission. This he was given in June, and with the Royal Sussex he fought at Loos in the following month. He was wounded in the battle, and was out in France until the end of 1916. As Brigade intelligence officer he part in the Battle of Nieuport in July 1917, and here won his Military Cross for valuable observation work. Early this year he was given command of a trench mortar battery with the rank of Captain. He had previously accepted a permanent commission. A former captain of the Stationers' Company's School at Hornsey, he was only 21 years of age at the time of his death.

Wednesday July 31st 1918

A Gallant Sussex Officer

The *"London Gazette"* announces the award of the Military Cross to the following Royal Sussex officer :-

T/2nd Lieutenant Edward Cecil Cutler, 7th Bn.

For conspicuous gallantry and devotion to duty when his platoon was attacked by strong enemy forces and almost completely surrounded. he showed great skill and coolness in rallying his men and beat off the attack. Next day, during a heavy enemy attack, he was severely wounded, but refused to allow himself to be taken away until the situation was restored and he had handed over command to an N.C.O.

Thursday August 1st 1918

M.C. Winners

The Military Cross has been awarded to the undermentioned officers of the Royal Sussex Regiment :-

T/Captain Ernest Clifton Gorringe, 7th Bn.

For conspicuous gallantry and devotion to duty during a very heavy attack against a bridge. Although almost surrounded by a superior force of the enemy, he succeeded in beating off all the attacks with heavy loss, and maintaining his position intact. His fine example and leadership had a most inspiring effect on all ranks.

T/Lieutenant (A/Captain) Alexander Douglas Hume, attd. Royal Fusiliers,

For conspicuous gallantry and devotion to duty in the field. He held a trench with both flanks exposed against repeated attacks, organising bombing parties and making blocks, and at no place, did the enemy enter his trench. Later withdrew, platoon by platoon, so skilfully that the enemy, who were up to his wire, did not discover the movement.

Friday August 2nd 1918

Sussex Officer's fine courage recognised

The Military Cross has been conferred on 2nd Lieutenant Herbert Cecil Mount, Royal Sussex Regiment, attd. M.G. Corps.

"For conspicuous gallantry and devotion to duty during a hostile attack, when he kept his guns in action, although the infantry on his flank had been temporarily overcome and were retiring. Leaving his guns in action he went back, re-organised the infantry, and leading them forward, formed a defensive flank, thus materially assisting in the defence of a line. When the order to withdraw was received he remained behind with his guns and covered the retirement. His fine courage and coolness were worthy of high praise."

Saturday August 3rd 1918

Gallant Sussex Officer

The Military Cross has been awarded to Lieutenant (T/Major) George Francis Osborne, 7th Bn. Royal Sussex Regiment.

For conspicuous gallantry and devotion to duty in the field. While in defence of a wood he went up to the front line, and, finding that the left flank was in danger, he returned to the reserve company, and led them up, and so disposed them that the enemy were driven back. He showed great ability and courage.

Wednesday August 7th 1918

Decorations for Sussex Soldiers

The *"London Gazette"* announces the award of a Bar to the Military Medal and Military Medals to the following Royal Sussex men :-

Bar to M.M.

No. SD/1084 Private (L/Corporal) John Curtis Perry, 11th Bn. (Tunbridge Wells)

M.M.

No. G/15513 Private William J. Anderson, 11th Bn. (Herts.)
No. SD/2612 C.Q.M.S. George Badcock, 13th Bn. (Eastbourne)
No. SD/1270 Private (L/Cpl.) Sidney Charles Boys, 11th Bn. (Eastbourne)
No. G/5228 L/Corporal (A/Cpl.) George Bramley, 2nd Bn. (South Norwood)
No. L/10479 Private (L/Cpl.) Albert Ernest Clevett, 2nd Bn. (Shoreham)
No. SD/3089 Sergeant George William Dudman, 13th Bn. (Fernhurst)
No. G/890 Corporal (A/Sgt.) Frank B.R. Ettridge, 2nd Bn. (Dedham)
No. G/17582 Private Walter E. Grover, 2nd Bn. (Folkestone)
No. SD/4822 Private (L/Cpl.) William Hunt, 11th Bn. (Eastbourne)
No. SD/5003 Private Richard Cecil Kelsey, 2nd Bn. (Hove)
No. G/14614 Private William John Kilbey, 2nd Bn. (Walthamstow)
No. SD/2723 Private Ernest Knight, 13th Bn. (Fishersgate)
No. G/17532 Pte. William H. Lee, 7th Bn. (Folkestone)
No. G/5140 Private (A/Cpl.) George T.H. Marney, 2nd Bn. (Lambeth)

No. SD/335 Pte. Henry Thomas Norman, 11th Bn. (Seaford)

No. G/14725 Private W. Reynolds, 13th Bn. (Norwich)
No. G/14877 Private Frederick Arthur Whittemore, 13th Bn. (Shefford)
No. G/17580 Private John W. Woolley, 2nd Bn. (Rainham)

Friday August 9th 1918

Sussex Officers Killed

Captain Stuart Keppel Reid, M.C. Order of the Nile 4th Class, died of wounds on the 29th July. Captain Reid won his M.C. in August, 1917, and his Order of the Nile, in March, 1917. Captain Arthur Nelson Hampton Weekes M.C. Royal Sussex Regiment, was among the local Sussex officers killed in the recent fighting, he was killed on the 29th July. He was the oldest son of the late Mr. Arthur Weekes, J.P., and Mrs. Weekes, of the Mansion House, Hurstpierpoint. He was a well know officer of the Territorial battalion, and his death will be keenly felt in the town with which the family has been associated for so long a period of time. He was 29 years of age and obtained his captaincy in September, 1916.

Shoreham Military Medal

Lance-Corporal A.E. Clevett, Royal Sussex Regiment, of 4, Aston Cottages, Shoreham-by-Sea, has been awarded the Military Medal for distinguished service at the Western front. Formerly in the employment of Messrs. Pullen-Burry Ltd., market-gardeners and fruit growers, of Sompting, he enlisted when war broke out, and has seen a great deal of service at the Western front: very fortunately having escaped injury so far. A brother has been wounded on one occasion.

Wednesday August 14th 1918

Sussex Soldiers Mentioned

A list of names of officers and other ranks who have been brought to the notice of the Secretary of State for War for valuable services rendered in connection with the war, they include :-

Crawfurd, Major & Bt. Lieutenant-Colonel P.E.P., A.O.D., (R of O) late Royal Sussex Regiment,
Ash, T/Captain C.D.   Bedfordshire Regiment, attd. Royal Sussex Regiment,
Goddard, Quartermaster & Hon. Captain N.C.
Wilberforce, Captain A.R.G. Royal Sussex Regiment (R of O)
Gooding, No. 265093 R.Q.M.S. (A/R.S.M.) W.A.
Nye, No. L/3238 R.S.M. A.
Greene, No. TR/10/4402 C.Q.M.S. E.S.G.

Where The "Sussex" Are

Correspondents describing the fighting in the great advance now in progress in France mention that the Sussex men, with Kent, Surrey and London battalions, are engaged at the extreme north end of the line, north of the Somme, between Dernacourt and Bray.

Friday August 16th 1918

No. 13042 L/Corporal W.T. Ball, M.M. (wounded and prisoner).
No. 3409 Corporal J.S. Waters, M.M. (prisoner).

Sergeant Hodges D.C.M.

The many friends of Sergeant George Hodges, Royal Sussex Regiment, of Haywards Heath, will regret to learn that he was dangerously wounded in the fighting on 10th August. He lies in a precarious condition in hospital at Rouen, but there are hopes of his recovery. The wound is in the head, inflicted by a shell. It is the third time Sergeant Hodges has been wounded.
He holds the D.C.M. and the Italian Medal. He was secretary of the Haywards Heath Conservative Club before the war.

Saturday August 17th 1918

Permission has been given by the King for members of the, Royal Sussex Regiment to wear decorations awarded them by the President of the French Republic for distinguished service in the course of the campaign is as follows :-

Croix de Guerre

Lt-Colonel W.C. Millward, D.S.O. 11th Bn.

Monday August 19th 1918

Award of the Medal Militaire

The award of the Decoration Militaire from the King of the Belgians was made upon :-

No. 12943 A/C./S.M. W. Larmer, Middlesex Regiment att. to the 2nd Bn. Royal Sussex Regiment., Acting Company Sergeant-Major Larmer comes from Willesden in northwest London.

Wednesday August 21st 1918

Captain McNair, V.C.

It was in February, 1916, when the 9th Battalion, of the Royal Sussex Regiment, led with brilliant courage, were showing the Germans what "Kitchener's chaps" were capable of, that, Captain Eric Archibald McNair won the Victoria Cross. He was then a subaltern. The award was announced the following month in these terms :-

For most conspicuous bravery. When the enemy exploded a mine, Lieutenant McNair and many men of two platoons were hoisted into the air, and many men were buried. But, though much shaken, he at once organised a party with a machine-gun to man the near edge of the crater and opened rapid fire on a large party of the enemy who were advancing. The enemy were driven back, leaving many dead, Lieutenant McNair then ran back for reinforcements, and sent to another unit for bombs, ammunition and tools to replace those buried. The communication trench being blocked, he went across the open under heavy fire, and led up the reinforcements the same way. His prompt and plucky action and example undoubtedly saved the situation.

Now comes the sad news of Captain McNair's death. In August, 1916, the gallant officer was severely wounded in the lungs. He was under treatment for a time at the London Hospital, and it was several months before he was again pronounced fit for service. Then he was put on probation for Staff work and went through a special course of instruction. Afterwards he served at home for a spell. In the early part of this year he again went on active service abroad, though not to the Western Front, and about six weeks ago he was invalided to a base hospital, where he passed away on 12th August.

An old Carthusian

Captain McNair, who was 24 years of age, was the younger son of Mr. George B. McNair, senior partner of Morgan and Co. solicitors, Calcutta. He was an old Carthusian, and previously was at Branksome Hall, Godmaling (Mr. Sylvester's). At Charterhouse he was head of school when he left in 1913 to become a Demy at Magdalen College, Oxford. He had already put in some service with the O.T.C. and on the outbreak of war his application for a commission in the Army was promptly granted. So he gave up, for the time being, at any rate, his intention of entering the Indian Civil Service, and donned khaki.

He was first appointed to the 10th Battalion of the Royal Sussex Regiment, but in August, 1915, was transferred to the 9th, and the next month he was in France, there to gain the highest decoration that the soldier can aspire to. Captain McNair has added lustre to the annals of the Royal Sussex Regiment, and his memory will be held dear for long years to come.

Tuesday August 27th 1918

Reward for Sussex Soldier

The following honour has been gazetted in recognition of distinguished services in connection with military operations in Mesopotamia :-

C.M.G.

Major & Bt. Lieutenant-Colonel George Charles Morphett, D.S.O.

Wednesday August 28th 1918

Cuckfield Medallist Killed

No. 111 Sergeant A.E. Selby, Royal Sussex Regiment, of Cuckfield was killed in action on 8th August, was the eldest son of Mr. and Mrs. E. Selby of Long Acre, Cuckfield. He was awarded the Military Medal for Meritorious Conduct 2 years ago.

Saturday August 31st 1918

Sussex Military Medallists

The Military Medal has been awarded to the following for bravery in the field :-

No. SD/3117 Private James Goldsmith, 4th Bn. Royal Sussex Regiment, (Alfriston)

Thursday September 5th 1918

D.C.M.'S for Royal Sussex N.C.O.'s

The *"London Gazette"* announces the award of the Distinguished Conduct Medal to the following :-

No. G/20400 C.S.M. (A/R.S.M.) H.M. Bird, 11th Bn. Royal Sussex Regiment, (Cork)

For conspicuous gallantry and devotion to duty on many occasions.

No. G/14923 Lance-Corporal (A/Cpl) J.A. Barnes, 11th Bn. Royal Sussex Regiment, (Elsworth)

For conspicuous gallantry and devotion to duty during a counter-attack. He led his two sections brilliantly, gained his objective, and then brought rifle and Lewis gun fire to bear on the enemy. He did fine work, and set a splendid example of cheerfulness and determination.

Monday September 9th 1918

Medals presented at Tunbridge Wells

At the Pump Room, Tunbridge Wells, yesterday morning, Brigadier-General de Falbe, presented ten awards gained by officers and men of the Home Counties Reserve Brigade in the presence of a large number of troops. In doing so he spoke of the fine example shown by the recipients, and added that there were countless gallant deeds that went unrecognised. The awards were as follows :-

No. G/5321 Private George E. Bartholomew,   M.M.   7th Bn. Royal Sussex Regiment,

On 3rd May, 1917, this man volunteered for special patrol duty. With two other men he went forward to reconnoitre a position of the enemy's line. They reached their objective, cleared out a superior force of the enemy, and held a portion of a captured trench until they were relieved nine hours afterwards. The bravery and devotion to duty by this man was a splendid example to all ranks.

No. G/16722 Private Charles S. Norman,   M.M.   11th Bn. Royal Sussex Regiment,

While acting as a stretcher-bearer he displayed exceptional courage and devotion to duty, repeatedly going back to bring in wounded. His coolness was an example to all ranks.

Tuesday September 10th 1918

More D.C.M. Awards

The King has been pleased to approve the award of the Distinguished. Conduct Medal to the following warrant officer, non-commissioned officers and men.

No. SD/1766 Sergeant Arthur Wilfred Golden, 12th Bn. Royal Sussex Regiment, (Worcester Park)

 For conspicuous gallantry and devotion to duty. During an enemy attack he, together with two Lewis gunners, jumped into an abandoned tank, started the engine, and moved forward to the part where the enemy was thickest. He checked the advance inflicted heavy casualties; and took fourteen prisoners. He operated the tank until he was badly wounded. His initiative, gallantry and coolness delayed the advance of the enemy for a considerable time.

No. G/4336 Private A. Harvey, 11th Bn. Royal Sussex Regiment, (Eastbourne)

For conspicuous gallantry and devotion to duty during a counter-attack. He rushed forward and killed two of the enemy who were mounting a machine-gun, thus enabling his platoon to continue its advance. His prompt and gallant action did much to make the attack a success.

No. G/3359 C.S.M. G.F. Head, 7th Bn. Royal Sussex Regiment, (Haslemere)

For conspicuous gallantry and devotion to duty. He led two platoons in an attack, and by his gallantry and brilliant leadership succeeded, in driving the enemy back and establishing his men in a commanding position.

No. SD/2446 Private James Henham, 12th Bn. Royal Sussex Regiment, (Paddock Wood)
For conspicuous gallantry and devotion to duty. With a Sergeant and Lance-Corporal he entered a tank, and by his coolness and accurate handling of a Lewis gun in the tank he was instrumental in checking the advance of the enemy, causing many casualties and taking fourteen prisoners.

Wednesday September 11th 1918

D.C.M. for Hurstpierpoint Sergeant

The King has approved the award of the Distinguished Conduct Medal to :-

No. L/8151 Sergeant H.A. Lewry, 1st Bn. Royal Sussex Regiment, (Hurstpierpoint)

For conspicuous gallantry and devotion to duty in leading an attack. When the company commander was killed, he took command, organised his men, and occupied the positions with great skill. His resource and coolness helped to a great extent towards the capture of the positions allotted to the battalion.

Friday September 13th 1918

Italian medals for Royal Sussex soldiers

The King of Italy has awarded the Bronze Medal for Military Valour for service in the war to the following :-

No. G/891 C.Q.M.S. Walter Harry Budgen, 7th Bn. (East Grinstead)
No. G/7827 Sergeant Benjamin Bull, 5th Bn. (Stony Stratford)

D.C.M for Royal Sussex Sergeant

The King has approved the award of the Distinguished Conduct Medal to :-

No. G/2084 Lance-Sergeant W.C. Pepper, 8th Bn. Royal Sussex Regiment, (Clapton)

For conspicuous gallantry and devotion to duty during an enemy attack. When in charge of two sections of a forward post he held on till gunners of the battery he was defending had been able to retire with their breech block. He then withdrew, and worked a machine-gun with great effect on the enemy.. Throughout he gave a fine display of fearlessness and devotion to duty.

Saturday September 14th 1918

More Sussex D.C.M. Winners

The Distinguished Conduct Medal has been conferred upon the following for gallantry :-

No. G/593 Private (L/Cpl.) C. Sprunt, 11th Bn. Royal Sussex Regiment, (near Saxmundham)

For conspicuous gallantry and devotion to duty. With a Sergeant and another man he manned a Lewis gun in a Tank, and by his accurate handling of the gun inflicted heavy casualties on the enemy and took fourteen prisoners.

No. S/2235 Private T.W. Stevens, 11th Bn. Royal Sussex Regiment, (Hove)

For conspicuous gallantry and devotion to duty. In taking a message alone the front-line posts under a raking shell, and machine-gun fire. Later, he went out under fire to one of our tanks, which was lying in, front of the line, set fire to it, and put it out of action. he showed wonderful coolness and rendered invaluable assistance throughout. the action.

No. G/200023 C. S.M. B.A. Stone, 13th Bn. Royal Sussex Regiment, (Bognor)

For conspicuous gallantry and devotion to duty. This W.O. who was in charge of a platoon, showed marked ability and great coolness throughout the operations. At a very critical period the tenacity with which he held the line with his men delayed the enemy, and enabled our troops to effect an orderly retirement, he himself, with his command, under shell fire of great intensity, only withdrawing on orders from his company officer. his good leadership inspired his men with confidence, and his courage and cheerfulness under most trying circumstances were the admiration of all ranks.

No. G/290873 C.S.M. C.E. Thomas, 8th Bn. Royal Sussex Regiment, (Battle)

For conspicuous gallantry and devotion to duty, this W.O. displayed conspicuous courage throughout two days hard fighting in defence of a post which he held to the last. By his own example of gallantry and coolness he kept his command well in hand when all the officers had become casualties. Under the stress of the circumstances the men broke temporarily on one occasion, but he rallied and re-organised them by his example, led. them back to the trenches. he was thus able to hand over the position intact to the troops sent ,to relieve him, the very large number of enemy casualties lying in front testifying to the stubborn nature in which it had been defended.

Military Medals and Bars

Gallant conduct in the face of the enemy has resulted in the following being awarded :-

Bar to M.M.

No. SD/2979 Private Percy Albert Nicholl, M.M., 13th Bn. Royal Sussex Regiment, (Brighton)
No. G/14877 Private Frederick Arthur Whittemore, M.M., 13th Bn. Royal Sussex Regiment, (Shefford)

M.M.

No. SD/4197 Corporal Ralph Ashford, 9th Bn. Royal Sussex Regiment, (Chard)
No. G/1548 Private Edwin Backshall, 8th Bn. Royal Sussex Regiment, (Firle)
No. G/8148 Private Herbert Bagge, 9th Bn. Royal Sussex Regiment, (Fulham)
No. G/16755 Private John W.H. Dunk, 9th Bn. Royal Sussex Regiment, (Hastings)
No. G/2498 Private Frank W. Evans, 8th Bn. Royal Sussex Regiment, (Maidenhead)

Monday September 16th 1918

Sussex Soldiers' medals

The Military Medal has been awarded the, following non- commissioned officers and men for bravery in the field :-

No. G/2432 Private Ernest Binstead, 8th Bn. Royal Sussex Regiment, (Haywards Heath)
No. G/5427 Corporal. Charles James Bliss, 9th Bn. Royal Sussex Regiment, (Bognor)
No. G/3212 Private. Joseph S. Bourne, 9th Bn. Royal Sussex Regiment, (Sussex)
No. G/6854 Private (L/Cpl.) John F. Brinkhurst, 11th Bn. Royal Sussex Regiment; (Crawley Down)
No. SD/5925 Corporal Thomas Burch, 11th Bn. Royal Sussex Regiment, (Adlington)

No. SD/3338 Lance-Corporal Alfred Ernest Durrant, 13th Bn. Royal Sussex Regiment, (Worthing)

Tuesday September 17th 1918

Award of the Bars to the D.S.O.

The following honours have been conferred for gallantry and devotion to duty in the field :-

Second Bar to D.S.O.

T/Lieutenant-Colonel Hugh Thomas Kay Robinson, D.S.O. and Bar., 13th Bn. Royal Sussex Regiment.,

For conspicuous gallantry and devotion to duty while commanding a composite battalion. He handled his battalion in such a way as to prevent the enemy entering a gap in the line, and so turning the right flank of the division. Later, when in command of another battalion, he, by skilful leadership and courageous example, caused the enemy's advance to be checked at a critical moment with heavy loss.
(D.S.O. gazetted 4th June, 1917. First Bar gazetted 17th December, 1917).

Bar to D.S.O.

Captain (T/Lt-Col.) Murray Victor Burrow Hill, D.S.O.,M.C. Royal Fusiliers attd. 9th Bn. Royal Sussex Regiment,

For conspicuous gallantry and devotion to duty during enemy attacks. He organised and personally led a counter-attack against a body of the enemy who were threatening to envelope the right flank of the brigade, and forced them to withdraw. He set a high example of cheerfulness, determination and good leadership.

(D.S.O. gazetted 25th August, 1917)

More Military Medals for Sussex Men

The *"London Gazette"* announce the award of the Military Medal to the following Royal Sussex Soldiers :-

No. G/2248 Lance-Corporal Arthur Furminger, 8th Bn. (Newick)
No. SD/3581 Private Thomas Golds, 13th Bn. (Haywards Heath).
No. G/17333 Private Philip A. Griston, 7th Bn. (North Walsham)
No. G120295 Corporal Walter Hammond Hadley, 9th Bn. (East Haddon)
No. L/17953 Private Bertie Holder, 11th Bn. (Brighton)
No. G/6426 Sergeant (A/ C.S.M.) David G. Honeysett, 11th Bn. (Eastbourne)
No. G/1 4365 Private William J. Izzard, 9th Bn. (Jarvis Brook)
No. G/16019 Private Oliver T. Leighton, 9th Bn. (Harrow)
No. G/16749 Private (L/Cpl.) William Luxford, 11th Bn. (Heathfield)

Wednesday September 18th 1918

Three Gallant Sussex Officers receive awards

The *"London Gazette"* announces the award of the D.S.O. to :-

Major (T/Lt.-Colonel) John Sheldon Woodruffe, 2nd Bn.

For conspicuous gallantry and devotion to duty in commanding his battalion in a very difficult situation, and under heavy fire during ten days operations. On one occasion he personally rallied and reformed troops under heavy shell fire, and led them to the attack, re-establishing the line at a very critical moment. He showed great gallantry in handling his command.

Awards of a Bar to the Military Cross includes the following : -

T/Captain Walter Hubert Baddeley, M.C.,

For conspicuous gallantry and devotion to duty during an enemy attack. He commanded his company with great skill and determination. He re-organised and directed his men in a masterly manner, and displayed fine powers of command.

 T/2nd Lieutenant (A/Captain) Horace Amon, M.C., 11th Bn.

For conspicuous gallantry and devotion to duty during an enemy attack. He organised a successful counter-attack, inflicting heavy casualties on the enemy and capturing prisoners and a machine-gun. He also made personal reconnaissance under heavy fire, and re-established contact with the troops on his right. By his courage and energy he set a fine example to his men.

Military Medals have been awarded to the undermentioned for bravery in the field :-

M.M.

No. G/3065 Sergeant Victor G. Maskell, 8th Bn. Royal Sussex Regiment, (Chippenham)
No. G/14047 Private Christopher T. Milton, 12th Bn. Royal Sussex Regiment, (Brighton)
No. G/17388 Private Owen Corby Morris, 11th Bn. Royal Sussex Regiment, (Northampton)
No. L/0924 Private Edward H. Paley, 9th Bn. Royal Sussex Regiment, (Hornsey)
No. G/5985 Private (L/Cpl.) Albert Parkes, 9th Bn. Royal Sussex Regiment, (Wolverhampton)
No. G/20582 Lance-Corporal James Philip Perkins, 8th Bn. Royal Sussex Regiment, (Croydon)
No. G/17658 Corporal Frank .C. Pestell, 9th Bn. Royal Sussex Regiment, (Clapham)
No. SD/3426 Private Herbert James Phillips, 13th Bn. Royal Sussex Regiment, (Brighton).
No. SD/3430 Sergeant Herbert C. Pocock, 13th Bn. Royal Sussex Regiment,
(Gt. Berkhampsted)
No. G/15961 Private Harry G. Pronger, 13th Bn. Royal Sussex Regiment, (Horsham)

Thursday September 19th 1918

More Military Medals for Sussex Soldiers
The *"London Gazette"* announces the award of the Military Medal to the following : -

No. SD/1737 Private Ellis Maurice Single, 11th Bn. Royal Sussex Regiment, (Paddington)
No. G/1440 Sergeant Isaac Y. Smith, 8th Bn. Royal Sussex Regiment, (Waldron)
No. G/16788 Private (L/Cpl.) William H. Spears, 11th Bn. Royal Sussex Regiment, (Rye)
No. G/2328 Private William A. Staines, 8th Bn. Royal Sussex Regiment, (East ham)
No. G/2165 Corporal Leonard .G. Standing, 8th Bn. Royal Sussex Regiment, (Worthing)
No. G/7671 Private Stanley D. Stokes, 9th Bn. Royal Sussex Regiment, (Deal)
No. G/12725 Private (L/Cpl.) Charles E. Taplin, 9th Bn. Royal Sussex Regiment, (Chichester)
No. G/17375 Private Arthur C. Taylor, 7th Bn. Royal Sussex Regiment, (Acton)
No. G/13582 Private Richard H. Weeks, 9th Bn. Royal Sussex Regiment, (East Fairleigh)
No. G/15623 Sergeant Harold William Whitaker, 13th Bn. Royal Sussex Regiment, (Dorking)
No. G/16762 Private (L/Cpl.) Sydney F. Wilkinson, 9th Bn. Royal Sussex Regiment, (Catford)
No. G/1741 Corporal Joseph Windmill, 8th Bn. Royal Sussex Regiment, (Tooting)

Friday September 20th 1918

The King has been pleased to approve of the award of the Bar to the Military Cross to be bestowed upon the following Royal Sussex officers : -

Bar to M.C.

T/2nd Lieutenant Douglas Walter Graham May, M.C., 9th Bn.

For conspicuous gallantry and devotion to duty. He made two daring reconnaissance's which enabled the situation to be cleared up. Later in the day he organised a counter-attack, and by his brilliant leadership and dash saved a critical situation.
(M.C. gazetted 22nd April 1918)

T/Captain Horace John White, M.C., 13th Bn.

For conspicuous gallantry and devotion to duty. When his company was ordered to cover the withdrawal of his battalion, with extreme skill and coolness he covered the withdrawal by means of his Lewis guns, he himself displayed great courage in crossing bullet swept zones to dispose his men to the greatest advantage. It was largely due to his military knowledge and complete contempt of danger that the remainder of his battalion was able to withdraw with but a few losses.
(M.C. gazetted 18th October, 1917)

The award of the Military Medal has been awarded for gallantry is announced in the *"London Gazette"* :-

M.M.

No. G/7008 Lance-Corporal A. Young, 8th Bn. Royal Sussex Regiment, (Glasgow)

Monday September 23rd 1918

Gallant Sussex Officers

To the undermentioned officers of the Royal Sussex Regiment, the Military Cross-has been awarded for gallantry in the field :-

M.C.

T/2nd Lieutenant (A/Captain) James Reuben Bradley, 12th Bn. attd. 7th Bn.

For conspicuous gallantry and devotion to duty. This officer was ordered with about forty men of the battalion to drive the enemy out of some woods which had been occupied. He had to lead the men over nearly 800 yards of open ground to reach the woods, which were infested with machine-guns, this he did with great dash, in spite of the fire, clearing the woods and killing a number of the enemy. This success was due to his energetic leading.

T/2nd Lieutenant Walter Henry Cater, 8th Bn.

For conspicuous gallantry and devotion to duty. When his platoon was cut off from the remainder of his company, he held on until practically surrounded by the enemy, and fought his platoon most skilfully with few casualties. He showed great courage and coolness.

Lieutenant Richard G. Cooper, 3rd Bn.

For conspicuous gallantry and devotion to duty. During a counter-attack by his battalion he went several times through heavy barrage to ensure the carrying out of orders he showed fine courage and devotion to duty.

2nd Lieutenant R. Hudson, 3rd Bn.

For conspicuous gallantry and devotion to duty in a raid on the enemy trenches, resulting in the capture of two prisoners. It was entirely owing to his leadership and example that the raid was successful.

Major D.M. Baker : Brighton

Major D.M. Baker has received the Military Cross, under the following circumstances "When in command of a battery he was slightly wounded, but refused to leave his battery till severely wounded a fortnight later. At one place the cross-roads were being heavily shelled and all his guns had come out of the gateway at this place. It was only through his coolness and gallantry that, all the guns were extricated."

Major Baker is the son of Mr. And Mrs. John Osborn Baker, Strathfield, Dyke Road, Brighton. He was educated at Brighton College, and was articled to the present Mayor of Brighton (Alderman H. Carden, J.P.) Major Baker enlisted in the first days of the war and has been on active service ever since. He has now recovered from his wounds and is back in the firing line again.

Thursday September 26th 1918

Shot down aeroplane with rifle

It is officially announced that the Military Cross has been conferred upon :-
T/2nd Lieutenant Richard John Boyes, 8th Bn. Royal Sussex Regiment,

For conspicuous gallantry and devotion to duty during an enemy attack; He re-organised men of his company and stragglers, dug a line and held off enemy attacks throughout the night and again in. The morning. He himself brought down with rifle fire, low flying enemy aeroplane which was directing artillery fire on the position. He set his men a fine example of courage and determination.

The *"London Gazette"* also announces the following award :-

M.C.

T/2nd Lieutenant Ernest James Hemsley, 12th Bn. Royal Sussex Regiment,

For conspicuous gallantry and devotion to duty. He led his platoon with great skill and dash under heavy machine-gun fire in a counter-attack, killing several of the enemy and taking several prisoners. His coolness and good leadership won the confidence of all ranks.

Friday September 27th 1918

The King has been pleased to approve of the award of the Military Cross to be bestowed upon the following Royal Sussex Officers :-

M.C.

Captain (A/Mjr.) Francis Louis du Moulin, 3rd Bn. Royal Sussex Regiment attd. 1st Bn. East Yorks.

For co-ordinating the withdrawal of the rearguard composed of various units, under heavy fire from three sides. He exhibited great coolness and ability, and a steady withdrawal was effected till the rearguard came into line with other troops more than a mile in the rear of their first position.

T/2nd Lt. Stephen Horscroft, Royal Sussex Regiment,

He kept his mortars in action under heavy fire until every round was fired, causing the enemy heavy casualties as he was massing for an attack, and greatly helping in spoiling his attack. He set a fine example of courage and determination.

Lt. Henry Hans L'Estrange, Royal Sussex Regiment,

Finding the flanks of his battalion had gone, he organised a defensive flank with his battery under very heavy shell and machine-gun fire. He did splendid work.

Saturday September 28th 1918

Military Crosses for Sussex Officers

The Military Cross has been awarded to the undermentioned officers for gallantry in the field :-

2nd Lieutenant John Alexander Davidson, 4th Bn.

For conspicuous gallantry and devotion to duty. He showed great skill and resource in command of a platoon. Later, owing to casualties, he took command of his company, of the whole line, and finally of his battalion. when relieved by a senior officer although nearly exhausted, he remained at duty, constantly exposing himself to heavy fire. Throughout ten days of strain and anxiety, his behaviour was a wonderful example of grit and determination.

("London Gazette" 16th September, 1918)

T/2nd Lieutenant Victor Richard Helps Ellis, Royal Sussex Regiment,

For conspicuous gallantry and devotion to duty. When a strong attack by the enemy pierced the line, causing our men to retire at one point, a party of fifty men, under an officer, was immediately sent forward to reinforce. Before this party got up, the officer in charge was severely wounded. This officer then dashed forward and took command, leading the men forward and re-establishing the line. His prompt action at a critical moment saved the situation.
("London Gazette 16th September, 1918)

2nd Lieutenant Donald Fraser, Royal Sussex Regiment,

For conspicuous gallantry and devotion to duty. By his personal efforts and example, while commanding his company, he repulsed strong enemy attacks. He showed fine skill and initiative in handling his men, and caused heavy casualties to be inflicted on the enemy.
("London Gazette" 16th September, 1918)

T/2nd Lt. Leonard William Hudson, Royal Sussex Regiment,

At a critical moment this officer led details of brigade headquarters forward in a determined counter-attack, saving the situation. The next day he rallied a party of 100 men, and held the position while the withdrawal of the remainder of the brigade was being affected. Throughout the operations he was in charge of the ammunition supply, which was satisfactorily maintained under most difficult circumstances.
("London Gazette" 16th September, 1918)

T/2nd Lieutenant James Mann, 9th Bn. Royal Sussex Regiment,

For conspicuous gallantry and devotion to duty. Through heavy enemy barrage he carried important messages to a forward company partly surrounded by the enemy, which resulted in the battalion being extricated from a very dangerous situation. He showed fine courage and determination and was later severely wounded while carrying a daring reconnaissance.
("London Gazette" 16th September, 1918)

2nd Lieutenant William Thomas Morrison, Royal Sussex Regiment,

For conspicuous gallantry and devotion to duty in command of a company. Orders to withdraw failed to reach his battalion, and although his left flank was exposed he clung to his position, inflicting heavy casualties on the enemy, only retiring when ordered. He was wounded, but refused to go back until he had extricated the whole company from a difficult position. His coolness and courage were the admiration of all ranks.
("London Gazette" 16th September, 1918)

T/2nd Lieutenant Percy Vinall Pullinger, Royal Sussex Regiment,

He put up a magnificent resistance to heavy enemy attacks, and. when surrounded cut his way through and withdrew his men, fighting, in good order. He displayed fine courage and initiative.
("London Gazette" 16th September, 1918)

 T/Captain Archibald Bernard Rewell, 9th Bn. Royal Sussex Regiment,

This officer put up a gallant and most determined resistance against successive enemy attacks, and chiefly owing to his fine courage and example the advance, of the enemy was checked.

("*London Gazette*" 16th September, 1918)

Lieutenant Arthur Curtis Wilmot Uloth, 3rd Bn.

For conspicuous gallantry and devotion to duty when brigade intelligence officer. He did valuable work on many occasions, obtaining information and helping to re-organise men. He led a mixed party in a counter-attack, and restored a dangerous situation. He showed great cheerfulness and courage, and set a fine example.

("*London Gazette*" 16th September, 1918)

Monday September 30th 1918

Gallant Defence

The Military Cross has been awarded for gallantry in the field to :-

T/Lieutenant Lawrence Daniel Moore, 8th Bn.

For conspicuous gallantry and devotion to duty. This officer, detailed to garrison a post in a switch, organised his platoon with great skill, facing the situation confidently, sending in good reports, and, when the enemy attacked in force, inflicted heavy casualties before withdrawing to the main line. He was wounded on the following day.

Wednesday October 2nd 1918

Sussex Officer runs gauntlet of machine-guns and 'plane

The Military Cross has been awarded for gallantry in the field to the undermentioned officers :-

T/2nd Lieutenant James Gordon Simpson, Royal Sussex Regiment,

For conspicuous gallantry and devotion to duty. Under very heavy fire, he successfully led his company in a counter-attack to their objective. He was twice wounded, but continued to encourage his men to advance. He set a fine example of devotion to duty and contempt for personal safety.

T/Captain High Sparks, 13th Bn. Royal Sussex Regiment,

For conspicuous gallantry and devotion to duty. This officer went up in charge of rations for the whole brigade. On approaching a village some miles behind the line held by the brigade, he found the enemy in possession. He halted the transport, and made a personal reconnaissance. Discovering that the brigade had retreated some distance to a flank, he got the rations up just after daybreak. He then found that his transport was between the enemy advanced troops and our own, so he led the transport at full gallop under heavy machine-gun fire till he reached or position, being followed by a low flying aeroplane, bombing and machine-gunning his column. Rations, water and ammunition were eventually delivered, thanks to his perseverance and initiative.

Thursday October 3rd 1918

Two Gallant Sussex Officers

Among the recipients of the Military Cross at the hands of the King at Buckingham Palace, was Lieutenant W.F. Howard, Sussex Yeomanry, son of Mr. C. Howard, East Street, Chichester. Lieutenant Howard went to Gallipoli as an N.C.O. in the Yeomanry, and while there his twin brother was killed. Since then he has seen much service in Egypt and Palestine. The official record of the distinction is as follows :-

He was in command of the leading wave of his Company on arrival at the final objective. When the enemy attacked he led three bayonet charges, kept intact, and advanced some 200 yards further, and established himself in a commanding position. He showed splendid courage and initiative.
Mr. C. Howard was at the investiture.

Wednesday October 9th 1918

Sussex Soldiers Medals

The *"London Gazette"* announces the award of the Military Medal for bravery in the field to :-

No. 20282 Sergeant A.J. Hersey, 8th Bn. (Raynes Park)

No. SD/80 Private Arthur Sydney Lightfoot, 9th Bn. (Eastbourne)

No. G/14848 Sergeant William C. Norman, 11th Bn. (Luton)

Thursday October 10th 1918

Military Medal Awards

The undermentioned have been awarded the Military Medal for bravery in the field :-

No. G/7896 Corporal Richard E. Stuart, 9th Bn. Royal Sussex Regiment, (Norwich)
No. G/2416 Sergeant Walter J. White, 8th Bn. Royal Sussex Regiment, (Woolwich)

Friday October 11th 1918

Local Soldiers gain further Honours

The following are among the decorations and medals awarded by the President of the French Republic at various dates to members of the British Forces for distinguished service rendered during the course of the campaign :-

Legion de Honner
Croix De Officer

Brevet Colonel (T/Brigadier-General) John Bartholomew Wroughton, C.M.G., 2nd Bn. Royal Sussex Regiment,

Croix de Guerre

Brevet Colonel (T/Brigadier-General) Alfred Edgar Glasgow, D.S.O., 8th Bn. Royal Sussex Regiment,
No. L Sergeant Charles Coates, M.M.,M.S.M. 8th Bn. Royal Sussex Regiment, (Brighton)
No. G/574 Sergeant Frederick James Ransom, M.M., 7th Bn. Royal Sussex Regiment, (Bexhill)

Medaille Militaire

No. 240935 Private (A/L/Cpl.) Edgar Buckwell, 5th Bn. Royal Sussex Regiment, (Plumpton)

Tuesday October 15th 1918

Award of the Military Cross

2nd Lt. Edgar James Hobbs, (16th Bn.) Royal Sussex Regiment,

For conspicuous gallantry and devotion to duty. With two men he successfully covered the withdrawal of his platoon. Noticing that his left-hand man was heavily engaged, he returned to his assistance and found him wounded and unconscious. In spite of a heavy bombing attack he succeeded in bringing the man away to a place of safety. His determination and courage were beyond praise.

Wednesday October 16th 1918

Medals for Sussex Men in Mesopotamia

The *"London Gazette"* announces the award of the Meritorious Service Medal to the following in recognition of valuable service rendered in the forces in Mesopotamia :-

No. L/9182 Sergeant L. Winchester, 1st Bn. Royal Sussex Regiment, (Ewhurst)

D.S.O. for Sussex Officer

The *"London Gazette"* announces the award of the Distinguished Service Order to Captain (T/Major) Henry Howard Johnson, 6th Bn. Royal Sussex Regiment, attd. Tank Corps.

For conspicuous gallantry and devotion to duty. During a long and arduous day's' fighting he followed the tanks, of which he was in command, on foot, running, one to the other, directing their operations with the greatest success.

He was indefatigable in his efforts, and by his personal reconnaissance of different points was enabled to manoeuvre his tanks in such a manner as to break off the resistance machine-guns which were holding up the infantry advance. During the whole day he was exposed to the heavy fire of artillery and machine-guns, and his devotion to duty was the admiration of all who saw him.

Thursday October 17th 1918

Military Medal presented at Horsham

From the Carfax bandstand at Horsham yesterday afternoon Private Edward Highgate, of the Royal Sussex Regiment, living at Manning's Heath, was publicly presented with the Military Medal.

A detachment of the R.G.A. from Roffey Camp lined up for the event, and those present included Colonel Nichols (Commandant of the Camp), Captain and Adjutant Holmes (Roffey Camp), Major William H. Goringe (Headquarters Staff, Royal Sussex Regiment, Horsham), and Captain and Adjutant H.C. Teague (3rd Volunteer Battalion, Royal Sussex Regiment). Mr. Edward I. Bostock, J.P., opened the proceedings, and the presentation was made by Colonel Nichols, who said the distinction was awarded for bravery in the field by volunteering to go into 'No Man's Land' and bringing back the wounded. He had great pleasure in making the presentation.

Private Highgate, who now holds the Military Medal with two Bars, said he was going back on Friday and he hoped when he returned again he would have gained an even higher decoration. While expressing the hope the war would soon be ended, he remarked that at any rate the Royal Sussex. Regiment were always ready to do their bit, to hold or to go over the top. He hoped they would be, to the front in the march into Berlin. Mr. Bostock cordially thanked Colonel Nichols for making the presentation.

Friday October 18th 1918

Military Cross

The King has been pleased to approve of the award of the Military Cross to be bestowed upon the following Sussex Officer :-

Lt. (A/Cpt.) V.H. Jaques, Royal Sussex Regiment, 3rd Bn. attd. 2nd Bn.

For conspicuous gallantry and dash during a raid on enemy trenches. The success of the aid was entirely due to his organisation and splendid leadership. After it was over he took a patrol and searched "No Man's Land" for three sniping men under persistent machine-gun and trench mortar fire.

Lt. Leslie Ward Lane, Royal Sussex Regiment,

For conspicuous gallantry and initiative when the enemy attempted a raid. As the enemy were withdrawing he collected a patrol, rushed out to cut them off, and made a very determined effort to reach one of them who was lying wounded near the enemy lines. At the moment he was prevented by bombs and close revolver fire from doing so, but later in the day he again took out a patrol and got his man, who had died meanwhile, thereby securing identification. He set a fine example of dash and gallantry throughout.

Arundel Military Medal winner killed

News has been received by Mr. & Mrs. H. Harwood, Orchard Place, Arundel, that one of their three soldier sons, Sergeant J. Harwood, M.M., royal Sussex Regiment, has been instantaneously killed. A high tribute to his excellent qualities has been paid by Lieutenant R.B. Mason, who, in a letter to the bereaved parents states that Sergeant Harwood was universally liked and respected, "As an N.C.O. he has been quite invaluable, and we knew he could always be trusted," adds the officer. "We feel we have lost a comrade whose place it will be impossible to fill."

Sergeant Harwood was a postal employee before the war, and was greatly liked by his fellows in civilian life. His brother Arthur has been wounded three times and has also won the Military Medal.

Monday October 21st 1918

More Military Crosses

The King has been pleased to approve of the award of the Military Cross to be bestowed upon two more Royal Sussex Officers, they are:-

T/2nd Lt. R. Waugh, 16th Bn.

While he was in charge of a small post covering a plank bridge over a river, the enemy pushed forward a machine-gun and opened enfiladed fire on his post. He and another man immediately went out and after throwing a bomb, rushed the gun, capturing two prisoners and scattering the detachment. But for his fine gallantry and promptitude the bridgehead position would have been untenable.

2nd Lt. B.J. Webber, 16th Bn.

For conspicuous gallantry and organising a small raid with artillery co-operation. When the barrage lifted he led the assault, arriving at each successive objective some distance ahead of the nearest man. The final objective was a house the shelling was heavy, and an enemy machine-gun was firing across the line of advance. Without hesitation he made for the house, and after completing his search of the ruins, withdrew his party, taking back three prisoners. The success of the raid was largely due to his fine courage and leadership.

Tuesday October 22nd 1918

Military Medal

The *"London Gazette"* announces the award of the Military Medal for bravery in the field to :-

No. G/596 Private (L/Cpl.) Charles E.V. Aish, 2nd Bn. Royal Sussex Regiment, (Yapton)

No. G/445 Corporal (A/Sergeant) George J. Farndale, 2nd Bn. Royal Sussex Regiment, (Portfield)
No. G/17541 Private Herbert Hatton, 2nd Bn. Royal Sussex Regiment, (Folkestone)
No. G/4424 Private Alfred J. Pascoe, 2nd Bn. Royal Sussex Regiment, (Islington)

Wednesday October 23rd 1918

Sussex Men earn D.C.M's

The following act of gallantry which earned the Distinguished Conduct Medal is published in the *"London Gazette"* :-

No. L/9010 T/S.M. HA Coles, 9th Bn. Royal Sussex Regiment, (Cocking)

For conspicuous gallantry and devotion to duty in the field. This W.O. has served his battalion for nearly three years as C.S.M. and R.S.M. He had previously been with another battalion until wounded. His consistent good work, especially in training young N.C.O.'s has been of great value.

No. G/1958 C.S.M. J.W. Tutt, M.M., 8th Bn. Royal Sussex Regiment, (Eastbourne)

For conspicuous gallantry and devotion to duty. He has always discharged his duties in the most efficient manner, and takes the greatest interest in the efficiency of the battalion. On one occasion he was wounded in the head by a bomb, but refused to go sick and carried on his duties. He has always set a fine example to the men.

Thursday October 24th 1918

More Honours for Sussex Soldiers

The following acts of gallantry for which the Distinguished Conduct Medal has been awarded to :-

No. G/240008 Sergeant W.H. Gilbert, 13th Bn. Royal Sussex Regiment, (Rye)

For conspicuous gallantry and devotion to duty for more than three years in the field.
He invariably showed remarkable coolness and courage under the heaviest fire, and his resources and splendid example have been of inestimable value.
No. L/7688 C.S.M. W. Herridge, 8th Bn. Royal Sussex Regiment, (Kemptown)

For conspicuous gallantry and devotion to duty. He has always displayed the keenest interest in his work, and has done much to contribute to the efficiency of the company. During his thirty months service with this battalion he has set a fine example to his men.

Steyning Military Medallist

The great British advance has enabled a Steyning man to achieve honour, Sergeant W. Spickernell, 16th Bn. Royal Sussex Regiment, son of Mr. & Mrs. Spickernell, "Melrose", College Hill, Steyning, has been awarded the Military Medal for :-

"For conspicuous gallantry and devotion to duty in action under heavy shell fire on 9th August."

He was then a corporal, but secured his promotion on that occasion. Twenty-three years of age, he was in private service when he enlisted during the first month of the war. He was at the Western Front until he received a shoulder wound, which developed into blood poisoning. Recovering, he was drafted to the East, and was at the fall of Jerusalem. Thence again sent to the Western Front and received a slight arm wound from a piece of shrapnel, but has quite recovered again, not having been sent home on this occasion.

Saturday November 2nd 1918

D.C.M Award

The award of the Distinguished Conduct Medal has been awarded to:-

No. 200172 Sergeant S.A. Constable, 4th Bn. Royal Sussex Regiment, (West Hoathly)

For conspicuous gallantry and devotion to duty. He collected and organised a company under heavy shell fire after all the officers in the neighbourhood had become casualties. By his utter disregard of danger and continued cheerfulness he set a splendid example to the men and inspired all with a feeling of confidence in the success of the advance.

No. 200342 Sergeant F. Pyle, 4th Bn. Royal Sussex Regiment, (Graffham, Sussex)

For conspicuous gallantry and devotion to duty in the field. He took command of his company when all the officers had become casualties and handled it with great skill and courage, his eagerness to advance acting like a tonic on his men when they were nearly exhausted. He was shot through the thigh while rushing an enemy machine-gun but went on to capture it, killing two of the enemy himself. Owing to loss of blood he was compelled to go back, but directed the advance to continue and handed over command to the next senior N.C.O. He behaved magnificently.

No. G/6010 Private F. Tallon, 2nd Bn. Royal Sussex Regiment, (Kendal)

For conspicuous gallantry and disregard of personal danger during a raid on the enemy lines. He saw one of the enemy running away with a light machine-gun on his shoulder, and immediately gave chase and followed him over the enemy second line. He fired at the man and made him drop the gun, which Private Tallon brought triumphantly back to his lines. Throughout the operation he showed splendid courage and initiative.

Tuesday November 3rd 1918

Infantry inspected at seaside

General Sir William Robinson, K.C.B., G.C.V.G., D.S.O., A.D.C., commanding the forces in Great Britain, paid a visit to a south coast town yesterday to inspect certain battalions of infantry in training there. The General was accompanied by Lieutenant-General C.L. Woolcombe, K.C.B., Commander-in-Chief of the Eastern Command, and a large staff of officers. The duties of the day were carried out with soldierly precision. There was a full battalion first on parade and the general salute was performed smartly, the preceding examination of the ranks during which period the band played a selection of music. This first event wound up with the march past. Going to another point a second battalion were put through their paces. The General reviewed each branch of trench activity from musketry, to gas warfare. Bayonet fighting over various obstacles, physical drill, including, of course, boxing, all were in their turn exhibited. The chief occurrence of the day was the bestowal of medals as follows –

Awarded the Military Medal.

No. G/10273 Sergeant George E. Vicary, 13th Bn. Royal Sussex Regiment,

For most conspicuous gallantry and good leadership in the Battle of Tower Hamlets on 26th September, 1917. He led his platoon into action most skilfully and fearlessly, and gained his objective and rapidly consolidated it. Throughout the whole operation he displayed courage, cheerfulness and dogged determination, with which spirit he successfully imbued his men, giving them an added sense of security in themselves. He volunteered to patrol the whole of the ground in front of his company's new positions, which he did for a distance of 250 yards.
There were present a number of leading residents to witness these presentations. The march past was a brilliant finale to the day's events.

Monday November 4th 1918

Horsham Soldier's reward for bravery

The following details are given by the *"London Gazette"* of the circumstances which led to the award of a Distinguished Conduct Medal to :-

No. 200318 Corporal E.J. White, 4th Bn. Royal Sussex Regiment, (Horsham.)

For conspicuous gallantry and devotion to duty in the field. He took command when all his officers and non-commissioned officers had become casualties. Under heavy fire and on his own initiative he re-organised the line with great skill and courage. At a critical period his grasp of the situation was largely responsible for the steadiness of his company in the advance.

Lance-Corporal H.J. Guiel wounded

Having been wounded in the left hip on 30th September, Lance-Corporal H.J. Guiel, of 16, Stanley Road, Worthing, is in hospital at Boulogne. A member of the Territorials, he was mobilised at the outbreak of hostilities in the Royal Sussex Regiment. He has been in France for two years and three months. He received the Military Medal a short time ago for "Most conspicuous bravery and devotion to duty in the battle of Ypres. He did splendid work as a battalion runner, delivering messages under heavy shell fire."

Thursday November 7th 1918

Sussex Soldiers Honoured

Permission has been given by the King for members of the Royal Sussex Regiment to wear decorations awarded them by the President of the French Republic for distinguished service in the course of the campaign is as follows :-

Decorations and Medals conferred by

THE PRESIDENT OF THE FRENCH REPUBLIC

Croix de Guerre

T/Captain Matthew James Manuai Makalua, 13th Bn.
No. L/8151 Sergeant-Major Harry Ambrose Lewry, D.C.M. (Hurstpierpoint)

Croix de Chevalier

Captain (T/Major) Harry Howard Johnson, Royal Sussex Regiment and Tank Corps.

Medaille Militaire

No. 265798 Private John Barford, M.M., (Bolton)

Saturday November 9th 1918

Military Crosses for Sussex Officers

Three more names have to, be added to the long scroll of fame which belongs to the Royal Sussex. They are those of Acting Captain Jack Chalmers Peskett, M.C., Lieutenant Henry Treacher, MC., and 2nd Lieutenant Archibald Victor Brown, M.C, To the first have been awarded Bars, to Military Crosses already won by them, and to the latter the Military Cross itself The *"London Gazette"* comments as follows on the awards :-

Lieutenant (A/Captain) Jack Chalmers Peskett, M.C.,

For marked courage and devotion to duty. As second in command he continually went forward to obtain information and clear up the situation. He never failed to carry out his task, under heavy fire, without regard to his personal safety, and his conduct throughout was beyond praise.
(M.C. gazetted 16th August, 1917)

T/Lieutenant Henry Treacher, M.C., 9th Bn.

For conspicuous gallantry and initiative. He went, with his runner, to the flank of the company that was being enfiladed by machine-gun fire, and working forward under heavy fire killed the gunner with a bomb and captured the gun. His skill and dash were worthy of great praise and saved many casualties.
(M.C. gazetted 1st January 1917)

T/2nd Lieutenant Archibald Victor Brown, 4th Bn.

He was shot in the hand early in the day, but refused to leave and led his company in, the advance under heavy fire, until again wounded in the body. After this, he carried on with, great courage, until he fainted from loss of blood. His personal example inspired his men with a spirit of emulation which helped them successfully through a most critical period.

Monday November 11th 1918

Another Sussex M.C.

The "*London Gazette*" gives the following details of the manner in which Lieutenant Reginald H. Fortescue, 3rd Bn. attd. 4th Bn. Royal Sussex Regiment, won the Military Cross.

For conspicuous gallantry and good leadership. He took command of two companies when all the officers had become casualties and re-organised them under heavy artillery fire. The success of the attack was largely due to his ability and chivalrous devotion to duty.

Wednesday November 13th 1918

Sussex Officer's Decoration

The King has given permission. To Major (A/Lieutenant-Colonel) John Meredith Hulton, D.S.O., Royal Sussex Regiment, attached Welsh Regiment, to wear the Order of the Nile, 3rd Class, bestowed upon him by the Sultan of Egypt, for distinguished services rendered during the course of the campaign.

Friday November 15th 1918

More Sussex Honours

The most recent honours list contains the names of a number of Royal Sussex men who have won the Military Medal. The following are the recipients :-

No. G/6977 Private Albert Golds, 2nd Bn. (Findon)
No. G/ 18982 Private Robert William Howlett, 2nd Bn. (Hammersmith)
No. L/7523 Private William E. Noakes, 16th Bn. (St. Leonards-on-Sea)
No. 320337 Private William Sanford, 16th Bn. (Thornton Heath)

Wednesday November 20th 1918

D.C.M. for Linfield Man

The Distinguished Conduct Medal has been conferred on Corporal C.A. Still for devotion to duty. Corporal Still formerly belonged to the Royal Sussex Regiment, is attached to the M.G Corps.

Saturday November 23rd 1918

Honours for Sussex Men

The *"London Gazette"* announces that the following honours have been conferred by the French President to British Forces for gallant service during the present campaign :

Croix de Guerre

Captain Rupert Charles Godfrey Middleton, M.C., Royal Sussex Regiment,

T/Lieutenant (A/Captain) Jack Chalmers Peskett, M.C., Royal Sussex Regiment,
T/2nd Lieutenant Isaac Leonard Read, Royal Sussex Regiment,
No. 200469 Private William George Douglas Langley, 4th Bn. Royal Sussex Regiment, (Chichester)
No. 200825 Corporal George Arthur Purver, 4th Bn. Royal Sussex Regiment, (Bognor)
No. 200484 Corporal Albert George Woolven, 4th Bn. Royal Sussex Regiment, (Horsham)

Medaille Militaire

No. 200172 Company-Sergeant Major Sydney Arthur Constable, 4th Bn. Royal Sussex Regiment, (West Hoathly)

"London Gazette" Tuesday November 26th 1918

The following are among the Decorations and medals awarded by the. Allied Powers at various dates to the British Forces for distinguished services rendered during the course of the campaign:—

His Majesty the King has given unrestricted permission in all cases to wear the Decorations and medals in question.

Decorations conferred by

THE PRESIDENT OF THE FRENCH REPUBLIC

Legion de Honneur
Croix de Chevalier

Temporary Major The Honourable Neville Stephen Lytton, O.B.E., 11th Bn.

Decorations and Medals conferred by

HIS MAJESTY THE KING OF ITALY

Order of St. Maurice and St. Lazarus

Officer

Major (A/ Lt-Col.) John Meredith Hulton, D.S.O., Royal Sussex Regiment, attd. Welsh Regiment (T. F).

Saturday November 30th 1918

Honour for Royal Sussex Officer

Among the decorations conferred by the king of Italy for distinguished service rendered during the campaign is : -

Order of the Crown of Italy

Major (Lt-Colonel) John Merideth Hulton, D.S.O., Royal Sussex Regiment, attd. Welsh Regiment,

Tuesday December 3rd 1918

A West Lavington Soldier's Military Medal

Mrs. Holden, of Royal Oak Cottage, West .Lavington, recently proceeded to Portsmouth to receive the Military Medal won by her son, Private E.V. Holden, Royal Sussex Marines, who was killed on 2nd April of this year. The young soldier joined the forces in September, 1914, and after serving on a ship which carried provisions to the Fleet in the North Sea, he volunteered for the firing line, and saw two years hard fighting in France before he met his death, Mrs, Holden's second son, Signaller W.J Holden, is in hospital in Doncaster suffering from wounds.

Friday December 6th 1918

Award of the D.C.M.

The *"London Gazette"* announces the award of the Distinguished Conduct Medal for gallantry to :-

No. G/1192 Sergeant A.W. Trevor, M.M., 7th Bn. Royal Sussex Regiment, (Portslade)

For conspicuous gallantry and fine leadership. He commanded a platoon in the leading wave of the attack and cleared up a pocket of the enemy who were delaying troops to his right, and captured two machine-guns and several prisoners. Later, he again led his platoon with the greatest courage, advancing over some three hundred yards of exposed ground under heavy machine-gun fire, and gained his objective.

Monday December 9th 1918

Military Cross Awarded

The *"London Gazette"* announces the award of the Military Cross to :-

2nd Lieutenant Arthur William Richardson, 4th Bn. Royal Sussex Regiment.

Conspicuous gallantry while commanding a patrol which was attacked by a superior force of the enemy and surrounded. Owing to his fine example of courage he succeeded in beating off that attack and accounting for several of the enemy.

Sussex Man's D.C.M.

The latest list of military awards contains the name of a Sussex soldier who has been awarded the Distinguished Conduct Medal :-

No. G/574 Sergeant F J Ransom, M.M. 7th Battalion, Royal Sussex Regiment, (Bexhill)
For conspicuous gallantry during an attack. All his officers having become casualties between the first and the second objectives, he re-organised the company and at the head of two platoons made a determined attack on the latter, accounting for three of the enemy himself It was due to his fine courage and leadership the second objective was taken.

"London Gazette" Wednesday December 11th 1918

His Majesty the KING has been graciously pleased to approve of the award of the Military Medal for bravery in the Field to the undermentioned Warrant Officers, Non-Commissioned Officers and Men:—

No. G/1777 Corporal W. Spickernell, 16th Bn. (Annington Mere)

Saturday December 21st 1918

Steyning Medallist

Joining the Army at the early age of 16 years, Private A F. Groome, Royal Sussex Regiment, a native of Steyning, but whose present home is in Brighton has been awarded the Military Medal for gallant work in getting wounded men to a place of safety under very fierce machine-gun fire and shell fire, showing, a fine example to all ranks. He has been wounded twice.

Monday December 23rd 1918

Sussex Men "Mentioned".

A further list of names of those mentioned in Sir Douglas Haig's latest dispatch includes the following from the county regiment :-

Lieutenant-Colonel (T/Brigadier-General) W.L. Osborn, C.M.G., D.S.O.,
Captain & Bt. Major Sir E.H. Preston, Bart. M.C.
Major & Bt. Colonel (T/Brigadier-General) J.B. Wroughton, C.M.G.
Captain H. Sayer, M.C., Sussex Yeomanry T.F.

Saturday December 28th 1918

Local Men "Mentioned"

Among the officers, non-commissioned officers and men mentioned in Sir Douglas, Haig's dispatch as worthy of special mention were the following :-

Royal Sussex Regiment

Adams, Lieutenant A. 5th Bn. (T.F.), attd. 16th Bn. (T.F.)
Chad, Lieutenant (A/Captain) TE. M.C.,   2nd Bn.
Chittenden, Lieutenant (A/Captain) H. F. M.C., 5th Bn. (T.F.) attd.1st Fd Surv. Bn. R.E.
Corral, Lieutenant (T/Major) W.R., M.C., Buffs. attd. 9th Bn.
Ellen, T/2nd Lieutenant W.P. 8th Bn.
Gillett, T/Lieutenant (A/Captain) R.H. attd. 10th L.T.M. Bty.
Hill, Captain (T/Lt.-Colonel) M.V.B. D.S.O., M.C. 5th Royal Fusiliers, Comdg. 9th Bn.
Hind, T/Captain R.C.D. M.C., 7th Bn.
Impey, Major (T/Lt.-Colonel) G.H., D.S.O., 7th Bn.
Lamotte Captain (Lt-Colonel) L., 2nd Bn. Commanding. 2nd Bn. York L.I.
Robinson, Lieutenant E.A.S. 6th Bn (T.F.) attd. 8th Bn.
Kay Robinson, T/Lt-Colonel H.T., D.S.O., 6th Bn. (T.F.) attd. 13th Bn.
Rothschild, T/Major G.F. M.C., 13th Bn. att. 2/10th Bn. London Regt.
Rothwell, Qmr. and T/Lieutenant E.N. 13th Bn. attd. 4th Bn. Ches. Regt. (T.F.)
Thomson, Captain (T/Lt.-Colonel) A.L., D.S.O., 7th Bn.
Turner, Captain (T/Major) M.T. M.C., 2nd Bn.
Woodruffe, Major (T/Lt.-Colonel) J.S., 2nd Bn. attd. 1st Bn. R, Newfoundland. Regt.
Bennett, No.30111 Corporal, E. 17th Bn., attd. 176th L.T.M. Bty.
Bray, No.5730 Private A. 9th Bn.
Hanlon, No.8562 C.Q.M.S. P.J. 7th Bn.
Hann, No. G/2121 Sergeant E.E. 7th Bn.
Humphrey, No. S/2385 C.Q.M.S. G. 16th Bn. (T.F.)
Humphrey, No. L/5863 R.Q.M.S. W. D.C.M., 2nd Bn.
Johnson, No. G/14968 Private W.G. 11th Bn.
Pearson, No. 266548 Sergeant S. 5th Bn. (T.F.)
Smith, No. G/2522 C.Q.M.S. H.P. 8th Bn.
Treadway, No. SD/2171 Corporal G. 14th Bn. (T.F.)

"London Gazette" Wednesday January 1st 1919

The following awards to officers of the Sussex Regiment are announced in the *"London Gazette"* and are for distinguished service in connection with military operations in France and Flanders :-

C.B.E. (Military Division)

Captain (T/Major) Montague Trevor Turner, 3rd Royal Sussex Regiment, (S.R.)

O.B.E. (Military Division)

Capt. Rev. Arthur Hamilton Boyd, M.C.,M.A. Army Chaplains Dept. 4th Bn. Royal Sussex Regiment,

M.B.E. (Military Division)

Lieutenant Thomas Wheatley Rose, M.C., 5th Bn. Royal Sussex Regiment,

D.S.O.

Captain & Bt. Major Sir Edward Hulton Preston, Bart. M.C.
T/Major George Francis Rothschild, M.C., 13th Bn. attd. 2/10th Bn. London Regt.

 Captain Humphrey Sayer, Sussex Yeomanry,

Thursday January 2nd 1919

Sussex Soldiers Rewards

The following decorations have been awarded Royal Sussex commissioned officers and non-commissioned officers for meritorious service :-

M.C.

 T/Lieutenant Cedric Blaker, 2nd Bn.

T/Captain Albert William Collingbourne, 9th Bn.

Lieutenant (T/Captain) James Edward Charles Langham, 5th Bn attd. 8th Bn.
Captain Harold Drummond Hillier, Gloucester Regt. attd.
Captain Leslie Phillips Marshall, West Yorks. attd.

D.C.M.

No. G1891 C.Q.M.S. W.H. Budgen, 7th Bn. (East Grinstead)
No. G/5828 A/Sergeant A.V. Coppard, 2nd Bn., (Hurst Green)
No. G/16014 Lance-Corporal A.J. Curd, 13th Bn. (Lancing)
No. G/3590 Sergeant A.J. Newnham, 9th Bn. (Dane Hill)

Saturday January 4th 1919

Honours for Sussex Men

The *"London Gazette"*, last night contained another list of military honours, the names of six Royal Sussex soldiers who have served in Egypt being included in it, one officer and five men. They are as follows :-

M.C.

Captain Reginald Douglas Jebb, 4th Bn. (T.F.)

In Italy

Awards to men who have served in Italy are also announced, as follows :-

Royal Sussex Regiment to be Brevet Lt.-Colonel

Major (Lt-Colonel) R.M. Birkett, D.S.O.

M.B.E.

Lieutenant (A/Captain) Frank Percival Twine, M.C., 5th Bn. (TF.)

M.C.

Lieutenant (T/Captain) William Edward Pears Done, 5th Bn. (T.F.)

D.C.M.

No. 240078 Corporal (A/Sgt.) A.J. Oyler, 5th Bn. (Rye)

M.S.M.

No. 240002 C.S.M. A.H. White, 5th Bn. (Hastings)
No. 240551 Sergeant H.J. Bannister, 5th Bn. (Rye)
No. 240405 Corporal R. Browning, 5th Bn. (East Grinstead)
No. 240355 Private (A/L/Cpl.) F. Isted, 5th Bn. (Ashburnham)

Monday January 6th 1919

Rewards for Home Service

The King has made the following appointments to the Order of the British Empire for valuable services rendered in connection with the war (Home Service) to be :-

O.B.E.

Major Henry Edmunds Matthews, 4th Battalion, Royal Sussex Regiment, (T.F.)

The King has approved the undermentioned rewards for valuable services rendered in connection with the war (Home Service).

To be Brevet Colonel

Lieutenant-Colonel Cecil G.H. Alers Hankey, Royal Sussex Regiment, 3rd Bn. Special Reserve,

To be Brevet Lieutenant-Colonel

Captain & Brigade Major (T/Lt-Col.) Jocelyn Brudenell, Earl of Chichester, Royal Sussex Regiment,

Worthing Soldier Decorated

For gallant conduct in bringing in wounded under heavy shell fire and machine-gun barrage on several occasions during the month of October, Private F. Slaughter whose home is at 15, Stanhope Road, Worthing, has been decorated on the field by General Higginson, commanding the 12th Division. Private Slaughter, who received the Military Medal enlisted in the Royal Sussex Regiment in the early part of the war.

Tuesday January 7th 1919

Last night's *"London Gazette"* notifies that the King has approved the grant of the Victoria Cross to Captain (A/Lt-Col.) Dudley Graham Johnson, D.S.O., M.C., South Wales Borderers, attached 2nd Battalion Royal Sussex Regiment. The gallant action for which the coveted honour was awarded is thus described :-

V.C.

For most conspicuous bravery and leadership during the forcing of the Sambre Canal on 4th November, 1918, The 2nd Infantry Brigade of which the 2nd Battalion, Royal Sussex Regiment formed part, was ordered to cross by the lock south of Catillon. The position was strong, and before the bridge could be thrown a steep bank leading up to the lock and a waterway about 100 yards short of the canal had to be crossed. The assaulting platoons and bridging parties, RE. on their arrival at the waterway were thrown into confusion by a heavy barrage and machine-gun fire, and heavy casualties were caused. At this moment Lt.-Colonel Johnson arrived, and, realising the situation, at once collected men to man the bridges and assist the R.E. and personally led the assault. In spite of his efforts heavy enemy fire again broke up the assaulting and bridging parties. Without any hesitation, he again re-organised the platoons and bridging parties and led them at the lock, this time succeeding in effecting a crossing, after which all went well. During all this time Lt-Colonel Johnson was under a very heavy fire, which, though it nearly decimated the assaulting columns, left him untouched. His conduct was a fine example of great valour, coolness and intrepidity, which added to his splendid leadership and the offensive spirit that he had inspired in his battalion, were entirely responsible for the successful crossing.

Italian Honours

General Cavan's Italian dispatch, quoted in last night' *"London Gazette"*, contains the following names mentioned by him for devotion to duty :-

Royal Sussex Regiment

Eberle, Major (A/Lt-Colonel) G.S.F.J. D.S.O., R.E. attd. Commanding. 5th Bn.
Birkett, Major R.M. D.S.O., (A/Lt.-Colonel, M.G. Corps.)
Brunskill, Lieutenant, G. 5th Bn.
Williams, Lieutenant (A/Captain) E.W. 5th Bn.
Bishop, No.240301 Private F. 5th Bn.
Cannon, No.240667 Sergeant G. 5th Bn.
Cosens, 240783 Private S. 5th Bn.
Furner, 240439 Private (A/L/Corporal) H.W. 5th Bn.
Turner, No. 240122 Sergeant R. 5th Bn.

Sussex Yeomanry

Mackay, Lieutenant J.E. attd. Remount Service.

Thursday January 9th 1919

D.C.M. for Lancing Man

The Distinguished Conduct Medal has been granted to Lance-Corporal A.J. Curd, Royal Sussex Regiment, son of Mr. and Mrs. R. Curd, Matfield, Penhill Road, Lancing. Lance-Corporal Curd is a young man of 23, has been in the Army two or three years, and has been wounded on two occasions. Prior to enlisting he worked for his father who is a market gardener.

Award of the D.C.M.

The award of the Distinguished Conduct Medal for gallantry is bestowed upon :-

No. 233460 Cpl. Arthur Allan W. Tribe, 16th Bn. Royal Sussex Regiment, attd. 74th Divisional Signal Company R.E.

For conspicuous gallantry near Templeux le Guerrard from September 17th, to 20th, 1918, he was continually laying forward and repairing telephone lines under heavy shelling and gas. During the attack on the 18th September, although suffering severely from gas poisoning, he followed the barrage, laying cable with the advancing troops, from time to time he sent back information from the front line that was of the utmost value.

Monday January 13th 1919

Awards for Gallant Service

A supplement to the *"London Gazette"* for Saturday contains many names of officers who have received awards for their gallantry and devotion to duty in the field. From them we extract the following :-

Bar to the D.S.O.

Captain (A/Lt-Col.) Dudley Graham Johnson, D.S.O. M.C., South Wales Borderers attd. 2nd Bn. Royal Sussex Regiment,

For conspicuous gallantry and devotion to duty in command of his battalion in the attack. The ground over which his battalion advanced was very difficult, but thanks to his careful dispositions, was successfully negotiated. He personally superintended the reorganisation after the objective was reached, and subsequently carried out a night attack, advancing some 1000 yards in the face of strenuous opposition. His skilful arrangements and conduct throughout inspiring the men under him with a splendid fighting spirit.

(D.S.O. gazetted 16th March 1915)

D.S.O.

Captain (A/Lt-Colonel) Arthur Lumley Thomson, Royal Sussex Regiment, Commanding. 7th Bn.

For conspicuous gallantry and good leadership while commanding his battalion in the attack. The ground over which his battalion advanced was very difficult, but thanks to his careful dispositions, was successfully negotiated. He personally supervised the reorganisations after the objective was reached, and subsequently carried out a night attack, advancing some thousand yards in the face of strenuous opposition. His skilful arrangements and conduct throughout inspired men under him with a splendid fighting spirit.

Bar to M.C.

T/Captain Geoffrey L Reckitt, M.C., 7th Bn. Royal Sussex Regiment,

For conspicuous gallantry during an attack. When units were in some confusion owing to the mist, on reaching the enemy third line he walked along the front and re-organised his company. He afterwards carried out a reconnaissance under heavy shell fire. Some days. later he again carried out daring reconnaissance's and gained information of great value regarding the enemy. Throughout the operations his fearlessness and devotion to duty were most marked.

Tuesday January 14th 1919

Military Cross for Royal Sussex Officer

Lieutenant Basil Hampton Charles Clark, 3rd Bn. attd. 7th Bn. Royal Sussex Regiment,

For conspicuous gallantry and devotion to duty during an attack. When the company on his left was held up, he led forward a platoon and captured 300 yards of enemy trench, together with eight machine-guns, two trench mortars and several prisoners: he personally killed an officer and three men. When forced to with draw by overwhelming numbers, he did so most skilfully, himself covering the retirement with a few men, and inflicting further losses on the enemy. His courage and able leadership were most marked.

Wednesday January 15th 1919

Awarded the Military Cross

A list issued last night for publication contained the names of more than two hundred officers and warrant officers who, by their gallant deeds on the battlefield, have earned for themselves the Military Cross. The three names which are appended are of interest in the county and the details of each officer will be read with pride.

Lieutenant (A/Capt.) Ronald Martin Howe, 3rd attd. 7th Bn. Royal Sussex Regiment,

For conspicuous gallantry and initiative. When the situation was obscure after an enemy attack, he made reconnaissance towards the enemy's lines under heavy shell fire and successfully assembled the leading companies in their positions ready for the attack next morning. The following evening he made another daring reconnaissance after which he personally led, his company into their position in the line. Although he lost all his officers within ten minutes of the attack commencing, he kept his own company and another company organised and ready to move at a moment's notice. He showed marked disregard of personal danger throughout.

T/2nd Lieutenant Sigmund Lotheim, 7th Bn. Royal Sussex Regiment,

For conspicuous gallantry and devotion to duty. He showed great courage in reorganising his company, which was heavily shelled when moving up to the line, and after his three senior officers were casualties he collected and brought on the company in a very short time without delaying the battalion. Later, though severely wounded, he stayed with his company until they had been collected and sent off to their new position, and personally reported that they had passed through and were all accounted for.

Lieutenant Reginald John Pring, 4th Bn. Royal Sussex Regiment, attd. 24th Bn. Royal Fusiliers,

He was in command of a company charged with dealing with any elements of enemy resistance which had been overlooked by the leading waves, and he carried' out his difficult and dangerous task with. great gallantry and, ability, the advance of the front line was entirely free from interference from the rear. He accounted for many enemy machine-guns and their teams.

Friday January 17th 1919

Gallant Men of Sussex

In a supplement to the *"London Gazette"* issued last night, there appears the names of two non-commissioned officers of the Royal Sussex Regiment who have gained awards for gallantry in the field. One of them, Sergeant A.W. Trevor, whose home is at Portslade, has already won the Distinguished Conduct Medal, and is now awarded a Bar to the medal. Sergeant E.J. Head, whose home is at Uckfield, has gained the D.C.M.

The announcements appear in the following terms :-

Bar to D.C.M.

No. G/1192 Sergeant AW. Trevor, D.C.M., M.M., 7th Bn. Royal Sussex Regiment, (Portslade)

For conspicuous gallantry near Meaulte on 22nd August, 1918. At the first objective he showed great initiative in clearing up dug-outs in which the enemy had collected, doing all single-handed. On reaching the final objective, seeing a party of the enemy on his flank, he went off by himself and returned with one officer and fourteen other rank prisoners. From the commencement of operations his courage and devotion to duty has continually been brought to notice.

(D.C.M. gazetted 5th December, 1918)

No. G/836 Sergeant E.J. Head, 7th Bn. Royal Sussex, (Uckfield)

For gallantry, near Becordel Becourt on 24th August, 1918. He took out a party of six men to investigate, a suspected machine-gun position. In spite of heavy machine-gun fire from the flank he succeeded, in making ,his way to the desired spot. from which he brought back fifteen prisoners. At Carnoy on 26th August, 1918, he continually organised bombing parties and succeeded in clearing several enemy bombing parties out of some trenches when the enemy were trying to bomb us out again, he held them up, and then rushing forward, killed four men dispersing the rest with a captured revolver and machine-guns.

Saturday January 18th 1919

His Majesty the KING has been graciously pleased to approve of the award of the Meritorious Service Medal to the following Warrant Officers, Non-Commissioned Officers and Men, in recognition of valuable service rendered with the Armies in France and Flanders: —

M.S.M.

S3/030182 Sgt.. Alex Clarence Cook, H.Q., 116th Inf. Bde. R.A.S.C. (Crawley Down).
(was SD/1297 11th Bn. Royal Sussex Regiment)

Monday January 20th 1919

Gallant Shoreham Man

Old Shoreham can now claim Company Sergeant-Major F. Wood, Royal Sussex Regiment, among its gallant Military Medallists. Formerly residing at Steyning, where several members of the family still are, his home is now at Old Erringham Farm Cottages. He is still only about 21 or 22 years of age, but has obtained both the Military Medal and the Croix de Guerre. He has been wounded twice, having recently got over his second injury.

Tuesday January 21st 1919

Sussex Men Decorated

A supplement to the *"London Gazette"* announces that the King has approved of the award of the Meritorious Service Medal to the following Warrant Officers, non-commissioned officers and men in recognition of valuable services rendered with the Armies in France and Flanders :-

M.S.M.

Royal Sussex Regiment

No. G/30740 Sergeant-Major J. Henderson, 17th Bn. (Irvine)
No. L/8712 Company Sergeant-Major W. Farrell 2nd Bn. (Stratford)

No. L/7788 Quartermaster-Sergeant W. Raby, 7th Bn. (Hawkhurst)

No. 200009 Quartermaster-Sergeant F. Seagrave, 4th Bn. (T.F.) (Horsham)
No. 200473 Sergeant C.G.B. Apps, 4th Bn. (T.F.). (Birmingham)
No. G/16007 Sergeant AS. Boniface, 13th Bn. (Pevensey)
No. G/3289 Sergeant A.C.R. Haynes, 9th Bn. (Brighton)
No. G/20338 Sergeant AT. Rolt, 8th Bn. (Wimbledon)
No. G/2712 Corporal P. Beckett, 5th Bn. (Felbridge)
No. G/S/57 Corporal H. Morrison, 7th Bn. (South Lambeth)

"London Gazette" Wednesday January 22nd 1919

M.I.D. (R.A.F.)

For valuable services rendered.

R.A.F. No. 31008 Lance-Sergeant Edwin Charles Jenks, (4th Bn. No. 1206) (East Grinstead)

Thursday January 23rd 1919

The Egyptian Campaign

A supplement to the *"London Gazette"* issued last night contains a list of names of those who have taken part in the campaign in Egypt and who have been mentioned in a dispatch forwarded by General Sir E.H.H. Allenby, G.C.B., G.C.M.G., the Commander-in-Chief. Those of local interest are as follows :-

Royal Sussex Regiment

Campbell, Captain E.R, 1/4th Battalion (T.F.)
Burk, No. L/6693 Sergeant J. 1/4th Battalion (T.F.)
Nye, No.200483 Sergeant H.W. 1/4th Battalion (T.F.)

Intelligence Corps.

Loder, Captain John de Vere,   4th Battalion Royal Sussex Regiment, (T. F.)

Friday January 24th 1919

Another Arundel Man gains Distinction

Yet another Arundel man has gained distinction for gallantry in battle, and the borough has now a long list of specially marked heroes.

The D.C.M. has been gained by Sergeant-Major Frederick Slaughter, 4th Royal Sussex Regiment, and youngest son of Mr. and Mrs. Slaughter, of the Abercrombie Inn. Before the war he was a member of the clerical staff of the Swallow Brewery, one of the Directors of which, it should be mentioned, is Major Guy Constable, M.C., whose associations with the "Fourth" are well known.

Sergeant-Major Slaughter took part in the landing at Sulva Bay, and was subsequently in the first and second battles of Gaza, the advance through Palestine, the fighting around Beersheba, and in. the battles of Khuweilfeh, Hebron, and Bethlehem. He was also present when the Turks were smashed up east of Jerusalem, and was one of those who entered the historic city. From Palestine he went to France with the "Fourth" in June last, and again saw very severe fighting.

A very promising and popular young man of 23 years, Sergeant-Major Slaughter will receive the hearty congratulations of a host of friends.

Monday January 27th 1919

Award of the Military Medal

No. G/1806 Sergeant Edwin J. Castle, 8th Bn.
"For Gallantry and devotion in the Field."
No. G/2249 Private Selby Reed, 8th Bn.
"For gallantry and devotion in the field."
No. 200106 Private Frank Rice, 4th Bn.
"For gallantry and devotion to duty in the field"
No. L/10483 Lance-Corporal Percy Shelley, 8th Bn.
"For gallantry and devotion to duty in the field"
No. 2008484 Corporal Albert G. Woolven, 4th Bn.
"For gallantry and devotion to duty in the field."

Award of the M.S.M.

The award of the Meritorious Service Medal has been made to :-

No. 492023 Corporal E.B. Whitehead, M.M. R.A.M.C. attd. 16th Bn.

Wednesday January 29th 1919

Military Medal for Kingston Man

Lance-Corporal P. Shelley, Royal Sussex Regiment, of 11, Kingston Terrace, Kingston-by-Sea, who was mentioned for gallantry and devotion to duty in August last, has been awarded the Military Medal. He has been wounded on three occasions.

Monday February 3rd 1919

D.S.O.

Capt.(A/Lt-Col.) Lewis Lamotte, 2nd Bn. Royal Sussex Regiment, attd. 2nd Bn. Yorkshire Light Infantry,

For conspicuous gallantry and devotion to duty at Herleville during the fighting of 23rd August, 1918. Thanks to his personal supervision his companies reached their objectives without serious loss, after destroying several machine-gun nests through the village. Throughout the day he was constantly among his men, suggesting improvements and preparing against counter-attacks. The success of the operation was largely due to his energy and judgement.

Bar to M.C.

The award of a Bar to the Military Cross has been bestowed upon the following Sussex officer :-

T/Lt. S.A. Andrews, M.C., 7th Bn. Royal Sussex Regiment,

For conspicuous gallantry near Carnoy, on August 26th 1918. He showed great courage in bombing a strongpoint from which the enemy were holding up the advance by heavy machine-gun fire. He led a few men forward, captured the gun, and killed five of the crew, enabling the remainder to advance and reach their objective. Throughout the operations from August 22nd/28th, his courage and leadership inspired all under his command.

(M.C. gazetted 8th October, 1917)

Tuesday February 4th 1919

Sussex Officer Decorated with M.C.

T/Lieutenant Victor Cecil Branson, 13th Bn. Royal Sussex Regiment,

For conspicuous gallantry near Becordel Becourt on 22nd August 1918, on patrol with a small party of men he entered the village of Becordel Becourt, then some 1,500 yards in front of our lines and discovered it to be free of the enemy. The same night, when the post of another company had been driven back, he immediately proceeded with two men, re-established the post, and at once pushed forward in pursuit of the enemy, obtaining a valuable identification some 80 yards in front of the post.

Thursday February 6th 1919

Two Gallant Officers

Announcement is made of the fact that the Military Cross has been awarded to the two undermentioned officers :-

Lieutenant Percy William Lovering, Royal Sussex Regiment, 3rd Bn. S. R. attd. 4th Bn. (T.F.)

For conspicuous gallantry and devotion to duty near Kemmel on 23rd September, 1918. As battalion intelligence officer, he went out by himself a distance of 400 yards to find out whether a crater was occupied by the enemy. As he saw no signs of them, he fetched up two men and climbed down into the crater to look in the dug-outs. He found and shot one of the enemy. Later on, going out again with six men, he found it strongly occupied, and returned after a bombing encounter, having gained valuable information.

T/Lieutenant Reginald Byron Mason, attd. Royal Sussex Regiment, 4th Bn. (T.F.)

For conspicuous gallantry and devotion to duty near Kemmel on 25th September, 1918. Two sections attempted to seize Spanbrockmohlen Crater, but were held up by machine-gun fire and snipers. He took out two more sections, and making skilful use of the ground crawled up to the post and killed four of the enemy, which enabled the party to occupy the crater.

Friday February 7th 1919

For Gallantry and Devotion

A supplement to the *"London Gazette"* issued last night, states that the Military Cross has been awarded the two undermentioned officers under the circumstances detailed :-

Lieutenant John Leslie Von Der Heyde, Royal Sussex Regiment, attd. Manchester Regiment, (Salonika)

For conspicuous gallantry and devotion to duty during the attack on the "P" ridge on 18th September, 1918. He was sent forward to ascertain the situation on the "P" ridge at a time when owing to dust and smoke, no observation was possible. He entered the enemy works alone, and, although subjected to very heavy machine-gun and trench mortar fire, returned with very valuable information.

Captain John Raymond Warren, 4th Bn. Royal Sussex Regiment, (T.F.)

For conspicuous gallantry and devotion to duty during operations near Kemmel on 1st September, 1918. In spite of determined opposition, he established his company in an advanced position, and, as neither of the units on the flank had come up, proceeded with the consolidation, and though almost surrounded, held on for many hours until reinforcements arrived. His grasp of the situation and determination were of great value.

Saturday February 8th 1919

A D.C.M. Award

A supplement to the *"London Gazette"*, issued last night, stated that the King has awarded the Distinguished Conduct Medal to No. L/8076 Corporal G. Hobday, 2nd Battalion, Royal Sussex Regiment, and ½nd King's African Rifles (Belfast), for services in connection with military operations in the British Forces in East Africa.

Monday February 10th 1919

KING'S COLOUR PRESENTED

Royal Sussex Battalion Honoured

The historical and interesting ceremony of the King's Colour to the 17th Battalion, Royal Sussex Regiment, by Major-General N. Smyth, V.C., C.B., their Divisional Commander, took place at Staple, in France, on Friday, 17th January. The battalion was drawn up with bayonets fixed, the companies in line forming three sides of a square on a field used as the battalion football ground. The fourth side of the square was occupied by the drums of the battalion piled on a carpet of camouflage net. The Divisional Commander was accompanied by the Brigade Commander, Brigadier-General T.Q. Cope, D.S.O., and Lieutenant-Colonel Westley, D.S.O. After the general salute on receiving the General, the cased Colour, in charge of the Colour Party, under Lieutenant C.R.M., Fry, was marched from the rear of the battalion to a position in the centre of the square.

The Colour was then placed against, the drums, and uncased by the Second-in-Command, Major A. Simkins, M.C. Then followed by the consecration of the Colour by the Chaplain, Captain, Griffin, who read the impressive prayer of consecration, followed by the Blessing. At the conclusion of the Blessing the Second-in-Command stepped forward and, lifting the, Colour from the drums, handed it to Major-General Smyth.

Receiving the Colour

Lieutenant Fry, commanding the Colour Party, now came forward, and, sinking on one knee, received the Colour from the General. Turning about he marched in slow time to his place, with the Colour Party the battalion being called to attention the while. A splendid address was given by the General, who said:-

Colonel Callard, officers, warrant officers, N.C.O.'s and men of the 17th battalion, Royal Sussex Regiment :- The King's Colour ,which has been consecrated by the Minister of, our Holy Faith, is a symbol, of Your loyalty to King George V and his successors, proved during the recent operations by your devotion to duty during the advance from St. Venant to the Aubers Ridge, which was followed by the liberation of Lille, and the forcing of the passage of the Scheldt.

A Glorious Record

The Royal Sussex Regiment was raised more than 200 years ago, and the regiment was in the war of the Spanish Succession at Gibraltar in 1704-5. The record of the regiment in the West Indies and on the American Continent is exceptionally distinguished, and its battle honours include Louisburg, Quebec, the crowing victory which made Canada a British colony in 1759, the capture of Martinique, 1762, Havannah in the same year, and St. Lucia 1778.

The regiment was at the victory of Maida, 1778. In Egypt, 1882, and in 1884, after crossing the Bavuda Desert in the Soudan, fought at Abu Klea Wells, where the British Square, opposed by odds of 20 to 1 were broken but reformed The conduct, the spirit, and discipline of the Royal Sussex Regiment has always been exceptionally good, and you have emulated the example of the old battalions. As a symbol of good service this King's Colour is entrusted to your keeping. England relies on you to ensure that no indiscipline shall tarnish the reputation the regiment has won.

Cherished in all Hearts

At the end of the address the battalion sloped arms, the Colour Party turned about, and the Colour unfurled at the carry, facing the battalion, was given the general salute. The Divisional hand played "God save the King", and the Colour Party, marching in slow time passed to its position in the ranks of the regiment. Thus ended a most impressive ceremony, the memory of which will always be cherished in the hearts of all ranks. The battalion in columns of four with the Colour flying in the centre of the battalion marched past the Divisional Commander, who had taken up his position at their saluting base in the village square.

After the march past "C" Company under the command of Captain Lilywhite, escorted the Colour and Colour Party to the house used as the Officers Mess, presented arms, while the Colour was carried in by Lieutenant Fry and placed in the stand provided for it in the mess room.

The General entertained

All the officers of the battalion afterwards gathered at the Officers Mess and had the pleasure of entertaining General Smythe and Brigadier-General Cope and their Staffs, when the health and success of the Regiment was toasted.

The 17th battalion of the Royal Sussex Regiment was formed in France in April and May, 1918, during the German spring offensive of that year.

The following were present at the ceremony :-

Major-General N.M. Smyth V.C., C.B., Brigadier-General T.G. Cope, D.S.O., Lieutenant-Colonel J.H.S. Westley, D.S.O., Captain S.P. Morgan, Captain R.H. Lupton, M.C., and Lieutenant G. Maycock, M.C.

The officers on parade with the battalion were :-

Lieutenant-Colonel N.L. Callard, Major A. Simkins, M.C., Captains J. Cartland and G. Lilywhite, Lieutenants J. Bottomley, N.E. Chadwick, H Lock, C.R.M. Fry, Lieutenant and Quartermaster Tulloch, and Second-Lieutenants H.W. Talbot, A.V. Frowen, F.H. Jenner, L.W. Hudson, M.C., F.J. Burrows, D. Carlisle, G.F. Cahill, R.E. Bennison, J.L. Cartwright, S.G. Sinclair, C. Redman, S.

Braybrook, R. Greenwood, G.D. Grant, E.J. Cherry, Lieutenant F.E. Webb, R.A.M.C., and Captain E.M. Griffin (Chaplain).

The Colour Party consisted of Lieutenant C.R.M. Fry, C.S.M. R Harris, C.S.M. J. Hoyle, C.S.M. E. Wilcox.

Wednesday February 12th 1919

Military Medal Awards

Sussex was well to the fore in a list of honours published in a supplement to the *"London Gazette"* last night, and men from different parts of the county serving in various regiments were shown to have received awards for gallantry in the field :-

Royal Sussex Regiment

Second Bar to M.M.

No. G/3833 Private Edwin Highgate, M.M., 7th Bn (Mannings Heath)
(M.M. gazetted 18th July, 1917, Bar 11th February, 1919)

Bar to M.M.

No. 200195 Private William Bateman, M.M., 4th Bn. (Littlehampton)
(M.M. gazetted 22nd March 1918)

No. G/2237 Corporal (L/Sergeant) Stephen A. Buckman, M.M., 7th Bn. (East Chiltington)
(M. M. gazetted 19th March, 1918).

No. G/3410 Private (L/Corporal) Charles Thomas Emery, M.M., 7th Bn. (Hove)
(M.M. gazetted 9th July, 1917),

No. G/128 Private Alfred L. Groves, M.M., 7th Bn. (Worthing)
(M.M. gazetted 25th April, 1918)

No. G/17333 Private Philip A. Griston, M.M., 7th Bn. (North Walsham)
(M.M. gazetted 13th September, 1918).

No. G/3833 Private Edwin Highgate, MM., 7th Bn. (Mannings Heath)
(M.M. gazetted 18th July, 1917)

No. G/16312 Sergeant James Simmonds, M.M., 7th Bn. (Turner's Hill)
(M.M. gazetted 11th February 1919)

Thursday February 13th 1919

The Seventh Royal Sussex

Thirty Military Medals Awarded

A feature of the supplement to the *"London Gazette"* issued last night was the number of men of the Royal Sussex Regiment who were named as recipients of the Military Medal for gallantry in the field. It will be noticed from the list which appears below that nearly all of them are men of the 7th Battalion.

Royal Sussex Regiment

No. G/1197 Private Frank T. Baker, 7th Bn. (Hastings)
No. G/6016 Private (L/Corporal) William Rufus Barwick, 7th Bn. (Wellingborough)
No. G/3002 Private Charles Bishop, 7th Bn. (Brighton)
No. G/12416 Private Harold J. Bone, 7th Bn. (Penge)
No. S/2143 Private (L/Corporal). Percy Booker, 7th Bn. (Stoke)
No. G/8355 Private Harry Brackpool, 7th Bn. (Southwick)
No. L/6040 Private (L/Corporal) H. Burchell, 7th Bn. (Petworth)
No. G/17180 Private Walter Camplin, 9th Bn. (Ackworth)
No. G/3910 Private John W. Carpenter, 7th Bn. (White Notley)
No. G/20476 Private Arthur S. Covey, 7th Bn. (Wonersh)
No. G/3725 Private F. Darcy, 7th Bn. (Horsham)
No. G/826 Corporal Frederick Dewell, 7th Bn. (Lower Walmer)
No. G/20477 Private Matthew Donald, 7th Bn. (Newmilns)
No. G/200077 Private Albert E. Francis, 4th Bn. (Horsham).
No. G/7231 Private Leonard Goodyer, 7th Bn. (Earlsfield)
No. G/19491 Private Harry E Knope, 7th Bn. (Stoke Newington)
No. SD/3861 Corporal Charles Harold Leppard, 7th Bn. (East Grinstead)
No. G/23613 Private Frank H. Moore, 7th Bn, (Brixton)
No. G/965 Private William G. Mustchin, 7th Bn. (Hove)
No. G/6355 Corporal Fred Packham, 7th Bn. (Crawley).
No. G/23625 Private Ernest A. Paine, 7th Bn. (Canonbury Road)
No. G/S/203 Private James C. Peck, 7th Bn. (King's Cross)
No. G/24875 Private Sidney Pepper, 7th.Bn. (Cromland)
No. G/20222 Private (L/Corporal) Frederick J. Reed, 7th Bn. (Ilford)
No. G/6312 Sergeant James Simmonds, 7th Bn. (Turner's Hill)
No. G/5070 Sergeant Frederick John Tooms, 7th Bn. (Rotherhythe)
No. G/780 Sergeant William C.J. Tulett, 7th Bn. (London, S.W.)
No. G/582 Private (L/Corporal) William J. Tulitt, 7th Bn. (Nuthurst)
No. G/23675 Private Thomas C. Waghorn, 7th Bn. (Dartford)
No. L/10237 Private Jack W. Wilmshurst, 7th Bn. (Hailsham)
No. G/7926 Private (L/Corporal) George F. Woolven, 7th Bn. (Acton)
No. G/8027 Corporal George W. Wright, 7th Bn. (Ore)

Monday February 17th 1919

Awards to Officers

A supplement to the *"London Gazette"* announces the following awards to officers of the Royal Sussex Regiment for service in the field.

D.S.O.

Lieutenant (A/Captain) Harry Roberts, M.C, 2nd Bn.

Bar to MC.

Lieutenant (A/Captain) Victor Henry Jaques, M.C., 3rd Bn. attd. 2nd Bn.
During an attack against the enemy's position north of the Ormignon River on September 18th, 1918, he handled his company throughout with conspicuous ability and displayed great gallantry. As soon as the second objective was reached, in addition to organising his own company, he went to other companies, and under heavy machine-gun fire made dispositions for those platoons where all their officers had become casualties. Later, when two platoons of another company were ordered to exploit forward he volunteered to go and supervise the operation and was wounded. Throughout his actions were marked by an utter disregard of danger.
(M.C. gazetted 15th October, 1918)

Lieutenant (A/Captain) John Isaac Mason, M.C., 2nd Bn.

For conspicuous energy and devotion to duty in the operations north of Gricourt on September 24th, 1918. His company was in support and became mixed with the front companies in the fighting. When the latter were fighting on the final objective he quickly organised a position in the rear to form a basis for consolidation.
Later, when the leading troops of the battalion on the left hand had been forced to retire, he went forward to the position still held by the leading troops to do what he could to help in a difficult situation. Later he took part in a counter-attack. When practically all the officers of the three companies had become casualties, he took command of the three companies and organised them as the outposts of the battalion sector. He worked untiringly throughout the operations, and was of very great assistance to the battalion.
(M.C. gazetted 3rd June, 1918)

Lieutenant Basil Charles Wright, M.C., 2nd Bn.

During operations on September 18th, 1918, near Pontrue, he commanded a platoon with great gallantry. On one occasion when the enemy was observed forming up to counter-attack, he charged with what men he could collect and dispersed the attack, inflicting casualties on the enemy. Throughout the battle he showed bold leadership and resource, and by keeping his platoon well in hand and using it with skill he materially assisted in the capture of the enemy positions with few casualties.
(M.C. gazetted 20th October, 1916)

M.C.

Lieutenant John Gatchel Hancock, 2nd Bn.

During the attack north of Gricourt, on September 24th, 1918, his platoon was one of the leading company. He reached his final objective, and though the troops on his left had been forced to withdraw he remained in this advanced position and sent back clear messages regarding it. Though isolated and some 600 yards in front of the remainder he did not withdraw until ordered to do so, and shortly afterwards showed great gallantry and dash in meeting an enemy counter-attack and getting severely wounded in the shoulder. He did fine work.

Tuesday 18th February 1919

Eight Gallant Officers

The supplement to the *"London Gazette"* issued last right gives the names of eight officers connected with the Royal Sussex Regiment, who have been awarded the Military Cross for their gallantry. They are :-

M.C.

2nd Lieutenant Edward Clements, 2nd Bn.

During an attack on the enemy near Pontru on 18th September, 1918, he led his platoon with great coolness and skill to the first objective. All the other officers having become casualties, he then took command of the company, and led them on to the second objective. He organised the company in the captured position under heavy machine-gun fire. On one occasion during the operations he, with a few men, rushed and bombed an enemy machine-gun which was holding them up. He showed marked courage and leadership.

Captain William Reid Dougal Cuthbertson, Sussex Yeomanry, attd.16th Bn.

When suddenly required to take command of his battalion on September 17th 1918, he handled it with skill and conspicuous success in the attack on the Quarries near Templeux le Guerrard on September 18th and again on September 21st when after a successful enfilade by machine-gun fire, in addition to being counter-attacked in front, he went forward and skilfully carried out the inevitable withdrawal of his front companies. He behaved most gallantly.

Lieutenant (A/Captain) Ernest Dolleymore, 6th Bn. attd. 2nd Bn.

During the operations against the enemy north of the D'Omignon River on September 18th, 1918, he handled his company with great skill. He was wounded at the commencement of the attack, but continued to lead his company, until they had gained the first objective, when he was again wounded. Nevertheless he re-organised his men under heavy machine-gun fire to continue the advance. He set a fine example of courage and leadership throughout.

Lieutenant Frederick Harry Fenton, attd. 4th Bn.

On September 29th 1918, at Wytschaete for conspicuous gallantry and devotion to duty. When the company was ordered to advance up the ridge to Wytschaete, he was detailed to take forward a patrol. On suddenly coming on an enemy gunnery officer, he immediately closed with him, disarmed him, and called on him to surrender with the enemy gun team who were with him.

The whole team of 11 other ranks then came out and surrendered to him single-handed. Throughout the operations he showed marked courage and leadership, thereby inspiring his brother officers and his men.

2nd Lieutenant Samuel Alexander Holwell Kirkby, 2nd Bn.

During an attack on the enemy near Pontru on September 18th 1918, he showed great gallantry and skill in handling his platoon, on one occasion going and assisting another company to repulse an enemy counter-attack. During the second attack at midnight, when all the officers of the company were killed, he assumed command and conducted the fighting with conspicuous gallantry, and made dispositions in a difficult situation to withstand possible enemy counter-attacks.

Captain Francis William Lascelles, Sussex Yeomanry, attd. 16th Bn.

For most conspicuous gallantry and devotion to duty at Quennemont Farm, September 21st 1918. He displayed the greatest coolness and gallantry in attacking and holding for six hours, under heavy fire, the position captured by the battalion. During this period he, personally organised and led several counter-attacks with the bayonet. Eventually, the position being almost completely surrounded and no reinforcements being available, he, though wounded in three places, organised the withdrawal of the remnants of the battalion through an extremely heavy barrage, being himself the last to leave the position. Previously at Templeux le Guerrard, he, with six men, personally attacked and made prisoners twenty-five of the enemy. Throughout the operations he showed a fine example of courage, coolness and resolution.

2nd Lieutenant William Lockett, 7th Bn. Cheshire Regiment, attd. 16th Bn.

For most conspicuous gallantry and devotion to duty at Quennemont Farm. Somme sector, on September 21st 1918. With a handful of men and a Lewis gun during the attack he engaged an enemy party of one officer and a large number of men and four machine-guns, and rendered invaluable service to the attacking troops by preventing the enemy completely surrounding them. The battalion was eventually almost surrounded, but though continually threatened by the enemy's superior numbers he held on for over five hours and only withdrew when his own party consisted only of himself and two other ranks, both wounded, and his ammunition was completely exhausted, he then fought his way out with the bayonet. By his action he undoubtedly very greatly assisted the attack and the withdrawal of the battalion.

T/2nd Lieutenant John Pannett, 2nd Bn.

During an attack on the enemy positions near Pontru on September 18th 1918, he led his platoon with great gallantry. When the second objective was reached he advanced to exploit a third objective, and he advanced to within 100 yards of the enemy position under heavy machine-gun fire. Later, he successfully dealt with an enemy counter-attack against his right flank. Again, during a night attack he led his platoon to their furthest objective and organised the position skilfully according to the situation and disregard of danger throughout were a fine example to all.

Wednesday February 19th 1919

Distinguished Conduct Medal

The Distinguished Conduct Medal has been awarded to the undermentioned local men. Last night's supplement to the *"London Gazette"* announces that the acts of gallantry for which the decorations have been awarded will be announced as early as practicable.

Royal Sussex Regiment

No. 315488 Corporal G. Aris, 16th Bn. (Eastbourne)
No. G/21770 Private W. Fordham, 16th Bn. (Whittlesea)
No. G/1899 A/Sergeant W. Pelling, 9th Bn. (Itchingfield)
No. 320069 L/Sergeant E. Sparkes, 16th Bn. (Bognor)
No. 2152 Private P. Weedon, M.M., 2nd Bn. (Arundel)

Saturday February 22nd 1919

Mesopotamian "Mentions"

A supplement to the *"London Gazette"* issued last night, makes mention of a large number of officers and men who are named by Lieutenant-General W.R. Marshall, Commanding Mesopotamian Expeditionary Force. Among them the following was noted the following :-

Royal Sussex Regiment

Dick, Major and Bt. Lt.-Colonel (T/Brig.-General) R.N.   D.S.O.
Leachman, Major and Bt. Lt.-Colonel G.E.   C.I.E.
Pearman, No.741 Private (A/C.S.M. Instr.) T.A. 1st Bn. attd. Army Gym Staff

Monday February 24th 1919

Recognition of Service

A supplement to the *"London Gazette"* announces that the King has approved of the award of the Meritorious Service Medal to a number of members of the Force. The following are of local interest :-

Royal Sussex Regiment

No. G/4657 Sergeant-Major. C. Amos, D.C.M., Depot (Faversham)
No. L/4369 Sergeant-Major J.R. Boniface, 3rd Bn. (Dover)
No. L/8913 Corporal (A/Sgt.) W. Gannon, 1st Bn. (Hastings)(India)
No. L/8928 Sergeant (A/S.M.) A. Gray, 1st Bn. (Shoreham)
No. L/3238 R/S/M. A. Nye, D.C.M., 4th Bn. (East Grinstead)
No. L/4503 Q.M.S. T.E. Lake, 3rd Bn. (Brighton)
No. 202015 Q.M.S. H.J. Bands, 4th Bn. (Rye)
No. L/6586 C.Q.M.S. B. Bosanquet, Depot (Belfast)
No. 265112 Corporal E.H. Buschell, 6th Bn. (Brighton)
No. 202015 Q.M.S. H.J. Rands, 4th Bn. (Rye)
No. TR/10/108102 Sergeant (A/C.Q.M.S.) G.H. Wilkinson, (Dover)
(now L/12183 Depot East Surrey Regiment)

Tuesday 25th February 1919

Meritorious Service

Although described in the official list as of Dover, Regimental Sergeant-Major Boniface, 3rd Battalion, Royal Sussex Regiment, who has been awarded the Meritorious Service Medal, is a Brightonian, having been born in Hampton Street. The R.S.M. is at present stationed at Newhaven.

Thursday February 27th 1919

The 7th Royal Sussex Regiment

PRESENTATION OF COLOURS

Official details were received yesterday of the presentation of Colours to the 7th Battalion Royal Sussex Regiment by his Royal Highness the Prince 6f Wales. The ceremony took place near Erre, at 10.30 on the morning of 4th February, when the Sussex men paraded with the Royal Fusiliers and the 5th Royal Berkshire Regiment, the constituting the 36th Infantry Brigade, under Brigadier-General C.S. Owen, C.M.G., D.S.O., The weather was bad, but the smartness and hearing of the Brigade on parade were excellent and called forth commendatory remarks. The Prince of Wales was received with the Royal Salute, and the Colours were consecrated by the senior Chaplain of the 12th Division, the Rev. H. P. Berkeley, MC., the Brigade forming part of the 12thh Division, commanded by Major-General H.W. Higginson, C.B., D.S.O., The senior Major of the 7th Royal Sussex handed the King's Colours to the Prince, from whom the senior Lieutenant received them, sinking to his knee.

Speech by the Prince

Addressing the Brigade, the Prince of Wales said :-

It gives me very great pleasure to be here today, and to have the honour to present the King's Colours to the battalion before me. You were raised in August, 1914, and came out to France in the 12th Division in May, 1915. Some hard fighting in minor engagements, and long periods of strenuous work in the trenches, you have taken a conspicuous part in the following battles :- Loos, Hohenzollern Craters, Somme, 1916, Arras, Cambrai, Somme, 1918, Epehy, and the German retreat to the Scheldt, which culminated in the final victory of our arms. I know full well that these Colours will always be honoured and cherished by you and that you will worthily uphold in the future, as you have always done in the past, the glorious traditions of the regiments to which you belong. These Colours are emblems of the heroic deeds which have been performed by your battalions. I now rust them to you, confident that you will guard them as worthy successors of those gallant soldiers who have so gloriously fallen in the service of their king and country.

Cheers and march past

The general salute was then given, and the Colours were carried to their places in the battalions while the band played "God save the King". This was followed by three cheers for the Prince of Wales, after which the Brigade marched past his Royal Highness in column. The day will always be memorable in the annals of these distinguished battalions of the 12th Division, which has played a conspicuous part in overthrowing the military power of Germany.

Tuesday March 4th 1919

Royal Sussex Officer's Honour

Last night's supplement to the *"London Gazette"*, announced Major and Bt. Lt-Colonel (T/Brig.-General) R.N. Dick, D.S.O., Royal Sussex Regiment, is to be a member of the Third Class, or Companion of the Order of St. Michael and St. George, for services rendered in connection with military operations in Mesopotamia.

Monday 10th March 1919

Awards for Royal Sussex Officers

A special supplement to the *"London Gazette"* announces the awards to the undermentioned officers of the Royal Sussex Regiment in recognition of their gallantry and devotion to duty in the field :-

D.S.O.

T/Lieutenant (A/Captain) Stephen Arthur Andrews, M.C., 7th Bn.

"Near Epehy, 18th September, 1918. For conspicuous gallantry and good work. His company was allotted the task of clearing the railway embankment of the enemy. Although enfiladed by machine-gun nests from the village, and having sustained heavy casualties, he personally led forward the remainder of his company, and was one of the very few to reach the objective. He then organised under very heavy fire and held the position until the situation was cleared up."

Bar to M.C.

Lieutenant (T/Captain) Michael Wallington, (Bt. Major) Royal Sussex Regiment, attd. 1st Infantry Brigade,
(M.C. gazetted 3rd June, 1916)

M.C.

Lieutenant Scott Langshaw Burdett, Special Reserve attd. 7th Bn. Royal Sussex Regiment,

For gallantry and devotion to duty near Ephey on 18th September, 1918. As battalion intelligence officer he was sent forward to discover the situation in front of the village. He made his way under very fire to the companies, and found men of all battalions considerably disorganised. He assisted the remaining company commander to reorganise his men.

2nd Lieutenant Leslie Guy Coxhead, 7th Bn. Royal Sussex Regiment,

For great gallantry near Ephey on 18th September. When the battalion was held up by severe machine-gun fire, and all the officers in the three companies had become casualties, he succeeded in rallying the men. He took command of all he could collect and led them forward, and assisted the company on his flank to maintain its position, thus materially helping the attacking troops to advance.

Tuesday March 11th 1919

It was announced last night in a supplement to the *"London Gazette"*, that the Military Cross had been bestowed upon the undermentioned officers of the Royal Sussex Regiment, in recognition of gallantry and devotion to duty in the field :-

M.C.

T/2nd Lieutenant Thomas Kelly, attd. 1st Bn. Hampshire Regiment,

For great gallantry and devotion to duty. On 24th October, 1918, at Monchaux, he seeing that a frontal attack on the village was impossible, took ten men to the left, and accompanied by Lieutenant Raynor entered the village, which was subsequently found to hold over 100 enemy and many machine-guns. He was mainly instrumental in capturing an enemy officer, through whom the enemy were made to surrender.

Lieutenant (T/Major) Charles Wilson Lundgren, Sussex Yeomanry, attd. 2/4th Yorks. and Lancs.

T/Captain Ralph Henry Lupton, attd. 17th Bn. Royal Sussex Regiment,

He handled his company with great gallantry and skill on 18th October, 1918, north of the village of Forest de Lille. After a long day's advance he pushed forward with energy, and gained much ground. Again, on the 20th, he drove back enemy posts across the river Scheldt. His reports throughout the whole advance were excellent.

T/2nd Lieutenant (A/Captain) William Edward Weeks, 17th Bn. Royal Sussex Regiment,

When in command he showed initiative and skill in leading his company. On 18th October, 1918, he pushed forward and captured the village of Forest de Lille, setting a fine example of dash and determination to his men. Again on the 20th October, he made a reconnaissance of the bank of the river Scheldt, under heavy fire, and sent back very valuable information.

The KING has been graciously pleased to confer the Territorial Decoration upon the undermentioned Officers of the Territorial Force who have been duly recommended for the same under the terms of the

Royal Warrant related 17th August, 1908, as modified by the Royal Warrant dated the 11th November, 1918: —

Major Henry E. Mathews 4th Bn. Royal Sussex Regiment,

Thursday March 13th 1919

Medals for Bravery
A supplement to the *"London Gazette"*, issued yesterday evening, contains notification of the following awards :-

D.C.M.

Royal Sussex Regiment

No. S/2159 Private W.H. Boulter, 2nd Bn. (Hastings)
No. S/2187 Private E.W. Burke, 2nd Bn. (Liverpool)
No. G/4728 Private (L/Corporal) F. Child, 2nd Bn. (Pulborough)
No. 320294 Sergeant W.O. Collis, 16th Bn. (Henfield)
No. G/1406 Private F.B. Evenden, M.M., 2nd Bn. (Waldron)
No. G/3755 Private H. Godden, 2nd Bn. (Eastbourne)
No. G/14183 Private (L/Corporal) S.R. Manthorpe, 2nd Bn. (Norwich)
No. L/10507 Corporal (A/Sergeant) A.J. Spurling, 2nd Bn. (Bethnall Green)
No. G/10402 Private (L/Corporal) A. Stoner, 2nd Bn. (Climping)
No. G/3147 Sergeant C.F. West, 7th Bn. (Arundel)

Friday March 14th 1919

Romanian Medal for Royal Sussex N.C.O.

Medaille Barbatie Si Credinta (3rd Class)

Lance-Corporal A. Cox, 2nd Bn. Royal Sussex Regiment,
"For services rendered during the war."

Sussex Officer Decorated

The following Royal Sussex Officer has been awarded the Territorial Decoration :-

Major Thomas H. Howard, 4th Battalion.
Major Henry E. Mathews 4th Battalion.

Saturday March 15th 1919

Military Medal Awards to the Royal Sussex Regiment

No. G/1379 Sergeant Frederick R. Bussell, 8th Bn. (Chichester)
No. 260055 Sergeant William T. Charman, 8th Bn. (Horsham)
"For gallantry and devotion to duty in action."
No. G/4215 Sergeant Frederick Westbrook, 8th Bn. (West Dean)
"For gallantry and devotion to duty in action."
No. 320027 Sergeant R.C.W. Wilmer, 16th Bn. (Broadstairs)

No. 266197 Corporal Percy W. Cornwell, 7th Bn. (Wadhurst)
No. G/1862 Corporal Frederick Flint, 16th Bn. (Crawley)
No. 315020 Private Arthur Hayhurst, 16th Bn. (Burnley)
No. G/315146 Private James Walter Mills, 16th Bn. (Littlehampton)
No. G/6421 Private Frederick Riggs, 8th Bn. (Bognor)

Saturday March 22nd 1919

Military Decorations Hastings

An interesting event took place at the Drill Hall, Middle Street, Hastings, on Thursday afternoon, when various soldiers received decorations for bravery on the field. The medals were distributed by Lieutenant-Colonel C.H.D. Lyon Campbell, who said he had the honour to present the medals conferred on them by the King. He also had to present a medal to 2nd Lieutenant P.H. Oxley, for his son, who had been killed in action. The following soldiers were decorated :-

M.M.

Corporal Robert H.W. Bryant, 5th Bn.
Private William Smith, 7th Bn.
2nd Lieutenant P.H. Oxley, for his son killed in action, (No. 5612 Cpl. P.J. Oxley, Lancers)

Friday March 28th 1919

Rendered Valuable Service

The names of the undermentioned have been brought to the notice of the Secretary of State for War for valuable services rendered in connection with the war, and when applicable an entry will be made in the records for service of officers and other ranks :-

Royal Sussex Regiment

No. 201040 Sergeant C.L. Barnes, 4th Bn.
Lieutenant-Colonel A. Bell-Irving, D.S.O., (R.P.)
Captain R.J.A. Betham,
Captain (T/Lt.-Colonel) A. Corbett,   Sussex Yeomanry.
Captain (T/Major) V.E.C. Dashwood, M.C.,   attd. M.G. Corps.
Major and Bt. Lt.-Colonel H.R. Lloyd, (R.P.)
Captain (A/Major) A.C. Maples, 4th Bn.
Major R.B. Otter-Barry,
T/Lieutenant C.D.B. Ross,

Saturday March 29th 1919

Brighton Officer's Distinction

Amongst the recipients of a Bar to the Military Cross from the hands of the King at the recent investiture at Buckingham Palace, was Captain Harry Treacher, of the Royal Sussex Regiment, who is the son of Mr. T. Treacher, 31, Stanford Avenue, Brighton, has now been demobilised.

Monday 31st March 1919

Military Medals

A supplement to the *"London Gazette"* gives particulars of the following awards :-

No. 202970 Corporal (L/Sgt.) William S. Castle, 5th Bn. (Lewes) (Italy)
No. 241145 Private Charles B. Clarke, 5th Bn. (Southend-on-Sea) (Italy)
No. 240722 Private (A/L/C pl.) Horace E. Heaseman, 5th Bn. (Hartfield) (Italy)
No. 240353 Sergeant William W. Rodway, 5th Bn. (Hotwell) (Italy)
No. 240877 Private (L/Cpl.) William J. Soanes, 5th Bn. (Buxted) (Italy)
No. 240137 Private Charles Steadman, 5th Bn. (Lewes) (Italy)

Wednesday April 2nd 1919

Local Award

A supplement to the *"London Gazette"* published yesterday, contains a long list of. awards by his Majesty the King of Italy to officers and men of the British Forces in Italy.

Order of the Crown of Italy

Major (T/Lieutenant-Colonel) Adrian Corbett, Sussex Yeomanry,

Thursday April 3rd 1919

Local Awards

A large number of awards to officers, find a place in a supplement to the *"London Gazette"*, published last night.

D.S.O.

Major and Bt. Lt.-Colonel Gerrard Evelyn Leachman, C.I.E., Royal Sussex Regiment, attached Political Department (Basra, Mesopotamia)

Bar to the M.C.

Lieutenant (A/Captain) Thomas Edward Chad, 2nd Bn. Royal Sussex Regiment, (Mesopotamia)

M.C.

Lieutenant Herbert Roland Bate, 6th Bn. Manchester Regiment, (T.F.) attd. 9th Bn. Royal Sussex Regiment,
T/Lieutenant Sidney John Arthur Bridger, 9th Bn. Royal Sussex Regiment,
Captain Eric John Burrows, 5th Bn. Manchester Regiment, (T.F.) attd. 9th Bn. Royal Sussex Regiment,

Friday April 4th 1919

Private B.J. Briggs, D.C.M., M.M.

Another illustration of the proverbial modesty of the British soldier has come to light in connection with the visit to the St. John's district of Withyham, of Private Bertie John Briggs, 2nd Battalion, Royal Sussex Regiment. He spent a few hours in former familiar surroundings on Wednesday, and was noticed to be wearing the ribbons of the Distinguished Conduct Medal and the Military Medal. This was the first intimation to his numerous friends in the locality of the distinctions he had gained for gallantry in the field.
He was severely wounded in the leg, early in the war, and subsequently spent many months recovering in England, but, volunteering for further active service, returned to France. Private Briggs, from the moment he was awarded the Military Medal, contrived to keep the fact a secret, and was similarly successful when as the result of further deeds in the field he won the Distinguished Conduct Medal. Now that the secret is out, St. John's residents are exceedingly proud and gratified at the double honour which Private Briggs has by his gallantry won for the district, and the proudest and the most pleased are the managers, teaching staff, and scholars of St. John's C.E. Elementary Schools, of which he is an "Old Boy".

How the awards were won

Private Briggs, who is the younger son of the late Mr. J.E. Briggs (formerly for many years headmaster of St. John's Schools and greatly respected and esteemed in the locality), upon leaving school was apprenticed to Mr. E.B. Pilbeam, builder and. decorator, London Road. When war broke out he was a member of the Crowborough Company of the 5th Battalion Royal Sussex Regiment (T.F.) and accompanied the regiment to France in February, 1915. The following year, while serving as a signaller, he was badly wounded in the leg, and returned to England. He proceeded to France a second time in the latter part of 1917, and was afterwards three times wounded. He was awarded the Military Medal in February, 1918, for holding the Germans back with a machine-gun operated from a motor side-car, he being at the time attached to the Motor Machine-gun Corps. During that and the following month he was four times mentioned in dispatches. Private Briggs was awarded the D.C.M., while serving with the 2nd Battalion, Royal Sussex Regiment, at Cambrai, for taking 28 German prisoners. After bringing them in he discovered that his sergeant had not returned with him, and under heavy shell fire went back into "No Man's Land", found him wounded, and brought him back to safety. He received the "ribbons" from Brigadier-General Brakes, G.O.C., at Woolwich. Private Briggs was demobilised a fortnight ago, and is at present staying in Tunbridge Wells. In honour of the distinctions won by Private B.J. Briggs the scholars of St. John's School will have a half-holiday today.

(Author's note :- there is no record of any Bertie John Briggs, Royal Sussex Regiment, or M.M.G.C. winning any of the above medals or M.I.D's.)

Rewards for Gallantry

The Military Cross has been awarded the following officers for gallantry and devotion to duty in the field, the citations will appear at a later date :-

Haigh, Lieutenant Arthur Duncan, 5th Bn. (T.F.)
Isaac, 2nd Lieutenant John Palmer, 4th Bn. (T.F.) attd. 2nd Bn.
Pearson, T/2nd Lieutenant William George Frederick, Royal Sussex Regiment,
Points, T/2nd Lieutenant Ernest John Douglas, 8th Bn.

Monday April 7th 1919

Belgian Decorations Awarded

The following are among the decorations awarded by the King of the Belgians to members of the British Forces, for distinguished service during the war.

Decoration Militaire

No. L/7922 Corporal Ernest Brown, M.M., 2nd Bn. Royal Sussex Regiment, (Fulham)
No. G/26443 Corporal Alfred Ernest Richardson, 8th Bn. Royal Sussex Regiment, (Sutton)
"For conspicuous gallantry and devotion to duty during operations."

Monday April 21st 1919

D.C.M. for East Grinstead Man

A supplement to the *"London Gazette"* announces that the Distinguished Conduct Medal has been awarded to No. SD/3861 Corporal (L/Sgt.) C.H. Leppard, M.M., 7th Bn. Royal Sussex Regiment, of East Grinstead, for gallantry and distinguished service in the field.

Thursday May 1st 1919

Royal Sussex Officer Mentioned

The name of T/Captain H. S. Cousens, 7th Bn. Royal Sussex Regiment, was included in a list of those brought to the notice for distinguished and gallant services and devotion to duty in France.

Tuesday May 6th 1919

An Eastbourne D.C.M.

At the meeting of the Eastbourne Council yesterday, the Mayor (Alderman C. O'Brien Harding J.P.) presented the Distinguished Conduct Medal to Sergeant Harris, of the Royal Sussex Regiment, and in doing so said it gave him a double pleasure because recipient was not only an Eastbourne man but a member of the Royal Sussex Regiment. They were glad to see Eastbourne men win distinction, and in this case where all the officers were killed, Sergeant Harris led the men. He congratulated him on the conduct which had won him the decoration, and which he (the Mayor) had pleasure in presenting (applause). Sergeant Harris was afterwards entertained to tea in the Mayor's Parlour.

(This probably refers to Corporal Aris 16th Bn. who won the D.C.M. and came from Eastbourne.)

Thursday May 15th 1919

Rose to Captain and won the M.C

Captain F. Peel, only son of Superintendent Peel, of Arundel, 4th Battalion, Royal Sussex Regiment, having been demobilised, is now serving as a Police Constable at Bognor. He joined up on 24th August, 1914, went with the regiment to Gallipoli, and was in the fighting at Sulva Bay. He then proceeded to Egypt, and was made Staff- Sergeant of a bombing party there. He received his commission on 1st July, 1917, and his Captaincy on 18th October, 1918. He was wounded in Egypt on 17th April, 1916. He was in the first battle of the Turkish right flank, when General Allenby took command, and he was awarded the MC., for services rendered in the field at the battle of Beersheba, Palestine, 31st October, 1917. This will be presented to him by the King at Buckingham Palace on the 22nd May. Police Constable Peel is only 24 years of age.

Monday May 19th 1919

Military Medal Awards

The King has been pleased to approve of the award of the Military Medal for bravery in the field to the following warrant officers, non-commissioned officers and men of the Royal Sussex Regiment :-

No. L/8212 Sgt. Frederick Clements, 2nd Bn. (Brighton)
No. G/ 14671 Sgt. Frank W. Coe, 2nd Bn. (Corbetts Tey)
No. 320336 Sgt. Albert O. Isbell, 16th Bn. (West London)
No. S/1118 Sgt. Frederick J.A. Knowles, 2nd Bn. (Tottenham)
No. 320121 Sgt. Charles E. Moller, 16th Bn. (Midhurst)
No. G/6601 Sgt. Joseph Henry Cook Watson, 2nd Bn. (Brede) (was SD/3041)
No. L/7519 Cpl. Albert J. Jennings, 2nd Bn. (Portsmouth)
No. G/8665 Cpl. (A/Sgt.) Leonard W. Lewis 2nd Bn. (Midhurst)
No. G/863 Cpl. Sidney Wackford, 2nd Bn. (Chichester)
No. G/18323 Pte. (A/Cpl.) George H. Amsbridge, 2nd Bn. (Wick)
No. L/9750 Pte. George R. Awcock, 2nd Bn. (Bolney)
No. G/6345 Pte. (A/Sgt.) John Bell, 2nd Bn. (Brighton)
No. G/408 Pte. William T. Blackman, 2nd Bn. (Felpham)
No. L/11120 Pte. Charles Henry Bray, 2nd Bn. (Redhill)
No. G/14662 Pte. (A/Cpl.) David Brewer, 2nd Bn. (Great Waltham)
No. G/6576 Pte. George A. Bryant, 2nd Bn. (Camber)
No. G/21174 Pte. Charles Burgoine, 2nd Bn. (Cranford)
No. G/19913 Pte. Robert Chapman, 2nd Bn. (Crostwick)
No. G/4852 Pte. Arthur Charles Cox, 2nd Bn. (Clapton Park)
No. G/18572 Pte. Ernest R. Cox, 2nd Bn. (Chelsea)
No. G/14678 Pte. Percy C. Day, 2nd Bn. (Forest Gate)
No. G/20078 Pte. George Dolman, 2nd Bn. (Stratford)
No. G/17539 Pte. (A/Cpl.) Thomas E. Franks, 2nd Bn. (Ash)
No. G/11000 Pte. Frederick H. Gordon, 2nd Bn. (Stone)
No. G/11961 Pte. Matthew Green, 16th Bn. (King's Lynn)

No. L/9902 Pte. Lawrence A. Gumbrill, 2nd Bn. (Littlehampton)
No. G/11224 Pte. Albert Gurry, 2nd Bn. (Sutton)
No. 202190 Pte. (A/Cpl.) Spencer Harold Hemsley, 2nd Bn. (Crowborough)
No. L/9003 Pte. (L/Cpl.) Frederick A. Hendley, 2nd Bn. (Heathfield)
No. 320344 Pte. Herbert R.N. Hillman, 16th Bn. (Hassocks)
No. G/19148 Pte. William A. Hyde, 9th Bn. (West Bromwich)
No. G/11019 Pte. Denis Lordan, 2nd Bn. (Bermondsey)
No. G/14619 Pte. Mark Percy Mann, 2nd Bn. (Ingatestone)
No. G/21502 Pte. Frederick J. Markwell, 16th Bn. (Enfield)
No. G/5865 Pte. (A/Sgt.) Thomas Matthias, 2nd Bn. (Wrexham)
No. SD/5779 Pte. (L/Cpl.) Stanley Richard Newman, 16th Bn. (Upper Tooting)
No. G/14627 Pte. Francis J. Nichols, 2nd Bn. (Yiewsley)
No. G/14821 Pte. (A/Cpl.) Joseph S. Pinckney, 2nd Bn. (Homerton)

No. G/6362 Pte. George Henry Ranger, 2nd Bn. (Newhaven)

No. L/10391 Pte. Harry E. Reed, 2nd Bn. (Lewes)
No. G/476 Pte. George A. Rudderham, 2nd Bn. (Fernhurst)
No. G/14822 Pte. (A/Cpl.) George C. Sears, 2nd Bn. (Forest Gate)

No. G/3898 Pte. Allan Seymour, 2nd Bn. (Jevington)

No. G/7967 Pte. (A/Cpl.) Arthur L. Simmonds, 2nd Bn. (Eastbourne)
No. G/21779 Pte. Ernest E. Sharpe, 16th Bn. (Newton)
No. G/19822 Pte. (L/Cpl.) James Smith, 2nd Bn. (Clapham)
No. L/11534 Pte. William Smith, 2nd Bn. (Glasgow)
No. L/8044 Pte. Arthur Stevens, 2nd Bn. (Worthing)
No. G/1701 Pte. Arthur Tapner, 2nd Bn. (Chichester)
No. S/1659 Pte. James Thompson, 2nd Bn. (Eastbourne)
No. L/7933 Pte. Arthur Valler, 2nd Bn. (Battersea)
No. G/1464 Pte. Frederick J.. Vigar, 2nd Bn. (Balcombe)
No. G/18972 Pte. Benjamin Wilson, 2nd Bn. (Harlesden)
No. 202163 Pte. Arthur Wilton, 2nd Bn. (Crowborough)

Italian Awards

The King of Italy has bestowed upon the following officers and N.C.O. gallantry awards for service during the war :-

Silver Medal for Gallantry

Lt. (A/Capt.) T.W. Rose, M.B.E., M.C., Royal Sussex Regiment, (T.F.)

Croce di Guerra

Bt. Lt-Col. (T/Lt-Col.) R.M. Birkett, D.S.O. Royal Sussex Regiment & M.G.C.
Lt. (T/Cpt.) William Edgar Pears Done, M.C., Royal Sussex Regiment, (T.F.)
T/2nd Lieutenant Norman Finn, Royal Sussex Regiment, (Service Battalion)
T/2nd Lieutenant Henri Fernand Hillebrand, Royal Sussex Regiment, (Service Battalion)
No. 240251 C.S.M. Arthur Charles Howard, 5th Bn. Royal Sussex Regiment, (Hastings)
No. 202066 Sergeant Edward Henry Swaine, 1/5th Royal Sussex Regiment, (Rye)

Thursday May 22nd 1919

Today at Buckingham Palace His Majesty the King presented the Military Cross to Captain F. Peel of the Royal Sussex Regiment, "For services rendered in the Battle of Beersheba, Palestine on the 31st October, 1917."

Tuesday May 27th 1919

Award of the D.S.O.

T/Capt. (A/Mjr.) George Henry Gilmore, M.C. & Bar. 8th Bn. Royal Sussex Regiment, attd. 2/10th Bn. Royal Scots, (Lewisham)

For conspicuous gallantry and good leadership in command of the left wing of the Detachment during operations from 25th January to 10th February, 1919. Thanks to his ability and presence of mind the retreat was carried out successfully. On 1st and 7th of February he took personal command of important reconnaissances, and directed operations which enabled the force to extricate itself from a difficult situation.

"London Gazette" Friday May 30th 1919

The KING has been graciously pleased to confer the Territorial Decoration upon the undermentioned Officers of the Territorial Force who have been duly, recommended for the same under the terms of the Royal Warrants dated 17th August, 1908, as modified by the Royal Warrant dated the 11th November, 1918. —

 Captain William H. Kenderdine, 4th Bn. Royal Sussex Regiment,

Major Charles V. Johnson, 6th Bn. Royal Sussex Regiment,

Friday May 30th 1919

Arundel Man's Awards

Arundel is proud, and has reason to be, one of its residents in the person of Mr. P. Weedon, of 2, Greystoke Terrace, Ford Road. When war broke out Mr. Weedon at once offered his services and joined the Royal Sussex Regiment. In January, 1915, he was sent to France, and saw service with the 2nd Battalion, for 3years and 10 months. He was first wounded in the fight thigh while crossing the Sambre Canal. In this fighting he put a German machine-gun out of action single-handed and also killed two Germans, for which he was awarded the Distinguished Conduct Medal. He was also awarded the Military Medal in 1916, for keeping up the line of communications while under heavy fire at Paschendale Ridge. Private Weedon went through with his regiment every big engagement that was fought during his 3 years and 10 months, and only reached Graylingwell Hospital, Chichester, a day before the Armistice was signed. He has now completely recovered, and is living with his parents at Ford Road, Arundel. He is single, and only 23 years of age.

"London Gazette" Tuesday June 3rd 1919

War Office,
5th June, 1919.

The Secretary of State -for War- has received the following despatch addressed-to the Chief of the General Staff, India, by Lieutenant-General Sir W. B. Marshall, K.C.B.,K.C.S.I., Commanding-in-Chief, Mesopotamian Expeditionary Force :

General Headquarters,
Mesopotamian Expeditionary Force,
7th February, L919.

Sir,

With reference to paragraph 39 of my despatch dated. 1st February, 1919, I have the honour to submit herewith a list of names of those officers, ladies, warrant and non-commissioned officers and men serving, or who have served, under my command, whose distinguished and gallant services and devotion to duty I consider deserving of special mention.

I have the honour, to be,
Sir,
Your obedient servant,

W.B. MARSHALL,
Lieut. -General Commanding-in-Chief,
Mesopotamian Expeditionary Force.

COMMANDS & STAFF

Maj. & Bt. Lt.-Col. George Charles Morphett,., C.M.G.,D.S.O., Royal Sussex Regiment,

POLITICAL DEPARTMENT

Maj. &.Bt. Lt.-Col. Gerrard Evelyn Leachman, C.I.E.,D.S.O., Royal Sussex Regiment,
The KING has been graciously pleased, on the occasion of His Majesty's Birthday, to give orders for the following promotions in, and appointments to, the Most Excellent Order of the British Empire, for valuable services rendered in connection with the War: —

To be Commanders of the Military Division of the said Most Excellent Order:—

C.B.E. (Military Division)

Lt.-Col. James Lewis Sleeman, attd. N.Z. Forces

O.B.E. (Military Division)

Captain Frederic Percy Joscelyne, M.C., R.A.M.C.
(was attached to 2nd Bn. The Royal Sussex Regiment)

Tuesday June 3rd 1919

Sussex recipients in First Gazette

In connection with the occasion of the anniversary of the King's birthday today, his Majesty has been pleased to confer a large number of decorations and awards upon officers and men of the British Services and ladies of the various Nursing Staffs for valuable war services rendered in connection with the military operations at Home and in the various theatres of war abroad.
The list are of a lengthy and comprehensive nature and are contained in various special supplements to the *"London Gazette"*. Today the local awards are given from the first list, that covering France and Flanders, as follows :-

ROYAL SUSSEX REGIMENT

C.B. (Third Class)

Major and Bt. Colonel (T/Brig-General) John Bartholomew Wroughton, C.M.G.

C.B.E. (Military Division)

Colonel Arthur Robert Gilbert, D.S.O.

C.M.G. (Third Class)

Major and Bt.-Col. (T/Brig-General) Alfred Edgar Glasgow. D.S.O.

T/Lieutenant-Colonel Bertram James Walker, D.S.O. 8th Bn.

O.B.E. Military Division)

Captain and Bt. Major George Herbet Blackett de Chair, M.C.

T/Major Mathew James Manuia Makalua,
Quartermaster and Captain Joseph Edward Clarke, 2/5th Bn.
Captain Frederick Alan Benson Nicholl, 3rd Bn. (Special Reserve)
Captain William Sydney Kemp Russell, 4th Bn. (T.F.)

D.S.O.

The award of the Distinguished Service Order has been bestowed upon the following officers

T/Major (A/Lt-Col.) Walter Hubert Baddeley, M.C. attd. 8th Bn. East Surrey Regiment,

T/Major (A/Lt-Col.) John Bigelow Dodge, D.S.C., Suffolk Regiment attd. 16th Bn. Royal Sussex Regiment,

Major (T/Lt-Col.) Herbert Ivor Powell-Edwards, Sussex Yeo. attd. 16th Bn.

Major Alfred Carlisle Sayer, M.C., Sussex Yeo. attd. 16th Bn.

M.C.

2nd Lieutenant George Bannell,. 8th Bn.
Captain John Cartland, R. Warks. Regt. Attd. 17th Bn.
Rev. Charles Cole-Hamilton, T/C. F., attd. 16th Bn.
Lieutenant (A/Captain) Basil Danells, Sussex Yeo. attd. 7th Bn. M.G.C.
T/Lieutenant Walter Parker Ellen, 8th Bn.
T/Lieutenant (A/Captain) Charles Henry Knight, 9th Bn.

D.C.M.

No. 30111 Sergeant E. Bennett, 17th Bn. attd. 176th L.T.M.B. (Clacton-on-Sea)
No. G/3291 Corporal D.G. Boast, 9th Bn. (Brighton)
No. 200131 C.S.M. Henry Catt, 4th Bn. (T.F.) (Steyning)
No. 200088 Sergeant S.D. Cluer, 4th Bn. (T.F.) (Bognor)
No. SD/3081 Corporal George H. Coles, 13th Bn. and. 101st L.T.M.B. (Haselmere)
No. 315371 Corporal C.B. Crane, 16th Bn. (Benges, Herts.)
No. 320426 Sergeant A. Lusted, 16th Bn. (Hailsham)
No. 3302 C.S.M. (A/R.S.M.) J. McClymont, 9th Bn. (Kirkholm)
No. 320311 Private E. Tattershall, 16th Bn. (Brighton)
No. 220506 A/C.S.M. J.W. Thompson, 16th Bn. (Leytonstone)
No. G/1680 Private (A/Cpl.) F. Turnbull, 2nd Bn. (Brighton)

M.S.M.

No. G/2381 R.Q.M.S. J.W. Boyce, 8th Bn. (Plaistow)
No. 320002 R.Q.M.S. S. Fennell, 16th Bn. (Chingford)
No. 320009 C.S.M. H.B. Cooper, 16th Bn. (Eastbourne)
No. 30922 C.S.M. J. Hoyle, 17th Bn. (Dulwich)
No. S/229 C.Q.M.S. J.A. Grimes, 8th Bn. (Lambeth)
No. L/8526 C.Q.M.S. P.J. Hanlon, 7th Bn. (Hastings)
No. G/1 742 C.Q.M.S. E.B. Maynard, 8th Bn. (Portsmouth)
No. 200692 C.Q.M.S. G. Woods, 4th Bn. (Horsham)
No. 263189 Sergeant W.T. Bennett, 17th Bn. (Whaleybridge)
No. 8594 Sergeant L. Douglas, 2nd Bn. (Lewes)
No. 9368 Sergeant W.T. Harris, 2nd Bn. (Kensington)
No. 201095 Sergeant G.E. James, 4th Bn. (Brighton)
No. 30258 Sergeant H.G. Nurse, 17th Bn. (Lambeth)
No. 200012 Sergeant C.T. Rapley, 4th Bn. (Arundel)
No. L/6600 Sergeant F. Spinney, 2nd Bn. (Hamworthy)
No. 310 Sergeant J. Turner, 7th Bn. (Durham)
No. G/20499 Sergeant D. Wilshere, 7th Bn. (Chorlton-cum-Hardy)
No. G/14893 Corporal (L/Sgt.) K.L. Willis, 7th Bn. (Hammersmith)
No. G/4514 Private T.E. Browning, 7th Bn. (Henfield)
No. G/14759 Private (Cpl) F. Franklin, 2nd Bn. (Walthamstow)
No. G/15918 Private A. Gearing, 8th Bn. (Bexhill)
No. G/16509 Private T.L. Higham, 9th Bn. (Lewes)
No. G/1936 Private R.C.R. Marshall, 8th Bn. (Tunbridge Wells)

The *"London Gazette"* announces that Captain William H. Kenderdine, 4th Bn. and Major Charles V. Johnson, 6th Bn. Royal Sussex Regiment, have been awarded the Territorial Decoration.

Wednesday June 4th 1919

Military Decorations for various Fronts

In connection with awards made by the King on the occasion of his birthday, yesterday, the second list of military decorations is published today. The awards are numerous, and are contained in several supplements to the *"London Gazette"*. The theatres of war covered are Italy, East Africa, Archangel and Mesopotamia, with the Royal Air Force covering all fronts. The awards for Sussex and the County Regiment are as follows :-

D.F.C. (France)

Captain Cecil Fawssett, 6th Bn. Royal Sussex Regiment and R.A.F.

SERVICES IN ITALY

O.B.E. (Military Division)

Quartermaster and Captain Harry Plews, 5th Bn. (T.F.)

M.B.E. (Military Division)

Lieutenant James Eugene Mackay, Sussex Yeomanry,
Lieutenant Sydney Stanley Joe Travers, Royal Sussex Regiment, (T.F.)

M.C.

Lieutenant (A/Captain) Harry Marshall Keen, Sussex Yeomanry, attd. 2nd. Bn. Royal Warwicks.

M.S.M.

No. 240007 C.Q.M.S. T.H. Tremaine, 5th Bn. (Five Ashes)
No. 240030 Sergeant G.H. Hodson, M.M., 5th Bn. (Robertsbridge)
No. 240080 Corporal (L/Sgt.) A.H. Noakes, 5th Bn. (Ore, Hastings)
No. 240096 Private (L/Cpl.) W.A. Hall, 5th Bn. (Five Ashes)

SERVICES IN NORTH RUSSIA

Archangel Command

M.S.M.

No. SD/2157 C.Q.M.S. HA. Coppard, 11th Bn. (South Norwood)
No. SD/258 C.Q.M.S. J.L. Warner, 11th Bn. (Eastbourne)

SERVICES IN MESOPOTAMIA

M.B.E. (Military Division)

Lieutenant (T/Captain) Francis Peete Musgrave, Sussex Yeomanry,

Thursday June 5th 1919

Final list of Decorations

In connection with the awards made by the King on the occasion of his birthday on Wednesday, two long lists have already been published of county, regiment and local recipients. Today the third and last list is given, being decorations for general war service in Egypt and Salonika, contained in several supplements of the *"London Gazette"* :-

For Services in Egypt

O.B.E. (Military Division)

Captain (T/Major) Geoffrey William Ridley, 4th Bn. Royal Sussex Regiment,

For Services in Salonika

M.B.E. (Military Division)

Lieutenant (A/Capt.) Charles John Strachan, Royal Sussex Regiment, (T.F.)

Services in connection with the War

O.B.E. (Military Division)

Major Harold Jellicorse, (R.P.)
Captain Arthur Roland George Wilberforce, (R.of O.)
Lieutenant-Colonel Robert Wilson. McKergow, Sussex Yeomanry,

M.B.E. (Military Division)

Captain Arthur Seymour Hamilton Dicker, 3rd Bn. (Special Reserve)
Major William Wellington Sandeman, (R.P.)
Lieutenant (A/Captain) Robert Charles Bean, 2/1st Sussex Yeomanry,

To be Brevet Lieutenant-Colonel

Major (T/Lt.-Colonel) G.H. Impey, D.S.O.

Major R.B. Otter-Barry,

Major R.H. Waithman, D.S.O.

M.S.M.

No. SR/714 R.Q.M.S. F.C, Funnell, 1st Bn. (Chichester) India
No. L/92OO Bandmaster C. Hindmarsh, 1st Bn. (Beaumaris) India
No. L/2764 Sergeant A.E. James, 1st Bn. (Chichester) India
No. L/9264 Sergeant (A/C.S.M.) G. Tutt, 1st Bn. (Brighton) India
No. L/8448 Private (L/Cpl.) A.E. Brown, 1st Bn. (Poynings) India

M.I.D.

Captain (T/Major) G.W. Ridley, 4th Bn. Royal Sussex Regiment,
T/Lieutenant (A/Capt.) K.B. Howard, Commanding 163rd L.T.M. Bty. Royal Sussex Regiment,

Saturday June 7th 1919

M.I.D.'s Italy

Royal Sussex Regiment

Captain H.R.W. Dawson, 5th Bn. (secc. M.G.C.)
T/Lt. A. St. John Frost, 5th Bn.
Lt. E.R. Gibson, 5th Bn.
Lt. (A/Capt.) J. Langridge, 5th Bn.
Lt. R. Maxwell, 5th Bn.
T/2nd Lt. F.T. Murray, 5th Bn.
Qmr. & Capt. H. Plews, 5th Bn.
No. 240529 Private (A/L/Cpl.) P.E.W. Beech, 5th Bn.
No. 240571 R.Q.M.S. A.W. Briggs, 5th Bn.
No. 202090 Private (A/L/Cpl.) E. Hill, 5th Bn.
No. 240073 Sergeant R. Holmwood, 5th Bn.
No. 202746 C.S.M. L. Wickens, 5th Bn.

Tuesday June 17th 1919

Henfield Man's Distinction

Private T.E. Browning, 7th Battalion, Royal Sussex Regiment, who won the Meritorious Service Medal, on the Western Front, is the elder son of Mr and Mrs. Peter Browning, Adur Cottage, Mockbridge, Henfield. He joined up in November, 1914, being at that time a gardener at Colemans Hatch and went to the Western front in 1915. He remained there ever since, excepting for one break of several months, while he was getting over two big wounds sustained at Cambrai. He is now 22. His younger brother, Percy, is a first-class stoker in the Royal Navy, and is at the Dardanelles having about two year's service to his credit.

Thursday June 19th 1919

Honours for Sussex Men

A supplement to the *"London Gazette"* gives a long list of recipients of the Military Medal with Bars- and Meritorious Service Medals Below are given the awards noted to local men :-

Second Bar to M.M.

No. G/3410 Corporal Charles Thomas Emery, M.M., 7th Bn. Royal Sussex Regiment, (Hove) (M.M. gazetted 9th July, 1917, 1st Bar gazetted 11th February, 1919.)

Bar to the M.M.

No. 874 Private William A. Carr, M.M, 7th Bn. Royal Sussex Regiment, (Kensington) (M.M. gazetted 9th July, 1917.)

M.M.

No. 200033 Sergeant Arthur Budd, 4th Bn. (Arundel)
No. G/3056 Private (L/Cpl.) Edward Bonner, 17th Bn. (Portsmouth)
No. S/2403 Sergeant Joseph Cahill, 17th Bn. (Roscrea)
No. 263106 Corporal (A/Sgt.) Harold Darnell 17th Bn. (Barnstaple)
No. G/10853 Sergeant Ernest R. Newport, 7th Bn. (Hastings)
No. 15965 Sergeant Charles W. Remnant, 7th Bn. (Petworth)
No. G/30949 Private (L/Cpl.) William Dunkerton, 17th, Bn. (Fence Houses)
No. G/1960 Private (L/Cpl.) George Farmer, 8th Bn. (Heathfield)
No. G/1848 Private (A/L/Cpl.) Mark Matthews, 8th Bn. (Cowfold)
No. G/30655 Private Hugh Murphy, 17th Bn. (Chryston)
No. G/30475 Private Walter Southgate, 17th Bn. (Chelmondiston)
No. G/12381 Sergeant George E. Search, 9th Bn. (Gravesend)
No. G/1041 Sergeant Frederick G. Sloper, 7th Bn. (Andover)
No. G/9353 Private William Thirst, 7th Bn. (Suffield)
No. G/30331 Corporal Walter J. Undrill, 17th Bn. (Cambridge)
No. L/9905 C.S.M. Walter J. Walls, D.C.M., 8thBn. (Woking)
No. G/2655 Corporal John L. Wheeler, 8th Bn. (Brighton)

Saturday June 21st 1919

The President of France has bestowed upon the following N.C.O's and Private, for gallant service during the war in France the Croix de Guerre :-

Croix de Guerre

No. 200650 Lance-Corporal George Baker, 4th Bn. Royal Sussex Regiment, (Horsham)
No. 201077 Private William Bolt, 4th Bn. Royal Sussex Regiment, (Worthing)
No. 200131 Company Sergeant-Major Henry Catt, 4th Bn. Royal Sussex Regiment, (Steyning)
No. G/14857 Sergeant Archibald Peacock, 4th Bn. Royal Sussex Regiment, (Clapham, Beds.)

Tuesday July 8th 1919

Deserving of Special Mention

For distinguished and gallant services and devotion to duty during the period 16th September, 1918, to 15th March, 1919, the following officers are considered by Sir Douglas Haig to be worthy of special mention :-

Royal Sussex Regiment

Major and Bt. Lt-Colonel (T/Lt-Colonel) J.S. Cameron, D.S.O.
Captain and Bt. Major G.H.B. de Chair, O.B.E., M.C.
Major and Bt. Colonel (T/Brig-General) A.E. Glasgow, D.S.O.
Major The Hon. J.S.R. Tufton, D.S.O., 3rd Bn. Royal Sussex Regiment, and 2nd Lieutenant 1st Life Guards,
Lieutenant (T/Captain) M. Wallington, M.C. & Bar
Major and Bt. Colonel (T/Brig-General) J.B. Wroughton, C.B.,C.M.G.

Sussex Yeomanry

Lieutenant H. Brown, attd. 16th Bn. Royal Sussex Regiment, (T.F.)
Major (T/Lt-Colonel) H.I. Powell-Edwards, D.S.O. attd. 16th Bn. Royal Sussex Regiment, (T.F.)
Captain, T.R. Edwards, attd. 16th Bn. Royal Sussex Regiment, (T.F.)

Lieutenant Cecil Charles Neeves.

Major A.C. Sayer, D.S.O.,M.C., attd. 16th Bn. Royal Sussex Regiment, (T.F.)

Wednesday July 9th 1919

Mentioned in Dispatches

Lieutenant S.A. Andrews, D.S.O., M.C. and Bar., 7th Bn. Royal Sussex Regiment, has been mentioned in dispatches for good work. This is the second time this officer has been mentioned in dispatches, the first occasion was on 15th November, 1917.

Friday July 11th 1919

Deserving of Special Mention

The following are mentioned by Sir Douglas Haig as deserving of special mention for distinguished and gallant services and devotion to duty during the period 16th September to 15th March, 1919.

Royal Sussex Regiment

Andrews, T/Lt. (A/Capt.) S.A., D.S.O. MC., 7th Bn.
Apperley, Capt. (A/Maj.) W.H.W., M.C., 2nd Bn.
Brooker, 2nd Lt. J.R., attd. 6th Bn. Dorset Regt.
Buckland, 2nd Lt. J.R., attd. 17th Bn.
Campbell, Lt. (T/Capt.) G.O.L., M. C., 3rd Bn. (S.R.)
Campion, Lt.-Col. W.R., D.S.O., T.D., 4th Bn. (T.F.)
Clarke, Qrmr. and Capt. J.E., attd. 7th Bn.
Coleman, T/Capt. H.C., M.C., 9th Bn.
Constable, Mjr. (T/Lt.-Col.) G.S. M.C., 4th Bn. (T.F.)
Cragg, T/Lt. A.B., 2nd Bn.
Dodge, T/Lt-Col. J.B. D.S.O.,D.S.C., attd. 16th. Bn. (T.F.)
Foster, T/Maj. T. 9th Bn.
Garner, T/Lt. C.C., 8th Bn.
Hill, T/Lt. G. 7th Bn.
Hill, Capt. (A/Lt.-Col.) M.V.B. D.S.O., 5th Bn. Royal Fusiliers, attd. 9th Bn.
Johnson, Major (A/Lt.-Col) D.G. V.C., D. S.O., M.C., South Wales Borderers att. 2nd Bn. (Commanding)
Lamotte, Capt. and Bt. Maj. (A/Lt.-Col.) L., D.S.O., 2nd Bn. and. 2nd Bn. York L.I
L'Estrange, Lt. (A/Capt.) H.H. M.C., attd. 73rd L.T.M. Bty.
Newton, T/Capt. C.V. M.C., 9th Bn.
Roberts, Lt. (A/Capt.) H., D.S.O., M.C., 2nd Bn
Russell, Capt. W.S.K., 4th Bn. (T.F.)
Solomon, T/Qrmr. and Capt. J., 8th Bn.
Walker, T/Lt-Col. B.J. D.S.O., 8th Bn.
Bamber, L/5648, C.S.M. (T/R.S.M.) W. 4th Bn. (T.F.)
Baxter, G/23248, Cpl. (A/Sgt.) J.H. 7th Bn.
Boniface, SD/3297, Sgt. V. 4th Bn. (T.F.)
Bryant, 315366, Sgt. B.H. 16th Bn. (T.F)
Bryce, 200142, C.Q.M.S. A. 4th Bn.   (T.F.).
Bull, G/7827, C.S.M. B. 5th Bn.
Butcherd, T/240633, Pte. (A/Sgt.) J.H. 7th Bn.

Charman, 6095, C.S.M. George Andrew (P.S.) attd. 16th Bn. (T.F.)

Cowley, G/2186, Sgt. (A/C.Q.M.S.) G.E. 6th Bn.
Dallaway, L/5908, C.S.M. (A/R.S.M.) J.H. D.C.M., 7th Bn.
Davey, 320053, Sgt. P.V. 16th Bn. (T.F.)
Dearlove, G/2377, Sgt. A. 3rd Bn.
Duck, 315173, Sgt. (A/C.Q.M.S.) J.G. l6th Bn. (T.F.)
Etherington, G/3733, C.Q.M.S. (A/R.Q.M S.) J. 9th Bn.
Gilchrist, G/30525, Sgt. A. 17th Bn.

Goodsell, SD/1168, Sgt. Augustus John 3rd Bn.

Grayson, G/30030, Pte. F. 17th Bn.
Gronheit, G/30807, Sgt. (A/C.Q.M.S.) A.L. 17th Bn.
Hammond, 18742, Sgt. R.P. 7th Bn. Royal West Kent, (now 31239)17th Bn.
Heasman, G/883, Sgt. E.H. 7tt Bn.
Hopkins, 200371, Sgt. A., 4th Bn. (T.F.)
Jones, G/2476, C.Q.M.S. C. 8th Bn.
Lenton, G/30645, Pte. (A/L/Cpl.) M.H. 17th Bn.
Licence, 200508, Cpl. (A/R.Q.M.S.), H. 4th Bn. (T.F.)
Lynch, G/2472, Pte. G.L. 8th Bn.
Marsh, G/1766, Cpl. H. 6th Bn.
Marshall, 6200, Pte. J. 2nd Bn.
McCarthy, G/19009, Pte. C.M. 9th Bn.
Morley, G/4320, Cpl. (A/Sgt.) G. 9th Bn.
Parker, 37077, Pte. L.H. 16th Bn. (T.F.)
Peterson, 315242, Sgt. (A/Clr.Sgt.) H.J. 16th Bn. (T.F.)
Ruff, 2410, Cpl. G.S. 2nd Bn.
Taylor, 8792, Pte. F. 2nd Bn.
Williams, G/1918, C.Q.M.S. H.H. 8th Bn.

Monday July 14th 1919

Distinguished Service

In a supplement to the *"London Gazette"*, in a dispatch from Sir Douglas Haig for distinguished service the undermentioned officer, of the Royal Sussex Regiment:-.

T/Captain F.E. Webb, M.B., R.A.M.C. attd. 17th Bn.

"London Gazette" **Tuesday July 15th 1919**

No. 66242 Pte. Albert Turton, M.M., 2/10th Bn., R. Scots (Sutton Bridge).

On 20th September, 1918, when the column commander wanted to regain touch with headquarters, and called for volunteers to row a boat some five miles through the shelled area and minefields, Lance-Corporal Turton immediately volunteered, and was given the despatch, and was also told to note the positions of the mines. In spite of shelling from river craft he steered his boat cleverly through the mines and delivered the despatch and a report on the position of the mines. His cool courage and ability were of very great service.

(Formerly No. 318 L/Corporal in 7th Royal Sussex Regiment)

Wednesday July 16th 1919

French awards for local Men

A special supplement to the *"London Gazette"* announces the award of certain decorations conferred by the President of the French Republic upon British officers, N.C.O.'s and men for distinguished services rendered during the course of the campaign.

His Majesty the King has given unrestricted permission to wear the decorations. The following local men have received the award of the Medaille d'Honneur avec glaives en Bronze.

Medaille d'Honneur avec glaives en Bronze

No. G/3291 Corporal Douglas Guy Boast,   9th Bn. Royal Sussex Regiment,

Monday July 21st 1919

ALLIES MARCH OF TRIUMPH

The Sussex Contingent

The 2nd Battalion Royal Sussex Regiment were represented in the March by the following officers, 'N.C.O.'s and men :-
Lieutenant-Colonel W.L. Osborn, C.B., C.M.G., D.S.O.,
(Commanding Composite Battalion, Southern Command)

Captain H. Roberts, D.S.O., M.C.
No. 9013 R.Q.M.S. W. Soughton, D.C.M.
No. 9258 Corporal J. Cope.
No. 11232 Corporal W. Francis.
No. 10479 Lance-Corporal A. Clevett, MM.
No. 11120 Lance-Corporal C.H. Bray, MM.
No. 13103 Lance-Corporal F. Turnbull, D.C.M.
No. 12195 Lance-Corporal A. Raynard, M.M.
No. 11937 Lance-Corporal R. Steele.
No. 10367 Lance-Corporal J. Hayler.
No. 10186 Lance-Corporal G. Barker.
No. 12184 Private R. Goacher, M.M.

No. 6588 Private W. Musselwhite.
No. 11290 Private A.E. Groome, M.M.
No. 13248 Private R. Apted.
No. 12702 Private J.W. Hodgson, D.C.M., M.M.
No. 6114 Private A. Routledge.
No. 6200 Private J. Marshall,
No. 10156 Private G. Packham.
No. 13302 Private H. Billington, D.C.M.
No. 12492 Private R. Chapman. M.M.
No. 11673 Private C.J. Boniface.
No. 13263 Private J.R. Rooke.
No. 13070 Private H. Winchester.
No. 12384 Private W. Smith.

In the detachment of *"Old Contemptibles"* the battalion was represented by No.12118 Lance-Sergeant E.J. Brown, D.C.M., M.M., D.M. Several of those taking part in the general portion given above possess the 1914 Star, while all have the 1915 Star.

Wednesday July 23rd 1919

A Bognor loss

Mrs. Stone, Melrose, Gordon Avenue, Bognor, has now received official notification from the War Office that her husband, R.S.M. B.A. Stone, D.C.M., 13th Battalion Royal Sussex Regiment, reported missing 26th April, 1918, is now presumed to have died on or after that date. R.S.M. Stone was a Sergeant in "G" Company 4th Battalion Royal Sussex Regiment on the outbreak of war, and after doing excellent service at home in helping to organise and train the 2/4 and 3/4 Battalions, was posted to the 13th Battalion Royal Sussex Regiment, France. He was promoted from C.S.M. to R.S.M., and gazetted with the D.C.M. in March, 1918, for conspicuous gallantry and good leadership. The report stated :-

This N.C.O. acted as platoon commander in No.1 Battalion of Colonel Hunt's Force. And displayed marked ability and coolness throughout the operations in handling his platoon at Bray-Sur-Somme. When his Company was ordered to support a unit in the, line, he advanced with his platoon under very heavy shell fire and only withdrew when. ordered to do so by his Company Commander.
His tenacity in holding the line with his platoon, in the face of very heavy shell fire, when other troops had withdrawn, undoubtedly delayed the advance of the enemy at a very critical period and enabled our troops to effect an orderly retirement. His good leadership throughout inspired the confidence of his men and was of the greatest assistance to his Company Commander. And his cheerfulness and courage under most trying conditions were an example to and admiration of all ranks.

The Adjutant of the regiment, when informing Mrs. Stone that her husband was missing, wrote :-

I can only express my sympathy, which must seem so little in your great anxiety You will be pleased to hear that your husband has won the D.C.M for gallantry and devotion to duty, and no one deserved it more than he. One feels honoured to work with such men, and I, as adjutant, feel the loss of one of the best Sergeant-Majors I have known.

Two popular brothers

It will no doubt be remembered that R.S.M. Stone's younger brother, Lieutenant V. Stone, Canadian Infantry, was killed in action in France on the 10th, November, 1917 He was among Canada's first sons to answer the call of the Mother Country, coming to England in 1915. After being gassed at Ypres he was offered Staff work at Hastings, this, however, he refused and obtaining a commission was soon back in the thick of the fighting. Both brothers were well-known at Bognor and Amberley, especially at the latter town, where they resided for a considerable number of years, and where their father, Mr. T, Stone, was schoolmaster. R.S.M. Stone leaves a widow and one little son, for whom much sympathy is felt.

Saturday July 25th 1919

Bar to the Military Medal

No. G/936 Private Joseph R. Selsby, M.M. 8th Bn. Royal Sussex Regiment,

"For conspicuous gallantry and devotion to duty during operations."

Monday July 28th 1920

Military Medallists

In Saturday's issue a list was given of eleven men of Sussex, who, having already won the Military Medal, have been awarded a bar to that medal. His Majesty, the King has also approved the award of the Military Medal to the following gallant Royal Sussex men :-

No. G/19396 Pte. Joseph Amsbury, 7th Bn. (Islington)
No. G/2712 Cpl. Percy Beckett, 8th Bn. (East Grinstead)
No. L/15550 Cpl. (A/Sgt) George Brewster, 17th Bn. (Gremsford).
No. G/475 Cpl. C.E. Bridger, 9th Bn. (Petworth)

No. G/1196 Pte. Harry T. Barber, 7th Bn. (Stone Cross)

No. G/2744 Henry Beecroft, 8th Bn. (Eltham)
No. G/1759 Pte. Jack Bridger, 8th Bn. (Bridhen)
No. G/8561 Pte. Frederick Briffett, 2nd Bn. (Bow)

No. G/150 Pte. Frederick Britt, D.C.M. 7th Bn. (Robertsbridge)

No. G/1920 Pte. (L/Cpl.) Arthur Brooke, 8th Bn. (Heathfield)
No. G/12072 Pte. John W. Bull, 7th Bn. (Strood)
No. G/18890 Pte. Ernest Caley, 2nd Bn. (St. Albans)
No. G/18575 Pte. Albert Cane, 2nd Bn. (Limehouse)
No. G/4536 Pte. Ernest H. Carver, 8th Bn. (Petworth)
"For conspicuous gallantry and devotion to duty during operations."
No. G/4312 Pte. Arthur Clarke, 8th Bn. (Manor Park).
"For conspicuous gallantry and devotion to duty during operations."

No. G/3523 Pte. Augustine A. Collier, 9th Bn. (Brighton)
No. G/4284 Pte. Frederick C. Cornish, 2nd Bn. (Lambeth)
No. G/18577 Pte. Alfred A. Cotton, 2nd Bn. (Bow)
No. G/19276 Pte. (A/Cpl.) George E. Davis, 6th Bn. (Walton)
No. G/2138 Pte. Nelson G. Dawson, 8th Bn. (Battle)
"For conspicuous gallantry and devotion to duty during operations."
No. G/14526 Pte. (L/Cpl.) Thomas C. Dix, 2nd Bn. (Alney)
No. G/10276 Pte. (L/Cpl.) William J. Durling, 9th Bn. (Wilmington)
No. G/1746 Pte. Sgt. Ernest E. Etherington, 8th Bn. (Petersfield)
No. G/7660 Cpl. (L/Sgt.) James A. Elphick, 7th Bn. (Tunbridge Wells)
No. G/15906 Pte. Alfred W. Farley, 2nd Bn. (Brighton)
No. G/1965 Pte. William Farrant, 8th Bn. (Polegate)
No. G/2430 Sgt. Hilling Goward, 8th Bn. (Haywards Heath)
"For conspicuous gallantry and devotion to duty during operations."
No. L/12184 Pte. Raymond P. Goacher, 2nd Bn. (Billingshurst)
No. G/6004 Pte. (A/Cpl.) George W. Gray, 2nd Bn. (Swanscombe)
No. G/16427 Pte. Albert Frank Groome, 9th Bn. (Steyning)
No. G/2455 Sgt. John J. Hunton, 8th Bn. (Kilburn.)
"For conspicuous gallantry and devotion to duty during operations."
No. G/17576 Pte. Geoffrey W. Harvey, 2nd Bn. (Whistable)
No. G/4153 Pte. Benjamin Hearn, 9th Bn. (Sheffield Park)
No. G/6359 Pte. Harry Hills, 2nd Bn. (Fishergate)
No. G/1857 Pte. (L/Cpl.) Arthur Jester, 8th Bn. (Cowfold)
No. 290480 Pte. Ernest A. Joyce, 9th Bn. (Rudgwick)
No. SR/120 Sgt. Albert Lee, 7th Bn. (Brighton)
No. L/8132 Sgt. Edward G. Lister, 7th Bn. (Belfast)
No. L/11570 Sgt. W.H. Lovering, 17th Bn. (Edmonton)
No. G/886 Sgt. Maurice Luff, 9th Bn. (Worplesdon)
No. G/7739 Pte. Henry J. Lade, 8th Bn. (Brighton)
"For conspicuous gallantry and devotion to duty during operations."
No. G/2836 Pte. (L/Cpl.) Thomas Leggatt, 8th Bn. (Brighton)
No.G14704 Pte. (L/Cpl.) Albert E. Lewis, 2nd Bn. (Maldon)
No. G/714 Sgt. Clifford J. Marshall, 7th Bn. (Chard)
No. G/839 Sgt. Ernest Munt, 7th Bn. (Laughton)
No. G/1898 Cpl. William H. Mason, 8th Bn. (Brighton)
No. G/2006 Pte. (L/Cpl.) Joseph Maguire, 7th Bn. (Brighton)
No. G/11824 Pte. (A/L/Cpl.) George L. Mann, 9th Bn. (Aldborough)
No.SD/4956 Pte. (L/Cpl.) Henry Martin, 16th Bn (Hollington)
No. G/19180 Pte. Robert Martin, 9th Bn. (Rawtenstall)
No. G/7050 Pte. Alex McFarlane, 8th Bn. (Ayr)
"For conspicuous gallantry and devotion to duty during operations."
No. L/6696 Pte. (A/Cpl.) John McKernan, 2nd Bn. (Motherwell)
No. G/2355 Pte. (L/Cpl.) Herbert E. Moger, 8th Bn (Lewes)
No. G/6281 Pte. Harry Moore, 2nd Bn. (Hastings)
No. G/2360 Cpl. Percy Newnham 8th Bn. (Westminston)
No. G/23694 Cpl. (L/Sgt.) Watson H. Onions, 7th Bn. (Blackheath)
No. G/30455 Pte. (L/Cpl.) John W. Oldham, 17th Bn. (New Sawley)
No. G/638 Sgt. Albert Parsons, 7th Bn. (West Chiltington)
No. G/2719 Sgt. William Penfold, 8th Bn. (Ditchling)
No. G/1432 Cpl. Robert H. Pierce, 9th Bn. (Beckley)
No. G/2591 Pte. (A/Cpl.) Charles T. Page, 8th Bn. (Lewes)
No. G/30964 Pte. Charles R. Poole, 17th Bn. (Gloucester,)
No. L/10747 Cpl. Charles Ranger, 7th Bn. (Wateringbury)
No. G/20443 Cpl. Alfred E. Richardson, 9th Bn. (Sutton)
No. G/9705 Cpl. Frederick P. Russell, 8th Bn. (Eastbourne)

No. G/1853 Pte. (L/Cpl.) Reginald Russell, 8th Bn. (Brentwood)
No. G/960 Pte. (L/Cpl.) John Saunders, 7th Bn. (Hove)
No. G/2396 Pte. (L/Cpl.) Percy Sayers, 8th Bn. (Partridge Green)
No. G/2010 Pte. Frederick J. Scrase, 8th Bn. (Hove)
No. G/1727 Pte. Frederick Slaughter, 7th Bn. (Worthing)
No. G/862 Pte. (L/Cpl.) Alfred J. Squires, 7th Bn. (East Lavant)
No. G/10553 Pte. John Stedman, 8th Bn. (Charlton)
"For conspicuous gallantry and devotion to duty during operations."
No. G/19341 Pte. Henry Theckston, 9th Bn. (Darwen)
No. G/31029 Pte. (A/Sgt.) Alfred T. Titcombe, 17th Bn. (North Kensington)
No. G/15792 Pte. John H. Troy, 8th Bn. (Crowborough)
No. G/2028 Cpl. (A/Sgt.) George W. Vale, 8th Bn. (Hackney)
"For conspicuous gallantry and devotion to duty during operations."
No. G/3147 Sgt. Charles F. West, D.C.M., 7th Bn. (Arundel)
No. G/5943 Sgt. Arthur Ernest Whitlock, 9th Bn. (Battersea)
No. G/101 Cpl. Edward G. Whitbread, 7th Bn. (Mayfield)
No. 320193 Cpl. Reginald E. Wild, 16th Bn. (Petersfield)
No. G/1865 Pte. Frederick J. Ward, 8th Bn. (Horsham)
No. G/2357 Pte. Arthur W. Wheeler, 8th Bn. (Brighton)
No. G/2621 Pte. George Woolgar, 8th Bn, (Shoreham)
No. G/30514 Pte. Norman L. Wright, 17th Bn. (Smullshaw)

Thursday July 31st 1919

The *"London Gazette"* announces the award of the Distinguished Service Order for conspicuous gallantry to :-

D.S.O.

Lieutenant (A/Capt.) Harry Roberts, M.C., 2nd Battalion Royal Sussex Regiment,

During the operations north of Gricourt on 24th September, 1918, he commanded the right front of the company of the battalion in the attack. After reaching the final objective and whilst the company was still somewhat disorganised from the attack, the enemy launched a counter-attack with about 400 men against the position occupied by this company.

He was out in front of the position when the counter-attack was first seen. He returned to his company and ordered the men to fire on the advancing enemy. As soon as he first saw the first wave of the enemy wavering he again blew his whistle and ordered the whole of the men in that area to fix bayonets and advance against the now advancing enemy. The total number of men at his disposal did not exceed 80. By this action he completely routed the counter-attacking enemy and captured many prisoners. Throughout this operation he was walking about fully exposed, and by his calm handling of the situation and skill in selecting the moment to dash pot against the enemy with the bayonet, was responsible for the thorough routing of a strong counter-attack and enabling the ground gained in the initial attack to be retained. During this advance he was severely wounded in the arm by a bullet fired at point-blank range, but in spite of this he remained with his company reorganising his men in defensive position and before being evacuated gave a full report of the situation to the battalion commander.

Bar to M.C.

T/Captain Alexander Campbell White-Knox, M.C., M.B., R.A.M.C., attd. 2nd Bn.

For conspicuous gallantry and devotion to duty. Throughout the operations north and south of the river D'Omignon, from September 18th to 24th, 1918. As medical officer of the battalion he organised and supervised the evacuation of the wounded in the most perfect manner, despite shell fire and gas. Besides superintending the work at the regimental aid post, he personally supervised the work of the stretcher-bearers with the leading waves of the assaulting troops. Owing to his energy and personal supervision, every wounded man was attended to and evacuated without delay. He did fine work.
(M.C. gazetted 1st January 1918)

T/Lieutenant Harold Quincey Rangecroft, M.C. attd. 1st Bn. Lancashire Fusiliers,

In the Ypres sector near Ghelune on September 30th, 1918, this officer in command of a company experienced very heavy rifle and machine-gun fire from an enemy pillbox. He organised and gallantly led a flanking attack on this pillbox under cover of Lewis gun-fire. The attack was completely successful and resulted in the capture of the pillbox, one officer and fifteen other ranks – without a casualty to his own force. He did fine work.
(M.C. gazetted 3rd June, 1918)

Friday August 1st 1919

Territorial Award

The award of the Territorial Efficiency Medal has been made to :-

No. 200033 L/Cpl. (A/Sgt.) A. Budd, 4th Bn. Royal Sussex Regiment,

Thursday August 7th 1919

Second Bar to Military Medal

No. 3833 Private Edwin Highgate, M.M. & Bar, 7th Bn. Royal Sussex Regiment,
(M.M. gazetted 18th July, 1917, 1st Bar gazetted 11th February 1919)

"London Gazette" Tuesday August 19th 1919

The KING has been graciously pleased to confer the Territorial Decoration upon the undermentioned Officers of the Territorial Force who have been duly recommended for the same under the terms of the Royal Warrants dated 17th August, 1908, as modified by the Royal Warrant dated the 11th November, 1918:—

Major (T/Lt.-Col.) Guy Sefton Constable, M.C. 4th Bn.
Reverend Arthur H. Boyd, O.B.E., M.C., M.A., attd. 4th Bn.

Gallant Hurst Man Killed

Regimental Sergeant-Major J. Simmons, D.C.M. Royal Sussex Regiment, eldest son of Mr. and Mrs. J. Simmons, of Goldbridge, Hurstpierpoint, has been killed during the fighting at the Western Front. A Territorial, he was in camp when war broke out, and was moved with his battalion. At the Dardanelles, he sustained a slight wound.

Going to Palestine subsequently he was, for gallantry at Gaza, awarded the D.C.M. He had been at Jericho, and later was transferred to the Western Front, where the gallant Territorial fell. He was a minister of the Parish Church choir, and was highly thought of by all who knew him.

Saturday August 23rd 1919

County Regiment "Mentions"

A list has been published of names brought before the Secretary of State for War, for valuable war services, and, when applicable, an entry will be made in the records of the officers and men mentioned. Those belonging to the County Regiment are as follows :-

Department of the Under-Secretary of State for War

Gudman, Major. C.B. 3rd (Vol.) Bn. (Lt-Col.) 3rd Bn.
Money, Major G.A. 5th (Vol.) Bn.
O'Donnell, Major G.B. 1st (Vol.) Bn.(Lt.-Col) Indian Army, R.P.)

Department of D.G. of Movements and Railways

Brooks, L/5413 C.S.M. F.B., Royal Sussex Regiment,

M.M.

Hann, Ernest E., G/2121 Sgt.. 7th Bn. (Hastings)
Buckland, William J., 200699 Pte. 9th Bn. (Holmwood)
Drake, George, 30168 Pte. (L/Cpl.) 17th Bn.. (Salford)
Fielder, Frederick G., G/2144 Pte. 8th Bn. (Hawkhurst)
Stobbart, Thomas R., G/1916 Pte, (A/Cpl.) 8th Bn. (Sanderstead)

Monday August 25th 1919

Allied Decorations and Medals

A supplement to the *"London Gazette"* publishes a long list of officers and men of the, Services who have been granted decorations and medals by the Allied Powers at various dates for distinguished services rendered during the course of various campaigns. His Majesty the King has given unrestricted permission in all cases to wear the awards. The local mentioned are as follows :-

Decorations conferred by the French Republic

Croix de Guerre

T/ Lieutenant (A/Captain) Walter Foster Barfoot, Royal Sussex Regiment,
(attd. 2nd Trench Mortar Battery).

Thursday August 28th 1919

War Service Home Commands Lists

The names of the following have been brought to the notice of the Secretary of State for War for valuable services rendered in connection with the war :-

Aldershot Command

53rd Battalion Royal Sussex Regiment

Lieutenant J.A. Carter,
T/Captain W.P.S. Jones,
Lieutenant (A/Capt.) A.H. Muirhead,
No. G/97864 C.S.M. F. Hurst,
No. G/165047 Sergeant J. Hall,
No. G/97866 Sergeant W. Peatfield, M.M.,
No. 57843 C.S.M. P.J. Rutherford,
No. 36198 C.Q.M.S. J. Sherwin,

Eastern Command

Lieutenant (A/Capt.) F.G. Box, Royal Sussex Regiment, (T.F.)
Lieutenant L.E. Cook, Royal Sussex Regiment,
Qmr. & Captain T.P. Field, (T.F.) attd. Royal Sussex Regiment,
Lieutenant (A/Capt.) G.R. Keep, (T.F.) attd. Royal Sussex Regiment,
T/Lieutenant A.E. Lawrence, Royal Sussex Regiment,
Major N.A. Layton, R.of O. Royal Sussex Regiment,
Lieutenant (A/Capt.) A.H.C. Lowe, Royal Sussex Regiment,
Qmr. & Major C. Philips, R. of O. Royal Sussex Regiment,
T/Major W.N. Porter, C.I.E., V.D., Royal Sussex Regiment,
No. 8601 Sergeant (A/C.S.M.) E. Warters, 2nd Bn. Royal Sussex Regiment,

Northern Command

Captain G.B. Mountford, M.C., 4th Bn. Royal Sussex Regiment,

Western Command 33rd Army Corps.

No. 181937 Private A.J. Barrow, 52nd Bn. Royal Sussex Regiment,
No. 41547 C.S.M. J. Bell, Royal Sussex Regiment,
No. 36121 Private (A/L/Sgt.) A.C. Bolitho, 52nd Bn. Royal Sussex Regiment,
No. G/41398 Corporal G.H. Butter, R.W. Kent attd. 51st Bn. Royal Sussex Regiment,
No. 36116 Private (A/Cpl.) J. Crowther 52nd Bn. Royal Sussex Regiment,
No. 36191 Private (A/Cpl.) E.W. Dade, R.S.Regt. attd. 51st Middlesex Regiment,
No. 36119 Private (A/L/Sgt.) C.A. Haynes, 52nd Bn. Royal Sussex Regiment,
No. 2568 Corporal (A/Sgt.) H.A.W. Judd, Middx. Regt. attd. 52nd Bn. R.S. Regt.
No. 6665 Corporal Ernest Henry Loveland 51st Bn. Royal Sussex Regiment,
No. G/41407 Corporal W. Martin, 51st Bn. Royal Sussex Regiment,
No. 1285 Sergeant A.E. Metcalfe, Middx. Regt. attd. 52nd Bn. Royal Sussex Regiment,
No. 41402 L/Sergeant A. Morgan, R.W.Kent attd. 52nd Bn. Royal Sussex Regiment,
No. L/1983 Sergeant J.A. Morton, R.W. Kent attd. 51st Bn. Royal Sussex Regiment,
No. 20431 Sergeant G. Morris, 3rd Bn. attd. 52nd Bn. Royal Sussex Regiment,
No. 36192 Private (A/L/Cpl.) B. O'Brien, 51st Middx. Regt. attd. Royal Sussex Regiment,
No. G/41370 Sergeant M. Parnell, 51st Bn. Royal Sussex Regiment,

No. 47224 Private T.J. Portch, 52nd Bn. Royal Sussex Regiment,

"London Gazette" Friday August 29th 1919

The names of the following have been brought to the notice of the Secretary of State for War for valuable services rendered in connection with the war :-

Captain & Flight Commander Aeroplane & Seaplane Alexander Evelyn Charlwood, Royal Sussex Regiment & R.F.C.

"London Gazette" Thursday September 4th 1919

The following are among the Decorations and Medals awarded by the Allied Powers at various dates to the British Forces for distinguished services rendered during the course of the campaign: —
His Majesty the King has given unrestricted permission in all cases to wear the Decorations and Medals in question.

Decorations Conferred by

HIS MAJESTY THE KING OF THE BELGIANS

Croix de Guerre

Captain William Sussex Grassett Bridger, 4th Bn. Royal Sussex Regiment,

Captain Rupert Charles Godfrey, Middleton, M.C., 4th Battalion, Royal Sussex Regiment,

Quartermaster and Lieutenant Ernest Norris Rothwell, Royal Sussex Regiment, (attached l/4th Battalion, Cheshire Regiment).
200036 Company Sergeant-Major Frederick Slaughter, D.C.M. 4th Battalion, Royal Sussex Regiment, (Arundel)

Friday September 5th 1919

Awards to Sussex Men

With reference to the announcement, says a supplement to the *"London Gazette"* of the award of the D.C.M. which appeared in the Gazette, 1st January this year, the following are the acts of gallantry which gained the award :-

No. G/391 C.Q.M.S. W.H. Budgen, 7th Bn. Royal Sussex Regiment, (East Grinstead)

For devotion to duty during the period 25th February to 16th September 1918. He set a fine example to all ranks by his determination and utter disregard of danger. On many occasions under heavy fire, he led his men in action with great gallantry, and as C.Q.M.S., never failed to get rations up to his company in spite of heavy shelling.

No. GS/828 A/Sgt. A.V. Coppard, 2nd Bn. Royal Sussex Regiment, (Hurst Green)

He served with the battalion for over three years, and for the greater part of that time was employed in the regimental scouts. At all times he did invaluable work. He carried out several patrols and brought back useful information, and his work and reports as an observer were of great assistance to his C.O. Both in and out of the lines the work of this N.C.O. was exemplary, and he set a fine example of gallantry and devotion to duty.

No. G/16014 L/Cpl. A.J. Curd, 13th Bn. Royal Sussex Regiment, (Lancing)

For conspicuous gallantry and devotion to duty during the second battle of the Somme. At St. Emilie, on 22nd March, when his runners had been killed in attempting to get in touch with battalion H.Q. he volunteered and reached battalion H.Q., afterwards returning with orders which enabled the company to withdraw to our lines with few casualties. From the 22nd to 27th March, 1918, when he was wounded, he repeatedly did good work under heavy machine-gun and rifle fire. His fine courage and cheerfulness were an example to all ranks.

No. L/8076 Cpl. G. Hobday, 2nd. Bn. Royal Sussex Regiment, attd. 1/2nd King's African Rifles, (Belfast)

For gallantry at Medo, on 12th April, 1918, in remaining at his post when wounded and thereby setting a fine example of courage to all ranks. In addition, he has commanded a platoon with exceptional ability and courage, and has been of the greatest assistance to his company commander.

No. GS/385 Sgt. C.F. Moody, M.M., 8th Bn. Royal Sussex Regiment, (Crofton Park)

He has been signalling sergeant of the battalion since its formation in 1914. It is entirely due to his untiring efforts that the signalling personnel of the battalion is efficient and competent at carrying out their work. He is out all hours of the day and night superintending the communications of the battalion, and at all times shows the greatest disregard for his personal safety under fire. He is a splendid example of keenness, efficiency and determination to those with him.

No. G/3590 Sgt. A.J. Newnham, 9th Bn. Royal Sussex Regiment, (Dane Hill)

For conspicuous gallantry on 21st March, 1918, when in charge of regimental transport. He went up five times in the day to brigade H.Q. at Hesbecourt, through heavy gas and H.E. bombardments. There were many casualties on the road, and many vehicles were prevented from getting up, but by his gallant and skilful example he succeeded in getting his transport up on every occasion. During the subsequent retreat his handling of the transport was infallible.

No. 240078 Cpl. (L/Sgt.) A.J. Oyler, 5th Bn. (P) Royal Sussex Regiment, (Rye) (Italy)

As Sergeant of the Divisional Observers he has performed much valuable work to the division, in the observance of enemy movement and the transmission of information under heavy shell fire. His conduct under these conditions has been gallant and absolutely fearless at all times, and no N.C.O. could have set a better example of courage and determination than has done.

No. 200036 C.Q.M.S. F. Slaughter, 4th Bn. Royal Sussex Regiment, (Arundel)

During the period 25th February to 17th September, 1918, he has carried out his duties with the greatest energy and zeal. During operations near Grand Rozoy, and in the line, he has superintended the distribution of rations to his company often under heavy fire, setting a fine example of devotion to duty. On one occasion near Kemmel in September, the driver of the limber on which he was taking up rations was wounded by a shell. Though unaccustomed to animals, he mounted and drove the limber himself, bringing up the rations to his company.

No. 11559 Private A. Wright, 17th Bn. Royal Sussex Regiment, (Painswick, Gloucester)

For most marked gallantry and devotion to duty. While acting as company runner he did good work in acting as our guide to our advanced posts in the line at Mercatel. He consistently took messages and led visiting patrols under heavy shell fire to our advanced posts during the attack and barrage. During the last period in the line he again did invaluable work under very trying circumstances in keeping communications open. When a man was wounded he bandaged him in the open under heavy shell fire.

"London Gazette" **Friday September 12th 1919**

The award of the Most Eminent Order of the Indian Empire has been bestowed by his Majesty the King, for Meritorious Service in connection with the war in India, upon :-

C.I.E.

Lt/Colonel Edward Leslie Mackenzie, D.S.O. 1st Bn. Royal Sussex Regiment,

The KING has been graciously pleased, on the occasion of His Majesty's Birthday, to give orders for the following promotions in, and appointments to, the Most Excellent Order of the British Empire, in recognition of distinguished services rendered in India in connection with the War. To be dated 3rd June, 1919: —

O.B.E. (Military Division)

Q/M. & Maj. George Gilpin, 1st Bn.
Lt.-Col. Brian Mansfield Hynes, R.S.R. Commanding 1/25th Bn. London Regiment,

Tuesday September 23rd 1919

Sussex Soldiers Decorated

The following decorations have been conferred by the King of Romania.

Croix de Virtue Militara (*1st Class*)

No. 320001 C.S.M. (A/R.S.M.) John Charles Sterry Balcombe, D.C.M., 16th Bn. Royal Sussex Regiment, (Brighton)

M.S.M.

The Meritorious Service Medal is awarded to :-

No. L/8349 Sgt. W.T. Pelham, 1st Bn. Royal Sussex Regiment, (Newhaven) (India)

Thursday September 25th 1919

Military Intelligence

Lieutenant W.G. Aukett, D.C.M., M.M., Royal Sussex Regiment, who has just been given his second star, belongs to the 3rd Battalion in which he was commissioned in November, 1917. he won the D.C.M., and the M.M., while serving in the ranks 1916-1917. He was latterly with the Machine Gun Corps.

Monday October 6th 1919

Bar to the M.C.

The award of a bar to the Military Cross was announced in the *"London Gazette"* and it was awarded to :-

Lt.(T/Capt.) Michael Wallington, Royal Sussex Regiment, Bt. Maj. 1st Infantry Brigade,

For gallant and distinguished conduct in the field. He has been brigade major since 16th October, 1917. On 17th October, at Vaux Andigny, when orders were issued for the attack to be continued, he rode to battalion headquarters of a regiment through heavy fire and explained the situation to the commanding officer, who was able to get his orders out in time for the operation. On many occasions he has shown resource, judgement and gallantry.

Sussex Soldiers Decorated

The Meritorious Service Medal has been awarded to the following in recognition of valuable services rendered with the British Forces in Russia :-

No. 290575 Sgt. (A/C.S.M.) H. Martin, 4th Bn. Royal Sussex Regiment, (Hastings) Archangel
No. SD/549 Cpl. W.A. Seall, 11th Bn. Royal Sussex Regiment, (Worthing) Murmansk

Wednesday October 8th 1919

The following are among the Decorations and medals awarded by the Allied Powers at various dates to the British Forces for distinguished services rendered during the course of the campaign: —

His Majesty the King has given unrestricted permission in all cases to wear the Decorations and medals in question.

Decorations conferred by THE PRESIDENT OF THE FRENCH REPUBLIC

Ordre du, Merite Agricole Chevalier

Late Lieutenant (Temporary Captain) Alfred John Sansom, 1/5th Battalion, Royal Sussex Regiment (Territorial Force).

Major The Honourable John Sackville Richard Tufton, D.S.O., 3rd Battalion, Royal Sussex Regiment (Special Reserve)

Legion d'Honneur
Croix de Guerre

200172 Company Sergeant-Major Sydney Arthur Constable, 4th Battalion, Royal Sussex Regiment (Territorial Force) (West Hoathly)

Tuesday October 21st 1919

Military Intelligence

Lieutenant Albert Brooke, M.M. Royal Sussex Regiment, who has retired, taking a gratuity, was a non-commissioned officer of nearly five years' service when the war opened in 1914. He got his commission for service in the field last year and prior to that had been mentioned in dispatches and awarded the Military Medal for gallantry.

Captain P.F. Drew, M.C. who has relinquished his temporary commission in the Royal Sussex Regiment, was a service battalion officer. He won the Military Cross in the fighting of 1917. (mentioned in dispatches).

Thursday October 23rd 1919

Local Honours

A supplement to the *"London Gazette"* published last night, gives a list of the recipients of the Military Medal awarded for bravery in the field in France and Flanders :-

Bar to M.M.

No. G/1746 Sgt. Ernest E. Etherington, M.M., 8th Bn. (Petersfield)

M.M.

No. 444517 Sgt. Frederick J. Snashall, 1/1st Sussex Yeomanry, (Brighton)

Tuesday October 28th 1919

Sussex Men Buried in France

Private H.J. Hook, who served in the Royal Naval Division and the 14th Fusiliers during the war, arrived home on leave from France at Brighton yesterday, his home being at 14, Southampton Street. Private Hook says that the bodies of several Sussex men have now been found, and have been interred with military honours.

Private H.R. Haywood No. 18005 Sergeant G.E. Bevan, D.C.M., No. 1849 Private P. Tolly, No. 10850 Private A.J. Blackman, No. 25306 Private T.H. Chapple, No. 1287 and Private A.V. Ward, No. 11964, are buried at Brie Cemetery, near Peronne. All belonged to the 2nd Battalion of the County Regiment, the following men of the 13th Battalion rest in hero's graves at Fins, near Nurlu : Corporal H.C.C. Ward, No. 17550, Private N. Privett, No. 16473, Lance-Corporal F. Penfolds, No. 16308, Private F. Green, No. 47766, Lance-Corporal A. Odell, No. 15640, Corporal J. Lee, No. 6617, Private B. Johnson, No. 14488, Lance-Corporal C. Fisher, No. 2037.

Friday November 7th 1919

"Good Old 74th"

This was the motto prominently displayed at Hove Town hall, yesterday evening, at the reunion dinner of the Sussex Yeomanry Old Comrades Association, and it reflected the spirit of camaraderie that invested the gathering. The Regiment has, of course, a war record to be proud of. With the 74th Division it was at Gallipoli, and subsequently saw service in Egypt, Palestine and France. Appropriately enough, the reunion was held on the anniversary of the battle of Sheria, Palestine, 6th November, 1917, in which the regiment took a leading part, and among those present yesterday evening were members who had travelled from Wales, Manchester , and various other parts of the country.
A presentation was made to former members by Major-General Girdwood, C.B., C.M.G. General Girdwood presented R.S.M. Balcombe, with the Distinguished Conduct Medal, remarking that it was won at Sheria (Palestine) for conduct in any other war would have gained the Victoria Cross.

To 2nd Lieutenant (formerly Sergeant) S. Hoad, the General presented him with the Military medal, saying he was the man responsible for the capture of a trench at Sheria, and that the thanks of the whole Brigade were due to him because it was the crux of the whole position. After his officers had been killed and men had fallen all around him he went gallantly on, and at the finish only 15 men were left out of the attacking platoon, yet they took 170 prisoners.

General Girdwood, also pinned on the breast of Pte. E. Tattershall, a Distinguished Conduct Medal, and in doing so said his Brigadier, General Kennedy had frequently spoken to him of his gallant conduct on the Somme in carrying dispatches under the heaviest rifle and shell fire.

All the recipients were loudly cheered and carried shoulder high to their seats after being decorated.

Territorial Decoration

The Territorial Decoration has been conferred on:-

Lieutenant-Colonel George S. Whitfeld, Sussex Yeomanry,
Major The Hon. Weetman H..M. Pearson, Sussex Yeomanry,

Tuesday November 11th 1919

Sussex Casualty

The latest War Office list of officer casualties contains that of Captain St. C.C. Tayler, M.C., Royal Sussex Regiment, attached R.F.C. who is shown as previously missing, now reported dead.

"London Gazette" Wednesday November 26th 1919

Decorations conferred by His Highness The Sultan of Egypt

Order of the Nile 4th Class

Captain (T/Mjr.) Geoffrey William Ridley, O.B.E. 4th Bn.(T.F.)

Wednesday November 26th 1919

From the supplement to the *"London Gazette"*, Decorations conferred by the President of the French Republic, the Croix de Guerre has been awarded to the following officer and men of the Royal Sussex Regiment :-

Lt. Reginald Henry Fortescue, M.C. 3rd Bn.

He distinguished himself by a tested bravery and his leadership qualities near Beugneux on 29th July, 1918. Lieutenant Fortescue, after the other officers had all been eliminated from the action, took command of two companies, and reformed them under concentrated artillery fire. By his skill, devotion to duty, and the skilful intelligence of his command, he made a considerable contribution to the success of the attack.

No. L/8212 Sgt. Frederick Clements, 2nd Bn. (Brighton)
No. 201812 Sgt. Albert Edward Field, 4th Bn. (T.A.) (Ticehurst)

Friday December 5th 1919

Gallant Men's Deeds

With reference to the announcement of the undermentioned awards which have already appeared in the *"London Gazette"*, the following are the acts of gallantry for which the awards were made. Many of them, it will be noticed, refer to Royal Sussex men :-

D.C.M.

No. S/2159 Pte. W.H. Boulter, 2nd Bn. (Hastings)

For most gallant conduct in the attack on the enemy positions on 24th September, 1918, north of Gricourt. He was No. 1 of a Lewis-gun team. When the enemy counter-attacked, he rushed forward alone into the open, go his gun into action, and inflicted many casualties on the enemy. his prompt action and utter disregard of danger undoubtedly helped save the situation at a very critical time.
No. S/2187 Pte. E.W. Burke, 2nd Bn. (Liverpool)

For marked gallantry and devotion to duty in the attack on Pontru on 18th September, 1918. He was a platoon runner, and though wounded, he refused to leave his platoon. In getting a message to one platoon he had to cross 200 yards of ground swept by very heavy machine-gun fire. Later part of his company had to withdraw slightly, he went forward 150 yards under machine-gun fire and carried a wounded man back to the unit. Throughout he behaved splendidly.

No. G/4728 Pte. (L/Cpl.) F. Child, 2nd Bn. (Pulborough)

For most conspicuous gallantry in the attack on enemy positions north of Gricourt on the 24th September, 1918. His platoon was held up by an enemy post on the flank. He immediately worked forward alone, killed several of the enemy, and forced the remainder to surrender.

His splendid action saved this critical situation, and throughout, his courage, cheerfulness, and ability to lead his platoon were most noticeable.

No. 320294 Sgt. W.O. Collis, 16th Bn. (Henfield)

For conspicuous gallantry and devotion to duty on 13th October, 1918, in the outpost line east of Quinquebus, when the enemy, under cover of a heavy barrage, succeeded in getting within bombing distance of his party. Although he was wounded in the leg, he directed the fire of his men with great success until everyone of them was a casualty. He continued firing himself until he was again wounded in the foot and thigh. His leadership and courage resulted in the enemy having to withdraw without being able to secure an identification. He has repeatedly given proof of his courage and initiative.

No. G/1406 Pte. F.B. Evenden, M.M., 2nd Bn. (Waldron)

For most conspicuous gallantry and determination during the attack on Pontru on 18th September, 1918. When the company was held up by machine-gun fire he went forward and with rifle grenades put the gun out of action. Later he led a raid on a trench and captured several machine-guns, and also greatly assisted the officer in repelling a counter-attack which was threatening a flank before the company had re-organised. His assistance in re-organisation was most invaluable. He set a splendid example of courage to all ranks.

No. G/3755 Pte. H. Godden, 2nd Bn. (Eastbourne)

For most conspicuous gallantry and devotion to duty in the attack on Pontru on 18th September, 1918. When his company was held up by enemy machine-gun fire he rushed forward and bombed and captured the machine-gun, thus making the way clear for the company to advance. During a halt in the advance for re-organisation he went forward through the protective barrage and obtained most valuable information. He set a splendid example of courage to all.

No. G/3833 Pte. (L/Cpl.) E. Highgate, M.M., 7th Bn. (Manning's Heath)

For marked gallantry and devotion to duty near Epehy on the 18th September, 1918. During the attack, five officers and a large number of men of the battalion were lying wounded in the open in full view of the enemy machine-gun nests 150 yards distance. This stretcher-bearer went out under sniping fire, and, unaided, bound up a large number of wounded of his company. He then in the space of one hour made seven journeys across this ground. The same evening he went out and succeeded in locating the bodies of three officers and thirty other ranks killed that morning. Throughout, his contempt for danger was splendid.

No. G/14813 Pte. (L/Cpl.) S.R. Manthorpe, 2nd Bn. (Norwich)

For most marked gallantry and good work in the attack on Pontru on the 18th September, 1918. When the platoon came under a very heavy machine-gun fire, he dashed forward through a gap in the wire, called on his section to follow, and jumped the trench and forced several enemy to surrender. When the enemy attempted to rush the trench from the rear, he told off some men to deal with there, and himself bombed his way up the trench, capturing three machine-guns and over twenty enemy. He showed splendid courage and determination.

No. L/10507 Corporal (A/Sgt.) A.J. Spurling, 2nd Bn. (Bethnal Green)

During the attack on the enemy positions north of Gricourt on 24th September, 1918, he was in command of a platoon which did good work. After reaching the final objective all the officers of the company became casualties, also many of the men. He organised the remainder of the company in advanced defensive positions. He remained in command of the company outposts for four days. His courage, determination and ability to command were most marked.

No. L/10462 Pte. ((L/Cpl.) A. Stoner, 2nd Bn. (Climping)

For most conspicuous courage and determination. During the attack on Pontru on the 18th September, 1918, he was in charge of a section which did excellent work. While capturing the enemy's trench he led his section in an bombing attack up the trench and cleared it of all the enemy, defeated a small local counter-attack, and then rushed a strongpoint, capturing ten prisoners. His fine action greatly assisted the advance of the remainder of the company.

No. G/3147 Sgt. C.F. West, 7th Bn. (Arundel)

For most conspicuous gallantry near Epehy on 18th September, 1918. When the battalion was held up and driven back during the morning, when his platoon was held up by machine-gun fire, he with a section rushed the post, captured the gun and killed the team. During re-organisation he rendered valuable assistance to his platoon officer. Throughout he set a fine example to his men.

"London Gazette" Tuesday December 9th 1919

The KING has been graciously pleased to give orders for the following promotions in and appointments to the Most Excellent Order of the British Empire, in recognition of valuable services rendered in connection with Military Operations in France and Flanders. To be dated 3rd June, 1919:-

M.B.E. (Military Division)

Q/M. & Capt. Alfred Eastick, 3rd Bn., Royal Sussex Regiment,

Wednesday December 10th 1919

M.C.

T/2nd Lt. William George Frederick Pearson, 8th Bn. Royal Sussex Regiment,

On 4th November, 1918, at Preux, he showed conspicuous gallantry and devotion to duty whilst employed in the repair of forward rods in the face of heavy machine-gun fire. He made the necessary reconnaissance of the road and the road was pushed forward and finally completed, under very difficult conditions.

Friday December 12th 1919

M.C.

Lt. (A/Capt.) Francis Locke Paddon, 4th Bn. Royal Sussex Regiment,

Saturday December 13th 1919

Gallant Deeds

With reference to the awards conferred as announced in the *"London Gazette"*, dated 2nd April last, the following are the statements of service for which the decorations were conferred :-

D.S.O.

Major and Bt. Lt.-Col. Gerrard Evelyn Leachman, C.I.E., 1st Bn. Royal Sussex Regiment, attd. Political Department (Mesopotamia).

For conspicuous gallantry and devotion to duty at Huwaish on 28th October, 1918, and again at Qaiyarah on 30th October, 1918. He displayed marked courage in personally reconnoitring in his own unarmoured car, under heavy fire, ground over which the heavier armoured cars could not move. He then returned to guide them to the attack. The success attained by these cars during the operations was largely due to his intimate knowledge of the country and fearless leading over trackless desert.

Bar to M.C.

Lt. (A/Capt.) Thomas Edward Chad, M.C., 2nd Bn.

During the operation of forcing the passage of the canal at the lock, two miles south of Catillon, on 4th November, 1918, he did conspicuous work under shell fire hurriedly getting the bridges man-handled by men of the assaulting troops on the spot, thus greatly assisting in getting the passage over the Canal effected. He has previously rendered valuable service.

(M.C. gazetted 1st January, 1917).

Lieutenant (A/Major) Albert Garnet Thomas, M.C., South Staffs. Regiment, attd. 5th Bn. Royal Sussex Regiment, (T.F.) (Italy)

For conspicuous gallantry and devotion to duty during the advance into enemy Austria between 1st/3rd November, 1918, particularly pushing forward supplies and tools to the troops under the most difficult circumstances regardless of enemy shell and machine-gun fire.
(M.C. gazetted 1st January 1917)

M.C.

Captain Eric John Burrows, 5th Bn. Manchester Regiment., (T.F.) attd. 9th Bn. Royal Sussex Regiment,

For marked gallantry and good leadership of his company in the attack on Wargnies-le-Grand, on 4th November, 1918. He received orders in the middle of the night to attack at 6 a.m. with his company on a front previously allotted to a whole battalion. He advanced in the leading line, and kept perfect control throughout the attack, dealing with each enemy post in a most able manner. His company captured seven machine-guns (three heavy), sixty prisoners, and three trench mortars.

Lieutenant Herbert Roland Bate, 6th Bn. Manchester Regiment, (T.F.) attd. 9th Bn. Royal Sussex Regiment,

He took over command of his company on the 2nd November, 1918, and led it with great gallantry and judgement throughout the attack on Wargnies-le-Grand on 4th November, 1918. It was due to his fine leadership through heavy enemy barrage that such great success was won.

T/2nd Lt. Sidney John Arthur Bridger, 9th Bn.

For conspicuous gallantry and good work in the attack on Wargnies-le-Grand, on 4th November, 1918. His skilful handling of his platoon resulted in the capture of the station and high ground commanding the main road bridge over the river. To achieve this, severe machine-gun fire had to be overcome, many prisoners captured, and two heavy machine-guns put out of action.

Lt. Arthur Duncan Haigh, 5th Bn. (TF.) (Italy.)

For gallantry and untiring energy during the advance into Austria, between the 1st/3rd November, 1918. He set a fine example when personally superintending the repair of the only forward road by his company, and rapidly pushed on this vitally important work with complete disregard of enemy shell fire.

2nd Lt. John Palmer Isaac, 4th Bn. (T.F.) attd. 2nd Bn.

During the operation of forcing the passage of the canal at the lock, two miles south of Catillon, on 4th November, 1918, he was seriously wounded in the arm before crossing the canal. Nevertheless, he continued to command his company, and led them forward to the first objective about a mile east of the canal, where he was ordered by the commanding officer to go to the dressing station. He showed great courage and determination.

T/Lt. Ernest John Douglas Points, 8th Bn.

On the 4th November, 1918, during the fighting at de Hecq, he was in charge of a platoon whose duty it was to make good the route to de Hecq, for the passage of guns and to remove obstacles. He went forward under enemy shelling with the advanced infantry and removed three mines which would have probably caused considerable damage. He also rendered great assistance to the guns by his skilful handling of a movable bridge.

Tuesday December 16th 1919

Military Intelligence

According to the Army List, the Royal Sussex Regiment, now consists of the 1st and 2nd (line) Battalions, the Depot, 3rd Special Reserve Battalion, the 4th, 5th, 6th, and 16th Territorial Battalions, and the 17th Service Battalion. The remainder of the other Battalions created during the war have disappeared.

Thursday December 18th 1919

Sussex Soldiers Decorated

The following decorations and medals have been conferred by the President of the French Republic :-

Croix de Guerre

T/Lieutenant Arthur Baker Cragg, 2nd Bn. Royal Sussex Regiment,

Medaille Militaire

No. L/8212 Sgt. Frederick Clements, M.M., 2nd Bn. Royal Sussex Regiment, (Brighton)

Friday January 1st 1920

The King has been graciously pleased to bestow the Order of the Companion of the Bath, Military Division to :-

C.B.

Colonel William Lushington Osborn, D.S.O.   Royal Sussex Regiment,

Monday January 5th 1920

North Russia

Rewards for Sussex Men

The King has approved of the following awards for bravery and valuable service with the British Forces in North Russia :-

M.S.M.

No. SD/241 R.Q.M.S. Norton Stevenson,   11th Bn. (Eastbourne)
No. SD/472 C.S.M. William John Stone, M.M.   11th Bn. (Abingdon)
No. G/25395 Pte. (A/Sgt.) J. Costa,   11th Bn. (Bayswater)

Serbia

M.I.D.

Lieutenant J.L. Von Der Heyde, M.C. (attd. 5th Bn. Manchester Regiment,)

Monday January 12th 1920

Award of the D.C.M.

The award of the Distinguished Conduct Medal for gallantry in the field has been bestowed upon :-

No. 315488 Corporal G. Aris, 16th Bn. (Eastbourne)

For most conspicuous gallantry, initiative and devotion to duty at Quennemont Farm on 2nd September, 1918. In a hand to hand encounter this non-commissioned officer accounted for ten of the enemy with the bayonet He also, through heavy rife and machine-gun fire, brought information back from the attacking line during the day. Though temporarily blinded in one eye he went forward again with messages for the front line, which by this time was practically surrounded.

No. L/7922 Corporal E.J. Brown, M.M. 2nd Bn. (Hammersmith)

During the operation of forcing the passage of the canal south of Vatillon, on 4th November, 1918, the bridge carrying crews and storming party became disorganised. He helped to rally the men under heavy shell fire, and also helped the sappers to get the bridge laid. He has shown consistent gallantry.

No. G/21770 Private W. Fordham, 16th Bn. (Whittlesea)

For most conspicuous gallantry and initiative at Quennemont Farm on 21st October, 1918. When his company had attacked the forward Hindenburg line he went forward alone across the open, which was being swept by the heaviest enemy artillery and motor-gun fire, to help in a wounded non-commissioned officer. Having succeeded in this he went out a second time to effect a rescue, and only returned on finding that the man was too seriously wounded to be moved.

No. G/899 Lance-Sergeant W. Pelling, 9th Bn. (Itchingfield)

For most conspicuous gallantry in the attack on Wargnies le Petit on 4th November, 1918. When the attack was held up by heavy machine-gun fire, he manoeuvred his Lewis gun into an exposed position, during which operation three of his section was killed. He alone maintained the position for five hours under very heavy fire, giving covering fire to a company coming up on his right.

No. 14822 Private (A/Cpl.) G.C. Sears, M.M. 2nd Bn. (Forest Gate)

During the forcing of the passage of the canal south of Catillon, on 4th November, 1918, he was the first man across the canal. He then rushed an enemy machine-gun post and shot three of the team, capturing the gun, with an officer and three men. Later, he advanced with four men against a defending house and captured a complete regimental staff.

No. 320069 Lance-Sergeant E. Sparkes, 16th Bn. (Bognor)

For conspicuous gallantry and powers of command. At Quennemont Farm, 21st September, 1918, all officers and senior non-commissioned officers of his company having become casualties, he took charge of the remnants of the company. He re-organised the withdrawal of his men under very heavy artillery, machine-gun and rifle fire, being himself the last of the company to leave the position. Throughout the operation he did splendid work.

No. 2152 Private F. Weedon, M.M., 2nd Bn. (Arundel)

During the forcing of the Canal south of Cattilion on 4th November, 1918, when the bridge carrying parties and storming parties had become disorganised owing to shelling, he rushed forward and displayed the greatest gallantry by standing on the top of the Lock Bank under heavy fire and firing about fifteen or twenty rounds at the enemy on the opposite side until he was wounds.

"London Gazette" **Monday January 12th 1920**

M.I.D.

(France)

Q/M. & Capt. G.W. Flint   4th Bn. Royal Sussex Regiment.

(Egypt)

Capt. P.S. Barlow, 5th Bn. att. 7th Field Survey Coy. R.E.
Capt. E.R. Campbell, 4th Bn.
No. 220099 Pte. (A/Sgt.)J. Piggott, 1/4th Bn.

"London Gazette" **Tuesday January 13th 1920**

The KING has been graciously pleased to confer the Territorial .Decoration upon the undermentioned officers, who have been duly recommended for the same under the terms of the Royal Warrant dated 17th August, 1908, as modified by the Royal Warrant dated 11th November, 1918: —

Maj. Sidney W. P. Beale. 4th Bn. Royal Sussex Regiment,
Maj. Charles R. B. Godman 4th Bn. Royal Sussex Regiment,

"London Gazette" **Wednesday January 14th 1920**

The KING has been graciously pleased to give orders for the following promotion in, and appointments to the Most Excellent Order of the British Empire, for valuable services rendered in connection with military operations in Siberia. Dated 3rd June, 1919: —

C.B.E. (Military Division)

Maj. (T/Lt-Col.) John Meredith Hulton, D.S.O.
R. Suss. R.

M.I.D. (Siberia)

No. 240691 A/L /Sgt. A. E . Ide,   4th Bn. R. Suss. R.

Saturday January 17th 1920

Afghanistan

Gallantry in India

Sussex Soldiers Decorated
The following awards have been made for gallantry and devotion to duty in the field with the British Forces in India :-

M.C.

2nd Lieutenant William John Hook, 1st Bn.

On 18th and 19th July, 1919, he on three occasions took out small parties to shift snipers. During the attack on Orange Patch Ridge, when some of the enemy penetrated his wire he showed great coolness and ability to command.

M.M.

No. L/8913 Cpl. (L/Sgt.) W. Gannon, 1st Bn. (Hastings)

"Orange Patch Ridge" In this action he was of the greatest assistance to his Company Commander. In the final assault he led the first half of the company and when the men were somewhat shaken as a result of passing through a heavy enfilade fire he steadied them and led them on. He made complete arrangements for consolidation of his position and showed judgement and coolness.

No. L/8674 Cpl. A. Oakley, 1st Bn. (Glasgow)

This N.C.O. was conspicuous for his courage and the manner in which he assisted his picquet commander in controlling fire and in observing the movements of the enemy. This N.C.O. also volunteered to out with his picquet commander and a small party on three occasions to clear out snipers.

No. G/20853 Pte. (L/Cpl.) J. Hughes, 1st Bn. (Wrexham)

The following is an extract of a letter received, General Sir A.A. Barrett, Commanding N.W.F.F. to G.O.C. 2nd Division, "I congratulate the men of the Royal Sussex on their gallant defence of their posts when largely outnumbered by the enemy. The change of name of Orange Patch to Sussex Ridge is approved.

The G.O.C. 2nd Division in forwarding this letter states :

"I desire to add my congratulations to those of the Force Commander to the garrisons of the Furthest Point (Sussex Ridge) and Barley Hill on the manner in which the defence of these posts was conducted and especially compliments the 1st Battalion The Royal Sussex Regiment on their continued success at Sussex Ridge."

Thursday January 22nd 1920

SIBERIA

M.S.M.

No. 240148 Sgt. G.T. Hopper, 4th Bn. Royal Sussex Regiment,

"London Gazette" Friday January 30th 1920

The KING has been graciously pleased to give orders for the following appointments to the Most Excellent Order of the British Empire, on the recommendation of the General Officer Commanding-in-Chief, Allied Forces, in recognition of valuable services rendered in connection with Military Operations in Archangel, North Russia. Dated 11th November, 1919 : —

O.B.E. (Military Division)

Maj. (T./Lt.-Col.) John Sheldon Woodruffe, D.S.O. Royal Sussex Regiment,

The KING has been graciously pleased to give orders for the following promotion in and appointments to the Most Excellent Order of the British Empire, on the recommendation of the General Officer Commanding-in-Chief, Allied Forces, in recognition of valuable services rendered in connection with military operations in Murmansk, North Russia.

Dated 11th November, 1919: —

O.B.E. (Military Division)

Maj. (T./Lt.-Col.) Albion Ernest Andrews, Hampshire Regiment att. Royal Sussex Regiment,

"London Gazette" Tuesday February 3rd 1920

The KING has been graciously pleased to give orders for the following appointments to the Most Excellent Order of the British Empire, on the recommendation of the Government of India, in recognition of valuable services rendered in connection with Military Operations in Bushire. Dated 3rd June, 1919: —

O.B.E. (Military Division)

Lt. Anderson Kirkwood Tennent, 2/6th Bn., Royal Sussex Regiment,

The names of the undermentioned have been brought to the notice of the Secretary of State for War by General H. S., Lord Rawlinson, G.C.B., G.C.V.O., K.C,M.G., A.D.C., Gen. General Officer

Commanding-in-Chief, Allied Forces, North Russia, for valuable and distinguished services rendered in connection with the operations in North Russia during the period 25th March to 26th September, 1919.

Dated 11th November, 1919:—

M.I.D.

ARCHANGEL

No. 290575 C.S.M. H. Martin, 4th Bn. Royal Sussex Regiment (T.F.).

The names of the undermentioned have been brought to the notice of the Secretary of State for War by General H. S., Lord Rawlinson, G.C.B., G.C.V.O., K.C.M.G., A.D.C., Gen., General Officer Commanding-in-Chief, Allied Forces, North Russia, for valuable and distinguished services rendered in connection with the Operations in North Russia during the period 1st March to 12th October, 1919. Dated 11th November, 1919:—

M.I.D.

MURMANSK

T/Capt. G. Salter, M.C., 11th Bn., Royal Sussex Regiment
T/Capt. E. L. Weale, M.C., 12th Bn., Royal Sussex Regiment
G/36737 Pte. (A./Sgt.) C. A. Bond , 11th Royal Sussex Regiment
SD/342 Cpl. George Page, 11th Bn. Royal Sussex Regiment
SD/94 Cpl. Herbert Page, 11th Bn., Royal Sussex Regiment
207625 Pte. (A./Sgt.) W. H. Reeks, 11th Bn.., Royal Sussex regiment
136709 Sgt. F. Scales, M.M., 11th Bn., Royal Sussex regiment
15240 L/Cpl. (A./.Sgt.) H. Scarff , 11th Bn. Royal Sussex Regiment
SD/546 Q.M.S. Arthur Stubbs, 11th Bn., Royal Sussex Regiment

His Majesty the King has been graciously pleased to approve of the award of the Military Medal to the undermentioned Warrant Officers, Non-Commissioned Officers and Men for bravery in the field, whose services have been brought to notice in accordance with the terms of Army Order 193 of 1919. To be dated 5th May 1919, unless otherwise stated:-

M.M.

No. T/203075 Pte. Charles Buss, 13th Bn. (Rye)

Thursday February 5th 1920

Sussex Soldiers Rewarded

The following awards have been granted for services in North Russia,

O.B.E. (Military Division)

Major (T/Lt.-Col.) John Sheldon Woodruffe, D.S.O., Royal Sussex Regiment,

Brought to the notice of Secretary of State for War

Gilmore, T/Captain (A/Major) G.H., D.S.O.,M.C.,
Salter, T/Captain E., 11th Bn.
Sparks, T/Captain E., 11th Bn.
Weale T/Capt. E.L. M.C. 12th Bn.
Woodruffe, Major (T/Lt.-Col.) J.S., D.S.O.
Bond, No. G/36737 Private (A/Sgt.) C.A., 11th Bn.
Martin, No. 290575 C.S.M. H., 4th Bn. (T.F.)
Page, No. SD/342 Corporal G., 11th Bn.
Page, No. SD/94 Corporal H., 11th Bn.
Reeks, No. 207625 Private (A/Sgt.) W.H., 11th Bn.
Scales, No. 136709 Sergeant F., M.M., 11th Bn.
Scarff, No. 15240 Lance-Corporal (A/Sgt.) H., 11th Bn.
Stubbs, No. SD/546 Q.M.S. A., 11th Bn.

Brought to the notice for Services with the British Forces in Persia

O.B.E. (Military Division)

Lieutenant (T/Mjr.) Albion Kirkwood Tennent, 2/6th Bn. Royal Sussex Regiment (T.F.)

Thursday February 26th 1920

It is officially announced in the *"London Gazette"* that the following are the acts of gallantry for which honours have been conferred on the following, France and Flanders being the war areas in which the awards were earned unless stated :-

D.C.M.

No. SD/3861 Corporal (L/Sgt.) C.H. Leppard, M.M. 7th Bn. Royal Sussex Regiment, (East Grinstead)

For conspicuous gallantry on the morning of 24th October, 1918. An attacking platoon of another battalion suffered heavily before they had gone 50 yards. Under very heavy machine-gun fire he went backwards and forwards, bringing in three badly wounded men, probably saving their lives, as no stretcher-bearers were available.

Saturday March 13th 1920

Gallant Deeds officially recorded

It is officially announced in the *"London Gazette"* that the following are the acts of gallantry for which honours have been conferred on the following, France and Flanders being the war areas in which the awards were earned unless stated :-

D.C.M.

No. G/3291 Corporal D.G. Boast, 9th Bn. Royal Sussex Regiment, (Brighton)

For conspicuous gallantry and devotion to duty as a runner during the operations around Cambrai from the 5th to 10th October, 1918. His work in maintaining communication with companies and Brigade Headquarters, and the way in which the runners under him were inspired by his example, contributed largely to the success of the operations.

No. 200131 C.S.M. Henry Catt, 4th Bn. Royal Sussex Regiment, (T.F.) (Steyning)

He has served with the battalion continuously throughout the war - Gallipoli, Palestine and France - and his work has always been admirable. He has set a fine example of efficiency and discipline in the line and out of it, and his coolness in action has on all occasions been remarkable.

No. 200088 Sergeant S. Cluer, 4th Bn. Royal Sussex Regiment, (T.F.) (Bognor)

He has served with the battalion throughout the war - Gallipoli, Palestine and France. His very cool in action, and as sergeant in command of stretcher-bearers has displayed marked courage and devotion to duty, particularly at Soissons, 1918.

No. SD/3081 Corporal George H. Coles, 13th Bn. Royal Sussex Regiment, (Haselmere)

During the advance across Kemmel and the Wytschaete Ridges, he commanded a section of guns after his officer had been killed. He rendered valuable support to a battalion in the taking of a crater. He has always displayed great courage and resource, which has undoubtedly inspired his comrades in action.

No. 315371 Corporal C.B. Crane, 16th Bn. Royal Sussex Regiment, (Benges, Herts.)

For conspicuous gallantry and devotion to duty. During an enemy raid on an isolated post near Wavrin, on 13th October, 1918, he was of great value to his platoon commander at a critical time. Although badly wounded he refused to leave his post until the enemy was repulsed. He has several times shown great skill in leading patrols.

No. 30111 Sergeant E. Bennett, 17th Bn. Royal Sussex Regiment, (Clacton-on Sea)

On the morning of 1st October, 1918, during the attack east of Laventi, he showed conspicuous gallantry and daring. He was in charge of a Stokes mortar and team, which had been called upon to engage an enemy machine-gun, which was holding up the advance. His gun not only silenced the machine-gun, but caused the crew to desert and leave the gun to be captured.

No. 320496 Sergeant A. Lusted, 16th Bn. Royal Sussex Regiment, (Hailsham)

For gallantry and devotion to duty, both in the outpost line at Sinjil-Palestine and in France. Especially so in front of Merville in July, 1918, he by his daring leadership brought about excellent results, including valuable information most helpful to the advance of the battalion.

No. 3302 C.S.M.(A/R.S.M.) J. McClymont 9th Bn. Royal Sussex Regiment, (Kirkcolm)

He has taken part in nearly all the engagements, and has on all occasions shown great coolness, energy and resource. As a Company Sergeant-Major during the last year he has proved himself very efficient and trustworthy, obtaining a very fine discipline in his company.

No. 320311 Private E. Tattershall, 16th Bn. Royal Sussex Regiment, (Brighton)

For gallant work as runner throughout the period covered by this despatch in Gallipoli and Palestine. On several occasions his has displayed great gallantry under fire by volunteering to go out, and link up broken telephone wires during bombardment.

No. 320506 Sergeant (A/C.S.M.) J.W. Thompson, 16th Bn. Royal Sussex Regiment, (Leytonstone)

He has always rendered most valuable service, in particular at the commencement of the advances at Richebourg l'Avoue, on 1st October, 1918. He was at all times quite untiring in his efforts and utterly regardless of personal safety.

No. G/1680 Private (A/Cpl.) F. Turnbull, 2nd Bn. Royal Sussex Regiment, (Brighton)

During the severe fighting of October, when in the operations east of Mazingheim, he displayed great gallantry, observing from a most advanced position the progress of the attack.

Supplement to the *"London Gazette"* Monday March 15th 1920

India Office
15th March, 1920
The following despatch from His Excellency the Commander-in-Chief in India regarding the operations against Afghanistan has been received from the Government of India: —

Army Headquarters, India,
Simla, the 1st November, 1919

FROM

HIS EXCELLENCY GENERAL SIR CHARLES CARMICHAEL MONRO,
G.C.B., G.C.S.I., G.C.M.G., A.D.C.
Commander-in-Chief- in India.
To

THE SECRETARY TO THE GOVERNMENT OF INDIA,
ARMY DEPARTMENT

Sir,
I have the honour to submit herewith, for the information of the Government of India, an account of the recent operations against Afghanistan.

OPERATION'S OF THE WAZIRISTAN FORCE.

48. On the 13th of July piqueting troops from Dakka experienced considerable opposition in taking up a position on the hills in the direction of Ghuzgai. The tribesmen were in strength and, offering favourable targets to our gun fire, suffered severely. In spite of the armistice conditions, Afghan officials were everywhere busy endeavouring to incite the tribesmen to rise. This culminated on the 16th July in a large gathering in the Bazar valley, estimated to be 10,000 strong. On the 18th, Ali Masjid was threatened and attacks were made on piquets in the Khaibar, one of which was rushed after stubborn resistance. The following night determined but unsuccessful attacks were made on the piquet line from Ali Masjid to Shagai, and as a result of the losses he had suffered in this fighting the enemy retired into the Bazar, valley, where he was bombed by aeroplanes and finally dispersed on the 19th. The General Officer Commanding, 2nd Division, brings to special notice the 1st Battalion, Royal Sussex Regiment, for their capture of a ridge to the south of Ali Masjiod on the 16th May, and for their defence of the same ridge on this occasion, as well as for consistently good work. On the early morning of the 22nd July a drive was carried out by a force of all arms of the 2nd Division across the Kajuri plain, by which gangs of Afridis harbouring in the plain were driven into the hills. On the 23rd a small action against a tribal gathering west of Dakka resulted in considerable enemy casualties. During the month of July the strength of the Mohmand lashkars at Hazarnao and Busawal varied in strength, but rose at one time to as many as 6,000 men. After a flying bridge across the Kabul river to Lalpura had been established, the sniping of Dakka camp practically ceased.

"London Gazette" Monday March 22nd 1920

The KING has been graciously pleased to confer the Territorial Decoration upon the undermentioned officers who have been duly recommended for the same under the terms of the Royal Warrant dated 17th August, 1908, as modified by the Royal Warrant dated 11th November, 1918: —

Captain Edwin P. Dawes (retired) 5th Bn. Royal Sussex Regiment,

Supplement to *"London Gazette"* Wednesday April 6th 1920

(3) *Offensive to cut of Dvina Force*
(25th January 5th April, 1919.)

This took the form of heavy attacks against Tarasevo, Shred Mekrenga and Morjegorskaya. Our forces were forced to evacuate Tarasevo, but the enemy suffered heavy defeats at Shred Mekrenga and Morjegorskaya. Actions at these places were successful owing to the personal bravery and power of leadership of Major G. H. Gilmore, D.S.O., M.C., and Lieut.-Colonel J. W. Carroll, C.M.G.,D.S.O. respectively. On several occasions the position was critical at both places, and it was solely due to the energy of these officers that our whole line had not to be withdrawn, which would have meant the collapse of the Dvina Force.

Thursday April 14th 1920

It is officially announced in the *"London Gazette"*, that the award of the Distinguished Conduct Medal is conferred on C.S.M. G. Manvell, of the Royal Sussex Regiment. The Citation reads as follows :-

No. 200004 C.S.M. (A/R.S.M.) G. Manvell, 4th Bn. Royal Sussex Regiment, (Brighton)

For gallantry and devotion to duty throughout the war. On all occasions he has shown great coolness under fire, and by his personal example has inspired all ranks. His services were particularly outstanding near Soissons on the 29th July, 1918, when he assisted in controlling the advance under heavy shell fire until himself was wounded.

Friday May 16th 1920

Meritorious Service Medal

A Meritorious Service Medal has been awarded to:-

No. L/12448 Pte. (A/Cpl.) A.E. Funnell, 3rd Bn. Royal Sussex Regiment,

Wednesday June 11th 1920

M.I.D.

T/Capt. George Henry Gilmore, D.S.O.,M.C. (Archangel)

"London Gazette" Tuesday July 13th 1920

The KING has been graciously pleased to confer the Territorial Decoration upon the undermentioned Officers, who have been duly recommended for the same under the terms of the Royal Warrant dated 17th August, 1908, as modified by the Royal Warrant dated 11th November, 1918: —

 Maj. William H. Gorringe, 4th Bn. Royal Sussex Regiment,

"London Gazette" Monday July 28th 1919

The following despatch from His Excellency the Commander-in-Chief in India on the part taken by India, including the Indian States, in the prosecution of the war, has been received from the Government of India: —
Army Headquarters, India.

Dated Delhi, 13th March, 1919.

From the Commander-in-Chief in India,
To the Secretary to the Government of India,
Army Department.

SIR,
In continuation of my despatch dated 20th August 1918, I have the honour to submit the following brief review of the part played by India, including the Native States, in the prosecution of the war:

55. In previous despatches I have expressed my gratitude, in the name of the Army in India, to the thousands of loyal and devoted workers who have contributed in various spheres of activity to the prosecution of the war, and now that the war has been brought to a successful conclusion, I cannot do more than reiterate that expression of thanks. The various departments of the Government of India, the heads and members of Provincial Governments, the Ruling Chiefs, Railway Administrations, Chambers of Commerce, Port Trusts and Municipalities, the Mercantile Marine, the numerous associations for the relief of distress and the care of the sick and wounded,—work in which the ladies of India have played a leading part,—the great nonofficial and commercial communities, and a host of individual workers,—one and all have laboured with conspicuous devotion. Last, and perhaps most important of all, I desire to express the great debt which, the Empire owes to the troops themselves, British and Indian, combatant and non-combatant, who have contributed so largely, often with their lives, to the attainment of the common end. A list of those whose services have been of particular value and whose assistance; and work I desire to bring specially to notice forms the subject of Appendix I of this despatch. I have the honour to be,

SIR,
Your obedient Servant,
C. C. MONRO, *General,*
Commander-in-Chief in India

"London Gazette" Tuesday August 3rd 1920

The King has been graciously pleased to approve of the undermentioned reward on the recommendation of the Government of India, for Distinguished Service in the Field in the Afghan War 1919. To be dated 1st January, 1920:-

M.C.

 Captain William Holderness, 1st Battalion, The Royal Sussex Regiment,

 Lieutenant-Colonel Frank William Frederick Johnson, D.S.O., 2/6th Battalion, The Royal Sussex Regiment.

 Lieutenant Reginald Francis Platt Orme, 1st Bn. Royal Sussex Regiment,

The names of the undermentioned Officers, Ladies, Warrant Officers, Non-commissioned Officers, Men and others have been brought to notice for distinguished service during the operations against Afghanistan by General Sir C.C. Monro, G.C.B., G.C.S.I., G.C.M.G., in his despatch, dated 1st November, 1919 (published, in the Supplement of the London Gazette dated 15th March, 1920) : —

1st Battalion, The Royal Sussex Regiment

Captain (acting Major) C. C. Malden
No. L/8913 Lance-Sergeant W. Gannon
No. 20853 Lance-Corporal J. Hughes
No. 8674 Corporal A. Oakley
No. 8840 Sergeant P. Pulling
No. 8581 Private H. Ruff
No. 9184 Sergeant L. Wood

No. L/8581 Pte. H.W. Ruff,   1st Bn.

Displayed great coolness and was most successful with his bombing, was also one of the party who volunteered to go out and clear off the snipers.

No. L/9184 Sgt. L. Wood,   1st Bn.

This N.C.O. was a splendid example to the remainder in the manner in which he used his rifle on snipers and showed marked ability and coolness in observation and control of fire, and throughout the whole action showed an absolute disregard to danger.

6th Battalion, The Royal Sussex Regiment.

No. 265492 Sergeant W. Knight
No. 21598 Private B. Middleditch

Supply and Transport Corps

No. 9310 Lance-Corporal (acting Sergeant) G. Upperton, 1st Battalion, The Royal Sussex Regiment (attached).

"London Gazette" Friday September 3rd 1920

His Majesty the KING has been graciously pleased to approve of the award of the Meritorious Service Medal to the undermentioned Warrant Officers, Non-commissioned Officers and Men in recognition of valuable services rendered in India in connection, with the War. Dated 3rd June, 1919 : —

M.S.M. (India)

No. L/8070 R.S.M. Steer, J S. 1st Bn. (Chichester).
No. L/9340 Coy./S.M. Barfoot, W. H. J., 1st Bn. (Elsted).
No. L/10325 Col.-Sgt. Gardner, A. 1st Bn. (Clapham Junction).
No. 2651663 Sgt. .(A./C/S.M.) Whinnett, A. 2/6th Bn. (Brixton)..
No. G/6466 Pte. Brooks, J. W. H., 1st Bn. (Brighton).
No. L/12909 Pte. (A./L./Sgt.) Lawley, W. F. 2/6th Bn. (Fulham).
No. 265717 Pte. (A./Sgt.) Singleton, J. S. 2/6th Bn. (Hull).
No. 266069 Pte. Wallis, W. H. 2/6th Bn. (Rotherhithe)

"London Gazette" Thursday September 30th 1920

The following are among the Decorations and Medals awarded by the Allied Powers at various dates to the British Forces for distinguished services rendered during the course of the campaign: —

His Majesty the King has given unrestricted permission in all cases to wear the Decorations and Medals in question.

DECORATIONS CONFERRED BY
THE PRESIDENT OF THE FRENCH REPUBLIC

Palmes Academie
Officier

Temporary Lieutenant Alec Francis Hervey, Royal Sussex Regiment.

"London Gazette" Tuesday October 12th 1920

The KING has been graciously pleased to confer the Territorial Decoration upon the undermentioned Officers, who have been duly recommended for the same under the terms of the Royal Warrant dated 17th August, 1908, as modified by the Royal Warrant dated 11th November, 1918: —

Lt.-Col. Barnard Thornton Hodgson, C.M.G.,V.D. 4th Bn. Royal Sussex Regiment,

"London Gazette" Friday October 15th 1920

The KING has been graciously pleased, on the occasion of the visit of His Royal Highness the Prince of Wales to Australia and New Zealand, to make the following promotions in and appointments to the Royal Victorian Order: —
To be dated 21st May, 1920

R.V.O. (Fourth Class)

Lieutenant-Colonel James Lewis Sleeman, C.B.E., Royal Sussex Regiment, Director of Military Training, Wellington.

"London Gazette" Wednesday October 20th 1920

His Majesty the KING has been graciously pleased to approve of the award of the Meritorious Service Medal to the undermentioned Warrant Officers, Non-Commissioned Officers and Men in recognition of valuable services rendered in India in connection with the War: —
(To be dated 3rd June, 1919)

M.S.M.

No. 8593 C.S.M. H. Bradford, 1st Bn. Royal Sussex Regiment (Eastbourne)

The Following White Russian awards 1918-1920 were not Gazetted

Order of St. Vladimir 4th Class with Swords

Major John Sheldon Woodruffe, O.B.E. Royal Sussex Regiment,
T/Capt. George Henry Gilmore, D.S.O., M.C. Royal Sussex Regiment,

Order of St. Anne 2nd Class with Swords

T/Capt. George Henry Gilmore, D.S.O., M.C. Royal Sussex Regiment,

Order of St. Anne 2nd Class

Brevet Lt-Col. Stanley de Vere Alexander Julius,

Medal of Zeal St. Stanilaus Ribbon

No. G/36877 Pte. (L/Cpl.) Walter Wood, 11th Bn. Royal Sussex Regiment,

The Soldier

If I should die, think only this of me :
That there's some corner of a foreign field
That is forever England. There shall be
In that rich earth a richer dust concealed,
A dust whom England bore, shaped, made aware,
Gave, once, her flowers to love, her ways to roam,
A body of England's, breathing English air,
Washed by the rivers, blest by the suns of home.

And think, this heart, all evil shed away,
A pulse in the eternal mind, no less,
Gives somewhere back the thought by England given,
Her sights and sounds; dreams happy as her day,
And laughter, learnt of friends ; and gentleness,
In hearts at peace, under an English heaven.

Victoria Cross Winners

Carter Nelson Victor C.S.M.	2th Bn.
Johnson Dudley Graham Lt-Col. D.S.O.,M.C.	2nd Bn.
McNair Eric Archibald Capt.	9th Bn.
McNeill John Carstairs Lt-Col.	107th Regt. of Foot

Victoria Cross Winners Who Died

Nelson Victor Carter V.C. Company Sergeant-Major SD/4 12th Bn. Friday 30th June 1916
Royal Irish Rifles Graveyard, Lavente, Pas de Calais, France
Grave Reference VI. C. 17.

Harry Wells V.C. Sergeant L/8088 2nd Bn. Saturday 25th September 1915
Dud Corner Cemetery, Loos, Pas de Calais, France
Grave Reference V. E. 2.

Eric Archibald McNair V.C. Captain 9th Bn. Monday 12th August 1918
Staglieno Cemetery, Genoa, Italy
Grave Reference I. B. 32.

K.C.B.

Fletcher *Sir* Henry Colonel Bart. V.D.	2nd V.B.
McNeill John Carstairs Mjr.-Gen. V.C.,C.B.,K.C.M.G.	

K.C.M.G.

McNeill John Carstairs Col. V.C.,C.B.,C.M.G.

C.B.

Donne Benjamin Doniethorpe Alsop Lt-Col.	1st Bn.
McNeill John Carstairs Lt-Col. V.C.,C.M.G.	
Vandeleur John Ormsby Colonel	1st Bn.
Wroughton John Bartholomew Bt. Colonel (T/Brig-General) C.M.G	2nd Bn.
Young James Charles Maj-Gen. (Colonel of the Regiment)	

C.M.G.

Bond Charles Earbery Mjr. D.S.O.	1st Bn.
Finlayson Robert A. Mjr. Kimberley Regiment	
Glasgow Alfred Edgar Mjr. & Bt.-Col. (T/Brig-General) D.S.O.	8th Bn.
Hodgson Barnard Thornton Lt-Col. V.D;T.D.	4th Bn.
Langham Frederick George Lt-Col. V.D.	5th Bn.
McNeill John Carstairs Lt-Col. V.C.	
Morphett George Charles Mjr. & Bt. Lt-Col.	7th Bn.
Osborn William Lushington Mjr. & Bt. Lt-Co. (T/Brig.) D.S.O.	7th Bn.
Panton John Gerald Lt-Col.& Bt. Col.	2nd Bn.
Somerville John Arthur Coghill Lt-Col.	
Villiers Evelyn Fontaine Mjr. (T/Lt-Col.) D.S.O.	1st Bn. Posted 2nd Bn.
Walker Bertram James T/Lt-Col.	2nd Bn.
Wroughton John Bartholomew Bt. Col. (T/Brig.) C.B.	2nd Bn.

C.I.E.

Leachman Gerrard Evelyn Mjr. & Bt. Lt-Col.	1st Bn.
Mackenzie Edward Leslie Lt-Col. D.S.O.	1st Bn.
Porter William Ninnis (Civilian)	

C.B.E.

Gilbert Arthur Robert Col. D.S.O.	1st Bn.
Turner Montague Trevor Capt. (T/Mjr.) M.C.	2nd Bn.
Sleeman James Lewis Mjr.	attd. N.Z. Forces
Hulton John Meredith Maj. (T/Lt-Col.) D.S.O.	4th Bn.

D.S.O.

Andrews S.A. T/Lt. (A/Capt.) M.C. & Bar	attd. 8th Bn. E/Surrey Rgt.	C	
Baddeley W.H. Lt-Col. M.C. & Bar	1st Bn.	C	B/H
Bellamy R. Lt.	3rd Bn. attd. M.G.C.	C	N/Y
Bidder H.F. Mjr. (T/Lt-Col.) Cmdg. 1st Bn. M.G.C.	7th Bn.	C	N/Y
Birkett R.M. Mjr. (T/Lt-Col.)	1st Bn.		N/Y
Bond C.E. Mjr. (T/Brig.) C.M.G.,D.S.O.	2nd Bn.		N/Y
Cameron J.S. Mjr.	4th Bn.		N/Y
Campion W.R. T/Lt-Col. T.D.		C	N/Y
Cassels F. Mjr.			N/Y
Clark P.L. T/2nd Lt. (A/Capt.)			N/Y
Coote-Brown W.C. T/Lt-Col.			N/Y
Cory E.J.D'A. Capt.	1st C.P.R.		B/H
Dick R.N. Lt-Col. (T/Brig-Gen.)	1st Bn.		B/H
Dodge J.B. T/Mjr. Lt-Col. Suffolk Regimen	attd. 16th Bn..		B/H
Foster T. T/Mjr.	9th Bn		B/H
Gilbert A.R Lt-Col. C.B.E.	1st Bn.		B/H
Gilmore G.H. T/Capt. (A/Mjr.) M.C. & Bar	8th Bn. attd. 2/10th R. Scots		B/H
Glasgow A.E. Mjr. (T/Lt-Col.)	8th Bn.	C	B/H
Green E.W.B. Lt-Col.	2nd Bn.		N/Y
Gwynne R.V. T/Mjr.	S/Yeo. Attd. R.W. Surreys.	C	
Harrison G.H. Lt-Col. Border Regiment	Cmdg. 11th Bn.	C	N/Y
Hill M.V.B. T/Lt-Col. M.C. 5th Bn. Royal Fusiliers & Bar	attd. 9th Bn.		B/H
Hulton J.M. Mjr. (A/Lt-Col.)	4th Bn.		N/Y
Impey G.H. Cpt. (T/Lt-Col.) & Bar	7th Bn.	C	N/Y
Johnson D.G. Lt-Col. V.C. D.S.O. M.C. S.W.B.	attd. 2nd Bn. Bar	C	N/Y
Johnson F.W.F. Lt-Col.	6th Bn.	C	B/H
Johnson H.H. Capt. (T/Mjr.)	6th Bn. & Tank Corps		B/H
Kay Robinson H.T. T/Mjr. (A/Lt-Col.) & 2 Bars	12th Bn. attd. 13th Bn.	C/C/C	N/Y
Lamotte L. Capt. (A/Lt-Col.)	2nd Bn. attd.2nd Bn. Y.L.I.	C	
Leachman G.E. Mjr. & Bt. Lt-Col. C.I.E.	Political Dept. (Mesopotamia)	C	
Mackenzie E.L. Lt-Col. D.S.O.,K.C.I.E.	1st Bn.	C	
MacRoberts N de Putron T/Lt (A/Capt.) M.C.	13th Bn.	C	
Millward W.C. T/Mjr. (Lt-Col.)	11th Bn.		B/H
Morphett G.C. Mjr	7th Bn.	C	
Osborn W.L. Mjr. (T/Lt-Col.)	7th Bn.		B/H
Powell-Edwards H.I.G. Mjr. (T/Lt-Col.)	16th Bn.		N/Y
Preston E.H. Bart. Capt. & Bt. Mjr. M.C.	2nd Bn.	C	N/Y
Roberts H. Lt. (A/Capt.) M.C.	2nd Bn.		N/Y
Rothschild G.F. T/Mjr. M.C.	13th Bn. attd. 2/10th Lon. Rgt.		B/H
Sayer A.C. Mjr. M.C.	16th Bn.		N/Y
Sayer H. Capt. M.C.	S/Yeo	C	N/Y
Sunderland M.S.J. Lt-Col.	2nd Bn.		N/Y
Terry R.J.A. Mjr. M.V.O.	2nd Bn.	C	B/H
Thomson A.L. Capt. (A/Lt-Col.)	Cmdg. 7th Bn.		N/Y
Tufton J.S.R. Mjr. The Hon.	3rd Bn.	C	N/Y
Villiers E.F. Mjr. (T/Lt-Col.) C.M.G.,D.S.O.	1st Bn. posted 2nd Bn.		N/Y
Waithman R.H. Mjr. (A/Lt-Col.)	2nd Bn.		B/H
Walker B.J. Capt. (T/Major)	8th Bn.		N/Y
Willet F.W.B. Mjr.	2nd Bn.	C	N/Y
Woodruffe J.S. Mjr. (T/Lt-Col.)	2nd Bn.		N/Y

Distinguished Service Order Winners Who Died

Hugh Thomas Kay Robinson D.S.O. & 2 Bars Lt-Colonel 12th Bn. attd. 13th Bn. Friday 26th April 1918
Tyne Cot Memorial, Zonnebeke, West-Vlaanderen, Belgium
Grave Reference Panel 86 to 88

Robert Joseph Atkinson Terry D.S.O.,M.V.O. Lt-Colonel 2nd Infantry Brigade R.S.R. Friday 1st October 1915
Noeux-Les-Mines Communal Cemetery, Pas de Calais, France
Grave Reference I. K. 14.

O.B.E.

Boyd Arthur Hamilton Capt. Rev. M.C.,M.A.	4th Bn.
Clarke Joseph Edward Q/M & Capt.	5th Bn.
de Chair George Herbert Blackett Capt. & Bt. Mjr.	2nd Bn.
Gilpin George. Q/M & Mjr.	1st Bn.
Hynes Brian Mansfield Lt-Col. Commanding	1/25 L.R.
Jellicorse Harold Mjr.	11th Bn.
Joscelyne Frederic Percy T/Capt.(A/Mjr.) M.C. R.A.M.C.	2nd Bn.
Lytton The Hon. Neville Stephen Mjr.	13th Bn.
Makalua Mathew James Manuia T/Mjr.	13th Bn.
McKergow Robert Wilson Lt-Col.	S/Yeo.
Nicholl Frederick Alan Benson Capt.	3rd Bn.
Plews Harry Q/M/ & Hon. Lt.	5th Bn.
Ridley Geoffrey W. Capt.	4th Bn.
Russell William Sydney Kemp Capt.	4th Bn.
Anderson Kirkwood Tennent Lt.	2/6th Bn.
Wilberforce Arthur Roland George Capt.	
Woodruffe John Sheldon Mjr. (T/Lt-Col.) D.S.O.	2nd Bn.

M.V.O.

Leachman Gerrard Evelyn Mjr. & Bt. Lt-Col.	1st Bn.
Mackenzie Edward Leslie Lt-Col. D.S.O.	
Porter William Ninnis (Civilian)	

M.V.O. Winner Who Died

Robert Joseph Atkinson Terry D.S.O.,M.V.O. Lt-Colonel 2nd Infantry Brigade R.S.R. Friday 1st October 1915
Noeux-Les-Mines Communal Cemetery, Pas de Calais, France
Grave Reference I. K. 14.

D.S.C.

Dodge John Bigelow Lt. R.N.V.R. (later Suffolk Regt. attd. 16th Bn. Royal Sussex Regiment)

M.B.E.

Andrews Albion Ernest Mjr. (T/Lt-Col. Hamp. Regt. attd.	
Bean Robert Charles Lt. (A/Capt.)	S/Yeo.
Dicker Arthur Seymour Hamilton Capt.	3rd Bn.
Eastwick Alfred Q/M & Capt.	3rd Bn.
Mackay James Eugene Lt.	S/Yeo.
Musgrave Francis Peete Lt. (T/Capt.)	
Rose Thomas Wheatley Lt. M.C.	5th Bn.
Sandeman William Wellington Capt.	
Strachan Charles John Lt. (T/Capt.)	
Travers Sydney Stanley Joe Lt.	
Twine Frank Percival Lt. (T/Capt.)	5th Bn.

Military Cross Winners

Name	Unit	Bar	Notes
Allen C.A. T/2nd Lt.	11th Bn.		Citation
Allen C.A. T/Lt. (A/Capt.)	11th Bn.	Bar	Citation
Ambler G. T/2nd Lt.	7th Bn. attd. 12th Bn.		Citation
Amon H. T/2nd Lt.	11th Bn.		Citation
Amon H. T/2nd Lt. (A/Capt.)	11th Bn.	Bar	Citation
Andrews S.A. T/2nd Lt. D.S.O.	12th Bn.		Citation
Andrews S.A. T/2nd Lt. D.S.O;M.C.	12th Bn.	Bar	Citation
Apperley W.H.W. Capt.	2nd Bn.		Citation
Baddeley W.H. T/Capt. D.S.O.	8th Bn.		Citation
Baddeley W.H. T/Capt. D.S.O.,M.C.	8th Bn.	Bar	Citation
Baker D.M. Mjr.	2nd Bn.		Citation
Baker E.A. 2nd Lt. (T/Capt.)	2nd Bn.		B/H
Ball H.J. C.S.M. (A/R.S.M.) No. 382	11th Bn.		Citation
Ballard C.W. T/Lt.	7th. Bn.		Citation
Bannell G. 2nd Lt.	8th Bn.		B/H
Barnes H.C. T/Lt.	2nd Bn. T.M.Bty.		Citation
Bartlett C. T/Lt.	13th Bn.		Citation
Bate H.R. Lt. 6th Bn. Manchester Regiment	attd. 9th Bn.		Citation
Batten P.W. 2nd Lt. (T/Lt. A/Capt.)	5th Bn.		Citation
Bennett W.H.P. T/2nd Lt.	13th Bn.		Citation
Best A.F. T/Capt.			B/H
Blakeney H.E.H. Lt. (T/Capt.)	2nd Bn.		N/Y
Blaker C. T/Lt.	2nd Bn.		N/Y
Bloomfield J. R.S.M. No. S/516	8th Bn.		N/Y
Blunden E.C. T/2nd Lt.	11th Bn.		Citation
Blunt H.E. Capt.	16th Bn.		Citation
Bolton C.O. T/Lt.	12th Bn.		Citation
Bowlby H.S. T/Capt.	7th Bn.		Citation
Boyd A.M. Rev. O.B.E. M.A.	4th Bn.		N/C
Boyes R.J. T/2nd Lt.	8th Bn.		Citation
Bradley J.R. T/2nd Lt. (A/Capt.)	12th Bn. attd. 7th Bn.		Citation
Branson V.C. T/Lt.	13th Bn.		Citation
Bridger S.J.A. T/Lt.	9th Bn.		Citation
Broughall H.S. T/2nd Lt.	7th Bn.		Citation
Brown A.J. 2nd Lt. (T/Capt.) & R.F.C.	6th Bn.		Citation
Brown A.V. T/2nd Lt.	4th Bn.		Citation
Buck S.T. T/Capt.	8th Bn.		N/Y
Burdett S.L. Lt.	7th Bn.		Citation
Burrows E.J. Capt. 5th Bn. Manchester Regiment	attd. 9th Bn.		Citation
Butcher B.N. C.S.M. D.C.M. No. 8881	2nd Bn.		Citation
Campbell G.O.L. 2nd Lt.	3rd Bn.		Citation
Cartland J. Capt. 8th Bn. R. Warks. Regiment	attd. 17th Bn.		B/H
Cassels J.S. T/2nd Lt.	11th Bn.		Citation
Cassy J.S. T/Capt.			Citation
Cater W.H. T/2nd Lt.	8th Bn.		Citation
Chad T.E. Lt. (A/Capt.)	2nd Bn.		N/Y
Chad T.E. Lt. (A/Capt.) M.C.	2nd Bn.	Bar	Citation
Chittenden H.F. 2nd Lt.			N/Y
Clark B.H.C. Lt.	3rd Bn. attd. 7th Bn.		Citation
Clarke T. 2nd Lt.	7th Bn.		Citation
Clements E. 2nd Lt.	2nd Bn.		Citation
Clements R.F. T/2nd Lt.	7th Bn.		Citation
Cockrell F.P. T/Capt.			N/Y
Cole A.H. T/2nd Lt.			Citation
Cole-Hamilton C. Rev. T/Capt. (Forces)	16th Bn.		B/H
Coleman H.C. Capt.	9th Bn.		N/Y
Collingbourne A.W. T/Capt.	9th Bn.		N/Y
Constable G.S. Capt.	4th Bn.		Citation
Cooper R.G. Lt.	3rd Bn.		Citation
Cornes L.G. T/2nd Lt.			Citation
Couldrey V.H. T/Lt.	13th Bn.		Citation
Courthope G.L. T/Mjr. M.P. T.D.	5th Bn.		B/H
Coxhead H.J. Capt.			B/H
Coxhead L.G. 2nd Lt.	7th Bn.		N/Y
Cuthbertson W.R.D. Capt.	16th Bn.		Citation
Cutler E.C. T/2nd Lt.	7th Bn.		Citation
Danells B. Lt. (A/Capt.) Sussex Yeomanry attd. 7th M.G.C.	S/Yeo & M.G.C.		B/H
Dashwood V.E.C. Lt.	2nd Bn.		N/Y
Davidson J.A. 2nd Lt.	4th Bn.		Citation
Dear F.H. 2nd Lt.	4th Bn.		Citation
de Chair G.B.H. Lt.	2nd Bn.		N/Y
de Jong K. Mjr.			N/Y

Name	Battalion	Bar	Award
Dibdin F.J.S. Lt. attd. 2nd Bn. Welsh Regiment	2nd Bn.		Citation
Dibdin F.J.S. Lt. M.C. attd. 2nd Bn. Welsh Regiment	2nd Bn.	Bar	Citation
Dolleymore E. Lt. (A/Capt.)	6th Bn. attd. 2nd Bn.		Citation
Done W.E.P. Lt. (A/Capt.)	5th Bn.		N/Y
Downes W.D. Capt. & Nigeria Regt.			N/Y
Drew P.F. T/Lt. (A/Capt.)			N/Y
Du Moulin F.L. Capt. attd. 1st Bn. E. Yorks.	3rd Bn.		Citation
Dyke J.N. T/2nd Lt.	11th Bn.		N/Y
Ellen W.P. T/Lt.	8th Bn.		B/H
Ellis E.S. Lt.	13th Bn.		Citation
Ellis V.R.H. T/2nd Lt.	11th Bn.		Citation
Evans S.G. Capt.			N/Y
Farrow H.J.R. T/Lt.	7th Bn.		Citation
Fazan E.A.E. Capt. R.A.M.C.	attd. 5th Bn.		N/Y
Fazan E.A.E. Capt. M.C. R.A.M.C.	attd. 5th Bn.	Bar	Citation
Feuchelle E.A. T/2nd Lt.			Citation
Fenton F.H. Lt.	4th Bn.		Citation
Fortescue R.H. Lt.	3rd Bn. attd. 4th Bn.		Citation
Foster A.D. T/Lt.	8th Bn.		Citation
Foy W.A. Lt.	1/4th Bn.		Citation
Fraser R. 2nd Lt.			Citation
Gammon K.W. T/2nd Lt.	11th Bn.		Citation
Gilmore G.H. T/Lt.	8th Bn.		B/H
Gilmore T.H. T/Capt.	8th Bn.	Bar	Citation
Goad C.E. T/Capt.	9th Bn.		Citation
Godwin E.T.H. T/Lt.			Citation
Gorringe E.C. T/Capt.	7th Bn.		Citation
Grant F.N. Capt.	5th Bn.		B/H
Haddon T.R. T/2nd Lt.	12th Bn.		Citation
Haigh A.D. Lt.	5th Bn.		Citation
Hall R.C. T/2nd Lt.	8th Bn.		Citation
Hall R.C. T/Lt.	8th Bn.	Bar	Citation
Hampton N.H. T/Capt. & Adjt.	8th Bn.		N/Y
Hancock J.D.G. Lt.			Citation
Harden E.J. T/2nd Lt. (A/Capt.)	13th Bn.		Citation
Hardy W.C. Capt.			Citation
Hemsley E.J. T/2nd Lt. attd. Royal West Surreys	12th Bn.		Citation
Hillier H. Capt. Gloucesters	attd. R.S.R.		B/H
Hind R.C.D. T/Capt.	7th Bn.		N/Y
Hobbs E.J. Lt.	2nd Bn.		N/Y
Hobbs E.J. 2nd Lt. S/Yeo	16th Bn.		Citation
Holdsworth M.J. Lt.	4th Bn.		B/H
Hook W.J. 2nd/Lt.	1st Bn.		Citation
Horsecroft S. T/2nd Lt.			Citation
Howard W.F. Lt.	16th Bn.		Citation
Howe R.M. Lt. (A/Capt.)	3rd Bn. attd. 7th Bn.		Citation
Hudson L.W. T2nd Lt.	13th Bn.		Citation
Hudson R. 2nd Lt.	3rd Bn.		Citation
Hume A.D. T/2nd Lt. (A/Capt.) attd. Royal Fusiliers	2nd Bn.		Citation
Hume A.D. T/2nd Lt. (A/Capt.) M.C. attd. Royal Fusiliers	2nd Bn.	Bar	Citation
Ireland L.A.F. T/Lt.	8th Bn.		N/Y
Isaac J.P. Lt.	4th Bn. attd. 2nd Bn.		Citation
Jaques V.H. Lt.	3rd Bn. attd. 2nd Bn.		Citation
Jaques V.H. Lt. (A/Capt.) M.C.	3rd Bn. attd. 2nd Bn.		Citation
Jebb R.D. Capt.	4th Bn.		N/Y
Johnson D.G. Lt-Col. V.C; D.S.O. South Wales Borderers.	Cmdg. 2nd Bn.		N/Y
Jones G.H. Lt.			B/H
Jones H.E. T/Lt.	13th Bn.		Citation
Jones T.A. Qmr. & Capt. D.C.M.	2nd Bn.		B/H
Joscelyne F.P. T/Capt. R.A.M.C.	attd. 2nd Bn.		Citation
Joy J. C.S.M. No. 8630	7th Bn.		Citation
Keen H.M. Lt. (A/Capt.) Sussex Yeomanry	attd. Roy. Warks.		B/H
Kelly T. T/2nd Lt.	attd. 1st Hamp. Regt.		Citation
Kemp G.L. T/Capt.	8th Bn.		B/H
Kirkby S.A.H. 2nd Lt.	2nd Bn.		Citation
Knight C.H. T/Lt. (A/Capt.)	9th Bn.		B/H
Knox A.C.W. T/Capt. R.A.M.C.	attd. 2nd Bn.		N/Y
Knox A.C.W. Capt. M.C. R.A.M.C.	attd. 2nd Bn.	Bar	Citation
Lane L.W. Lt.	2nd Bn.		Citation
Langham J.E.C. Lt. (T/Capt.)	5th Bn. attd. 8th Bn.		N/Y
Lascelles F.W. Capt.	16th Bn.		Citation
Lavering P.W. Lt.	3rd Bn. attd. 4th		Citation
Lawrence C.H. T/2nd Lt.			Citation
L'Estrange H.H. Lt.			Citation

Name	Unit	Bar	Notes
Le Hardy W.H.C. Capt.	7th Bn.		Citation
Leavens F.C. C.S.M. No. S/327			N/Y
Lewis H.S. Lt.	11th Bn.		Citation
Lewis H.S. T/Capt. M.C.	11th Bn.	Bar	Citation
Lockett W. Lt. 7th Bn. Cheshire Regiment	attd. 16th Bn.		Citation
Lothiem S. T/2nd Lt.	7th Bn.		Citation
Lott H.C. T/Capt.	3rd Bn. attd. 4th Bn.		N/Y
Lovering P.W. Lt. M.C.	4th Bn.		06/02/19
Lucas A. T/2nd Lt.	16th Bn.		Citation
Lundgren C.W. Lt. (T/Mjr.) Sussex Yeomanry	attd. 2/4th Y & Lancs.		Citation
Lupton R.H. T/Capt.	17th Bn.		Citation
MacRoberts N. de Putron Lt. D.S.O.	13th Bn.		Citation
MacRoberts N. de Putron Lt. D.S.O. M.C.	13th Bn.	Bar	Citation
McCracken N. T/2nd Lt.	7th Bn.		Citation
Mann J. T/2nd Lt.	9th Bn.		Citation
Marshall L. Capt. West Yorks.	attd. R.S.R.		B/H
Marsland J. T/Lt.	8th Bn.		Citation
Mason C.S. T/Lt.	2nd Bn.		Citation
Mason J.I. Lt. (A/Capt.)	2nd Bn.		B/H
Mason J.I. Lt. (A/Capt.) M.C.	2nd Bn.	Bar	Citation
Mason R.B. T/Lt.	4th Bn.		Citation
May D.W.G. T/2nd Lt.	9th Bn.		Citation
May D.W.G. T/2nd Lt. M.C	9th Bn.		Citation
Maycock G.L. T/Lt.	11th Bn.		B/H
Middleton R.C.G. Capt.	4th Bn.		N/Y
Mitchell C.L. T/2nd Lt.	11th Bn.		Citation
Moody L.L. T/2nd Lt.	12th Bn.		Citation
Moore L.D. T/Lt.	8th Bn.		Citation
Morrison W.T. 2nd Lt.			Citation
Mount H.C. Lt. Attd. M.G.C.			Citation
Mountford G.B. 2nd Lt.	attd. K.R.R.C.		Citation
Nagle G. T/2nd Lt.	7th Bn.		Citation
Newton C.V. Lt. (A/Capt.)	9th Bn		Citation
Nickalls M. Capt. S/Yeo.	16th Bn.		N/Y
Norton W.C. T/Capt.	9th Bn.		B/H
Orme R.F.P. Lt.	1st Bn.		N/C
Osborne G.F. Lt. (T/Mjr.)	7th Bn.		Citation
Osmaston R.S. 2nd Lt. & 23d Squadron. R.F.C.	3rd Bn. attd. 2nd Bn.		Citation
Paddon F.L. Lt. (A/Capt.)	4th Bn.		N/C
Paget J.O. T/Capt.			B/H
Pannett J. T/2nd Lt.	2nd Bn.		Citation
Pearson W.G.F. T/2nd Lt.	8th Bn.		Citation
Peel F.C. T/2nd Lt.	4th Bn.		Citation
Peskett J.C. T/Lt.	4th Bn.		Citation
Peskett J.C. A/Capt. M.C.	4th Bn.	Bar	Citation
Points E.J.D. T/2nd Lt.	8th Bn.		Citation
Powell-Edwards W.G.H. Capt.	16th Bn.		Citation
Preston E.H. Capt. D.S.O.	2nd Bn.		B/H
Prince G.W. 2nd Lt.	7th Bn.		Citation
Pring R.J. Lt. attd. 2/4th Bn. Royal Fusiliers	4th Bn.		Citation
Pullinger V.B. T.2nd Lt.			Citation
Rangecroft H.Q. T/Lt. attd. 1st Bn. Lancs. Fusiliers			B/H
Rangecroft H.Q. T/Lt. M.C. attd. 1st Bn. Lancs. Fus.		Bar	Citation
Ratcliff W.P. T/Lt.			Citation
Reckitt G.L. T/Capt.	7th Bn.		Citation
Reckitt G.L. T/Capt. M.C.	7th Bn.	Bar	Citation
Reid S.K. Capt.	4th Bn.		Citation
Rewell A.V. T/Capt.	9th Bn.		Citation
Richardson A.W. 2nd Lt.	4th Bn.		Citation
Richardson V. 2nd Lt. attd. King's Royal Rifle Corps.	4th Bn.		Citation
Roberts E.P. 2nd Lt. (T/Lt.) & R.F.C.	2nd Bn.		Citation
Roberts H. 2nd Lt. (A/Capt.)	13th Bn.		B/H
Rose T.W. Lt. M.B.E.	5th Bn.		Citation
Rothschild G.F. T/Capt. D.S.O.	13th Bn.		B/H
Rumsby R.W. T/2nd Lt.	9th Bn.		Citation
Rutter D.C. Lt. (T/Capt.) 43rd Squadron R.F.C.	2nd Bn. attd. 9th Bn.		Citation
Sadler H. 2nd Lt.	7th Bn.		N/Y
Sainton F.C. 2nd Lt. (T/Capt.)	7th Bn.		Citation
Salter G. T/2nd Lt.	2nd Bn.		Citation
Saxon H. T/Capt.	11th Bn.		Citation
Sayer A.C. Mjr. D.S.O.	3rd Bn.		Citation
Sayer H. Capt. D.S.O.	16th Bn.		B/H
Shackel G.M. Capt.	16th Bn.		Citation
Simpson J.G. T/2nd Lt.			Citation
Simpson J.G. T/2nd Lt.			Citation

Skipworth B.W. Lt. attd. 9th Bn. M.G.C.	3rd Bn. att. 9th Bn.		Citation
Somerville H.A. 2nd Lt. & 82nd Squadron R.F.C.	M.G.C.		Citation
Sparks H. T/Capt.	13th Bn.		N/Y
Stace W.A. C.S.M. No. 3461	13th Bn.		Citation
Story H.H. T/2nd Lt.			Citation
Sutton E.G. T/Lt.	13th Bn.		Citation
Tayler St. C.C. 2nd Lt. attd. 80th Squadron R.F.C.	7th Bn.		Citation
Taylor H.F. Lt. (T/Capt.)	7th Bn.		Citation
Thomas A.G. Lt. (A/Mjr.) South Staffs.	attd. 5th Bn.	Bar	Citation
Thomas A.G. Lt. (A/Mjr.) M.C. South Staffs.	attd. 5th Bn.		Citation
Thomas G.F. Capt.	5th Bn.		N/Y
Treacher H.L. T/Lt.	9th Bn.	Bar	Citation
Treacher H.L. T/Lt. M.C.	9th Bn.		N/Y
Turner M.T. Capt.	2nd Bn.		N/Y
Twine F.P. Lt. M.B.E.	5th Bn.		Citation
Uloth A.C.W. Lt.	3rd Bn.		Citation
Vidler A.G.A. T/2nd Lt. (A/Capt.)	2nd Bn.		Citation
Von der Heyde J.L. Lt. attd. Manchester Regt. (Salonika)	2nd Bn.		Citation
Wallington M. Lt. (T/Capt.)			B/H
Wallington M. Lt. (T/Capt.) Bt. Mjr. M.C. 1st Infantry Brigade	4th Bn.		Citation
Walter C.G. 2nd Lt.	16th Bn.		Citation
Warren J.R. Capt.		Bar	Citation
Waugh R. T/2nd Lt.	16th Bn.		Citation
Weale E.L. T/2nd Lt. (A/Capt.)	4th Bn.		Citation
Webber B.J. 2nd Lt. C de G (F)	17th Bn.		Citation
Weekes A.N.H. Capt.	3rd Bn. att. 9th Bn.		Citation
Weeks W.E. T/2nd Lt. (A/Capt.)	13th Bn.		Citation
Welham H.G. 2nd Lt.	13th Bn.		Citation
White H.J. T/2nd Lt.	12th Bn.		Citation
White H.J. T/Lt. M.C.			Citation
White P. C.S.M. (A/R.S.M.) No. 6404	5th Bn.	Bar	N/Y
Whitely C.A.F. T/2nd Lt. attd. R.F.C.	6th Bn.		Citation
Whiteman B. 2nd Lt.	7th Bn.		N/Y
Wilkins C.H. Lt.		Bar	B/H
Williams W.J. Rev. T/Chaplin to the Forces 4th Class	2nd Bn.		N/Y
Winter N. 2nd Lt. (T/Lt.)	2nd Bn.		B/H
Woodrow A.B. T/2nd Lt.	2nd Bn.		Citation
Wright B.C. 2nd Lt.	11th Bn. attd. 7th Bn.		Citation
Wright B.C. Lt. M.C.			Citation
Wright J.A. Lt. M.C.			B/H
Wyatt R.J.P. T/Capt.	1/4th Bn.		B/H
Wyatt R.J.P. T/Capt. M.C.	1/4th Bn.		Citation
Young R.C. T/2nd Lt.			Citation
Young R.P. Lt.			Citation

Military Cross Winners Who Died

Charles Willard Ballard M.C. Captain 7th Bn. Sunday 25th November 1917
Cambrai Memorial, Louverval, Nord, France
Grave Reference Panel 7

Hugh Cyril Barnes M.C. Captain 2nd Bn. T.M.B. R.S.R. Sunday 21st July 1918
Loos Memorial, Pas de Calais, France
Grave Reference Panel 69 to 73

Cyril Bartlett M.C. Major 13th Bn. Wednesday 14th November 1917
Outtersteene Communal Cemetery Extension, Bailleul, Nord, France
Grave Reference II. B. 56.

William Henry Pope Bennett M.C. 2nd Lieutenant 13th Bn. Sunday 3rd March 1918
Thiepval Memorial, Somme, France
Grave Reference Pier and Face 7C

Harold Ernest Blunt Capt. M.C. Sussex Yeomanry Sunday 16th February 1919
Ath Communal Cemetery, Ath, Hainaut, Belgium
Grave Reference B. 17.

Bernard Norris Butcher M.C; D.C.M. C/ Sergeant-Major 6391201 2nd Bn. Tuesday 16th August 1921
Hove Old Cemetery Sussex
Grave Reference E. 18.

Walter Henry Cater M.C. 2nd Lieutenant 8th (Pioneer) Bn. Friday 16th August 1918
St. Sever Cemetery, Rouen, France
Grave Reference B. 5. I

Reginald Francis Clements M.C. Lieutenant 7th Bn. Wednesday 14th August 1918
Morlancourt British Cemetery No. 2, Somme, France
Gave Reference B. 9.

W.D. Downes M.C. Captain R.S.R. at. H.Q. Nigeria Regt. R.W.A.F.F. Thursday 5th August 1920
Kaduna Civil Cemetery, Nigeria
Grave Reference (Not given)

Francis Louis Du Moulin M.C. Lt-Colonel 3rd Bn. att. 1st Bn. East Yorks. Thursday 7th November 1918
Berlaimont Communal Cemetery, Nord, France
Grave Reference (Not given)

Victor Richard Helps Ellis M.C. 2nd Lieutenant 11th Bn. Sunday 28th April 1918
Tyne Cot Cemetery, Zonnebeke, West-Vlaanderen, Belgium
Grave Reference Panels 86 to 88

Alfred David Foster M.C. Captain 8th Bn. Saturday 5th May 1917
St. Martin Calvaire British Cemetery, St. Martin-Sur-Cojeul, Pas de Calais, France
Grave Reference 1. B. 18.

William Archibald Foy M.C. Lieutenant 1/4th Bn. Tuesday 5th November 1917
Beersheba War Cemetery, Israel
Grave Reference G. 75.

Edward Clifton Gorringe M.C. Captain 7th Bn. Thursday 5th September 1918
Peronne Communal Cemetery Extension, STE Radegonde, Somme, France
Grave Reference III. M. 2.

Ferris Nelson Grant M.C;M.I.D. Capt.   5th Bn. Sunday 9th May 1915
Le Touret Memorial
Panel 20 and 21.

Ernest James Hemsley M.C. 2nd Lieutenant 12th Bn. Wednesday 4th September 1918
Grootebeek British Cemetery, Reninghelst, Poperinge, West-Vlaaderen, Belgium
Grave Reference G. 1.

John Marsland M.C. Lieutenant 8th (Pioneer) Bn. Monday 23rd July 1917
Dickebusch New Military Cemetery Extension, Ieper, West-Vlaanderen, Belgium
Grave Reference I. A. 8.

Leonard Leighton Moody M.C. 2nd Lieutenant 12th Bn. Friday 30th June 1916
Loos Memorial, Pas de Calais, France
Grave Reference Panel 69 to 73

Gilbert Nagle M.C. Captain (Adjutant) 7th Bn. Thursday 5th July 1917
Faubourg D'Amiens Cemetery, Arras. Pas de Calais, France
Grave Reference V. J. 2.

Robert Shirley Osmaston M.C. Captain 3rd Bn. attd. 23rd Sqdn. R.F.C. Monday 24th September 1916
Beaval Communal Cemetery, Somme, France
Grave Reference A. 18.

Stuart Keppel Reid M.C. O. of Nile (4th Class) Captain 4th Bn. Monday 29th July 1918
Vauxbuin French National Cemetery, Ainse, France
Grave Reference II. A. 1

Victor Richardson M.C. Lieutenant 4th Bn. Saturday 9th June 1917
Hove Old Cemetery, Sussex
Grave Reference H. A. 56

Donald Campbell Rutter Capt. M.C. 9th Bn. & 43rd Sqdn. R.F.C. Thursday 7th June 1917
Tyne Cot Cemetery, Zonnebeke, West-Vlaanderen, Belgium
Grave Reference LVIII. A. 15.

Francis Charles Sainton M.C. Captain 2nd Bn. Thursday 18th April 1918
Woburn Abbey Cemetery, Cuinchy, Pas de Calais, France
Grave Reference I. G. 23.

Bernard William Skipworth M.C. Lieutenant 3rd Bn. att. 9th Bn. M.G.C. Thursday 25th April 1918
Tyne Cot Memorial, Zonnebeke, West-Vlaanderen, Belgium
Grave Reference Panel 86 to 88

Henry Arthur Somerville M.C. Lieutenant 13th Bn. attd. 82nd Sqdn. R.F.C. Thursday 28th March 1918
Dompierre French National Cemetery, Oise, France
Grave Reference 88

Eric Guy Sutton M.C. Lieutenant 7th Bn. Saturday 8th April 1916
Vermelles British Cemetery, Pas de Calais, France
Grave Reference II. D. 20.

St. Cyprian Churchill Tayler M.C. Captain attd. 80th Sqdn. R.F.C. Sunday 17th March 1918
Arras Flying Services Memorial, Arras, France

Arthur Curtis Wilmot Uloth M.C. Lieutenant 3rd Bn. Thursday 19th September 1918
Doingt Communal Cemetery Extension, Somme, France
Grave Reference I. C. 6.

Arthur Nelson Weekes M.C. Captain "B" Coy. 1/4th Bn. Monday 29th July 1918
Raperie British Cemetery, Villemontorie, Ainse, France
Grave Reference IX. E. 8.

Harry George Welham M.C. Lieutenant 3rd Bn. att. 9th Bn. Monday 4th September 1918
Wargnies-Le-Petit Communal Cemetery, Nord, France
Grave Reference In South-East Part

John (Jack) Armer Wright M.C;M.I.D. Lieutenant 11th Bn. att. 7th Bn. Wednesday 18th September 1918
Epehy Wood Farm Cemetery, Epehy, Somme, France
Grave Reference I. B. 12.

Robert Percival Young M.C. Lieutenant 1/4th Bn. Monday 17th December 1917
Jerusalem War Cemetery. Israel

D.F.C

Candy John Geoffrey Sadler Lt. attd. R.F.C.
Fawssett, Cecil Capt. 6th Bn. Royal Sussex Regiment & R.A.F.

Distinguishes Conduct Medal Winners

Adams A. L/Cpl.	5968	2nd Bn.	Citation
Aris G. Cpl.	315488	16th Bn.	Citation
Aukett W.G. C.S.M. M.M.	SD/2219	12th Bn.	Citation
Bailey A. Pte.	2424	5th Bn.	Citation
Balcombe J. C.S.M.	320001	16th Bn.	Citation
Baldwin A. Cpl.	3603	1st Bn.	Citation
Barnard F. C.S.M.	10145	9th Bn.	Citation
Barnes J.A. L/Cpl.(A/Cpl.)	G/14923	11th Bn.	Citation
Bartlett J. A/C.S.M.	3841	9th Bn.	Citation
Beale A. Pte.	7440	2nd Bn.	Citation
Bennett E. Sgt.	30111	17th Bn.	Citation
Bevan G.E. Pte. (A/Cpl.)	S/1849	2nd Bn.	Citation
Billington H. Pte.	G/6346	11th Bn.	Citation
Bird H.M. C.S.M. (A/R.S.M.)	G/20400	11th Bn.	Citation
Boast D.G. Cpl.	G/3291	9th Bn.	Citation
Bonney L. A/Sgt.Major	5474	9th Bn.	Citation
Boulter W.H. Pte.	S/2159	2nd Bn.	Citation
Britt H. Pte.	G/150	2nd Bn.	Citation
Brown E.J. Cpl. M.M.	7922	2nd Bn.	Citation
Bryant P. Cpl.	200353	4th Bn.	Citation
Budd R. Sgt.	SD/270	11th Bn.	Citation
Budgen W.H. C.Q.M.S.	G/981	7th Bn.	Citation
Burke E.W. Pte.	S/2187	2nd Bn.	Citation
Burt A. Sgt.	G/8542	2nd Bn.	Citation
Bush R. Cpl.	SD/3741	13th Bn.	Citation
Butcher B.N. C.S.M.	8881	2nd Bn.	Citation
Catt H. C.S.M.	200131	4th Bn.	Citation
Cheesman R. Pte.	206	7th Bn.	Citation
Child F. Pte. (L/Cpl.)	G/4728	2nd Bn.	Citation
Clay C.C.P. L/Sgt.	9157	2nd Bn.	Citation
Clift J. Pte.	1166	1st Bn.	Citation
Cluer S.D. Sgt.	200088	4th Bn.	Citation
Coles G.H. Cpl.	SD/3081	13th Bn.	Citation
Coles H.A. T/R.S.M.	L/9010	9th Bn.	Citation
Collis W.O. Sgt.	320294	16th Bn.	Citation
Compton G. Sgt. M.M.	SD/658	11th Bn.	Citation
Constable S.A. Sgt.	200172	4th Bn.	Citation
Coppard A.V. Sgt.	GS/828	2nd Bn.	Citation
Couchman W. Sgt.	L/9107	2nd Bn.	Citation
Cowstick S.E. Pte.	1440	1st Bn.	Citation
Crane C.B. Cpl.	315371	16th Bn.	Citation
Curd A.J. L/Cpl.	G/16014	13th Bn.	Citation
Dadswell F. Pte.	SD/1022	11th Bn.	Citation
Dale E. Pte.	688	1st Bn.	Citation
Dallaway J. C.S.M.	5908	2nd Bn.	Citation
Day J. Pte.	4633	2nd Bn.	Citation
Deeprose C.J. C.S.M.	9117	2nd Bn.	Citation
Dell A.J. L/Cpl.	L/10537	9th Bn.	Citation
Dennett W.C. L/Sgt.	3192	9th Bn.	Citation
Elphick P.G. Sgt.	240048	5th Bn.	Citation
Evenden E. Pte. M.M.	G/1406	2nd Bn.	Citation
Fairhall F.C. Cpl.	10228	13th Bn.	Citation
Finucane A. Sgt.	3762	2nd Bn.	Citation
Fordham W. Pte.	G/21770	16th Bn.	Citation
Fowler C. Cpl. M.M.	SD/2909	13th Bn.	Citation
Gates T. Sgt.		1st Bn.	Citation
Gilbert W.H. Sgt.	240008	13th Bn.	Citation
Gill J. Pte.	3697	1st Bn.	Citation
Gill J. Pte.	914	2nd Bn.	Citation
Godden H. Pte.	G/3757	2nd Bn.	Citation
Golden A.W. Sgt. M.M.	SD/1766	11th Bn.	Citation
Green E.J. Sgt.	SD/874	11th Bn.	Citation
Haines E. A/S/Major P.S.	L/4040	5th Bn.	Citation
Hammond E.A. C.S.M.	SD/2922	13th Bn.	Citation
Harvey A. Pte.	G/4336	11th Bn.	Citation
Head E.J. Sgt.	G/836	7th Bn.	Citation
Head G.F. C.S.M. M.S.M.	G/3359	9th Bn.	Citation

Name	Number	
Hearn R.W. R.Q.M.S.	3952	Citation
Heaseman J. Pte.	2205	Citation
Henham J. Pte.	SD/2446	Citation
Herridge W. C.S.M.	L/7688	Citation
Highgate E. L/Cpl. M.M. & 2 Bars	G/3833	Citation
Hobday G. Cpl.	L/8076	Citation
Hodges G. Sgt.	G/3303	Citation
Hollobone F.W. Sgt.	SD/421	Citation
Hughes W.C. Cpl.	3058	Citation
Humphrey W. C.S.M.	5863	Citation
Johnston H.E. Sgt.	320096	Citation
Jupp M.G. Pte.	3238	Citation
Kenward C.S. Cpl. (A/Sgt.)	1366	Citation
King J. Sgt.	10187	Citation
Langley J. Sgt.	9650	Citation
Leppard C.H. Cpl. (L/Sgt.) M.M.	SD/3861	Citation
Lewry H.A. Sgt.	8151	Citation
Lusted A. Sgt.	320496	Citation
Mallett G.W. Pte.	15256	Citation
Manthorpe S.R. Pte. (L/Cpl.)	G/14183	Citation
Manvell W. C.S.M. (A/R.S.M.)	200004	Citation
Maudling F. Pte.	4591	Citation
Marillier F.C.J. Sgt. (2nd Lt.)	9275	Citation
McClymont J. C.S.M. (A/R.S.M.)	3302	Citation
Moody C.F. Sgt. M.M.	GS/385	Citation
Moore F. L/Cpl.	4256	Citation
Moss E.W. Cpl.	20230	Citation
Mullett M.R. C.S.M.	L/5079	Citation
Neiderauer G. Sgt.	8853	Citation
Neville C. Pte.	4634	Citation
Newnham A.J. Sgt.	G/3590	Citation
Nye A. C/Sgt.	L/3238	Citation
Oatley B.J. A/C.S.M.	SD/537	Citation
Ockleford A. L/Sgt.	5118	Citation
Othen W. L/Sgt.	318	Citation
Oyler A.J. Cpl. (A/Sgt.)	240078	Citation
Page H. A/C.S.M.	600	Citation
Paine C.	1434	Citation
Pelling F.L. Pte.	56078	Citation
Pelling W. A/Sgt.	G/899	Citation
Pepper W.C. L/Sgt.	G/2048	Citation
Pittman C. Q.M.S.		Citation
Prevett R. A/Cpl.	541	Citation
Pyle F. Sgt.	200342	Citation
Rainsford W.F. Sgt./Major	6489	Citation
Ransom F.J. Sgt. M.M.	G/574	Citation
Rawding S. Sgt.	15305	Citation
Roberts H. C.Q.M.S.	766	Citation
Ross P.T. Trpr.	16484	Citation
Russell J. Cpl.	SD/345	Citation
Sanderson J.W. Sgt.	4307	Citation
Sawyer F.G. Cpl. (A/Sgt.)	9815	Citation
Say T.H. Pte.	5792	Citation
Scrase T. L/Cpl.	4297	Citation
Sears G.C. Pte. (A/Cpl.) M.M.	14822	Citation
Short H. L/Cpl.	1052	Citation
Simmons J. C.S.M.	200087	Citation
Sippetts A. L/Sgt.	SD/4159	Citation
Slaughter F. C.Q.M.S.	200036	Citation
Sloan R.H.S. A/Cpl.	10094	Citation
Smethurst W.R. Sgt.	4708	Citation
Smith E.A. L/Cpl.	15007	Citation
Snaith A. Sgt.	2055	Citation
Soughton W. C.S.M.	9013	Citation
Sparkes E. L/Sgt.	320069	Citation
Spicer F.G.J. Sgt.	7946	Citation
Sprunt C. Pte. (L/Cpl.)	SD/593	Citation
Spurling A.J. Cpl. (A/Sgt.)	L/10507	Citation
Startup F. T/Sgt.	7422	Citation
Stevens T.W. Pte.	SD/2235	Citation
Stone B.A. C.S.M.	200023	Citation
Stoner A. Pte. (L/Cpl.)	L/10462	Citation

Name	Number	Battalion		
Tallon F. Pte.	L/6010	2nd Bn.		Citation
Tattershall E. Pte.	320311	16th Bn.		Citation
Thomas C.E. C.S.M.	290873	8th Bn.		Citation
Thompson J.W. A/C.S.M.	320506	16th Bn.		Citation
Thwaits S.M. Sgt./Mjr.		1st Bn.		Citation
Tilling W.S. T/Cpl.	1401	2nd Bn.		Citation
Toney E.E. Cpl.	17832	7th Bn.		Citation
Trevor A.W. Sgt. M.M.	G/1196	7th Bn.		Citation
Trevor A.W. Sgt. D.C.M. M.M.	G/1196	7th Bn.		Citation
Tribe A.A.W. Sgt. M.M.	233460	74th D.Sig. RE		Citation
Trussler E.G.C. Drmr.	3355	9th Bn.		Citation
Turnbull F. Pte. (A/Cpl.)	G/1680	2nd Bn.	Bar	Citation
Tutt J.W. C.S.M. M.M.	G/1958	8th Bn.		Citation
Waghorn O. Pte. (L/Cpl.)	2373	5th Bn.		Citation
Walls W.J. C.S.M. M.M.	L/9905	13th Bn.		Citation
Ward G. Sgt.	424	5th Bn.		Citation
Weal H. T/Sgt.	8396	2nd Bn.		Citation
Webb W. Sgt. (A/C.Q.M.S.)	16925	2nd Bn.		Citation
Weedon P.L. Pte. M.M.	S/2152	2nd Bn.		Citation
Welch G. Cpl.	15987	13th Bn.		Citation
West C.F. Sgt. M.M.	G/3147	7th Bn.		Citation
Westgate A. Sgt.	SD/251	11th Bn.		Citation
Weston A.E. C/Sgt.	2697	1st Bn.		Citation
Weston G. Cpl.	2382	1st Bn.		Citation
Weston G. Pte.	1981	5th Bn.		Citation
White E.J. Cpl.	200318	4th Bn.		Citation
White P. C.S.M.	2003	12th Bn.		Citation
Williams C.O. L/Cpl. (A/Cpl.) M.M.	16259	12th Bn.		Citation
Woodward S.H. Sgt.	SD/2826	13th Bn.		Citation
Woollard H. Sgt.	SD/3049	13th Bn.		Citation
Worley F. Sgt.	SD/555	11th Bn.		Citation
Wright A. Pte.	L/11559	17th Bn.		Citation
Yeomans F.W. L/Cpl.	G/1671	8th Bn.		Citation

Distinguished Conduct Medal Winners Who Died

Frederick Barnard D.C.M. Company Sergeant-Major 10145 9th Bn. Thursday 12th April 1917
Arras Memorial, Pas de Calais, France
Grave Reference Addenda Panel

James Bartlett D.C.M. Company Sergeant-Major 3841 17th Bn. Saturday 26th October 1918
Eastbourne (Ocklynge) Cemetery, Sussex
Grave Reference I. 49.

George Edward Bevan D.C.M. Sergeant S/1849 2nd Bn. Wednesday 18th September 1918
Brie British Cemetery, Somme, France
Grave Reference I. F. 9.

Robert Budd D.C.M. Sergeant SD/270 11th Bn. Sunday 3rd September 1916
Villers-Bretonneux Military Cemetery, Somme, France
Grave Reference IIIA. F. II.

Alexander Burt D.C.M. Sergeant G/8542 2nd Bn. Thursday 14th September 1916
Heilly Station Cemetery, Mericourt-L'Abbe, Somme, France
Grave Reference IV. C. 71

Bernard Norris Butcher M.C; D.C.M. Company Sergeant-Major 6391201 2nd Bn. Tuesday 16th August 1921
Hove Old Cemetery, Sussex
Grave Reference E. 18.

Reginald Cheesman D.C.M;M.M. Private 206 7th Bn. Thursday 5th October 1916
Heilly Station Cemetery, Mericourt-L'Abbe, Somme, France
Grave Reference IV. J. 23.

Guy Compton D.C.M; M.M. 2nd Lieutenant 9th Bn. Thursday 26th July 1917
Ypres (Menin Gate) Memorial, Ieper, West-Vlaanderen, Belgium
Grave Reference Panel 20

Walter Couchman D.C.M. Sergeant L/9107 2nd Bn. Monday 1st May 1916
Maroc British Cemetery, Nord, France
Grave Reference I. A. 16.

Alfred James Dell D.C.M. Lance-Corporal L/10537 9th Bn. Sunday 24th March 1918
Pozieres Memorial, Somme, France
Grave Reference Panel 46 and 47

Frederick Charles Fairhall D.C.M. Sergeant L/10228 7th Bn. Sunday 25th November 1917
Cambrai Memorial, Louverval, Nord, France
Grave Reference Panel 7

James Gill D.C.M. Private GS/SR/914 2nd Bn. Wednesday 17th March 1915
Brown's Road Military Cemetery, Festubert, Pas de Calais, France
Grave Reference IV. B. 4.

Edwin James Green D.C.M. Company Sergeant-Major SD/874 11th Bn. Sunday 21st October 1916
Regina Trench Cemetery, Grandcourt, Somme, France
Grave Reference IX. M. 23.

Alec Harvey D.C.M. Private G/4336 7th Bn. (was 2nd Bn.) Wednesday 18th September 1918
Epehy Wood Farm Cemetery, Epehy, Somme, France
Grave Reference II. B. 17.

William Charles Hughes D.C.M. Sergeant G/3058 9th Bn. Friday August 18th 1916
Thiepval Memorial, Somme, France
Grave Reference Pier and Face 7C

Henry Edward Johnson D.C.M. 2nd Lieutenant 16th Bn. Saturday 16th March 1918
Jerusalem War Cemetery, Israel
Grave Reference O. 43.

James King (Keegan) D.C.M. Sergeant L/10187 7th Bn. Saturday 4th March 1916
Loos Memorial, Pas de Calais, France
Grave Reference Panel 69 to 73

Frederick Charles Jermens Marillier D.C.M. 2nd Lt. 2nd Bn. Friday 30th October 1914
Ypres Memorial (Menin Gate) Memorial, Ieper, West-Vlaanderen, Belgium
Grave Reference Panel 20

Robert Prevett D.C.M. Sergeant G/541 "B" Coy. 7th Bn. Friday 6th October 1916
Dartmoor Cemetery, Becordel-Becourt, Somme, France
Grave Reference II. D. 29.

Frederick Ransom D.C.M.,M.M., C de G Sergeant G/574 7th Bn. Tuesday 8th October 1918
St. Sever Cemetery Extension, Rouen, Seine-Maritime, France
Grave Reference S. II. I. 20.

John Simmons D.C.M. Regimental Sergeant-Major 200087 1/4th Bn. Monday 29th July 1918
Raperie British Cemetery, Villemontorie, Ainse, France
Grave Reference IX. E. 3.

Robert Henry Stewart Sloan D.C.M. Corporal L/10094 2nd Bn. Monday 24th July 1916
Daours Communal Cemetery Extension, Somme, France
Grave Reference I. C. 12.

Bernard Alfred Stone D.C.M. Regimental Sergeant-Major TF/200023 13th Bn. Friday 26th April 1919
Tyne Cot Memorial, Zonnebeke, West-Vlaanderen, Belgium
Grave Reference Panel 86 to 88

Military Medal Winners

Name	Number	Battalion		Notes
Aish C.E.V. Pte.	G/595	2nd Bn.		
Allchorn E.W. Pte. (A/Sgt.)	SD/24	11th Bn.		Citation
Alston G. Sgt.	SD/2213	12th Bn.		
Amsbridge G.G. Pte. (A/Cpl.)	G/18323	2nd Bn.		
Amsbury J. Pte.	G/19396	7th Bn.		
Anderson W.J. Pte.	G/15513	11th Bn.		
Arnold G. Pte.	240130	5th Bn.		
Ashford R. Cpl.	SD/4197	9th Bn.		
Ashford W.A. Sgt.	SD/138	11th Bn.		
Atkinson H. Pte.	SD/5966	11th Bn.		
Attree E.C. Sgt.	L/6430	8th Bn.		
Aukett W.G. C.S.M. D.C.M.	SD/2219	12th Bn.		Citation
Aungier H. Pte.	G/6625	7th Bn.		
Aungier H. Pte. M.M.	G/6625	7th Bn.	Bar	
Avis G.J. Pte.	SD/733	11th Bn.		
Awcock G.R. Pte.	L/9750	2nd Bn.		
Back H.J. L/Cpl.	20332	8th Bn.		
Backshall E. Pte.	G/1548	8th Bn.		
Badcock G. C.Q.M.S.	SD/2621	13th Bn.		
Bagge H. Pte.	G/8148	9th Bn.		
Bailey A. Pte.	G/15036	11th Bn		Citation
Bailey A. Pte.	SD/2854	13th Bn.		Citation
Bailey W.B. Sgt.	G/6339	9th Bn.		
Bailey W.J. L/Cpl.	G/2776	8th Bn. was 13th Bn.		Citation
Baker F.T. Pte.	G/1197	7th Bn.		
Baker H.J. Pte.	SD/2365	11th Bn.		Citation
Baker S.C. Pte.	SD/1830	12th Bn.		Citation
Baker W. Sgt.	8344	7th Bn.		
Balcombe T. Pte.	SD/3730	13th Bn.		Citation
Ball C.E. L/Cpl.	SD/3521	13th Bn.		Citation
Ball T.J. Cpl. (A/Sgt.)	SD/32	11th Bn.		
Ball W.T. Pte.	G/13042	9th Bn.		
Ball W.T. Pte. (L/Cpl.) M.M.	G/13042	9th Bn.		Citation
Banks E.R. Sgt.	G/22	7th Bn.		
Banks E.R. Sgt. M.M.	G/22	7th Bn.		
Barber H.T. Pte.	1196	7th Bn.	Bar	
Barfield T. Pte.	G/15104	12th Bn.		
Barford J. Pte.	265798	2nd Bn.		
Barham F. Pte.	G/2691	8th Bn.		
Barker L. L/Cpl.	SD/5743	11th Bn.		
Bartholomew G.E. Pte.	5321	7th Bn.		
Barwick W.R. Pte. (L/Cpl.)	G/6016	7th Bn.		Citation
Bassett H. L/Cpl.	G/260026	13th Bn.		Citation
Bateman W. Pte.	200195	4th Bn.		
Bateman W. Pte. M.M.	200195	4th Bn.		
Beale A.W. Sgt.	931	7th Bn.		
Beall T.H. Pte.	G/648	7th Bn.	Bar	
Beckett P. Cpl. M.S.M.	G/2712	8th Bn.		
Beecroft H. Pte.	G/2744	8th Bn.		
Beeney A. Pte.	SD/573	11th Bn.		
Beeney J. Pte.	8522	9th Bn.		
Bell D. Pte.	5918	2nd Bn.		
Bell J. Pte. (A/Sgt.)	G/6345	2nd Bn.		
Belton H.S.B. Pte.	SD/1655	12th Bn.		
Belton J.T. Pte.	10729	2nd Bn.		
Bennett F.E. L/Cpl. (A/Cpl.)	G/2835	8th Bn.		Citation
Bilham J.E. L/Cpl.	G/16213	12th Bn.		
Billing R.D. Pte. (L/Cpl.)	6278	9th Bn.		
Billings A.C. L/Cpl.	SD/1790	12th Bn.		Citation
Bingham B.C. Pte.	SD/1686	11th Bn.		
Binstead E. Pte.	G/2432	8th Bn.		
Bird J. Pte.	S/2033	7th Bn.		Citation
Bishop C. Pte.	G/3002	7th Bn.		
Bishop J. Pte.	SD/400	11th Bn.		
Blackman W.A. Pte.	G/408	2nd Bn.		
Bliss C.J. Cpl.	G/5427	9th Bn.		Citation
Blunden C.H. Pte.	G/15882	11th Bn.		
Bone H.J. Pte.	G/12416	7th Bn.		
Boniface W. Cpl.	G/15888	13th Bn.		Citation
Bonner E. Pte. (L/Cpl.)	G/3056	17th Bn.		

Name	Service No.	Battalion	Bar	Citation
Booker P. Pte. (L/Cpl.)	S/2143	7th Bn.		
Booth W. L/Cpl.	SD/390	11th Bn.		
Boreham W. Sgt.	SD/1220	12th Bn.		
Boswell A.E. Pte.	200630	4th Bn.		
Bough E. Pte.	G/19554	11th Bn.		
Bourne J.S. Pte.	3212	9th Bn.		
Bowers E. Pte.	2313	5th Bn.		
Boys S. Pte. (L/Cpl.)	SD/1270	11th Bn.		
Brackpool H. Pte.	G/8355	7th Bn.		
Bramley G. L/Cpl. (A/Cpl.)	G/5228	2nd Bn.		
Bray C.H. L/Cpl.	L/11120	2nd Bn.		
Brewer D. Pte. (A/Cpl.)	G/14662	2nd Bn.		
Brewer J. Sgt.	200176	17th Bn.		
Brewster G. Cpl. (A/Sgt.)	L/11550	17th Bn.		
Bridger C.E. Cpl.	G/475	9th Bn.		
Bridger J. Pte.	G/1759	8th Bn.		
Bridger P.W. Pte.	4017	7th Bn.		
Bridger R.W. Pte.	320124	16th Bn.		
Bridle C.W. L/Cpl.	G/1767	8th Bn.		
Briffett F. Pte.	G/18561	2nd Bn.		
Brinkhurst J.F. Pte. (L/Cpl.)	SD/6854	11th Bn.		
Britt F. Pte.	G/160	7th Bn.		
Brooke A. Pte. (L/Cpl.)	G/1920	8th Bn.		
Brown C.E. Pte.	999	7th Bn.		
Brown E.J. Cpl. D.C.M, D.M.	L/7922	2nd Bn.		
Brown E.J. Pte.	SD/1157	11th Bn.		
Bryant G.A. Pte.	G/6576	4th Bn.		
Bryant R.H.W. Cpl.	240665	5th Bn.		
Buckland W.J. Pte.	200699	9th Bn.		
Buckman S.A. Cpl.	G/2237	9th Bn.		
Buckman S.A. Cpl. (L/Sgt.) M.M.	G/2237	7th Bn.	Bar	Citation
Buckwell E.V. Sgt.	G/358	8th Bn.		
Buckwell J. Sgt.	S/384	8th Bn.		
Budd A. Sgt.	200033	4th Bn.		
Bull J.W. Pte.	G/12072	7th Bn.		
Bullock R. Pte.	1022	2nd Bn.		
Bunce E.C.A. Sgt.	G/2489	8th Bn.		
Bunker J. Pte.	G/1997	8th Bn.		
Burch T. Cpl.	SD/5925	7th Bn.		
Burchell H. Pte. (L/Cpl.)	L/6040	7th Bn.		Citation
Burden F. Pte.	7835	2nd Bn.		
Burgess S. Sgt.	6995	2nd Bn.		
Burgoine C. Pte.	G/21174	2nd Bn.		
Burn H.T. Cpl.	7692	9th Bn.		
Buss C. Pte.	T/203075	13th Bn.		
Bussell F.R. Sgt.	G/1379	8th Bn.		Citation
Bustin F.G. L/Cpl.	G/202396	11th Bn.		
Butcher W. Cpl.	184	7th Bn.		
Caesar G. L/Sgt. (A/Sgt.) M.S.M.	G/2379	8th Bn.		
Cahill J. Sgt.	S/2403	17th Bn.		
Caley E. Pte.	G/18890	2nd Bn.		
Camplin W. Pte.	G/17180	9th Bn.		
Cane A. Pte.	G/18575	2nd Bn.		
Carpenter J.W. Pte.	G/3910	7th Bn.		
Carr W.A. Pte.	874	7th Bn.		
Carr W.A. Pte. M.M.	874	7th Bn.	Bar	Citation
Carver E.H. Pte.	G/4536	8th Bn.		Citation
Castle E.J. Sgt.	G/1806	8th Bn.		
Castle W.S. Cpl. (L/Sgt.)	202970	5th Bn.		
Catchpole A.G. Sgt.	5420	2nd Bn.		
Chambers C.G.T. L/Cpl.	SD/2641	13th Bn.		Citation
Chandler F. Pte.	G/15802	11th Bn.		
Chapman R. Pte.	G/19913	2nd Bn.		Citation
Chapman R. Pte.	12492	2nd Bn.		
Charman W.T. Sgt.	260055	8th Bn.		
Cheeseman D. L/Cpl.	G/2235	8th Bn.		
Cheeseman J. Cpl.	6814	9th Bn.		
Chittenden W.R. Sgt.	3477	9th Bn.		
Chittenden W.R. Sgt.	3477	13th Bn.		
Clark G.H. Pte.	G/241483	8th Bn.		Citation
Clarke A. Pte.	G/4312	5th Bn.		
Clarke C.B. Pte.	241145	5th Bn.		
Clarke H.C. Pte.	G/16117	12th Bn.		
Clayton H.R. Pte.	5197	7th Bn.		

Name	Number	Battalion		
Clements F. Sgt. MM (F)	L/8212	2nd Bn.		
Clevett A.E. Pte. (L/Cpl.)	L/10479	2nd Bn.		
Clinch W. L/Cpl.	6815	7th Bn.		
Coates C. Sgt. M.M.,M.S.M.,C de G)	L/5391	8th Bn		Citation
Coates R. Pte.	G/12419	7th Bn.		
Cockett H.E. Pte.	SD/1017	11th Bn.		
Cockett H.E. Pte. M.M.	SD/1017	11th Bn.	Bar	
Coe F. W. Sgt.	G/164671	2nd Bn.		
Collier A.A. Pte.	G/3523	9th Bn.		
Collins F. Cpl.	3071	9th Bn.		Citation
Compton G. Sgt. D.C.M.	SD/658	11th Bn.		
Cook B. Pte.	200344	4th Bn.		
Cooper A. Cpl. (L/Sgt.)	G/218	7th Bn.		
Cooper F.A. Pte.	SD/5095	13th Bn.		Citation
Corbett E.F.J. Pte. (L/Cpl.)	L/9837	2nd Bn.		
Cornish F.C. Pte.	G/4284	2nd Bn.		Citation
Cornwell P.W. Cpl.	266197	7th Bn.		
Cosham H.E. Pte.	823	7th Bn.		Citation
Cosstick W.T. Pte.	SD/2872	13th Bn.		
Cotton A.A. Pte.	G/18577	2nd Bn.		
Covey A.S. Pte.	G/20476	7th Bn.		
Coward H. Sgt.	G/2430	8th Bn.		
Cox A.C. Pte.	G/4852	2nd Bn.		Citation
Cox E.R. Pte.	G/18572	2nd Bn.		
Cox R.E. Cpl. (A/Sgt.)	SD/503	11th Bn.		Citation
Cramp A. Pte.	G/18184	13th Bn.		
Crawford F.O. Sgt. S/Yeomanry	21529	10th Bn. R.W.S.		
Dabson B. Pte.	3268	5th Bn.		
Dale W. Sgt.	240396	5th Bn.		
Dancy F. Pte.	G/3725	7th Bn.		
Dann N. L/Cpl.	G/1955	8th Bn.		Citation
Darnell H. Cpl. (A/Sgt.)	263106	17th Bn.		
Daughtry J. Cpl. (A/Sgt.)	G/2424	8th Bn		Citation
Davey A.H. L/Cpl.	SD/1189	11th Bn.		
Davies C. Pte.	SD/2896	13th Bn		
Davies G.T. Sgt.	2398	5th Bn.		
Davis C. Pte.	315374	16th Bn.		
Davis G.E. Pte. (A/Cpl.)	19276	6th Bn.		
Dawes C.J. Pte.	G/202330	13th Bn.		
Dawson N.G. Pte.	G/2138	8th Bn.		
Day P.C. Pte.	G/14678	2nd Bn.		
Deeprose V.E.T. L/Cpl.	G/12300	11th Bn.		
Delves G.F. Cpl.	L/6255	2nd Bn.		
Delves G.F. Cpl. M.M.	L/6255	2nd Bn.	Bar	
Dendy E.J. Pte. (L/Cpl.)	G/150	7th Bn.		Citation
Dennett M.S.S. L/Cpl. (A/Cpl.)	G/9750	8th Bn.		
Dewell F. Cpl.	G/826	7th Bn.		
Dick Q.W.A. Pte.	3628	9th Bn.		
Dickerson T.W. Pte. (L/Cpl.)	G/14842	9th Bn.		
Dinnage W. Cpl.	G/938	7th Bn.		
Diplock H.R. Sgt.	L/9685	8th Bn.		Citation
Dix T.C. Pte. (L/Cpl.)	G/14526	2nd Bn.		
Dolman G. Pte.	G/20078	2nd Bn.		
Donald M. Pte.	G/20477	7th Bn.		
Drake G. Pte. (L/Cpl.)	30168	17th Bn.		
Drewery H.W. L/Cpl.	G/1792	8.th Bn		
Drury C.A. L/Cpl.	SD/1523	12th Bn.		Citation
Dudman E. L/Cpl.	601	7th Bn.		
Dudman G.W. Sgt.	SD/3089	13th Bn.		
Duke J.H.G. Cpl. (L/Sgt.)	SD/145	13th Bn.		
Dunk A. Pte. (L/Cpl.)	7648	2nd Bn.		
Dunk A.E. Pte.	8681	2nd Bn.		
Dunk J.W.H. Pte.	G/16755	9th Bn.		
Dunkerton W. Pte. (L/Cpl.)	G/30940	17th Bn.		
Dunningham J. Pte.	G/5979	11th Bn.		
Durling W. Pte. (L/Cpl.)	G/10276	9th Bn.		
Durrant A.E. L/Cpl.	SD/3338	13th Bn.		
Dybell C.W. Cpl.	G/15263	11th Bn.		
Eade W.J. Pte.	SD/1180	7th Bn.		
Eaton F. Pte.	G/10998	2nd Bn.		
Edwards C. Pte.	G/10998	2nd Bn.		Citation
Edwards E. L/Cpl.	SD/2904	13th Bn.		
Elphick J.A. Cpl. (L/Sgt.)	G/7660	7th Bn.		
Elphick W. L/Cpl.	SD/990	11th Bn.		
Emerson J.A. L/Cpl.	G/1999	8th Bn.		

Name	Number	Battalion			
Emery C.T. Pte.	G/3410	7th Bn.			
Emery C.T. Pte. (L/Cpl.) M.M.	G/3410	7th Bn.	Bar		
Emery C.T. Cpl. M.M.	G3410	7th Bn.		Bar	
Emsley F.M. Pte.	G/2726	8th Bn.			
Emsley R. Pte.	SD/3340	13th Bn.			Citation
Emsley R. Pte.	SD/3340	13th Bn.	Bar		
Etherington E.E. Sgt.	G/1746	8th Bn.			
Etherington E.E. Sgt. M.M.	G/1746	8th Bn.		Bar	
Ettridge F.B.R. Cpl. (A/Sgt.)	G/890	2nd Bn.			
Evans A.J. Sgt.	G/764	7th Bn.			
Evans F.W. Pte.	G/2498	8th Bn.			
Evans J. Pte.	G/946	7th Bn.			
Evenden F. Pte. D.C.M.	G/1406	2nd Bn.			
Farley A.W. Pte.	G/15906G	2nd Bn.			
Farmer G. Pte. (L/Cpl.)	/1960	8th Bn.			
Farmer I.H. Cpl.	SD/1883	12th Bn.			
Farndale G.J. Cpl. (A/Sgt.)	G/445	2nd Bn.			
Farrant A. Cpl. (L/Sgt.)	SD/305	9th Bn.			
Farrant W. Pte.	G/1965	8th Bn.			
Faulkner B. Pte.	G/15224	11th Bn.			
Field A.J. Pte.	G/16124	12th Bn.			Citation
Fielder F.G. Pte	G/2144	8th Bn.			
Finch J.J.G. Pte.	G/8950	2nd Bn.			
Firth H. Cpl.	SD/3341	13th Bn.			
Fishenden H.E. Pte.	SD/307	11th Bn.			
Fishenden H.E. Pte. M.M.	SD/307	11th Bn.	Bar		
Flint F. Cpl.	G/1862	13th Bn.			Citation
Ford A.S. Pte.	SD/3101	13th Bn.			
Foster C. Pte.	G/4481	8th Bn.			
Foster J.W.S. Sgt.	3062	2nd Bn.			
Foster P. Pte.	G/15408	12th Bn.			
Fowler C. Cpl. D.C.M.	SD/2909	13th Bn.			
Francis A.E. Pte.	G/200077	4th Bn.			
Franks T.E. Pte. (A/Cpl.)	G/17539	2nd Bn.			
Fuller A. L/Cpl.	G/2192	8th Bn.			
Fuller C. Sgt.	5786	9th Bn.			
Fuller F. Pte.	10190	2nd Bn.			
Fuller L. Pte.	8145	9th Bn.			
Furminger A. L/Cpl.	G/2248	8th Bn.			
Gannon W. Cpl. (L/Sgt.)	L/8913	1st Bn.			
Gardiner P.J. Pte.	5946	2nd Bn.			
Gardner G.F. Pte.	G/202406	12th Bn.			
Gardner H. Pte.	3322	9th Bn.			
Gardner H. L/Cpl.	320212	16th Bn.			
Garton A.G.M. A/Cpl.	G/15414	12th Bn.			
Gaston C.H. Pte.	2664	5th Bn.			
Gates W.A. Sgt.	1489	5th Bn.			
Gibbs G.W. Pte.	SD/1885	12th Bn.			
Gibson A. L/Cpl.	SD/5509	13th Bn.			
Giles J.C. Sgt.	SD/1039	11th Bn.			
Glenister H. Pte.	1264	7th Bn.			
Goacher R.P. Pte.	L/12184	2nd Bn.			
Goble E.G. L/Sgt.	SD/1341	12th Bn.			
Goddard J.H. Pte.	2238	7th Bn.			
Golden A.W. L/Sgt. D.C.M.	SD/1766	11th Bn.			
Golds A. Pte.	G/6977	2nd Bn.			
Golds T. Pte.	SD/3581	13th Bn.			
Golds W.B. Sgt.	L/9958	7th Bn.			
Goldsmith J. Pte.	SD/3117	4th Bn.			
Goodyer L. Pte.	G/7231	7th Bn.			
Gordon F.H. Pte.	G/11000	2nd Bn.			
Goward H. Sgt.	G/2430	8th Bn.			
Gratwick S.F. Pte.	232	7th Bn.			
Gray G.W. Pte. (A/Cpl.)	G/6004	2nd Bn.			
Green M. Pte.	G/11961	16th Bn.			
Green R. Pte.	G/14952	12th Bn.			
Grenyer W.D. L/Cpl.	SD/1691	12th Bn.			
Griffin F. Pte.	G/6697	9th Bn.			
Grimstead E.G. Sgt.	200140	4th Bn.			
Griston P.A. Pte.	G/17333	7th Bn.			
Griston P.A. Pte. M.M.	G/17333	7th Bn.	Bar		

Name	Number	Battalion		Notes
Groome A.F. Pte.	G/16427	9th Bn.		
Grover W.E. Pte.	G/17582	2nd Bn.		
Groves A.L. Pte.	G/1282	7th Bn.		
Groves A.L. Pte. M.M.	G/1282	7th Bn.	Bar	
Guiel H.J. Pte.	G/17829	12th Bn.		
Guilford G.H. L/Cpl.	SD/185	11th Bn.		
Gumbrill L.A. Pte.	L/9902	2nd Bn.		
Gurry A. Pte.	G/11224	2nd Bn.		
Guttridge R. L/Cpl.	SD/2691	13th Bn.		
Guy A.H. L/Cpl.	320464	16th Bn.		Citation
Guymer J. Pte.	G/11601	2nd Bn.		
Hadley W.H. Cpl.	G/20295	9th Bn.		
Hammond G.C. Sgt.	G/2219	8th Bn.		
Hann E.E. Sgt.	G/2121	8th Bn.		
Harding S.J. L/Sgt.	3182	9th Bn.		
Harman E.A. Pte.	402	7th Bn.		Citation
Harris A.J. Pte.	G/390	8th Bn.		Citation
Harris G.C. Cpl.	320024	16th Bn.		
Harrold W.P.G. L/Sgt.	SD/2698	13th Bn.		
Hart J. L/Cpl.	2340	5th Bn.		
Harvey G.W. Pte.	G/17576	2nd Bn.		
Harwood J. Cpl. (A/Sgt.)	200236	4th Bn.		
Hatton H. Pte.	G/17541	2nd Bn.		
Hawkett H. L/Cpl. (A/Cpl.)	G/2499	8th Bn.		
Hayes J. Sgt. (A/C.Q.M.S.)	71	7th Bn.		
Hayhurst A. Pte.	315020	16th Bn.		Citation
Hayter J.B. Pte.	SD/3600	13th Bn.		
Hayward W.H. Pte.	141	7th Bn.		
Hearn B. Pte.	G/4153	9th Bn.		
Heaseman H.E. Pte. (A/L/Cpl.)	240722	5th Bn.		
Heathfield C.W. L/Cpl.	SD/194	11th Bn.		Citation
Heise A.W. Cpl.	G/3186	11th Bn.		
Hemsley H. Pte.	L/9919	2nd Bn.		
Hemsley H. Pte.	L/9919	2nd Bn.	Bar	
Hemsley S.H. Pte. (A/Cpl.)	202190	2nd Bn.		
Hendley F.A. Pte. (L/Cpl.)	L/9003	2nd Bn.		
Hendry W. L/Cpl.	G/350	7th Bn.		
Henty J. Cpl.	10060	2nd Bn.		
Hermitage E. Pte.	G/16429	13th Bn.		
Hersey A.J. Sgt.	G/29282	8th Bn.		
Highgate E. Pte. D.C.M.	G/3833	7th Bn.		
Highgate E. Pte. D.C.M.,M.M.	G/3833	7th Bn.	Bar	
Highgate E. Pte. D.C.M.,M.M.	G/3833	7th Bn.	Bar	
Hillman H.R.N. Pte.	320344	16th Bn.		
Hills H. Pte.	G/6359	2nd Bn.		
Hoad E. Pte.	200365	4th Bn.		
Hoad S. Sgt.	320034	16th Bn.		
Hodson G.H. Sgt. M.S.M.	240030	5th Bn.		
Holder B. Pte.	L/7953	7th Bn.		
Hollands A.E. Pte.	200869	4th Bn.		
Holman R. L/Cpl.	G/545	8th Bn.		
Honeysett D.G. Sgt. (A/C.S.M.)	G/6426	11th Bn.		
Hopkins R.J. Cpl. (A/Sgt.)	SD/1056	11th Bn.		
Horcroft A. L/Cpl.	1659	2nd Bn.		
Horne A.W. Sgt.	1312	7th Bn.		
Horne A.W. Sgt. M.M.	1312	7th Bn.	Bar	
Horton H.E. Pte.	SD/320	11th Bn.		
Horton H.J. Cpl.	200269	4th Bn.		
Howlett R.W. Pte.	G/18982	2nd Bn.		
Hughes F. Pte.	5845	2nd Bn.		
Hughes J. Pte. (L/Cpl.)	G/20853	1st Bn.		
Humphrey M.A. Pte.	G/2554	8th Bn.		Citation
Hunt C. Sgt.	710	9th Bn.		
Hunt W. Pte. (L/Cpl.)	SD/4822	11th Bn.		
Hunton J.J. Sgt.	2455	8th Bn.		Citation
Hutchings J. Pte.	G/16137	12th Bn.		
Hyde W.A. Pte.	G/19148	9th Bn.		
Isard E. Pte.	16763	9th Bn.		
Isbell A.D. Sgt.	320336	16th Bn.		
Isted S. Pte.	3788	7th Bn.		

Name	Number	Battalion	Award
Izzard W.J. Pte.	16763	9th Bn.	
Jarvis C.H. Sgt.	5928	9th Bn.	
Jeffery T.R. Pte.	G/3878	8th Bn.	
Jenkinson W.G. Pte.	G/17862	12th Bn.	
Jenkinson W.G. L/Cpl. M.M.	G/17862	12th Bn.	Bar
Jennings A.J. Cpl.	L/7519	2nd Bn.	
Jester A. Pte. (L/Cpl.)	G/1857	8th Bn.	
Johncox J. L/Cpl.	G/2344	8th Bn.	Citation
Jordan H. Cpl.	G/15449	12th Bn.	
Josland A.E. Pte.	G/11362	7th Bn.	
Joyce E.A. Pte.	290480	9th Bn.	
Kelsey R.C. Pte.	SD/5003	2nd Bn.	
Kent C.W. L/Cpl.	6014	2nd Bn.	
Kennard E.S. Pte.	G/17822	8th Bn.	
Kenward E.S. Pte.	SD/3381	8th Bn.	
Key J.W. Cpl. (A/Sgt.)	G/6271	11th Bn.	
Kibbey G.H. L/Sgt.	SD/1973	12th Bn.	
Kilbey W.J. Pte.	G/14614	2nd Bn.	
Kimber A.F. Sgt.	8165	2nd Bn.	
King A.W. Pte.	1891	5th Bn.	
Knight A.C. Cpl.	8835	2nd Bn.	
Knight E. Pte.	SD/2723	13th Bn.	
Knight H.H. L/Cpl. (A/Cpl.)	G/10803	8th Bn.	Citation
Knight R. L/Cpl.	SD/2947	13th Bn.	
Knope H.E. Pte.	G/19491	7th Bn.	
Knowles F.J.A. Sgt.	G/1118	2nd Bn.	Citation
Lade H.J. Pte.	G/7739	8th Bn.	
Laker E.G. Pte.	G/849	8th Bn.	
Laming C.J. Pte.	9992	2nd Bn.	
Larby G. Cpl.	9977	2nd Bn.	Citation
Lassetter C.F. L/Cpl.	SD/1535	12th Bn.	
Laughton W. Sgt.	1393	9th Bn.	
Lawrence H.J. Pte.	4758	7th Bn.	
Lawrence R. A/Sgt.	7	7th Bn.	
Lee A. Sgt. M.S.M.	SR/120	7th Bn.	
Lee W.H. Pte.	G/17535	2nd Bn.	
Leggatt T. Pte. (L/Cpl.)	G/2836	8th Bn.	
Leighton O.T. Pte.	G/6091	9th Bn.	
Leppard C.H. Cpl. (L/Sgt.) D.C.M	SD/3861	7th Bn.	
Lewis A. Pte. (L/Cpl.)	G/14704	2nd Bn.	
Lewis L.W. Cpl. (A/Sgt.)	G/8665	2nd Bn.	
Light G. Pte.	G/5742	8th Bn.	
Lightfoot A.S. Pte.	SD/80	9th Bn.	
Linford A.W. Sgt.	G/20279	12th Bn.	
Link B.T. Pte. (Cpl.)	260092	9th Bn.	
Lintott R. Cpl.	6812	9th Bn.	Citation
Lisher C.A. Pte.	SD/2137	13th Bn.	
Lister E.G. Sgt.	L/8132	7th Bn.	
Littlewood C.W.E. L/Cpl.	15459	12th Bn.	
Lloyd J. L/Cpl.	SD/1070	11th Bn.	
Lock C.F. Pte. (A/L/Cpl.)	320204	16th Bn.	
Lordan D. Pte.	G/11091	2nd Bn.	
Lovell B. Pte. (L/Cpl.)	G/17522	8th Bn.	
Lovering W.H. Sgt.	L/11570	17th Bn.	
Lucas T. L/Cpl.	G/16046	13th Bn.	
Luff M. Sgt.	G/886	9th Bn.	
Lusted G. Sgt.	1647	5th Bn.	
Luxford W. Pte. (L/Cpl.)	G/16749	11th Bn.	
Madgwick A.E. L/Cpl.	5638	2nd Bn.	Bar
Madgwick A.E. L/Cpl. M.M.	5638	2nd Bn.	
Maguire J. Pte. (L/Cpl.)	2006	7th Bn.	
Mann F.J. Pte.	G/2200	8th Bn.	
Mann G.L. Pte. (A/L/Cpl.)	G/11824	9th Bn.	
Mann M.P. Pte.	G/14619	2nd Bn.	
Mant J. L/Cpl.	5325	9th Bn.	
Manvell E.J. Sgt.	G/2519	8th Bn.	
Markwell F.J. Pte.	G/21502	16th Bn.	
Marney G.T.H. Pte. (A/Cpl.)	G/5140	2nd Bn.	
Marshall C.J. Sgt.	G/714	7th Bn.	
Martin H. Pte. (L/Cpl.)	SD/4956	16th Bn.	
Martin R. Pte.	G/19180	9th Bn.	
Martin W.E. L/Cpl.	10147	9th Bn.	
Martin W.J. L/Cpl.	G/18218	13th Bn.	

Name	Number	Battalion		
Maskell G.T. Pte.	G/2067	8th Bn.		
Maskell V.G. Sgt.	G/3065	9th Bn.		
Mason C. Pte.	G/20450	11th Bn.		
Mason F. Pte.	SD/2244	12th Bn.		
Mason W.H. Cpl.	G/1898	8th Bn.		
Masters F. Sgt.	SD/3745	13th Bn.		
Matthias T. Pte. (A/Sgt.)	G/5865	2nd Bn.		
Matthews M. Pte. (A/L/Cpl.)	G/1848	8th Bn.		
Maughan H. Pte.	G/266	7th Bn.		
Mayes C.P. Pte. (A/L/Cpl.)	333	7th Bn.		
McCormick C. Pte.	G/10322	13th Bn.		
McFarlane A. Pte.	G/7050	8th Bn.		Citation
McKernan J. Pte. (A/Cpl.)	L/6696	2nd Bn.		
Milbourne W.A. Cpl.	SD/2183	12th Bn.		
Mills G. Pte.	SD/1409	12th Bn.		Citation
Mills G. Sgt. M.M.	SD/1409	2nd Bn. Was 12th Bn.	Bar	
Mills J.W. Pte.	315146	16th Bn.		
Mills T. Cpl. (A/Sgt.)	SD/3905	11th Bn.		
Milton C.T. Pte.	G/14047	11th Bn.		
Milton W.J. Pte.	G/15594	12th Bn.		
Mitchell J.E. Pte.	SD/1641	12th Bn.		Citation
Mitchell J.E. Pte. M.M.	SD/1641	12th Bn.	Bar	Citation
Moger H.E. Pte. (L/Cpl.)	G/2355	8th Bn.		
Mole J. L/Sgt.	G/14845	13th Bn.		
Moller C.E. Sgt.	320121	13th Bn.		
Moody C.F. Sgt. D.C.M.	S/385	16th Bn.		
Moore F.H. Pte.	G/23613	8th Bn.		
Moore H. Pte.	6281	7th Bn.		
Moore W. Pte.	10651	2nd Bn.		
Morris O.C. Pte.	G/17388	2nd Bn.		
Munt E. Sgt.	G/839	7th Bn.		
Murphy H. Pte.	G/30655	17th Bn.		
Mustchin W.G. Pte.	G/965	7th Bn.		
Newham L. Pte.	G/6435	13th Bn.		
Newman K. Sgt.	G/1603	8th Bn.		Citation
Newman S. Pte.	G/19621	12th Bn.		
Newman S.R. Pte. (L/Cpl.)	SD/5779	16th Bn.		
Newnham P. Cpl.	G/2630	8th Bn.		
Newport E.R. Sgt.	G/10853	7th Bn.		
Newport H.W. Pte.	7684	7th Bn.		
Nicholl P.A. Pte.	SD/2979	13th Bn.		
Nicholl P.A. Pte. M.M.	SD/2979	13th Bn.	Bar	
Nichols F.J. Pte.	G/14627	2nd Bn.		
Nicholls F.V. Pte.	G/124	7th Bn.		
Noakes S. Cpl.	SD/878	11th Bn.		
Noakes W.E. Pte.	L/7523	16th Bn.		
Norman C.S. Pte.	G/16722	11th Bn.		
Norman H.T. Pte.	SD/335	11th Bn.		
Norman W.C. Sgt.	G/14848	9th Bn.		
Offler J.W. Pte.	2205	2nd Bn.		
Oldham J.W. Pte. (L/Cpl.)	G/30455	17th Bn.		
Oliver G.F. Pte.	G/6356	12th Bn.		
Onions W.H. Cpl. (L/Sgt.)	G/23694	7th Bn.		
Osborne W.J. Sgt.	G/415	7th Bn.		
Packham C. Sgt. (A/C.S.M.)	SD/458	11th Bn.		Citation
Packham F. Cpl.	G/16355	7th Bn.		Citation
Page C.T. Pte. (A/Cpl.)	G/2591	8th Bn.		
Paine E.A. Pte.	G/23625	7th Bn.		
Paley E.H. Pte.	L/0924	9th Bn. attd. 73rd W.B. H.Q.		
Parkes A. Pte. (L/Cpl.)	G/5985	9th Bn.		
Parsons A. Sgt.	G/638	7th Bn.		
Parvin F.H. Pte.	SD/3663	13th Bn.		
Pascoe A.J. Pte.	G/4424	2nd Bn.		
Pascoe A.W. Pte.	G/16245	12th Bn.		
Patrick F.J. Pte.	SD/879	11th Bn.		
Pattenden K. L/Cpl.	1046	5th Bn.		Citation
Pattenden W.T. Pte.	1626	5th Bn.		
Peacock A.N. L/Sgt.	524	7th Bn.		
Peacock J.G. L/Sgt.	325	7th Bn.		
Peck J.C. Pte.	GS/203	7th Bn.		
Pelham W.T. Sgt.	L/8349	1st Bn.		
Pell H. Sgt.	SD/338	11th Bn.		
Penfold W. Sgt.	G/2719	8th Bn.		

Name	Number	Battalion	
Penticost J. Pte.	726	7th Bn.	
Pepper S. Sgt.	G/24875	7th Bn.	
Percival J. Pte.	G/9418	13th Bn.	
Perkins J.P. L/Cpl.	G/20582	8th Bn.	
Perkins W. Pte.	G/1826	8th Bn.	Citation
Perry J.C. Pte. (L/Cpl.)	SD/1084	11th Bn.	
Perry J.C. L/Cpl. M.M.	SD/1084	11th Bn.	
Pestell F.C. Cpl.	G/17658	9th Bn.	
Philips T.S. Pte.	5877	7th Bn.	
Phillips H.J. Pte.	SD/3426	13th Bn.	
Picton F. Cpl.	290	7th Bn.	
Pierce R.H. Cpl.	1432	9th Bn.	
Pinckney J.S. Pte. (A/Cpl.)	G/14821	2nd Bn.	
Pink A. Pte.	6382	9th Bn.	
Pocock H.C. Sgt.	SD/3430	11th Bn.	
Poile W. Pte.	G/2184	8th Bn.	
Poole C.R. Pte.	G/30964	17th Bn.	
Porteous D.R. Pte.	G/22923	7th Bn.	
Porter E.G.C. Cpl.	G/223	7th Bn.	
Potiphar J.E. Pte.	G/17894	12th Bn.	
Preston G.W. Pte.	684	7th Bn.	
Price L.S. Pte.	G/1787	8th Bn.	
Pronger H.G. Pte.	G/15961	13th Bn.	
Pullinger B.C. Cpl.	2595	5th Bn.	Citation
Randall J. Pte.	4438	7th Bn.	
Ranger C. Cpl.	L/10747	7th Bn.	
Ranger G.H. Pte.	G/6362	2nd Bn.	
Ransom F.J. Sgt. D.C.M.	G/574	7th Bn.	
Rapley A. Pte.	7471	9th Bn.	
Raynard A. L/Cpl	G/2159	8th Bn.	
Read E.B. Pte. (A/Sgt.)	10298	2nd Bn.	Citation
Read H.S. Pte.	G/14161	12th Bn.	
Redman C.B.W. Pte.	G/20417	11th Bn.	
Reed H.H.E. Pte.	L/10391	2nd Bn.	
Reed F.J. Pte. (L/Cpl.)	G/20222	7th Bn.	
Reid S. Pte.	G/2249	8th Bn.	Citation
Relf R. L/Cpl.	G/2321	8th Bn.	
Relf-West T.F. Cpl. (A/Sgt.)	G/2244	8th Bn.	
Remnant C.W. Sgt.	15965	7th Bn.	
Renshaw H.H. Cpl.	G/15777	11th Bn.	
Reyland W.T. Pte.	G/11249	13th Bn.	
Reynolds W. Pte.	G/14725	13th Bn.	
Rice F. Pte.	200106	4th Bn.	
Rice L.S. Pte.	G/1787	4th Bn.	
Rich E.J. L/Cpl.	SD/1123	11th Bn.	
Richardson A.C.T. Pte.	200627	4th Bn.	
Richardson A.E. Cpl.	20443	8th Bn.	
Richardson C. Sgt.	L/6885	8th Bn.	
Richold A.A. C.Q.M.S.	4867	7th Bn.	Citation
Riggs F. Pte.	G/6421	8th Bn.	
Ripley J. Pte.	SD/1547	12th Bn.	
Robbins W.H.M. L/Cpl.	200304	4th Bn.	
Rodway W.W. Sgt.	240353	5th Bn.	
Rose S.R. Sgt.	SD/2119	12th Bn.	Citation
Rossiter G.S. Cpl.	G/1996	8th Bn.	
Route P.A. L/Cpl.	SD/1178	11th Bn.	
Rovery L. Sgt.	4199	7th Bn.	
Rowlands L.S. Pte.	G/16744	11th Bn.	
Rudd J.W. Pte. (L/Cpl.)	G/6071	2nd Bn.	
Rudderham G.A. Pte.	G/476	2nd Bn.	
Ruff H.W. Pte.	L/8581	1st Bn.	
Russell F.P. Cpl.	G/9705	8th Bn.	
Russell R. Pte. (L/Cpl.)	G/1853	8th Bn.	
Salmon W. L/Cpl.	G/15534	11th Bn.	
Sanford W. Pte.	320387	16th Bn.	
Sargent G.A. L/Cpl.	SD/1171	11th Bn.	
Saunders J. Pte. (L/Cpl.)	G/960	7th Bn.	
Sayers P. Pte. (L/Cpl.)	G/2396	8th Bn.	

Name	Number	Battalion		
Scott E. Pte.	G/2267	8th Bn.		Citation
Scott H.C. Pte.	SD/3225	13th Bn.		
Scott P.W. Pte.	8368	7th Bn.		
Scrase F.J. Pte.	G/2010	8th Bn.		
Scutt G.A. Pte. (L/Cpl.)	9447	2nd Bn.		
Search G. Sgt.	G/12381	9th Bn.		
Searle C. Cpl. (A/Sgt.)	L/8558	2nd Bn.		
Sears G.C. Pte. (A/Cpl.) D.C.M.	G/14822	2nd Bn.		
Selby A.E. A/Sgt.	111	7th Bn.		
Selsby J.R. Pte.	G/936	7th Bn.		
Selsby J.R. Pte. M.M.	G/936	7th Bn.	Bar	Citation
Seymour A. Pte.	G/3898	2nd Bn.		Citation
Sharp G. Pte.	SD/1456	12th Bn.		Citation
Sharpe E.E. Pte.	G/21779	16th Bn.		
Shearing W.E. Pte.	SD/736	11th Bn.		
Shelley P. Pte. (L/Cpl.)	L/10486	8th Bn.		Citation
Sheppard A.R. Sgt.	SD/3229	13th Bn.		
Sheppard W.H. Pte.	SD/232	11th Bn.		
Sherwood A. Pte.	SD/5137	12th Bn.		
Shine T. Pte.	315248	16th Bn.		
Shirley F.E. Pte.	G/15756	11th Bn.		
Shonfield H.A. Sgt.	S/2	8th Bn.		
Short W. Pte.	G/2605	8th Bn.		
Shotter W. Pte.	G/17761	13th Bn.		
Simmonds A.L. Pte. (A/Cpl.)	G/7967	2nd Bn.		
Simmonds J. Sgt.	G/16312	7th Bn.		
Simmonds J. Sgt. M.M.	G/16312	7th Bn.	Bar	
Single E.M. Pte.	SD/737	11th Bn.		
Sivyer H.G. Cpl.	2946	9th Bn.		
Skinner R.E. Sgt.	G/2004	8th Bn.		
Slaughter F. Pte.	G/1727	7th Bn.		
Sloane G. Pte.	SD/363	11th Bn.		Citation
Sloper F.G. Sgt.	G/1041	7th Bn.		
Smith D. L/Cpl. (A/Cpl.)	4742	2nd Bn.		Citation
Smith I.J. Sgt.	G/1440	8th Bn.		
Smith J. Pte. (L/Cpl.)	G/18822	2nd Bn.		
Smith J. Pte. (L/Cpl.)	G/19872	12th Bn.		Citation
Smith J.Y. Pte.	10515	7th Bn.		
Smith W. Pte.	L/11534	2nd Bn.		
Smith W. Pte.	18236	7th Bn.		
Snashall F.J. Sgt.	(297) 444517	1/1st S Yeo.		
Soanes W. Pte. (L/Cpl.)	240877	5th Bn.		
Southgate W. Pte.	G/30475	17th Bn.		
Spears W.H. Pte. (L/Cpl.)	G/16788	11th Bn.		
Spickernell W. Cpl.	G/1777	16th Bn.		
Squires A.J. Pte. (L/Cpl.)	G/862	7th Bn.		
Staines W.A. Pte.	G/2328	8th Bn.		
Standing L.G. Cpl.	G/2165	8th Bn.		
Stanford C. Sgt.	SD/3463	13th Bn.		Citation
Stannard J. Pte.	G/2376	7th Bn.		
Stapley G.A. Sgt.	G/2795	8th Bn.		
Steadman C. Pte.	240137	5th Bn.		
Stedman J. Pte.	G/10553	8th Bn.		
Stemp W.H. Pte.	G/2091	8th Bn.		
Stenning A. Pte.	S/2156	8th Bn.		
Stevens A. Pte.	L/8044	2nd Bn.		
Still E. Cpl.	1657	2nd Bn.		
Stobbart T.R. Pte. (A/Cpl.)	G/1916	8th Bn.		
Stockbridge S.C. Sgt.	SD/1332	13th Bn.		
Stokes S.D. Pte.	G/7671	9th Bn.		
Stone F. Sgt.	2376	5th Bn.		
Stone W.J. L/Sgt.	SD/472	11th Bn.		
Storey W. Pte.	G/15312	13th Bn.		
Stringer E. Cpl.	G/1834	8th Bn.		Citation
Stuart R.E. Cpl.	G/7896	9th Bn.		
Stubbings H.T. Pte.	G/15647	13th Bn.		
Stunt A. Sgt.	G/2117	8th Bn.		
Swallow W.L. Pte.	G/2371	8th Bn.		

Name	Number	Battalion		
Taplin C.E. Pte. (L/Cpl.)	G/12725	9th Bn.		
Tapner A. Pte.	G/1701	2nd Bn.		
Taylor A.C. Pte.	G/17375	7th Bn.		
Taylor H. Pte.	L/8114	2nd Bn.		
Taylor H.S. Pte.	G/15759	11th Bn.		
Taylor W.H. Pte.	G/16080	13th Bn.		
Taylor W.H. Pte. M.M.	G/16080	13th Bn.	Bar	
Taylor W.T. Pte.	SD/4109	13th Bn.		Citation
Tester A.E. L/Cpl.	200784	4th Bn.		
Tester J. L/Cpl.	8513	2nd Bn.		
Theckston H. Pte.	G/19341	9th Bn.		
Theobald W.J. Pte.	G/201699	13th Bn.		
Thirst W. Pte.	G/9353	7th Bn.		
Thompsett F.H.G. L/Cpl.	SD/3029	13th Bn.		
Thompsett F.H.G. L/Sgt. M.M.	SD/3029	13th Bn.	Bar	
Thompson J. Pte.	S/1659	2nd Bn.		
Thorns R.W. Pte.	SD/3475	13th Bn.		
Tickner G.W. Sgt.	3125	9th Bn.		
Titcombe A.T. Pte. (A/Sgt.)	G/31029	17th Bn.		
Todman J. L/Cpl.	722	9th Bn.		
Tomlinson H. Pte.	200517	4th Bn.		
Tomlinson H. Pte.	5594	9th Bn.		
Toogood S. L/Cpl.	SD/5649	13th Bn.		
Tooms F.J. Sgt.	G/5070	7th Bn.		
Towner T.W. L/Cpl.	1912	5th Bn.		
Trevor A.W. Sgt. D.C.M. & Bar	G/1192	7th Bn.		
Tribe A.A.W. Sgt. D.C.M.	233460	16th Bn. att. 74th D.Sig. Coy.		
Troy J.H. Pte.	G/15792	R.E.		
Tucker E. Pte. (A/Cpl.)	L/9249	8th Bn.		
Tulett W.C.J. Sgt.	G/780	2nd Bn.		
Tulitt W.J. Pte. (L/Cpl.)	G/582	7th Bn.		
Turner C. Pte.	9501	7th Bn.		
Turner H. L/Cpl.	320117	1st Bn. att. 'Z' Div. Sig. Coy.		
Turner J.F. Cpl. (A/Sgt.)	G/20296	16th Bn.		
Turrell C.W. Pte.	4071	12th Bn.		
Turton A. Cpl.	318	9th Bn.		
Tutt J.W. C.S.M. D.C.M.	G/1958	7th Bn.		
Undrill W.J. Cpl.	G/3033	8th Bn.		
Upton E.J. Sgt. (2nd Lt.)	7318	17th Bn.		
Vale G.W. Cpl. (A/Sgt.)	G/2028	2nd Bn.		Citation
Valler A. Pte.	L/7933	8th Bn.		
Vicary G.E. Sgt.	L/10273	2nd Bn.		Citation
Vidler W.G. Pte.	SD/3039	13th Bn.		
Vigar A.L.J. Pte.	320387	11th Bn 16th Bn.		
Vigar F.J. Pte.	G/1464	2nd Bn.		
Vigor J. L/Sgt.	G/2194	8th Bn.		
Wackford S. Cpl.	S/863	2nd Bn.		
Wade E.W. Pte. (A/L/Cpl.)	9316	2nd Bn.		
Waghorn T.C. Pte.	G/23675	7th Bn.		
Waldron W.H.S. L/Cpl.	SD/3503	13th Bn.		
Walker J. Pte.	200673	13th Bn.		
Walls W.J. C.S.M. M.M.	L/9905	4th Bn.		
Ward F.J. Pte.	G/1865	8th Bn.		
Waters G.C.F. L/Cpl. A/Cpl.)	G/16390	8th Bn.		
Waters J.S. Cpl.	SD/3409	13th Bn.		Citation
Watson J.E. Cpl. (A/Sgt.)	SD/1916	12th Bn.		
Watson J.H.C. Sgt.	G/6601	11th Bn.		
Weedon P.L. Pte. D.C.M.	S/2152	2nd Bn.		
Weeks R.H. Pte.	G/13582	2nd Bn.		
Weeks-Pearson E.E. Cpl.	G/18000	9th Bn.		Citation
Weller A.G. Cpl.	G/18247	13th Bn.		
Wells H. L/Cpl.	SD/1559	13th Bn.		Citation
Wells J.A. L/Cpl. (A/Cpl.)	SD/5416	12th Bn.		
West C.F. Sgt. D.C.M.	G/3147	7th Bn.		
West H. Sgt.	SD/1740	13th Bn.		
West L. Pte.	SD/2819	13th Bn.		Citation
Westbrook F. Sgt.	G/4215	8th Bn.		
Wheeler A.W. Pte.	G/2357	8th Bn.		
Wheeler J.L. Cpl.	G/2655	8th Bn.		
Whitaker H.W. Sgt.	G/15623	13th Bn.		
Whitbread E.G. Cpl.	G/101	7th Bn.		

Name	Number	Battalion	Award	
Whitehead E.B. Cpl.	492023	R.A.M.C. attd. 16th Bn.		
Whitcher L. Cpl.	546	9th Bn.		
White P.A.C. Pte.	725	7th Bn.		
White W.H. Pte.	SD/5772	13th Bn.		
White W.J. Sgt.	G/2416	8th Bn.		
Whiteman A.G. Sgt.	G/20293	12th Bn.		
Whittemore F.A. Pte.	G/14877	13th Bn.		
Whittemore F.A. Pte. M.M.	G/14877	13th Bn.	Bar	
Whiting R.S. Sgt.	200346	4th Bn.		
Whitlock A.E. Sgt.	SD/5943	9th Bn.		
Whitton P.H. Pte.	SD/373	11th Bn.		
Wilcock C.J. L/Cpl.	G/12966	12th Bn.		
Wild R.E. Cpl.	320193	16th Bn.		
Wileman A.H. Sgt.	G/19825	11th Bn.		
Wilkinson H.S. Pte. (A/Sgt.)	SD/751	11th Bn.		
Wilkinson S.F. Pte. (L/Cpl.)	G/16762	9th Bn.		
Williams C.O. Pte. D.C.M.	G/16259	12th Bn.		
Wilmer R.C.W. Sgt.	320027	16th Bn.		
Wilmshurst C.A. Sgt.	225	5th Bn.		
Wilmshurst J.W. Pte.	L/10237	7th Bn.		
Wilmshurst T. Pte.	G/1664	8th Bn.		
Wilson A.R. Pte.	1677	5th Bn.		
Wilson B. Pte.	G/18972	2nd Bn.		
Wilson J. Pte.	322	7th Bn.		
Wilson J. Pte. M.M.	322	7th Bn.	Bar	
Wilton A. Pte.	202163	2nd Bn.		
Wimborn R.C.V. L/Cpl.	G/1721	8th Bn.		Citation
Windebank A. Pte.	G/15655	13th Bn.		
Windmill J. Cpl.	G/1741	8th Bn.		
Wood L. Sgt.	L/9184	1st Bn.		Citation
Woolgar G. Pte.	G/2621	8th Bn.		
Woollam A.S. Pte.	SD/1510	12th Bn.		
Woollard C. Pte.	G/14899	13th Bn.		
Woolley C. Pte.	L/10472	2nd Bn.		
Woolley J.W. Pte.	G/17580	2nd Bn.		
Woolley J.W. Pte. M.M.	G/17580	2nd Bn.	Bar	
Woolven A.G. Cpl.	200484	4th Bn.		
Woolven G.F. Pte. (L/Cpl.)	G/17926	7th Bn.		
Worcester E. L/Cpl.	5345	3rd Bn. was 13th Bn.		
Wratten G.A. Pte.	G/1962	8th Bn.		
Wright G.W. Cpl.	G/18027	7th Bn.		
Wright N.L. Pte.	G/30514	17th Bn.		
Young A. A/Sgt.	1483	2nd Bn.		
Young A. L/Cpl.	G/7008	8th Bn.		
Young G.T. A/Sgt.	G/1599	2nd Bn.		
Younger W. Cpl.	39396	7th Bn.		

Military Medal Winners Who Died

Horace Atkinson M.M. Private G/5966 11th Bn. Wednesday 26th September 1917
Tyne Cot Memorial, Zonnebeke, West-Vlaanderen, Belgium
Grave Reference Panel 86 to 88

William Bridger Bailey M.M. Sergeant G/6339 9th Bn. Saturday 23rd March 1918
Pozieres Memorial, Somme, France
Grave Reference Panel 46 & 47

Charles Edward Ball M.M. Lance-Sergeant SD/3521 13th Bn. Sunday 3rd September 1916
Hamel Military Cemetery, Beaumont-Hamel, Somme, France
Grave Reference I.E.41.

Lawrence Barker M.M. Sergeant SD/5743 11th Bn. Wednesday 3rd April 1918
Roisel Communal Cemetery Extension, Somme, France
Grave Reference III E. 10.

William Rufus Barwick M.M. Lance-Corporal G/6016 7th Bn. Monday 26th August 1918
Peronne Road Cemetery, Maricourt, Somme, France
Grave Reference IV. H. 2.

Alfred William Beale M.M. Sergeant G/931 7th Bn. Monday 9th April 1917
Arras Memorial, Pas de Calais, France
Grave Reference Bay 6

Thomas Herman Beall M.M. Private G/648 "B" Coy. 7th Bn. Wednesday 27th March 1918
Pozieres Memorial, Somme, France
Grave Reference Panel 46 & 47

James Bird M.M. Private   S/2033 7th Bn. Friday 7th July 1916
Thiepval Memorial, Somme, France
Grave Reference Pier and Face 7C

James Bishop M.M. Private SD/400 11th Bn. Monday 23rd October 1916
Contay British Cemetery, Contay, Somme, France
Grave Reference IV C 29

Charles James Bliss M.M. Sergeant   G/5427 9th Bn. Monday 4th November 1918
Cross Roads Cemetery, Nord, France
Grave Reference I F 7

Charles Henry Blunden M.M. Lance-Corporal   G/15882 11th Bn. Wednesday 3rd April 1918
Pozieres Memorial, Somme, France
Grave Reference   Panel 46 & 47

Percy William Bridger M.M. Private G/4017 7th Bn. Tuesday 3rd May 1917
Arras Memorial, Pas de Calais, France
Grave Reference Bay 6

Ernest James Brown M.M. Lance-Corporal SD/1157 11th Bn. Thursday 12th October 1917
Hamel Military Cemetery, Beaumont-Hamel, Somme, France
Grave Reference II B 11

George Caesar M.M.,M.S.M. Sergeant G/2379 "C" Coy. 8th Bn. Wednesday 7th August 1918
Ribemont Communal Cemetery Extension, Somme, France
Grave Reference II B 8

Alfred George Catchpole M.M. Sergeant L/5420 2nd Bn. Saturday 9th September 1916
Thiepval Memorial, Somme, France
Grave Reference Pier and face 7 C

Frederick C. Chandler M.M. Private G/15802 11th Bn. Friday 7th December 1917
Nine-Elms British Cemetery, Poperinghe, Poperinghe, West-Vlaanderen, Belgium
Grave Reference IX D 10

George Herbert Clarke M.M. Private TF/241483 13th Bn. Friday 18th October 1918
Tyne Cot Memorial, Zonnebeke, West-Vlaanderen, Belgium
Grave Reference Panel 86 to 88

Horace Edward Cockett M.M. & Bar Private SD/1017 11th Bn. Wednesday 3rd April 1918
Pozieres Memorial, Somme, France
Grave Reference Panel 46 & 47

John Daughtry M.M. Lance-Corporal G/2424 8th Bn. Sunday 1st October 1916
Thieval Memorial, Somme, France
Grave Reference Pier and Face 7C

Horace Reginald Diplock M.M. Sergeant L/9685 8th Bn. Saturday 8th September 1918
Duhallow A.D.S. Cemetery, Ieper, West-Vlaaanderen, Belgium
Grave Reference I C 7

Alfred Ernest Durrant M.M. Corporal 3338 4th Bn. Wednesday 4th September 1918
Messines Ridge British Cemetery, Mesen, West-Vlaanderen, Belgium
Grave Reference V B 41

William John Eade M.M. Private SD/1180 7th Bn. Monday 20th May 1918
Mailly Wood Cemetery, Somme, France
Grave Reference II M 1

Arthur James Evans M.M. Sergeant G/764 7th Bn. Friday 7th July 1916
Serre Road Cemetery No 2., Somme, France
Grave Reference XV B 16

Isaac Henry Farmer M.M. Sergeant SD/1883 2nd Bn. Thursday 24th October 1918
St. Sever Cemetery Extension, Rouen, Seine-Maritime, France
Grave Reference S. II. KK. 6.

Alfred Samuel Ford M.M. Private SD/3101 13th Bn. Friday 30th June 1916
Loos Memorial, Pas de Calais, France
Grave Reference Panel 69 to 73

Percy John Gardiner M.M. Lance-Corporal G/5946 "D" Coy. 2nd Bn. Saturday 9th September 1916
Serre Road Cemetery No. 2, Somme, France
Grave Reference XXXI. J. 7.

Herbert Gardner M.M. Lance-Corporal TF/32012 16th(S/Yeo.)Bn. Thursday 3rd October 1918
Le Chateau Memorial Cemetery, Nord, France
Grave Reference I. B. 157.

Arthur Gibson M.M. Lance-Corporal SD/5509 13th Bn. Saturday 4th August 1917
Etaples Military Cemetery, Pas de Calais, France
Grave Reference XXII. O. 24.

Arthur Wilfred Golden D.C.M.,M.M. Sergeant SD/1766 11th Bn. Wednesday 24th April 1918
St. Sever Cemetery Extension, Rouen, Seine-Maritime, France
Grave Reference P. IX. N. 11A

Richard Guttridge M.M. Lance-Corporal SD/2691 13th Bn. Sunday 24th March 1918
Abbevillle Communal Cemetery Extension, Somme, France
Grave Reference I. B. 28.

Joseph William Guymer M.M. Private G/11601 2nd Bn. Sunday 13th October 1918
Vadencourt British Cemetery, Maissemy, Ainse, France
Grave Reference III. A. 5.

Walter Hammonds Hadley M.M. Sergeant G/20295 9th Bn. Monday 4th November 1918
Villers-Pol Communal Cemetery Extension, Nord, France
Grave Reference C.2.

George Charles Hammond M.M. Sergeant 2219 8th Bn. Friday 7th February 1919
Esnes Communal Cemetery, Nord, France
Grave Reference 3.

Walter Philip Gordon Harrold M.M. Lance-Sergeant SD/2698 13th Bn. Sunday 3rd September 1916
Thiepval Memorial, Somme, France
Grave Reference Pier and Face 7C

Albert William Heise M.M. Sergeant SD/3186 11th Bn. Saturday 27th April 1918
Tyne Cot Memorial, Zonnebeke, West-Vlaanderen, Belgium
Grave Reference Panel 86 to 88

Spencer Harold Hemsley M.M. Corporal 202190 "A "Coy. 2nd Bn. Saturday 27th September 1918
Brie British Cemetery, Somme, France
Grave Reference IV. D. 10.

William Hendry M.M. Private G/350 7th Bn. Thursday 2nd November 1916
Agny Military Cemetery, Pas de Calais, France
Grave Reference F. 49.

Robert William Howlett M.M. Private G/18982 2nd Bn. Wednesday 23rd October 1918
Highland Cemetery, Le Cateau, Nord, France
Grave Reference V. B. 1.

Richard Cecil Kelsey M.M. Private SD/5003 2nd Bn. Tuesday 24th September 1918
Vis-en-Artois Memorial, Pas de Calais, France
Grave Reference Panel 6

Alfred William Linford M.M. Company Sergeant-Major G/29279 12th Bn. Thursday 25th September 1917
Tyne Cot Memorial, Zonnebeke, West-Vlaanderen, Belgium
Grave Reference Panel 86 to 88

Charles Alfred Lisher M.M. Private SD/2137 13th Bn. Friday 8th March 1918
Fins New British Cemetery, Sorel-Le-Grand, Somme, France
Grave Reference IV. C. 31

Thomas Lucas M.M. Lance-Corporal G/16046 13th Bn. Thursday 21st March 1918
Pozieres Memorial, Somme, France
Grave Reference Panel 46 and 47

Mark Percy Mann M.M. Private G/14619 2nd Bn. Tuesday 24th September 1918
Vis-en-Artois Memorial, Pas de Calais, France
Grave Reference Panel 6

Ernest James Manvell M.M. Sergeant G/2579 8th Bn. Saturday 23rd March 1918
Chauny Communal Cemetery British Extension, Ainse, France
Grave Reference 3. A. 3.

Thomas Matthias M.M. Sergeant SD/3745 13th Bn. Tuesday 24th September 1918
Vadencourt British Cemetery, Maissemy, Ainse, France
Grave Reference IV. F. 2.

Henry Maughan M.M. Lance-Corporal G/266 7th Bn. Sunday 25th November 1917
Cambrai Memorial, Louveral, Nord, France
Grave Reference Panel 7

James Walter Mills M.M. Private 315146 "B" Coy. 16th Bn. Monday 7th October 1918
St. Sever Cemetery Extension, Rouen, Seine-Maritime, France
Grave Reference S. II. I. 9.

Owen Corby Morris M.M. Private 17388 7th Bn. Sunday 26th August 1918
Peronne Road Cemetery, Maricourt, Somme, France
Grave Reference IV. H. 3.

Walter Jesse Osborne M.M. Sergeant G/415 7th Bn. Wednesday 21st November 1917
Tincourt New British Cemetery, Somme, France
Grave Reference II. G. 13.

James Philip Perkins M.M. Lance-Corporal G/20582 8th Bn. Wednesday 23rd October 1918
Highland Cemetery, Le Cateau, Nord, France
Grave Reference IV. C. 10.

William Poile M.M. Private G/2184 8th Bn. Friday 12th April 1918
St. Sever Cemetery Extension, Rouen, Seine-Maritime, France
Grave Reference P. VII. K. 7A.

Dennis Reid Porteous M.M. Private G/22923 7th Bn. Thursday 28th March 1918
Pozieres Memorial, Somme, France
Grave Reference Panel 46 and 47

George William Preston M.M. Corporal G/684 7th Bn. Tuesday 20th November 1918
Cambrai Memorial, Louveral, Nord, France
Grave Reference Panel 7

Herbert Henry Renshaw M.M. Corporal G/15777 "B" Coy. 11th Bn. Tuesday 25th September 1917
Hooge Crater Cemetery, Ieper, West-Vlaanderen, Belgium
Grave Reference IX. F. 4.

Joseph Ripley M.M. Private SD/1547 12th Bn. Saturday 4th November 1916
Contay British Cemetery, Contay, Somme, France
Grave Reference III. E. 32.

Henry Charles Scott M.M. Private SD/3225 13th Bn. Friday 30th June 1916
St. Vaast Post Military Cemetery, Richebourg-L'Avoue, Pas de Calais, France
Grave Reference III. G. 9.

Albert Edward Selby M.M. Sergeant G/111 "A" Coy. 7th Bn. Thursday 8th August 1918
Beacon Cemetery, Sailly-Laurette, Somme, France
Grave Reference II. G. 9.

Frederick Edward Shirley M.M. Private G/15756 11th Bn. Tuesday 31st October 1916
Theipval Memorial, Somme, France
Grave Reference Pier and Face 7C

Ernest Stringer M.M. Sergeant G/1834 8th (Pioneer) Bn. Tuesday 14th May 1918
Ribemont Communal Cemetery Extension, Somme, France
Grave Reference I. M. 6.

Arthur Tapner M.M;M.I.D. Private G/1701 2nd Bn. Monday 12th October 1918
Vadencourt British Cemetery, Maissemy, Ainse, France
Grave Reference II. A. 7.

Archibald Edmund Tester M.M. Lance-Corporal 200784 1/4th Bn. Wednesday 7th November 1917
Beersheba War Cemetery, Israel
Grave Reference A. 18.

John Tester M.M. Lance-Corporal L/8513 2nd Bn. Sunday 20th August 1916
Thiepval Memorial, Somme, France
Grave Reference

William Thirst M.M. Private G/9353 "B" Coy. 7th Bn. Friday 4th October 1918
Suffield (St. Margaret) Churchyard, Norfolk
Grave Reference North of Church

H. Tomlinson M.M. Private SD/5594 9th Bn. Saturday 6th April 1918
Le Cateau Memorial Cemetery. Nord, France
Grave Reference I. B. 10.

Sidney Toogood M.M. Lance-Corporal SD/5649 13th Bn. Thursday 27th September 1917
Tyne Cot Memorial Zonnebeke, West-Vlaanderen, Belgium
Grave Reference Panel 86 to 88

John Frank Turner M.M. Sergeant G/20296 8th Bn. Thursday 21st March 1918
Pozieres Memorial, Somme, France
Grave Reference Panel 46 and 47

William Henry S. Waldron M.M. Lance-Sergeant SD/3503 13th Bn. Wednesday 1st August 1917
Brandehoek New Military Cemetery, Vlamertinghe, Ieper, West-Vlaanderen, Belgium
Grave Reference IV. C. II.

Leonard West M.M. Private SD/2819 13th Bn. Tuesday 31st July 1917
Ypres (Menin Gate) Memorial, Ieper, West-Vlaanderen, Belgium
Grave Reference Panel 20

Frederick Arthur Whittemore M.M. & Bar Private G/14877 7th Bn. Monday 26th August 1917
Carnoy Military Cemetery, Carnoy, Belgium
Grave Reference Z. 13.

Arthur Harold Wileman M.M. Sergeant G/14877 11th Bn. Sunday 28th April 1918
Tyne Cot Memorial, Zonnebeke, West-Vlaanderen, Belgium
Grave Reference Panel 86 to 88

Henry Sydney Wilkinson M.M. Sergeant SD/751 11th Bn. Monday 30th October 1916
Warloy-Baillon Communal Cemetery Extension, Somme, France
Grave Reference VIII. C. 6.

Arthur Young M.M. Sergeant G/1483 2nd Bn. Saturday 9th September 1916
Thiepval Memorial, Somme, France
Grave Reference Pier and Face 7C

George Thomas Young M.M;M.I.D. Sergeant G/1599 2nd Bn. Saturday 9th September 1916
Thiepval Memorial, Somme, France
Grave Reference Pier and Face 7C

V.D.

Aitkins F.W. Mjr.	1st C.P.R.
Bartelot Sir W.B. Bart. Hon. Col. C.B.	2nd V.B
Bloomfield J.A. Hon. Mjr. & Adj.	2nd V.B
Campion W.H. Mjr. & Hon. Lt-Col.	2nd V.B
Caudle A.W.W. Surg-Lt. Rtd.	2nd V.B
Clarke J.C. Capt. Rtd.	1st V.B
Clarke C.S. Lt-Col. & Hon. Col.	1st V.B
Cortis A. Qm & Hon. Capt.	2nd V.B
Currie E.R. Very Rev. A/ Ch. M.A.	1st C.P.R.
Eden A. Rev. A/Chaplain	1st C.P.R.
Fletcher Sir H. Lt-Col. & Hon. Col.	2nd V.B
Gell A.F. Mjr. & Hon. Lt-Col.	1st V.B.
Harrison E.R. Capt. & Hon. Mjr.	2nd V.B
Hawken G.L.L. Surgeon-Lt. Rtd.	2nd V.B
Helme R.M. Mjr. & Hon. Lt-Col.	2nd V.B
Henty A. Capt. & Hon. Mjr.	2nd V.B
Henty E. Capt. & Hon. Mjr.	2nd V.B
Hodgson B.T. Lt-Col. C.M.G.	(2nd V.B.) 5th Bn.
King G.L. Capt. & Hon. Mjr.	1st V.B.
Langham F G Lt-Col. C.M.G.	5th Bn.
Lewis C.F. Bde. Surg. Lt-Col.	2nd V.B
Lister J.J. Capt. & Hon. Mjr.	2nd V.B
Livesay J.R. Capt. & Hon. Mjr.	1st V.B
Malden H.C. Capt. & Hon. Mjr. Rtd.	1st V.B
Mostyn E.H.J.D. Mjr. Hon. Lt-Col.	2nd V.B
Norfolk H. Duke of Mjr. & Hon. Lt-Col. K.G.	2nd V.B
Oxley J.S. Capt. & Hon. Mjr.	1st V.B
Pearless J.R. Lt. & Hon. Capt. Rtd..	1st V.B
Porter W N T/Mjr. C.I.E.	
Richardson A. Lt-Col. & Hon. Col.	1st C.P.R.
Scott E.E. Capt. Rtd.	2nd V.B.
Selmes C.A. Capt. & Hon. Mjr.	1st C.P.R.
Southwell H.K. Rev. A/Ch. M.A.	1st V.B.
Stuckey W. Capt.	1st V.B.
Shaft G.T. Capt. & Hon. Mjr.	2nd V.B.
Tamplin W.C. Lt-Col. & Hon. Col.	2nd V.B.
Turner S.D. Hon. Mjr. & Adj.	1st C.P.R.
Verrall H.J. Mjr. & Hon. Lt-Col.	1st V.B.
Verrall H. Hon. Col.	1st V.B.
Weston S.T. Qm & Hon. Mjr.	1st C.P.R.
Woolley A.C. Mjr. & Hon. Lt-Col.	1st V.B.
Wyatt H.H. Rev. & Hon Ch. M.A.	1st V.B.

T.D.

Beale Sidney W.P. Mjr.	4th Bn.
Boyd Arthur H. Rev. O.B.E.,M.C.,M.A.	4th Bn.
Campion William Robert Mjr. (A/Lt-Col.) D.S.O	4th Bn..
Constable Guy Sefton Mjr. (T/Lt-Col.) M.C	5th Bn..
Cory Edward John Capt. D.S.O	1st C.P.R.
Courthope George Loyd Mjr. M.C.	4th Bn.
Constable Guy Sefton Mjr. (T/Lt-Col.)	4th Bn.
Dawes Edwin P. Captain (retired).	4th Bn.
Gorringe William H. Mjr.	5th Bn.
Godman Charles R.B. Mjr.	4th Bn.
Hodgson Barnard T. Lt.-Col. C.M.G.,V.D.	4th Bn.
Holmes Leonard Mjr.	6th Bn.
Howard Thomas H. Mjr.	4th Bn.
Johnson Charles V. Mjr.	4th Bn.
Kenderdine William H. Capt.	4th Bn.
Langham Edward Hennah Mjr.	5th Bn.
Mathews Henry E. Mjr.	4th Bn.
Messel Leonard Charles Capt. & Hon. Mjr.	4th Bn.
Norfolk Henry Duke of, K.G.,G.C.V.O. Cmdg.	2nd V.B.
Moore Ernest Gresham Capt. & Hon. Mjr.	4th Bn.
Pearson Weetman H.M. Mjr. The Hon.	S/Yeo.
Whitfield George S. Lt-Col.	S/Yeo.

Mentioned in Despatches

Name	Number	Battalion
Adams A. Lt.		5th Bn.
Aldridge C.P. Capt.		1st Bn.
Aldridge F.R. R.Q.M.S.	142	
Alexander G.R. T/2/Lt.		
Alexander J.W.R. 2/Lt.		
Amos C. Sgt./Mjr. (3)		3rd Bn.
Andrews P. Sgt.	1512	
Andrews S.A. Lt. D.S.O.,M.C. (2)		7th Bn.
Apperley W.H.W. Capt. M.C. (2)		2nd Bn.
Armitage F.G. T/2/Lt. (A/Lt.)		
Ash C.D. T/Capt. Beds Regt. attd. R.S.R.		
Ashby J.R. Mjr.		
Ashworth H.S. Capt. (T/Lt-Col.) (1)		
Atkinson L. de B. 2/Lt.		
Atree B. Pte.	8745	2nd Bn.
Baddeley W.H. Capt. (2)		
Balcombe J.C. C.S.M.	320001	
Baldwin A. Cpl.		1st^t Bn.
Bamber W. C.S.M.	L/5648	4th Bn.
Banham J.J. T/2/Lt.		
Barford J. Pte.	265798 (was 1415)	1st Bn.
Barlow P.S. Capt.		5th Bn.
Barnes C.L. Sgt.	201040	4th Bn.
Barrow A.J. Pte.	181937	52nd Bn.
Bartlett C. T/Capt.		
Batt J. Sgt.	6961	2nd Bn.
Baxter J.H. Cpl..	G/23248	7th Bn.
Beale A.W. L/Sgt.	931	
Beale S.W.P. Mjr.		
Beech P.E.W. Pte.	240529	5th Bn.
Bell J. C.S.M.	41547	
Bellamy R. Lt.		1st Bn
Bell-Irving A. Lt-Col. D.S.O.		
Bennett E. Cpl.	30111	17th Bn.
Bennett F. Cpl.	653	
Betham R.J.A. Capt. (2)		
Bidder H.F. Mjr. (T/Lt-Col)		
Birkett R.M. Mjr. (T/Lt-Col.) D.S.O. (3)		7th Bn.
Blackman W. Sgt.	1164	
Blake F.W.E. Capt. 3rd attd.1st		3rd Bn.
Blakeney H.E.H. Lt.		1st Bn.
Blease A. Pte. (Vol.Coy)		2nd Bn.
Bliss D. Sgt.	240178	1st Bn.
Blois-Johnson T.G. Col. C.M.G. Punjabis		
Bloomfield J. R.S.M.	S/516	
Bolitho A.C. Pte. (A/L/Sgt.)	36121	
Bond C.A. Pte. (A/Sgt.)	G/36737	52nd Bn.
Bond C.E. Mjr.7 Bt. Col. (T/Brig) C.M.G.,D.S.O. (7)	L/4369	11th Bn.
Boniface J.R. R.S.M.	SD/3297	
Boniface V. Sgt.		
Box F.G. Lt.	G/2381	4th Bn.
Boyce J.W. R.Q.M.S.	5730	
Bray A. Pte.	4017	
Bridger P.W. Pte.	240751	9th Bn.
Briggs A.W. R.Q.M.S.		
Brooker J.R. 2/Lt.	L/5413	5th Bn.
Brooks F.B. C.S.M.	G/2316	
Brown C.E. Pte.		
Brown G.L. Lt.		
Brown H. Lt.	315366	1st Bn.
Bryant B.H. Sgt.	200142	16th Bn.
Bryce A. C.Q.M.S.		16th Bn.
Buckland J.R. 2/Lt.	200699	4th Bn.
Buckland W.J. Pte.	891	17th Bn.
Budgen W.H. Sgt. (2)	G/7827	9th Bn.
Bull G. C.S.M.	7835	
Burden F. Pte.	6995	5th Bn.
Burgess S. Sgt.	L/6693	2nd Bn.
Burk J. Sgt.	9843	2nd Bn.
Busby F. Cpl.	G/1379	4th Bn.
Bussell P.R. Cpl.	T/240633	2nd Bn.
Butcherd J.H. Pte. (A/Sgt)	G/41398	7th Bn.

Name	Number	Unit
Butter R.W. Cpl. R.W.K. attd.		51st Bn.
Café C.H.W. Lt-Col.		2nd Bn.
Caldwell R. McK 2/Lt.		S/Yeo.
Cameron J.S. Mjr. & Bt. Lt-Col. D.S.O. (4)		4th Bn.
Campbell E.R. Capt.		4th Bn.
Campbell G.O.L. T/Capt. M.C. (2)		3rd Bn.
Campion W.R. Lt-Col.) D.S.O.,T.D.,M.P. (3)		4th Bn.
Carter J.A. Lt.		2nd Bn.
Cassels F. Mjr.		
Cassy J.S. T/Capt. M.C.		
Catmur H.A.F.V. 2/Lt.		
Catt H. C.S.M.	200131	
Chad T.E. Lt. M.C		
Charlwood A.E. Capt. & Flight Commander		R.F.C.
Charman G.A. C.S.M.	6095	16th Bn.
Cheal W.H. C.Q.M.S.	2643	5th Bn.
Chittenden H.F. Lt. M.C.		
Clark P.L. 2/Lt. D.S.O.		7th Bn.
Clarke J.E. Q/M & Hon. Lt. (2)		3rd Bn.
Clarke S.R. Mjr.		2nd Bn.
Clay C.C.P. L/Sgt.	9157	1st Bn.
Clements E. Sgt.	9214	9th Bn.
Coleman H.C. T/Capt. M.C.		
Collins F. Cpl.	3071	4th Bn.
Constable G.S. Mjr. (T/Lt-Col.) M.C.		
Cook L.E. Lt.		1st Bn.
Cook TH. Pte.	1814	
Cooling J.H. T/Capt.		
Coote-Browne W. Mjr. (T/Lt-Col.)		
Coppard A.V. Pte. (A/Sgt.)	828	S/Yeo
Corbett A. Capt. (T/Lt-Col.) (2)		9th Bn.
Corral W.R. Lt. (T/Mjr.) M.C. Buffs attd.		1st Bn.
Cosens G. Sgt. (A/Sgt/Mjr.)	6536	6th Bn.
Courthorpe G.L. Capt.		7th Bn.
Cousens H.S. T/Capt.		6th Bn
Cowley G.E. Sgt. (A/C.Q.M.S.)	G/2186	
Coxhead H.J. T/Capt.		2nd Bn.
Cragg A.B. T/2/Lt. (2)		2nd Bn.
Crane J.W. Sgt.	G/2652	
Crawfurd P.E.P. Mjr. & Bt. Lt-Col.		2nd Bn.
Crispin H.T.C. Lt-Col.		52nd Bn
Crowther J. Pte.	36116	
Cutting E.W. Sgt.	560	51st M.R
Dade E.W. Pte. (A/Cpl.) attd. Mdx. Regt.	36191	7th Bn.
Dallaway J.H. C.S.M. D.C.M.	L/5908	2nd Bn.
Dashwood V.E.C. Capt. (T/Lt-Col.) M.C. (3)		16th Bn
Davey P.V. Sgt.	320053	
Davies G.T. Sgt.	2398	5th Bn.
Dawson H.R.W. Capt.		2nd Bn.
de Chair G.H.B. Capt.& Bt. Mjr. O.B.E.,M.C. (3)		3rd Bn.
Dearlove A. Sgt.	G/2377	2nd W.R
Dibden F.J.A. Lt. attd. Welsh Regt.		
Dick R.N. Mjr. & Bt. Lt-Col. (T/Brig.) D.S.O. (2)		3rd Bn.
Dicker A.S.H. Capt.		2nd Bn.
Diplock T. Sgt.	6868	16th Bn
Dodge J.B. T/Lt-Col. D.S.O.,D.S.C.		17th Bn.
Dolleymore E. 2/t. (A/Capt.)		
Donne B.D.A. Lt-Col.		1st Bn.
Drake G. Pte.	30168	
Dray W. Sgt.	8427	2nd Bn.
Drew P.F. T/2?lt. (A/Capt.)		
du Moulin L.E. Mjr.		1st Bn.
Duck J.G. Sgt. (A/C.Q.M.S.)	315173	16th Bn
Edwards T.R. Capt.		16th Bn
Ellen W.P. T/2/Lt		8th Bn.
Ellis R.V.H. T/2/Lt.		
Etherington J. C.Q.M.S.	G/3733	9th Bn.
Evans S.G. Capt.		3rd Bn.
Eve J. Sgt.	8962	
Farmer G.S. T/2/Lt.		
Farrell W. Sgt.	L/8712	
Farrer S.J. T/2Lt.		
Fazan E.A.C. Capt. M.B. R.A.M.C.		5th Bn.
Fennell S. R.Q.M.S	320002	

Name	Number	Battalion
Fenton F.H. 2/Lt. (A/Capt.)		
Field C.A. Capt.		8th Bn.
Field T.P. Q/M & Capt.		4th Bn.
Fielder F.G. Pte.	G/2144	8th Bn.
Finch L.H.K. Lt.		2nd Bn.
Finlayson R.A. Mjr. C.M.G. (2)		
Fitzhugh V.M. T/Capt.		
Flint C.W. Q/M & Capt.		
Foord S. Sgt.	451	
Foster P.G. T/2/Lt.		
Foster T. T/Mjr. (2)		9th Bn.
Frost A. St. John A. T/Lt.		5th Bn.
Gannon W. L/Sgt.		1st Bn.
Garner C.C. T/Lt. (2)		8th Bn.
Gates T. Sgt/Drmr.		1st Bn.
Gibson E.R. Lt.	G/30525	5th Bn.
Gilbert A.R. Brevet Mjr. (2)		1st Bn.
Gilchrist A. Sgt.		17th Bn.
Gillett R.H. T/Lt. (A/Capt.)		
Gilmore G.H. T/Capt. D.S.O.,M.C. (2)		
Glasgow A.E. Mjr. & Bt. Lt-Col (T/Brig.) D.S.O. (6)		8th Bn
Glenny EB. T/2/Lt.		
Goddard N.C. Q/M & Hon. Capt.	265093	
Godwin E.T.H. T/Lt. M.C.	SD/1168	9th Bn
Gooding W.A. R.Q.M.S.		
Goodsell A.J. Sgt.	G/30030	3rd Bn.
Grant F.N. Capt.		5th Bn.
Grayson F. Pte.	TR/10/4402	17th Bn.
Green E.W.B. Lt-Col. D.S.O. (5)	G/30807	2nd Bn.
Greene E.S.G. C.Q.M.S.		
Gronheit A.L. Sgt.(A/C.Q.M.S.)	452	17th Bn.
Gudman C.B. Mjr.(Lt-Col)	G/165047	3rd V. Bn
Hall H.F. Cpl.	now 31239	
Hall J. Sgt.		
Hammond R.P. Sgt. 18742 7th Bn. R.W.K.	936	17th Bn.
Hampton N.H. T/Capt.	8562	
Hams W.T. Sgt.	G/2121	
Hanlon P.J. C.Q.M.S. (2)		7th Bn.
Hann E.E. Sgt. (2)	36119	7th Bn.
Harden E.J. T/2/Lt. (A/Capt.)	3359	
Haynes C.A. Pte.		51st Bn..
Head G.F. Sgt.	G/883	
Heagerty W.T. T/Mjr.	L/7688	
Heasman E.H. Sgt.	200276	7th Bn.
Herridge W. C.S.M.	759	
Hersee C.H. Sgt..	G/16509	
Hewson H.C. Sgt.	202090	
Higham T.L. Pte.		
Hill E. Pte.		5th Bn.
Hill E.A. T/Capt.	2223	
Hill G. T/Lt.		7th Bn.
Hill L. L/Cpl	20752	5th Bn.
Hill M.V.B. Capt. (T/Lt-Col.) M.V.B.,D.S.O.R Fus. (3)		9th Bn.
Hillman E. Pte.		
Hind R.C.D. T/Capt. (3)		7th Bn.
Hobbs E.J. 2/Lt.		2nd Bn.
Hodgson B.T. Lt-Col. C.M.G.		1st Bn.
Holderness W. Capt.		
Holdsworth M.J. 2/Lt.	8861	
Holland A. 2/Lt.	G/3416	
Hollingdale F. Pte.	240073	2nd Bn.
Holman W.H. Sgt.	200371	
Holmwood R. Sgt.		5th Bn.
Hopkins A. Sgt.	1864	4th Bn.
Hornblower T.B. Capt.		5th Bn.
Howard A.C. Sgt.		
Howard K.B. T/Lt. (A/Capt.)		
Hughes J. L/Cpl.	S/2385	1st Bn.
Hulton J.M. Mjr. (A/Lt-Col.) C.B.E.,D.S.O. (2)	L/5863	4th Bn.
Humphrey G. C.Q.M.S.	G/97864	16th Bn.
Humphrey W. R.Q.M.S. D.C.M.	2105	2nd Bn
Hurst F. C.S.M.	8779	
Hygate H.P. Cpl.	240017	

Name	Number	Battalion
Hyland H. Cpl.	8779	2nd Bn.
Hyland R.J. Sgt.	240017	
Ide A.E. A/L/Sgt	240691	4th Bn.
Impey G.H. Mjr.(T/Lt-Col.) D.S.O. (3)		7th Bn.
Ireland L.A.F. T/2/Lt.		
Jebb R.D. Lt.		
Johnson DG. Mjr. (A/Lt-Col.) V.C.,D.S.O.,M.C.		2nd Bn.
Johnson F.W.F. Lt-Col. D.S.O. (2)		2/6th Bn.
Johnson W.G. Pte. (2)	G/14968	11th Bn.
Jones C. C.Q.M.S.	G/2476	8th Bn.
Jones H.E. T/Lt.		
Jones T. Sgt.	4746	
Jones T.A. Q/M & Hon. Lt. M.C.,D.C.M. (3)	was 2871	was 1st Bn. now 2nd Bn
Jones W.P.S. T/Capt.		
Judd H.A.W. Cpl.	2568	52nd Bn
Kay Robinson H.T. T/Lt-Col. D.S.O. (3)		13th Bn.
Keep G.R. Lt.		
Kemp G.L. T/Lt.		
Kemp W.H. Sgt.		1st Bn.
Kenward H.J. Clr/Sgt.	5/2198	5th Bn.
Kimber A.F. Sgt.	8166	2nd Bn.
King R.N.R. Lt.		3rd Bn
Kitchen W.S. Sgt.	1458	1st Bn.
Knight W. Sgt.	265492	6th Bn.
Lamotte L. Capt. (Lt-Col.) D.S.O. Cmdg 2 York L.I. (2)		2nd Bn.
Langdon J.F.P. Mjr.(T/Lt-Col.) (2)		
Langham E.H. Mjr. T.D.		
Langham F.G. Lt-Col. V.D.		5th Bn
Langham J.E.C. Lt.		
Langridge J. Lt.		5th Bn.
Lapworth C. T/2/Lt.		
Lawes W.A. Sgt.	240045	
Lawrence A.E. T/Lt.		
Layton N.A. Mjr.		
Leachman G.E. Mjr.& Bt. Lt-Col. C.I.E. (3)		1st Bn.
Lee A. Sgt. 120		
Lenton M.H. Pte.	G/30645	17th Bn.
Lewry H.A. Sgt.		1st Bn.
Licence H. Cpl. (A/R.Q.M.S.)	200508	4th Bn.
Lissiman H.C. T/2/Lt.		
Lloyd H.R. Mjr. & Bt. Lt-Col.		
Lockhart J. Pte.		1st Bn.
Loder R.E.. Lt. (T/Capt.) (1)		
Loder J. de Vere Capt.		
Long S.W. R.Q.M.S.	118	4th Bn.
Lott H.C. T/Capt. (2)		
Love A. Pte. (A/Sgt.)	5949	8th Bn.
Loveland E. Cpl.	6665	51st Bn.
Lowe A.H.C. Lt.		
L'Strange H.H. Lt. M.C.		
Lundgren C.W. T/Mjr.		S/Yeo
Lupton R.H. T/Lt.		
Lusted G. Sgt.	1647	
Lynch G.L. Pte.	G/2472	8th Bn.
Mackenzie E.L. Lt-Col. D.S.O. (2)		1st Bn.
MacRoberts N. de Putron T/Lt. D.S.O;M.C.		
Malden C.C. Capt. (A/Mjr.)		1st Bn.
Maples A.C. Capt.		4th Bn.
March Earl of Col.		3rd Bn.
Marsland J. T/2/Lt.		
Marsh H. Cpl.	G/1766	6th Bn.
Marshall J. Pte.	6200	2nd Bn.
Martin H. C.S.M.	290575	4th Bn.
Martin J. Pte.	8261	2nd Bn.
Martin W. Cpl.	G/41407	51st Bn
Mathews H.E. Capt.		
Maxwell R. Lt.		5th Bn.
May R.T. T/Capt.		
Maycock G. T/Lt.		
McArthur D. Sgt.	9	
McCarthy C.M. Pte.	G/19009	9th Bn.
McIvor A.R. T/Capt.		
Meade H.W. T/Capt.		8th Bn.
Meaton H.J. C.Q.M.S.	202870	

Name	Number	Battalion
Metcalf A.E. Sgt. Mdx. Regt. attd.	1285	52nd Bn
Middleditch B. Pte.	21598	6th Bn.
Middleton R.C.G. Lt. M.C.		
Millward W.C. Mjr. (A/Lt-Col.) D.S.O. (2)		
Minns W. Pte.	8149	2nd Bn
Money G.A Mjr.		5th Bn
Montresor E.H. Capt.		1st Bn
Moody C.F. Sgt. M.M.	S/385	8th Bn.
Morey G. Cpl.	G/4320	9th Bn.
Morgan A. L/Sgt. R.W.K. attd.	41402	52nd Bn.
Morphett G.C. Bt. Lt-Col. D.S.O. (2)		1st Bn.
Morris G. Sgt.	20431	3rd Bn. attd. 51st Bn.
Morton J.A. Sgt.	L/1983	52nd Bn.
Mountford G.B. Capt. M.C.		4th Bn
Muirhead A.H. Lt.		
Mullett M.R. C.S.M.	L/5079	
Murray F.T. T/2/Lt.		5th Bn.
Musgrave F.P. Lt.		S/Yeo
Neeves C.C. Lt.		S/Yeo
Nelson S. Sgt.	10023	
Newnham A.J. Sgt.	3590	
Newton C.V. T/Capt. M.C. (2)		9th Bn.
Noakes A. Cpl.	1461	
Nutley A. C.S.M.	254	7th Bn.
Nye A. R.S.M. (2)	L/3238	
Nye H.W. Sgt.	200483	4th Bn.
Oakley A. Cpl.	8674	1st Bn.
O'Brien B. Pte. 51st Mdx Regt. attd.	36192	51st Bn
Ockleford A. L/Sgt.	551	1st Bn
Ockleford A. L/Sgt.	5118	1st Bn.
O'Donnell G.B. Mjr. (Lt-Col. Indian Army)		1st V. Bn
O'Neill F.R. Capt. (A/Mjr.) (2)		
Osborn W.L. Mjr. (T/Brig.) D.S.O. (4)		7th Bn.
Osborne G.F. Lt-Col. (T/Brig.) C.M.G.,D.S.O. (3)		
Otter-Barry R.B. Mjr.		
Owen A.G.L. Lt.		2nd Bn.
Owen H.S. T/2/Lt. (T/Capt.)		
Page G. Cpl.	SD/342	11th Bn.
Page H. Cpl.	SD/94	11th Bn.
Paine C.W. C.S.M.	5391	
Panton J.G. Lt-Col.		1st Bn.
Papilon P.R. Capt.		3rd Bn.
Parker L.H. Cpl.	37077	16th Bn.
Parkes A. Pte.	5985	
Parnell M. Sgt.	G/41370	51st Bn.
Patching E.G. Lt.		
Pearman T.A. Pte. (A/C.S.M. Instr.) Army Gym Staff	741	
Pearce O.D. 2/Lt.		
Pearce R. Hon. Lt. & Q/M (2)		1st Bn.
Pearson S. Sgt.	266548	5th Bn.
Pemberton Sgt.		3rd Bn.
Penfold P. Cpl.	3378	1st Bn.
Peterson H.J. Sgt.	315242	16th Bn.
Philips C. Q/M & Mjr.		
Piggott J. Pte. (A/S/Sgt.)	200099	1/4th Bn.
Pittman C. .Q.M.S.	1807	1st Bn.
Plews H. Q/M & Hon. Lt. (3)		5th Bn.
Pollard-Urquhart W.E. Lt.		1st Bn.
Portch T.J. Pte.	47224	51st Bn.
Porter W.N. T/Mjr. C.I.E;V.D.		
Powell-Edwards H.I.G. Mjr. (T/Lt-Col.) D.S.O.		16th Bn.
Preston E.H. Sir Capt. & Bt. Mjr. Bart. M.C. (3)		2nd Bn.
Pulling P. Sgt.	8840	1st Bn.
Raby W. R.Q.M.S.	7788	
Ramsbotham G.B. Lt.		3rd Bn.
Ratcliff W.P. T/2/Lt.		
Read E.B. Sgt.	10208	2nd Bn.
Reeks W.H. Pte. (A/Sgt.)	207625	11th Bn.
Richardson J. Sgt.	L/8256	2nd Bn.
Ridley G.W. T/Mjr. (2)		4th Bn.
Roberts H. Lt. D.S.O;M.C.		2nd Bn.
Robertson R. Drmr.	8225	1st Bn.
Robins W.G. Cpl.	298	5th Bn.

Name	Number	Bn.
Robinson E.A.S. Lt.		6th Bn.
Robinson F.W.T. Capt.		1st Bn.
Rodway W.W. Sgt.	240353	
Rolt A.T. Sgt.	20338	
Rose E. Sgt.	SR/399	
Rose T.W. Lt. M.C.		5th Bn.
Ross C.D.B. T/Lt.		
Ross F. Sgt.		V. Coy
Rothschild G.F. T/Mjr. M.C.		13th Bn.
Rothwell E.N. Q/M & T/Lt.		13th Bn.
Rowe H. L/Cpl.	7009	2nd V. Bn.
Rowland J.T. Pte	7366	1st Bn.
Ruff G.S. Cpl	2410	2nd Bn.
Ruff H. Pte.	8581	1st Bn.
Russell W.S.K. Capt.		4th Bn.
Rutherford P.J. C.S.M.	57843	
Salter E. T/Capt. M.C.		11th Bn.
Sanger-Davis F.M. Lt.		
Sansom A.J. Lt. (A/Lt-Col.)		
Saxby W. Sgt.	3963	1st Bn.
Say T.H. Pte.	5792	1st Bn.
Sayer A.C. Mjr. D.S.O.,M.C. (2)		16th Bn.
Sayer H. Capt. M.C. (2)		S/Yeo
Scales F. Sgt. M.M.	136709	11th Bn.
Scarff H. L/Cpl. (A/Sgt.)	15240	1th Bn.
Scrase T. Cpl.	3	1st Bn.
Secrett A.R. R.Q.M.S.		
Shackel G.M. T/Capt.		
Sherwin J. C.Q.M.S.	36198	
Simmonds H.C.C. Sgt.	200449	4th Bn.
Simmons J. C.S.M.	200087	4th Bn.
Smethurst W.R. Sgt.	4708	2nd Bn.
Smith H.P. C.Q.M.S. (2)	G/2522	8th Bn.
Snaith A. Sgt.	2055	1st Bn.
Solomon J. T/Q/M & Hon. Lt. (3)		8th Bn.
Sparks E. T/Cap.		11th Bn.
Sparks H. T/Capt.		
Stapley G.A. Cpl.	G/2795	
Stevens E.W. Pte.	1249	2nd Bn.
Stevenson N. R.Q.M.S.	241	
Stewart H.E. T/Capt.		
Still C.A. L/Cpl. 8811	now 74116	M.G.C.
Still T. Pte.	L/10035	2nd Bn.
Stillwell S. Cpl.	3341	
Stobbart T.R. Pte.	G/1916	8th Bn.
Stripp J. Pte.		1st Bn.
Stubbs A. Q.M.S.	SD/546	11th Bn.
Sunderland. M. S. J. Mjr.		1st Bn.
Sutton T. Lt.		7th Bn.
Swain B.F. T/Q/M & Hon Lt.		V. Coy
Symes F.H. Pte.		
Tapner A. Pte. M.M.	G/1701	2nd Bn
Taylor F. Pte.	8792	2nd Bn.
Tennent A.K. Lt. (T/Mjr.)		6th Bn.
Terrey G.E. 2/Lt.		S/Yeo
Terry R.J.A. Mjr. M.V.O.,D.S.O. (2)		2nd Bn.
Tester W.A. Pte.	6940	2nd Bn.
Thomson A.L. Capt. (T/Lt-Col.) D.S.O.		7th Bn.
Thomwaite J.D. T/Lt.		
Thorpe T.H. Lt.		
Thwaits S. Sgt./Mjr.		1st Bn.
Ticehurst W. Clr./Sgt.	3443	1st Bn.
Tisdall C.H. T/2/Lt.		
Trafford L.J. Capt.		1st Bn.
Treadway G. Cpl.	SD/2171	14th Bn.
Tremaine T.H. Clr/Sgt.	24007	
Trowbridge S. C..M.S.	6948	
Tufton J.S.R. Mjr. The Hon. D.S.O.		3rd Bn.

Name	Number	Battalion
Tunnell J. Cpl.	1073	5th Bn.
Turner C. Spr	9501	
Turner M.T. Capt. (2)		3rd Bn.
Twine F.P. 2/Lt		
Upperton G. L/Cpl. (A/Sgt.)	9310	1st Bn.
Vaughan L. Mjr.		
Vandeleur J.O. Col.		1st Bn.
Verrall C.F. Lt		2nd Bn.
Villiers E.F. Mjr. D.S.O. (5)		1st Bn.
Von Der Hyde J.L. Lt. attd. 5th Man. Regt.		2nd Bn.
Waithman R.H. Mjr. (A/Lt-Col.)		
Walker B.J. T/Lt-Col. D.S.O. (2)		8th Bn.
Wallington M. Lt. M.C. (3)		
Ward B.T. T/Capt.	8601	
Warters E. Sgt. (A/C.S.M.)		2nd Bn.
Wayman R.C. Clr./Sgt. (2)		1st Bn.
Weale E.L. T/Capt. M.C.		12th Bn.
Webb F.E. T/Capt. M.B. R.A.M.C.		17th Bn.
Webber J.C. 2/Lt.	L/9068	16th Bn.
Wedge A. Pte.	2697	2nd Bn.
Weston A.E. Clr./Sgt.	2382	1st Bn
Weston G. Cpl.		1st Bn.
Wheatley E.B. T/2/Lt. (A/Capt.)		
Whitehead H.M. 2/Lt.	202746	
Wickens L. C.S.M.		
Wilberforce A.R.G. Capt.		5th Bn.
Wilkie A.B. Mjr.		
Willett F.W.B. Mjr.(A/Lt-Col.) D.S.O. (3)	G/1918	4th Bn.
Williams H.H. C.Q.M.S.	512	2nd Bn.
Williams O. C.S.M.	9182	8th Bn.
Winchester L. Cpl.		9th Bn.
Winterton E.E. Capt.		1st Bn.
Wood A.H. Capt.	9184	1st Bn.
Wood L. Sgt.	240465	1st Bn.
Woodgate J.W. Sgt.		5th Bn.
Woodruffe J.S. Mjr. (T/Lt-Col.) (2)		2nd Bn.
Woodhams T. Capt.		7th Bn.
Wright J.A. T/2/Lt.		
Wroughton J.B. Mjr. & Bt. Col. (T/Brig.) C.M.G. (8)	G/1599	2nd Bn.
Yeates A.W. Cpl. (A/Sgt.)	200303	
Young G.T. T/Cpl M.M.		2nd Bn.
Young, N.E. T/Captain M.C.		

Mentioned In Despatches Winners Who Died

Gordon R. Alexander, 2/Lt. M.I.D. 2nd Bn attd. 13th Bn. Tuesday 24th April 1917
Fifteen Ravine British Cemetery, Villers-Plouich
IV. I. 12.

Hugh Stirling Ashworth, Lt-Col. M.I.D., C de G. (French) Commanding 4th Bn. Monday 26th March 1917
Jerusalem Memorial
Panels 26 and 27.

Lewis De Burgh Atkinson, Capt. M.I.D. 2nd Bn Wednesday 16th August 1916
Thiepval Memorial
Pier and Face 7 C.

Joseph John Banham, Mjr. M.I.D. 9th Bn. Wednesday 27th March 1918
Pozieres Memorial
Panel 46 and 47.

Cyril Barlett, Mjr. M.C.,M.I.D. 13th Bn. Wednesday 14th November 1917
Outtersteene Communal Cemetery Extension, Bailleul
II. B. 56.

Alfred William Beale, Sgt. M.M.,M.I.D. G/931 7th Bn. Monday 9th April 1917
Arras Memorial
Bay 6.

Cyril Edward Brown Pte. G/2316 M.I.D. 8th Bn. Thursday 13th September 1917
Mendinghem Military Cemetery
IV. D. 21.

Frank Busby Cpl. N0. 9843 M.I.D. 2nd Bn. Tuesday 26th January 1915
Le Touret Memorial
Panel 20 and 21.

Charles Percy Parker Clay, Sgt. 9157 D.C.M., M.I.D., Cross of St. George, 3rd Class (Russia).
 2nd Bn. Sunday 9th May 1915 Le Touret Memorial
Panel 20 and 21.

Harry Albert Frederick Catmur, Lt. M.I.D. 3rd Bn. Saturday 1st July 1916
Thiepval Memorial
Pier and Face 7 C.

Hugh Trevor Crispin, Lt-Col. M.I.D. Commanding 2nd Bn. Friday 30th October 1914
Ypres (Menin Gate) Memorial
Panel 20.

T. Diplock, Sgt. No. 6868 M.I.D. 2nd Bn. Thursday 8th October 1914
Villers –En- Prayeres Communal Cemetery
C. 5.

W. Farrell C.S.M. L/8712 M.I.D., M.S.M. "C" Coy. 2nd Bn. Monday3oth September 1918
Brookwood Cemetery
Y. 181664.

Percy George Foster, 2/Lt. M.I.D. 2nd Bn. 7th Bn. Sunday 2nd April 1916
Hastings Cemetery, Sussex
E. H. O29.

Ferris Nelson Grant, Capt. M.C.,M.I.D. 5th Bn. Sunday 9th May 1915
Le Touret Memorial
Panel 20 and 21.

Arthur Leslie Gronheit Sgt. G/30807 M.I.D. 17th Bn. Monday 7th July 1919
Archangel Allied Cemetery (buried Semenovka (Bereznik) Cemetery Extension).
Sp. MemorialB55.

Harry Francis Hall, Cpl. G/452 M.I.D. 7th Bn. Wednesday 22nd May 1918
St. Sever Extension, Rouen
Q. III. F. 24.

William Thomas Heagerty, Mjr. M.I.D. 13th Bn Wednesday 31st January 1917
Lijssenthoek Military Cemetery
X. A. 3.

Harold Philip Hygate, L/Sgt. SD/2105 M.I.D. 7th Bn.   Monday 23rd September 1918
Doingt Communal Cemetery Extension
I. D. 6.

Hugh Thomas Kay Robinson Lt-Col. 12th Bn. attd. 13th Bn. D.S.O.,M.I.D.   Friday 26th April 1918
Tyne Cot Memorial
Panel 86 to 88.

Gerrard Evelyn Leachman, Lt-Col. C.I.E.,D.S.O.,M.I.D. 1st Bn Thursday 12th August 1920
Baghdad (North Gate) War Cemetery Iraq
XIV. C. 1.

Robert Egerton Loder, Lt. (T/Capt.) M.I.D. 1/4th Bn. Thursday 29th March 1917
Deir El-Belah War Cemetery
C. 73.

Frederick Charles Jennens Marillier, 2/Lt, D.C.M.,M.I.D. formerly (9275) Friday 30th October 1914
Ypres (Menin Gate) Memorial
Panel 20.

J. Marsland Lt. M.C.,M.I.D. 8th (Pioneer) Bn. Monday 23rd July 1917
Dickebusch New Military Cemetery Extension
I. A. 8.

Horace Warren Meade, Capt. M.I.D. 8th Bn. Thursday 13th July 1916
Peronne Road Cemetery, Maricourt
I. E. 30.

H.J. Meaton, C.Q.M.S. No.202870 M.I.D.   Wednesday 11th December 1918
Brighton (Lewes Road) Borough Cemetery
KB. 41.

W.H. Minns, L/Cpl. L/8149 2nd Bn. M.I.D.   Friday 15th January 1915
Le Touret Memorial
Panel 20 and 21.

Ernest Henry Montresor, Lt-Col.   Cmdg. 2nd Bn. Monday 14th September 1914
La Ferte-sous-Jouarre Memorial
France

George Boudrie O'Donnell, Lt-Col. M.I.D.   Royal Defence Corps Monday 20th October 1919
Brighton City Cemetery (Bear Road)
ZIW. 70.

John Gerald Panton Col. C.M.G.,M.I.D. Tuesday 7th December 1915
Brookwood Cemetery
X. 176775.

William Edward Pollard-Urquhart, Lt. M.I.D. 1st Bn. M.I.D. Sunday 18th April 1915
Delhi Memorial (India Gate)
Face 1-23.

Ernest William Stevens Pte. No. G/1249 M.I.D.   2nd Bn.   Sunday 10th October 1915
Bethune Town Cemetery France
IV.F.3.

Thomas Still Pte. M.I.D. "A" Coy 2nd Bn. Monday 14th September 1914
La Ferte –sous-Jouarre Memorial
France

Robert Joseph Atkinson Terry Lt.-Col. D.S.O.,M.V.O., M.I.D. 2nd Infantry Brigade R.S.R. Friday 1st October 1915
Noeux-Les-Mines Communal Cemetery, Pas de Calais, France
Grave Reference I. K.14.

Christopher Francis Verrall Lt.   M.I.D. 2nd Bn. Tuesday 22nd December 1914
Le Touret Memorial
Panel 20 and 21

Meritorious Medal Winners

Andrews P. Sgt.	SD/1512	12th Bn.	
Amos C. S/Major D.C.M.	G/4657	Depot	
Apps C.G.B. Sgt.	200437	4th Bn.	
Aylmore A. Sgt.	425	7th Bn.	
Bannister H.J. Sgt.	240551	5th Bn.	
Barfoot W.H.J. C.SM.	L/9340	1st Bn.	INDIA
Beckett P. Cpl. M.M.	G/2712	8th Bn.	
Beedham H. Sgt.	G/15374	12th Bn.	
Bennett W.T. Sgt.	263189	17th Bn.	
Boniface A.S. Sgt.	G/16007	13th Bn.	
Boniface J.R. R.S.M.	L/4369	3rd Bn.	
Bosanquet B. C.Q.M.S.	L/6586	Depot (2nd Bn.)	
Boyce J.W. R.Q.M.S.	G/2381	8th Bn.	
Bradford H. C.S.M.	8593	1st Bn.	INDIA
Brooks J.W.H. Pte.	G/6466	1st Bn.	INDIA
Brown A.E. Pte. (L/Cpl.)	8448	1st Bn.	INDIA
Browning R. Cpl.	240405	5th Bn.	
Browning T.E. Pte.	G/4514	7th Bn.	
Buschell E.H. Cpl.	265112	6th Bn.	INDIA
Caesar G. Sgt. M.M.	G/2379	8th Bn.	
Coates C. Sgt. M.M.	L/5391	8th Bn.	
Coleman C. C.Q.M.S.	929	7th Bn.	
Cook A.C. Sgt. was SD/1297	S3/030182	116th Inf. Bde.	
Cooper H.B. C.S.M.	320009	16th Bn.	
Coppard H.A. C.Q.M.S.	SD/2157	11th Bn.	MURMANSK
Costa W. Pte. (A/Sgt.)	G/25395	11th Bn.	MURMANSK
Douglas L. Sgt.	8594	2nd Bn.	
Eve J. Sgt.	8926	2nd Bn.	FRANCE
Evershed P. Sgt.	4673	3rd Bn.	GALLANTRY
Farrell W. C.S.M.	L/8712	2nd Bn.	
Fennell S. R.Q.M.S.	320002	16th Bn.	
Franklin E. Pte. (Cpl.)	G/14759	2nd Bn.	
Funnell A.E. Pte. (A/Cpl.)	L/12448	3rd Bn.	
Funnell F.C. R.Q.M.S.	SR/714	1st Bn.	INDIA
Gannon W. Cpl. (A/Sgt.)	L/8913	1st Bn.	INDIA
Gardner A. C/Sgt.	L/10325	1st Bn.	INDIA
Gearing A. Pte.	G/15918	8th Bn.	
Gray A. Sgt. (A/S/Mjr.)	L/8928	1st Bn.	INDIA
Grimes J.A. C.Q.M.S.	S/229	8th Bn.	
Hall W.A. Pte. (L/Cpl.)	240096	5th Bn.	
Hanlon P.J. C.Q.M.S.	L/8526	7th Bn.	
Harris W.T. Sgt.	9368	2nd Bn.	
Haynes A.R.C. Sgt.	G/3289	9th Bn.	
Head G.F. C.S.M. D.C.M.	3359	9th Bn.	FRANCE
Henderson J.R. A/S/Major	G/30740	17th Bn.	
Higham T.L. Pte.	G/16509	9th Bn.	
Hills W.A. Sgt.	SD/3134	13th Bn.	
Hindmarsh C. Bandmaster	L/9200	1st Bn.	INDIA
Hodson G.H. Sgt. M.M.	240030	5th Bn.	
Holman W.H. Sgt.	G/3416	4th Bn.	GALLANTRY
Hopper G.T. Sgt.	240148	4th Bn.	SIBERIA
Hoyle J. C.S.M.	30922	17th Bn.	
Hunter A. Sgt.	SD/808	11th Bn.	FRANCE
Isted F. Pte. (A/L/Cpl.)	240335	5th Bn.	
James A.E. Sgt.	L/2754	1st Bn.	INDIA
James G.E. Sgt.	201095	4th Bn.	FRANCE
Lake T.E. Q.M.S.	L/4503	3rd Bn.	
Lawley W.F. Pte. (A/L/Sgt.)	L/12909	2/6th Bn.	
Lee A. Sgt. M.M.	120	7th Bn.	
Long S.W. Q.M.S.	118	7th Bn.	
Marshall R.C.R. Pte.	G/1936	8th Bn.	
Martin H. Sgt. (A/C.S.M.)	290575	4th Bn.	ARCHANGEL
Maynard E.B. C.Q.M.S.	G/1742	8th Bn.	
Morrison H. Cpl.	GS/57	7th Bn.	
Nelson S. Sgt.	10023	2nd Bn.	FRANCE
Noakes A.H. Cpl. (L/Sgt.)	240080	5th Bn.	
Nurse H.G. Sgt.	30258	17th Bn.	
Nye A. T/S/Major D.C.M.	L/3238	4th Bn.	
Palmer J. Sgt.	240112	5th Bn.	
Puxty F.C. Sgt.	240288	5th Bn.	

Raby W. Q.M.S.	L/7788	7th Bn.	
Rands H.J. Q.M.S.	202015	4th Bn.	
Rapley C.T. Sgt.	200012	4th Bn.	
Rolt A.T. Sgt.	G/20338	8th Bn.	
Seagrave F. Q.M.S.	200009	4th Bn.	
Seall W.A. Cpl.	SD/549	11th Bn.	MURMANSK
Singleton J.S. Pte. (A/Sgt.)	2651663	2/6th Bn.	INDIA
Spinney F. Sgt.	L/6600	2nd Bn.	
Standing F.A. C.S.M.	SD/859	11th Bn.	FRANCE
Steer J.S. R.S.M.	L/8070	1st Bn.	INDIA
Stevenson N. R.Q.M.S.	SD/241	11th Bn.	MURMANSK
Stone W.J. C.S.M.	SD/472	11th Bn.	MURMANSK
Taylor R.A. Sgt.	S/391	8th Bn.	FRANCE
Terry H. Sgt.	3474	13th Bn.	FRANCE
Tremaine T.H. C.Q.M.S.	240007	5th Bn.	
Turner J. Sgt.	310	7th Bn.	
Tutt G. Sgt. (A/C.S.M.)	L/9264	1st Bn.	INDIA
Wallis W.H.	266069	2/6th Bn.	INDIA
Warner J.L. C.Q.M.S.	SD/258	11th Bn.	MURMANSK
Whinnett A. A/C.S.M.	2651663	2/6th Bn.	INDIA
White A.H. C.S.M.	240002	5th Bn.	
Willis K.L. Cpl. (L/Sgt.)	G/14893	7th Bn.	
Wilshere D. Sgt.	G/20449	7th Bn.	
Winchester L. Sgt.	L/9182	1st Bn.	INDIA
Woods G. C.Q.M.S.	200692	4th Bn.	
Yeates A.W. Cpl. (A/Sgt.)	200303	4th Bn.	

Meritorious Service Medal Winner Who Died

Percy Evershed M.S.M. Sergeant SD/4673 13th Bn. Tuesday 28th May 1918
Peronne Communal Cemetery Extension, Ste Radegonde, Somme, France
Grave Reference Memorial I.

Divisional Commander's Certificate for Gallantry

G/2774 Pte. Charles Edwards,	8th Bn.
G/ 2554 Pte. Martin Archibald Humphrey,	8th Bn.
G/2715 Pte. Francis William Austin,	8th Bn.
G/17713 Pte. Arthur Matten,	16th Bn.

Divisional Commanders Certificate for Gallantry who Died

Charles Edwards, Private G/2774 8th Bn. Tuesday 31st July 1917
Lijssenthoek Military Cemetery
Grave Reference XVI. J. 13A

Foreign Award Winners

Belgian

Ordre de Leopold de La Couronne

Ordre de Leopold II (4th Class)

Officer

Wroughton J.B. Bt. Lt-Col. (T/Col.) C.M.G.		2nd Bn.

Chevalier

Cameron J.S. Major D.S.O.		2nd Bn.
Tufton J.R.S. Maj. The Hon. D.SO.		3rd Bn.
Grant A.J.S. Lt.		4th Bn.

Croix de Guerre

Wroughton J.B. Bt. Col. (T/Brig-Gen.) C.M.G.		2nd Bn.
Tufton J.R.S. Maj. The Hon. D.S.O.		3rd Bn.
Bridger W.S.G. Capt.		4th Bn.
Grant A.J.S. Lt.		4th Bn.
Chegwyn W.H. Pte.	G/5827	2nd Bn.
Goward H. Sgt.	G/2430	8th Bn.
Griffiths C. Sgt.	L/8498	2nd Bn.
Holmes R.C. Cpl.	2322	5th Bn.
Mackellow F. Sgt.	240012	5th Bn.
Middleton R.C.G. Capt. M.C.		4th Bn.
Rayner J. J. Sgt.	S/375	8th Bn.
Rothwell E.R. Qm & Lt.		4th Bn.
Slaughter F. C.S.M. D.C.M.	200036	4th Bn.
Tucker E. L/Sgt.	L/9249	2nd Bn.
Watt I.W.B. Cpl.	SD/3487	2nd Bn.
White R. Sgt.	SD/3490	11th Bn.
Wood C.W. Sgt.	SD/558	2nd Bn.
Wood F. Sgt.	G/7243	2nd Bn.

Decoration Militaire

Brown E. Cpl. D.C.M.,M.M.	L/7922	2nd Bn.
Coppard A.V. Pte. (A/Cpl.)	G/828	2nd Bn.
Richardson A.E. Cpl. M.M.	G/204423	9th Bn.

Egyptian

Order of the Nile (3rd Class)

Hulton J.M. Mjr. (A/Lt-Col.) D.S.O.	4th Bn.

Order of the Nile (4th Class)

Reid S.K. Lt. (T/Capt.) M.C.	4th Bn.
Ridley G.W. Capt. (T/Mjr.) O.B.E.	4th Bn.

Order of Osmanieh 3rd Class

Donne B.D.A. Mjr.	1st Bn.

3rd Class Medjidieh

Donne B.D.A. Capt. & Bt. Mjr.	1st Bn.

4th Class Medjidieh

Donne B.D.A. Capt.	1st Bn.
Kelly W.F. Mjr & Bt Lt-Col.	1st Bn.
Williams-Freeman G.C.P. Capt.	1st Bn.
Skinner F. St. Duthus Lt.	1st Bn.

French

Legion de Honneur Croix de Officer

Wroughton J.B. Bt. Col. (T/Brig.-Gen.) C.M.G.   2nd Bn.

Croix de Chevalier

Cameron J.S. Mjr. D.S.O.		2nd Bn.
Johnson H.H. D.S.O. Capt. (T/Mjr.)		6th Bn.
Lytton The Hon. N.S Mjr. O.B.E.		11th Bn.
Pelham H.L. The Hon. Lt.		2nd Bn.
Stewart H.E. T/Capt.		8th Bn.

Ordre du, Merite Agricole, Chevalier

Sansom A.J. Lt. (T/ Capt.)		4th Bn.
Tufton J.S.R. Mjr. The Hon. D.S.O.		3rd Bn.

Medaille d'Honneur avec glaives en Bronze

Boast D.G. Cpl.   G/3291   9th Bn.

Palmes Academic Officier

Hervey A.F. T/Lt.

Croix de Guerre

Name	Number	Bn.	
Ashworth H.S. Lt-Col.		4th Bn.	
Barfoot W.F. T/Lt. (A/Capt.)			Citation
Constable S.A. C.S.M. D.C.M.	200172	2nd Bn.	
Cragg A.B. T/Lt.		4th Bn.	
Fortescue R.H. Lt. M.C.		7th Bn.	
Glasgow A.E. Bt. Col (T/Brig-Gen.)		8th Bn.	
Johnson H.H. Capt. (T/Mjr.)		6th Bn.	
Makalua M.J.M. T/Capt.		13th Bn..	
Middleton R.C.G. Capt. M.C.		4th Bn.	
Millward W.C. Lt-Col. D.S.O.		11th Bn.	
Peskett J.C. T/Lt. (A/Capt.) M.C.		4th Bn.	
Read I.L. T/2nd Lt.		4th Bn.	
Baker G. L/Cpl.	200650	4th Bn.	
Bolt W. Pte.	201077	4th Bn.	
Catt H. C.S.M.	200131	4th Bn.	
Clements F. Sgt. M.M.	L/8212	2nd Bn.	
Coates C. Sgt. M.M.,M.S.M.	L/5391	8th Bn.	
Collis W.O. L/Cpl. D.C.M.	320494	16th Bn.	
Field A.E. Sgt.	201812	4th Bn.	
Halley J.C. A/Sgt.	6035	2nd Bn.	
Langley W.D.G. Pte.	9650	4th Bn.	
Lewry H.A. C.S.M. D.C.M.	L/8151	1st Bn.	
Peacock A. Sgt.	G/14857	7th Bn.	
Purver G.A. Cpl.	200825	4th Bn.	
Ransom F.J. Sgt. D.C.M., M.M.	G/574	7th Bn.	
Sansom A.J. Lt.		5th Bn.	
White R.G. Sgt.	SD/3490	11th Bn.	
Woolven A.G. Cpl. M.M.	200484	4th Bn.	

Medal Militaire

Name	Number	Bn.	
Barfield T. Pte. M.M.	15104	2nd Bn.	
Barford J. Pte.	265798	6th Bn.	
Buckwell E. Pte. (A/L/Cpl.)	240935	5th Bn.	
Chillman J. Sgt.	1381	2nd Bn.	
Clements F. Sgt. M.M.	L/8212	2nd Bn.	Citation
Constable S.A. C.S.M. D.C.M.	200172	4th Bn.	
Dale J.S. Pte.	SD/1212	12th Bn.	
Holland F.G. Sgt.	806	2nd Bn.	
Larmer W. C.Q.M.S. Middlesex Regiment, attd. R.S.R.	L/12718	2nd Bn.	
Webber B.J.T. R.S.M.	320007	16th Bn.	

Italian

Officer of the Order of the Crown of Italy

Whitfield G.S. Lt-Col. T.D. Sussex Yeomanry		16th Bn.
Hulton J.M. Mjr. (A/Lt-Col.) D.S.O.		
Corbett A. Mjr. (T/Lt-Col.) Sussex Yeomanry		16th Bn.

Cavalier of the Order of St. Maurice and St. Lazarus

Dick R.N. Bt. Lt-Col.		1st Bn.

Croce di Guerra

Birkett R.M. Bt. Lt-Col. (T/Lt-Col.) D.S.O.	22	7th Bn.
Done W.E.P. Lt. (T/Capt.) M.C.		5th Bn.
Finn N. T/2nd Lt.		
Hillebrand H.E.F. T/2nd /Lt.		
Howard A.C. C.S.M.	240251	5th Bn.
Swaine E.H. Sgt.	202066	1/5th Bn.

The Silver Medal for Military Valour

Alexander J.R.W. 2nd Lt.		2nd Bn.
Rose T.W. Lt. (A/Capt.) M.B.E., M.C.		5th Bn.

The Bronze Medal for Military Valour

Budgen W.H. C.Q.M.S. D.C.M.	G/891	7th Bn.
Bull B. Sgt.	G/7827	5th Bn.
Hodges G. Sgt. D.C.M.	L/3303	7th Bn.
Yeomans F.W. Cpl. D.C.M.	G/1671	8th Bn.

Montenegro

Order of Dunilo (3rd Class)

Osborn W.L. Mjr. (T/Brig.-Gen.) C.B., D.S.O.		7th Bn.

Romanian

Medaille Barbatie Si Credinta (3rd Class)

Cox A.C. L/Cpl. M.M.	G/4852	2nd Bn.

Croix de Virtue Militara

Balcombe J.C.S. C.S.M. (A/R.S.M.) D.C.M.	320001	16th Bn.

Russian

Order of St. Vladimir (4th Class with Swords)

Woodruffe J.S. Mjr. O.B.E.		
Gilmore G.H. T/Capt. D.S.O.,M.C.		8th Bn.

Order of St. Anne (2nd Class with Swords)

Wroughton J.B. Mjr. (T/Col.) C.M.G.		2nd Bn.
Gilmore G.H. T/Capt. D.S.O.,M.C.		8th Bn.

Order of St. Anne (2nd Class)

Julius S de Vere A. Bt. Lt-Col.

Cross of the Order of St. George (3rd Class)

Clay C.P.P. Sgt. D.C.M.	9157	2nd Bn.

Cross of the Order of St. George (4th Class)

Robins W.G. Cpl.	298	5th Bn.

Medal of St. George (4th Class)

Beale A. Bandsman (Sgt.) D.C.M.	7440	2nd Bn.
Burrell H. Sgt.	5535	2nd Bn.

Medal of Zeal (St. Stanislaus Ribbon)

Wood W. Pte. (L/Cpl.)	G/36877	11th Bn.

Serbian

Gold Medal

Budd W.A. L/Cpl. (A/Sgt.)	695	4th Bn.

Silver Medal

Knapp A. Pte.	1349	4th Bn.

Foreign Award Winners Who Died

Hugh Stirling Ashworth Croix de Guerre (French) Lt-Colonel Commanding 4th Bn. Monday 26th March 1917
Jerusalem Memorial, Israel
Grave Reference Panels 26 and 27

Herbert Lytleton Pelham Legion of Honneur, Croix de Chevalier, (French) Lt. The Hon. Monday 14th September 1914
Vendresse British Cemetery, Ainse, France
Grave Reference 1.C.15.

Charles Percy Parker Clay, Sgt. 9157 M.I.D., Cross of St. George, 3rd Class (Russian). 2nd Bn
Sunday 9th May 1915
Le Touret Memorial
Panel 20 and 21.

Stuart Keppel Reid M.C., Order of Nile (4th Class) Captain 4th Bn. Monday 29th July 1918
Vauxbuin French National Cemetery, Ainse, France
Grave Reference II. A. 1.

Alfred John Sansom Ordre du, Merite Agricole, Chevalier (Belgian) Lt-Col. Thursday 5th July 1917
Faubourg D'Amiens Cemetery, Arras
Grave Reference V.J.1

Henry Edward Stewart Legion of Honneur, Croix de Chevalier (French) Captain 8th Bn. Friday 1st June 1917
Sunken Road Cemetery, Boisleux-St. Marc, Pas de Calais, France
Grave Reference I. F. 14.

Alphabetical Index

Adams A. L/Cpl. D.C.M.	17/05/16
Adams A. Lt. M.I.D.	28/12/18
Aglionby J.O. Capt. Rev. M.C.,M.A., attd. R.S.R.	05/06/17
Aish C.E.V. Pte. M.M.	21/10/18
Aitkins F,W. Mjr. V.D.	29/11/92
Aldridge C.P. Capt. M.I.D.	10/09/01
Aldridge F.R. R.Q.M.S. M.I.D.	20/12/17
Alexander G.R. T/2nd Lt. M.I.D.	28/02/18
Alexander J.W.R. 2nd Lt. Silver Medal (Italy).,M.I.D.	04/01/2017,28/05/18
Allchorn E.W. Pte. (A/Sgt.) M.M.	08/01/17
Allen C.A. Mjr. M.C.	22/12/2016,16/08/17,27/09/17,10/01/18,18/02/18
Alston G. Sgt. M.M.	22/08/16
Ambler G. T/2nd Lt. M.C	21/08/16,25/02/18
Amsbridge G.G. Pte. (A/Cpl.) M.M.	19/05/19
Amon H. T/2nd Lt. (A/Capt.) M.C.	19/10/17,09/03/18,18/09/18
Amos C. S/Major D.C.M.,M.S.M.,M.I.D.	29/07/02, 24/12/19,25/02/19
Amsbury J. Pte. M.M.	28/07/19
Anderson W.J. Pte. M.M.	07/08/18
Andrews A.E. Mjr. (T/Lt-Col.) M.B.E. attd. R.S.R.	30/01/20
Andrews P. Sgt. M.S.M.,M.I.D.	20/12/17,18/06/18
Andrews S.A. Lt. (A/Capt.) D.S.O.,M.C.,M.I.D.	19/10/17,15/11/17,09/03/18,03/02/19,10/03/19,09/07/19,11/07/19
Apperley W.H.W. Capt. M.C., M.I.D.	20/10/17,19/01/18,26/04/18,11/07/19
Apps C.G.B. Sgt. M.S.M.	21/01/19
Apted R. Pte. (Victory Parade)	21/07/19
Aris G. Cpl. D.C.M.	19/02/19,06/05/19,12/01/20
Armitage F.G. 2nd Lt. (A/Lt.) M.I.D.	23/05/17
Arnold G. Pte. M.M.	05/11/17
Ash C.D. T/Capt. M.I.D. Bedford Regt. attd. R.S.R.	14/08/18
Ashby J.R. Mjr. M.I.D.	27/02/17
Ashby J.W.F.W. Mjr. T.D.	02/09/13
Ashford R. Cpl. M.M.	14/09/18
Ashford W.A. Sgt. M.M.	20/02/17
Ashworth H.S. Capt. (T/Lt-Col.) C de G (F)., M.I.D.,	02/12/16,22/05/17,14/01/18
Atkinson H. Pte. M.M.	19/10/17
Atkinson L. de B. 2nd Lt. M.I.D.	04/01/17
Atree E.C. Sgt. M.M.	21/11/17
Attree B. Pte. M.I.D.	23/06/15
Aukett W.G. C.S.M. D.C.M.,M.M.	22/08/16,27/03/17,25/09/19
Aungier H. Pte. M.M.	22/09/16,22/02/17
Austin F.W. Pte. Div.Com.Cert.for Gallantry	21/10/16
Avis G.J. Pte. M.M.	14/03/18
Awcock G.R. Pte. M.M.	19/05/19
Aylmore A. Sgt. M.S.M.	18/06/18
Back H.J. L/Cpl. M.M.	05/01/18
Backshall E. Pte. M.M.	14/09/18
Badcock G. C.Q.M.S. M.M.	07/08/18
Baddeley W.H. Lt-Col. D.S.O.,M.C.,M.I.D.	23/05/17,17/08/17,20/12/17,18/09/18,03/06/19
Bagge H. Pte. M.M.	14/09/18
Bailey A. Pte. No. 15036 M.M.	08/01/17
Bailey A. Pte. No. 2424 D.C.M.	23/10/16,30/01/17,04/01/17,14/02/17
Bailey A. Pte. No. 2854 M.M.	22/08/16
Bailey W.B. Sgt. M.M.	22/08/17
Bailey W.J. L/Cpl. M.M.	21/09/16,23/10/16
Baker C. Lt. M.C.	02/01/19
Baker D.M. Mjr. M.C.	25/09/18
Baker E.A. 2nd Lt. (T/Capt.) M.C.	03/06/16
Baker F.T. Pte. M.M.	13/02/19
Baker G. L/Cpl. C de G (F)	21/06/19.
Baker H.J. Pte. M.M.	08/01/18,29/01/18
Baker S.C. Pte. M.M.	22/08 16
Baker W. Sgt. M.M.	16/06/17
Balcombe J.C. C.S.M. D.C.M.	14/01/18,30/03/18,23/09/19,07/11/19
Balcombe T. Pte. M.M.	20/05/16,11/08/16
Baldwin A. Cpl. D.C.M.,M.I.D.	18/07/02,31/10/02
Ball C.E. L/Cpl. M.M.	22/08/16,29/08/16
Ball H.J. C.S.M. (A/R.S.M.) No. 382 M.C.	18/10/17,09/03/18
Ball T.J. Cpl. (A/Sgt.) M.M.	08/01/17
Ball W.T. Pte. (L/Cpl.) M.M.	19/07/17

Name	Date
Ballard C.W. T/Lt. M.C.	11/07/19
Bamber W. C.S.M. (T/R.S.M.) M.I.D.	04/01/17
Banham J.J. T/2nd Lt. M.I.D.	14/09/16, 14/05/18
Banks E.R. Sgt. M.M..	03/06/19
Bannell G. 2nd Lt. M.C.	04/01/19
Bannister H.J. Sgt. M.S.M.	28/07/19
Barber H.T. Pte. M.M.	18/04/17, 16/07/17
Barfield T. Pte. M.M., M.M.(F)	25/08/19
Barfoot W.F. T/Lt. (A/Capt.) C de G (F)	03/09/20
Barfoot W.H.J. C.S.M. M.S.M.	25/02/18, 20/05/18, 07/11/18
Barford J. Pte. M.M., M.M.(F)., M.I.D.	18/07/17
Barham F. Pte. M.M.	21/07/19
Barker G. L/Cpl. (Victory Parade)	10/10/17, 19/10/17, 09/05/18
Barker L. A/Sgt. M.M.	12/01/20
Barlow P.S. Capt. M.I.D.	06/06/17, 10/07/17
Barnard F. C.S.M. D.C.M.	28/03/19
Barnes C.L. Sgt. M.I.D.	18/09/17, 30/07/18
Barnes H.C. T/Lt. M.C.	05/09/18
Barnes J.A. L/Cpl. (A/Cpl.) D.C.M.	28/08/19
Barrow A.J. Pte. M.I.D.	21/07/17, 09/09/18
Bartholomew G.E. Pte. M.M.	29/11/92
Barttletot –B Sir W. Lt-Col. & Hon. Col. Bart. V.D.	19/10/17, 20/12/17, 09/03/18
Bartlett C. T/Lt. M.C., M.I.D.	05/01/18, 18/04/18
Bartlett J. A/C.S.M. D.C.M.	13/02/19
Barwick W.R. Pte. (L/Cpl.) M.M.	30/01/18
Bassett H. L/Cpl. M.M.	03/04/19, 13/12/19
Bate H.R. Lt. M.C. 6th Bn. Manch. Regt.	23/03/18, 12/02/19
Bateman W. Pte. M.M.	23/06/15
Batt J. Sgt. M.I.D.	18/02/18, 20/07/18
Batten P.W. 2nd Lt. (T/Lt./A/Capt.) M.C.	11/07/19
Baxter J.H. Cpl. (A/Sgt.) M.I.D.	18/01/15, 26/08/15, 23/09/15, 13/01/20
Beale A. Pte. D.C.M., Medal of St. George (Russia)	16/06/16, 15/09/17
Beale A.W. Sgt. M.M., M.I.D.	14/01/18
Beale S.W.P. Mjr. T.D; M.I.D.	10/07/17, 30/04/18
Beall T.H. Pte. M.M.	05/06/19
Bean R.C. Lt. (A/Capt.) M.B.E. S/Yeo	21/07/19, 28/07/19
Beckett P. Cpl. M.M., M.S.M.	07/06/19
Beech P.E.W. Pte. (A/L/Cpl.) M.I.D.	28/07/19
Beecroft H. Pte. M.M.	08/06/18
Beedham H. Pte. M.S.M.	19/10/17
Beeney A. Pte. M.M.	10/07/17
Beeney J. Pte. M.M.	11/12/16
Bell D. Pte. M.M.	28/08/19
Bell J. C.S.M. No. 41547 M.I.D.	19/05/19
Bell J. Pte. (A/Sgt.) No. G/6345 M.M.	10/09/01, 27/09/01
Bellamy R. Lt. D.S.O., M.I.D.	28/03/19
Bell-Irving A. Lt-Col. D.S.O., M.I.D.	08/01/17
Belton H.S.B. Pte. M.M.	07/08/16, 11/08/16
Belton J.T. Pte. M.M.	28/12/18, 03/06/19, 13/03/20
Bennett E. Sgt. D.C.M., M.I.D.	20/12/17
Bennett F. Cpl. No. 653 M.I.D.	28/05/17
Bennett F.E. L/Cpl. (A/Cpl.) M.M.	18/12/17, 24/04/18, 25/0418
Bennett W.H.P. 2nd Lt. M.C.	03/06/19
Bennett W.T. Sgt. M.S.M.	31/05/18
Best A.F. T/Capt. M.C.	16/06/16, 28/03/19
Betham R.J.A. Capt. M.I.D.	23/09/16, 28/10/19
Bevan G.E. Sgt. D.C.M.	20/12/17, 02/01/18
Bidder H.F. Mjr. (T/Lt-Col.) M.C., M.I.D.	30/01/18
Bilham J.E. L/Cp. M.M.	10/07/17
Billing R.D. Pte. (L/Cpl.) M.M.	19/10/17
Billings A.C. Cpl. M.M.	06/03/18, 21/07/19
Billington H. Pte. D.C.M.	15/11/17, 29/01/18
Bingham B.C. Pte. M.M.	16/09/18
Binstead E. Pte. M.M.	05/09/18
Bird H.M. C.S.M. (A/R.S.M.) D.C.M.	14/09/16
Bird J. Pte. M.M.	01/01/16, 04/01/17, 19/01/18, 18/02/18, 26/04/18, 25/05/18
Birkett R.M. Mjr. (T/Lt-Col.) D.S.O.	04/01/19, 07/01/19, 09/05/19
Bishop C. Pte. M.M.	13/02/19
Bishop F. Pte. No. 240301 M.I.D.	07/01/19
Bishop J. Pte. M.M.	30/10/16, 08/01/17
Blackman W. Pte. No. 1164 M.I.D.	04/01/17
Blackman W.A. Pte. M.M.	19/05/19
Blake F.W.E. Capt. M.I.D.	10/09/01
Blaker C. T/Lt. M.C.	02/01/19

Blease A. Pte. M.I.D.	19/10/01
Bliss C.J. Cpl. M.M.	16/09/18
Bliss D. Sgt. M.I.D.	31/05/18
Blakeney H.E.H. Lt. (T/Capt.) M.C.,M.I.D.	11/12/15,14/01/16
Bloomfield J. R.S.M. No. S/516 M.C.,M.I.D.	04/01/17,03/01/18
Bloomfield J.A. Hon. Mjr. & Adj. V.D.	24/01/93
Blunden C.H. Pte. M.M.	22/11/17,29/01/18
Blunden E.C. T/2nd Lt. M.C.	27/01/17
Blunt H.E. Capt. M.C.	05/07/18
Boast D.G. Cpl. D.C.M., Medaille de Honneur (F)	03/06/19,16/07/19,13/03/20
Bolitho A.C. Pte. (A/L/Sgt.) M.I.D.	28/08/19
Bolt W. Pte. C de G (F)	21/06/19.
Bolton C.A. Q/M/ & Hon. Lt. M.I.D.	17/01/18
Bolton C.O. T/Lt. M.C.	21/08/16
Bond C.E. Mjr. (T/Brig.) C.M.G.,D.S.O., M.I.D.	10/09/01,31/10/02,05/11/02,09/10/14,23/06/15,01/01/16, 12/12/17,21/05/18
Bond C.A. Pte. (A/Sgt.) M.I.D.	30/01/20,05/02/20
Bone H.J. Pte. M.M.	13/02/19
Boniface A.S. Sgt. M.S.M.	21/01/19
Boniface C.J. Pte. (Victory Parade)	21/07/19
Boniface J.R. R.S.M. M.S.M.,M.I.D.	30/11/16,27/02/17,24/02/19,25/02/19
Boniface V. Sgt. M.I.D.	11/07/19
Boniface W. Cpl. M.M.	29/01/18
Bonner E. Pte. (L/Cpl.) M.M.	19/06/19
Bonney L. A/S/M. D.C.M.	03/06/16,22/06/16,04/06/17
Booker P. Pte. (L/Cpl.) M.M.	13/02/19
Booth W. L/Cpl. M.M.	11/08/16
Boreham W. Sgt. M.M.	19/10/17
Bosanquet B. C.Q.M.S. M.S.M.	24/02/19
Boswell A.E. Pte. M.M.	23/03/18,09/04/18
Bough E. Pte. M.M.	15/03/18,11/04/18
Boulter W.H. Pte. D.C.M.	13/03/19,05/12/19
Bourne J.S. Pte. M.M.	16/09/18
Bowers E. Pte. M.M.	22/09/16
Bowlby H.S. T/Capt. M.C.	27/09/16
Box F.G. Lt. (A/Capt.) M.I.D.	28/08/19
Boyce J.W. R.Q.M.S. M.S.M.,M.I.D.	20/12/17,03/06/19
Boyd A.H. Capt. Rev. O.B.E.,M.C.,M.A.,T.D.	18/02/15,19/08/19
Boyes R.J. T/2nd Lt. M.C.	26/08/18
Boys S. Pte. (L/Cpl.) M.M.	07/08/18
Brackpool H. Pte. M.M.	13/02/19
Bradford H. C.S.M. M.S.M.	20/10/20
Bradley J.R. T/2nd Lt. (A/Capt.) M.C.	23/09/18
Bramley G. L/Cpl. (A/Cpl.) M.M.	07/08/18
Branson V.C. T/Lt. M.C.	04/02/19
Bray A. Pte. M.I.D.	28/12/18
Bray C.H. L/Cpl. M.M.	19/05/19,21/07/19
Brewer D. Pte. (A/Cpl.) M.M.	19/05/19
Brewer J. Sgt. M.M.	22/03/18
Brewster G. Cpl. (A/Sgt.) M.M.	28/07/19
Bridger C.E. Cpl. M.M.	28/07/19
Bridger J. Pte. M.M.	28/07/19
Bridger P.W. Pte. M.M.,M.I.D.	23/05/17,10/07/17
Bridger R.W. Pte. M.M.	22/03/18
Bridger S.J.A. T/Lt. M.C.	03/04/19,13/12/19
Bridger W.S.G. Capt. C de G (B)	04/09/19
Bridle C.W. L/Cpl. M.M.	15/12/16
Briffett F. Pte. M.M.	28/07/19
Briggs A.W. R.Q.M.S. M.I.D.	07/06/19
Brinkhurst J.F. Pte. (L/Cpl.) M.M.	16/09/18
Britt F. Pte. M.M.	28/07/19
Britt H. Pte. D.C.M.	30/03/18
Brooke A. Lt. M.M.	28/07/19,21/10/19
Brooker J.R. 2nd Lt. M.I.D.	11/07/19
Brooks F.B. C.S.M. M.I.D.	23/08/19
Brooks J.W.H. Pte. M.S.M.	03/09/20
Broughall J.S. T/Lt. M.C.	23/09/16,20/11/16
Brown A.E. Pte. (L/Cpl.) M.S.M.	05/06/19
Brown A.J. 2nd Lt. (T/Capt.) M.C. & R.F.C.	25/06/18
Brown A.V. 2nd Lt. M.C.	09/11/18
Brown C.E. Pte. No. G/2316 M.I.D.	20/12/17
Brown C.E. Pte. No. 999 M.M.	02/09/16
Brown E.J. Cpl. L/7922. D.C.M.,M.M.,D.M.(B)	12/01/16,07/04/19,12/01/20
Brown E.J. Pte. No. SD/1157 M.M.	22/08/16
Brown G.L. 2nd Lt. M.I.D.	20/05/18

Name	Date
Brown H. Lt. M.I.D.	08/07/19
Brown S.L. 2nd Lt. M.I.D.	20/05/18
Browning R. Cpl. M.S.M.	04/01/19
Browning T.E. Pte. M.S.M.	03/06/19,17/06/19
Brunskill G. Lt. M.I.D.	07/01/19
Bryant B.H. Sgt. M.I.D.	11/07/19
Bryant G.A. Pte. M.M.	19/05/19
Bryant P. Cpl. D.C.M.	18/08/17
Bryant R.H.W. Cpl. M.M.	05/11/17,22/03/19
Bryce A. C.Q.M.S. M.I.D.	11/07/19
Buck S.T. T/Capt. M.C.	15/09/17,03/01/18
Buckland J.R. 2nd Lt. M.I.D.	11/07/19
Buckland W.J. Pte. M.M.	23/08/18
Buckman S.A. Cpl. (L/Sgt.) M.M.	22/03/18,12/02/19
Buckwell E. Pte. (A/L/Cpl.) M.M.(F)	11/10/18
Buckwell E.V. Sgt. M.M.	21/07/17
Buckwell J. Sgt. M.M.	23/10/16
Budd A. Sgt. M.M., T.E. Medal	19/06/19,01/08/19
Budd R. Sgt. D.C.M.	28/07/16
Budd W.A. L/Cpl. (A/Sgt.) Gold Medal (Serbia)	16/02/17
Budgen W.H. C.Q.M.S. D.C.M., Bronze Medal (Italy).,M.I.D.	23/05/17,20/12/17,13/09/18,02/01/19,05/09/19
Bull B. C.S.M. Bronze Medal for Valour (Italy).,M.I.D.	13/09/18,11/07/19
Bull J.W. Pte. M.M.	28/07/16
Bullock R. Pte. M.M.	11/12/16
Bunce E.C.A. Sgt. M.M.	13/12/17
Bunker J. Pte. M.M.	16/05/17,28/05/17
Burch T. Cpl. M.M.	16/09/18
Burchell H. Pte. (L/Cpl.) M.M.	13/02/19
Burden F. Pte. M.M.,M.I.D.	16/06/16,12/10/16,04/04/17
Burdett S.L. Lt. M.C.	10/03/19
Burgess S. Sgt. M.M.,M.I.D.	18/02/15,12/10/16
Burgoine C. Pte. M.M.	19/05/19
Burk J. Sgt. M.I.D.	23/01/19
Burke E.W. Pte. D.C.M.	13/03/19,05/12/19
Burn H.T. Cpl. M.M.	28/10/16
Burrell H. Sgt. Medal of St. George (Russia)	26/08/15
Burrows E.J. Capt. M.C. 5th Bn. Manch. Regt.	03/04/19,13/12/19
Burt A. Sgt. D.C.M.	11/10/16,21/10/16
Busby F. Cpl. M.I.D.	23/06/15
Buschell E.H. Cpl. M.S.M.	24/02/19
Bush R. Cpl. D.C.M.	21/08/16
Buss C. Pte. M.M.	30/01/20
Bussell F.R. Sgt. M.M.,M.I.D.	23/05/17,15/03/19
Bustin F/G/ L/Cpl. M.M.	11/04/18
Butcher B.N. C.S.M. D.C.M.,M.C.	01/07/15,27/09/16,20/11/16,30/11/16
Butcher W. Cpl. M.M.	02/09/16,03/07/17
Butcherd J.H. Pte. (A/Sgt.) M.I.D.	11/07/19
Butter G.H. Cpl. M.I.D.	28/08/19
Caesar G. L/Sgt. (A/Sgt.) M.M.,M.S.M.	28/05/17,08/06/18
Café C.H.W. Lt-Col. M.I.D.	07/06/98
Cahill J. Sgt. M.M.	19/06/19
Caldwell R. McK. 2nd Lt. (T/Lt.) M.I.D. S/Yeo.	16/06/16
Caley E. Pte. M.M.	28/07/19
Cameron J.S. Mjr. (T/Lt-Col.) D.S.O., C/ de Chev. (B & F)	25/02/15,01/01/16,14/01/16,04/04/16,12/12/17, 21/05/18,08/07/19
Campbell E.R. Capt. M.I.D.(2)	23/01/19,12/01/20
Campbell G.O.L. T/Capt. M.C., M.I.D.	21/10/16,20/12/17,11/07/19
Campion W.H. Lt-Col. & Hon. Col. C.B.,V.D.	29/11/92,26/06/02
Campion W.R. Lt-Col. M.P.,D.S.O.,T.D.,M.I.D.	20/12/17,02/01/18,11/07/19
Camplin W. Pte. M.M.	13/02/19
Candy J.G.S. Lt. attd. R.F.C.	03/06/19
Cane A. Pte. M.M.	28/07/19
Carpenter J.W. Pte. M.M.	13/02/19
Carr W.A. Pte. M.M.	21/07/17,17/06/19
Carter J.A. Lt. M.I.D.	28/08/19
Carter N.V. C.S.M. V.C.	11/09/16,03/05/17
Cartland J. Capt. M.C. 7th Bn. R. Warks. attd.	10/02/19,03/06/19
Carver E.H. Pte. M.M.	28/07/19
Cassels F. Mjr. D.S.O.,M.I.D.	20/12/17,02/01/18
Cassels J.S. T/2nd Lt. M.C.	15/11/16
Cassy J.S. T/Capt. M.C.,M.I.D.	22/12/16,04/01/17
Castle E.J. Sgt. M.M.	27/01/19
Castle W.S. Cpl. (L/Sgt.) M.M.	31/03/19
Catchpole A.G. Sgt. M.M.	23/10/16
Cater W.H. T/2nd Lt. M.C.	23/09/18
Catmur H.A.F.V. 2nd Lt. M.I.D.	04/01/17

Catt H. C.S.M. D.C.M.,M.I.D.,C de G(F).	14/01/18,03/06/19,21/06/19,13/03/20
Caudle A.W.W. Surg-Lt. V.D.	09/08/98
Chad T.E. Lt. (A/Capt.) M.C.,M.I.D.	03/01/17,07/02/17,28/12/18,03/04/19,13/11/19
Chambers C.G.T. L/Cpl. M.M.	22/08/16,30/11/16
Chandler F. Pte. M.M.	05/01/18,29/01/18,21/05/18
Chapman R. Pte. No. 12492 M.M.	21/07/19
Chapman R. Pte. No. G/19913 M.M.	19/05/19
Charman G.A. C.S.M. M.I.D.	11/07/19
Charman W.T. Sgt. M.M.	15/03/19
Cheal W.H. C.Q.M.S. M.I.D.	25/05/18
Cheeseman D. L/Cpl. M.M.	08/10/17,05/11/17
Cheeseman J. Cpl. M.M.	28/10/16,01/11/16
Cheesman R. Pte. D.C.M.	15/04/16,29/04/16
Chegwyn W.H. Pte. C de G (B)	13/07/18
Child F. Pte. (L/Cpl.) D.C.M.	13/03/19,05/12/19
Chillman J. Sgt. M.M. (F)	16/07/17.
Chittenden H.F. Lt. M.C.,M.I.D.	02/01/17,03/01/17,28/12/18
Chittenden W.R. Sgt. M.M.	28/10/16
Clark B.H.C. Lt. M.C.	14/01/19
Clark J.C. Capt. V.D.	29/11/92
Clark P.L. T/2nd Lt. (A/Capt.) D.S.O.,M.I.D.	18/12/17,24/04/18,25/05/18
Clarke A. Pte. M.M.	28/07/19
Clarke C.B. Pte. M.M.	31/03/19
Clarke C.S. Lt-Col. & Hon. Col. V.D.	19/11/01
Clarke G.H. M.M.	29/01/18
Clarke H.C. Pte. M.M.	19/10/17
Clarke J.E. Q/M & Capt. O.B.E.,M.I.D.	16/06/16,01/01/17,03/06/19,11/07/19
Clarke S.R. Lt-Col. & Hon. Col. M.I.D.	29/07/02
Clarke T. T/2nd Lt. M.C.	20/11/17,23/03/18
Clay C.C.P. Sgt. D.C.M.,M.I.D., C of St. Geo. (R)	19/10/14,07/11/14,26/08/15
Clayton H.R. Pte. M.M.	21/07/17
Clements E. 2nd Lt. M.C.	18/02/19
Clements E. Sgt. M.I.D.	20/05/16
Clements F. Sgt. M.M.,M.M.(F).,C de G(F)	19/05/19,26/11/19,18/12/19
Clements R.F. T/2nd Lt. M.C.	14/05/18
Clevett A.E. Pte. (L/Cpl.) M.M.	07/08/18,09/08/18,21/07/19
Clift J. Pte. D.C.M.	06/05/84
Clinch W. L/Cpl. M.M.	2810/16,01/11/16
Cluer S.D. Sgt. D.C.M.	03/06/19,13/03/20
Coates C. Sgt. M.M.,M.S.M.,C de G (F).	22/12/16,18/06/18,11/10/18
Coates R. Sgt. M.M.	13/12/17
Cockett H.E. Pte. M.M.	19/10/17,05/11/17
Cockrell F.P. T/Capt. M.C.	03/01/18
Coe F.W. Sgt. M.M.	19/05/19
Cole A.H. T/2nd Lt. M.C.	19/01/18,26/04/18
Cole-Hamilton C. Rev. T/Capt. M.C. attd. R.S.R.	03/06/19
Coleman C. C.Q.M.S. M.S.M.	08/06/18
Coleman H.C. Capt. M.C.,M.I.D.	03/01/18,11/07/19
Coles G.H. Cpl. D.C.M.	03/06/19,13/03/20
Coles H.A. T/R.S.M. D.C.M.	31/05/18,23/20/28
Collier A.A. Pte. M.M.	28/07/19
Collingbourne A.W. T/Capt. M.C.	02/01/19
Collins F. Cpl. M.M.,M.I.D.	16/06/16,28/10/16
Collis W.O. Sgt. D.C.M.,C de G (F).	22/05/17,13/03/19,05/12/19
Compton G. Lt. D.C.M.,M.M.	11/07/16,21/07/16,30/11/16,07/08/17
Constable G.S. Mjr. (T/Lt-Col.) M.C.,T.D.,M.I.D.	21/06/17,17/08/17,12/06/18,24/01/19,11/07/19,22/08/19
Constable S.A. C.S.M. D.C.M.,M.M. (F).,C de G (B)	02/11/18,32/11/18,26/11/19
Cook A.C. Sgt. M.I.D. as S3//030182 R.A.S.C.	18/01/19
Cook B. Pte. M.M.	22/03/18
Cook L.E. Lt. M.I.D.	28/08/19
Cook T.H. Pte. M.I.D.	20/05/18
Cooling J.H. T/Capt. M.I.D.	04/01/17
Cooper A. Cpl. (L/Sgt.) M.M.	22/03/18,28/03/18
Cooper F.A. Pte. M.M.	22/08/16
Cooper H.B. C.S.M. M.S.M.	03/06/19
Cooper R.G. Lt. M.C.	23/09/18
Coote-Brown W.C. T/Lt-Col. D.S.O.,M.I.D.	20/12/17,02/01/18
Cope J. Cpl. (Victory Parade)	21/07/19
Coppard A.V. A/Sgt. D.C.M., M.I.D., D.M.(B)	23/05/17,26/05/17,16/04/18,02/01,19,05/09/19
Coppard H.A. C.Q.M.S. M.S.M.	04/06/19
Corbett A. Mjr. (T/Lt-Col.) M.I.D., O. O Crown of Italy	27/02/17,28/3/19,02/04/19
Corbett E.F.J. Pte. (L/Cpl.) M.M.	25/02/18
Cornes L.G. T/2nd Lt. M.C.	19/10/17,11/03/18

Cornish F.C. Pte. M.M.	28/07/19
Cornwell P.W. Cpl. M.M.	15/03/19
Corral W.R. Lt. (T/Mjr.) M.I.D.	28/12/18
Cortis A. Qm & Hon. Capt. V.D.	29/11/92
Cory E.J.D'A. Capt. D.S.O.,T.D.,M.I.D.	10/09/01,27/09/01,14/05/09
Cosens G. Sgt. (A/S/Mjr.) M.I.D.	13/03/18
Cosham H.E. Pte. M.M.	02/09/16
Cosstick W.T. Pte. M.M.	08/01/17,13/01/17
Costa W. Pte. (A/Sgt.) M.S.M.	05/01/20
Cotton A.A. Pte. M.M.	28/07/19
Couchman W. Sgt. D.C.M.	14/01/16,13/03/16
Couldrey V.H. T/Lt. M.C.	18/12/17,24/04/18
Courthope G.L. T/Mjr. M.P.,M.C.,T.D.,M.I.D.	23/06/15,21/01/16
Cousens H.S. T/Capt. M.I.D.	01/05/19
Covey A.S. Pte. M.M.	13/02/19
Cowley G.E. Sgt. (A/C.Q.M.S.) M.I.D.	11/07/19
Cowstick S.E. Pte. D.C.M.	25/08/85
Cox A.C. L/Cpl. M.M., Medal Barbatie Si Credinta (Rom)	14/03/19,19/05/19
Cox E.R. Pte. M.M.	19/05/19
Cox R.E. Cpl. (A/Sgt.) M.M.	02/12/16,01/01/17,08/01/17,16/08/17
Cox W.J. Cpl. M.M.	01/12/17
Coxhead H.J. T/Capt. M.C.,M.I.D.	04/01/17,05/06/17
Coxhead L.G. 2nd Lt. M.C.	08/03/19
Cragg A.B. T/Lt. M.I.D; C de G (F)	04/01/17,11/07/19,18/12/19
Cramp A. Pte. M.M.	05/11/17
Crane C.B. Cpl. D.C.M.	03/06/19,13/03/20
Crane J.W. Sgt. M.I.D.	23/05/17
Crawford F.O. Sgt. M.M. S/Yeo.	20/03/17
Crawfurd P.E.P. Mjr. Bt. Lt-Col. M.I.D.	11/06/18,14/08/18
Crispin H.T. Lt-Col. M.I.D.	10/11/14,18/02/15
Crowther J. Pte. (A/Cpl.) M.I.D.	28/08/19
Curd A.J. L/Cpl. D.C.M.	02/01/19,09/01/19,05/09/19
Currie E.R. Very Rev. A/Ch. V.D.	15/11/04
Cuthbertson W.R.D. Capt. M.C.	18/02/19
Cutler E.C. T/2nd Lt. M.C.	31/07/18
Cutting E.W. Sgt. M.I.D.	20/12/17
Dabson B. Pte. M.M.	11/12/16
Dade E.W. Pte. (A/Cpl.) M.I.D	28/08/19
Dadswell F. Pte. D.C.M.	28/07/16
Dale E. Pte. D.C.M.	25/08/85
Dale J.S. Pte. M.M. (F)	02/05/17
Dale W. Sgt. M.M.	10/07/17
Dallaway J.H. C.S.M. D.C.M.,M.I.D.	30/11/16,11/07/19
Danells B. Lt. (A/Capt.) M.C. S/Yeo	03/06/19
Dann N. L/Cpl. M.M.	23/10/16,04/1/16
Darcy F. Pte. M.M.	13/02/19
Darnell H. Cpl. (A/Sgt.) M.M.	19/06/19
Dashwood V.E.C. Capt. (T/Mjr.) M.C.,M.I.D.	19/10/14,18/02/15,19/02/15,25/02/15,28/03/19
Daughtry J. L/Cpl. M.M.	23/10/16
Davey A.H. L/Cpl. M.M.	11/12/16
Davey P.V. Sgt. M.I.D.	11/07/19
Davidson J.A. 2nd Lt. M.C.	28/09/18
Davies C. Pte. M.M.	22/08/16
Davies G.T. Sgt. M.M.,M.I.D.	16/06/16,13/11/16
Davis C. Pte. M.M.	22/03/18
Davis G.E. Pte. (A/Cpl.) M.M.	28/07/19
Dawes C.J. Pte. M.M.	29/01/18
Dawes E.P. Capt. T.D.	22/03/20
Dawson H.R.W. Capt. M.I.D.	07/06/19
Dawson N.G. Pte. M.M.	28/07/19
Day J. Pte. D.C.M.	09/07/98
Day P.C. Pte. M.M.	19/05/19
De Chair G.H.B. Capt. Bt. Mjr. O.B.E.,M.C.,M.I.D.	18/02/15,19/02/15,25/02/15,12/12/17,03/06/19,0/07/19
de Jong K. Mjr. M.C.	02/01/17
Dear F.H. 2nd Lt. M.C.	05/02/18,09/07/18
Dearlove A. Sgt. M.I.D.	11/07/19
Deeprose C.J. C.S.M. D.C.M.	05/01/18,18/04/18
Deeprose V.E.T. L/Cpl. M.M.	29/01/18
Dell A.J. L/Cpl. D.C.M.	18/08/17,02/04/18
Delves G.F. Cpl. M.M.	12/10/16
Dendy E.J. Pte. (L/Cpl.) M.M.	22/03/18,21/05/18
Dennett M.S.S. L/Cpl. (A/Cpl.) M.M.	29/01/18
Dennett W.C. L/Sgt. D.C.M.	29/11/15

Denyer A.A. T/2nd Lt. M.C. Yorks. and Lancs.	26/04/17
Dewell F. Sgt. M.M.	13/02/19
Dibdin F.J.S. Lt. M.C. attd. 2nd Bn. Welsh Regt.	23/06/15,15/11/16
Dick Q.W.A. Pte. M.M.	17/11/16,22/11/16
Dick R.N. Bt. Lt-Col. (T/Brig.) C.M.G.,D.S.O., M.I.D., Cavalier of the Order of St. Mark & St. Lazarus (Italy)	14/09/06,23/12/16,01/09/17,08/02/18,13/03/18, 04/03/19,22/02/19
Dicker A.S.H. Capt. O.B.E.,M.I.D.	16/06/16,15/03/18,05/06/19
Dickerson T.W. Pte. (L/Cpl.) M.M.	04/04/18
Dinnage W. Cpl. M.M.	22/03/18
Diplock H.R. Sgt. M.M.	15/09/17,20/09/17,10/10/17,07/01/18
Diplock T. Sgt. M.I.D.	19/10/14
Dix T.C. Pte. (L/Cpl.) M.M.	28/07/19
Dodge J.B. Mjr. (T/Lt-Col.) D.S.O.,D.S.C.,M.I.D. Suffolk Regt. attd.	08/11/15,03/06/19,11/07/19
Dolleymore E. Lt. (A/Capt.) M.C.,M.I.D.	20/12/17,18/02/19
Dolman G. Pte. M.M.	19/05/19
Donald M. Pte. M.M.	13/02/19
Done W.E.P. Lt. (T/Capt.) M.C.,M.I.D., Croce de Guerra (Italy)	04/01/19,19/05/19,31/05/19
Donne B.D.A. Lt-Col. C.B.,M.I.D.,3rd & 4th Class Medjidieh (Egypt)	23/10/85,17/01/90,15/08/93,29/11/00;16/04/01
Douglas L. Sgt. M.S.M.	03/06/19
Downes W.D. Capt. M.C. & Nigeria Regt.	03/01/18
Drake G. Pte. M.M.	23/08/19
Dray W. Sgt. M.I.D.	23/06/15
Drew P.F. T/Lt. (A/Capt.) M.C.,M.I.D.	23/05/17,03/01/18,21/10/19
Drewery H.W. L/Cpl. M.M.	21/07/19
Drury C.A. L/Cpl. M.M.	22/08/16
du Moulin F.L. Capt. M.C. attd. 1st Bn. East Yorks.	27/08/18
du Moulin L.E. Mjr. (Bt. Lt-Col) M.I.D.	08/05/01,10/09/01,27/09/09
Duck J.G. Sgt. (A/C.Q.M.S.) M.I.D.	11/07/19
Dudman E. L/Cpl. M.M.	14/09/16
Dudman G.W. Sgt. M.M.	07/08/18
Duke J.H.G. Cpl. (L./Sgt.) M.M.	19/10/17
Dunk A. Pte. (L/Cpl.) M.M.	11/12/16
Dunk A.E. Pte. M.M.	12/10/16
Dunk J.W.H. Pte. M.M.	14/09/18
Dunkerton W. Pte. (L/Cpl.) M.M.	19/06/19
Dunningham J. Pte. M.M.	29/01/18
Durling W. Pte. (L/Cpl.) M.M.	28/07/19
Durrant A.E. L/Cpl. M.M.	16/09/18
Dybell C.W. Cpl. M.M.	08/01/17
Dyke J.N. T/2nd Lt. M.C.	18/12/17,24/04/18
Eade W.J. Pte. M.M.	26/04/18,30/05/18
Eastwick A. Q/M. & Capt. M.B.E.	30/01/20
Eaton F. Pte. M.M.	25/02/18
Eberle G.S.F.J. Mjr. (A/Lt-Col.) D.S.O.,M.I.D.	07/01/19
Eden A. Rev. A/Ch. V.D.	29/11/92
Edwards C. Pte. Div. Com. Cert. For Gallantry	21/10/16
Edwards E. L/Cpl. M.M.	20/10/17
Edwards T.R. Capt. M.I.D.	08/07/19
Ellen W.P. T/Lt. M.C.,M.I.D.	28/12/18,03/06/19
Ellis E.S. Lt. M.C.	21/08/16
Ellis V.R.H. T/2nd Lt. M.C.,M.I.D.	20/12/17,28/09/18
Elphick J.A. Cpl. (A/C/Sgt.) M.M.	28/07/19
Elphick P.G. Sgt. D.C.M.	03/11/16,05/01/18,18/04/18
Elphick W. L/Cpl. M.M.	29/01/18
Emerson J.A. L/Cpl. M.M.	28/05/17
Emery C.T Cpl. M.M.	10/07/17,12/02/19,19/06/19
Emsley F.M. L/Cpl. M.M.	21/11/17
Emsley R. Pte. M.M.	22/08/16,08/01/17,07/01/18
Etherington E.E. Sgt. M.M.	28/07/19,23/10/19
Etherington J. C.Q.M.S. (A/R.Q.M.S.) M.I.D.	11/07/19
Ettridge F.B.R. Cpl. (A/Sgt.) M.M.	07/08/18
Evans A.J. Sgt. M.M.	14/09/16
Evans F.W. Pte. M.M.	14/09/18
Evans J. Pte. M.M.	02/03/18,04/04/18
Evans S.G. Capt. M.C.,M.I.D.	16/06/16,02/01/17
Eve J. Sgt. M.S.M.,M.I.D	04/01/17,19/06/18
Evenden F.B. Pte. D.C.M.,M.M.	22/12/17,25/02/18,13/03/19,05/12/19
Evershed P. Sgt. M.S.M. (Gallantry)	12/03/17
Fairhall F.C. Cpl. D.C.M.	18/08/17
Farley A.W. Pte. M.M.	28/07/19
Farmer G. Pte. (L/Cpl.) M.M.	19/06/19
Farmer G.S. T/2nd Lt. M.I.D.	25/05/18
Farmer I.H. Cpl. M.M.	03/11/17,29/01/18

Farndale G.J. Cpl. (A/Sgt.) M.M.	23/10/18
Farrant A. Cpl. (L/Sgt.) M.M.	04/04/18
Farrant W. Pte. M.M.	28/07/19
Farrell W. C.S.M. M.S.M.,M.I.D.	20/12/17,21/01/19
Farrer S.J. T/2nd Lt. M.I.D	04/01/17
Farrow H.J.R. T/Lt. M.C.	18/2/18,20/07/18
Faulkner B. Pte. M.M.	29/01/18
Fawssett C. Capt. D.F.C. & R.F.C.	04/06/19
Fazan E.A.C. Capt. M.C.,M.I.D. R.A.M.C. attd. 5th Bn	01/1101/16,14/01/16,05/02/18,08/07/18
Fenchelle E.A. T/2nd Lt. M.C.	22/12/16
Fennell S. R.Q.M.S. M.S.M.,M.I.D.	14/01/18,03/06/19
Fenton F.H. Lt. M.C.,M.I.D.	25/05/18,18/02/19
Field A.E. Sgt. C de G (F)	26/11/19
Field A.J. Pte. M.M.	20/10/17,20/05/18
Field C.A. Capt. M.I.D.	14/01/18
Field T.P. Q/M & Capt. M.I.D.	28/08/19
Fielder F.G. Pte. M.M.	23/08/19
Finch J.J.G. Pte. M.M.	25/02/18
Finch L.H.K. Lt. M.I.D.	18/02/15
Finlayson R.A. Mjr. C.M.G.,M.I.D.	16/04/01,19/04/01,27/02/17
Finucane A. Sgt. D.C.M.	09/07/98
Firth H. Cpl. M.M.	20/10/17
Fishenden H.E. Pte. M.M.	20/02/17,25/02/18,11/03/18
Fitzhugh V.M. T/Capt. M.I.D.	01/01/16
Fletcher H. Sir Col. Bart. K.C.B.,V.D.	29/11/92,16/10/10
Flint C.W. Q/M & Capt. M.I.D.	12/01/20
Flint F. Cpl. M.M.	15/03/19
Foord S. Sgt. M.I.D.	04/0/17
Ford A.S. Pte. M.M.	11/08/16
Fordham W. Pte. D.C.M.	19/02/19,12/01/20
Fortescue R.H. Lt. M.C.,C de G (F)	11/11/18,26/11/19
Foster A.D. T/Lt. M.C.	21/10/16,15/05/17
Foster C. Pte. M.M.	20/09/17
Foster J.E. T/2nd Lt. M.I.D.	16/06/16
Foster J.W.S. Sgt. M.M.	11/12/16
Foster P. Pte. M.M.	20/10/17
Foster P.G. T/2nd Lt. M.I.D.	16/06/16
Foster T. T/Mjr. M.I.D.	20/12/17,11/07/19
Fowler C. Cpl. D.C.M.,M.M.	21/08/16,29/01/18
Foy W.A. 2nd Lt. M.C.	17/08/17
Francis A.E. Pte. M.M.	13/02/19
Francis W. Cpl. (Victory Parade)	21/07/19
Franklin F. Pte. (Cpl.) M.S.M.	03/06/19
Franks T.E. Pte. (A/Cpl.) M.M.	19/05/19
Fraser D. 2nd Lt. M.C.	28/09/18
Frost A. St .John T/Lt. M.I.D.	07/06/19
Fuller A. L/Cpl. M.M.	06/02/18
Fuller C. Sgt. M.M.	31/07/17
Fuller F. Pte. M.M.	11/12/16
Fuller L. Pte. M.M.	28/10/16,03/07/17
Funnell A.E. Pte. (A/Cpl.) M.S.M.	12/05/20
Funnell F.C. R.Q.M.S. M.S.M.	05/06/19
Furminger A. L/Cpl. M.M.	17/09/18
Furner H.W. Pte. (A/L/Cpl.) M.I.D.	07/01/19
Gammon K.W. T/2nd Lt. M.C.	26/08/16
Gannon W. Sgt. M.M.,M.S.M.,M.I.D.	24/02/19,17/01/20,03/08/20
Gardiner P.J. Pte. M.M.	07/08/18,11/08/16
Gardner A. C/Sgt. M.S.M.	03/09/20
Gardner G.F. Cpl. M.M.	05/11/17
Gardner H. L/Cpl. No. 320212 M.M.	22/03/18
Gardner H. Pte. No. 3322 M.M.	11/08/16
Garner C.C. T/Lt. M.I.D.	25/05/18,11/07/19
Garton A.G.M. A/Cpl. M.M.	27/03/17
Gaston C.H. Pte. M.M.	13/11/16
Gates T. Sgt. D.C.M.	31/10/12
Gates W.A. Sgt. M.M.	13/11/16
Gearing A. Pte. M.S.M.	03/06/19
Gell A.F. Mjr. & Lt-Col. V.D.	09/11/97
Gibbs G.W. Pte. M.M.	08/01/17,13/01/17
Gibson A. L/Cpl M.M.	05/11/17

Gilbert A.R. Col. C.B.E.,D.S.O.,M.I.D.	29/11/00,10/09/01,31/10,02,03/06/19
Gilbert W.H. Sgt. D.C.M.	08/06/18,24/10/18
Gilchrist A. Sgt. M.I.D.	11/07/19
Giles J.C. Sgt. M.M.	20/10/17
Gill J. Pte. No. 3697 D.C.M.	19/04/01
Gill J. Pte. No. 914 D.C.M.	02/07/15
Gillet R.H. T/Lt. (A/Capt.) M.I.D.	28/12/18
Gilmore G.H. T/Capt. (A/Mjr.) D.S.O.,M.C. & Bar.,(2) M.I.D. O of St. Vladimir 4th Class with Swords, O of St. Anne 2nd Class with Swords (R)	05/06/17,27/07/17,27/05/19,05/02/20
Gilpin G. Q/M & Mjr. O.B.E.	12/09/19
Glasgow A.E. Bt. Lt-Col. (T/Brig.) C.M.G.,D.S.O.,M.I.D.,C de G (F)	01/01/16,03/06/16,16/06/16,04/06/17,12/12/17,21/05/18, 11/10/18,03/06/19,08/07/19
Glenister H. Pte. M.M.	06/09/16,22/09/16
Goacher R.P. Pte. M.M.	21/07/19,28/07/19
Goad C.E. T/Capt. M.C.	27/07/17
Goble E.G. L/Sgt. M.M.	08/01/17
Goddard J.H. Pte. M.M.	22/09/16
Goddard N.C. Q/M & Hon. Capt. M.I.D.	14/08/18
Godden H. Pte. D.C.M.,M.M.	13/03/19,05/12/19
Godman C.R.B. Mjr. T.D.	13/01/20
Golden A.W. L/Sgt. D.C.M.,M.M.	08/01/17,10/09/18
Goldie G.L. Lt-Col. K.C.B.	28/06/61
Golds A. Pte. M.M.	15/11/18
Golds T. Pte. M.M.	14/06/18,17/09/18
Golds W.B. Sgt. M.M.	22/03/18
Goldsmith J. Pte. M.M.	31/08/18
Gooding W.A. R.Q.M.S. (A/R.S.M.) M.I.D.	14/08/18
Goodsell A.J. Sgt. M.I.D.	1/07/19
Godwin E.T.H. Lt. M.C.,M.I.D.	09/11/15,01/01/16
Goodyer L. Pte. M.M.	13/02/19
Gordon F.H. Pte. M.M.	19/05/19
Gorringe E.C. T/Capt. M.C.	01/08/18
Goringe W.H. Mjr. T.D.	13/07/20
Goward H. Sgt. M.M.,C de G (B)	16/07/18,28/07/19
Grant A.J.S. Lt. Chevalier de la Couronne (B).,C de G (B)	25/09/17,12/05/18
Grant F.N. Capt. M.C.,M.I.D.	23/06/15,25/06/15
Gratwick S.F. Pte. M.M.	14/09/16
Gray A. Sgt. (A/S/Mjr.) M.S.M.	24/02/19
Gray G.W. Pte. (A/Cpl.) M.M.	28/07/19
Grayson F. Pte. M.I.D.	11/07/19
Green E.J. Sgt. D.C.M.	21/08/16,07/08/17
Green E.W.B. Lt-Col. D.S.O., M.I.D.	10/09/01,19/10/14,18/02/15,19/02/15,01/01/16,16/06/16
Green M. Pte. M.M.	19/05/19
Green R. Pte. M.M.	20/10/17
Greene E.S.G. C.Q.M.S. M.I.D.	14/08/18
Grenyer W.D. L/Cpl. M.M.	22/08/16
Griffin F. Pte. M.M.	04/04/18
Griffiths C. Sgt. C de G (B)	13/07/18
Grimes J.A. C.Q.M.S. M.S.M.	03/06/19
Grimstead E.G. Sgt. M.M.	21/07/17
Griston P.A. Pte. M.M.	17/09/17,12/02/19
Gronheit A.L. Sgt. (A/C.Q.M.S.) M.I.D.	11/07/19
Groome A.F. Pte. M.M.	21/12/18,21/07/19,28/07/19
Grover W.E. Pte. M.M.	08/08/18
Groves A.L. Pte. M.M.	26/04/18,12/02/19
Gudman C.B. Mjr. (Lt-Col.) M.I.D.	23/08/19
Guiel H.J. Pte. M.M.	20/10/17,04/11/18
Guildford G.H. L/Cpl. M.M.	30/01/18
Gumbrill L.A. Pte. M.M.	19/05/19
Gurry A. Pte. M.M.	19/05/19
Guttridge R. L/Cpl. M.M.	30/01/18
Guy A.H. L/Cpl. M.M.	22/03/18
Guymer J. Pte. M.M.	28/02/18
Gwynne R.V. T/Mjr. D.S.O. S/Yeo.	18/04/17
Haddon T.R. T/2nd Lt. M.C.	23/04/18
Hadley W.H. Cpl. M.M.	17/09/18
Haigh A.D. Lt. M.C.	04/04/19,13/12/19
Haines A.E. A/S/Mjr. (P.S.) D.C.M.	12/12/16
Hall H.F. Cpl. M.I.D.	25/05/18
Hall J. Sgt. M.I.D.	28/08/19
Hall R.C. T/Lt. M.C.	21/10/16,27/09/17,10/01/18
Hall W.A. Pte. (L/Cpl.) M.S.M.	04/06/19
Halley J.C. A/Sgt. C de G (F)	02/05/17

Hammond E.A. C.S.M. D.C.M.	15/11/16
Hammond G.C. Sgt. M.M.	20/09/17
Hammond R.P. Sgt. M.I.D.	11/07/19
Hampton N.J. T/Capt. & Adj. M.C.,M.I.D.	23/05/17,03/06/18
Hancock J.D.G. Lt. M.C.	17/02/19
Hanlon P.J. C.Q.M.S. M.S.M.,M.I.D.	04/01/17,28/12/18,03/06/19
Hann E.E. Sgt. M.M.,M.I.D.	28/12/18,23/8/19
Harden E.J. T/2nd Lt. (A/Capt.) M.C.,M.I.D.	18/12/17,20/12/17,24/04/18
Harding S.J. L/Sgt. M.M.	28/10/16
Hardy W.H.C. Capt. M.C.	19/02/18,22/07/18
Harman E.A. Pte. M.M.	03/07/17
Harris A.J. Pte. M.M.	22/12/16
Harris G.C. Cpl. M.M.	06/02/18
Harris W.T. Sgt. M.S.M.,M.I.D.	23/05/17,03/06/19
Harrison E.R. Capt. & Hon. Mjr. V.D.	11/01/10
Harrison G.H. Lt-Col. D.S.O., Cmdg. 11th Bn. R.S.R.	01/01/17
Harrold W.P.G. L/Sgt. M.M.	22/08/16
Hart J. L/Cpl. M.M.	13/11/16
Harvey A. Pte. D.C.M.	10/09/18
Harvey G.W. M.M.	28/07/19
Harwood J. Cpl. (A/L/Sgt.) M.M.	22/03/18,18/10/18
Hatton H. Pte. M.M.	22/10/18
Hawken G.L.L. Surg-Lt. V.D.	14/05/97
Hawkett H. L/Cpl. (A/Cpl.)	05/01/18
Hayes J. Sgt. (A/C.Q.M.S.) M.M.	22/09/16
Hayhurst A. Pte. M.M.	15/03/19
Hayler J. L/Cpl. (Victory Parade)	21/07/19
Haynes A.R.C. Sgt. M.S.M.	21/01/19
Haynes C.A. Pte. (A/L/Sgt.) M.I.D.	28/08/19
Hayter J.B. Pte. M.M.	11/08/16
Hayward W.H. Pte. M.M	20/02/17
Head E.J. Sgt. D.C.M.	17/01/19
Head G.F. Sgt. D.C.M.,M.S.M.,M.I.D.	04/01/17,19/06/18,10/09/18
Heagerty W.T. T/Mjr. M.I.D.	04/01/17
Hearn B. Pte. M.M.	28/07/19
Hearn R.W. R.Q.M.S. D.C.M.	03/06/16,22/06/16,07/08/16
Heaseman H.E. Pte. (A/L/Cpl.) M.M.	31/03/19
Heaseman J. Pte. D.C.M.	14/01/16,13/03/16
Heasman E.H. Sgt. M.I.D.	11/07/19
Heathfield C.W. L/Cpl. M.M.	11/12/16
Heise A.W. Cpl. M.M.	16/10/17,20/10/17
Helme R.M. Capt. & Hon. Mjr. V.D.	31/10/99
Hemsley E.J. T/2nd Lt. M.C.	26/09/18
Hemsley H. Pte. M.M.	12/10/16,16/05/19
Hemsley S.H. Pte. (A/Cpl.) M.M.	19/05/19
Henderson J.R. A/S/Major	21/01/19
Hendley F.A. Pte. (Cpl.) M.M.	19/05/19
Hendry W. L/Cpl. M.M.	14/09/16
Henham J. Pte. D.C.M.	10/09/18
Henty A. Capt. & Hon. Mjr. V.D.	29/11/92
Henty E. Capt. & Hon. Mjr. V.D.	29/11/92
Henty J. Cpl. M.M.	11/12/16
Hermitage E. Pte. M.M.	20/10/17
Herridge W. C.S.M. D.C.M.,M.I.D.	20/12/17,31/05/18,24/10/18
Hersee C.H. Sgt. M.I.D.	06/07/17
Hersey A.J. Sgt. M.M.	09/10/18
Hervey A.F. T/Lt. Palmes Academie Officier (France)	30/09/20
Hewson H.C. Sgt. M.I.D.,	11/03/18,25/05/18
Higham T.L. Pte. M.S.M.,M.I.D.	25/05/18,03/06/19
Highgate E. L/Cpl. D.C.M.,M.M.	21/07/17,20/09/17,17/10/18,12/02/19,05/12/19
Hill E.A. T/Capt. M.I.D.	25/05/18
Hill E. Pte. (A/L/Cpl.) M.I.D.	07/06/19
Hill G. T/Lt. M.I.D.	11/07/19
Hill L. L/Cpl. M.I.D.	23/06/15,25/06/15
Hill M.V.B. T/Lt-Col. D.S.O.,M.C.,M.I.D.	27/08/17,20/12/17,17/09/18,28/12/18,11/07/19
Hillebrand H.F. T/2nd Lt. Croce di Guerra (Italy)	19/05/19
Hillier H.D. Capt. M.C. Gloucester Regt. attd. R.S.R.	03/01/18,11/03/18,02/02/19
Hillman E. Pte. M.I.D.	25/05/18
Hillman H.R.N. Pte. M.M.	19/05/19
Hills H. Pte. M.M.	28/07/19
Hills W.A. Sgt. M.S.M.	19/06/18
Hind R.C.D. T/Capt. M.C.,M.I.D	16/06/16,04/01/17,03/01/18,28/12/18
Hindmarsh C. Bandmaster M.S.M	05/06/19

Name	Dates
Hoad E. Pte. M.M.	19/12/17,22/03/18
Hoad P. Cpl. D.C.M.	02/10/00
Hoad S. Sgt. M.M.	22/03/18,07/11/19
Hobbs E.J. 2nd Lt. M.C. S/Yeo. 16th Bn.	15/10/18
Hobbs E.J. 2nd Lt. M.C.,M.I.D., 2nd Bn.	01/01/16,14/01/16
Hobday G. Cpl. D.C.M. attd. 1/2nd King's African Rifles	08/02/19,05/09/18
Hodges G. Sgt. D.C.M., Bronze Medal for Honour (Italy)	27/09/16,28/05/17
Hodgson B.T. Lt-Col. C.M.G.,V.D.,T.D.,M.I.D.	05/03/01,11/06/18,08/07/18,12/10/20
Hodson G.H. Sgt. M.M.,M.S.M.	13/11/16,04/06/19
Holder B Pte. M.M.	22/07/18,17/09/18
Holderness W. Capt. M.I.D.	20/07/19
Holdsworth M.J. Lt. M.C.,M.I.D.	04/01/17,08/06/18
Holland A. 2nd Lt. M.I.D.	25/05/18
Holland F.G. Sgt. M.M.(F)	02/05/17
Hollands A.E. Pte. M.M.	11/04/18
Hollingdale F. Pte. M.I.D.	18/02/15
Hollobone F.W. Sgt. D.C.M.	21/08/16
Holman W.H. Sgt. M.S.M. (Gallantry).,M.I.D.	27/02/17,12/03/17
Holman R. L/Cpl. M.M.	13/12/17
Holmes L. Mjr. T.D.	26/05/14
Holmes R.C. Cpl. C de G (B)	15/07/18
Holmwood R. Sgt. M.I.D.	07/06/19
Honeysett D.G. Sgt. (A/C.S.M.)	17/09/18
Hook W.J. 2nd Lt. M.C.	17/01/20
Hopkins A. Sgt. M.I.D.	11/07/19
Hopkins R.J. Cpl. (A/Sgt.)	08/01/17
Hopper G.T. Sgt. M.S.M.	22/01/20
Horcroft A. L/Cpl. M.M.	03/06/16,07/08/16,30/11/16
Horne A.W. Sgt. M.M.	22/09/16,19/06/17
Horsecroft S. T/2nd Lt. M.C.	27/09/18
Horton H.E. Pte. M.M.	08/01/17
Horton H.J. Cpl. M.M.	22/03/18
Howard A.C. C.S.M. No. 240251 Croce di Guerra (Italy)	19/05/19
Howard A.C. Sgt. No. 1864 M.I.D.	04/01/17
Howard K.B. T/Lt. (A/Capt.) M.I.D.	05/06/19
Howard T.H. Mjr. T.D.	14/03/19
Howard W.F. Lt. M.C. S/Yeo.	02/01/18,03/10/18
Howe R.M. Lt. (A/Capt.) M.C.	15/01/19
Howlett R.W. Pte. M.M.	15/11/18
Hoyle J. C.S.M. M.S.M.	10/02/19,03/06/19
Hudson L.W. T/2nd Lt. M.C	28/09/18
Hudson R. 2nd Lt. M.C.	25/09/18
Hughes F. Pte. M.M.	03/06/16
Hughes J. Pte. (L/Cpl.) M.M.	16/01/20,17/01/20
Hughes J. L/Cpl. M.I.D.	03/08/20
Hughes S. Cpl. M.M. Royal West Surrey's	10/10/17
Hughes W.C. Sgt. D.C.M.	31/03/16,22/05/16,09/09/16
Hulton J.M. Mjr. (A/Lt-Col.) C.B.E., D.S.O., Order of Nile 3rd Class (Egypt).,Officer of the Order of Crown of Italy.,M.I.D.(2)	03/06/16,14/01/18,31/05/18,07/06/18,15/06/18,13/11/18,26/11/18,30/11/18,01/01/19,14/01/20
Hume A.D. T/2nd Lt. (A/Capt.) M.C. attd. Royal Fusiliers	04/06/18,01/07/18
Humphrey G. C.Q.M.S. M.I.D.	28/12/18
Humphrey M.A. Pte. Div. Com. Cert. For Gallantry	21/10/16
Humphrey W. C.S.M. D.C.M.,M.I.D.	14/02/17,28/12/18
Hunt C. Sgt. M.M.	17/11/16
Hunt W. Pte. (L/Cpl.) M.M.	08/07/16
Hunter A. Sgt. M.S.M.	19/06/18
Hunton J.J. Sgt. M.M.	28/07/19
Hurst F. C.S.M. M.I.D.	28/08/19
Hutchings J. Pte. M.M.	30/01/18
Hyde W.A. Pte. M.M.	19/05/19
Hygate H.P. Cpl. M.I.D.	25/05/18
Hyland H. Cpl. M.I.D.	23/06/15
Hyland R.J. Sgt. M.I.D.	20/12/17
Hynes B.M. Lt-Col. O.B.E.	12/09/19
	14/01/20
Ide A.E. A/L/Sgt. M.I.D.	16/06/16,01/01/17,04/01/17,26/07/18,28/12/18,05/06/19
Impey G.H. Mjr. (T/Lt-Col.) D.S.O. , M.I.D.	04/01/17,03/01/18
Ireland L.A.F. T/Lt. M.C.,M.I.D.	04/04/19,13/12/19

Isard E. Pte. M.M.	31/07/17
Isbell A.D. Sgt. M.M.	19/05/19
Isted F. Pte. (A/L/Cpl.) M.S.M.	04/01/19
Isted S. Pte. M.M.	19/06/19
Izzard W.J. Pte. M.M.	17/09/18
James A.E. Sgt. M.S.M.	05/06/19
James G.E. Sgt. M.S.M	03/06/19
Jaques V.H. Lt. (A/Capt.) M.C.	18/10/18,17/02/19
Jarvis C.H. Sgt. M.M.	17/11/16
Jebb R.D. Lt. (T/Capt.) M.C.,M.I.D.	01/01/16
Jeffery T. R. Pte. M.M.	05/11/17
Jellicorse H. Mjr. O.B.E.	05/05/19
Jenkinson W.G. L/Cpl. M.M.	08/01/17,25/02/18
Jennings A.J. Cpl. M.M.	19/05/19
Jester A. Pte. (L/Cpl.) M.M.	28/07/19
Johncox J. L/Cpl. M.M.	23/10/16
Johnson C.V. Mjr. T.D.	30/05/19,03/06/19
Johnson D.G. Lt-Col. V.C.,D.S.O.,M.C.,M.I.D., Cmdg. 2nd Bn. R.S.R.	02/01/18,07/01/19,13/01/19,11/07/19
Johnson F.W.F. Lt-Col. D.S.O.,M.I.D.	20/05/18,10/06/18,28/07/19
Johnson H.H. Capt. (T/Mjr.) D.S.O., Croix de Chevalier (F)	16/10/18,07/11/18
Johnson W.G. Pte. M.I.D.	25/05/18,28/12/18
Johnston H.E. Sgt. D.C.M.	30/03/18
Jones C. C.Q.M.S. M.I.D.	11/07/19
Jones G.H. Lt. M.C.	05/06/17,04/07/17
Jones H.E. T/Lt. M.C.,M.I.D.	23/05/17,19/10/17,09/03/18
Jones T. Sgt. M.I.D.	01/01/16
Jones T.A. Q/M. & Hon. Capt. M.C.,D.C.M., M.I.D.	10/09/01,27/09/01,23/06/15,25/06,15,03/06/16, 01/01/17,04/01/17
Jones W.P.S. T/Capt. M.I.D.	28/08/19
Jordan H. Cpl. M.M.	20/10/17
Joscelyne F.P. T/Capt. O.B.E., M.C. R.A.M.C. attd. 2nd Bn. R.S.R	28/07/16,03/06/19
Josland A.E. Pte. M.M.	01/01/18
Joy J. C.S.M. M.C.	22/12/16
Joyce E.A. Pte. M.M.	28/07/19
Judd H.A.W. Cpl. (A/Sgt.) M.I.D.	28/08/19
Julius S de Vere A Bt. Lt-Col. Order of St. Anne 2nd Class (R)	No Date Available Not Gazetted
Jupp M.G. Pte. D.C.M.	31/03/16,22/05/16,09/09/16,11/09/16
Kay Robinson H.T. T/Lt-Col. D.S.O.,M.I.D.	04/01/17,04/06/17,24/07/17,18/12/17,24/04/18, 25/04/18,07/05/18,25/05/18,17/09/18,28/12/18
Keen H.M. Lt. (A/Capt.) M.C. S/Yeo.	04/06/19
Keep G.R. Lt.(A/Capt.) M.I.D.	28/08/19
Kelly T. 2nd Lt. M.C. attd. 1st Bn. Hampshire Regt.	11/03/19
Kelly W.F. Mjr. & Bt. Lt-Col. 4th Class Medjidieh (Egypt)	06/10/85
Kelsey R.C. Pte. M.M.	08/08/18
Kemp G.L. T/Captain M.C.,M.I.D.	04/01/17,31/05/18
Kemp W.H. Sgt. M.I.D.	10/09/01
Kenderdine W.H. Capt. T.D.	30/05/19,03/06/19
Kent C.W. L/Cpl. M.M.	12/10/16
Kenward C.S. Cpl. (A/Sgt.) D.C.M.	06/06/17,10/07/17,04/05/18
Kenward E.S. Pte. M.M.	06/02/18
Kenward H.J. C/Sgt. M.I.D.	16/03/18
Key J.W. Cpl. (A/Sgt.) M.M.	28/01/18
Kibbey G.H. L/Sgt. M.M.	08/01/17
Kilbey W.J. Pte. M.M.	08/08/18
Kimber A.F. Sgt. M.M.,M.I.D.	16/06/16,12/10/16
King A.W. Pte. M.M.	13/11/16
King G.L. Capt. & Hon. Mjr. T.D.	22/04/04
King (Keegan) J. Sgt. D.C.M.	11/10/15,11/12/15,24/03/16
King R.N.R. Lt. M.I.D.	16/06/19
Kirkby S.A.H. 2nd Lt. M.C.	18/02/19
Kitchen W.S. Sgt. M.I.D.	20/05/18
Knapp A. Pte. Silver Medal (Serbia)	16/02/17
Knight A.C. Cpl. M.M.	12/10/16
Knight C.H. T/Lt. (A/Capt.) M.C.	03/06/19
Knight E. Pte. M.M.	08/09/17,08/07/18
Knight H.H. L/Cpl. (A/Cpl.) M.M.	05/11/17
Knight R. L/Cpl. M.M.	22/08/16,07/01/18
Knight W. L/Sgt. No. 200105 M.I.D.	14/01/18
Knight W. Sgt. No. 265492 M.I.D.	03/08/20

Knope H.E. Pte. M.M.	13/02/19
Knowles F.J.A. Sgt. M.M.	19/05/19
Knox A.C.W. Capt. M.C., M.B., R.A.M.C. attd. 2nd Bn. R.S.R.	03/01/18,17/02/19
Lade H.J. Pte. M.M.	28/07/19
Lake T.E. Q.M.S. M.S.M.	24/02/19
Laker E.G. Pte. M.M.	24/06/17,21/07/17
Laming C.J. Pte. M.M.	28/10/16
Lamotte L. Capt. & Bt. Mjr. (A/Lt-Col.) D.S.O;M.I.D.	28/12/18,03/02/19,11/07/19
Lane L.W. Lt. M.C.	18/10/18
Langdon J.F.P. Mjr. (T/Lt-Col.) M.I.D.	16/06/16
Langham E.H. Mjr. M.I.D.,T.D.	07/07/16,15/05/17
Langham F.G. Lt-Col. V.D.,C.M.G.,M.I.D.	19/06/0623/06/15,25/06/15
Langham J.E.C. Lt (T/Capt.) M.C.,M.I.D.	20/12/17,23/05/18,02/01/16
Langley J. Sgt. D.C.M.	15/04/16,10/10/16
Langley W.G.D. Pte. C de G (F)	23/11/18
Langridge J. Lt. (A/Capt.) M.I.D.	07/06/19
Larby G. Cpl. M.M.	03/06/16
Larmer W. C.Q.M.S. M.M. (F) Middx. Regt. attd. 2nd Bn. R.S.R.	17/08/18
Lascelles F.W. Capt. M.C. S/Yeo. attd. 16th Bn. R.S.R.	18/02/19
Lassetter E.R. L/Cpl. M.M.	22/08/16
Laughton W. Sgt. M.M.	10/07/17
Lawes W.A. Sgt. M.I.D.	31/05/18
Lawley W.F. Pte. (A/L/Sgt.) M.S.M.	03/09/20
Lawrence A.E. T/Lt. M.I.D.	28/08/19
Lawrence C.H. T/2nd Lt. M.C.	20/11/17,25/03/18
Lawrence H.J. Pte. M.M.	14/09/16
Lawrence R. A/Sgt. M.M.	22/09/16
Leachman G.E. Mjr. Bt. Lt-Col. C.I.E.,D.S.O.,M.I.D.	29/07/02,14/07/16,23/12/16,22/02/19,03/04/19,03/06/19, 13/12/19
Leavens F.C. C.S.M. No. S/329 M.C.	02/01/17
Lee A. Sgt. M.M.,M.S.M.,M.I.D.	23/05/17,19/06/18,28/07/19
Lee J.V. Lt. M.C. S/Yeo.	04/01/18
Lee W.H. Pte. M.M.	07/09/18
Leggatt T. Pte (L/Cpl.) M.M.	28/07/19
Leighton O.T. Pte. M.M.	17/09/18
Lenton M.H. Pte. (A/L/Cpl.) M.I.D.	11/07/19
Leppard C.H. Cpl. (L/Sgt.) D.C.M.,M.M.	13/02/19,21/04/19,26/02/20
L'Estrange H.H. Lt. (A/Capt.) M.C.,M.I.D.	27/09/18,11/04/19
Lewis A. Pte. (L/Cpl.) M.M.	29/11/92
Lewis C.F. Surg-Lt.-Col. V.D.	28/07/19
Lewis H.S. T/Capt. M.C.	26/06/16,27/09/17
Lewis L.W. Cpl. (A/Sgt.)	19/05/19
Lewry H.A. S/Mjr. D.C.M.,M.I.D.,C de G (F)	20/05/18,11/09/18,07/11/18
Lewry J.H.A. Sgt. M.I.D.	20/05/18
Licence H. Cpl. (A/R.Q.M.S.) M.I.D.	11/07/19
Light G. Pte. M.M.	25/02/18
Lightfoot A.S. Pte. M.M.	09/10/18
Linford A.W. Sgt. M.M.	27/03/17
Link B.T. Pte.(Cpl.) M.M.	06/11/17
Lintott R. Cpl. M.M.	28/10/16,01/11/16
Lisher C.A. Pte. M.M.	02/10/17,20/10/17,21/03/18
Lissiman H.C. T/2nd Lt. M.I.D.	25/05/18
Lister E.G. Sgt. M.M.	28/07/19
Lister J.J. Capt. Ho. Mjr. V.D.	16/02/97
Littlewood C.W.E. L/Cpl. M.M.	20/10/17
Livesay J.R. Capt. & Hon. Mjr. V.D.	29/11/92
Lloyd H.R. Mjr. Bt. Lt-Col. M.I.D.	17/08/06,28/03/19
Lloyd J. L/Cpl. M.M.	20/10/17
Lock C.F. Pte. (L/Cpl.) M.M.	22/03/18
Lockett W. Lt. M.C. 7th Bn. Cheshire Regt. attd. 16th Bn. R.S.R.	18/02/19
Lockhart J. Pte. M.I.D.	18/07/02
Loder R. E. Lt. (T/Capt.) M.I.D.	02/12/16,14/01/18
Loder J. De Vere Capt. M.I.D.	23/01/19
Long W. Q.M.S. M.S.M.,M.I.D.	04/01/17,06/06/17
Lordan D. Pte. M.M.	19/05/19
Lotheim S. T/2nd Lt. M.C.	15/01/19
Lott H.C. T/Capt. M.C.,M.I..D.	01/01/16,16/06/16,02/01/17
Love A. Pte. (A/Sgt.) M.I.D.	23/05/17
Loveland E. Cpl. M.I.D.	28/08/19

Lovell B. Pte. (L/Cpl.) M.M	03/06/19
Lovering P.W. Lt. M.C..	06/02/19
Lovering W.H. Sgt. M.M.	28/07/19
Lowe A.H.C. Lt. (A/Capt.) M.I.D.	28/08/19
Lucas A, T/2nd Lt. M.C.	18/02/18,22/07/18
Lucas T. Cpl. M.M.	20/10/17, 18/02/18
Luff M. Sgt. M.M.	28/07/19
Lundgren C.W. Lt. (T/Mjr.) M.C.,M.I.D. S/Yeo.	12/06/18,11/03/19
Lupton R.H. T/Capt. M.C.,M.I.D.	04/01/17,10/02/19,11/03/19
Lusted A. Sgt. D.C.M.,M.I.D.	03/06/19,13/03/20
Lusted G. Sgt. M.M.,M.I.D.	16/06/16,13/11/16
Luxford W. Pte. (L/Cpl.) M.M.	01/06/18,17/09/18
Lynch G.L. Pte. M.I.D.	11/07/19
Lytton N.S. Mjr. The Hon. O.B.E., Chevalier (F)	07/06/18,26/11/18
Mackay J.E. Lt. M.B.E.,M.I.D.	07/01/19,04/06/19
Mackellow F. Sgt. C de G (B)	15/07/18,16/07/18
Mackenzie E.L. Lt-Col. C.I.E.,D.S.O.,M.I.D.	10/09/01,27/09/01,05/07/16,12/09/19
MacRoberts N. de Putron Lt. (A/Capt.) D.S.O.,M.C.	26/06/16,28/07/16,20/11/16,27/09/17,20/12/17,10/01/18
Madgwick A.E. L/Cpl. M.M.	11/12/16,18/04/17
Maguire J. Pte. (L/Cpl.) M.M.	28/07/19
Makalua M.J.M. T/Capt. O.B.E.,C de G (F)	07/11/18,03/06/19
Malden C.C. Capt. (A/Mjr.) M.I.D.	03/08/20
Malden H.C. Capt. & Hon. Mjr. V.D.	29/11/92
Mallett G.W. Pte. D.C.M.	23/10/17,30/01/18
Mann F.J. Pte. M.M.	31/07/17
Mann G.L. Pte. (A/L/Cpl.) M.M.	28/07/19
Mann J. T/2nd Lt. M.C.	28/09/18
Mann M.P. Pte. M.M.	19/05/19
Mant J. L/Cpl. M.M.	03/06/16
Manthorpe S.R. Pte. (L/Cpl.) D.C.M.	13/03/19,05/12/19
Manvell E.J. Sgt. M.M.	26/02/18,17/04/18
Manvell G. C.S.M. (A/R.S.M.) D.C.M.	14/04/20
Maples A.C. Capt. (A/Mjr.) M.I.D.	28/03/19
March C.H., Earl of Col. A.D.C. C.B.,M.I.D.	29/07/02,31/10/02,05/11/02
Marillier F.C.J. Sgt. (2/ Lt) D.C.M.,M.I.D.	19/10/14,07/11/14,10/11/14,03/12/14
Markwell F.J. Pte. M.M.	19/05/19
Marney T.H. Pte. (A/Cpl.) M.M.	08/08/18
Marsh H. Cpl. M.I.D.	11/07/19
Marshall C.J. Sgt. M.M.	28/07/19
Marshall J. Pte. M.I.D.	11/07/19,21/07/19
Marshall L.P. Capt. M.C.	03/01/18,11/03/18,02/01/19
Marshall R.C.R. Pte. M.S.M.	03/06/19
Marsland J. Lt. M.C.,M.I.D.	23/05/17,31/07/17,17/08/17
Martin H. Pte. (L/Cpl.) No. SD/4956 M.M.	28/07/19
Martin H. Sgt. (A/C.S.M.) No. 290575 M.I.D.,M.S.M.	06/10/19,30/01/20
Martin J. Pte. M.I.D.	23/06/15
Martin R. Pte. M.M.	28/07/19
Martin W. Cpl. M.I.D.	28/08/19
Martin W.E. L/Cpl. M.M.	03/06/16
Martin W.J. L/Cpl. M.M.	06/11/17
Maskell G.T. Pte. M.M.	15/12/16
Maskell V.G. Sgt. M.M.	18/09/18
Mason C. Pte. M.M.	31/01/18
Mason C.S. Lt. M.C.	15/11/16
Mason F. Pte. M.M.	11/08/16
Mason H.L. Sgt. South Wales Brdrs. Presentation of M.M.	21/05/18
Mason J.I. Lt. (A/Capt.) M.C.	31/05/18,17/02/19
Mason R.B. T/Lt. M.M.	18/10/18,06/02/19
Mason W.H. Cpl. M.M.	28/07/19
Masters F. Sgt. M.M.	30/01/18
Mathews H.E. Capt. (T/Mjr.) T.D.,M.I.D.	27/02/17,11/03/19
Matten A. Pte. Div. Com. Cert. For Gallantry	20/05/18
Matthews H.E. Mjr. O.B.E.	06/01/19
Matthews M. Pte. (A/L/Cpl.) M.M.	19/06/19
Matthias T. Pte. (A/Sgt.) M.M.	19/05/19
Maudling F. Pte. D.C.M.	09/07/98
Maughan H. Pte. M.M.	21/07/17
Maxwell R. Lt. M.I.D.	07/06/19
May D.W.G. T/2nd Lt. M.C.	23/04/18,20/09/18
May R.T. T/Capt. M.I.D.	16/06/16
Maycock G.L. Lt. M.C.,M.I.D.	23/05/17,05/06/17,10/02/19

Mayes C.P. Pte. (A/L/Cpl.) M.M.	22/09/16
Maynard E.B. C.Q.M.S. M.S.M.	03/06/19
McArthur D. Sgt. M.I.D.	20/12/17
McCarthy C.M. Pte. M.I.D.	11/07/19
McClymont J. C.S.M. (A/R.S.M.) D.C.M.	03/06/19,13/03/20
McCormick C. Pte. M.M.	06/11/17
McCracken N. T/2nd Lt. M.C.	19/07/17
McFarlane A. Pte. M.M.	28/07/19
McIvor A.R. T/Capt. M.I.D.	16/06/16
McKergow R.W. Lt-Col. O.B.E. S/Yeo.	05/06/19
McKernan J. Pte. (A/Cpl.) M.M.	28/07/19
McNair E.A. Capt. V.C.	31/03/16,22/06/16,09/09/16,21/08/18
McNeill J.C. Mjr.-Gen V.C.,K.C.B.,K.C.M.G.,C.B.,C.M.G.	16/08/64,23/12/70,31/03/76,17/08/80,08/12/82
Meade H.W. T/Capt. M.I.D.	01/01/16
Meaton H.J. C.Q.M.S. M.I.D.	16/03/18
Messel L.C.R. Capt. & Hon. Mjr. TD.	15/03/12
Metcalfe A.E. Sgt. M.I.D.	28/08/19
Middleditch B. Pte. M.I.D.	03/08/20
Middleton R.C.G. Capt. M.C.,M.I.D.,C de G (F)&(B)	06/07/17,04/01/18,14/01/18,23/11/18,04/09/19
Milbourne W.A. Cpl. M.M.	20/10/17
Mills G. Sgt. M.M.	22/08/16,14/05/18
Mills J.W. Pte. M.M.	15/03/19
Mills T. Cpl. (A/Sgt.) M.M.	20/10/17
Millward W.C. Mjr. Bt. Lt-Col. D.S.O;M.I.D..,C de G (F)	23/05/17,29/10/17,20/12/17,20/03/18,17/08/18
Milton C.T. Pte. M.M.	18/09/18
Milton W.J. Pte. M.M.	20/10/17
Mitchell C.L. T/2nd Lt. M.C.	15/11/16
Mitchell J.E. Pte. M.M.	21/09/17,20/10/17,23/11/17,25/02/18
Moger H.E. Pte. (L/Cpl.) M.M.	28/07/19
Mole J. L/Sgt. M.M.	06/11/17
Moller C.E. Sgt. M.M.	19/05/19
Money G.A. Mjr. M.I.D.	23/08/19
Montresor E.H. Capt. M.I.D.	29/07/02
Moody C.F. Sgt. D.C.M.,M.M.,M.I.D.	15/12/16,14/01/17,05/09/19
Moody L.L. 2nd Lt. M.C.	26/06/16
Moore E.G. Capt. & Hon. Mjr. T.D.	10/01/11
Moore F. L/Cpl. D.C.M.	31/03/16,22/05/16,09/09/16
Moore F.H. Pte. M.M.	13/02/19
Moore H. Pte. M.M.	28/07/19
Moore L.D. Lt. M.C.	30/09/18
Moore W. Pte. M.M.	12/10/16
Morgan A. L/Sgt. M.I.D.	28/08/19
Morley G. Cpl. (A/Sgt.) M.I.D.	11/07/19
Morphett G.C. Bt. Lt-Col. C.M.G.,D.S.O., Legion of Honneur (F).,M.I.D.	29/07/02,23/12/16,27/08/17,01/09/17,13/03/18,27/08/18, 03/06/19
Morris G. Sgt. M.I.D.	28/08/19
Morris O.C. Pte. M.M.	18/09/18
Morrison H. Cpl. M.S.M.	21/01/19
Morrison W.T. 2nd Lt. M.C.	28/09/18
Morton J.A. Sgt. M.I.D.	28/08/19
Moss E.W. Cpl. D.C.M.	01/04/18
Mostyn E.H.J.D. Lt-Col. T.D.,M.I.D.	09/11/97,27/02/17
Mount H.C. 2nd Lt. M.C. attd. M.G.C.	01/08/18
Mountford G.B. Capt. M.C.,M.I.D.	17/08/17,28/08/19
Muirhead A.H. Lt. (A/Capt.) M.I.D.	28/08/19
Mullett M.R. C.S.M. D.C.M.,M.I.D.	04/01/17,06/06/17,10/07/17
Munt E. Sgt. M.M.	28/07/19
Murphy H. Pte. M.M.	19/06/19
Murray F.T. T/2nd Lt. M.I.D.	07/06/19
Musgrave F.P. Lt. (T/Capt.) O.B.E.,M.I.D. S/Yeo.	13/03/18,04/06/19
Musselwhite W. Pte. (Victory Parade)	21/07/19
Mustchin W.G. Pte. M.M.	13/02/19
Nagle G. Capt. M.C.	15/04/16,12/07/17
Neeves C.C. Lt. M.I.D.	08/07/19
Neiderauer G. Sgt. D.C.M.	01/07/15
Nelson S. Sgt. M.S.M.,M.I.D.	23/05/17,20/06/18
Neville C. Pte. D.C.M.	02/10/00
Newham L. Pte. M.M.	06/11/17

Name	Date(s)
Newman K. Sgt. M.M.	22/12/16
Newman S. Pte. M.M.	30/01/18
Newman S.R. Pte. (L/Cpl.)	19/05/19
Newnham A.J. Sgt. D.C.M.,M.I.D.	20/12/17,02/01/19,05/09/19
Newnham P. Cpl. M.M.	25/06/18,28/07/19
Newport E.R. Sgt. M.M.	19/06/19
Newport H.W. Pte. M.M.	22/09/16
Newton C.V. Lt. (A/Capt.) M.C.,M.I.D.	17/08/17,25/05/18,11/07/19
Nicholl F.A. Capt. O.B.E.	03/06/19
Nicholl P.A. Pte. M.M.	30/01/18,14/09/18
Nicholls F.V. Pte. M.M.	22/09/16
Nichols F.J. M.M.	19/05/19
Nickalls M. Capt. M.C. S/Yeo. attd. 16th Bn. R.S.R.	04/01/18
Noakes A. Cpl. (L/Sgt.) M.I.D.	23/05/17
Noakes A.H. Cpl. (L/Sgt.) M.S.M.	04/06/19
Noakes S. Cpl. M.M.	22/08/16,29/08/16
Noakes W.E. Pte. M.M.	15/11/18
Norfolk H. Duke of Mjr. & Hon. Lt-Col. K.G;K.G.M.V.O;V.D.	29/11/92,14/04/03
Norman C.S. Pte. M.M.	20/10/17,09/09/18
Norman H.T. Pte. M.M.	07/09/17
Norman W.C. Sgt. M.M.,C de G (F)	09/10/18,23/11/18
Norris F. Pte. C de G (F)	23/11/18
Norton W.C. T/Capt. M.C.	31/03/16,03/06/16
Nurse H.G. Sgt. M.S.M.	03/06/19
Nutley A. C.S.M. M.I.D.	01/01/16
Nye A. R.S.M. D.C.M.,M.S.M.,M.I.D.	10/09/01,27/09/01,14/08/18,24/02/19
Nye H.W. Sgt. M.I.D.	23/01/19
Oakley A. Cpl. M.I.D.	03/08/20
Oatley B.J. A/C.S.M. D.C.M.	23/10/17,30/01/18
O'Brien B. Pte. (A/L/Cpl.) M.I.D.	28/08/19
Ockleford A. L/Sgt. No. 551 M.I.D.	07/05/01
Ockleford A. L/Sgt. N0. 5118 D.C.M.,M.I.D.	10/09/01,27/09/01
O'Donnell G.B. Mjr. 1st Bn.(Vol.) Lt-Col. (I. A.) M.I.D.	20/05/18,23/08/19
Offler J.W. Pte. M.M.	03/06/16,07/08/16
Oldham J.W. Pte. (L/Cpl.) M.M.	28/07/19
Oliver G.F. Pte. M.M.	20/10/17
O'Neill F.R. 2nd Lt. (T/Capt.) M.I.D.	04/01/17,25/05/18
Onions W.H. Cpl. (L/Sgt.) M.M.	28/07/19
Orme R.F.P. Lt. M.C.	03/08/20
Osborn W.L. Mjr. Bt. Lt-Col. (T/Brig.) C.B.,C.M.G.,D.S.O., Order of Dunilo 3rd Class Montenegro).,M.I.D.	01/01/16,15/04/16,06/06/16,01/01/17,03/01/17, 10/03/17,15/05/17,2/12/17,21/07/19
Osborne G.F. Lt. (T/Mjr.) M.C.,M.I.D.	04/01/17,25/05/18,03/08/18
Osborne W.J. Sgt. M.M.	18/08/17
Osmaston R.S. Capt. M.C. & 23rd Sqdn. R.F.C.	17/05/16,02/10/16
Othen W. L/Sgt. D.C.M.	25/08/85
Otter-Barry R.B. Mjr. M.I.D.	1906,28/03/19,05/06/19
Owen A.G.L. Lt. M.I.D.	16/06/16
Oxley J.S. Capt. & Hon. Mjr. T.D.	19/11/07
Oyler A.J. Cpl. (A/Sgt.) D.C.M.	04/01/19,05/09/19
Packham C. Sgt. (A/C.S.M.) M.M.	07/08/17,12/10/17,20/10/17
Packham F. Cpl. M.M.	13/02/19
Packham G. Pte. (Victory Parade)	21/07/19
Paddon F.L. Lt. (A/Capt.) M.C.	12/12/19
Page C.T. Pte. (A/Cpl.) M.M.	28/07/19
Page G. Cpl. M.I.D.	30/01/20,05/02/20
Page H. A/C.S.M. D.C.M.	03/06/16,22/06/16
Paget J.O. T/Capt. M.C.	31/05/18
Paine C. Pte. D.C.M.	25/08/85
Paine C.W. C.S.M. (A/R.S.M.) M.I.D.	20/12/17
Paine E.A. Pte. M.M.	13/02/19
Paley E.H. Pte. M.M.	18/09/18
Palmer J. Sgt. M.S.M.	08/06/18
Pannett J. T/2nd Lt. M.C.	18/02/19
Panton J.G. Lt-Col. C.M.G.,M.I.D.	08/05/01,29/06/06
Papillon P.R. Capt. M.I.D.	29/07/02
Parker L.H. Pte. M.I.D.	11/07/19
Parkes A. Pte. (L/Cpl.) M.M.,M.I.D.	25/05/18,18/09/18
Parnell M. Sgt. M.I.D.	28/08/19
Parsons A. Sgt. M.M.	28/07/19
Parsons F.C. Capt. & Hon. Mjr. V.D.	16/02/97
Parvin F.H. Pte. M.M.	11/08/16

Pascoe A.J. Pte. M.M.	22/10/18
Pascoe A.W. Pte. M.M.	30/01/18
Patching E.G. Lt. M.I.D.	15/06/18,21/06/18
Patrick F.J. Sgt. M.M.	08/01/17,16/06/17
Pattenden K. L/Cpl. M.M.	22/09/16,04/11/16
Pattenden W.T. Pte. M.M.	16/09/16,28/11/16,11/12/16
Peacock A. Sgt. C de G (F)	21/06/19.
Peacock A.N. Sgt. M.M.	11/09/16,14/09/16
Peacock J.G. Sgt. M.M.	15/09/16
Pearce R. Q.M. & Hon. Lt. M.I.D.	10/09/01
Pearless J. R. Lt. & Hon. Capt. V.D.	29/11/92
Pearman T.A. Pte. M.I.D.	22/02/19
Pearson W.H.M. Mjr. T.D. S/Yeo.	07/11/19
Pearson S. Sgt. M.I.D.	28/12/18
Pearson W.G.F. T/2nd Lt. M.C.	04/04/19,10/12/19
Peatfield W. Sgt. M.M.,M.I.D.	28/08/19
Peck J.C. Pte. M.M.	13/02/19
Peel F.C. T/2nd Lt. M.C.	05/02/18,05/07/18,15/05/19,22/05/19
Pelham H.L. Lt. The Hon. (Adj.) Croix de Chevalier (F)	12/10/14
Pelham W.T. Sgt. M.S.M.	23/09/18
Pell H. Sgt. M.M.	20/10/17
Pelling F.L. Pte. D.C.M. S/Yeo. attd. M.G.C.	23/04/18
Pelling W. A/Sgt. D.C.M.	19/02/19,12/01/20
Pemberton Sgt. M.I.D.	29/07/02
Penfold P. Cpl. M.I.D.	10/09/01
Penfold W. Sgt. M.M.	28/07/19
Penticost J. Pte. M.M.	19/06/17
Pepper S. Pte. M.M.	13/02/19
Pepper W.C. L/Sgt. D.C.M.	13/09/18
Percival J. Pte. M.M.	20/10/17
Perkins J.P. L/Cpl. M.M.	18/09/18
Perkins W. Pte. M.M.	23/10/16
Perry J.C. Pte. (L/Cpl.) M.M.	20/02/17,07/08/18
Peskett J.C. T/Capt. M.C.,C de G (F)	17/08/16,09/11/18,05/11/18,23/11/18
Pestell F.C. Cpl. M.M.	18/09/18
Peterson H.J. Sgt. (A/C/Sgt.) M.I.D.	11/07/19
Philips C. Mjr. & Q/M. M.I.D.	28/08/19
Philips T.S. Pte. M.M.	17/07/18
Phillips H.J. Pte. M.M.	18/09/18
Picton F. Cpl. M.M.	14/09/16
Pierce R.H. Cpl. M.M.	28/07/19
Piggott J. Pte. (A/S/Sgt.) M.I.D.(2)	15/06/18,12/01/20
Pinckney J.S. Pte. (A/Cpl.) M.M.	19/05/19
Pink A. Pte. M.M.	11/08/16
Pittman C. C.Q.M.S. D.C.M.,M.I.D	29/07/02,31/10/02
Plews H. Q/M & Hon. Lt. O.B.E. M.I.D.	01/01/16,23/05/17,26/05/17,04/06/19
Pocock H.C. Sgt. M.M.	18/09/18
Poile W. Pte. M.M.	30/01/18
Points E.J.D. T/Lt. M.C.	04/04/19,13/12/19
Pollard-Urquhart W.E. Lt. M.I.D.	05/07/16
Poole C.R. Pte. M.M.	28/07/19
Portch T.J. Pte. M.I.D.	28/08/19
Porteous D.R. Pte. M.M.	27/04/18
Porter E.G.C. Cpl. M.M.	22/03/18
Porter W.N. T/Mjr. C.I.E.,V.D.,M.I.D.	21/04/04,22/03/18
Potiphar J.E. Pte. M.M.	19/12/17,25/04/18
Powell-Edwards H.I.G. Mjr. (T/Lt-Col.) D.S.O.,M.I.D.	03/06/19,08/07/19
Powell-Edwards W.G.H. Capt. M.C.	05/02/18,10/07/18
Preston E.H. Capt. Bt. Mjr. Bart. D.S.O.,M.C.,M.I.D.	23/06/15,03/06/16,15/05/17,13/12/17,23/12/18,01/01/19
Preston G.W. Pte. M.M.	21/07/17
Prevett R. A/Cpl. D.C.M.	23/09/16,25/10/16
Price L.S. Pte. M.M.	20/09/17
Prince G.W. 2nd Lt. M.C.	20/07/17
Pring R.J. Lt. M.C. attd. 24th Bn. Royal Fusiliers	15/01/19
Pronger H.G. Pte. M.M.	18/09/18
Pulling P. Sgt. M.I.D.	03/08/20
Pullinger P.V. T/2nd Lt. M.C.	28/09/18
Pullinger B.C. Cpl. M.M.	13/11/16
Purver G.A. Cpl. C de G (F)	23/11/18
Puxty F.C. Sgt. M.S.M.	08/06/18
Pyle F. Sgt. D.C.M.	02/11/18

Name	Date
Raby W. R.Q.M.S. M.S.M.,M.I.D.	20/12/17,21/01//19
Rainsford W.F. S/Major D.C.M.	03/06/16,22/06/16,07/07/16
Ramsay D.G. 2nd Lt. (T/Lt.) M.I.D.	18/02/14
Ramsbotham G.B. Lt. M.I.D.	01/01/16
Randall J. Pte. M.M.	17/07/18
Rands H.J. Q.M.S. M.S.M.	24/02/19
Rangecroft H.Q. T/Lt. M.C. attd. 1st Bn. Lancs. Fusiliers	31/05/18,31/07/19
Ranger C. Cpl. M.M.	28/07/19
Ranger G.H. Pte. M.M.	19/05/19
Ransom F.J. Sgt. D.C.M.,M.M.,C de G (F)	04/04/18,11/10/18,09/12/18
Rapley A. Pte. M.M.	11/12/16
Rapley C.T. Sgt. M.S.M.	03/06/19
Ratcliff W.P. T/Lt. M.C.,M.I.D.	23/05/17,19/10/17,13/03/18
Rawding S. Sgt. D.C.M.	07/03/18
Raynard A. L/Cpl. M.M.	21/07/17,21/0719
Rayner J.J. Sgt. C de G (B)	15/07/18
Read E.B. Sgt. M.M.,M.I.D.	16/06/16,12/10/16
Read H.S. Pte. M.M.	20/10/17
Read I.L. T/2nd Lt. C de G (F)	23/11/18
Reckitt G.L. T/Capt. M.C.	15/05/18,13/01/19
Redman C.B.W. Pte. M.M.	20/10/17
Reed F.J. Pte. (L/Cpl.) M.M.	13/02/19
Reed H.E. Pte. M.M.	19/05/19
Reed S. Pte. M.M.	27/01/19
Reeks W.H. Pte. (A/Sgt.) M.I.D.	30/01/20,05/02/20
Reid S.K. Capt. M.C.,Order of the Nile 4th Class (Egypt)	10/03/17,17/08/17,09/08/18
Relf R. L/Cpl. M.M.	30/06/17,21/07/17
Relf-West T.F. Cpl. (A/Sgt. M.M.	06/11/17
Remnant C.W. Sgt. M.M.	19/06/19
Renshaw H.H. Cpl. M.M.	20/10/17
Rewell A.B. T/Capt. M.C.	28/09/18
Reyland W.T. Pte. M.M.	26/02/18
Reynolds W. Pte. M.M.	08/08/18
Rice F. Pte. M.M.	27/01/19
Rice L.S. Pte. M.M.	20/09/17
Rich E.J. L/Cpl. M.M.	08/01/17
Richardson A. Lt-Col. & Hon.-Col. V.D.	19/11/01
Richardson A.C.T. Pte. M.M.	23/06/17,21/07/17
Richardson A.E. Cpl. M.M., D.M. (B)	23/11/18,28/07/19
Richardson A.W. 2nd Lt. M.C.	09/12/18
Richardson C. Sgt. M.M.	22/12/16
Richardson J. Sgt. M.I.D.	23/06/15
Richardson V. 2nd Lt. M.C. attd. K.R.R.C.	19/06/17
Richold A.A. C.Q.M.S. (A/C.S.M.) M.M.	22/09/16
Ridley G.W. Capt. (T/Mjr.) O.B.E.,M.I.D.,O of the Nile 4th Class	15/06/18,05/06/19,26/11/19
Riggs F. Pte. M.M.	15/03/19
Ripley J. Pte. M.M.	08/01/17
Robbins W.H.M. L/Cpl. M.M.	22/03/18
Roberts E.P. 2nd Lt. (T/Lt.) M.C;D.C.M. No. 3 Corps. Sqdn.	05/03/17
Roberts H. C.Q.M.S. D.C.M.	14/01/16,21/01/16,13/03/16
Roberts H. Lt. (A/Capt.) D.S.O.,M.C.,M.I.D.	05/06/17,25/02/18,17/02/19,11/07/19,21/07/19,31/07/19
Robertson R. Drummer M.I.D.	18/07/02
Robins W.G. Cpl. Order of St. George 4th Class (Russia).,M.I.D.	23/06/15,25/06/15,26/08/15,16/04/17
Robinson E.A.S. Lt. M.I.D.	28/12/18
Robinson F.W.T. Capt. D.S.O.,M.I.D.	10/09/01,27/09/01,29/02/02
Rodway W.W. Sgt. M.M.,M.I.D.	31/05/18
Rogers F. A/Bombadier 113th H.B. R.G.A. Presentation of M.M.	21/05/18
Rolt A.T. Sgt. M.S.M.,M.I.D.	25/05/18,02/01/19
Rooke J.R. Pte. (Victory Parade)	28/12/18
Rose E. Sgt. M.I.D.	10/09/01,27/09/01,29/02/02
Rose H. Sgt. No.10223 Medal of St. George 1st Class (Russia)	16/05/17
Rose S.R. Sgt. M.M.	21/07/17
Rose T.W. Lt. M.B.E.,M.C., Silver Medal for Gallantry (Italy).,M.I.D.	27/11/16,06/08/17,31/05/18,19/05/19
Ross C.D.B. T/Lt. M.I.D.	28/03/19
Ross F. Sgt. M.I.D.	10/09/01
Ross P.T. Tpr. D.C.M.	27/09/01
Rossetter G.S. Cpl. M.M.	12/05/17,28/05/17
Rothschild G.F. T/Mjr. D.S.O.,M.C.,M.I.D.	05/06/17,28/12/18,01/01/19
Rothwell E.N. Q/M. & T/Lt. M.I.D.,C de G (B)	28/12/18,04/09/19
Route P.A. L/Cpl. M.M.	18/04/17
Routledge A. Pte. (Victory Parade)	21/07/19
Rovery L. Sgt. M.M.	22/09/16
Rowe H. L/Cpl. M.I.D.	10/09/01
Rowland J.T. Pte. M.I.D.	20/05/16
Rowlands L.S. Pte. M.M.	20/10/17

Rudd J.W. Pte. (L/Cpl.) M.M.	26/02/18
Rudderham G.A. Pte. M.M.	19/05/19
Ruff G.S. Cpl. M.I.D.	11/07/19
Ruff H. Pte. M.I.D.	03/08/20
Rumsby R.W. T/2nd Lt. M.C.	17/08/17
Russell F.P. M.M.	28/07/19
Russell J. Cpl. M.M.	28/07/16
Russell R. Pte. (L/Cpl.) M.M.	28/07/19
Russell W.S.K. Capt. O.B.E.,M.I.D.	03/06/19,11/07/19
Rutherford P.J. C.S.M. M.I.D.	28/08/19
Rutter D.C. Lt. (T/Capt.) M.C. & 43rd Sqdn. R.F.C.	12/05/17,05/03/18
Sadler H. 2nd Lt. M.C.	02/01/17,03/01/17
Sainton F.C. 2nd Lt. (T/Capt.) M.C.	15/11/16
Salmon W. L/Cpl. M.M.	15/11/16
Salter G. T/2nd Lt. M.C.,M.I.D.	22/12/16,30/01/20,05/02/20
Sanderson J.W. Sgt. D.C.M.	13/03/16
Sandeman W.W. Mjr. O.B.E.	05/06/19
Sanford W. Pte. M.M.	15/11/18
Sanger-Davis F.M. Lt. M.I.D.	31/05/18
Sansom A.J. Lt. (T/Capt.)(A/Lt-Col.) M.I.D. Chevalier (B)	23/05/17,08/10/19
Sargent G.A. L/Cpl. M.M.	20/02/17
Saunders J. Pte. (L/Cpl.) M.M.	28/07/19
Sawyer F.G. Cpl. (A/Sgt.) D.C.M.	14/02/17
Saxby W. Sgt. M.I.D.	29/07/02
Saxon H. T/Capt.) M.C.	27/07/17
Say T.H. Pte. D.C.M.,M.I.D.	10/09/01,27/09/01
Sayer A.C. Mjr. D.S.O.,M.C.,M.I.D.	14/01/18,05/07/18,03/06/19,08/07/19
Sayer H. Capt. D.S.O.,M.C.,M.I.D. S/Yeo. attd. 16th Bn. R.S.R.	03/06/16,14/07/16,23/12/18,01/01/19
Sayers P. Pte. (L/Cpl.) M.M.	28/07/19
Scales F. Sgt. M.I.D.	30/01/0,05/02/20
Scarff H. Cpl. M.I.D.	30/01/20,05/02/20
Scott E. Pte. M.M.	23/10/16
Scott E. Capt. V.D.	29/11/92
Scott H.C. Pte. M.M.	11/08/16
Scott P.W. Pte. M.M.	19/06/17
Scrase.F.J. Pte. M.M.	28/07/19
Scrase T. L/Cpl. D.C.M.,M.I.D.	27/09/01,31/10/02
Scutt G.A. Pte. (L/Cpl.) M.M.	12/10/16,07/01/18
Seagrave F. Q.M.S. M.S.M.	04/01/19,21/01/19
Seall W.A. Pte. M.S.M.	06/10/19
Search G. Sgt. M.M.	19/06/19
Searle C. Cpl. (A/Sgt.) M.M.	26/02/18
Sears G.C. Pte. (A/Cpl.) D.C.M.,M.M.	19/05/19,12/01/20
Secrett A.R. R.Q.M.S. M.I.D.	23/05/17
Selby A.E. Sgt. M.M.	22/09/16,28/08/18
Selmes C.A. Capt. & Hon. Mjr. .D.	30/08/07
Selsby J.R. Pte. M.M.	22/09/16,25/07/19
Seymour A. Pte. M.M.	19/05/19
Shackel G.M. T/Capt. M.C.,M.I.D.	23/05/17,27/07/17
Shaft G.T. Capt. & Hon. Mjr. V.D.	29/11/92
Snaith A. Sgt. D.C.M.,M.I.D.	10/09/01,27/09/01
Snashall F.J. Sgt. M.M. 1st/1st S/Yeo.	23/09/19
Soanes W. Pte. (L/Cpl.) M.M.	31/03/19
Sharp E.E. Pte. M.M.	19/05/19
Sharp G. Pte. M.M.	22/08/16
Shearing W.E. Pte. M.M.	08/01/17,30/01/18
Shelley P. Pte. (L/Cpl.) M.M.	27/01/19
Sheppard A.R. Sgt. M.M.	08/01/17
Sheppard W.H. M.M.	11/12/18
Sherwin J. C.Q.M.S. M.I.D.	28/08/18
Sherwood A. Pte. M.M.	08/01/17
Shine T. Pte. M.M.	28/06/18
Shirley F.E. Pte. M.M.	08/01/17,15/12/17
Shonfield H.A. Sgt. M.M.	31/07/17
Short H. L/Cpl. D.C.M.	15/04/16
Short W. Pte. M.M.	21/09/16,23/10/16
Shotter W. Pte. M.M. (deleted "L/G" 19/06/17)	11/12/16,19/06/17
Simmonds A.L. Pte. (A/Cpl.) M.M.	19/04/19
Simmonds H.C.C. Sgt. M.I.D.	14/01/18,19/02/18,22/08/19
Simmonds J. Sgt. M.M.	07/02/19
Simmons J. C.S.M. D.C.M.,M.I.D.	14/01/18,19/01/18,19/08/19
Simpson J.G. T/2nd Lt. M.C.	23/10/17,30/01/18
Single E.M. Pte. M.M.	19/09/18
Singleton J.S. Pte. (A/Sgt.) M.S.M.	03/09/20

Name	Dates
Sippetts A. L/Cpl. D.C.M.	23/10/17,30/01/18
Sivyer H.G. Cpl. M.M.	31/07/17
Skinner F. St. Duthus Lt. 4th Class Medjidieh (Egypt)	30/08/87
Skinner R.E. Sgt. M.M.	06/02/18
Skipworth B.W. Lt. M.C. attd. 9th Bn. M.G.C.	28/11/17,10/04/18
Slaughter F. C.Q.M.S. D.C.M.	21/08/16,24/01/19,04/09/19,05/09/19
Slaughter F. Pte. M.M.	06/01/19,28/07/19
Sleeman J.L. Lt-Col. C.B.E;M.V.O.	03/06/19,15/10/20
Sloan R.H.S. A/Cpl. D.C.M.	21/08/16
Sloane G. Pte. M.M.	20/10/17
Sloper F.G. Sgt. M.M.	19/06/19
Smethurst W.R. Sgt. D.C.M.,M.I.D.	23/06/15,17/11/15,20/04/16
Smith D. L/Cpl. (A/Cpl.) M.M.	23/10/16,03/07/17
Smith E.A. L/Cpl. D.C.M.	23/10/17,31/01/18
Smith H.P. C.Q.M.S. M.I.D	25/05/18,28/12/18
Smith J.Y. Sgt. N0. G/1440 M.M.	01/06/18,19/09/18
Smith J. Pte. (L/Cpl.) No. 19872 M.M.	20/10/17
Smith J. Pte. (L/Cpl.) No. G/18822 M.M.	19/05/19
Smith Y.J. Pte. M.M. No. 10515	19/06/17,20/06/17,08/05/18
Smith W. Pte. No. 12384 (Victory Parade)	21/07/19
Smith W. Pte. No. 18236 M.M.	18/06/18,18/07/18,22/03/19
Smith W. Pte. No. L/11534 M.M.	19/05/19
Snaith A. Sgt. D.C.M.,M.I.D.	10/09/01,27/09/01
Snashall F.J. Sgt. M.M. 1st/1st S/Yeo.	23/10/19
Soanes W. Pte. (L/Cpl.) M.M.	31/03/19
Solomon J. T/Q.M. & Capt. M.I.D..	23/05/17,20/12/17,11/07/19
Somerville H.A. 2nd Lt. M.C. & 83rd Squadron R.F.C.	19/10/17,09/03/18
Somerville J.A.C. Lt.-Col. C.M.G.	01/01/18
Soughton S. C.S.M. D.C.M.	22/06/16,30/11/16,21/07/19
Southgate W. Pte. M.M.	19/06/19
Southwell H.K. Rev, A/Ch. M.A., V.D.	04/09/06
Sparkes E. L/Sgt. D.C.M.	19/02/19,12/01/20
Sparks H. T/Capt. M.C.,M.I.D.	25/05/18,02/10/18
Spears W.H. Pte. (L/Cpl.) M.M.	19/09/18
Spicer F.G.J. Sgt. D.C.M.	14/02/17,04/06/17
Spickernell W. Cpl. M.M.	24/10/18,15/11/18
Spinney F. Sgt. M.S.M.	03/06/19
Sprunt C. Pte. (L/Cpl.) D.C.M.	14/09/18
Spurling A.J. Cpl. (A/Sgt.) D.C.M.	13/03/19,05/12/19
Squires A.J. Pte. (L/Cpl.) M.M.	28/07/19
Stace W.A. C.S.M. No. 3461 M.C.	14/01/18
Staines W.A. Pte. M.M.	19/09/18
Stamp W.H. Pte. M.M.	21/07/17
Standing F.A. C.S.M. M.S.M.	26/06/18
Standing L.G. Cpl. M.M.	19/09/18
Stanford C. Sgt. M.M.	08/01/17,03/07/17
Stannard J. Pte. M.M.	31/07/17
Stapley G.A. Sgt. M.M.,M.I.D.	23/05/17,06/11/17
Startup F. Sgt. D.C.M.	14/01/16,13/03/16,23/06/16
Steadman C. Sgt. M.M.	31/03/19
Stedman J. Pte. M.M.	28/07/19
Steele R. L/Cpl. (Victory Parade)	21/07/19
Steer J.S. R.S.M. M.S.M.	03/09/20
Stemp W.H Pte. M.M.	21/07/17
Stenning A. Pte. M.M.	26/02/18
Stevens A. Pte. M.M.	19/05/19
Stevens E.W. M.I.D.	16/06/16
Stevens T.W. Pte. D.C.M.	14/09/18
Stevenson N. R.Q.M.S. M.S.M.,M.I.D.	20/12/17,03/01/20
Stewart H.E. T/Capt. L de H, Croix de Chevalier (F).,M.I.D.	23/05/17,16/07/17
Still C.A. L/Cpl. D.C.M.,M.I.D.	25/05/18,20/11/18
Still E. Cpl. M.M.	12/10/16
Still T. Pte. M.I.D.	19/10/14,20/10/14,06/11/14
Stillwell S. Cpl. (A/L/Sgt.) M.I.D.	23/05/17
Stobbart T.R. Pte. (A/Cpl.) M.M.	23/08/19
Stockbridge S.C. Sgt. M.M.	20/10/17
Stokes S.D. Sgt. M.M.	19/09/18
Stone B.A. C.S.M. D.C.M.	26/06/18,14/09/18,23/07/19
Stone F. Sgt. M.M.	13/11/16
Stone W.J. L/Sgt. M.M.,M.S.M.	20/10/17,03/01/20
Stoner A. Pte. (L/Cpl.) D.C.M.	13/03/19,05/12/19
Storey W. Pte. M.M.	30/01/18
Story H.H. T/2nd Lt. M.C.	15/11/16
Stringer E. Cpl. M.M.	23/09/16,23/10/16,23/05/18

Name	Date
Stripp J. Pte. M.I.D.	10/09/01
Stuart R.E. Cpl. M.M.	10/10/18
Stubbings H.T. Pte. M.M.	30/01/18
Stubbs A. Q.M.S. M.I.D.	06/11/17
Stuckey W. Capt. V.D.	21/07/93
Stunt A. Sgt. M.M.	06/11/17
Sunderland M.S.J. Lt-Col. D.S.O.	25/08/85,12/04/89
Sutton E.G. T/Lt. M.C.,M.I.D.	04/10/15,01/1101/16,14/04/16
Swain B.F. T/Q.M. & Hon. Lt. M.I.D.	23/05/19
Swaine A.C. C.S.M. Croce di Guerra (Italy)	19/05/19
Swallow W.L. Pte. M.M.	06/11/17
Symes F.H. Pte. M.I.D.	10/09/01
Tallon F. Pte. D.C.M.	02/11/18
Tamplin W.C. Mjr. & Hon. Lt-Col. V.D.	29/11/92
Taplin C.E. Pte. (L/Cpl.) M.M.	19/09/18
Tapner A. Pte. M.M.,M.I.D	20/12/17,19/05/19
Tattershall E. Pte. D.C.M.	03/06/19,07/11/19,13/03/20
Tayler St. C.C. 2nd Lt. M.C. attd. 80th Squadron R.F.C.	27/09/17,14/01/18,28/03/18,11/11/19
Taylor A.C. Pte. M.M.	19/09/18
Taylor F. Pte. M.I.D.	11/07/19
Taylor G.D. Pte. M.M. Royal Irish Rifles	01/05/18
Taylor H. Pte. M.M.	01//12/17,26/02/18,01/05/18
Taylor H.F. Lt. (T/Capt.) M.C.	20/07/17,25/07/17
Taylor H.S. Pte. M.M.	08/01/17
Taylor R.A. Sgt. M.S.M.	20/06/18
Taylor W.H. Pte. M.M.	20/10/17,25/02/18
Taylor W.T. Pte. M.M.	11/08/16
Tennent A.K. Lt. O.B.E.	03/03/20
Terrey G.E. 2nd Lt. M.I.D. S/Yeo. attd. Devonshire Regt.	12/06/18
Terry H. Sgt. M.S.M.	20/06/18
Terry R.J.A. Mjr. M.V.O.,D.S.O.,M.I.D.	22/06/14,23/06/15,26/06/15,22/10/15,01/01/16
Tester A.E. L/Cpl.	21/07/17,06/02/18
Tester J. L/Cpl. M.M.	07/08/16,11/08/16,21/06/17
Tester W.A. Pte. M.I.D.	18/02/15
Theckston H. Pte. M.M.	28/07/19
Theobald W.J. Pte. M.M.	06/11/17
Thirst W. Pte. M.M.	19/06/19
Thomas A.G. Lt. (A/Mjr.) M.C. South Staffs. attd. R.S.R.	01/01/17,13/12/19
Thomas C.E. C.S.M. D.C.M.	14/09/18
Thomas G.F. Capt. M.C.	27/11/16
Thompsett F.H.G. L/Sgt. M.M.	08/01/17,19/10/17,03/11/17
Thompson J. Pte. M.M.	19/05/19
Thompson J.W. A/C.S.M. D.C.M.	03/06/19,13/03/20
Thomson A.L. Capt. (T/Lt-Col.) D.S.O.,M.I.D.	28/12/18,13/01/19
Thorns R.W. Pte. M.M.	08/01/17
Thornthwaite J.D. T/Lt. M.I.D.	25/05/18
Thorpe T.H. Lt. M.I.D.	31/05/18
Thwaites S. S/Mjr. D.C.M.	27/09/01
Thwaits S.M. S/Mjr. D.C.M.,M.I.D.	10/09/01,27/09/01
Ticehurst W. C/Sgt. M.I.D.	10/09/01
Tickner G.W. Sgt. M.M.	31/07/17
Tilling W.S. T/Cpl. D.C.M.	17/11/15
Tisdall C.H. T/2nd Lt. M.I.D.	16/06/16
Titcombe A.T. Pte. (A/Sgt.) M.M.	28/07/19
Todman J. L/Cpl. M.M.	10/07/17
Tomlinson H. Pte. No. 200517 M.M.	02/04/18
Tomlinson H. Pte. No. SD/5594 M.M.	22/08/17
Toney E.E. Cpl. D.C.M.	03/05/18
Toogood S. L/Cpl. M.M.	20/10/17
Tooms F.J. Sgt. M.M.	13/02/19
Towner T.W. L/Cpl. M.M.	13/11/16
Trafford L.J. Capt. (his Majority)	25/08/85
Travers S.S.J. Lt. M.B.E.	04/06/19
Treacher H.L. T/Lt. M.C.	02/01/17,09/11/18,29/03/19
Treadway G. Cpl. M.I.D.	28/12/18
Tremaine T.H. C.Q.M.S. M.S.M.,M.I.D.	20/12/17,04/06/19
Trevor A.W. Sgt. D.C.M.,M.M.	01/08/16,06/12/18,16/01/19,17/01/19
Tribe A.A.W. Sgt. D.C.M.,M.M.	05/01/18,05/02/18,09/01/19
Trowbridge S. C.Q.M.S. M.I.D.	25/05/18
Troy J.H. Pte. M.M.	28/07/19
Trussler E.G. Drummer D.C.M.	14/02/17
Tucker E. Cpl. (L/Sgt.) No. L/9249 M.M.,C de G (B)	12/10/16,16/07/18

Tufton J.S.R. Mjr. The Hon. D.S.O.,O. De Leo. Chev.(B)., C de G. (B)., Chevalier., (F)., M.I.D.	01/01/16,14/01/16,12/03/18,08/07/19,08/10/19 13/02/19
Tulett W.C.J. Sgt. M.M.	13/02/19
Tulitt W.J. Pte. (L/Cpl.) M.M.	23/06/15
Tunnell J. L/Cpl. M.I.D.	03/06/19,21/07/19,13/03/20
Turnbull F. Pte. (A/Cpl.) D.C.M.	09/02/17,12/05/17
Turner C. Pte. M.M.,M.I.D.	22/02/18
Turner E. Pte. (1914 Ribbon)	22/03/18
Turner H. L/Cpl. M.M.	03/06/19
Turner J. Sgt. M.S.M.	16/01/18
Turner J.F. Cpl. (A/Sgt.) M.M.	16/05/17,04/01/18,08/01/18,28/12/18,01/01/19
Turner M.T. Capt. C.B.E.,M.C.,M.I.D.	07/01/19
Turner R. Sgt. M.I.D.	24/01/93
Turner .D. Hon. Mjr. & Adj. V.D.	11/12/16
Turrel C.W. Pte. M.M.	14/09/16,16/07/19
Turton A. Cpl. M.M. (D.C.M. 66242 2/10 Royal Scots)	31/05/19
Tutt G. Sgt. (A/C.S.M.) M.S.M.	03/06/16,06/06/18,23/10/18
Tutt J.W. C.S.M. D.C.M., M.M.	04/01/17,04/01/18,04/01/19
Twine F.P. Lt. O.B.E.,M.C.,M.I.D.	28/09/18
Uloth A.C.W. Lt. M.C.	19/06/19
Undrill W.J. Cpl. M.M.	03/8/20
Upperton G. L/Cpl. (A/Sgt.) M.I.D.	12/10/16
Upton E.J. Sgt. (2nd Lt.) M.M.	28/07/19
Vale G.W. Cpl. (A/Sgt.) M.M.	19/05/19
Valler A. Pte. M.M.	25/08/85
Vandeleur J.O. Col. C.B. Cmdg. 1st Bn.	25/08/85
Vaughan L. Mjr. M.I.D.	20/05/18
Verrall C.F. Lt. M.I.D.	18/02/15
Verrall H. Hon. Col. V.D.	29/11/92
Verrall H.J. Mjr. & Hon. Lt-Col. V.D.	29/11/92
Vicary G.E. Sgt. M.M.	30/01/18,03/11/18
Vidler A.G.A. T/2nd Lt. (A/Capt.) M.C.	19/10/17,12/03/18
Vidler W.G. Pte. M.M.	11/12/16
Vigar A.L.J. Pte. M.M.	22/03/18
Vigar F.J. Pte. M.M.	19/05/19
Vigor J. L/Sgt. M.M.	06/02/18
Villiers E.F. Mjr. (T/Lt-Col.) C.M.G.,D.S.O.,M.I.D.	10/09/01,27/09/01,18/02/15,23/06/15,01/01/16,03/03/16, 16/06/16,30/11/16,15/03/18
Von der Heyde J.L. Lt. M.C.,M.I.D., attd. Man. Regt.	15/10/18,07/02/19
Wackford S. Cpl. M.M.	19/05/19
Wade E.W. Pte. (L/Cpl.) M.M.	12/10/16
Waghorn O. Pte. (L/Cpl.) D.C.M.	01/07/15,06/09/15
Waghorn T.C. M.M.	13/02/19
Waithman R.H. Mjr. (T/Lt-Col.) D.S.O.,M.I.D.	18/02/15,20/12/17,02/01/18
Waldron W.H.S. L/Cpl. M.M.	20/02/17
Walker B.J. T/Lt-Col. C.M.G.,D.S.O.,M.I.D.	15/09/17,25/05/18,31/05/18,03/06/19,11/07/19
Walker J. Pte. M.M.	21/07/17
Wallington M. Lt. (T/Capt.) Bt. Mjr. M.C; M.I.D. 1st Inf. Brigade	03/06/16,03/01/17,24/01/17,13/12/17,10/03/19,08/07/19,06/10/19
Wallis W.H. Pte. M.S.M.	03/09/20
Walls W.J. C.S.M. D.C.M.,M.M.	10/07/17,24/06/19
Walter C.G. 2nd Lt. M.C.	09/03/18
Ward B.T. T/Capt. M.I.D., London Regt. attd. R.S.R.	16/06/16
Ward F.J. Pte. M.M.	28/07/19
Ward G. Sgt. D.C.M.	27/09/16,10/10/16,21/05/18
Warner J.L. C.Q.M.S. M.S.M.	04/06/19
Warren J.R. Capt. M.C.	07/02/19
Warters E. Sgt. (A/C.S.M.) M.I.D.	28/08/19
Waters G.C.F. L/Cpl. (A/Cpl.) M.M.	30/01/18
Waters J.S. Cpl. M.M.	20/10/17,20/11/17,16/09/18
Watson J.E. Cpl. (A/Sgt.)	30/01/18
Watson J.H.C. Sgt. M.M.	19/05/19
Watt I.W.B. Sgt. C de G (B)	16/07/18,20/07/18,29/07/18
Waugh R. T/2nd Lt. M.C.	21/10/18
Wayman R.C. C/Sgt. M.I.D.	10/09/01,29/07/02
Weale E.L. T/2nd Lt. (A/Capt.) M.C.,M.I.D.	19/10/17,09/03/18,30/01/20,05/02/20
Weale H. T/Sgt. D.C.M.	21/08/16
Webb F.E. T/Capt. M.B. M.I.D., R.A.M.C. attd. 17th Bn. R.S.R	10/02/19,11/07/19
Webb W. Sgt. (A/C.Q.M.S.) D.C.M.	23/05/17

Webber B.J.T. 2nd Lt. M.C.,M.M. (F)	14/02/17
Webber J.C. T/2nd Lt. M.I.D.	22/05/17,21/10/18
Weedon P.L. Pte. D.C.M.,M.M.	26/02/18,19/02/19,30/05/19,12/01/20
Weekes A.N.H. Capt. M.C.,M.I.D.	17/01/18,23/07/8,09/08/18
Weeks R.H. Pte. M.M.	19/09/18
Weeks W.E. T/2nd Lt. (A/Capt.) M.C.	11/03/19
Weeks-Pearson E.E. Cpl. M.M.	06/11/17
Welch G. Cpl. D.C.M.	23/10/17,24/10/17,30/01/18
Welham H.G. 2nd Lt. M.C.	17/08/17
Weller A.G. Cpl. M.M.	13/12/17
Wells H. L/Cpl. M.M.	28/08/16
Wells H. Sgt. V.C.	19/11/15
Wells J.A. L/Cpl. (A/Cpl.) M.M.	28/02/18
West A.J.G. Sgt. Commendation	03/05/16
West C.F. Sgt. D.C.M.,M.M.	13/03/19,28/07/19,05/12/19
West H. Sgt. M.M.	20/10/17
West L. Pte. M.M.	22/08/16
Westbrook F. Sgt. M.M.	15/03/19
Westgate A. Sgt. D.C.M.	07/03/18
Weston A.E. C/Sgt. D.C.M.,M.I.D.	10/09/01,27/09/01
Weston G. Cpl. D.C.M.,M.I.D.	10/09/01,27/09/01
Weston G. Pte. D.C.M.	14/01/16,21/01/16,13/03/16
Weston S.T. Qm. & Hon. Mjr. V.V.	29/11/92
Wheatley E.B. T/2nd Lt. (A/Capt.) M.I.D.	23/05/17
Wheeler A.W. Pte. M.M.	28/07/19
Wheeler J.L. Cpl. M.M.	19/06/19
Whinnett A. C.S.M. M.S.M.	03/09/20
Whitaker H.W. Sgt. M.M.	19/09/18
Whitbread E.G. Cpl. M.M.	28/07/19
Whitcher L. Cpl. M.M.	17/11/16
White E.J. Cpl. D.C.M.	04/11/18
White H.J. T/Lt. M.C.	19/10/17,09/03/18,20/09/18
White P. C.S.M.(A/R.S.M.) No. 6404 M.C.	04/01/18
White P. C.S.M. No.2003 D.C.M.	21/08/16
White P.A.C. Pte. M.M.	22/09/16
White R. Sgt. C de G (F)	16/07/18
White W.H. Pte. M.M.	20/10/17
White W.J. Sgt. M.M.	10/10/18
Whitehead E.B. Cpl. M.M., R.A.M.C. attd. 16th Bn. R.S.R.	22/03/18
Whitehead H.M. 2nd Lt. (T/Lt.) M.I.D.	25/05/18
Whitely C.A.F. T/2nd Lt. M.C. attd. R.F.C.	21/08/16,06/11/16
Whiteman A.G. Sgt. M.M.	29/01/18
Whiteman B. 2nd Lt. M.C.	02/01/17
Whitfield G.S. Lt-Col. O of the Order of the Crown of Italy, T.D.	01/09/17,07/11/19
Whiting R.S. Sgt.(A/C.S.M.) M.M.	23/01/18,22/03/18
Whitlock A.E. Sgt. M.M.	28/07/19
Whittemore F.A. Pte. M.M.	08/08/18,14/09/18
Whitton P.H. Pte. M.M.	20/02/17
Wickens L. C.S.M. M.I.D.	07/06/19
Wilberforce A.R.G. Capt. O.B.E.,M.I.D.	14/08/18,05/06/19
Wilcock C.J. L/Cpl. M.M.	19/12/17
Wild R.E. Cpl. M.M.	28/07/19
Wileman A.H. Sgt. M.M.	30/01/18
Wilkie A.B. Mjr. M.I.D.	16/03/18
Wilkins C.H. Lt. M.C.	31/05/18
Wilkinson G.H. Sgt. (A/C.Q.M.S.) M.S.M.	24/02/19
Wilkinson H.S. Pte. (A/Sgt.) M.M.	12/12/16,08/01/17
Wilkinson S.F. Pte. (L/Cpl.) M.M.	19/09/18
Willett F.W.B. Mjr. (A/Lt-Col.) D.S.O.,M.I.D.	01/01/16,14/01/16,04/01/17,23/05/17
Williams C.O. L/Cpl. (A/Cpl.) D.C.M.,M.M.	07/03/18,08/01/19
Williams E.W. Lt. (A/Capt.) M.I.D.	23/05/17,07/01/19
Williams H.H. C.Q.M.S. M.I.D.	11/07/19
Williams O. C.S.M. M.I.D.	16/06/16
Williams W.J. Rev. M.C. T/Chaplin 4th Class attd. 7th Bn.	02/01/18
Williams-Freeman G.C.P. Capt. 4lh Class Medjidieh (Egypt)	06/10/85
Willis K.L. Cpl. (L/Sgt.) M.M.	03/06/19
Wilmer R.C.W. Sgt. M.M.	15/03/19
Wilmshurst C.A. Sgt. M.M	03/06/16,16/06/16
Wilmshurst J.W. Pte. M.M.	16/11/16,13/02/19
Wilmshurst T. Pte. M.M.	06/11/17
Wilshere D. Sgt. M.S.M.	03/06/19
Wilson A.R. Pte. M.M.	22/09/16
Wilson B. Pte. M.M.	19/05/19
Wilson J. Pte. M.M.	02/09/16,08/01/17,27/03/17

Wilton A. Pte. M.M.	19/05/19
Wimborn R.V.C. L/Cpl. M.M.	21/09/16,23/10/16
Winchester H. Pte. (Victory Parade)	21/07/19
Winchester L. Sgt. M.S.M.,M.I.D.	13/03/18,16/10/18
Windebank A. Pte. M.M.	08/01/17
Windmill J. Cpl. M.M.	19/09/18
Winter N. 2nd Lt. (T/Lt.) M.C.	05/06/17
Winterton E. Earl Capt. (T/Mjr.) M.I.D.	14/01/18
Wood A.H. Capt. (T/Mjr.) M.I.D.	16/06/16
Wood C.W. Sgt. C de G (B)	16/07/18
Wood F. C.S.M. M.M.,C de G (B)	13/07/17,16/07/17,26/07/18,18/01/19
Wood L. Sgt. M.I.D.	03/08/20
Wood W. Pte. (L/Cpl.) Medal of Zeal St. Stanislaus Ribbon	No date available Not Gazetted
Woodgate J.W. Sgt. M.I.D.	31/05/18
Woodhams G. Lt. (T/Capt.) M.I.D.	01/01/16,08/01/16,16/06/16
Woodrow A.B. T/2nd Lt. M.C.	18/12/17,25/04/18
Woodruffe J.S. Mjr. (T/Lt-Col.) O.B.E.,D.S.O.,M.I.D,	18/09/18,28/12/18,05/02/20
Order of St. Vladimir 4th Class (R)	No date not Gazetted
Woods G. C.Q.M.S. M.S.M.	03/06/19
Woodward S.H. Sgt. D.C.M.	21/08/16
Woolgar G. Pte. M.M.	28/07/19
Woollam A.S. Pte. M.M.	08/01/17
Woollard C. Pte. M.M.	06/11/17
Woollard H. Sgt. D.C.M.	22/11/17,07/03/18
Woolley A.C. Mjr. & Hon. Lt-Col. V.D.	15/09/08
Woolley C. Pte. M.M.	26/02/18
Woolley J.W. Pte. M.M.	08/08/18,19/05/19
Woolven A.G. Cpl. M.M.,C de G (F)	23/11/18,27/01/19
Woolven G.F. Pte. (L/Cpl.) M.M.	13/02/19
Worcester E. L/Cpl. M.M.	06/11/17
Worley F. Sgt. D.C.M.	07/03/18
Wratten G.A. Pte. M.M.	06/02/18
Wright A. Pte. D.C.M.	05/09/19
Wright B.C. Lt. M.C.	21/10/16,17/02/19
Wright G.W. Pte. M.M.	13/02/19
Wright J.A. T/Lt. M.C.,M.I.D	20/12/17,31/05/18
Wright N.L. Pte. M.M.	28/07/19
Wroughton J.B. T/Brig. C.B.,C.M.G., Legion of Honneur (F).,Ordre of Leopold 4th Class (B).,C de G (B).,Order of St. Anne 2nd Class with Swords (Russia).,M.I.D.	19/10/14,23/06/15,25/06/15,16/06/16,01/01/17,03/01/17, 16/02/17/16/05/17,27/07/17,01/12/17,12/12/17,20/12/17, 12/03/18,11/10/18,23/12/18,03/06/19,08/07/19
Wyatt H.H. Rev. Hon. Ch. M.A;V.D.	24/01/93
Wyatt R.J.P. T/Capt. M.C.	02/01/18,29/07/18
Yeates A.W. Cpl. (A/Sgt.) M.S.M.,M.I.D.	28/05/17,06/07/17
Yeomans F.W. L/Cpl. D.C.M., Bronze Medal for Valour (Italy)	21/10/16,23/10/16,28/05/17
Young A. A/Sgt. No.1483 M.M.	03/06/16,07/08/16
Young A. L/Cpl. No. G/7008 M.M.	20/09/18
Young G.T. A/Sgt. M.M.,M.I.D.	16/06/16,12/10/16
Young J.C. Maj-Gen. C.B.	04/06/17
Young N.E. T/Capt. M.I.D.	25/05/18
Young R.C. T/2nd Lt. M.C.	22/12/16,01/01/17
Young R.P. Lt. M.C.	23/07/18

Honours and Awards 1921-1966

Dedication

This book is dedicated to Captain Reginald Anthony Alston-Roberts-West, M.C., 5th & 1st Battalions Royal Sussex Regiment, who has kindly allowed me to use his memoirs to describe incidents during the Second World War.

And to all the Officers and Men of The Royal Sussex Regiment who served and fought in the service of their Country 1921-1966. Heroes all, the mentioned and rewarded and to the unsung whose deeds went unnoticed and unmentioned.

For the Fallen

"They went with songs to the battle, they were young,
Straight of limb, true of eye, steady and aglow;
They were staunch to the end against odds uncounted,
They fell with their faces to the foe.

They shall grow not old, as we that are left to grow old;
Age shall not weary them, nor the years condemn.
At the going down of the sun and in the morning
We will remember them."

Kohima Epitaph

When You Go Home, Tell Them Of Us And Say,
For Your Tomorrow, We Gave Our Today.'

Acknowledgements

With grateful acknowledgement to the British Library Newspapers (Colindale), the National Archives (Kew), the Chairman and Trustees of The Royal Sussex Regiment Museum Trust, and Colonel R.R. McNish, (Roussillon Barracks, Chichester), Alan Readman, Assistant County Archivist, for the use of the Royal Sussex Regimental Archives (County Hall, Chichester), Colin Wood (Crawley Down), Keith Fuller (Newhaven), Captain R.A. Alston-Roberts-West M.C., Captain Murray Gillings, Major John Ainsworth, Corporal Ken Flint, Bert Maile and all ex-members of the Regiment and their families who contributed, also to Alan Brown of the Airborne Forces Museum (Aldershot)) and the Commonwealth War Graves Commission, without whose assistance this book could not have been compiled. Excerpt is from the poem "For the Fallen" by Laurence Binyon (1869-1943). The Kohima Epitaph verse is attributed to John Maxwell Edmonds (1875-1958), and is thought to have been inspired by the epitaph written by Simonides to honour the Greek who fell at the Battle of Thermopylae in 480BC. The final poem "The Soldier" is by Rupert Brook (1887-1915). These acknowledgements cover the period 1921-1966.

Bibliography

Many of the listings in the *"London Gazette"* for the 1939-1945 war are mis-indexed and some names have been omitted. So while a regimental/battalion diary states that person was awarded a particular medal or M.I.D. it is not always possible to trace it in the *"London Gazette"*. There is even one instance of a 9th Battalion N.C.O. who won a Military Medal in 1944/5 and it is not gazetted until 1950. Many of the Foreign awards are not gazetted until a few years after the war.

Many of the *"Citations"* (recommendations) were destroyed by the Army as no longer required, so all the *"Citations"* within this book are all I have been able to trace, (25 Honours/Medal Awards and 270 M.I.D. *"Citations"* unavailable).

My sources of references apart from the *"London Gazette"*, were Battalion diaries, the memoirs of Captain R.A. Alston-Roberts-West M.C., Captain Murray Gillings' *'The Shiny Ninth'* book, Major John Ainsworth from his book on The Royal Sussex Regiment, *'The Last Twenty Years 1948-1967'*, Ken Flint's personal diary *'In the Shadow of Shamsan'*,(Aden) and Colonel R.R. McNish for the use of his article on the 133 Brigade at El Alamein, the *"Sussex Daily News,"* the *"Brighton and Hove Gazette"* and the *"Brighton and Hove Herald"* also other local newspapers and my primary list of awards is from the *'Roussillon Gazette'* compiled after the war, and the West Sussex Record Office.

For a description of the 7th Bn. and 109th L.A.A. Regiment, read the *'Roussillon Gazette' December 1946*. For more on the Suez conflict, in depth detail is given in the *'Roussillon Gazette' Spring 1952* and the *'Roussillon Gazette' Summer 1965* for more details on the Aden campaign. For a fuller description of the 133 Brigade at El Alamein read the *'Roussillon Gazette' Winter 1993*. The Airborne Forces Museum for supplying the names of award winners of the 10th Battalion The Parachute Regiment who fought in Italy (1943) and Arnhem (1944) and the 9th Battalion The Parachute Regiment who fought in Northwest Europe (1944) Normandy Invasion and the River Rhine crossing.

All dates shown in the various medal lists are *"London Gazette"* dates. As the newspapers of the time had very little in them about individual Regiments/Battalions or the conditions they fought under, I have used *"memoirs"* and the *9th Battalion* book to describe events surrounding the awards of the officers and men of the Royal Sussex Regiment, and some of the places in which they served and fought from various articles in the *Roussillon Gazette*.

There were three other battalions, 8th Battalion was formed out of the original Local Defence Volunteers and served on guard duties in England. It was a relatively short-lived formation as were the 50th Battalion, formed at Seaford to supply drafts to other battalions. The 70th Battalion, formed in

September 1940, helped to defend vulnerable points in Sussex, Surrey, and Kent, and later provided drafts for overseas duty but these were short lived and did not see active service.

Forewords

When I suggested to Richard Buckman that his book should have a Foreword it was the idea that someone of more exalted rank, who had enjoyed close contact with The Royal Sussex in wartime, should be invited to contribute. Alas, after half a century, this notion was, I realised, somewhat optimistic. Those heroic figures are no longer with us ....Which is why the reader will have to be content with a mere platoon commander in the knowledge that even they are becoming a rare breed. However it is not the Foreword which is important, but the Contents and these deserve your unqualified recommendation.

The readers first impression might be that he is about to wade through one hundred and thirty odd pages listing medal recipients and Mentioned in Despatches, interesting but not much more entertaining than reading a directory. That impression could not be more wrong for Mr. Buckman has skilfully interlaced his Citations with press reports, photographs, extracts from books and letters as well as personal accounts of engagements and field conditions by those who were there at the time. This treatment is particularly effective in covering the North Africa and Italian campaigns and I have learned more about them in this book than I have from reading more prestigious authors. As for the Burma campaign, although I knew the majority of the men decorated I had never had the chance to read their Citations. Capt. R.A. Alston-Roberts-West, M.C. and other contributors tell the story as it really was for the men on the ground at the sharp end of combat. And what a story it is. From 1939 to 1946, including bars to medals already received, the Regiment won no less than one hundred and sixty gallantry awards comprising of one Victoria Cross, fourteen Distinguished Service Orders (plus two bars), seven Distinguished Conduct Medals, fifty-five Military Crosses (plus three bars), seventy-seven Military Medals (plus one bar). This is in addition to the innumerable Mentions in Despatches and also excludes miscellaneous honours bestowed to field commanders and other ranks.

As befits the senior battalion of the Regiment, the 1st Battalion collected the highest number of awards (3 D.S.O.'s, 23 M.C.'s and 35 M.M.'s) – a total of sixty-one. They were followed some way behind by the 9th with thirty-three awards. (1 D.S.O., 1 U.S. Silver Star, 1 U.S. Bronze Star, 8 M.C.'s and 22 M.M.'s). Inevitably the 1st Battalion must have suffered a correspondingly high casualty rate, being in action longer than any of the others. The 9th Battalion's casualty rate was mercifully low and that reflects the main difference between those two theatres of war. Whilst conditions in North Burma may have been marginally worse, we never had to face battles on the scale of El Alamein or Monte Cassino.

It is a pity – though no fault of the compiler – that we have so little information about the Royal Sussex battalions in France prior to the Dunkirk evacuation. Presumably all war diaries were destroyed and few people had time for writing. We know that the 2nd, 4th, and 5th Battalions were all in the 133 Brigade and suffered heavy losses in the withdrawal to Dunkirk. It was the survivors of the 2nd recuperating at Chichester, without arms or equipment, who were placed under the command of Lt-Col. (later Field Marshal) Gerald Templer and sent to Ross-on-Wye to form the nucleus of the 9th Battalion. They were destined to come under American command and fight further from home than any other British troops. In 37 Brigade the 7th Battalion ordered to defend Lens, was overrun and many of them killed or taken prisoner... The 6th, sent to support them, were overtaken by events and were lucky to get out of France from St. Nazaire, a distance of 600 km. from Lens – before the Germans arrived. The 7th, who had won seven medals in the limited time they were allowed, were never reconstituted as Infantry but the 6th Battalion became part of the 3rd Infantry Division and was later converted to motorised Infantry as part of the 9th Armoured Division under general Paget. "You are my future cutting edge in Europe", he told them, but this forecast proved somewhat premature, both for himself and the 6th, who never left the U.K. again. So once more their luck held because in 1943 they were equipped with the Crusader and Covenant tanks, now officially acknowledged as the worst ever built.

Richard Buckman is to be congratulated not only for the endless hours he must have spent in amassing all this data but also for putting it together so as to make a very readable book which should be required reading for all members of The Royal Sussex Regiment and their descendants.

         Capt. M. Gillings, Ex 9th Bn.
           Diss, Norfolk.

           July 2002

Although The Royal Sussex Regiment went into the history books in December 1966 on merging with the County Regiments of Surrey, Kent and Middlesex to form the new Queen's Regiment, there are many ex-members still alive who hold the achievements of their old regiment in high esteem.

This labour of love by Richard Buckman has produced an excellent reference book on the Military Honours and Awards by members of The Royal Sussex Regiment between 1921-1966 and he is to be congratulated on the results of his diligent research. I know of no similar reference book and it complements the Rolls of Honour displayed in the Regimental Chapel of St. George in Chichester Cathedral of those who fell in the 1st and 2nd World Wars.

                      Colonel J. Buckeridge,
                     Late The Royal Sussex Regiment.

                          September 2002

Battle Honours

The Royal Sussex Regiment

"**Gibraltar, 1704-5,**" "**Louisbourg, 1758,**" "**Quebec, 1759,**" "**Martinique,**" ""**Havannah, 1762,**" "**St. Lucia, 1778,**" "**Maida, 1806**""**Egypt, 1882,**" "**Abu Klea,**" "**Nile, 1884-85,**" "**South Africa, 1900-02,**" "Mons," "**Retreat from Mons,**" Marne, 1914, 1918," "Aisne, 1914," "Armentieres, 1914," **Ypres, 1914, 1917, 1918,**" "Gheluvelt," "Nonne Bosschen," "Givenchy, 1914," "Aubers," "Loos," **Somme, 1916, 1918,**" "Albert, 1916, 1918," "Bazentin," "Delville Wood," "Pozieres," "Flers-Courcelette," "Morval," "Theipval," "Le Transloy," "Ancre Heights," Ancre, 1916,1918," "Arras, 1917,1918," "Vimy, 1917," "Scarpe, 1917," "Arleux," "Messines, 1917," **Pilckem,**" "Langemarck, 1917," "Menin Road," "Polygon Wood," "Broodseinde," "Poelcapplle," "Passchendaele," "Cambrai, 1917,1918," "St. Quentin, "Bapaume, 1918," "Rosieres," "Avre," "Lys," "Kemmel." "Scherpenberg," "Soissonnais-Ourcq," "Amiens," "Drocourt-Queant," **Hindenburg Line,**" "Epehy," "St. Quentin Canal," "Beaurevoir," "Courtrai," "Selle," "Sambre," "France and Flanders, 1914-1918," "Piave," "Vittorio, Vento," **Italy, 1917-18,**" "Sulva," "Landing at Sulva," "Scimitar Hill," **Gallipoli, 1915,**" "Rumani," "Egypt, 1915-17," "Gaza, "El Mughar," "Jerusalem," "Jericho," "Tell 'Asur," "Palestine, 1917-18," **N.W. Frontier India, 1915,1916-17,**" "Murman, 1918-19," **Afghanistan, 1919.**" 'Defence of Escaut,' 'Amiens, 1940,' 'St. Omer-La Basse,' 'Foret de Nieppe', **'North-West Europe,' 1940,**' 'Karora-Marsa Taclai,' 'Cub Cub,' 'Mescelit Pass,' 'Keren,' 'Mt. Enghiahat,' 'Massawa,' **'Abyssinia 1941,' 'Omars,'** 'Benghazi,' **'Alam el Halfa,' 'El Alamein,' 'Akarit,'** 'Djebel el Meida,' 'Tunis,' **'North Africa 1940-43,'** 'Cassino 11,' 'Monastery Hill,' 'Gothic Line,' 'Pian de Castello,' 'Mont Reggiano,' **'Italy, 1944-45,'** 'North Arakan,' 'Pinwe,' 'Shweli,' **'Burma 1943-45.'**

Battle Honours emblazoned on the Colours are shown in heavy type.

Motto

Honi soit qui mal y pense

Nothing succeeds like Sussex

Colonel-in-Chief

HM Queen Juliana of the Netherlands June 30th 1953 - December 31st 1966

Allied Colonel-in-Chief

HM Queen Juliana of the Netherlands December 31st 1966 - March 24th 2004 (Her death)

Colonels of the Regiment

1914–1926 Maj-Gen. James Charles Young, C.B. (April 28th)
1926–1941 Brig-Gen. William Lushington Osborn, C.B., C.M.G., D.S.O. (July 10th)
1941–1942 Brig. Richard Maule Birkett, D.S.O. (July 30th)
1942–1953 Brig. Thomas Francis Vere Foster, C.B.E., M.C. (December 1st)
1953–1963 Gen. Sir Lashmer Gordon Whistler, G.C.B., K.C.B. K.B.E., C.B., D.S.O. (December 1st)
1963–1966 Brig. John Blackwood Ashworth, C.B.E., D.S.O. (July 4th)

Honorary Colonel

4th/5th Bn. (Cinque Ports) (T.A.)

1966 -1967 Rt. Hon. Sir Robert Menzies, K.T., P.C., C.H., Q.C., F.R.S., LL.M., LL.D., D.C.L., D.Sc. (June 1st 1966 - March 31st 1967)

Nicknames of the regiment:- The Orange Lilies, The Haddocks and The Iron Regiment.

Marches of the Regiment

1st Bn. Quick March :- The Royal Sussex
2nd Bn. Quick March:- The Lass of Richmond Hill
5th Bn. then 4/5th Bn. (Cinque Ports) :- Let the Hills Resound
Regimental Slow March :- Roussillon

After 1948 The Royal Sussex and The Lass of Richmond Hill were combined as one score.

Dispositions of The Royal Sussex Regiment 1939-1945

1st Bn.

03/09/39-14/08/40 23rd Infantry Brigade in Egypt, Delta and Suez Canal Area.
22/11/40 Came under command of the 7th Indian Brigade, 4th Indian Infantry Division in Egypt.
30/12/40 Arrived in the Sudan.
26/04/41 Embarked for Egypt.
30/04/41 Arrived in Egypt and proceeded to the Western Desert.
26/02/42 Returned to Egypt from Libya.
31/03/42 Sailed for Cyprus.
25/08/42 Returned to Western Desert.
31/03/43 Arrived in Tunisia.
08/07/43 Returned to Egypt.
13/09/43 Arrived in Palestine.
16/11/43 Returned to Egypt.
09/12/43 Arrived in Italy.
03/11/44 Arrived in Greece.
08/07/45 Ceased to be under command of the 7th Indian Infantry Brigade. 4th Indian Infantry Division.
19/07/45-31/08/45 Arrived in Austria, part of 61st Lorried Infantry Brigade.

2nd Bn.

03/09/39–08/04/40 United Kingdom.
09/04/40–30/05/40 France & Belgium, 133rd Brigade. 44th (Home Counties) Division.
31/05/40–30/05/42 United Kingdom.
31/05/42–24/07/42 At Sea, enroute to Egypt via the Cape.
24/07/42 133rd Infantry Brigade, 10th Armoured Division, X Corps. 8th Army, Middle-East.
29/12/42 Absorbs 4th Battalion in newly constituted Battalion.
02/04/43 Came under command of the 24th Indian Infantry Brigade, 6th Indian Infantry Division on arrival in Iraq from Egypt.
02/03/44 Arrived in Persia.
13/06/44 Arrived in Palestine.
24/08/44 Arrived in Iraq.
30/03/45 Arrived in Persia.
08/07/45 Ceased to be under command of the 24th Indian Infantry Brigade and came under command Persia Area.

{After El Alamein, 10th Bn. Parachute Regiment A.A.C. was formed from 2nd Bn. and volunteers from the 4th and 5th Bn.'s in December 1942 at Kabrit, they fought in Italy 1943 and at Arnhem 1944, the reconstituted 2nd Bn. goes to Persia as part of Paiforce.}

4th Bn.

03/09/39-07/06/40 France & Belgium, 133rd Brigade. 44th (Home Counties) Division.
08/06/40-31/05/42 United Kingdom.
31/05/42-24/07/42 At sea, enroute to Egypt via the Cape.
24/07/42 133rd Brigade, 10th Armoured Division, X Corps. 8th Army, Middle-East.
29/12/42 Transferred to newly constituted 2nd Battalion.

5th Bn.

07/10/39-07/06/40 France & Belgium, 133rd Brigade. 44th (Home Counties) Division.

08/06/40-31/05/42 United Kingdom.
31/05/42-24/07/42 At sea, enroute to Egypt via the Cape.
24/07/42 133rd Brigade, 10th Armoured Division, X Corps. 8th Army, Middle-East.
29/12/42 Assumes title of 4/5th Battalion T.A.

4/5th Bn.

01/01/43 New Battalion comes into effect.
01/02/43 Came under command of the 27th Indian Infantry Brigade, 6th Indian Infantry Division on arrival in Iraq from Egypt.
17/04/43 Arrived in Persia.
26/09/43 Arrived in Iraq.
28/03/44 Arrived in Palestine.
24/05/44 Arrived in Persia.
16/04/45 Arrived in Iraq. No further change.

6th Bn.

07/10/39-21/04/40 United Kingdom, Formed out of the 4th Bn., 37th Infantry Brigade. 12th Division.
22/04/40-07/06/40 37th Infantry Brigade, France, 12th Division.
08/06/40-31/08/45 213th Independent Infantry Brigade (Home).

7th Bn.

07/10/39-21/04/40 United Kingdom, Formed out of 5th Bn., 37th Infantry Brigade. 12th Division.
22/04/40-07/06/40 37th Infantry Brigade, 12th Division, France.
08/06/40-19/11/41 United Kingdom.
20/11/41-12/06/44 Due to heavy losses and many of whom became P.o.W.'s the Battalion is converted to 109th Light Anti-Aircraft Regt. R.A. (The Royal Sussex Regiment) South Coast, United Kingdom.
13/06/44-30/09/44 Normandy
01/10/44-28/02/45 Holland
01/03/45-07/05/45 Germany

9th Bn.

07/10/40-14/07/42 212th Independent Infantry Brigade.
15/07/42 Converted to 160th Royal Armoured Corps. Regiment. In October sent to Burma via Brazil and South Africa as part of 267th Indian Armoured Brigade.
01/04/43 Re-converted to 9th Bn. Royal Sussex at Poona and came under command of the 72nd Infantry Brigade.
16/02/44 Moved to the Arakan.
28/04/44 72nd Independent Infantry Brigade re-designated 72nd Indian Infantry Brigade. 36th Division.
16/07/45 Ceased to be under command of the 72nd Indian Infantry Brigade. 36th Division.
20/07/45 Arrived in Dharapuram Camp and came under command of the 74th Indian Infantry Brigade, 25th Indian Infantry Division. No further change.

10th Bn.

26/10/40-17/09/42 219th Independent Infantry Brigade. (Home) (10th Independent Beach Brigade)
18/09/42-24/10/43 203rd Independent Infantry Brigade. (Home) (10th Independent Beach Brigade)

Honours and Awards 1921-1966

"London Gazette" Thursday March 31st 1921

The KING has been graciously pleased to confer the Territorial Decoration upon the undermentioned Officers under the terms of the Royal Warrant dated 13th October, 1920: —

Major Eric Alfred Charles Fazan, M.C. 5th Bn.

"London Gazette" Friday April 1st 1921

The KING has been graciously pleased to sanction, the following promotions in and appointments to the Order of the Hospital of St. John of Jerusalem in England: —

As Esquires.

Maj. (T/Lt-Col.) James Lewis Sleeman, C.B.E.,M.V.O.

"London Gazette" Thursday June 4th 1921

The KING has been graciously pleased, on the occasion of His Majesty's Birthday, to give directions for the following promotions in and appointments to the Most Distinguished Order of Saint Michael. and Saint George: —

To be Ordinary Members of the Third or Companions, of the said Most Distinguished Order: —

C.M.G.

Major James Lewis Sleeman, C.B.E.,M.V.O., (527)

In recognition of services as Director of Military Training, New Zealand Military Forces.

"London Gazette" Wednesday June 10th 1921

The names of the undermentioned Officers, Ladies, Warrant Officers, Men and others have been brought to notice for distinguished service during the operations in Waziristan, 1919-20, by Gen. Sir O.C. Monro, G.C.B., G.C.S.I., G.C.M.G., in the despatch dated August 1st, 1920. (Published in the (Supplement of the London Gazette dated December 8th, 1920): -

M.I.D.

No. 3 Wireless Signal Squadron

No. 6711 Pte. W. Lovell, Ist Bn. The Royal Sussex Regiment, attached

"London Gazette" Monday June 28th 1921

The KING has been graciously pleased to confer the Territorial Decoration upon the undermentioned Officers under the terms of the Royal Warrant dated 13th October, 1920-:

Maj. Thomas Bartleet Hornblower, 5th Bn.

"London Gazette" Friday August 19th 1921

**DECORATIONS CONFERRED
BY HIS MAJESTY THE EMPEROR OF JAPAN**

Order of the Rising Sun

4th Class

Major John Meredith Hulton, C.B.E., D.S.O

"London Gazette" Monday February 4th 1922

**DECORATIONS CONFERRED
BY HIS MAJESTY THE EMPEROR OF JAPAN**

Order of the Sacred Treasure (3rd Class)

Major James Lewis Sleeman, C.M.G.,C.B.E.,M.V.O. (527)

"London Gazette" Tuesday July 4th 1922

The KING has been graciously pleased to confer the Territorial Decoration upon the undermentioned Officers under the terms of the Royal Warrant dated 13th October, 1920: —

Major John Raymond Warren, M.C. 4th Bn.

"London Gazette" Saturday 2nd June 1923

The KING has been graciously pleased, on the occasion of His Majesty's Birthday, to give orders for the following promotions in, and appointments to, the Most Honorable Order of the Bath:-

C.B.

Lieutenant-Colonel, Brevet Colonel Alfred Edgar Glasgow, C.M.G.,D.S.O. 2nd Bn.

M.B.E.

Captain Thomas Picton M.C., Adj. 7th Bn. Royal Welsh Fusiliers, (T.A.)

"London Gazette" Tuesday June 12th 1923

The names of the undermentioned have been brought to notice for distinguished service during the operations in Waziristan, April, 1921, to December, 1921, by His Excellency General Lord Rawlinson of Trent, G.C.B., G.C.V.O., K.C.M.G., A.D.C. Gen., Commander-in-Chief in India, in the dispatch dated 24th May, 1922. (Published in the Supplement to the London Gazette dated 4th December, 1922,):—

M.I.D.

Lieutenant Robert Hawkins Rohde, (5550) The Royal Sussex Regiment, attd. M.G.C.

"For distinguished service during the operations in Waziristan, April 1921."

"London Gazette" June 3rd 1927

The KING has been pleased, on the occasion of His Majesty's Birthday, to give orders for the following promotions in, and appointments to, the Most Excellent Order of the British Empire :—

To be Officers of the Military Division of the said Most Excellent Order:—

O.B.E.

 Major John Raymond Warren, M.C., T.D., 4th Battalion

"London Gazette" August 25th 1927

The KING has been graciously pleased to confer the Territorial Decoration upon the undermentioned Officers under the terms of the Royal Warrant dated 13th Oct. 1920: —

 Qm & Capt. William Frederic Wraight, 4th Bn.

"London Gazette" Tuesday January 1st 1929

The KING has been graciously pleased to sanction the following promotions in and appointments to the Venerable Order of the Hospital of St. John of Jerusalem: —

As Commanders

Lieut.-Colonel James Lewis Sleeman, C.M.G.,C.B.E., M.V.O.   (527)

"London Gazette" Friday March 1st 1929

The KING has been graciously pleased to confer the Territorial Decoration upon the undermentioned Officers under the terms of the Royal Warrant dated 13th October, 1920: —

Capt. Joseph Edward Herbert Mostyn (Ret.). 4th Bn.

"London Gazette" Friday November 1st 1929

The KING has been graciously pleased to confer the Territorial Decoration upon the undermentioned Officers, under the terms of the Royal Warrant dated 13th Oct. 1920:—

Capt. Alexander John Stevenson Grant, (23442) 5th Bn.

"London Gazette" Friday February 20th 1931

The KING has been graciously pleased to confer the Territorial Decoration upon the undermentioned Officers under the terms of the Royal Warrant dated 13th October, 1920: —

Major Bernard Whiteman, M.C. 5th Bn.

"London Gazette" Tuesday June 23rd 1931

The KING has been graciously pleased to sanction the following promotions in and appointments to the Venerable Order of the Hospital of St. John of Jerusalem:—

As Knights of Justice

Colonel James Lewis Sleeman, C.M.G.,C.B.E.,M.V.O.

"London Gazette" Friday May 6th 1932

The names of the undermentioned have been brought to notice by His Excellency, General Sir Philip Chetwode, Bart., G.C.B., K.C.M.G.,D.S.O., Commander-in-Chief in India, for distinguished services rendered in connection with military operations on the North West Frontier of India, during the period October, 1930—March, 1931:—

M.I.D.

Corporal (Staff Sergeant) James G. Hoare, 2nd Battalion, The Royal Sussex Regiment and Indian Corps of Clerks.

"London Gazette" Wednesday January 1st 1936

The KING has been graciously pleased to give orders for the following promotions in, and appointments to, the Most Honourable Order of the Bath:—

To be Ordinary Members of the Civil Division of the Third Class, or Companions of the said Most Honourable Order:—

C.B.

Colonel James Lewis Sleeman, C.M.G., C.B.E.,M.V.O. (527)

"London Gazette" Thursday November 19th 1937

The KING has been graciously pleased to confer the Territorial Decoration upon the undermentioned Officer under the terms of the Royal Warrant dated 13th October, 1920: —

Major Bayard Sorby Hissey, (23448)   5th Bn.

"London Gazette" Thursday June 8th 1939

The KING has been graciously pleased, on the occasion of the Celebration of His Majesty's Birthday, to give orders for the following promotions in, and appointments to, the Most Excellent Order of the British Empire :—

M.B.E.

To be Members of the Military Division of the said Most Excellent Order :—

No. 6392311 C.S.M. Leonard Frederick Divall, 1st Battalion, The Royal Sussex Regiment

"London Gazette" Friday December 22nd 1939

The names of the undermentioned have been brought to notice by the General Officer Commanding the British Forces in Palestine and Trans-Jordan in recognition of distinguished services rendered in connection with the operations in Palestine during the period 1st April to 30th July 1939: —

M.I.D.

Commands and Staff

Major Douglas Reginald E. Shaw,   1st Bn.   (12820)

Tuesday June 18th 1940

M.C. FOR SUSSEX OFFICER

OUTSTANDING LIAISON WORK

Second-Lieutenant (A/Lt.) Patrick Edward Xenophon Turnbull of The Royal Sussex Regiment has been awarded the Military Cross.

When most of the communications had to be carried by dispatch rider or liaison officer under hazardous conditions, Lieutenant Turnbull acting as liaison officer was quite outstanding, states the War Office. Nothing was too much trouble for him by day or night. However difficult the situation he was always prepared to start at once and he carried out his duties with intelligence and determination.

Linfield Officer's Death

Second-Lieutenant Edward Percy Reid Jourdain, The Royal Sussex Regiment, attached Anti-Tank Company, whose death is announced, was the second son of Mr. and Mrs. H.J. Jourdain, of "The Welkin", Linfield, and was 24 years old. He received his commission in the Territorial Army in 1938.

Monday July 8th 1940

Pretended to be a German

SUSSEX MAN WINS M.C.

An officer of The Royal Sussex Regiment, who passed through the German lines by night by pretending to be a German patrol has been awarded the M.C. On 20th May, Second-Lieutenant Eric Chisholm Sevenoaks, on returning from patrol was cut off by enemy tanks and came under heavy fire. He concealed his men in a thick wood and himself made several reconnaissances.

Finding he was completely surrounded by enemy armoured fighting vehicles, and motorized units, he kept his men under cover and eventually succeeded in withdrawing them, without loss, through German outpost lines by night by pretending to be a German patrol.

He showed great courage, initiative and coolness in a difficult situation, says the War office in announcing 23 immediate awards by the Commander-in-Chief of the B.E.F.

All-Round Sportsman

Second-Lieutenant E.C. Sevenoaks is a son of Mr. and Mrs. W.H. Sevenoaks, of 9 Lascelles Terrace, Eastbourne. He was educated at Beaumount College, Windsor, and served in the O.T.C. there. After leaving school, he joined a Territorial Battalion of The Royal Sussex Regiment.

He was in business in London and abroad and had to return from abroad owing to bad health. He was on the Reserve of Officers and was recalled to the Army on the outbreak of war. Second-Lieutenant Sevenoaks is an all-round sportsman and, like his father, is a very keen tennis player. He has played in several of the tournaments at Eastbourne, Hastings and Bexhill and played tennis for the Devonshire Park Club.
His brother, Mr. D.V. Sevenoaks, in an officer in the Royal Berkshire Regiment.

"London Gazette" Thursday July 11th 1940

The KING has been graciously pleased to approve of the undermentioned awards for gallant and distinguished services in action in connection with recent operations.:—

D.S.O.

Major (A/Lt-Col.) Farrar Robert Horton Morgan, Border Regiment, (14595) Commanding 5th Bn. Royal Sussex Regiment,

For conspicuous ability and leadership in command of his Battalion. During the 27 & 28 May, his Battalion greatly reduced by casualties held a long sector at Rouge Croix. No reserve except the carrier platoon was available. By his skilful dispositions, by his personal example of bravery where enemy pressure was heaviest and by his very able use of his carrier platoon, he maintained his line intact against heavy enemy attacks both by A.F.V;'s and infantry.

Major (A/Lt-Col.) Lashmer Gordon Whistler, 4th Bn. (13017)

For consistent display of courage, ability and power of command under very severe conditions. During the whole of the fighting in which his battalion was engaged both on the Escaut and Caestre he gave a fine example of coolness under fire and ability to instil confidence and resolution into those under him. Throughout he kept firm control of his Battalion which was in consequence always ready for the heavy and unexpected calls made upon it.
In particular he conducted with outstanding skill the defence of Caestre. Although his Northern flank was completely unprotected, he held the position against A.F.V.'s and infantry supported by heavy artillery fire for two days until finally ordered to withdraw. This withdrawal he carried out successfully and without loss.

M.C.

Captain Joseph Simpson Magrath,   4th Bn. (42679)

For distinguished conduct. As Company Commander, Captain J.S. Magrath was a continual example to his men. He was always present when there was danger and encouraged his men by word of mouth and example. During the fighting at Caestre his work was particularly praiseworthy. His rapid reorganisation of the defences in very difficult circumstances was of the highest standard throughout. He maintained his position in spite of repeated attacks by A.F.V.'s and infantry.

Lieutenant Frederick Morley Smith, (110692) R.A.M.C. attd. 4th Bn.

On 21st May, 1940 between 1400 and 1700 hours, the Battalion lay in Anseghem village awaiting orders to move forward. The village came under very heavy shell fire and numerous casualties occurred. Lieutenant Smith whose first experience of shell fire it was, displayed the greatest coolness and courage ending to the wounded with complete disregard to his own safety. Later in the day Lieutenant Smith continued to deal with the casualties in and around the R.A.F. again under heavy shell fire with great personal courage and cheerfulness. His behaviour throughout was exceptional.

A recommendation for an immediate award was forwarded to Bde. HQ on 21 May. During the period 25-28 May at Caestre, Lt. Smith again showed the same high qualities of courage and coolness during very heavy shelling of his R.A.P. and I was prepared to recommend him again for the M.C. if the first recommendation had failed.

2nd Lieutenant Ivor Malcolm Austin,   (71265) 5th Bn.

For conspicuous gallantry, resource and initiative on 28 May 1940 at Rouge Croix. When the line was temporarily broken under very heavy fire, he rushed forward a section of his carriers, restored the position, holding practically a whole Company front and putting out of action a large number of the enemy. He held on until ordered to withdraw. Only himself and one of his drivers remained, all others being killed or wounded.

It was largely owing to his magnificent effort with the line of the Strazeele-Caestre road was kept intact.

(was PoW at Oflag V11.C.)

2nd Lieutenant John Baptiste De Manio, (100313) 7th Bn. (T.A.)

This officer, together with Sgt. Hollands, 7 Bn. displayed great courage and coolness when about 1100hrs. on 20 May 1940 an enemy aircraft was shot down one mile from Bray. Both went immediately to the place where the plane had fallen. Sergeant Hollands entered the plane first despite the fact that it was burning fiercely and that ammunition was exploding. He was eventually ordered away by an officer. 2/Lt. De Manio then arrived and entered the machine, pulled the pilot out and removed his identification papers and personal belongings. A number of British and French soldiers were standing some distance away and 2/Lt. De Manio set them a fine example of courage and coolness under extremely dangerous conditions.

His own irreverent account from his autobiography, "Life Begins Too Early."

"The Calvados was a great success, however. Almost too much so, because the average British soldier has never heard of the stuff, and as always they start by despising anything with which they are unfamiliar, be it people or drink. We were a merry lot – for a little while.

It was while we were in this orchard that I watched Abbeville, which was close by, being dive-bombed. It was a pretty horrid sight: everything going up in smoke and flame all over the place, and those 'stukas' screaming down like great black birds, getting bigger and bigger the nearer they got to the ground. Not only did their engines scream, but they had special sirens fixed to the wings to make them scream all the more, as if they were not frightening enough already.

One of them got a little bit too cheeky and either he could not pull out of his dive in time, or he got shot up. Whatever happened he hit the ground with a resounding thump only a quarter of a mile from our orchard. It just shows you what a state we were all in because I got a medal just for being nosy. Naturally, curiosity sent me speeding over to this plane to have a look. It was burning merrily and there was a lot of bangers and squibs going off inside, which I suppose was ammunition exploding.

It occurred to me there might be someone still alive in there, so I heaved out a couple of dead Germans, who turned out to be very dead indeed. All I could do was collect up their papers and maps just in case they might be of some help to us. By that time the local populace had arrived. Disappointed though they undoubtedly were at finding their prey dead, they were, nevertheless, not deterred from smashing the lifeless bodies to pieces with clubs, pitchforks, shotguns, boots and anything they could lay their hands on. I was so revolted and sickened by this time that I very nearly shot some of them myself. But looking back on it, I suppose it is not an unreasonable way to behave if your houses, farms, wives and children are being blown to pieces."

2nd Lieutenant Edward Percy Reid Jourdain, (79264) 4th Bn. (T.A.)

2/Lt. Jourdain showed great personal courage both at the battle of Audenarde and again at Caestre. At the latter place he was continually in action with his guns encouraging the crews and working as one of the crew. He carried out all my orders with great cheerfulness and determination and was a splendid example to all who came in contact with him. He displayed a great ability in moving his guns under fire and keeping them in action.

2nd Lieutenant Peter Henry Rubie, (74658) 7th Bn. (T.A.)

For gallant conduct under fire. As Carrier Platoon Commander 2/Lt. Rubie was always in the forefront of any action. His behaviour at all times and under all conditions as of the highest order. At Merville after having placed a section of carriers in a position to cover the Battalion, he personally went forward to see for himself the position in front. His conduct is spoken of with the highest praise by many N.C.O.'s and men of the Battalion.

D.C.M.

No. 6397264 Sgt. Darrell Ernest Hollands,   7th Bn. (Bath)

France/Belgium 1940: This N.C.O., together with an Officer (2/Lt. De Manio, J.B.) displayed great courage and coolness when, at about 1100 hours, on the 20 May, 1940, an enemy aircraft was shot down about one mile from Bray. Both went immediately to the place where the plane had fallen.
Sgt. Hollands arrived first and despite the fact that the plane was burning fiercely, that ammunition was exploding inside, and that three unexploded bombs were lying near the flames, he entered the plane without hesitation and brought out the machine-gun. He was about to re-enter in an endeavour to bring out the pilot when he was ordered away by 2/Lt. H.C.T. Robinson, 6th Bn. Royal Sussex, who had arrived at the scene. A large number of British and French soldiers were standing some distance away and 2/Lt. De Manio and Sgt. Hollands set them a very fine example of courage and coolness under extremely dangerous conditions.
(He later won a D.S.O. as a Lt.(T/Capt.)(194123) Royal Tank Regiment, Royal Armoured Corps. "L/G" May 4th 1943 for North Africa.)

No. 1061601 Sergeant Arthur Cyril Knapp, 5th Bn.

France/Belgium 1940: For exceptional determination, coolness and courage demonstrated on several occasions during the fighting 23/29 May, 1940. On one occasion at Stazeele on May 27th he went back in the face of intense enemy shelling and machine-gun fire to find a fellow Sergeant who had been hit and carried him back. At Monte des Cats on 29th he dragged four wounded men to safety and tended them during heavy shelling and dive bombing. Throughout he showed complete disregard of his personal safety, and was an example to those under his command. When the shelling was hottest he was seen playing a mouth organ to encourage his men.

No. 5669089 C.S.M. William Connell, 4th Bn.

France/Belgium 1940: The above named W.O. was C.S.M. of "A" Coy. On May 21st, 1040, the Battalion was waiting orders at Anseghem, when it came under heavy shell fire. In "A" Company there were several casualties, including two stretcher-bearers attached to the Company whose stretchers were at the time on the Company truck.
C.S.M. Connell on his own initiative, having helped to steady the Company whose first experience of shell fire this was, went in search of the truck and stretchers. After a time he returned dragging to stretchers behind him. He then organised the evacuation of the wounded to a cellar, himself helping to carry them.
The whole area was being heavily shelled throughout. C.S.M. Connell's calmness and steadiness under fire, of which it was his first experience, his initiative and complete disregard of personal danger were an inspiration to all around him, and were of the greatest value in steadying the Company as well as the means of getting the wounded to safety.
In subsequent action at Caestre this W.O.'s behaviour was of equally high standard. During the march to Dunkirk with only one Officer with the Company his leadership and cheerfulness contributed to the eventual safe arrival of the Company.

M.M.

No. 4385843 L/Corporal Robert Binnington, 4th Bn. (Dunkirk)

On 28th May, 1940, this N.C.O. lead a reconnoitring patrol from "A" Coy. And returned with valuable information. On 28/29 May, the section under command of L/Cpl. Binnington became detached from its Platoon during the course of a small local advance to secure a defensive line round the village of Caestre. On his return to the village, L/Cpl. Binnington failed to find his platoon or Coy., as the Bn. Had meanwhile marched off to Mont des Cats. He therefore with his section occupied his previous defensive positions till dawn. He then obtained information from elements of 5th Bn. Royal Sussex who were left in the area that the order had been given to make for Dunkirk. He found an abandoned lorry, loaded his section and some stragglers from 5th Royal Sussex on to it, and drove to within 10 miles of Dunkirk. As he had no maps and only very vague information, I consider this a most praiseworthy example of initiative and leadership. With the exception of one man lost during the night, he got his section safely on the beach at Dunkirk and thence to England.

No. 63988745 Private Harold Croft, 2nd Bn. (Peacehaven)

Private Croft was the driver of the Mortar Ammunition Truck at the battle of Audenarde. As occasion required and often under heavy shell and machine-gun fire he drove his truck to the Mortar position with fresh ammunition. Finally he drove his truck to the position over completely open country and evacuated both guns and crew under heavy machine-gun and artillery fire.
This Private took part in the evacuation from Dunkirk, and when under heavy fire, courageously risked his life to save his comrades. He "scuttled" his lorry so that it could not fall into enemy hands.

No. 6399092 Private Wilfred George Wilson, 5th Bn.

For leadership and determination on the Strazeele-Caestre road on 27 May 1940. Private Wilson who had on that day been appointed to command a section, took up a position in some farm buildings. Largely due to his high qualities of leadership and determination all enemy attempts to get in to the building were frustrated, despite the fact that the enemy surrounded the place and using such subterfuge as calling out in English for admittance. He held on until the early hours of the next day when a general withdrawal was ordered, the extricating his men without casualties.

Friday August 2nd 1940

PEACEHAVEN M.M.

RISKED LIFE TO SAVE COMRADES

The first Peacehaven resident to be awarded a decoration for gallantry is Private Harold Croft, Royal Sussex Regiment, youngest son of Mrs. Croft, of "St. Anne's", Bramber Avenue, Peacehaven. Private Croft, a transport driver who received a Military Medal, took part in the evacuation from Dunkirk, and when under heavy fire, courageously risked his life to save his comrades. He "scuttled" his lorry so that it could not fall into enemy hands. Private Croft came through without a scratch.

"London Gazette" Tuesday August 20th 1940

The KING has been graciously pleased to approve of the undermentioned awards for gallant and distinguished services in action in connection with recent operations:—

M.M.

No. 6398354 Corporal Wilfred Herbert Eric Goodhall, 7th Bn.

At Amiens on May 20/21 and succeeding days this N.C.O. was with 2/Lt. E.C. Sevenoaks 7th Bn. and displayed courage and initiative of a very high order. Though at times surrounded by enemy tanks and infantry, and repeatedly under heavy fire from artillery and L.M.G. he made several reconnaissance in a fearless manner, and brought back reliable information which greatly assisted in getting the party away safely. In addition his cheerfulness throughout did a great deal towards sustaining the men's confidence and spirits.

Monday August 26th 1940

FOR GALLANTRY IN ACTION

EAST GRINSTEAD MAN WINS M.M.

The First East Grinstead man to win the Military Medal during the war is Sergeant W.H.E. Goodhall, of The Royal Sussex Regiment. The award was won for gallantry in action in France. Sergeant Goodhall's home is 9 Ship Street, East Grinstead.

"London Gazette" Friday December 20th 1940

The names of the undermentioned have been brought to notice in recognition of distinguished services in connection with operations in the field, March-June, 1940.

M.I.D.

Captain (A/Mjr.) John Blackwood Ashworth, 4th Bn. (47519)

This officer acted as my adjutant throughout the period February 1940 to the end of active operations. His thoroughness, coolness in action and efficiency largely contributed to the efficiency of the Battalion in action and to the smoothness of its movements in and out of battle.

Lieutenant (Q/M.) Frank Angell, 4th Bn. (125650)

This officer acted as Quartermaster from March to the end of active operations. His consistent good work throughout largely contributed to the excellent state of the clothing and equipment of the Battalion in France and to its maintenance in a state of efficiency. His handling of rations etc. in action was of very high order and food was always produced when it was humanly possible to do so.

2nd Lieutenant John Maurice Drage, (76028) 4th Bn.

This officer acted as Liaison Officer between H.Q. 133 Inf. Bde. And 4th and 5th Battalions Royal Sussex. This duty he carried out excellently under all conditions of danger. His reports were accurate and his work admirable. A considerable portion of his duties was carried out under quite considerable artillery fire.

No. 6398985 P.S.M. L. Leeder, 4th Bn.
(not gazetted, taken from Battalion records)
This Warrant Officer was in command of a platoon of a Rifle Company throughout active operations. His personality and cheerfulness at all times kept his men at a very high standard of efficiency. He carried out very important patrols and gained much valuable information on several occasions.

No. 6400343 Lance-Corporal William Reginald J. Brown, 4th Bn.

This N.C.O. was in charge of "A" Echelon transport and at all times showed initiative and courage under fire. L/Cpl. Brown was left in charge of the Coy's transport which was bombed and set on fire. L/Cpl. Brown was buried and temporarily unconscious but soon recovered and collected the Coy. Drivers together with other men of the Battalion. Altogether he mustered a party of seven and under his sole command he marched the party safely to Dunkirk.

No. 6401777 Lance-Corporal Albert Walter Dench,   4th Bn.

He was instrumental in the rescue of 20 soldiers of the East Lancashire Regiment, who had been trapped South of the Lys after all bridges had been blown. He swam the canal several times personally rescuing 5 and in fact being responsible for the rescue of all. Although the enemy were not actually in sight, they could be expected at any moment.

No.5667269 Corporal (L/Sgt.) Thomas Walter B. Denmead,   4th Bn. (Battle)

At the battle around Caestre, L/Sgt. Denmead as a result of casualties, was left in command of his Platoon during an attack by A.F.V.'s. He took charge with complete confidence and personally organised the fire of two A/Tank Rifles against the enemy A.F.V.'s which were within 400 yards of his position. His example was most heartening to the men of his company and was largely instrumental in their steadiness in very trying circumstances.

No. 6402284 Private Richard H. Foster,   4th Bn.

Both in the battles of Anseghem and Caestre, the above named man acted as an orderly between Battalion H.Q. and his own Company H.Q.

No. 6399510 Private Harry Newnham,   4th Bn.

At Caestre the above named soldier acted as an orderly between Battalion H.Q. and his own Company H.Q. At all times he was ready to carry orders and messages under shell fire without regard to his own personal safety, and in fact constantly did so.

No. 6399347 Private Thomas Stanley,   4th Bn.

During the actions at Caestre he was performing the duties of signal clerk and he did this in a most exemplary manner. He was always ready to collect orderlies or to convey messages himself under fire. His devotion to his duties and his actions, being carried out without any regard to his own safety, were a constant example to those around him.

Lieutenant-Colonel Edward Keith Beavan Wannop, (45350) 6th Bn.

Major (A/Lt-Col.) Patrick J.M. Ellison,   2nd Bn.

Major (T/Lt-Col.) Samuel Alexander Holwell Kirkby, M.C.

Major Christopher Francis Ashburner Nix, 4th Bn. (35771)

Throughout the period spent in France and Belgium this officer commanded a Coy of the Battalion. The Coy was always in an excellent fighting condition and never wavered under any circumstances. I attribute this to the fine leadership and example set by Major Nix whose tactical ability and complete coolness under fire were of inestimable value to me and his Company.

Major Cyril Reid Peckitt, (15229) 2nd Bn.

Major James Stuart Cassels, M.C. (13193) 7th Bn.
(since died)

Captain (A/Mjr.) F.W. Bedford,

Major Alexander John Stevenson Grant, T.D., (23442) 5th Bn.

"For rearguard actions at Dunkirk"

Captain William Robert Ellen, 5th Bn

For his magnificent work during the actions in the period 23/29 May 1940. Entirely regardless of his personal safety throughout, he set a splendid example of selfless devotion to duty, remaining calm, collected and efficient under the heaviest fire and in the most difficult circumstances.

Captain Hugh John C. Taylor,

Captain Edward Gerald Hollist, 4th Bn. (44064)

Captain Ronald Hennah Langham, 5th Bn. (38113)

Lieutenant & Q/M Percy John Hanlon, (69631) 2nd Bn

2nd Lieutenant Harold George Castle, (102541) 6th Bn.

On May 29th 1940 2/Lt. Castle was in charge of about 60 men holding the northern bank of the canal running north-east from Wulpen. Throughout the day in spite of machine-gun fire and heavy mortar bombardment from the enemy he held his position and brought well directed rifle fire to bear on the enemy concentrations and small parties attempting to cross the canal. His energy, resource and total disregard of personal danger set a fine example and played a large part in preventing the enemy from crossing the canal.

2nd Lieutenant Garrick Dermod Bowyer, 7th Bn. (72780)

No. 6391344 R.S.M. Richard Froude, 2nd Bn. (since died)
No. 6395706 R.S.M. William C. Evans,
No. 6394041 C.S.M. Thomas P. Simmonds,
No. 5876732 C.S.M. Arthur S. Izzard,
No. 5669740 Sergeant C.J. Harwood,
No. 6397014 Corporal H. Ayling,
No. 6398967 Corporal Leslie J. Saunders, 4th Bn.
No. 5501274 Private Cyril Thomas English,
No. 6396792 Corporal G. Hawkins,
No. 6400647 Private William G. Nutter,

No. 6399289 Private Ernest W.A. Ide, 4th Bn.

No. 5439968 Private F.A. Robey,

No. 6399326 Private George Webb, 2nd Bn.

For gallant conduct under fire. Throughout operations but particularly during the fighting around Merville, this soldier continually showed complete disregard of danger. He was instrumental in the collection of wounded under fire. His extreme high spirits at all times and under all conditions of fire and exhaustion were an example and inspiration to his comrades.

The KING has been pleased to approve of the undermentioned awards in recognition of gallant conduct in action with the enemy: —

M.C.

2nd Lieutenant Eric Chisholm Patrick Sevenoaks, (63782) 7th Bn. Royal Sussex Regiment, (Lancefield, Cumberland)

On 20 May 1940 this officer took out a patrol of one platoon on a recce through Salouel near Amiens, and on to the high ground West of the village. He obtained much valuable information as to the enemy's dispositions and strength which he communicated to his Company Commander. On his way back, his patrol encountered enemy tanks and came under heavy fire. He concealed his men in a thick wood and himself made several recces in order to find a way back, but without success.

When 2/Lt. Sevenoaks realised he was completely surrounded by the enemy AFV's and motorized units, he kept his men under cover and eventually succeeded in withdrawing them without loss through the German outpost lines. He spent many hours within a few yards of German armoured units and passed through German outpost lines by night by pretending to be a German patrol.

Having got through the German lines he continued his march through heavy shelling and eventually contacted French troops after marching throughout the night.

He showed courage, initiative and coolness in a difficult situation and set his men a very fine example in determination.

2nd Lieutenant (A/Lt.) Patrick Edward Xenophon Turnbull, (39499) 4th Bn. Royal Sussex Regiment, G.H.Q. Liaison Officer lent to Petreforce.

Most of the communications from Petreforce was done through D.R. of liaison officer and very often under hazardous conditions. Lieutenant Turnbull was quite outstanding in these duties. Nothing was too much trouble for him, by day or night. Whatever the situation was, he was prepared to start at once and carried out his duties with intelligence and determination.

"London Gazette" Wednesday January 1st 1941

The KING has been graciously pleased to approve the following Awards: —

The Medal of the Military Division of the Most Excellent Order of the British Empire, for Meritorious Service: —

B.E.M. (Military Division)

No. D/1580 Orderly Room Sergeant Albert Ernest Brown,

"London Gazette" Friday January 28th 1941

The KING has been graciously pleased to approve that the following be Mentioned for distinguished services in the field:-

M.I.D. ESCAPE AND EVASION AND SPECIAL OPERATIONS

No. 6400527 L/Cpl. Raymond Victor Lewis-Clements, 7th Bn.
No. 832419 Pte. W. C. Burgess, 7th Bn.

Prior to Capture

On the 18 May the Bn. was in their positions at ST. SAENS and was moved to the MAGINOT LINE to relieve the 51st Div. On the way to AMIENS, the train came under heavy fire and they lost about half their strength. The rest of the Bn. left the train and hid in a wood for two days on the north side of AMIENS.

Capture

On the third day the advancing Germans came into contact with them and after severe fighting, in which there were many casualties the rest of the Bn. was forced to surrender.

L/Cpl. Lewis-Clements was wounded in the back and so saw little of the actual surrender. Pte. Burgess was run down by a German tank and suffered from bruises for 6 weeks. They both were taken by American Ambulance (manned by Americans) to a hospital in AMIENS where they spent 6 weeks; but, during this period, the hospital was shelled and they were moved to another in the same town.

Escape

About 3/4 July they were moved to a camp at DOULLENS. They left AMIENS with about 6000 P/W, mostly French, but on the march were able to slip away. They met a farmer who took them to his farm and lodged them there for a fortnight (about 1km from DOULLENS).

After this they decided to make for SWITZERLAND via ALBERT, but on their way they met an Englishman who advised them not to go; so they returned to DOULLENS and spent a further week at the farm at which they had been previously.

They then decided to make for SPAIN through unoccupied France and made their way to AMIENS. Soon after they left this town, they came across an enormous gun, hidden in a wood, some 2km south of AMIENS, which, judging by its calibre and direction of fire, must have been shelling England. They continued on to CLERMONT and then on to FLEURINS and 4 kms. beyond saw a big German airfield, well camouflaged.

From FLEURINS they carried on into PARIS and while wandering around the streets got lost but eventually came across the American Red Cross, by whom they were given 400 frs. One of the Society took them in the underground out of PARIS.

From outside PARIS, they went on by way of ORLEANS to VIERZON. At VIERZON, which is half in unoccupied France and half in occupied France, they entered a cafe to which they had been directed to by two demobilised French soldiers (they told them what they were trying to do), and the proprietor of this cafe led them through some ruined buildings across the line, while one of his employees kept watch for German patrols.

From then on to the Spanish frontier, they had little trouble, their route being CHATEAUROUX AND GEURET. Here they met a French Infantry captain who took them in his car to CLERMONT FERRAND and then on to PERIGUEX, where he left them; but, before leaving them, he got in touch with the Mayor and persuaded him to give them tickets to PERPIGNAN. From PERPIGNAN they walked by way of FORT VENDRES and due south crossed the border without incident.

Once they had crossed the frontier, however, the Spaniards arrested them and after a stay at FORT BOU, they were taken to FIGUREAS, where they met P.S.M. Clubbs.

Sunday February 9th 1941

1st Bn. Royal Sussex Regiment seized Karora and Mersa Taclai, a small roadside 30 miles inside Eritrea. 100 prisoners taken. The tiny port of Mersa Taclai had possibilities for the supply of petrol by dhows and coasters as the consumption by the columns operating in the area would be enormous.

Monday February 10th 1941

The 1st Bn. Royal Sussex still lead the column, seized Elghena, 30 miles inland from Mersa Taclai. A mobile column of "C" Coy Royal Sussex and a carrier platoon are ordered to encircle the Italian lines and cut their communications.

"London Gazette" Tuesday February 11th 1941

The KING has been graciously pleased to approve that the following be mentioned for distinguished services in the field in Somaliland:-

M.I.D.

Lt. (A/Capt.) John Belford Arthur Glennie, 1st Bn. (63600)

Wednesday February 12th 1941

1st Bn. Royal Sussex are delayed for 48 hours due to soft sand, dried river beds and inaccurate handkerchief maps. They succeed in cutting the road 3 miles south of Cub Cub, and capture an Italian Field Cashier with two large chests of lire.

Wednesday February 19th 1941

"BACK FROM THE DEAD"

ROYAL SUSSEX OFFICER IS P.O.W.

Major L.W. Lane, M.C., Royal Sussex Regiment, who was reported killed, is now officially reported a prisoner of war.
(was PoW at Oflag V11. C/H.)

Saturday February 22nd 1941

Cub Cub is taken, 430 prisoners and a number of light artillery pieces and a large supply dump are captured.

London Gazette" Friday March 7th 1941

The KING is graciously pleased to approve the undermentioned awards in recognition of distinguished services in the field :-

D.C.M.

No. 6397485 Lance-Sergeant Archibald Tilling,   7th Bn. (Chichester)

Prior to Capture

On 19 May 40 the 7 Royal Sussex were travelling by train to Abbeville, when they were bombed just outside Amiens and were ordered to take up defensive positions. They remained here during the night.

Capture

On the morning 20 May, the Germans increased their attack and Tilling was hit in the thigh. In spite of this he continued for some time to fire on a machine-gun post, and eventually managed to crawl to the temporary field dressing station, where stretcher-bearers were attending to the wounded. About an hour later the station was surrounded by German tanks and a German officer demanded their surrender. As all ammunition was exhausted, those of the wounded that could walk did so. All stragglers were rounded up by armoured vehicles and collected at the dressing station.
The Germans were heavily armed and adopted a menacing attitude throughout the interrogation on Unit, Bde, Div and strength of Army. Questions were also put on the armament of the R.A.F. About 40 P/W were put into tanks or armoured vehicles and 4 wounded (of which Tilling was one) were left under armed guard at the FDS, during this time there was no medical attention, food or water.

Escape

That night Tilling discussed escaping with another P/W but the latter decided against it. Tilling who was determined to escape, eluded the guard, crawled down the road in a ditch and eventually found an abandoned bicycle, on which he free-wheeled for about 2 miles into the next village. Here he fainted and was picked up by two villagers, who put him in a handcart at first then a car and drove him to Beauvais to the French hospital.
On 23 May Tilling was taken from Beauvais to Paris by a French ambulance and admitted to the Bichot Hospital. On the same day, he was evacuated to a French Military Hospital- France-Mussulman at Bobigny (Seine) and remained at this hospital until 13 June. During this period he was operated upon and the bullet in his thigh extracted. On 13 June he was evacuated to Clermont Ferrand in an ambulance train and put into a large school which was being used as a hospital. During the time he spent there, he was disguised as a French soldier and was moved from hospital to hospital in order not to come under suspicion.
From here he was sent to a convalescent home at Gravanche about 5 kms from Clermont Ferrand. At Gravanche there was a large aerodrome. From here he was sent back to Clermont Ferrand to another hospital-Hospital St. Hilaire-where he tried to persuade the M.O. in charge to discharge him but was not successful.
On 9 August, with the help of an Irish nurse, he managed to persuade the M.O. to discharge him and was given a railway warrant to Marseilles. When he reached Marseilles he went to the American Consul and was passed on to the Annexe which was the unofficial British Consulate, after a period he was interned in Fort St. Jean.

During his internment, a scheme was in progress whereby British soldiers should become Poles, be given Polish passports and obtain visas to Portugal and Spain. The plan fell through. In the fort he contacted C.S.M. Moir and with him, they approached a man, giving him 1,000Frs for a passage to Oran. When the time came for them to board the ship, the captain asked them for a further sum of money, which they were unable to give, so had to come off the French troop carrier. However, they managed to get back 500Frs of the 1,000Frs they had paid originally.

After this they returned to the Poles again, who by then had another scheme and had managed to obtain a boat "SS Storm"- but after waiting about 10 days on board ship, they heard that the scheme had fallen through, as the Poles were unable to obtain permission for the boat to leave the harbour.

Tilling then decided to try and get to Spain, so took the train to Perpignan and walked over the mountains near le Perthus. In Spain he travelled at night by side-roads and passed through Figueras and on to Gerona. Just outside Gerona, he was arrested by the Guardian Civil and asked for papers, when he produced the British Emergency Certificate given to him by the American Consul at Marseilles, he was taken to the Police Station and from there put in prison.

He was removed to Figueras where he remained for 10 days. His next prison was Castillo in Figueras where he remained for a week. From Castillo he was transferred to the concentration camp at Cevera for 10 days and then sent on to Miranda del Ebro where he remained until he was released and sent to Gibraltar via Madrid.

Escaped Prisoner of War: Captured near Amiens 20 May 1940 and escaped same day. Interned Fort St. Jean, Vichy France. Left Gibraltar 19 November 1940. Arrived United Kingdom 4 December 1940. Recommendation for Distinguished Conduct Medal based on interrogation report dated 5 December 1940, now in the Public Record Office (Reference WO 373 reel 60).

Saturday March 15th 1941

Royal Sussex N.C.O. awarded D.C.M.

Lance-Sergeant Archibald Tilling, Royal Sussex Regiment, has been awarded the Distinguished Conduct Medal for distinguished services in the field.

"London Gazette" Tuesday April 1st 1941

The KING has most graciously pleased to award the following promotion, in and appointment to the Most Excellent Officer of the British Empire in recognition of distinguished service in the Middle East during the period August 1939 to November 1940.

C.B.E. Military Division)

Colonel Thomas Francis Vere Foster, M.C. (3175) (Late Royal Sussex)

An officer of the highest professional ability who has done valuable service on the staff of the B.T.E. for a long period. Has worked successfully and untiringly both before and after the outbreak of War problems arising from the Implementation of the Anglo-Egyptian Treaty and the organisation of the British Civil Community in Egypt to meet an emergency.
Has done excellent work in connection with raising of new units and in the co-ordination of Welfare work for the Troops.

The KING has most graciously pleased to approve that the following be Mentioned for distinguished service in the Middle East during the period August 1939 to November 1940.

M.I.D.

1st Bn.

Lieutenant (Q/M) Charles Henry Pocock, (169609)
No. 6398857 Lance-Corporal A.F. Edwards
No. 6398458 Corporal (Local Sergeant) S. Doidge,
No. 6396474 Private Percival Gordon Brown,

"London Gazette" Tuesday April 29th 1941

The KING has been graciously pleased to approve that the following be Mentioned for distinguished service in the field :-

Commands and Staff

M.I.D.

Maj. (T/ Lt.-Col.) Lashmer Gordon Whistler, D.S.O. (13017).

"London Gazette" Friday 2nd May 1941

The KING has been graciously pleased to approve that the following be Mentioned for distinguished service in the field :-

M.I.D. (M.E.)

Lt. (T/Capt.) Francis John Ronald, (67904) 1st Bn.

"London Gazette" Friday 18th July 1941

The KING has been graciously pleased to approve the undermentioned awards in recognition of gallant and distinguished services in the Middle East :—

M.M.

No. 6011748 Corporal Sidney John De Ville,   1st Bn.   (Boreham) (attd. 'L' detachment S.A.S.)

This N.C.O. has shown the utmost disregard for his personal safety and on many occasions caused the enemy severe casualties. At the action of Mersa Taclai on 10th February 1941, whilst in command of a carrier, by his initiative rounded up a machine-gun post thereby saving many casualties. On 21st march 1941 when an enemy plane was shot down between the lines north of Keren, this N.C.O. went forward within a very short distance of the enemy's lines and captured the pilot who had "baled out".

Saturday July 19th 1941

The KING has approved of the following award in recognition of distinguished and gallant service in East Africa :-

Military Medal

No. 6011748 Corporal Sidney John De Ville,   1st Bn.   (Ipswich)

Wednesday August 27th 1941

RESCUE FROM MINEFIELD

ROYAL SUSSEX MEN MENTIONED

The gallant action of soldiers have been specially brought to the notice in orders by Lieutenant-General B.C.T. Paget, CB. D.S.O. M.C., Army Commander, South Eastern Command.
On the 16th June, 1941 when in charge of the guard, Corporal Duncan Elgar Wood, Royal Sussex Regiment, heard cries for help, and on investigating, found a private soldier lying wounded in the centre of a minefield.
Corporal Wood entered the minefield, and went up to the wounded man. Having found that the latter's injuries made him incapable of assisting in his own removal, Corporal Wood called to his aid one of the three privates whom he had brought with him, namely Private S. Talbot. Corporal Wood and Private Talbot then carried the wounded private to safety.
The minefield was at Fairlight near Hastings, East Sussex.

"London Gazette" Tuesday October 28th 1941

The KING has graciously pleased to approve the award of the George Medal in recognition of conspicuous gallantry in carrying out hazardous work in a brave manner.

No. 6403801 Corporal Duncan Elgar Wood, 5th Bn.   (Crayford, Kent)
No. 6409686 Private Steven Talbot, 5th Bn.   (Dublin)

Corporal Wood was in charge of a guard on the 16th June 1941, when he heard someone crying out for help. On making investigation he found that the cries came from a soldier who was lying in the centre of a minefield. The soldier had been severely injured by the explosion of one of the mines. Although there was no safety track visible and the mines were covered up by long grass, Corporal Wood promptly entered the minefield and went up to the injured man. On observing that the latter's condition prevented him from being removed single-handed, Corporal Wood called upon Private Talbot to assist him. Although Private Talbot was unaware of the position of the mines, he immediately entered the minefield and went to Corporal Wood's assistance. Together they succeeded in carrying the injured man to a safe place, where further assistance was available.
Both Corporal Wood and Private Talbot displayed great courage, initiative, and complete disregard for their own safety in entering the minefield in order to rescue the injured soldier.

(Private S. Talbot transferred to the "Buffs" on the 6th September, 1941, the "L/G" shows him as the "Buffs".)

Saturday November 22nd 1941

1 Royal Sussex are directed to open the assault on Omar Nuovo, they embussed and moved off with 2 Squadrons from the 42nd Royal Tank Regiment.

"From an Indian Army Public Relations officer who was there."

"As we crossed the desert that morning, we could her the rumble and crashes as the artillery and bombers laid on. The little carriers of the Royal Sussex lead, followed by the tanks with their pennants flying. Immediately behind the tanks came the leading companies of the infantry in lorries. Behind them, Brigade Headquarters. Then came the remainder of the Royal Sussex, and following, more tanks, lorries and carriers for 4/16 Punjabi attack, until as far as the eye could reach the plain was filled with fighting machines speeding into battle. I had just said 'Trafalgar must have been like this' when a whizz and a crash showed the enemy ranging on us. On the horizon upright black streaks marked the telescopic ladders of his artillery observers. We had had no hope of concealing ourselves on a plain as flat and bare as a billiard table".

As the Royal Sussex neared Omar Nuovo, the carriers dashed for a previously reconnoitred gap in the minefield. It proved a trap, a hedge of mines had been sown, four tanks and three carriers were blown up. The infantry was pressing hard behind, the officer rallied his remaining carriers and charged across the minefield. The tanks followed in behind, the Royal Sussex then exited their lorries, formed up and raced into enemy positions, 500 yards ahead. In a short fierce fight, the attack won home. From slit trenches and heavily manned strong-points the Italian soldiers emerged, their arms upraised in surrender. Within two hours the battle was won and over 1,500 prisoners taken.

Friday December 12th 1941

FOLLOWING UP IN LIBYA

ROYAL SUSSEX REPEL TANKS

Persistent harassing of the Axis Forces in Libya on Wednesday resulted in the enemy being pushed still further west and north-west of El Adem, stated yesterday's Cairo communiqué. A Nazi Tank attack on Sikhs, Punjabis and the Royal Sussex Regiment was driven off. In The past two days the Nazis have lost at least 75 tanks. In addition to the ten mentioned in yesterday's communiqué, it was stated in authoritative circles in London that our patrols in the coastal area located and destroyed 38 tanks in workshops, apart from the 27 reported to have been destroyed on Wednesday. The opposing forces are now preponderously Italian, and there is no information in London that General Rommel has been able to get any reinforcements.

Wednesday December 17th 1941

Quentin Reynolds Says- Salute to the Brighton Boys

Quentin Reynolds, postscript speaker and Daily Express reporter, returned to London last night by way of Moscow, Kuibishev and Cairo. He had a hundred stories to tell. "But", he said, "there is only one story I want to tell you about the war in the desert. It is the story of the Royal Sussex - the Brighton Boys.

"These Brighton Boys were hemmed in the desert by the Germans, by tanks and by land mines. You know what land mines are - you put your foot on a piece of smooth sand and you are blown to eternity. "Well, The Royal Sussex Regiment, the Brighton Boys, bust their way through that string of land mines and engaged the line of tanks. They got through to the other side and I want to tell you that I think the Royal Sussex are the real heroes of the Western Desert.

"All the time I have been away, I have seen nothing more impressive than the way they went into battle in the desert, which means the battle of the tank and the land mines, with the bayonet and were content. These are the boys for my money."

Friday December 19th 1941

SIX ROYAL SUSSEX MEN

AWARDS FOR GALLANTRY

Cairo Thursday

General Auchinleck, C-in-C. Middle East, has made some immediate awards for gallantry in action during operations in the Western Desert, including the following :-

M.C.

Captain Peter Michael Jermyn Harrison, 1st Bn. (73141)
Lieutenant Derrick William Gaylard, 1st Bn. (99819)
Captain Leonard Bapty, M.B. R.A.M.C. attd. 1st Bn. (119899)

D.C.M.

No. 6397782 Corporal Albert William Talmey, 1st Bn.

M.M.

No. 6391608 Sergeant E. Conroy,   1st Bn.
No. 6400007 Private J. Cunningham, 1st Bn.
No. 6408377 Private S.H. Young,   1st Bn.

Saturday December 20th 1941

M.C. for Hove Town Clerk's Son

Captain Peter Michael Jermyn Harrison, who has been awarded the Military Cross by General Auchinleck, C-in-C Middle East, for gallantry in action during operations in the Western Desert, is the son of Mr. W. Jermyn Harrison, Town Clerk of Hove. He is 24. A native of Hove, Captain Harrison was educated at Wykeham House School, Worthing, and afterwards at Lancing College. He chose an Army career, and went straight from Lancing to Sandhurst in 1935.
He passed out high in the list, and was gazetted to The Royal Sussex Regiment in 1937, and was sent to Egypt. He returned home on sick leave in January, 1939, but had returned to Egypt before the outbreak of war.
He was wounded recently in the fighting at Sidi Omar, and it was for his gallantry on that occasion that he has been decorated. Mr. Jermyn Harrison told the Sussex daily News : yesterday : "I have heard from my son, and he described the fighting at Sidi Omar. Previously we had received a wire from him saying "Slight wound in right leg, otherwise very fit."

"London Gazette" Tuesday December 30th 1941

The KING has given orders for the following appointments and awards in recognition of distinguished service in the Middle-east, (including Egypt, East Africa, Western Desert, the Sudan, Greece, Crete, Syria and Tobruk) during the period February 1941 to July 1941.

O.B.E. (Military Division)

Major (T/Lt-Col.) John Leslie Von Der Heyde, M.C.   (31719)

He is A.A.G. 2nd Echelon during the periods of rapid expansion and reorganisation, he has done excellent work in the face of many great difficulties.

M.B.E. (Military Division)

Captain (T/Mjr.) John Keele Haselden, (46405) 1st Bn.

This officer was transferred to be D.A.Q.M.G. (M), Haifa on 16 July 1941. Prior to this date he had for a period of 18 months worked unceasingly in Alexandria on Movements, of which he was the senior representative for most of the time. He was unfailingly tactful, particularly careful about detail and controlled a very large number of movements into and out of Alexandria with accuracy and despatch.

C.S.M. (A/R.S.M.) William Frederick Lyons, (6395377) 1st Bn. (attd. 50 M.E. Commando) (Littlehampton)

This W.O. has been a member of M.E. Commandos since their inception. He was, previous to joining this depot, C.S.M. to 50 M.E. Commando. His services in the field with that unit gained the highest praise from all concerned. Since being appointed R.S.M. to this Depot he has carried out his duties with outstanding energy and efficiency.

The KING has been graciously pleased to approve that the following be Mentioned in recognition of distinguished services in the Middle East (including Egypt, East Africa, The Western Desert, The Sudan, Greece, Crete, Syria and Tobruk) during the period February, 1941, to July, 1941: -

M.I.D.

Commands and Staff

Colonel Thomas Francis Vere Foster, C.B.E.,M.C. (3175)
(Late Royal Sussex)

1st Battalion

Captain Geoffrey Arthur Phelps, (36752) 1st Bn.

Major Douglas Reginald E. Shaw, (12820) 1st Bn.
(also M.I.D. "L/G" 22/12/39)

No. 6398043 C.Q.M.S. R. Albert, 1st Bn.

Between November 1941 and April 1942 this Warrant Officer has done exceedingly good work in connection with the preparations of accommodation for units returned from active operations in the Western Desert. He thought only of the comfort of the troops to be accommodated and to meet this end, spared himself nothing to ensure success and leave no room for complaint. The preparation of the camps meant long hours of work but the completion of the job was uppermost in his mind.

No. 6395892 Sergeant (A/S/Sgt.) William A. Pack, 1st Bn.
No. 6398059 Lance-Corporal F.A. Brown, 1st Bn.

"London Gazette" Friday January 23rd 1942

The KING has been graciously pleased to approved the following awards in recognition for gallant and distinguished service in the Middle East :-

M.C.

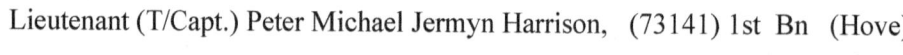

Lieutenant (T/Capt.) Peter Michael Jermyn Harrison, (73141) 1st Bn (Hove)

During the nights of 20/21 November 1941 while the battalion was occupying a position West of Libyan Omar, this officer carried out two patrols into the enemy's area, entailing truck and foot moves and brought in useful information. In the attack Sidi Omar Nouvo on 22 November, Captain Harrison displayed great courage and devotion to duty. After his Coy Comd. was wounded and though wounded himself he continued to command his Coy and small detachments of others with skill.
By his offensive action and planning he forced some 180 of the enemy to surrender on the final objective. Throughout the period 20/22 November, Captain Harrison has shown the greatest devotion to duty and has been an example to all ranks. Despite his wound he remained at his post until ordered to return to the A.D.S.

Lieutenant Derrick William Gaylard, (99819) 1st Bn. (Homedale, Manor Way, South Croydon)

During the attack on Sidi Omar Nouvo on 22 November 1941, Lieutenant Gaylard was commanding the Carrier Platoon, and was ordered to lead the 'I' Tanks on to the left of the objective. Just short of the objective, the carriers met an enemy minefield. Lieutenant Gaylard, immediately, under heavy fire searched for a gap and when this could not be found, did not hesitate to cross the minefield.

During this, three of his carriers were blown up. On 23 November he carried out two patrols to locate enemy positions South of Sidi Omar, and during the second his carrier was destroyed by Anti-Tank gun fire, but he managed to return to the Battalion. Throughout this action this officer has displayed great coolness and dash, and his conduct in action deserves the highest praise.

Captain Leonard Bapty, M.B. R.A.M.C. (119899) attd. 1st Bn. (Victoria, British Columbia)

During the attack on Sidi Omar Nouvo on 22 November 1941, Captain Bapty was the Medical Officer attached to the 1 Royal Sussex Regiment. The R.A.P. was in an exposed place and subject to continual and intense artillery fire. With great calmness and skill, Captain Bapty continued to attend the wounded of which some 87 passed through his hands in less than 24 hours.
His complete disregard for his own personal safety, and his coolness and continued devotion to duty were beyond all praise, and were an example to those around him.

D.C.M.

No. 6397782 Corporal Albert William Talmey, 1st Bn.

North Africa: During the attack on Sidi Omar Nuovo on 22 November 1941, Cpl. Talmey, although suffering from several wounds continued to fight and lead his men forward. Finally when unable through weakness to go further forward himself, he gave covering fire with a Bren gun and so enabled two men to get forward and capture an enemy post. The courage and devotion to duty shown by this N.C.O. were beyond all praise.

M.M.

No. 6391608 Sergeant Ernest Conroy, 1st Bn. (18, Alfred St. Northampton)

During the attack on Sidi Omar Nouvo on 22 November 1941, Sergeant Conroy was Platoon Sergeant of No. 11 Platoon of "B" Coy. Although painfully wounded through the mouth, he carried on until the objective was taken, taking over command of his platoon when the Platoon Commander went to command the Coy. His determination not to give up and his leadership were an inspiration to all others who witnessed his conduct.

No. 6400007 Private John Cunningham, 1st Bn. (attd. "L" S.A.S.) (8 Claraden St. Southwick)

During the attack on Sidi Omar Nouvo on 22 November 1941, Private Cunningham's section was held up by a Breda machine-gun. Alone and in the face of heavy fire, this private soldier went forward and put the post out of action with a grenade. The initiative and courage of this soldier was a fine example to all around him.

No. 64083777 Private Stanley Herbert Young, 1st Bn. (15 Fitzroy Rd. Lewes)

During the attack on Sidi Omar Nouvo on 22 November 1941, Private Young the No. 1 Bren Gunner maintained his gun in action though exposed to heavy and light Breda fire on a ridge. Any movement immediately brought down fire, but despite this and the fact the previous No. 1 gunner had only just been killed, he opened fire whenever opportunity offered. This private soldier's bravery and determination was an example to all.

Saturday January 24th 1942

TWO SUSSEX HEROES

GALLANTRY IN THE DESERT

The London Gazette last night contained the names of 50 officers and men who have been awarded honours or mentioned for gallantry and distinguished services in the Middle East and South West Pacific. There are three D.S.O's, eleven M.C's, five D.C.M.'s, nineteen Military Medals, eight Indian D.S.M's, one Indian Order of Merit (Second Class), three mentions for distinguished service.

Brighton Man

The Distinguished Conduct Medal has been awarded to Corporal Albert William Talmey, of The Royal Sussex Regiment, of Henry Street, Brighton, whose courage and devotion to duty were beyond praise. Although suffering from several wounds during the attack on Sidi Omar on 22nd November, he continued to fight and lead his men forward. When unable, through weakness, to go further forward himself, he gave covering fire with a Bren gun and enabled two men to get forward and capture an enemy post.

Lives at Southwick

Private John Cunningham, of The Royal Sussex Regiment, whose home address is Claraden Street, Southwick, has been awarded the Military Medal for initiative and courage. His section was held up by a Breda machine-gun, but alone and under heavy fire he put the post out of action with a grenade.

The KING has approved the following award for gallant and distinguished service in the Middle-East:-

Military Medal

No. 6398463 Lance-Corporal F.W. Hall,

"London Gazette" Tuesday February 24th 1942

The KING has been graciously pleased to approved the following awards in recognition for gallant and distinguished service in the Middle East :-

Bar to D.S.O.

Major (T/Lt-Col.) Geoffrey Charles Evans, D.S.O. (12895)
Royal Warwickshire Regiment, Commanding 1st Bn. Royal Sussex

On 21st November 1941 Colonel Evans and his Battalion attacked and captured Omar Nuovo with a degree of dash and coverage worthy of the very highest traditions of the British Army. Though tanks were held up mines and 88 mm. guns for some time, Colonel Evans and his men were undeterred and successfully continued the attack in spite of heavy losses.

The splendid and bold leadership of this officer gave his men an example which they eagerly followed. Throughout the further advance and the capture of Martuba this officer continued to show the greatest dash and initiative.

"London Gazette" **Thursday February 26th 1942**

The KING has been graciously pleased to confer " The efficiency Decoration " upon the following officers of the Territorial Army: —

Colonel (Hon. Colonel) James Lewis Sleeman, C.B.,C.M.G.,C.B.E., M.V.O. (527)

Wednesday April 22nd 1942

Royal Sussex M.C. wounded

W.S./Lieutenant D.W. Gaylard, Royal Sussex Regiment, who was awarded the Military Cross in January, in recognition of gallant and distinguished service in the Middle East, is reported wounded, in an official casualty list issued today.

"London Gazette" **Thursday April 23rd 1942**

The KING has been graciously pleased to approved the following awards in recognition for gallant and distinguished service in the Middle East :-

M.C.

2nd Lieutenant George Parker Bidder, (156504) 1st Bn.
(Henley-on-Thames)

During the break-out from Benghazi by a column of the 7th Indian Infantry Brigade, 2nd Lieutenant Bidder was commanding the Carrier Platoon. About 1000hrs. on 29th January 1942 when the column was in the vicinity of Amtelat, an enemy column escorted by tanks was seen moving down the escarpment from the East and turning North. The carrier platoon was ordered to attack and destroy the vehicles without becoming engaged with the tanks.

2nd Lieutenant Bidder with six carriers carried out the operation with such skill that he succeeded in checking the following without a single casualty to personnel or vehicles:-

14 Italians killed
1 Italian officer and 27 O.R.'s made prisoner
1 Lorry captured in good running order
8 M.G.'s, 6 lorries and 1 Anti-Tank gun destroyed
800 gallons of diesel oil destroyed

The initiative and offensive spirit of this officer were deserving of very high praise.

M.M.

No. 6397604 Sergeant William Richard Rasell,   1st Bn. (Haywards Heath)

During the break-out from Benghazi by a column of the 7th Indian Infantry Brigade, Sergeant Rasell was Platoon Sergeant of the Carrier Platoon. At about 1000hrs. on 29th January 1942 in the vicinity of Amtelat, the Carrier Platoon was ordered to attack an enemy column. Although fired upon at point-blank range by an Anti-tank gun, Sergeant Rasell did not hesitate to take his carrier straight towards it and after killing the crew, destroyed the gun. The courage and offensive spirit of the N.C.O. were way beyond all praise and set a magnificent example to all around him.

No. 6398463 Lance-Corporal Frank William Hall,   1st Bn. (Petts Wood)

During the break-out from Benghazi by a column of 7th Indian Infantry Brigade, Lance-Corporal Hall was Medical Orderly to the Battalion. On 29th January 1942 the column was subjected to severe and very accurate dive-bombing and M.G. attacks which caused a number of casualties. With complete calm and outstanding efficiency, Lance-Corporal Hall assisted the Medical Officer in dealing with and evacuating casualties. Having no ambulance, this N.C.O. devised an ingenious method of loading two 3 ton vehicles to make the badly wounded comfortable from a further 150 miles of bad desert going. For two days and nights this N.C.O. never left the wounded, attending to their wants and keeping them cheerful. The devotion to duty of this N.C.O. was a subject of comment among his comrades, and this together with the calm he displayed under exceptionally trying circumstances were worthy of the highest praise.

Monday April 27th 1942

Military Medal

A Sussex soldier has been awarded the Military Medal in recognition of gallant and distinguished service in the Middle East.

No. 6397604 Sergeant W.R. Rasell,   (Haywards Heath)

Thursday April 30th 1942

Sussex Men at Sidi Omar

M.M. Sergeant's Letter Home

"I have had bags of fun with Old Jerry; in fact, the regiment has rather a grand name now."
This is a passage in a letter from Sergeant William Richard Rasell, of The Royal Sussex Regiment, who has been awarded the Military Medal for distinguished services in the Middle East, to his father, Mr. W.R. Rasell, 54a South Road, Haywards heath, and the late Mrs. Rasell. The letter continues :-

"We had rather an exciting time at Sidi Omar …. It was broadcast about the famous Southern County Regiment who took Sidi Omar against terrific odds. I don't think anyone could praise the boys enough for the grand way they all went in."

"My carriers finished up in front of the light tanks, and so did the infantry, after having crossed minefields under terrific shell fire &c. The boys never wavered or stopped. It really was a sight on can never forget, yet never likely to see again. We lost some good friends, but I sure guess 'old Jerry' lost more."

He adds that he has recovered from his last wounds; "In fact, have been in several battles since." After leaving St. Wilfrid's School, Sergeant Rasell was an employee of Rice Bros., Saddlers & Co., South Road, until his enlistment in 1935. He is 29.

"London Gazette" **Tuesday May 12th 1942**

The KING has been graciously pleased to give orders for the following appointment to the Most Excellent Order of the British Empire in recognition of distinguished services in the field: —

M.B.E. (Military Division)

Lieutenant Richard Edward Hope Parkinson, (88370) 4th Bn.

In May, 1940, when this officer's Battalion was vacating its position at Caestre, he was left behind with a small detachment to act as rearguard. Acting on instructions he later withdrew, only to find that he was unable to get through to re-join his Battalion, so with two men, in uniform and carrying arms, they headed west walking at night only and hiding during the day.

After a fortnight's journey they reached the forest of Hazebrouck where they were joined by another soldier who was in civilian clothes. The party journeyed on through St. Omer to Wivernes, and one evening they were overtaken by a German cycle patrol, which opened fire on them whilst they were scattering, killing one man. They were later joined by two more soldiers at Licqes, where they were befriended by the villages and guided to a hide-out at Guines, which they all had to leave after a week as a result of being sighted by some German gunners. In the confusion of fleeing, Lieutenant Parkinson and another soldier lost sight of the remainder of the party.

The next month was spent in searching for a boat in the Pas de Calais district, but they were unsuccessful and the frustration of numbers of German Anti-Aircraft gunners compelled them to leave. They then made their way South and at Barbure-Sure-Conche they met four other British soldiers who were waiting help from an organisation which assisted British soldiers to escape. They were told to remain in hiding till summoned, but after a time they lost faith in the scheme and set off for Lille where they again got in touch with the organisation, whose Headquarters was in Roubaix.

Three weeks later they were guided to Marseilles, crossing the Line of Demarcation in a goods train with the help of French railway employees. Lieutenant Parkinson remained in Marseilles at St. Hippolyte from June to September 1941, in order to assist in the organisation of escapes. He escaped from there himself in September 1941, and after two attempts he reached Spain, from whence he was repatriated in December 1941.

"London Gazette" **Tuesday June 30th 1942**

The KING has been graciously pleased to approve that the following be Mentioned in recognition of gallant and distinguished services in the Middle East during the period July, 1941 to October, 1941:-

M.I.D.

Lieutenant (T/Capt.) James Conwy Morgan, (47361) 1st Bn.
Lieutenant Kenneth Stephen Horace Wilson, (141036) 1st Bn.

Wednesday August 5th 1942

Sussex Men in Egypt

YEOMANRY AND INFANTRY

In a recent telegram from Cairo, mention was made of the fair men of Sussex being among the troops engaged, and it is now permissible to state that the units serving in North Africa include the Sussex Yeomanry and The Royal Sussex Regiment.

"London Gazette" Wednesday September 9th 1942

The KING has been graciously pleased to approve the following awards in recognition of gallant and distinguished services in the Middle East during the period November, 1941 to April, 1942 : —

M.C.

Captain (T/Mjr.) Robert Essex Staveley Shinkwin, (63601) 1st Bn. (Rochester)

During the attack on Sidi Omar Nuovo on 28th November 1941, Major Shinkwin was commanding "B" Coy. When the Coy was held up on a prominent ridge by heavy and accurate Mortar, H.M.G. and rifle fire, he cooly organised his Coy and attempted to outflank the enemy. When this failed, despite the heavy fire, he walked back and obtained the aid of a tank which enabled the Coy to occupy a good position. He was later wounded when forward observing the enemy position. Throughout this action this officer's coolness and complete disregard for his personal safety was the mainstay of the Coy and an inspiration to all ranks.

M.M.

No. 6396042 Corporal Patrick Christopher Anthony Brennan, 1st Bn.

During the attack on Sidi Omar Nuovo on 22nd November 1941, Corporal Brennan was i/c Stretcher-bearers "B" Coy. When the Coy was held up on a prominent ridge, this N.C.O. continually exposed himself to heavy and accurate fire, to tend the wounded. Particularly on one occasion when a mortar bomb wounded two men, Corporal Brennan immediately went forward to their assistance in an area which the enemy had already put approximately 30 large mortar bombs.

Throughout this period this N.C.O. showed the greatest devotion to duty and a complete disregard of danger.

M.I.D.

No. 6398043 W.O.II. (G.Q.M.S.) R. Albert 1st Bn.

Thursday September 10th 1942

Battle in Libya : British Troops' Gallantry

By an Indian Army Official Observer

"During the last two days of enforced leisure if not peace in Sidi Omar Nuovo, I have been able to gather further details to supplement what I saw myself of the capture of the fortress by an English Southern County Regiment on Friday last, I have also had ample opportunity to study the ground (there is a small piece of slit trench, every stone in the bottom of which I have examined almost microscopically) and the more I think of it I am convinced that even in this tremendous battle this is a feat of arms which will stand out not only in the regimental history but in the story of the campaign as a whole. For the importance of the taking of this immensely strong position is only equalled by the dash and determination with which it was taken.

The attack was put in from the north to south through the back door. The tanks were to move to a start line three and a half miles north of Sidi Omar with the battalion carriers under command. They were to move across the start line twenty minutes before an intensive artillery preparation of ten minutes. The only mistake I made was in saying that the carriers followed the tanks. In fact is was the little Bren carriers which led, and the young officer in charge of them not only brought the monsters up to the first objective in spite of two of his carriers being blown up almost immediately, but then proceeded to lead them on to the second, showing the greatest coolness and courage throughout.

The battalion was to cross the start line in trucks at zero hour and was to debus some seven hundred yards short of the enemy defences. The plan was to attack two defended localities, A and B, with two companies each, and one company from the left ; two companies were then to go through and take the third objective, Sidi Omar itself, which, I must repeat, is not a place but the map reference of part of a defensive system. A mortar detachment was to move in carriers in close support of each inner flank company and an anti-tank troop in the rear of both columns. As the battalion got ready in the assembly area the carriers and tanks could be seen going forward under heavy shell fire, and I have already described how we got a full ration ourselves round Brigade Headquarters, a few hundred yards behind the start line.

Nevertheless, when the battalion moved up on to the line at 11.47 every man was in good heart and high spirits and cheered the Brigadier when he came up to see them off and wish them good luck. In actual fact they debussed only four hundred yards short of the enemy and crossed the line ten minutes after noon. Unfortunately there was an unallocated minefield about eighty feet deep on the line of the advance, and although some tanks managed to get through several were blown up. Despite this and the fact that two company commanders leading the columns were killed and a third wounded, the men, seventy percent of whom come from the county whose name the Regiment bears, went forward unhesitatingly, at times in front of the tanks, and no storm troops in the world could have pressed on with greater dash.

There was, for example, a corporal who continued to lead his section although he had been several times wounded, and when too weak from loss of blood to stand gave covering fire with his Bren gun until an enemy machine-gun post had been silenced. There was an officer, a platoon commander who, hit in both knees, staggered to his feet and went on until he was shot in the head within fifteen yards of the enemy. The men on either side of whom were also killed but the trenches ahead were captured by the rest of platoon. There was a gunner major who came up with a battalion commander instead of sending an F.O.O. and was seen leading the infantry to the attack waving his cap and shouting them on.

There was a private, a number one Bren gunner, who kept his gun in action in spite of the fact that the previous number one had just been killed and that the slightest movement brought down heavy and accurate fire from heavy and light Bredas. There was a corporal in charge of stretcher-bearers of a company held up on the ridge. He continually exposed himself tending the wounded, and when two men were hit by a mortar bomb immediately went forward to their assistance in an area in which the enemy had dropped approximately thirty large mortar bombs.

There was a company commander who, when his company was held up and an attempt to outflank the enemy had failed, calmly walked back amidst a hail of bullets, found a tank and led it on foot to deal with the opposition. These are only a few of the stories of individual courage and coolness, and, as always, there were many acts of gallantry which passed unnoticed in the heat of the action. Strong point by strong point the position was cleared with the aid of single tanks, and by 2.20, that is to say in just over two hours objective A on the left had been captured while objectives B on the right and C in the centre, but further on, were half taken. At this time only fourteen men of this company remained unwounded.

The position now held by three companies, was an isolated hill behind which were some 300 of the enemy with heavy mortars, anti-tank guns and machine-guns, who were still offering a determined resistance. With the aid of a tank and a 3-inch mortar rushed up in a carrier this pocket was cleared by 5.30. The number of prisoners taken was 300 and the number of the party which took them was thirty! On the right, in front of "C" Company, the enemy continued sniping but a light tank was dispatched, and this tank and the remaining fourteen of the company rounded up another 300. By darkness the whole of the fortress was in our hands.

Fortunately the casualties had not proved as nearly heavy as was first feared, but tragic though it was to walk round in the twilight and count our dead it was inspiring to see that every man had died with his face to the enemy and that most of them had died within a few yards of the enemy trenches. One last story which was told me by the battalion commander is worth repeating. A wounded corporal was lying in the open during the advance still under heavy fire. As the colonel passed he raised his hands and pointed to the silent enemy gun. "See that so-and-so, sir," he said, "I put that blank out of with a couple of bombs." Today, in spite of some further experiences which I hope to report in a further despatch when they are past history and the shells are no longer zooming overhead as they were when I began to write, and are likely to do so at any moment, the battalion is in great heart. "Look out, chum, major road ahead," was the last remark I happened to overhear from the slit trench next to mine as someone, roaring along in a captured Italian truck with his turned to observe a nearby shell burst, drove into a large crater. The British soldier has not changed much since the last war."

This narrative shows the action from which awards to Captain Shinkwin, M.C., Captain Harrison, M.C., Lieutenant Gaylard, M.C., Captain Bapty, R.A.M.C., M.C., Sergeant Talmey, D.C.M., Sergeant Conroy, M.M., Corporal Brennan, M.M., Private Cunningham, M.M., Private Young, M.M. were made.

Friday September 11th 1942

The King has approved the following award for gallant and distinguished service in the Middle-East :-

Military Medal

Corporal (A/Sgt.) P.C.A. Brennan,   (Dublin)

"London Gazette" Tuesday September 29th 1942

The King has been graciously pleased to approve the following award in recognition of gallant and distinguished service in the field :-

Military Medal (Escapee)

No. 6899188 Corporal George Russell Wheeler,
(St. Nazaire, attd. to SS Bde. No. 2 Commando)

Corporal Wheeler along with Lance-Corporal R.W. Sims, S.L.I. took part in combined operations against St. Nazaire on the 27th march 1942. When it became clear that re-embarkation was impossible, they were instructed to fight their way into the new town in the hope of getting into the country. Early next day they succeeded in entering the new town, where they hid until midnight in a dried up drain underneath a house, where which they found later to be next door to the German Kommandatur. In the moonlight they then made their way through the streets and into the open country, where, whilst hiding in a haystack they were discovered by a Frenchman, who took them to a farmhouse, where they were given food, clothes and money.

For the next fortnight they made their way towards the line of demarcation, being sheltered, fed and directed at the various farmhouses at which they called. On the 13th April, they were conducted to the River La Creuse by the sister of a farmer who had previously sheltered them, and who herself trying to escape from German occupied France. Dodging the patrols they succeeded in crossing the river in spite of the fact that the water came up to their chests and was flowing swiftly.

They had their clothes dried at a nearby farm and continued their journey south to Chaumussay where, at another farm, they received further hospitality in the form of food and shelter. From here they went to La Bousse where they discovered a chateau, the owner of which was very pro-British. After giving them a good dinner and a room in his private suite, he gave them 200 Francs and directed them to Chateaurox which they reached by bus.

As the bus was entering Chateauroux , they saw from a window a notice 'English spoken here' outside a café. They went in, and the owner who had previously lived in England found out the train times and fares to Toulouse for them, gave them wine and showed them where to buy bread. On the way to the bakers they met a Belgian boy of 16 or 17 who had been living in the refugee camp in the town and who asked whether he might accompany them. They consented to this, and with the Belgian, who bought the tickets for them, they took the train to Toulouse the next morning. In Toulouse they were put in touch with an organisation which arranged for their eventual return to this country.

The KING has been graciously pleased to approve that the following be Mentioned in recognition of gallant and distinguished services in the Middle East:—

M.I.D.

Major & Q/M. John Samuel Steer,   (37526) 2nd Bn.

Friday October 23rd 1942

E Alamein, 5th Battalion

"C" Coy and Anti-tank Coy take up positions on Miteirya Ridge to lengthen the line of the 2nd Battalion. "A" & "B" Coys support Royal Engineers clearing the mine-fields. 27th October, "A" Coy on right, "C" Coy on left with "B" in reserve set off. Battalion reach objective by midnight but are pinned down by heavy shell-fire. They lose contact with 4th Battalion on the left but maintain contact with 2nd Battalion on the right. They remain in a defensive position until the 5th November when a general breakout is established at El Alamein.

At 2300 hours, the brigade advanced: 5 Royal Sussex left, objective SNIPE, 4 Royal Sussex on the right, objective WOODCOCK and 2 Royal Sussex in reserve. Their departure was accompanied by wishes of good luck laced with Scottish oaths from the forward Highland positions, while waiting tank crews assured them that if they took their objectives the tanks would advance through them in the morning, a thought that cheered the infantry on their way. The 2nd Battalion were further cheered with a Rum issue that arrived, just before they left, "with the compliments of the Commander of the Highland Division". Some days later, the Royal Sussex Brigade were to have further cause to thank the Highland commander.

In the 5th Battalion the two leading companies were A on the right and C on the left, commanded respectively by Captain Dave Richards and Captain John Stanton. Both companies soon encountered enemy machine-gun and mortar fire but pressed on. A Company, at about seven hundred yards from the start, reached trenches from which some of the enemy troops fled as they approached. They fired on them, but were unable to catch them in the darkness. A few hundred yards further on, having completed their planned number of paces, the leading platoons dug in. C Company on the left encountered much stiffer opposition. About half-way to their objective they ran into strong German defences, including some dug-in tanks. These were dealt with by soldiers who climbed aboard and dropped grenades through open hatches. Entrenched infantry were encountered next. Some fought and then surrendered, others fled in the darkness. In places fighting was bitter, with our soldiers being lured on with cries of "Kamerad" only to be fired upon at close range. Mounting casualties, (including two platoon commanders killed) dust and darkness inevitably led to disorganisation and after 800 yards or so the surviving officers and N.C.O.'s were leading small groups of men from differing sub-units. Stanton found himself with Sergeant Wickham, a rifleman and two Bren gunners. He led them on a dash of some 200 yards to high ground which he took to be the objective. Meanwhile Lieutenant Douglas Sladden, led five riflemen in a flanking move to the same objective, fortunately not grenading Stanton who had got there before him. In the close quarter fighting that ensued on the strongly held position, Stanton, Sladden, Wickham and Cox, one of the Bren gunners, were severely wounded. The other gunner, Woods, and Elbrow, a rifleman were killed. The two surviving soldiers were sent back by Sladden for reinforcements, but they never returned. Too weak to offer resistance, the four wounded men were later given first aid by the Germans who cautiously returned in strength. They lay in the open through the following day while a tank battle raged over them. Regrettably the Crusader tanks of 24 Armoured Brigade were driven back and the following night the four were made prisoner and evacuated.

Meanwhile A and B Companies and Battalion H.Q. dug in on the forward slope to the right of the line of advance of C Company, which had lost about 80% of its fighting strength, including all its officers. The battalion anti-tank guns were brought up and dug in, while the 3" mortars put down retaliatory fire. The 4th Battalion led by Lieutenant-Colonel Ronald Murphy had initially encountered no enemy during their advance. However, their axis clipped the edge of ABERDEEN (held by 1 Gordons) a position of which they had no warning. Challenged in a guttural tones, the 4th opened fire wounding a Highlander. This unfortunate misunderstanding was sorted out after a short delay. The advance continued for nearly 3000 yards before cross-fire from the left fell on the two leading companies. Captain John Harrison, leading D Company in reserve, immediately wheeled his company and assaulted the source of fire with two of his platoons. On closing, the enemy was found to a close leaguer of panzers. The resulting battle decimated D Company with Harrison and many others killed. Nonetheless, their sacrificial action had diverted fire from A and C Companies who had at last found the enemy and captured 200 prisoners and five 88mm guns. By then the battalion had advanced two miles to find WOODCOCK, and Murphy ordered them to dig in. They were now isolated from the rest of the brigade. The ground was very hard and by dawn the men were in shallow scrapes but with their anti-tank guns prominent above ground.

As the sky lightened, tanks were detected approaching from all around. Only three of the battalion's 6 pounders had been able to find their way forward and these opened fire. They were picked off by the German gunners within half an hour. Next to be destroyed were the battalion's and gunner FOO's radio trucks. The battalion was deep in enemy territory and out of contact with everyone.

The Panzers closed in on the unprotected infantry, who waited for our armour to appear and save the day, as promised the previous evening. None came, and before they were crushed, the survivors were obliged to surrender. Among the many killed was Ronald Murphy. Patrols from 1 Armoured Division at Point 32 detected the battalion in its final throes but it transpired that their local commander has considered it unwise to commit his troops so far forward. And Jasper Booty, adjutant of the 2nd Battalion, recalls the frustration of seeing, through his binoculars, the enemy overrunning the 4th Battalion, and being unable to bring down fire without inflicting casualties on our own troops.

The Salient

The morning of 28th October found the 5th Battalion on the left, dug in on a forward slope, secure but unable to move due to hostile artillery and sniper fire. Due to C Company losses, the battalion was echeloned back on the left. The 2nd Battalion was brought up on their right, thus extending the line. During the recce which preceded this move, Lieutenant-Colonel Kenneth Hooper was shot dead by a sniper as he viewed the ground with Captain Keith Tucker, OC A Company. His place was taken by Major Christopher Nix, lately 2 IC of the 4th Battalion.

On the extreme right, the survivors and rear details of the 4th Battalion were taken under command of the 2nd Battalion and formed a defensive flank. Thus 133 Brigade now occupied a salient some 1500 yards deep to the south of the KIDNEY feature. Among the 5th Battalion on the forward slope, casualties rose from constant shelling and sniping. The carrier platoon under Captain Graham Jelley made several gallant forays for re-supply and casualty evacuation, but after several of their vehicles were hit by 88's, these operations were suspended until darkness. Captain Harry Hayes, the adjutant, was killed when answering a call in the radio truck. Lieutenant-Colonel Gerald Bowser, the brigade staff captain recalls the circuit going dead when the 88mm shell struck Hayes' vehicle. However, it was not all one-sided. That night 2nd Battalion mounted a series of patrols to destroy sniper positions and locate others for treatment by our guns and mortars. The following day the battalion had the satisfaction of accepting the surrender of 41 members of 115 Panzer Grenadier Regiment, shelled out of their position. By a happy coincidence, the gunners that provided this fire were from 98 (Surrey and Sussex Yeomanry) Field regiment.

On 29th October, Brigadier Lee ordered the forward troops to withdraw some 500 yards to the reverse slope of the Kidney Ridge which they did that night. As they withdrew, the 5th Battalion was obliged to abandon two of its anti-tank guns. Later, a patrol from B Company having established that the enemy had not re-occupied the position, Lieutenant May took a towing vehicle forward and carefully retrieved the guns one at a time. After withdrawal the Brigade, under constant shellfire, occupied the ground between 5 Black Watch and 1 Gordons. On 31st October it was placed under command of the Highland Division. For operation SUPERCHARGE.

Thus it fell to 133 Brigade to attack again and assist the final breakthrough; but under very different conditions of command to those of 27th October. SUPERCHARGE was to strike the enemy with the Highland Division on the left and the New Zealand Division on the right. 133 Brigade under command of 51 Division was to advance and form a hard shoulder protecting the left flank. The 2nd and 5th Battalions were, respectively, given the task of re-capturing WOODCOCK and SNIPE on the nights of 1st and 2nd November. In the words of Captain Roly Langham, OC C Company, 2 Royal Sussex, "WOODCOCK and SNIPE had held up the whole Eighth Army for over a week and it was therefore an honour for the Battalion to be allotted one of these objectives."

These operations contrasted sharply with those of 27 October. Each move was carefully controlled and operated from a firm base, with Highland and Royal Sussex battalions mutually supporting each other. The operation was covered by massive close artillery fire, with Bofors firing tracer overhead to guide units to their objectives. Thus although in the darkness and chocking dust sub-units sometimes lost direction, errors did not multiply. 2 Royal Sussex took WOODCOCK on the night of 1st November with the 5th swinging south to take SNIPE the following night. Again, there was close quarter fighting, this time mainly with Italians. Langham, who was wounded in this attack, remarked that the Germans appeared to have abandoned their positions under the artillery barrage while their allies had stuck to their posts before surrendering. In the words of Christopher Nix "the attack was completely successful, although I had some very anxious moments. The Battalion was magnificent and fairly tore into the enemy and after an hour's hand-to-hand fighting on the enemy position, all opposition died away." The number of prisoners taken by the Brigade was estimated at over 500.

Nix later found four burnt-out mortar carriers of the 4th battalion on WOODCOCK proving that the battalion had been on their objective. The gratification of avenging the 4th's fate of 28th October needs no amplification.

Despite being committed to an imprecise, dispersed and over hasty operation, 133 Brigade's achievements were significant: (a) 4 Royal Sussex re-opened a breach in the axis anti-tank screen started by 2 KRRC, which the enemy was forced to close, hence his violent reaction as 28th October dawned.

The resources expended in terms of fuel, ammunition and track mileage, and destruction of his anti-tank guns, was in pursuance of Montgomery's policy of attrition.

(b) 133 Brigade's salient during the following days maintained the enemy's sensitivity in the KIDNEY sector, tying down and expending his resources. Second, to consider the operations of 1st/2nd November. The precision with which these attacks were planned by Freyberg and Wimberley had been mentioned. This precision certainly ensured success. 133 Brigade, although reduced to a strength of two battalions, played a vital part in this battle. Remembering that its soldiers had already suffered heavily on 27th/28th and had defended the salient for four days, their achievement in re-capturing WOODCOCK and SNIPE is noteworthy. Their success allowed the Royal to break out to the south west which persuaded Rommel that the battle was lost.

THE BATTLE OF EL ALAMEIN

(Memoirs of Capt. A-R-West, 5th Bn.)

On the 23rd we heard that in the evening the long expected offensive was going to start. We were also told that it was going to be the biggest show yet seen in Africa and that at 2130 hrs the barrage was due to start. That night I was to go down and inspect the wire perimeter round the bastion for breaks which had been damaged by shellfire. I went round with Nobby Clarke and found the dead handler's pliers which he had been holding when he accidentally stepped back and trod on an anti-personnel mine. I found only one gap of fifty yards and having measured the distance from the house gap and went to report to Nobby the second in command. He was standing by a derelict Honey tank and we sheltered by it as the shells came near.

We were on the famous Kattara Track probably the closest part of the line to the enemy. Jerry was only 700 yards away. I was told to get back to Vic Arnett's 'stand to' positions for day time with the remainder of my men before the barrage as Vic's area was very short. Our watches were wrong however and the great barrage started whilst we were talking. 'Zero Hour' had come. All along the line the front the guns spewed up turning night into day. We were the point of a salient and our job was to lie quiet whilst the attacks went in from the north and south. One battery had a gun which fired short and shells landed in and around the bastion. I met later in hospital an officer of that battery and he apologised to me. We had great satisfaction in seeing our guns crash into Jerry's line, sometimes sending up a series of flashed as booby-traps on the wire were set off. Our own machine-guns usually opened up as we came home and brought down fire on us. I reached the truck which had the engine running. The driver leapt out of his slit trench and we were off.

I went over to Vic's dugout when we arrived and spent most of the night drinking and making hot coffee on his captured stove. We watched the colossal barrage and speculated on the outcome. Suddenly Jerry opened up on us. We dived back in again for cover as his area had a bad reputation. We could not sleep that night at all and just went on making coffee and smoking till the dawn, even then the barrage had not stopped completely. The next morning I went back with my platoon to our normal positions. From then on we just sat back and waited for the expected break-through. Our task had been changed, we were not going to man the bastion after all.

For three days we did not get much news except that the French had been pushed off Himeimat. We saw the 'Boston Bus Service' go every hour over our lines, this was a wonderful sight for sore eyes. To the north a big tank battle was going on and lasted four days. I used to go up with Major Shinkwin and Nobby into an O.P. on the ridge and watch the battle in the distance in the direction of Fuka air field. The rumbling of big guns went on continuously and quite often we saw a tank burning, it is a nasty sight to see a great pillar of black smoke curling upwards and knowing that some wretches were probably inside. It was like watching the Aldershot tattoo only people were really being killed all the time. As we did not have much news except occasionally the B.B.C. we could not tell how much progress had been made. Probably people in London were much better informed than ourselves only a few thousand yards away.

Captain Upton came up with the rations to join 'A' Company which meant we were over strength so I was posted to 'C' Company who were all packing up. I was left as I/C. Rear party. Apparently the

"Breakthrough" had come, partly pushed through by 5th Infantry Brigade near Miteirya Ridge. We were to go round to join them and expand the gap. I was given a message to take to 69th Brigade H.Q. which had taken over the headquarters of 7th Infantry Brigade. Having done that I came back to the little camp of the rear party. It was hard to sleep that night as there was a battery of 25 pounders nearby who kept up a regular show during the night. We moved the next morning and I had a new batman, Coleman. Wallace had gone back to 'B' Echelon as I had reckoned he was too old to be kept running about with me. He had served me very well and I told him to get a good job at the base. He was 42 when he came out with the 5th Battalion. I had great difficulty in getting him away from the 1st Battalion and regretted taking him. Eventually he became the senior padre's batman at Division H.Q. Having arrived at 'C' Company's 'A' Echelon we waited for darkness to move up with the rations. Whilst waiting we had a short snooze in the midday sun despite the flies.

The journey was made in twilight and we followed a gap in a big minefield with the aid of a tape. We could see either side of the gap various objects which we were told were the latest Jerry booby-traps one example of which was two high explosive aerial bombs tied together and connected to a trip wire. It soon became very dark and with every shattering bump of the springs of the 15 cwt we felt very naked and noisy. Having reached a place from which we had to walk to carry our rations and ammunition. The artillery seemed to make louder and more permanent noises, it seemed impossible that Jerry had not heard us and sure enough tracer came out of the distance and started spraying in amongst us. I wondered how on earth it hit no one as it was trained on the gap through which we had come. The bullets seemed about three feet off the ground and made a nasty cheap sort of pop, they were probably fired at extreme range because some of the pots and pans were dented and not pierced. It was very hard not to stop laughing aloud as there were many grunts of uncomfortable bodies struggling forward with cumbersome boxes. Such was the good news of the break-through appreciated that all the men were cheerful.

Once we reached Italian sangars we sat down and had a smoke whilst grimy hands were thrust forward with greasy plates to reach the cold tea and 'M' and 'V' ration. By the light of a fag-end the men read the mail to each other. Letters seemed to mean so much more in time of peril and every word was memorialised for the rest of the next day. Such sentences as "I hope you are well and safe" seemed to take on a new import. We were told that it was impossible to move in daylight as our positions were in full view, so the chaps before us, the 1/4 Essex had said they had not moved certainly as the positions were filthy and the smell dreadful. I began to feel weak. The next morning I was called over to Company H.Q. to meet the Commander, Jack De Manio but he had left a message to say he had gone forward with Nick Hanmer to locate the Breda which had troubled us that night before. I could see them both about 200 yards away lying flat on the ground observing the wire in front of them. Then the phone rang and he C.O. spoke. He asked me what was happening and told me to lay on smoke from the three inch mortars just behind me and also get the Company ready to move forward.

Apparently we should have moved the night before but not moved because we had had no signal. I myself was very much out of the picture having just joined a new company and wished I had seen Jack before he went off. However I started to get people ready and lay on the smoke when luckily the sergeant major who had been watching the two in front told me to look and we saw them get up on their feet and walk up to the wire and then turn round towards us. The enemy had gone for there was silence. I went up to meet Jack and told him what had happened and he told me to get ready for an early move. Jack said the enemy had gone during the night and we were to follow up. We 'C' Company would move with 'B' Company on our right. 'B' Company was out to the side and must have over a mile away level with us. All this time the Swedes with their disinterest in the enemy had been strolling about washing and smoking quite oblivious of being in an area which the Essex had claimed was very hot, too hot to move about in daytime. Anyhow, now after the order to move we were strapping equipment on and getting ready for an advance. Most of us had had no breakfast being a (soya link?) no one was much interested. Many ate as they went. We fixed bayonets as we went and fanned out. As we had to walk through a minefield we had to go through in single file. 14th Platoon, my Platoon was to go last.

The wire in front stretched to our left and right as far as we could see. Jack let us through the minefield with a compass. My Platoon was on the right once we got through luckily with no casualties. After about twenty minutes hard walking the right hand section observed one or two figures on the skyline, soon we could see a company. I shouted to Jack and we headed half right to meet them and I saw Ben Clegg the Company Commander in his balaclava and knew we were O.K., it was 'B' Company alright advancing like ourselves in extended order. He waved to us and we went on.

After about five miles our left-hand Platoon stopped and on the sky line we saw two armoured cars. Whose were they? One of them was flying pennants the other looked like a Jerry. We had no anti-tank weapons with us at all, nor did we know the recognition pennants for the day. As it happened the Company had arrived among some small mounds of sand and we crouched down expecting an avalanche of some kind hate directed at us. The cars came towards us with their turrets trained towards the centre of the company where Jack and myself were, thinking up all the recognition points we had ever known. From their actions we guessed the cars were ours and a minute later we were quite certain, phew! With a sigh of relief we pushed on.

We passed an 88mm with its piece spiked and came upon some dugouts. The '88' looked like a naval coast defence gun with a well-constructed emplacement but even so I should not have liked to man it with a barrage of 25 pounders trained on it. We halted about a mile further on, in the centre of a Jerry strong hold. The position was covered with loot, soon everyone was searching clumps of clothing for personal belongings, cameras etc. I found a nice little dump of Jerry parachute boots and spent a few minutes selecting a comfortable pair. My own boots were very uncomfortable and so I gave them to a chap in my Platoon who coveted them, his own he had thrown away having worn them out on the rocks. I found soap and a huge supply of razor blades. One of the men gave me a camera no doubt he had found a very good one himself. I gave my batman a watch and we also found some German and Italian coins which we kept as souvenirs. One item shook me that was a newspaper dated October 16th it was now November the 4th. The paper was the 'Volkischer Beobachter' printed in Berlin. I found some Greek stamps which I sent off home at the end of the month from hospital. Most of these had been printed under German occupation.

The parachutists who had occupied these positions had looted most of Europe judging by their possessions. There were photographs of girls in France, Holland, Yugoslavia and Greece amongst the stuff we found. What was better still than all the bric-a-brac was food and water. We were very thirsty too and found the Jerry lemonade powder very interesting. Jack had set himself up in a very comfortable fly proof dugout and we listened to a nearby tank battle on the radio. We spent a very comfortable night in warm dugouts. I lay in some ex-German officer's shelter reading his maps and thinking about what we had seen and done. This particular shelter was beautifully made, complete with a wooden roof to prevent the sandbags falling in, it even had new flypaper too.

During the afternoon of the next day we were told to go back into reserve as we had advanced too far, in fact four miles too far. Our Company had taken no prisoners but that had not been our fault. Some had been taken by 'B' Company and some by the Raj. Rif. on our left. In fact they had twenty and had been taken only a few yards away. Once back in our former positions we brewed up. As I had made the decision about the ration lorry forward, we had gone without food.

The decision had been either to bring up the rations in a lorry at night or wait till the morning, seeing that we had lost one lorry on the minefield. I had told the C.S.M. to wait till the morning and now we were eating our first meal for some hours although some of us had shared out a few tins of looted food.

I felt very ill after supper and lay down. My illness had been going on for about three days, in fact the night when I had moved up to join Jack. I did not know what was wrong either. I could eat very little and that made me sick. That night as it was November the 5th, Jack, Nick and myself, the three Platoon Commanders fired Verey lights into the air as it was Guy Fawkes night. The lights were Jerry loot and provided many minutes of amusement as some of us had never seen them before being daylight signals and whistling lights. Apparently the same celebrations were going on all the way down the line. The South Africans in particular had gone round units asking for flares for experimental purposes which were now being fulfilled much to the chagrin of the suckers who had handed them over. In the distance Jerry dumps were going up all over the place. The whole of that night was noisy and the enemy was in mass retreat. One particular dump was very awe inspiring and pretty, it contained star shells, flak and Verey ammunition and was a fitting conclusion to the celebrations. We waited three days for transport to take us forward to mop up. During the time we occupied ourselves in examining enemy weapons and defences. The Breda which had shot us up was amongst these items, the actual position included two 47/32mm Breda infantry guns as well as a dozen L.M.Gs. One odd coincidence of war occurred when I went to examine a three tonner which had blown up on the Kattara track only two hundred yards away. Ongoing over the equipment inside I came across a map case belonging to Eggerton Savoy (5th Battalion the Royal Sussex Regiment) the track had blown up on a mine in the road, another vehicle a Dingo had tried to over-take and had blown up the other side of the road.

When the transport did arrive we made a firm base from which to start "salvaging the battlefield" i.e. to collect all useful war material. This became a great competition for different companies who tried to excel each other in their finds. I was detailed to lead the Company, followed up by every available one of our trucks in which to put our loot. We went out armed in case we met any resistance. Jack had told us the night before how the battle was going and we were all in good spirits. We found masses of guns of all calibres, our company alone brought back 16 47/32mm Breda infantry guns, 100 rifles and countless thousands of rounds of ammunition, three large field guns, signal cable in drums. The next few days we pushed further afield. In fact we would set out for a whole day, often going miles over virgin desert to come across some hospital or position. I got to know the ground very well for twenty miles all round. Our dump became bigger than those of the other companies. On the fourth day we found a graveyard of tanks near Sidi Raman. There were perhaps forty to fifty burned-out or destroyed tanks mostly Italian light models. We brought one back, a Spa that would almost work and had to leave it ten miles from our base as the touring hawser snapped when it was getting dark. By now the dump was beginning to grow very large and certain vehicles became the pride of the companies. One day we found an Italian diesel four tonner loaded with ammunition, this we brought back intact except for a battery. There were three ME 109s which had been shot down all within a mile of a Boston. One of them was the latest type. I found it fascinating touring the desert. One of the most interesting days was when we found a hospital for to the south near the Kattara Depression which was deserted. On the ground leading down to the Depression we found three Italian armoured cars which had been burned-out. These had apparently been shot up from the air as there was no marks of tanks or other vehicles. Inside one of the cars the whole crew sat seated as if in action. On tapping the side of the car they all collapsed into a heap of dust. Very gruesome!

It was soon ordained that the Brigade should go for a rest to Hamman beside the sea and some way back. It was now the 16th and Jack threw a party in the company mess. Victor Rich had joined us and spent most of his time in rigging up a first class mess out of captured materials. Cookie had also joined us and was shortly leaving to become D.A.P.M. With us that night were George Taylor, Ben Clegg, Desmond Thornton, Jack, Nick, Victor and myself who was too ill to drink. I went to bed early feeling dreadful. I was to take the advance party off in the morning. I heard that later that night Jack had gone back with the officers of 'B' Company for a drink in their mess and on the way back had lost the track in his 15 cwt., he had spent the night in the back very cold. The two companies were only about three hundred yards away from each other but nevertheless in the desert one often got lost even for the most trifling voyages to the lavatory.

The morning I left was bitterly cold and especially at six in the morning it was not the best hour for one who was virtually a walking invalid. We passed nearby the tank battleground at Sidi Raman and came on to the main coast road. All along the road there was large convoys carrying supplies up to the victorious Eighth Army. At last we arrived near Hamman, there being nothing of interest except a few mud huts there. We reconnoitred a place south of the road suitable for a camp for the Company. Unfortunately we were not allowed to go by sea as the area was full of mines and marshy. Having arrived we brewed up but I could not drink nothing. I lay down in my bivouac feeling ghastly not knowing why. Cole managed to produce a cup of cocoa from the driver of a broken down vehicle which had been mixed up in an accident on the road to Mersa Matruh. That night the rest of the company arrived. I was given a message to say that I would be going on a short course at Brigade Headquarters the next morning. I arrived early and met Major Showers of the 1/2 Gurkhas who was running the course on tactics in the desert. I could not concentrate and that night was the last night I was on my feet until February 10th. the next morning I sent Cole over to the Adjutant apologising for my absence saying that I was ill. The only thing I could eat was mustard, I could not smoke but drink water now. The next day Tom Reilly came to see me and gave me a couple of pills. He told me he would be back soon. He did not come back for another two days. Nick used to see me every evening and tell me he was getting ready to go to Siwa Oasis. Tom Reilly came again, he said he would offer to send me to hospital but rashly I said I would be better in the morning. Alas the night came I could hardly move and my camp bed broke. That night was agony, most awful pains came from my stomach.

In the afternoon of the next day Tom arrived with his ambulance and pushed me in. I said goodbye to Cole and Tom stuck a cigarette in my mouth saying goodbye and don't be away too long my boy, with his usual Scottish accent. I think Tom was known by everyone in the Battalion and loved by them.

Monday October 5th 1942

On the night of 5/6 October, two platoons of "B" Coy under Captain B.B. Clegg, attacked strongly defended enemy observation posts. In a dashing assault six sangars were taken and enemy casualties numbered about 30. Nine Sussex were missing and seventeen wounded.

Prime Minister Winston Churchill sent his congratulations to the Royal Sussex on this occasion.

Monday November 9th 1942

Gallant Fight By Royal Sussex

Cairo, Friday

Along the field telephone system on the El Alamein front flashed the message, "Well done the Sussex." It came from the General Commanding the British Armoured Division, and it was sent to one of his brigadiers.

Behind the four brief words of praise is a story of magnificent courage and determination. The Royal Sussex had been set a task as hard as any set to any troops in the present fighting – and they succeeded brilliantly. They had captured two vital features, driving a wedge into enemy lines.

They Fought for a Week

It was obvious that the Germans would make a determined effort to win back this vital ground. At dawn the enemy attacked with tanks and they overran some forward troops. They shelled the Sussex line and raked it with machine-gun fire.

The Royal Sussex held on grimly. They were cut off. Out there in the lonely salient the Sussex fought for a week. Then the crisis passed. British and Dominion troops advanced in the north, and the right flank was secured.
They were relieved and withdrawn.

"Sticky position"

The story of the fight was told by Private Harvey, of Bexhill. "The attack was thrilling," he said. "Our gunners had prepared the way for us. We found heaps of enemy dead in their deep slit trenches. We didn't occupy those trenches. We knew the enemy would have fixed lines on them.
"On the first morning of their isolation, the position of the Royal Sussex was indeed sticky. The ground to their rear was under continuous fire, and no vehicle could reach them."
They couldn't get shovels up to us, so we had to dig new holes for ourselves with our tin hats, our hands, anything," said Private Harvey.

Colonel at the Gun

"And we dug them, too – we dug for our lives. For three days nothing could reach us. Only Bren carriers could come up, and then at great risk. We lived hard – very hard. Shelling and mortar fire was always heavy, and always we were being sniped at from some derelict tank. But we settled back down to it and gave them back more than they gave us.
We crowned it today by taking 20 prisoners. The Colonel himself manned the Bren gun which drove them from their holes." – Exchange Telegraph Co.

First In North Africa

Battalions of The Royal Sussex Regiment were among the first of our troops to reach North Africa and they took a prominent part in the capture of Sidi Barrani in December, 1940. In the following month they were in action in Eritrea, and after the fall of Keren they returned to the Western Desert.

"London Gazette" Tuesday 17th November 1942

The KING has been graciously pleased to confer "The Efficiency Decoration" upon the following officers of the Territorial Army: —

Col. (T/Brig.) Richard John Penfold Wyatt, M.C. (T.A.R.O.) (35594)
Capt. (T/Mjr.) (A/Lt-Col.) Francis W. Bedford, (7907)

Tuesday November 17th 1942

Panzers Fleeing To Tripoli

ITALIAN OFFER TO ROYAL SUSSEX REGIMENT

[From Reuter's Special Correspondent]
          CAIRO, Monday.

British long-range fighters, flying from the R.A.F.'s newly won airfields at Martuba, are already strafing Rommel's dwindling panzers as far away as El Agheila, on the Gulf of Sirte – the farthest point British troops have ever reached inside Libya. Twice we have recoiled from El Agheila – where Cyrenaica ends and Tripolitania begins – but this time it looks as though General Montgomery is going straight through.
Martuba, 60 miles beyond Tobruk and 175 miles from Benghazi, has some of the finest landing grounds in Africa. From this splendid new base the R.A.F. is keeping up its harassing attacks on the retreating enemy. Allied airmen report that the Axis transport is still "advancing" westwards along the coast road towards Tripoli.
Vehicles and grounded aircraft were destroyed, and heavy casualties inflicted on enemy personnel in a heavy attack on the El Agheila-Agenabia area, while 60 miles west of Aalo over 20 vehicles were destroyed.

Benghazi Bombed

Allied heavy bombers in a night attack on Benghazi Harbour scored hits on the Mole, and the fire following a tremendous explosion could be seen 60 miles away. The Axis is still putting up only slight air opposition. The R.A.F. shot down a Heinkel 111 while U.S. heavy bombers shot down a M.E. 109 and damaged several other planes. American fighter activity had "a most successful sweep" against the retreating enemy, U.S. Army Middle East Headquarters reported today.
Rommel's forces are racing as hard as they can for Tripoli, and any attempt they may make to defend

Agheila sector will only be a rearguard action. It is clear the remnants of the Afrika Korps. Are not offering any resistance, but making the fastest pace they can in their long retreat towards Tripolitania.

Offered To Collect Prisoners

The readiness of many of the enemy troops to become prisoners is illustrated by the story about an Italian captain captured east of Matruh, who said that there were 150 German and Italian soldiers waiting a few away. As the Royal Sussex Regiment operating in this region had no vehicles for transporting prisoners, the Italian captain offered to solve the problem, "I can easily get you 15 of our lorries in working order," he said. "I will get you the vehicles and the drivers. All that you have to do then is collect the prisoners." In charge of a solitary officer, a convoy of 15 Italian lorries, driven by Italians, went out to pick up the prisoners and take them to the British camps. – Reuter

Derna Next

Now that the British have occupied Martuba, there is every likelihood that the occupation of Derna, about 15 miles to the N.W., will follow immediately, possibly today, says Afl, the Independent French News Agency. The whole of Cyrenaica will then have been cleaned up, for it seems very improbable that the enemy will hold on to Benghazi. - Reuter

"London Gazette" Thursday November 26th 1942

The KING has been graciously pleased to approve the following awards in recognition of gallant and distinguished services in the Middle East: —

M.C.

Captain Benjamin Beattie Clegg, (226920)   2nd Bn. (South Bank, Yorks.)

When orders were originally received to raid a strong enemy outpost at Pt. 62 Ruweisat Ridge, Captain Clegg was entrusted with the task of reconnoitring the position to watch the enemy movements and to ascertain the nature of the defences. This he did on four nights preceding the operation, it was largely due to his accurate report that many casualties were inflicted on the enemy.
On the night 5/6 October 1942 he led the assaulting forces which completely cleared the enemy outpost, killing or severely wounding at least 28 of the enemy. He, himself, led one section against the main enemy sangar and killed the occupants with grenades and pistol fire. Although wounded in the hand by a bullet fired at point-blank range he ensured that the enemy position was cleared and then gave orders or the withdrawal of the raiding force. His leadership, bravery and devotion to duty were the main reasons for ensuring the success of the operation.

M.M.

No. 6403983 Corporal James Bungard, 1st Bn. (Hartfield)

On the night 5/6 April 1942 Corporal Bungard was in charge of a section forming part of a raiding force which attacked an enemy outpost surrounded by wire and anti-personnel mines. On advancing to the attack all his section except one man became casualties through anti-personnel mines. He however went forward and alone attacked a sangar from which a L.M.G. was firing on men of another section who were attempting to negotiate another wire obstacle. He threw a grenade through a slit in the sangar and killed the garrison of three. His bravery and devotion to duty saved the lives of many men of the raiding party and materially assisted in the success of the operation.

No. 6403088 Private Alec James Paterson, 1st Bn. (Seaford)

On the night 5/6 April 1942, Private Paterson was a member of a raiding party which attacked an enemy outpost located in sangars surrounded by wire and anti-personnel mines. He bayoneted two men, one of whom was about to open fire with a T.S.M.G. When his section Commander was seriously wounded by fire from an automatic weapon he also bayoneted the firer. He then attempted to assist his section Commander to safety, but was fired on by a L.M.G. from another sangar. He immediately left the N.C.O. charged the sangar with the intention of silencing the gun, when it was put out of action by another soldier. His bravery and devotion to duty was instrumental in overcoming the opposition in the main sangar, thus reducing casualties to the raiding party and contributing to the success of the whole operation.

"London Gazette" Tuesday December 15th 1942

The KING has been graciously pleased to approve that the following be Mentioned in recognition of gallant and distinguished services in the Middle East during the period November, 1941, to April, 1942:-

M.I.D. (M.E.)

Captain (T/Mjr.) Oswald Charles Johnston, (47613) (k.i.a.)
Lieutenant (T/Capt.) Harry Samuel Pollington, (137737)
Lieutenant (T/Capt.) Thomas Chamber Windsor Roe, (121387)
      Lieutenant (Qr. Mstr.) Charles Henry Pocock, (169609)

No. 6397589 Lance-Sergeant H. George,
No. 13048186 Corporal D. Beaton,
No. 6397152 Corporal T. Fowler,
No. 6398261 Corporal J. Gumbrell,
No. 6391476 Private H. Randall,

"London Gazette" Thursday December 17th 1942

The KING has been graciously pleased to approve the following award in recognition of gallant and distinguished services during operations at Madagascar : —

M.M.

No. 4032286 Sergeant Anthony Reginald Seymour, Royal Sussex Regiment, attd. King's African Rifles,
(Sidley, near Bexhill-on-Sea)

"A French 65mm gun opened fire at a range of 75 yards. The platoon commander was severely wounded, three Askari were killed and several others wounded. Five Askari went straight for the gun under heavy rifle fire and machine-gun fire. Through Sergeant Seymour's gallantry and devotion to duty the gun was silenced and the crew captured."

"London Gazette" Thursday January 7th 1943

The KING has been graciously pleased to approve the following awards in recognition of gallant and distinguished services in the field: —

M.C. (Escapee)

Lieutenant (T/Capt.) Rupert Joseph Fuller, (50209) 5th Bn. Royal Sussex Regiment, (R of O)

This officer escaped with two others from Stalag V1 B at Dossel near Warburg on 30th August 1942. They started working on schemes for escape in April and the whole camp had similar ideas. In fact there was a suggestion at one time that all the officers in the camp should attempt escape at the same time. This fortunately was given up.
An apparatus consisting of a ladder 11 feet long with a duck-board at the top to be launched across the space between the two rows of wires was prepared secretly. On the night of the escape, diversions were made in other parts of the camp to cover the escape.
Hiding by day and walking by night, the here officers went via, Paderborn, Bielefeld, Dissen, Lengerich and finally crossed the Dutch frontier on 14 September. The Dutch, though nervous of doing so were anxious to help in every possible way and the three officers with this assistance finally reached a place in Holland at the end of September where they were put in touch with an organization which arranged for their escape through Belgium and France.

M.M. (Escapee)

No. 6399046 Private Frederick Harry Trigg, 4th Bn.
(attd. 2 Commando, Special Service Brigade) (Haywoods Heath)

Private Trigg was attached to 2 Commando for operation 'Musketoon'. This highly successful operation resulted in the destruction of the important electric power plant at Glomfjord in Norway on the night 20th October 1942. Private Trigg throughout showed skill and resolution. He spent, in all, twelve days in enemy-occupied country and eventually made his escape in spite of great exhaustion and hardship.

The written account of the escape.

"We left our home port on 11th September 1942 and disembarked four days later. After the operation, which took place successfully on the night of 20th September, we climbed up to the huts behind Glomfjord power station. Captain Black then told the rest of us to climb the hill as best we could and get away. We divided into two parties, Smith, O'Brian, Christiansen, Fairclough and Trigg going up to the right and the others to the left. However Captain Black called Smith back to administer morphine to a man who had been wounded.
The four of us carried on for four hours up the mountain till 0600 hours on the 21st September when we reached the south side of a valley leading to Storglomvatnet Lake. We had abandoned our haversacks and everything but two colts and our emergency rations. We had two compasses apart from the small compasses in the aid boxes. Christiansen had a large scale map.
The river was deep and rapid and we were on the wrong side of it as the Storglomvanet lake blocked our way east. Christiansen managed to cross with difficulty but shouted to us not to follow him. He was in much stronger form than we were, he was agile as a goat and was going strong when we last saw him again. He still had the map. We now had a compass between the three of us, Christiansen having taken one with him. We were very tired and hungry and we ate all our emergency rations in twenty minutes. We went on down the south side of a valley and during the afternoon had to lie low because four

Messerschmitts and a Heinkel came to look for us. In the evening we were able to cross the river where it reaches the lake and skirted round the north side of the lake.

We walked all night and by Tuesday morning the 22nd September we reached a road going north and south just to the south of South Bjeliaa Lake. It was an appalling journey through snow and blizzard 5,000 feet up. On the road O'Brian approached a farmhouse and came out again with a parcel of food, bread, butter, cheese. After eating this we waded across a stream and up into the woods. O'Brian thought he saw four Germans and we hid in some rocks for an hour. We then marched up the hill (385417 GSGS 4090 K.14) and Sergeant O'Brian lost the remaining compass. We continued, but the following evening we found we had gone in a circle and dropped with exhaustion. We made a big fire and slept there all that night. O'Brian went down to a valley thinking he was going east. We followed him the next day the 23rd September but never saw him again. We went to a second farmhouse at 1200 hours, where they fed us and gave us sandwiches for the journey. They pointed at the valley down which we had come as being the way to Sweden. We had, in fact come down the valley we had previously gone up. We set off again up the same valley and climbed all that night. At the top we passed a woodman's hut. We climbed over to the other side of the mountain, but we were so exhausted that we went back to the hut which we had reached at dawn on the 24th of September. We found some stale cheese, coffee and flour in it. Trigg made some doughnuts, fried the cheese and made some coffee. We slept until midday.

Despairing of getting to Sweden without help, we returned once more to the road intending to go to the farm again but got lost. We decided to follow the road north and came to another farm near South Bjeliaa Lake. The man who opened the door spoke English but was very frightened and said there was a German patrol on the road south. We carried on north along the road and after a few minutes the farmer followed us on a bicycle and told us to go to his parent's house which he pointed out east of the road. We went there and they gave us some socks. Then the son arrived and said he would find a guide for the next morning. He gave us a haversack each full of food and a bottle of milk. He took us a mile further up to another farm from where bedding, pillow and blankets were provided for us in a loft.

At 0500 hours on the 25th September he took us to the top of a hill, gave us a small compass on top of a pen and told us to march east. He drew a rough map showing the route to the north of a lake where we should see some telegraph poles. We were told to follow the line of these, but not too closely, as there was a hut nearby where there was thought to be a Quisling. When we got near the poles, we saw in the snow some tracks of commando boots which we followed but these came to an end and we never picked them up again.

When we got to the Mo-Bod road we had some trouble crossing the river. A motorcyclist passed by on the road, we ducked and were not seen. We eventually found a boat and crossed the river, we made a fire on the top of the hill that night. It was very cold indeed with snow six inches deep. We went to sleep but kept waking up with the cold and making the fire up. The following dawn the 26th September we again set out climbing a very high peak about 5,000 feet. It was sheer rock and we were scared, sometimes snow up to our chests. We eventually got down into a valley intending to keep to valleys in future. We followed this valley down to the Junkerdal-Craddis road, there we found a farm and they gave us food. It was at this farm that we met a man who was to guide us over the frontier. He took us to a friend's house a mile along the stream.

There we had another feed and went to bed at 1500 hours, the guide went out to make arrangements to get us across that night. He woke us at 1800 hours giving them another meal and sandwiches, we left at 0900 hours and went up to his sister's house at Skiati. We had more food there at 200 hours, and left at 2300 hours. The guide and his brother-in-law then accompanied us over the frontier and left us three hundred yards the other side. This was at 0230 hours, the 27th September, they told us to follow the telegraph poles for eight miles to some friends of theirs at Merkenes. The country here is very wooded and we could not have found the house unless we had been directed. We met nine Norwegian refugees here.

We were taken down the Lakes by motorboat and rowing boats to Jackvik where we stayed two days and were disinfected. This consisted of a Turkish bath, having our hair closely cropped, the hair scraped of our bodies and our clothes fumigated. Then we were taken to Jokkmokk where we were interrogated by a Swedish Intelligence Officer, Lieutenant Levi. We said we had escaped from a prisoner of war camp in Norway. Afterwards we discovered that there was no such camp for British prisoners of war but the Swedes did not ask too many questions. Orders then came from Stockholm that we were to be passed through immediately. We were taken to the Legation there and left by plane on the 6th of October, arriving at Leuchars on the 7th October 1942."

"London Gazette" Thursday January 28th 1943

The KING has been graciously pleased to approve the following awards in recognition of gallant and distinguished services in the Middle East: —

M.M.

No. 6396807 Private Walter King, 2nd Bn.

During an attack on the enemy strongpoint known as "Woodcock" (map reference 865296) on the night 1/2 November 1942, Private King was advancing with his Coy when an enemy L.M.G. opened fire at close range, Private King was badly wounded, one of his legs receiving a whole burst of fire. Although in great pain from this wound, he continued to go forward, hopping on one leg, he went straight to the enemy post and bayoneted the three occupants of the trench manning the L.M.G. Only then did he allow the Coy Stretcher-Bearers to attend his wounds. The outstanding gallantry and determination of this action by Private King enabled the advance to continue without further casualties and was of the utmost value in maintaining the momentum of the attack.

Saturday January 30th 1943

Sussex Military award

The King has been pleased to approve the following award in recognition of gallant and distinguished service in the Middle East :-

M.M.

No. 6396807 Private Walter King,

"London Gazette" Thursday February 18th 1943

The KING has been graciously pleased to give orders for the following promotions in, and appointments to, the Most Excellent Order of the British Empire, in recognition of gallant and distinguished services in the Middle East during the period May, 1942 to October, 1942: —

M.B.E. (Military Division) (Egypt)

Major & Q/M John Samuel Steer, (37526) 2nd Bn.

Major Steer has for the past two years been C.O. of 157 Suez Transit camp. During this period he has carried out his duties with the utmost energy, drive and initiative despite exceptional administrative difficulties. By his utter disregard for any personal consideration Major Steer has earned an unchallenged reputation amongst units in transit including troops of all the Allied Forces.

"London Gazette" **Thursday February 25th 1943**

The King has been graciously pleased to approve the following awards for gallant and distinguished service in the Middle-East :-

M.C.

Captain (T/Mjr.) Ronald Hennah Langham, (38113) 5th Bn. (Reading)

This officer commanded one of the Rifle Coys. During the initial phase of the operations from 23 October-5 November 1942 with outstanding courage and skill, and with a complete disregard for his own safety. On no less than three occasions, when his company was subjected to very heavy fire and bombing, his calmness and courage, were manfully responsible for rallying his men when they had become disorganised by the enemy fire.
On 29/30 October, when his company was holding a key position at Pt. 33, the skill and determination with which he handled his company and his aggressive actions, were responsible for silencing many snipers and a M.G. post, and for taking many prisoners.
On 1/2 November, during a night attack carried out by the Bn. on a strong point known as "Woodcock", he led his company in hand to hand fighting and displayed the highest courage. Though wounded, he continued in command of his Coy. Until the position had been consolidated, and only then allowed his hand to be dressed. Subsequently he was seriously wounded and had to be evacuated.

Captain Graham Milton Jelley, (137222) 5th Bn. (Dallington, Northampton)

On 28/29 October 1942, the Battalion of which this officer is O i/c Carrier Platoon, was occupying a very exposed position on the forward slope of a prominent feature, and movement was impossible due to heavy and accurate M.G. and artillery fire, and sniping. The fire was so heavy that it was not possible to get water and rations up to the forward Coys by carrying parties, except at great loss in personnel.
This officer organised his carriers and himself led the sections forward to each coy with the necessary supplies. He was continually under Small arms fire, as well as Anti-personnel shells from Anti-tank Guns, which detect his movements in the moonlight. His carrier was destroyed under him, but he transferred to another, and when his task was completed he went back and recovered his damaged vehicle in the face of the enemy.

M.M.

No. 6407127 Private Daniel Syphas, 2nd Bn.

On 29/30 October, the Coy to which Private Syphas was attached as a stretcher-bearer, was holding a very exposed position in the vicinity of Pt 33, the whole area being under heavy and continuous M.G. and artillery fire, and accurate sniping. With complete disregard for his own safety, Private Syphas moved about this exposed area during the whole period tending wounded and bringing many into the R.A.P.
On one occasion a sergeant was wounded by a bullet from an M.G. firing on a fixed line, but despite the grave risk of going into this dangerous zone on which any movement was fired upon, Private Syphas jumped out of his trench, went over to the sergeant, dressed his wounds and brought him in.

His consistent bravery and devotion to duty were an inspiration to all those around him. And fully deserves the award asked for.

Saturday February 27th 1943

Royal Sussex at El Alamein

"COURAGE LOYALTY AND GUTS"

The part played by The Royal Sussex Regiment in the battle of El Alamein was the subject of a striking tribute in a letter sent to Colonel F.G. Langham, C.M.G. by Sergeant E. Beaney, and old Royal Sussex man.
Sergeant Beaney, in his letter, which was read at yesterday's annual meeting of the Regimental Association, said he would like it to be known what a great show the officers, n.c.o's and men of the Regiment put up at El Alamein.
"Their courage, loyalty, guts and devotion to duty under hellish conditions", he wrote, "is something of which they and the people of Sussex can be proud."

It explained the meaning of the "bulldog breed", Sergeant Beaney wrote, adding "Ask Jerry".

Wednesday March 17th 1943

Royal Sussex Commando's M.M.

At a recent investiture at Buckingham Palace, the recipients of honour included Frederick Trigg, of 4th Bn. The Royal Sussex Regiment, who, with John Fairclough, of the Grenadier Guards, both members of a Commando, received the Military Medal. They would not disclose what they had won the medals for.

"London Gazette" Tuesday March 23rd 1943

The KING has been graciously pleased to confer " The Efficiency Decoration " upon the following officers of the Territorial Army: —

The Royal Sussex Regiment

Maj. Alfred Eric Percival Bridge (24420) 4th Bn.
Capt. John Eric Parris (33282) 5th Bn.

Friday March 26th 1943

Sussex Hero Went to Palace with Mother and Bride

Last week at Buckingham Palace, Private Frederick Harry Trigg, 1, Beach Cottages, St. John's Road, Haywards Heath, received from his Majesty the King, the Military Medal which has been awarded him for gallantry and bravery while on Special Service in the field. He was accompanied to the Palace by his mother, and by the bride whom only seven days previously he had married in Scotland, Miss Jean Hazlett, of 16, Broom Crescent, Ochiltree, Ayrshire.

A Territorial

Private Trigg was born at 1, Beach Cottages, and his father was a Petty Officer in the Navy; he came right through the last war without a scratch. For four years Private Trigg has been in the 4th Royal

Sussex Territorials when they were mobilized for this war, he previously being a milk roundsman in the employ of Mr. J.L. Felix, South Road. He is an Old Boy of St. Wilfrid's School, played for St. Wilfrid's F.C., and plays Army football now. Friends who have seen the film "Next of Kin" may have spotted him in it.

Wednesday April 7th 1943

The attack on El Meida kopje at 0400 hours by "D" Coy followed by "B" and "C" Coys worked their way to the ridge of the escarpment. Within 30 minutes El Meida and 600 yards of the western end of the anti-tank ditch had been captured along with about 300 German prisoners.
The attack on the anti-tank ditch was at its height and the left flank Brigade was pinned down, a platoon of Royal Sussex went round to the rear of the ditch and charged with bayonets, capturing four L.M.G's and some prisoners.

"London Gazette" Thursday April 22nd 1943

The King has been graciously pleased to approve the following awards for gallant and distinguished service in the Middle-East :-

Bar to D.S.O.

Lt-Colonel Lashmar Gordon Whistler, D.S.O., (13017) 4th Bn.

From 28 Jan until 10 Feb Brigadier Whistler in command of 131 Bde. Was in charge of operations along the coast road West of Tripoli. He conducted these operations with great skill, forced the enemy back 70 miles and inflicted much damage and casualties to their rearguards. Always in front himself, he set a high example of courage and determination. His was the driving force which sustained the momentum of the advance over 14 days. Frequently under shellfire, often bombed and machine-gunned from the air, constantly recconnaisssancing over ground known to be un-cleared of mines, he showed complete disregard for all his personal safety and an inspiring example to all ranks to get on and overcome all difficulties.
His skill and bold leadership was reflected throughout the Bde. which he led so successfully.

"London Gazette" Tuesday May 4th 1943

The KING has been graciously pleased to approve that the following be Mentioned in recognition of gallant and distinguished services in the field: —

M.I.D. (M.E.) ESCAPE AND EVASION AND SPECIAL OPERATIONS

No. 6398332 Private Reginald James Ballard, 5th Bn.

I was captured between ST OMER and HAZEBROUK on 28 May, 40. I was taken to HAZEBROUK, whence the column of P/W began marching next day, I escaped with Pte. Bryant of my unit (S/P.G. (F) 120) and another soldier on 7 June near CAMBRAI by slipping away from the column. We reached Etaples about 19 June and were sheltered at a farm till about 8 or 9 Aug, when we and other British soldiers set of for UNOCCUPIED France in small groups. I was recaptured at FRENCHQ on 9 Aug with two soldiers named LONGMAN and

JOHNSON who, I believe, are now in GERMANY. We were taken to MONTREUIL and thence to LILLE, where we were put into what had been a French barracks.

I escaped with Pte. LAKE (S/P.G. (F) 534) on 4 Sep by scaling a wall and dropping 15 feet into a backyard. We were sheltered in a cafe in LILLE from 12 Sep to 27 Nov, when we left for UNOCCUPIED France with a Frenchman who was trying to reach the U.K.

We travelled by train via AMIENS and PARIS to CLERMONT FERRAND, where we stayed a month at a French Demobilisation centre. About 29 Dec we went to VICHY, where the U.S. Consul gave us 1500 frs. Each for clothes and fare to MARSEILLES (arrived 31 Dec).

After three days in a hotel we went to MORT ST. JEAN, where internment was very lax. When the camp moved to ST. HIPPOLYTE (about 7 Jan 1941) I remained at a cafe in MARSEILLES. At a seaman's mission I met Dvr. CLAYTON (S/P.G. (F) 993) who invited me to join a party to ORAN. The other members of the party were Sgt, TURNER R.O.A.C; Sgt. KNIGHT (S/P.G. (-) 986). I believe the arrangements were made by Capt. MURCHIE (S/P.G. (-) 681).

We were arrested on 26 Jan 41 in ORAN, where we were five or six weeks in prison, and were afterwards interned at CARNOT, MEDEA, AUMALE and LAGHOUAT. We were released on 12 Nov 42.

At LAGHOUAT I got out on the tunnel escape scheme on 7 Jun 42 but was recaptured after covering 15 km with two companions. About a month later I again got out of the camp in a party which included L/Cpl. DAVIES (S/P.G. (Tunisia) 999) and four others. I was liberty for about six hours.

Wednesday May 12th 1943

A German Officer of a Panzer Division arrived at Royal Sussex Headquarters to arrange for a surrender of a Panzer Grenadier Regiment. The following morning at 0600 hours 3,000 Germans lay down their arms. Later on of the morning 13th May, the Royal Sussex reached Ste. Marie du Zit and rounded up another 500 prisoners.

Wednesday June 2nd 1943

Royal Sussex Officer Took Von Arnim Prisoner

COUNTY REGIMENT'S NOTABLE PART IN THE AFRICAN CAMPAIGNS

"YOU GOT THROUGH BECAUSE YOU WERE BOLD"

An officer of The Royal Sussex Regiment received the surrender of General von Arnim during the fighting in Tunisia just before the close of the victorious campaign. This fact is revealed in an account of the part played by the County Regiment not only in the fighting in Tunisia but also in the campaigns in the Western Desert and Eritrea.
A battalion of the Regiment was in the Middle East at the beginning of the war, and as part of the 4th Indian Division it fought in East Africa until the conquest of Eritrea. After the fall of Keren, Asmara and Massowa, the Division returned to the Western Desert in the spring of 1941 to help to halt the first Axis counter-offensive.
The Royal Sussex was the British battalion of the Indian Infantry Brigade which advanced from Port Sudan southward along the Red Sea coast, threatening Keren from the north. Consequently it took no part in the assault on the mountain fortress and does not appear in the accounts of the actual fighting.

But the movement counted for something in the final abandonment by the Italians of their remaining defences and the flight into Abyssinia.

Decisive Action

In September, 1941, the Royal Sussex were again on the western frontier of Egypt, preparing for the second invasion of Cyrenaica, under General Auchinleck. They were heavily engaged in the drive northwards behind the Axis strongholds west of the border wire, Sidi-Omar, Libyan Omar and Sidi Omar Nuovo were captured, and later Rommel's massed raid was defeated and driven back westwards. At Sidi Omar Nuovo The Royal Sussex did splendid work. The taking of the place was a fine achievement, and its successful defence later against German tanks and guns was one of the decisive actions of the campaign. About 40 Mark111 tanks attacked from all sides of the position in turn. They charged repeatedly and got within 300 yards of our infantry. They left 16 wrecked tanks behind when they withdrew, having accomplished nothing.

In the next phase of the battle The Royal Sussex were part of a division which swept north and then west along the Trigh Capuzzo. This movement did much to convince Rommel that the campaign was lost and he must evacuate Cyrenaica. In the advance through Tobruk, Gazala, Derna, and Cyrene and Barce to Benghazi the Royal Sussex had much hard fighting. It was they who swooped upon the aerodrome at Derna, captured many enemy aircraft on the ground, and shot down six out of eight Junker transport planes which came in to land a half-light. Previously the battalion had been attacked many times by dive-bombers and had replied with Bren gun and rifle fire.

From Benghazi, when Rommel counter-attacked in January, the Brigade to which the Royal Sussex belonged broke out after being cut off. It drove south and then turned east, marching 200 miles through the desert, beating off enemy attacks, and bringing with it – when it reached the Gazala-Bir-Hacheim area – many prisoners. In a message of congratulation General Auchinleck said : "You got through because you were bold-always be bold."

From Mareth to Cape Bon

In General Montgomery's great victory they fought on the decisive north sector when the break-through was made. A detachment of the Regiment reoccupied the Siwa Oasis. When the Eighth Army reached Tunisia they were called upon once more. In the Mareth Line battle their division forced the Hallouf Pass, and in 60 hours' fighting in difficult, mountainous country cleared the area between Hallouf and Foum Tatahoume, capturing Toujane, Zelton and Mamata. The advance on E Hama and these successes turned the whole Mareth position.

After the Eighth Army's capture of Enfidaville the Royal Sussex were amongst the troops transferred to the First Army in the Medjez el Bab area and joined in the great decisive thrust down the Medjerda valley to Tunis. The Cape Bon Peninsular was sealed off by the division with which the Royal Sussex had fought for two years, sharing in its victories. It helped to break down the last defences and captured many thousands of Axis prisoners. General von Arnim's surrender was made to an officer of the Regiment.

Proud History

The Royal Sussex Regiment (the old 35th Foot) or "The Orange Lilies" – a nickname which dates from the capture of Quebec when the men of Sussex destroyed the famous Royal Roussillion Regiment of the French Army and took their colours, which bore lilies of gold – was raised in 1701 by the Earl of Donegal. The Archduke Charles, whose claims to the Spanish throne were supported by Great Britain, thanked the Regiment for its part in the defence of Barcelona in 1706.

It stormed Quebec in 1759; the first British flag flown on the Island of Malta (in 1800) was the King's Colour of the Regiment; it fought at Maida and Waterloo; and for years in India during the Mutiny.

The Royal Sussex served in the South African War from 1899-1902, and their bass drum – being the only drum of its kind in the Army which had survived the advance – had to be passed from regiment to regiment to play for the march past of the Army before Lord Roberts at Pretoria. Twenty-three battalions of the Regiment fought in the 1914-1918 war, and casualties amounted to 6,800. The 2nd battalion formed part of the thin screen of British infantry which alone stood between the German Armies and the Channel in the autumn of 1914.

"Times"

HOW VON ARNIM SURRENDERED

Royal Sussex Badge Recognised

From our own correspondent
CAIRO June 8th

One of the most interesting sidelights on the collapse of the German Armies is given by the account issued here today of the circumstances in which General Von Arnim gave himself up to our forces.
When Arnim and his staff officers approached the British troops under the protection of a white flag on May 12 and signified their willingness to surrender, the German commander immediately recognised the cap badge of the troops awaiting him. They were those of The Royal Sussex Regiment, and Lieutenant-Colonel J.B. Glennie, their commander, who stepped forward to await him, was greeted by the German general with the words : "I fought against your regiment in the last war," a coincidence which appeared to give Arnim some relief from the emotion of the ceremony.
The surrender took place in an unnamed wadi some 10 miles north of Zaghouan, where Arnim and his staff had been sheltering in the later stages of the North Africa battle. Major Bryant, of The Royal Sussex, whose home is in Cheam, Surrey, was riding with the advanced guard and his battalion's carriers were some distance in front. The battle was still in progress and the carriers were held up by the fire of 20mm guns.

WHITE FLAG IN THE CAR

"It was essential to get the mortars up to them quickly as possible, so we went straight down the road and caught the carriers about 10.30," Major Bryant said. "A few moments before we reached them two German staff cars came along with a white flag, and the occupants told the carrier officer that they wanted to see the army commander. They also asked that fire should cease until they had returned from their mission.
"I told them that this was impossible, as we had orders to push on. Eventually I agreed to wait 10 minutes until they found the battalion commander. The carrier commander, Captain Peter Cavallier, escorted them back, and we waited 10 minutes and then proceeded. We had gone on another 10 miles when another German staff car bearing a white flag came along. It contained two officers who asked that we should wait until the mission returned. I decided to wait another 10 minutes in case any orders came by wireless. A motor-cyclist came into view and gave himself up. He stayed with me until the Germans turned and made off, when he turned back also. We followed him.

SINGING PRISONERS

"Soon we came to German H.Q. in the wadi. Some German officers were getting their men together so that they could surrender. They formed into squares and were addressed by their officers. They then gave three 'Heils', and began marching away, singing at the top of their voices.
There were thousands of them. I wirelessed the commanding officer, who came up, and we then realized that Arnim had a couple of furnished caravans."
Of the surrender, Lieutenant-Colonel Glennie said "von Arnim looked tired after the strain of the last few weeks. He recognised my cap badge and said that he had fought my regiment in the last war. I reminded him that the Germans themselves had called it the 'iron regiment'. Our divisional and corps. commanders arrived to take the formal surrender, and von Arnim and his staff were escorted away."
It is understood that Arnim's caravans are being taken to India for inspection there.

"London Gazette" Tuesday June 15th 1943

The KING has been graciously pleased to approve the following awards in recognition of gallant and distinguished services in North Africa: —

M.M.

No.6405479 Private Raymond Reginald James Weller, att. 3rd Bn. Para. Regt. Army Air Corps. (Haywards Heath)

For most conspicuous gallantry and devotion to duty in DJEBEL ABIOD Sector.

On 13 Mar 43 this soldier while under command of 1st Bn. Parachute Regiment, was acting as scout to his section which was taking part in a counter-attack on a 1st Bn. Position. A very heavy burst of MG fire was encountered but Pte. Weller pushed straight on and managed to snipe and kill the gunner. Shortly afterwards he was grenaded but showing the greatest coolness he continued to advance firing from the hip and shouting encouragement to his section and derision at the enemy. It was largely due to the courage and dash of this soldier that the counter-attack was successful.

"London Gazette" Thursday June 17th 1943

The KING has been graciously pleased to approve the following awards in recognition of gallant and distinguished services in the Middle East: —

D.S.O.

T/Lt-Colonel Charles Edward Anson Firth, (24722)   The Gloucestershire Regiment   (Ceylon)

Lt-Colonel Firth commanding the 1st Bn. Royal Sussex Regiment during the night attack on the hills at Akarit. This operation was one of the upmost difficulty owing to the nature of the country. Early on in the battle, Colonel Firth had three Coy commands, his Battalion I/O, most of his Bn. Signals and his Adjutant killed or wounded. Realising the extreme gravity and the difficulties of this situation and knowing that the whole Army plan depended on his success in securing the vital Meida feature, Colonel Firth personally went up to his Coys, in some cases personally led them and at all times displayed to officers and men of the Division an inspiring example of courage and cool skill.

His gallant conduct, his coolness and utter disregard of danger in the heavy shell and small arms fire of this battle at night in the mountains led to the successful capture of the vital Meida feature by the appointed time.

Major (T/Lt-Col.) John James McCully, (32030) 5th Bn. (Cranbrook)

Throughout the past period of operations from 23 October-5 November, Lt-Colonel McCully has displayed a very high order of leadership and calmness under fire, in the face of the most difficult conditions. On the night 27/28 October, his Battalion was ordered to carry out a night attack, with but the scantiest preparations, and in the face of heavy opposition. Owing to the circumstances beyond Lt-Colonel McCully's control the Battalion did not quite reach its objective and found itself next morning holding a very exposed position under heavy and accurate small arms and artillery fire. Despite this, however, they held for a day and a half before being withdrawn. It was mainly due to Lt-Colonel McCully's coolness and leadership that the Battalion got as far as it did, and then maintained itself there for so long. Subsequently, on the night 1/2 November, his Battalion carried out another night attack and once again this officer's leadership and his complete disregard of his own safety were instrumental in making this attack successful.

D.C.M.

No. 553755 Sergeant Sidney George John Davies,   4th Bn. (Rustington)

North Africa: On 28 October, 1942, No. 553755 Sergeant Davies was in command of a Troop of A/Tank guns, which, with a few infantry were all that remained of his Battalion after it had been attacked by enemy tanks in a very exposed and isolated position known as "Woodcock", and over-run.
This small detachment held an advanced position just behind a low ridge at Pt. 33. Later in the day, four enemy tanks appeared over the ridge and brought heavy fire to bear on the detachment.
Sgt. Davies, however ran to one of the guns and acting as No. 1 engaged them knocking out three German Mk.111 tanks and causing the fourth an Italian Mk.13, to surrender. His coolness under fire and his gallant conduct undoubtedly prevented the enemy from breaking through the position at a spot where its consequences would have jeopardised the safety of the rest of the Brigade.
(Military Medal Recommended)

M.M.

No. 6401005 Private Eric Eaton, 4th Bn. (Herne Bay)
On 28 October 1942 Private Eaton went up to the forward Coys to evacuate some severely wounded men. The whole area was subjected to intense shell and machine-gun fire. Private Eaton eventually succeeded in getting back to the R.A.P. in a carrier. On the following day, it was necessary to evacuate a man who was in a critical condition, to the A.D.S. It was not possible for ambulances to approach the R.A.P. owing to it being shelled.
Private Eaton drove the man to the A.D.S. in a 15 cwt. Truck and in doing so, contributed in saving the man's life. Private Eaton subsequently drove several times between the R.A.P. and the A.D.S. to bring up valuable medical supplies, food and water. Private Eaton displayed most commendable gallantry and devotion to duty throughout the action, without thought for his own personal safety, and in doing so, was an inspiration to all his comrades.

No. 6400335 Sergeant Dennis George Wells, 5th Bn. (Ninfield)

On the night of the 27 October 1942, the Mortar Officer was missing during a night attack. Since when this N.C.O. has been in command of the Platoon and has carried out his duties with zeal and marked ability. On the 28/29 October, while in an exposed position, he was able to get his mortars into action against an enemy Anti-Tank gun and thus able to assist in the operation of carriers bringing up supplies. His leadership and devotion to duty on numerous occasions have been a source of inspiration to his men. On 2 November, while an Infantry Battalion and tank attack on the enemy was taking place on the flank, the tank came dangerously within range of an 88mm Anti-tank gun, with mortar H.E. and smoke, and was so able to blind the gun and so save severe casualties amongst the tanks. This enemy post soon afterwards blew up their gun and vacated the post.

No. 6403785 Sergeant Henry George White, 5th Bn.   (Balham)

On the night 27/28 October 1942, 5 Royal Sussex Regiment was carrying out a night attack on a locality known as SNIPE in conjunction with 2 Royal Sussex Regiment on the right. Owing to the darkness and loss of direction, a gap opened between these battalions, and it was vitally important to the operation that touch should be re-gained at once. This N.C.O. volunteered to effect liaison with a small patrol. Despite heavy and accurate fire on fixed lines over part of the area to be traversed, and the fact that part of it was held by the enemy, this N.C.O. successfully led his patrol through, established touch with the Battalion on the right, and then re-joined his own unit. On a second occasion later in the operation, he successfully carried out a similar patrol work at a critical stage, under conditions of grave danger, and was always to the fore in volunteering for any difficult or dangerous work.
His cheerfulness and complete disregard for his own safety, set a very high example and undoubtedly inspired the men to follow his example.

Tuesday June 22nd 1943

BOTH WINNERS OF THE M.C.

News has been received in Brighton that Lieutenant Lawrence William Weeks, of the Royal Sussex Regiment has been awarded the Military Cross, and has also been promoted to the rank of Captain. By a remarkable coincidence Captain Weeks' father, Mr. William E. Weeks, the well-known solicitor, also served as an officer of the Royal Sussex Regiment in the last war and was awarded the Military Cross. It is thought that the honour of father and son both serving in the same regiment and both winning the M.C. is exceptional. Captain Lawrence Weeks, who is 24 years of age, was born in Brighton and educated at the Brighton, Hove and Sussex Grammar School. He was on the eve of taking his final examination as a solicitor to become a member of his father's firm when he joined up as a recruit, and after a few months training was commissioned into the Royal Sussex Regiment, and went overseas in 1940.

As it is well known, the Sussex Regiment went through the thick of fighting in North Africa, took part in the capture of von Arnim and 300,000 Germans.

Thursday June 24th 1943

Sussex Major read Dickens in Heat of Battle

Now sitting up in bed in a South African military hospital is Major R.H. Langham, the Royal Sussex Regiment, who was awarded the Military Cross recently for conspicuous gallantry at El Alamein last October. For eight months he has had his left arm in plaster, soon it will be well again.

When Major Langham led his company into action to attack the now famous "Kidney Ridge" feature, he took with him a copy of "Pickwick Papers." For 12 days his battalion held the ridge under tremendous fire, and throughout that time he set a magnificent example of courage to his men.

Quite early in the battle his colonel was killed near to him, and later, when his company was dive-bombed, shelled, and under mortar and anti-tank fire, he showed unequalled spirit. When things got really bad, and our men were forced to get down into their shallow trenches, Major Langham could been seen quietly reading his "Pickwick Papers." At other times he was out on patrol with his men, or helping to bring in the wounded.

So successful was one of his patrols of five men that on 29th October it returned from a daylight raid of the enemy trenches with 50 men and an anti-tank gun crew as prisoners-all Germans.

Wounded He Carried On

On the night of 1st November, Major Langham led his company forward in another night attack. This was the one in which the Royal Sussex attacked the central sector of the German line, together with the 51st Highland Division. During the advance Major Langham's company came under enemy fire early, and a bullet shot his compass from his hand and shattered his thumb.

Yet he carried on commanding his company with his wound roughly bandage, and after taking part in fierce hand-to-hand fighting, ascertained that the Germans and Italians in his sector had all been killed or captured.

He then supervised the digging in of his company, and prepared for a likely counter-attack, nor would he give up his command until he was forced to the following evening, when a direct shell-burst shattered his collar bone.

Major Langham was formerly Magistrates' Clerk to the Borough of Reading. His home is at Wargreaves, reading, and at present his wife and two years old son, Nicholas, are living at Langton Green, Stonewall Park Road, Tunbridge Wells. The son of Colonel F.G. Langham, the Hastings Magistrates' Clerk, he was recently visited in hospital by his brother, Commander Guy Langham, R.N., who was awarded the O.B.E. in the last New Year's Honours List.

"London Gazette" Thursday June 24th 1943

ROYAL SUSSEX MEN

The King has been graciously pleased to approve that the following be Mentioned in recognition for gallant and distinguished services in the Middle East during the period 1st May, 1942 to 22nd October, 1942 :-

COMMANDS AND STAFF
Colonel Thomas Francis Vere Foster, C.B.E., M.C.   (3175)   (Late Royal Sussex Regiment)

INFANTRY

ROYAL SUSSEX REGIMENT (Ist Bn.)

Lieutenant (T/Capt.) Vincent Warwick Calmady-Hamlyn (64149)

Lieutenant Charles Henry Covington, (164693)
No. 2027714 Sergeant Jack A. Longthorne
No. 5626241 Private (A/Cpl.) G.E. Field
No. 6395113 Private T. West

Monday June 28th 1943

Colonel John Leslie Von der Heyde, who has just been promoted to the rank of Brigadier, is a Brighton man. In 1914 he joined the 6th battalion of the Royal Sussex Regiment, and after serving some time obtained his commission, receiving the Military Cross and being mentioned in dispatches. He then became a Staff Captain and afterwards Brigade Major, and subsequently G.O.S. 111, of a division.
On peace being declared, he served on two occasions as Adjutant to the 1st Battalion Royal Sussex Regiment, and also as Adjutant to the 4th Battalion Royal Sussex Regiment. He was promoted Captain in 1929, and Major in 1938, and served in Palestine, being awarded the Palestine Medal and Clasp.
At the outbreak of the present war he was stationed in Egypt on the Staff and appointed D.A.A.G. Promoted Lieutenant-Colonel and appointed A.A.G., he was shortly afterwards promoted again to the acting rank of Colonel and received the O.B.E. in December, 1941. On 16th April, 1943, he was promoted to the war substansive rank of Lieutenant-Colonel, Temporary Colonel and acting Brigadier.

"London Gazette" Thursday July 8th 1943

The KING has been graciously pleased to approve die following awards in recognition of gallant and distinguished services in the Middle East: —

M.C.

Captain Geoffrey William Hawkes, (129367) 1st Bn.

As Liaison officer from HQ 7 Infantry Brigade, attached to 1 Royal Sussex Regiment during the night 5/6 April 1943 for the attack on Djebel el Meida and on the Anti-Tank ditch defences for earthworks. From 0040 hrs. 6 April, the Battalion continuing to advance under heavy mortar and machine-gun fire throughout the night and Captain Hawkes' coolness was an example to all ranks. Just before first light, seeing that fire was still coming from the right of the Battalion objective, he collected together a party of men, ordered them to fix bayonets and led them forward to clear the remainder of the objective. They did this after some resistance and they captured several prisoners and a troop of 75mm guns.

Captain Hawkes then assisted in getting these guns into action against the enemy on the right flank who were holding up the 50 Division attack. His party was then shelled and heavily fired on by machine-guns, the latter he silenced with rifle fire.

Captain Hawkes bravery, initiative and leadership very substantially contributed to the successful operation of the right of the Battalion's objective, which in turn prevented the force from the rear being eliminated in the 50 Division attack.

Captain Sidney Joseph Fowler Upton, (90925) 1st Bn.

On the night 5/6 April 1943, Captain Upton was commanding B Coy. R.S.R. during the attack and capture of the Djebel el Meida NW of Wadi Akarit. At 0040hrs while still in close night formation the battalion came under intense mortar fire and M.M.G. fire and Captain Upton was wounded by a splinter in the leg, which though superficial was exceedingly painful.

The Battalion was immediately ordered to change direction, which presented great difficulties owing to the pitch darkness, the precipitous nature of hill country and heavy and accurate enemy fire. In spite of this Captain Upton kept complete control over his Company.

Throughout the rest of the night, when under heavy and constant mortar fire, and in spite of considerable pain in his leg, this officer set an outstanding example of coolness, courage and determination. At dawn he led his Coy. In exploiting the success of the Battalion clearing many pockets of resistance.

The bravery and powers of personal leadership and endurance shown by Captain Upton during the night and the following day when under M.G. and shell fire were beyond all praise, and his bearing under difficult and dangerous conditions in keeping with the highest traditions of the service.

Captain Lawrence William Weeks, (155698) 1st Bn.

On the night 5/6 April 1943 during the attack on Djebel el Meida feature NW of Wadi Akarit, this officer showed outstanding courage, coolness and resource in the face of heavy enemy fire under the most difficult conditions. "D" Coy. in which Captain Weeks was then platoon commander was leading the Coy. to attack the objective. Owing to violent mortar fire before it had deployed to attack there was some disorganisation and the Bn. had to wheel sharply to move towards its objective.

"D" Coy. was then ordered to push on towards the objective known to be strongly held by the enemy. In the pitch darkness and owing to the precipitous nature of the ground, two platoons of "D" Coy. lost touch. Captain Weeks, however, who had become responsible for navigation, unerringly led his platoon and Coy. on to the foot of the objective. This was done in spite of heavy mortar and M.G. fire.

At 0445hrs. while awaiting the final order to assault, the company commander was killed. Captain Weeks immediately took over command and when our Artillery concentration ceased, led his men with great dash and captured the objective in the face of stubborn resistance.

Using Djebel el Meida feature as a base, he then started clearing enemy posts in the vicinity, taking many prisoners. He held on and reorganised the position until the arrival of the rest of the Battalion in spite of continuous enemy fire.

The initiative, powers of leadership and bravery under fire displayed by this officer were beyond all praise and were largely instrumental in the final success by his Battalion.

Captain Frederick Wallace Phillips, Chaplain, (128829) 1st Bn.

As unit Chaplain, Captain Phillips accompanied 1 Royal Sussex Regiment on the night approach to, and capture Djebel el Meida on 5/6 April 1943. On reaching area 105522 the Battalion came under heavy mortar and machine-gun fire which continued throughout the night. Captain Phillips, who was attached to the R.A.P. immediately assisted the M.O. in tendering and ministering to the wounded even though the R.A.P. was under continuous mortar fire which wounded many of those inside.
Wherever help was needed in bringing wounded he always went out and assisted, though there was much machine-gun fire. When dawn was breaking Captain Phillips helped carry away the wounded who were under direct observation of the enemy on feature 094513. He then accompanied the R.A.P. to the SW end of the Anti-Tank ditch and continued to do his work. Later this was subjected to a shelling by heavy enemy guns and Captain Phillips frequently left the R.A.P. during the shelling to help bring in the wounded.
His bravery and devotion to duty, and coolness under fire, set a fine example and gave confidence to all ranks.

Captain Thomas Reilly, M.B. R.A.M.C. (114190) 1st Bn.

As unit Medical Officer, Captain Reilly accompanied the 1 Royal Sussex Regiment on the night approach to, and capture Djebel el Meida on 5/6 April 1943. On reaching area 105522 the Battalion came under heavy mortar and machine-gun fire which continued throughout the night. Captain Reilly immediately set up his R.A.P. and attended to all wounded, which included many from other units of the Brigade. The R.A.P. was under continuous mortar fire throughout the night, and many of those inside were wounded, Captain Reilly continued with his duties with great courage and coolness.
As dawn was breaking it was apparent that the R.A.P. was in direct view of the enemy on the feature 094513 and that it would shortly be subjected to aimed machine-gun fire. Captain Reilly therefore organised carrying parties from troops in the vicinity and called forward transport so that the large number of casualties was cleared before light. He then rejoined the Battalion and set up his R.A.P. again at the SW end of the Anti-tank ditch and resumed his work and to give aid to the more seriously wounded before they could be moved to the R.A.P.
His bravery and devotion to duty set an example and gave confidence to all and in addition his organising abilities saved further casualties and many lives.

Bar to M.M.

No. 6403983 Sergeant James Bungard, M.M. 1st Bn.

On the night 5/6 April 1943, during the attack by 1 Royal Sussex Regiment on the Djebel el Meida Hill NW of Wadi Akarit. While acting as Platoon Sergeant, this N.C.O. showed courage, initiative and devotion to duty of the highest order. His Coy was under very heavy and accurate mortar fire in a wadi in pitch darkness. He showed the greatest coolness in rallying his platoon and helping them together in the advance over very difficult country in the darkness.
He led his men to the wadi up a steep hillside with great dash and it was largely due to his leadership and determination to close with the enemy that his platoon captured its objective. At dawn, not content with this he led some of his platoon well beyond the objective to the next ridge. where his party captured 4 enemy field guns and their crews. During the consolidation period 6 April, he was always to the forefront under heavy enemy fire, cooly directing fire from the exposed positions without any regard to his personal safety. Throughout the action he showed the highest qualities of leadership and was an inspiration to all around him.
(M.M. gazetted 26/11/42)

M.M.

No. 6392527 C.S.M. Joseph Greenfield, 1st Bn.

During the night 5/6 April 1943, the attack by 1 Royal Sussex Regiment on Djebel el Meida Hill NW of Wadi Akarit, this W.O. showed courage, initiative and devotion to duty of the highest order. His Coy was under intense mortar and shell fire for the whole of the night and early next morning. During this period they had to carry out a complicated night march and attack over precipitous hillsides in the pitch darkness. In spite of continuing heavy and accurate mortar and machine-gun fire, C.S.M. Greenfield gave the greatest assistance to his Coy Commander by visiting all parts of the Coy and ensuring that there was no confusion in the darkness.

He showed outstanding dash and determination during the attack on the Coy objective, setting an example to all ranks. At dawn during re-organisation he continually moved about in the open visiting forward platoons and urging them on, completely ignoring heavy and accurate enemy fire. His presence was a source of inspiration to the entire Coy.

The conduct of this W.O. is worthy of the highest praise. His determination to close with the enemy and his complete disregard of his personal safety, in doing so became a byword among the men of his Coy.

(Recommended for the D.C.M.)

No. 13048241 Corporal Douglas Ronald George Coppard, 1st Bn.

On the night 5/6 April 1943 during the attack by 1 Royal Sussex Regiment on Djebel el Meida Hill, NW of Wadi Akarit, this N.C.O. showed the greatest courage, initiative and devotion to duty. While under very heavy mortar fire in a narrow wadi, a bomb burst in the middle of his platoon, killing his platoon commander, wounding his platoon sergeant and several of the men.

Out of the confusion caused by this in pitch darkness, Corporal Coppard immediately took command, rallied the platoon and led it forward over very difficult country under continuous mortar and shell fire. He led his platoon to the attack up a steep hillside with great dash and captured his objective. He immediately started to consolidate and then and all the next day showed great ability as a commander in the handling of his platoon.

He showed complete disregard of his own safety under heavy fire when visiting and encouraging his sections. His conduct throughout the whole of this difficult operation was worthy of the highest praise.

No. 6398674 L/Corporal James Henry Hickman, 1st Bn.

On the night of 5/6 April 1943 during the attack by 1 Royal Sussex Regiment on Djebel el Meida Hill NW of Wadi Akarit, this N.C.O. showed courage, initiative, leadership and devotion to duty of the highest order. He was N.C.O. I/C of Bn. No.11 W/T Set which was carried on a stretcher by 8 men. Very early on a mortar bomb wounded 6 of these, the Signal Sergeant and temporarily knocked out the Signal Officer.

In the confusion caused by this in pitch darkness L/Corporal Hickman took complete control, detailed 6 men as carriers and moved forward with the set up a wadi under intense and accurate mortar fire. Later finding one of the W/T batteries missing he returned under heavy fire and brought it up. It is entirely due to his coolness and control of the situation when so many of the signal section were wounded and his determination to get it there over very difficult country, under heavy fire, that the set was brought safely to the objective.

Not content with this – just before first light he volunteered to join a party of men under an officer to attack and mop up the enemy posts in the Anti/tank ditch on the right of the Battalion objective.

He showed great dash in a bayonet charge which cleared the enemy.

In this action his determination to close with and kill the enemy was outstanding. His conduct throughout the whole action is worthy of the highest praise.

No. 6398680 Private Benjamin Ives, 1st Bn.

During the night 5/6 April 1943 at Djebel el Meida. Private Ives showed great devotion to duty as a stretcher bearer. Although himself wounded he continued to attend to other wounded under intense mortar and machine-gun and shell fire. He was without regard for his own personal safety throughout and was finally wounded again and taken to the R.A.P.

No. 6408272 Private Neill Wait Mackinlay, 1st Bn.

During the night 5/6/April 1943 at Djebel el Meida, Private Mackinlay showed outstanding courage and coolness under incessant mortar, shell and machine-gun fire. For five hours he continually went out from the R.A.P. and rescued wounded of his own and other units. His assistance was invaluable to the R.M.O. and a source of encouragement to others, and a comfort to the wounded. His sole aim was the rescue, care and comfort of the wounded with complete disregard of his own safety. As a result of his gallant actions undoubtedly many lives were saved.

No. 6402589 Private Ernest George Peacock, 1st Bn.

On the night 5/6 April 1943 during 1 Royal Sussex Regiment night attack on Djebel el Meida NW of Wadi Akarit, Private Peacock showed courage, coolness and devotion to duty of the highest order. He was attached to "B" Coy as a stretcher bearer. Throughout the night (for 5 hours) the Coy was under intense and accurate mortar and shell fire in a narrow rocky wadi, which considerably increased their splinter effect. Showing supreme contempt of all this fire and without regard for his own safety, rendered first aid to the wounded throughout. He carried or dragged away wounded to places of safety one after the other. The whole of the next day he continued to end the wounded under heavy shell fire and by his courageous action undoubtedly saved many lives.

No. 6408187 Private Edward Rossitter,   1st Bn.

On the night 5/6 April 1943 during 1 Royal Sussex Regiment attack on Djebel el Meida NW of Wadi Akarit, Private Rossitter showed courage, dash and initiative of the highest order. His Coy was under very heavy and accurate mortar fire in a narrow wadi. He showed great coolness and complete disregard for his own safety and was a great help to his Platoon Commander and Platoon Sergeant, in rallying and re-organising the platoon during a difficult change of direction which had to be made in the darkness. In the subsequent advance and attack on the objective he showed great dash and determination to close with and kill the enemy. Throughout next day he showed great coolness under heavy fire during consolidation, his fearless conduct was a very fine example to the rest of his platoon and is worthy of the highest praise.

Friday July 9th 1943

Hartfield Man's M.M.

Among Middle East awards announced in the London Gazette last night, is the Military Medal to Corporal (A/Sgt.) James Bungard, M.M. Royal Sussex Regiment, of Hartfield. He wins the award for the second time, for he gained it originally in the attack on the Ruweisat Bridge.

Saturday July 10th 1943

Military Awards

FURTHER SUSSEX HONOURS

The King has been pleased to approve the following awards in recognition of gallant and distinguished services in the Middle East :-

M.C.

Captain Geoffrey William Hawkes, (129367) (Shrewsbury)
Captain Sidney Joseph Fowler Upton, (90925) (Bognor Regis)
Captain Thomas Reilly, M.B. (114190) (Bonnybridge)
Captain Lawrence William Weeks, (155698) (Hove)

Bar to M.M.

No. 6403983 Corporal James Bungard, M.M.

M.M.

No. 6392527 C.S.M. Joseph Greenfield,
No. 13048241 Corporal Douglas Ronald George Coppard,
No. 6398674 L/Corporal James Henry Hickman,
No. 6398680 Private Benjamin Ives,
No. 6408272 Private Neill Wait Mackinlay,
No. 6402589 Private Ernest George Peacock, (Cas. 19/02/44)
No.6408187 Private Edward Rossiter,

Wednesday July 21st 1943

M.M. for Applesham Man

Congratulations are due to Private E.G. Peacock, of Valley Barn Cottages, Applesham, near Shoreham, on being awarded the Military Medal. He has been serving in the Royal Sussex with the Eighth Army in the Middle East, and the photograph was taken in the desert. Before joining up, he was a stockman to Mr. W.O. Passmore, of Applesham and worked at the farm since he left school at Henfield. He has done heroic work as a stretcher-bearer.
He was first commended two months after landing, and secondly this year, receiving the medal in June. He has a brother and two sisters in the Services.

"London Gazette" Thursday August 5th 1943

The KING has been graciously pleased to approve the following awards in recognition of gallant and distinguished services in Tunisia: —

D.S.O.

Brigadier Manley Angell James, V.C.,M.C. (9531)
Late Royal Sussex Regiment,

He commanded his brigade, with considerable success. He stopped the enemy attack on Beja, and the fact that the Hampshires fought so well must be attributed to a great extent on his personal leadership. Personally brave as a lion, he was at the same time careful and solicitous about he committed his troops. His difficulties were not lightened by the fact that all through the campaign he was suffering from ear trouble, from which anybody with less guts would have gone sick at an early stage of the operations.

"London Gazette" Thursday August 19th 1943

The KING has been graciously pleased to confer " The Efficiency Decoration " upon the following officers of the Territorial Army.—

Lieutenant-Colonel (T/Col.) Geoffrey Vidal Heriz-Smith, O.B.E.,M.C. (36031) of The Royal Sussex Regiment.

Wednesday September 22nd 1943

Military Appointment

To be Colonel, The Royal Sussex Regiment.

Colonel (acting Brigadier) T.F.V. Foster, C.B.E.,M.C. retired pay, Reserve of Officers (re-employed), with effect from December 1, 1942, in succession to the late Colonel (Hon. Brigadier) R.M. Birkett, D.S.O.

"London Gazette" Thursday September 23rd 1943

The KING has been graciously pleased to approve that the following be Mentioned in recognition of gallant and distinguished services in North Africa:-

M.I.D.

No. 6403057 Private William M. Tyler, Royal Sussex Regiment

Monday October 4th 1943

Royal Sussex Meeting Overflows

EIGHT ARMY GENERAL'S MESSAGE

Major-General F.I.S. Tuker, C.B., D.S.O., O.B.E., General Officer Commanding the famous 4th Indian Division of the immortal Eighth Army in North Africa, visited Brighton yesterday and met with a rousing reception at the Dome, packed with a large audience and among whom were relatives and friends of the men of The Royal Sussex Regiment which played such a gallant and conspicuous part in the defeat and rout of the German Armies in North Africa from Tobruk to Tunis. The overflow crowd outside the Dome which heard the General's speech by broadcast was as large again as within.
The General was received by the Mayor of Brighton (Captain B. Dutton Briant) and the Mayoress, the Mayor of Hove (Clr. A.H. Clarke) and the Mayoress, the Town Clerk of Brighton (Mr. J.G. Drew, O.B.E.), Ald. H.W. Aldrich, J.P., the Deputy Constable of Sussex (Captain W.J. Hutchinson), Colonel Frank Eastwood (Commanding 15th Sussex Home Guard), and Mr. Albert Prior (Ministry of Information, Brighton).

Some of the Fiercest Fights

"A message from the men of the Sussex Regiment in North Africa" was the text of the General's address, which in fact amounted to a military and technical description in brief of the campaign in North Africa in which the 4th Indian Division played so a notable part, and the particular exploits of The Royal Sussex regiment from Eritrea to Tunis.
In the course of this narrative the speaker quoted actual description supplied by staff officers of some of the fiercest battles in which the Royal Sussex took part, such as those at Keren Massowa, Sidi-Omar,

Benghazi, El Alamein and the Mareth Line, Akarit, Garcia, Enfidaville and Teboursouk, down to the capture of von Arnim and staff and the triumphal entry into Tunis.

Not the least interesting part of the General's address was that in which he requested relatives and friends of the following officers and N.C.O.'s to see him after the meeting with the object of imparting any special information in his power : Major Sidney Joseph Fowler Upton, M.C., Lieutenant Kenneth Frank Wheeler, Captain Lawrence William Weeks, M.C., Lieutenant Arthur Geoffrey Flavell, Lieutenant Sidney Fase, Lieutenant Guy Patrick Douglas John Nugent, Lieutenant Richard Peter Cooper, R.S.M. Herbert Frank Philllips, C.S.M. Charles William Friday, C.S.M. Charles Albert Fleet, C.S.M. Leonard Edward Brett, C.S.M. Ronald Wells, C.S.M. William James Fleet, C.S.M. Arthur James Cox and C.Q.M.S. Arthur George Davey.

Royal Sussex Awards

The General also referred to the high percentage of awards won by the Royal Sussex , including :-

Lieutenant-Colonel G.C. Evans, Bar to the D.S.O.
Captain P.M.J. Harrison, M.C.
Captain L. Bapty, R.A.M.C., M.C.
Sergeant A. Talmey, D.C.M.
Private S.H. Young, M.M.
Major R.E.S. Shinkwin, M.C.
Captain D.W. Gaylard, M.C.
Sergeant E. Conroy, M.M.
Private J. Cunningham, M.M.

Tribute to General Montgomery

There were, of course, some reverses, concluded the distinguished soldier (who is on Old Boy of Brighton College), but General Montgomery was a man who took the view that "no matter what happens, the enemy has to be beaten, and," remarked General Tuker, "after meeting our chaps a few times the enemy came to the conclusion that the only thing was to be beaten" (cheers). A vote of thanks to Major-General Tuker was seconded by Colonel Eastwood and accorded with acclamation at the instance of the Mayor of Brighton, who presided over the proceedings.

"London Gazette" Thursday October 14th 1943

The KING has been graciously pleased to give orders for the following promotions in, and appointments to, the Most Excellent Order of the British Empire, in recognition of gallant and distinguished services in the Middle East: —

C.B.E. (Military Division)

Brigadier John Leslie Von der Heyde, O.B.E.,M.C. (31719)

This officer has been in charge of 2nd Echelon for two years, during which time he has expanded it several times as the MEF has increased. He has been responsible for the capacity of 2nd echelon to expand and retain, as it does, the efficiency which it continues to display. Colonel Von der Heyde has shown marked qualities of sound judgement and organising ability, coupled with the capacity of making his large organisation an efficient, well balanced and happy team, the administration of which is excellent.

This officer's service in organising the despatch of drafts to 8th Army (during el Alamein battle and subsequent) have contributed greatly to the successful reinforcing of that Army.

M.C.

Captain Stephen Edward Pritchard, R.A.Ch.D. (4th Class) (72201) 4th Bn.

This officer was the Chaplain attached to 4th Bn. Royal Sussex Regiment, during the phase of the operations from 23 October-5 November 1942. Throughout the whole of this period, he set a very high example of devotion to duty, in assisting the wounded and carrying out the burial of those who had been killed. The greater part of this work was carried out amongst the forward Coys, over very exposed ground under heavy and accurate small arms and artillery fire, but despite this, Captain Pritchard carried on with a complete disregard for his own personal safety.

His courage and calmness under fire were an inspiration and a source of confidence to all those around him and have become a subject of general comment amongst the men of the Battalion.

T/Captain David Richards, (91119) 5th Bn.

This officer during the period of the present hostilities, has led his Coy with zeal and determination which has had a most beneficial effect upon the successful issue. during night attacks on 27 October and on 1 November 1942, he has shown marked leadership and bravery. While in a "laager" on the night 28 October, the Battalion was attacked by enemy machine-guns and snipers and he organised his Coy in such a manner that the enemy was successfully kept at bay and the safety of the Battalion was maintained. Whilst passing through a minefield on the same night, when his men were being blown up on anti-personnel mines, he kept his head and his Coy was able to negotiate the obstacle.

His personal leadership and determination when under fire, has enabled the Battalion to press forward in the face of opposition and gain its objective on two separate occasions.

Saturday October 16th 1943

Middle East Honours For Sussex

The King has been pleased to approve the following awards for gallant and distinguished service in the Middle East :-

C.B.E. (Military Division)

Brigadier John Leslie Von der Heyde, O.B.E.,M.C. (31719)

BRIGHTON OFFICER

Brigadier Von der Heyde is a member of a well-known family in Sussex, and before the war was serving with his regiment in Egypt. At that time the Royal Sussex and the King's Royal Rifles comprised the Canal Brigade, and Major Von der Hyde, as he was then, was Staff Captain for the Brigade.
Afterwards he became D.A.A.G., and then A.A.G., and promoted to the rank of Colonel, and in June of this year he became a Brigadier.

Former Territorial

He was commissioned in the Royal Sussex Regiment in 1917, after service in the Territorials. He was appointed adjutant and served in the Middle East during the last war. Brigadier Von der Heyde is the son of the late Major Von der Heyde and Mrs. Von der Heyde of Brighton. He married at St. Peter's, Brighton, in May, 1930, Miss Sybil Marjorie Buckwell, youngest daughter of the late Mr. J.C. Buckwell, a former Mayor of Brighton, and Mrs. Buckwell, of Springfield Road, Brighton.

M.C.

Lieutenant (T/Capt.) David Richards, (9119) 5th Bn. (Bexhill)

"London Gazette" **Thursday October 21st 1943**

The KING has been graciously pleased to confer " The Efficiency Decoration " upon the following officers of the Territorial Army: —

Major (A/Lt-Col.) Christopher Francis Ashburner Nix, (35771) 4th Bn.

"London Gazette" **Thursday November 25th 1943**

The KING has been graciously pleased to give orders for the following promotions in, and appointments to, the Most Excellent Order of the British Empire, in recognition of gallant and distinguished services in the Middle East: —

M.B.E. (Military Division)

Lt. (T/Capt.) Archibald Philip Edwards, (124222) 1st Bn. (Colwyn Bay)

During the period 18 February 1943 to 31 May 1943 which included the operations at the Mareth Line, Wadi Akarit, Embidaville and Tunis, this officer performed outstanding service as Staff Captain of 7 Ind. Inf. Bde. Working often under the most adverse and difficult conditions he never once failed to carry put his task with the utmost efficiency and cheerfulness. The hill operation in which these Bde. Was engaged often involved rapid improvisation of the "Q" arrangements at very short notice. The fact that these arrangements never failed was largely due to the untiring efforts of this officer. All units had very great confidence in him and the success of the Bde. Could not have been achieved without his devoted and skilful work.

"London Gazette" **Thursday December 16th 1943**

The KING has been graciously pleased to approve the following awards in recognition of gallant and distinguished services in Burma and on the Eastern Frontier of India: —

M.C.

Lt. George Henry Borrow, (228394) attd. 13th Bn. King's Regiment, (Diss, Norfolk)

Throughout the operations in Burma from mid-February to mid-May 1943, Lieutenant Borrow acted as Intelligence Officer to HQ No. 2 Group. He insisted on accompanying the expedition despite the fact that he was suffering from jaundice. The continued privations and hardships of the campaign prevented him from ever recovering his health in the course of it, and in the latter stages he suffered intensely from internal disorders, general weakness and a malady which attacked his legs and made marching extremely difficult and painful.
Despite the effects of these serious inroads upon a stage of health already poor, he showed throughout

the campaign a superb example of doggedness and courage which aroused the admiration of every officer and man who saw him. And inspired them all to emulate his magnificence endurance. His work as I.O. not only did not suffer from his bad state of health, but would have been remarkable for its thoroughness and efficiency in ordinary circumstances, while his behaviour under fire was exemplary. His high spirits helped immensely to carry the party with which he was travelling, through most arduous trials until the British lines were reached, when, after an example of steadfastness and endurance which cannot often been surpassed, he finally collapsed.

The KING has been graciously pleased to approve that the following be Mentioned in recognition of gallant and distinguished services in Burma and on the Eastern Frontier of India:—

M.I.D.

W.O.1 (S/Cdr.)(A/Cdr.) William Nightingale,   attd. I.A.C.C.

Thursday December 30th 1943

Honour the 7th Royal Sussex

HOW THEY CHECKED A PANZER DIVISION

This is both a very old and a new story. It is old, for it tells of the action of the 7th Battalion of the Royal Sussex Regiment which resulted in checking the advance of a German Panzer Division for six or seven hours on the afternoon of the 20th May, 1940. It is a new story because it has only just come out of a prison camp in Germany, whence it was brought to this country by a repatriated prisoner in the form of a report which bears the pass of the German Camp Censor.
On 18th May, 1940, the 7th Royal Sussex entrained for Lens, and just outside Amiens became the target for a heaving bombing attack. In all some 100 of the 500 members of the regiment were casualties. The survivors were doubled off into a small wood less than half a mile away from the railway and there reorganised.

They Stood Alone

Next day, refugees in an unbroken stream poured down the road to Poix. By the afternoon of the 20th, several reports had been received that the Germans were in Amiens in force. The stream of refugees was now but a thin trickle, and it was clear that the Royal Sussex were left without support of the Allied troops who had been in the vicinity. They stood alone in the face of the German advance.
The Commanding Officer called his company commanders together and explained that, as he had received no orders, it was his intention to hold the ground to the last. The Battalion, on a front about a quarter of a mile long, was drawn up before the Amiens-Rouen road. Early in the afternoon the enemy made contact, and mortar and shell fire soon developed.

Refused to yield ground

Shortly after three o'clock, an enemy attack was launched against the battalion's centre, and soon it was decided to attempt to relieve pressure there and drive the enemy back by advancing one reserve company and the company on the right of the line, while relying on the remaining reserve company to conform from the right flank. Within a few minutes battle developed and continued for some two hours. The Royal Sussex fought with dogged valour and refused to yield ground. The companies which had come to the relief of the centre of the line, despite the heavy odds against them, refused to capitulate until late in the afternoon, when they were virtually overwhelmed by enemy tanks.

Forced to surrender

At 5.30 the Commanding Officer, who had been making a tour of the battalion's positions, met on the right of the battalion a group of 20 men who reported numbers of enemy tanks. He organised them into two sections and led them on to the high ground, and himself went forward to try and ascertain the situation. He had almost reached the crest when he found himself faced by several enemy tanks which suddenly appeared on his right, by which, though not until an hour later, he was forced to surrender.
The gallant resistance had been an amazingly successful bluff. It was certain that a force which amounted to little more than half the strength of a full battalion could not, more than momentarily hold the ground against a panzer division with any real prospect of success.

Enemy's Advance Delayed

As the Commanding Officer himself observed, if the Germans had known the real situation, they could have cleared the Sussex positions in five minutes. In fact, however, the desperate and unflinching defence offered by the battalion succeeded in delaying the enemy's advance for a least six hours and that meant until next morning.
The Royal Sussex had given splendid effect to those instructions given by the Commanding Officer to his company commanders : "Our original orders were to proceed to Lens. That is impossible. We have no orders to go back. Therefore we stay where we are."
It remains to add that the panzer division which encountered this small force of British troops, was commanded by no less a leader than General Rommel.

Rommel In Command

During a parade at Offlag IX A/H Spangenburg, Germany, Oberleutnant Richter, who was with General Rommel's division, recognised the Commanding Officer of the 7th Royal Sussex, and admitted to him that the German formation had travelled 70 kms. since dawn on the 20th May, and that this had been their first serious resistance they met. He added that because of the gallantry shown by this tiny force, his division was checked in its advance until daylight on the 21st May.
General Rommel himself was admitted to be personally in command of the operation, and the Commanding Officer of the Royal Sussex was in fact handed over to him on being taken prisoner.

"London Gazette" **Thursday January 13th 1944**

The KING has been graciously pleased to approve the following awards in recognition of gallant and distinguished services in Italy:—

2nd Bar to D.S.O.

T/Brigadier Lashmer Gordon Whistler, D.S.O. (13017) 1st Bn. (Chichester)

This officer was in command of 131 Brigade and led the advance of 7th Armoured Division. From Carva Terreni followed it North Side of Mount Vesuvius. He showed fine qualities of leadership and utter disregard for the enemy's fire. His personal example was instrumental in maintaining the momentum of the advance through much difficult country well defended by the enemy. He was always to be found right in front ascertaining for himself the exact situation and planning and organising the next move. His attitude throughout the advance inspired all under his command with the utmost confidence and led to the successful results.

M.C.

Capt. (T/Major) Anthony Gervase Ryshworth-Hill, (76924) attd. Yorks & Lancs.

At La Millina on 22nd September, Major Ryshworth-Hill was ordered to capture this village. In spite of at least eight concrete pillboxes and numerous machine-gun nests, he manoeuvred his infantry company into position astride the German line of communications and dominated the bridge of LA Millina by daylight. For 24 hours he remained in possession of the bridge and prevented all German movements near the bridge. During the night 24th/25th he attacked the German positions in the houses south of the bridge, taking 32 prisoners, including an officer. He then organised the removal of charges and explosives from the bridge.

The KING has been graciously pleased to approve that the following be Mentioned in recognition of gallant and distinguished services in the Middle East: —

M.I.D.

Captain (T/Major) Edwin Albert Hanchard Goodwin, (173431) (R of O)
Captain Denis Richard Courtenay Hayes, (130053) 5th Bn. (k.i.a.)
　　Captain Charles William Sidney Johnson, (138167)

Lieutenant (T/Capt.) Norman Fletcher Bates, (171956)
Lieutenant (T/Capt.) Keith Oliver Tucker, (78997)
Lieutenant Christopher Peter Browne, (138160) 5th Bn. (k.i.a.)
No. 737437 C.S.M. Basil Norman Baker,
No. 6398703 Sergeant (A/W.O.11) (C.S.M.) R.E. Wells,
No. 6398625 Sergeant J. Betts,
No. 6398115 Sergeant Charles E.D. Bristow,
No. 6403653 Sergeant George Henry Homden,
No. 6394866 Corporal L. Murphy,
No. 6401176 Private (A/Cpl.) G. Priddle,
No. 5505141 Lance-Corporal C.W. Elliott,
No. 6403870 Private A.A. Bone,
No. 5505188 Private Percy Clifford Marks, 5th Bn. (k.i.a.)
No. 5573831 Private H.R. White,
No. 6400234 Sergeant Thomas Cyril Bentley, Mortar Platoon 10th Bn. Para. Regt. A.A.C.
No. 6400067 Private (A/Cpl.) William Garibaldi, 10th Bn. Para. Regt. A.A.C.

Friday January 14th 1944

Sussex Officer's Gallantry in Italy

T/Brigadier Lashmer Gordon Whistler, Royal Sussex Regiment, of Chichester, is awarded a second bar to the Distinguished Service Order.
In the advance round the north of Mt. Vesuvius this officer (says the citation) was always in front ascertaining the situation for himself and planning the next move.

Brigadier L.G. Whistler is in his 46th year, he is the son of Lieutenant-Colonel A.E. Whistler, late of the Indian Army, and Mrs. Whistler, of Upperton Road, Eastbourne, and he married at Eastbourne Parish Church, in 1926, Miss Esme Winifred Keighly, daughter of the late Mr. George Keighly and Mrs Keighly, of Hartington Mansions, Eastbourne.

He received his commission in September, 1917, and was wounded twice while serving in France and Belgium in the last war. From 1929 to 1933 he was Adjutant of the 5th (Territorial Army) Battalion of the Royal Sussex Regiment at Hastings.

Saturday January 15th 1944

Sussex M.C. Held Bridge

For his gallantry in capturing a German held bridge in Italy the M.C. has been awarded to Captain (Temporary Major) Anthony Gervase Ryshworth-Hill, of Tunbridge Wells.

MENTIONS

The following members of The Royal Sussex Regiment have been mentioned in dispatches for gallant and distinguished service in the Middle East :-
Captain (T/Major) E.A.H. Goodwin, 173431 (R of O)
Captain D.R.C. Hayes, 130053 (k.i.a.)
Captain C.W.S. Johnson, 138167
Lieutenant (T/Capt.) N.F. Bates, 171956
Lieutenant (T/Capt.) K.O. Tucker, 78997
Lieutenant C.P. Browne, 138160 (k.i.a.)
W.O. 11 C.S.M. B.N. Baker, 737437
Sergeant (A/W.O.11) (C.S.M.) R.E. Wells, 6398703
Sergeant J. Betts, 6398625
Sergeant C.E.D. Bristow, 6398115
Sergeant G.H. Homden, 6403653
Corporal L. Murphy, 6394866
Private (A/Cpl.) G. Priddle, 6401176
Lance-Corporal C.W. Elliott, 5505141
Private A.A. Bone, 6403870
Private P.C. Marks, 5505188 (k.i.a.)
Private H.R. White, 5573831

Saturday January 22nd 1944

Royal Sussex Colonel Named

"We Stay Where We Are" Order At Amiens

Publication has been permitted of the fact the Commanding Officer of the Battalion of The Royal Sussex Regiment which at Amiens on 20th May, 1940, barred the way for several hours to a German Panzer division commanded by General Rommel, was Lieutenant-Colonel Ronald Gethen, M.C. Prior to the war he had commanded a Territorial Battalion of the Regiment.

"Wintons," Folders Lane, Burgess Hill, is Colonel Gethen's home, and has been since 1935 when he moved from Lewes Road, Haywards Heath. His interest in local life is shown by the fact that before the war he ran the gymnastic club at Scaynes Hill.

The full story of the action has already been told in the Sussex Daily News. The gallant resistance of the Royal Sussex proved an amazingly successful bluff for, as Colonel Gethen himself observed, if the Germans had known the real situation they could have cleared the Royal Sussex positions in five minutes. As it was, the Battalion's stand delayed the enemy's advance for at least six hours. Colonel

Gethen's instructions were "Our original orders were to proceed to Lens. That is impossible we have no orders to go back. Therefore we stay where we are."

"London Gazette" Thursday January 27th 1944

The KING has been graciously pleased to approve the following awards in recognition of gallant and distinguished services in Italy: —

M.M.

No. 6397316 Lance-Sergeant Ernest Edward William Goldsmith, 1st Bn. (Special Raiding Squadron) (Winchelsea)

In the fighting South of Termoli on the 3rd October 1943, L/Sergeant Goldsmith led his sub-section with great daring and initiative and when one of his officers was wounded, tended him himself and evacuated him under fire. In subsequent operations when large numbers of men had been wounded he immediately dashed forward under fire to their assistance and organised stretcher parties to evacuate them. Later when ordered to hold an important section of the line he took up a position on top of 500 gallons of petrol although under heavy fire, as this was the only place from which he could carry out his task. Throughout he showed a very high standard of leadership and his courage was a constant inspiration to his men.

"London Gazette" Thursday February 10th 1944

The King has been graciously pleased to approve of the following awards in recognition of gallant and distinguished service in Burma :-

M.C.

Lieutenant (T/Capt.) Hubert Arthur Christopher Edelsten, (109220) attd. 4th Bn. 14th Punjab Regiment. (Balcombe)

This officer captured a Japanese position with his Company on 1 Dec 1943 at Mauguaw North. He secured a large amount of most valuable documents and equipment. His personal recce prior to the action and the preparation for the approach of his Company through very dense jungle was carried out thoroughly and most efficiently two nights before. He led the Company through this thick jungle with such skill that the enemy were definitely caught by surprise. When fired on by light automatics at a range of 30 yards and by L.M.G. up in a tree, also by mortar fire, he immediately organised a Blitz party of two platoons and captured the position.
His personal example was of the highest order. He searched the area most thoroughly with his Company knowing that enemy gunfire might be expected at any moment and sent back over three mule loads of captured documents, one L.M.G., one 2" mortar and other equipment. Enemy gunfire came down very accurately on to his position just as the Company was moving clear of it.
In the weeks prior to this action Captain Edelsten carried personal reconaissances involving considerable risk behind the enemy outpost line. The cutting out operation on Awtanbyin West achieved surprise and success was due to his enterprise and bold recces.

Thursday February 17th 1944

Monte Cassino first assault

"D" Coy Royal Sussex in the lead an attack of a ridge at night, the forward platoons worked round a barricade of boulders a gained a foothold on the slopes of Pt. 593. From the cover of sangars and foxholes dug in the rocky ledges the Germans defended with Spandau fire and grenades. The consolidation platoon dashed round the rocks and destroyed two Spandau nests, many men became casualties, the officer leading them was wounded but established himself in a ditch outside the walls of the fort. The Company Commander managed to reach the summit but heavy fire stopped the rest of the platoons from reaching their officers.

"A" Coy went forward as reinforcements but again many became casualties due to the incessant heavy fire from the German defenders. "C" Coy then joined the fight and for a short time it looked as though the Sussex would carry the day. Unfortunately at a critical point in the attack three green Very lights, the signal for a Sussex withdrawal lit the sky, these were fired by the Germans and had the desired effect on the Royal Sussex. "D" Coy relinquished its hold of the crest and fell back, "B" Coy then on detecting the ruse formed up for another assault, but again incessant heavy fire prevented any ground being retaken, the Royal Sussex having to retire to their original jump off point.

"London Gazette" Thursday February 24th 1944

The KING has been graciously pleased to approve the. following awards in recognition of gallant and distinguished services in Italy. —

M.C.

Lieutenant (T/Capt.) Patrick Michael Mordaunt, (164690) attd. 5th Bn. Hampshire Regiment, (Dublin)

On the night of the 14-15 October 1943, Captain Mordaunt was ordered to carry out an attack on a position some 800 yards North of the Volurno. This attack was unopposed, and he was therefore ordered to advance to a line of the canal three miles away. His Coy carried out this advance and took a position the other side of the canal. At dawn they were heavily shelled and counter-attacked by infantry and a tank at very close quarters. A Coy was then sent up to support them and was so heavily mortared that they had to withdraw.

A further Coy was unable to get within two miles of Captain Mordaunt's position, so that he was left in complete isolation and in grave danger of envelopment by the enemy. In spite of this Captain Mordaunt held on to his position until the C.O. of his Bn. was able to regroup at nightfall. During the night Captain Mordaunt's Coy was again heavily counter-attacked but he did not withdraw his Coy behind the canal until his position had become quite untenable and his C.O. was satisfied that the remainder of the Bn.'s positions were secure.

When he did eventually withdraw across the canal in the face of heavy enemy opposition, Captain Mordaunt personally supervised the withdrawal, which was carried out in an excellent manner. Throughout this action Captain Mordaunt's courage and complete disregard for his own safety was a stirring example to his men.

Saturday March 4th 1944

Hove Officer Wounded

Capt. L.W. Weeks, M.C.

News was received yesterday (Friday) by Mr. and Mrs. W.E. Weeks, of Montefiore Road, Hove, that their son, Captain Lawrence William Weeks, M.C., of the Royal Sussex Regiment, has been seriously wounded. A telegram from the Under-Secretary of State for War states that reports received from the Central Mediterranean area intimate that Captain Weeks has been seriously wounded and placed on the dangerously ill list suffering from a shell wound of the thigh, with complications. It is a sad coincidence that he was wounded on his 25th birthday.

Captain Weeks won the Military Cross last year for distinguished service with the Middle East Forces, and in gaining his decoration he emulated the achievement of his father, who won the M.C. with the Royal Sussex Regiment in the 1914-1918 war.

His many friends in Brighton and Hove, and those of his parents, will join in the earnest wish that better news will be forthcoming soon.

Wednesday March 8th 1944

M.C. Son of Brighton Solicitor Dies of Wounds

Mr. William E. Weeks (the well-known solicitor) and Mrs. Weeks, of Montefiore Road, Hove, have received news of the death of their only son, Captain Lawrence William Weeks, M.C., on his 25th birthday, as a result of wounds received while in action in Italy.

Born in Brighton, Captain Weeks was educated at the Brighton, Hove and Worthing Grammar School. He joined his father's firm (Messrs. J. Lord Thompson and Weeks) and just passed his final examination to qualify as a solicitor when he joined up. After a few months training he was commissioned in The Royal Sussex Regiment, and went overseas in 1940.

He saw service throughout the arduous battles of North Africa and took part in the capture of Von Arnim and 300,000 Germans.

Official Citation

The official citation when he was awarded the M.C. in 1943 said :-

"The initiative, powers of leadership and bravery under fire displayed by this officer were beyond all praise and were largely instrumental in the final success gained by his battalion."

This refers to the occasion in April, 1943, during the attack on the Djebel el Meida feature, when, his commander having been killed. Captain (then Lieutenant) Weeks took over command and with great dash captured the objective in the face of stubborn enemy resistance.

Captain Weeks' father, Mr. William Weeks, was also in The Royal Sussex Regiment, serving from 1914-18, and he, too, was awarded the M.C.

The young captain had numerous friends in Brighton and Hove, particularly in golfing circles. Quite early in his sporting career he was runner-up in the championship of the Dyke Golf Club, of which his father is now the Hon. Secretary. He was well know also on the East Brighton course, and was holder of many competition trophies.

Wednesday March 15th 1944

1st Battle of Cassino (Memoirs of Capt. A-R-West, 1st Bn.)

It is impossible to describe the 1st Battle of Cassino without explaining the layout and order of battle prior to March 15th. The object of the battle was to open up Route 6 (the road that led to Rome). To do this Cassino town had to be taken together with the immediate overlooking heights which included Castle Hill, the Monastery, 435 Hangman's hill (so called) because the gallows like object (which was the remains of the aerial railway), certain other heights such as 569, 593 and Albaneta House, 449 were all intermediate objectives in the taking of the Monastery. The troops to be used were the New Zealand Corps (known as the Spadger Force), 2nd New Zealand Division and 4th Indian supported by additional medium and heavy artillery and Armoured Brigade of the New Zealand Corps.

A great aerial bombardment consisting of 600 medium and heavy bombers was going to flatten Cassino town and neutralise the Monastery. It was hoped that armour would break through the Route 6 as soon as possible thus making the battle fluid. Strategically would it was hoped alleviate the situation an Anzio when the 5th Army would roll up the road to Rome. Against this the Germans had what was called the Gustav Line and behind that the Adolf Hitler Line manned by some of the finest troops in Italy. I will try and describe how the battle went as regards 7th Indian Infantry Brigade who were right hand troops in the order of battle and upon them hinged the Allied Assault. On the right lay the French Expeditionary Corps and I have already described their sector. The left boundary lay from Phantom Ridge, down the new tank track constructed by our sappers, exclusive of Cairo village and across the Rapido.

At the head of this tank track was 7th Brigade Recce Squadron under Malcom Cruikshank. This consisted of a troop of Sherman and another of Honeys, the whole force was to come under command of a New Zealand Armoured Squadron. The expedition was to be a surprise and a diversion. It was hoped that if they were ever needed they might turn the tide against the heights for the Germans who be amazed to see tanks in their O.Ps. 7th Brigade order of battle were Royal Sussex, 2nd Camerons, 4/16 Punjabs, 4/6 Raj. Rifles, 1/2 and 2/7 Gurkhas. The 2nd Camerons and 57 Light Anti-Aircraft were acting as porters. 7th Brigade objectives were 593, 449 and Monastery. 5th Brigade order of battle was 1/4 Essex, 1/6 Raj. Rifles and 1/9 Gurkhas. 11th Brigade as can be seen were all under command of 7th Brigade. 5th Brigade main objectives were Hangmans Hill and Castle Hill and Hill 222, these lay further round to the left and above Cassino Town.

The New Zealand Division were (i) to take the town (ii) to take the railway station which entailed crossing the Rapido. Theoretically all objectives taken would mean the end of the battle but it was hoped and thought by everyone that all formations would mutually assist each other by taking objectives and if one could not succeed successive pressure from another quarter would force us to success. As will be seen each objective held out for too long and nothing cracked in the expected way so the battle was a failure but not a defeat. The great attack was scheduled for early morning, March 15th. The night of 14/15th was moonlight hand quiet. All orders and movements of troops had been completed prior to the battle. We all felt that the impending battle was coming off because we had been so long cooped up on the hill and we felt that in a few hours we should find ourselves driving up the road to Rome instead of hiding in and out of slit trenches.

On the 14th the code word "Bradman" was received and we knew everything was ready. At eight-thirty the sound of bombers was very close. Forward troops had been withdrawn to avoid all chances of their being hit. There was a great air expectancy as thousands of Allied eyes gazed upwards and many conjectures were formed as to the surprise that Jerry would get. Onwards came the drone and then we saw them. Large Fortresses in formation, squadrons of Mitchells were there as well. Then we heard the swish and roar of falling bombs, sometimes we could see them pouring down and then the whole ground appeared to erupt. I could not see the town of Cassino, only the Monastery top. Then I heard a succession of what sounded like loud Japanese crackers. Soon after a huge cloud of smoke covered the scene of operations, then I realized why the bombers were flying so high (10,000 feet), they were just above smoke which must have reached many thousands of feet.

The continuous noise was terrible and many bombs appeared by the sound to drop nearer us. One terrible sight I shall never forget was a formation of Mitchells which started to come towards the Monastery from behind our lines, when they reached our 'B' Echelon area the other side of the valley they let go their bombs. We could see the bombs falling starting from the leader. We all watched speechless with rage and impotence. Gloomily we heard the crack of the explosions and saw about four or fires start, these went on for a good few minutes. As a whole, the bombardment had been immensely exciting and had raised our spirits. We knew that 7th Brigade had not much to do and now it was the turn of 5th Brigade and the Kiwis. Hourly we waited for results and they were not long in coming. Success and success, most of the town was in our hands by midday and the Kiwis had crossed the Rapido

At 1700 hrs the Essex went to relieve them on Castle Hill. All this sounded very good then we heard that the armour was having difficulty over the bomb craters. Next we heard that the Continental Hotel was proving an obstacle, there we heard that the Gurkhas were making excellent progress at 2200 hrs the 1/6 Raj. Rifles set off. 24 hours thus passed, still we heard that same story about the enormous bomb craters which seemed to keep creeping in. We all knew the saying that no news means good news and we hoped it was right. It was decided to commit our surprise weapon the 'mountain climbing tanks' to battle. This we all thought would turn the tide of battle.

The tanks went in and caused alarm and consternation amongst the Germans as we found out by hearing on the wireless that "Allied tanks had broken through" in terms of panic. But the tanks met very bad going, they ground on through machine gunning and shelling but there was no infantry to follow up and what success and surprise they had was soon lost. One by one the tanks got knocked out and the operation was called off. I went with Brigadier Lovett to visit 7th Brigade Recce Squadron afterwards. Beside a twisting track we found violets growing, the Brigadier was determined to get some and we did. Malcolm Cruikshank and his tanks were laid up after the battle at the head of the track. Whilst we were up there we saw the marks of the needle-gun on the Shermans in certain places they had penetrated the armour. Whilst on the way back someone from Phantom Ridge played about with a Spandau which sent up bits of dirt above us.

Each day we awaited the good news which never came. We used to watch the planes which dropped supplies to the 1/9 Gurkhas on Hangmans Hill (they cooked chapatis at Foggia). Sometimes they never seemed to get enough supplies and the Germans got many instead. On two occasions I watched dive bombing on the Monastery from the Royal Sussex H.Q. in the house over the crest near Hill 593. We heard that the Castle walls had collapsed and that Battalion H.Q. of 4/6 Raj. Rifles was out of action, then we heard about the Gurkhas on Hangmans Hill and we knew the battle had failed......

"London Gazette" **Thursday April 6th 1944**

The KING has been graciously pleased to approve that the following .be Mentioned in recognition of gallant and distinguished services in the Middle East: —

M.I.D.

T/Brigadier J.L. Von der Heyde, O.B.E.,M.C. (31719)
Captain (T/Mjr.) A.C. Bryant, (33024) R. of O.
Captain (T/Mjr.) David Richards, M.C. (91119)
Lieutenant (T/Capt.) Hector Samuel Burnard, (175799)

Lieutenant (T/Capt.) Benjamin Dalton, (105089)

No. 6391134 R.S.M. William George Alce,
No. 6404010 Corporal (A/Sgt.) B.B. Hiscock,
No. 6403507 Lance-Sergeant Reginald W. Jenkins,
No. 6404065 Corporal Thomas Alfred C. Aylward,

Corporal Aylward and friends.

Monday April 10th 1944

Royal Sussex at Cassino

THRILLING STORY OF ITS TOUGHEST EXPERIENCE

A Battalion of the Royal Sussex Regiment which fought in Eritrea and the Western Desert has gone through the toughest time it has ever had in the hill features north-west of Cassino. It has done difficult jobs before, but the men looking back are likely to reckon this spell as one of the hardest.

A Reuter special correspondent in a telegram dated "Before Cassino, Saturday," says:-

"When an Indian formation went into the line the Royal Sussex took over a feature known as 'The Snake's Head.' We cleared up a bit, and hastily built some low walled defences," a company said, "The track to this feature was not even fit for mules. It was steep and slippery. The first night only 30 out of 240 mules laden with supplies and ammunition got through. From the very start we envisaged this of running dangerously short of ammunition if we expended our stores lavishly.

"The track ran through a gully which received more than usual attention from German artillery, and in consequence earned the name "Death Valley". Movement was impossible by day.

Sussex Men's Washing

"Sussex men can't sit all day behind their defences and keep still. They must come out and they must hang their washing around. This naturally resulted in casualties. The battalion found a strong bomb-proof German pillbox with comfortable bunk, and used it as headquarters. The Americans who were there before them had named it "Kesselring Castle"

On the night following the bombing of Cassino Monastery by Allied planes the Royal Sussex went in to capture a hill feature, a high tableland with sides dropping away sheer. On the top the ruins of an ancient rampart provided excellent defensive positions for the enemy.

Deluge of Grenades

"As the Sussex boys went in the German started deluging the slope with sticks of grenades and small arms fire from behind the rampart. The fire was more than had been expected and the job turned out to be too big for one battalion. Amid confused yelling some of the Germans were also shouting in English. With tommy-guns and grenades clearing their way the company fought its way on to the flat top of the hill. The position had been definitely been knocked out, but the company had been reduced in strength and the Germans later on managed to infiltrate through again.

Subaltern's Bravery

"It was then that 2nd Lieutenant Dennis Cox, of Duke's Walk, St. Margaret's, Middlesex, showed exceptional bravery. He had been seriously wounded in the leg by a direct hit from a German grenade, and was lying among three dead Germans, two of whom he himself had killed. When the company commander came to the spot he ordered Cox to be evacuated, but Cox said he would fight on. Sometime later he was hit again by two German grenades bursting close to him. At last a corporal lifted him on his shoulders and brought him down the hill.

Call For Aid

"Assistance was asked for the hard pressed company, whose ammunition was nearly exhausted, and it came, but the Germans added to the already confused situation by sending up quantity of Verey lights, and the attack was finally called off. Then set in a period of so called 'quiet'. This quiet proved a heavy drainage on the battalion. 'Casualties were quite unusual for a quiet period', said one company commander. 'We were so close to the Germans that we couldn't even call for help from our own artillery for fear of hitting our own men.'

'The grim game of chucking grenades at each other and shooting at anyone who raised his head above his own defences went on between the two sides without a break. The battalion had a short spell of 'rest' but they were resting in 'Death Valley', only 800 yards behind their lines. It was good as being in the line.

They came back to their positions when the recent large scale offensive operations against Cassino began.

"London Gazette" Thursday April 20th 1944

The King has been graciously pleased to confer the "Efficiency Decoration" upon the following officer of the Territorial Army :-

Major (T/Lt.-Colonel) Francis Frazer Haddock, (39985) 4th Bn.

Tuesday April 25th 1944

Sussex Major Killed

Mr. And Mrs. H. McD. Edelsten, of Bramble Hill, Balcombe, have received official notification that their only son, Major Hubert Arthur Christopher Edelsten, M.C., has been killed in action while serving on the Arakan Front, Burma. Major Edelsten who was 27 years of age, was a member of the Royal Sussex Territorials at the outbreak of war and went to France with the B.E.F. serving with the 6th Battalion, the Royal Sussex Regiment. After the fall of France he made good his escape from Nantes about a week after the evacuation of Dunkirk. He afterwards went to India, and saw service on the North-West Frontier, before going to Burma.

He was awarded the Military Cross for gallant and distinguished service.

"London Gazette" Thursday April 27th 1944

The KING has been graciously pleased to approve the following awards in recognition of gallant and distinguished services in North Africa: —

M.C.

Lieutenant (T/Capt.) Harold Vere Holden-White, (162512) Royal Sussex Regiment.

No. 2 Special Boat Section Unit – Oran Landings.
Assault on port by H.M.S. Walney and H.M.S. Harland, 8th November 1942.

A/Captain H.V. Holden-White was in command of the Special Boat Section Unit which was detailed to carry out dangerous and delicate operations in conjunction with an assault on the port of Oran. He was in charge of the party operating from H.M.S. Walney on foldboats and displayed courage and initiative of a high order in attacking with small torpedoes a French destroyer which was leaving port, and it is believed that one hit on the vessel was obtained.

Thursday May 25th 1944

Sussex Officer Killed

A/Captain G.H. Borrow, Royal Sussex Regiment, who last year was awarded the Military Cross for gallant and distinguished service in the Burma Campaign.

"London Gazette" Thursday June 8th 1944

The KING has been graciously pleased, on the occasion of His Majesty's Birthday to give orders for the following appointments to the Most Excellent Order of the British Empire: —

King's 15th Birthday Honours List

M.B.E. (Military Division)

Captain (T/Major) Peter Spencer Hadley, (88627) 4th Bn.

For outstanding ability and devotion to duty. Major Hadley is a most efficient and tireless Staff Officer who has been indefatigable in everything he has undertaken. By his high example, cheerfulness and foresight he has greatly helped in the smooth running of the system of command within the Brigade, and all ranks have derived great benefit from his ideas, teaching and initiative.

B.E.M. (Military Division)

No. 6396504 Private Edward George Tomlin, 2nd Bn. attd. 10th Bn. Parachute Regiment,

Private Tomlin after serving seven years with the Colours, mostly in India where he gained an I.G.S. Medal, was recalled at the outbreak of war to the Royal Sussex Regiment. He then served in France and the Western Desert at El Alamein. When his Battalion of the Royal Sussex Regiment was converted to a Parachute Battalion, he was one of the first to volunteer and was a strong influence in causing many others to do so.

At this time he was well overage, being nearly 40, and although injured on one of his first jumps, he insisted on carrying on and by his example and cheerful good humour was the greatest encouragement to the younger men of the unit, which then only consisted of 200 Royal Sussex men. He is now employed as a storeman and nobody could wish for a better one, efficient, cheerful, helpful and reliable. He has done a number of years of excellent service and is now a much respected member of this unit and an example to all ranks.

"London Gazette" Thursday June 15th 1944

The KING has been graciously pleased to approve the following awards in recognition of gallant and distinguished services in Italy : —

M.M.

No. 793925 Private Sydney George Avey, 1st Bn. 111 Coy. A.M.P.C.

Escapes from Camp 73 (Carpi) Italy

The entire camp was taken over on 9 Sep 43 by the Germans, who disarmed the Italian guards and put them in the cells. P/W were given no food or water for three days' after the German's arrival. On 14 Sep 43 the P/W were marched to the station for entrainment to Germany, and a number escaped enroute.

"London Gazette" Tuesday June 20th 1944

DECORATION CONFERRED BY THE PRESIDENT OF THE POLISH REPUBLIC

Order of Polonia Restituta
Third Class

Lt-Col. (Local Colonel) George Herbert Blackett De Chair, O.B.E.,M.C. (24056)

"London Gazette" Thursday June 22nd 1944

The KING has been graciously pleased to approve the following awards in, recognition of gallant and distinguished services in Burma:—

M.C.

Captain (T/Mjr.) James Maynard Cash, (174342) 9th Bn. (Saffron Walden)

Mayu Range Arakan 26/03/44

T/Major Cash commanded "B" Coy during this successful assault on the Sausage Feature. He led his Coy with outstanding courage and it was largely due to his determination that this precipitous and strongly defended feature was captured. In succeeding phase, determined enemy counter-attacks were beaten off, and the objective held. Throughout these actions T/Major Cash's personal example and courage was an inspiration to the whole Coy.

M.M.

No. 14203602 L/Corporal Charles Edward Davis, 9th Bn. (London E.1)

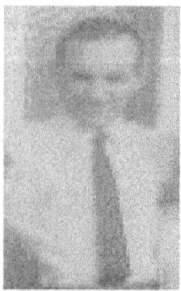

During the attack on the Sausage feature, L/Corporal Davis as Section Commander showed very great bravery and leadership in the assault and consolidation of his objective which was accomplished in the face of heavy fire from enemy mortars and L.M.G.'s Later he carried badly needed ammunition under continuous enemy fire and succeeded in maintaining the section position in very difficult circumstances. Throughout L/Corporal Davis displayed coolness, courage and leadership of high order and his conduct was an example to all ranks.
(picture circa 1966)

No. 5342055 Corporal George Francis Taylor,   9th Bn. (London N.8)

During the assault on the Sausage Feature, Corporal Taylor was Platoon Commander during the action. He led his platoon on to the objective in the face of fierce enemy L.M.G. fire and quickly consolidated his position. He then personally directed 2in. mortar and L.M.G. fire on a bunked position enfilading his platoon position. He showed great courage and leadership during the whole action

Extract from the "Shiny Ninth"

The two tunnels, half way along the road from Maungdaw to Buthidaung and the Kalapanzin Valley, had originally been cut for a light railway but had been dismantled by the river navigation company who owned it and a road laid over the track. The Mayu range rises to over a 1,000 feet at this point and the Japs had built three formidable defences dominating the locality, strong enough to be called fortresses, which they were.
The first already mentioned, was Razabil, including the infamous "Tortoise" feature, the second was Letwadet seven miles to the North-West, and the third the twin tunnels, one of which was to be the target for 72 Bde. Before the battle had even begun Major Neil Selkirk, commanding "A" Coy, had been killed on patrol.
On March 26th, supported by artillery, 72 Bde. launched their attack on the West tunnel with "B" Coy Royal Sussex (Major R. Cash) and "B" Coy S.W.B. leading. The Royal Sussex company reached their objective without much serious resistance and sent a success signal back at 1043 hours but from then on they were subjected to sustained mortar and grenade attack, incurring heavy casualties.
"B" Coy were again attacked in the night but the enemy withdrew in the face of grenades and L.M.G. fire. "C" Coy then took over two features, Dog and X-Ray, from the Glosters and they were shelled, sustaining two casualties. The tunnel was finished off by the S.W.B. supported by the tanks of the Dragoons, one of which fired a round straight up the tunnel mouth, blowing up the ammunition stored inside and causing a certain amount of havoc for the Japanese. In the ensuing confusion the Welsh rushed the tunnel and it was secured.
(L/Sgt. R.C. Hollingdale was also awarded the M.M. for this action, "L/G" 08/02/45)

The KING has been graciously pleased to confer " The Efficiency Decoration" upon the following officers of the Territorial Army.

Captain Ronald Hennah Langham, M.C. (58113) 5th Bn.

Tuesday July 11th 1944

In the afternoon of the 11 July, the 1 Royal Sussex passed through the lines held by the Gurkhas on San Maria di Tiberina and advanced along the crest of the ridge. With Divisional and Corps. Artillery supplying smoke cover in the exposed positions, by 2200 hours 1 Royal Sussex were within a mile of their objective and encountering fierce and heavy resistance. "A" Coy came into the fight, but its Commander was killed and the advance halted. At dawn the following day a patrol discovered that the enemy had withdrawn from the village. The village was occupied by the Royal Sussex and a platoon sent out to seize Mont Cedrone an important lookout which was blocking the advance of 10 Brigade along the west side of the River Tiber.

Friday July 14th 1944

Royal Sussex Officer killed

Captain Murray James Angus Dickson, M.C. (138855) 1st Bn.

"London Gazette" Thursday July 20th 1944

The KING has been graciously pleased to approve the following awards in recognition of gallant and distinguished services in Italy: —

D.S.O.

Captain (T/Mjr.) Benjamin Dalton, 1st Bn. (105089) (London N.W.6)

During the night 16/17 February 1944 in the area Pt. 593 west of Cassino, Major Dalton personally led two platoons of his Coy in a night attack on to the top of the Pt.593 feature. The enemy were entrenched in their rocky country behind steep walls and their position was stronger than expected. Major Dalton's Coy came under very heavy L.M.G. and grenade fire and sustained heavy casualties. This officer however personally led on the survivors and practically obtained his objective after very heavy hand to hand battle with grenades.

His men by now had run out of grenades and were exposed to heavy enemy grenade fire. Major Dalton, although wounded and under heavy fire, regardless of his own safety organised a further supply of grenades and led his men again to the attack. In spite of his dashing leadership, heavy enemy fire causing further casualties stopped him from penetrating the enemy position, and his men had run out of grenades.

The Battalion Commander ordered a withdrawal, on this order being given Major Dalton personally supervised the evacuation of the wounded and completely regardless of his own safety, he carried out a search of "No Man's Land" under very heavy fire to find out if any of his Coy who might be lying wounded. He personally helped several men back to our lines and was the last of his Coy to return. Although wounded in the leg he refused to be evacuated and remained to command his Coy in their positions 80 yards from the enemy for a total of 21 days before being relieved. The courage and devotion to duty of this officer both during the night attack and the subsequent long period with his Coy in the line is worthy of the highest praise.

His magnificent leadership and example throughout was an inspiration to his Coy for the whole very trying time.

M.C.

Captain Ernest John Bowmer, M.B. R.A.M.C. (139727) 114th Field Ambulance,

During the operations in the hill area known North of Cassino from 15-19 February 1944, this officer showed outstanding courage and devotion to duty under most difficult and hazardous conditions. From 15-17 February, while preparations were being made for the Bde. Attack on the monastery of Montecassino, he personally organised and laid out the system of medical evacuation for the Bde. This had to be done over an area of very steep and precipitous country which came under intense enemy shell and mortar fire during this period. Captain Bowmer worked day and night without rest and often under enemy fire.

At the same time a considerable number of casualties were being inflicted on units of the Bde. While they were moving into position, Captain Bowmer was constantly on the spot where enemy fire was thickest and our casualties were heaviest, both giving assistance to unit M.O.'s and working on his own. His conduct and personal gallantry during this period were of a high order while his organising skill was outstanding. After the attack on the monastery on the night 17/18 February this officer again showed the most extraordinary personal courage and devotion to duty.

Casualties during the night had been very heavy in 3 battalions and their evacuation from forward positions, now more than ever exposed to intense M.G., mortar and shell fire, became a most serious and urgent problem. For two days and nights Captain Bowmer worked unceasingly without thought of rest, food or his own personal safety. He assisted unit M.O.'s, organised stretcher parties, rendered first aid and reported frequently to Bde. H.Q. on the progress of the evacuation.

His movements to and from the R.A.P.'s brought him constantly under the heaviest fire from all weapons both by day and night, but he was not in the least deterred. He set a magnificent example and inspired all those working with him with a determination to complete the task. There is no doubt that the skill and devotion to duty of this officer were directly responsible for saving a large number of lives. His personal bravery and endurance under intense enemy fire were beyond all praise and became a byword throughout the whole Bde.

(Although not attached to 1st Bn. he administered first aid to the Battalion wounded, see Battles round Cassino, 'Memoirs' of Capt. A.R. Alston-Roberts-West for details.)

M.M.

No. 6403616 Corporal (A/Sgt.) Thomas Sidney Andrews, 1st Bn. Regimental Military Police, (Leytonstone)

On 28th February 1944, Sergeant Andrews of the Provost Wireless
Traffic Control Section received orders to connect Villa Traffic Post to Cairo Traffic Post by telephone and lay the necessary wire. This communication was vital in order to warn vehicles approaching the Cairo Circuit of enemy shelling, and to allow vehicles to proceed safely through the circuit only when shelling had temporarily slackened. The Cairo circuit is a vital link for maintenance of forward troops. He commenced work at about 0900hrs. and completed laying the line during the morning, but owing to heavy shelling the line required continuous repairs.

For three days Sergeant Andrews tested and repaired many cuts in the line under constant shell fire, and, with complete disregard for his personal safety, he kept this vital communications in working order. On the second day whilst running a new section of wire from his Jeep, it was blown up by a mine, and although considerably shaken by concussion kept up his patrol of the circuit and repairs to the telephone line during the day, and insisted on continuing his work the next day.

He was soon after posted to command 5 Bde. Det. Provost so that in his own words, "He could keep an eye on the Cairo Circuit", and on the 17th March, he was seriously wounded in the vicinity of Villa. He was an inspiration to all those who worked with him.

No.5573770 Lance-Sergeant Walter Edward Osman, 1st Bn. (Wroughton, Wilts.)

'During the night 16/17 February 1944 in the area Pt 593 West of Cassino, Corporal Osman took part in the night attack onto the top of the Pt 593 feature. The enemy were strongly entrenched in rocky positions and behind steep walls. Despite heavy and effective L.M.G. fire and a hail of rifle and stick grenades, which caused heavy casualties, this N.C.O. by his outstanding courage and leadership got the remnants of his Section to his objective and destroyed an enemy L.M.G. Post.

Later, when ordered to withdraw, Corporal Osman, accompanied by his Company Commander under heavy L.M.G. and grenade fire on a search for causalities lying in "No Man's Land". With complete disregard for his personal safety he carried back a badly wounded N.C.O. who was a heavy man, to our own lines though under very heavy fire.

Throughout the action and the subsequent 3 weeks in very close contact with the enemy, the courage, devotion to duty and disregard to his own safety of this N.C.O. was beyond all praise and an inspiration to all around him.'

No. 6403958 Corporal Walter George Gould, 1st Bn. (Fordingham, Hants.)

'During the night 16/17 February 1944 in the area Pt 593 West of Cassino, Corporal Gould's Company took part in a night attack onto the top of the Pt 593 feature. Corporal Gould was N.C.O. i/c Company Stretcher Bearers. The Company reached the top but sustained heavy casualties. The enemy continued to bring heavy L.M.G. fire and rifle grenade fire onto our forward positions as well as continuously throwing stick grenades. Under this heavy fire, Corporal Gould, with complete disregard for his personal safety went forward to exposed positions and personally carried back the wounded Platoon Commander of the forward platoon. Having done this, he returned again and again and successfully evacuated other wounded men from positions swept by bullets and under a hail of rifle and stick grenades.

His personal efforts undoubtedly saved many lives. Throughout this action he showed courage, devotion to duty of the highest order. On several occasions during the subsequent period of 3 weeks in the line in close contact with the enemy, he tended wounded men in full view of the enemy and exposed to fire from enemy snipes. His conduct throughout was an inspiration to his fellow stretcher bearers and is worthy of the highest praise.

No. 6406678 Lance-Corporal William Joseph Chapman, 1st Bn. (London S.W.6)

'During the nights 15/16 and 16/17 February 1944 in the area Pt 593 West of Cassino, Lance-Corporal Chapman was N.C.O. i/c "C" Company Stretcher Bearers. On each night the Company attacked the top of the Pt 539 feature where the enemy were strongly entrenched. On both nights, casualties in his Company were heavy.

This N.C.O. showed exceptional coolness, courage and powers of organisation in evacuating wounded under heavy fire. He himself was always where the fight was thickest, cooly tending the wounded and arranging their evacuation quite regardless of his own safety under a hail of bullets, rifle grenades and stick grenades. On his Company withdrawing, he himself searched "No Man's Land", still under heavy fire, for any further wounded.

He brought in three men and would not return finally to his own lines until he was satisfied that there were no further wounded out there. On the next morning he attempted to recover some of the dead but was driven back by heavy fire. Five days later this N.C.O. was wounded by a sniper while tending a wounded man in the open, close to the enemy.

The courage, devotion to duty and self-sacrifice displayed by this N.C.O. throughout is worthy of the highest praise. He was an inspiration to his fellow stretcher bearers throughout a very trying period.

No. 6401002 Private William George Edward Goodsell, 1st Bn. (Bexhill)

'During the period 13th February to 4th March 1944 in the area between Cairo and Pt 593 West of Cassino, Private Goodsell was in charge of "A" Company mules. His work was of a very exhausting and hazardous nature, as every night it entailed taking his mules three miles up a very narrow mountain track and through a very deep valley which was continually heavily shelled and mortared, up to his Company position within 100 yards of the enemy.

The track alternated between being frozen, in which case the steep sides of the mountain made it a perilous journey for mules – or being boggy in which case the going was appalling and in the rocky parts extremely slippery. In spite of all these difficulties, Private Goodsell never failed to get his Company mules through. On the night 25/26 February 1944 when returning with his mules, after supplying the Company, he came under heavy shell-fire. Two Indian muleteers with him were wounded. Private Goodsell showed great courage and complete disregard for his own safety by carrying one Indian and supporting the other over a distance of 800 yards through a narrow valley to an R.A.P. under a veritable hail of shells and mortar bombs. After resting at the R.A.P. a few minutes he attempted to return to get his mules, but was forbidden to do so by an officer on account of the heavy shelling and the fact that the mules would have stayed.

The courage and resourcefulness, and complete disregard of danger shown by Private Goodsell throughout the whole period was a fine example to all those engaged in the extremely arduous duty of keeping the Battalion supplied.

No. 6403747 Private Edward Percy Moreton, 1st Bn. (London S.W.11)

'During the night 16/17 February 1944 in the area Pt 593 West of Cassino, Private Moreton took part in a night attack onto the top of the Pt 593 feature where the enemy were strongly entrenched in rocks and behind steep walls. His platoon and the platoon on his left suddenly came under very heavy L.M.G. fire and a hail of rifle and stick grenades which caused heavy casualties. Without hesitation, Private Moreton charged forward firing his Bren from the hip and killed the crew of an L.M.G. which were causing heavy casualties to the platoon on his left.

This gallant action by this soldier allowed the advance in that area to continue. Later in the action, when the Company were held up by a steep wall and had run out of grenades – a withdrawal was ordered and Private Moreton whose Bren had run out of ammunition searched for wounded and quite regardless of his own safety carried a man back to our lines under a hail of bullets and grenades. Regardless of the heavy fire he returned again and again to help the wounded back.

The courage and devotion to duty displayed by this soldier throughout the attack and the subsequent period of 21 days in the line was a shining example to all around him.

Saturday July 22nd 1944

Military Awards to Sussex Men

The King has been pleased to approve the following award for gallant and distinguished service in Italy:-

D.S.O.

Captain (T/Mjr.) Benjamin Dalton, 1st Bn.

M.M.

No. 6403616 Sgt. T.S. Andrews,		1st Bn.
No. 5573770 L/Sgt. W.E. Osman,		1st Bn.
No. 6403958 Cpl. W.G. Gould		1st Bn.
No. 6406678 L/Cpl. W.J. Chapman,		1st Bn.
No. 6401002 Pte. W.G.E. Goodsell,		1st Bn.
No. 6402724 Pte. E.P. Moreton,		1st Bn.

"London Gazette" Thursday August 3rd 1944

The KING has been graciously pleased to approve that the following be Mentioned in recognition of gallant and distinguished services in the field: —

M.I.D. (Italy)

No. 6436367 Private J. Davies, 1st Bn.

Saturday August 5th 1944

Mentioned in Dispatches

Mentioned in dispatches in recognition of gallant and distinguished service in the field :-

No. 6436367 Private J. Davies,

"London Gazette" Thursday August 24th 1944

The KING has been graciously pleased to approve the following immediate award's in recognition of gallant and distinguished services in Italy: —

D.S.O.

Major (T/Lt-Col.) Robert Oliver Vere Thompson, (30951) (Fairford, Glos.) Commanding 1/6th East Surrey Regiment, since killed in action (to be dated 6th June, 1944)

Lt-Col. Thompson commanded his Battalion from the time it made an assault crossing over the River Cari at 2345 hrs. on 11th May 1944, until the final mopping up at Cassino on the morning of 18th May 1944. The outstanding success achieved by this Battalion throughout the battle was largely due to this Officers able and thorough work in the planning stages and to his personal example, energy and determination during the operation itself. During the assault crossing nearly all the assault boats were sunk or carried away by the current, but Lt-Col. Thompson by his drive, encouragement and personal courage ensured the construction of 2 flying ferries without which neither the St of his Battalion not the following Battalions could have crossed the river. During the vital 12th May, his Battalion hung on to its objective, despite the most determined enemy efforts to dislodge them and drive them back into the river. During the whole action Lt-Col. Thompson's cool judgement, leadership and personal example had a very considerable effect on the troops under his command.

On 17th and 18th May, his Battalion advanced with great dash and speed and finally cleared Cassino of the remnants of the enemy. The spirit, dash and magnificent fighting qualities of his Battalion reflected very great credit on this Officer's personality and leadership.

Lieutenant Denis Harry Cox, (210789) 1st Bn. (Twickenham)

On the night 16/17 February 1944 in the area Pt 593 west of Cassino, Lieutenant D.H. Cox and his Platoon took part in a night attack with the rest of his Company ("D" Coy) onto the top of the Pt 593 feature. The feature was extremely rocky and broken up by very large boulders which made deployment difficult and bunching almost inevitable. It was strongly held by the enemy, Lieutenant Cox's Platoon was initially in reserve with orders to follow close to the two leading Platoons and be prepared for "mopping up" or any other task which might arrive. The two leading Platoons came under intense Spandau fire and showers of rifle grenades which caused heavy casualties. In the right hand Platoon, the Platoon Commander, Platoon Sergeant and all Second in Commands were killed and the left hand Platoon feared little better. After trying to get on, those two Platoons were pinned down. Fire was still very heavy and the situation critical.

The fire was chiefly coming from an enemy strongpoint on the top of Pt 539, slightly to the right. The Company Commander decided to send Lieutenant Cox's Platoon to try and wipe out this strongpoint but before he could order this, Lieutenant Cox himself arrived with his Platoon and fully realising the critical situation said "Hadn't I better have a crack at that place?" indicating the enemy strongpoint. He immediately went forward with his Platoon and came intense Spandau fire and a veritable hail of rifle grenades causing heavy casualties, he told his Platoon to take cover and stay down. He himself then crawled forward a distance of 70 yards to attack the enemy strongpoint single-handed. Lieutenant Cox with the greatest gallantry and extreme dash then charged the strongpoint single-handed and knocked out two Spandau posts killing the crews with grenades and Tommy-gun.

In performing this extremely gallant action he was badly wounded in the leg. His batman who by now had followed him up alone unordered, tried to evacuate him but Lieutenant Cox refused all aid and shouted to his Platoon to come up and consolidate. This they did promptly and were met on top by a further hail of rifle grenades and heavy Spandau fire which had all by now been turned onto the captured position. At this stage Lieutenant Cox was twice again wounded but still refused to be evacuated. He lay on the ground cooly and calmly giving detailed orders to his men for consolidation of the position.

In spite of being in great pain and still under intense fire his orders were clear and detailed, and his coolness, calmness and cheerfulness had a tremendous steadying effect on his men during what was a difficult time.

During this time he refused three time to be evacuated, and only finally evacuated by the direct orders of his Company Commander in order to save him dying through loss of blood. Throughout the action the inspired and outstanding devotion to duty and the complete disregard of personal safety displayed by Lieutenant Cox was a shining example and superb inspiration to all around him. His magnificent conduct is worthy of the highest praise and must rank very high among all the deeds of gallantry performed by the British Army.

(Forwarded and recommended for V.C.)

(There are two independent accounts of his action in WD 373)

M.C.

Lt. (T/Capt.) Reginald Anthony Alston-Roberts-West, (114111) 1st. Bn. (Hove)

During the period 11th February 1944 to 28th March 1944 in the hills north of Cassino, this officer showed great courage and devotion to duty while acting as Liaison Officer attached to the Bde. HQ. From 12-20 February, during which time the Bde. attacked the Monastery at Monte Cassino the Battalion HQ. Of the 1st Royal Sussex Regiment was situated in a most exposed area in full view of the enemy. The route from Bde. HQ. To Bn. HQ. Was subject to the most intense mortaring and shelling both by day and by night, and part of the route was constantly harassed by enemy snipers and machine-guns firing at close range.

Owing to the telephone cables frequently being out and the failure of wireless communications, it had become necessary for Captain West to make many journeys on foot between Bde. HQ. And Bn. HQ. At all times these journeys were extremely hazardous and Captain West frequently came under heavy machine-gun, mortar and shell fire. In spite of this he never once failed to complete his mission and showed himself willing at all times to repeat the journey as often as necessary. His courage, endurance, cheerfulness and devotion to duty during a very difficult period of operations were quite outstanding and a very fine example.

From 21st February to 25th March, Captain West was frequently called upon both by day and night to take orders and messages to the forward Battalions. The fact that he was required to do this meant that all other means of communications had failed owing to the results of heavy enemy fire in the area. His journeys were at all times hazardous, but again he never once failed to carry out his task. On the nights 26/27 and 27/28 March the Brigade was relieved by another formation, Captain West was sent down the hill to organise the policing of the route or the incoming units. This involved remaining the whole night in the valley which was frequently subjected to the most violent enemy shelling and mortaring.

Every track junction and road had to be accurately registered and the enemy brought down very heavy concentrations of fire at intervals throughout both nights. In spite of this Captain West went about his work calmly and efficiently and with no thought of his personal safety. It was largely due to the gallant work of this officer that a very difficult relief was carried out successfully.

The example of determination and courage set by this officer during a long and difficult period was quite outstanding.

M.I.D.

Major John Blackwood Ashworth, (47519) 4th Bn.
No. 4545640 Private (A/Cpl.) A.L. Smith, 1st Bn.
No. 6412155 Private F. Jeffery, 2nd Bn. attd. 10th Bn. Parachute Regt. A.A.C.

BATTLES ROUND CASSINO

(Memoirs of Capt. A-R-West, 1st Bn.)

We left Baia Latina for the Cassino front on 10th February by night. After a long trip with no lights and in a terrible rain we arrived at San Michele on the (11th of February). It was about two in the morning and everyone was drenched, we could not light any fires as we were in full view of the enemy who overlooked us from the other side of the Rapido Valley. If fact, wherever one walked on could be seen from the slopes of Monte Cassino. Dick Wheaton, Pip and I broke into a farmhouse and procured some boards so that we could sleep off the floor. We had no bedding. We had found small pieces of loot such as two umbrellas and some eggs. I shall not forget seeing the childlike gleam of delight on Dick's face as we broke open a lock of a box. We were like children sharing the spoils of war while outside was being fought one of the grimmest battles of the war.

The 11th, we split up Brigade H.Q. into mule parties and moved off by night. I went on ahead with Bill Stewart to Recce the new Brigade H.Q. which was across the Rapido and overlooking the little village of Cairo. Everything seemed very very quiet except for the purr of the jeep engines. It was a bright moonlight too. We crossed the Rapido without any trouble and parked our jeeps behind a few houses at the new H.Q. there were only four vehicles as it was not deemed that there would be any more cover. The tracks were very narrow and there was scarcely any room for any more vehicles to park. Shortly the place was going to be congested with mules and we must not attract any attention. I was sent back on foot to Cairo to bring up the mules and the marching party who were expected soon.

I waited at the cross roads and saw several American six wheelers come through and followed by their mule train which mounted up the hill the way I had come and on past Brigade H.Q. to the American positions investing the Monastery. The six wheelers came back to turn round as they could go no further. It was difficult for them to turn in the narrow mountain streets. The village of Cairo was very damaged and every available house was occupied with troops whether the house was damaged or not. I remember whilst waiting at the cross roads an American G.I. Joe said to me "I shouldn't stay there son, it's one of the hottest spots on earth". This seemed odd as everything was so quiet and it was hard to see the shell holes with the moon overhead. It was hard to keep away as this was the rendezvous and everyone had to pass it. Nevertheless I waited in a house on the corner where other guides had arrived for the companies of the Brigade. I talked to Jack Snell (later taken prisoner) and we got into a six wheeler which had been parked outside partly to keep warm and to smoke.

Then we were so cold that we went into another house where there were some Americans warming themselves by a fire. They invited us in and Jack passed his cigarettes round. We started discussing Cassino, the Americans had been there six weeks and could make no progress. We met a chap outside who admitted he was a deserter and said he would not go back in those hills again. After what seemed an age the Brigade column started to arrive. Finally the whole Brigade H.Q. arrived I explained about splitting up the mules and the American officer in charge refused to have them split up. He sent all he could back empty. We still had a long way to go. However after much confusion we arrived. Most of the heavy stuff had been dumped by the crossroads.

We still had a few mules and many people got their blankets that night also a bit of food which Pip and I managed to bring up in our jeeps. Boakes was my batman and he helped me a lot. Pip was a real soldier and never failed anyone. I would have done anything for him I think if I was under his command. About three 'o clock someone started an attack, anyhow Jerry started putting down everything he had on us. The hillside was most picturesque and an awful sight to behold. Great gouts of flame were bursting everywhere above and below the group of buildings. Everyone got as near below ground as they could. There were five of us in one slit trench.

I was from bottom up with my legs, my head and shoulders were level with Boakes above ground. To make things worse my little jeep 'Gremlin' had its engine running and the exhaust was pouring into our faces. We were all swearing but no one could or would get out to turn it off. Pip and I were going to take the jeeps back as they were bound to be hit and we had orders from Bill Stewart to save them. I think we made one more trip bringing up supplies I then took Freddie's jeep back as I could not get mine out, the place was too narrow. When I got back with Pip, the awful cacophony was still going on wherever we were the shells seemed to burst from at the crossroads. Mike Lea arrived in his jeep and was just in time to share our slit trench.

He did not stay long with his orders. Poor chap I felt very sorry for him visiting us at the time. The roads were most unsafe especially if one did not know the way well. I am afraid he did not get the welcome he should have had. My own jeep I found was hit several times and was a complete wreck 'Gremlin' had had it. We managed to make the last trip back with Pip and one of his signallers, three jeeps in all. The road was congested with stray mules and wrecked vehicles, however we got down after running over bit and pieces. What a horrible noise a dying mule makes when passing over in a jeep. There had been several direct hits on the track. We spent a good hour in getting down the track, perhaps it was only half a mile in all but we were in and out of jeeps at the worst of the stonks depending on the shelling.

When we got down dawn was breaking. It was no better in Cairo. We sheltered in a house and the next door had a direct hit. By then we were used to anything. I saw several burning six wheelers including the one I had sat in a few hours back. After breakfast the shelling stopped and all was quiet and we walked up to Brigade. That short drive was the last time I was to use a vehicle until the end of March. We moved into a field and started digging a trench. I got a few hours rest on the Brigadier's bed but developed cramp. In the odd collection of houses round us lived a brigade of Americans who were very bomb happy when we arrived. This was very understandable because they had been there six weeks on those hills living in appalling conditions. How they ever got up there we wondered hard.

There is no doubt that the American soldier is very brave but there seemed to be so few of them up at the front. We found out the reason of the bad dose of the shelling. There had been a German attack in the morning and this had been beaten off by the Americans, luckily for us. We were due to relieve an American Division or what was left of them. It amounted to less than a brigade, so each of our Battalions would take over a Regimental front. I remember going up the hill with Colonel Glennie and the Battalion to take over from some of the 34th Texas Division. It was very dark and there was still some snow. We wound our way up a terrible steep incline and the C.O. waited for the Battalion to catch up. Whilst waiting I saw two Americans sitting down on some boxes under a blanket, they wanted me to share their blanket and water bottle as they saw I was sweating.

It was bitterly cold but hot work climbing but I was really thankful of this small welcome. They told me it was an unhealthy spot. I was very glad of a smoke under the blanket. The Yanks said they were going to issue a grenade to every soldier who came up as part of the relief stores. After ten minutes I decided to walk on to the H.Q. which was a little Ersatz Pill Box. If I had known then what a hot spot those two Americans had been sitting in I would not have insured their lives for 6d. I had the greatest respect for their valour. What few of the infantrymen I had met were unmistakable warriors. I suppose we always base our opinions of the other countries on the worst types but I have learnt my lesson. The American fighter is tough, zealous, sentimental though what is more progressive. Nothing is too good for him. In the H.Q. I met various personalities of the Texan Division. The place was eighteen foot square and crowded out, there must have been about seventeen in all. This was due to the relief taking place that night. The relief was an extraordinary show, some of the Americans had to be carried back from their weapon pits, one chap I met had frostbite on his foot.

The Americans left us a lot of their kit and plenty of food which was very generous of them. The relief was soon as no one was desirous of remaining a minute longer than necessary. On our part we were keen to get to sleep being tired after an exhausting march. The night luckily was quiet. I slept in a bunk with George Harper the Adjutant after drinking many cups of American coffee. It seemed that the Americans whilst on this hill had been slogging away almost daily at the Monastery, in fact at eleven o' clock each morning. The Germans must have known someone else was opposite for he did not get his usual attacks. One American told me had got very close before they had to withdraw. We asked him if people had taken much notice of the so-called neutrality of the Monastery which was so much in the public eye.

He told us that nobody took much notice of the neutrality signs the Germans had displayed and also one particular 'Monk' who was accustomed to fire his Spandau at meal times from a window on the second floor. I do not know whether it was ever discovered if 1st Parachute Division had put up signs proclaiming the neutrality of the Monastery, anyhow there was much bitterness felt at the opinion of certain bishops at home who whilst sitting in nice easy armchairs and complained of the damage to sacred buildings by Allied Forces. Kesselring's Castle or so the pill box H.Q. we were in was called was so named because it was said that the great Marshal had visited it. Anyhow the place was beautifully made and had curtains and bunks.

The piece de resistance was the painting for a scene in Goethe's Faust and Mephistopheles shown in all his glory. A house farther up the path and over the crest which later became Battalion H.Q. and R.A.P. alternatively was in full view of the Monastery. It was said that when the Americans were there they did not use the front door because when it was opened the departing guest would be met by a hail of Spandau fire. Whether this had been so, I have never discovered anyhow the Germans must have given up this sport because the Royal Sussex were always going in and out sometimes even they shook their blankets, full view or no. A Red Cross flag used to be hung up on that part of the house which was used as an R.A.P. One usually entered or was asked to enter by the back, having crawled through brushwood. This operation was not comfortable as there were many American dead which had not been buried.

Also lower down there was a corpse on the steps as one jumped down to enter. Italian houses as a rule had very stout walls and bad roofs, this house was no exception. The house had been badly damaged and was very smelly. At times it became a risky operation to go to the lavatory which was usually done at night and was certainly a very brief operation. One American captain had told me that they had had already two truces with the Germans so as to give each side time to collect the wounded. This seems very strange in modern warfare, but I have seen many strange things. The last truce had been on the morning after we had moved into Cairo in the morning after the German attack which had so stubbornly been held back by the Americans. The Germans then had been 1st Parachute Division who were fanatics and about the best enemy Division the 4th Indian Division ever faced. They had entrenched themselves up in the hills and had many supporting weapons which were ideal for the job of defence.

The famous 'Nebelwerfer' which we had met before in Tunisia was one of the most awful. We nicknamed it the 'Organ Grinder' because of its noise. It was no wonder that so many mysteries were attached to this evil sport in front of the Monastery. Soon after the takeover of the Royal Sussex, Brigade H.Q. moved up to a certain little house half way up the hill. This particular house it was reputed was not marked on any map. The first few days we slept in bivouacs round about until the bad weather flooded us out and so we moved into the house. My own was flooded out so I slept in the mess with Fred, my batman and the cook and mess staff. This little room was paradise to us, the ceiling leaked and also it was not black out proof, however we had a very small table and four or five chairs and everyone from Brigade H.Q. except the brigadier and the brigade major came to feed in turn.

The Brigadier and Bill Stewart had their food brought to them in the Ops. room next door. Somebody found a lot of crockery buried and we used that. Most people slept on stretchers until they were needed and never seen again. One day Corporal Robinson one of the clerks was killed at the entrance to the mess (a tiny little splinter from a mortar shell hit him next to me) and the cook's assistant Bert got wounded, after that we had the door sandbagged up Corporal Robinson should have been home a long time ago and it was a great loss to us all who knew him to hear of his sudden death. A few days before he had rushed out to put out a fire which had started among some mortar bombs which had been hit. Needless to say, those pits were never used again as such as they had been responsible for Jerry bringing down a withering fire on our main track which was our lifeline. I suppose the mortars had been spotted from Monte Cairo which directly overlooks us.

This track was always trouble especially during large scale moves. Evacuation of the wounded and supply columns used this even during the hours of daylight as well as mules and visitors. We did not know until later on that the enemy had observation on us from three sides. Very often Jerry used to fire on us from the direction of Monte Gifalis and this gave us the impression of being shelled by our own guns. Truly, this was a very nasty sector and we always got complements and shell reps giving curious bearings mostly sound bearings which was very inaccurate due to the echo in the mountains. About this time the C.R.A. started the Division Counter Mortar Organisation which was a godsend to us. We had medium guns to help neutralise Jerry's persistent artillery as well. It was encouraging to hear one our own stonks going down on Jerry and the relief it caused us was hard to express on paper. Several attacks had been put in to capture Hill 593 which was a dominant peak of which we held a portion.

We could take this hill but never hold it for long. Some said it had been a castle and would show you what did look like a wall round it. It is hard to imagine that so many could and live around that terrible place. I suppose the Germans must have been just as uncomfortable and restless in their portion of the hill. The weather was so bad that we had to wait until March 15th for a full scale attack. February 23rd had been scheduled but the weather had been so bad for the bombers. This we found hard to understand but apparently the landing grounds at Foggia were in a bad condition due to the rain and also because the bombers wanted to bomb from a high altitude with good visibility.

During all this period we had been losing many valuable men due to enemy action on our tracks. Several times Jerry sent over propaganda pamphlets written in bad Hindi. On one day our own gunners fired a lot of propaganda shells as well and the wind brought them back; on the same day at the same time Jerry fired his own lot so that there was a lot of paper floating about. Actually, the Germans had used very high brow Hindi and many of the Indian troops, in fact the majority had been unable to read with understanding. One of the outstanding points to my mind were the medical services. Any man so unfortunate enough to get wounded badly had a most awful journey back; if he was lucky he would get his wound dressed after the stonk was over and be carried to a dressing station then he would have to wait his turn for treatment from a perpetually exhausted team whilst others would be waiting to be carried back.

The process of carrying back under fire was most gruelling, yet the stretcher bearers worked miracles not to jolt their passengers on the journey down the steep hill. There were various stretcher posts at which he bearers were changed otherwise it would not have been possible for them to do more than about three journeys a day to the A.D.S. at the foot of the hill. Again at the A.D.S. which was a very hot corner, Ernie Bower was over parked also under observation and near Jeep head, sometimes elapsed before transport was available to clear the casualties across the valley (about six miles under fire) to the A.D.S. (Advanced Dressing Station). Four hours was about bogey to evacuate a casualty to be taken out of range of the enemy guns and in a bed. This meant many men risking their lives under all kinds of bad conditions.

No wonder there were many decorations for the Medics and they really deserved them. Some of the bravest of the latter I have seen are the American Field Servicemen who are volunteers. They were never in the news but always to be found in sectors where the fighting was thickest. The Americans had a dressing station quite close to our own and this lay on a fork track which led back to the village of Cairo. Our own advanced dressing station was in the valley at the foot of the track leading up to our awful residence, it became a jeep head for the ambulance jeeps. The next building belonged to the gunners (anti-tank) who were operating mortars and counter mortar battery. The building was known as the Plasterer's Arms on account of the pasting it use to get.

The gunners had painted a very nice signboard which swung in the shell blasts. Jimmy James our supply officer lived in it for it had become jeep head for all supplies and mules. Further down the track towards the barracks the sappers took up residence and later on 5th Brigade. The period of waiting for the big attack in March was interspersed with abortive raids. Brigadier Lovett was one of the greatest commanders I have ever met. He would visit everybody during the worst of times and was always cheerful, yet heaven knows how many times he escaped death. I used to be frightened every time I went up to the battalion myself and would plan my path depending on the current days stonking, for there were no places that Jerry could not and had not touched. The Royal Sussex had made two unsuccessful bids against Hill 593 in February soon after arrival and where they were asked to try again February 17/18th the big 7th Brigade attempt General Tuker the G.O.C. who was in hospital sent a signal wishing them success and said for the Honour of the Battalion it must be taken, so vital was it. Actually, it had been taken and lost by bad chance for in the moment of success Jerry had given the signal to withdraw that had been by 'D' Company.

In this action Lieutenant Cox received the D.S.O. That had been the second bid and now for the third, most of the company commanders lay wounded. The big attack as planned for the night of 17/18th would include Battalions from the other two Brigades and under Command of Brigadier Lovett. The

1/2 Gurkhas and the 1/9 Gurkhas were to assault the Monastery. 4/6 Ray Rifles supported by the Royal Sussex were to take 593. The 4/16 would give supporting fire whilst two companies of 1/6 were in reserve. The 2nd Camerons were supplying porters to man handle supplies, the 57th Lt. A.A. where helping the stretcher bearers. I went up in the evening before with orders and on the way back I found a troop of mules and they asked me to guide them down the track. I passed Nicol and Loftus Totterham of the 1/2 Gurkhas who swore at the mules. A few hours later I was sent up again when the attack had started to find out the form it was just before light.

I went up to the house on the crest and crept forwards above to the new H.Q. near to 593. I met the L.O. of the 1/9 who was looking for his battalion. In the valley to the left and before the Monastery there was considerable machine gun fire when I approached my own Battalion H.Q. I was very nearly shot by our own troops like an unfortunate signaller (Corporal Dale) the day before. However, on the Hill 593 everybody was crammed together. It resembled a market place with numerous wireless sets and signallers and everybody talking and swearing and then Jerry started firing his rifle grenades. The C.O. of the 4/6 gave the Royal Sussex then under his command orders to move back to the house which was near H.Q. Even this was crowded out as a R.A.P. (Regimental Aid Post) so Colonel Glennie gave orders to move back his H.Q. to Kesselring's Castle. Jerry started to mortar.

We all seemed to sense the attack had not gone off well. The C.O.'s batman Blundell saved our feelings by cooking some beans and coffee on his little primus stove but once again we knew that 1st Parachute Division had beaten us. This was only a bitter disappointment and we knew that we should soon have another go at the Monastery. Mail was very indifferent from England and when it did arrive we used to get letters saying that we were lucky to be in Sunny Italy also there were strikes in the mines in England, altogether we were not too pleased with things in general.

Life in the mess was never monotonous and we used to watch everything being cooked with great interest as food was at a premium. We had several mules of our own which brought our rations and water from the well in the Bowl. The 'Bowl' was a hollow of a bowl shape in which units used to rest, if one could use this term, rest; it was within five minutes up the hill from Brigade H.Q. In the middle of this was a well which was used sometimes. This used to dry up, at other times the enemy made the journey difficult by mortaring the track to it. Quite often Jerry used to send over shells which made pink smoke, why we never discovered, unless it was for ranging, anyhow we could be seen from so many places.

One day our signals officer Pip Mott was hit on the chin by a splinter from one of these and he was stitched up by Ernie Bowmer on one of his visits to the mess and this operation was watched by the mess. It must have been very painful for Pip and we made him laugh with our rude comments as the doctor only had large needles. Needless to say Ernie produced some rum, only a little tot but it was wonderful. Ernie used to visit us frequently more often than not with his little bottle of cheer. Ernie (He got the M.C.) was an amazing little chap who seemed absolutely tireless.

He was responsible for our excellent medical services under very trying conditions. If he had not been there, there would have been many more casualties who would have died of wounds. Time soon arrived for the big attack and when it arrived we were living under the conditions mentioned. By now we all keen to get it over with come what may.

Friday August 25th 1944

The King has been pleased to approve the following award for gallant and distinguished service in Italy :-

Immediate Decoration

D.S.O.

Major (T/Lt-Col.) Robert Oliver Vere Thompson,   (30951) (Fairford, Gloucester)
attd. 1/6th Royal East Surreys

Lt. Denis Harry Cox, (210789) 1st Bn. (Twickenham)

M.C.

Lt. (T/Capt.) Reginald Anthony Alston-Roberts-West, (114111) 1st Bn. (Hove)

M.I.D.

Major John Blackwood Ashworth, (47519) 4th Bn.
No. 4545640 Private (A/Cpl.) A.L. Smith, 1st Bn.

Saturday August 26th 1944

1 Royal Sussex enter Urbino, the entire inhabitants lined the streets and gave an enthusiastic welcome to the troops.

"London Gazette" Thursday August 31st 1944

The KING has been graciously pleased to approve the following awards in recognition of gallant and distinguished services in Normandy: —

Major William Thyrkel Woodruffe, (64610) attd. 5th Bn. East Yorks.

On 18 June 1944, Major Woodruffe's Company made an attack upon the village of Longraye at 1630 hours. Immediately after crossing the start line the Company was met by machine-gun and heavy mortar fire. After about 40 minutes the two forward platoons succeeded in working round the flank of the village. Major Woodruffe ordered the reserve platoon to advance through the village itself.
At the South end of the village the Company came under very heavy machine-gun fire at short range from high ground on its left rear, and from an enemy tank. Major Woodruffe moved about constantly rallying his men, directing fire, and himself giving covering fire with a mortar. He finally moved forward almost alone to try and contact his forward sections as all communications had broken down. Although part of his equipment was shot away and his ammunition on fire, he continued to move about in the open under heavy aimed fire from machine-guns and mortars with complete disregard for danger, and by his fine leadership and personal example succeeded in rallying his Company, which had suffered heavy casualties from enemy fire and counter-attack.

Sunday September 10th 1944

"D" Coy 1 Royal Sussex advanced from Pian di Castello village to seize Cemetery Hill to the north, with "B" Squadron 6 Royal Tank Regiment they are able to dislodge the German defenders and take about 20 prisoners. Later that night two troops of tanks and "C" Coy 1 Royal Sussex in close support behind a Corps. barrage move north towards Onferno which is beyond Cemetery Hill. 1 Royal Sussex seized their objective and consolidated their positions to await enemy counter-attacks. The Royal Sussex ably aided by the tanks repelled five attempts to repel them.

"London Gazette" Thursday September 21st 1944

The KING has been graciously pleased to approve the following awards in recognition of gallant and distinguished services in Italy: —

M.C.

Lt. Murray James Angus Dickson, (138855) 1st Bn. (Etchingham)

At 0420 hrs. on the morning 26th May 1944, "D" Company, 1st Bn. The Royal Sussex Regiment carried out a raid on Le Piane, a small village between Arielli and Ceccho, known to be occupied by the enemy. The object was to secure identification, the right forward Platoon commanded by Lt. Dickson searched their half of the village and was then fired on from a group of houses 400 yards to the north along the ridge known as July. Lt. Dickson, disappointed at finding no enemy in Le Piane and realising the importance of capturing a prisoner, on his own initiative quickly rallied two of his section and pushed straight through to July.

The Platoon having passed August, came under heavy Spandau fire and suffered casualties and two badly injured men were lying in an exposed position. Lt. Dickson with complete disregard for his own personal safety rushed across and dragged the first man to a position of safety. In doing this he was wounded in the side, regardless of this he went back for the second man whom he reached and found dead.

Under cover of Bren fire, he and a few men then rushed the enemy in July with Tommy guns, forcing the enemy to withdraw to June, 200 yards further along the ridge. He then took up a position near July, and engaged the enemy who was in strength in June and were firing at his force with a least two Spandaus. He realised that his section were too weak to make another assault, he therefore remained in position at July until his ammunition was completely exhausted. Although in a weak and exhausted condition, he continued to direct his force until ordered to withdraw.

M.M.

No. 6401368 Lance-Sergeant Thomas Alfred Gardner, 1st Bn. (Balcombe)

On the morning of the 26th May 1944, during the raid by "D" Coy 1 R.S.R. on the village of Le Piane, 18 Platoon was ordered to clear the South half of the village. The plan was for 9 Section, commanded by L/Sergeant Gardner to clear the houses East of the track running through the village, and for 7 Section to clear those West of the track. 6 Section to remain with Platoon "H" in reserve. The assault opened and 9 Section immediately came under fire from a Spandau in a house. L/Sergeant Gardner got his Bren gun into action and shouted for assistance of the Piat Mortar.

He himself worked the remainder of his section round the right flank and rushed the house, driving the enemy out with Tommy guns and grenades. He searched rapidly through the house but all the enemy had evacuated. Meanwhile another Spandau had opened up on the house. The Platoon Commander moved his H.Q. and Reserve and engaged the enemy. L/Sergeant Gardner with 9 Section made a rapid left flanking movement and assaulted the house. Once again the enemy eluded him and withdrew via "mouse holes". L/Sergeant Gardner then saw fire coming from 'G' which was holding up the advance of the reserve section and without hesitation he rushed this strongpoint, with two of his men and succeeded in completely demoralising the enemy who fled under cover of smoke. L/Sergeant Gardner by his dash, initiative and quickness of decision, completely demoralised and routed the enemy. Throughout the engagement, his leadership and courage were an inspiration to his Section, he himself being always in the lead, and in the thick of battle.

No. 6402864 Private Charles James Willard, 1st Bn.   (Devizes)

On the morning 26th May 1944, during the raid by "D" Coy 1st Royal Sussex Regt., on Le Piane, having cleared the North half of the village and finding no enemy, pressed on with two Sections towards the group of buildings known as 'July', 400 yards North along the ridge, from where they were being fired on by enemy Spandaus. This force, with casualties, pushed on doggedly right in the face of enemy fire. Finally this light section was forced to go to ground about 100 yards from 'July' having lost their commander and four others, and coming under close range enemy automatic fire. The Commander of the left section who beside himself had only three men left, ordered his Bren group of which Private Willard was the No. 2 to engage the enemy. The gun was got into action, and the Platoon Commander and Section Commander were able to dash forward a few yards and hurl two 77 smoke grenades which put up a partial screen. Private Willard to the left, seized this opportunity to dash forward on his own initiative a distance of about 80 yards in the face of enemy's fire and hurl Mills grenades into the windows from which the enemy were firing, thus silencing both guns and enabling the remainder of the force to move up. Private Willard by his superb, individual effort, not only silenced two enemy Spandaus but inflicted casualties and put the remainder of the enemy force to flight. His initiative and promptness of action maintained the momentum of the advance at a critical stage when a stalemate seemed inevitable. His gallantry undoubtedly saved further casualties amongst his comrades who were pinned down by the enemy's fire.

Friday September 22nd 1944

The King has been pleased to approve the following award for gallant and distinguished service in Italy:-

M.C.

Lt. Murray James Angus Dickson, (138855) 1st Bn. (Etchingham)

M.M.

No. 6401368 Lance-Sergeant T.A. Gardner, 1st Bn.
No. 6402864 Private C.J. Willard, 1st Bn.

Sunday September 24th 1944

On the night of 24/25 September 1 Royal Sussex crossed the River Marecchia and seized Gemmiano on its western bank.

Sunday October 1st 1944

(Memoirs of Capt. A-R-West, 1st Bn.)

The Royal Sussex were going to put in an attack on the Reggiano Ridge further to the west of Tribola. The attack did not come off till the 1st of October when a barrage of 340 guns was fired and the Battalion went in with the Camerons then under command for the battle. Little opposition was met but fifty prisoners were taken. Every calibre of gun available from 25 pounders to 7.2 howitzers had been used for an hour's fierce barrage. Soon after the 2/11 put in an attack further left which proved unsuccessful, they had tried to take Borghi and suffered for it instead. It was obvious that the line was becoming stabilized and would remain much the same for the winter owing to the appalling weather.

"London Gazette" Thursday October 19th 1944

The KING has been graciously pleased to approve the following awards in recognition of gallant and distinguished services in North West Europe: —

No. 6398348 Company Quarter-Master-Sergeant Leonard Arthur Graham, 9th Bn. Parachute Bn. 3rd Parachute Bde. 6th Airborne Division, Army Air Corps (Manchester).

St. Come, 9th June 44

On 9th June 44, whilst holding a vital piece high ground, the Battalion was attacked in strength. CQMS Graham was in charge of a machine-gun post and was wounded shortly after the attack was commenced. Although knocked into a ditch he crawled back and continued to fire the gun. A few minutes later he was wounded again, and again knocked into the ditch. Once again he crawled back to the gun and continued to fire it. A short he was wounded yet a third time and collapsed while attempting to reach the gun again. His determination to stick to his post and his complete disregard of his own wounds, set an example to the remainder of the men worthy of the best traditions of the Army.

Saturday October 28th 1944

Premier's Tribute

THE ROYAL SUSSEX REGIMENT

Military and civic pageantry of a kind to which the town has long been a stranger marked the ceremony of conferring the Freedom of the County Borough of Brighton upon The Royal Sussex Regiment yesterday. The day's proceedings were carried out with dignity worthy of the occasion, the outstanding events being the gatherings in the Council Chamber at the town Hall, at which the formal resolution giving effect to the will of the Council was passed, and in the Dome, where the actual presentation was made.

The scarlet of the Aldermen and the mazarin blue of the Councillors, with the Military, Naval and Air Force uniforms of many high ranking officers of the services, made the scene in the Council Chamber a brilliant one. A further touch of colour was provided by a vase of chrysanthemums on the Mayoral desk.

The Public Gallery was completely occupied by khaki clad officers and men of the Royal Sussex Regiment. Prominent seats were allotted to the Sussex Members of Parliament, among whom were Lieutenant-Colonel A. Marlowe and Flight Lieutenant W. Teeling (Members for Brighton), Rear-Admiral T.P.H. Beamish (Member for Lewes) and Colonel R.S. Clarke (Member for East Grinstead), who also represented the Sussex Yeomanry Association).

Welcomes

The company first rose, at the call of Ald. J. Talbot Nanson, who acted as M.C., to welcome Sussex Mayors – all wearing their chains of office. They were the Mayors of Eastbourne (Ald. Miss A. Hudson), Lewes (Ald. C.D. Crisp, O.B.E.) Arundel (Cr. R.W. Pearson, M.B. M.C.) Hove (Cr. A.H. Clarke), Bexhill (Cr. W.H. Hughes) and Worthing (Cr. E.R. Willoughby). The last five were accompanied by their Mayoress'. A few minutes later a similar tribute was paid to the official guests – the Lord Lieutenant (Lord Leconfield), the Duke of Norfolk, the High Sheriff (Mr. Basil Ionides), Sir George Boughy, Bart. (Chairman of the East Sussex County Council) and Lady Anderson.

The Mayoral procession, headed by the mace-bearer with the mace, was a most impressive one. A striking feature was the Colours of the Regiment borne by a young officer, who was followed by Lieutenant-General Sir Kenneth Anderson, K.C.B., M.C. (Commanding the South-Eastern District), and Brigadier-General W.L. Osborn, C.B., C.M.G., D.S.O. (acting Colonel of the Regiment). Behind the Mayor walked the Recorder (Sir Charles Doughty, K.C.), the Town Clerk Mr. J.G. Drew, O.B.E.) and the Clerk of the Peace (Mr. G.S. Godfree), in wigs and gowns.

In Recognition of Great Traditions

The Mayor moved the resolution to confer "in recognition of the great traditions of the Regiment since its formation in 1701, its splendid record and gallant services more especially during the present war in North Africa, Italy and North-West Europe, and of the close associations which have so long existed between the Regiment and this Borough."

In doing so his Worship recalled that the Prime Minister was Joint Honorary Colonel with General Osborn of the 4th and 5th Battalions (now amalgamated) and read the following message:-

"As Joint Honorary Colonel of the 4/5th Battalion The Royal Sussex Regiment, I am proud that the Borough of Brighton is thus honouring the Regiment with its Freedom. I wish it were possible for me to be with you today so that I could thank you personally on behalf of the Battalion. It is no small distinction to be Freeman of a town, already famous, which for five years has shared with others on the South Coast the honour of standing in the forefront of the battle. I send my best wishes both to Brighton and to the members of the Royal Sussex Regiment who are united by this bond."

WINSTON S. CHURCHILL

His Worship went on to speak of the Regiment's great record, mentioning among other things that it captured von Arnim in North Africa and that von Arnim, who had fought against the Royal Sussex in the last war, called it "the iron regiment". He detailed the links between Brighton and the Regiment and incidentally described how the Regiment was entertained when it was stationed in the town 48 years ago. Then the surplus of the fund raised by the inhabitants for the purpose of "a large silver milk jug" for the officers mess (laughter) which was still among the regimental plate. "All the inhabitants of Brighton", he concluded, "are one with us in conferring the freedom."

After General Osborn and the Mayor had signed the Roll of Freedmen and the Town Clerk had read the statutory declaration, General Osborn thanked the Council in a few simple but heartfelt words.

"You have taken the lead in the County of Sussex in honouring the County Regiment," he said, "On behalf of the officers, n.c.o's and men of the Regiment I give you our sincere thanks." Since Dunkirk, he said the Regiment had fought in Eritrea, Abyssinia, El Alamein, Libya, Tunisia, Sicily, Italy and the Far East. It would take some time to acquaint such widely spread units with the news of Brighton's tribute to their fighting qualities, but he was sure they would be inspired by such recognition of their deeds.

The ceremony concluded with a silent tribute to the men of the regiment who had made the supreme sacrifice.

Monday November 6th 1944

Royal Sussex Regiment

The Mayor of Brighton has received the following telegram from an overseas Battalion of the Royal Sussex Regiment :-

"All ranks reciprocate greetings on the occasion of conferring Freedom County Borough on Regiment."

Lieutenant-Colonel Ellen.

"London Gazette" Thursday November 9th 1944

The KING has been .graciously pleased to approve the following awards in recognition of gallant and distinguished services in the field: —

M.C. (1940)

Captain Richard Brian de Fontenne Sleeman, (50239) 2nd Bn.
(was PoW at Oflag V11 C/H.)

Recommended by Captain H. Pozner, R.A.M.C., and Captain & Q/M. P.J. Hanlon.

For the greatest devotion to duty during the period 22nd/29th May 1940. With four Commanding Officers killed, or wounded, in succession, he carried the whole direction of the Battalion on his shoulders during a difficult withdrawal and subsequent to a defensive position. Although suffering both from stomach trouble and a shrapnel wound to the leg, he refused to go sick. He carried on in spite of three nights without sleep, and at the end, having ordered the Medical Officer and Quartermaster to get away, he remained with one man at Battalion H.Q. until taken prisoner early on the morning of May 29th. His courage and example were of the highest standard throughout.

"During the period of May 21st/22nd his conduct and work under heavy shell fire were of the highest order, and thoroughly endorse the above account as characteristic of Captain Sleeman's work all the time he was my Adjutant."

(signed) P.J. M. Ellison. Lt-Col.

"The only person, I thought, who was absolutely superb was Brian. He was a man of action, highly strung, and yet he had to remain in one spot the whole time, with the complete direction of the Battalion upon his own shoulders. During the last few days he was in pain from his stomach trouble, he had been caught in the leg with a piece of shrapnel, a thing which I found out only after a lot of questioning, and he hadn't slept for three nights. He could have got away with me, and yet he preferred to stay behind to have a last shot at the Jerries. I think that after I'd got my wounded away and he'd told me to go whilst there was still a chance, he was really fighting-mad.
You know, with his responsibility, he deserved something, because that job was worse than any of ours."

Extract from a letter dated 8th January 1941 to Colonel Ellison from Captain H. Pozner, R.A.M.C.

The KING has been graciously pleased to approve that the following be Mentioned in recognition of gallant and distinguished services in Sicily: —

M.I.D.

No. 6404085 Private Christopher S. Seller, 1st Bn.

Friday November 10th 1944

The King has been graciously pleased to approve the following awards in recognition of gallant and distinguished service :-

M.C.

Major Richard Brian de Fontenne Sleeman, (50239) 2nd Bn.

"London Gazette" Thursday November 16th 1944

The King has been graciously pleased to approve the following awards in recognition of gallant and distinguished service in Burma :-

M.C.

Major Kenneth Leslie Callender, (164699) 9th Bn.

In N. Burma on night 4/5 August 1944, prior to the attack on the feature known as Hill 60, Major Callender was ordered to move his Coy to take up a position on the Eastern slope of Hill 60. It was not known at this time whether the enemy were still in position of this area or not. Major Callender personally carried out a recce of this position and finding part of the feature unoccupied he continued his recce until he located the enemy positions. By his skill he succeeded in locating the enemy positions nearest to his Coy at the same time remaining undetected by the enemy. Major Callender returned to his Coy and at once occupied the position without opposition.
At 0400hrs. 5 August, Major Callender received orders to clear the enemy from Hill 60, Major Callender advanced at once with his Coy but soon came under heavy fire and was held up, the enemy being in

stronger positions and greater strength than was anticipated. At dawn both forward platoons found themselves in exposed positions pinned down by the fire from enemy machine-guns. Major Callender with complete disregard for his own safety, worked his way forward under enemy fire and personally organised the withdrawal of these two platoons. Major Callender also supervised the evacuation of the wounded until this had been completed, during which time Major Callender remained under constant enemy fire.

By skilful handling of his Coy and his personal gallantry he extricated his Coy from an extremely precarious position with far fewer casualties than they may have expected. The action of this Coy materially assisted the final capture of Hill 60.

T/Major Francis William Seymour Stanbrook, (249251)   9th Bn.

At 0230hrs. on 6th August 1944 Lieutenant Stanbrook "D" Coy was in position approximately 150 yards. North of the Japanese defended locality known as Hill 60. This position was taken up during darkness and the ground between the two positions was unknown. At 0230hrs. Lieutenant Stanbrook was ordered to take a patrol forward to ascertain the strength and disposition of the enemy. This he accomplished over very difficult country and in darkness bringing back valuable information as to the strength of the enemy.

At 0400hrs. two fighting patrols were detailed to approach the Japanese position and if no opposition or slight was encountered, patrols were to occupy and hold them.

One of these patrols was commanded by Lieutenant Stanbrook, by excellent groundwork he had led his patrol to within 30 yards of the enemy positions unobserved when fire was opened some 1000 yards distant. The patrol was now observed and heavy M.G. and L.M.G. and grenade fire was opened. By personal example he led the patrol to within 15 yards of the Japanese trenches. Here the patrol was counter-attacked twice, both of which were repelled. A hidden L.M.G. now enfiladed the patrol and it withdrew. Lieutenant Stanbrook's conduct throughout was excellent, in the close quarter withdrawal his example and personal bravery did much to aid the patrol which by now was being sniped from the other flank and casualties were constant.

He remained under fire until the last of the patrol were brought into safety and helped bring out the last wounded. At 0800hrs. he took "C" Coy back over the same route to a forming up point from where they were to assault. Throughout the action this officer showed a high degree of courage and devotion to duty.

M.M.

No. 6410995 Private Alexander Walter Gentle   9th Bn. (Cheshunt)

During the attack on Hill 60 near Sekmaw on 5 August 1944 Private Gentle was No.1 on the section L.M.G. His Coy had almost reached the summit of Hill 60 when an enemy Machine-gun opened up in the rear of the Coy at close range, temporarily halting the advance of the Coy. Private gentle moved quickly to a flank across fire-swept ground, stalked the enemy machine-gun and wiped out the post single-handed, killing 4 Japs and capturing the gun. His prompt action enabled the remainder of the Coy to successfully attain their objective. In a subsequent action on 17 August, Private Gentle was in the forward position of his platoon covering the road into Thaikwagon.

At 0300hrs. a Jap fighting patrol, about 30 strong attacked his post. They were driven off but during the two hours they tried again and again to overcome the position. In spite of many casualties in his Section, Private Gentle continually engaged the enemy with his L.M.G. When his ammunition was exhausted, Private Gentle remained by his gun dodging Jap grenades until some more ammunition arrived. Eventually the enemy was compelled to withdraw leaving 6 dead in front of his post. If Private Gentle's Section had not held their post the Coy position would have been jeopardised. The courage and absolute steadiness of this private soldier has been an example to all ranks.

No. 6412104 Private William Eric Selbourne, 9th Bn. (London N.15)

In N. Burma on the night 4/5 August 1944 prior to the attack on the feature known as Hill 60, Private Selbourne was No. 1 on his Section L.M.G. and was a member of a fighting patrol recceing enemy positions on the Eastern slope of Hill 60. Very soon the patrol came under heavy and accurate machine-gun fire which pinned the patrol to the ground. Private Selbourne on his own initiative taking with him the No. 2 worked his way through thick scrub to a position which enfiladed the enemy positions. Very soon Private Selbourne became the target of enemy fire, his No. 2 was killed almost at once, but by constantly changing his position to deceive the enemy he succeeded in maintaining a steady and accurate fire on the enemy position.

Private Selbourne was continually under enemy fire and was wounded in the leg but continued to engage the enemy during which time the patrol managed to disengage itself. Private Selbourne was now alone and in spite of his wound succeeded in making his way back to his Coy.

Private Selbourne displayed great initiative in moving around the enemy position, and later, courage and determination although wounded in engaging the enemy, and it was very largely due to his action that his patrol disengaged itself and brought back vital information.

No. 6407586 Private Arthur William White, 9th Bn. (Midhurst)

In N. Burma on the night 18/19 August 1944, Private White was performing the duties of No. 1 of his section L.M.G. Private White's Section Post was the forward post in his Coy which was covering the approaches to Thaikwagon village captured the previous day. At 0100hrs. this position was attacked by an enemy raiding party numbering between 30 or 40. A party of the enemy rushed Private White's position. He engaged the enemy and with his first burst of fire killed 3. The third enemy body fell on top of his L.M.G. and prevented him firing it again.

Another of the enemy charged Private White with a bayonet, Private White kicked him in the stomach, temporarily putting his enemy out of action. Meanwhile the Section Post on his right had been overrun, Private White remained at his post and endeavoured to get his L.M.G. into action again in the course of which Private White received 4 bayonet wounds.

Eventually Private White got his L.M.G. into action again and engaged such enemy as was still in the vicinity. By his tenacity, courage and resourcefulness he played no small part in driving off the enemy raiding party.

The KING has been graciously pleased to confer "The Efficiency Decoration" upon the following officers of the Territorial Army:-

Lieutenant-Colonel Edward Keith Beavan Wannop, (45350) 6th Bn.
Captain (T/Mjr.) Rex Anthony E. Hillman, (2717)

Monday December 4th 1944

Japs Routed By The Royal Sussex

Battle of Pinwe

Men of The Royal Sussex Regiment in North Burma, under the command of Major Bobby Cash, routed a Japanese suicide charge near the railway line from Myitkyina in the jungle corridor. As the Sussex men moved forward a riot of shooting burst out and Japanese came running madly towards them.

Evidently the Japanese had crept from their bunkers during the night, prepared to attack at dawn. To get the Japanese in the open is the British warrior's dream. Private Denis Clark, Henley-on-Thames, was in bed when the shooting began, for he was not concerned in the initial attack.

Reaching for his Bren gun, as he saw two of the enemy rushing towards him, he killed both of them, then a third, and though his mare had been killed, wounded four more Japs.

Orgy of Shooting

In the orgy of shooting, Corporal Victor Connetta, of Battersea, scored the biggest bag by shooting nine of the enemy, some at a few yards range. Then, in a lull, Connetta stripped and cleaned his Bren. Private George Fuller, of Binfield, Berks., scattered a bunch of Japanese, but one of the enemy stalked him, finally shattering Fuller's Bren with bullets, but Fuller continued firing despite splinters in his face and one eye.
In a short time the jungle was quiet again. The suicide charge had cost the Japanese 60 dead and probably over 100 casualties in all.

The awards following the battle of Pinwe were presented by General Festing, the recipients being Major J.J. Dickson, (M.C.) Corporal A. Harris, Corporal J. Govier, Corporal V. Conetta, Private F.C. Stoneham, Private C.A. Colesby, Private J.W. Cox and Private S. Powell, (M.M.'s), Private J.E. Maynard received a Certificate of Gallantry.

Extract from the "Shiny Ninth"

The Battle of Pinwe

Operations began on November 9th with a routine order to advance down the railway line, which was our usual axis, with the South Wales Boarders astride the road to the Battalion's left, the objective being to occupy Hpapan and Pinwe and push towards the rail junction at Naba. About a quarter of a mile from Hpapan the leading platoon (8 Platoon of "A" Coy, under Lt. Neal) was fired on but succeeded in entering the village without much further trouble and were able to report it clear, whereupon the remainder of "A" Coy moved up to occupy Hpapan. The remainder of the Battalion were concentrated just South of Mintha, short of "A"'s starting position when at 1030 they were dived bombed by U.S. Thunderbolts which were supposed to be supporting the S.W.B. on the road. There were sixteen casualties, including two killed.
"D" Coy reinforced by "B" Coy then went forward but were held up by heavy fire from a chaung 1,000 yards South of Hpapan. Both Coys were withdrawn.
Next day, "C" Coy tried unsuccessfully to what "D" and "B" had failed to do the day before and it was also withdrawn temporarily. After a concentration of artillery and heavy fire from the Manchesters, "A" Coy were ordered to make a right flanking attack on "Stourbridge" by moving down a chaung about half a mile to the West of Hpapan which ran into "Stourbridge" and advance along the South bank to the railway bridge.
The attack was carried out by Major Dickson and his men to such good effect that some of the enemy were caught out of their bunkers and disposed of, John Dickson was able to exert direct control on the last stages of the fire fight and destroy the remaining pockets of resistance. It was a model company attack which could not have been bettered at a battle school demonstration.
Private Harris, Corporal Tasker, Sergeant Myerscough, Private Govier, Sergeant Smith, Sergeant Herman and the stretcher-bearer Private Powell, all distinguished themselves.

"London Gazette" Thursday December 7th 1944

The KING has been graciously pleased to approve the following awards in recognition of gallant and distinguished services in Italy: —

M.C.

Lieutenant (T/Capt.)(A/Mjr.) Tom Dixon, (189367) attd. 5th Bn. The Buffs. (Redcar)

On 23rd June 1944 this Battalion moved to an assembly point area near Pescia at approximately 0800hrs. They were immediately subjected to extremely heavy shelling from artillery, mortar and hebelwerters, which continued throughout the day. In the evening the Battalion was ordered to force the crossing of the River Pescia, zero hour being fixed for 1830hrs. The shelling had now increased in intensity and the situation was made more difficult by an enemy machine-gun which started to fire enfilade from the right flank across the ground over which the attacking troops had to pass.

Major Dixon was commanding the right hand leading Company for the attack and despite extreme heavy shelling and machine-gun fire he rallied his men together and lead them forward into the attack. By his great determination and powers of leadership he led his men on, and together with the Company on his left crossed the river and made a bridge-head secure. Forty-six prisoners of whom six were officers, an enemy Infantry gun, limbered up ready to move, a wireless set almost intact and a Panther tank were captured by the Company. This magnificent result was entirely due to Major Dixon's determination to gain his objective and to his brilliant leadership under the most difficult conditions.

Friday December 8th 1944

Helped to capture Kalewa
Battersea Soldier accounts for nine Japs

While listening to an account of a battle between British and Japanese forces in Burma broadcast during the 12 o'clock news on Sunday a Battersea family were surprised to hear the announcer mention the name of Private Victor Conetta, who, "during the fighting, had killed nine of the enemy."

The surprised listeners were the family of Pte. Conetta, who lives at 19 Taybridge Road, Battersea. The story told was that of East African troops, who after an advance through the Myitta Gorge in Burma, had thrown the Japanese defenders out of the key Chindwin River port of Kalewa, one of the main centres for downstream traffic to Mandalay, 150 miles to the south-east.

Men of the Royal Sussex Regiment, under Major Bobby Cash, were instrumental in repulsing a suicidal Japanese charge in which the enemy had 100 casualties, 60 of them dead. Pte. Conetta without thought of personal safety, accounted for nine Japs, and so played an important part in the capture of Kalewa.

Within five yards of Japs

A letter sent by Pte. Conetta and received by his family the day after the broadcast tells of another incident of the campaign. Pte. Conetta and his comrades advanced under a withering fire from enemy guns. As they drew nearer the firing stopped. The men continued to advance until they were within five yards of the Jap positions. They were then ordered to lie "doggo" for a while in preparation for a final attack. Just then the enemy opened fire again with all he had. Knowing that their position was perilous and that they must not reveal their location the men remained still and silent for over an hour. After that they were told to withdraw. As they tried desperately to get back to their lines three enemy machine-gun posts took a mounting toll of lives. Pte. Conetta attacked the posts with hand grenades, and after killing ten Japs managed to silence the guns. Unfortunately however, he was soon injured in the back. He got back safely to the British lines, and, with his comrades, was told that they were to have a week's rest.

Basnett Road School

Pte. Conetta is aged 21. He was born at 1 Wickersley road, Battersea, and was educated at Basnett Road School, where he was well known as a keen athlete. In civilian life he worked with his father as a parquet floor layer. Pte. Conetta volunteered for the Army in 1942, and after 15 months in this country was sent to India, and later to the Burma front

Of the Japs he writes: "They are everything that is cunning and crafty. In battle they will wait for you to reveal yourself and then fire at you with everything they have. They are detestable and ignorant fighters."

Pte. Conetta has four sisters and five brothers. They are : Mrs. Winnie Yianoppolus; Joseph Conetta, aged 26, a war worker; Ernst Conetta, aged 23, a Bevin boy for the past six months ; Henry Conetta, aged 20 ; John Conetta, aged 17, a transport engineer ; Laura Conetta, aged 15, a war worker ; Michael Conetta, aged 14, who has just left school ; and Lena Conetta, aged 12.

Monday December 11th 1944

The King has been pleased to approve the following award for gallant and distinguished service in Italy:-

M.C.

Major T. Dixon, attd. 5th Bn. The Buffs,

"London Gazette" Thursday December 21st 1944

The King has been graciously pleased to approve the following award in recognition of gallant and distinguished service in Italy :-

D.S.O.

Major (T/Lt-Col.) John Bedford Arthur Glennie, (63600) 1st Bn. (Newton Abbot)

During the period 13th January 1944 to 30th April 1944, this officer, firstly in the Orsogna sector and then in the Cassino area showed the greatest gallantry and devotion to duty whilst commanding his Battalion under the most arduous and trying conditions. Lt-Col. Glennie's battalion occupied the central sector on the Orsogna Front line in January 1944. Here his excellent leadership and tactical knowledge were prominent in the efficient way in which he handled his men and very quickly organised his defensive positions.
Working with untiring zeal and cheerfulness, under the worst possible weather conditions and in an area which was perpetually under heavy mortar and artillery fire, Lt-Col. Glennie repeatedly, with no thought of personal safety, went right forward to his Companies.
His battalion sector on the Casino Front in the Pt 593 area was a most exacting one, isolated, within 80 yards of the enemy and where his Battalion HQ. Had of necessity to be right forward, right in the forward Company area. The Battalion sector was continually subjected to intense enemy small arms, mortars and artillery fire. All this time Lt-Col. Glennie showed great courage and powers of leadership by visiting his Companies and Platoons frequently, often going through a hail of fire to do so, and imbuing in all his personnel an offensive spirit of a very high order which was present until the Brigade was relieved at the end of March.
He was wounded early in February but refused to be evacuated and by his cheerfulness, fearlessness and devotion to duty inspired all under his command. Lt-Col. Glennie has commanded his Battalion very well for over a year, during which time he has answered all the calls made upon him with unfailing and untiring readiness to do what was required of him and his battalion.
The example he has set in courageous leadership is one worthy of the highest traditions of the service.

Lt-Colonel John Blackwood Ashworth, (47519) 4th Bn. (Hove)
Commanding 1/5 Bn. Queen's Royal Regiment.

At Lonquilles on 7 August 44 the 1/5 Bn. Queen's Royal Regiment, commanded by Lt-Col. Ashworth were ordered to move to the support of another Bn. who were in the area at the crossroads at 879471. The country was extremely difficult for movement and the crossroads were under constant heavy shell fire but by expert handling and continued exposure to the enemy fire, Lt-Col. Ashworth succeeded in accomplishing his task. He decided to take up his position near the village of Compadre Valcon Grain and whilst doing so two Coys had great trouble in penetrating the very thick woods through which they had to pass. They immediately lost touch and Lt-Col. Ashworth at great risk to himself and with no thought for his safety set off in a Jeep to "step up" the communications. Throughout the operations

carried out
under the most adverse conditions believable, this officer led his men with cool, calm courage, and by his example his men were cheered and encouraged to complete their hazardous task.

M.M.

No. 6402963 Private Hector Percy Eather, 1st Bn.

6402963 Private Hector Eather, 1st Bn. The Royal Sussex Regiment, has been a Regimental Signaller since 1941. He was with the Battalion throughout the campaigns in Eritrea and the Western Desert. He was wounded at Wadi Akarit. He accompanied the Unit to Italy and was with the Battalion on the Orsogna front during January 1944. On 10th February 1944, the 1st Bn. The Royal Sussex Regiment took over a sector on the Cassino Front near Pt 539, it remained in this sector for a first period of 22 days, followed by a rest in a counter-attack role, 900 yards from the front line for 20 days, finishing with a short spell of 5 days once again in the front line, a total of 47 days.

The country was difficult being extremely mountainous and rocky, and progress was made more difficult by the very inclement weather over a long period. As a result of the 4th Indian Division's attack on the Monastery, enemy activity was very brisk. The 1st Bn. The Royal Sussex regiment, were occupying positions well within observation of the enemy, in some cases, only a matter of 80 to 100 yards separated the opposing lines.

The enemy shelled and mortared all available means of approach and the slightest sign of movement, especially by day, immediately brought down accurate Spandau and rifle grenade fire. As a direct result of the continuous enemy activity, lines of communications were constantly being destroyed and it required bravery of the highest order in any man called upon to make the necessary repairs. Private Eather in his capacity of Signal Linesman, was with the Battalion during the whole of this time. He was continually repairing broken lines of communication by night and by day and he seemed to be utterly regardless of fear, even when he himself was the target of enemy fire – he carried out his job quietly and conscientiously and it was largely due to his untiring efforts that a system of communications was kept open and working during that period.

On many occasions, he volunteered for this duty when volunteers were called for and his courage and cheerfulness was an example to all who were with him. Although no incident of a specific nature can be quoted, it was quite obvious to all those who saw Private Eather work – that only a man of the most courageous nature and devotion to duty could possibly have accomplished the difficult tasks that were imposed upon him – he was entirely regardless of his own safety and was never content till the work was completed to his own satisfaction.

Bar to M.C. (N.W.E.)

Captain (T/Mjr.) Peter Henry Rubie, M.C., (74658) 7th Bn. attd. 49th Reconnaissance Regiment R.A.C.   (Staines)

On 4th September 1944 "B" Squadron was on reconnaissance to find the position and strength of the outer defences of Le Havre in the area of Octeville. The ground was open and the enemy had observation posts covering most of the approaches. Two troops were sent forward to reconnoitre the area forward of St. Barthelemy and came under heavy and accurate machine-gun and shell fire. Major Rubie went forward and extricated these two troops and personally led two other troops forward to the same area to continue reconnaissance.

His men were again subjected to heavy fire and further casualties resulted, but Major Rubie who was continually in the forefront and throughout the day showed great gallantry and complete disregard for enemy fire, was an inspiration to his men whose morale remained of the highest throughout a very testing operation. Major Rubie continued for the remainder of the day to direct vigorous and aggressive patrols forward until he was satisfied that the full information about the

enemy in the area had been obtained. Major Rubie showed complete contempt for enemy fire.
(M.C. gazetted 20/11/40)

M.C. (Normandy)

Decorated by Field-Marshall B.L. Montgomery, Nijmegen, October 1944

Lieutenant (A/Capt.) Peter Wilfred Burrell Thompson,   (203059)
6th Bn. Royal Sussex Regiment, attd. 9th Bn. Durham Light Infantry,
(Birmingham)
(actual Citation not found)

On the 13 June 1944, Captain Thomson was in command of 'A' Coy, when he was ordered to make an exploratory attack on the German positions. He came under attack and was wounded but he was able to extricate his Coy. He was taken prisoner but as he and the Germans sheltered in the roadside, he was able to persuaded the Germans to surrender. This they agreed to do providing that they would decide when.

This he agreed to, later as the fighting became fiercer and as the Devons' attacked, Captain Thomson was asked to go out holding a white flag on a pole whilst being covered by heavily armoured Germans, and to shout to the oncoming troops that it was a British officer who held the flag.

When the Devons' arrived, the 30 to 40 heavily armed German troops then surrendered to Captain Thomson, who led them back to captivity and was himself then taken to the R.A.P. to have his wounds dressed.

For this action the Military Cross was possibly awarded.
Conformation of these events were verified by Captain J.J. Casey, 9th Bn. Durham Light Infantry.

Captain Thomson's father, Lieutenant-Colonel A.L.B. Thomson commanded the 7th Bn. in the last war, in which he was awarded the D.S.O. for conspicuous gallantry and good leadership.

Wednesday December 27th 1944

M.C. for former Eastbourne P.C.

His former colleagues in the Eastbourne Division of the Sussex Police Force have received news that P.C. Kenneth Leslie Callender, now a Major in the 9th Bn. Royal Sussex Regiment serving in Burma, has received the immediate award of the Military Cross.

"London Gazette" Monday January 1st 1945

The KING has been graciously pleased to give orders for the following promotions in, and appointments to, the Most Excellent Order of the British Empire: —

M.B.E. (Military Division)

Major Cyril Reed Peckitt, (15229) 2nd Bn.

(Citation not found)

Captain (T/Major) John Bewley Atkinson (189366)
(Citation not found)

"London Gazette" Thursday January 11th 1945

The KING has been graciously pleased to approve that the following be Mentioned in recognition of gallant and distinguished services in Italy:—

M.I.D.

Major (T/Lt-Col.) Victor Henry Jaques, M.C. (131287) 1st Bn.
Major (T/Lt-Col.) Joseph Simpson Magrath, M.C. (42679) 1st Bn.
Captain (T/Mjr.) Leslie Charles Cook, (149841) 1st Bn.
Lieutenant (T/Capt.) James Roy Anderson, (153258) 1st Bn.
Lieutenant Anthony Gouldsmith, (179803) 1st Bn.
Lieutenant Robert Norman Geall (255776) 10th Bn. Para. Regt. A.A.C.
No. 6190062 R.S.M. Herbert Frank Phillips, 1st Bn.
No. 6408392 Private L.E. Marsh, 1st Bn.
No. 6399794 Private R. Shield, 1st Bn.
No. 6400272 Private Leonard Whaymand, 1st Bn.

Monday January 15th 1945

Mentioned for Gallantry

The King has approved that the following be mentioned in recognition of gallant and distinguished services in Italy :-

Royal Sussex Regiment

Major (T/Lt-Colonel) V.H. Jaques, M.C., Major (T/Lt-Colonel) J.S. Magrath, M.C., Captain (T/Major) L.C. Cook, Lieutenant (T/Captain) J.R. Anderson, Lieutenant A. Gouldsmith, W.O. 1 (R.S.M.) H.F. Phillips, Private L.E. Marsh, Private R. Shield, Private L. Whaymand.

Thursday January 18th 1945

British Over Irrawaddy

As announced officially today, substantial forces of the British 36th Division are across the Irrawaddy. It is the most southerly crossing in force yet made in this campaign. Farther north, of course, the river has been crossed both by American and Chinese troops. The Irrawaddy at the point where the crossing took place is a magnificent stream, some 500 yards broad, shallow and slow moving at this time of the year. Gilded Burmese dagobas (Buddhist shrines), their bells tinkling in the breeze, stand on the bank, and in the distance are the mountain ranges which cup the Irrawaddy plain. The weather just now is superb. All day long, once the morning mists are dispelled the sun beats down out of a clear, light-blue sky and the air is warm, fresh, and invigorating.
The first crossing was made on the morning of December 14 in sampans by a small party of The Royal Sussex Regiment. On the next day the rest of the battalion began to cross. The leading company commander hauled up a Union Jack. A three day patrol penetrated far to the south-east and established contact with bearded Americans of the so-called Mars Force.

Raft and Mules

On Boxing Day I watched other units crossing. By that time engineers, both British and Indian, had made rafts with rubber boats and saved Japanese pontoons. Powered by outboard engines, these were transporting a variety of cargo across. One pontoon had been made into a tug with an engine taken out of a jeep and a propeller and transmission gear made in some Indian electrical and mechanical engineer's workshops. Mules were some across, and two mules, particularly strong and intrepid swimmers, were used to tow a sampan loaded with supplies. A detachment of The Royal Sussex Regiment on the farther bank were recovering from the effects of a Christmas which everyone agreed had been a triumph for the Royal Indian Army Service Corps. and the American transport pilots who flew in all good things. This small detachment alone, aided by some gunners, put away one pig, 12 geese, and 24 ducks, as well as five bottles of beer for each man. Their Christmas Day had apparently been spent as follows :- In the morning a football match and then church service with carols: in the afternoon a sampan regatta on the Irrawaddy, followed by another football match: in the evening a pwe- a Burmese entertainment with eight Burmese dancing girls and six Burmese musicians: finally a concert with various turns by men in the detachment and community singing round the camp fire.

"London Gazette" Thursday 25th January 1945

The KING has been graciously pleased to approve that the following be Mentioned in recognition of gallant and distinguished services in Italy: —

M.I.D.

No. 6408614 Corporal A. St. C. Maslin, 1st Bn.

"London Gazette" Thursday February 1st 1945

The KING has been graciously pleased to approve the award of the VICTORIA CROSS to:—

Victoria Cross

Captain Lionel Ernest Queripel   (108181) 2nd Bn. (Tunbridge Wells)

2 I/C 'A' Coy. 10th Bn. 4th Para. Bde. 1st Airborne Division.

"In Holland on 19th September, Captain Queripel was acting as commander of a composite company of three parachute battalions. At 14:00 hours on that day his company was advancing along a main road which was on an embankment towards Arnhem. The advance was conducted under continuous medium machine-gun fire which, at one period, was so heavy that the company suffered considerable losses.

"Captain Queripel at once proceeded to reorganise his force crossing and re-crossing the road, while doing so under extremely heavy and accurate fire. During this period he carried a wounded sergeant to the Regimental Aid Post under fire and was himself wounded in the face."

"Captain Queripel then led a party against the strongpoint holding up the advance. This strongpoint consisted of a captured British anti-tank gun and two machine-guns.

Despite the extremely heavy fire directed at him, Captain Queripel succeeded in killing the crews of the machine-guns and re-capturing the anti-tank gun. As a result the advance was able to continue."

"Later the same day Captain Queripel, finding himself cut off with a small party of men, took up a position in a ditch. By this time he had received further wounds in both arms. Regardless of his wounds and of the very heavy mortar and Spandau fire he continued to inspire his men to resist with hand grenades, pistols and a few remaining rifles."

"As, however, enemy pressure increased, Captain Queripel decided that it was impossible to hold the position any longer and ordered his men to withdraw. Despite their protests he insisted on remaining behind to cover their withdrawal with his automatic pistol and a few remaining grenades. This is the last time he was seen."

Friday February 2nd 1945

Royal Sussex Officer awarded the V.C.

The award of the Victoria Cross to an officer of the Royal Sussex Regiment was announced last night. The recipient of the award is Captain Lionel Ernest Queripel, the 24 years old son of Colonel L.H. Queripel, D.S.O., of Warwick Park, Tunbridge Wells. It is the first V.C. won by a member of the Regiment during the present war, and it was gained when Captain Queripel was serving with the 1st Airborne Division at Arnhem.

The citation reads :-

"In Holland on 19th September, Captain Queripel was acting as commander of a composite company of three parachute battalions. At 14:00 hours on that day his company was advancing along a main road which an on an embankment towards Arnhem. The advance was conducted under continuous medium machine-gun fire which, at one period, was so heavy that the company suffered considerable losses.
"Captain Queripel at once proceeded to reorganise his force crossing and re-crossing the road, while doing so under extremely heavy and accurate fire. During this period he carried a wounded sergeant to the Regimental Aid Post under fire and was himself wounded in the face."
"Captain Queripel then led a party against the strongpoint holding up the advance. This strongpoint consisted of a captured British anti-tank gun and two machine-guns.
Despite the extremely heavy fire directed at him, Captain Queripel succeeded in killing the crews of the machine-guns and re-capturing the anti-tank gun. As a result the advance was able to continue."

Inspired his men

"Later the same day Captain Queripel, finding himself cut off with a small party of men, took up a position in a ditch. By this time he had received further wounds in both arms. Regardless of his wounds and of the very heavy mortar and Spandau fire he continued to inspire his men to resist with hand grenades, pistols and a few remaining rifles."
"As, however, enemy pressure increased, Captain Queripel decided that it was impossible to hold the position any longer and ordered his men to withdraw. Despite their protests he insisted on remaining behind to cover their withdrawal with his automatic pistol and a few remaining grenades. This is the last time he was seen."

Fought at El Alamein

Captain Queripel went through all the fighting to El Alamein, served in Italy and then Arnhem. His father, Colonel Leslie Herbert Queripel, D.S.O., Royal Artillery, took part in the Boxer Rebellion, in 1900, and also served in Mesopotamia, France and Russia during the last war. His father was Colonel A.E. Queripel and his great-grandfather was also a soldier.
Captain Queripel showed high military qualities in the Marlborough College O.T.C. in which he was an officer.

"London Gazette" Thursday February 8th 1945

The KING has been graciously pleased to give orders for the following promotions in, and appointments to, the Most Excellent Order of the British Empire, in recognition of gallant and distinguished services in Burma and on the Eastern Frontier of India: —

M.B.E. (Military Division)

Major (T/Lt-Col.) Thomas Chamber Windsor Roe,   (121387) (Hove)

During the Arakan operations 1943/44, Lt-Col. Roe was D/Q of this Div. And his skill, energy, patience, perseverance, and disregard of fatigue were a password in the Div. When 7 Div. Were cut off from the outside existence only W/T links with the outside world was through these H.Q.'s and Lt-Col. Roe was on the set night and day for many days arranging for their air supply and other means of assistance. If it is not too much to say that the seriousness of the situation was greatly reduced through this officer's devotion to duty. During the Imphal operations Lt-Col. Roe was promoted A/Q. of the Div. And as such his gift for organisation and his untiring efforts have done much to assist the success of the operations. Prior to moving to the Arakan this Div. Has reorganised twice and done two overseas moves which have placed a great strain on this officer and added to his great service to the Div., which deserves recognition.

M.M.

No. 796696 Sergeant Harold Luxford,   1st Bn.   (Brighton)

"During the early afternoon of Wednesday 12th June 1944, Sergeant Luxford was Platoon Sergeant of 11 Platoon, in an attack directed against Col de Fabri feature. This N.C.O. led his men into the attack on the more exposed left flank and in the face of heavy machine-gun fire and succeeded in reaching his objective. This success was not achieved without some casualties, which were further increased by a concentration of shell and mortar fire to which his position was now subjected. Sergeant Luxford, seeing that some of his men were badly wounded and in need of immediate attention, without hesitation dashed into the open and commenced to carry casualties to the cover afforded by the ridge now occupied by his Platoon.

While so engaged, the enemy counter-attacked with the utmost determination, sergeant Luxford with complete coolness rallied several men to his assistance and opposed the assault with such effect that the enemy were put to flight, leaving their dead and wounded upon the field. The promptness of action and the initiative shown by this N.C.O. undoubtedly saved his Company from a serious reversal which was likely to jeopardise the whole attack.

His complete disregard for his own personal safety and his care for his wounded comrades is worthy of the highest praise and was a stirling example of supreme courage and devotion to duty.

No. 64023427 Sergeant Leslie Sydney Douglas Morley,   1st Bn. (L.R.D.G.)   (Reigate)

On 14th June 1944, Sergeant Morley was one of a patrol of L.R.D.G. dropped by parachute in the Arezzo area to obtain information. Soon after landing the patrol was attacked and split up. Sergeant Morley evaded capture and took to the hills. During the next few weeks he made detailed reconnaissance of enemy movements and positions, in spite of active enemy measures against partisans and escaped Allied P.O.W's in that area. He also harassed the enemy so far as he was able to do so without assistance.

Two attempts at re-joining our forces with urgent information were unsuccessful, but at the third attempt he crossed the lines and reported to HQ. 4th Indian Division. Sergeant Morley immediately volunteered to assist as a guide and was sent to the 1/9th Gurkha Rifles, who were about to enter the area from which he had come. He was able to give this Battalion valuable and detailed information about the enemy and the country, and he guided them at night onto an objective without the enemy's knowledge. Throughout Sergeant Morley displayed the greatest determination to evade capture, to gather information and to return to our lines so that this information could be put to the best use.

In September 1944, whilst under command of Land Forces Adriatic, Sergeant Morley was captured by a German E-Boat. Again he showed magnificent determination, initiative and total disregard for danger. He escaped and is once more back with L.R.D.G.

(Owing to the secret nature of these operations it is requested that no publication be made.)
(See also extract from WD 373 Reel 9 from the Lt-Col. Commanding 1/9th Gurkha Rifles.)

No. 6407683 L/Sergeant Reginald Claude Hollingdale, 9th Bn. (Petworth)

Mayu Range, Akaran, February/May 1945.
During the attack on the 'Sausage' feature above the Western Tunnel, the section led by L/Sergeant Hollingdale came under intense enemy L.M.G. fire. Although wounded L/Sergeant Hollingdale led his section forward and captured the objective. He refused to be evacuated until the section had reorganised, and he had seen supplies and reinforcements arrive up, and the position consolidated. He displayed great courage and leadership throughout the operations.

No. 5577443 Private Harold George Owen, 9th Bn. (Bristol 7)

During the attack on the 'Sausage' feature above the Maungdaw-Buthidaung Road, Private Owen led the way under fire past the mouth of the Tunnel and forced his way up through dense undergrowth and precipitous slopes to his objective.

Although exhausted on arrival he immediately attacked a Japanese fox-hole single-handed, killing the occupants. He then advanced further up the slopes and established himself in a vacated Japanese fox-hole which he held in the face of enemy L.M.G. fire and periodic sniping.

Throughout the operations this soldier has shown great skill in exterminating the enemy and has displayed courage and initiative above his rank.

Friday February 9th 1945

Royal Sussex in Paiforce

HONOURED CHAPTER IN WAR ANNULS

Persia and Iraq will not, in this war, figure in The Royal Sussex Regiment's long list of battle honours, but Paiforce (Persia and Iraq Command) will fill an honoured chapter in its annuls (writes a Military Observer).

For over two years men of The Royal Sussex Regiment – men of a regular battalion and of a Territorial battalion that has the honour to claim Mr. Winston Churchill as its Honorary Colonel – have been serving there. They came straight from the Western Desert where, at Alamein and Bare Ridge, they had played their part in the breaking of Rommel's last assault on Alexandria.

They came to Paiforce expecting that those same qualities that broke Rommel's drive would be required to meet a fresh German swing southwards through the Caucasus. That was not to be, however; the Germans were routed before Stalingrad, and in consequence the whole purpose and function of Paiforce became changed from that of an operational to that of a garrison command.

Protecting the Lines

For two years now the role of Paiforce has been to keep clear the lines of communications by which arms and supplies have flowed through the Persian Gulf to Russia. The fact that since Paiforce was formed four million tons of goods have passed over the lines of communication proves how successfully it has fulfilled that role.

For the protection of those lines the men of The Royal Sussex Regiment have been in part responsible. It has been unspectacular work that the Regiment has done under the command of Colonel (now Brigadier) J.J. McCully, D.S.O. Lt-Col. C.F.A. Nix, and Lt-Col. W.R. Ellen, but its value cannot be denied. It has been work by no means without its incidents.

Paiforce, as a new command, had few amenities at the start. The country was not fully mapped, information on local conditions had to be acquired by experience and the Sussex during their first months, learned many lessons about a climate that ranges from the extremes of cold. Sussex men when they return, will have many stories to tell of how, during their first winter in Persia, their tents night after night were flooded out, and of how, in their first summer in the Southern Iraq Desert,
they were scorched day after day by the blazing heat.

Guard of Honour for Shah

Much of their work has been monotonous, but it has been no less strenuous on that account for they have had to keep themselves fully fit and trained as fighting men for the day when they will be required for active service in another front. Guard duties at Teheran – they had the privilege of providing a Guard of Honour for the Shah and Shareen of Persia – and the protection of the convoy routes, have alternated with periods of intense training in desert fighting and mountain warfare.

The Paiforce battalions of the Royal Sussex are as ready to go into action today at a moment's notice as they were when they landed in Egypt nearly three years ago now to break Rommel's drive.

Saturday February 10th 1945

Local Military Awards

The King has been pleased to approve the following awards for distinguished services in Burma, Italy and on the Eastern Frontier of India :-

M.B.E.

Major (T/Lt-Col.) Thomas Chamber Windsor Roe, (121387)   (Hove)

M.M.

No. 6407683 Sergeant Reginald Claude Hollingdale,   1st Bn. (Petworth)
No. 796696 Sergeant Harold Luxford,   1st Bn.   (Brighton)

Friday February 16th 1945

Royal Sussex in Burma fighting

For the part he played in the final and successful battle for the North Burma "railway corridor," Corporal Albert Harris, of The Royal Sussex Battalion with Major-General Frank Festing's 36th Division has been awarded the M.M. He was also promoted from private immediately after the battle.

The final "railway corridor" battle came at Pinwe where the Japanese were determined to hold on as long as possible. They held off the division for some weeks. Gradually they were forced out.

In one fight The Royal Sussex put in a flanking attack on Japanese bunker positions, Corporal Harris led his section along the railway line and caught the Japanese trying to escape. Later in the battle, when

the leading company of The Sussex was cut off, he and his section tried to reach them.
The platoon in front of his section were shot up by the Japanese and forced to retire, but Corporal Harris kept his section within a few yards of the enemy, holding the ground until relief came.
(M.M. gazetted 22/03/45)

"London Gazette" Thursday February 22nd 1945

The KING has been graciously pleased to give orders for the following promotions in, and appointments to, the Most Excellent Order of the British Empire, in recognition of gallant and distinguished services in the field : —

O.B.E. (Military Division) (Italy)

Lt-Colonel Hubert Cudlipp, (210790) 1st Bn.

This officer has been Chief Editor of all editions of the Union Jack since the first publication of that paper some 18 months ago. This task, which carries great responsibility, has been adequately performed by Lt-Colonel Cudlipp who has shown not a considerable initiative in the setting up of the paper in many places and its procurement from many sources of all types of news which has proved both interesting and instructive for the troops.
In view of the efficient way in which this officer has carried out his task, I consider he is worthy of recognition.

M.B.E. (Military Division) (M.E.)

No. 6398914 R.S.M. Harold Fleet, attd. 2 G.H.Q. Signals,

As senior British W.O. in cipher at AFHQ, has shown outstanding organising ability and devotion to duty in dealing with heavy cipher traffic. He was recently in charge of the Prime Minister's traffic, and earned a special commendation for his work.

Friday February 23rd 1945

Sergeant H. Luxford, M.M., Royal Sussex Regiment wounded.

"London Gazette" Thursday March 1st 1945

The KING has been graciously pleased to approve the following awards in recognition of gallant and distinguished services in North West Europe: —

M.C.

Lieutenant Allan Reginald Chittenden, (278354) attd. 5th Bn. Wiltshire Regiment,

On 22nd July 1944 Lieutenant Chittenden was commanding a platoon in "A" Coy during the attack on Maitot. On reaching the objective it was found that the bulk of the enemy positions were along the hedgerows to the right and consisted of at least a Coy dug in. Lieutenant Chittenden immediately organised his platoon and assaulted the positions, clearing the entire area. By skilful leadership and quick reactions this officer made a complete success of a very dangerous situation.
The King has been graciously pleased to approve the following awards for gallant and distinguished service in the field :-

M.M. (Escapee)

No. 6397126 Private James Nicholas Mack, 1st Bn.

Although Mack avoided capture for five days after his unit had been surrounded at Benghazi, he was apprehended on 2 Feb 1942. At the time of the Italian Armistice he was imprisoned at Monturano (Camp 70) and, obeying the orders of the Senior British Officer, did not try to escape until the Germans arrived. On 27 Sep 1943, when P/W were being transferred to Germany, Mack hid in a tree and left the camp the same night. After an unsuccessful attempt to penetrate the lines, he worked for the Italians for three months. Apprehended by the Fascists, and sent to a camp at Arrezzo on 4 March 1944, he bluffed the German guards into believing that he was an Italian workman.

He returned to the Teramo area to form a guerrilla group which did useful work harassing the Germans and fascists until Polish troops arrived on 23 June 1944. A member of his band paid tribute to his zeal, ability and powers of leadership in the following terms.

"I joined the rebels and found this Englishman whose actual name was JAMES MACK – his unit and No. is 6397126 Corporal J. Mack 1st Bn. Royal Sussex Regiment. He I know personally well was outstanding; showing good zest and leadership; and got a real good disciplined band together, smashing many German trucks on the roads during the night. I stayed with this band until the end. He is the best man I have ever come across in my experience of war".

Monday March 5th 1945

Field Marshall B.L. Montgomery holds an investiture at Bishop's College, Weert, Holland. Among those present is Captain P.W.B. Thomson, 6th Bn. Royal Sussex Regiment attached to 9th Bn. Durham Light Infantry, to receive his Military Cross which he won last June in the Normandy Campaign with the D.L.I.
("L/G" 21/12/44)

"London Gazette" Thursday March 8th 1945

The KING has been graciously pleased to approve the following awards for distinguished and gallant services in Italy :-
M.C.

Lieutenant Gerald Bryan Burnett, (240419) (Crowborough) attd. 9th Bn. Royal Fusiliers

On the morning of 5th September 1944, the Battalion crossed the River Conca, "B" Coy who were leading, were slowed up by the necessity for clearing up some parties of the enemy before further advance, and "A" Coy, of which Lieutenant Burnett was the leading Platoon, came into the lead. On the advance up towards Croce, considerable opposition was met from enemy machine-gun posts, and it was imperative to act quickly to avoid large numbers of casualties throughout the Company. Without hesitation Lieutenant Burnett lead his Platoon forward in a charge, and with them destroyed at once the Spandau posts.

Later, on the night of 7th September 944, Lieutenant Burnett was in command of 15 men engaged in clearing some houses, he was supported by tanks and the streets were swept persistently by snipers with machine-guns and rifles. Eventually the tanks proved unable to silence the opposition and hen some were struck by enemy bazookas, they withdrew.

It was then that Lieutenant Burnett by his untiring leadership, and complete disregard or his own safety in leading his men from one enemy post to the next, clearing up opposition without further assistance, and established himself firmly in the enemy's place. Lieutenant Burnett's personal example throughout the fighting has been an inspiration to his men, and his prompt action has saved the Company in many dangerous situations.

T/Major Peter Reginald Cavalier, (124221) 1st Bn. (Market Weston, Norfolk)

Major Cavalier has displayed great qualities of leadership, determination, and devotion to duty during the heavy fighting in which his Battalion has been recently involved. On the morning of 30th August 1944, "B" Coy. Commanded by Major Cavalier, was called upon to reinforce "C" Coy in the area of the road junction at Piave di Cagna when very heavy opposition had been encountered. Major Cavalier moved his Company with such speed and decision through heavy concentrations of shell and mortar fire that the enemy was completely surprised by this unexpected show of strength and suffered severe losses in the subsequent counter-attacks which were repulsed.

Throughout the advance and during the subsequent heavy fighting on the ridge, Major Cavalier could be seen directing and encouraging his men regardless of the heavy shell, mortar and later small arms fire to which he was subjected. During the early stages of the action he was wounded by a mortar bomb to the head but ignoring the pain he continued in command of his Company, as he realised the tenseness of the situation and the vital importance of holding, at all costs, the ground he had occupied.

It was largely due to Major Cavalier's fine personal example that the vital ground was, in fact, held. His actions throughout the battle were a source of inspiration to the men under his command and materially contributed to the success of the operation.

Lieutenant Richard Albert Roach, (324671) 1st Bn. (London S.W.1)

On the 10th September 1944, "C" Coy. 1st Bn. The Royal Sussex Regiment, was ordered to attack and seize Pt 573 (MR 526760) and this was successfully carried out in spite of enemy opposition. During this attack, Lieutenant Roach's Platoon captured 12 enemy prisoners, Lieutenant Roach himself pursuing and capturing the enemy officers. After heavy shelling and mortaring, the enemy launched a series of strong counter-attacks during the night 10/11th September 1944. The estimated strength of the enemy being a Company of approximately 50 men.

The main weight of these counter-attacks was launched against No. 15 Platoon commanded by Lieutenant Roach, who held the forward position on Pt 573. At approximately 0200hrs Platoon HQ and two sections were cut off and isolated from the remainder of the Company until 0400hrs, when the enemy was driven off with losses. During this period, Lieutenant Roach, with complete disregard to his own personal safety, and although coming under heavy enemy small arms fire, on several occasions dashed forward and hurled grenades at the enemy thoroughly disorganising them. When he discovered Platoon HQ and two sections were isolated from the remainder of the Company, he ordered his men to remain at their posts and to prevent at all costs the enemy overrunning his positions.

Throughout this action Lieutenant Roach set an inspiring example to his men by his courage and devotion to duty and his positions remained intact until the enemy was finally driven off.

M.M.

No. 5626378 Private Leonard Jack Bryant, 1st Bn. (Plymouth)

During the action of Piave di Castello, on 12th September 1944, Private Bryant was a signaller in "B" Coy, which was holding a hill feature about 400 yards north of the village. This feature was heavily shelled during the day and night, causing casualties, and invariably breaking the telephone line, Private Bryant again and again, frequently under heavy shell, mortar and small arms fire, and without any orders, went out to repair the lines. The maintenance of these lines was vital during this period, Private Bryant's disregard for personal danger and devotion to duty, was of the highest order, and his courage set a fine example to the rest of the men in the Company.

No. 6149840 Corporal Joseph Robert Horwood, 1st Bn. (Pembroke)

On 30th August 1944, during an attack by No. 13 Platoon, on a vital road junction just south of Piave di Cagna, (MR 8465), Corporal Horwood and his Section ascending across a very steep wadi, had to clear houses and consolidate on a hill fifty yards further on. The complete move was carried out with such speed and efficiency that the enemy had no idea where this section was situated. This was proved when on the following night the enemy counter-attacked in strength, and chose as his line of approach the ridge where Corporal Horwood's Section was positioned. On two occasions the enemy tried to get to the main positions, but each time this section held its fire until the enemy were almost on the Section's position, and then broke up the enemy attacks.

The following day, the enemy shelled and mortared the position constantly, but Corporal Horwood maintained complete control over the situation, and by sniping prevented the enemy from consolidating on a feature overlooking the Platoon's position. In all, this Section accounted for five enemy killed.

No. 6411433 Private Francis Simmons, 1st Bn. (Bognor Regis)

During the advance from Auditore to Piave di Castello, Private Simmons was a driver of one of the R.A.P. Stretcher Jeeps. The leading Companies were held up by a road crate and mines, and came under heavy and continuous shell and mortar fire, and sustained casualties from the shelling, and anti-personnel mines. Private Simmons in his Jeep, made six journeys to evacuate these casualties. This was alone in broad daylight along a road on a forward slope, under close and direct observation by the enemy, which was being shelled. With complete disregard for his personal safety and without being ordered to do so. Private Simmons went backwards and forwards over this road evacuation the severely wounded as quickly as possible.

Many of these casualties were caused by small anti-personnel mines, most of whom had a foot blown off. By their evacuation, he enabled them to have immediate medical attention, which undoubtedly saved many lives.

No. 6399670 Corporal Leonard Frank White, 1st Bn. (Crowborough)

During the advance from Urbino to Piave di Cagna, on 29th August 1944, Corporal White was in the leading Honey tank of the Battalion, which was held up at Pt 8456452, by craters in the road. Corporal White went forward, on foot, with the Commander of the Honey's, and was ordered to recce a route to by-pass the hole in the road. This he proceeded to do, by himself on foot, during his recce, he suddenly came upon a dug in Spandau Post, manned by two gunners. Although only armed with a revolver, with great presence of mind and bravery he at once attacked the post, at point-blank range, killing both occupants. He then returned, and reported the situation, and gave his recce report. By his courage and initiative, he greatly assisted our troops to occupy the feature as this Spandau post covered the only approach to the position.

Shortly afterwards, continuing this action, he engaged from his Honey tank a German 75mm Anti-tank gun, which was firing from our left flank at our honeys, but Corporal White's fire eventually neutralised the German 75mm, thereby enabling our tanks, and carriers to move up the road to the forward Infantry positions. All through this operation, Corporal White displayed great personal courage, and initiative, which materially assisted in the successful conclusion of the operation.

No. 6408649 A/Corporal Cyril Herbert Wilson, 1st Bn. (Tonbridge)

On 30th August 1944, Corporal Wilson was leading a Section of No. 13 Platoon in an attack on a heavily defended road junction near the village of Piave di Cagna in the outskirts of the Gothic Line. Early in the action, the Platoon came under withering fire from a strong Spandau post on the crest of an almost perpendicular slope, the Platoon was forced to a stop. At once Corporal White realised that unless the post was put out of action the whole attack might fail, his Section was now reduced to four men but without hesitation he dashed forward and led his men up the slope. The speed and determination of this audacious assault carried Wilson and his men to the crest where he found that the enemy outnumbered his small party by four to one.

He pressed straight in and personally killed two Germans. The enemy fled in confusion, leaving one more dead in the position and two more were captured together with the Spandau and ammunition. The splendid courage of Corporal Wilson and his determination to press on and destroy the enemy at all costs were an inspiration to all ranks and played a vital part in the success of the action and the advance of the Battalion.

Friday March 9th 1945

American Honour For Hove Officer
A Hove officer, Major Merrick Cockell, who has been serving with the Royal Sussex Regiment in Burma for two and a half years, has recently been honoured by our American allies with the award of the American Silver Star medal.

Major Cockell's wife, who lives at "Morecote" Hill Brow, Dyke Road, Hove, received a cable on Monday from her husband's commanding officer informing her of the award, but giving no details of the nature of the action which merited it. Mrs. Cockell has also received a letter from her husband, who is at present in hospital, but he made no mention of his medal.

Eagerly Awaiting Details

The Silver Star is, however, the third highest American Service award, and Mrs. Cockell is eagerly awaiting further details. She is especially proud and delighted as she has many friends and relations living in America. Major Cockell is the son of the late Major Charles Cockell and Mrs. Oswald Hempson, of Esher, Surrey, and was educated at Hurstpierpoint College, where he was a member of the O.T.C. He joined the Grenadier Guards in 1939, and in May, 1940, he was commissioned in The Royal Sussex Regiment, having received his training at Sandhurst.

With this award Major Cockell brings an unusual honour to his battalion which has already distinguished itself during the campaigns in Burma and of which he has always been very proud.

Thursday March 14th 1945

Royal Sussex To The Fore

It was announced from S.E.A.C. H.Q. yesterday, that men of the Royal Sussex Regiment took a big share in a brilliant outflanking action through the jungle which ended in the capture of Mong Mit, Burma communication centre 15 miles south-east of Myitson, and 17 miles north-east of the ruby-mine town of Mogok.

The Sussex men stormed up a precipitous hill feature known as Hill 800, so close behind the deadly artillery barrage that they could feel the shell blasts.

After the capture of the hill they took to the jungle where, although they had to hack their way through, they advanced two or three miles a day, and captured three villages.

One column of Major-General Frank W. Festing's 36th Division has been operating on its own for three months it is now revealed. Starting from Tigyaing, on the Upper Irrawaddy, in December, this column pushed east, and then south supplied throughout from the air.

Stiff Fighting In Mandalay

Street fighting in Mandalay, where 19th Indian ("Dagger") Division troops continue to clear the city against stiff opposition, was reported yesterday. Troops of the 19th Division, the ("Dagger") Division, in a swift push from Mandalay, have captured Maymyo, 40 miles north-east of Mandalay.

Since men of the Fourth Corps. broke out of the Irrawaddy bridgehead, and rushed across the country to Meiktila, inflicting more losses on the Japanese than were suffered in the whole 1942 retreat from Burma, the Japanese have recovered from their surprise, and are building up their forces.

"Times"

Mong Mit taken by 36th Division

Mong Mit the capital of Shan State of the same name and an important communications centre 195 miles north-north-east of Mandalay, has been captured by troops of the 36th British Division by a swift outflanking movement which deceived the Japanese. It is a town of 5,000 inhabitants. 15 miles south-east of Myitson where the 36th Division established a bridgehead across the Shwcli river, and 17 miles north-east of Mogok.

Striking through dense jungle along the Nammeik Chaung instead of taking the main track from Myitson, British infantry cut their way forward through country that the Japanese though impassable. Indian engineers followed the leading infantry, turning the path into a jeep track and bulldozers manned by Indian and Americans made the path into lane for motor traffic. Men of The Royal Sussex Regiment led for much of the way.

"London Gazette" Friday March 22nd 1945

The KING has been graciously pleased to approve the following awards in recognition of gallant and distinguished services in North West Europe: —

M.C.

T/Captain Geoffrey Derek Hodgson, (78964) 4th Bn.
(attd. Dorsetshire Regiment) (Hassocks)

Near Tripsrath on 20 Nov 44 after a Battalion attack to clear a large wood, during the consolidation period, the whole Battalion area was subjected to constant and heavy shell and mortar fire. As A/Tank Platoon Commander, Captain Hodgson worked steadily and imperturbably, despite numerous air bursts, for over four hours without thought of taking cover recce routes for his guns through thick woods and personally directing the manhandling of his guns into position.

Had it not been for the magnificent work and splendid example set by this officer the Battalion might well have had to withstand a counter-attack by enemy tanks without A/Tank guns.

By his courage and devotion to duty, his guns were in position before such an attack developed, and contributed very considerably in sustaining the morale of the men.

The KING has been graciously pleased to approve the following awards in recognition of gallant and distinguished services in Burma: —

M.C.

T/Major John James Dickson, (96192) 9th Bn. (attd. 5 Commando)

On 10th November 1944 near Hpapan, Major Dickson was in command of a company ordered to attack and capture a strong enemy bunkered position on the banks of a river. The position contained a high proportion of machine-guns and mortars, and it was obvious that Major Dickson was faced with a difficult task. This task he fulfilled with conspicuous skill and gallantry, both the planning and execution of the operation being a model of their kind. Leading the company himself he put in a most determined attack from the flank, rolling up the enemy position bunker by bunker and finally causing the remnants of the enemy to flee in disorder leaving behind them much new equipment.

Major Dickson was always to the fore himself wherever the attacked showed signs of slowing down, and by his personal example of courage and offensiveness ensured the success of the attack. On the following day, Major Dickson once more displayed exceptional skill and bravery when his company bumped the main enemy defences covering Pinwee. His company came under heavy machine-gun and shell fire, suffering casualties. In very trying circumstances Major Dickson exhibited a coolness and personal example of courage.

M.M.

No. 14497662 Private Christopher Alfred Colesby, 9th Bn. (London N.1)

On 14th November 1944, during an attack on our positions near Pinwee, Private Colesby exhibited exceptional courage and initiative in the performance of his duties as stretcher-bearer. The enemy pressed home his attack with such determination that, aided by the dense jungle, he was able to bring up several L.M.G.'s and a M.M.G. within 25 yards of our perimeter.
The recovery of wounded under these conditions presented great difficulties. Any movement brought bursts of automatic fire from the enemy guns at almost point-blank range. Whilst the other stretcher-bearers wavered Private Colesby with complete disregard for his own safety decided to make the attempt and at the same time carry forward reserve ammunition.
Ignoring the bursts of automatic fire directed at his every movement he succeeded in delivering his ammunition and in attending to five wounded men. Inspired by his example, other men then made their way forward and assisted him in getting the wounded to the rear. Again on 23rd November 1944, in subsequent operations North of Pinwee, this man exhibited the same disregard for his own safety in bringing back a wounded man from within 15 yards of an enemy L.M.G.

No. 6418677 Private Victor Conetta, 9th Bn. (London S.W. 11)

On the morning 14th November 1944, near Pinwee, the enemy launched a counter-attack on one of our Battalion positions. The main weight of this attack fell on the sector held by the Coy of which Private Conetta was a member. In the early stages of the attack Private Conetta fired his L.M.G. to great effect with coolness and determination, although he was being mortared and was constantly under the fire of an enemy M.M.G. and a L.M.G. at almost point-blank range.
By his action all further efforts by the enemy to close in on the position failed. Later, when our counter-attack was launched, the enemy had worked their automatics through the very thick jungle to within 25 yards of our perimeter. In the face of this withering fire our counter-attack in this sector first wavered but Private Conetta, on his own initiative and alone, crawled forward with his Bren gun, carrying his magazines in his pockets to within 15 yards of the enemy M.M.G.
With great coolness and an utter disregard of the fire to which he was being subjected, he got his gun behind a tree stump and proceeded systematically to wipe out all the members of the M.M.G. crew and their escort. In all he killed 10 Japanese, including the officer commanding the M.M.G. detachment before capturing the M.M.G. itself.
Inspired by his example, the rest of the section resumed their attack. Later, by his quickness in engaging fleeing targets he accounted for 6 more of the enemy who would otherwise have escaped. Throughout the next 10 days until he was wounded on 24th November 1944, he displayed conspicuous bravery in every action in which he took part.

No. 14517101 Private John William Cox, 9th Bn. (Erith)

On 14th November 1944, the enemy put in a strong attack on the Battalion positions near Pinwee. Private Cox was No. 2 of an L.M.G. crew on a sector of the Battalion perimeter which was particularly heavily attacked. Very early in the action his No. 1 was wounded. Soon afterwards Private Cox was hit in the arm by a Jap bullet. Despite this he took over the L.M.G. and fired it with great coolness, ignoring the heavy fire directed at him.

It was not long before he sustained a second wound, being hit through the fingers, not daunted he carried on and continued to hold off all attempts of the enemy to close in on his post. By now it was obvious that the enemy were making particularly strenuous efforts to eliminate his L.M.G. and Private Cox was wounded a third time by a Jap bullet in the shoulder. It was not until he received his fourth wound, in the throat, that he was compelled to relinquish his gun, but by that time he had succeeded in bringing the enemy attack on his post to a standstill.

His courage, determination and refusal to give in to his wounds undoubtedly saved a dangerous situation on his sector of the Battalion front.

No. 5391495 A/Corporal Joseph Govier, 9th Bn. (Brill, Bucks.)

On 10th November 1944, near Hpapan, Private Govier's Coy was ordered to attack and capture a strong enemy position on the banks of a chaung. At the start of the attack Private Govier was a member of the 2" Mortar Detachment in Platoon H.Q., but before the attack had progressed very far his platoon was held up by a particularly strong bunker. As the country was unsuitable for the deployment of a 2" mortar, Private Govier, on his own initiative dashed forward and seizing a L.M.G., charged at the bunker firing at the hip.

He killed two enemy inside the bunker thereby enabling his platoon to overrun it. He then relinquished his borrowed L.M.G., but a few minutes later the platoon was again held up by another bunker. Without waiting for orders, Private Govier once again took offensive action on his own initiative. Working round to a flank he threw grenades at the bunker to such good effect that he forced three enemy occupants out into the open where they were at once killed by platoon fire from the front.

By his prompt and courageous actions Private Govier assisted very materially in the success of the whole attack.

No. 6411142 A/Corporal Albert Harris, 9th Bn. (London W.2)

On 10th November 1944, near Hpapan, Private Harris's Coy was ordered to attack and capture a strong enemy bunker position on the bank of a small river. Private Harris was No. 1 Section L.M.G. of the right hand assaulting platoon. On encountering the first bunker there was a pause in the attack, until Private Harris dashed forward firing his L.M.G. from the hip.

He killed three Japanese and by his prompt action restored the momentum of the attack. Continuing the advance he crossed the railway line in pursuit of the fleeing Japanese, giving them no chance to reorganise and make a further stand. Throughout this action he displayed and admirable offensive spirit, and grasped every opportunity of killing the enemy and keeping them on the run.

On 23rd November 1944, near Pinwee, Private Harris's Coy was ordered to break through the main enemy position and come to the assistance of the leading Coy which had been cut off. Private Harris was in command of one of the leading sections when contact was made. The enemy had held his fire until we were within 10 yards of his L.M.G.'s. In the face of this fire the section on either side of Private Harris began to fall back. Private Harris, however, refused to be driven off from the ground which he had won and held on where he was with his section. By his courage and determination under heavy fire he enabled a difficult situation to be restored.

No. 6412096 Private Sidney John Powell, 9th Bn. (Kenton)

On 10th November 1944, during an attack on a strong enemy bunkered position near Hpapan, Private Powell was a stretcher-bearer attached to the Coy carrying out the attack. In the course of the attack one of our Bren gunners was very seriously wounded in close proximity to an enemy bunker containing an L.M.G. With total disregard for his own safety, Private Powell dashed forward to attend to the wounded man. Placing his own body between the wounded man and the L.M.G., he applied a tourniquet and remained shielding the man until the bunker had been captured by our own troops.

On the following day, near Pinwee, Private Powell was attached to the same Rifle Coy when it was held up by the main enemy defensive position astride the railway. The Coy was pinned to the ground by heavy M.M.G. and L.M.G. fire. The enemy then began to shell the Coy with a quick-firing gun, all the shells falling accurately within the Coy area. One of the first shells landed in Coy H.Q. wounding Private Powell in the head and body. Disregarding his own wounds, Private Powell immediately set about assisting the seriously wounded. He moved from one casualty to another despite the shelling, and, as fresh casualties occurred, he repeatedly crossed the railway line under L.M.G. fire to attend the men on the other side.

Throughout, Private Powell displayed magnificent courage and undoubtedly saved the lives on many of his comrades. His own wounds were dressed last of all.

No. 6412116 Private Frederick Charles George Stonham, 9th Bn. (Cobham)

On 17th November 1944, near Pinwee, Private Stonham's platoon was leading platoon in a Coy attack on an enemy road block. The enemy position was strongly held by M.M.G.'s and L.M.G.'s on the bank of a small river. Private Stonham crossed the river to the enemy's side alone with his Platoon Commander. Immediately they came under automatic fire from a range of 20 yards. The officer almost at once sustained a very severe wound and was unable to move.

Meanwhile, the enemy fire had isolated Private Stonham and his Platoon Commander from the remainder of the platoon, which was unable to cross the river. Under this heavy fire Private Stonham managed to drag the officer who was much heavier than himself, back across the river. They were still in an very exposed position and unable to reach the rest of the platoon, but Private Stonham managed to signal back for stretcher-bearers.

Then he attended to his Platoon Commander's wounds. When the stretcher-bearers failed to come forward in what seemed a reasonable time, he very carefully camouflaged the officer with leaves and undergrowth, and crawled back to hasten the stretcher-bearers. Returning with them he assisted in getting the officer to the rear.

The whole operation, which took some time, was carried out under very heavy fire. Later in the same day, volunteers were called for to go on a O.P., Private Powell volunteered for the task, and with a small escort crept forward and threw smoke grenades with such accuracy that the artillery were able to destroy the enemy strong-point which he thus indicated.

Certificate of Gallantry

Private J.E. Maynard, 9th Bn.
(War Diary 3rd February 1945)

The KING has been graciously pleased to approve that the following be Mentioned in recognition of gallant and distinguished services in North West Europe:—

M.I.D.

No. 6397417 W.O. 11 Thomas E. Rayner, 109th L.A.A. Regt. R.A. (& 7th Bn.)
No. 6397342 Gunner Leslie V. Foster, 109th L.A.A. Regt. R.A. (& 7th Bn.)
No. 6399663 Gunner Edward J. Illman, 109th L.A.A. Regt. (& 7th Bn.)
No. 6390313 Sergeant Walter H. Lambird, Royal Corps. of Signals
A/Major-General Lashmer Gordon Whistler, D.S.O. (13017)
Captain Frank Norman Shippam, (180207)

Saturday March 24th 1945

M.B.E. for Warnham R.S.M.

One of six serving brothers and son of an ex-R.S.M. in the Royal Sussex Regiment, R.S.M. Fleet, has been awarded the M.B.E. for "Gallantry and distinguished services in Italy." His parents, Mr. and Mrs. W. Fleet, of Friday Street, Warnham, have learned of their son's decoration in one of his letters home.

"London Gazette" Thursday March 29th 1945

The KING has been graciously pleased to give orders for the following appointments to the Most Honorable Order of the Bath, in recognition of gallant and distinguished services in North-West-Europe: —

C.B. (Military Division)

T/Brigadier Lashmar Gordon Whistler, D.S.O. (13017)
(Citation not found)

The KING has been graciously pleased to approve the award of the British Empire Medal (Military Division), in recognition of gallant and distinguished services in North West Europe, ,to the undermentioned : —

B.E.M. (Military Division) (Arnhem)

No. 5573750 Corporal Robert Charles Longman, 2nd Bn. attd. 10th Bn. Parachute Regiment, (Selby)

Corporal Longman has been employed as PRI Clerk since August 1940 to the 2nd Bn. The Royal Sussex Regiment, and to this unit since its formation in January 1943. Throughout the whole of this period he has carried out his duties with zeal, complete thoroughness and attention to detail.
His intimate knowledge of all the Battalion accounts has been of inestimable value during the frequent changes of the officers responsible for them.
On the many occasions when he has been called upon to handle the local purchases and deal with the

cash accounts he has shown himself utterly trustworthy and reliable. He went to the Western Desert with the 2nd Bn. The Royal Sussex regiment in July, 1942 and was transferred to 10th Bn. The Parachute Regiment in January 1943. He performed long and arduous journeys to Alexandria in search of comforts for the Battalion, and his work here was invaluable in keeping up the morale of the unit. When the Battalion went to Italy in September 1943, he again rose to the occasion and the men's' needs were looked after.

Again in September 1944, when the Battalion went to Arnhem, he had laid up his stocks of welfare goods and had he been able to link up, the men would have been well satisfied. It is largely due to his initiative, his ability and unceasing efforts that the welfare of the Battalion has been so well organised and successful.

Tuesday April 3rd 1945

The king has been pleased to approve the following award for gallant and distinguished service in North-West Europe :-

M.C.

Captain G.D. Hodgson, (78964)   attd. Dorset Regiment,

"London Gazette" Thursday April 5th 1945

The KING has been graciously pleased to approve that the following be Mentioned in recognition of gallant and distinguished services in Burma and on the Eastern Frontier of India: —

M.I.D.

T/Lieutenant-Colonel Derrick Hewitt Oliver, (33736) 9th Bn.
T/Major Leonard Charles Beecher, (164700) 9th Bn.
Lieutenant Ian Myles Frisby, (308955) 9th Bn.

Lieutenant Norman Eric Hulme, (256584) 9th Bn.
(Listed under Lancashire Fusiliers)

No. 6398489 C.S.M. F.J. Powell, 9th Bn.

No. 6408005 Sergeant A.R. Simmons, 9th Bn.

No. 5629505 A/Corporal H. Steer, 9th Bn.

No. 6408017 Private T.J. Spencer, 9th Bn.

The King has been pleased to grant unrestricted permission for the wearing of the following decoration which has been conferred on the under-mentioned person in recognition of distinguished services in the cause of the Allies :-

**DECORATIONS CONFERRED BY THE PRESIDENT OF
THE UNITED STATES OF AMERICA**

Silver Star (Immediate)

Major Charles Merrick Campbell Cockell, (130495) "C" Coy 9th Bn.

This was for his part in the attack on Hill 60 in August 1944.

Bronze Star (Immediate)

No. 6457417 R.S.M. Herbert Norman Brockless, 9th Bn.

This was for his part in the attack on Hill 60 August 1944.

1MM 1145ms Cipher 11 Jan 45

General Sultan wishes make following immediate awards of American decorations to personnel of 36 Div for gallantry in Burma operations. The Silver Star decoration to WS/Capt. (T/Major) Charles Merrick Campbell Cockell 130495. Royal Sussex.
The Bronze Star decoration to WO 1 RSM Herbert Norman Brockless (Royal Sussex)

Recommendations have support this HQ and concurrence Supreme Allied Commander. Individuals are not being recommended for British awards for same action.
Request approval to be given soonest possible as American authorities are anxious for early bestowal of these awards.

Saturday April 7th 1945

M.I.D.

The following members of the 9th Bn. Royal Sussex Regiment have been mentioned in dispatches for services in Burma and on the Indian Frontier :-

T/Lieutenant-Colonel D.H. Oliver, D.S.O., Major S.G. Neal, Major J.M. Cash, M.C., T/Major L.C. Beecher, Captain B.H. Chow, Captain F.R. Mansell, Captain J.E. Bridge, Captain N.E. Hulme, Captain I.C. McArthur, Lieutenant I.M. Frisby, W.O.I. F.J. Powell, W.O.II. R.E. Newton, Sergeant A.R. Simmons, Sergeant L.W. Wallis, Sergeant J. Barratt, Sergeant A.J. Rogers, Sergeant W.G. Leech, Sergeant R. Cadwallader, Sergeant A.F. Everson, Sergeant D.A.J. Mockford, Lance-Sergeant R.J.L. Smith, Sergeant C. Plested, Corporal H. Steer, Corporal A. Wildash, Corporal C.A. Saunders, Lance-Corporal B. Wyeth, Private A.J. Spencer, Private N. Burnham.

Certificate of Gallantry

Private J.E. Maynard, 9th Bn.

Tuesday April 10th 1945

Lewes Soldier saved Many Lives

KILLED IN ACTION AFTER WINNING M.M.

"By his courageous action he undoubtedly saved many lives."
This is an extract from the citation regarding the award of the Military Medal to Lance-Corporal Ernest George Peacock, son of Mr. And Mrs. E.G. Peacock, of 73, Ashcombe Farm, near Lewes. Mr. And

Mrs. Peacock recently attended an investiture at Buckingham Palace and received at the hands of the King, the medal which their son had earned by his self-sacrifice.

Unfortunately L/Cpl. Peacock was killed last year while bringing in a wounded comrade. The deed which won him the Military Medal was performed at the battle of Wadi Akarit, North Africa, during the night of 5th/6th April, 1943, and is described as follows in official citation:-

"On the night of 5th/6th April 1943, during the night attack on the Djebel el Meida hill, north-west of Wadi Akarit.

Private (as he was then) Peacock showed courage, coolness and devotion to duty of the highest order. He was attached to "B" Company (of The Royal Sussex Regiment) as a stretched bearer. Throughout the night the Company was under intense mortar and shell fire in narrow rocky wadis. Showing supreme contempt of this fire, Private Peacock rendered first aid to the wounded removing them to places of safety. The whole of the next day he continued to tend the wounded under heavy shell, and by his courageous action undoubtedly saved many lives."

Lance-Corporal Peacock, who was 26, joined the 1st Bn. Royal Sussex Regiment as a stretcher-bearer at the outbreak of the war.

"London Gazette" **Thursday April 12th 1945**

The KING has been graciously pleased to approve the following awards in recognition of gallant and distinguished services in North West Europe:—

M.C.

Major Henry Jervis Jourdain, (165751)
attd. 2nd Bn. Monmouthshire Regiment,

On 4 Jan 45, the Bn. had been ordered to attack the Bois de Hampteau and the village of Rendeux Bas in the Ardennes. Major Jourdain was commanding "A" Coy whose task it was to attack Southwards from the village of Hampteau towards Rendeux, while other Coys cleared the Bois de Hampteau itself. Major Jourdain's attack progressed well until, on rounding a bend in the rod, stiff enemy opposition was encountered in the vicinity of a strongly constructed and well sited road-block, protected by a number of Spandau groups and two dug in tanks.

Hard fighting followed throughout the afternoon and evening but though casualties were inflicted on the enemy and an attack by him on a troop of our tanks was beaten off by the Coy, the final objective was not secured. Major Jourdain was painfully wounded early in the action but contrived to command his Coy with great skill and determination. Under trying conditions of intense cold and very difficult steep wooded country, he launched a second attack on the road-block area.

This met with little further success and the Coy was ordered by the C.O. to disengage preparatory to fresh Bn. attack. This was launched under cover of darkness at 0600 hrs on 5 Jan 45. even stiffer opposition was met, but Major Jourdain persisted in his efforts to secure the road-block, until it was clear that a wide outflanking attack was the only effective course of action.

Throughout this action, Major Jourdain displayed the finest possible fighting spirit, a great tactical skill and cool personal courage that inspired his Coy under extremely trying conditions. He refused to take any notice of his wound until his Coy was relieved, and remained at duty ever since. Though the final objective of the Bn. was not achieved, yet without his fine example and leadership, it is doubted if the attack would have progressed as far as it did.

The KING has been graciously pleased to confer "The Efficiency Decoration" upon the following officers of the Territorial Army: —

Captain (T/Mjr.) Jack Gordon Wagener, (41353)

Wednesday April 18th 1945

Military Medal

For displaying great personal courage and initiative on the Italian Front, a Crowborough corporal, Corporal Frank White, of the Royal Sussex Regiment has been awarded the Military Medal.

"London Gazette" Thursday April 19th 1945

The KING has been graciously pleased to give orders for the following promotions in, and appointments to, the Most Excellent Order of the British Empire, in recognition of gallant and distinguished services in Italy: -

O.B.E. (Military Division)

A/Colonel Victor Henry Jaques, M.C. (131287) (Cranbrook)

Up to and during the period 1 May to 31 August 1944, Lt-Col. Jaques was responsible for the administrative planning and representation at Adv. H.Q. A.A.I. This called for extremely responsible and detailed work requiring co-ordination with all branches of the Staff and services. In his capacity as Administrative Representative at Adv. H.Q. he was owing to the considerable distance between Adv. And Main H.Q. frequently called upon to report the Administrive situation to the General Staff and take such immediate decisions as were necessitated. He performed his duties in a most zealous manner and by his ability and willingness to accept responsibility contributed in a large measure to the successful functioning of Adv. H.Q. so far as the administrative aspect was concerned.

M.B.E. (Military Division)

No. 6190062 R.S.M. Herbert Frank Phillips,   1st Bn. (London S.W. 11)

This W.O. who has thirty years continuous service, has been R.S.M. of the Bn. since May 1943. During the successful operations on the Adriatic Sector in May and June 1944, the Upper Tiber Valley in July and August 1944 and during the most recent operations which included the assault and penetration of the Gothic Line positions. R.S.M. Phillips has been solely responsible for the supply of ammunition to the forward Coys of the Bn.
This task he has carried out admirably and through his efforts there has never been the slightest shortage of ammunition even during the most difficult phases of the operations. During the course of the operations in the Upper Tiber Valley ammunition invariably had to be carried to the forward Coys up exceedingly difficult mountain tracks necessitating the use of jeeps and mules. For the most part, these tracks were under shell and mortar fire and usually owing to enemy observations - had to be negotiated at night. This made them doubly dangerous and trips took as long as five or six hours. On such occasions, whenever there was the slightest possibility of the ammunition column going astray due to either enemy fire or dangerous tracks at night, or to a combination of both, R.S.M. Phillips always led the column personally. These occasions were the rule rather than the exception.
Typical of his conduct, is the occasion during these operations when a treacherous narrow road was being heavily shelled several vehicles had been forced into the ditch blocking the road and there was some confusion. R.S.M. Phillips immediately took charge and remained standing cooly directing traffic and getting the vehicles back on the road. The shelling continued heavily throughout but R.S.M. Phillips' fine example very soon restored confidence and averted casualties and delay at an important time. In the more recent operations, in breaking through the Gothic Line R.S.M. Phillips in addition to his normal duties, supervised the evacuation of casualties from forward Coy positions under conditions caused by enemy fire, heavy rain and mud, which could hardly have been worse.

Throughout the operations and during the previous Cassino operations February 1944, during periods of heavy enemy opposition and extreme weather conditions, by his sympathetic understanding of the men, by his courage, cheerfulness and devotion to duty R.S.M. Phillips has been an inspiration to all ranks.

Friday April 20th 1945

The King has been pleased to approve the following award or gallant and distinguished service :-

O.B.E.

Colonel Victor Henry Jaques, M.C.

M.B.E.

R.S.M. Herbert Frank Phillips

Wednesday April 25th 1945

The King has been pleased to approve the following award for gallant and distinguished service in the Middle-East :-

Military Cross

For his courage and devotion to duty at Tripsrath, last November, an officer of the Royal Sussex Regiment, Captain Geoffrey Derek Hodgson, of Hassocks, has been awarded the M.C. After a battalion attack to clear a wood, the battalion came under heavy fire. As commander of an anti-tank platoon, Captain Hodgson worked steadily, despite the shells for over four hours, and without thought of taking cover to find routes through the woods for his guns and then personally directed their positioning.

"London Gazette" Thursday April 26th 1945

The KING has been graciously pleased to approve that the following be Mentioned in recognition of gallant and distinguished services in Burma: —

M.I.D.

T/Captain George Henry Borrow, M.C. (228394) (k.i.a.) (A.D.C. to Brig. Orde Wingate)

(Attached Nigerian Regiment)

T/Major Lionel William Skipworth Tayler, (52239)
A/Captain Peter Coombe Harris, (153261)
Lieutenant Leslie Philip Banfield, (265869)
Lieutenant Joseph Kilner Tabrar Earle, (276359)
Lieutenant Charles Henry Mercer, (265871)
No. 6398407 C.S.M. F. Hill,

The KING has been graciously pleased to approve the following awards in recognition of gallant and distinguished services in Italy: —

M.M.

No. 14657022 L/Corporal Ernest Edward Brockhurst, 1st Bn. (Poling)

On 25 September 1944 a platoon of "B" Coy went on patrol to locate enemy defences on Monte Reggiano. L/Corporal Brockhurst was Second in Command of a Section leading the advance. The patrol was ambushed and subjected to very heavy fire from Spandau, rifle grenades and mortars resulting in severe casualties and temporary disorganisation. Several members of L/Corporal Brockhurst's Section were killed, including the Section Commander.

This N.C.O. at once took charge and rallying the remainder of the section he pressed on to achieve the object of the patrol. The enemy fire increased in intensity, but, displaying a courage and devotion to duty which inspired his men, he led them forward. Passing through a belt of Spandaus, some of which were pouring out a hail of bullets at a distance of only fifteen yards, the section got behind the enemy positions.

L/Corporal Brockhurst located at least nine of these positions before leading his section back to our lines. He then at once went out again and indicated the enemy positions to his Coy Commander with great accuracy. As a result our supporting tanks and artillery were able to engage the enemy with devasting results.

The coolness and courage of this junior N.C.O. are worthy of the highest praise. His undaunted determination to obtain information which resulted in the complete destruction of enemy positions undoubtedly contributed greatly to the success of the subsequent attack.

"London Gazette" **Thursday May 10th 1945**

The KING has been graciously pleased to approve that the following be Mentioned in recognition of gallant and distinguished services in North-West Europe:-

M.I.D.

No. 6406413 Gunner L. Donaghy, 109th L.A.A. Regt. R.A. (& 7th Bn.)
No. 6395578 W.O.11 E. Jordan, Royal Corps of Signals

M.I.D. (Arnhem)

No. 6400234 Sgt. Thomas Cyril Bentley, 2nd Bn. (10th Bn. Para Reg. A.A.C.)
No. 1463360 Pte. G. Harwood, 2nd Bn. (10th Bn. Para Reg. A.A.C.)
No. 6400271 Sgt. A.L. Sparkes, 2nd Bn. (10th Bn. Para Reg. A.A.C.)
No. 5573779 Cpl. L. Waite, 2nd Bn. (10th Bn. Para Reg. A.A.C.)

Thursday May 31st 1945

Sussex Troops In Unique Exercise

Men of a battalion of The Royal Sussex Regiment, now serving in Paiforce (Persia and Iraq Command), have recently taken part in a training exercise that may well claim to be unique (writes a Military Observer) in so far as it constituted the first occasion on which British and Indian troops have undertaken a series of manoeuvres side by side with their Iraqi brothers – in – arms.

The scheme had been planned and devised by the General Staff of Iraq Army for the training of one of its divisions, and the exercise was held in the north-east corner of Iraq.

The exercise, which lasted for a fortnight, was a very thorough test of military knowledge and efficiency. Mechanical transport, apart from jeeps, could be little employed owing to the nature of the ground; mules had to used, and long marches undertaken with full equipment; there were mountains to be climbed and rivers to be forded; the days were as hot as the nights were cold and, with a strong wind blowing, many of the men's faces had begun to peel and blister before the exercise was half-way through. The conclusion of the exercise, which was visited by H.R.H. the Regent of Iraq, was attended by various festivities. On the last day the military band from Mosul played a programme of English songs as the men cleaned up after a day's work. It was a pleasant sight to see the men of Sussex, many of them bare to the waist, their chests and backs burnt as brown as the canvas of their bivouacs, eating their evening meal and listening to the songs they had learned to love in England beside the Downs.

"London Gazette" **Thursday June 14th 1945**

The KING has been graciously pleased, on the occasion of the Celebration of His Majesty's Birthday, to approve the award of the British Empire Medal (Military Division) to the undermentioned :

B.E.M. (Military Division)

No. 7810834 Sergeant William Percy Vinall, 1st Bn. The Royal Sussex Regiment

"London Gazette" **Thursday June 21st 1945**

The KING has been graciously pleased to give orders for the following promotions in, and appointments to, the Most Excellent Order of the British Empire, in recognition of gallant and distinguished services in North West Europe: —

M.B.E. (Military Division)

T/Major Eric Chisholm Sevenoaks, M.C. (63782) 7th Bn. (Lancefield, Cumberland)

This officer has been SO(L) at H.Q. 1st Canadian Army throughout the campaign in N.W.E. His work at all times has been efficient and accurate. He has shown himself to be thoroughly reliable and can be counted on to complete whatever task he is given no matter what the circumstances. His devotion to duty is exceptional. In recent months this officer has shown that he has benefited greatly from his practical experience in liaison work and he is now playing an increasingly important part in the successful functioning of the Liaison Branch of the General Staff at this H.Q.

M.C.

Lieutenant Ronald Morris Williams, (187071) attd. 4th Bn. Royal Welch Fusiliers.

In the attack on Ibbenburen on the night 5/6 April 1945, Lieutenant Williams lead the leading platoon in the assault. The enemy consisted of very tough Officer cadets and N.C.O.'s, who were completely determined not to give in and fought with fanatical fury. Against machine-gun posts manned by these stubborn enemy Lieutenant Williams led attack after attack. On more than one occasion he personally led the assault on a house containing enemy and by his skilful leadership and dash quickly succeeded in reaching his objective. With morning light, the enemy most of whom had gone to ground to avoid our bombardment became active all over town. Some infiltrated Lieutenant Williams platoon area. He quickly made a plan to dislodge them, and put it in to execution with such vigour that the enemy was quickly driven out. In spite of the fact that the enemy was armed with telescopic sights and were thus able to pick out the officers easily from their men, he led the attack and did so with a dash that carried him and his men into the house with an irresistible momentum – Lieutenant Williams personally killed many Germans and quickly overpowered the remainder. Under his inspiring leadership his men fought magnificently. Early in the assault Lieutenant Williams was wounded in the leg, but he continued to direct operations until the enemy was completely eliminated and the platoon position firmly established. By his personal example, courage and fortitude he did much to win the battle for his Company – his conduct was quite outstanding.

M.M.

No. 6398404 Sergeant Frank Arthur Worthington, (attd. No. 6 Commando)

At Wesel on 24th March 1945, Sergeant Worthington was in charge of a small defensive position on the outskirts of the city when he saw an enemy bicycle patrol coming towards him at a range of 1000 yards. The patrol suddenly turned off down a side-street and disappeared from view. Realising they were heading for a part of town which had not yet been consolidated, Sergeant Worthington acted immediately and sent a runner to tell his Troop Commander of his action.

He then left a skeleton force in the defensive position and taking the remaining eight of his men he set off to ambush the patrol. He struck the side of the road just in time to meet the patrol head-on and fired on them from houses by the side of the road. Eight of the enemy were killed or wounded, five taken prisoner and the remainder fled. Sergeant Worthington himself was wounded at the start bur refused to hand over or even have his wound dressed until the action was over and the patrol brought back. By this successful action and by his own initiative, gallantry and immediate action, Sergeant Worthington liquidated the enemy patrol and prevented them from running into another unit who were just then at that awkward stage prior to consolidation.

The KING has been graciously pleased to approve the following awards in recognition of gallant and distinguished services in Burma: -

Bar to M.C.

T/Major John James Dickson, M.C. (96192) 9th Bn.

On 27 February 1945, Major Dickson was ordered to capture the feature known as Hill 800 near Myitson. This feature commanded the line of advance of the whole Bde., and captured enemy documents disclosed that the enemy attached great importance to its retention. Major Dickson scored tactical surprise y attacking up a precipitous face, through dense jungle and avoiding the easier slopes which offered obvious lines of approach.

The attack was met by L.M.G. and sniper fire, Major Dickson, seeing that some men in the leading sections were wavering, owing to the barrage of our own guns falling short, at once went forward himself and became the spearhead of the attack. With cool courage and determination he personally led his Coy to the crest of the hill where the leading platoons were again held up by L.M.G. fire from the far end of the ridge.

Rapidly grasping the situation, he called for additional artillery fire and committed the reserve platoon to a left flanking attack. This attack was put in with such skill and determination that it met with instant success and the enemy fled, leaving one officer and 5 Jap other ranks on the field, together with an L.M.G., packs and other equipment, which showed that the position was a least a Coy one. It was due to this officer's outstanding courage, initiative and superb leadership, combined with tactical skill of a very high order, which enabled the feature to be captured with the loss of very few casualties of our own troops.

(M.C. gazetted 22/04/45)

M.C.

A/Major Christopher Hunt, (148571) 9th Bn. (Llanrhidian, Swansea)

On 14 February 1945, Major Hunt's Coy formed part of the bridgehead over the Shweli River near Myitson. Between the 14/18 February the bridgehead was subjected to considerable shelling and was under continual fire from grenades, L.M.G.'s and mortars. Major Hunt's Coy held a large perimeter with one platoon of another Battalion under command. During the entire battle this officer showed outstanding leadership and initiative, combined with courage and a coolness in action that was an inspiration to all ranks who were present. With complete disregard to his own safety he moved continuously from platoon to platoon encouraging and inspiring confidence in his men at a critical stage of the battle.

On 16 February, at considerable risk to himself he organised the recovery of a wounded man of the attached platoon. Under covering fire from one of his L.M.G.'s he went forward himself, throwing smoke grenades, undercover of which he assisted in carrying the wounded man.

At a later stage in the battle, when men's nerves were strained, and a fresh attack seemed imminent, he restrained his men from opening fire prematurely and when the enemy emerged from the jungle he himself killed several of the leading enemy, thereby being largely instrumental in breaking up this fresh attack. At the close of the battle, this officer showed considerable skill and ability in organising the re-grouping of his Coy. He carried through his plan in the face of considerable enemy fire, extricating his Coy from a difficult position without suffering a casualty.

During the action, this officer showed leadership and courage combined with tactical skill of a high order.

M.M.

No. 6405175 Corporal Percy Lawrence Glover, 9th Bn. (Haywards Heath)

On February 15th 1945, Corporal Glover's section formed part of the Coy holding the bridgehead over the Shweli river near Myitson. For three days this N.C.O.'s section was heavily attacked by superior forces. On one occasion, when his section had been depleted in numbers in order to form a patrol, the enemy tried to rush his position. Corporal Glover immediately seized a Bren gun and drove off the enemy. He then went forward alone and pursued the enemy with grenades. He repeated this again the following day. After the attacks had been beaten off, three enemy dead were found in front of his position, and, in addition, many had been wounded.

During all this time he also crawled to exposed positions with ammunition, water and rations. His coolness and courage in action under considerable fire was an inspiration to all ranks, and in no small way contributed to the successful withdrawal of his Coy from the bridgehead.

No. 6209984 Sergeant Harry Ernest Herman, 9th Bn. (London N.17)

On 27th February 1945, during the assault on the precipitous jungle-covered feature known as Hill 800, Sergeant Herman was Platoon Sergeant of the right forward assaulting platoon. Attacking through thick jungle, the assault was retarded through a number of our own shells falling short only a few yards in front of the leading troops.

The Platoon Commander became a casualty and was unable to continue, Sergeant Herman at once ran forward and called upon the platoon to follow him. With considerable dash and determination, combined with tactical skill, he brought the platoon to the objective. The first opposition being overcome, this N.C.O. again in the lead directed his platoon to the centre of the enemy's position.

The attack was pressed with such skill and determination that the enemy did not wait for the final assault, but broke and fled, leaving 15 packs and other equipment in the position. Sergeant Herman charged forward alone and pursued the enemy down the further slope of the hill, inflicting further casualties on them with bayonet and grenades.

It was due in no small measure to this N.C.O.'s outstanding courage and leadership, combined with his tactical skill, that Hill 800 was successfully taken.

No. 14650172 Lance-Corporal Albert John Picard, 9th Bn. (London W. 9)

During an attack on the precipitous feature known as Hill 800, on 27th February 1945, L/Corporal Picard was No. 1 of the Bren gun on the left hand leading platoon. The attack was carried out through thick jungle under artillery barrage 50 yards ahead of the leading troops. Some shells fell short only 10 yards in front of L/Corporal Picard's section and several men wavered.

This N.C.O. at once cheered his men on and took the lead himself. The section continued the assault through tangled creepers and up bare rock where hands and feet had to be used to maintain balance. On reaching the crest of the hill, an enemy L.M.G. was encountered, the crew of which was hastily endeavouring to turn the gun on to our leading troops. L/Corporal Picard charged forward alone, and, firing his Bren gun from the hip, knocked out the Jap L.M.G. killing the crew. Further on toward the centre of the Jap position, further enemy was encountered. These were destroyed by L/Corporal Picard and his section. The Coy was now held up for an hour by persistent and stubborn L.M.G. and rifle fire from the farthest tip of the feature. Again, L/Corporal Picard worked his way forward alone, whilst endeavouring to outflank the enemy, was wounded, but he continued to maintain his gun in action until another member of his section was able to work his way forward and relieve him.

It was largely due to this N.C.O.'s determination and outstanding leadership in the face of considerable opposition that Hill 800 was successfully captured.

No. 5350852 Lance-Corporal William George Rogers, 9th Bn. (Reading)

On 15th February 1945, Private Rogers' Coy was assisting to hold the bridgehead over the Shweli river, near Myitson, when the enemy put down a road block behind the Coy, which was temporarily surrounded. Private Rogers was No. 1 of a Bren gun covering an enemy approach to the Coy position. For three days, Private Rogers maintained his gun in action and intense enemy L.M.G. and sniper fire. His first No. 2 was wounded by his side, and a second was killed. In order to avoid further casualties, Private Rogers maintained his gun in action single-handed.

During this period he killed five of the enemy himself, and it was due in no small measure to his courage and initiative that the enemy were held off, and his Coy was later successfully withdrawn from the bridgehead.

Saturday June 23rd 1945

Military Medal

The King has been pleased to approve of the following award for distinguished and gallant service in Burma :-

Corporal Percy Lawrance Glover, 9th Bn. (Haywoods Heath)

"London Gazette" Thursday June 28th 1945

The KING has been graciously .pleased to give orders for the following promotions in, and appointments to, the Most Excellent Order of the British Empire, in recognition of gallant and distinguished services in Italy: —

O.B.E. (Military Division)

T/L/Colonel Edwin Albert Hanchard Goodwin, (163317) 1st Bn. (London N.1)

Lt-Col. Goodwin has been employed as an A.Q.M.G. on H.Q. 3 District for six months. During this time the size of the District has more than doubled and now has a ration strength of 350,000 and an area of 60,000 square miles. Lt-Col. Goodwin has been responsible for all accommodation throughout the District. Not only has this entailed accommodating existing personnel, but he has recently had to plan for reception of five major Formations. In addition, accommodation and building for extensive increases to Base Depots and Installations has been his responsibility. On all occasions Lt-Col. Goodwin has tackled every problem with an enthusiasm and drive that has achieved a prompt and satisfactory solution. I strongly recommend Lt-Col. Goodwin for O.B.E.

M.B.E. (Military Division)

T/Captain Homi Toni Boga, (307388) 1st Bn. (London W.1)

Captain Boga has been Liaison Officer at H.Q. 28 Inf. Bde. During many months of active service. As such he been called upon to make vital journeys which have frequently been difficult and sometimes hazardous, but never has he failed to carry out his task in the most cheerful and energetic manner. In October 1944 he was promoted and appointed SLO, in this capacity he has not only been at great assistance to the Staff, but he organised and personally supervised a most efficient system of Traffic Control in the forward areas. The success of this latter task may be measured by the fact that despite appalling weather conditions and in the face of consistent enemy shelling of roads and tracks there has never been an occasion when the smooth and steady flow of supporting weapons and supplies for the forward troops has been seriously dislocated. Captain Boga has inspired the officers and men who are his assistants with the same spirit of cheerful efficiency and reliability in the face of danger, and has earned for himself a reputation which is endorsed by all with whom he is associated.

The KING has been graciously pleased to give orders for the following promotions in, and appointments to, the Most Excellent Order of the British Empire, in recognition of gallant and distinguished services in Burma: —

O.B.E. (Military Division)

Lieutenant-Colonel Thomas Chamber Windsor Roe, (121387) (Hove)

Throughout the period under review, Lt-Col. Roe, as A.A. & Q.M.G. of the Division, has been responsible for the prompt and regular provision of ammunition and supplies, the evacuation of casualties, the organisation of movement and the one thousand and one other items included in the administration of a Division. The efficiency with which these tasks were carried out in the most adverse monsoon weather and bad roads was largely responsible for the good health and high morale of all ranks and did much to ensure the success of the operations.

The KING has been graciously pleased to approve the following awards in recognition of gallant and distinguished services in Italy: —

D.S.O.

Lt-Colonel Geoffrey Arthur Phelps, (36752) 1st Bn.

During the Gothic Line Battle, in which the 1st Royal Sussex Regt. Fought almost continually and in previous battles Lt-Colonel Phelps showed the greatest gallantry and devotion to duty whilst commanding his battalion. Firstly Lt-Colonel Phelps' battalion was one of the first battalions to reach the Gothic Line proper, near Auditore, after considerable fighting. His battalion column, supported by armour, captured several enemy localities including the ancient of Urbino and smashed through to form a flank well to the West of Auditore. This fierce and resolute thrust drew almost the whole of the enemy artillery fire and thereby enabled other units to breach the actual Gothic Line defences.

The column seized Fieve di Cagna ridge under a hail of artillery, mortar and small-arms fire from three sides. The enemy counter-attacked fiercely, but was beaten off in several hand to hand encounters. The success of this operation was entirely due to Lt-Colonel Phelps, who working with untiring zeal, courage and cheerfulness, under perpetual artillery, mortar and small-arms fire, repeatedly went right forward to the head of his column. This conduct was an inspiration to all.

Secondly, after the eventual penetration of the Gothic Line, his battalion supported by armour, attacked and seized the Piane di Castello feature which was of vital importance to the Divisional plan. This attack entailed seizing an intermediate ridge, crossing a heavily mined river and fighting up the long slopes of the ridge. The attack was fiercely opposed and determined fighting took place, the battalion taking over 40 prisoners.

During the four day occupation of the objective the battalion was resolutely counter-attacked many times, but all these were beaten off with heavy losses. All this time Lt-Colonel Phelps showed great courage and powers of leadership, visiting his Coys frequently, often going through heavy fire with an offensive spirit of a very high order.

Subsequently his battalion supported by armour attacked and seized the Reggiano ridge, beyond the River Rubicon. All this fighting was in torrential rain and bitterly opposed. His battalion had now been reduced by casualties to three weak Coys, but despite these disheartening conditions, Lt-Colonel Phelps kept the morale of his battalion high, and by the dash and ferocity of their attack on Reggiano captured many prisoners.

That the spirit of the battalion was so high at the end of this gruelling six weeks was largely due to the unflagging spirit and tireless energy of Lt-Colonel Phelps.

M.M.

No. 6403993 Sergeant George Alfred Percy Martin, 1st Bn. (Lewes)

Throughout the operations in the Gothic Line. September/October 1944, this N.C.O. set a high standard of courage, initiative and devotion to duty as a Mortar Section Commander, and in charge of O.P's. During the Gothic Line period he repeatedly manned O.P.'s many of them in exposed positions for long periods. He showed great coolness and presence of mind whenever his O.P. was under enemy shelling and mortaring.

In the Piane di Castello operation, Sergeant Martin's work was consistently outstanding and set a high example to all ranks. He was under fire for long periods. When not running an O.P. he organised and maintained the entire mortar position.

On 3rd September, he took out a line in the face of heavy fire and maintained communications. By his indifference to danger, he maintained communications during a critical phase of the operations. On 6th September, Sergeant Martin, with complete disregard for his own safety went out under fire to one of his platoon, who had been severely wounded by a shell bursting near the mortar pit.

Sergeant Martin crawled backwards with the casualty, got him under cover and temporarily dressed his wounds which were bleeding freely. By his gallant conduct and prompt action he undoubtedly enabled the man to have the earliest possible attention at the R.A.P. Sergeant Martin has been with the Battalion for four years having served in all the Regiments campaigns from the Western desert 1940 to the Gothic

Line 1944.
He has been with the Mortar Section Platoon since the beginning of the Italian campaign. Throughout the hard fighting in the Adriatic Sector, Cassino, Upper Tiber Valley and the Gothic Line, he has always shown cheerfulness, keenness in all circumstances and great devotion to duty.

The skill, energy and determination shown by this officer, throughout these operations has been beyond all praise and is eminently deserving of recognition.

Saturday June 30th 1945

The King has been pleased to approve the following award for distinguished and gallant service :-

Military Medal

Sergeant George Alfred Percy Martin, 1st Bn. (Lewes)

"London Gazette" Thursday July 12th 1945

The KING has been graciously pleased to approve the following awards in recognition of gallant and distinguished services in Burma: —

D.S.O.

T/Lieutenant-Colonel Derrick Hewitt Oliver, (33736) 9th Bn. (Chichester)

On 12 November 1944, the Bde. was advancing S of Mawlu, with two Battalions down the road, and Lt-Col. Oliver's Battalion down at the railway, about a mile to the West. Strong opposition was encountered on both axis, but by the night of 13 November, the enemy outposts had been driven back to their main line of defence. Lt-Col. Oliver's Battalion took a position astride the railway in very thick jungle. During the night, the whole Battalion area was shelled and mortared and casualties occurred to men and mules. It became quite obvious that the enemy intended to put in a strong counter-attack, but it was quite impossible to estimate which direction it would come from as there had been sniping and movement all round the perimeter.
Lt-Col. Oliver also knew that he could expect no help from the rest of the Bde., who were already heavily involved on the other axis. The Japs attacked on all sides at daybreak, with a strong battalion. The orders for this attack found later in the day on a dead Jap officer, directed that the British force holding the railway should be annihilated, or they should die in the attempt. They poured automatic fire from all angles into our perimeter, and until midday kept up their fanatical attacks. In spite of casualties, the Battalion held all their ground.
Lt-Col. Oliver, regardless of danger, constantly moved round his Coys, encouraging the men, directing the defence and ensuring their ammunition supply. About midday, the attacks appeared to be weakening, and Lt-Col. Oliver immediately organised a counter-attack with one Coy. This caught the enemy by surprise, they were located in a Chaung re-organising, a barrage of 2" and 3" mortars was brought down on them, and the Coy charged with the bayonet. The enemy fled in confusion, leaving 50 dead, and many more bodies were discovered later in the area.
In the meantime, another Battalion of the Bde. On the road to the East, had been encircled and were being hard pressed, the Japs having cut their water supply, also the road behind them. It was essential that the road be opened as ammunition was becoming low and the men were suffering from thirst. Lt-Col. Oliver immediately detached two Coys from his perimeter and attacked the roadblock behind the other Battalion. The Japs were mostly killed and the road re-opened, and supplies rushed through. The success of the day was very largely due to Lt-Col. Oliver's quick appreciation of the situation on the railway, and his immediate counter-attack, thus enabling him to send Coys to the relief of the other Battalion.

During the many previous engagements, particularly at Hill 60 and Thaikwagon in August, Lt-Col. Oliver has shown himself to be an exceptional leader of men. He is quite unmoved by danger to himself and his clear-headed orders under adverse conditions, give his men the greatest confidence.

"London Gazette" **Thursday July 19th 1945**

The KING has been graciously pleased to approve that the following be Mentioned in recognition of gallant and distinguished services in Italy: —

M.I.D. 1st Bn

T/Major Archibald Philip Edwards, M.B.E. (124222)
T/Major Charles Paul Genillard, (129366)
T/Major Kenneth Stephen Horace Wilson, (141036)
T/Major Thomas Jocelyn Faulconer Wisden, (97236)
Captain Hugh Mannington M.B. (71741)
T/Captain John William Howard Shaw, (203806)
Lieutenant Charles Alan Powell, (284563)
No. 6398209 Colour-Sergeant R.H. Foreman,
No. 6391441 Private J. Owens,
No. 6403012 Private H. Thrift,

The KING has been graciously pleased to approve that the following be Mentioned in recognition of gallant and distinguished services in Burma: —

M.I.D. 9th Bn.

T/Captain Harold Richard Clarke Curtis (274994)
No. 5337445 Sergeant Frederick Richard Allen, (k.i.a.)
No. 6408083 A/Sergeant Arthur Frederick Everson, (k.i.a.)
No. 6396611 L/Sergeant Frederick George Crunden, (k.i.a.)

No. 6407374 L/Sergeant Charles Selby, (k.i.a.)

"London Gazette" **Thursday July 26th 1945**

The KING has been graciously pleased to approve the following awards in recognition of gallant and distinguished services in the field: —

D.C.M. (Escapee)

No. 7011496 Sergeant Samuel Herbert Cooke, 2nd Bn.

Escaped Prisoner of War : Sgt. Cooke was captured at Hazebrouck on 27 May 1940 and was imprisoned in Stalag VIII B (Lamsdorf), Germany, for the whole of the period of his captivity. He made five attempts to escape before finally reaching Warsaw in the summer of 1944. His first attempt was in November 1940, after timing the sentries, he got through the wire at night and walked 30 kilometres. He was recaptured the next morning and punished with 14 days cells.

In April 1941 he volunteered to take a working party to Hindenburg, with the idea of escaping into Poland. He walked away from the cookhouse without any difficulty and hid in trains which carried him to within 5 miles of Krakow. He walked into the city to find a helper, whose address had been given to him, but was halted by a German patrol asking for papers and was thus recaptured. He was again punished with 14 days cells and bread and water.

His third attempt was made October 1942, when with two other P/W he cut the wire. Sgt. Cooke separated from his companions outside the camp and after walking in circles was captured the following day by police.

In September 1943, while on a working party at Ratibor, for which he had volunteered in order to escape, Cooke removed the distinguishing paint patch from his overalls and walked out of the main gate undetected. He reached Berlin by train but having no papers, was arrested by the Control at the station. His punishment on return was 21 days cells, and he was warned that he would be shot should he attempt to escape again. However, six weeks later Sgt. Cooke escaped for the fifth time. He and two men went to draw coal from the dump outside the main camp just before the sentries changed. When the men returned Cooke stayed in the forest. Towards evening he was apprehended by some guards off duty and was brought back to the camp.

Sgt. Cooke's final escape was effected in April 1944. He had obtained money by selling chocolates and cigarettes to the German guards: wearing civilian clothes acquired from Poles and carrying food given him by the British Medical Officer, Sgt. Cooke cut the wire and got away on the night of 22 April 1944. Travelling by rail and on foot, he reached the German-polish frontier, which he crossed in dense forest. Poles assisted him on his way and, on reaching Warsaw, he went to an address that one of them had given him. Here he was well cared for, fed and given identity papers and money. Two months after his arrival there he assisted the distribution of arms to the resistance party in the city.

In August 1944 Cooke decided to join the Russians, who were then advancing in the direction of Warsaw. This he did, against the advice of his host, and after long interrogations and imprisonment by the Russians, who needed a great deal of convincing that he was English, Sgt. Cooke was finally handed over to the British in Moscow on 22 September 1944.

M.M. (Escapee)

No. 6403919 Lance-Sergeant Alfred Clarence Searson, (attd. 2 Commando, PoW & Escapee)
(St. Nazaire)

After being taken prisoner along with Lance-Sergeant R. Bradley, Royal Berkshire Regt. and Private J. Brown, Ex Argyll and Sutherland Highlanders, on 28th March 1942, they were sent to Germany. On 17th August 1942, using a stolen file, Searson, Brown and another prisoner of war cut through the window bars and escaped from Stalag V111 B. they had been at liberty for four days when they were caught as they slept in a wood.

Their second attempt was made at the beginning of October 1942, wearing overalls, old caps and rucksacks, they posed as civilian workmen, but their disguise was penetrated the next day. For punishment they were sent to stone quarries near Bunzlau, and when they refused to work, received instead nine days in the cells, prior to their return to the main camp. Although Brown succeeded in leaving Greiffenberg working camp in March 1943, he was arrested at Gorlitz because the dye from his overcoat stained his face and neck. He was sent back to Stalag V111 B where he again met Searson who had in the meantime helped two other prisoners of war to leave a working camp at Sternberg, and had acquired money and clothing in July 1943, from a factory at Freiheit-Johannesburg. Accompanied by Bradley, he travelled by train to Engen, and the two men were nearing the Swiss frontier when they were caught and once more returned to Stalag V111 B. Brown who had waited another month to acquire a civilian jacket, was detected as he was leaving the factory on 12th August 1943.

By October 1943, Brown, Bradley and Searson had completed their preparations for a combined effort. At this time they were employed at Wossswalda, and while the guards were having a meal the three men forced the door lock with a bent nail, walked to the station, and travelling on slow trains reached Tuttlingen unchallenged. Completing the remainder of the journey on foot, they crossed into Switzerland near Hofenacker on 25th October 1943.

"London Gazette" Thursday August 9th 1945

The KING has been graciously pleased to approve that the following be Mentioned in recognition of gallant and distinguished service in North-West Europe: —

M.I.D.

No. 6403307 Bombardier Cyril Roy Downham, 109th L.A.A. Regt. R.A. (& 7th Bn.)
A/Major-General Lashmer Gordon Whistler, C.B. D.S.O. (13017) 4th Bn.
T/Captain Arthur Allen Atkins, (130315)
Lieutenant Raymond Alfred Daniels, (284757) attd. 7th Hampshire Regiment

"London Gazette" Thursday August 23rd 1945

The KING has been graciously pleased to approve the following awards in recognition of gallant and distinguished services in Italy: —

M.C.

T/Major John Neville Crawford, (98330) (Bedford) attd. 1/5th Mahratta Light Infantry,

On the 9th April 1945 at 1920 hrs. Major Crawford's Coy assaulted and captured the East bank of the Senio river. The Coy which was to pass through his and assault the West bank suffered very casualties including the Coy Commander and became disorganised. Quickly realising the situation which was becoming critical, Major Crawford personally leading one of his platoons, waded the river under very heavy mortar and small arms fire and established a footing on the West bank. At this juncture he was severely wounded in the stomach.
In spite of being in great pain, Major Crawford continued to direct the operations in the immediate neighbourhood and called for and directed artillery fire on to a large party of enemy forming up for a counter-attack, thereby breaking it up and forcing the enemy to withdraw.
It was entirely Major Crawford's magnificent example of initiative, leadership, devotion to duty and complete disregard of personal danger that enabled the West bank to be captured and held at a very critical period, thereby ensuring the future success of the operations.

Saturday 1st September 1945

Rottingdean Major Awarded M.C.

Gallantry in an action in Italy, during which he was wounded but refused aid and continued to lead his company, has been rewarded by the bestowal of the Military Cross upon Major Charles Paul Genillard, of the Royal Sussex Regiment, the eldest son of Mr and Mrs C. Genillard, of the Rookery, Dean Court Road, Rottingdean.
Major Genillard has served throughout the Italian campaign, and the story of the action in which he won the M.C. is graphically told in the official citation. On April 20, 1945, the battalion was ordered to strike north from Mascarina in order to by-pass heavy enemy resistance that was being encountered by a battalion of the Lancashire Fusiliers to the west. This task fell to a company commanded by Major Genillard.

"Throughout the day," states the citation, "the company advanced against stiffening opposition, meeting innumerable pockets of resistance and being continually harassed by snipers in the high grass.

With leading Troops

"Major Genillard was always with his leading troops throughout this action, and was an inspiration to all those who saw him, due to his example and complete disregard of his own safety. In this action he was hit by a shell splinter in the back and refused all aid and continued to command and lead his company to the final objective."

On two separate occasions after he was wounded, and although in great pain, he himself led attacks on Spandau positions, forcing the crews to surrender. It was not until the final objective was gained that Major Genillard allowed his wound to be dressed, and even then would not be evacuated.

"The effect of this action was to loosen the opposition on the left of the battalion, enabling the general advance to continue," adds the citation. "Had it not been for the great courage and inspired leadership of Major Genillard it would never have been possible for one company to carry out this rapid advance, and any slowing up of the rate of advance would have allowed the enemy to occupy already prepared positions."

Running an Officers' Club

Apart from this exploit, Major Genillard was mentioned in dispatches about 18 months ago. Now he is in Austria, where, in a beautiful private residence on a lakeside, he is running an officers; club with an Austrian and Hungarian staff of 54. Major Genillard who joined the Royal Sussex Regiment at the outbreak of war, is an old Varndeanian, and was formerly in the office of Messrs. Gates, McCully & Buckwell, solicitors, of Brighton.

His brother, Flight Lieutenant Gaston Genillard, also joined up at the beginning of hostilities and has spent three years overseas. He too, has been wounded. The brothers met in Italy, just after the fall of Naples, for the first time in three years.

"London Gazette" Thursday September 13th 1945

The KING has been graciously pleased to approve the award of the British Empire Medal (Military Division) to the undermentioned, in recognition of gallant and distinguished services in Burma:—

B.E.M. (Military Division)

No. 6407531 A/Sergeant Edwin Bulmer Portlock, 9th Bn. (Haywards Heath)

On 9 November 44, on the first day of the advance southwards from Mawlu, Sergeant Portlock, a Junior Signal N.C.O. in charge of a detachment, was ordered to take command of the Signal Platoon. Owing to sickness and battle casualties, culminating in the death of the A/Platoon Commander within a few hours of the start of the advance, it was necessary for Sergeant Portlock to assume full responsibility for the Battalion's communications at very short notice.

The advance down the country towards Pinwe was a difficult one and imposed a great strain upon the depleted Signal Platoon. Sergeant Portlock however, discharged his new responsibilities so well that throughout this phase of operations signal communications never failed except through enemy action. In spite of his inexperience and undeterred by unavoidable shortages of stores, he successfully completed a fine job of work and earned the admiration of the Battalion. His cool and level-headed handling of his platoon under fire, added to his own untiring energy and personal courage, was deserving of high praise.

The KING has been graciously pleased to approve the following awards in recognition of gallant and distinguished services in Burma: —

M.C.

T/Major Rayman Dudley Stuart Hogben, (180204) 9th Bn. (attd. 3/4th Bn. Bombay Grenadiers)

During the period under review, 16 August-15 November 1944, this officer has been in command of "D" Coy 3/4 Bombay Grenadiers. His company has performed the duties of close protection to the tanks and on occasions advance guard to the leading brigade. Throughout the recent operations the outstanding performance of this company has been a direct reflection of Major Hogben's leadership and coolness under fire.

Typical of his conduct on several occasions was the action to take Bombay Grenadier Hill on 26 October, when Major Hogben's Coy was acting as close protection to 3 troops of tanks who were in support of 22 King's African Rifles. The attack originally planned for 0830 hours was postponed for one hour due to dive bombing causing heavy casualties, but by 1500 hours the feature had not been taken.

Realizing the necessity to capture and consolidate the position before darkness and owing to the fact that no command could be established with the leading companies of 22 K.S.R., a plan was made by Major Hogben in conjunction with the tank command, Major Hogben personally lead his Coy in this attack which was made at the point of a bayonet. This was so successful that the enemy hurriedly left the position leaving behind a quantity of arms and ammunition.

His personal courage, leadership and complete disregard for his own safety has throughout been an inspiration to all ranks.

Tuesday September 18th 1945

O.B.E. (Military Division) (Italy)

Lieutenant-Colonel Edwin Albert Hanchard Goodwin, (173431) 1st Bn.

D.S.O. (Italy)

Lieutenant-Colonel Geoffrey Arthur Phelps, (36752) 1st Bn.

"London Gazette" Thursday September 20th 1945

The KING has been graciously pleased to give orders for the following promotions in, and appointments to, the Most Excellent Order of the British Empire in recognition of gallant and distinguished services in Italy:—

M.B.E. (Military Division)

T/Major James Alec Day, (183335)

During the past months Captain Day has commanded Headquarters Company with great ability. He has also been responsible for the welfare of the Battalion and has worked continuously to obtain the maximum comfort and best conditions available for the benefit for the troops in this Unit. This has been an extremely difficult and trying task, during the recent period of semi-active service, with the possibility of hostilities breaking out at a moment's notice. It necessitated frequent moves, often at short notice, and the establishing of many small detachments over a large area of the country. This, coupled with extreme weather conditions of snow and sleet, and a hostile attitude of the local population, made Captain Day's task of welfare extremely difficult, but all the more necessary.

However, Captain Day, working unceasingly and untiringly, frequently making long journeys by jeep, sometimes completely through the night in appalling weather, to collect and deliver welfare goods, achieved excellent results and by so doing made considerably easier the difficult task, which had to be carried out by the troops during this unfortunate period.

Throughout the Gothic Line ops Sep-Oct 44, Captain Day commanded B Coy with conspicuous ability, initiative and bravery. He was responsible not only for making the daily rations for fwd areas but he volunteered to make additional journeys for the welfare of the troops. These journeys were all under constant enemy observation and heavy fire, but Captain Day showed complete disregard for his safety. He also overcame appalling weather conditions and bad communications. Although routes were frequently blocked and bridges collapsed, this officer made long and dangerous detours. He showed great determination and has never once failed to reach his objectives.

By his continuous devotion to duty, on no single day were the troops in the line without rations, and whenever essential comforts, such as cigarettes, were available, Captain Day took them forward.

The welfare of the troops, both in and out of the line, has been his constant aim. Given an emergency commission in 1940, Captain Day, who joined the Regiment as a boy, has served continuously for 19 years. His work in all the Battalion's ops from the Western Desert 1940, to Italy 1944 including CASSINO, where he commanded a rifle Coy, has always been marked by courage, cheerfulness and selfless devotion to duty.

The King has been pleased to approve the following award for distinguished and gallant service :-

M.M.

No. 6401944 Corporal Cecil Buss, 1st Bn. (L.R.D.G.) (Heathfield)

On 14th June 1944 Corporal Buss was a member of a patrol which was dropped by parachute near Arezzo. His patrol officer and sergeant were both captured soon after landing but Corporal Buss by his coolness and determination led the remainder of the patrol through many difficulties safely to our own lines. In August 1944 Corporal Buss was captured by E-Boats when rowing in a small boat off the coast of Dalmatia. After being held for some days by the enemy he escaped and safely reached our own lines after a long hazardous march.

In October 1944 he was dropped by parachute near Florina in Greece as part of a patrol sent in to disrupt the enemy's withdrawal. On this operation he was the senior N.C.O. of a party which blew the main Florin-Kozani road so successfully that the R.A.F. were able to inflict severe casualties on an enemy convoy of vehicles and troops. Throughout these operations Corporal Buss has shown outstanding qualities of leadership and courage and his complete disregard for his own personal safety has been a magnificent example to other members of his patrol.

The KING has been graciously pleased to approve the following awards in recognition of gallant and distinguished services at Arnhem.: —

Bar to M.C.

T/Captain Benjamin Beattie Clegg, M.C. (226920)   2nd Bn. attd. B Coy 10th Bn. Parachute Regt. A.A.C. (Tunbridge Wells)

On the afternoon of 19th September 1944 at Arnhem Captain Clegg took over command of "B" Coy 10 Bn. By then only one Subaltern Officer was left. Almost immediately he had to conduct a very difficult disengaging manoeuvre across a very exposed piece of ground which was covered by M.G.'s and Mortar fire. Captain Clegg by his personal example and leadership and complete disregard of all personal danger managed to withdraw his Coy in good order and with a minimum of casualties. At dusk the same day the enemy launched a very strong attack against 10 Bn.'s new positions, and before the Bn. had time to dig in properly.

It was largely due to Captain Clegg's example in moving from section to section, particularly where the fighting was fiercest, and encouraging the men to greater efforts that the enemy was unable to break through. Again, in the late morning of the 20th September, Captain Clegg led his Coy in a most spirited bayonet attack in the final stages of which he personally attacked and destroyed a German M.G. Post. In the late afternoon the Bn. now sorely depleted in strength, was ordered to attack and capture a cross-roads held by the enemy on the Divisional perimeter at Osterbeck. To secure the cross-roads it was necessary to clear eight houses and their gardens. Captain Clegg personally led the assault and cleared three of these houses against bitter opposition from the enemy. In the third house he was very seriously wounded in the jaw by M.G. fire, but insisted on carrying on until all the enemy were exterminated, and the three houses cleared and organised in a state of defence.

During this time he was losing a great deal of blood and was in great pain. He finally consented to have his wounds dressed and had just handed over his Coy to the Senior Sergeant when he collapsed. From the time he landed until he collapsed, Captain Clegg, in this period of very bitter and confused fighting carried out his duties in an exemplary manner. The leadership of this very gallant officer was outstanding with his own personal courage and complete disregard of danger an inspiration and example to all his men.
(M.C. gazetted 26/11/42)

D.C.M.

No. 6400234 Sergeant Thomas Cyril Bentley, 2nd Bn. attd. Mortar Platoon 10th Bn. Parachute Regiment, (Caversham)

At Oosterbeek on 20 Sept 44, Sergeant Bentley who had already shown conspicuous bravery in hand to hand fighting since he dropped on 18 Sept, was in charge of a detachment of soldiers, using the top floor of a house as a O.P. in the hard pressed North-Eastern corner of the Divisional perimeter. The position was held by the remnants of the Bn. about 50 strong, continually under fire and frequently being attacked. From this O.P. he not only directed killing fire on the enemy, but received information vital to the defences, which he was obliged to take back to his C.O. under fire from the enemy on each occasion. When the side of the house was blown in by a S.P. Gun at point blank range, he fell from the top floor to the basement but crawled out and carried on from outside. He was shot at again more than once that day, but set a magnificent example of determination to carry on, and during the afternoon was responsible for the discovery of regular infiltrating movements from an advanced quarter, soon after another attack overran the Battalion H.Q. house, the C.O. was wounded and the few men there were captured.

The mortars were lost. That night Sergeant Bentley led a patrol into the enemy occupied area and brought the mortars out, operating them from then on, often under heavy fire, under the personal direction of the Brigadier, for whom they were the last two in the Brigade.

It is difficult to praise too highly this N.C.O.'s courage, coolness, endurance and confidence and to underestimate his contribution, both material and morale in difficult situations.

The KING has been graciously pleased to approve that the following be Mentioned in recognition of gallant and distinguished services at Arnhem: —

M.I.D.

No. 6400067 Lance-Corporal William Garibaldi, 2nd Bn. attd. 10th Bn. Parachute Regt. A.A.C. (k.i.a.)

"For rescuing men under heavy enemy machine-gun, small arms fire and mortars, and taking them to safety in his armoured carrier until he was killed."
(actual Citation missing, this is a report from men after the war whom he had rescued.)(1st M.I.D. 14/01/44)

M.I.D. (Arnhem) (Escapee)

No. 6395864 C.S.M. Robert Edward Grainger, 2nd Bn. attd. 10th Bn. Parachute Regt. A.A.C.

After being wounded in the ear on the night 19 September 1944, Grainger was taken to a civilian hospital at Wolfheze. A week later, when this hospital was being evacuated in response to orders issued by the Germans, Grainger and two other paratroopers were led out by members of the Dutch Red Cross, who pretended that were escorting lunatic patients. The three men were taken towards Ede, where they went into the woods. Almost immediately they found shelter and were hidden by various civilians until their journey to Allied lines was arranged.
On 19 and 21 October 1944, Grainger accompanied by an officer on extensive reconnaissance to find a route for the immediate mass evacuation of Allied service personnel. When this took place on 22 October 1944, Grainger and the officer acted as guides, and it was to a large extent due to their excellent work that sixty men reached safety.

"London Gazette" Thursday September 27th 1945

The KING has been graciously pleased to approve that the following be Mentioned in recognition of gallant and distinguished services in Burma: —

M.I.D.

9th Bn.

T/Major James Maynard Cash, M.C. (174342)
T/Major Frederick Rosser Mansell, (129363)
T/Major Warwick Thompson, (203808)
T/Captain John Edward Maurice Bridge, (174244)
T/Captain Joseph Alexander Anthony Chodzko, (165749)
T/Captain Raymond Hebert Clow, (164689)

T/Captain Harold Vere Holden White, (162512)
Lieutenant Michael Benedict Morphy, (186157)
Lieutenant Stanley George Neal, (268155)
No. 6403457 Sergeant Ronald Cadwallader,
No. 5342411 A/Sergeant J.J. Barrett,
No. 6407882 A/Sergeant J.W. Foster,
No. 6408047 A/Sergeant L.W. Wallis,
No. 5335399 Corporal Albert C. Wildash,

No. 5351082 L/Corporal Douglas Ben Jeffrey Wyeth, (k.i.a.)

No. 5958799 Private Neville F. Burnham,

"London Gazette" Thursday October 11th 1945

The KING has been graciously pleased to give orders for .the following promotions in, and appointments to, the Most Excellent Order of the British Empire, in recognition of gallant and distinguished services in North-West Europe:-

M.B.E. (Military Division)

Lieutenant Reginald William Farrant, (181699) (attd. No. 3 Special Forces Detachment)

As Administrive Officer of No. 3 Special Forces Detachment, Lieutenant Farrant has during the last fifteen months carried out his duties in exemplary manner. Although within this Detachment there was no possibility of his promotion he has worked abnormally long hours with consistent cheerfulness. His complete dependability, remarkable application to detail and the deep interest that he took in the welfare of his men, contributed in a large degree to the successful working of this detachment.

"London Gazette" Thursday October 18th 1945

The King has been graciously pleased to approve the following awards in recognition of gallant and distinguished services in Italy: —

M.C.

T/Major Francis Waldemar Firminger, (265375)   attd. 2/5th Queen's Royal Regiment, (London S.W. 20)

Throughout the operations from the landings at Menate to the capture of Venice, Major Firminger was in command of "C" Coy 2/5 Bn. Queen's Royal Regiment. His resolute leadership and untiring energy resulted in a series of highly successful actions of his Coy. On 11th April his Coy landed from Fantails in the flooded area N.E. of Menate. The actual landing was made some 2000 yards further East than intended, and owing to thick smoke and the confusing network of dykes the Coy had some difficulty in locating its original objective. Difficulties were increased by the fact that there were still enemy in areas which were expected to be securely in our hands.

In spite of these initial setbacks Major Firminger personally led his Coy forward in a most determined manner, reaching Menate at it South end. It was then necessary to clear the whole village, approximately a mile long in order to reach his Coy objective. He was set against stubborn opposition, it was a long job as there were a number of damaged houses in which the enemy had left snipers and determined groups of men with Spandaus.

Major Firminger, working first with one platoon and then with another was always present when opposition was heaviest and it was entirely due to his efforts that the whole village was cleared house by house and the bridge secured by early afternoon. This rapid and decisive action forced two enemy Spandau guns to withdraw from the area just North of the Menate bridge shortly before "A" and "B" Coys approached from the North, the area which the guns were covering. "C" Coy made a large contribution to the 250 prisoners taken by the Bn. on this day.

Throughout all subsequent actions by "C" Coy. Major Firminger displayed the same qualities of leadership and indifference to danger. At Filo and again at Rovigo, and the Brenta bridge this officer led his Coy in a magnificent manner and no praise is too much. His work has always been outstanding.

T/Major Charles Paul Genillard, (129366) 1st Bn. (Rottingdean)

On 20th April, 1945, the Battalion was ordered to strike north of Mascarina in order to by-pass heavy enemy resistance that was being encountered by the 2nd Battalion of the Lancashire Fusiliers to the west. This task fell to "D" company, commanded by Major Genillard, who, throughout the day, advanced against stifling opposition, meeting innumerable pickets of resistance and being harassed by snipers in the high grass.

Major Genillard was with his leading troops throughout this action and his example and complete disregard to his own safety were an inspiration to all. He was hit by a shell splinter in the back, but refused aid and continued to command and lead his company to the final objective.

On two separate occasions later he was wounded, and it was not until the final objective was gained that Major Genillard allowed his wound to be dressed, and even then to be evacuated. Had it not been for the great courage and inspired leadership of Major Genillard it would never have been possible for one company to carry out this rapid advance, and any slowing up would have allowed the enemy to occupy already prepared positions."

Monday October 22nd 1945

Sussex Military Award

The King has been pleased to approve the following award for gallant and distinguished service in Italy

M.C.

T/Major Charles Paul Genillard, (129366) (Rottingdean)

"London Gazette" Thursday November 1st 1945

The KING has been, graciously pleased to give orders for the following appointments to the Most Excellent Order of the British Empire, in recognition of gallant and distinguished services in the field:-

M.B.E. (Military Division)

Escapee

Lieutenant Albert Edwin Baker, (240394) 2nd Bn. attd. B Coy 10th Bn. Parachute Regiment A.A.C.

Lieutenant Baker was prisoner whilst wounded near Arnhem on 15 September 1944. After remaining in hospital at Erjelo for five weeks he was put on a hospital train for transfer to Germany. His boots had been removed, but by a trick he persuaded a guard to return them. When he considered the guards were sufficiently sleepy he swung his feet out of bed, smashed the window and threw himself out. Although the train was travelling at approximately 30mph, his practice in parachute jumping enabled him to "land" without serious injury. He concealed himself until the train had passed and then found a more secure hiding place. The next morning, carrying a sack and a stick, he passed several parties of Germans unchallenged and continued to Holten.

Whilst receiving shelter from civilians he gave instructions to members of the Underground in the use of explosives and on one occasion during an R.A.F. raid blew up a railway track. Moving to the Martenbergh area, he again took part in sabotage activities and on 25 march 1945 had to swim a canal under fire from both Dutch and the Germans when the enemy interrupted the laying of explosives. Lieutenant Baker met advancing Allied forces on 4 April 1945.

"London Gazette" Thursday November 8th 1945

The KING has been graciously pleased to approve that the following be Mentioned in recognition of gallant and distinguished service in North-West
Europe: —

M.I.D. (N.W. Europe)

The KING has been graciously pleased to approve that the following be Mentioned in recognition of gallant and distinguished service in North-West Europe: —

No. 6394257 W.O.1 John W. Loten, 109th L.A.A. Regt. R.A. (& 7th Bn.)
No. 6401395 Sergeant Harold Morris, 109th L.A.A. Regt. R.A. (& 7th Bn.)
No. 6402059 Bombadier W.J. Cole, 109th L.A.A. Regt. R.A. (& 7th Bn.)
T/Captain Gerald Patrick Robert Anslow, (132415)
T/Captain Frank Alan Day, (183336)

Friday November 9th 1945

Sultan's Palace for Royal Sussex Regiment

Singapore Thursday

A luxury house is now a leave hostel for men of the Royal Sussex Regiment, on garrison duties in Northern Malaya, thanks to the Sultan of Kedah, who offered the use of his mansion at Penang, jewel island of the Orient, off the Malayan Peninsular. There is everything desirable in the mansion, from refrigerators, radio sets and armchairs, to fine beds and the best cutlery. The troops even have morning tea in bed. Private Daw, of Waldron takes the men in a commandeered Japanese bus around the island's beauty spots, bathing places, cinemas and dance halls. Local nurses are invited to the weekly dances held in the hostel.-
Reuter

"London Gazette" Thursday November 15th 1945

The KING has been graciously pleased to approve the following awards in recognition of gallant and distinguished services in Burma: —

M.M.

No. 6401696 Sergeant Neville Elijah Sampson, 9th Bn. (Worthing)

Sergeant Sampson has served with distinction during the last six months, during which time his courage and leadership has been a continual source of inspiration to his Platoon, which he has commanded in battle on a number of occasions. On the 14th November 1944 during the fighting near Pinwe, the enemy counter-attacked the Battalion perimeter, and after the attack had been halted, Sergeant Sampson was ordered to take his Platoon out and annihilate a party of six enemy who had withdrawn to cover and were sniping his Coy. He displayed such resource and tactical skill in handling his platoon that two of the enemy were stalked and killed and the rest driven into the fire lines of our own machine-guns which killed the remaining four.

On the 23rd November 1944, when his Platoon were ordered to patrol and pinpoint enemy positions on the Gyobin chaung, he successfully accomplished this difficult task in the face of both L.M.G. and rifle fire. During the withdrawal of the Platoon, six of the enemy attempted to follow it up. Sergeant Sampson halted his Platoon, made a quick reconnaissance, and laid two ambushes. A few minutes later an enemy party walked into his well concealed positions and were promptly killed, Sergeant Sampson himself accounting for two of the enemy. By his resource and initiative on this patrol he obtained the information which enabled artillery concentration to be put down quickly on enemy held positions and a successful attack to be launched the next day. Throughout the Battalion operations this N.C.O. has shown outstanding qualities of leadership, determination and great personal gallantry in action.

No. 6403457 Sergeant Ronald Cadwallader, 9th Bn. (Portslade)

During the last six months Sergeant Cadwallader as Platoon Sergeant has set a splendid example of leadership and devotion to duty. He has invariably been the first to volunteer for every patrol that has been sent out by his Coy. In action his courage and disregard for his own personal safety has been unsurpassed. On the 15th November 1944 near Pinwe his Platoon was attacked by a superior force of the enemy and several of his men were badly wounded and laying in the open. With disregard for his own safety, this N.C.O. crawled forward under L.M.G. fire and succeeded in bringing his men into the R.A.P. He was himself badly wounded whilst carrying out this action. Throughout the subsequent engagement the bearing and action of this N.C.O. was of a high order, and it was in no small way due to his courage and leadership that the enemy were beaten off and the Platoon perimeter held intact. Only when the action was over did Sergeant Cadwallader allow his own wounds to be attended to.

"London Gazette" Thursday November 29th 1945

The KING has been graciously pleased to give orders for the following appointments to the Most Excellent Order of the British Empire, in recognition of gallant and distinguished services in the field:-

M.B.E. (Military Division)

No. 5485467 R.S.M. Joseph Edward Eames, 7th Bn.

Served with the Battalion from its inception at the start of the outbreak of war. This W.O. was instrumental in helping lay the foundations of sound discipline and in training and building up a healthy structure of N.C.O.'s, in spite of the almost complete lack of any real experience amongst those from whom he had to draw. This assistance in training young officers was also of great importance.

He set a fine example to all his departments and patience at all times went into guiding the number of young recruits. This example carried on in full, when, on the weekend 18/20 May 1940 the Battalion entirely alone in a French sector, just west of Amiens, was attacked by General Rommel's Panzer Division, a very great deal is owing to this fine old soldier (who had been a regular and was 52 years old at the time) for the manner in which all ranks carried out their orders and held their ground until he and other survivors had no alternative to being taken prisoner.

After being taken prisoner, he escaped with some others on the first evening 20 May, but were overtaken by armoured car 24 hours later. I recommend this W.O. be awarded the M.B.E.
(was PoW at Stalag XX.A.)

The King has been graciously pleased to approve the following awards in recognition of gallant and distinguished service in the field :-

M.C.

A/Captain Charles Hughlings Jackson, (38234) 7th Bn. (Guilford, Surrey)

On 20 May 1940 this officer commanding "A" Coy 7th Battalion, at about 13.00 hours an enemy tank attack developed without warning just as the Coy found itself in a position out in the open some 300 yards ahead of the rest of the Battalion. In spite of shelling, mortaring and persistent M.G. fire his Coy held its ground until the survivors, numbering 32 finally forced to concede at almost 18.00 hours.

The Battalion was without any support of any kind, Anti-tank rifles were useless, as enemy tanks were "medium", none of the men were more than half trained and scarcely any had been under fire before. Despite all efforts on the part of the rest of the Battalion to reform or to extricate "A" Coy was frustrated by enemy fire.

This officer although himself wounded several times was primarily responsible for his Coy holding out for five hours which undoubtedly bluffed the enemy and delaying his advance at this point for nearly half a day. For conspicuous bravery in an isolated position and for his fine example, I recommend that this officer be awarded the Military cross.

The KING has been graciously pleased to approve that the following be Mentioned in recognition of gallant and distinguished service in North-West Europe: —

M.I.D.

T/Captain George Herbert Cook, 7th Bn. (97137)

Near Amiens on 20 May 1940, Captain Cook commanding H.Q. Coy 7 Royal Sussex Regiment, although suffering from shock as the result of bombing in a troop train on 18 May, showed outstanding gallantry in the defence of our exposed position against tank attack. His actions and example even after being twice wounded, definitely continued the ability of the Battalion (entirely unsupported) to hold up the enemy. (100 tanks under General Rommel), actually delaying them for nineteen hours.)

(was recommended for M.C.)
(was PoW at Hospital du Valde Grace, Paris)

Captain Hugh Mannington, M.B. (71741) attd. 7th Bn.

As Medical Officer to 7 Royal Sussex Regiment from its inception at the outbreak of war, this officer was tremendous in his work and the welfare of the men of this unit. In the constantly changing personnel he was always up to date with his work. The good health of the Battalion owes much to the work of

Captain Mannington.
Finally on 18 May when the Battalion was bombed in a train just west of Amiens, this officer though seriously wounded, with the greatest coolness, showing a large degree of devotion to duty. I recommend this officer for Mention in Despatches.

Lieutenant (Q/M) George Thomas William Blackwell   (89293) 7th Bn. (k.i.a.)

As Quartermaster of a newly formed Battalion he was the most tireless, loyal and conscientious officer in this post that it was possible to have. The high standard of supplies in clothing (replacement so far as it was available) was largely due to the efforts of this officer.

He was unfailingly cheerful and hard working until he was killed by enemy bombing of the train in which the Battalion was on, on 18 May 1940. For his unfailing loyalty and devotion to duty I recommend that this officer be Mentioned in Despatches.

No. 6401391 C.Q.M.S. Robert Cecil Lowles, C Coy. 7th Bn.
(since commissioned)

Was "C" Coy C.Q.M.S. having no previous experience in this work, this man assumed the duties of C.Q.M.S. as a Lance-Corporal at the end of 1939. His department was always an example of perfect orderliness and correction. On May 18 after the battalion had suffered casualties by being bombed whilst in a train, he assumed the duties of R.Q.M.S. to my complete satisfaction – until on 20 May he led a platoon of men into action against Rommel's Panzer Division with great gallantry. For the loyalty, courage and devotion to duty of this Staff Sergeant, I recommend that he be Mentioned in Despatches.

No. 6393734 Sergeant Samuel Henry Barnard, A Coy.7th Bn.(k.i.a.)

During the engagement with General Rommel's Panzer Division just west of Amiens on 20 May, this N.C.O. was in command of No. 7 Platoon "A" Coy who were placed ahead of the rest of the Battalion and took the first shock. During the afternoon's battle he reported to his Company Commander that all the men in his platoon had been killed. His Company Commander told him to return to his position, collect all the dead men's ammunition and carry on.

This order he promptly carried out with unhesitating obedience and so set an excellent example to the men. Shortly afterwards this N.C.O. was killed at his post. Subsequently his Company Commander was only able to trace one member of No. 7 Platoon as a survivor. I recommend this N.C.O. to be Mentioned in despatches. (If any suitable posthumous award is available I feel some greater recompense than an M.I.D. should be given.)
(D.C.M. recommended on later letter)

No. 6401438 Sergeant Frederick E. Morling, 7th Bn. (Seaford)

This N.C.O. carried out a high standard of work in 1939 and early part of 1940 as Pioneer Sergeant in training his men. On the weekend 18/20 May 1940 this N.C.O. showed the greatest coolness under battle bombing and shell fire and set a fine example. On 20 May when the Battalion was attacked he showed great courage and even after being taken prisoner, he succeeded in escaping almost at once but was overtaken by an armoured car 24 hours later.

For the excellent example set by this N.C.O. at all times and for his courage and devotion to duty, I recommend that he be Mentioned in Despatches.
(was PoW at Stalag XX.A.)

No. 6402487 Private Anthony G. Verth, 7th Bn.

This battalion Stretcher-Bearer on May 18 when the Battalion received heavy casualties when bombed in a train just west of Amiens and again on the afternoon of May 20 when the Battalion was attacked by a German armoured force, this man's devotion to duty in tending the wounded under fire was an inspiration to all who witnessed his behaviour.

It was remarked that he might have been taken for the Medical Officer himself, so quick and efficient was the aid he tendered. (The M.O. was wounded and his sub was killed).

I recommend that this man be Mentioned in Despatches.

(was PoW at Stalag XX.A.)

(Sergeant Beesley, C.S.M. J. Bell, C.S.M. Fry, C.Q.M.S. S.C. Laurie, were also recommended for M.I.D.'s. R.Q.M.S. Aston was recommended for a B.E.M. but no recommendations were sent to Brigade for scrutiny by the Brigadier-General. See W.D. 373 reel 57 for all relevant paperwork on recommendations to the 7th Bn.)

The KING has been graciously pleased to approve that the following be Mentioned in recognition of gallant and distinguished services in Italy: —

M.I.D.

1st Bn.

T/Lieutenant-Colonel Alfred John Odling-Smee, (34483)
T/Major Gerald Charles Mather Bowser, (66324)
T/Major Robert Wilfred Sidney Carrington, (68799)
T/Major John Neville Crawford, M.C. (98330)
A/Major Francis Walderman Firminger, M.C. (265375)
Captain Arthur Roy Rees, (197271)
T/Captain Anthony Gouldsmith, (179803)
T/Captain Godfrey Somerset How, (189957)
T/Captain William Maurice Lee, (187070)
T/Captain David Charles Stratten, (182278)
T/Captain Felix Ivor Webster, (242760)
Lieutenant Ronald Mayr Silver, (243964)
Lieutenant Peter J.C. Wyndham, (295507)

Lt. P.J.C. Wyndham,

No. 6398615 C.S.M. George R.A. Coates,
No. 6404241 A/C.S.M. E.T. Church,
No. 6406032 A/Sergeant A. Brown,
No. 6392926 L/Sergeant C. Knight,
No. 6403829 Corporal Leslie W. Barnett,
No. 641327 L/Corporal Cyril R.C. Leggatt,
No. 6406645 L/Corporal J. Pasiful,
No. 5626379 L/Corporal William G. Tolley,
No. 6412573 Private Julian Flexer,
No. 14534767 Private G. Holmes,

Saturday December 1st 1945

General Slim's Farewell to "Forgotten Army"

Today the 14th Army, largest single Army of the World War, and in which The Royal Sussex Regiment played a prominent part, disbands and passes into history. This was the Army that smashed the myth of Japanese "invincibility", after one of the most amazing campaigns ever fought. Statistics give little idea of the grandeur of the achievement of these men of the Fourteenth, the "Forgotten Army." Their victory was not only over the Japanese, but over the terrain, the jungle and the climate; over malaria and dysentery. There were no roads, save those they built themselves, no railways, and few towns of any size.

KILLED 120,000 Japs

The 14th Army killed well over 120,000 Japs, or more than seven times as many as its own dead. It held the longest battle-line in the war – from the Bay of Bengal north to where India and Burma border on China – and in its last ten months of operations it covered more than one thousand miles.
Here are further facts and figures about the Fourteenth given by South-East Asia Command :-
In 1944 and 1945 the 14th Army was approximately 1,000,000 strong. Just before the fall of Rangoon, it had about 500,000 fighting men at its disposal – although all were not necessarily deployed at one time.
The 14th Army was the first army to plan and execute the movement of whole infantry divisions by air. In March 1944, the 5th and 7th Indian Divisions were flown complete from Arakan to the Central Front. In the same month the Chindits were taken by air 200 miles behind Japanese lines.
General Sir William Slim, Commander of the 14th Army – "Uncle Bill" to his forces – yesterday bade farewell, cables a Reuter correspondence from Singapore.
"When you were first formed," he said in an Order of the Day, "I told you that you could become one of the best known armies the British Empire ever had and so you did. Inheriting a legacy of defeat and disaster, constantly short of equipment and men, you, by your stubborn courage, your skill and, above all, by your refusal to be beaten by man or nature, achieved a success few though possible.
"Work and fight as you did in Arakan, at Imphal, and through Burma. Remember you were the 14th Army and never say die. As long as you live, you may be proud of your old army.
"I send each of one you my thanks, my admiration and my confidence that in peace and in war, the men and women of the 14th Army will play a noble part."
The 14th grew out of the rearguard of Indian Divisions, known as the Burma Corps. Which "Bill" Slim led out of Burma into India in the retreat of 1942.
It fought in some of the worst conditions in the world. Through tropical jungle and torrential monsoon rain, and across two great rivers, the Chindwin and the Irrawaddy, before the liberated Mandalay and Rangoon.
The 14th Army fought and killed more Japanese soldiers ever put in the field, and killed more Japanese soldiers than were accounted by all the Allied Forces in the Pacific theatre. More than 100,000 dead were actually counted. Twenty V.C.s were won by the Indian Army alone.

"London Gazette" Thursday December 13th 1945

The KING has been graciously pleased to give orders for the following promotions in, and appointments to, the Most Excellent Order of the British Empire, in recognition of gallant and distinguished services in Italy: —

O.B.E. (Military Division)

 T/Lieutenant-Colonel Alfred John Odling-Smee, (34483) (Kingsbridge) Commanding 5th Bn. The Buffs.

Lieutenant-Colonel Odling-Smee assumed command of the 5th Bn. The Buffs in November 1944. The Battalion was below standard in efficiency, and the morale of the officers and men was very low. The conditions in the Appenines under which the Battalion was serving were appalling. Lt-Colonel Odling-Smee has shown the greatest patience in building up the Battalion. By his keen sense of humour and knowledge of man-management, he has succeeded in improving the Battalion beyond all recognition. The morale is high and the general unit administration is now on very sound lines. During the recent operations, the Battalion were not fortunate to take part in any spectacular engagement but they were continuously undertaking difficult and unpleasant tasks.

Every action was completed successfully, and Lt-Col. Odling-Smee deserves the greatest credit for his leadership. His fine example of personal courage and endurance was reflected throughout the Battalion. Since the end of actual hostilities, he has done excellent work in the administration of prisoners of war and surrendered personnel.

M.B.E. (Military Division)

Lieutenant (Q/M) Herbert Ivor Blackmore, (301158) 1st Bn. (London W.10)

During the period April 1945 to the present time, Lieutenant Blackmore has been Q/M. of the Bn. and he has carried out his duties with great initiative and ability. This period has been a most difficult one, with the Bn. gradually spreading over an increasing wide area of Northern Macedonia, in order to compete with its task of restoring the country to its normal standards of law and order and security. This has necessitated many Coy and pl detachments from the mountains in the North with few and bad communications, to the sea in the South. The detachments vary between 20 and 100 miles from Bn. H.Q., and present an extremely difficult admin. Problem. However, so efficiently has Lt. Blackmore carried out his duties as Q/M. that not once has the smallest and most distant detachment has been wanting in supplies and stores. Supply and maintenance of the Bn. a great enough problem in itself, has by no means been the only task with which Lt. Blackmore has had to compete.

He has been responsible for transporting UNRA relief supplies, (food and clothing), and for their distribution to many of the Greek villages which have been severely stricken, not only by the enemy occupation, but also by civil war. The return of large numbers of refugees on the cessation of hostilities made this a very necessary and extremely urgent task. The distances involved have been greater than the already stretched Bn. supply routes, but by Lt. Blackmore's organising ability and unceasing hard work this important task has been successfully carried out, thereby greatly contributing to the early relief and rehabilitation of this area of Greece.

Lt. Blackmore has served continuously with the Bn. throughout the whole of the war. In 1940 and 1941, in Eritrea and the Western Desert, he was a C.S.M. of a rifle company. He continually showed a complete disregard for his own personal safety and carried out many patrols and raids into enemy lines and strong-points, as well as playing a conspicuous part in two major Bn. attacks on prepared and well fortified enemy positions.

In 1942 he became R.Q.M.S. a post he successfully filled during Alamein and the advance to Tunis. In July 1943 he became Q/M. of the Bn. and has served as such through the Italian Campaign from Cassino to the Gothic Line operations to the present day. During all these long and difficult years of war Lt. Blackmore has constantly displayed a high standard of courage, cheerfulness, and devotion to duty, which has been an inspiration to all ranks of the Bn.

The KING has been graciously pleased to approve the award of the British Empire Medal (Military Division), in recognition of gallant and distinguished services in Italy, to the undermentioned: —

B.E.M. (Military Division)

No. 6396368 C.Q.M.S. James Parks, 1st Bn. (Chichester)

During his three years continuous service overseas C.Q.M.S. Parks has shown outstanding devotion to duty and powers of leadership beyond those normally expected of a N.C.O. His work has been no less outstanding during the difficult operations in Greece, where his remarkable administrative ability has been invaluable to the battalion and a real contribution to Anglo-Greek relations.

On many occasions his company has been on detachment during the Battalion's control duties on the Yugoslav-Bulgarian frontiers. He has spent many long periods over and above his normal duties distributing UNRA clothing, food and medical supplies, and the rehabilitation of refugees. Before UNRA was established in Northern Greece C.Q/.M.S. Parks company was instructed to deliver urgent supplies of clothing to some of the most distressed areas of Greece.

Immediately he knew that this responsibility was to fall on his company, C.Q.M.S. Parks entirely on his own initiative went to the most remote frontier villages, organised committees, obtained all the necessary information regarding population, sizes, and the numbers of people normally resident in the villages but who were then away as refugees.

When the clothing arrived C.Q.M.S. Parks worked long periods and travelled several hundreds of miles to supervise the delivery and thus saw that there was a fair distribution. He issued no fewer than three thousand pieces of clothing in three days to the grateful villages.

Later his company were responsible for the resettlement of refugees. By his hard work, by his superb administration ability and by his sympathy and tact, he overcame many difficulties inseparable from the return of people to villages ruthlessly damaged and burnt by the Bulgarians. C.Q.M.S. Parks always saw that there was adequate transport and food available.

His continual search for information about damaged buildings, missing people, orphans requiring care and treatment, has been of outstanding value to the Greek civilian authorities. At Cassino where he was a platoon sergeant his courage and determination were a constant inspiration to his men. Twice in three days he commanded his platoon when his officer became casualties.

The KING has been graciously pleased to confer "The Efficiency Decoration" upon the following officers of the Territorial Army.

Captain Maurice E. Few, (40294) 7th Bn.
(was a PoW at Oflag V11.C/H.)

"London Gazette" **Thursday December 20th 1945**

The KING has been graciously pleased to approve that the following be Mentioned in recognition of gallant and distinguished services in the field:—

M.I.D.

Captain John Burder, (40998)

"London Gazette" Tuesday January 1st 1946

The KING has been graciously pleased to give orders for the following promotions in, and appointments to, the Most Excellent Order of the British Empire:—

M.B.E. (Military Division)

T/Captain James Vernon Lee, M.C. (133695)
(Citation not found)

"London Gazette" Thursday January 10th 1946

The KING, has been graciously pleased to approve that the .following be Mentioned in recognition of gallant and distinguished services in Burma: —

M.I.D. 9th Bn.

T/Major Rayman Dudley Stuart Hogben, M.C. (180204) 9th Bn. attd. 4th Bn. Bombay Grenadiers

A/Major John Rescorla Moon, (96437)

No. 6209984 A/C.Q.M.S Harry Ernest Herman, M.M.
No. 6407875 A/Sergeant Horace F. Felix,
No. 6411812 A/Sergeant William Gilbert Leech, *(in lieu of M.M.)*

No. 6406286 A/Sergeant Donald Archibald John Mockford,

No. 6408035 A/Sergeant E.G. Turner,
No. 6404210 L/Sergeant Maurice John Steadman, (k.i.a.)

"During a counter-attack on a Japanese machine-gun post a member of another platoon was very badly wounded, L/Sergeant Steadman immediately went to his assistance with no regard for his own safety. Another machine-gun opened up and he was instantaneously killed."

No. 6408154 Corporal J. O'Neill,

No. 5576992 L/Corporal Thomas John Richard. Hiscocks,

No. 5350828 Private G.E. Fuller,
Capt. Ian Colin McArthur, (164773) Royal Sussex Regiment,
(Listed in "L/G" as being in Essex Regiment)

Monday January 14th 1946

MENTIONED IN DISPATCHES

The King has approved the following awards for gallant and distinguished services in Burma, of personnel of the 9th Bn. Royal Sussex Regiment :-

M.I.D.

T/Major R.D.S. Hogben, M.C., A/Major J.R. Moon, A/C.Q.M.S. H.E. Herman, M.M., A/Sergeant E.G. Turner, Lance-Sergeant M.J. Steadman, (k.i.a.) Corporal J. O'Neill, Lance-Corporal T.J.R. Hiscocks, Private G.E. Fuller.

"London Gazette" Thursday January 17th 1946

The KING has been graciously pleased to give orders for the following promotions in, and appointments to, the Most Excellent Order of the British Empire, in recognition of gallant and distinguished services in Burma:—

M.B.E. (Military Division)

T/Major Gerald Edelshain, (197096) 9th Bn. attd. 19th Hyderabad Regiment, (Hove)

This officer has been employed with 15 Indian Corps. as DAQMG for the past seven months. He has carried out 'Q' duties in the field with quite outstanding ability. The success of the Mayu operations in December & January 1944/5 from the 'Q' aspect was largely due to this officer's work, for a considerable period he was sole 'Q' representative at Tac H.Q. and during operations his initiative, foresight and ability to plan ahead were quite exceptional and well above average.

The KING has been graciously pleased to approve the award of the British Empire Medal (Military Division), in recognition of gallant and distinguished services in Burma, to the undermentioned: —

B.E.M. (Military Division)

No. 6398576 A/C.S.M. Bertie Reginald White, 9th Bn. (Wells)

During the period under review (16 Feb-15 May 45) and for the past three years this W.O. has been running the clerical side of the Orderly Room of this unit. Throughout both Kaladan campaign (Jan 44-Jun 44 & Sep 44-Feb 45) this W.O. has been indefatigable in spite of the most adverse conditions of fatigue, weather and enemy action, and his keenness and sense of duty has been an inspiration to his colleagues. Throughout his time in the orderly room nothing has been too much trouble for him and for hid complete devotion to duty.

The KING has been graciously pleased to approve the following awards in recognition of gallant and distinguished services in Burma: —

M.C.

T/Captain Maurice Arthur Jack Budd, (200854) 9th Bn. (attd. "V" Force) (Southren, Hants.)
During the period under review, Captain Budd operating continuously with clandestine small patrols behind enemy lines in the Ramnee and Taungup-Sandoway areas, has provide a constant flow of valuable information regarding enemy concentrations and movements. On one occasion knowing that the enemy were aware of his presence behind their lines and were hunting him, he remained and completed his task and then succeeded in withdrawing his patrol without loss. Throughout Captain Budd has performed his duties with unfaltering steadfastness and without personal regard, displaying a standard of courage and devotion to duty of a high order.
I strongly recommend him for the award of the Military Cross.

M.M.

No. 6407552 Lance-Sergeant Ronald Leslie Smith, 9th Bn. (High Wycombe)

L/Sergeant Smith has served with his Bn. throughout the whole of the campaign, during which he has set a fine example of courage and determination at all times. At Stourbridge chaung near Hrapan in November 1944, he commanded the leading section of the assault platoon against a strong enemy position over difficult country. This N.C.O. led the assault with grim determination and personally killed two of the enemy.
At Hill 800, on 27th February, South of Myitson, Sergeant Smith again led one of the assault sections, the attack was made up steep broken country under a barrage. Sergeant Smith was the first man of the platoon over the crest of the hill, and into the enemy position, again killing two of the enemy himself. During the campaign, this N.C.O. has killed more of the enemy than any other man of the Coy. He has proved himself a reliable and courageous patrol leader on numerous occasions, and his frequent gallant actions deserve recognition.

The KING has been graciously pleased to approve that the following be Mentioned in recognition in recognition of gallant and distinguished services in Italy: —

M.I.D.

T/Captain William Maurice Lee, (187070) 1st Bn.

Saturday 19th January 1946

AWARD FOR SUSSEX OFFICER

M.B.E. (Military Division)

T/Major Gerald Edelshain, (Hove)

"London Gazette" Thursday January 24th 1946

The KING has been graciously pleased to give orders for the following promotions in, and appointments to the Most Excellent Order of the British Empire, in recognition of gallant and distinguished services in North. West Europe :-

M.B.E. (Military Division)

T/Captain Arthur Allen Atkins, (13015) (Cambridge)

Captain Atkins has held the appointment of GSO111 5L of C Sub Area throughout the present campaign, from early June in Normandy till the end of hostilities when this information was responsible for the administration of Units and Formations comprising Maasforce, in addition to its routine activities as an L of C sub Area. In Normandy, 5l of C Sub Area was responsible for the organisation and administration of the RMA which during its peak period comprised 6888 Units, and a total of approx. 240,000 all ranks. Captain Atkins was the only G Staff Officer on this H.Q., and on his shoulders alone fell the responsibility for security and operational moves of this mass of troops.

In addition he was responsible for the security and dispersal of several thousands of prisoners in transit, as well as 2 P/W camps. The security of P/W's during the Ardennes offensive was a problem of considerable magnitude. Later, as the RMA decreased in size, large numbers of French and Algerian Pioneers were introduced in replacement of British personnel. The co-ordination of security in the Normandy enclave with only a few troops available was in itself a task of no mean order. Throughout this period, with so much administration to attend to, Captain Atkins was of necessity left very much to his own.

His resourcefulness and enthusiasm was beyond all praise. In Holland in April 1945, when this Sub Area took over the administration of the Maasforce, Captain Atkins was again the only GSO, and such was responsible for the co-ordination and interpretation of operations as between H.Q. 5L of Sub Area administering the forward troops and H.Q. Maasforce, the operational H.Q. This was in addition to his routine duties in the Sub Area's L of C commitment. This task was so ably done that the H.Q. was always completely in the operational picture, and on some occasions were closer to the true state of affairs than other formations more directly concerned with operations.

Throughout the campaign Captain Atkins has done more than would normally be expected of an officer of his rank and status. Moreover, his quite exceptional interest, enthusiasm and devotion to duty have been an inspiration and instilled confidence in individuals and units alike. This has gone a long way towards the success of the administration of this H.Q. and the smooth working of L of C.

For this quite exceptional, sustained and cheerful effort, I recommend the M.B.E.

The KING has been graciously pleased to approve the following awards in recognition of gallant and distinguished services in North West Europe ::—

M.C.

Lieutenant Raymond Alfred Daniels, (284757) attd. 7th Hampshire Regiment,

Lieutenant Daniels commanded a platoon in a rifle coy from 12 July 1944 until he was wounded at Cloppenburg 13 April 1945. He has continually displayed the highest standard of leadership and devotion to duty in action, and his good example and personal disregard of danger, of which the following examples are but typical, has always been a source of great inspiration to his men.

On 28 March during the operation in the Milldigen-Megchelen area when his platoon was held up by intense and accurate M.G. fire and heavy shelling, while attacking a group of houses held by paratroopers, this officer showed great skill and powers of leadership in working his platoon forward until at last he was able to close with and completely rout the enemy post, capturing several prisoners.

On the next day this officer's platoon was ordered to cross a small river and to establish a bridge-head on the far bank. In the face of enemy paratroopers which covered the crossing from the far bank, 2nd

Lieutenant Daniels led his platoon across the river with great dash, carrying out a scramble crossing over the remains of the bridge, which involved hanging on by the arms from a girder.

On reaching the opposite bank he quickly collected his platoon together and successfully led it on the assault of the enemy positions, capturing nine prisoners.

Again at Cloppenburg on 13 April 1945, Lieutenant Daniels' platoon became involved in very heavy house to house fighting against determined resistance from paratroopers. Due to the close nature of the fighting fine SP was impossible. Each house was strongly held and it is was entirely due to this officer's dash, leadership and great courage that progress was able to be made, against opposition of such calibre. It was while leading his platoon in an assault that Lieutenant Daniels was severely wounded in the face and head and had to be evacuated, refusing to leave however until he had organised and handed over his platoon.

The KING has been graciously pleased to confer "The Efficiency Decoration" upon the following officers of the Territorial Army: —

Captain Stanley William Harold Pickworth, (43287) (T.A.R.O.)

"London Gazette" Thursday February 14th 1946

The KING has been graciously pleased to approve that the following be Mentioned in recognition of gallant and distinguished services in the field : —

M.I.D.

Lieutenant Philip Godfrey Stibbe, (203807)

"London Gazette" Thursday February 21st 1946

The KING has been graciously pleased to approve that the following be Mentioned in recognition of gallant and distinguished services in the field: —

M.I.D. (N.W.E.)

2nd Lieutenant R.D. Waters (86483) 2nd Bn.
(was a PoW at Oflag V11. C/H.)

"London Gazette" Thursday April 4th 1946

The KING has been graciously pleased to approve that the following be Mentioned in recognition of gallant and distinguished services in North-West Europe:-

M.I.D.

Royal Regiment of Artillery

T/Maj. John Theodore Mayer, (13851) 109th L.A.A. Regt. R.A. (& 7th Bn.)
T/Capt. Charles Brian Godsell Turner (105324) 109th L.A.A. Regt. R.A
T/Capt. Ronald Henry Vaughan-Williams, (186160) 109th L.A.A. Regt. R.A. (& 7th Bn.)
No. 6396257 W.O. II Frederick W. Doidge, 109th L.A.A. Regt. R.A. (& 7th Bn.)
No. 6396495 W.O.11 George W. Lilley, 109th L.A.A. Regt. R.A. (& 7th Bn.)
No. 6399765 Sergeant Ralph Libby, 109th L.A.A. Regt. R.A. (& 7th Bn.)
No. 6406193 L/Bombardier Leslie P. Wright, 109th L.A.A. Regt. R.A. (& 7th Bn.)

Royal Sussex Regiment

A/Major-General Lashmer Gordon Whistler, (13017)

T/Lieutenant-Colonel Topham Donald Hood, (52421)

This officer landed with 36 Brick in OPERATION OVERLORD as MLO. For many weeks he was responsible for the military operation of MIKE beach, and it was mainly due to his indefatigable efforts that the flow of large numbers of reinforcement vehicles across the beach was maintained with smoothness and efficiency. He later moved to Calais and December was appointed CC 112 Transit Camp when it was in the process of formation. During this difficult period he once again showed unusual imagination and ability, and with his unsurpassed energy and unceasing efforts was an inspiration of all with whom he came in contact. The undoubted success of the leave transit camp was due to a large extent to this officer's exceptional enthusiasm and skill, and to his ceaseless devotion to duty.

A/Lieutenant-Colonel Vernon Maitland Fallowfield-Cooper, (98352)
T/Major David Fordyce Beardshaw, (138384)

T/Major Jack Gordon Wagener, T.D. (41353)

T/Captain William Sydney Eade, (164694)

Lieutenant Leonard James Hayes, (177728)

Lieutenant Geoffrey Fiennes Trotman, (323896)

"London Gazette" Thursday May 9th 1946

The KING has been graciously pleased to approve that the following be Mentioned in recognition of gallant and distinguished services in Burma :—

M.I.D.

9th Bn.

T/Lieutenant-Colonel Thomas Chamber Windsor Roe, M.B.E. (121387) (Hove)
T/Major Michael Charles Selfe Langdon, (162067)
T/Captain Eric George de Salvo Hall, (176196)
Lieutenant Michael Benedict Morphy, (186157)
No. 6394462 R.S.M. Leslie C. Hookway,
No. 6397850 C.S.M. E.S. Hammond,
No. 6404600 L/Sergeant Cecil Plested,

"London Gazette" Thursday May 23rd 1946

The KING has been graciously pleased to approve that the following be Mentioned in recognition of gallant and distinguished services in the Mediterranean Theatre: —

M.I.D.

T/Lieutenant-Colonel Joseph Cowderoy Hodgson, (88046)
T/Major Frank Ian H.H. Thompson, (91452)
T/Captain George Henry Launcelot Harpur, (148570)

Lieutenant John Buckeridge, (269397)

Lieutenant Frederick Henry Christmas, (207770)
Lieutenant Enrique Carlos Cuss, (289892)
Lieutenant Albert Wilfred Lester, (315391)
Lieutenant Henry Leonard Rolington, (251293)
Lieutenant Norman William Trott, (308456)
No. 6398242 C.S.M. Albert G. Davey,
No. 5666799 A/Sergeant Charles W. Pinkham,
No. 6403771 A/Sergeant Reginald F. Turner,
No. 849522 Corporal Herbert G.N. Godley,

Saturday May 25th 1946

ROYAL SUSSEX REGIMENT AWARDS

The King has approved the following awards for gallant and distinguished services in the Mediterranean Theatre :-

M.I.D.

T/Lieutenant-Colonel J.C. Hodgson,
T/ Major F.I.H.H. Thompson,
T/Captain G.H.L. Harpur,
Lieutenant J. Buckeridge,
Lieutenant F.H. Christmas,
Lieutenant E.C. Cuss
Lieutenant A.W. Lester,
Lieutenant H.L. Rolington,
Lieutenant N.W. Trott
W.O. 11 A.G. Davey,
A/Sergeant C.W. Pinkham,
A/Sergeant R.F. Turner,
Corporal H.G.N. Godley,

"London Gazette" Tuesday 4th June 1946

The KING has been graciously pleased, on the occasion of the Celebration of His Majesty's Birthday, to signify his intention of conferring the Honour of Knighthood upon the following:—

K.B.E.

Colonel James Lewis Sleeman, C.B., C.M.G., C.B.E., M.V.O., T.D., (527)
Chief Commissioner, St. John Ambulance Brigade Overseas.

"London Gazette" Thursday June 6th 1946

The KING has been graciously pleased to approve the following awards in recognition of gallant and distinguished services in Burma: —

M.M.

No. 6407875 Sergeant H. Frederick Felix, 9th Bn.

During the period under review February 1944/May 1945, Sergeant Felix was in action with "C" Coy. On 19th November 1944 during the action at Pinwe a platoon of "C" Coy was ordered to attack and destroy an enemy position in which the Japanese were well dug in. Sergeant Felix was in command of a section in which to force a crossing and destroy the enemy. By excellent fieldcraft Sergeant Felix succeeded in bringing his platoon into a favourable position from which to make an assault. By this time the enemy had realised his intention and he and his men came under concentrated fire of both heavy and light automatic fire from the enemy positions.

In spite of intense opposition, Sergeant Felix led his section into the attack with such skill and determination that he succeeded in forcing a crossing and reached the outer defences of the Japanese locality, only to be beaten back by a withering cross-fire from the left flank. During this close quarter withdrawal across the Chuang, Sergeant Felix's conduct was exemplary. Having reformed his section Sergeant Felix showing great courage and determination led his section in two further attacks, but without success. Sergeant Felix then received the order to withdraw.

Having rejoined his platoon which by this tome reforming, he discovered that one of his men, Corporal Huggett was missing. Sergeant Felix immediately went out by himself, saw Corporal Huggett lying wounded in the Chaung under enemy guns. Without regard for his own safety, Sergeant Felix worked his way down towards the wounded man, only to be met by concentrated fire of Japanese small arms and automatics. He succeeded in reaching the wounded man who was in great pain.

Showing incredible tenacity and courage, Sergeant Felix succeeded by excellent ground –work in dragging the wounded man into the jungle, and having reached the safety of cover, he was able to carry Corporal Huggett back to the stretcher-bearers.

Throughout the whole of the North Burma campaign, Sergeant Felix fought many actions with a bravery and skill which endeared him to the men he led and instilled in them new courage and tenacity by his example. On many occasions Sergeant Felix was responsible for the success of many hard tasks allotted to his unit. Sergeant Felix is both a courageous man and a gallant leader, always he has been to the forefront in battle and, when confidence has been lacking, by his inspiration and leadership, he has turned the tide of many a difficult situation.

By his conduct in the past Sergeant Felix has shown himself deserving of the highest praise, and by his example, courage and sound judgement he has endeared himself to all the soldiers who have fought with him during the many months of hard fighting in the North Burma Campaign.

No. 5351042 Private Dennis Clark, 9th Bn.

During the period under review, Feb 44 - May 45, Private Clark proved himself a soldier of the highest order and the men whom he has commanded in battle owe much to his great spirit and his outstanding courage. At Pinwe on 14th November 1944 the Bn. concentration area was heavily engaged by a strong Japanese force, supported by light and heavy M.G. fire. The enemy attacked with great determination and tenacity. The main strength of the enemy attack was launched against "C" Coy's front, and a great deal of bitter fighting ensued in this sector. Private Clark was a Bren gunner in one of the forward positions which ran parallel to the railway line.

In the early stages of the attack Private Clark's Bren gun position was pinpointed by the enemy, and became the object of several determined charges by the enemy. Private Clark succeeded in beating off all these attacks and accounted for a considerable number of enemy when his No. 2 was severely wounded beside him. Private Clark continued to fire his Bren gun while at the same time doing what he could for his wounded comrade. On several occasions the position threatened to be overrun, but Private Clark stuck to his post with such tenacity that the enemy found it impossible to penetrate the defences in this sector.

Undoubtedly Private Clark's courage and extreme devotion to duty saved a breakthrough in this area and was instrumental in avoiding what might have developed into a very serious position. On 17th January 1945, whilst on patrol Private Clark's section was ambushed by a party of four enemy concealed in the jungle, Private Clark who was on the flank of his section immediately rushed to the attack, firing his Bren gun from the hip killing all four of the enemy. Throughout the whole of the North Burma Campaign, Private Clark was an inspiration to these men who served with him – on many occasions his example and extreme disregard for his own personal safety have encouraged other men to follow his example, and often he has been responsible for the success of his section when they have been hard pressed in extreme difficulty.

"London Gazette" Thursday June 13th 1946

The KING has been graciously pleased, on the occasion of the Celebration of His Majesty's Birthday, to give orders for the following promotions in, and appointments to, the Most Excellent Order of the British Empire:—

To be Additional Commanders of the Civil Division of the said Most Excellent Order: —

C.B.E. (Civil Division)

Colonel Victor Henry Jaques, O.B.E., M.C.,
Attached to the Staff of the Supreme Allied Commander, South East Asia.
(Citation not found)

O.B.E. (Military Division)

T/Lieutenant-Colonel Trevor George Corry Evans (97144)
(Citation not found)

M.B.E. (Military Division)

No. 6398407 R.S.M. Frank Hill,
(Citation not found)

"London Gazette" Thursday June 20th 1946

The KING has been graciously pleased to approve that the following be Mentioned in recognition of gallant and distinguished services in the field: —

M.I.D.

T/Captain Geoffrey Ferncombe Jordan, (143729) 4th Bn.

"London Gazette" Thursday August 29th 1946

The KING has been graciously pleased to approve that the following be Mentioned in recognition of gallant and distinguished services in the field: —

M.I.D. (Netherlands East Indies)

No. 6401712 Gunner Harold Laurence John Martin, 79/21st L.A.A. Regt. R.A. (posthumous)

(formerly of the 5th & 7th Bns. The Royal Sussex Regiment)

He was captured by the Japanese with B.H.Q. A&C Troops 79/21 L.A.A. Regt. R.A. in Timor, Netherlands East Indies on 23 February 1942. He was interned at Oesapa-Besar P.O.W. Camp near Koepang. He broke out of the camp on several expeditions into the jungle endeavouring to contact friendly natives etc. with a view to engineering an escape to Australia.

I last saw him in September 1942 when he left the camp and his absence was this time detected by the enemy. I ordered him, by messages which were delivered outside to him, to remain hidden in the jungle until a favourable opportunity occurred for him to be smuggled back into the camp. However, about 23 September 1942, all the P.O.W's at Oesapa-Besar were transhipped to Batavia, Java and contact was never re-established with Gunner Martin.

I therefore only know in September 1942 he was alive, free and on duty in the South-West part of Timor. May I suggest you check with the Australian Military Authorities regarding the fate of this Gunner as he was accompanied on this expedition by Corporal Armstrong, "D" Coy 2/40 Bn. A.I.F. of "Sparrow Force", Timor, whose fate at that time was unknown.

Gunner Martin showed resource, initiative, coolness, devotion to duty and great courage during the expeditions referred to. These were all carried out at great personal risk. I quote one occasion when accompanied by Cpl. Armstrong, they were surprised by a Japanese patrol of three men when 25 miles away from the P.O.W. Camp. The Japanese were killed by Mills bomb and Jack-knife by these two O.R.'s. He volunteered for these duties and I recommend that notice of his conduct be brought before the proper authority.

> J.P.H. Dempsey, Major, R.A.
> O.C. 79th L.A.A. Bty. R.A.
>
> Oct 1941 – Nov 1945

M.I.D. (N.W.E.) (Escapees)

Lieutenant Alan Elfast Claude Leake, (79304) 4th Bn.

Lieutenant Leake was captured in Belgium in October 1940.
In June 1941 he and another officer prepared to escape but their plan was vetoed by the Senior British Officer because their attempts would have endangered Polish P/W's.
During 1943, Lieutenant Leake and some other officers attempted to escape through the Commandant's house. So that he could reconnoitre the house first, Lieutenant Leake insulted a guard and was taken before the commandant. The escapers were discovered, however, and Lieutenant Leake served six months in Graudenz. On the way to Graudenz he escaped from the train but was forced to give himself up three days later.
During his captivity he was involved in constructing a number of tunnels but they were all unsuccessful. He has been commended by Major-General Fortune for his escape work.
(was a PoW at Oflag V11. C/H.)

No. 5438571 Private Thomas Harry Smith, 7th Bn.

Smith was captured at Amiens on 20th May 1940. In autumn 1942 with three companions, he escaped from a farm near Luderan Grudenz. They were recaptured by military police in a Polish village. In summer 1943, Smith escaped from a farm at Bairsee near Bromberg. After five days liberty he was recaptured whilst trying to get food from a working party.
In spring 1944, Smith and a companion escaped from a goods yard. They were free for three days before being picked up by a patrol near Kotonterz. At Bairsee, Smith walked away from a farm in the middle of the day in uniform. He was recaptured two days later.
As a result of his attempts to escape, Smith was sent to Gros Waltz. Here he was one of fifteen P/W's who broke down the wall of a small outhouse. He was free for three days and was caught whilst obtaining food from a British working party.
On 19th January 1945, when being marched from Thorn, Smith and a companion escaped and managed to reach the Russian lines.
(was a PoW at Stalag XXA.)

"London Gazette" September 12th 1946

The KING has graciously been pleased to approve that the following be Mentioned in recognition of gallant and distinguished service while Prisoners of War :-

M.I.D. (N.W.E.)

No. 6395903 Sergeant Hedley Owen Tupper, 109th L.A.A. Regt. (Royal Sussex) R.A.

"London Gazette" Thursday September 19th 1946

The KING has been graciously pleased to approve that the following be Mentioned in recognition of gallant and distinguished services in Burma: —

M.I.D. 9th Bn.

T/Major Geoffrey Alastair Nisbet Boyne, (73142)
T/Major Eric George de Salvo Hall, (176196)

T/Major Leslie John Ring, (289878)
T/Captain Joseph Alexander Anthony Chodzko, (165749)
T/Captain James Peter Paget Gibbs, (153257)
Lieutenant Arthur William Butcher, (279007)
Lieutenant Richard George Peter Wharton, (330711)
No. 6407951 C.S.M. R. Newton,
No. 6404636 Sergeant R.A.R. Burdfield,

 No. 6411812 Sergeant William Gilbert Leech,

No. 6407543 Sergeant H.J. Rogers,
No. 6408035 Sergeant E.G. Turner,
No. 6408047 Sergeant L.W. Wallis,
No. 6407552 A/Sergeant R.L.J. Smith,
No. 5576992 Corporal Thomas John Richard Hiscocks,
No. 6408154 Corporal J. O'Neill,
No. 6407985 Corporal Arnold Hugh Rowe,

 No. 6399711 Corporal Cecil Albert Saunders,

No. 14646041 L/Corporal B. Cohen,
No. 5350800 Private J. Clark,

"London Gazette" Thursday November 7th 1946

S.E. Asia Special Operations

The King has been graciously pleased to approve the following award in recognition of gallant and distinguished service while engaged in special operations in S.E. Asia :-

D.S.O.

 A/Colonel Victor Henry Jaques, C.B.E., O.B.E., M.C. (131287)
(Citation not found)

He was head of an S.E.O. group, part of Force 136.

The King has graciously pleased to approve that the following be Mentioned in recognition of gallant and distinguished service whilst engaged in special operations in South East Asia :-

M.I.D.

T/Major Robert (Robin) de Lisle King, (67150) 1st Bn.

Saturday November 9th 1946

D.S.O. FOR ROYAL SUSSEX COLONEL

The King has been pleased to approve the following awards in recognition of gallant and distinguished services while engaged in special operations in S.E. Asia :-

D.S.O.

A/Colonel Victor Henry Jaques, C.B.E.,O.B.E., M.C.

M.I.D.

T/Major Robert de Lisle King,

"London Gazette" Tuesday November 12th 1946

The following Officers are awarded the Efficiency Medal (Territorial); —

Maj. Hugh Mannington, M.B. R.A.M.C. (71741).attd.

"London Gazette" Thursday November 14th 1946

The KING has been graciously pleased to approve that the following be Mentioned in recognition of gallant and distinguished services in the field: —

M.I.D. (N.W.E.) (Escapees)

No. 6401735 W.O.111 H.E. Franks, 2nd Bn.

Whilst at Stalag 344, Lamsdorf, Franks was in charge of security. For his good work in this connection he has been commended by a British Officer, the Camp Leader and three colleagues.
In addition, on many occasions he sent valuable information to England by secret means.
(was a PoW at Stalag V111.B.)

No. 6402352 Private H. Seymour, 2nd Bn.

Seymour was captured at Dunkirk on 2nd June 1940 and imprisoned in Germany. He escaped from the march through Belgium and was free for five days before being recaptured by Germans.
On 10th October 1942, a colleague and Seymour escaped from a working party at Gleiwitz by cutting the wire surrounding the billet but were caught two days later on a train at Beuthen, by railway police. After an unsuccessful attempt at Troppau in April 1943, Seymour escaped in civilian clothes with three others on 14th July 1943 by prising a hole in the latrine roof, but they were recaptured after seven days in Czechoslovakia.
When the Germans evacuated the camp in January 1945, Seymour and three others hid and were left behind, but became P/W's ten days later as the Germans returned. Seymour made two more escapes before the final one from a column of march heading for Moosberg on 23rd April 1945.
With two others he hid in a house in Kofering where he was liberated by the Allies on 27th April 1945.
(was a PoW at Stalag V111.B.)

Saturday November 16th 1946

MENTION FOR MEN

The King has been pleased to approve the following awards in recognition of gallant and distinguished services in the field :-

M.I.D.

W.O.111 (P.S.M.) H.E. Franks,
Private H. Seymour,

"London Gazette" Thursday November 28th 1946

The following Officers are awarded the Efficiency Medal (Territorial)

Capt. Sidney Joseph Fowler Upton M.C. (90925)
Lt. (T/Capt.) Graeme Ramsey Keith Gordon, (269314)
Lt. Arthur Stanley Shadbolt (314185)

"London Gazette" Thursday December 12th 1946

The following Officers are awarded the Efficiency Medal (Territorial)

Lt. Edward John Leeder, (285868)

"London Gazette" Wednesday January 1st 1947

The KING has been graciously pleased to give orders for the following appointment to the Most Excellent Order of the British Empire : —

O.B.E. (Military Division)

T/Lieutenant-Colonel Claude Hector Dewhurst, (39037) 1st Bn.

Lieutenant-Colonel Dewhurst has for the past year been acting G.S.O.(1) General Staff Intelligence, and as such is responsible for coordinating the work of all sections of G.S. (1) and for liaison with para-military and Allied Intelligence bodies. He has done invaluable work, not only in the collection of intelligence from every possible source, but in its dissemination by means of books, pamphlets and summaries. His personality and capacity for continuous hard work have achieved outstanding results; and his profound knowledge of the problems of Palestine in particular, and the Middle east as a whole, have been quite invaluable.

He has been recommended for an award on five previous occasions.

T/Lieutenant-Colonel Gerald Edward Thornton, (13003) 2nd Bn.

This officer has been Assistant Commandant of the Small Arms School, Sauger since September 1943. During the strenuous training of the war years he has set an outstanding example of keenness, loyalty, determination and objectiveness.

He is a master of Weapon Training to which he has devoted his lifetime. His knowledge of all weapons (Infantry) is profound, and it has been of the greatest possible value to the Army, especially in the matter of weapon trials and the writing of official pamphlets.

The proficiency of the SAS after the many vicissitudes it has passed through in recent times can be directly attributed to the outstanding efficiency, enthusiasm and devotion to duty of this most valuable officer.

"London Gazette" Thursday January 9th 1947

The following Officers are awarded the Efficiency Medal (Territorial)

Capt. Frederick Henry Joseph Maxse, (38995)
Lt. Donald William Smalley, (352409)

"London Gazette" Thursday January 16th 1947

**DECORATIONS CONFERRED BY HIS ROYAL HIGHNESS
THE PRINCE REGENT OF BELGIUM**

Croix de Guerre 1940, with Palm

No. 6401092 L/Bombardier Leslie Charles Crossfield, 109th L.A.A. Regt. (Royal Sussex) R.A.

L/Bdr. Crossfield set a particularly high standard of discipline and cheerfulness during his Bty's deployment on the bridge over the RIVER MAAS near Berg where it was deployed shortly after the initial crossing had finally evicted the Germans from Belgian territory in this area.

"London Gazette" Thursday February 6th 1947

The following Officers are awarded the Efficiency Medal (Territorial)

Lt. (Hon. Capt.) Ronald Arthur Reynolds, (281837)

"London Gazette" Friday February 21st 1947

The following Officers are awarded the Efficiency Medal (Territorial)

Lt. (Hon. Capt.) George Herbert Cook   (97137)
Lt. (Hon. Capt.) Robert Kenneth Milne   (88067)

"London Gazette" Thursday March 6th 1947

The following Officers are awarded the Efficiency Medal (Territorial)

Lt. Harold Douglas Thornton, (186159)

"London Gazette" Thursday March 20th 1947

DECORATIONS CONFERRED BY HER MAJESTY THE QUEEN OF THE NETHERLANDS

Bronze Lion

T/Capt. Brian Dean Carr (138170) 2nd Bn. attd. 10th Bn. Parachute Regt. A.A.C.

Lieutenant Carr jumped near Arnhem on 17th September as part of the advance group of 10th Battalion the Parachute Regiment. His task was to mark and defend the rendezvous for the battalions drop on the next day. When he arrived at the dropping zone on the morning of the 18th, the chosen Rendezvous was held by about a platoon of the enemy. Lieutenant Carr had 8 men, and it was five hours at least until the battalion would arrive. He attacked with his small force, seized the Rendezvous from the enemy and held it against counter attack until the battalion arrived. To do so demanded a very high degree of courage, activity and determination from this officer, but failure would have meant disorganisation for the battalion on its arrival and Lieutenant Carr did not hesitate to offer battle against heavy odds and at great personal risk to secure the successful arrival of the whole. His prolonged defence of the objective, once gained, made even greater demands than the assault, and is worthy of high praise.

When the 10th Battalion was forced to withdraw from near the Dreijenseweg blocking line on the 19th September, Lieutenant Carr stayed behind to help the Medical Officer evacuate the wounded. German troops overtook them and Carr, together with Lieutenant Dodd of the Mortar Platoon who had also stayed behind, were forced to hide and eventually became separated. Dodd was later killed, but Carr successfully evaded capture and later returned to England after reaching the Allied lines.

The following Officers are awarded the Efficiency Medal (Territorial)

Capt. (T/Mjr.) David Richards, M.C. (91119)
Lt. (T/Capt.) Alan Glover, (138163)

"London Gazette" Friday April 18th 1947

The following Officers are awarded the Efficiency Medal (Territorial)

Capt. (now T/Maj.) Benjamin Dalton, D.S.O. (105089)
Lt. (Hon. Capt.) Edmund Watter N.S. Clarke (74805)

"London Gazette" Friday May 2nd 1947

The following Officers are awarded the Efficiency Medal (Territorial)

Lt. (now Capt.) Garrick D. Bowyer (72780) R.A. (was 7th Bn. then 109th L.A.A. (Royal Sussex) R.A.)

"London Gazette" Friday May 30th 1947

The following Officers are awarded the Efficiency Medal (Territorial)

Capt. John Burder, (40998)

"London Gazette" Thursday June 26th 1947

The KING has been graciously pleased to give orders for the following promotions in, and appointments to, the Most Excellent Order of the British Empire, in recognition of gallant and distinguished services in the Netherlands East Indies prior to 30th November, 1946: —

O.B.E. (Military Division)

Major John Lionel Chapman, (40032) 1st Bn.
(Citation not found)

The KING has been graciously pleased to approve the award of the British Empire Medal (Military Division), in recognition of gallant and distinguished services in the Field, prior to September, 1945, to the undermentioned: —

B.E.M. (Military Division)

No. 881623 Private James Owen Martin, 2nd Bn.

For his escaping abilities whilst a prisoner of war.

"London Gazette" Tuesday August 12th 1947

The following Officers are awarded the Efficiency Medal (Territorial).

Capt. (Hon. Maj.) Kenneth Piers Hickman (67439)

"London Gazette" Friday September 12th 1947

The KING has been graciously pleased to confer the "Efficiency Decoration" upon the following Officers of the Territorial Army.

Capt. Edward Ernest Greenough, M.C. (50031) (T.A.R.O.)
Maj. (Q/M.) Edward James Upton, M.M. (11848)

"London Gazette" Friday September 25th 1947

**DECORATIONS CONFERRED BY HIS ROYAL HIGHNESS
THE PRINCE REGENT OF BELGIUM**

Commander of the Order of the Crown with Palm.
Croix de Guerre 1940 with Palm.

T/Major-General Lashmer Gordon Whistler, C.B., D.S.O. (13017), late The Royal Sussex Regiment.

Major-General Whistler commanded the 3rd British Infantry Division in the operations in Belgium resulting of the crossing of the ESCAULT canal at LIEGE ST ALBERT on 18 September 1944 and the subsequent advance north east to clear Belgium of the enemy.
It was essential to attack the Germans on the ESCAULT canal quickly to prevent them from consolidating their position. The Division was accordingly moved from France at short notice and was faced with the difficult task of an assault crossing at night with very little time for preparation.
Major-General Whistler's fine qualities as a divisional commander ensured the success of this difficult operation. His quick grasp of the situation, his energy, drive and determination, and his clear and complete orders so inspired his subordinates that the operation was carried through without a hitch in the face of determined opposition, and was a great contribution to the quick liberation of that part of Belgium.

Chevalier of the Order of Leopold 11 with Palm,
Croix de Guerre 1940 with Palm.

T/Mjr. Patrick John Lowry Powell, (97605) 109th L.A.A. (Royal Sussex) R.A.

Major Powell's Bty was detached from the Regt. And deployed in defence of the bridge over the RIVER MAAS near BERG shortly after the initial crossing which finally evicted the Germans from this area. Major Powell commanded his Bty. Capably and well during this period.

"London Gazette" Friday November 7th 1947

The following Officers are awarded the Efficiency Medal (Territorial) 2nd Clasp: —

Lt. Harold William Phillips (203800).

"London Gazette" Friday November 14th 1947

The KING has been pleased to grant unrestricted permission for the wearing of the following decorations which have been conferred on the undermentioned personnel in recognition of distinguished services in the cause of the Allies: —

DECORATIONS CONFERRED BY THE PRESIDENT OF THE UNITED STATES OF AMERICA

Bronze Star (Arnhem)

No. 6395864 C.S.M. Robert Edward Grainger, 2nd Bn. attd. D Coy 10th Bn. Parachute Regiment,

During two days of heavy and enforced fighting on the 18th and 19th September 1944 in the woods West of Arnhem this C.S.M.'s company was heavily engaged and suffered a large number of casualties in officers and men. C.S.M. Grainger was continually in the forefront of the battle leading and encouraging the men, and by his devotion to duty was an example to all. Later, when himself was wounded he attempted, under heavy fire and across completely open ground to rescue the company clerk who had been wounded. He was later taken to a hospital in enemy hands and showed great initiative in escaping and evading captivity for over four weeks.

When it became necessary to patrol the river front with a view to crossing, C.S.M. Grainger went with Captain Wainwright for this task. This necessitated two long and extremely difficult night patrols through and area very strongly held. The final success of this evacuation was very largely due to the skill and determination of this patrol.

"London Gazette" Thursday January 1st 1948

The KING has been graciously pleased to give orders for the following promotions in, and appointments to, the Most Excellent Order of the British Empire: —

M.B.E. (Military Division)

Major & Q/M Percy John Hanlon, (69631) 2nd Bn.

This officer has served continually without a break in The Royal Sussex Regiment since 1906, a total of 41 years. During this period Major Hanlon has put the Regiment before everything else. By his zeal and efficiency he was given accelerated promotion from Captain to Brevet Major in July 1944, and was promoted to substantive rank in April 1945.

Not only is this officer thoroughly efficient at his work but also was a fine athlete and keen shot. He trained the Battalion team for many years and was a competitor at Bisley this year, and although by many a year the oldest competitor he got into the Army 50.

Through the whole period of this officer's career in the Army he has received nothing but excellent reports both while R.S.M. and Quartermaster. His whole life has been the Army and one of his chief aims has been to foster the Regimental spirit.

"London Gazette" Friday January 30th 1948

The following officers are awarded the Long Service and Good Conduct Medal (Military), without Gratuity —

Lt (now Hon Capt.) Arthur James Steer (163060) 109th L.A.A. Regt. R.A. (& 7th Bn.)

"London Gazette" Friday June 11th 1948

The following Officers are awarded the Efficiency Medal (Territorial).

Lt. Maurice James Mason, (278011)

"London Gazette" Friday June 25th 1948

The following Officers are awarded the Efficiency Medal (Territorial).

Lt. Desmond Carlisle, (277621)

"London Gazette" Friday July 30th 1948

The following Officers are awarded the Efficiency Medal (Territorial) 1st Clasp.

Lt. (T/Capt.) Paul Arthur Cockram, (343084)

The following Officers are awarded the Efficiency Medal (Territorial).
Lt. Douglas Bryan Mosley, (273971)

"London Gazette" Friday September 3rd 1948

The following Officers are awarded the Efficiency Medal (Territorial).

Lt. Norman Henry James Clarke, (256638)

"London Gazette" Friday September 17th 1948

The KING has been pleased to grant unrestricted permission for the wearing of the following decorations which have been conferred on the undermentioned personnel in recognition of distinguished services in the cause of the Allies.

DECORATIONS CONFERRED BY THE PRESIDENT OF THE UNITED STATES OF AMERICA

Silver Star (Italy)

No. 6401551 Colour Sergeant Henry Clifford Biggs, 1st Bn.

For gallantry in action, during the period 14 February 1944, to 26 March 1944, near Cassino, Italy. While his company held mountain positions, Company Quartermaster Sergeant Biggs supervised the supply of his unit by mule pack over narrow, precipitous and rocky mountain trails. The tracks were often frozen and at other times extremely boggy, making it an arduous physical feat to cover the distance.
In addition of natural difficulties the enemy shelled the trails nightly. Despite all dangers and difficulties, Company Quartermaster Sergeant Biggs made trips each night up the hazardous, shell-swept slope to his company's position within 80 yards of the enemy. His courage, energy, and devotion to duty were essential factors in maintaining the morale of his company in combat.

DECORATIONS CONFERRED BY His ROYAL HIGHNESS THE PRINCE REGENT OF BELGIUM

Chevalier of the Order of the Crown

T/Captain Maurice Emmanuel Levey, (284615)

"London Gazette" Friday October 8th 1948

The following Officers are awarded the Efficiency Medal (Territorial).

Lt. David George Packham, (341872)

"London Gazette" Friday November 12th 1948

The following Officers are awarded the Efficiency Medal (Territorial).

Lt. Maurice Charles Elliott, (320533)

"London Gazette" Saturday January 1st 1949

The KING has been graciously pleased to give orders for the following promotions in, and appointments to, the Most Excellent Order of the British Empire: —

M.B.E. (Military Division)

Major Reginald Gower Samworth, (77409) 1st Bn. *(Citation not found)*

"London Gazette" Tuesday January 4th 1949

The KING has been graciously pleased to sanction the following Promotions in, and Appointments to, the Venerable Order of the Hospital of St. John of Jerusalem:—
As Commanders (Brothers)

Major Richard Brian de Fontenne Sleeman, M.C.

"London Gazette" Friday January 7th 1949

The KING has been graciously pleased to approve that the following be Mentioned in recognition of gallant and distinguished Services in Palestine during the period 27th March, 1947 to 26th September, 1947: —

M.I.D.

Major Peter Maurice Lawson, (153960) 1st Bn.
Captain Albert Holmes Goodall, (378345) 1st Bn.

"London Gazette" Friday January 21st 1949

The following Officers are awarded the Efficiency Medal (Territorial).

Lt. Denys Gerald Winton Apthorpe, (Deceased) (105087)

"London Gazette" Friday March 4th 1949

The following Officers are awarded the 1st Clasp to the Efficiency Medal (Territorial).

Lt. Michael Benedict Morphy, (186157)

The following Officers are awarded the Efficiency Medal (Territorial).

Lt. (T/Capt.) Stephen Robert Ablett, (2296400) (now R.A.)

"London Gazette" Friday March 25th 1949

The following Officers are awarded the Efficiency Medal (Territorial).

Lt. Eric John Berlyn, (99781)
Lt. (Hon. Capt.) Arthur Paul Edward Camden Egerton-Savory, (138850)

"London Gazette" **Friday April 1st 1949**

The following Officers are awarded the Efficiency Medal (Territorial).

Lt. (Hon. Capt.) Peter John Pafford, (162506)

"London Gazette" **Friday April 8th 1949**

The KING has been graciously pleased to approve that the following be Mentioned in recognition of gallant and distinguished services in Malaya during the period 1st July 1948 to 31st December 1948.

M.I.D.

Major Peter Rogers Richards,   (358068) 1st Bn.

"London Gazette" **Friday April 22nd 1949**

The following Officers are awarded the 1st Clasp to the Efficiency Medal (Territorial).

Capt. (Hon. Mjr.) Harry Philip Durant, (132180)

The following Officers are awarded the Efficiency Medal (Territorial).
Capt. (Hon. Mjr.) Harry Philip Durant, (132180)
Lt. Derrick William Gaylard, M.C. (Deceased) (99819)
Lt. (Hon. Mjr.) Frank Arthur James, (143969)

"London Gazette" **Friday June 17th 1949**

The following Officers are awarded the Efficiency Medal (Territorial).
Capt. Rowland Jack Page, (198838)

"London Gazette" **Friday August 12th 1949**

The following Officers are awarded the Efficiency Medal (Territorial).

Lt. Frank Harbord, (160408)

"London Gazette" **Friday September 9th 1949**

The Following officers are awarded the Long Service and Good Conduct Medal (Military) without gratuity (the date of qualification is shown in brackets).

Lt. (Qr.-Mstr.) Eric Oswald Robinson, (358659)
(12th Feb. 1947)

"London Gazette" **Friday October 14th 1949**

DECORATIONS CONFERRED BY His MAJESTY THE KING OF THE HELLENES

Distinguished Service Medal

T/Mjr. Harold George Castle (102541), The Royal Sussex Regiment.

Throughout the Bn's stay in Greece the services of Maj Castle in re-establishing the Govt's authority and directing relief supplies to the most deserving were outstanding. His tact and determination for fair play won him the respect and even the affection of the most reactionary elements in MACEDONIA. He first displayed his great abilities when acting as liaison officer between H.M.G. Consul General in SALONIKA Mr. Ropp C.M.G. and Gen. Bavivdiz. He was present during their fateful conference at the R. AXIOS which but for his indefatigable efforts might not have taken place. Again on 24 Feb 45 this officer led the first Br. Force to KILKIS to gain first-hand information of conditions in E.A.M. dominated territory. The reception accorded him and the troops under his command was menacing, but by dint of much parleying between Maj Castle and local leaders of E.A.M. good relations was established even so far as to an excellent official dinner given to the Br. Officers in their honour. From the shrewd conclusions drawn by Maj Castle in his detailed report of this operation much valuable planning for the future was made easier. When the Bn. moved from the SALONIKA area to DRAMA this officer was made entirely responsible for investigating all stories of atrocities and persecutions. By his diligent untiring and necessary fearless probing much that might have remained a canker in the side of the GREEK GAST was removed in the remote and Mountain regions of W MACEDONIA. After many days of careful reconnaissance of villages in the BULGARIAN frontier area, Maj Castle established a Coy Det on the 22 April in the devastated village of LEVKOYIA the centre of a large area in which local inhabitants had fled their village in fear of marauding gangs of bandits. By the intensive patrolling of his troops and continuous unearthing of ELAS arms Maj Castle restored confidence and a normal way of life in this region. It was during this period that he undertook the fair distribution of UNRA supplies of food and clothing. No simple task in this E.A.M. territory. On his return to DRAMA in May Maj Castle treated with ANTON TSOUS the nationalist leader and through his shrewd, determined yet tactful handling of this colourful personality much valuable assistance was gained from him in running stocks of arms and bandits to earth.

T/Mjr. Philip Hilary Jones (180206), The Royal Sussex Regiment.
(Citation not found)

The following Officers are awarded the Efficiency Medal (Territorial).

Lt. Wilfred Gordon Elms, (105090)
Lt. (Hon. Capt.) Edward Brassey Newson, (129365)

"London Gazette" Friday November 4th 1949

The following Officers are awarded the Efficiency Medal (Territorial).

Capt. (Hon. Mjr.) Harry Oswald Cox, (160547)

"London Gazette" Friday December 9th 1949

The KING has been graciously pleased to give orders for the following promotions in, and appointments to, the Most Excellent Order of the British Empire in recognition of gallant and distinguished services in Malaya during the period 1st January, 1949, to 30th June, 1949: —

M.B.E. (Military Division)

Lieutenant & Q/M. Herbert Norman Brockless, (6457417) 1st Bn.

Singapore Oct 46 to Dec 49

Lieutenant H.N. Brockless, Royal Sussex Regt. was appointed Quarter Master to GHQ ALFSEA, now FARELF, on 11/10/46, and is still so employed.

Although he is not responsible for Barrack and Accommodation Stores, the Quarter Master, in addition to the normal Regimental had until the end of May 1949 a heavy additional commitment of 135 married quarters to ration. In addition now, he is still responsible for 3 Officers Messes, one large WO & Sgts' Mess 2 WRAC Messes besides a large British Other Ranks Mess. All these have had to be rationed and fuelled. The breaking down from bulk, cutting up and issuing, has been, and still is, entirely his responsibility.

When Lieutenant Brockless was appointed QM to this GHQ the strength was approx. 500 Officers and 1100 men and WRAC living in 22 Messes (twenty-two). The administration was still on wartime accounting, and the resultant contraction to the present strength involves much additional work to bring this GHQ back to peacetime accounting. It has necessitated working long hours, and much time spent outside working hours.

Another responsibility of the QM is the execution of all minor work and repairs at this GHQ. The Unit Pioneers are under his direct control and are responsible for the complete signing of this GHQ and much are the portioning and alterations to offices of the many Branches and Directorates.

The Hygiene Section is also controlled by the QM. Besides the general cleanliness of the Barracks, the Hygiene Section to undertake all outside DDT Block spraying 135 married quarters. These additional commitments have to be supervised in addition to his normal work as Quartermaster, with the results that often his work is carried on outside working hours.

Lieutenant Brockless has served under me for 18 months. His capacity for work is unlimited. Possessing a cheerful disposition, and all ways anxious to assist or help anybody, his name is practically a household word in this GHQ for real solid work, always carried on time, and always ready to co-operate.

As is often the case much of his work is unnoticed and possibly taken for granted. As his Commanding Officer I know that much of his work has been performed by him alone. Sometimes with a indifferent or shorthanded staff he has still maintained a high standard of efficiency. The Quarter Master's stores in its complete layout is demonstrated officially by the School of Administration FARELF as what a model QM should be.

I rate Lieutenant Brockless as above the average Unit Quarter Master, and in my opinion he has rendered outstanding work to this GHQ since he was appointed Quarter Master. Moreover, it is solid work, which in my opinion worthy of recognition. I therefore to recommend Lieutenant Brockless for the award of the Member of the British Empire.

"London Gazette" **Tuesday December 13th 1949**

The following Officers are awarded the Efficiency Medal (Territorial).

Capt. (Hon. Mjr.) Peter Reginald Cavalier, M.C. (124221)

"London Gazette" **Tuesday January 2nd 1950**

The KING has been graciously pleased to give orders for the following promotions in, and appointments to, the Most Excellent Order of the British Empire: —

O.B.E. (Military Division)

Major Alexander John Stevenson Grant, T.D. (23442) 4/5th Bn. (T.A.)
(Citation not found)

"London Gazette" Friday February 24th 1950

The King has graciously pleased to approve the undermentioned award, in recognition of gallant and distinguished service in Burma during the period 10th November 1944 to 15th February 1945, in lieu of Mentioned in Despatches published in *"London Gazette"* 10th January 1946.

M.M. (Burma 1944/1945)

No. 6411812 Sergeant William Gilbert Leech, 9th Bn.
(In place of M.I.D. awarded 10/01/46, Citation not found)

Friday February 24th 1950

The Royal Humane Society Bronze Medal

Corporal E. Brazier, 4th/5th (C.P.) Bn. The Royal Sussex Regiment,
For the rescue of two boys from a minefield at Fairlight on the night 23rd/24th February, 1950.

"London Gazette" Thursday March 24th 1950

The Following officers are awarded the Long Service and Good Conduct Medal (Military) without gratuity (the date of qualification is shown in brackets).

Lt. (T/Mjr.) Patrick Michael Mordaunt, M.C. (164690)

"London Gazette" Thursday March 31st 1950

The KING has been graciously pleased to confer the award of the "4 Clasps" to the "Territorial Efficiency Decoration" upon the following Officers: —

Mjr. Alexander John Stevenson Grant, T.D. (23442) 4/5th Bn.

"London Gazette" Friday April 14th 1950

The following Officers are awarded the 1st Clasp to the Efficiency Medal (Territorial).

Lt. Albert Brett, (326745)

The following Officers are awarded the Efficiency Medal (Territorial).
Lt. (now T. Maj.) James Roy Anderson, (153258)
Lt. (now Capt.) David Michael Charles Burrough, (99792) (now R.A.P.C.)

"London Gazette" Friday April 21st 1950

The KING has been graciously pleased to confer the award of the 1st Clasp to the "Territorial Efficiency Decoration" upon the following Officers: —

Capt. (Hon. Mjr.) John Osborne Lintott, (64452) 4th Bn.
Capt. (Hon. Mjr.) Alfred Alan Roberts, (91120) 4th Bn.
Capt. (Hon. Mjr.) Garrick D. Bowyer, (72780) (was 7th Bn. then 109th L.A.A. (Royal Sussex)) R.A.

The KING has been graciously pleased to confer the award of the "Territorial Efficiency Decoration" upon the following Officers: —

Lt-Col. Ronald Gethen, M.C. (86687)
Mjr. Vernon Maitland Fallowfield-Cooper, (98352)
Mjr. Cyril Reid Peckitt, M.B.E. (15229)
Capt. (Hon. Mjr.) Randle Frederick Hicks Darwall Smith, (94624)
Capt. (Hon. Mjr.) Kenneth Piers Hickman, (67439)
Capt. (Hon. Mjr.) Geoffrey Derek Hodgson, M.C. (78964)
Capt. (Hon. Mjr.) Walter Ketton Hubbard, (91890)
Capt. (T/Mjr.) Peter Tavener Miller, (39804) (k.i.a.)
Capt. (Hon. Mjr.) Robert Rickman Penney, (69305)
Capt. (T/Mjr.) David Richards, M.C. (91119)
Capt. (Hon. Mjr.) Sidney Joseph Fowler Upton, M.C. (90925)
Capt. (Q/M) George W. Ayling, (75926)
Lt. (Hon. Capt.) Edmund Watter N.S. Clarke, (74805)
Lt. (Hon. Capt.) George Herbert Cook, (97137)
Lt. (Hon. Capt.) Denis Howard de Pass, (74079)
Lt. (Hon. Capt.) Robert Kenneth Milne, (88067)
Lt. William Henry Rogers, (42300)

"London Gazette" **Friday May 26th 1950**

The following Officers are awarded the 1st Clasp to the Efficiency Medal (Territorial).

Capt. (Hon. Mjr.) Edward John Leeder, (285868)

"London Gazette" **Thursday June 8th 1950**

The KING has been graciously pleased to give orders for the following promotions in, and appointments to, the Most Excellent Order of the British Empire:—

O.B.E. (Military Division)

T/Colonel Alexander Charles Clayton, (20161) (Rtd.)

O.C. Transit Camp

I was G.O.C. British Troops India in 1947 and early 1948. I first met Col. Clayton in a British Transit Camp outside Bombay through which passed the great portion of withdrawing British Units. As the withdrawal neared completion a large number of families were also passed through his establishment and another at DEOLALI. Amongst these families were there a large number emigrating to Australia. Almost at the last moment certain difficulties arose with the Australian Government and it became necessary to retain these families in a holding in India and pass them out as occasion permitted. This produced a very difficult position as I, as British Commander, had leave at the appointed time and this organisation had to be set up and left behind in India on a very indefinite basis indeed.
I had known Col. Clayton in the past so approached him to remain and be Commandant and this camp that was named the British Holding Camp. In spite of being a long time away from and knowing full well the difficulties ahead Col. Clayton volunteered to remain.
He was given an extremely small staff and had to utilise the Transistees to carry out all duties. Although

I only saw the beginning of this establishment I understand that it was brought to a successful conclusion in December 1948.

There is no doubt there would have been serious difficulties had Col. Clayton not volunteered. That the project was a success shows the excellent work and devotion to duty displayed by Col. Clayton.

"London Gazette" **Tuesday June 20th 1950**

The KING has been graciously pleased to confer "The Territorial Efficiency Decoration with 1st Clasp" upon the following officers:—

Mjr. Francis H. Rogers, (30149)
Capt. (Hon. Mjr.) Thomas Marsland Hole, (63126)

The KING has been graciously pleased to confer the award of the "Territorial Efficiency Decoration" upon the following Officers: —

Lt. (Hon. Capt.) Hugh Charles Hughes, (72944)

"London Gazette" **Friday November 17th 1950**

The KING has been graciously pleased to confer The Cadet Forces Medal upon the following officers of the Cadet Forces:

Sussex
A/Mjr. Emil August Bruder (344038) (now C.C.F.).
A/Mjr. Robert Wallace Harvey (275250).

The KING has been graciously pleased to confer The Cadet Forces Medal upon the following officers who completed the qualifying period whilst serving with the Cadet Forces: —

Sussex

Arthur Wheeler (275282) (formerly A/Lt.-Col.).
Percy Victor Wilkins (280806) (formerly A/Capt.).

"London Gazette" **Tuesday December 12th 1950**

The KING has been graciously pleased to confer the award of "3 Clasps" to the Territorial Efficiency Decoration upon the following officers: —

COMMANDS AND STAFF

Col. Sir James Lewis Sleeman, Kt., C.B., C.M.G.,C.B.E.,M.V.O., T.D., M.A. (527)
(late Herefordshire Regt.)

"London Gazette" **Friday December 15th 1950**

The KING has been graciously pleased to confer The Cadet Forces Medal upon the following officers of the Cadet Forces:-

Sussex

A/Lt.-Colonel Leonard Norman Phillips, M.C. (275279)

"London Gazette" Monday January 1st 1951

The KING has been graciously pleased to give orders for the following promotions in, and appointments to, the Most Excellent Order of the British Empire:—

M.B.E. (Military Division) (Aden)

Captain Charles Emberton Brook, (202477) 1st Bn.

Captain Brook has been Staff Officer to this, the Regular Commissions Board and to No. 1 R.C.B. and one Travelling Board overseas over the past four tears. He has served five different Major-Generals with commendable loyalty and devotion to duty, (Gen. V. Eveleigh, C.B.,D.S.O.,O.B.E., Gen. D.H. Pratt, C.B.,D.S.O.,M.C., Gen. C.E.N. Lomax, C.B.,C.B.E.,D.S.O.,M.C., Gen. H.P.M. Berney-Flicklin, C.B.,M.C., Gen. F.R.G. Matthews, C.B.,D.S.O.)

He has been, and still is, a quite exceptional example of uprightness and loyalty to all the candidates, civilians, cadets, Emergency Commissioned Officers and others who come before the board.

His charming manner and unfailing willingness to help to the uttermost over the most humble of question or requirement of the Candidates has made him not only admired and liked by all, but he has demonstrated to those thousands (6,000) ho have come in contact with him what a good, loyal officer should be; thereby enhancing in the eyes of the nation the reputation of the Army.

His perfect turn-out and correct manner is an example to all who come in contact with him, both young and old. He never spares himself for one second, always putting duty before self, and even after a serious accident he returned to duty in advance of when he should. He has, in addition to his exceptional work with the regular Commissions Board, given trusty and true service to the Army over a great period of years and his work with a Beach Group in Italy was of the highest order.

Over and above his work in personal contact with candidates he has had immense correspondence with Fathers, Mothers, Guardians and Headmasters of boys due to come before the RCB over the matter of changing dates of appearance. In each case he has shown great personal interest and consideration. Be it a telegram at the last moment or a telephone call late at night, he never fails to satisfy the Parent or Guardian and to leave a pleasant feeling towards the Army. His relationship with all is outstanding and his personal interest in the welfare of Other Ranks employed at the RCB alone is worthy of commendation.

A man of the highest principles who stands out as a shining example to all as a man who knows what loyalty and sense of duty mean and puts them into practice.

The KING has been graciously pleased to give orders for the following appointments to, the Most Excellent Order of the British Empire:—

M.B.E.

Major Ian Edmund Snell, (219870) 1st Bn. Military Assistant to Resident Adviser, Mukalla, Aden Protectorate. *(Citation not found)*

"London Gazette" Thursday February 16th 1951

The following officers are awarded the Long Service and Good Conduct Medal (Military) without gratuity. (The date of the qualification is shown in brackets).

Capt. (Q.M.) Herbert Norman Brockless, M.B.E. (363956)
(17th May 1950)

"London Gazette" Thursday February 23rd 1951

The KING has been graciously pleased to confer the award of the Cadet Forces Medal upon the following Serving officers of the Cadet Forces: —

Sussex

A/Lt.-Col. Hedley John Bonfield (now C.C.F.) (122689).
A/Capt. Thomas Arthur Hunnisett (298340).

"London Gazette" March 16th 1951

The KING has been graciously pleased to confer the award of the Cadet Forces Medal upon the following Serving officers of the Cadet Forces: —

Sussex

A/Capt. Thom Miles Potter (275256).

"London Gazette" April 17th 1951

The KING has been graciously pleased to confer the award of the Cadet Forces Medal upon the following serving officers of the Cadet Forces.
Sussex

A/Mjr. Charles Albert Mortimer   (275255)

"London Gazette" Friday June 29th 1951

The following Officers are awarded the Efficiency Medal (Territorial).

Lt. Laurence Harry Allen, (281155)
Lt. (Hon. Capt.) Terence John Power, (137328)

"London Gazette" Friday July 31st 1951

The King has been graciously pleased to approve the following award, in recognition of gallant and distinguished service :-

George Medal

Captain Ronald Victor Harley, (243086)

On the 21st February 1951, No. 243086, Captain R.V. Harley Royal Sussex Regiment, attached Royal Army Ordnance Corps. was on duty at No. 3 Central Ammunition Sub-Depot Hampstead Norris (Bramley), supervising the receipt of ammunition. He was in the sorting shed when a 25pdr. Ammunition exploded and injured six soldiers of the Royal Pioneer Corps. one of whom died later. The blast was so violent that it blew another shell to pieces, reduced many more to a dangerous condition, started a fire, and blanketed the area with smoke.
Captain Harley immediately ordered all the men out of the building, leaving it to himself only when he could see no more personnel. He re-entered the building almost immediately to find some injured men running out. Without hesitation he went right up to the scene of the explosion which was still enveloped

in smoke, and saw flames. He ordered a soldier who was at his side (No. 1441727) Pte. L.K. McGarrigle, Royal Pioneer Corps. to fetch fire appliances, and himself went further into the smoke where he found a badly injured soldier staggering about.

By this time another helper had arrived and Captain Harley, after seeing that the injured soldier was being evacuated, ran to the office next door to call the ambulance and fire Brigade. Next he saw that all the casualties were being attended to, and ordered the most serious cases be taken to hospital straight away in a unit vehicle. Then he again went to the scene of the explosion to check up that the fire was out and that there were no further casualties, and finally ordered a roll call to see that all his personnel had been accounted for.

Captain Harley, owing to his proximity to the explosion suffered considerably from its effects; he had seen the wounded men and heard their screams, and was fully aware of the possibility of further detonations taking place. In spite of this he showed bearing and leadership of the very highest order, and undoubtedly his exemplary behaviour affected the discipline of the men under his command in their efforts to extinguish the fire and succour the casualties under very hazardous conditions.

"London Gazette" Tuesday 14th August 1951

The KING has been graciously pleased to confer the award of the "Territorial Efficiency Decoration" upon the following Officers: —

Captain (Hon. Major) Charles Howard Simmons, (94973) (T.F.) (was 109th L.A.A. R.A.)

The following Officers are awarded the Efficiency Medal (Territorial).
Lt. (Hon. Capt.) Warren Clarke Wallace, (247802)

"London Gazette" Tuesday 25th September 1951

The following Officers are awarded the Efficiency Medal (Territorial).

Lt. (Hon. Capt.) Norman William Trott, (308546)

"London Gazette" Monday October 19th 1951

The KING has been graciously pleased to approve that the following be Mentioned, in recognition of gallant and distinguished services in Malaya, during the period 1st January to 30th June, 1951: —

M.I.D.

Brigadier Claude Hector Tarver, D.S.O., (380334)
"In recognition of gallant and distinguished services in Malaya."
The KING has been graciously pleased to confer the award of the "Territorial Efficiency Decoration" upon the following Officers: —

Hon. Lt. Edward A. Ree, (91608) (Deceased)

Tuesday December 4th 1951

Eleven Killed in Canal Zone Clashes

Royal Sussex Men to the Rescue

A company of The Royal Sussex Regiment played a part in one of two clashes between British troops and Egyptians yesterday. In these a corporal of the British Military Police and six Mauritians were killed, a British major is missing presumed killed, and a Royal Engineer is missing.

The bodies of four Egyptians, including three policemen, were found, while 25 Egyptians were taken prisoner. A British Army communiqué last night said that the British corporal was deliberately shot in the back. He died in hospital.

The Egyptian Minister of the Interior, Serag El Din Pasha, told Parliament that nine Egyptians were killed and 62 injured. These he said, were hospital figures. The first clash occurred at 11.30 when a party of 20 Royal Engineers were sniped at by terrorists as a petrol point on the fringe of the desert outside the town of Suez was being moved inside the Canal Zone perimeter.

"They did not return the fire, for a lack of a target", said a spokesman, but later about 50 "trigger-happy" Egyptian police arrived and started firing. They also used petrol bombs and grenades. A company of about 60 men from the First Battalion The Royal Sussex Regiment, went out with Bren carriers to bring them in.

Heard Firing and Stopped Car

At about 12.30 pm. The Assistant Provost-Marshal of Suez returning from the British Consulate with a military police escort heard the firing and stopped his car to speak to an Egyptian police officer. It was then that the military police corporal was shot in the back.

The firing lasted until 2.30 pm. And when the Royal Sussex men drove away, four Egyptians were found dead. The 25 prisoners, also taken away, included a policeman.

The second incident occurred at 4.30 p.m., when a light van and a three-ton lorry were ambushed at the Suez railway crossing in the same area. They were fired on and an incendiary bomb was thrown. It was this clash that the six Mauritians were killed and the major and other rank reported missing. The commanding officer of the Mauritians, visiting the scene, found nothing but the burned vehicles.

Wednesday December 5th 1951

Royal Sussex Regiment in Suez Clash

Fighting flared up in the Suez Canal Zone yesterday, when 40 Egyptians fired on men of The Royal Sussex Regiment who were driving through the town in three Bren gun carriers. One officer and one other rank were wounded, and "at least " 20 Egyptians killed or wounded. The shooting occurred soon after Brigadier Greenacre, commander of the British Garrison in Suez, met the Egyptian Governor of the city to discuss Monday's battle.

"London Gazette" Sunday December 28th 1951

The KING has been graciously pleased to confer the award of the 1st and 2nd Clasps to the Territorial Efficiency Decoration upon the following officers:—

Mjr. Maurice E. Few, T.D. (40294)

1951-1952

(Korea)

A number of Reservists were called up for the Korean War and some officers and soldiers of the Regiment served in Korea with other regiments, notably with the 1st Battalion The Middlesex Regiment and some with the Royal Fusiliers and also the Glosters.

"London Gazette" Tuesday January 1st 1952

The KING has been graciously pleased to give orders for the following appointment to the Most Excellent Order of the British Empire:—

K.B.E. (Military Division)

Lieutenant-General Lashmer Gordon Whistler, C.B.,D.S.O.,DL. (13017)

O.B.E. (Military Division) (BOAR)

Lieutenant-Colonel Richard Brian de Fontenne Sleeman, (50239) 1st Bn.

Lieutenant-Colonel Sleeman has been British Chief of Staff – lately re-titled Secretary – at the allied Kommandatura in Berlin for more than two years. During this time he has on many occasions had to work a very high pressure in dealing with rapid successions of Commandant's meetings caused by Berlin emergencies of one kind or another.

The task of agreeing recorded decisions on behalf of the Commandants with two Allies is a hard and complicated one requiring not only a very accurate staff work but much tact and patience. By his untiring energy through many long hours of work and by his intelligent and efficient staff work he has done much to improve the machinery of the Allied Kommandatura and its relationship with the Berlin City Authorities. He has also, by his ability and character, fostered extremely good and close relationships with the U.S. and French Delegations in Berlin.

British prestige has been greatly enhanced by his conduct of business in the Allied Kommandatura in which he has exceeded his formal duties to such a degree that he has been accepted as a natural leader by all delegations. In fact he has shown devotion to duty that he has made an outstanding contribution to the orderly and efficient Government of the City of Berlin.

"London Gazette" Tuesday February 19th 1952

The QUEEN has been graciously pleased to confer the award of The Territorial Efficiency Decoration upon the following officers:—

Maj. (Hon. Lt-Col.) Trevor George Corry Evans, (97144).

 Capt. (Hon. Maj.) Peter Spencer Hadley, M.B.E. (88627). 4th Bn.

"London Gazette" Tuesday March 4th 1952

The following Officers are awarded the Efficiency Medal (Territorial).

Capt. Anthony Glyn Jones, (219869)

"London Gazette" Friday April 4th 1952

The QUEEN has been graciously pleased to give orders for the following promotion in, and appointments to, the Most Excellent Order of the British Empire, in recognition of gallant and distinguished conduct:—

M.B.E. (Military Division) (Suez)

 Lieutenant Patrick Galloway Grattan, (362231) 1st Bn.

In a very sharp action his platoon dispersed an Egyptian terrorist force to relieve a detachment of the Buffs, cut off while guarding the water filtration plant on the outskirts of Suez town.

The QUEEN has been graciously pleased to confer the award of the Cadet Forces Medal upon the following former officers of the Cadet Forces: —

ARMY CADET FORCE

Sussex

 Stephen John Hoskins (275252) (formerly A/Maj.).

"London Gazette" Friday May 23rd 1952

The following Officers are awarded the Efficiency Medal (Territorial).

Lt. John Alan Turner, (240479) (now Capt. R.A.)

The following officers are awarded the Long Service and Good Conduct Medal (Military) without gratuity. (The date of the qualification is shown in brackets.)

Capt. Edward Ansell, (167647) (28 June 1945)

"London Gazette" Thursday June 5th 1952

The QUEEN has been graciously pleased, on the occasion of the Celebration of Her Majesty's Birthday, to give orders for the following promotions in, and appointments to, the Most Excellent Order of the British Empire: —

M.B.E. (Military Division) (Suez)

Major Philip Sidney Newton, (108180) 1st Bn.

Major Newton has been the only DAQMG in this District HQ. During the period under review. The problem with which he has had to deal have included in particular the accommodation and maintenance of the very large number of troops that have been brought into the District. During this time there has been an acute shortage of transport and virtually no labour, so that improvisation has been the rule rather than the exception. All this particularly at a Grade 11 level has involved a very great deal of meticulous and detailed hard work. Not only has Major Newton worked tirelessly for very long hours and often late into the night, but he has also shown that he can make sound and realistic decisions, and has hesitated to do so. Moreover he has taken pains to appreciate each problem from the unit's point of view and has been willing to shoulder any amount of extra work and trouble in order to serve them. In brief his has risen to the occasion in this present emergency but has not only got through a great deal more work than is normally expected of one man, but has also accepted responsibility to a far greater degree than is normally expected from an officer of his rank.

Date Unknown (1952) (Suez)

G.O.C. Egypt's Commendation for Bravery

No. 6402157 Sergeant Walter Stanley John Smith, 1st Bn.

He commanded a detachment from his platoon defending the railway signal box on the outskirts of Suez town. They were being continually sniped at by terrorists operating from the native quarter, but through his leadership, initiative and coolness he silenced the terrorist fire.

"London Gazette" Tuesday June 10th 1952

The QUEEN has been graciously pleased to confer the award of The Territorial Efficiency Decoration and 1st Clasp upon the following officers: —

Capt. Percy Nugent Claridge, (62495)

"London Gazette" Tuesday July 22nd 1952

The following Officers are awarded the Efficiency Medal (Territorial).

Lt. (Hon. Capt.) Douglas Eric Stephens, (137322)

"London Gazette" Friday October 10th 1952

The Queen has graciously pleased to approve the following award in recognition of gallant and distinguished conduct :-

Queen's Commendation For Brave Conduct (Suez)

Lieutenant David Anthony Graeme Blaxter, (407761) 1st Bn.

He led his platoon under fire to recover the bodies of the Mauritian soldiers killed in an ambush and on the following day recovered the body of the British sergeant from the Sweet Water Canal.

"London Gazette" Friday September 12th 1952

The following Officers are awarded the Efficiency Medal (Territorial).

Lt. Cedric Raymond Knaggs, (258394) (now Capt. R.A.E.C.)

"London Gazette" Friday November 25th 1952

The QUEEN has been graciously pleased to confer the award of the Cadet Forces Medal upon the following serving officers of the Cadet Forces: —
Sussex

A/Capt. Paul Francis Heatherley (275234)
Lt. Leslie Joseph Hagel (298546)

Monday January 19th 1953

The Men of Sussex are Coming Home

Duke of Norfolk to welcome them

The men of Sussex are coming home. With a distinguished record of service behind it, the 1st Battalion The Royal Sussex Regiment is due to arrive at Southampton from the Middle East on February 4.

And the thankful words on the lips of the wives and families, who will cheer the arrival of the troopship Empire Ken from the quayside, will be : "It's been a long time ....."

For it has been a long time since the battalion left for overseas on its present tour of duty in 1936. Their duty abroad has only been broken by a few months in 1948-49, when the men returned home to be amalgamated with the 2nd Battalion at an historic ceremonial parade at Chichester.

For the men on their way home it will be a time of looking back – remembering the proud moments in their full tour of duty in the canal Zone.

There was a time when .... The battalion had the privilege of mounting a guard of honour on His late Majesty King Abdulla at Aqaba.

There was a time when .... During the crisis months in Egypt in the autumn and winter 1951-52, the battalion was stationed at Suez and later moved to Ismalia. After duties on road blocks and railway guards it was to a great part due to the bearing, turnout and discipline of the battalion that confidence of the civilian population of Ismalia was so quickly restored.

There was the time when .... Close relations with the Arab Legion were always maintained. Many of the officers of the regiment served in the legion, and Brigadier McCully, who had been with both battalions of the regiment for many years, commanded 2nd Infantry Brigade, Arab Legion.

In addition to many National Servicemen who will be making their first voyage home as part of a unit, there will be about 90 officers and men who joined the battalion in July, 1949. Many National Servicemen have changed their engagements to become regular soldiers.

The battalion which will be welcomed at the quayside by the Duke of Norfolk, Lord Lieutenant of Sussex, accompanied by Brigadier T.F.V. Foster, Colonel of the Regiment, will move to Fowler Barracks, Perham Down, Tidworth, where it is to be stationed. Leave for most men will start shortly after their arrival at Tidworth.

The battalion is commanded by Lt-Col. J.B. Ashworth, with Major R.B. de F. Sleeman as second in command.

Monday February 6th 1953

Cheers, Tears End The 10-Day Trip

And For Some It Was "First Time Back" For 3 Years

A great cheer went up from the troop decks of the Empire Ken as she nosed through the mist of Southampton Water on Saturday afternoon. Aboard were 450 officers and men of the 1st Battalion The Royal Sussex Regiment, home from the Middle East after a safe, uneventful 10-day passage.

The band of the regiment, overcoated and alone on one of the top decks, thumped into action, and as the white-painted trooper drew closer "Sussex by the Sea." The 1914-18 war marching song, drifted across the calm water.

From the quayside came an answering cheer, almost an echo, from parents, wives and relatives, some of whom had waited in the cold sunlight nearly four hours for this moment.

There was a flutter of Union Jacks; telescopes and binoculars were raised. There were shouts of recognition and babies were held aloft, pawing at the cold air as they mimicked their excited mothers.

A Chirp from The Tug Neptune

Shouts of laughter came from the ship for a burly Pay Corps. sergeant who marched up the quayside bellowing across the narrow strip of water at comrades onboard. Even the tiny tug Neptune, snuffling around the bows of the "Ken", had a sense of the occasion and chirped on her siren.

The troops cheered for the newsreel cameramen and hung over the rails, rows of blue berets over cheeky faces and khaki overcoats.

Watchful, Tactful and Tough

When the colonel said they had had a busy time he did not over-estimate. The Battalion was in Egypt at the time of the riots and in Ismalia. They had to be watchful, tactful sometimes tough.
But they upheld the tradition of their Regiment and added lustre to its glorious achievements.
Two officers, Major P.S. Newton and Captain P.G. Grattan, received M.B.E.'s during their tour and Lieutenant D.A.G. Blaxter was awarded a Mention in Dispatches and Sergeant Smith the G.O.C.'s Mention.
Early yesterday the Battalion disembarked and went by train to Tidworth. By last night they were all on leave.

"London Gazette" Tuesday April 24th 1953

The QUEEN has been graciously pleased to approve that the following to be Mentioned in recognition of gallant and distinguished services in Korea, during the period 1st July to 31st December, 1952:-

M.I.D.

Major Peter Maurice Lawson, (153960) 1st Bn.
(M.I.D. 7th January, 1949, Palestine)

"London Gazette" Thursday May 1st 1953

The Queen has been graciously pleased to approve that the following be Mentioned in recognition of gallant and distinguished services in Malaya, during the period 1st July to 31st December, 1952:-

M.I.D.

Captain Terence Michael Carter, (346875) 1st Bn.

"London Gazette" Monday June 1st 1953

The QUEEN has been graciously pleased, on the occasion of Her Majesty's Coronation, to give orders for the following promotions in, and appointments to, the Most Excellent Order of the British Empire:-

M.B.E. (Military Division)

Major John Richard Guy Stanton (95305)

Period covered August 51- 31 December 52

The progress of Air trooping since its inception in 1951 has made Malta one of the busiest Air Trooping junction in the world.
This officer is responsible for all movements of personnel stores and vehicles in and out of Malta. He has had to contend with the constant disruption of programmes by international crises, weather and the un-serviceability of aircraft.
He has with never-failing patience and zeal left no stone unturned to maintain the smooth flow of traffic and has ensured all ranks of the Service have conveyed to their destination expeditiously and with the maximum of comfort possible. This has entailed careful planning, long and irregular hours, unceasing vigilance and an entirely unselfish devotion to the interests of Her Majesty's Service.
His tenacity, devotion, and leadership has inspired those who work under him and produced the maximum of efficiency and benefit to the Service.

Captain Frank Alan Day   (183336)

Salisbury Plain District 1 Nov 49 to 11 Nov 52

Deputy Assistant Quarter Master General (Maint)

Captain/T. Major F.A. Day has been employed for the past three years as D.A.Q.M.G. (Maint), Headquarters, Salisbury Plain District. During this period his work has been of a very high order. In a District which is concerned with training of the Reserve Army, he has worked far harder and longer hours than normally expected of a second grade staff officer. During the Training Season he seldom left his desk before 10pm, and on Saturdays regularly finished work after midnight. This was caused by the problems of the reception and despatch of Z Reservists of which this District alone handled some 47,0000 during the 1952 Training Season. Major Day devoted himself whole-heartedly to the successful training and administration of these men together with the Territorial Army. The success which has attended the training of the Reserve Army and Z Reservists in this District during the past three years can be said to be due in a large measure to Major Day's devotion to duty.

In addition to the tasks mentioned above, Major Day has taken a pride in the efficient administration of the regular units in the District and has not spared himself in ensuring that these units, so far as lay in his power, wanted for nothing

He also found time to devote to the personal welfare of the troops of this HQ in addition to his other work.

"London Gazette" **Tuesday June 30th 1953**

The QUEEN has been graciously pleased to give orders for the following appointment:-

Her Majesty The Queen of The Netherlands as Colonel-in-Chief The Royal Sussex Regiment.

"London Gazette" **Tuesday September 8th 1953**

The QUEEN has been graciously pleased to confer the award of The Territorial Efficiency Decoration upon the following officers:—

Mjr. (Hon. Lt.-Col.) Donald Thomas Davis, (87619)
The following Officers are awarded the Efficiency Medal (Territorial).

Lt. David James Ablett, (229639)

Wednesday September 16th 1953

Dutch Honour for Sussex Colonel

Her Majesty the Queen of the Netherlands has bestowed the honour of a Commander in the Hulsorde Van Orange, on Brigadier T.F.V. Foster, C.B.E., M.C., Colonel of the Royal Sussex Regiment, who headed a deputation from the Regiment which Her Majesty received at Soestdjokj Palace on September 16th, 1953. In connection with her appointment as Colonel-in-Chief of the Regiment. The Netherlands Ambassador, Mr. D. U. Stikker, conferred the decoration on Brigadier Foster at the Netherlands Embassy in the presence of the Dutch Service Attaché.

"London Gazette" Friday September 25th 1953

The following officers are awarded the Long Service and Good Conduct Medal (Military) without gratuity. (The date of qualification is shown in brackets):—
Lt. (now Hon. Capt.) Basil Walter Herbert Wyard (183337)
(20th Dec. 1940).

"London Gazette" Saturday November 3rd 1953

The QUEEN has been graciously pleased to confer the award of the Army Emergency Reserve Decoration upon the following officers:—

Major Noel Harold Ormerod, (75939)
(now Maj. Reg. Comm.)

"London Gazette" Friday November 20th 1953

The QUEEN has been graciously pleased to confer the award of the 2nd Clasp to the Territorial Efficiency Decoration upon the following officers: —

Capt. (Hon. Maj.) Rex Anthony E. Hillman, T.D. (2717) (Rtd.)

"London Gazette" Saturday December 1st 1953

The Queen has been graciously pleased to confer the award of Army Emergency Reserve Decoration on the following officers :-
Captain John George Cook Macpherson, (76278) (Major Reg. Comm)

"London Gazette" Saturday December 8th 1953

The QUEEN has been graciously pleased to approve the following awards in recognition of gallant and distinguished services in Korea during the period 1st January to 30th June, 1953: —

M.M.

No. 22549787 Corporal Michael Montague Garrett,   1st Bn.   (attd. 1st Bn. Royal Fusiliers.)

Corporal Garrett, a 20 year old N.C.O., has been in 'D' Company throughout the time the battalion has been in Korea. He has at all times shown himself utterly reliable and always ready and eager to undertake any task however dangerous. He has volunteered for every patrol his platoon has been detailed to carry out and his platoon commander has had, in fact, to ensure that he is only given his fair share, although his keenness and efficiency have always made him an extremely valuable patrol number.

On the night of 8/9 April 1953, Corporal Garrett commanded a standing patrol of three men which occupied a position on a spur about 300 yards in front of the forward platoon of D Company. Early in the night enemy movement was heard to a flank and Corporal Garrett, deciding that he was likely to be cut off, moved his patrol to another position from where he passed back continuous information to his platoon commander and at the same time directed mortar fire on to the area where the movement was occurring. He then moved his standing patrol back to its original position. Throughout this time Corporal Garrett's cool and efficient handling of his patrol were a fine example of leadership and initiative.

On the night of 31 May, 1953, Corporal Garrett succeeded in establishing a standing patrol on a feature to the West of the Hook position, in spite of the fact that efforts to establish this patrol the two previous nights had been unsuccessful, since any movement brought down heavy enemy mortar fire. Shortly after taking up his position the Company on the Hook behind the patrol was heavily mortared. Corporal Garrett quickly located the enemy mortar but was unable to direct counter mortar fire due to an intervening hill. Although sounds of enemy movement had been heard in the vicinity of the patrol, Corporal Garrett with complete disregard for his own safety, moved forward to the next hill from where he coolly and skilfully directed fire until the enemy mortar was silenced.

In these two actions he displayed leadership, determination and skill far beyond his rank and years. At all times during the period Corporal Garrett has displayed unfailing courage and devotion to duty and the example he has set has earned him the admiration and respect of all ranks who have served with him.

"In these two actions he displayed leadership, determination and skill far beyond his rank and years. At all times, Corporal Garrett has displayed unfailing courage and devotion to duty and the example he has set has earned him the admiration and respect of all ranks who have served with him."

Tuesday December 11th 1953

Corporal wins M.M. for Korea Actions

The award was announced last night of the Military Medal to 20 year old Corporal Michael Montague Garrett, The Royal Sussex Regiment, of 3, Dolphin Terrace, Shoreham, for serving in Korea. The citation refers to Corporal Garrett's courage in operations with patrols he commanded on the nights April 8 and May 31 this year. In both actions he directed mortar at the enemy.

"In these actions he displayed leadership, determination and skill far beyond his rank and years, says the citation.

"At all times….. Corporal Garrett has displayed unfailing courage and devotion to duty and the example he has set has earned him the admiration and respect of all ranks who have served with him.."

Corporal Garrett, who was born in Brighton, joined the Army as a regular in February, 1951. After service in the Canal Zone he volunteered for Korea. When he last wrote to his parents he was stationed in Kure, Japan. He hopes to return home in October, 1954.

Was Injured

When he was seven he was seriously injured by an unknown substance after picking up a container on the Downs. He spent three years in hospital, but completely recovered. Before joining the Army he worked for Messrs. Beves and Co.'s timber yard in Shoreham. He was a sergeant in the Cadets.

He has been wounded in Korea.

Mrs. Garrett said last night : "We are very proud of him. We did not know he had won a medal. He has not said anything about the action." She showed a reporter a musical box which she has received from her son last week, commenting : "He is the best son in the world."

"London Gazette" Friday January 1st 1954

The QUEEN has been graciously pleased to approve the award of the British Empire Medal (Military Division) to the undermentioned : —

B.E.M. (Military Division)

No. 6398414 C.Q.M.S. Leonard George Marchant, S.A.S.C. Late Royal Sussex 1931-41

C.Q.M.S. Marchant joined the Royal Sussex Regiment in February 1934 and transferred to the Small Arms School Corps. In August 1941 on the 6th August 1949 he joined the Proof and Experimental Establishment, Pendline, as C.Q.M.S. and has shown outstanding ability in performance of his duties. Owing to the complex nature of the Inter Service Unit his work has entailed the maintenance of ledgers etc. which are normally the duty of an R.Q.M.S.

He has also handled personnel of all services and civilians to the best advantage under difficult conditions.

In matters to do with the Establishment out of working hours he has greatly benefited the people living on the estate by his activities in connection with entertainments and general well-being of Pendline. He is well known at Bisley as an expert shot and is an all-round sportsman.

He is a fine type of man whose devotion to duty and sterling character has set an example to all personnel at Pendline.

Friday 30th April 1954

Queen Elizabeth The Queen Mother presented new colours to the 1st Battalion, The Royal Sussex Regiment (the 35th Foot), on the cricket ground at Arundel Castle on Saturday. She had travelled by road from Badminton on Friday and spent the night at Arundel Castle as the guest of the Duke and Duchess of Norfolk.

After receiving a royal salute, she inspected the battalion, accompanied by Lieutenant-General Sir Lashmer Whistler, K.B.E.,C.B.,D.S.O., colonel of the regiment, and Lieutenant-Colonel J.B. Ashworth, commanding officer. Then followed the trooping of the old colours, presented in 1928 by the Duke of Gloucester, and as they were borne off the band played *Auld Lang Syne*.

Before presentation of the new colours, carried by Lieutenant D.A.G. Blaxter, which are of hand-embroidered silk and took four months to make at a cost of £200, they were consecrated by the Assistant Chaplain-General, the Rev. K.A. Puntan, O.B.E. In her address to the battalion the Queen Mother referred to the fine tradition of the regiment. She had a special word for the members of the Sussex Home Guard who were on parade.

Among those present at the ceremony were the Duke and Duchess of Norfolk, Brigadier-General C.F. Pahud de Mortagnes, representing Queen Juliana of the Netherlands, who is the colonel-in-chief of the regiment, and Colonel P.T.A. Goosens, Netherlands Military Attaché.

In the afternoon the battalion returned to the cricket field to receive the Freedom of the borough of Arundel from the Mayor, Ald. A.G. Whittaker. After the ceremony, the battalion marched through the flag-decked streets of the town with fixed bayonets.

On Sunday the old colours of the 2nd Battalion (the 107th Foot) were laid up in St. George's Chapel, Chichester Cathedral. These were the colours which the 2nd Battalion had from 1926 until its amalgamation with the 1st Battalion two years ago.

The old colours of the 1st Battalion will be taken later this year to Gibraltar and laid up there. The first battle honour of the regiment, formed in 1701, was Gibraltar, 1704-5, and it is felt that the laying-up of the colours there will cement the link between Gibraltar and Sussex.

Monday May 3rd 1954

M.S.M.

Air Commodore G.B. Dacre pins the Meritorious Service Medal on R.S.M. F.H. Nash, of 7th Cadet Battalion, The Royal Sussex Regiment. He got it in recognition of his service in the regular Army. R.S.M. Nash is the battalion's A.A.I.

Saturday May 8th 1954

Order of the House of Orange

At Tidworth, on 8th May, the following were invested in the classes of the Order shown, by Her Majesty Queen Juliana, Colonel-in-Chief, The Royal Sussex Regiment :

Grand Officer

Lieutenant-General Sir Lashmer Gordon Whistler, K.B.E.,C.B.,D.S.O.

Officer

Lieutenant-Colonel John Blackwood Ashworth, D.S.O.
Lieutenant-Colonel John Lionel Chapman, O.B.E.
Major Richard Gordon Harrison Stanton,

Chevalier First Class

Captain Nigel Bedingfield Knocker,

Gold Medal of Honour

R.S.M. Ronald George Lucas, (436174)

"London Gazette" Friday June 4th 1954

The QUEEN has been graciously pleased to confer the award of the "Territorial Efficiency Decoration" upon the following Officers: —
Mjr. Peter McGennis Bulwer, (186171)
(later Lt-Col. In R.S.R.)

"London Gazette" Friday June 11th 1954

The QUEEN has been graciously pleased to confer the award of the Cadet Forces Medal upon the following officers:—

Sussex

A/Lt.- Col. Henry C. Burchett

The QUEEN has been graciously (pleased to confer the award of the Cadet Forces Medal upon the following former officers of the Cadet Forces: -

Sussex

Hon. Maj. Charles Percival Basil Shippham (283149) Retired

"London Gazette" Tuesday July 20th 1954

The QUEEN has been graciously pleased to confer the award of the "Territorial Efficiency Decoration" upon the following Officers: —

Mjr. George Joseph Langridge, (184768)

"London Gazette" Friday October 1st 1954

The following officers are awarded the Long Service and Good Conduct Medal (Military) without gratuity. (The date of the qualification is shown in brackets.)

Capt. (QM) Stanley John Omar Mowbray, (279165)
(3rd Nov. 1943)

Monday October 25th 1954

Royal Sussex Colours Laid Up

From our correspondent Oct. 24.

The colours of the 1st Battalion, The Royal Sussex Regiment, which bear the battle honour *"Gibraltar, 1704/5"* were ceremoniously laid up in the historic King's Chapel here this evening joining the colours of four other regiments which took part in the capture or subsequent siege of Gibraltar. Before today's service the colours were paraded under the old walls of the fortress, marched up the main street of the city, and saluted for the last time outside the chapel. The Governor of Gibraltar was present at the service and the lesson was read by Lieutenant-Colonel Sir Lashmar Whistler, G.O.C. Western Command, who is Colonel of The Royal Sussex Regiment.
The scheme under which the King's Chapel has become the shrine of units of her majesty's armed forces who took part in the capture and subsequent defence of Gibraltar was initiated nearly seven years ago by the then Governor, General Sir Kenneth Anderson. Colours previously laid up are those of the Grenadier and Coldstream Guards, the Royal Northumberland Fusiliers (Fighting Fifth), and the Plymouth Division, Royal Marines.

"London Gazette" Tuesday October 26th 1954

The QUEEN has been graciously pleased to approve the award of the British Empire Medal (Military Division), in recognition of distinguished services in Malaya during the period 1st January to 30th June, 1954:—

B.E.M. (Military Division)

No. 6397816 Sergeant William Abel Redford, The Royal Sussex Regiment
(attached The Queen's Royal Regiment (West Surrey)

Sergeant Redford has continued to be quite outstanding in the performance of his duties since his last citation. For six years as Regimental Provost Sergeant he has held a position of great responsibility and trust, and never once has he fallen below the very highest standard. Due in large measure to his example and efforts, a very high standard of discipline has been achieved in the Battalion, and he commands a degree of respect and popularity which are quite unusual. Since arriving in Malaya, in particular, he has made it his business that young soldiers are prevented in getting into trouble under conditions strange to them; in this his success has been exceptional. As he draws to the end of his long service with the Army his influence for good attains its maximum, and he remains a quite outstanding example of a smart, loyal and efficient Non Commissioned Officer.

The QUEEN has been, graciously pleased to confer the award of the Territorial Efficiency Decoration upon the following officers :—

Capt. Lewis Bernard Haines, (197285)

"London Gazette" Saturday January 1st 1955

The QUEEN has been graciously pleased to give orders for the following promotions in, and appointments to, the Most Honourable Order of the Bath: —

To be Ordinary Members of the Military Division of the second Class, or Knights Commanders of the said Most Honourable Order :—

K.C.B.

Lieutenant-General Sir Lashmer Gordon Whistler, K.B.E., CB., D.S.O. (13017), late Infantry (Colonel, The Royal Sussex Regiment).

"London Gazette" Friday April 29th 1955

The QUEEN has been graciously pleased to confer the award of the "Territorial Efficiency Decoration" upon the following Officers: —

Lt. Ivor Malcolm Austin, M.C. (71265)

"London Gazette" Tuesday May 31st 1955

QUEEN has been graciously pleased to approve that the following be Mentioned in recognition of distinguished service in Malaya during the period 1st July to 31st December, 1954:—

M.I.D.

Major John Humphrey Woodrow, (77647) 1st Bn.
Lieutenant Robert John Morris, (422279) 1st Bn.

"London Gazette" Thursday June 9th 1955

The QUEEN has been graciously pleased, on the occasion of the Celebration of Her Majesty's Birthday, to give orders for the following promotions in, and appointments to, the Most Excellent Order of the British Empire:—

M.B.E. (Military Division)

Major Harold Edward Roy Watson, (153264) 1st Bn.

Major Watson has been responsible for the preparation of 'Q' policy Directives and Instructions affecting all Commands at Home and overseas. In addition he has had special responsibility for all major policy matters affecting N.A.A.F.I., and for sponsoring N.A.A.F.I. matters in the War Office. Owing to pressure of other work on his immediate superiors he has worked to a large extent without direct or close supervision and has handled matters that would normally have been undertaken by a first grade staff officer. His responsibilities in connection with N.A.A.F.I. have been exceptionally onerous owing to problems that have arisen in connection with redeployment in MELF and reduction and withdrawals respectively of the garrisons in Korea and Trieste, as well as the operations in progress in Malaya and East Africa.

The quality of his work much of which had had to be undertaken outside of official working hours has been exceptionally high. In particular the General Manager of N.A.A.F.I. Major-General Sir Randle Feildon, has written specially to the War Office, drawing attention to the exceptionally high standard of work performed by Major Watson in his duties on N.A.A.F.I.'s behalf.

The QUEEN has been graciously pleased, on the occasion of the Celebration of Her Majesty's Birthday, to approve the award of the British Empire Medal (Civil Division) to the undermentioned:-

B.E.M. (Civil Division)

Frank Henry Nash, Regimental Sergeant Major, Cadet Battalion, Royal Sussex Regiment. (Chichester, Sussex.) *(Citation not found)*

"London Gazette" Tuesday June 28th 1955

The following Officers are awarded the Efficiency Medal (Territorial).

Lt. Clive E. Woodbridge, (94365)

"London Gazette" Friday August 12th 1955

The following Officers are awarded the Efficiency Medal (Territorial).

Lt. (Hon. Capt.) William Burdon Gillott, (124223)

"London Gazette" Friday September 2nd 1955

The QUEEN has been graciously pleased to confer the award of the "Territorial Efficiency Decoration" upon the following Officers: —

Lt. (Hon. Capt.) Andrew Leonard Pitman, (73738)

The QUEEN has been graciously pleased to confer the award of the 1st Clasp to the "Territorial Efficiency Decoration" upon the following Officers: —

Lt. (Hon. Capt.) A.L. Pitman, (73738)

"London Gazette" Tuesday October 25th 1955

The QUEEN has been graciously pleased to confer the award of the "Territorial Efficiency Decoration" upon the following Officers: —

Capt. John Ivan Warren Walton, (73348)

"London Gazette" Friday November 18th 1955

The following Officers are awarded the Efficiency Medal (Territorial).

Capt. (Hon. Mjr.) George Albert McGowan, (137324)

"London Gazette" Tuesday April 10th 1956

The following officers are awarded the Cadet Forces Medal:-

A/Capt. Arthur George Barber, (332598)

"London Gazette" Tuesday May 1st 1956

The QUEEN has been graciously pleased to confer the award of the "Territorial Efficiency Decoration" upon the following Officers: —

Lt. (Hon. Capt.) St. John George Auguste Sechiari, (91765) (Rtd.)

"London Gazette" Thursday May 31st 1956

The QUEEN has been graciously pleased, on the occasion of the Celebration of Her Majesty's Birthday, to give orders for the following promotions in, and appointments to, the Most Excellent Order of the British Empire: —

O.B.E. (Military Division)

Major John Bedford Arthur Glennie, D.S.O. (63600) 1st Bn.

This officer has been responsible for the work involved in the preparation, control and subsequent analysis of some six major outdoor and indoor exercises. In each case the intentions of the Director- The General Officer Commanding – were fully carried out. As a result a large part of the Army – both Regular and Territorial has received sound, interesting and realistic tactical training. In addition this officer's branch has been responsible for the coordination of the successful C.C.P. and A.C.F. camps in this command and for the Command pre-Staff College Courses which have been of such assistance in raising the standard of candidates.

His personal share in this has been a large one. He has added to his marked professional qualities an extremely conscientious devotion to the task in hand, and unswerving determination to overcome all obstacles and infectious enthusiasm. The high standard thus set has been an example to all those whom he has worked and evoked a cooperation without which the successful training of many thousands of individuals and a number of formations would not have been possible.

1956-57 Korea (Peace-keeping Force)

From July 1956 to September 1957, The Royal Sussex served under the auspices of the United Nations in Korea, and were the last British Regiment to leave. As the Battalion's tour of duty came to a close, two events took place which clearly showed how successful its stay had been. First, the Commanding Officer was summoned to report to the Commander-in-Chief U.S. Forces in Korea who informed him that the President of the United States had awarded him the Distinguished Service Medal for the outstanding contribution the Battalion had made to the United Nations Forces during its stay in Korea. He added, with profound regret, that the award had been 'disallowed' by the British Foreign Office. Then later the 21st (Gimlet) Infantry Regiment paraded, complete with Tank Company, its three Battalions and Regimental Staff with its Regimental Commander who insisted on Colonel Sleeman inspecting the Regiment and taking its farewell salute at a march past. In his closing remarks, the Regimental Commander conveyed the gratitude to the 1st Royal Sussex for their co-operation and friendship during their stay with his Regiment. On the 27th July the Battalion embarked at Inchon in H.T. *Asturias* to the sound of the U.S. Army Band, bound for Gibraltar.

"London Gazette" Friday July 27th 1956

The following officers are awarded the Cadet Forces Medal:—

Sussex

A/Capt. Herbert Frank Williams   (340445)

"London Gazette" Tuesday July 31st 1956

The following Officers are awarded the Efficiency Medal (Territorial).

A/Capt. Herbert Frank Williams, (340445)

"London Gazette" Friday November 30th 1956

The following officers are awarded the Cadet Forces Medal:-

A/Capt. Arthur Frank Masterman, (344253)

"London Gazette" Tuesday January 1st 1957

The QUEEN has been graciously pleased to give orders for the following promotions in, and appointments to, the Most Honorable Order of the Bath: —

G.C.B.

Lieutenant-General Sir Lashmer Gordon Whistler, K.C.B.,K.B.E.,C.B,D.S.O.,DL.   (13017)

"London Gazette" Tuesday January 15th 1957

The QUEEN has been graciously pleased to confer the award of the 1st Clasp to the "Territorial Efficiency Decoration" upon the following Officers: —

Mjr. Peter McGennis Bulwer, (186171)

"London Gazette" Tuesday May 14th 1957

The QUEEN has been graciously pleased to confer the award of the "Territorial Efficiency Decoration" upon the following Officers: —

Capt. (Hon. Mjr.) Charles Patrick Maule Hunting, (75878) (now T.A.R.O.)

"London Gazette" Friday May 24th 1957

The following officers are awarded the Cadet Forces Medal:-

A/Mjr. Dennis Archer Smith, (351026)

"London Gazette" Tuesday July 30th 1957

The following Officers are awarded the Efficiency Medal (Territorial).

Lt. (Hon. Capt.) Percy Robert William Carter, (295665)

"London Gazette" Tuesday November 12th 1957

The QUEEN has been graciously pleased to confer the award of the "Territorial Efficiency Decoration" upon the following Officers: —

Capt. Denis Horace Hoad, (354551)
Capt. (Hon. Mjr.) O.R. Stevenson, (68730) (Rtd.)

The QUEEN has been graciously pleased to confer the award of the 1st Clasp to the "Territorial Efficiency Decoration" upon the following Officers:-

Capt. (Hon. Mjr.) O.R. Stevenson, (68730) (Rtd.)

"London Gazette" Friday November 22nd 1957

The following Officers are awarded the Efficiency Medal (Territorial).

Lt. (Hon. Mjr.) Edward Cuthbert May, (148958)

Sussex

The following officers are awarded the Cadet Forces Medal:-

A/Capt. Frederick William Eaves, (351604)

"London Gazette" Wednesday January 1st 1958

The QUEEN has been, graciously pleased, on the advice of Her Majesty's Ghana Ministers, to give orders for the following promotion in, and appointments to, the Most Excellent Order of the British Empire: —

O.B.E.

Major (T/Lt-Col.) Benjamin Dalton, (105089) 1st Bn.
On loan to the Government of Ghana.
(Citation not found)

"London Gazette" Friday 10th January 1958

The QUEEN has been graciously pleased to confer the award of the 2nd Clasp to the "Territorial Efficiency Decoration" upon the following Officers: —

Lt.-Col. Alfred Eric Percival Bridge, T.D. (24420) (Rtd.)

"London Gazette" Friday January 31st 1958

The following officers are awarded the Cadet Forces Medal:—

Sussex

A/Capt. Reginald Charles Edward Allen, (404265)

"London Gazette" Tuesday March 18th 1958

The following Officers have qualified and. Are recommended for the award of the 2nd Clasp to the Territorial Efficiency Decoration:—

Maj. (Hon. Lt.-Col.) Christopher Francis Ashburner Nix, T.D. 4/5th Bn. (3151771) (now T.A.R.O.)
The following Officers have qualified and are recommended for the award of the 1st Clasp to the Territorial Efficiency Decoration:—

Maj. (Hon. Lt.-Col.) Christopher Francis Ashburner Nix, T.D. 4/5th Bn. (3151771) (now T.A.R.O.)

"London Gazette" Thursday June 12th 1958

The QUEEN has been graciously pleased, on the occasion of the Celebration of Her Majesty's Birthday, to give orders for the following promotions in, and appointments to, the Most Excellent Order of the British Empire: —

C.B.E. (Military Division)

Brigadier-General Claude Hector Tarver, D.S.O.   (380334)

Brigadier-General Tarver brought to this senior Intelligence appointment a wealth of experience and knowledge which he has unsparingly applied, with tact and skill. Both in the office and with outside contacts of which he has may. He has taken a lot of trouble to get to know the foreign Military Attaches and to win their confidence, thus achieving excellent results. He continues to devote a great deal of extra time and effort to a detailed study of the Intelligence organisation in the War Office, and in Whitehall, and has shown where economies can be made without serious loss of output. He has achieved a continuing improvement in the quality of the work and has made and continues to make, an outstanding contribution to the Intelligence field.

O.B.E. (Military Division)

Lieutenant-Colonel Peter Michael Jermyn Harrison, M.C. (3517) 4/5th Bn. (T.A.)

Lieutenant-Colonel Harrison was commissioned into The Royal Sussex Regiment from RMC Sandhurst in 1937. He served at various Regimental and Staff appointments during the last war and was awarded the M.C. for gallantry during the fighting in the Western Desert.

In August 1949 Lieutenant-Colonel Harrison resigned his commission as a Regular Officer, chiefly because it was found that one of his children was medically unfit to live in overseas stations. Immediately however, he joined the T.A. as a Temporary Major and thus made available to it the wide experience and knowledge he had acquired during his service throughout the world in peace and war. This knowledge and experience proved invaluable to his new unit and he was of the greatest assistance to his Commanding Office in the training of both National Service soldiers and Territorial Volunteers.

On 1 June 1956 Lieutenant-Colonel Harrison was appointed to command his unit, 4/5th Battalion The Royal Sussex Regiment (T.A.) Since when he has devoted himself tirelessly to the well-being and efficiency of the Battalion. He spends several evenings each week visiting his Companies and also gives most of his weekends to training or other military activities. In fact it appears at times he must be neglecting his business and family affairs in the interests of the T.A. He maintains an excellent liaison with his local Civil Authority and is a great help to them in organising joint military and Civil Defence training exercises. He also finds time to give valuable and extensive assistance to many Cadet Units in Sussex.

Lieutenant-Colonel Harrison's efforts have produced the results to be expected, he is respected by his Battalion, it is happy and efficient, and its recruiting intake for volunteers is already amongst the highest in the Division, and are continuing to rise. It is strongly recommended that because of his outstanding service and personal example be rewarded by his appointment to the Officer of the British Empire.

Roussillon Gazette

Quebec Day Saturday September 13th 1958

General Sir Lashmar Gordon Whistler, G.C.B.,K.B.E.,D.S.O. presented the Meritorious Service Medal to Colour-Sergeant (Drum Major) Frederick James B. Powell in the Sergeants Mess at the Roussillon Barracks in Chichester.

"London Gazette" Friday September 19th 1958

The QUEEN has been graciously pleased to confer the award of the Territorial Efficiency Decoration upon the following officers:-

Capt. Kenneth Patrick Bent, (58541) (now T.A.R.O.).

"London Gazette" Tuesday September 30th 1958

The following officers are awarded the Cadet Forces Medal:-

Berkshire

A/Capt. Francis William Seymour Stanbrook, M.C. (249251) (formerly 9th Bn. R.S.R.)

Sussex

Lt. Edward George Hart, (430542)

Wednesday October 1st 1958

Queen Juliana of the Netherlands graciously received in audience at Soestdjijk Palace, the Colonel of the Regiment, Lieutenant-Colonels J.B.A. Glennie, D.S.O.,O.B.E. and P.M.J. Harrison, O.B.E.,M.C., Major P.S. Newton, M.B.E., and R.S.M. D. Houghton. At the commencement of the audience she invested Lieutenant-Colonels Glennie and Harrison and Major Newton with the insignia of Officers of the Order of the House of Orange, and R.S.M. Houghton with the Gold Medal of the same order. Lieutenant-Colonel R.B. de F. Sleeman, O.B.E.,M.C., was also honoured with the insignia of an Officer of the Order of the House of Orange in his absence.

Order of the House of Orange

Officer

Lieutenant-Colonel John Bedford Arthur Glennie, D.S.O.,O.B.E.
Lieutenant-Colonel Peter Michael Jermyn Harrison, O.B.E.,M.C.
Lieutenant-Colonel Richard Brian de Fontenne Sleeman, O.B.E.,M.C.
Major Philip Newton, M.B.E.

Gold Medal

R.S.M. Dennis George Houghton, (6405069)

"London Gazette" Thursday January 1st 1959

The QUEEN has been graciously pleased to give orders for the following promotions in, and appointments to, the Most Excellent Order of the British Empire:-

To be Ordinary Members of the Military Division of the said Most Excellent Order:-

No. 6391134 Warrant Officer Class II William George Alce, The Royal Sussex Regiment, Territorial Army.

Service in the 4/5th (Cinque Ports) Bn. Period covered 1947-1958.

WO (ORQMS) Alce joined the Regular Army (Royal Sussex Regiment) in December 1919. In January 1936, after 17 years' service, he was appointed RSM of this Battalion as a Regular Soldier. Continuing in this appointment on the outbreak of war he saw service with the B.E.F., returned to England and helped to reform the Battalion. Proceeding with the unit to the Middle East he remained with the Battalion throughout the Alamein operations until being appointed RSM of GHQ Middle East Land Forces in 1944

He was discharged from the Regular Army in 1945, and immediately the Territorial Army was reformed in 1947 he enlisted in this Battalion and was appointed Orderly Room Sergeant in the rank of WO11. He has served in this appointment continuously since that date.

Due to his prior experience in the Territorial Army and this Battalion his help in re-establishing it as a volunteer unit was quite outstanding. He was well known to many pre-war members and he was instrumental in obtaining them as volunteers.

With the introduction of National Service he became responsible for the documentation of more than 1500 National Servicemen who have passed into the unit to date. During this time he has served under five Adjutants, and it is entirely due to his selfless loyalty and application to duty that the Documentation Inspection reports of the unit have invariably been never less than good, with several "excellent" "above average" and "very high standard" gradings.

In order to achieve this standard and quite regardless of his own personal interests he has attended at least 500 drills each year and every week-end when required.
He plays a noteworthy part in all social and sporting activities in the unit. He is an active member of the Rifle Club and for the last three years has won major prizes in the Battalion Rifle Meetings. Unaided he voluntarily carries out statistical duties at the Sussex County Rifle Association Services Meetings.

In all his activities he plays an outstanding part in the life of the Battalion, is an example to all ranks, and typifies to a high degree all that is the very best in service life.

London Gazette" **Friday July 17th 1959**

The following Officers are awarded the Long Service and Good Conduct Medal (Military) without Gratuity.
(The date of qualification is shown in brackets):

Capt. (Q.M.) Ronald George Lucas, (436174)
(14th July 1957)

"London Gazette" **Tuesday July 28th 1959**

The following officers are awarded the Cadet Forces Medal:-

Sussex

A/Mjr. John Harold Germain Parsons, (182850)

"London Gazette" **Tuesday March 29th 1960**

The following officers are awarded the Efficiency Medal (Territorial):-

Lt. (now Mjr.) Jack Thomas Walker, (203372)
(now Reg. Commn.).

"London Gazette" Tuesday May 17th 1960

The QUEEN has been graciously pleased to conifer the award of the Territorial Efficiency Decoration upon the following officers:-

Capt. (A/Mjr.) Bryan Morrison Barron, (387069).

"London Gazette" Saturday June 11th 1960

The QUEEN has been graciously pleased, on the occasion of the Celebration of Her Majesty's Birthday, to give orders for the following promotion in, and appointments to, the Most Excellent Order of the British Empire:-

M.B.E. (Military Division)

Major Douglas Arthur Banks, (375571) 1st Bn.
On loan to the Government of the Federation of Malaya. (Citation not found)

"London Gazette" Friday July 15th 1960

The QUEEN has been graciously pleased to confer the award of the Territorial Efficiency Decoration upon the following officers:-

Capt. Michael Hatton James, (341908)

"London Gazette" Friday September 16th 1960

The QUEEN has been graciously pleased to confer the award of the Territorial Efficiency Decoration upon the following officers:-

Mjr. Richard Frederick George Shaw, (352068)

Capt. (Hon. Mjr.) John Walton Gooddy, (78487)
(now T.A.R.O.).

"London Gazette" Friday November 29th 1960

The following officers are awarded the Efficiency Medal (Territorial):-
A/Capt. David Wilson Freeman Bradshaw, (389351)

"London Gazette" Thursday December 31st 1960

The QUEEN has been graciously pleased to give orders for the following promotions in, and appointments to, the Most Excellent Order of the British Empire:

M.B.E.

Captain (Q/M) Robert Edward Grainger, (438724) 17th Bn. Parachute Regiment (T.A.) (9 D.L.I.)

Captain Grainger joined The Royal Sussex Regiment as a Boy in 1927. He served in India for nine years, returning to England in 1936. He went overseas with the B.E.F. in 1939, as a sergeant in the same regiment, and was evacuated through Dunkirk in 1940.

He served in the Middle East and took part in the Battle of Alamein. He transferred to the Parachute Regiment in 1942 in the rank of C.S.M. He served at Taranto and in North Africa, with the 10th Battalion. His war time service ended with the operations at Arnhem as a C.S.M. in 10 Para, for which he was awarded the American Bronze Star. He became R.S.M. of 2 Para in 1945, and served in Palestine. He became Quarter master of 3 Para in 1954 and served in Cyprus and at Suez.

In 1958 he was appointed Quartermaster of 17 Para (T.A.) (9 D.L.I.). The Battalion is located in Felling, Newcastle, Gateshead, Hartlepool and Stockton. At the time of his appointment, an indifferent standard of administration existed. Now, the present high standard of administrative efficiency achieved by his department is a direct result of the enthusiasm, skill, judgement and sheer hard work with which he has applied himself to his job during the past two years. The fact that staff is short and limited to specific hours did not deter him. It merely encouraged him to work longer hours himself.

It can be said without hesitation that the efficiency and general well-being of the Battalion can to a considerable extent be attributed to the efforts of Captain Grainger. During recent months he has had to bear alone a most serious domestic worry. His courageous approach to this problem and his refusal to allow personal preoccupations to interfere in any way with his duty have inspired the limited number who know the circumstances he faces.

For example, the unit has just completed an annual camp, the success of which largely depended on resourceful and imaginative quarter mastering. He was an outstandingly success. This was to be expected but it is particularly noteworthy when one considers his own personal difficulties. He has served for 33 years in the Regular Army, never failing to maintain the highest standard. He much richly deserves the award of the M.B.E. for which he is strongly recommended.
(M.I.D. 20th September 1945)

"London Gazette" **Tuesday March 14th 1961**

The QUEEN has been graciously pleased to confer the award of the Territorial Efficiency Decoration upon the following officers :-

Mjr. John Roy Harding, (402745)

"London Gazette" **Tuesday March 28th 1961**

The following officers are awarded the Cadet Forces Medal:-

A/Capt. Cecil Arthur Vidler, (395420)

"London Gazette" **Friday May 26th 1961**

The following officers are awarded the Cadet Forces Medal:-

Sussex

A/Mjr. Arthur Victor Patrick Wye (395763)

"London Gazette" Friday July 28th 1961

The following officers are awarded the Cadet Forces Medal:-

Sussex

A/Capt. Stanley Albert Beattie, (395778)
A/Capt. Francis Herbert Medcalf, (275024)

"London Gazette" Tuesday September 19th 1961

The QUEEN has been graciously pleased to approve the award of the Military Cross to the undermentioned -:

M.C. (Congo)

2nd Lieutenant David William Durrant Peatfield, (467042) The Royal Sussex Regiment serving with Ghana forces in the Congo.

2/Lieut. Peatfield was serving with the 2nd Battalion The Ghana Regiment of Infantry which formed part of the United Nations Forces in the Congo. He was the leading platoon commander of a company which was ambushed at about 10 p.m. on the night of the 28th April, 1961. The resulting action continued for an hour during which they were subjected to intense rifle, machine-gun and mortar fire. Displaying great devotion to duty and gallantry, Peatfield led his men and personally assisted in the removal of road blocks.

In the confusion which reigned while the convoy moved slowly through the ambush some men who had taken cover by the roadside were left behind. Lieut. Peatfield bravely went back, despite sporadic enemy fire, and got them out of danger. His courage and leadership inspired the troops and contributed greatly to the successful way in which the company fought through the ambush.

"London Gazette" Tuesday October 27th 1961

The following Officers are awarded the Long Service and Good Conduct Medal (Military) without Gratuity.

(The date of qualification is shown in brackets):-

Lt. (Q.M) Leonard Frederick Smitherman, (463506)
(2nd July 1961)

"London Gazette" Friday November 17th 1961

The QUEEN has been graciously pleased to confer the award of the Territorial Efficiency Decoration upon the following officers:-

Capt. Harry Malcolm MacNicol, (362080)

"London Gazette" Monday January 1st 1962

The QUEEN has been graciously pleased to give orders for the following promotions in, and appointments to, the Most Excellent Order of the British Empire:-

C.B.E. (Military Division)

Brigadier John Blackwood Ashworth, D.S.O. (47519)

Brigadier Ashworth has been Director of Military Training since June 1959. During this period progress towards an All Regular Army has brought about great changes in the Training Organisation and these have posed many problems for the Training Staff in the war Office. The detailed investigation and solution to many of these problems has fallen to Brigadier Ashworth, who has applied himself to the task with the greatest energy and enthusiasm. He has throughout set a fine example to the whole Directorate, and his sound judgement has been invaluable.

Amongst the major problems with which he has been particularly concerned are the introduction of the new syllabus at Sandhurst, extensive developments at the Royal Military College of science, and improvements in recruit training. In addition, Brigadier Ashworth has given unstintingly of his time and effort to further the Adventure training and assistance to the National Youth Organisations, while he has also taken almost entirely upon himself the task of furthering Civil defence training in both the regular and Territorial Armies.

To all these activities Brigadier Ashworth has devoted himself untiringly without any thought of personal convenience. For over two years he has shouldered a very large share of the reporting for the detailed work in connection with training of the Army. He has needed little direction and on his own initiative has made an outstanding contribution.

His loyalty, dependability and trusted advice have been of the greatest help to successive Director Generals of Military training. His work in this particular appointment and throughout a long and distinguished career both in Command and on the Staff is highly deserving of recognition.

O.B.E. (Military Division)

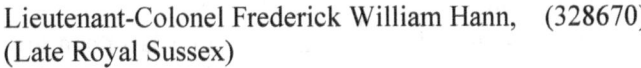

Lieutenant-Colonel Frederick William Hann, (328670)
(Late Royal Sussex)

Background

After Boys Service and 14 years' service in the ranks of The Royal Sussex Regiment, he was given an Emergency Commission in 1942 and subsequently a Regular (Q/M) Commission.

In 1957 he joined the Duke of York's Royal Military School as Adjutant and Quartermaster. In this appointment his duties are threefold; As adjutant as Q/M and as Messing Officer; in fact he virtually carried the administrative work of the school on his own shoulders. The widening of the school curriculum and the increase in its out-of-school activities have thrown an ever increasing burden on him, which he has always accepted with outstanding willingness and efficiency.

In 1959 owing to the temporary loss of the Executive Officer from the Establishment he had to undertake further duties. The load was then more than any one man could undertake but he strove so gallantly and cheerfully working long hours for seven days a week that nobody realised the strain he was bearing until he suffered a partial breakdown in health.

Since his recovery he has continued and still continues to carry out his work with exceptional zeal and efficiency and never spares himself. In addition to his official duties, he takes great trouble to foster good relations with the Old Boys of the school. His house is almost a free hotel for Old Boys visiting the school and the happy relations existing between the school and the Old Boys Association are largely due to him.

A man so loyal and devoted to duty does not exist. His own outstanding service over the past 4 years much deserves recognition.

M.B.E. (Military Division)(Congo)

Captain John Michael Howlett Johnson, (421201) 1st Bn.
On loan to the Government of Ghana

This officer has acted as Adjutant to the Ghanaian Commanding Officer as first appointment as a Commanding Officer. He has always shown the utmost tact, a great capacity for hard work and considerable patience. He has welded the young officers together into a fine team and due to him the relationship between Ghanaian and British has been consistently good in the battalion. A young man of the very highest integrity who has never spared himself, either in Ghana or in the Congo. It has been largely due to his efforts that the standard of discipline and efficiency of the 1st Bn. Ghana Regiment has been consistently high.

The QUEEN has been graciously pleased to approve the award of the British Empire Medal (Military Division) to the undermentioned :-

B.E.M. (Military Division)

No. 6402157 Sergeant Walter Stanley John Smith, 1st Bn.
(Unit Pay Sergeant)

Sergeant Smith has served the Royal Sussex Regiment and his Corps. exceptionally well and loyally during his 22 years' service.

In particular, during the last five years he has created a record for saving, both at the Depot of The Royal Sussex Regiment where he served for four years and for a year in the 1st Bn. which was unequalled in the British Army.

Through his own personal enthusiasm and leadership he ensured during 1938/39 at the Depot that 100% of the records, both Regular and National Servicemen opened a Post Office Savings account whilst under training and by 1959 he had converted all the permanent staff as well. It is a tribute to his enthusiasm for the National cause which he fostered with such outstanding results, that the last member of the permanent staff to be converted was the C.Q.M.S. who had 33 years' service and was within a year of retirement. He has conducted this self-appointed campaign in this battalion, where many of the soldiers had come from other Depots and succeeded in raising the percentage of personnel serving to 80%.

He practiced what he preached and he also set the highest standards of integrity and loyalty throughout his service. His cheerful and robust figure is now sadly missing from the battalion as he has left on completion of his service but the effects of his good work will remain as a target for the future.
(G.O.C. Commendation for Brave Conduct in Suez 1952)

Saturday April 14th 1962

Her Majesty Queen Juliana of the Netherlands, Colonel-in-Chief of the Royal Sussex Regiment, presented General Sir L.G. Whistler, G.C.B,.K.C.B.,K.B.E.,CB,DSO, Colonel of the Regiment, with the Knight Grand Cross of the Order of the House of Orange.

"London Gazette" Saturday June 2nd 1962

The QUEEN has been graciously pleased, on the occasion of the Celebration of Her Majesty's Birthday, to give orders for the following appointments to the Most Excellent Order of the British Empire:-

O.B.E.(Military)

Lieutenant-Colonel Robert de Lisle King, (67150) 1st Bn.
On loan to the Government of the Federation of Malaya
(Citation not found)

The QUEEN has been graciously pleased, on the occasion of the Celebration of Her Majesty's Birthday, to approve the award of the British Empire Medal (Military Division to the undermentioned:-

B.E.M. (Military Division)

No. 22221010 Colour-Sergeant Ronald Cullen, 1st Bn.

He has done exceptionally well as Drum-Major during the last 10 years and especially during the last 2 years in Northern Ireland and Sussex, where he has become a character of renown, due particularly to his great height, fine bearing and magnificent handling of his Mace. This was very evident at the World Football Match in Belfast between Northern Ireland and Greece, where he and the Band and Drums left the ground to prolonged cheers at the conclusion of their engagement in Ulster. He has been in the Battalion and Northern Ireland this year including Trooping the Queen's Colour on H.M. Birthday the 260th Anniversary Parade in Belfast, Trooping the Regimental Colours and the Ceremony of receiving the freedom of Belfast. In all these his own performance at the front of the parade has produced admiring cheers.

He has undoubtedly brought further renown and reputation to his Regiment which he has served with such loyalty and sense of devotion to duty during so many years and he has done a great deal towards producing the good publicity required for recruiting in the Army. Almost the first question asked by spectators prior to a parade is always, "Have you still got that wonderful Drum-Major?"

This is testimony enough of the goodwill and reputation which he has created by his presence and hard work.

"London Gazette" Tuesday September 18th 1962

The QUEEN has been graciously .pleased to confer the award of the 2nd Clasp to the Territorial Efficiency Decoration upon- the following officers:-

Lt.-Col. Peter McGennis Bulwer, T.D. (186171)

"London Gazette" Friday November 16th 1962

The QUEEN has been graciously pleased to confer the award of the 1st Clasp to the Territorial Efficiency Decoration upon the following officers:-

Lt-Col. George Joseph Langridge, T.D. (184768)

"London Gazette" Tuesday March 19th 1963

CANCELLATION

The Efficiency Medal (Territorial)

The *London Gazette* Supplement No. 39546 of 23rd May 1952

INFANTRY

Royal Sussex Regiment

Lt. John Alan Turner, (240479) (now Capt. R.A.).

"London Gazette" Friday May 31st 1963

The Queen is graciously pleased to award the following in recognition of gallant and distinguished services in Brunei:-

M.I.D.

Lieutenant David Cuthbert McNeill, (459297) 1st Bn.

"London Gazette" Saturday June 8th 1963

The QUEEN has been graciously pleased, on the occasion of the Celebration of Her Majesty's Birthday, to give orders for the following promotions in, and appointments to, the Most Excellent Order of the British Empire:-

C.B.E. (Military Division) (Brunei)

Brigadier-General John Belford Arthur Glennie, D.S.O., O.B.E. (63600)

Brigadier Glennie was holding the appointment of Brigadier-General Staff, G.H.Q. when the rebellion broke out in Brunei on the 8th December 1962. He was appointed, without any notice to take command of the joint Naval, Army and Airforce in the course of being despatched to Borneo Territories. He left on the 9th December with an improvised headquarters and a force assigned from a variety of different sources. He arrived when the situation was very obscure and the Civilian Government and administration had broken down. He had to take the initiative and responsibility for operations to restore the situation.

It was under Brigadier Glennie's leadership and direction that the units of the Force established control in Brunei town, relieved Limborg, Kuala Belait, Lewas, Tutong and Muara; and brought about the end of the offensive phase of the revolt.

It was Brigadier Glennie who set in motion the rapid follow up of the security forces, coordinating his own force with what remained of the local Police forces, to cut off and mop up the rebels. This was an essential measure for the future peace of the territories and it was Brigadier Glennie's skilful appreciation, leadership and drive which led to the successful launching of this second phase of the operations.

During the campaign Brigadier Glennie had under his command the equivalent of six major Army units and substantial Naval and Air forces. Throughout he exercised responsibility far exceeding and appropriate to his rank as Brigadier.

During his period in command, Brigadier Glennie has displayed outstanding ability, judgement and leadership. It is largely through his skilful handling of the exceptionally difficult situation that the revolt was brought quickly under control.

"London Gazette" **Thursday September 19th 1963**

The following officers are awarded the Cadet Forces Medal:-

Sussex

Lt (A/Capt.) Ernest Ronald Wood, (395904)

November 1963

Order of the House of Orange

Officer

Lt-Colonel Douglas Challenor Snowdon, T.D. (73947)

"London Gazette" **Friday January 17th 1964**

The QUEEN has been graciously pleased to confer the award of the 1st Clasp to the Territorial Efficiency Decoration upon the following officers:-

Maj. Denis Harold Hoad, T.D. (354551)

"London Gazette" **Tuesday January 28th 1964**

The following officers are awarded the Cadet Forces Medal:-

Sussex

Lt. (A/Capt.) Francis Henry Freeman, (446085)

"London Gazette" **Friday November 27th 1964**

The following officers are awarded the Cadet Forces Medal:-

Sussex

Lt. (A/Mjr.) Kenneth Bryant, (311878)

"London Gazette" Friday January 1st 1965

The QUEEN has been graciously pleased to give orders for the following promotions in, and appointments to, the Most Excellent Order of the British Empire:-

C.B.E. (Military Division)

Colonel Robert de Lisle King, O.B.E. (67150) 1st Bn.

For determination, steadfastness and unremitting devotion to duty as Garrison Commander, British Guiana since 6 December 1963. During this time Colonel King's leadership of this garrison has never faltered and with a small staff he has competed to the very best of his ability with the manifold problems of operations, reinforcements and logistics arising from the current emergency in the Colony. The calm, steady and resolute behaviour of the British soldier in support of the Civil Power in British Guiana and the morale and temper of the Garrison after months of strain are much to this officer's credit.

The Governor of British Guiana has commented as follows :-

"2/. I would be very happy to support a recommendation for Colonel R. de Lisle King for an award in the New Year Honours List of 1965. I can readily endorse the citation as regards the period of my governorship since 7 March 1964.

3/. In addition to the qualities and achievements of Colonel King, which are mentioned in your citation it has been particularly helpful to the task in British Guiana, that Colonel King is an excellent "team" officer. His cooperation with me and, I believe with the Commissioner of Police, has been of a high order."

Brigadier Robert Eric Loder, (52600)

Brigadier Loder was commissioned into The Royal Sussex Regiment in 1931 and is to be retired early in 1965 after 34 years' service.
Prior to the last war he served in India, Australia and the United Kingdom. In 1940 he was captured in France and was a prisoner of war for five years, but despite this great handicap Brigadier Loder was quick to rehabilitate himself and passed through Staff College within a year.
Since then he has served in various command and staff appointments at Home and abroad; he was Head of the Commonwealth Liaison Mission in Korea in 1961/2.
As Deputy Commander 43 (Wessex) Division/District he has frequently had responsibilities in excess of those normally expected of an officer of his rank and has discharged these with enthusiasm, loyalty and efficiency. As Commander of Gloucester and Somerset Sub District, he has been outstandingly successful in command and has taken much trouble and time to establish excellent relations with the many civilian organisations and bodies with whom he has dealings in the counties concerned.
During the last two years he has been responsible for the most successful military displays in the Bristol and Taunton Army Weeks, which have been of considerable benefit to the Army. Brigadier Loder has devoted his life unselfishly and unquestionably to the Army and to his country throughout his service.

O.B.E. (Military Division)

Lieutenant-Colonel James Roy Anderson, (153258) 1st Bn.

By the end of April 1971 Brigadier Anderson will have completed over six years service in Kenya in the last decade. He served with the 3rd Bn. King's African Rifles 1961-63. He was put in command of 11th Bn. King's African Rifles after its mutiny in 1964 and he reorganised and retrained it to become 1st Bn. Kenya Rifles. From April 1967 – May 1969 he was Chief of Staff to the Kenyan Armed Forces under Major-General Penfeld. In June 1969 he became Commander of the three British Training Teams. It is principally on his performance in the last appointment that I comment here, though he did an excellent job as Chief of Staff, and it was largely because of this that all concerned wanted him in his present post.

Anderson is a outspoken forthright soldier but with charm an tact and throughout his Kenyan service he has been respected – particularly by African officers, for his honesty and fairness. He has their complete confidence and understands them as well as any European can hope to.

Nothing in Africa runs smoothly or to plan. Idleness, inertia and inefficiency bedevil the government and the Armed Forces. The fact that the three Training Teams have functioned well, without major snags and, most important, without apparently ruffling Kenyan feathers is largely due to Anderson's tactful hand on the reins and a quick eye to spot trouble before it occurs.

His relationship with Major-General Ndelo, Kenya's Chief of Defence Staff, is personal and close. The emergence of Ndelo from the background of being a Regimental Sergeant Major to be coming a much respected Major-General of considerable stature owes much to Anderson's sound advice, close friendship and moral support.

In addition to commanding the Training Teams and advising the Armed Forces, Anderson had frequently been brought into Cabinet – level meetings and has been asked to produce policy papers on a number of matters which would not be normally considered soldier's business. All these things he has taken in his stride with unfailing good humour and efficiency.

That he will be sadly missed by the Kenyans is unquestioned. I too will miss his reliable and well-reasoned advice. I believe that his contribution to both Kenyan and British interests have been great. As the above remarks make clear Anderson has done much more than his job description suggest, and he has never limited himself to the normal call of duty.

"London Gazette" **Tuesday March 16th 1965**

The QUEEN has been graciously pleased to confer the award of the Territorial Efficiency Decoration upon the following officers:-

Mjr. Michael Anthony George Roberts, (436234)
Capt. (A/Mjr.) Eldred David Englebright Wakefield, (416296)

Saturday April 3rd 1965

Sussex men cheer for a change in Aden

There was a cheer from hundreds of Sussex men last week. They were soldiers of the 1st battalion The Royal Sussex Regiment in Malta, and the happy incident occurred when they were told on a special parade that they were to have a change of scenery by a short spell in Aden.
The battalion will move this month to relieve a squadron of the Royal Air Force regiment for six months. There was more cheering when the commanding officer, Lieutenant-Colonel D.C. Snowdon, stated that

they had been authorised to wear royal blue hosetops. Previously when wearing shorts the soldier had to wear plain khaki hosetops, so in future the battalion will present a rather more colourful spectacle. At the moment the battalion is busy carrying out the various types of training that will suit the conditions found in Aden. The advance party will be moving out to Aden very soon, and the main body of the battalion will follow towards the end of the month.

Friday April 30th 1965

On the occasion of her Birthday at the Soestdjijk Palace, Queen Juliana of the Netherlands graciously bestowed upon the following Officers and Warrant Officers the Order of the House of Orange.

Order of the House of Orange

Commander

Brigadier John Blackwood Ashworth, C.B.E., D.S.O.

Officer

Lieutenant-Colonel Jack Thomas Walker,
Lieutenant-Colonel David E.C. Russell,

Gold Medal

R.S.M. F. Webb, 1st Bn.
O.R.Q.M.S. W.G. Alce, 4/5th Bn. (T.A.)

Friday June 11th 1965

Royal Sussex men on security work in Aden

The 1st Battalion, The Royal Sussex Regiment, who moved from Malta to Aden in April for a six month tour, to relieve a squadron of the R.A.F. Regiment, have been joined by officers and men of the Territorial Army Emergency Reserve – the Ever Readies.
All companies will receive a number of ever readies, who will work alongside regular soldiers in all departments of the battalion.
The battalion are engaged on patrolling, guarding, and searching duties in the Aden area, and "B" Company recently found a quantity of arms and ammunition hidden in a village. Each company will take it in turns to go 'up country' to Mukeiras for a fortnight, and there will take part in a type of soldering totally different from the internal security work they are more used to in Aden.
Mukeiras, on top of a 7,000ft. plateau, is a camp 100 miles North of Aden and five miles south of the Yemen border, and the climate there is cool and invigorating, in contrast to that which the battalion have been accustomed. The camp is shared by a British infantry company and a detachment of the Federal Regular Army.
Recent V.I.P.'s visiting the battalion in Aden have included, on different occasions, the Chief of Staff Designate, Field Marshal Sir Richard Hull, and the Commander-in-Chief, Lieutenant-General Sir Charles Harington. Each watched the work in connection with internal security.

"London Gazette" Saturday June 12th 1965

The QUEEN has been graciously pleased, on the occasion of the Celebration of Her .Majesty's Birthday, to give orders for the following promotions in, and appointments to, the Most
Excellent Order of the British Empire :-

M.B.E. (Military Division)

Major Stanbrook is a dedicated A.C.F. Officer, whose services over the past nineteen years have been outstanding. These services include detachment commander, area commander and his present appointment as County Training Officer. In addition to his normal duties he has planned and organised several successful adventure expeditions in the Welsh Mountains and Dartmoor.

His sense of duty can be measured by an incident some years ago when he was seriously injured in a motor accident with cadets. The War Office restricted his activities during convalescence to sedentary duties only, but in order to overcome this restriction he volunteered to arrange his own insurance cover during cadet training.

Major Stanbrook is prominent in Berkshire County Youth Work, where his services are particularly sought in connection with the Duke of Edinburgh's Award. Major Stanbrook was awarded the M.C. in Burma. This in itself makes him a subject of admiration. He couples with this distinction a quiet and unassuming nature together with a courtesy, efficiency and selflessness which attract the highest admiration and respect from officers and cadets alike.

Major Stanbrook well deserves such an award and it would be very much appreciated by every person not only in the A.C.F. but by all connected with the service of youth in this county.

Friday June 18th 1965

Sussex Ever Readies are in the Sun

Flown from England to trouble spot

Unsung and unheralded a group of Sussex men have made history in the past two or three weeks. They have been whisked away from the changing conditions of an English summer to the searing heat of an Arabian desert.

The men are from local Territorial army units and were among a group known as the Ever Readies. They were recently flown out from this country to join the 1st Battalion The Royal Sussex Regiment who recently left Malta for duty in the Aden trouble spot.

About 35 men have gone from various units in Sussex and they are among a total of about 175 who were called up from the Home Counties Brigade, which covers Kent and Sussex.

Extra Bounty

The Ever Readies are Territorial soldiers who agree to accept a condition to be sent anywhere at any time, subject to their serving a maximum of six months in any one year.

For this they receive an additional bounty of £150 a year, plus a £50 extra allowance when they are actually called.

Among those who went are five from "D" Company 4/5th Battalion R.S.R. (T.A.) whose headquarters are at the new T.A. Centre in North Street, Lewes.

Local Men

They are: Sergeant Derek Bickmore, a postman, of Uckfield, Corporal Ken Flint, a cartographer for SeeBoard, of Lewes, Corporal Tony Cruttenden, a postman, of Uckfield, Corporal Tony Bennett, a shop owner, of Eastbourne, and Corporal Ray Packham, a brewers drayman, of Brighton.

The first news of the men is now getting back home and Major Dennis Hoad, O.C. of "D" Company said the men were engaged chiefly on security and guard duties at the Battalion's base just outside

Aden. They went off after a short spell at the brigade depot in Aden.
They are doing foot and motor patrols, and were engaged in cordon and search work in suspected areas. Corporal Flint is on signal work.

Tented camp

Major Hoad said: "They are certainly fully committed out there and conditions are not all that good. They are in a tented camp in the desert, where the temperature goes up to 110 degrees. They sleep in tents, with concrete bases.

"From reports we have received they seem to be enjoying themselves and the Regulars have been impressed by the high standard of training attained by the men."

First-hand information of the "guinea pigs" came from the new P.S.I. at the Lewes headquarters, Colour-Sergeant Ted Courtredge, who was with the 1st Battalion and put the Ever Readies through their first week of training and acclimatisation.

4/5th Bn. The Royal Sussex Regiment (T.A.) in action

Friday July 7th 1965

Lieutenant J.J. Smith, 'A' Coy, led a patrol "up-country" with T.A.E.R. and Regulars of the 1st Battalion The Royal Sussex Regiment, that laid a successful ambush on a patrol of dissident tribesmen. They killed four of the dissidents (and recovered two bodies) and wounded four others. A private of the Buff's T.A. was slightly wounded and was airlifted to Steamer Point Hospital. For this action Lieutenant Smith has been awarded the Military Cross.

Saturday August 21st 1965

A British infantry battalion – the 1st Battalion, Coldstream Guards – is to be moved temporarily from the Rhine Army to replace a battalion in Aden. The members of the battalion will serve for six months in Aden before returning to Iserlohn. They are to replace The Royal Sussex in October, when the latter complete a six month tour in Aden and return to Malta. The Royal Sussex, normally a two company battalion, have had attached to them a company of "Ever Readies" from the Territorial Army Emergency Reserve while they have been in Aden.

There are four British infantry battalions in Aden, among them the 2nd Battalion, Coldstream Guards, which has one company in Mauritius and which will be replaced towards the end of the year by the Welsh Guards. Duties for the four battalions are divided between mounting internal security guards in Aden itself and keeping watch on the frontier, where they combine operations with the battalions of the Federal Regular Army.

Wednesday October 25th 1965

Fighting Ever Readies back from Aden

Britain's first serving ever Readies returned home yesterday. Fifty-five men who had served in Aden since May landed at Gatwick and were paid off at their Canterbury depot. After seven days' leave they will be back in civilian jobs. The formal title is Territorial Army Emergency Reserve. It was founded two years ago. The men agree to serve in any trouble spot for six months in support of the Regular Army.

The only officer, Major Michael Roberts, 34, of Goldstone Crescent, Hove, is a city insurance assessor. The other men include fitters, draughtsmen, office workers, labourers and gardeners.

Twice wounded

Some, including Pte. Cyril Barrett, 23, milk roundsman, of Hounslow, who as twice wounded, are willing to serve again. Pte. Barrett was wounded by dissident tribesmen when on patrol in an Aden suburb. "I would go back if the wife would let me." He said.

Other views were held by Pte. David Clark, 23, of Montague Road, Hendon, a buyer. "I would not have missed the experience," he said. "It gave most of us who had never done National Service a chance to go out and see the world. But once is enough. It was really pretty rough and I certainly wouldn't want to go back to Aden."

World war veteran

The oldest soldier was Cpl. Ken Flint, 41, draughtsman, of Priory street, Lewes, Sussex, who served in the Second World War. He would go again if permitted. "I just like soldering," he said. The men are entitled to a bounty of £150, but many had already received much of this. The average pay received yesterday was about £100.

Pte A. Bedford, 35, scaffolder, of East Hill, Wandsworth, who drew the highest bounty of £137 10s 0d, has a baby son he had never seen.

The men had been serving with the 1st Battalion The Royal Sussex Regiment in Aden. By Friday 114 Ever Readies will have returned from Aden. Another 60 are due back before Christmas from Aden, Cyprus and Borneo.

Saturday October 30th 1965

Successful peace-keeping work in Aden

Eastbourne men figure in the return of the 1st Battalion The Royal Sussex Regiment, to Malta after six months' peace-keeping duty in Aden. Another is among the "Ever Readies" who have returned home after helping the battalion there.

Major-General J.E.F. Willoughby, General Officer Commanding Middle East Land Forces, visited the battalion to wish the men farewell, and among those to whom he spoke was Colour Sergeant Ron Avery, of 145 Ringwood Road, Eastbourne.

"You have done a wonderful job," he told them. "You arrived in Aden when it was at its hottest, politically as well as climatically. You leave it as the weather cools and, thanks to you, as tension eases."

The battalion was brought up to strength in Aden by the mobilisation of over 100 Territorial Army Emergency reservists, the "Ever Readies", who, leaving their jobs, their families and homes have worked with the regulars in a successful peace-keeping role in the Middle eastern trouble spot.

One of the Army's many jobs in Aden is to prevent hostile tribesmen, or "dissidents", from smuggling arms across the boundary between Aden Protectorate and the Yemen – the armed groups which are claiming land within the protectorate.

Mountain bases

For much of the time they were engaged in observation work in the Radfan Mountains, where the Army had mountain top bases with the homely sounding code names of "Hotel 10", "Monksfield" and "Piccadilly". At other times as support patrols at El Mahala where the Army is building a main road to Dala.

Thursday January 21st 1966

G.O.C.'s Commendation for Bravery (Aden)

The Commander-in-Chief Commends

For exemplary conduct, beyond the normal call of duty, at Mansura, Aden State on night 12/13 August 1965 and directs that an appropriate entry be made in his record of service.

Aden
Date 21 Jan 1966

No. 23228618 Corporal Anthony J. Cruttenden, 4/5th Bn. (Cinque Ports T.A.) The Royal Sussex Regiment,

"London Gazette" Tuesday January 25th 1966

The Queen has been graciously pleased to approve the undermentioned award for gallantry in Aden :-

M.C.

Lieutenant Joseph James Smith, (468118) 5th Bn. The Middlesex Regiment, (Duke of Cambridge's Own) T.A. serving with The Royal Sussex Regiment,

On 6th July 1965, Lieutenant Smith, who was commanding the Piccadilly picquet, manned by 3 Platoon, A Company 1 Royal Sussex Regiment, led an ambush patrol towards the top of the steep rise known as Ludgate Hill.
The ambush was in fact sited to intercept dissidents moving along the track leading to the Wadi Taim, however at 2120 hours a small party of dissidents were observed past the ambush positions. Lieutenant Smith quietly redeployed his ambush and opened fire on the party of dissidents at a range of about 75 yards. Two of the dissidents were seen to fall whilst the remainder scattered and returned the fire of the patrol wounding one of its members.
Lieutenant Smith then called for Artillery fire on the path of retreat of the dissidents. He himself rendered first aid to the wounded soldier and withdrew his patrol to Piccadilly. He then ordered periodic harassing fire to be brought down on the area of the attack to prevent the dissidents recovering the bodies.
At 0600 hours the next morning he took his patrol back to the scene of the ambush where he recovered two dead Arabs. It subsequently transpired that four dissidents were killed and two wounded.
It is considered that Lieutenant Smith, a Territorial Army Emergency Reserve Officer, who had only recently joined his battalion displayed outstanding courage and skill in the circumstances that would have tested a more experienced Officer.

"London Gazette" Friday January 28th 1966

The following offices are awarded the Cadet Forces medal:-

Sussex

2nd Lt. Leslie Avon Whitlam, (471868)

"London Gazette" Wednesday March 16th 1966

The QUEEN has been graciously pleased to confer the award of the Territorial Efficiency Decoration upon the following officers:-

Capt. (A/Mjr.) Derek Charles Carter, (424067)

Monday June 8th 1966

Order of the House of Orange

Officer

Lieutenant-Colonel John Buckeridge,
Lieutenant-Colonel Edward Gerald Hollist, (Retired)

Gold Medal

R.S.M. R. Pace,

"London Gazette" Saturday June 11th 1966

THE QUEEN has been graciously pleased, on the occasion of the Celebration of Her Majesty's Birthday, to give orders for the following promotions in, and appointments to, the Most Excellent Order of the British Empire:-

M.B.E. (Military Division)

T/Captain Roger James Lester Sherrin, (467631) 1st Bn. attd. Royal Brunei Malay Regiment, *(Citation not found)*

"London Gazette" Friday June 17th 1966

TERRITORIAL ARMY

The Right Honourable Sir Robert MENZIES, K.T., P.C., C.H., Q.C., F.R.S., LL.M., LL.D., D.C.L., D.Sc., is appointed Honorary Colonel, 4th/5th Battalion (Cinque Ports) Royal Sussex Regiment (T.A.), 1st June 1966, in an existing vacancy.

"London Gazette" Friday July 15th 1966

The QUEEN has been graciously pleased to confer the award of the Territorial Efficiency Decoration upon the following officers:-

Home Counties Brigade

Royal Sussex

Mjr. Michael William Howard Buckingham, (435886)

"London Gazette" Friday July 29th 1966

The following officers are awarded the Cadet Forces Medal:-

Sussex

Lt. Thomas Joseph Garside, (360027)

Thursday December 29th 1966

The Royal Sussex March Out

As the old year gives way to the new, the Army will "ring out" The Royal Sussex Regiment and ring in the 3rd Battalion, The Queen's Regiment (Royal Sussex). The change will take place at a brief vesting ceremony at Howe Barracks, Canterbury, on Saturday (11.30). After an eventful history going back to 1701, The Royal Sussex is being merged with three other regiments of the Home Counties Brigade to form a new large regiment, The Queen's Regiment.
Queen Juliana of the Netherlands will retain her link with The Royal Sussex by becoming an "Allied Colonel-in-Chief." Princess Marina, Duchess of Kent becomes Colonel-in Chief of the new large regiment. Neither will be able to attend Saturday's ceremony, and the salute will be taken by the Colonel of the Regiment, Lieutenant-General Sir Richard Craddock. Last Post will be sounded as the Home Counties Brigade flag is lowered and Reveille as the flag of The Queen's Regiment is raised.

Saturday December 31st 1966

Death and Birth

A Fanfare sounded at Howe Barracks, Canterbury, today to mark the passing of four infantry regiments, steeped in tradition, including The Royal Sussex Regiment. Down from their mastheads for the last time came the four regimental standards, to be replaced a few moments later by the standard of the new Queen's Regiment.
The Royal Sussex Regiment has combined with the Queen's Surrey Regiment, the Queen's Own Buffs, Royal Kent Regiment and the Middlesex Regiment, with Princess Marina, Duchess of Kent, as Colonel-in Chief.
The Queen, in a message, said that she felt sure that the new regiment would be worthy of the traditions of all the regiments from which it had been formed. The Royal Sussex in the new set-up, will become the Third Battalion, Queen's Regiment (Royal Sussex). Queen Juliana of the Netherlands, formerly Colonel-in-Chief of The Royal Sussex Regiment, will be the battalion's Allied Colonel.
Lieutenant-Colonel John Buckeridge of The Royal Sussex Regiment commanded the parade and a contingent from the Regiment was led by Captain Mark Tarver. Taking the salute, along with Lieutenant-General Sir Richard Craddock, Colonel of the new regiment, was Brigadier J.B. Ashworth, Deputy-Colonel of the Third Battalion (Royal Sussex).

SUPPLEMENT TO THE LONDON GAZETTE, 3RD JANUARY 1967

INFANTRY

The Queens Regiment

REGULAR ARMY

By virtue of the provisions of the Royal Warrant dated 6th November 1966 (published in Army Order 62 of 1966 all officers of the Land Forces belonging to The Queen's Royal Surrey Regiment (2nd, 31st and 70th), The Queen's Own Buffs. The Royal Kent Regiment (3rd, 50th and 97th), The Royal Sussex Regiment (35th and 107th) and The Middlesex Regiment (Duke of Cambridge's Own) (57th and 77th) are transferred to The Queen's Regiment with effect from 31st December 1965.
The undermentioned Officers relinquish their appointments, 31st Dec. 1966 on re-organisation of the Home Counties Brigade:-

Lt.-Gen. Sir Richard Craddock, K.B.E.,C.B.,D.S.O., Deputy Col., The Queen's Own Buffs, The Royal Kent Regiment
Maj.-Gen. F. J. C. Piggott, C.B.,C.B.E.,D.S.O., Col., The Queen's Royal Surrey Regiment
Brig. J. B. Ashworth, C.B.E.,D.S.O., Colonel, The Royal Sussex Regiment
Maj.-Gen. C. M. M. Man, O.B.E.,M.C., Col., The Middlesex Regiment

Lt.-Gen. Sir Richard Craddock, K.B.E.,C.B.,D.S.O., is appointed Col., The Queen's Regiment

31st Dec. 1966, on formation

The undermentioned Officers. are appointed Deputy Cols., The Queen's Regiment, 31st Dec. 1966, on formation:-

Maj.-Gen. F. J. C. Piggott, C.B.,C.B.E.,D.S.O., Deputy Col. The Queen's Regiment (Queen's Surreys)
Maj.-Gen. C. H. Tarver, C.B.,C.B.E.,D.S.O. Deputy Col. The Queen's Regiment (Queen's Own Buffs)
Brig. J. B. Ashworth, C.B.E.,D.S.O., Deputy Col. The Queen's Regiment (Royal Sussex)
Maj.-Gen. C. M. M. Man, O.B.E.,M.C., Deputy Col. The Queen's Regiment (Middlesex)

"London Gazette" **January 3rd 1967**

The QUEEN has been graciously pleased to give orders for the appointments of :-

Her Majesty The QUEEN OF THE NETHERLANDS as Allied Colonel-in-Chief, The Queen's Regiment (Royal Sussex), 31st Dec. 1966.

Monday March 6th 1967

Royal Sussex Colours Laid Up

Another chapter in the history of The Royal Sussex Regiment was written at Chichester Cathedral when the colours of the 4th/5th (Cinque Ports) Battalion (T.A.) were laid up in the St. George's Chapel.
The Duke of Norfolk, Lord Lieutenant of the county and a former officer in The Royal Sussex, led the worship.
A handful of men in the huge congregation were in his company at Dunkirk. A larger number were at El Alamein and in the Western Desert. A few veterans were at Loos, the Marne, the Somme....

Led by a Royal Engineers (T.A.) band, the battalion marched through Chichester carrying the regimental and Queen's colours. The Mayor (Cr. Harry Bell) took the salute in front of the city council's headquarters.

Extra seats were brought into accommodate the congregation who came from all over Sussex and listened to the Dean (the Very Rev. Walter Hussey) trace the history of the Sussex Volunteers and of The Royal Sussex Regiment (T.A.).

History

The colours being laid up, he said, defined the period in the history from 1908 to 1967, less than the span of a man's life and yet a period which had seen two world wars.
"They were wars which brought such terrible suffering and loss that we can only pray and work that they will never be repeated."
War divided peoples' minds in a special way. It was horrible and far-reaching in its effects on those who fought in it, perhaps became futile in its consequences.
At the same time it produced splendid acts of courage and unselfish devotion to duty for which we could not be entirely ungrateful.
"We would wish that such standards might be shown in the days of peace," said the dean.
The dean said the Volunteers were raised by William Pitt as a defence against threatened invasion by Napoleon. Later in 1859, in view of the threat by Napoleon 111, they were organised throughout Sussex and affiliated to The Royal Sussex Regiment.

Volunteered

In the South African War, they went overseas for the first time to fight alongside Regular soldiers.

The pattern was repeated in this century, and despite the many changes which had taken place the name "Volunteers" would live on in the Sussex Volunteers of the Queen's Regiment.

Brig. J.B. Ashworth, Deputy Colonel of the Queen's Regiment (Royal Sussex), read the lesson and later he and Lt-Col. J.T. Walker, commanding officer of the 4th/5th Battalion took the colours from the colour party, carried them to the altar rails and handed them to the dean, who laid them on the altar.

The colours were those presented to the regiment by the Duke of Norfolk at Hove in 1960. They replaced the colours of the 4th battalion, laid up in Horsham Parish Church, and of the 5th Battalion, laid up in St. Cement's Church, Hastings.

Footnote: Although the battalion is being disbanded in its present form, it continues in two new reserve battalions, the 5th and 9th Battalions of the Queen's Regiment. The company of the 5th Battalion, which retains the name Cinque Ports, will be based at Hastings.

"London Gazette" Thursday April 6th 1967

INFANTRY
THE QUEEN'S REGIMENT

Honorary Colonels Army Emergency Reserve and Territorial Army

The Rt. Hon. Sir Robert Menzies, K.T., P.C., C.H., Q.C., F.R.S., 5th (Volunteer) Battalion,
The Queen's Regiment.
Maj. The Duke of Norfolk, K.G., P.C., G.C.V.O., 9th (Territorial) Battalion,
The Queen's Regiment (Royal Sussex).

The Soldier

If I should die, think only this of me :
That there's some corner of a foreign field
That is forever England. There shall be
In that rich earth a richer dust concealed ;
A dust whom England bore, shaped, made aware,
Gave, once, her flowers to love, her ways to roam,
A body of England's, breathing English air,
Washed by the rivers, blest by the suns of home.

And think, this heart, all evil shed away,
A pulse in the eternal mind, no less,
Gives somewhere back the thought by England given ;
Her sights and sounds; dreams happy as her day;
And laughter, learnt of friends ; and gentleness,
In hearts at peace, under an English heaven.

Victoria Cross

Queripel L.E. Capt. 10th Bn. Para. Regt. A.A.C.　　　108181　　　Citation　　　Arnhem

Victoria Cross Winner who Died

Lionel Ernest Queripel, V.C. Capt. No. 108181   10th Bn. Para. Regt. A.A.C.
Tuesday, 19th September 1944
Cemetery: Arnhem Oosterbeek War Cemetery, Netherlands
Grave Ref: 5. D. 8.

G.C.B.

Whistler L.G. Lt-Gen. K.C.B.,K.B.E.,CB.,D.S.O.　　　13017　　　N/Y

K.C.B.

Whistler L.G. Lt-Gen. ,CB.,K.B.E.,D.S.O.　　　13017　　　N/Y

K.B.E.

Sleeman J.L. Col. C.B.,CM.G.,C.B.E.,M.V.O.,T.D.　　　527　　　B/H
Whistler L.G. Lt-Gen. CB.,D.S.O.　　　13017　　　N/Y

C.B.

Glasgow A.E. Brig-Gen. C.M.G.,D.S.O.　　　　　　B/H
Sleeman J.L. Col. C.M.G.,C.B.E.,M.,V.O.,T.D.　　　527　　　N/H
Whistler L.G. Mjr.-Gen.　 D.S.O.　　　13017　　　N.W.E.

C.M.G.

Sleeman J.L. Mjr. C.B.E., M.V.O.,T.D.　　　527　　　B/H

C.B.E.

Name	Bn.	No.		Citation	Location
Ashworth J.B. Brig-Gen.	4th Bn.	47519		Citation	Italy
Foster T.V.F. Brig-Gen.	1st Bn.	3175		Citation	M.E.
Glennie J.B.A. Lt-Col. O.B.E.	1st Bn.	63600		Citation	Brunei
Jaques V.H. Col. C.B.E.,M.C.		131287		N/Citation	S.E. Asia
King R. de L. Col. O.B.E.	1st Bn.	67510		Citation	Brit. Guiana
Loder R.E. Brig-Gen.	1st Bn.	52600		Citation	N/Y
Von der Heyde J.L. Brig-Gen. O.B.E., M.C	1st Bn.	31719		Citation	M.E.

D.S.O.

Name	Bn.	No.		Citation	Location
Ashworth J.B. Lt-Co.	4th Bn.	47529		Citation	N/Y
Cox D.H. Lt.	1st Bn.	210789		Citation	Italy
Dalton B. Mjr.	1st Bn.	105089		Citation	Italy
Evans G.C. Mjr. (T/Lt-Col.) D.S.O.	1st Bn.	12895	Bar	Citation	M.E.
Firth C.E.A. Mjr. (T/Lt-Col.)	1st Bn.	24722		Citation	M.E.
Glennie J.B.A. Lt-Col.	1st Bn.	63600		Citation	Italy
James M.S. Brig-Gen. V.C.	2nd Bn.	9531		Citation	Tunisia
Jaques V.H. Col. C.B.E,O.B.E.,M.C.	1st Bn.	131287		N/Citation	S.E. Asia
McCully J.J. Maj. (T/Lt-Col.)	5th Bn.	32030		Citation	M.E.
Morgan F.R.M. Mjr.	5th Bn.	14595		Citation	France
Oliver D.H. Lt-Col.	9th Bn.	36752		Citation	Burma
Thompson R.O.V. Lt-Col.	1st Bn.	30951		Citation	Italy
Whistler L.G. Mjr. (/Lt-Col.)	4th Bn.	13017	& Bars	Citations	France/M.E./Italy

D.S.O Winner Who Died

Robert Oliver Vere Thompson, D.S.O. Lt-Col., No. 30951, Wednesday, 7th June 1944
Cemetery: Rome War Cemetery, Italy
Grave Ref: II. E. 16

O.B.E.

Name	Bn.	Number	Citation	Location
Anderson J.R. Lt-Col.	1st Bn.	153258	Citation	Kenya
Chapman J.L. Mjr	1st Bn.	40032	N/Citation	S.E.Asia
Clayton A.C. T/Col.	1st Bn.	20161	Citation	B/H
Cudlipp H. Lt-Col.	1st Bn.	210790	Citation	Italy
Dalton B. Lt-Col.	1st Bn.	105089	N/Citation	Italy
Dewhurst C.H. T/Lt-Col.	1st Bn.	39037	Citation	Ghana
Glennie J.B.A. Mjr. C.B.E., D.S.O.	1st Bn.	63600	Citation	B/H
Goodwin E.A.H. Lt-Col.	1st Bn.	173471	Citation	Italy
Grant A.J.S. Mjr. T.D.	1st Bn.	23442	N/Citation	N/Y
Harrison P.M.J. Lt-Col. M.C	4/5th Bn.	3517	Citation	Italy
Jaques V.H. Lt-Col. O.B.E.,M.C	1st Bn.	131287	Citation	Italy
King R. de L. Lt-Col.	1st Bn.	67150	Citation	Italy
Odling-Smee A.J. Lt-Col.	4th Bn.	34483	Citation	B/H
Roe T.C.W. Lt-Col. M.B.E.	1st Bn.	121387	Citation	Italy
Sleeman R.B. de F. Mjr. M.C.	1st Bn.	50239	Citation	Burma
Thornton G.E. Lt-Col.	2nd Bn.	13003	Citation	N/Y
Von der Heyde J.L. T/Lt-Col. C.B.E., M.C	1st Bn.	31719	Citation	M.E.
Warren J.R. Mjr. M.C.,T.D.	4th Bn.		N/Citation	B/H

M.B.E.

Name	Bn.	Number	Citation	Location
Alce W.G. O.R.Q.S.M.	1st Bn.	6391134	Citation	B/H
Atkins A.A. Capt.	1st Bn.	130315	Citation	N/W.E.
Atkinson J.B. Capt.		189336	N/C	N/Y
Baker A.E. Lt.	2nd Bn.	240394	Citation	Arnhem
Banks D.A. Mjr.	1st Bn.	375571	N/Citation	B/H
Blackmore H.I. Lt. & QM.	1st Bn	301158	Citation	Italy
Boga H.T. Capt.	1st Bn.	307338	Citation	Italy
Brockless H.N. Capt. & QM.	9th Bn.	6457417	Citation	Burma
Brook C.E. Capt.	1st Bn.	202477	Citation	N/Y
Day F.A. Capt.	1st Bn.	183336	Citation	Q/C
Day J.A. Mjr.	1st Bn.	183335	Citation	Italy
Divall L.F. C.S.M.	1st Bn.	6392311	N/Citation	B/H
Eames J.E. R.S.M.	7th Bn.	5485467	Citation	N.W.E.
Edelshain G. T/Mjr.	9th Bn.	197096	Citation	Burma
Edwards A.P. Capt.	1st Bn.	124222	Citation	M.E.
Farrant R.W. Lt.		181699	Citation	N.W.E.
Fleet H. R.S.M.	1st Bn.	6398914	Citation	M.E.
Grainger R.E. Mjr.		438724	Citation	N/Y
Grattan P.G. Lt.	1st Bn.	362231	N/Citation	Suez
Hadley P.S. Capt. (T/Maj.)	4th Bn.	88627	Citation	B/H
Hanlon P.J. Mjr. & QM.	2nd Bn.	69631	Citation	N/Y
Haselden J.K. Mjr.	1st Bn.	46405	Citation	M.E.
Hill F. R.S/M.		6398407	N/Citation	B/H
Johnson J.M.H. Capt.	1st Bn.	421201	Citation	N/Y
Lee J.V. T/Capt. M.C.		133695	N/Citation	N/Y
Lyons W.F. C.S.M. (A/R.S.M.)	1st Bn.	6395377	Citation	M.E.
Newton P.S. T/Mjr.	1st Bn.	108180	Citation	Suez
Parkinson R.E.H. Lt.	4th Bn.	88370	Citation	France
Peckitt C.R. Mjr.	2nd Bn.	15229	N/Citation	N/Y
Phillips H.F. R.S.M.	1st Bn.	6190062	Citation	Italy
Picton T. Mjr. M.C.			N/Citation	B/H
Roe T.C. Mjr. (T/Lt-Col.)	9th Bn.	121387	Citation	Burma
Samworth R.G. Mjr.	1st Bn.	77409	N/Citation	N/Y
Sevenoaks E.C. Mjr. M.C.	7th Bn.	63782	Citation	France
Sherrin R.L.J. T/Capt.	1st Bn.	467631	N/Citation	B/H
Snell I.E. Mjr.	1st Bn.	219870	N/Citation	Aden
Stanbrook F.W.S. Mjr. M.C.	9th Bn.	249251	Citation	Burma
Stanton J.R.G. Mjr.	1st Bn.	95305	Citation	Q/C
Steer J.S. Mjr. & QM.	2nd Bn.	37526	Citation	Egypt
Watson H.E.R. Mjr.	1st Bn.	153264	Citation	B/H

M.B.E. Winner who Died

Richard Edward Hope Parkinson M.B.E. Capt. No. 88370 4th Bn.
Wednesday 4th November 1942
Cemetery: El Alamein War Cemetery, Egypt
Grave Ref: XX1X. H. 5.

M.C.

Name	Bn.	Number		Theatre	
Alston-Roberts-West R.A. Capt.	1st Bn.	114111		C	Italy
Austin I.M. 2nd Lt.	5th Bn.	71265		C	France
Bapty L. Capt. M.B. R.A.M.C.	1st Bn.	119899		C	Italy
Bidder G.D. 2nd Lt.	1st Bn.	156504		C	M.E.
Borrow G.H. A/Capt.	9th Bn.	228394		C	Burma
Bowmer E.J. Capt. M.B. R.A.M.C.		139727		C	Italy
Budd M.A.J. Capt.	9th Bn.	200854		C	Burma
Burnett G.B. Lt. attd. 9th Bn. R. Fus.		240419		C	Italy
Cash J.M. Mjr.	9th Bn.	174342		C	Burma
Cavalier P.R. Maj.	1stBn.	124221		C	Italy
Chittenden A.R. Lt. attd. 5th Bn. Wilts. Rgt.		278354		C	N.W.E.
Clegg B.B. Capt.	2nd Bn.	226920		C	M.E.
Clegg B.B. Capt. M.C. 10th Para. Regt.	2nd Bn.	226920	Bar	C	N.W.E.
Crawford J.N. Maj. attd. 1/5th Mahratta L/Inf.		98330		C	Italy
Daniels R.A. Lt. attd. 7th Bn. Hants. Rgt.		284757		C	N.W.E.
De Manio J.B. 2nd Lt.	7th Bn.	100313		C	France
Dickson J.J. Maj.	9th Bn.	96192	& Bar	C/C	Burma
Dickson M.J.A. Lt.	1st Bn.	138855		C	Italy
Dixon T. Mjr. attd. 5th Bn. The Buffs.		189367		C	Italy
Edelsten H.A.C. T/Capt. attd. 14th Punjab Regt.	6th Bn.	109220		C	Burma
Firminger F.W. Maj. attd. 2/5th Queens Ryl. Rgt.		265375		C	Italy
Fuller R.J. Lt. (T/Capt.)	5th Bn.	50209		C	N.W.E.
Gaylard D.W. Lt.	1st Bn.	99819		C	M.E.
Genillard C.P. T/Mjr.	1st Bn.	129366		C	Italy
Harrison P.M.J. Capt.	1st Bn.	73141		C	M.E.
Hawkes G.W. Capt.	1st Bn.	129367		C	M.E.
Hodgson G.D. Capt.		78964		C	N.W.E.
Hogben R.D.S. Maj.	9th Bn.	180204		C	Burma
Holden-White H.V. Lt. (T/Capt.)	1st Bn.	162512		C	Oran
Hunt C. Maj.	9th Bn.	148571		C	Burma
Jackson C.H. Capt.	7th Bn.	38234		C	France
Jelley G.M. Capt.	5th Bn.	137222		C	M.E.
Jourdain E.P.R. 2nd Lt.	4th Bn.	79264			France
Jourdain H.J. Maj. attd. 2nd Bn. Monmouth Regt.		165751		C	N.W.E.
Langham	2nd Bn.	38113		C	France
Magrath J.S. Capt.	4th Bn.	42679		C	France
Mordaunt P.M. Capt. Attd. 5th Hants. Rgt.		164690		C	Italy
Peatfield D.W.D. 2nd Lt.	1st Bn.	467042		C	Congo
Phillips F.W. Capt.	1st Bn.	128829		C	M.E.
Pritchard S.E. Capt.	4th Bn.	72201		C	M.E.
Reilly T. Capt. M.B.R.A.M.C.	1st Bn.	114190		C	Italy
Richards D. Lt. (T/Capt.)	5th Bn.	91110		C	M.E.
Roach R.A. Lt.	1st Bn.	324671		C	Italy
Rubie P.H. 2nd Lt	7th Bn.	74658		C	France
Rubie P.H. Capt. T/Mjr. M.C. 49th Recce Regt.		74658	Bar	C	France
Ryshworth-Hill A.G. Capt.	2nd Bn.	76924		C	Italy
Sevenoaks E.C. 2nd Lt.	7th Bn.	63782		C	France
Shinkwin R.E.S. Mjr.	5th Bn.	63601		C	M.E.
Sleeman R.B. de F. Mjr.	2nd Bn.	50239		C	France
Smith F.M. Lt. R.A.M.C.	4th Bn.	110692		C	France
Smith J.J. Lt. 5th Bn. Middx. Rgt. attd.	1st Bn.	468118		C	Aden
Stanbrook F.W.S. Mjr.	9th Bn.	249251		C	Burma
Thomson P.W.B. Lt.	6th Bn.	203059		C	N.W.E.
Turnbull P.E.X. 2nd Lt. (A/Lt.)	4th Bn.	39499		C	France
Upton S.J.F. Capt.	1st Bn.	90925		C	M.E.
Weeks L.W. Lt.	1st Bn.	155698		C	M.E.
Williams R.M. Lt. attd. 4th Ryl Welch Rgt.		187071		C	N.W.E.
Woodruffe W.T. Maj.	6th Bn.	64610		C	France

Military Cross Winners who Died

George Henry Borrow, M.C. Capt., No. 228398 9th Bn.   Friday, 24th March 1944
Cemetery: Arlington National Cemetery, Virginia, U.S.A.
Grave Ref: Sec. 12. Coll. Grave 288

Maurice Arthur Jack Budd, M.C. Major, No. 200854 9th Bn. Friday, 23rd November 1945
Cemetery: Gauhati War Cemetery, India
Grave Ref: 3. E. 2.

Alan Reginald Chittenden, M.C. Lt., No. 278354 Saturday, 5th August 1944
Cemetery: St. Manvieu War Cemetery, Cheux, Calvados, France
Grave Ref: VIII. G. 16.

Murray James Angus Dickson, M.C. Capt., No. 138855 1st Bn. Thursday, 13th July 1944
Cemetery: Arezzo War Cemetery, Italy
Grave Ref: III. D. 14.

Hubert Arthur Christopher Edelsten, M.C. Capt., No. 109220 6th Bn. attd. 4th Bn. 14th Punjab Regt. Wednesday, 5th April 1944
Cemetery: Rangoon Memorial, Myanmar
Grave Ref: Face 14.

Derrick William Gaylard, M.C. Capt., No. 99819 1st Bn. Tuesday, 6th April 1943
Cemetery: Sfax War Cemetery, Tunisia
Grave Ref: VII. E. 20.

Edward Percy Reid Jourdain, M.C. 2ndLt., No. 79264 4th Bn. Saturday, 15th June 1940
Cemetery: Ghent City Cemetery, Ghent, Oost-Vlaanderen, Belgium
Grave Ref: 18. 3. 8.

Lawrence William Weeks, M.C. Capt., No.155698 1st Bn. Tuesday, 22nd February 1944
Cemetery: Cassino War Cemetery, Italy Grave Ref: I. C. 3.

Distinguished Conduct Medal

Bentley T.C. Sgt.	10th Bn. A.A.C.	6400234	Citation	Arnhem
Connell W. C.S.M.	4th Bn.	5669089	Citation	France
Cooke B.H. Sgt.	2nd Bn.	7011496	Citation	Escapee/Germany
Davies B.G. Sgt.	4th Bn.	553755	Citation	M.E.
Hollands D.E. Sgt.	7th Bn.	6397624	Citation	France
Knapp A.C. Sgt.	5th Bn.	1061601	Citation	France
Talmey a. CPL.	1ST Bn.	6397782	Citation	M.E.
Tilling A.. L/Sgt.	7th Bn.	6397485	Citation	Escapee/France

George Medal

Harley R.V. Capt.	1st Bn.	243086	Citation
Talbot S. Pte.	5th Bn.	6409686	Citation
Wood D.E. Cpl.	5th Bn.	6403801	Citation

Military Medal

Name	Rank	Bn	Number		Award	Location
Andrews T.S.	Sgt.	1st Bn.	6403616		C	Italy
Avey S.G.	Pte.	1st Bn.	793925		C	Italy
Binnington R.	L/Cpl.	4th Bn.	4385843		C	Dunkirk
Brennan P.C.	Sgt.	1st Bn.	6396042		C	M.E.
Brockhurst E.E.	Cpl.	1st Bn	14657022		C	Italy
Bryant L.J.	Pte.	1st Bn.	5626378		C	Italy
Bungard J.	Sgt.	1st Bn.	6403983	&Bar	C/C	M.E.
Buss C.	Cpl.	1st Bn	6401944		C	Italy
Cadwallader R.	Sgt.	9th Bn.	6403457		C	Burma
Chapman W.J.	L/Cpl.	1st Bn.	6406678		C	Italy
Clark D.	Pte.	9th Bn.	5351042		C	Burma
Colesby C.A.	Pte.	9th Bn.	14497662		C	Burma
Conetta V.	Pte.	9th Bn.	6418677		C	Burma
Conroy E.	Sgt.	1st Bn.	6391608		C	M.E.
Coppard D.R.G.	Sgt.	1st Bn.	13048241		C	M.E.
Cox J.W.	Pte.	9th Bn.	14517101		C	Burma
Croft H.	Pte.	4th Bn.	6398745		C	Dunkirk
Cunningham J.	Pte.	1st Bn.	6400007		C	M.E.
Davis C.E.	L/Cpl.	9th Bn.	14203602		C	Burma
De Ville S.J.	Cpl.	1st Bn.	6411748		C	East Africa
Eather H.P.	Pte.	1st Bn.	6402963		C	Italy
Eaton E.	Pte..	4th Bn.	6401005		C	M.E.
Felix H.F.	Sgt.	9th Bn.	6407875		C	Burma
Gardner T.A.	Sgt.	1st Bn.	6401368		C	Italy
Garrett M.M.	Cpl.	1st Bn.	22549787		C	Korea
Gentle A.W.	Pte.	9th Bn.	6410995		C	Burma
Glover P.L.	Cpl.	9th Bn.	6405175		C	Burma
Goldsmith E.E.W.	L/Sgt.	1st Bn.	6397316		C	Italy
Goodhall W.H.E.	Pte.	7th Bn.	6398354		C	Dunkirk
Goodsell W.G.E.	Pte.	1st Bn.	6401002		C	Italy
Gould W.G.	Cpl.	1st Bn.	6403958		C	Italy
Govier J.	Pte.	9th Bn.	5391495		C	Burma
Graham L.A.	C.Q.M.S.	9th Bn. A.A.C.	6398348		C	N.W.E.
Greenfield J.	C.S.M.	1st Bn.	6392527		C	M.E.
Hall F.W.	L/Cpl.	1st Bn.	6398463		C	M.E.
Harris A.	Cpl.	9th Bn.	6411142		C	Burma
Herman H.E.	Sgt.	9th Bn.	6209984		C	Burma
Hickman J.H.	L/Cpl.	1st Bn.	6398674		C	M.E.
Hollingdale R.C.	Sgt.	9th Bn.	6407683		C	Burma
Horwood J.R.	Cpl.	1st Bn.	6149840		C	Italy
Ives B.	Pte.	1st Bn.	6398680		C	M.E.
King W.	Pte.	2nd Bn.	6396807		C	M.E.
Leech W.G.	Sgt.	9th Bn.	6411812		N/C	Burma
Luxford H.	Sgt.	1st Bn.	796696		C	Italy
Mack J.N.	Pte.	1st Bn.	6397126		C	Escapee
Mackinlay N.W.	Pte.	1st Bn.	6408272		C	M.E.
Martin G.A.P.	Sgt.	1st Bn.	6403993		C	Italy
Moreton E.P.	Pte.	1st Bn.	6402747		C	Italy
Morley L.S.D.	Sgt.	1st Bn.	6402427		C	Italy
Osman W.E.	Sgt.	1st Bn.	5573770		C	Italy
Owen H.G.	Pte.	9th Bn.	5577443		C	Burma
Paterson A.J.	Pte.	1st Bn.	6403088		C	M.E.
Peacock E.G.	Pte.	1st Bn.	6402589		C	M.E.
Picard A.J.	L/Cpl.	9th Bn.	14650172		C	Burma
Powell S.J.	Pte.	9th Bn.	6412096		C	Burma
Rasell W.R.	Sgt.	1st Bn.	6397604		C	M.E.
Rogers W.G.	L/Cpl.	9th Bn.	5350852		C	Burma
Rossiter E.	Pte.	1st Bn.	6408187		C	M.E.
Sampson N.E.	Sgt.	9th Bn.	6401696		C	Burma
Searson A.C.	Sgt.		6403917		C	St. Nazaire
Selbourne W.E.	Pte.	9th Bn.	6412104		C	Burma
Seymour A.R.	Sgt.		4032286		C	Madagascar
Simmons F.	Pte.	1st Bn	6411433		C	Italy
Smith R.L.J.	L/Sgt.	9th Bn.	6407552		C	Burma
Stonham F.C.G.	Pte.	9th Bn.	6412116		C	Burma
Syphas D.	Pte.	2nd Bn.	6407127		C	M.E.

Taylor G.F. Pte.	9th Bn.	5342055	C	Burma
Trigg F.H. Pte.	4th Bn.	6399046	C	Norway
Weller R.R.J. Pte.	10th Bn. A.A.C.	6405479	C	M.E.
Wells D.G. Sgt.	5th Bn.	6400335	C	M.E.
Wheeler G.R. Cpl.		6399188	C	St. Nazaire
White A.W. Pte.	9th Bn.	6407586	C	Burma
White H.G. Sgt.	5th Bn.	6403785	C	M.E.
White L.F. Cpl.	1st Bn.	6399670	C	Italy
Willard C.J. Pte.	1st Bn.	6402864	C	Italy
Wilson C.H. Pte.	1st Bn.	6408649	C	Italy
Wilson W.G. Pte.	5th Bn.	6399092	C	Dunkirk
Worthington F.A. Sgt		6398404	C	N.W.E.

Military Medal Winners who Died

Thomas Sidney Andrews, M.M. Sgt. No. 6403616, 1st Bn. Friday, 17th March 1944
Cemetery: Cassino War Cemetery, Italy
Grave Ref: III. E. 5.

Robert Binnington, M.M. Sgt. No. 4385843, 4th Bn. Tuesday, 27th October 1942
Cemetery: El Alamein War Cemetery, Egypt
Grave Ref: VI. B. 26.

James Bungard, M.M.& Bar, Lt., No. 315398, Essex Regt. Wednesday, 6th September 1944
Cemetery: Montecchio War Cemetery, Italy
Grave Ref: II. B. 16

Sidney John De Ville, M.M. L/Sgt. No. 6011748, 1st Bn. Wednesday, 15th July 1942
Cemetery: Heliopolis War Cemetery, Egypt
Grave Ref: 2.D. 3.

Ernest George Peacock, M.M. L/Cpl. No. 6402589. 1st Bn. Saturday, 19th February 1944
Cemetery: Cassino War Cemetery, Italy
Grave Ref: XVIII. G. 2.

Frederick Harry Trigg, M.M. Pte. No. 6399046, 1st. Bn. Wednesday, 16th February 1944
Cemetery: Cassino Memorial, Italy
Grave Ref: Panel 7.

Arthur William White, M.M. Pte. No. 6407586, 9th Bn. Sunday, 22nd October 1944
Cemetery: Digboi War Cemetery, India
Grave Ref: 3. D. 5.

B.E.M.

Brown A.E. Sgt.	1st Bn.	D/1580	N/Citation	N/Y
Cullen R. Clr-Sgt.	1st Bn.	2221010	Citation	B/H
Longman R.C. Cpl.	2nd Bn.	553750	Citation	Arnhem
Marchant L.G. C.Q.M.S.	2nd Bn.	6398414	Citation	N/Y
Martin J.O. Pte.	2nd Bn.	881623	Citation	N.W.E.
Nash F.H. R.S.M.	7th Cdt Bn.		N/Citation	B/H
Park J. C.Q.M.S.	1st Bn.	6396368	Citation	Italy
Portlock E.B. Sgt.	9th Bn.	6407531	Citation	Burma
Redford W.A. Sgt.	1st Bn.	6397816	Citation	Malaya
Smith W.S.J. Sgt.	1st Bn.	6402157	Citation	B/H
Tomlin E.G. Pte.	2nd Bn.	6396504	Citation	B/H
Vinall W.P. Sgt.	1st Bn.	7810834	N/Citation	B/H
White B.R. C.S.M.	9th Bn.	6398576	Citation	Burma

Territorial Decoration   (inc. Clasps)

Name	Bn.	Number
Austin I.M. M.C. Lt.	5th Bn.	71265
Ayling G.W. Capt. (Q/M)		75926
Barron B.M. Capt. (A/Mjr.)		387069
Bedford F.W. Capt. (T/Mjr.) (A/Lt-Col.)		7907
Bent K.P. Capt.		58541
Bridge A.E.P. Mjr.		24420
Buckingham M.W.H. Mjr.		435886
Bulwer P. McG. Mjr.		186171
Burder J. Capt.		40998
Carter D.C. Capt. (A/Mjr.)		424067
Claridge P.N. Capt.	7th Bn.	62495
Clarke E.W.N.S. Lt. (Hon. Capt.)		74805
Cook G.H. Lt. (Hon. Capt.)		97137
Davis D.T. Mjr. (Hon. Lt-Col.)		87619
De Pass Lt. (Hon. Capt.)	5th Bn.	74079
Evans T.G.C. Mjr. (Hon. Lt-Col.)	7th Bn.	97144
Fazan E.A.C. Mjr. M.C.,	5th Bn.	97137
Few M. E. Capt.	5th Bn.	40294
Foster T.F.V. Col. C.B.E.,M.C.		3175
Gooddy J.W. Capt. (Hon. Mjr.)		78487
Grant A.J.S. Capt.		23442
Greenough E.E. Capt. M.C.		50031
Haddock F.F. Mjr.		88627
Hadley P.S. Capt. (Hon. Mjr.)		39985
Haines L.B. Capt.		197285
Halsall J.A.L. Capt. (Hon. Mjr.)		402745
Harding J.R. Mjr.	5th Bn.	90292
Heriz-Smith G.V. Lt-Col. O.B.E.,M.C.		36031
Hickman K.P. Capt. (Hon. Mjr.)	5th Bn.	67439
Hillman R.A.E. Capt.	5th Bn.	2717
Hissey B.S. Mjr.		23448
Hodgson G.D. M.C. Capt. (Hon. Mjr.)		78964
Hoad D.H. Mjr.		354551
Hole T.M. Capt. (Hon. Mjr.)	4th Bn.	63126
Hornblower T.B. Mjr.	5th Bn.	
Hubbard W.K. Capt. (Hon. Mjr.)	4th Bn.	91890
Hughes H.C. Lt. (Hon. Capt.)		7944
Hunting C.P.M. Capt. (Hon. Mjr.)		75878
James M.H. Capt.		341908
Langham R.H. Capt. M.C.	5th Bn.	38113
Langridge G.J. Mjr.		184768
Lintott J.O. Capt. (T/Mjr.)		64452
MacNicol H.M. Capt.		362080
Maxse F.H.J. Capt.		38995
Miller P.T. Capt. (T/Mjr.)		39804
Milne R.K. Lt. (Hon. Capt.)		88067
Mostyn J.E.H. Capt. (Ret.)	4th Bn.	
Nix C.F.A. Mjr.	4th Bn.	35771
Parris J. E. Capt.		30149
Penney R.R. Capt. (Hon. Mjr.)		69305
Pickworth S.W.H. Capt.		43287
Pitman A.L. Lt. (Hon. Capt.)		73738
Ree E.A. Hon. Lt.		91608
Richards D. M.C. Capt. (T/Mjr.)		91119
Roberts A.A. Capt. (Hon. Mjr.)		33282
Roberts M.A.G. Mjr.		436234
Rogers F.H. Mjr.		43287
Rogers W.H. Lt.		42300
Sechiari St.J. G.A. Lt. (Hon. Capt.)		401698
Shaw R.F.G. Mjr.		352068
Simmons C.H. Capt.		94973
Sleeman J.L. Col. C.B,.C.M.G.,C.B.E.,M.V.O.		527
Stevenson O.R. Capt. (Hon. Mjr.)		68730
Upton E.J. Mjr. M.M. (Q/M)		11848
Upton S.J.F. M.C. Capt. (Hon. Mjr.)	4th Bn.	90529
Wagener J.G. Capt.	5th Bn.	41353
Wakefield E.D.E. Capt. (A/Mjr.)		416296
Walton J.I.W. Capt.		73348
Wannop E.K.B. Lt-Col.	5th Bn.	45350
Warren J.R. Mjr. M.C.,	4th Bn.	
Whiteman B. Mjr. M.C.	5th Bn.	
Woodbridge C.E. Lt.		94365
Wraight W.F. Qmr. & Hon. Capt.	4th Bn.	
Wyatt R.J.P. M.C. Col. (T/Brig.)		35594

Efficiency Medal (Territorial) (inc. Clasps)

Ablett D.J. Lt.	229639
Ablett S.R. Lt. (T/Capt.)	229640
Allen L.H. Lt.	281155
Anderson J.R. Lt. (T/Mjr.)	153258
Apthorpe D.G.W. Lt.	105087
Berlyn E.J. Lt.	99781
Bowyer G.D. Capt.	72780
Brett A. Lt.	326745
Burrough D.M.C. Capt.	99792
Carter P.R.W. Lt. (Hon. Capt.)	295665
Cavalier P.R. M.C. Capt. (Hon. Mjr.)	124221
Carlisle D. Lt. (Hon. Capt.)	227617
Clarke E.W.N.S.	74805
Clarke N.H.J. Lt.	256638
Cockram P.A. Lt. (T/Capt.)	343084
Cook G.H. Lt. (Hon. Capt.)	97137
Cox H.O. Capt. (Hon. Mjr.)	160547
Dalton B. Capt. (T/Mjr.) D.S.O.	105089
Durant H.P. Capt. (Hon. Mjr.)	132180
Egerton-Savory A.P.E.C. Lt. (Hon. Capt.)	138850
Elliott M.C. Lt.	320533
Gaylard D.W. M.C. Lt.	99819
Gillott W.B. Lt. (Hon. Capt.)	124223
Glover A. Lt. (T/Capt.)	138163
Gordon G.R.K. Lt. (T/Capt.)	269314
Harbord F. Lt.	160408
Hickman K.P. Capt. (Hon. Mjr.)	67439
Hughes Lt. (Hon. Capt.) H. C.	72944
James F.A. Lt. (Hon. Mjr.)	43969
Jones A.G. Capt.	219869
Knaggs C.R. Capt.	258394
Leeder E.J. Lt.	285863
Mannington H. Capt. M.B.	71741
Mason M.J. Lt.	278011
May E.C. Lt. (Hon. Mjr.)	148958
McGowan G.A. Capt. (Hon. Mjr.)	137324
Milne R.K. Lt. Hon. Capt.	88067
Morphy M.B. Lt.	186157
Moseley D.B. Lt.	273971
Newson E.B. Lt. (Hon. Capt.)	129365
Packham D.G. Lt.	341872
Pafford P.J. Lt. (Hon. Capt.)	162506
Page R.J. Capt.	198838
Phillips H.W. Lt.	203800
Power T.J. Lt. (Hon. Capt.)	137328
Reynolds R.A. Lt. (Hon. Capt.)	281837
Shadbolt A.S. Lt.	314185
Smalley D.W. Lt.	352409
Stephens D.E. Lt. (Hon. Capt.)	137322
Thornton H.D. Lt	186159
Trott N.W. Lt. (Hon. Capt.)	308546
Turner J.A. Capt.	240479
Walker J.T. Mjr.	203372
Wallace W.C. Lt. (Hon. Capt.)	247802
Williams H.F. A/Capt.	340445

Army Emergency Reserve Decoration

Ormerod N.O.H. Mjr.	1st Bn.	75939
Macpherson J.G.C. Capt.	1st Bn.	76278

Mentioned in Despatches

Name	Bn.	Number		Theatre
Albert R. C.Q.M.S.	1st Bn.	6398043	C	M.E.
Alce W.G. R.S.M.	5th Bn.	6391134		M.E.
Allen F.R. Sgt.	9th Bn.	5337445		Burma
Anderson J.R. Capt.	1st Bn.	153258	C	Italy
Angell F. Lt. (Q.M.)	4th Bn.	125650	C	France
Anslow G.P.R. Capt.	109th L.A.A.	132415		N.W.E.
Ashworth J.B. Lt-Col. D.S.O.	4th Bn.	47519		France & M.E.
Atkins A.A. Capt. M.B.E.		130315		N.W.E.
Ayling H. Cpl.	1st Bn.	6397014		France
Aylward T.A.C. Cpl.	1st Bn.	6404065		M.E.
Baker B.N. R.S.M.	1st Bn.	737437		Italy
Ballard R.J. Pte.	1st Bn.	6398332	C	M.E.
Banfield L.P. Lt.	9th Bn.	265869		Burma
Barnard S.H. Sgt.	7th Bn.	6393734		France
Barnett L.W. Cpl.	1st Bn.	6403829		Italy
Barrett J.J. Sgt.	9th Bn.	5342411		Burma
Bates N.F. Capt.	1st Bn.	171956		Italy
Beardshaw D.F. Mjr.		138384		N.W.E.
Beaton D. Cpl.		13048186		M.E.
Bedford F.W. Mjr.		7907		France
Beecher L.C. Mjr.	9th Bn.	162700		Burma
Bentley T.C. Sgt.	10th Bn. A.A.C.	6400234		M.E./N.W.E.
Betts J. Sgt.	1st Bn.	6398625		Italy
Blackwell G.T.W. Lt. & Q/M.	7th Bn.	89293		France
Bone A.A. Pte.	1st Bn.	6403870		Italy
Borrow G.H. Lt. M.C.	9th Bn.	228394		Burma
Bowser G.C.M. Mjr.	1st Bn.	66324		Italy
Bowyer G.D. 2nd Lt.	109th L.A.A.	72780		France
Boyne G.A.N. T/Mjr.	9th Bn.	73142		Burma
Bridge J.E.M. Capt.	9th Bn.	174244		Burma
Bristow C.E.D. Sgt.	1st Bn.	6398115		Italy
Brown A. Sgt.	1st Bn.	6406032		Italy
Brown F.A. L/Cpl.	1st Bn.	6398059		M.E.
Brown P.G. Pte.	1st Bn.	6396474		M.E.
Brown W.R.J. L/Cpl.	4th Bn.	6400343		France
Browne C.P. Lt.	5th Bn.	138160		Italy
Bryant A.C. Mjr.	5th Bn.	33024		M.E.
Buckeridge J. Lt.	1st Bn.	269397		Italy
Burder J. Capt.	1st Bn.	40998		Italy
Burdfield R.A.R. Sgt.	9th Bn.	6404636		M.E.
Burgess W.C. Pte.	7th Bn.	832419	C	M.E.
Burnard H.S. Capt.	5th Bn.	175799		Burma
Burnham N.F. Pte.	9th Bn.	598799		Burma
Butcher A.W. Lt.	9th Bn.	279007		
Cadwallader R. Sgt.	9th Bn.	6403457		Burma
Calmady-Hamlyn V.W. Capt.	1st Bn.	64149		M.E.
Carrington R.W.S. Mjr.	1st Bn.	68799		Italy
Carter T.M. Capt.	1st Bn.	346875		Malaya
Cash J.M. Mjr. M.C.	9th Bn.	174342		Burma
Cassels J.S. Mjr. M.C	7th Bn.	13193	C	France
Castle H.G. 2nd Lt.	6th Bn.	102541		France
Chodzko J.A.A. Capt	9th Bn.	165749		Burma
Christmas F.H. Lt.	1st Bn.	207770		Italy
Church E.T. C.S.M.	1st Bn.	6404241		Italy
Clarke J. Pte.	9th Bn.	5350800		Burma
Clow R.H. Capt.	9th Bn.	164689		Burma
Coates G.R.A. C.S.M.	1st Bn.	6398615		Italy
Cohen B. L/Cpl.	9th Bn.	14646041		Burma
Cole W.J. Bdr.	109th L.A.A.	6402059		N.W.E.
Cook G.H. Capt.	7th Bn.	97137	C	France
Cook L.C. Capt.	1st Bn.	149841		M.E. & Italy
Covington C.H. Lt.	1st Bn.	164693		M.E.
Crawford J.N. Mjr.	1st Bn.	98330		Italy
Crunden F.G. Sgt.	9th Bn.	6396611		Burma
Curtis H.R.C. Capt.	9th Bn.	274994		Burma
Cuss E.C. Lt.	1st Bn.	289892		Italy

Name	Unit	Number		Theatre
Dalton B. Capt. D.S.O.	5th Bn.	105089		M.E.
Daniels R.A. Lt.		284757		N.W.E.
Davey A.G. C.S.M.	1st Bn.	6398242		Italy
Davies J. Pte.	1st Bn.	6436367		Italy
Day F.A. T/Capt.	1st Bn.	183336		N.W.E.
de Salvo Hall E.G.	9th Bn.	176196		Burma
Dench A.W. L/Cpl.	4th Bn.	6401777	C	France
Denmead T.W.B. Sgt.	4th Bn.	5667269	C	France
Doidge J.W. W.O.11	109th L.A.A.	6396257		N.W.E.
Doidge S. Cpl.	1st Bn.	6406413		M.E.
Donaghy L. Gnr.	109th L.A.A.	6398458		N.W.E.
Downham C.R. Bmdr.	109th L.A.A.	6403307		France
Drage J.M. 2nd Lt.	4th Bn.	76028		France
Eade W.S. Capt.		164964		N.W.E.
Earle J.K.T. Lt.	9th Bn.	267359		Burma
Edwards A.F. L/Cpl.	1st Bn.	6398857		M.E.
Edwards A.P. Mjr. M.B.E.	1st Bn.	124222		Italy
Ellen W.R. Capt.	5th Bn.		C	France
Elliot C.W. L/Cpl.	1st Bn.	505141		Italy
Ellison P.J.M. Mjr. (A/Lt-Col.)	2nd Bn.	15273		France
English C.T. Pte.		5501274		France
Evans W.C. R.S.M.		6395706		France
Everson A.F. Sgt.	9th Bn.	6408083		Burma
Fallowfield-Cooper V.M. A/Lt-Col.	7th Bn.	98352		N.W.E.
Field G.E. Cpl.	1st Bn.	5626241		M.E.
Felix H.F. Sgt.	9th Bn.	6407875		Burma
Firminger F.W. Mjr. M.C.	1st Bn.	265375		Italy
Flexer J. Pte.	1st Bn.	6412573		Italy
Foreman R.H. C/Sgt.	1st Bn.	6398209		Italy
Foster J.W. Sgt.	1st Bn.	6407882	C	Italy
Foster L.V. Gnr.	109th L.A.A.	6397342		N.W.E.
Foster R.H. Pte.	4th Bn.	6402284		France
Foster T.F.V. Brig-Gen	1st Bn.	3175		M.E.
Fowler T. Cpl.	1st Bn.	6397152	C	M.E.
Franks H.E. W.O.111	2nd Bn.	6401735		N.W.E.
Frisby I.M. Lt.	9th Bn.	308955		Burma
Froude R. W.O.1	2nd Bn.	6391344		France
Fuller G.E. Pte.	9th Bn.	5350828		Burma
Garibaldi W. L/Cpl.	10th Bn. A.A.C.	6400067	C	M.E./Arnhem
Geall R.N. Lt.	10th Bn. A.A.C.	255776		Italy
Genillard C.P. Maj. M.C.	1st Bn.	129366		Italy
George H. L/Sgt.	1st Bn.	6397589		M.E.
Gibbs J.P.P. T/Capt.	9th Bn.	153257		Burma
Glennie J.B.A. Lt-Col. D.S.O	1st Bn	630600		M.E.
Godley H.G. Cpl.	1st Bn.	849522		Italy
Goodall A.H. Capt.	1st Bn.	378345		Palestine
Goodwin E.A.H. Mjr. O.B.E.	1st Bn.	173431		Italy
Gouldsmith A. A/Capt.	1st Bn.	179803		Italy
Grainger R.E. C.S.M.	1st Bn.	6395864		Arnhem
Grant A.J.S. Mjr. T.D.	2nd Bn.	23442		France
Gumbrell J. Cpl.	1st Bn.	6398261		M.E.
Hammond E.S. C.S.M	9th Bn.	6397850		Burma
Hanlon P.J. Mjr. & Q/M	2nd Bn.	69631		France
Harpur G.H.L. Capt.	1st Bn.	148570		Italy
Harris P.C. Capt.	9th Bn.	153261		Burma
Harwood C.J. Sgt.	A.A.C.	5669740		France
Harwood G. Pte.	2nd Bn.	1463360		Arnhem
Hawkins G. Cpl.		6396792		M.E.
Hayes D.R.C. Capt.	5th Bn.	130053		Italy
Hayes L.J. Lt.		177728		N.W.E.
Herman H.E. Sgt. M.M.	9th Bn.	6209984		Burma
Hill F. C.S.M.	9th Bn.	6398407		Burma
Hiscock B.B. Sgt.	5th Bn.	6404010		Italy
Hiscocks T.J.R. L/Cpl.	9th Bn.	5576992		Burma
Hoare J.G. Cpl. (S/Sgt.)	1st Bn.			India
Hodgson J.C. Lt-Col.	1st Bn.	88046		Italy
Hogben R.D.S. Mjr. M.C.	9th Bn.	180204		Burma

Name	Unit	Number		Theatre
Holden White H.V. Capt.	9th Bn.	162512		Burma
Hollist E.G. Lt-Col.	4th Bn.	44064		France
Holmes G. Pte.	1st Bn.	14534767		Italy
Homden G.H. Sgt.	1st Bn.	6403653		Italy
Hood T.D. T/Lt-Col.		52421	C	N.W.E.
Hookway L.C. R.S.M.	9th Bn.	6394462		Burma
How G.S. T/Capt.	1st Bn.	189957		Italy
Hulme N.E. Capt.	9th Bn.	256584		Burma
Ide E.W.A. Pte.	4th Bn.	6399289		France
Illman G.J. Gnr.	109th L.A.A.	6399663		N.W.E.
Izzard A.S. C.S.M.		5876732		France
Jaques V.H. Lt-Col. ,D.S.O.,M.C.	1st Bn.	131287		Italy
Jeffery F. Pte.	10th Bn. A.A.C.	6412155		Italy
Jenkins R.W. Sgt.	5th Bn.	6403507		M.E.
Johnson C.W.S. Capt.	1st Bn.	138167		Italy
Johnston O.C. Mjr.	1st Bn.	47613		M.E.
Jordan E. W.O.11	Royal Signals	6395578		N.W.E.
Jordan G.F. T/Capt.	4th Bn.	143729		N.W.E.
King R. de L. T/Mjr.	1st Bn.	67150		S.E.Asia
Kirkby S.A.H. Lt-Col. M.C.	6th Bn.	14469		France
Knight C. Sgt.	1st Bn.	6392926		Italy
Lambird W.H. Sgt.	R.C.S.	6390313		N.W.E.
Langdon M.C.S. Mjr.	9th Bn.	162067		Burma
Langham R.H. Capt. M.C.	2nd Bn	38113		France
Lawson P.M. Mjr	1st Bn.	153960		Pale/ Korea
Leake A.E.C. Lt.	2nd Bn.	79304		N.W.E.
Lee W.M. Capt.	1st Bn	187070		Italy
Leech W.G. Sgt.	9th Bn.	6411812		Burma
Leeder L. P.S.M.	4th Bn.	6398985		France
Leggatt C.R.C. L/Cpl.	1st Bn.	6412327		Italy
Lester A.W. Lt.	1st Bn.	315391		Italy
Lewis-Clements R.V. L/Cpl.	7th Bn.	6400527		M.E.
Libby R. Sgt.	109th L.A.A.	6399765	C	N.W.E.
Lilley G.W. W.O. 11	109th L.A.A.	6396495		N.W.E.
Longthorne J.A. Sgt.	1st Bn.	2027714		M.E.
Loten J.W. W.O.1	109th L.A.A.	6394257		N.W.E.
Lovell W. Pte.	1st Bn.	6711		India
Lowles R.C. C.S.M.	7th Bn.	6401391	C	France
Magrath J.S. Lt-Col. M.C.	1st Bn.	42679		Italy
Mannington H. Capt. M.B.	7th Bn.	71741		France
Mannington H. Capt. M.B.	1st Bn.	71741	C	Italy
Mansell F.R. Mjr.	1st Bn.	129363		Italy
Marks P.C. Pte.	5th Bn.	5505188		Italy
Marsh L.E. Pte.	1st Bn.	6408392		Italy
Maslin A., St. C., Cpl.	1st Bn.	6408614		Italy
Martin H.L.J. Gnr.	7th Bn.	6401712		East Indies
Mayer J.T. T/Maj.	109th L.A.A.	13851	C	N.W.E.
McArthur I.C. Capt.	9th Bn.	16473		Burma
McNeill D.C. Lt.	1st Bn.	459297		Brunei
Mercer C.H. Lt.	9th Bn.	265871		Burma
Mockford D.A.J. A/Sgt.	9th Bn.	6406286		Burma
Moon J.R. Mjr.	9th Bn.	96437		Burma
Morgan J.C. Capt.	1st Bn.	47361		M.E.
Morling F.E. Sgt.	7th Bn.	6401438		France
Morphy M.B. Lt.	9th Bn.	186157	C	Burma
Morris H. Sgt.	109th L.A.A.	6401395		N.W.E.
Morris R.J. Lt.	1st Bn.	42279		Malaya
Murphy L. Cpl.	1st Bn.	6394866		Italy
Neal S.G. Lt.	9th Bn.	268155		Burma
Newnham H. Pte.	4th Bn.	6399510		France
Newton R.E. C.S.M.	9th Bn.	6407951	C	Burma
Nightingale W. WO1	I.A.A.C.			Burma
Nix C.F.A. Mjr.	4th Bn.	35771		France
Nutter W.G. Pte.		6400647	C	France
Odling-Smee A.J. Lt-Col. O.B.E.	2nd Bn.	34483		Italy
Oliver D.H. T/Lt-Col. D.S.O.	9th Bn.	33736		Burma
O'Neill J. Cpl.	9th Bn.	6408154		Burma
Owens J. Pte.	1st Bn.	6391441		Italy
Pack W.A. Sgt. (A/S/Sgt.)	1st Bn.	6395892		M.E.
Pasiful J. L/Cpl.	1st Bn.	6406645		Italy

Name	Unit	Number		Theatre
Peckitt C.R. Mjr.	2nd Bn.	15229		France
Phelps G.A. Mjr. D.S.O.	1st Bn.	36752		M.E.
Phillips H.F. R.S.M.	1st Bn.	6190062		Italy
Pinkham C.W. A/Sgt.	1st Bn.	5666799		Italy
Plested C. Sgt.	9th Bn.	6404600		Burma
Pocock C.H. Lt. (Q.M.)	1st Bn.	169690		M.E.
Pollington H.S. Capt.	1st Bn.	137737		M.E.
Powell C.A. Lt.	1st Bn.	284563		Italy
Powell F.J. C.S.M.	9th Bn.	6398489	C	Burma
Priddle C. Cpl.	1st Bn.	6401176		Italy
Randall H. Pte.	1st Bn.	6299476		M.E.
Rayner T.E. W.O.11	109th L.A.A.	6397417		N.W.E.
Rees A.R. Capt.	1st Bn.	197271		Italy
Rhode R.E. Lt.	1st Bn.	5550		Waziristan
Richards D. Capt. M.C.	9th Bn.	91119		Burma
Richards P.R. Mjr.	1st Bn.	358068		Malaya
Ring L.J. Mjr.	9th Bn	289878		Burma
Robey F.A. Pte.		5439968		France
Roe T.C.W. Lt-Col. O.B.E.,M.B.E.	1st Bn.	121387		M.E.
Rogers H.J. A/Sgt.	9th Bn.	6407543		Burma
Rollington H.L.. Lt.	1st Bn.	251293		Italy
Ronald F.J. Lt. (T/Capt.)	1st Bn.	67904		M.E.
Rowe A.H. Cpl.	9th Bn..	6407985		Burma
Saunders C.A. Cpl.	9thBn.	6399711		Burma
Saunders C.T. Cpl.	4th Bn.	6398967		France
Selby C. Sgt.	9th Bn.	6407374		Burma
Seller C.S. Pte.	1st Bn.	6404085		Sicily
Seymour H. Pte.	2nd Bn.	6402352		N.W.E.
Shaw D.E.R. Mjr.	1st Bn.	12820		Pal/M.E.
Shaw J.W.H. Capt..	1st Bn.	203806		Italy
Shield R. Pte.	1st Bn.	6399794		Italy
Shippham F.N. Capt.		180207		N.W.E.
Silver R.M. Lt.	1st Bn.	243914		Italy
Simmons A.R. Sgt.	9th Bn.	6408005		Burma
Simmonds T.F. C.S.M.		6394041		France
Smith A.L. Cpl.	1st Bn.	4545640		Italy
Smith R.L.J. Sgt.	9th Bn.	6407552		Burma
Smith T.H. Pte.	7th Bn.	5438571		N.W.E.
Sparkes A. Sgt.	2nd Bn.	6400271		Arnhem
Spencer T.J. Pte.	9th Bn.	6408017		Burma
Stanley H. Pte.	4th Bn.	6399347		France
Steadman M.J. Sgt.	9th Bn.	6404210		Burma
Steer J. Cpl.	9th Bn.	5629505		Burma
Steer J.S. Mjr. (QM)	1st Bn.	37526		M.E.
Stibbe P.G. Lt.	1st Bn.	203807		Italy
Stratten D.C. Capt.	1st Bn.	182278		Italy
Tarver C.H. Brig.	1st Bn.	380334		Malaya
Tayler L.W.S. Mjr.	9th Bn.	52239		Burma
Taylor H.J.C. Capt.		42139		France
Thompson F.I.H.H. Mjr.	1st Bn.	91452		Italy
Thompson W. Mjr.	1st Bn.	203808		Italy
Thrift H. Pte.	1st Bn.	640312		Italy
Tolley W.G. L/Cpl.	1st Bn.	5626379		Italy
Trotman G.F. Lt.		323896		N.W.E.
Trott N.W. Lt.	1st Bn.	308456		Italy
Tucker K.O. Capt.	1st Bn.	78997		Italy
Tupper H.O. Sgt.	R.A.	6395903		N.W.E.
Turner C.B.G. T/Capt.	109th L.A.A.	105234		N.W.E.
Turner E.G. Sgt.	9th Bn.	6408035		Burma
Turner R.F. Sgt.	1st Bn.	6403771		Italy
Tyler M.W. Pte.		6403057		N. Africa
Vaughan-Williams T/Capt.	109th L.A.A.	186160		N.W.E.
Verth A.G. Pte.	7th Bn.	6402487	C	France
Von der Hyde J.L. Brig. O.B.E.,M.C		31719		M.E.
Wagener J.G. T/Mjr. T.D.				
Waite L. Cpl.	4th Bn.	41153		N.W.E.
Wallis L.W. Sgt.	2nd Bn.	5573779		Arnhem
Wannop E.K.B. Lt-Col.	9th Bn.	6408047		Burma
Waters R.D. Capt	6th Bn.	45350		France
Webb G. Pte.	2nd Bn.	86483		France
Webster F.I. Capt.	2nd Bn.	6399326	C	France
Wells R.E. C.S.M.	1st Bn.	242760		France
West T. Pte.	1st Bn.	6398703		Italy
Wharton R.G.P. Lt.	1st Bn.	6395113	C	Italy
	9th Bn.	330711		M.E.

Whaymand L. Pte.	1st Bn.	6400272	Burma
Whistler L.G. A/Mjr-Gen D.SO.	4th Bn.	13017	M.E./Italy/N.W..E.
White H.R. Pte.	1st Bn.	5573831	N.W.E.
White H.V.H. Capt. M.C.	1st Bn.	162512	Italy
Wildash A.C. Cpl.	9th Bn.	5335399	Burma
Wilson K.S.H. T/Mjr.	1st Bn.	141036	M.E./Italy
Wisden T.J.F. T/Mjr.	1st Bn.	97236	Italy
Woodrow J.H. Mjr.	1st Bn.	77647	Malaya
Wright L.P. L/Bdr.	109th L.A.A.	6406193	N.W.E.
Wyeth D.B.J. Cpl.	9th Bn.	5351082	Burma
Wyndham P.C.J. Lt.	1st Bn.	295507	Italy

Mentioned In Dispatches Winners who Died

Frederick Richard Allen, Sgt. No. 5337445, 9th Bn. Saturday, 5th August 1944
Cemetery: Taukkyan War Cemetery, Myanmar
Grave Ref: 7. G. 4.

Samuel Henry Barnard, Sgt. No. 6393734, 7th Bn. Monday, 20th May 1940
Cemetery: Abbeville Communal Cemetery Extension, Somme, France
Grave Ref: Plot 9. Row F. Grave 11.

George Thomas William Blackwell, Lt. (Q/M), No. 89293, 7th Bn. Saturday, 18th May 1940
Cemetery: Abbeville Communal Cemetery Extension, Somme, France
Grave Ref: Plot 9. Row D. Grave 9.

Christopher Peter Browne, Lt. No. 138160, 5th Bn. Tuesday, 27th October 1942
Cemetery: El Alamein War Cemetery, Egypt
Grave Ref: XVIII. E. 21.

Norman Frederick Burnham, L/Cpl. No. 5958799, 9th Bn. Monday, 29th January 1945
Cemetery: Rangoon Memorial, Myanmar
Grave Ref: Face 14.

James Stuart Cassels, M.C. Major, No. 13193 7th Bn. Tuesday, 21st May 1940
Cemetery: Morvillers-St. Saturnin Churchyard, Somme, France

Charles Henry Covington, Lt. No. 164693, 1st Bn. Saturday, 22nd November 1941
Cemetery: Halfaya Sollum War Cemetery, Egypt
Grave Ref: 6. D. 3.

Frederick George Crunden, L/Sgt. No. 6396611, 9th Bn. Saturday, 5th August 1944
Cemetery: Taukkyan War Cemetery, Myanmar
Grave Ref: 7. G. 5.

Arthur Frederick Everson, Sgt. No. 6408083, 9th Bn. Sunday, 6th August 1944
Cemetery: Taukkyan War Cemetery, Myanmar
Grave Ref: 7. A. 22.

Richard Froude, R.S.M. No. 6391344, 2nd Bn. Wednesday, 22nd May 1940
Cemetery: Adegem Canadian War Cemetery, Maldegem, Oost-Vlaanderen, Belgium
Grave Ref: 3. AB. 1.

William Garibaldi, L/Cpl. No. 6400067, 10th Bn. A.A.C. Wednesday, 20th September 1944
Cemetery: Arnhem Oosterbeek War Cemetery, Netherlands
Grave Ref: 5. D. 14.

Denis Richard Courtenay Hayes, Capt. No. 130053, 5th Bn. Thursday, 29th October 1942
Cemetery: El Alamein War Cemetery, Egypt
Grave Ref: XVIII. E. 17.

Thomas John Richard Hiscock, L/Cpl. No. 5576992, 9th Bn. Thursday, 1st November 1945
Cemetery: Taiping war Cemetery, Malaysia
Grave Ref: 3.

Oswald Charles Johnston, Major No. 47613, 1st Bn. Saturday, 22nd November 1941
Cemetery: Halfaya Sollum War Cemetery, Egypt
Grave Ref: 6. B. 3.

Percy Clifford Marks, Pte. No. 5505188, 5th Bn. Friday 30th October 1942
Cemetery: El Alamein War Cemetery, Egypt
Grave Ref: XVIII D. 25.

Samuel Alexander Howell Kirkby Col. Commands and Staff General Staff Friday 28th May 1943
Alderbury (St. Mary) Churchyard
Grave Ref: P.C.S.

Harold Laurence John Martin, Gnr. No. 6401712, 79/21st L.A.A. Regt. R.A. Sunday 13th June 1943
Cemetery: Kranji War Cemetery, Singapore Memorial, Singapore
Grave Ref: Column 25.

Charles Selby, L/Sgt. No. 6407374, 9th Bn. Sunday, 6th August 1944
Cemetery: Taukkyan War Cemetery, Myanmar
Grave Ref: 7. A. 23.

Frank Norman Shippam, Capt. No. 180207, attd.1/7th Middx. Regt. Monday, 10th July 1944
Cemetery: La Delivrande War Cemetery, Douvres, Calvados, France
Grave Ref: VII. A. 2.

Maurice John Steadman, Sgt. No. 6404210, 9th Bn. Thursday, 23rd November 1944
Cemetery: Taukkyan War Cemetery, Myanmar
Grave Ref: 6. J. 10.

Douglas Ben Jeffrey Wyeth, L/Cpl. No. 5351082, 9th Bn. Wednesday, 22nd November 1944
Cemetery: Taukkyan War Cemetery, Myanmar
Grave Ref: 7. H. 22.

Certificate of Gallantry

Maynard J.E.	9th Bn.	5351714		Burma

Queen's Commendation For Bravery

Blaxter D.A.G. Lt.	1st Bn.	407761	Citation	Suez

G.O.C.'s Commendation for Bravery

Cruttenden A.J. Cpl.	4/5th Bn.	23228618	Citation	Aden
Smith W.S.J. Sgt.	1st Bn.	402157	Citation	Suez

American Awards

Silver Star

Biggs H.C. C/Sgt	1st Bn.	6401551	Citation	Italy
Cockell C.M.C. Mjr.	9th Bn.	30495	Immediate	Burma

Bronze Star

Brockless H.N. Lt. & Q.M.	9th Bn.	6457417	Immediate	Burma
Grainger R.E. C.S.M.	10th Bn. A.A.C.	6395864	Citation	Arnhem

Belgian Awards

Commander of the Order of the Crown with Palm, Croix de Guerre 1940 with Palm

Whistler L.G. Mjr.-Gen. CB.,D.S.O.   13017   Citation

Chevalier of the Order of the Crown

Levey M.E. T/Capt.   284615   N/Citation

Chevalier of the Order of Leopold 11 with Palm, Croix de Guerre 1940 with Palm

Powell P.J.L. T/Mjr.   97605   109th L.A.A. R.A   Citation

Croix de Guerre 1940, with Palm

Crossfield L.C. L/Bmdr   6401092   109th L.A.A. R.A.   Citation

Dutch Awards

Bronze Lion

Carr B.D. T/Capt.   138170   10th Bn. Para. Regt. A.A.C.   Citation

Greek Awards

Distinguished Service Medal

Castle H.G. T/Maj.   102541   Citation
Jones P.H. T/Maj.   180206   N/Citation

Japanese Awards

Order of the Sacred Treasure (3rd Class)

Sleeman J.L. Mjr. C.M.G.,C.B.E,.,M.V.O.,T.D.   527

Order of the Rising Sun (4th Class)

Hulton J.M. Mjr. C.B.E.,D.S.O.

Polish Award

Order of Polonia Restituta (3rd Class)

De Chair G.H.B. Lt-Col. O.B.E.,M.C.   24056

Meritorious Service Medal

Nash F.H. R.S.M.
Powell F.J.B. C/Sgt.   6394395

Long Service and Good Conduct Medal

Brockless H.N. M.B.E. Capt. (Q/M)   363956
Lucas R.G. Capt. (Q/M)   436174
Mordaunt P.M. Lt. (T/Mjr.) M.C.   164690
Mowbray S.J.O. Capt. (Q/M)   279165
Robinson E.O. Lt. (Q/M)   358659
Smitherman L.F. Lt. (Q/M)   463506
Steer A.J. Lt. (Hon. Capt.)   163060
Wyard B.W.H. Lt. (Hon. Capt.)   **183337**

Cadet Forces Medal

Allen R.C.E. A/Capt.	404265
Barber A.G. A/Capt.	332598
Beattie S.A. A/Capt.	395778
Bonfield H.J. A/Lt-Col.	122689
Bradshaw D.W.F. A/Capt.	389351
Bruder E.A. A/Mjr.	344038
Bryant K. Lt. (A/Mjr.)	311878
Burchett H.C. A/Lt.-Col.	
Crook S. A/Capt.	275246
Dobson N.A. 2nd Lt.	426746
Eaves F.W. A/Capt.	351604
Freeman F.H. Lt. (A/Capt.)	446085
Garside T.J. Lt.	360027
Hagel L.J. Lt.	298546
Hart E.G. Lt.	430542
Harvey R.W. A/Mjr.	275250
Heatherley P.F. A/Capt.	275234
Hoskins S.J. was A/Mjr.	275252
Hunnisett A. Lt. (Hon. Capt.	298340
Masterman A.F. A/Capt.	344253
Medcalf F.H. A/Capt.	255024
Mortimer C.A. A/Mjr.	275255
Parsons J.H.G. A/Mjr.	182850
Phillips L.N. Lt-Col.	275279
Potter T.M. A/Capt.	283149
Shippham C.P.B. Hon. Mjr.	275256
Smith D.A. A/Mjr.	351026
Stanbrook F.W.S. A/Capt.	249251
Vidler C.A. A/Capt.	395420
Wheeler A. was A/Lt-Col.	275282
Wilkins P.V. was A/Lt-Col..	280806
Williams H.F. A/Capt.	340445
Wood E.R. Lt. (A/Capt.)	395904
Wye A.V. A/Mjr.	395763

Order of the House of Orange (Netherlands)

Knight Grand Cross

Whistler L.G. Gen. G.C.B.,K.C.B.,C.B.,K.B.E..,D.S.O.

Grand Officer

Whistler L.G. Gen. G.C.B.,K.C.B.,C.B.,K.B.E.,D.S.O.

Commander

Ashworth J.B. Lt-Col. D.S.O.,C.B.E.
Foster T.F.V. Brig-Gen. C.B.E.,M.C.,

Officer

Ashworth J.B. Lt-Col. D.S.O.,C.B.E.
Buckeridge J. Lt. [Col.
Chapman J.L. Lt-Col. O.B.E.
Glennie J.B.A. Lt-Col. D.S.O.,C.B.E.,O.B.E.
Harrison P.M.J. Capt. O.B.E,M.C,
Harrison-Stanton R.G. Mjr.
Hollist E.G. Lt-Col.
Newton P.S. T/Mjr. M.B.E
Russell D.E.C. Lt-Col.
Sleeman R.B. de F. Mjr. O.B.E.,M.C
Snowdon D.C. Lt-Col. T.D.
Walker J.T. Lt-Col.

Chevalier First Class

Knocker N.B. Capt.

Gold Medal

Alce W.G. O.R.Q.M.S.	6391134
Houghton D.G. R.S.M.	6405069
Lucas R.G. R.S.M.	436174
Webb F. R.S.M.	14380376

Royal Humane Society Bronze Medal

Brazier E. Cpl.   4/5th Bn.

Index

Ablett D.J. Lt. E.M. — 08/09/53
Ablett S.R. Lt. (T/Capt.) E.M. — 04/03/49
Albert R. C.Q.M.S. (G.Q.M.S.) (6398043) M.I.D. — 30/12/41,09/09/42
Alce W.G. O.R.Q.S.M. M.B.E., M.I.D., Gold Medal — 6/04/44,01/01/59,30/04/65
Allen F.R. Sgt. M.I.D. — 19/07/45
Allen R.C.E. A/Capt. C.F.M. — 31/01/58
Alston-Roberts-West R.A. Capt. M.C. — 24/08/44
Anderson J.R. Capt. O.B.E., Eff. Medal, M.I.D. — 11/01/45,14/04/50,01/01/65
Andrews T.S. Sgt. M.M. — 20/07/44
Angell F. Lt. & Q/M. M.I.D. — 20/12/40
Anslow G.P.R. Capt. M.I.D. — 08/11/45
Apthorpe D.G.W. Lt. E.M. — 21/01/49
Ashworth J.B. Lt-Col. D.S.O.,C.B.E.,M.I.D. — 20/12/40,24/08/44,21/12/44,08/05/54,01/01/62, 30/04/65,09/08/45,11/08/45,24/01/46

Atkins A.A. Capt. M.B.E.,M.I.D. — 11/07/45
Atkinson J.B. Capt. M.B.E. — 01/01/45
Austin I.M. 2nd Lt. M.C.,T.D. — 11/07/40,29/04/55
Avey S.G. Pte. M.M. — 15/06/44
Ayling G.W. Capt. (Q/M) T.D. — 21/04/50
Ayling H. Cpl. M.I.D. — 20/12/40
Aylward T.A.C. Cpl. M.I.D. — 06/04/44

Baker A.E. Lt. M.B.E. — 01/11/45
Baker B.N. R.S.M. M.I.D. — 13/01/44
Ballard R.J. Pte. M.I.D. — 04/05/43
Banks D.A. Mjr. M.B.E. — 11/06/60
Bapty L. Capt. M.C.,M.B. R.A.M.C. — 19/12/41,23/01/42
Barber A.G. A/Capt. C.F.M. — 10/04/56
Barnard S.H. Sgt. M.I.D. — 29/11/45
Barnett L.W. Cpl. M.I.D. — 27/09/45
Barrett J.J. Sgt. M.I.D. — 11/01/44,15/01/44
Barron B.M. Capt. (A/Mjr.) T.D. — 17/05/60
Bates N.F. Capt. M.I.D. — 04/04/46
Beardshaw D.F. Mjr. M.I.D. — 15/12/42
Beaton D. Cpl. M.I.D. — 20/12/40
Beattie S.A. A/Capt. C.F.M. — 28/07/61
Bedford F.W. Mjr. M.I.D. — 17/11/42,05/04/45
Beecher L.C. Mjr. M.I.D. — 05/04/45,20/09/45
Bent K.P. Capt. T.D. — 19/09/58
Bentley T.C. Sgt. D.C.M. ,M.I.D. — 13/01/44,10/05/45,20/09/45
Betts J. Sgt. M.I.D. — 23/04/42
Bidder G.D. 2nd Lt. M.C. — 11/07/40
Biggs H.C. C/Sgt. Silver Star — 17/09/48
Binnington R. L/Cpl. M.M. — 13/12/45
Blackmore H.I. Lt. & Q/M. M.B.E. — 29/11/45
Blaxter D.A.G. Lt. Q.C .for B. — 10/10/52
Boga H.T. Capt. M.B.E. — 28/06/45
Bone A.A. Pte. M.I.D. — 13/01/44,15/01/44
Bonfield H.J. A/Lt-Col. — 20/02/51
Borrow G.H. Lt. M.C.,M.I.D. — 16/12/43,25/05/44,26/04/45
Bowmer E.J. Capt. M.C.,MB. R.A.M.C. — 20/07/44
Bowser G.C.M. Mjr. M.I.D. — 29/11/45
Bowyer G.D. Capt. M.I.D., Eff. Medal & Clasp — 20/12/40,25/05/47,21/04/50
Boyne G.A.N. T/Mjr. M.I.D. — 19/08/46
Bradshaw D.W.F. A/Capt. C.F.M — 29/11/60
Brazier E. Cpl. R.H.S.B.M. — 24/02/50
Brennan P.C. Sgt. M.M. — 09/09/42,11/09/42
Brett A. Lt. E.M. — 14/04/50
Bridge A.E.P. Mjr. T.D. — 25/03/43,10/01/58
Bridge J.E.M. Capt. M.I.D. — 27/09/45
Bristow C.E.D. Sgt. M.I.D. — 13/01/44,15/01/44
Brockhurst E.E. Cpl. M.M. — 26/04/45
Brockless H.N. Lt. & Q/M. M.B.E.,B.S.,LS&GC — 05/04/45,09/12/49,16/02/51
Brook C.E. Capt. M.B.E. — 01/01/51
Brown A. Sgt. M.I.D. — 29/11/45
Brown A.E. Sgt. B.E.M. — 01/01/41
Brown F.A. L/Cpl. M.I.D. — 30/12/41
Brown P.G. Pte. M.I.D. — 01/04/41
Brown W.R.J. L/Cpl. M.I.D. — 20/12/40
Browne C.P. Lt. M.I.D. — 13/01/44,15/01/44
Bruder E.A. A/Mjr. C.F.M. — 17/11/50
Bryant A.C. Mjr. M.I.D. — 06/04/44
Bryant K. Lt. (A/Mjr.) C.F.M. — 27/11/64
Bryant L.J. Pte. M.M. — 08/03/45
Buckeridge J. Lt.[Col. M.I.D. — 23/05/46,25/05/46,08/06/66
Buckingham M.W.H. Mjr. T.D. — 15/07/56
Budd M.A.J. Capt. M.C. — 17/01/46
Bulwer P. McG. Mjr. T.D. — 04/06/54,15/01/57,18/09/62

Bungard J. Sgt. M.M.	26/1/42,08/07/43,09/07/43,10/07/43
Burchett H.C. A/Lt-Col. C.F.M.	08/06/54
Burder J. Capt. T.D.,M.I.D.	20/12/45,30/05/47
Burdfield R.A.R. Sgt. M.I.D.	19/09/46
Burgess W.C. Pte. M.I.D.	31/01/41
Burnard H.S. Capt. M.I.D.	06/04/44
Burnett G.B. Lt. M.C.	08/03/45
Burnham N.F. Pte. M.I.D.	27/09/45
Burrough D.M.C. Capt. Eff. Medal	14/04/50
Buss C. Cpl. M.M.	20/09/45
Butcher A.W. Lt. M.I.D.	19/09/46
Cadwallader R. Sgt. M.M.,M.I.D.	07/04/45,27/09/45,15/11/45
Callender K.L. Mjr. M.C.	16/11/44
Calmady-Hamlyn V.W. Capt. M.I.D.	24/06/43
Carlisle D. Lt. E.M.	25/06/48
Carrington R.W.S. Mjr. M.I.D.	29/11/45
Carr B.D. T/Capt. Bronze Lion (Dutch)	20/04/47
Carter D.C. Capt. (A/Mjr.) T.D.	15/03/66
Carter P.R.W. Lt. (Hon. Capt.) E.M.	30/07/57
Carter T.M. Capt. M.I.D.	01/05/53
Cash J.M. Mjr. M.C.,M.I.D	22/06/44,27/09/45
Cassels J.S. Mjr. M.C.,M.I.D.	20/12/40
Castle H.G. T/Maj. M.I.D..D.S.M. Greece	20/12/40,14/10/49
Cavalier P.R. Maj. M.C.,E.M.	08/03/45,13/12/49
Chapman J.L. Mjr. O.B.E.	26/06/47,08/05/54
Chapman W.J. L/Cpl. M.M.	20/07/44
Chittenden A.R. Lt. M.C.	01/03/45
Chodzko J.A.A. Capt. M.I.D.	27/09/45,19/09/46
Chow R.H. Capt. M.I.D.	27/09/45
Christmas F.H. Lt. M.I.D.	23/05/46,25/05/46
Church E.T. C.S.M. M.I.D.	29/11/45
Claridge P.N. Capt. T.D.	10/06/52
Clark D. Pte. M.M.	06/06/46
Clarke J. Pte. M.I.D.	19/09/46
Clarke E.W.N.S. Lt. (Hon. Capt.) T.D.,E.M.	18/04/47,21/04/50
Clarke N.H.J. Lt. E.M.	03/09/48
Clayton A.C. T/Col. O.B.E.	08/06/50
Clegg B.B. Capt. M.C.	05/10/42,27/11/42,20/09/45
Clow R.H. T/Capt. M.I.D.	27/09/45
Coates G.R.A. C.S.M. M.I.D.	29/11/45
Cockell C.M.C. Maj. U.S. Silver Star	05/04/45
Cockram P.A. Lt. (T/Capt.) E.M.	30/07/48
Cohen B. L/Cpl. M.I.D.	19/09/46
Cole W.J. Bdr. M.I.D.	08/11/45
Colesby C.A. Pte. M.M.	22/03/45
Conetta V. Pte. M.M.	22.03/45
Connell W. C.S.M. D.C.M.	11/07/40
Conroy E. Sgt. M.M.	19/12/41,23/01/42
Cook G.H. Capt. T.D.,E.M.,M.I.D.	29/11/45,21/02/47,21/04/50
Cook L.C. Capt. M.I.D.	06/04/44,11/01/45
Cooke S.H. Sgt. M.I.D.	26/07/45
Coppard D.R.G. Sgt. M.M.	08/07/43,10/07/43
Covington C.H. Lt. M.I.D.	24/06/43
Cox D.H. Lt. D.S.O.	24/08/44
Cox H.O. Capt. (Hon. Mjr.) E.M.	04/11/49
Cox J.W. Pte. M.M.	22/03/45
Crawford J.N. T/Maj. M.C.,M.I.D.	23/08/45,29/11/45
Croft H. Pte. M.M.	11/07/40,02/08/40
Crook S. A/Capt. C.F.M.	29/06/51
Crossfield L/Bmdr. C/G with Palm, Belgium	16/01/47
Crunden F.G. Sgt. M.I.D.	19/07/45
Cruttenden A.J. Cpl. G.O.C'S C for B.	21/01/66
Cudlipp H. Lt-Col. O.B.E.	22/02/45
Cullen R. Drum-Major B.E.M.	02/06/62
Cunningham J. Pte. M.M.	19/12/41,23/01/42,24/01/42
Curtis H.R.C. Capt. M.I.D.	19/07/45
Cuss E.C. Lt. M.I.D.	23/05/46,25/05/46
Dalton B. Mjr. D.S.O.,O.B.E.,E.M.,M.I.D.	06/04/44,20/07/44,18/04/47,01/01/58
Daniels R.A. Lt. M.C.,M.I.D.	09/08/45,11/08/45,24/01/46
Darwall-Smith R.F.H. Capt. (Hon. Mjr.) T.D.	21/04/50
Davey A.G. C.S.M. M.I.D.	23/05/46,25/05/4
Davies J. Pte. M.I.D.	03/08/44
Davies S.G. Sgt. D.C.M.	17/06/43
Davis C.E. L/Cpl. M.M.	22/06/44
Davis T.D. Mjr. (Hon. Lt-Col.) T.D.	08/09/53
Day F.A. Capt. M.B.E., M.I.D.	08/11/45,01/06/53
Day J.A. Maj. M.B.E.	20/09/45
De Chair G.H.B Lt-Col. O.B.E.,M.C., Order of Restituta 3rd Class, Poland	20/06/44
De Manio J.B. 2nd Lt. M.C.	11/07/40
de Pass D.H. Lt. (Hon. Capt.) T.D.	21/04/50
de Salvo Hall E.G. Capt. M.I.D.	09/05/46,19/09/46
Dench A.W. L/Cpl. M.I.D.	20/12/40

Denmead T.W.B. Sgt. M.I.D.	20/12/40
De Ville S.J. Cpl. M.M.	18/07/41,19/07/41
Dewhurst C.H. T/Lt-Col. O.B.E.	01/01/47
Dickson J.J. Maj. M.C.	22/03/45,21/06/45
Dickson M.J.A. Lt. M.C.	21/09/44,22/03/45,21/06/45
Divall L.F. C.S.M. M.B.E.	13/06/49
Dixon T. Mjr. M.C.	07/12/44
Dobson N.A. 2nd Lt. C.F.M.	28/01/66
Doidge J.W. W.O.11 M.I.D.	04/04/46
Doidge S. Cpl. M.I.D.	01/04/41
Donaghy L. Gnr. M.I.D.	10/05/45
Downham C.R. Bmdr. M.I.D.	09/08/45
Drage J.M. 2nd Lt. M.I.D.	20/12/40
Durant H.P. Capt. (Hon. Mjr.) E.M.	22/04/49
Eade W.S. Capt. M.I.D.	04/04/46
Eames J.E. R.S.M. M.B.E.	29/11/45
Earle J.K.T. Lt. M.I.D.	26/04/45
Eather H.P. Pte. M.M.	21/12/44
Eaton E. Pte. M.M.	17/06/43
Eaves F.W. A/Capt. C.F.M.	22/11/57
Edelshain G. T/Mjr. M.B.E.	17/01/46,19/01/46
Edelsten H.A.C. T/Capt. M.C.	10/02/44,25/04/44
Edwards A.F. L/Cpl. M.I.D.	01/04/41
Edwards A.P. Mjr. M.B.E.,M.I.D.	25/11/43,19/07/45
Egerton-Savory A.P.E.C. Lt. (Hon. Capt.) E.M.	25/03/49
Ellen W.R. Capt. M.I.D.	20/12/40
Elliot C.W. L/Cpl. M.I.D.	13/01/44,15/01/44
Ellison P.J.M. Mjr. (A/Lt-Col.) M.I.D.	20/12/40
Elliott M.C. Lt. E.M.	12/11/48
Elms W.G. Lt. E.M.	14/10/49
English C.T. Pte. M.I.D.	24/04/42
Evans G.C. Mjr. (T/Lt-Col.) D.S.O.	19/02/52
Evans T.G.C. Mjr. (Hon. Lt-Col.) O.B.E., T.D.	20/12/40,13/06/46
Evans W.C. R.S.M. M.I.D.	20/12/40
Everson A.F. Sgt. M.I.D.	19/07/45
Fallowfield-Cooper V.M. A/Lt-Col. T.D.,M.I.D.	04/04/46,21/04/50
Farrant R.W. Lt. M.B.E.	11/10/45
Fazan E.A.C. Mjr. M.C.,T.D.	31/03/21
Felix H.F. Sgt. M.M.,M.I.D.	10/0/46,06/06/46
Few M.E. Capt. T.D. & Clasps	13/12/45,28/12/51
Field G.E. Cpl. M.I.D	24/03/43
Firminger F.W. Maj. M.C.,M.I.D.	18/10/45,29/11/45
Firth C.E.A. T/Lt-Col. D.S.O.	17/12/43
Fleet H. R.S.M. M.B.E.	22/02/45,24/03/45
Flexer J. Pte. M.I.D.	29/11/45
Foreman R.H. C/Sgt. M.I.D.	19/07/45
Foster J.W. Sgt. M.I.D.	27/09/45
Foster L.V. Gnr. M.I.D.	22/03/45
Foster R.H. Pte. M.I.D.	20/12/40
Foster T.F.V. Brig-Gen. C.B.E.,M.C., M.I.D.	01/04/41,30/12/41,24/06/43,22/09/43, 16/09/53
Fowler T. Cpl. M.I.D.	15/12/42
Franks H.E. W.O.111 M.I.D.	14/11/46,16/11/46
Freeman F.H. Lt. (A/Capt.) C.F.M.	28/01/64
Frisby I.M. Lt. M.I.D.	05/04/45
Froude R. W.O.1 M.I.D.	20/12/40
Fuller G.E. Pte. M.I.D.	10/01/46,14/01/46
Fuller R.J. Lt. (T/Capt.) M.C.	07/01/43
Garibaldi W. L/Cpl. M.I.D. 10th Bn. A.A.C.	13/01/44,20/09/45
Gardner T.A. Sgt. M.M.	07/01/43
Garrett M.M. Cpl. M.M.	08/12/53,15/12/53
Garside T.J. Lt. C.F.M.	29/07/66
Gaylard D.W. Lt. M.C.,E.M.	19/12/41,23/01/42,24/04/42,22/04/49
Geall R.N. Lt. M.I.D. 10th Bn. A.A.C.	11/01/45
Genillard C.P. Maj. M.C.,M.I.D.	19/07/45,18/10/45,22/10/45
Gentle A.W. Pte. M.M.	16/11/44
George H. L/Sgt. M.I.D.	15/12/42
Gethen R. Lt-Col. M.C.,T.D.	21/04/50
Gibbs J.P.P. T/Capt. M.I.D.	12/08/55
Gillott W.B. Lt. (Hon. Capt.) E.M.	19/09/46
Glasgow A.E. Brig-Gen. C.B.,C.M.G.,D.S.O.	02/06/43
Glennie J.B.A. Lt-Col. D.S.O.,C.B.E.,O.B.E.,M.I.D Officer of the Order of the House of Orange	11/02/41,21/12/44,31/05/56,01/10/58,08/06/63
Glover A. Lt. (T/Capt.) E.M.	20/03/47
Glover P.L. Cpl. M.M.	21/06/45,23/06/45
Godley H.G. Cpl. M.I.D.	23/05/46,25/05/46
Goldsmith E.E.W. L/Sgt. M.M.	27/01/44
Goodall A.H. Capt. M.I.D.	07/01/49
Goody J.W. Capt. (Hon. Mjr.) T.D.	16/09/60
Goodhall W.H.E. Pte. M.M.	20/08/40,26/08/40
Goodsell W.G.E. Pte. M.M.	20/07/44

Name	Dates
Goodwin E.A.H. Lt-Col. O.B.E.,M.I.D.	13/01/44,15/01/44,28/06/45,18/09/45
Gordon G.R.K. Lt. (T/Capt.) E.M.	28/11/46
Gould W.G. Cpl. M.M.	20/07/44
Gouldsmith A. A/Capt. M.I.D.	11/01/45,29/11/45
Govier J. Pte. M.M.	20/03/45
Graham L.A. C.Q.M.S. M.M.	19/10/44
Grainger R.E. Capt. M.B.E.,M.I.D.,U.S. B.S.	20/09/45,14/11/47,31/12/60
Grant A.J.S. Mjr. M.B.E.,M.I.D.,T.D.	01/11/29,20/12/40,02/01/50,31/03/50
Grattan P.G. Lt. M.B.E.	04/04/52
Greenfield J. S/Mjr. M.M.	08/07/43,10/07/43
Greenough E.E. Capt. M.C.,T.D.	12/09/47
Gumbrell J. Cpl. M.I.D.	15/12/42
Haddock F.F. Mjr. (T/Lt-Col.) T.D.	20/04/44,24/04/44
Hadley P.S. Capt. (T/Mjr.) M.B.E.,T.D.	08/06/44,19/02/52
Hagel L.J. Lt. C.F.M.	21/11/52
Haines L.B. Capt. T.D.	26/10/54
Hall F.W. L/Cpl. M.M.	23/04/42,24/04/42
Hammond E.S. C.S.M. M.I.D.	09/05/46
Hanlon P.J. Mjr. & Q/M. M.B.E., M.I.D.	20/12/40,01/01/48
Hann F.W. Lt-Col. O.B.E.	01/01/62
Harbord F. Lt. E.M.	12/08/49
Harding J.R. Mjr. T.D.	17/03/61
Harley R.V. Capt. G.M.	31/07/51
Harpur G.H.L. Capt. M.I.D.	23/05/46,25/0/46
Harris A. Cpl. M.M.	22/03/45
Harris P.C. Capt. M.I.D.	26/04/45
Harrison P.M.J. Capt. O.B.E,M.C,	19/12/41,20/12/41,23/01/42,12/06/58,01/10/58
Harrison-Stanton R.G. Mjr. O of Orange Order	08/05/54
Hart E.G. Lt. C.F.M.	30/09/58
Harvey R.W. A/Mjr. C.F.M.	17/11/50
Harwood C.J. Sgt. M.I.D.	20/12/40
Harwood G. Pte. M.I.D.	10/05/45
Haselden J.K. Maj. M.B.E.	30/12/41
Hawkes G.W. Capt. M.C.	09/07/43,10/07/43
Hawkins G. Cpl. M.I.D	20/12/40
Hayes D.R.C. Capt. M.I.D.	13/01/44,15/01/44
Hayes L.J. Lt. M.I.D.	04/04/46
Heatherley P.F. A/Capt. C.F.M.	21/11/52
Heriz-Smith G.V. Lt-Col. (T/Col.) O.B.E.,M.C.,T.D.	19/08/43,21/08/43
Herman H.E. Sgt. (A/C.Q.M.S.) M.M.,M.I.D.	21/06/45,10/01/46,14/01/46
Hickman J.H. L/Cpl. M.M.	08/07/43,10/07/43
Hickman K.P. Capt. (Hon. Mjr.) T.D.,E.M.	12/08/47,21/04/50
Hill F. R.S.M. M.B.E.,M.I.D.	26/04/45,13/06/46
Hillman R.A.E. Capt. (T/Mjr.) T.D.	16/11/44,18/11/44,24/11/53
Hiscock B.B. Sgt. M.I.D.	06/04/44
Hiscocks T.J.R. L/Cpl. M.I.D.	10/01/46,14/01/46,19/09/46
Hissey B.S. Mjr. T.D.	19/11/37
Hoad D.H. Capt. T.D.	12/11/57,17/01/64
Hoare J.G. Cpl. (S/Sgt.) M.I.D.	06/05/32
Hodgson G.D. Capt. M.C. ,T.D.	22/03/45,21/04/50
Hodgson J.C. Lt-Col. M.I.D.	23/05/46,25/05/46
Hogben R.D.S. Maj. M.C.,M.I.D.	13/09/45,10/01/46,14/01/46
Holden-White H.V. Lt. (T/Capt.) M.C.,M.I.D.	24/04/44,27/09/45
Hole F.H. Mjr. T.D.& Clasps	26/06/50
Homden G.H. Sgt. M.I.D.	11/07/40
Hollands D.E. Sgt. D.C.M.	13/01/44,15/01/44
Hollingdale R.C. Sgt. M.M.	08/02/45
Hollist E.G. Lt-Col. M.I.D.	20/12/40,08/06/66
Holmes G. Pte. M.I.D.	29/11/45
Hood T.D. T/Lt-Col. M.I.D.	04/04/46
Hookway L.C. R.S.M. M.I.D.	09/05/46
Hornblower T.B. Mjr. T.D.	28/06/21
Horwood J.R. Cpl. M.M.	08/03/45
Hoskins S.J. was A/Mjr. C.F.M.	04/04/52
Houghton D.G. R.S.M.	01/10/58
How G.S. T/Capt. M.I.D.	29/11/45
Hubbard W.K. Capt. (Hon. Mjr.) T.D.	21/04/50
Hughes H.C. Lt. (Hon. Capt.) T.D.	20/06/50
Hulme N.E. Capt. M.I.D	05/04/45
Hulton J.M. Mjr. C.B.E.,D.S.O. O of R Sun 4th Cl.	19/09/21
Hunnisett A. Lt. (Hon. Capt.) C.F.M.	20/02/51
Hunt C. Maj. M.C.	21/06/45
Hunting C.P.M. Capt. (Hon. Mjr.) T.D	14/05/57
Ide E.W.A. Pte. M.I.D.	20/12/40
Illman E.J. Gnr. M.I.D.	22/03/45
Ives B. Pte. M.M.	08/07/43,10/07/43
Izzard A.S. C.S.M. M.I.D.	20/12/40
Jackson C.H. Capt. M.C.	29/11/45
James F.A. Lt. (Hon. Mjr.) E.M.	22/04/49
James M.A. Brig-Gen. V.C.,M.C.	05/08/43
James M.H Capt. T.D.	15/07/60
Jaques V.H. Col. D.S.O.,C.B.E.,O.B.E.,M.C..,M.I.D.	11/01/45,19/04/45,13/06/46,07/11/46,09/11/46

Name	Date
Jeffery F. Pte. M.I.D.	24/08/44
Jelley G.M. Capt. M.C.	25/02/43
Jenkins R.W. Sgt. M.I.D.	17/06/43
Johnson C.W.S. Capt. M.I.D.	06/04/44
Johnson J.M.H. Capt. M.B.E.	13/01/44,15/01/44
Johnston O.C. Mjr. M.I.D.	01/01/62
Jones A.G. Capt. E.M.	15/12/42
Jones P.H. T/Maj. D.S.M. Greece	14/10/49
Jordan E. W.O.11 M.I.D.	04/03/52
Jordan G.F. T/Capt. M.I.D.	10/05/45
Jourdain E.P.R. 2nd Lt. M.C.	18/06/46
Jourdain H.J. Maj. M.C.	11/07/40,12/04/45
King R. de L. T/Mjr. C.B.E.,O.B.E.,M.I.D.	07/11/46,09/11/46,02/06/62,01/0/65
King W. Pte. M.M.	28/01/43,30/01/43
Kirkby S.A.H. Lt-Col. M.C.,M.I.D.	20/12/40
Knaggs C.R. Capt. E.M.	12/02/52
Knapp A.C. Sgt. D.C.M.	11/07/40
Knight C. Sgt. M.I.D.	29/11/45
Knocker N.B. Capt.	08/05/54
Lambird W.H. Sgt. Royal Corps Sigs. M.I.D.	22/03/45
Lane L.W. Mjr. M.C.	19/02/41
Langdon M.C.S. Mjr. M.I.D.	09/05/46
Langham R.H. Maj. M.C.,M.I.D.	20/12/40,25/02/43,24/06/43,22/06/44
Langridge G.J. Mjr. T.D.	20/07/54,16/11/62
Lawson P.M. Mjr. M.I.D.	07/01/49,24/04/53
Leake A.E. Lt. M.I.D.	29/08/46
Lee J.V. T/Cpt. M.C.	01/01/46
Lee W.M. Capt. M.I.D.	29/11/45,17/01/46
Leeder E.J. Lt. E.M.	12/12/46,26/05/50
Leech W.G. Sgt. M.M.,M.I.D.	10/01/46,19/09/46,24/02/50
Leeder L. P.S.M. (M.I.D. Not Gazetted)	11/07/40
Leggatt C.R.C. L/Cpl. M.I.D.	29/11/45
Lester A.W. Lt. M.I.D.	23/05/46,25/05/46
Levey M.E. T/Capt. Chev of the Ord. Of the Crown	17/09/48
Lewis-Clements R.V. L/Cpl. M.I.D.	31/01/41
Libby R. Sgt. M.I.D.	28/01/41
Lilley G.W. W.O.11 M.I.D.	04/04/46
Lintott J.O. Capt. (Hon. Mjr.) T.D.	21/04/50
Loder R.E. Brig-Gen. C.B.E.	01/01/65
Longman R.C. Cpl. B.E.M	29/03/45
Longthorne J.A. Sgt. M.I.D.	24/06/43
Loten J.W. W.O.1 M.I.D.	08/11/45
Lovell W. Pte. M.I.D.	10/06/21
Lowles R.C. C.S.M. M.I.D.	29/11/45
Lucas R.G. R.S.M. O of H/O G.M.,LS&GC	08/05/54,17/07/59
Luxford H. Sgt. M.M.	08/02/45
Lyons W.F. R.S.M. M.B.E.	30/12/41
Mack J.N. Pte. M.M.	01/03/45
Mackinlay N.W. Pte. M.M.	08/07/43,10/07/43
Macpherson J.G.C. Mjr. A.E.R.D.	01/12/53
MacNichol H.M. Capt. T.D.	17/11/61
Magrath J.S. Lt-Col. M.C.,M.I.D.	11/07/40,11/01/45
Mannington H. Capt. M.B.E.M.,M.I.D. R.A.M.C.	19/07/45,29/11/45,12/11/46
Mansell F.R. Mjr. M.I.D.	27/09/45
Marchant L.G. C.Q.M.S. B.E.M.	01/01/54
Marks P.C. Pte. M.I.D.	13/01/44,15/01/44
Marsh L.E. Pte. M.I.D.	11/01/45
Martin G.A.P. Sgt. M.M.	28/06/45,30/06/45
Martin H.L.J Gnr. M.I.D.	29/08/46
Martin J.O. Pte. B.E.M.	26/06/47
Maslin A., St. C., Cpl. M.I.D.	25/01/45
Mason M.J. Lt. E.M.	12/06/48
Masterman A.F. A/Capt. C.F.M.	30/11/56
Maxse F.H.J. Capt. T.D.	09/01/47
May E.C. Lt. (Hon. Mjr.) E.M.	22/11/57
Mayer J.T. T/Mjr. M.I.D. 109th L.A.A. R.A.	04/04/46
Maynard J.E. Pte. C.O.G.	04/04/4622/03/45
McArthur I.C. Capt. M.I.D.	22/03/45
McCully J.J. Maj. (T/Lt-Col.) D.S.O.	10/01/46
McGowan G.A. Capt. (Hon. Mjr.) E.M.	17/06/43
Mockford D.A.J. A/Sgt. M.I.D.	18/11/55
McNeill D.C. Lt. M.I.D.	21/04/50
Medcalf F.H. A/Capt. C.F.M.	28/07/61
Mercer C.H. Lt. M.I.D.	28/05/63
Miller P.T. Capt. (T/Mjr.) T.D.	26/04/45
Milne R.K. Lt. (Hon. Capt.) T.D.,E.M.	21/02/47,21/04/50
Moon J.R. Mjr. M.I.D.	10/01/46,14/01/46
Moreton E.P. Pte. M.M.	20/07/44
Morgan F.R.H. Mjr. (A/Lt-Col.) D.S.O.	11/07/40
Morgan J.C. Capt. M.I.D.	30/06/42
Morley L.S.D. Sgt. M.M.	08/02/45
Morling F.E. Sgt. M.I.D.	29/11/45

Mortimer C.A. A/Mjr. C.F.M.	17/04/51
Morphy M.B. Lt. E.M.,M.I.D.	27/09/45,09/05/46,04/03/49
Morris H. Sgt. M.I.D.	08/11/45
Morris R.J. Lt. M.I.D.	31/05/55
Mordaunt P.M. Capt. M.C.,LS&GC	24/02/44,24/03/50
Moseley D.B. Lt. E.M.	30/07/48
Mostyn J.E.H. Capt. (Ret.) T.D.	01/03/29
Mowbray S.J.O. Capt. (Q/M) LS&GC	01/10/54
Murphy L. Cpl. M.I.D.	13/01/44,15/01/44
Nash F.H. R.S.M. B.E.M., M.S.M.	03/05/54,09/06/55
Neal S.G. Lt. M.I.D.	27/09/45
Newnham H. Pte. M.I.D.	20/12/40
Newson E.B. Lt. (Hon. Capt.) E.M.	14/10/49
Newton R.E. C.S.M. M.I.D.	19/09/46
Newton P.S. T/Mjr. M.B.E.,	05/06/52,01/10/58
Nightingale W. R.S.M. M.I.D.	16/12/43
Nix C.F.A. Mjr. M.I.D.,T.D.	20/12/40,21/10/43,18/03/58
Nutter W.G. Pte. M.I.D.	20/12/40
Odling-Smee A.J. Lt-Col. O.B.E.,M.I.D.	29/11/45,13/12/45
Oliver D.H. T/Lt-Col. D.S.O.,M.I.D.	05/04/45,12/07/45,14/07/45
Ormerod N.H. Mjr. A.E.R.D.	03/11/53
O'Neill J. Cpl. M.I.D.	10/01/46,14/01/46,19/09/46
Osman W.E. Sgt. M.M.	20/07/44
Owen H.G. Pte. M.M.	08/02/45
Owens J. Pte. M.I.D.	19/07/45
Pace R. R.S.M. O of H/O G.M.	08/06/66
Pack W.A. Sgt. (A/S/Sgt.) M.I.D.	30/12/41
Packham D.G. Lt. E.M.	08/10/48
Pafford P.J. Lt. (Hon. Capt.) E.M.	01/04/49
Page R.J. Capt. E.M.	17/06/49
Parks J. C.Q.M.S. B.E.M	13/12/45
Parkinson R.E.H. Lt. M.B.E.	12/05/42,15/05/42
Parris J.E. Capt. T.D.	25/03/43
Parsons J.H.G. A/Mjr. C.F.M.	28/07/59
Pasiful J. L/Cpl. M.I.D.	29/11/45
Paterson A.J. Pte. M.M.	26/11/42
Peacock E.G. Pte. M.M.	08/07/43,10/07/43,21/07/43
Peatfield D.W.D. 2nd/Lt. M.C.	19/09/61
Peckitt C.R. Maj. M.B.E.,T.D.,M.I.D.	20/12/40,01/01/45,21/04/50
Penney R.R. Capt. (Hon. Mjr.)	21/04/50
Phelps G.A. Lt-Col. D.S.O.,M.I.D.	30/12/41,31/12/41,28/06/45,18/09/4508/07/43
Phillips F.W. Capt. M.C. Chaplain	08/07/43
Phillips H.F. R.S.M. M.B.E.,M.I.D.	11/01/45,19/04/45
Phillips H.W. Lt. E.M.	21/06/45
Phillips L.N. Lt-Col. C.F.M.	15/12/50
Picard A.J. L/Cpl. M.M.	04/11/47
Picton T. Capt. M.B.E.	02/06/23
Pickworth S.W.H. Capt. T.D.	31/01/46
Pinkham C.W. A/Sgt. M.I.D.	23/05/46,25/05/46
Pitman A.L. Lt. (Hon. Capt.) T.D.	02/09/55
Plested C. Sgt. M.I.D.	09/05/46
Pocock C.H. Lt. & Q/M. M.I.D.	01/04/41,15/12/42
Pollington H.S. Capt. M.I.D.	15/12/42
Portlock E.B. Sgt. B.E.M.	13/09/45
Potter T.M. A/Capt. C.F.M.	16/03/51
Powell C.A. Lt.	19/07/45
Powell F.J. C.S.M. M.I.D.	05/04/45
Powell F.J.B. C/Sgt. M.S.M.	13/09/58
Powell P.J.L. T/Mjr. Chev of O Leo 11 with Palm, C de G with Palm 1940, Belgium	25/09/47
Powell S.J. Pte. M.I.D.	22/04/45
Power T.J. Lt. (Hon. Capt.) E.M.	29/06/51
Priddle C. Cpl. M.I.D.	13/01/44,15/01/44
Pritchard S.E. Capt. M.C. Chaplain	14/10/43
Queripel L.E. Capt. V.C.	01/01/45,02/01/45
Randall H. Pte. M.I.D.	15/12/42
Rasell W.R. Sgt. M.M.	23/04/42,27/04/42,30/04/42
Rayner T.E. W.O.11 M.I.D.	22/03/45
Redford W.A. Sgt. B.E.M.	26/10/54
Ree E.A. Hon. Lt. T.D.	19/10/51
Rees A.R. Capt. M.I.D.	29/11/45
Reilly T. Capt. M.C.,M.B. R.A.M.C.	08/07/43,10/07/43
Reynolds R.A. Lt. (Hon. Capt.) E.M.	06/02/47
Richards D. Capt. M.C.,T.D.,M.I.D.	14/10/43,06/04/44,20/03/47,21/04/50
Richards P.R. Mjr. M.I.D.	08/04/49
Ring L.J. T/Mjr. M.I.D.	19/09/46
Roach R.A. Lt. M.C.	08/03/45

Name	Date(s)
Roberts A.A. Capt. (Hon. Mjr.) T.D.	21/04/50
Roberts M.A.G. Mjr. T.D.	16/03/65
Robey F.A. Pte. M.I.D.	20/12/40
Robinson E.O. Lt. (Q/M) LS&GC	09/09/49
Roe T.C.W. Lt-Col. O.B.E.,M.B.E.,M.I.D.	15/12/42,08/02/45,08/02/45,28/06/45,09/05/46
Rogers F.H. Mjr. T.D.	20/06/50
Rogers H. J. A/Sgt. M.I.D.	19/09/46
Rogers W.G. L/Cpl. M.M.	21/06/45
Rogers W.H. Lt. T.D. & Clasps	21/04/50
Rohde R.E. Lt. M.I.D.	12/06/23
Rolington H.L. Lt. M.I.D.	23/05/46,25/05/46
Ronald F.J. Lt. (T/Capt.) M.I.D.	02/05/51
Rossiter E. Pte. M.M.	08/07/43,10/07/43
Rowe A.H. Cpl. M.I.D.	19/09/46
Rubie P.H. Capt. T/Mjr. M.C.	11/07/40,21/12/44
Russell D.E.C. Lt-Col.	30/04/65
Ryshworth-Hill A.G. Capt. (T/Mjr.) M.C.	13/01/44,15/01/44
Sampson N.E. Sgt. M.M.	15/11/45
Samworth R.G. Mjr. M.B.E.	01/01/49
Saunders C.A. Cpl. M.I.D.	19/09/46
Saunders L.J.. Cpl. M.I.D.	20/12/40
Searson A.C. Sgt. M.M.	26/07/45
Sechiari St.J. G.A. Lt. (Hon. Capt.) T.D.	01/05/56
Selbourne W.E. Pte. M.M.	16/11/44
Selby C. Sgt. M.I.D.	19/07/45
Seller C.S. Pte. M.I.D.	09/11/44
Sevenoaks E.C. Maj. Lt. M.B.E., M.C.	18/06/40,20/12/40,21/06/45
Seymour A.R. Sgt. M.M.	17/12/42
Seymour H. Pte. M.I.D.	14/11/46,16/11/46
Shadbolt A.S. Lt. E.M.	28/11/46
Shaw D.R.E. Mjr. M.I.D.	22/12/39,30/12/41,31/12/41
Shaw J.W.H. Capt. M.I.D.	19/07/45
Shaw R.F.G. Mjr. T.D.	16/09/60
Sherrin R.L.J. T/Capt. M.B.E.	11/06/66
Shield R. Pte. M.I.D.	11/01/45
Shinkwin R.E.S. Mjr. M.C.	09/09/42
Shippam C.P.B. Hon. Mjr. C.F.M.	08/06/54
Shippam F.N. Capt. M.I.D.	22/03/45
Silver R.M. Lt. M.I.D.	29/11/45
Simmons A.R. Sgt. M.I.D.	05/04/45
Simmons C.H. Capt. (Hon Mjr.) T.D.	14/07/51
Simmons F. Pte. M.M.	08/03/45
Simmonds T.P. C.S.M. M.I.D.	20/12/40
Sleeman J.L. Col. C.B,C.M.G.,K.B.E.,C.B.E.,M.V.O.,T.D.	01/04/21,04/06/2106/02/22,01/01/2923/06/31
Order of the Sacred Treasure 3rd Class, Japan	01/01/36,26/02/42,04/06/46,12/12/50
Sleeman R.B. de F. Mjr. O.B.E.,M.C.	09/11/401/01/52,04/01/49,01/10/58
Snowdon D.C. Lt-Col. T.D.	Nov. 63
Smalley D.W. Lt. E.M.	09/01/47
Smith A.L. Cpl. M.I.D.	24/08/47
Smith D.A. A/Mjr. C.F.M.	11/07/40
Smith F.M. Lt. M.B. M.C. R.A.M.C.	25/01/66
Smith J.J. Lt. M.C.	17/01/46,19/09/46
Smith R.L. Sgt. M.M.,M.I.D.	29/08/46
Smith T.H. Pte. M.I.D.	27/10/61
Smith W.S.J. Sgt. B.E.M.,G.O.C's Comm for Bravery	1952,01/01/62
Smitherman L.F. Lt. (Q/M) LS/GC	27/10/61
Snell I.A. Mjr. M.B.E.	01/01/51
Sparkes A.L. Sgt. M.I.D.	10/05/45
Spencer T.J. Pte. M.I.D.	05/04/45
Stanbrook F.W.S. Mjr. M.B.E.,M.C.,C.F.M.	16/11/44,30/09/58,12/06/65
Stanley H. Pte. M.I.D.	20/12/40
Stanton J.R.G. Mjr. M.B.E.	01/06/53
Steadman M.J. Sgt. M.I.D.	10/01/46,14/01/46
Steer H. Cpl. M.I.D.	05/04/45
Steer A.J. Lt. (Hon. Capt.) Long Service & Good Conduct	30/01/48
Steer J.S. Maj. & Q/M. M.B.E., M.I.D.	29/09/42,18/02/43
Stephens D.E. Lt. (Hon. Capt.) E.M.	22/07/52
Stevenson O.R. Capt. (Hon. Mjr.) T.D.	12/11/57
Stibbe P.G. Lt. M.I.D	14/02/46
Stonham F.C.G. Pte. M.M.	22/03/45
Stratten D.C. Capt. M.I.D.	29/11/45
Syphas D. Pte. MM.	25/02/43
Talbot S. Pte. G.M.	27/08/41,28/10/41
Talmey A. Cpl. D.C.M.	19/12/42,23/01/42,24/01/42
Tarver C.H. Brig. C.B.E.,M.I.D.	19/10/53,12/06/58
Tayler L.W.S. Mjr. M.I.D.	26/04/45
Taylor G.F. Pte. M.M.	22/06/44
Taylor H.J.C. Capt. M.I.D.	20/12/40
Thompson F.I.H.H. Mjr. M.I.D.	23/05/46,25/05/46
Thompson R.O.V. Lt-Col. D.S.O.	24/08/44
Thompson W. Mjr. M.I.D.	27/09/45

Thomson P.W.B. Lt. M.C.	21/12/44
Thornton G.E. T/Lt-Col. O.B.E.	01/10/47
Thornton H.D. Lt. E.M.	06/02/47
Thrift H. Pte. M.I.D.	19/07/45
Tilling A. L/Sgt. D.C.M.	07/03/41,16/03/41
Tolley W.G. L/Cpl. M.I.D.	29/11/45
Tomlin E.G. Pte. B.E.M.	08/06/44
Trigg F.H. Pte. M.M.	07/01/43,17/03/43,26/03/43
Trotman G.F. Lt. M.I.D.	04/04/46
Trott N.W. Lt. E.M., M.I.D.	23/05/46,25/05/46,25/09/51
Tucker K.O. Capt. M.I.D.	13/01/44,15/01/44
Tupper H.O. Sgt. M.I.D. R.A.	12/09/46
Turnbull P.E.X. 2nd Lt. (A/Lt.) M.C.	18/06/40,20/12/40
Turner C.B.G. T/Capt. M.I.D.	04/04/46
Turner E.G. Sgt. M.I.D.	10/01/46,14/01/46,19/09/46
Turner J.A. Capt. E.M.	23/05/52,19/03/63
Turner R.F. Sgt. M.I.D.	23/05/46,25/05/46
Tyler M.W. Pte. M.I.D.	24/09/43
Upton E.J. Mjr.(Q/M) M.M. T.D.	12/09/47
Upton S.J.F. Capt. M.C.,T.D.	09/07/43,10/07/43,04/10/43,28/11/46,12/09/47,21/04/50
Vaughan-Williams R.H. Capt. M.I.D.	04/04/46
Verth A.G. Pte. M.I.D.	29/11/45
Vidler C.A. A/Capt. C.F.M.	28/03/61
Vinall W.P. Sgt. B.E.M.	14/06/45
Von der Heyde J.L. Brig. C.M.G,C.B.E. O.B.E.,M.C.,M.I.D.	30/12/41,28/06/43,14/10/43,16/10/43,06/04/44
Wagener J.G. T/Mjr. M.I.D.,T.D.	12/04/45,04/04/46
Waite L. Cpl. M.I.D.	10/05/45
Wakefield E.D.E. Capt. (A/Mjr.)	16/03/65
Walker J.T. Lt-Col. E.M., O of H/O	29/03/60,30/04/65
Wallace W.C. Lt. (Hon. Capt.) E.M.	14/08/51
Wallis L.W. Sgt. M.I.D.	27/09/45,19/09/46
Walton J.I.W. Capt. T.D.	25/10/55
Warren J.R. Mjr. O.B.E.,M.C.,T.D.	04/07/22,03/06/27
Wannop E.K.B. Lt-Col. M.I.D.,T.D.	04/07/22,20/12/40,16/11/44,18/11/44
Waters R.D. Capt. M.I.D.	21/02/46
Watson H.E.R. Mjr. M.B.E.	09/06/55
Webb F. R.S.M.	30/04/65
Webb G. Pte. M.I.D.	20/12/40
Webster F.I. Capt. M.I.D.	29/11/45
Weeks L.W. Lt. M.C.	08/07/43
Weller R.J.R. Pte. A.A.C. M.M.	22/06/43,09/07/43,10/07/43,04/03/44,08/03/44
Wells D.G. Sgt. M.M.	15/06/43
Wells R.E. C.S.M. M.I.D.	13/01/44,15/01/44
West T. Pte. M.I.D.	24/06/43
Wharton R.G.P. Lt. M.I.D.	19/09/46
Whaymand L. Pte. M.I.D.	11/01/45
Wheeler A. was A/Lt-Col.	17/11/50
Wheeler G.R. Pte. M.M.	29/09/42
Whistler L.G. Gen. G.C.B.,K.C.B.C.B.,K.B.E..,D.S.O., M.I.D,, Commander of the Order of the Crown with Palm Croix de Guerre 1940 with Palm ,Belgium	11/07/40,29/04/41,22/04/43,13/01/44,14/01/44, 22/03/45,29/03/45,09/08/45,11/08/45,04/04/46,25/09/47, 01/01/52,08/05/54,01/01/55,01/01/57,14/04/62
White A.W. Pte. M.M.	16/11/44
White B.R. C.S.M. B.E.M.	17/01/46
White H.G. Sgt. M.M.	17/06/43
White H.R. Pte. M.I.D.	13/01/44,15/01/44
White L.F. Cpl. M.M.	31/07/56
Whiteman B. Mjr. M.C.,T.D.	20/02/31
Wildash A.C. Cpl. M.I.D.	07/04/45,27/09/45
Wilkins P.V. A/Capt. C.F.M.	17/11/50
Willard C.J. Pte. M.M.	21/09/44,22/09/44
Williams H.F. A/Capt. E.M., C.F.M.	27/07/56,31/07/56
Williams R.M. Lt. M.C.	21/06/45
Wilson C.H. Pte. M.M.	08/03/45
Wilson K.S.H. T/Mjr. M.I.D.	30/06/42,19/07/45
Wilson W.G. Pte. M.M.	11/07/40
Wisden T.J.F. T/Mjr. M.I.D.	19/07/45
Wood D.E. Cpl. G.M.	28/10/41
Wood E.R. Lt. (A/Capt.) C.F.M.	29/11/63
Woodbridge C.E. Lt. T.D.	28/06/55
Woodrow J.H. Mjr. M.I.D.	31/05/55
Woodruffe W.T. Maj. M.C.	31/08/44
Worthington F.A. Sgt. M.M.	21/06/45
Wraight W.F. Q/M & Capt. T.D.	25/08/27
Wright L.P. L/Bdr. M.I.D.	04/04/46
Wyard B.W.H. Lt. (Hon. Capt.) L/Service & Good Conduct	25/09/53
Wyatt R.J.P. Hon. Brig. M.C. ,T.D.,D.L.	17/11/42
Wye A.V. A/Mjr. C.F.M.	26/05/61
Wyeth D.B.J. Cpl. M.I.D.	27/09/45
Wyndham P.C.J. Lt. M.I.D.	29/11/45
Young S.H. Pte. M.M.	19/12/41,23/01/42

The Royal Sussex Regiment

Prisoners of War 1940-1945

No.	Rank	Name	Battalion	Country	Camp No.	Pow No.
6402240	S/Sgt.	Eustace Lewis Abbey	4th Bn.	Germany	Stalag IV B. Muhlberg	260963
5727605	Pte.	Kenneth Charles Adams	7th Bn.	Poland	Stalag XX A. Thorn	4830
71885	Capt.	John F Ainsworth	2nd Bn.	Germany	Oflag VII B. Eichstaat (Fuchstaat)	203
6400079		George Ernest Alderton	2nd Bn.	Poland	Stalag B.A.B. 20 Kedzierzyn-Kozle	20110
6403305		George Wallace Allcorn	7th Bn.	Poland	Stalag 344 Lamsdorf	479
129361	Capt.	Michael Richard Allden	1st Bn.	Germany	Oflag V A. Weinsberg	2957
176893	Lt.	G L Allen	4th Bn.	Germany	Oflag V A. Weinsberg	2712/32
6403294	Pte.	H Allen	7th Bn.	Poland	Stalag XXI V.Z.A. Posen	3336
6395123	P.S.M.	Ralph James Allen	2nd Bn.	Poland	Stalag 344 Lamsdorf	10143
6396009	Pte.	A Ancell	2nd Bn.	Poland	Stalag 344 Lamsdorf	7327
6404224	Pte.	George Stanley Andrews	4th Bn.	Germany	Stalag IV A. Hohenstein	252394
6397411	Sgt.	W Andrews	1st Bn./50 Commando	Germany	Stalag 383 Hohen Fels	12558
6401449	L/Cpl.	Albert Edward Apps	5th Bn.	Poland	Stalag XX B. Malbork	18879
6401970	Pte.	William Herbert Ashby	2nd Bn.	Poland	Stalag XX B. Malbork	1598
6403417	Pte.	R J Ashdown	4th Bn.	Germany	Stalag IV D/Z	249547
6401202	L/Cpl.	A Ashley	4th Bn.	Germany	Stalag IX A. Altenburg	141782
6399180	Bdsm.	F W Austen	2nd Bn.	Poland	Stalag XX (5) Thorn	13784
71265	2/Lt.	Ivor Malcolm Austin	5th Bn.	Germany	Oflag VII B. Eichstaat (Fuchstaat)	891
6399293	Cpl.	A C Avann	2nd Bn.	Poland	Stalag XX B. Malbork	8465
6400452	Pte.	A S Ayling	4th Bn.	Czechoslovakia	Stalag IV C Bystrice	258590
6398726	Pte.	Edward Francis Ayling	4th Bn.	Czechoslovakia	Stalag IV C. Bystrice	250650
75926	Lt. (Qmr.)	George William Ayling	7th Bn.	Germany	Oflag IX A/H Spangenberg	35012
6406523	L/Cpl.	C Baddock	4th Bn.	Germany	Stalag IV D/Z Annaburg	249741
6400228	Pte.	C E Bailey	1st Bn.	Poland	Stalag 344 Lamsdorf	34573
6400318	Pt.	W T Bailey	7th Bn.	Poland	Stalag XX B. Malbork	8319
6398362	Pte.	A Baker	1st Bn.	Poland	Stalag VIII B. Cieszyn	77232
6400143	Pte.	F Baker	4th Bn.	Germany	Stalag IV D.Z. (Annaburg)	249747
64063863	L/Cpl.	F C Baker	4th Bn.	Germany	Stalag IV F. (Hartmansdorf Chemnitz)	249983
5622049	Pte.	G G Baker	2nd Bn.	Poland	Stalag 344 Lamsdorf	11475
6401847	Pte.	K Balaam	2nd Bn.	Poland	Stalag B.A.B. 20 Kedzierzyn-Kozle	109191
6401965	Pte.	E R Baldy	7th Bn.	Poland	Stalag XX A Thorn Podgorz	5797
5622193	Pte.	A E Ball	4th Bn.	Poland	Stalag 344 Lamsdorf	9792
6401605	Pte.	S W Ball	5th Bn.	Poland	Stalag 344 Lamsdorf	10350
96964	2/Lt.	John Bruce Ballard	7th Bn.	Poland	Oflag VII B. Eichstaat (Fuchstaat)	96964
6403102	Pte.	S Banfield	4th Bn.	Czechoslovakia	Stalag IV C. Bystrice	251017
6400080	Pte.	Bertie Leonard George Barker	2nd Bn.	Poland	Stalag 344 Lamsdorf	13707
6403358	L/Cpl.	Donald T F Barker	4th Bn.	Poland	Stalag 344 Lamsdorf	
6397100	Pte.	L E Barker	2nd Bn.	Poland	Stalag XX B. Malbork	20230
5501272	Pte.	R D Barnes	5th Bn.	Germany	Stalag IX C. Mulhausen Bad Sulza	31149
6399436	Pte.	F W Barr	1st Bn.	Poland	Stalag VIII B. Cieszyn	127049
7010300	L/Cpl.	J Barr	2nd Bn.	Germany	Stalag III A Luckenwalde	1171
5255715	Pte.	G C Bartholomew	1st Bn.	Germany	Stalag XI A. Altengrabow	142548
6401850	Pte.	D W Barton	2nd Bn.	Poland	Stalag XX B. Malbork	19319
6394542	Pte.	R A Barwick	2nd Bn.	Poland	Stalag 344 Lamsdorf	3123
5667541	Pte.	G W Bayliss	4th Bn.	Poland	Stalag 344 Lamsdorf	15145
6396651	Pte.	G H Bean	2nd Bn.	Poland	Stalag XX B. Malbork	12289
6404111	Cpl.	Ronald Alfred Beck	4th Bn.	Germany	Stalag IV B. Muhlberg (Elbe)	252117
6401091	Pte.	J H Bedford	2nd Bn.	Poland	Stalag 344 Lamsdorf	2358
14218904	Pte.	Sydney Beet	1st Bn.	Germany	Stalag XI A. Altengrabow	142173
5727861	Pte.	Leslie Allen Belam	7th Bn.	Poland	Stalag XX A. Thorn	
6400305	L/Cpl.	N R Bennett	5th Bn.	Poland	Stalag XX A. 2 Thorn	11811
6401824	Pte.	J G Benson	2nd Bn.	Poland	Stalag 344 Lamsdorf	10781
6398096	Pte.	William Walter Bentley	1st Bn.	Germany	Stalag IV B. Muhlberg (Elbe)	260943
6399184	Pte.	R Bergin	1st Bn.	Germany	Stalag XIII C. Hammelberg am Main	15076
99781	2/Lt.	Eric John Berlyn	7th Bn.	Germany	Oflag VII B. Eichstaat (Fuchstaat)	486
6396480	Pte.	F C Bicknell	2nd Bn.	Poland	Stalag XX A. 3.A. Thorn	12451
6404230	Pte.	G H Billingham	4th Bn.	Germany	Stalag IV D. Torgau (Elbe)	250249
6403277	Pte.	G Billings	7th Bn.	Poland	Stalag VIII B. Cieszyn	3773
5615537	Pte.	R G Billington	4th Bn.	Poland	Stalag VIII B. Cieszyn	10841
6401177	Pte.	S A Bishop	5th Bn.	Poland	Stalag XX B. Malbork	12903
6401851	Pte.	V H Bishop	2nd Bn.	Germany	Stalag 344 Lamsdorf	15655
6403895	Pte.	George H Blaber	1st Bn.	Germany	Stalag 357 Oerbke	260613
6401982	Pte.	H J Blackman	2nd Bn.	Poland	Stalag XX B. Malbork	8654
5727656	Pte.	W Blows	7th Bn.	Poland	Stalag XX A. 5. Thorn	10
1304899	Pte.	G F Bond	1st Bn.	Poland	Stalag 344 Lamsdorf	30102
6397146	Pte.	W H Bond	2nd Bn.	Germany	Stalag 344 Lamsdorf	10491
6399064	Pte.	J E Boniface	2nd Bn.	Germany	Stalag 344 Lamsdorf	10734
6396044	Pte.	William George A Boniface	2nd Bn.	Germany	Stalag 344 Lamsdorf	10494
6400460	Pte.	J R Booth	5th Bn.	Poland	Stalag XX A. (7) Thorn	11181
5501318	Pte.	Thomas William Bosanquet-Bryant	5th Bn.	Germany	Stalag 344 Lamsdorf	15748
6087581	Pte.	V Bostrom	4th Bn.	Germany	Stalag IV D. Torgau (Elbe)	250593
6400638	Pte.	F C Bourne	7th Bn.	Poland	Stalag 344 Lamsdorf	4749
6403286	Pte.	Gordon Horace Bourner	7th Bn.	Poland	Stalag XXI B.1. Szubin	
6410936	Pte.	N Bowers	4th Bn.	Germany	Stalag IV A. Hohenstein	258264
6404116	L/Cpl.	A D Boxall	4th Bn.	Germany	Stalag IV G. Oschatz	249289
6397266	Pte.	William Henry Braine	attd. 101st Coy R.E.	Poland	Stalag XX B. Malbork	15059
6392549	CQMS	Harold George Brassfield	5th Bn.	Germany	Stalag 383 Hohen Fels	19351
6406003	L/Cpl.	Fred Farnsworth Brassington	4th Bn.	Czechoslovakia	Stalag IV C. Bystrice	252118
6399165	Sgt.	Albert Edward Braund	2nd Bn.	Germany	Stalag 383 Hohen Fels	11321
6404236	Pte.	Leonard Claude Bray	4th Bn.	Germany	Stalag IV A. Hohenstein	252216
6394901	Pte.	Sidney Herbert Braybrooks	2nd Bn.	Poland	Stalag VIII C. Konin-Zaganski	10857
5809	Mjr.	James Leighton Breeds	4th Bn.	Germany	Oflag IX A/H. Spangenburg	217
3240030	Pte.	J Bridges	2nd Bn.	Poland	Stalag 344 Lamsdorf	8655
6475755	Pte.	W L Bridges	4th Bn.	Germany	Stalag IV D/Z Annaburg	249518
6400208	Pte.	S H Brigden	4th Bn.	Poland	Stalag 344 Lamsdorf	1167
6398917	Pte.	Ernest George A Briggs	2nd Bn.	Czechoslovakia	Stalag IV C Bystrice	3
5729056	Pte.	T H Brindley	4th Bn.	Germany	Stalag IV D/Z Annaburg	249554
6403148	Pte.	N E Broad	4th Bn.	Germany	Stalag IV F. Hartmansdorf Chemnitz	258785
6400911	Pte.	E Broadbridge	4th Bn.	Germany	Stalag IV B. Muhlberg (Elbe)	262748
562259	Pte.	A E Brockway	2nd Bn.	Poland	Stalag XX B. Malbork	5340
6402019	Pte.	W F Brooke	2nd Bn.	Poland	Stalag XX A. Thorn Podgorz	9496
5501250	L/Cpl.	Edward Charles Brookman	5th Bn.	Poland	Stalag XX B. Malbork	19673
6398650	Pte.	J Brooks	1st Bn.	Germany	Stalag VII A. Moosburg (Isar)	129831
5728001	Pte.	J R Brooks	7th Bn.	Poland	Stalag XX B. Malbork	10251
6399782	Pte.	J Broomfield	5th Bn.	Poland	Stalag XX B. Malbork	1234
6402383	Pte.	A C Brown	7th Bn.	Germany	Stalag 344 Lamsdorf	16030
6410636	Pte.	A J Brown	4th Bn.	Czechoslovakia	Stalag IV C Bystrice	295483
6401798	L/Cpl.	J Brown	7th Bn.	Poland	Stalag 344 Lamsdorf	3992
5439411	Pte.	J T Brown	7th Bn.	Poland	Stalag XX B. Malbork	10293
6398666	Cpl.	Robert Macdonald Brown	1st Bn.	Germany	Stalag 111D.	

Service No.	Name	Battalion	Country	Camp	PoW No.
6397256	Pte. E A J Bryant	2nd Bn.	Poland	Stalag XX B. Malbork	12307
6401856	Pte. E C Bryant	2nd Bn.	Poland	Stalag VIII B. Cieszyn	4735
6401901	Pte. L Buck	1st Bn.	Germany	Stalag IV G Oschatz	131444
6401066	Pte. H W Budd	2nd Bn.	Poland	Stalag VIII B. Cieszyn	2236
6403267	Pte. Edwin T A Bull	7th Bn.	Poland	Stalag XX B. Malbork	10420
6398836	Pte. J Bullen	1st Bn./50 Commando	Germany	Stalag IV D. Torgau (Elbe)	12474
6401045	Pte. F S Burbridge	2nd Bn.	Poland	Stalag VIII B. Cieszyn	1725
40998	Capt. John Burder M.I.D.	4th Bn.	Germany	Oflag IX A/Z. Rotenburg an der Fulda	495
6403103	Pte. Keith Ian C P Burgess	4th Bn.	Germany	Stalag IV G Oschatz	131443
6401990	Pte. S C Burggy	2nd Bn.	Poland	Stalag 346 B.A.B. 21. Blechammer	1617
6400359	Pte. F J Burns	5th Bn.	Poland	Stalag XX B. Malbork	17658
193769	2/Lt. Peter Michael Burns	4th Bn.	Germany	Oflag V A. Weinsberg	2713
99792	2/Lt. David Michael Charles Burrough	7th Bn.	Germany	Oflag VII B. Eichstaat (Fuchstaat)	2602
6399651	Pte. H J Buss	7th Bn.	Poland	Stalag VIII B. Cieszyn	3337
6401819	Pte. J G Butcher	2nd Bn.	Poland	Stalag XX B. Malbork	9653
6141740	Pte. J R Butler	2nd Bn.	Poland	Stalag 344 Lamsdorf	5031
6411276	Pte. J W Butterworth	4th Bn.	Germany	Stalag IV G. Oschatz	249312
3961866	Pte. Thomas Eli F Byng	2nd Bn.	Germany	Stalag B.A.B. 20. Kedzierzyn-Kozle	10441
1832025	Pte. J Byrnes	4th Bn.	Germany	Stalag IV G. Oschatz	258894
6401868	Pte. Arthur Richard Cadey	2nd Bn.	Poland	Stalag XX A. Thorn Podgorz	9054
77938	2/Lt. John Boucicault de S Calthrop	5th Bn.	Germany	Oflag 79 Brunswick	769
6403314	Pte. Joseph Noel Campany	7th Bn.	Germany	Stalag 344 Lamsdorf	15211
6401807	Pte. George H Campbell	7th Bn.	Germany	Stalag 344 Lamsdorf	14109
6406800	Pte. Cyril J. A. Carey	4th Bn.	Germany	Stalag IV F. Hartmansdorf Chemnitz	258309
6401029	Pte. A G Carley	4th Bn.	Germany	Stalag 344 Lamsdorf	15484
6403539	L/Cpl. Arthur Henry F Carpenter	4th Bn.	Poland	Stalag 344 Lamsdorf	35465
105088	2/Lt. James Dean Carr		Germany	Oflag VII B. Eichstaat (Fuchstaat)	226
6343972	Sgt. S J Carr	4th Bn.	Germany	Stalag IV B. Muhlberg (Elbe)	260595
6404240	Pte. Harry Edward Castleman	4th Bn.	Germany	Stalag IV D/Z Annaburg	249521
6396543	Pte. W P Challis	2nd Bn.	Poland	Stalag XX A. Thorn Podgorz	12446
6084459	L/Sgt. F A Chambers	4th Bn.	Germany	Stalag IV B. Muhlberg (Elbe)	229180
6286925	Pte. A Champion	2nd Bn.	Poland	Stalag XX B. Malbork	6718
6400772	Pte. R J Chandler	4th Bn.	Germany	Stalag IV D/Z Annaburg	249411
5728134	Pte. R G Chapman	7th Bn.	Poland	Stalag XX B. Malbork	2558
6400141	Pte. M E Charman	4th Bn.	Germany	Stalag IV F. Hartmansdorf Chemnitz	250188
6402822	Pte. H Chatfield	4th Bn.	Czechoslovakia	Stalag IV C Bystrice	252208
6397524	Pte. William Arthur J Chatfield	1st Bn.	Germany	Stalag IV D. Torgau (Elbe)	259788
13048227	Pte. Reginald William Cheese	1st Bn.	Austria	Stalag XVII A. Kaisersteinbruck Bei Bruck	15351
6394494	L/Sgt. W Chevis		Poland	Stalag 357 Oerbke (near Fallingbostel)	10986
6401861	Pte. P R Chivers	2nd Bn.	Poland	Stalag XX B. Malbork	8653
6630701	P.S.M. Eric Albert Clark	2nd Bn.	Poland	Stalag XX B. Malbork	
6402901	Pte. R E Clarke	2nd Bn.	Austria	Stalag 398 Papping (near Ling)	154867
4855239	A/Sgt. T Cleaver	4th Bn.	Germany	Stalag IV B. Muhlberg (Elbe)	227260
5439362	Pte. L G Clements	7th Bn.	Poland	Stalag XX B. Malbork	5205
6402083	Cpl. R Clements	4th Bn.	Germany	Stalag IV B. Muhlberg (Elbe)	260524
6396304	L/Cpl. E G Clifton	2nd Bn.	Germany	Stalag 344 Lamsdorf	14728
6406401	Pte. Samuel George A. Coates	1st Bn.	Germany	Stalag IV A. Hohenstein	258311
13048233	Pte. S P C R Cobb	1st Bn.	Czechoslovakia	Stalag IV C Bystrice	253514
6400134	Pte. Harold Douglas Cobby	2nd Bn.	Poland	Stalag XX B. Malbork	11446
6399284	Pte. William H Cogger	5th Bn.	Germany	Stalag 344 Lamsdorf	11117
6403985	Pte. B Colbourne	1st Bn.	Germany	Stalag IV G. Oschatz	253611
6403271	Pte. D F Coles	7th Bn.	Poland	Stalag XX B. Malbork	8842
5827035	Pte. L Collins	2nd Bn.	Poland	Stalag VIII B. Cieszyn	13732
6400000	Pte. M Collins	7th Bn.	Poland	Stalag XX A. Thorn	9543
6282522	Pte. Sidney Collins	4th Bn.	Poland	Stalag XX I B. Cieszyn	
95484	Lt. Michael R Colyer		Germany	Oflag VII B. Eichstaat (Fuchstaat)	238
6471499	Pte. W F Condon	4th Bn.	Germany	Stalag III A. Luckenwalde	34134
7010624	Pte. B Connolly	2nd Bn.	Germany	Stalag III A. Luckenwalde	20181
5727891	Pte. A D Cook	7th Bn.	Poland	Stalag 344 Lamsdorf	4015
6398123	Pte. R F Cook	5th Bn.	Poland	Stalag XX B. Malbork	11248
7011496	Pte. Samuel Herbert Cooke D.C.M.	2nd Bn.	Germany	Stalag 344 Lamsdorf	
6401954	Pte. B T Cooksley	7th Bn.	Poland	Stalag XX A. Thorn	9542
5501281	Pte. Edgar F E Coombs	5th Bn.	Germany	Stalag IV A. Hohenstein	258462
6397719	Pte. C E Cooper	1st Bn.	Germany	Stalag 357 Oerbke (near Fallingbostel)	30095
6397513	Sgt. J F Cooper	2nd Bn.	Germany	Stalag 344 Lamsdorf	10489
6401025	Pte. O Cooper	4th Bn.	Germany	Stalag IV F. Hartmansdorf Chemnitz	229312
17220	Pte. G M Coskin	4th Bn.	Poland	Stalag XX A. Thorn	11637
6406404	Pte. D Costello	4th Bn.	Germany	Stalag IV F. Hartmansdorf Chemnitz	259760
6397147	Pte. Harry Frederick Cottle	4th Bn.	Poland	Stalag XX B. Malbork	1541
6401956	Pte. James Richard Coughlan	4th Bn.	Germany	Stalag IV B. Muhlberg (Elbe)	249508
6409502	Pte. F W Coutts	1st Bn.	Germany	Stalag XI A. Altengrabow	142637
6400714	Pte. E G Cox	4th Bn.	Poland	Stalag XX B. Malbork	11277
6403234	Pte. F G Cox	7th Bn.	Poland	Stalag XX A. Thorn	11565
5672584	Pte. R H Cox	5th Bn.	Germany	Stalag IX B. Fallingbostel	140771
14551708	Pte. Douglas Percy Creasey	1st Bn.	Germany	Stalag IV A. Hohenstein	131011
6197192	Pte. William Joseph Crème	2nd Bn.	Poland	Stalag XX A. Thorn	12662
6397770	Pte. Charles George Crittenden	2nd Bn.	Poland	Stalag XX B. Malbork	8117
6396460	Pte. H S Crocker	2nd Bn.	Germany	Oflag VII B. Eichstaat (Fuchstaat)	87
6403275	Pte. J Crook	4th Bn.	Czechoslovakia	Stalag IV C Bystrice	251648
95482	2/Lt. Francis Harry A. Crouch	2nd Bn.	Germany	Oflag VII B. Eichstaat (Fuchstaat)	244
6404945	L/Cpl. E Crump	4th Bn.	Germany	Oflag IV C. Saalhaus Colditz	250634
6400301	Pte. James Edward Cruttenden	1st Bn.	Poland	Stalag XX A. Thorn	8690
5668595	Pte. Lawrence Henry Cullen		Germany	Stalag XX B. Malbork	192
64117127	Pte. A C Curd	1st Bn.	Poland	Stalag VIII A. Cieszyn	131442
6403479	Pte. Ernest Thomas E Curd	4th Bn.	Germany	Stalag IV D/Z Annaburg	249798
6400378	Pte. Harold Henry Cutting	5th Bn.	Germany	Stalag IX C. Mulhausen Bad Sulza	16301
6403283	Pte. B J Dadswell	7th Bn.	Poland	Stalag XX B. Malbork	10391
4686185	Sgt. J Daley	4th Bn.	Germany	Stalag IV B. Muhlberg (Elbe)	260560
5616899	L/Cpl. R S Darby	4th Bn.	Germany	Stalag IV B. Muhlberg (Elbe)	251738
6403194	Cpl. Alfred Charles D G Daughtrey	7th Bn.	Poland	Stalag XX A. Thorn	5811
33664	Capt. Aubrey Claude Davidson-Houston	2nd Bn.	Germany	Oflag VII B. Eichstaat (Fuchstaat)	246
5728162	Pte. D J Davis	7th Bn.	Poland	Stalag XX A. Thorn	
5434132	Pte. Geoffrey William T Davis	7th Bn.	Germany	Stalag B.A.B. 20. Kedzierzyn-Kozle	6008
6395814	Pte. L S Davis	2nd Bn.	Poland	Stalag XX A. Thorn	13871
6011825	Cpl. R G Davison		Poland	Stalag 344 Lamsdorf	1021
14241846	L/Cpl. H F Daw	1st Bn.	Austria	Stalag XVIII A. Wolfsberg (Karnten)	6720
792815	L/Cpl. F Deacon	2nd Bn.	Poland	Stalag B.A.B. 20. Kedzierzyn-Kozle	12684
5435539	Pte. E Deakin	7th Bn.	Poland	Stalag 344 Lamsdorf	15493
6398260	Pte. H F Dean	1st Bn.	Germany	Reserve-Lazerett (PoW Hospital) Obermassfeld	52189
6403312	Pte. R C Dean	7th Bn.	Poland	Stalag 344 Lamsdorf	18088
6474705	Pte. A W Deeks	4th Bn.	Germany	Stalag IV F. Hartmansdorf Chemnitz	228775
5439307	Pte. Albert Leslie Dell	7th Bn.	Poland	Stalag XX A. Thorn	
6404021	Pte. Ronald E De Lara	1st Bn.	Germany	Stalag IV D/Z. Annaburg	227438
6401777	L/Cpl. Albert Walter Dench M.I.D.	4th Bn.	Germany	Stalag IV B. Muhlberg (Elbe)	229060
3530140	Pte. Samuel Dentith		Germany	Stalag IV A. Hohenstein	
6399802	Pte. L D Denyer	2nd Bn.	Poland	Stalag VIII B. Cieszyn	2298
6401096	Pte. P H Denyer	2nd Bn.	Poland	Stalag XX B. Malbork	12725
6402254	Pte. E F Dickson	5th Bn.	Poland	Stalag XX A. Thorn	1958
5727109	Pte. S J Dinmore	7th Bn.	Poland	Stalag 344 Lamsdorf	15415
6401267	Pte. W G Ditton		Poland	Stalag 344 Lamsdorf	25808
162504	A/Capt. Timothy Charles Donavan	4th Bn.	Germany	Oflag 79 Brunswick	3335
13048268	Pte. J W Dorsett	4th Bn.	Germany	Oflag IV C Colditz	249376
6402899	Pte. C A Douch	4th Bn.	Germany	Stalag IV C. Bystrice	253642
6082779	Sgt. T Dowd	7th Bn.	Germany	Stalag 383 Hohen Fels	758

6404955 Cpl. G R Drake		4th Bn.	Germany	Stalag IV F. Hartmansdorf Chemnitz	251422
6915461 Pte. H J Drake		4th Bn.	Germany	Stalag IV G. Oschatz	251421
6395806 Pte. W Driscoll attd. Pioneer Corps.			Germany	Stalag XI B. Fallingbostel	140329
6397774 Pte. J Dudman		2nd Bn.	Poland	Stalag 344 Lamsdorf	11132
6401820 Pte. W A Dudman		2nd Bn.	Poland	Stalag XX B. Malbork	750
6408346 Pte. J Dunkerton		1st Bn.	Poland	Stalag 344 Lamsdorf	220593
6404136 Pte. A F Durrant		4th Bn.	Germany	Stalag IV F. Hartmansdorf Chemnitz	260113
6401561 Cpl. Douglas John F. B. Durston		7th Bn.	Poland	Stalag 344 Lamsdorf	16326
5501255 Pte. James Edward Dyer			Poland	Stalag 344 Lamsdorf	12930
54855467 W.O.1 James Edward Eames		7th Bn.	Germany	Stalag 357 Oerbke (near Fallingbostel)	5604
6394854 L/Cpl. R Eason		2nd Bn.	Poland	Stalag 344 Lamsdorf	17057
6402432 Pte. Albert George Edney		7th Bn.	Poland	Stalag XX B. Malbork	10421
63950009 Pte. C H Edwards		2nd Bn.	Poland	Stalag 344 Lamsdorf	12131
6395723 Sgt. Harold H. Edwards		1st Bn.	Poland	Stalag 317 Markt Pongua	39010
6398094 Pte. Alexander Leonard Vernon Elliott		2nd Bn.	Poland	Stalag XX B. Malbork	13785
6401417 Pte. Horace Maurice A. Elliott		4th Bn.	Germany	Stalag IV F. Hartmansdorf Chemnitz	228736
105090 2/Lt. Wilfred Gordon Elms			Germany	Oflag VII B. Eichstaat (Fuchstaat)	259
6939301 Cpl. Reginald Victor Elphick		2nd Bn.	Poland	Stalag 344 Lamsdorf	10490
5728011 Pte. J Ester		1st Bn.	Poland	Stalag 344 Lamsdorf	4806
6404101 L/Sgt. Harold George Etheridge		2nd Bn.	Poland	Stalag VII A. Moosburg (Isar)	139074
6396830 Pte. Robert J. Etherton		2nd Bn.	Poland	Stalag 344 Lamsdorf	13243
6397846 Pte. S. Etherton		1st Bn.	Germany	Stalag IV F. Hartmansdorf Chemnitz	259775
6399196 Pte. Charles A. Everley		1st Bn.	Czechoslovakia	Stalag IV C. Bystrice	226585
2025638 C.S.M. Daniel J Fallshaw		4th Bn.	Germany	Stalag 357 Oerbke (near Fallingbostel)	260446
6473463 Pte. J L Farrell		4th Bn.	Germany	Stalag IV D. Torgau (Elbe)	275341
6399298 Sgt. E Farrow		4th Bn.	Germany	Stalag 357 Oerbke (near Fallingbostel)	299199
6398310 Cpl. P C Faulkner		4th Bn.	Germany	Stalag 344 Lamsdorf	15611
6398418 Pte. T Feist		1st Bn.	Poland	Stalag VIII C. Konin-Zaganski	76939
162505 Lt. Norman William Reed Felstead		1st Bn.	Germany	Oflag V A. Weinsberg	2718
40294 Capt. Maurice E. Few		7th Bn.	Germany	Oflag VII B. Eichstaat (Fuchstaat)	902
6976526 Cpl. William J Fiddis		4th Bn.	Poland	Stalag 344 Lamsdorf	82200
7343128 Cpl. Raymond Filmer		1st Bn.	Poland	Stalag 344 Lamsdorf	21573
6396337 Pte. Harry Filtness		2nd Bn.	Poland	Stalag 344 Lamsdorf	10495
6396357 Pte. R Finch		2nd Bn.	Poland	Stalag XX B. Malbork	20757
6400249 Pte. B Fisher		2nd Bn.	Poland	Stalag XX B. Malbork	13007
5727495 Pte. E B Fisher		7th Bn.	Poland	Stalag 344 Lamsdorf	3931
6396154 Pte. Lloyd George Fitsell		2nd Bn.	Poland	Stalag XX A. 3 Thorn	12469
6397703 Pte. Leonard John Fletcher		2nd Bn.	Germany	Stalag B.A.B. 20 Kedzierzyn-Kozle	19311
7011517 Pte. J J Flood		2nd Bn.	Poland	Stalag III A. Luckenwalde	1175
6397996 Cpl. S R Foord		attd. Infantry Base Depot	Poland	Stalag XXI B.Z. Szubin	5189
862484 Pte. W C Foord		5th Bn.	Poland	Stalag XX A. Thorn	19019
6475845 Pte. L A Forbes		4th Bn.	Germany	Stalag IV G. Oschatz	250095
6403161 Pte. R Foster		7th Bn.	Poland	Stalag 344 Lamsdorf	709
6410987 Pte. J Fowler		4th Bn.	Germany	Stalag IV F. Hartmansdorf Chemnitz	249982
296998 Lt. Edward Foy		attd. 2nd Devons	Germany	Oflag 79 Brunswick	409
6402027 Pte. Sidney Lester France		4th Bn.	Czechoslovakia	Stalag IV C. Bystrice	252214
6402252 Pte. D F Franks		5th Bn.	Poland	Stalag XX A. Thorn	64301
6401735 P.S.M. H E Franks		2nd Bn.	Poland	Stalag 344 Lamsdorf	10775
6404623 Pte. C J Freeman		1st Bn.	Czechoslovakia	Stalag IV C. Bystrice	258273
6398282 Cpl. A E French		1st Bn.	Czechoslovakia	Stalag IV C. Bystrice	258955
6394552 Sgt. A H Fuller		7th Bn.	Germany	Stalag 357 Oerbke (near Fallingbostel)	259934
6395035 Pte. J Fuller		2nd Bn.	Poland	Stalag 344 Lamsdorf	10550
50209 Capt. Robert Joseph Fuller M.C.		5th Bn.	Germany	Oflag VII B. Eichstaat (Fuchstaat	905
6398220 Pte. W C Furnell		1st Bn.	Germany	Stalag XI B. Fallingbostel	140422
6396085 Pte. W L Gadd		2nd Bn.	Poland	Stalag XX B. Malbork	9294
6401947 Pte. A Gander		7th Bn.	Poland	Stalag XX B. Malbork	3586
6403190 Pte. H R Gardiner		2nd Bn.	Poland	Stalag XX B. Malbork	7424
6399489 Pte. Douglas Francis M. Gardner		1st Bn.	Germany	Stalag IV B. Hohenstein	258146
5723527 Pte. C V Garland		7th Bn.	Poland	Stalag 344 Lamsdorf	14020
6395895 Pte. C P Garvey		2nd Bn.	Poland	Stalag VIII A. Gorlitz	9722
6403874 Pte. Reginald Northern Gasking		1st Bn.	Poland	Stalag 344 Lamsdorf	220733
6138359 Pte. Edward Charles Gatcum		2nd Bn.	Poland	Stalag 357 Oerbke (near Fallingbostel)	19313
6403931 Pte. Edward Reginald Geall		1st Bn.	Germany	Stalag IV A. Hohenstein	260416
86687 Lt/Col. Ronald Gethen		7th Bn.	Germany	Oflag IX A/H Spangenburg	272
6403374 Pte. F A Gibbs		1st Bn.	Germany	Stalag IV B. Muhlberg (Elbe)	253610
6410689 Pte. T A Gibbs		4th Bn.	Poland	Stalag 344 Lamsdorf	30525
6307841 Pte. G E Gilbert		2nd Bn.	Poland	Stalag XX B. Malbork	8466
5729427 Pte. C E Giles		4th Bn.	Germany	Stalag IV D. Torgau (Elbe)	251665
6401123 Pte. R G Gillett		7th Bn.	Poland	Stalag XX A. V. Thorn	8689
6401175 Pte. R E Gillis		7th Bn.	Poland	Stalag 344 Lamsdorf	708
6403220 Pte. E Glasby		7th Bn.	Poland	Stalag XX B. Malbork	8611
6397459 L/Cpl. Albert J. Glason		2nd Bn.	Poland	Stalag 344 Lamsdorf	10074
6396546 Pte. Albert John Glazier		2nd Bn.	Germany	Stalag 344 Lamsdorf	37159
64016146 L/Sgt. D Glover		7th Bn.	Poland	Stalag XX A. Thorn	7506
6409380 Pte. J W Glover		1st Bn.	Germany	Stalag XI A. Altengrabow	142726
6395604 Pte. J Glue		1st Bn.	Germany	Stalag IV A. Hohenstein	21695
6406943 Cpl. E W Goble		4th Bn.	Germany	Stalag IV B. Muhlberg (Elbe)	251351
6396524 Pte. Albert William Godley		4th Bn.	Poland	Stalag VIII B. Cieszyn	17
6399098 Sgt. Donald John Godley			Germany	Stalag 383 Hohen Fels	16000
6401567 Pte. F A Goldsmith		7th Bn.	Poland	Stalag VIII B. Cieszyn	7152
6401567 Pte. George A. Goldsmith		7th Bn.	Poland	Stalag 344 Lamsdorf	7152
6398214 Pte. Harold W. Goldsmith		2nd Bn.	Germany	Stalag XII A. Limburg	25972
6410691 Pte. R S Goldsmith		4th Bn.	Czechoslovakia	Stalag IV C. Bystrice	259456
6402253 Pte. A Goodsell		4th Bn.	Poland	Stalag 344 Lamsdorf	43768
203061 2/Lt. David Hugh Goodson		4th Bn.	Germany	Oflag XII B. Hadamar	273
6399325 Pte. Victor D Goodwin		2nd Bn.	Poland	Stalag 344 Lamsdorf	11535
5728161 Pte. Philip Joseph Goold		7th Bn.	Poland	Stalag VIII B. Cieszyn	3731
6405844 Pte. T Gordon		4th Bn.	Germany	Stalag IV D.Z. Annaburg	249726
5727883 Pte. A J Gould		7th Bn.	Germany	Stalag IX C. Mulhausen Bad Sulza	3860
6401631 Pte. Roy T P Gould		5th Bn.	Poland	Stalag 344 Lamsdorf	15679
6395359 Pte. A Goulthorp		2nd Bn.	Poland	Stalag XXI A. Schildberg	
6404263 Pte. Leslie Kitchener Grace		4th Bn.	Germany	Stalag IV D. Torgau (Elbe)	59956
6400217 Pte. W L Gray		4th Bn.	Poland	Stalag 346 B.A.B. 21. Blechammer	1475
6401315 Pte. A J Green		4th Bn.	Poland	Stalag 344 Lamsdorf	9708
6402248 Cpl. D A Green		4th Bn.	Germany	Stalag IV B. Muhlberg (Elbe)	
6404830 Jack Gilbert J. Green		1st Bn.	Germany	Stalag IV D/Z Annaburg	228025
6401676 Pte. P A Green		5th Bn.	Poland	Stalag 344 Lamsdorf	10285
6395131 Pte. W S Green		2nd Bn.	Poland	Stalag XX B. Malbork	7706
6399376 Pte. W Greene		2nd Bn.	Poland	Stalag 344 Lamsdorf	166
6393653 C.S.M. F P Greenfield		2nd Bn.	Poland	Stalag 344 Lamsdorf	37162
6398065 Cpl. Arthur Betram Grigg		2nd Bn.	Poland	Stalag VIII B. Cieszyn	10647
6396778 Pte. E W Groves		2nd Bn.	Poland	Stalag 344 Lamsdorf	743
6396808 Pte. G Gurr		2nd Bn.	Germany	Stalag IX C. Mulhausen Bad Sulza	31099
6399513 Sgt. Gilbert Henry D. Hagger		5th Bn.	Poland	Stalag 344 Lamsdorf	9768
5718241 Pte. Leslie Thomas Haiek		7th Bn.	Poland	Stalag 344 Lamsdorf	4819
64113184 Pte. John Henry Haladay		4th Bn.	Germany	Stalag IV F. Hartmansdorf Chemnitz	253159
5501300 Pte. E G Hall		5th Bn.	Poland	Stalag 344 Lamsdorf	10264
2041961 Pte. F J E Hall		2nd Bn.	Poland	Stalag XX B. Malbork	6720
6397788 Pte L F Hall		2nd Bn.	Poland	Stalag XX B. Malbork	7703
5501300 Pte. R G Hall		5th Bn.	Poland	Stalag 344 Lamsdorf	10264
6408578 Pte. C Halstead		4th Bn.	Austria	Stalag XVII A. Kaisersteinbruck Bei Bruck	153432
6402677 L/Cpl. Theodore Frederick G. Hamblin		1st Bn.	Germany	Stalag XI A. Altengrabow	142552
6403933 Pte. Harry S Hamer		1st Bn.	Germany	Stalag IV A. Hohenstein	260432
7011484 Pte. E Hamilton		2nd Bn.	Poland	Stalag III A. Luckenwalde	142248

Service No. & Name	Bn.	Country	Camp	POW No.
6411156 Pte. Samuel Edward Hamilton	1st Bn.	Germany	Stalag X1 A. Altengrabow	114158
6399546 Pte. A G Hammond	4th Bn.	Germany	Stalag IV D. Torgau	251714
6401385 Pte. B Hampton	5th Bn.	Poland	Stalag XX A. 7. Thorn	20638
6404268 Pte. J E Hands	4th Bn.	Germany	Stalag IV B. Muhlberg (Elbe)	260974
3965166 Pte. J M Hannan	7th Bn.	France	Hospital Bergin, St. Mande Paris	
6400083 Pte. David R. Hannant	2nd Bn.	Germany	Stalag IV B. Muhlberg (Elbe)	10936
6404149 Cpl. A S Harding	4th Bn.	Germany	Stalag 357 Oerbke (near Fallingbostel)	250306
5671261 Pte. Frederick John P. Harding	4th Bn.	Poland	Stalag XX B. Malbork	539
6400054 Pte. J R Harding	2nd Bn.	Poland	Stalag XX B. Malbork	9329
6390326 C.Q.M.S. Samuel G. Harding	2nd Bn.	Germany	Stalag 357 Oerbke (near Fallingbostel)	11302
6397780 Pte. W A Harding	2nd Bn.	Poland	Stalag XX B. Malbork	36811
6399307 L/Cpl. E J Hardick	2nd Bn.	Poland	Stalag 344 Lamsdorf	3121
5439964 Pte. Kenneth William Harper	7th Bn.	Poland	Stalag XX B. Malbork	1126
6400320 Pte. Stanley Jesse Harriott	5th Bn.	Poland	Stalag 344 Lamsdorf	10492
5509243 Pte. F B Harris	1st Bn.	Germany	Stalag XI A. Altengrabow	142302
6397874 Pte. Joseph Richard Harris	2nd Bn.	Germany	Stalag 344 Torgau (Elbe)	47967
6397392 C.S.M. R Harris	4th Bn.	Germany	Stalag IV B. Muhlberg (Elbe)	261049
6402404 Pte. V A Harrison	7th Bn.	Poland	Stalag VIII B. Cieszyn	434
P/62939 2/Lt. Richard Gordon Harrison-Stanton		Germany	Oflag VII B. Eichstaat (Fuchstaat)	853
6396329 Sgt. J H W Hart	2nd Bn.	Poland	Stalag 344 Lamsdorf	11382
5727667 Pte. William Arthur Hart	7th Bn.	Poland	Stalag XXI B.H. Szubin	3932
6408534 Pte. L F Hartfield	4th Bn.	Germany	Stalag VI D/Z Annaburg	249563
115619 Lt. Bedford Anthony Hartnell		Germany	Stalag VII B. Eichstaat (Fuchstaat)	1174
6398438 Pte. John E H Harvey	1st Bn.	Germany	Stalag 344 Torgau (Elbe)	228474
6402296 Pte. G S Hawkins	2nd Bn.	Poland	Stalag 344 Lamsdorf	10903
6403291 Pte. N F W G Hayes	1st Bn.	Poland	Stalag 344 Lamsdorf	220767
6411401 Pte. R A Haynes	4th Bn.	Germany	Stalag IV F. Hartmansdorf Chemnitz	261176
3910379 Pte. Thomas E Haynes	1st Bn.	Germany	Stalag XI A. Altengrabow	142533
6399055 Pte. Edgar Charles Hayward	5th Bn.	Poland	Stalag 344 Lamsdorf	10694
6401799 Pte. G Hayward	7th Bn.	Poland	Stalag XX B. Malbork	10423
315393 Lt. Alan Heaps	1st Bn.	Germany	Oflag IX A/Z. Rotenburg an der Fulda	2025
5439928 Pte. A H Heard	7th Bn.	Poland	Stalag XXI B.H. Szubin (20)	4721
6400252 Pte. Lionel D Hearsey	2nd Bn.	Poland	Stalag 344 Lamsdorf	11133
76693 2/Lt. John Heasman	5th Bn.	Germany	Stalag VII B. Eichstaat (Fuchstaat)	575
6469322 Pte. Stanley J Hempsted	4th Bn.	Germany	Stalag IV G. Oschatz	249201
6403384 L/Cpl. E S Herbert	4th Bn.	Germany	Stalag IV D. Torgau (Elbe)	250616
6404026 Pte. C Herriot	1st Bn.	Germany	Stalag IV A. Hohenstein	248387
6398254 Drmr. George William Hewlett	1st Bn.	Germany	Stalag IV D. Torgau (Elbe)	262778
6401325 Pte. E W Hickman	7th Bn.	Poland	Stalag 344 Lamsdorf	4695
6401900 L/Cpl. Edward J Hickmott	4th Bn.	Germany	Stalag IV D. Torgau (Elbe)	249874
6397999 Sgt. R Hicks	4th Bn.	Germany	Stalag IV B. Muhlberg (Elbe)	260977
6403233 Pte. F J Hillman	7th Bn.	Poland	Stalag 344 Lamsdorf	361
6400758 Pte. J E Hillman	4th Bn.	Czechoslovakia	Stalag IV C. Bystrice	259458
6397427 Pte. Henry Samuel G. Hills	2nd Bn.	Poland	Stalag 344 Lamsdorf	17179
6307858 Pte. L Hills	2nd Bn.	Poland	Stalag 344 Lamsdorf	11443
6399749 Pte. George Thomas Hoad	2nd Bn.	Poland	Stalag 344 Lamsdorf	2354
6397194 Pte. George P. Hoather	4th Bn.	Germany	British Labour Camp Wittenberg	1247
6397211 Pte. J G Hockley	2nd Bn.	Poland	Stalag VIII A. Gorlitz	11534
6400088 Cpl. T Hodd	2nd Bn.	Poland	Stalag XX A. Thorn	7696
6396010 Pte. E P Hodges	2nd Bn.	Germany	Stalag IX C. Mulhausen Bad Sulza	3871
6400894 Pte. F Hodges	7th Bn.	Poland	Stalag 344 Lamsdorf	77884
6401809 Cpl. T Hodges	7th Bn.	Germany	Stalag 383 Hohen Fels	5172
6398075 Sgt. S Hodgson	1st Bn.	Austria	Stalag 317 Markt Pongua	39009
117119 2/Lt. David Cuthbert Lyall Holland	7th Bn.	Germany	Oflag VII B. Eichstaat (Fuchstaat)	531
6403652 Pte. R J Holland	1st Bn.	Czechoslovakia	Stalag IV C. Bystrice	251604
6402046 Pte. Donald Augustus Holliman	4th Bn.	Czechoslovakia	Stalag IV C. Bystrice	251804
4545902 Pte. Edgar Hollingworth	4th Bn.	Germany	Stalag IV B. Muhlberg (Elbe)	
6402180 Pte. W G Holmes	4th Bn.	Poland	Stalag 344 Lamsdorf	15779
6398431 Sgt. Alfred Charles Honeysett	1st Bn.	Germany	Stalag 383 Hohen Fels	6013
6401275 Pte. C Honeysett	5th Bn.	Poland	Stalag XX B. Malbork	12554
6395361 C.S.M. A E Hood	2nd Bn.	Germany	Stalag 383 Hohen Fels	11300
6400851 Pte. F W Hook	7th Bn.	Poland	Camp 2 CB	2281
6399443 Pte. L Hook	2nd Bn.	Poland	Stalag 344 Lamsdorf	14719
6398250 Cpl. David W Hooker	1st Bn.	Austria	Stalag XVIII A. Wolfsberg (Karnten)	6949
6469330 Pte. Norman William H. Hoole	4th Bn.	Germany	Stalag IV F. Hartmansdorf Chemnitz	249833
2023893 Pte. W F Hooper	attd. No. 2 Commando	Germany	Stalag 357 Oerbke (near Fallingbostel)	18689
6395265 Pte. John Hope	2nd Bn.	Poland	Stalag XX B. Malbork	9326
6403896 Pte. G F Hopkins	1st Bn.	Germany	Stalag IV F. Hartmansdorf Chemnitz	260934
6403228 Pte. J Hopkins	7th Bn.	Poland	Stalag 344 Lamsdorf	3335
6401189 Pte. P W Hopkins	4th Bn.	Austria	Stalag XVIII A. Wolfsberg (Karnten)	8250
6398645 Pte. James A Hopwood	1st Bn.	Czechoslovakia	Stalag IV C. Bystrice	252068
6466744 Pte. Thomas H Hopwood	4th Bn.	Germany	Stalag IV D. Torgau (Elbe)	263101
5573705 Pte. William Horlick	4th Bn.	Poland	Stalag 344 Lamsdorf	263101
6007092 Pte. C W Horn	1st Bn.	Czechoslovakia	Stalag IV C. Bystrice	258623
6397149 Sgt. J H Hornsby	2nd Bn.	Poland	Stalag 344 Lamsdorf	16811
5668367 Cpl. S W House	attd. 133rd Inf. Bde (H/Q).	Germany	Stalag 383 Hohen Fels	13186
6939943 Pte. F W Hughes	7th Bn.	Poland	Stalag 344 Lamsdorf	4748
6398754 Pte. L A Hull	5th Bn.	Poland	Stalag 344 Lamsdorf	10695
6401931 Pte. J R Humphrey	7th Bn.	Poland	Stalag 344 Lamsdorf	16325
6306871 Cpl. R J Humphrey	2nd Bn.	Poland	Stalag 383 Hohen Fels	20280
6401914 Pte. Gordon Derek Hunnisett	2nd Bn.	Germany	Stalag XX B. Malbork	2359
6411018 Pte. A C Hunt	4th Bn.	Czechoslovakia	Stalag IV C. Bystrice	252228
2571089 Pte. T W Hunt	4th Bn.	Germany	Oflag IV C. Saalhaus Colditz	249412
6397828 Pte. W J Hunt	2nd Bn.	Poland	Stalag XX A. Thorn	8464
639276 L/Cpl. Louis Frank Huntly	7th Bn.	Poland	Stalag XX B. (21) Malbork	5062
6400607 Pte. C F Hurd	5th Bn.	Germany	Stalag 344 Lamsdorf	34873
63598 Lt. James Frederick Huxford		Germany	Oflag VII B. Eichstaat (Fuchstaat)	294
6469589 Pte. R W Hyland	4th Bn.	Poland	Stalag 344 Lamsdorf	221386
6475509 Pte. Jack Henry Iddiols	4th Bn.	Poland	Stalag 344 Lamsdorf	31400
6402451 Pte. Reginald Douglas G. Inkpin	7th Bn.	Poland	Stalag 344 Lamsdorf	1374
6396747 Pte. J H Inman	2nd Bn.	Poland	Stalag 344 Lamsdorf	12940
6400381 Pte. George Edward Irving	5th Bn.	Poland	Stalag 344 Lamsdorf	10331
6398922 Pte. J W Irving	5th Bn.	Poland	Stalag 344 Lamsdorf	448
6395909 Pte. L S Isaac	2nd Bn.	Poland	Stalag XX A. Thorn	124444
6397367 Pte. G E Isted	5th Bn.	Poland	Stalag XX A. Thorn	64311
6401513 Pte. W Ives	5th Bn.	Poland	Stalag VII B. Cieszyn	1685
6393074 Sgt. C Jackson	2nd Bn.	Germany	Stalag IV B. Muhlberg (Elbe)	261140
38234 Lt. Charles Hughlings Jackson M.C.	5th Bn.	Germany	Oflag V I B. Eichstaat (Fuchstaat)	1194
6404164 Cpl. G A Jackson	4th Bn.	Germany	Stalag IV B. Muhlberg (Elbe)	252070
6911269 S/Sgt. G R Jackson	4th Bn.	Germany	Stalag IV B. Muhlberg (Elbe)	263781
6401881 Pte. Phillipus Johannas P. Jacobs	2nd Bn.	Poland	Stalag 344 Lamsdorf	10493
5622562 Pte. D G James		Poland	Stalag 344 Lamsdorf	18064
6401738 Pte. Peter J Jarman		Poland	Stalag XXI D. Poznan	4746
6402093 Pte. D Jeal	4th Bn.	Czechoslovakia	Stalag IV C. Bystrice	251801
5667449 Pte. H F Jenkins	5th Bn.	Poland	Stalag VIII B. Cieszyn	36484
6403507 L/Sgt. Reginal W. Jenkins M.I.D.	1st Bn.	Germany	Stalag VII A. Moosburg (Isar)	127866
6403240 Pte. C R Jenner	7th Bn.	Poland	Stalag VIII B. Cieszyn	3334
5668894 C.S.M. W Johnson	4th Bn.	Germany	Stalag IV B. Muhlberg (Elbe)	229602
6393123 Pte. A F Jones	2nd Bn.	Poland	Stalag 344 Lamsdorf	6202
6401295 Pte. A N Jones	4th Bn.	Germany	Stalag IV B. Muhlberg (Elbe)	263896
6400278 Pte. H Jones	2nd Bn.	Poland	Stalag XX A. Thorn	8388
6399365 Cpl. H A Jones	2nd Bn.	Germany	Stalag 383 Hohen Fels	9016
6399652 Pte. L Jones	5th Bn.	Poland	Stalag XX A. Thorn	12413
143729 Mjr. Geoffrey Ferncombe Jordan	4th Bn.	Germany	Oflag VA. Weinsberg	2714/32

Service No.	Name	Bn.	Country	Camp	Number
6387157	S/Sgt. W Juden	4th Bn.	Germany	Stalag IV F. Hartmansdorf Chemnitz	249981
6475921	Pte. C Just	4th Bn.	Czechoslovakia	Stalag IV C. Bystrice	251844
6402455	Pte. Frank Harold Keable	7th Bn.	Poland	Stalag 344 Lamsdorf	14106
6398938	Pte. Thomas Gerald Keeley	1st Bn.	Poland	Stalag VIII C. Konin Zaganski	77063
6400275	Pte. Victor R Kembrey	2nd Bn.	Poland	Stalag XX B. Malbork	8463
6395762	Pte. F H Kent	2nd Bn.	Poland	Stalag 344 Lamsdorf	14240
6908555	Pte. Arthur Thomas Kilbee	7th Bn.	Poland	Stalag 344 Lamsdorf	15465
5669468	L/Cpl. Albert Leonard G. King	5th Bn.	Poland	Stalag 344 Lamsdorf	13727
6394548	Pte. C C King	2nd Bn.	Poland	Stalag XX A.C. Thorn	9291
6400084	Pte. D G King	2nd Bn.	Poland	Stalag XX A. Thorn	12831
6398548	Pte. V J King	2nd Inf. Base Depot.	Poland	Stalag 344 Lamsdorf	6480
6401263	Pte. Henry James Kingsland	7th Bn.	Poland	Stalag XX I B. Szubin	
6396963	Pte. Wilfred Norman Kingsland	1st Bn.	Germany	Stalag 357 Oerbke (near Fallingbostel)	9301
6395393	Pte. E J Kingston	2nd Bn.	Poland	Stalag XX B. Malbork	9292
5666681	Cpl. H E Kingston	5th Bn.	Poland	Stalag 344 Lamsdorf	359
6402656	Pte. T B Kinnard	2nd Bn.	Poland	Stalag XX B. Malbork	16009
6406280	Pte. F T Knight	4th Bn.	Germany	Stalag IV F. Hartmansdorf Chemnitz	250397
6401574	Pte. J G Knight	7th Bn.	Poland	Stalag 346 B.A.B. 21. Blechammer	4747
6397677	L/Cpl. J H Knight	4th Bn.	Czechoslovakia	Stalag IV C. Bystrice	251988
6397205	Pte. L Knight	2nd Bn.	Poland	Stalag XX B. Malbork	11529
6402316	Pte. S R Knight	5th Bn.	Poland	Stalag VIII A. Gorlitz	6137
6402556	Pte. A W Knott	5th Bn.	Poland	Stalag XX B. Malbork	19408
6401426	L/Cpl. E G Laker	4th Bn.	Czechoslovakia	Stalag IV C. Bystrice	252108
6399043	Pte. H Laker	4th Bn.	Germany	Stalag XI B. Fallingbostel	140599
5728156	Pte. F T Lamb	7th Bn.	Poland	Stalag XXI B.H. Szubin	4061
572814	Pte. A H Lambert	7th Bn.	Poland	Stalag 344 Lamsdorf	4825
5728144	Pte. Harold Henry Lancaster	7th Bn.	Poland	Stalag VIII B. Cieszyn	2544
6401649	Pte. A J Lane	7th Bn.	Poland	Stalag XX B. Malbork	3575
6401332	Pte. G Langridge	7th Bn.	Poland	Stalag 344 Lamsdorf	1378
64000105	L/Cpl. Norman Charles Larkings	5th Bn.	Germany	Stalag 383 Hohen Fels	11249
6394887	C.Q.M.S. D Lavender	1st Bn.	Germany	Stalag 357 Oerbke (near Fallingbostel)	9391
6400242	Pte. J R Lawrance	2nd Bn.	Poland	Stalag 344 Lamsdorf	2297
647007	Pte. V Lawrence	4th Bn.	Germany	Stalag IV A. Hohenstein	250030
6968068	C.Q.M.S. S C Lawrie	7th Bn.	Poland	Stalag XXI B. Szubin	
6401966	Pte. W H Lawson	6th Bn.	Poland	Stalag 344 Lamsdorf	18576
79304	2/Lt. Alan Elfast Claude Leake M.I.D.	4th Bn.	Germany	Oflag IX A/H. Spangenberg	600
6401210	Pte. A G Leaney	4th Bn.	Poland	Stalag 344 Lamsdorf	35204
6402239	Pte. Frank Le Beau	5th Bn.	Poland	Stalag XX A. Thorn	20277
6401093	Pte. W J Lee	7th Bn.	Poland	Stalag XX B. Malbork	2689
6397327	Pte. Frank William Lefevre	4th Bn.	Czechoslovakia	Stalag IV C. Bystrice	251057
7527881	L/Cpl. Thomas H. Legg	7th Bn.	Poland	Stalag XXI A. Schildberg (now called Ostrzeszow)	125
6401070	Pte. Donald James Leggatt		Poland	Stalag XX A. Thorn	14989
6400231	Pte. D C Lendrum	2nd Bn.	Poland	Stalag XX A. Thorn	9478
6398459	L/Sgt. R Lenton	1st Bn.	Germany	Stalag XI A. Altengrabow	139489
837587	L/Cpl. Douglas George Leppard	1st Bn.	Germany	Stalag XI A. Altengrabow	142278
6403666	Pte. J J Levy	4th Bn.	Germany	Stalag IV G. Oschatz	251420
6403192	Pte. A Lievers	7th Bn.	Poland	Stalag 344 Lamsdorf	3939
6146988	Pte. S J Lines		Austria	Stalag XVIII A. Wolfsberg (Karnten)	7709
6397551	Pte. H Loade	2nd Bn.	Poland	Stalag 344 Lamsdorf	42442
6400950	L/Cpl. J W Lockyer	5th Bn.	Poland	Stalag 344 Lamsdorf	117
52660	Capt. Robert Eric Loder	2nd Bn.	Germany	Oflag VII B. Eichstaat (Fuchstaat)	315
6402537	Pte. H G Long	2nd Bn.	Poland	Stalag XX B. Malbork	8657
6402161	Pte. Freeman Alexander Longlands	5th Bn.	Poland	Stalag 344 Lamsdorf	15801
6403221	Pte. A W Lord	7th Bn.	Poland	Stalag 344 Lamsdorf	2532
4804996	Pte. F Lord	1st Bn.	Germany	Stalag VIII A. Gorlitz	87085
6402461	Pte. A C S Lovell	7th Bn.	Poland	Stalag 344 Lamsdorf	724
5727950	Pte. G Lowe	7th Bn.	Poland	Stalag 344 Lamsdorf	15547
3599158	Pte. William Henry Loxley		Poland	Stalag VIII A. Gorlitz	11908
6397769	L/Sgt. Edwin Victor Luff	1st Bn.	Austria	Stalag XVIII A. Wolfsberg (Karnten)	7696
6402319	Pte. W Lunn	5th Bn.	Poland	Stalag XX B. Malbork	11269
6398870	Pte. Charles L Lusted	1st Bn.	Poland	Stalag 344 Lamsdorf	11217
6402113	Sgt. J R Macfarlane	4th Bn.	Germany	Stalag VIII A. Gorlitz	80707
6401916	Pte. A J Macklin	7th Bn.	Poland	Stalag 344 Lamsdorf	5608
6401437	Pte. T Magrath	5th Bn.	Poland	Stalag XX B. Malbork	12340
6396076	Cpl. F Maguire	5th Bn.	Germany	Stalag 383 Hohen Fels	9513
5671912	Pte. E V Main	5th Bn.	Poland	Stalag XXI D. Poznan	5839
6402146	Cpl. T Major	4th Bn.	Czechoslovakia	Stalag IV C. Bystrice	252119
6411473	Pte. J H Malthouse	4th Bn.	Germany	Stalag IV D/Z Annaburg	
6403269	Cpl. A E Mankelow	7th Bn.	Poland	Stalag 344 Lamsdorf	5009
883276	Pte. L G Manktelow	1st Bn.	Germany	Stalag XI A. Altengrabow	142522
6397799	Cpl. William A J Manley	2nd Bn.	Germany	Stalag 357 Oerbke (near Fallingbostel)	10990
6399428	L/Cpl. H Mann	2nd Bn.	Poland	Stalag 344 Lamsdorf	17055
5501315	Pte. E T Manning	5th Bn.	Poland	Stalag XX B. Malbork	1946
6399796	Pte. Sidney D. Manser	7th Bn.	Germany	Oflag VII B. Eichstaat (Fuchstaat)	624
640099	Pte. F P Mansfield	4th Bn.	Poland	Stalag 344 Lamsdorf	15209
6404340	Pte. L C H Mansfield	4th Bn.	Germany	Stalag IV F. Hartmansdorf Chemnitz	258956
6398677	Pte. D Marchant	1st Bn.	Poland	Stalag 344 Lamsdorf	29204
6401090	Pte. E R Marchant	5th Bn.	Poland	Stalag 344 Lamsdorf	14049
6400233	Pte. R I Marchant	2nd Bn.	Poland	Stalag XX B. Malbork	11445
6393619	Sgt. A Marsh	5th Bn.	Germany	Stalag 383 Hohen Fels	111
6401529	L/Cpl. E G Marsh	7th Bn.	Poland	Stalag XX A. Thorn	7173
6085118	Pte. J Marsh	2nd Inf. Base Depot	Poland	Stalag XX A. Thorn	19666
6404287	L/Cpl. H S Marshall	4th Bn.	Germany	Oflag IV B. Konigstein	249597
6399170	Cpl. J Marshall	2nd Bn.	Germany	Stalag 357 Oerbke (near Fallingbostel)	12450
5505189	L/Cpl. C E Martin	5th Bn.	Germany	Stalag IV F. Hartmansdorf Chemnitz	260155
639889	Pte. H Martin	1st Bn. attd. 52 Commando	Germany	Stalag IIIA. Luckenwalde	12631
881623	Pte. J O Martin	2nd Bn.	Poland	Stalag 344 Lamsdorf	14089
6402540	Pte. W J Martin	5th Bn.	Poland	Stalag XX B. Malbork	5969
6402505	Pte. J E Mason	7th Bn.	Poland	Stalag XX A. Thorn	8843
6397437	Pte. H D Masters	2nd Bn.	France	Feldpost FS 112	7686
14402634	Pte. C Mather	1st Bn.	Poland	Stalag 344 Lamsdorf	137916
6303212	Pte. R J Mathieson	7th Bn.	Poland	Stalag 346 B.A.B. 21. Blechammer	2235
6403973	Pte. D Matthews	1st Bn. attd. 52 Commando	Austria	Stalag XVIII A. Wolfsburg (Karnten)	7842
6399800	Pte. V G May	4th Bn.	Germany	Stalag IV F. Hartmansdorf Chemnitz	258640
3956161	Cpl. Joseph Henry Maughin	5th Bn.	Germany	Stalag IX C. Mulhausen Bad Sulza	31221
6404848	Pte. R A Mayell	1st Bn.	Czechoslovakia	Stalag IV C. Bystrice	253010
836780	Pte. F F McIver	2nd Bn.	Poland	Stalag XX A. 7. Thorn	11193
6979863	Pte. E McKendrick	5th Bn.	Poland	Stalag XX B. Malbork	14004
6411469	Pte. F C McNeill	4th Bn.	Germany	Stalag IV G. Oschatz	249294
6404177	Pte. E W Medhurst	4th Bn.	Germany	Stalag IV F. Hartmansdorf Chemnitz	250404
5501345	Pte. A W Merritt	5th Bn.	Poland	Stalag 344 Lamsdorf	42980
6400752	Pte. R P Merritt	4th Bn.	Germany	Stalag IV F. Hartmansdorf Chemnitz	228722
6403273	Pte. William George Metherell	7th Bn.	Poland	Stalag 344 Lamsdorf	3332
6308510	Pte. A C Meyer	5th Bn.	Poland	Stalag XX B. Malbork	3446
6399321	Cpl. Douglas Miles	2nd Bn.	Germany	Stalag 383 Hohen Fels	1241
6401286	Pte. E W Miles	7th Bn.	Poland	Stalag 346 B.A.B. 21. Blechammer	3576
6399650	Pte. R H Miles	5th Bn.	Poland	Stalag 344 Lamsdorf	10263
6402471	Pte. S Miles	7th Bn.	Poland	Stalag 344 Lamsdorf	4724
6404178	Pte. A Milham	4th Bn.	Germany	Stalag IV F. Hartmansdorf Chemnitz	249822
770361	Pte. A J C Miller	2nd Bn.	Poland	Stalag VIII B. Cieszyn	2886
6474151	Pte. E A Miller	4th Bn.	Germany	Stalag IV A. Hohenstein	
6396598	L/Cpl. F A Miller	2nd Bn.	Poland	Stalag 344 Lamsdorf	11531
3455628	Pte. R Mills	4th Bn.	Czechoslovakia	Stalag IV C. Bystrice	258112
6398081	Cpl. S J Mills	2nd Bn.	Poland	Stalag 344 Lamsdorf	10486

Service No.	Name	Battalion	Country	Camp	POW No.
641065	Pte. E J Milsom	4th Bn.	Poland	Stalag 344 Lamsdorf	28932
6402474	Pte. E A Minter	7th Bn.	Poland	Stalag XX A. Thorn	10489
6403349	Pte. J Mitchell	7th Bn.	Poland	Stalag XX B. Malbork	725
6403213	Pte. J H Mitchell	7th Bn.	Poland	Stalag VIII B. Cieszyn	3333
6403682	Pte. A.A. Model	1st Bn.	Germany	Stalag IV F. Hartmansdorf Chemnitz	229064
6404182	Pte. G Monk	4th Bn.	Germany	Stalag IV D. Torgau (Elbe)	262959
2044010	Pte. V C Monk	2nd Bn.	Poland	Stalag 344 Lamsdorf	13708
5510149	Pte. E A Monks	1st Bn.	Germany	Stalag XI A. Altengrabow	14225
240677	Lt. Bertie Durie Moody		Germany	Oflag 79 Brunswick	1957
6403208	Pte. A J Moore	7th Bn.	Poland	Stalag XXI B. Szubin	3310
6400183	Pte. Frederick R. D. Moore	5th Bn.	Poland	Stalag 344 Lamsdorf	14747
7011582	Pte. J M.M. Moore		Germany	Stalag III A. Luckenwalde	1190
5727637	Pte. Leslie G B Moore	7th Bn.	Poland	Stalag 344 Lamsdorf	4694
6401393	Pte. R V Moore	7th Bn.	Poland	Stalag XX B. Malbork	7437
6403684	Pte. W Morbin	4th Bn.	Czechoslovakia	Stalag IV C. Bystrice	252102
6396693	Pte. Thomas Alfred Mordle	2nd Bn.	Poland	Stalag 344 Lamsdorf	2216
6396749	Pte. S J Morley	2nd Bn.	Germany	Stalag IX C. Mulhausen Bad Sulza	1505
6401438	Sgt. Frederick Ernest Morling M.I.D.		Germany	Stalag 383 Hohen Fels	5605
6399360	Pte. R A Morgan	1st Bn.	Poland	Stalag VIII C. Konin Zaganski	77062
6402330	Pte. R J Morgan	4th Bn.	Germany	Stalag IV D. Torgau (Elbe)	260355
6402330	Pte. R V Morgan		Poland	Stalag VIII C. Konin Zaganski	10853
6396749	Pte. S J Morley	2nd Bn.	Germany	Stalag IX C. Mulhausen Bad Sulza	1505
6402024	Pte. C W Morris	4th Bn.	Germany	Stalag IV A. Hohenstein	252215
6462539	Pte. L T Morris	4th Bn.	Austria	Stalag XVII A. Kaiserteinbruck Bei Bruck	153616
6393003	Pte. J H Moss	2nd Bn.	Poland	Stalag 344 Lamsdorf	3865
4540662	Pte. W Motley	4th Bn.	Germany	Stalag IV F. Hartmansdorf Chemnitz	259255
4386213	L/Sgt. Thomas L Mowbray	4th Bn.	Germany	Stalag IV B. Muhlberg (Elbe)	260958
6411910	Pte. Cyril G. Mugridge	1st Bn.	Germany	Stalag XI A. Altengrabow	142386
18627	Mjr. Arundel Keith Mumford	2nd Bn.	Germany	Oflag IX A/H. Spangenberg	333
6402475	Pte. J S Murdock	7th Bn.	Germany	Stalag IX C. Mulhausen Bad Sulza	1353
5728146	Pte. M J Murphy	7th Bn.	Germany	Stalag III A. Luckenwalde	354
6400611	Pte. Denys C. Murrell	7th Bn.	Poland	Stalag XX B. Malbork	7395
6396783	Pte. W H Murrell	5th Bn.	Poland	Stalag XX B. Malbork	16084
6397425	Pte. Harry R. H. Murwald	2nd Bn.	Poland	Stalag 344 Lamsdorf	11532
4543155	Pte. Philip Roland Nalley	4th Bn.	Germany	Stalag IV G. Oschatz	249301
6400139	Pte. Edward Phil Napper	5th Bn.	Poland	Stalag XX A. Thorn	10626
6396122	Pte. W G Neale	2nd Bn.	Germany	Stalag 344 Lamsdorf	37158
6397801	L/Cpl. Henry James S. Neary	2nd Bn.	Poland	Stalag 344 Lamsdorf	15858
3127955	Pte. M Nesbitt	2nd Bn.	Germany	Stalag III A. Luckenwalde	1174
5501340	Pte. F H Newman	5th Bn.	Poland	Stalag XX B. Malbork	12827
6397789	Pte. F L Newman	2nd Bn.	Poland	Stalag XX A. Thorn	6719
6402415	Pte. A H Newnham	7th Bn.	Poland	Stalag XX B. Malbork	10432
6395143	Sgt. John William P. Newton	1st Bn.	Austria	Stalag XVIII A. Wolfsberg (Karnten)	9381
6401872	Pte. D A P S Nicholson	2nd Bn.	Poland	Stalag XX A. Thorn	9433
6402332	Pte. A H Niles	5th Bn.	Poland	Stalag 344 Lamsdorf	10556
6400313	Pte. Henry James Nixey	4th Bn.	Poland	Stalag 344 Lamsdorf	5964
6397720	Pte. A F Noble	1st Bn. attd. 50 Commando	Germany	Stalag IV F. Hartmansdorf Chemnitz	12570
6402105	Pte. Leslie Arthur Norgate	4th Bn.	Germany	Stalag IV F. Hartmansdorf Chemnitz	249867
6411500	Pte. O T Norris	4th Bn.	Germany	Stalag IV G. Oschatz	249256
6402012	Cpl. A C North	4th Bn.	Germany	Stalag IV B. Muhlberg (Elbe)	252361
6475595	Pte. A Norton	4th Bn.	Germany	Stalag XI B. Fallingbostel	140095
7010990	Pte. M Nugent	2nd Bn.	Poland	Stalag XX B. Malbork	9831
6307787	Pte. George A Nuttall	2nd Bn.	Poland	Stalag 344 Lamsdorf	14746
6401259	Pte. F W Oak	5th Bn.	Poland	Stalag XX A. Thorn	19426
6403196	Pte. H Oakley	7th Bn.	Poland	Stalag XX A. Thorn	14553
6407955	Cpl. J O'Brien	1st Bn.	Germany	Stalag VIIA. Moosburg an der Isar	132879
3965415	Pte. D P O'Callaghan	7th Bn.	Germany	Stalag III A. Luckenwalde	4347
6395369	Cpl. W F O'Connor	2nd Bn.	Germany	Stalag 383 Hohen Fels	1320
6404294	Pte. W Oldfield	4th Bn.	Czechoslovakia	Stalag IV C. Bystrice	250398
6397141	Pte. Ernest George William Olive	2nd Bn.	Poland	Stalag 344 Lamsdorf	13808
6976577	Pte. J O'Neill	2nd Bn.	Germany	Stalag III A. Luckenwalde	11328
6399004	Pte. James Reginald E Oram	5th Bn.	Poland	Stalag 344 Lamsdorf	17182
75939	Mjr. Noel Howard Ormerod	4th Bn.	Germany	Oflag XII B. Hadamar	349
6402985	L/Cpl. G W Osborn	4th Bn.	Germany	Stalag IV F. Hartmansdorf Chemnitz	250626
5347198	Pte. J H Pace	2nd Bn.	Germany	Stalag IV D/Z Annaburg	249615
6401889	Pte. E V Page	5th Bn.	Poland	Stalag 344 Lamsdorf	18145
6399405	Pte. H P Page	2nd Bn.	Poland	Stalag VIII B. Cieszyn	5029
6403187	Pte. P G Page	7th Bn.	Poland	Stalag XX B. Malbork	4288
6403187	Pte. S G Page	7th Bn.	Germany	Stalag VII A. Moosburg (Isar)	129809
6400610	Pte. George Henry Paige	5th Bn.	Poland	Stalag XX B. Malbork	9052
6397822	Pte. V Paige	2nd Bn.	Poland	Stalag XX B. Malbork	8462
6394463	Pte. R F Pankhurst	2nd Bn.	Poland	Stalag XX A. 2. Thorn	9519
6400530	Pte. F E Pannett	5th Bn.	Poland	Stalag 344 Lamsdorf	10696
6401626	Pte. George E. Parbery	7th Bn.	France	Hospital Begin, St. Mande, Seine	
71157	Capt. Peter J A Parish	1st Bn.	Germany	Oflag VII B. Eichstaat (Fuchstaat)	3396
6401108	Sgt. Ronald Robert R. Parish	5th Bn.	Germany	Stalag 383 Hohen Fels	19824
6396772	Pte. Harold H. Parker	2nd Bn.	Poland	Stalag 344 Lamsdorf	10574
6402693	Pte. John Frederick Henry Parker	2nd Inf. Base Depot	Poland	Stalag VI A. Hemer/Iserlohn	
6403440	Pte. M E Parkes	1st Bn.	Germany	Oflag V A. Weinsburg (Wurtemburg)	22005
5438450	Pte. Samuel G. Parpworth	7th Bn.	Poland	Stalag XX A. Thorn	358
6397742	Sgt. Ronald Allen Parris	4th Bn.	Poland	Stalag 344 Lamsdorf	220979
6083960	L/Cpl. Dennis F. Parsonage	4th Bn.	Germany	Stalag IV B. Muhlberg (Elbe)	251805
6404341	Pte. G Parsons	5th Bn.	Germany	Stalag IV A. Hohenstein	247982
14536793	Pte. George William C. Parsons	1st Bn.	Germany	Stalag IV D. Torgau (Elbe)	131008
6402188	Pte. J A Patching	5th Bn.	Poland	Stalag 344 Lamsdorf	11627
3965195	Pte. William Victor Patten	7th Bn.	Poland	Stalag XX B. Malbork	4356
6401302	Pte. W E Pattenden	4th Bn.	Germany	Stalag IV D. Torgau (Elbe)	253673
6395355	Cpl. Albert Stephen Pavey	2nd Bn.	Germany	Stalag 357 Oerbke (near Fallingbostel)	1318
5728721	Pte. Isaac Pavodler	4th Bn.	Germany	Stalag IV F. Hartmansdorf Chemnitz	279811
6406016	Pte. J W Payne	4th Bn.	Germany	Stalag IV D/Z Annaburg	249428
6404369	Pte. R F Payne	4th Bn.	Czechoslovakia	Stalag IV C. Bystrice	258105
6400630	Pte. T F Payne	4th Bn.	Germany	Stalag 344 Lamsdorf	221336
6406017	Pte. S J Peacock	4th Bn.	Germany	Stalag IV B. Muhlberg (Elbe)	249115
2878734	Pte. Raymond Basil B. Peat	2nd Bn.	Poland	Stalag XX A. Thorn	10079
3965137	Pte. E Pedraglio	7th Bn.	Poland	Stalag 344 Lamsdorf	4350
6401586	Pte. W H Peel	5th Bn.	Poland	Stalag XX B. Malbork	12375
6400371	Pte. James A. Pellen	4th Bn.	Czechoslovakia	Stalag IV C. Bystrice	252109
6391191	C.S.M. P A Pelling	4th Bn.	Germany	Stalag IV B. Muhlberg (Elbe)	260992
6397798	Pte. F G Perrin	2nd Bn.	Poland	Stalag VIII A. Gorlitz	14118
6398234	Pte. A J Peters	1st Bn.	Germany	Stalag IV B. Muhlberg (Elbe)	250488
6402508	Pte. G H Peters	7th Bn.	Germany	Stalag XXI B. Szubin	3314
6398087	Pte. S J Pettitt	1st Bn.	Germany	Stalag 357 Oerbke (near Fallingbostel)	260612
6398321	Pte. C F Phillips		Germany	Stalag 344 Lamsdorf	15208
6395671	Pte. R T Phillips	2nd Bn.	Poland	Stalag XXI A. Schildberg	3030
5501235	Pte. S G Phillips	5th Bn.	Poland	Stalag XX B. Malbork	9183
6389323	Pte. W G Phillips	2nd Bn.	Poland	Stalag XX A. Thorn	12680
6394532	Pte. William James Phillips	2nd Bn.	Poland	Stalag XX B. Malbork	7705
6399323	Pte. W M Phillips	2nd Bn.	Poland	Stalag XX A. Thorn	12680
6406298	Pte. B Philpot	4th Bn.	Germany	Stalag IV F. Hartmansdorf Chemnitz	249955
6401950	Pte. W G Pierce	7th Bn.	Poland	Stalag 344 Lamsdorf	4745
6401104	Pte. George Edward Piggott		Poland	Stalag 344 Lamsdorf	449
6401521	Pte. George Albert Edward Pilbeam	5th Bn.	Germany	Stalag IV G. Oschatz	249322
39650303	Pte. John William Plater	7th Bn.	Germany	Stalag 344 B.A.B. 20 Kedzierzyn-Kozle	5816
6403433	Pte. F E Plowright	4th Bn.	Germany	Stalag IV A. Hohenstein	253570

Service No.	Name	Battalion	Country	Camp	Number
6400086	Pte. S Plumridge	2nd Bn.	Poland	Stalag XX A. Thorn	
6398664	Pte. William James Plumridge	1st Bn.	Austria	Stalag XVIII A. Wolfsberg (Karnten)	5463
169069	Lt. Charles Henry Pocock	1st Bn.	Germany	Oflag V A. Weinsberg	2961
6404195	L/Cpl. A F Pooley	4th Bn.	Germany	Stalag IV B. Muhlberg (Elbe)	
6403897	Pte. J Pooley	1st Bn.	Austria	Stalag XVII A. Kaisersteinbruck Bei Bruck	155164
6401961	Pte. W Pope	7th Bn.	Poland	Stalag 344 Lamsdorf	5069
5438543	Pte. R D Porter	7th Bn.	Poland	Stalag XX A. Thorn	7738
6396791	A/Cpl. A E Potter	4th Bn.	Poland	Stalag 344 Lamsdorf	221301
6396868	Pte. R C Potter	2nd Bn.	Germany	Stalag 383 Hohen Fels	5968
6398652	Pte. A G Potts	1st Bn.	Germany	Stalag IV A. Hohenstein	258145
6407970	L/Cpl. A G Preston	4th Bn.	Poland	Stalag 344 Lamsdorf	221169
3905838	Pte. Albert Edward Prideaux	1st Bn.	Germany	Stalag 357 Oerbke (near Fallingbostel)	29726
1852	Mjr. T Prince	2nd Bn.	Germany	Oflag IX A. Spangenburg Bei Kassel	353
6397855	Pte. P Pritchard	2nd Bn.	Poland	Stalag 344 Lamsdorf	12775
3965158	Pte. R M Pritchard	7th Bn.	Poland	Stalag XXI B. Szubin	
6403998	Pte. Cecil Frederick Putland	1st Bn.	Germany	Stalag VII A. Moosburg (Isar)	127951
64000973	Pte. Sidney John Puttick	4th Bn.	Germany	Stalag VII A. Moosburg (Isar)	
229779	Lt. David John Pye	attd. Army Air Corps.	Germany	Oflag VII B. Eichstaat (Fuchstaat)	1635
6396469	Pte. Sydney Leonard Quickenden	2nd Bn.	Poland	Stalag VIII B. Cieszyn	13276
6399722	Pte. Cecil Stanley Quinnell	2nd Bn.	Poland	Stalag 344 Lamsdorf	1008
6473748	Pte. J T Ramsey	4th Bn.	Czechoslovakia	Stalag IV C. Bystrice	251647
5439277	Pte. Percival Arthur Randlesome	7th Bn.	Poland	Stalag VIIIB. Cieszyn	4905
6406479	L/Cpl. John L Ranford	1st Bn.	Germany	Stalag XI A. Altengrabow	142305
6406302	Pte. Walter William Ratcliffe	4th Bn.	Austria	Stalag XVIII A. Wolfsberg (Karnten)	39807
6469419	Pte. W H Rawlings	4th Bn.	Germany	Stalag IV G. Oschatz	249200
6401930	Pte. E G Read	4th Bn.	Poland	Stalag 344 Lamsdorf	221381
5727657	Pte. Norman Kenneth Read	7th Bn.	Poland	Stalag 344 Lamsdorf	3732
6395640	L/Cpl. R G Read	4th Bn.	Germany	Stalag IV D/Z. Annaburg	249292
6411088	Pte. Sidney John Reaveley	4th Bn.	Germany	Stalag IV B. Muhlberg (Elbe)	260462
6411089	Pte. E H Redgrave	4th Bn.	Germany	Stalag IV A. Hohenstein	251377
91608	Lt. Edward Anton Ree	5th Bn.	Germany	Oflag VII B. Eichstaat (Fuchstaat)	638
6402751	L/Cpl. D A Reed	1st Bn.	Germany	Stalag XI A. Altengrabow	142418
6397816	Pte. William A Redford	2nd Bn.	Poland	Stalag XX B. Malbork	7697
6436345	Pte. C Rice	Special Service Battalion	Poland	Stalag 344 Lamsdorf	25328
6402063	Pte. S G Rice	4th Bn.	Germany	Stalag IV G. Oschatz	251424
6397114	Sgt. D E Richardson	7th Bn.	Poland	Stalag 344 Lamsdorf	4996
6400869	Pte. J Richardson	7th Bn.	Poland	Stalag 346 B.A.B. 21. Blechammer	5087
6399917	Pte. N L G Richardson	4th Bn.	Poland	Stalag XX A. Thorn	11617
6400812	Pte. R Richardson	7th Bn.	Czechoslovakia	Stalag IV C. Bystrice	252213
6397320	L/Sgt. R A Richardson	7th Bn.	Germany	Stalag IX C. Mulhausen Bad Sulza	31287
P/102382	Lt. David Forster Roberts	2nd Bn.	Germany	Oflag VII B. Eichstaat (Fuchstaat)	358
6404306	Pte. Frederick William Arthur Robinson	4th Bn.	Germany	Stalag IV D/Z. Annaburg	249502
6400365	Pte. E Rodmell	5th Bn.	Poland	Stalag XX B. 2 A. Malbork	20640
6296202	Pte. Clifford Albert Rollings	2nd Bn.	Poland	Stalag XX B. Malbork	11214
640339	Pte. Charles George Romain	7th Bn.	Poland	Stalag XX A. Thorn	7178
6397940	C.Q.M.S. E W Rooke	1st Bn.	Austria	Stalag 317 Markt Pongua	39011
5666833	Pte. C F Roper	5th Bn.	Poland	Stalag XX A. Thorn	11702
6403942	Pte. S J Rose	1st Bn.	Poland	Stalag VIII C. Konin Zaganski	77064
6396321	Pte. B H Rouse	2nd Bn.	Poland	Stalag 344 Lamsdorf	10670
5727634	Pte. R J Rowden	7th Bn.	Poland	Stalag 344 Lamsdorf	4696
6403236	Pte. C V Rowe	7th Bn.	Poland	Stalag XX B. Malbork	10135
6399217	Cpl. Donald Sidney J Ruff	4th Bn.	Germany	Stalag IV F. Hartmansdorf Chemnitz	250115
6398732	Cpl. R Rumble	4th Bn.	Germany	Stalag 357 Oerbke (near Fallingbostel)	50159
6403259	Pte. C Rumsey	7th Bn.	Poland	Stalag XX A. 2A. Thorn	20099
6396741	Sgt. Norman G Ryan	2nd Bn.	Germany	Stalag VI A. Hemer/Iserlohn	
5668911	Pte. E Salathiel	5th Bn.	Poland	Stalag 344 Lamsdorf	11346
6402528	Pte. Pte. H T Sales		Poland	Stalag XX A. Thorn	1698
6396402	Pte. F C Sandalls	7th Bn.	Poland	Stalag XX A. 62. Thorn	10136
6398979	Pte. Victor J A Sandalls	4th Bn.	Czechoslovakia	Stalag IV C Bystrice	251924
88657	Capt. Peter Douglas Sanday	4th Bn.	Germany	Oflag V A. Weinburg (Wurtemburg)	3259
6394780	Cpl. H W Sanders	2nd Bn.	Germany	Stalag 383 Hohen Fels	12974
6402722	Pte. Arthur Ernest Sandles	2nd Inf. Base Depot	Poland	Stalag XXI D. Poznan	1688
6400479	Pte. C H Sands	7th Bn.	Poland	Stalag VIII B. Cieszyn	1688
6396362	L/Cpl. H R Sands	2nd Bn.	Germany	Stalag 344 Lamsdorf	14087
6404307	Pte. A W Satchell	4th Bn.	Germany	Stalag IV F. Hartmansdorf	228737
6436354	Sgt. George Victor Saunders	attd. 10 Commando	Germany	Stalag 111 (Sagan)	
2695314	Cpl. G F Saye	2nd Bn.	Germany	Stalag VI D. Annaburg	
6402736	Pte. J J Sergent		Poland	Stalag XXI B. Szubin	
39655254	Pte. A J Schneider	7th Bn.	Poland	Stalag XX B. Malbork	5799
4544332	Pte. G Schofield	4th Bn.	Germany	Stalag IV G. Oschatz	249258
6402204	Pte. Cyril John Schooley	5th Bn.	Germany	Stalag 344 Lamsdorf	11764
6411099	Pte. C A Scott	4th Bn.	Germany	Stalag IV A. Hohenstein	251378
6403925	Sgt. Douglas Gordon M Scott	1st Bn.	Germany	Stalag VII A. Moosburg an der Isar	128072
6401949	Dmr. R C Scott	7th Bn.	Poland	Stalag XX B. Malbork	9541
6398038	Sgt. Henry George Scovell	1st Bn.	Germany	Stalag IV B. Muhlberg (Elbe)	227986
5439106	Pte. F Seagrove	7th Bn.	Germany	Stalag VIII B. Cieszyn	14710
6401304	Pte. S H Seall	4th Bn.	Czechoslovakia	Stalag IV C. Bystrice	258893
6396876	Pte. A W Seaman	2nd Bn.	Germany	Stalag 344 Lamsdorf	11744
6406487	Pte. John Clements Search	1st Bn.	Austria	Stalag XVII A. Kaisersteinbruck Bei Bruck	155253
6401059	Sgt. H Seville	4th Bn.	Germany	Stalag IV B. Muhlberg (Elbe)	260924
6402352	Pte. Patrick H. Seymour M.I.D.	5th Bn.	Poland	Stalag 344 Lamsdorf	13175
6402121	Pte. E C Sharp	4th Bn.	Czechoslovakia	Stalag IV C. Bystrice	251782
110011	2/Lt. Sydney William Grant Shaw		Germany	Oflag IX A/Z. Rotenburg an der Fulda	1202
6406488	Pte. J Sheehan	1st Bn.	Austria	Stalag XVII A. Kaisersteinbruck Bei Bruck	153722
6396634	Pte. J M Short	4th Bn.	Germany	Stalag IV F. Hartmansdorf	258694
6401194	Pte. R G Short	4th Bn.	Czechoslovakia	Stalag IV C. Bystrice	251733
6402057	J H Silver	4th Bn.	Czechoslovakia	Stalag IV C. Bystrice	251874
6470415	Pte. H T Simmonds	4th Bn.	Germany	Stalag IV G. Oschatz	249306
6402719	Pte. D W Simmons	1st Bn.	Germany	Stalag IV F. Hartmansdorf	260302
6399282	Pte. W H Simmons	2nd Bn.	Germany	Stalag 344 Lamsdorf	10549
6398981	L/Cpl. J Sinden	5th Bn.	Poland	Stalag XXI B. Szubin	
6406311	Pte. F E Sired	4th Bn.	Germany	Stalag IV G. Oschatz	251423
5726399	Pte. P Skeffington	7th Bn.	Poland	Stalag XX B. Malbork	11105
6085447	Pte. P H Skinner	2nd Bn.	Poland	Stalag XX A. 3.A. Thorn	12826
6403545	Pte. Wilfred George E Skipper	1st Bn.	Germany	Stalag IV F. Hartmansdorf	253900
182282	2/Lt Douglas Leon Sladden	5th Bn.	Germany	Oflag V A. Weinsberg	2751
50239	Capt. Richard Bryan de Fontenne Sleeman	2nd Bn.	Germany	Oflag VII B. Eichstaat (Fuchstaat)	
6400997	Cpl. Leslie J Smeeth	4th Bn.	Germany	Stalag VIII A. Gorlitz	15396
6398067	Pte. A Y Smith	1st Bn.	Austria	Stalag XVII A. Wolfsberg	9339
6403008	Pte. D C Smith	4th Bn.	Germany	Stalag IV F. Hartmansdorf	250680
6399366	Pte. E Smith	1st Bn.	Germany	Stalag VIII A. Gorlitz	77060
6401937	Pte. F Smith	7th Bn.	Poland	Stalag VIII B. Cieszyn	2690
6394637	Pte. George A Smith		Germany	Dulag Luft Wetzlar	1774
6398997	Pte. George R P Smith	4th Bn.	Germany	Stalag IV D/Z.	249748
6401440	Pte. G W Smith	7th Bn.	Poland	Stalag 344 Lamsdorf	2988
6402356	Pte. H Smith	5th Bn.	Germany	Stalag 344 Lamsdorf	14048
6391449	Pte. H S Smith		Poland	Stalag 344 Lamsdorf	7385
6398262	Cpl. H V Smith	1st Bn.		Stalag 357 Oerbke	
7262283	Sgt. James Kitchener R. Smith	1st Bn.	Poland	Stalag 344 Lamsdorf	35361
5501246	Pte. L G Smith	5th Bn.	Germany	Stalag 344 Lamsdorf	47595
6400359	Pte. S F Smith	5th Bn.	Poland	Stalag XXI A. 721. Schildberg	
6410777	Pte. S V F Smith	4th Bn.	Germany	Stalag IV B. Konigstein	249375
5438571	Pte. Pte. Thomas Harry Smith	7th Bn.	Poland	Stalag XX A. Thorn	
4545911	Pte. Thomas Snelson	4th Bn.	Poland	Stalag 344 Lamsdorf	34824

Service No.	Name	Unit	Country	Camp	Number
6411482	Pte. A Snewing		Germany	Stalag IV F. Hartmansdorf	253152
6399218	Sgt. P South		Germany	Stalag 357 Oerbke	13218
6401244	L/Cpl. W Southgate	4th Bn.	Germany	Stalag IV B. Konigstein	250590
6474213	Pte. Thomas C Spackman	4th Bn.	Germany	Stalag IV A. Hohenstein	248529
5501264	Pte. B W Sparkes	5th Bn.	Germany	Stalag 344 Lamsdorf	10298
6396837	Pte. Ernest Alfred Speer	2nd Bn.	Germany	Stalag 344 Lamsdorf	13359
6398451	Pte. R C Spencer	2nd Bn.	Poland	Stalag B.A.B. 21. Blechammer	4405
5727556	Pte. C G Spice	7th Bn.	France	Hospital Begin St. Mande Seine	
6400737	Pte. Thomas Edward Spilsted	5th Bn.	Germany	Stalag VI A. Lazarette 22A. Hemer/Iserlohn	4757
6403289	Pte. Percy A V Spooner	7th Bn.	Poland	Stalag B.A.B. 21. Blechammer	21
4545718	Pte. Matthew Bagnall Spoors	4th Bn.	Germany	Stalag IV D. Torgau (Elbe)	260129
6402225	Pte. James Mark Springett	5th Bn.	Germany	Stalag III D. Berlin	110760
545307	Pte. George Alfred Springthall		Poland	Stalag 344 Lamsdorf	10921
6396922	Pte. Alfred E Standen	5th Bn.	Poland	Stalag VIII B. Cieszyn	370
6473780	Cpl. A P. Standen	1st Bn.	Germany	Stalag VII A. Moosburg an der Isar	133952
6088919	Sgt. Victor Charles Standen	4th Bn.	Germany	Stalag IV B. Muhlberg (Elbe)	269877
6404313	Cpl. Maurice William Stanford	4th Bn.	Germany	Stalag IV B. Muhlberg (Elbe)	252341
6397995	Pte. T Stanford	1st Bn.	Austria	Stalag XVII A. Kaisersteinbruck Bei Bruck	153520
95305	Capt. John Richard G. Stanton	5th Bn.	Germany	Oflag VII B. Eichstaat (Fuchstaat)	279
6396517	Cpl. T W Stedman	2nd Bn.	Poland	Stalag XX B. Malbork	12325
6403443	Pte. David Kenneth E. Steel	1st Bn.	Germany	Stalag IV F. Hartmansdorf	252704
6399974	Pte. A J Steer	4th Bn.	Czechoslovakia	Stalag IV C. Bystrice	
5670130	Pte. R Steer	5th Bn.	Poland	Stalag XX A. Thorn	
6399334	Pte. George L. Stephens	2nd Bn.	Poland	Stalag XX B. Malbork	5030
6401592	Pte. W C Stephens	7th Bn.	Poland	Stalag 344 Lamsdorf	9461
6401778	Pte. Ernest John Stidder	7th Bn.	Poland	Stalag XX B. Malbork	10527
6399747	Pte. C Still	4th Bn.	Austria	Stalag XVII A. Kaisersteinbruck Bei Bruck	
6399413	Pte. J R Stillwell	1st Bn.	Germany	Stalag VII A. Moosburg an der Isar	35239
6398073	Pte. Ernest John G. Stolton	2nd Bn.	Germany	Stalag 344 Lamsdorf	12976
6392721	Pte. C A Stone	2nd Inf. Base Depot	Poland	Stalag VIII B. Cieszyn	7263
6403201	Pte. C M Stoner	7th Bn.	Poland	Stalag VIII B. Cieszyn	710
64000626	Pte. R M Stones	4th Bn.	Germany	Stalag IX B. Bad Orb-Wegscheide	3915
6402509	Pte. Pte. F A Stonestreet	7th Bn.	Poland	Stalag XX B. Malbork	10653
6394830	P.S.M. Maurice Henry G. Stonestreet	2nd Bn.	Poland	Stalag 344 Lamsdorf	11596
6398751	L/Cpl. F Stonham	7th Bn.	Poland	Stalag B.A.B. 21. Blechammer	4744
4624470	Pte. A E Storey	4th Bn.	Germany	Stalag IV B. Muhlberg (Elbe)	249210
6394319	P.S.M. W Stott	2nd Bn.	Germany	Stalag 344 Lamsdorf	10488
6401142	Pte. L E J Streeter	2nd Bn.	Poland	Stalag B.A.B.21. Blechammer	3297
6396619	L/Cpl. R H Streeter	4th Bn.	Germany	Stalag IV B. Muhlberg (Elbe)	252148
6400560	Pte. Arthur Leonard George Stretton	7th Bn.	Poland	Stalag XX B. Malbork	11553
6399936	Pte. W V Stringer	1st Bn.	Germany	Stalag XI A. Altengrabow	142285
6402586	Pte. E Stubbington	2nd Inf. Base Depot	Poland	Stalag 344 Lamsdorf	1686
6396534	Pte. Alfred Ernest A. Stubbs	4th Bn.	Poland	Stalag XX B. Malbork	12595
5727518	Pte. Phillip Eric Summerton	7th Bn.	Poland	Stalag 346 B.A.B. 21. Blechammer	3855
6406652	Pte. George Albert C. Sutliff	4th Bn.	Germany	Oflag IV C. Saalhaus Colditz	250514
6403400	Pte. Thomas Harold Swainland	4th Bn.	Germany	Stalag IV B. Muhlberg (Elbe)	261018
6476513	Pte. Ronald Patrick Swale	4th Bn.	Germany	Stalag VIII A. Gorlitz	33917
6403326	Pte. Douglas Swift	7th Bn.	Poland	Stalag XXI B.Z. Szubin/Stalag 344 Lamsdorf	4043
6396635	Pte. Dennis W Sworn	2nd B.	Poland	Stalag 344 Lamsdorf	4828
6396421	Pte. W P Symons	2nd Bn.	Poland	Stalag XX B. Malbork	8683
6400568	Pte. F E Tandy	1st Bn.	Germany	Stalag VII A. Moosburg an der Isar	124771
6402571	Pte. E Taylor	5th Bn.	Poland	Stalag XX A. Thorn	11268
6403556	Pte. J Taylor	1st Bn.	Germany	Stalag IX B. Fallingbostel	140477
6403905	Pte. R J Taylor	1st Bn.	Austria	Stalag XVIII A. Wolfsberg	7914
6402238	Pte. Thomas F A Taylor	5th Bn.	Poland	Stalag B.A.B. 20 Kedzierzyn-Kozle	9097
5668585	Cpl. Idris Teague	5th Bn.	Poland	Stalag XXI B.Z. Szubin	
6404318	Pte. A Tenner	4th Bn.	Germany	Stalag IV F. Hartmansdorf	253509
5439313	Pte. D Terrell	7th Bn.	Poland	Stalag XX B. Malbork	4903
6402654	Pte. E J Tester	1st Bn.	Austria	Stalag XVIII A. Wolfsberg	332
6496769	L/Cpl. George William Theis	1st Bn.	Austria	Stalag XVII A. Kaisersteinbruck	153517
6398298	L/Cpl. T Thew	1st Bn.	Poland	Stalag 344 Lamsdorf	30165
6397998	Sgt. S C Thomas	7th Bn.	Germany	Stalag 383 Hohen Fels	4684
5501241	Cpl. W J Thomas	5th Bn.	Germany	Stalag 357 Oerbke (Elbe)	19444
3965389	Pte. D L G Thompson	7th Bn.	Poland	Stalag 344 Lamsdorf	79174
6394883	Pte. R E Thompson	2nd Bn.	Poland	Stalag XX A. 2a Thorn	19941
6396595	Pte. F Thomsett	2nd Bn.	Poland	Stalag XX B. Malbork	7389
5728186	Pte. V W Thurgood	7th Bn.	Poland	Stalag XX B. Malbork	4006
6398795	Sgt. J E Ticehurst	5th Bn.	Germany	Stalag VII B. Eichstaat (Fuchstaat)	5647
6398206	C.Q.M.S. C A Tickner	1st Bn.	Germany	Stalag IV B. Muhlberg (Elbe)	227941
6411123	Pte. D B Tippett	4th Bn.	Germany	Stalag IV F. Hartmansdorf	250005
2208028	R.S.M. Charles Bernard Tobutt	4th Bn.	Germany	Stalag IV B. Muhlberg (Elbe)	229101
6398402	Pte. H Todd	1st Bn.	Germany	Stalag IV A. Hohenstein	2225
6401772	Pte. H F Todd	5th Bn.	Poland	Stalag XX B. Malbork	12338
6401772	Pte. C.E. Tomsett	5thBn.	Poland	Stalag XX A . 1. Thorn	18433
6396595	Pte. F. Tomsett	2nd Bn.	Poland	Stalag XX A. 100. Thorn	7389
6396803	Pte. H G Tonge	2nd Bn.	Germany	Stalag III A. Luckenwalde	7699
5439758	Pte. William Robert R. Tonkin	7th Bn.	Poland	Stalag XX B. Malbork	3914
6401265	Pte. Edward F Tourle	5th Bn.	Poland	Stalag 344 Lamsdorf	7318
6397894	Pte. K R Town	1st Bn.	Poland	Stalag 344 Lamsdorf	77118
6400026	Pte. Frank Herbert Tree	2nd Bn.	Poland	Stalag XX B. Malbork	16092
6407215	Sgt. W G Tring	2nd Bn.	Poland	Stalag XXI D. Poznan	4376
5724788	Pte. W H Tuck	4th Bn.	Germany	Stalag IV F. Lamsdorf	250581
6411128	Pte. William P J Tucker	4th Bn.	Czechoslovakia	Stalag IV C. Bystrice	252131
6400273	Pte. V R C Tuff	2nd Bn.	Germany	Stalag 344 Lamsdorf	10782
6397804	Pte. F A Tuffin	2nd Bn.	Germany	Stalag 344 Lamsdorf	14088
6397560	L/Cpl. W E Tull	2nd Bn.	Germany	Stalag IV A. Hohenstein	11063
214586	Lt. Douglas Elborough Turner	4th Bn.	Germany	Oflag V A. Weinsburg (Wurtemburg)	2754
6402372	Pte. E C Turner	5th Bn.	Poland	Stalag 344 Lamsdorf	12060
6396372	Pte. H T Turner	7th Bn.	Poland	Stalag 344 Lamsdorf	850
6401672	Pte. S A Twine	4th Bn.	Germany	Stalag VII A. Gorlitz	80006
6411620	Pte. Alfred Charles R. Twitchen	4th Bn.	Germany	Stalag IV D/Z. Annaburg	249791
6472846	Pte. John E. Vanstavaren	4th Bn.	Czechoslovakia	Stalag IV C. Bystrice	251886
6396745	Pte. William V. Veness	2nd Bn.	Poland	Stalag 344 Lamsdorf	12683
6395482	Pte. A C Verey	2nd Bn.	Germany	Stalag 344 Lamsdorf	10701
6402487	Pte. Anthony G. Verth M.I.D.	7th Bn.	Poland	Stalag XXA. Thorn	
5626474	Pte. Kenneth George Viant	1st Bn.	Germany	Stalag IX A. Altengrabow	142357
6286997	Pte. L A Vicarey	5th Bn.	Poland	Stalag XX A. 3.A. Thorn	12414
6403079	Pte. George Edward Vooght	4th Bn.	Germany	Stalag IV F. Hartmansdorf	250657
6476105	Pte. C V Vorley	4th Bn.	Germany	Stalag IV D/Z. Annaburg	249735
6402554	Pte. S G Walsh	1st Bn.	Germany	Stalag IV G. Oschatz	12035
6398047	Pte. James Eric R. Walter	2nd Bn.	Poland	Stalag 344 Lamsdorf	14779
6399361	Pte. D H Walters	2nd Bn.	Poland	Stalag 344 Lamsdorf	11533
6408259	Pte. J A Walters	2nd Bn.	Germany	Stalag IV D/Z. Annaburg	249719
762398	Pte. A Walton	2nd Bn.	Poland	Stalag VIII B. Cieszyn	1314
6396325	Pte. A H Want	2nd Bn.	Poland	Stalag 344 Lamsdorf	14086
6396839	Sgt. H J Ward	2nd Bn.	Poland	Stalag 344 Lamsdorf	15067
6402515	Pte. Michael Herbert Warden	7th Bn.	Poland	Stalag XX A. Thorn	9843
6411130	Pte. R S Ware	4th Bn.	Germany	Stalag IV F. Hartmansdorf Chemnitz	250003
6397670	Cpl. George Frederick Wares	1st Bn.	Poland	Stalag VIII A. Gorlitz	80587
6397089	Pte. R B Wares	4th Bn.	Poland	Stalag 344 Lamsdorf	30049
182279	Lt. Francis Edmund Warneford	4th Bn.	Germany	Oflag 79 Brunswick	2711/32
6397777	Pte. Henry George Warner	2nd Bn.	Poland	Stalag 344 Lamsdorf	
6396886	Pte. W Warnes	2nd Bn.	Poland	Stalag XX B. Malbork	242
6401800	L/Cpl. J A Warr	7th Bn.	Poland	Stalag 344 Lamsdorf	15701

Service No.	Name	Battalion	Country	Camp	POW No.
6473811	Pte. Pte. G H Warren	4th Bn.	Poland	Stalag 344 Lamsdorf	27980
6469477	Cpl. J R Warwick	4th Bn.	Poland	Stalag 344 Lamsdorf	29459
803825	Pte. Charles William Washer	1st Bn.	Germany	Stalag VI B. Nieuweschans Emsland	77188
6400090	Pte. J Washer	2nd Bn.	Poland	Stalag XX B. Malbork	7408
6408049	Pte. R S Waterhouse	4th Bn.	Poland	Stalag 344 Lamsdorf	30141
6084038	L/Cpl. F E Waters	4th Bn.	Poland	Stalag 344 Lamsdorf	30894
86483	Lt. Reginald D Waters M.I.D.	2nd Bn.	Germany	Oflag VII B. Eichstaat (Fuchstaat)	892
153264	Mjr. Harold Edward Roy Watson	1st Bn.	Germany	Stalag VII A. Moosburg (Isar)	
6396324	Pte. H Watts	2ndBn.	Poland	Stalag XX B. Malbork	12682
6399847	Pte. W G Watts	2nd Bn.	Germany	Stalag 344 Lamsdorf	10722
4542380	Pte. L Webb	4th Bn.	Poland	Stalag 344 Lamsdorf	29525
6402073	Pte. A E Webster	4th Bn.	Poland	Stalag 344 Lamsdorf	11563
6399818	Pte. M Webster	2nd Bn.	Poland	Stalag XX A. Thorn	
6396768	Cpl. H D Weller	2nd Bn.	Germany	Stalag 383 Hohen Fels	12975
6398992	Pte. H Wells	1st Bn.	Germany	Stalag IV A. Hohenstein	258143
6402275	Pte. Leonard W S Wescombe	2nd Bn.	Poland	Stalag XX B. Malbork	19589
6400511	Pte. F E West	4th Bn.	Poland	Stalag VIII B. Cieszyn	80909
6399708	Pte. F J West	4th Bn.	Poland	Stalag 344 Lamsdorf	28979
5728138	Pte. S A West	7th Bn.	Poland	Stalag VIII B. Cieszyn	
6083792	Pte. R H Westgate	4th Bn.	Poland	Stalag 344 Lamsdorf	28995
6411132	Pte. J Whalley	4th Bn.	Poland	Stalag 344 Lamsdorf	30766
6395695	Pte. H Whamand	2nd Bn.	Poland	Stalag XX A. Thorn	8656
6404069	Pte. B Wheatley	1st Bn.	Czechoslovakia	Stalag IV C. Bystrice	259241
5499855	Pte. S A Wheeler	5th Bn.	Poland	Stalag VIII C. Konin Zaganski	80089
6400107	Pte. C J White	4th Bn.	Germany	Stalag IX C. Mulhausen Bad Sulza	31185
6395882	R.S.M. E W White	1st Bn.	Germany	Stalag XI A. Altengrabow	139003
5728136	Pte. F White	7th Bn.	Poland	Stalag XX B. Malbork	3730
3965240	Pte. F E White	7th Bn.	Poland	Stalag XX B. Malbork	3907
6400307	L/Cpl. Frederick Robert George White	4th Bn.	Poland	Stalag XX A. 3.A. Thorn	13250
6395274	Cpl. G A White	4th Bn.	Poland	Stalag 344 Lamsdorf	28912
6398253	Pte. H White	1st Bn.	Poland	Stalag 344 Lamsdorf	30442
6405761	Pte. Sidney Ernest .J White	4th Bn.	Poland	Stalag 344 Lamsdorf	222154
6411135	Pte. W A White	4th Bn.	Germany	Stalag IV B. Muhlberg (Elbe)	261397
6474433	Pte. G Whitear	4th Bn.	Poland	Stalag VIII C. Konin Zaganski	80106
6400027	Pte. Lucien Roy Whitebrook	2nd Bn.	Poland	Stalag XX B. Malbork	7698
6399170	Pte. James Edward S. Whiteman	2nd Bn.	Poland	Stalag XX A. 2.A. Thorn	20339
5566044	Pte. Edgar John Whitlock	5th Bn.	Poland	Stalag 344 Lamsdorf	12688
6396829	Pte. Thomas Francis George Whitwell	2nd Bn.	Poland	Stalag XX A. Malbork	7707
5728169	Pte. Victor W. Wickenden	7th Bn.	Germany	Stalag B.A.B. 20. Kedzierzyn-Kozle	16015
6394912	Pte. F H Wickham	5th Bn.	Germany	Stalag 357 Oerbke (near Fallingbostel)	229055
4625917	Pte. W J Wilkins	4th Bn.	Poland	Stalag VIII C. Konin Zaganski	80955
3599427	Pte. G W Wilkinson		Poland	Stalag VIII B. Cieszyn	17934
6400900	Pte. G A Willard	5th Bn	Czechoslovakia	Stalag IV C. Bystrice	3443
3965175	Pte. A H Williams	7th Bn.	Poland	Stalag VIII B. Cieszyn	4357
57278169	Pte. E P Williams	7th Bn.	Poland	Stalag 344 Lamsdorf	4804
5439768	Pte. R Williams	7th Bn.	Germany	Stalag 383 Hohen Fels	4722
3595526	Pte. F Williamson		Poland	Stalag VIII B. Cieszyn	12484
6400282	Pte. Pte. A Willis	2nd Bn.	Poland	Stalag XX A. Thorn	976
5501219	Pte. Ronald S G Willoughby	5th Bn.	Poland	Stalag XX A. Thorn	64312
6404330	L/Cpl. William E G Willsdon	4th Bn.	Poland	Stalag 344 Lamsdorf	30703
6340437	Pte. G H Wilson	2nd Bn.	Poland	Stalag XX B. Malbork	7704
69148	Capt. Laurence N H Wilson		Germany	Oflag VII B. Eichstaat (Fuchstaat)	3389
5727498	L/Cpl. R A H Wilson	7th Bn.	Poland	Stalag VIII B. Cieszyn	759
3965186	Pte. T Wilson	7th Bn.	Poland	Stalag VIII B. Cieszyn	3451
410812	Pte. Walter George T. Wilson	4th Bn.	Germany	Stalag IV D/Z. Annaburg	226655
6399559	Pte. D Wiltshire	4th Bn.	Poland	Stalag 344 Lamsdorf	15368
6468883	Pte. Raymond G. Windscheffel	4th Bn.	Poland	Stalag VIII B. Cieszyn	30695
6402233	Pte. Frederick Jack Wingfield	5th Bn.	France	St. Pol-sur-Turnoise	
6394598	Pte. F Winsor	4th Bn.	Germany	Stalag IX C. Mulhausen	11315
6538913	Pte. H H Wise	2nd Bn.	Poland	Stalag 344 Lamsdorf	1317
3965290	Pte. J H Witton	7th Bn.	Poland	Stalag XX B. Malbork	12985
6400293	Pte. A Wood	2nd Bn.	Poland	Stalag 344 Lamsdorf	12751
6398227	Pte. Walter Albert Wood	2nd Bn.	Czechoslovakia	Stalag IV C. Bystrice	
94365	Lt. Charles Edward Woodbridge	1st Bn.	Germany	Oflag V A. Weinsberg (Wurtemburg)	2764
5501327	Pte. L A Woodford	5th Bn.	Germany	Stalag IX C. Mulhausen	3667
180210	Lt. Athelstan Rex Woods		Germany	Oflag V A. Weinburg (Wurtemburg)	2708
6411140	Pte. W P Woods	4th Bn.	Poland	Stalag 344 Lamsdorf	30459
6402691	L/Sgt. Charles Woolgar	1st Bn.	Poland	Stalag XX A. 3.A Thorn	
6396338	Pte. S E Woolgar	2nd Bn.	Poland	Stalag XX A. 3.A. Thorn	
3965264	Pte. Kenneth L Woolley	7th Bn.	Poland	Stalag VIII B. Cieszyn	
6399274	Pte. M Woolvin	4th Bn.	Germany	Stalag IV A. Hohenstein	229791
66873	Capt. Stephen Bache Wortham		Germany	Oflag VII B. Eichstaat (Fuchstaat)	396
6005454	Cpl. George John M Wright	7th Bn.	Germany	Stalag 383 Hohen Fels	2572
6395911	Pte. Geoffrey Denzil B. Wyard	2nd Bn.	Germany	Stalag 344 Lamsdorf	11742
6398240	L/Sgt. F J Young	1st Bn.	Austria	Stalag 317 Pongua	39226

All the Prisoners of War captured in North Africa and Italy were originally held as PoW's in Italy, they were later transferred to Austria, Germany and Poland in January 1944 when the Allied invasion of Italy was succeeding in driving the Germans out.

Early repatriations

14395 Capt. Leslie Ward Lane, M.C. 2nd Bn. Oflag VII C/H. 30921
T/Capt. George Herbert Cook, M.I.D. 7th Bn. (was PoW at Hospital du Valde Grace, Paris)
6403343 Pte. F. Akehurst, 7th Bn. (was PoW at Hospital Begin St. Mande, Seine)
6401134 Pte. H.A. Christian, 7th Bn. (was PoW at Hospital Begin St. Mande, Seine)
6403317 Pte. S.J. Crouch, 7th Bn. (was PoW at Stalag XX A. 7388)
6397163 Pte. Sidney J.J. Jordan, 7th Bn. (Amiens)
7011187 Pte. P. Lennon, 2nd Bn.
6396152 J.S. Mepham, 2nd Bn. (was PoW at Ambulance Chirugical Lourde, 422, Sana d'Helfant, Pas de Calais)
6401626 Pte. G. E. Parbery, 7th Bn. (was PoW at Hospital Begin St. Mande, Seine)
6401886 Pte. C F Stevens, 5th Bn. (was PoW at Hospital de Boussu Mons, Belgium)
6401794 Pte. F.A.W. Sexton, 7th Bn. (was Pow at Hospital 69 Rue de Paris, St. Lo Manche, Seine)
3965320 Pte. R. F. Virrells, 7th Bn. (was PoW at Hospital Begin St. Mande, Seine)

Escapees

6402352 Pte. Patrick H. Seymour, M.I.D. 2nd Bn. Stalag 344 Lamsdorf
Escaped three times the final one from a column of march heading for Moosberg on 23rd April 1945.

5438571 Pte. Thomas Harry Smith, 7th Bn. Stalag XXA (Thorn)
Escaped three times the last time on 19th January 1945, when being marched from Thorn, Smith and a companion escaped and managed to reach the Russian lines.

6401561 Cpl. Douglas John F. B. Durston   7th Bn. Stalag 344 Poland
Escaped from temporary camp at Piaski, Poland, whilst being evacuated from working camp attached to Stalag VIIIB; evacuated to UK via Odessa.

6403339 Pte. C G Romain   7th Bn. Stalag VIB
Escaped from column of march en route for Magdeburg, Germany, and contacted Allied Forces.

50209 Capt. Rupert Joseph Fuller, M.C. 5th Bn.
Escaped from Germany via Holland, Belgium and France to Spain.

6398332 Pte. Reginald James Ballard 5th Bn.
Escaped from Germans in France; escape from Vichy France to French North Africa; internment in French North Africa until released by Allied Forces.

6395507 L/Cpl. H Phillips
Escaped from France to Spain.

6399582 Pte. E Bryant
Escaped from France to Spain.

832419 Pte. W Burgess
Escaped from France to Spain.

6400527 L/Cpl. Raymond Victor Lewis-Clements
Escaped from France to Spain.

6397485 L/Sgt. Archibald Tilling, D.C.M. 7th Bn.
Escaped from France to Spain then to Gibralta.

Died as PoW

5727861 Pte. Leslie Allen Belam, 7th Bn. Poland Stalag XX A. Thorn, (died 19/02/41 Krakow Rakowiki Cemetery)
6398666 Cpl. Robert Macdonald Brown, 1st Bn. Germany Stalag 111D. Berlin (died 21/06/44 Berlin 1939-1945 War Cemetery)
6630701 P.S.M. Eric Albert Clark, 2nd Bn. Poland Stalag XX B. Malbork (died 15/12/40 Malbork Commonwealth Cemetery)
6282522 Pte. Sidney Collins, 4th Bn. Poland Stalag XX I B. Cieszyn (died 26/04/40 Krakow Rakowicki Cemetery)
5439307 Pte. Albert Leslie Dell, 7th Bn. Poland Stalag XX A. Thorn (died 14/04/43 Krakow Rakowicki Cemetery)
6397703 Pte. Leonard John Fletcher,, 2nd Bn. Germany Stalag B.A.B. 20 Kedzierzyn-Kozle (11/04/45 Durnbach War Cemetery)   19311
6397874 Pte. Joseph Richard Harris, 2nd Bn. Germany Stalag 344 Torgau (Elbe)(died 20/02/45 Prague War Cemetery)   47967
5727667 Pte. William Arthur Hart, 7th Bn. Poland Stalag XXI B.H. Szubin (39 died 29/10/42 Posen Old Garrison Cemetery) 3932
6402389 Pte. Thomas A. Horner, 7th Bn. Louvel Hospital, Amiens, (died 29/06/42 Berlin Cemetery)
6401263 Henry James Kingsland, 7th Bn. Poland Stalag XX I B. Szubin (died 10/09/42 Krakow Rakowicki Cemetery
6400139 Pte. Edward Phil Napper, 5th Bn. Poland Stalag XX A. Thorn (died 26/05/42 Malbork Commonwealth Cemetery)   10626
6402693 Pte. John Frederick Henry Parker, 2nd Inf. Base Depot Poland Stalag VI A. Hemer/Iserlohn (died 26/08/44 Krakow Rakowicki Cemetery)
6394532 Pte. William James Phillips, 2nd Bn. Poland Stalag XX B. Malbork (25/03/45 Berlin 1939-1945 War Cemetery)   7705
6400359 Pte. S F Smith, 5th Bn. Poland Stalag XXI A. 721. Schildberg (died 01/04/42 Krakow Rakowicki Cemetery)
6394883 Pte. R E Thompson, 2nd Bn. Poland Stalag XX A. 2a Thorn (2) Malbork Commonwealth Cemetery)   19941
6399818 Pte. M Webster, 2nd Bn. Poland Stalag XX A. Thorn (died 20/09/41 Malbork Commonwealth Cemetery)
6396829 Pte. Thomas Francis George Whitwell, 2nd Bn. Poland Stalag XX A. Malbork (died 11/04/45 Berlin 1939-1945 War Cemetery)   770
6398227 Pte. Walter Albert Wood, 2nd Bn. Czechoslovakia Stalag IV C. Bystrice, (died 12/12/41 Prague War Cemetery)

Japanese Prisoners of War

6392490 WOII William James Leaney, attd. 2nd Bn. Loyal Regiment, Singapore, captured 15 Feb 1942
6409214 Pte. Henry Edward Pickering, captured 18 May 1942

Both repatriated after the end of the war.

Roll of Honour

1939-1947

and

1950-1953

Algeria

Archer Alan Gerald Valentine Capt. No. 124139 1st Bn. 25/08/43
El Alia Cemetery
Grave ref: 12. D. 29.

Mooney Francis Pte. No. 6399106 1st Bn. 23/07/43
Dely Ibrahim Cemetery
Grave ref: 4. K. 9.

Westbury Arthur William Pte. No. 3965346 1st Bn. between 27/08/44 and 28/08/44
Dely Ibrahim Cemetery
Grave ref: 2. J. 6.

Bangladesh

Armstrong Lindsey Crawford Lt. No. 149381 attd. 1st Bn. Sierra Leone Regt. R.W.A.F.F. 10/04/44
Chittagong War Cemetery
Grave ref: 7. D. 8.

Lynn Sidney Frank Pte. No. 6406968 attd. No. 5 Commando 10/04/44
Chittagong War Cemetery
Grave ref: 7. C. 11.

Miles Albert Frederick Pte. No. 14828687 9th Bn. 23/03/45
Maynamati War Cemetery
Grave ref: 3. B. 15.

Belgium

Abrams Jack Samuel Sgt. No. 6394641 2nd Bn. 22/05/40
Esquelmes War Cemetery
Grave ref: V. B. 42.

Bangs Jack Philip Laurence Lt. No. 302327 attd. Gloucestershire Regt. 03/11/44
Geel War Cemetery
Grave ref: 111. C. 42.

Barham Herbert George Cpl. No. 6398990 5th Bn. between 10/05/40 and 16/06/40
Adegem Canadian War Cemetery
Grave ref: 1. AB. 8.

Barnfield William Ernest L/Sgt. No. 5494160 4th Bn. 21/05/40
Anzegem Communal Cemetery
Grave 4

Beirne Joseph Pte. No. 6398893 2nd Bn. 22/05/40
Esquelmes War Cemetery
Grave ref: VI. A. 24.

Birchall Frank Thomas Pte. No. 6401549 5th Bn. 23/05/40
White House Cemetery, St. Jean-les Ypres
Grave ref: 1. L. 4.

Booth Thomas Harry L/Sgt. No. 6397614 22/05/40
Esquelmes War Cemetery
Grave ref: VI. B. 31.

Bridger Harold Frederick Pte. No. 6399214 5th Bn. 22/05/40
Esquelmes War Cemetery
Grave ref: V. B. 43.

Brooks Albert Harry Sgt. No. 1664494 5th Bn. 22/05/40
Adegem Canadian War Cemetery
Grave ref: i. AB. 2.

Browning Frederick Pte. No. 6398789 4th Bn. 21/05/40
Gijzelbrechtegem Churchyard
Grave 5

Checksfield Alfred H. L/Sgt. No. 6397259 2nd Bn. 23/05/40
Esquelmes War Cemetery
Grave ref: VI. B. 29.

Clarke George Thomas Sgt. No.6395122 2nd Bn. 23/05/40
Esquelmes War Cemetery
Grave ref: V. B. 34

Deeprose Percy Frank L/Cpl. No.6394196 2nd Bn. 23/05/40
Adegem Canadian War Cemetery
Grave ref: I. AB. 9.

Edwards George Alfred Pte. No. 6399598 2nd Bn. 23/05/40
White House Cemetery, St. Jean-les Ypres
Grave ref:

Finch Ernest Allen Pte. No. 6402596 4th Bn. 25/05/40
Nine Elms British Cemetery
Grave ref: 16. C. 5.

Fletcher Thomas Charles Cpl. No. 6399549 5th Bn. 22/05/40
Grave ref: I. AB. 3.

Froude Richard R.S.M. M.I.D. No. 6391344 2nd Bn. 22/05/40
Adegem Canadian War Cemetery
Grave ref: III. AB. 1.

Gallop John Arthur Pte. No. 792084 2nd Bn. 22/05/40
Esquelmes War Cemetery
Grave ref: VI. A. 23

Gardner Richard John L/Cpl. No. 5668683 22/05/40
Adegem Canadian War Cemetery
Grave ref: II. AB. 4.

Goodger John James Pte. No. 6396597 2nd Bn. 22/05/40
Duiksmuide Communal Cemetery
Grave 845

Haste George W. Pte. No. 6396582 2nd Bn. 22/05/40
Esquelmes War Cemetery
Grave ref: VI. B. 30

Hemmings Trevor Charles Frederick Pte. No. 6402300 4th Bn. 21/05/40
Anzegem Communal Cemetery
Grave 9

Hewett Ronald Sidney L/Cpl. No. 6402255 5th Bn. 22/05/40
Adegem Canadian War Cemetery
Grave ref: II. AB.1

Hickman Frederick John Pte. No. 6401489 4th Bn.   21/05/40
Gijzelbrechtegem Churchyard
Grave 4

Holcombe Arthur W.O.11 No. 6393623 2nd Bn.   16/06/40
Brussels Town Cemetery
Grave ref: X. 12 10.

Jenner William Edward W.O.11 No. 2206518 5th Bn.   22/05/40
Adegem Canadian War Cemetery
Grave ref: II. AB. 12

Jourdain Edward Percy Reid M.C. 2/ Lt. No. 79264 4th Bn.   15/06/40
Gent City Cemetery
Grave ref: 18. 03. 8.

Parish William Joseph Pte. No. 6397501 2nd Bn.   21/05/40
Gijzelbrechtegem Churchyard
Grave 2

Parker Kenneth Sidney Pte. No. 5501230 5th Bn.   23/05/40
Adegem Canadian War Cemetery
Grave ref: II. AB. 3.

Pelling Sidney Pte. No. 6400098 2nd Bn.   24/05/40
Schorisse Communal Cemetery
Grave 3

Pilbeam Frederick J.T. Pte. No. 6400680 5th Bn.   16/06/40
Esquelmes War Cemetery
Grave ref: V. B. 52

Price E.T. L/Sgt. No. 6397432 2nd Bn.   22/05/40
Esquelmes War Cemetery
Grave ref: V. B. 50

Prynn Arthur Robert C/Sgt. No. D/30127 Unk/Bn.   02/12/44
Brussels Town Cemetery
Grave ref: X. 26. 46.

Rainbow Sidney Frank Cpl. No. 817275 2nd Bn.   29/05/40
Adegem Canadian War Cemetery
Grave ref: II. AB. 10.

Read Leslie Ronald Pte. No. 5667114 5th Bn.   22/05/40
Adegem Canadian War Cemetery
Grave ref: I. AB. 12

Rooker William George Cpl. No. 5669309 5th Bn.   between 10/06/40 and 16/06/40
Adegem Canadian War Cemetery
Grave ref: II. AB. 9.

Slowe Edward Patrick Lt. No. 90597 5th Bn.   23/05/40
Adegem Canadian War Cemetery
Grave ref: I. AB. 11

Smith Cecil Pte. No. 6398814 4th Bn.   23/05/40
Adegem Canadian War Cemetery
Grave ref: VI. AA. 5.

Snaith George Frank Pte. No. 6396411 5th Bn.   16/06/40
Adegem Canadian War Cemetery
Grave ref: I. AB. 1.

Standing William John Pte. No. 6400285 2nd Bn.   22/05/40
Esquelmes War Cemetery
Grave ref: VI. B. 26.

Sugg Lester E. Pte. No. 5668999 5th Bn.   16/06/40
Esquelmes War Cemetery
Grave ref: V. B. 47.

Taylor John Thomas Pte. No. 6398600 5th Bn. 22/05/40
Adegem Canadian War Cemetery
Grave ref: II. AB. 8.

Turnbull Richard Dominic Pte. No. 6400600 5th Bn. 16/06/40
Cement House Cemetery
Grave XVII B. 8.

Turner Ronald Arthur Pte. No. 6401339 5th Bn. 22/05/40
Adegem Canadian War Cemetery
Grave ref: I. AB. 4.

Watson Gerald Arthur Capt. No. 64042 4th Bn. 21/05/40
Anzegem Communal Cemetery
Grave 10.

Webber Harold L/Cpl. No. 6402132 2nd Bn. 28/05/40
Esquelmes War Cemetery
Grave ref: VI. A. 22.

Winter John Edward Sgt. No. 6397795 2nd Bn. 21/05/40
Gijzelbrechtegem Churchyard
Grave 1

Cyprus

Barnard Arthur Henry Pte. No. 6398236 1st Bn. 12/07/42
Nicosia War Cemetery
Grave ref: 5. B. 11.

Czech Republic

Harris Joseph Richard Pte. No. 6397874 2nd Bn. 20/02/45
Prague War Cemetery
Grave ref: IV. D. 4.

Wood Walter Albert Cpl. No. 6398227 2nd Bn. 12/12/41
Prague War Cemetery
Grave ref: IV. D. 8.

Egypt

Agus Robert Pte. No. 4544130 5th Bn. 03/11/42
El Alamein War Cemetery
Grave ref. XVIII. F. 23.

Allcorn James Ernest Harold Cpl. No. 6397546 1st Bn. 31/01/42
El Alamein War Cemetery
Column 61

Allen George Mompesson Lt. No. 197198 2nd Bn. 03/11/42
El Alamein War Cemetery
Grave ref: XVII. X, 15.

Appleyard David William Pte. No. 6470772 4th Bn. 27/10/42
El Alamein War Cemetery
Grave ref: XIX. A. 7.

Arthur William Henry Pte. No. 6403619 1st Bn. 24/11/42
Halfaya Sollum War Cemetery
Grave ref: 5. D. 1.

Ashdown Robert Charles William Cpl. No. 6403031 5th Bn. 29/10/42
El Alamein War Cemetery
Grave ref: XIII. D. 9.

Baker John Victor Pte. No. 6400212 1st Bn. 22/11/41
Halfaya Sollum War Cemetery
Grave ref: 6.E. 3.

Baker Robert Leonard W.O.11 No. 6398049 1st Bn. 22/11/41
Halfaya Sollum War Cemetery
Grave ref: 6.E. 3.

Ball David George L/Sgt. No. 6088912 4th Bn. between 27/10/42 and 28/10/42
El Alamein War Cemetery
Grave ref: XXII. H. 1.

Barbour John Cpl. No. 7011605 2nd Bn. 02/11/42
El Alamein War Cemetery
Grave ref: XVIII. C. 9.

Barson William Cpl. No. 4543324 4th Bn. 01/09/42
El Alamein War Cemetery
Grave ref: XII. F. 1.

Beale David John Pte. No. 6400575 5th Bn. 27/10/42
Alamein Memorial
Column 61.

Beeton Alexander James Pte. No. 6011028 1st Bn. 22/11/41
Halfaya Sollum War Cemetery
Grave ref: 6. E.1.

Bell Fred Pte. No. 6396130 1st Bn. 22/11/41
Halfaya Sollum War Cemetery
Grave ref: 6. D. 6.

Bing Walter Frederick Pte. No. 6401980 2nd Bn. 31/10/42
El Alamein War Cemetery
Grave ref: XIV. E. 10.

Binnington Robert Sgt. M.M. No. 4385843 4th Bn. 27/10/42
El Alamein War Cemetery
Grave ref: VI. B. 26

Blackmore Alfred Nelson L/Cpl. No. 5670104 1st Bn. 22/11/41
Halfaya Sollum War Cemetery
Grave ref: 6.D. 5.

Blyth George Thomas Pte. No. 6408546 1st Bn. 22/11/41
Halfaya Sollum War Cemetery
Grave ref: 6. G. 4.

Bone Charles Edward Pte. No. 5505235 5th Bn.
El Alamein War Cemetery
Grave ref: XVIII. B. 18.

Bourne Alfred Henry Pte. No. 6410935 4th Bn. between 27/10/42 and 28/10/42
Alamein Memorial
Column 61.

Bourne Charles Alfred Pte. No. 6400808 4th Bn. 27/10/42
El Alamein War Cemetery
Grave ref: XIX. A. 4.

Bovingdon Reginald William Pte. No. 6102682 5th Bn.
Alamein Memorial
Column 61

Bradbury Norman Percival Pte. No. 5346984 2nd Bn. 28/10/42
Alamein Memorial
Column 61

Brading Leslie Stephen Pte. No. 5502187 5th Bn. 27/10/42
El Alamein War Cemetery
Grave ref: XVIII. E. 22.

Brambley William Frank Pte. No. 5499076 27/10/42
El Alamein War Cemetery
Grave ref: XVIII. E. 24.

Bravant Leslie Gerrard Pte. No. 5436193 2nd Bn. 22/11/42
Tel el Kebir War Memorial Cemetery
Grave ref: I. C. 2.

Breeds Ronald Clifford Pte. No. 6403035 4th Bn. between 27/10/42 and 28/10/42
Alamein Memorial
Column 61.

Bridger William Percival Pte. No. 6402565 1st Bn. 14/11/42
Alamein Memorial
Column 61

Britt Stanley L/Cpl. No. 6402919 4th Bn. 28/10/42
El Alamein War Cemetery
Grave ref: XIX. A. 12.

Brogden Charles Pte. No. 5504079 5th Bn. 27/10/42
El Alamein War Cemetery
Grave ref: XVIII. E. 23.

Brooks Albert George Pte. No. 6410633 2nd Bn. 26/10/42
El Alamein War Cemetery
Grave ref: XIII. G. 3.

Brooks Godfrey George Pte. No. 6403425 1st Bn. 30/10/40
Cairo War Memorial Cemetery
Grave ref: P. 272.

Broomfield Reginald Frederick Pte. No. 5496619 5th Bn. 28/10/42
El Alamein War Cemetery
Grave ref: IX. A. 19.

Brown Arthur George Pte. No. 5573415 2nd Bn. 28/10/42
Alamein Memorial
Column 62.

Brown Bertie Pte. No. 6470894 2nd Bn. 30/10/42
El Alamein War Cemetery
Grave ref: Joint grave XVII. F. 15.

Brown Charles Edward Pte. No. 13048206 1st Bn. 22/11/41
Halfaya Sollum War Cemetery
Grave ref: 6. D. 7.

Browne Christophe Peter Lt. M.I.D. No. 138160 5th Bn. 27/10/42
El Alamein War Cemetery
Grave ref: XVIII. E. 22.

Bryant Leslie James Pte. No. 6403875 1st Bn. 22/11/41
Halfaya Sollum War Cemetery
Grave ref: 6. B. 6.

Bull Tom Pte. No. 6402103 2nd Bn. 29/10/42
El Alamein War Cemetery
Grave ref: III. G. 14.

Bunch Sidney Lewis Sgt. No. 6401454 5th Bn. 27/10/42
Alamein Memorial
Column 61

Burgess Albert Edward Pte. No. 6408378 1st Bn. 22/11/41
Halfaya Sollum War Cemetery
Grave ref: 6. D. 8.

Burgess Arthur Harold Cpl. No. 6404120 4th Bn. 28/10/42
El Alamein War Cemetery
Grave ref: XXXI. F. 22.

Burningham Albert Gordon Lt. No. 224922 5th Bn. 27/10/42
Alamein Memorial
Column 61.

Bush Reginald Harold Arthur Pte. No. 6404003 1st Bn. 15/06/41
Tel el Kebir War Memorial Cemetery
Grave ref: 3. O. 1.

Canning Albert Edward Cpl. No. 6396348 1st Bn. 22/11/41
Halfaya Sollum War Cemetery
Grave ref: 6. D. 4.

Cantillon Michael   Pte. No. 6410946 4th Bn. 27/10/42
El Alamein War Cemetery
Grave ref: XIX. A. 13.

Catlin Christopher Alfred Pte. No. 6406037 2nd Bn. 25/10/42
 El Alamein War Cemetery
Grave ref: VI. A. 15.

Chalcraft Charles Henry Lt. No. 5505102 5th Bn. 03/11/42
El Alamein War Cemetery
Grave ref: VI. G. 3.

Charman William Henry L/Sgt. No. 6394868 4th Bn. 28/10/42
El Alamein War Cemetery
Grave ref: Joint grave XVIII. B. 1.

Chase Robert Edwin Cpl. No. 6398641 1st Bn. 22/11/41
Halfaya Sollum War Cemetery
Grave ref: 6. B. 2.

Chatfield Cyril Donald Pte. No. 6403883 1st Bn. 22/11/41
Halfaya Sollum War Cemetery
Grave ref: 6. E. 6.

Chidgey Albert Edward Pte. No. 5568362 2nd Bn. 01/11/42
El Alamein War Cemetery
Grave ref: XVIII. C. 8.

Chilman Edward Henry Sgt. No. 6397175 2nd Bn. 25/10/42
El Alamein War Cemetery
Grave ref: XI. F. 10.

Chopping Walter Frederick Pte. No. 6394408 2nd Bn. 01/12/43
Suez War Memorial Cemetery
Grave ref: 3. E. 2.

Clarke William Frederick Pte. No. 6398223 1st Bn. 24/10/42
El Alamein War Cemetery
Grave ref: XXXI. C. 13.

Comber Sidney Pte. No. 6398573 4th Bn. 30/10/42
El Alamein War Cemetery
Grave ref: XXIII. B. 2.

Cook Harold Pte. No. 6397195 2nd Bn. 24/1042
El Alamein War Cemetery
Grave ref: VI. A. 20.

Cook Ronald James L/Cpl. No. 55505113 5th Bn. 28/10/42
El Alamein War Cemetery
Grave ref: V. H. 14.

Coomber Leslie Richard Pte. No. 6407606 5th Bn. 27/10/42
El Alamein War Cemetery
Grave ref: XVIII. E. 16.

Cooper William John Pte. No. 6407037 5th Bn. 02/11/42
El Alamein War Cemetery
Grave ref: XVIII. F. 17.

Cottrill Eric Cpl. No. 4545843 5th Bn. 29/10/42
El Alamein War Cemetery
Grave ref: XXII. H. 24.

Covington Charles Henry Lt. M.I.D. No. 164693 1st Bn. 21/11/41
Halfaya Sollum War Cemetery
Grave ref: 6. D. 3.

Creasey Frederick William Pte. No. 6403962 1st Bn. 24/11/41
Halfaya Sollum War Cemetery
Grave ref: 21. E. 1.

Croft Gilbert Lawrence Pte. No. 6402123 2nd Bn. 29/10/42
El Alamein War Cemetery
Grave ref: XVIII. B. 13.

Crouch William Cyril Cpl. No. 6395785 2nd Bn. 03/11/42
El Alamein War Cemetery
Grave ref: IX. A. 17.

Daughtrey Albert Cpl. No. 6397544 1st Bn. 19/02/41
Ismailia War Memorial Cemetery
Grave ref: 1. C. 8.

Davies Norman George Capt. No. 138161 2nd Bn. 28/10/42
Alamein Memorial
Column 61.

Davis Ben Pte. No. 6402642 1st Bn. 13/11/40
Cairo War Memorial Cemetery
Grave ref: P. 279.

Daw Frederick Charles Pte. No. 873234 1st Bn. 04/03/41
Ismailia War Memorial Cemetery
Grave ref: 1. C. 8.

Dawson Frank Edgar Pte. No. 6403864 2nd Bn. 26/10/42
El Alamein War Cemetery
Grave ref: XIX. A. 8.

Deacon Horace James Capt. No. 171955 1st Bn. 22/11/41
Halfaya Sollum War Cemetery
Grave ref: 6. E. 2.

Denham Cyril Charles Pte. No. 6403483 1st Bn. 22/11/42
Halfaya Sollum War Cemetery
Grave ref: 6. B. 7.

Deville Sidney John L/Sgt. M.M. No. 6011748 1st Bn. 15/07/424
Heliopolis War Cemetery
Grave ref: 2. D. 3.

Doyle Sydney Joseph Sgt. No. 6397836 1st Bn. 22/11/41
Halfaya Sollum War Cemetery
Grave ref: 6. E. 9.

Duff John Edward Sidney Creighton 2/Lt. No. 130859 1st Bn. 28/09/40
Ismailia War Memorial Cemetery
Grave ref: 2. B. 3.

Earwaker Robert Roy Sgt. No. 6404253 4th Bn. 28/10/42
El Alamein War Cemetery
Grave ref: XIX. A. 11.

Edwards Eric John Cpl. No. 6399445 2nd Bn. 02/11/42
El Alamein War Cemetery
Grave ref: XIX. A. 17.

Edwards Ronald Isaac Cpl. No. 6404098 1st Bn. 05/10/42
Alamein Memorial
Grave ref: Column 61.

Elbrow Albert Harold Pte. No. 6396071 5th Bn. 01/11/42
Alamein Memorial
Grave ref: Column 62.

Ellis George William Pte. No. 6401112 Army Catering Corps. attd. 5th Bn. 27/10/42
El Alamein War Cemetery
Grave ref: XVIII. E. 14.

Fellows Reginald Thomas Cpl. No. 6400361 5th Bn. 28/10/42
El Alamein War Cemetery
Grave ref: XVIII. E. 19.

Fiddler Relf Herbert Pte. No. 5500808 5th Bn. 29/10/42
Alamein Memorial
Grave ref: Column 62.

Fletcher John Wilfred Pte. No. 55055285 5th Bn. 02/11/42
Alamein Memorial
Grave ref: Column 62.

Ford Frederick William Pte. No. 6403355 1st Bn. 17/08/41
Tel el Kebir War Memorial Cemetery
Grave ref: 3. K. 4.

Fuller Edward Henry Pte. No. 6401925 1st Bn. 22/11/41
Halfaya Sollum War Cemetery
Grave ref: 6. G. 9.

Galloway Alfred Sydney Pte. No. 4626073 2nd Bn. 02/11/42
El Alamein War Cemetery
Grave ref: V. F. 4.

Garman George Thomas Pte. No. 6400253 2nd Bn. 28/10/42
El Alamein War Cemetery
Grave ref: V. C. 16.

Garner Sidney Pte. No. 6398802 2nd Bn. 23/08/40
Ismailia War Memorial Cemetery
Grave ref: 2. C. 2.

Gartrell Wilfred L/Cpl. No. 6403832 5th Bn. 09/11/42
Alexandria (Hadra) War Memorial Cemetery
Grave ref: 4. B. 14.

Gearing Arthur Stanley Pte. No. 6407677 1st Bn. 05/10/42
Alamein Memorial
Column 62

Glassenbury Bert Pte. No. 6403580 1st Bn. 24/01/42
Heliopolis War Cemetery
Grave ref: 1. D. 27.

Goddard Gerad Pte. No. 6404335 4th Bn. 28/10/42
El Alamein War Cemetery
Grave XIX. A. 5.

Golding Albert Pte. No. 6399212 2nd Bn. 01/11/42
Alamein Memorial
Column 62.

Goldring Edward Charles Pte. No. 6404032 1st Bn. 02/05/42
El Alamein War Cemetery
Grave ref: XXXII. B. 10.

Goodsell George L/Cpl. No. 6398294 1st Bn. 22/11/41
Halfaya Sollum War Cemetery
Grave ref: 6. D. 2.

Green Horace John Cpl. No. 6460435 4th Bn. 28/10/42
Alamein Memorial
Column 61.

Griffiths Reginald Allenby Douglas L/Cpl. No. 6402909 4th Bn. between 27/10/42 and 28/10/42
El Alamein War Cemetery
Grave ref: XVIII. C. 4.

Gulland Ronald Alfred Pte. No. 6402292 2nd Bn. 30/10/42
El Alamein War Cemetery
Grave ref: Joint grave XVII. F. 15.

Haffenden Robert Harold L/Cpl. No. 6398041 1st Bn. 22/11/41
Halfaya Sollum War Cemetery
Grave ref: 6.G. 10.

Hall Eric Newman Cpl. No. 6404620 1st Bn. 12/09/43
Moascar War Cemetery
Grave ref: 2. B. 9.

Hamilton Edward Thomas George Pte. No. 550448 5th Bn. 03/11/42
El Alamein War Cemetery
Grave ref: XVIII. C. 17.

Hamilton Ernest Albert L/Cpl. No. 6398838 1st Bn. 22/11/41
Halfaya Sollum War Cemetery
Grave ref: 6. E. 8.

Hancock Francis Lewis Pte. No. 562312 2nd Bn. 25/10/42
El Alamein War Cemetery
Grave ref: IX. B. 1A.

Hare Charles Colville Lt. No. 228395 5th Bn. 27/10/42
El Alamein War Cemetery
Grave ref: III. F. 4.

Harrington Walter Frederick 2/Lt. No. 203803 1st Bn. 21/09/42
El Alamein War Cemetery
Grave ref: XXVII. A. 6.

Harris Ronald William Cpl. No. 6403901 5th Bn. 03/11/42
El Alamein War Cemetery
Grave ref: XVIII. C. 13.

Harrison George Henry L/Cpl. No. 5505159 5th Bn. 01/11/42
El Alamein War Cemetery
Grave ref: XX. A. 18.

Harrison John Vellacot Capt. No. 138165 4th Bn. 27/10/42
El Alamein War Cemetery
Grave ref: XVIII. C. 15.

Hart Arthur George L/Cpl. No. 5505160 5th Bn. 27/10/42
Alamein Memorial
Column 61.

Hart William John Pte. No. 5509416 5th Bn. 03/11/42
El Alamein War Cemetery
Grave ref: XVII. F. 12.

Hatton John Ernest Edward Pte. No. 5505162 5th Bn. 27/10/42
Alamein Memorial
Column 62.

Hayes Dennis Richard Courtney Capt. M.I.D. No. 130053 5th Bn. 29/10/42
El Alamein War Cemetery
Grave ref: XVIII. E. 17.

Hayward Charles James Pte. No. 5505165 5th Bn. 30/10/42
Alamein Memorial
Column 62.

Hazelden Jack Pte. No. 6898632 1st Bn. 25/11/41
Halfaya Sollum War Cemetery
Grave ref: 5. D. 4.

Hill John Stephen L/Cpl. No. 6403432 1st Bn.
El Alamein War Cemetery
Grave ref: XVII. A. 8.

Hilton William Seymour Pte. No. 5386526 22/11/41
Halfaya Sollum War Cemetery
Grave ref: 6. G. 7.

Hoare Edward Pte. No. 6409663 4th Bn. 27/10/42
Alamein Memorial
Column 62.

Hodge Bertie Pte. No. 6402827 4th Bn. 22/11/41
Halfaya Sollum War Cemetery
Grave ref: 6. G. 8.

Hodgson Sidney Pte. No. 4545858 1st Bn. 05/10/42
Alamein Memorial
Column 62.

Holder Edgar George Pte. No. 6401419 4th Bn. 29/10/42
El Alamein War Cemetery
Grave ref: XXIII. E. 3.

Holderness Frederick Pte. No. 6403502 4th Bn. 01/09/42
El Alamein War Cemetery
Grave ref: XII. F. 26.

Holland Cecil Laurence Pte. No. 6401647 5th Bn. 30/10/42
El Alamein War Cemetery
Grave ref: XII. H. 5.

Hooles Sidney Arthur L/Cpl. No. 6406275 1st Bn. 06/10/42
El Alamein War Cemetery
Coll. Grave XXIV. B. 1.

Howe Ernest Henry Pte. No. 6403505 1st Bn. 24/11/41
Halfaya Sollum War Cemetery
Grave ref: 6. D. 1.

Hunt William Charles Pte. No. 5348070 2nd Bn. 29/10/42
Alamein Memorial
Column 62.

Isaac Gwilym Sgt. No. 5568670 2nd Bn. 25/10/42
El Alamein War Cemetery
Grave ref: XI. E. 1.

Jackson George William Pte. No. 6398747 1st Bn. 24/11/41
Halfaya Sollum War Cemetery
Grave ref: 5. D. 2.

Jenkins Albert Pte. No. 6403121 1st Bn. 05/10/42
El Alamein War Cemetery
Grave ref: XXV. H. 11.

Jenkins Joseph Pte. No. 6402977 10th Bn. Para. Regt. A.A.C. 03/02/43
Fayid War Cemetery
Grave ref: 5. A. 1.

Jenkinson Alfred Pte. No. 5340801 2nd Bn. 28/10/42
El Alamein War Cemetery
Grave ref: III. E. 18.

Johnson George Cpl. No. 6400153 5th Bn. 02/11/42
El Alamein War Cemetery
Grave ref: IX. J. 26.

Johnston Oswald Charles Mjr. M.I.D. No. 47613 1st Bn. 22/11/41
Halfaya Sollum War Cemetery
Grave ref: 6. B. 3.

Jones Ernest Victor Sgt. No. 5668960 5th Bn. 28/10/42
El Alamein War Cemetery
Grave ref: XVIII. E. 8.

Jones George William Thomas Pte. No. 6399271 5th Bn. 27/10/42
Alamein Memorial
Column 62

Kenward John William L/Cpl. No. 6399903 5th Bn. 28/10/42
El Alamein War Cemetery
Grave ref: XVIII. B. 20.

Kenyon Vincent Stanley Pte. No. 6398644 1st Bn. 22/11/41
Halfaya Sollum War Cemetery
Grave ref: 6. E. 7.

King Edward Cpl. No.6404006 1st Bn. 21/09/42
El Alamein War Cemetery
Grave ref: XXVII. A. 7.

King Reginald Cpl. No. 6407987 5th Bn. 03/11/42
Alamein Memorial
Column 61.

Kirk Frederick John Pte. No. 64722388 2nd Bn. 06/11/42
El Alamein War Cemetery
Grave ref: IX. A. 16.

Knapp Jack Alwyn Claud Pte. No. 6399028 4th Bn. 28/10/42
Alamein Memorial
Column62.

Lidgett Ivor Frank Pte. No. 5506229 5th Bn. 28/10/42
Alamein Memorial
Column 62.

Lucas Edward Arthur Pte. No. 5342644 2nd Bn. 25/10/42
El Alamein War Cemetery
Grave ref: VI. A. 19.

Lyle Peter Anthony Lt. No. 184152 4th Bn. 27/10/42
El Alamein War Cemetery
Grave ref: XVIII. C. 12.

Lyons James Henry Pte. No. 6410169 2nd Bn. 31/10/42
El Alamein War Cemetery
Grave ref: IX. A. 18.

Macey Charles Edward Pte. No. 5501355 5th Bn. 27/10/42
El Alamein War Cemetery
Grave ref: XVIII.A. 19.

Mansfield Percy Jack Pte. No. 6460236 4th Bn. 27/10/42
El Alamein War Cemetery
Grave ref. XXII. H. 3.

Manville Frederick Edward Duncan 6393646 5th Bn. 27/10/42
El Alamein War Cemetery
Grave ref: XVIII. C. 21.

Marks Percy Clifford Pte. M.I.D. No. 5505188 5th Bn. 30/10/42
El Alamein War Cemetery
Grave ref: XVII. D. 25.

Marten Sidney John Pte. No. 6401239 4th Bn. 02/11/42
El Alamein War Cemetery
Grave ref: XVIII. C. 6.

Martin James Pte. No. 6412160 2nd Bn. 19/08/42
Heliopolis War Cemetery
Grave ref: 2. F. 13.

Martin John Barlow Pte. No. 6404000 1st Bn. 22/11/41
Halfaya Sollum War Cemetery
Grave ref: 6. G. 1.

Maxwell Ernest Pte. No. 6411049 4th Bn. 27/10/42
El Alamein War Cemetery
Grave ref: XIX. A. 2.

Miles Eric Leslie Pte. No. 6403524 4th Bn. between 27/10/42 and 28/10/42
Alamein Memorial
Column 62.

Miles Sidney John Richard Pte. No. 6398544 1st Bn. 19/10/41
Tel el Kebir War Memorial Cemetery
Grave ref: 3.H. 3.

Mills Charles Ernest Capt. No. 137738 1st Bn. 25/09/42
El Alamein War Cemetery
Grave ref: XIX. B. 8.

Mills Percy Pte. No. 6398054 1st Bn. 12/09/42
Alamein Memorial
Column 62.

Mitten Thomas Edward Pte. No. 6400016 1st Bn. 29/01/42
Alamein memorial
Column 62.

Monk Frederick James L/Cpl. No. 4545098 4th Bn. 24/10/42
El Alamein War Cemetery
Grave ref: VI. A. 16.

Moore Leslie Charles Pte. No. 6403596 1st Bn. 22/11/41
Halfaya Sollum War Cemetery
Grave ref: 6. G. 5.

MacGregor Dennis Richmond Grant Lt. No. 124224 1st Bn. 22/11/41
Halfaya Sollum War Cemetery
Grave ref: 6. B. 4.

Nicholls William Thomas Sgt. No. 6397534 2nd Bn. 30/10/42
El Alamein War Cemetery
Grave ref: III. F. 22.

Nicholson Leslie James Pte. No. 6411495 5th Bn. 27/10/42
El Alamein War Cemetery
Grave XVIII. E. 18.

Nightingale Douglas Arthur James Cpl. No. 6399684 2nd Bn. 02/11/42
Alamein Memorial
Column 61.

Osborne Arthur Ernest Pte. No. 5503289 5th Bn. 27/1042
El Alamein War Cemetery
Grave ref: XVIII. C. 10.

Pack Cyril Raymond Pte. No. 5505198 5th Bn. 01/09/42
El Alamein War Cemetery
Grave ref: XXV. B. 18.

Parker George Cecil Pte. No. 6408162 5th Bn. 01/11/42
El Alamein War Cemetery
Grave ref: XVIII. E. 12.

Parkinson Richard Edward Hope Capt. M.B.E. No.88370 4th Bn. 04/11/42
El Alamein War Cemetery
Grave ref: XXIX. H. 5.

Pelling Frederick Walter L/Cpl. No. 6400011 1st Bn. 29/05/41
Ismailia War Memorial Cemetery
Grave ref: 4. B. 6.

Pelling James Valentine Pte. No. 6398266 1st Bn. 22/11/41
Halfaya Sollum War Cemetery
Grave ref: 6. B. 1.

Peters John Raymond Pte. No. 6406748 1st Bn. 31/08/42
El Alamein War Cemetery
Grave ref: XII. G. 7.

Philpott Leonard Joseph Pte. No. 5555204 5th Bn. 27/10/42
Alamein Memorial
Column 62

Philps William Alfred Cpl. No. 5505204 5th Bn. 01/11/42
El Alamein War Cemetery
Grave ref: XVIII. E.5.

Poore Roy Charles Pte. No. 5573669 2nd Bn. 27/10/42
El Alamein War Cemetery
Grave ref: V. G. 19.

Potter William Cyril Pte. No. 5573774 2nd Bn. 03/11/42
Heliopolis War Cemetery
Grave ref: 2. E. 31.

Preen Joseph James Sgt. No. 6396008 2nd Bn. 29/12/42
Fayid War Cemetery
Grave ref: 1.C. 24.

Prodger Thomas Victor Pte. No. 6398157 1st Bn. 21/09/42
El Alamein War Cemetery
Grave ref: XXVII. A. 5.

Pumphrey Thomas John Pte. No. 6404091 1st Bn. 23/11/41
Halfaya Sollum War Cemetery
Grave ref: 6. E. 10.

Ralph Thomas James Pte. No. 6403536 1st Bn.
Halfaya Sollum War Cemetery
Grave ref: 6. G. 6.

Ray Arthur James Pte. No. 5053813 5th Bn. 01/09/42
El Alamein War Cemetery
Grave ref: XIII. D. 17.

Reynolds Robert Frederick Verdun Pte. No. 6404300 4th Bn. 27/10/42
El Alamein War Cemetery
Grave ref: IX. J. 15.

Roberts Geoffrey Pte. No. 643743 4th Bn. 22/12/42
Heliopolis War Cemetery
Grave ref: 3. H. 9.

Roberts Samson Pte. No. 6404727 2nd Bn. 28/10/42
El Alamein War Cemetery
Grave ref: XVIII. C. 3.

Sadler Peter Henry Lt. No. 137329 2nd Bn. 25/10/42
El Alamein War Cemetery
Grave ref: IX. B. 3A.

Sands William Henry Pte. No. 6395776 1st Bn. 09/11/42
Alexandria (Hadra) War Memorial Cemetery
Grave ref: 4. B. 12.

Scotford George Sgt. No. 6395046 4th Bn. 27/10/42
El Alamein War Cemetery
Grave ref: XIX. A. 6.

Scott Horace George Cpl. No. 6398601 1st Bn. 22/11/41
Halfaya Sollum War Cemetery
Grave ref: 6. E. 4.

Scott James Pte. No. 5501278 4th Bn. 27/10/42
El Alamein War Cemetery
Grave ref: XIX. A. 1.

Scrase Frederick Henry John Pte. No. 6398896 1st Bn.
Alamein Memorial
Column 62.

Simmons Victor Alfred Pte. No. 6407356 2nd Bn. 30/10/42
El Alamein War Cemetery
Grave ref: XVIII. B. 5.

Simpson George Vivian L/Cpl. No. 6403007 2nd Bn. 02/11/42
El Alamein War Cemetery
Grave ref: XVIII. C. 7.

Slater John William Pte. No. 6104110 5th Bn. 02/11/42
El Alamein War Cemetery
Grave ref: XIX. A. 25.

Sloman Douglas George Pte. No. 6403894 1st Bn. 23/05/41
El Alamein War Cemetery
Grave ref: XII. C. 10.

Smith Frank Henry Pte. No. 6412175 1st Bn. 06/08/42
Heliopolis War Cemetery
Grave ref: 2. E. 11.

Smith Paul Eric Pte. No. 6401227 5th Bn. 31/10/42
El Alamein War Cemetery
Grave ref: III. F. 12.

Smith Ronald Anthony Pte. No. 6013396 1st Bn. 06/10/42
El Alamein War Cemetery
Grave ref: Coll. Grave XXIV. B. 1.

Southgate Edward Pte. No. 6411113 4th Bn. 27/10/42
El Alamein War Cemetery
Grave ref: XVIII. C. 4.

Steed Herbert Pte. No.6406872 5th Bn. 29/10/42
El Alamein War Cemetery
Grave ref: XXII. H. 20.

Stone Arthur Percy Pte. No. 6407177 5th Bn. 27/10/42
Alamein Memorial
Column 62.

Sullivan George Pte. No. 6403604 1st Bn. 12/12/40
Cairo War memorial Cemetery
Grave ref: P. 289.

Swatton William Ferguson L/Sgt. No. 6400976 4th Bn. 28/10/42
El Alamein War Cemetery
Grave ref: XIX. A. 10.

Taylor Thomas Walter Cpl. No. 63984201st Bn. 22/11/41
Halfaya Sollum War Cemetery
Grave ref: 6. G. 2.

Thornton John Michael Edward Pte. No. 5500599 5th Bn. 02/09/42
El Alamein War Cemetery
Grave ref: XIII. J. 14.

Thynne Joseph John Pte. No.6404884 1st Bn. 05/10/42
Alamein Memorial
Column 62.

Tilley Alfred Pte. No. 5342805 1st Bn. 02/11/42
El Alamein War Cemetery
Grave ref: XVII. F. 9.

Tiltman Alec Howard Pte. 6404066 No. 1st Bn. 05/10/42
Alamein Memorial
Column 62.

Tucker Albert Peter Pte. No. 6398285 1st Bn. 31/01/42
Alamein Memorial
Column 62.

Turner Alfred John Pte. No. 6405584 5th Bn. 27/10/42
Alamein Memorial
Column 62.

Tutty Cecil Vernon Pte. No. 6150050 5th Bn. 27/10/42
Alamein Memorial
Column 62.

Upton Albert Gordon Pte. No. 604015 1st Bn. 22/11/41
Halfaya Sollum War Cemetery
Grave ref: 6. D. 9.

Wardell Patrick William Pte. No. 5507380 5th Bn. 04/11/42
Alexandria (Hadra) War Memorial Cemetery
Grave ref: 4. C. 16.

Weir Frank Leonard Sgt. No. 6400692 4th Bn. between 27/10/42 and 28/10/42
Alamein memorial
Column 61.

Whitely Jack Pte. No. 4539615 4th Bn. 01/09/42
El Alamein War Cemetery
Grave ref: XII. H. 17.

Whitmore Thomas William Pte. No. 5890362 2nd Bn. 25/10/42
El Alamein War Cemetery
Grave ref: XI. F. 12.

Whittaker Ronald George Pte. No. 6406332 1st Bn.
Halfaya Sollum War Cemetery
Grave ref: 11. E. 4.

Wild James Scullion Pte. No. 5572729 1st Bn. 24/09/42
Moascar War Cemetery
Grave ref: 1. C. 16.

Willard George Frederick Pte. No. 6404044 1st Bn. 21/09/42
El Alamein War Cemetery
Grave ref: XXV. F. 28.

Willard John Albert L/Cpl. No. 6404214 4th Bn. 27/10/42
El Alamein War Cemetery
Grave ref: XIX. A. 9.

Willcox John George Pte. No. 6406512 4th Bn. 27/10/42
El Alamein War Cemetery
Grave ref: V. G. 20.

Willett Hubert Clive Lt. No. 172262 4th Bn. 27/10/42
Alamein Memorial
Column 61.

Willett Ronald Frederick Pte. No. 6398385 1st Bn. 22/11/41
Halfaya Sollum War Cemetery
Grave ref: 6. G. 3.

Williams Richard Pte. No. 6400055 1st Bn. 22/11/41
Halfaya Sollum War Cemetery
Grave ref: 15. B. 10.

Wiseman Alfred Daniel Pte. No. 5337297 1st Bn. 02/11/42
Alamein Memorial
Column 62.

Withall Harold James Pte. No. 6399345 1st Bn. 16/07/40
Ismailia War Memorial Cemetery
Grave ref: 1. C. 3.

Woolgar Charles L/Sgt. No. 6402691 1st Bn. 21/09/42
El Alamein War Cemetery
Grave ref: XXVII. A. 4.

Woolgar Laurence George Pte. No. 2571372 1st Bn. 22/11/41
Halfaya Sollum War Cemetery
Grave ref: 6. E.5.

Yeates William Edward Pte. No. 6398587 1st Bn. 02/11/42
Moascar War Cemetery
Grave ref: 1. E. 1.

Young William Herbert Pte. No. 5504821 5th Bn. 27/10/42
El Alamein War Cemetery
Grave ref: XVIII. E. 20.

Youngs Frank Pte. No. 6399314 1st Bn. 28/01/42
Alamein Memorial
Column 62.

Eritrea

Ashenden Spencer Charles Sgt. No. 6464470 1st Bn. 27/07/41
Asmara War Cemetery
Grave ref: 2. E. 4.

Axell Charles Henry Cyril Pte. No. 6398499 1st Bn. 11/04/41
Asmara War Cemetery
Grave ref: 2. E. 5.

Boreham Leslie Charles Pte. No. 6404074 1st Bn. 08/04/41
Asmara War Cemetery
Grave ref: 2. G. 4.

Carver Alfred James Pte. No. 6399015 1st Bn. 08/04/41
Asmara War Cemetery
Grave ref: 2. F. 3.

Cornell William James Pte. No. 6403709 1st Bn. 08/04/41
Asmara War Cemetery
Grave ref; 2. G. 6.

Fadden James Pte. No. 6404068 1st Bn. 08/04/41
Asmara War Cemetery
Grave ref: 2. G. 10.

Fitzgerald Daniel David Godfrey L/Cpl. No. 6398860 1st Bn. 08/04/41
Asmara War Cemetery
Grave ref: 2. C. 1.

Gillespie Conrad Ernest Pte. No. 6403494 1st Bn. 08/04/41
Asmara War Cemetery
Grave ref: 2. F. 2.

Goldsmith Percy Pte. No. 6399120 1st Bn. 27/03/41
Keren War Cemetery
Grave ref: 4. C. 14.

Hampshire George Frederick William Pte. No. 6399154 1st Bn. 08/04/41
Asmara War Cemetery
Grave ref: 2. F. 1.

Heavers Ronald Thomas Pte. No. 6399810 1st Bn. 09/04/41
Asmara War Cemetery
Grave ref: 2. G. 8.

Huntly Clifford Bernard L/Cpl. No. 6398658 1st Bn. 19/03/41
Keren War Cemetery
Grave ref: 4. C. 15.

Kemp Sidney Pte. No. 6402980 1st Bn. 08/04/41
Asmara War Cemetery
Grave ref: 2. G. 5.

Luff Reginald Harry Arthur Sgt. No. 6398517 1st Bn. 08/04/41
Asmara War Cemetery
Grave ref: 2. F. 6.

Munro Ronald Pte. No. 6403688 1st Bn. 08/04/41
Asmara War Cemetery
Grave ref: 2. F. 5.

Paget William Edward Sydney 2/Lt. No. 130054 1st Bn. 08/04/41
Asmara War Cemetery
Grave ref: 2. G. 3.

Rusbridge Edmund George Samuel Pte. No. 6399905 1st Bn. 08/04/41
Asmara War Cemetery
Grave ref: 2. F. 7.

Smith Charles Leslie Pte. No. 6402750 1st Bn. 08/04/41
Asmara War Cemetery
Grave ref: 2. E. 7.

Smith Harold Victor Pte. No. 6398760 1st Bn. 08/04/41
Asmara War Cemetery
Grave ref: 2. G. 9.

Spooner Frederick William Pte. No. 6402362 1st Bn. 08/04/41
Asmara War Cemetery
Grave ref: 2. F. 4.

Tuppen Raymond Pte. No. 6398919 1st Bn. 27/03/41
Keren War Cemetery
Grave ref: 4. C. 13.

Walls George Henry Pte. No. 6398610 1st Bn. 08/04/41
Asmara War Cemetery
Grave ref: 2. G. 7.

Ethiopia

Campbell William Alexander Sgt. No. 6397101 1st Bn. 25/05/41
Addis Ababa War Cemetery
Grave ref: 2. B. 15

France

Abrahamowicz Richard George   Pte. No. 6436363 No. 10 Commando   07/06/44
Bayeux Memorial
Panel 15, Column 1.

Abrahams George   Pte. No. 5438562 7th Bn. 20/05/1940
Dunkirk Memorial
Column 63.

Acres Barnard Henry John   Pte. No. 6401272 7th Bn. 18/05/1940
Abbeville Communal Cemetery Extension
Plot 9. Row D. Grave 1.

Adsett George David Pte. No. 6410372 9th Bn. Para. Regt. A.A.C. 06/06/44
Bayeux Memorial
Panel 18. Column 1.

Andrews Reginald Gilbert   Pte. No. 5727493 7th Bn. between 19/05/40 and 12/06/40
Dunkirk Memorial
Column 63.

Apted Eric   Pte. No. 6400171   4th Bn. 28/05/40
Meteren (Mont-des-Cats) Communal Cemetery
Grave 15

Arenstein Hans   L/Corporal No. 6436352 No. 10 Commando   10/08/44
Ranville War Cemetery
Grave ref: 1A.M.4.

Arrow Walter Jack Pte. No. 6403243 7th Bn. 20/05/40
Abbeville Communal Cemetery Extension
Plot 9. Row F. Grave 13.

Atkinson Charles Joseph Pte. No. 5727920 7th Bn. between 21/05/40 and 09/06/40
Abbeville Communal Cemetery Extension
Plot 9. Row F. Grave 5.

Aukett Ernest John Rollison Pte. No. 839044 2nd Bn. between 10/05/40 and 28/05/40
Hazebrouck Communal Cemetery
Plot 4. Row A. Grave 11.

Aylward Frederick Alfred Pte. No. 6401783 6th Bn. 20/05/40
Pont-de-Metz Churchyard
Plot 4. Row A. Grave 21.

Baker Graham Edward Pte. No. 6401844   Unk/Bn.   between 03/06/40 and 23/06/40
Dunkirk Memorial
Column 63

Baldock Albert Jesse Pte. No. 6402241 4th Bn. 27/05/40
Caestre Communal Cemetery
Plot 5. Row A. Grave 5.

Bampton Sidney Thomas Pte. No. 5668673 5th Bn. 04/06/40
Bertenacre Military Cemetery, Fletre
Plot 2. Row G. Grave 1.

Banham Henry John Pte. No. 5622487 Unk/Bn. 07/06/40
Neufchatel-en-Bray Communal Cemetery
Grave ref: Mil. Plot, Row 1, Grave 7.

Barnard Samuel Henry Sgt. M.I.D. No. 6393734 7th Bn. 20/05/40
Abbeville Communal Cemetery Extension
Plot 9. Row F. Grave 11.

Barnes Ernest Charles Pte. No. 6397106 2nd Bn. between 26/05/40 and 04/06/40
Dunkirk Memorial
Column 63

Barnes Ronald Jack Pte. No. 6403295 7th Bn. between 21/05/1940 and 23/06/1940
Dunkirk Memorial
Column 63

Barnett Moses Pte. No. 6399659 4th Bn. between 10/05/40 and 31/05/40
Dunkirk Town Cemetery
Plot 2 Row 1 Joint grave 2.

Batchelor Walter Jack Pte. No. 6401974 2nd Bn. between 24/05/40 and 04/06/1940
Le Grand Hasard Military Cemetery, Morbeccque
Grave ref: Sp. Mem. 6. B. 1.

Bazely William James Pte. No. 5728157 7th Bn. 20/05/40
Abbeville Communal Cemetery Extension
Plot 9. Row F. Grave 12.

Bell John W.O.11 No. 6391060 7th Bn. 08/10/40
Viroflay New Communal Cemetery
Row B. Grave 2.

Bevan William George Hamilton Pte. No. 5501319 5th Bn. 16/06/40
Dunkirk Memorial
Column 64

Bevis George Henry L/Cpl. No. 5728071 7th Bn. between 18/05/40 and 20/05/40
Abbeville Communal Cemetery Extension
Plot 9. Row F. Grave 7.

Bishop John Frederick Pte. No. 6401732 7th Bn. 20/05/40
Dunkirk Memorial
Column 64

Blackford Ronald Alfred Pte. No. 5727698 7th Bn. between 21/05/40 and 12/06/40
Abbeville Communal Cemetery Extension
Plot 9. Row F. Grave 15.

Blackwell George Thomas William Lt. M.I.D. No. 89293 7th Bn. 18/05/40x
Abbeville Communal Cemetery Extension
Plot 9. Row D. Grave 2.

Blakemore Stanley Charles Bernard Pte. No. 6401981 2nd Bn. 28/05/40
Hazebrouck Communal Cemetery
Plot 4. Row A. Grave 16.

Bolingbroke Stanley Pte. No. 6412488 9th Bn. Para. Regt. A.A.C. 20/08/44
La Delivrande War Cemetery, Douvres
Grave ref: I. H. 2.

Booker Ernest Pte. No. 6401986 2nd Bn. 28/05/40
Hazebrouck Communal Cemetery
Plot 4. Row A. Grave 15.

Boorer John Alfred Pte. No. 6400572   4th Bn. 28/05/40
Caestre Communal Cemetery
Plot 5. Row B. Grave 5.

Boote John L/Bmdr. No. 10560586   359 Bty. 109 L.A.A. R.A. (7th Bn. The Royal Sussex Regiment) 17/09/44
Bayeux War Cemetery
Grave ref: 1.D.1.

Boxall Leonard James Pte. No. 6400619 4th Bn. 28/05/40
Lille Southern Cemetery
Plot 5. Row E. Grave 23.

Brain Clifford Edward Gnr. No. 111058598 109 L.A.A. R.A. (7th Bn. The Royal Sussex Regiment) 22/09/44
Bayeux War Cemetery
Grave ref: 1.A.10.

Bravery William John Pte. No. 6079433 2nd Bn. 27/05/40
Dunkirk Memorial
Column 64

Brett Frederick George Pte. No. 6399911 5th Bn. 16/06/40
Bertenacre Military Cemetry, Fletre
Plot 2. Row F. Grave 11.

Brett Jack Pte. No. 6400726 5th Bn. 21/05/40
Bertenacre Military Cemetry, Fletre
Plot 2. Row F. Grave 21.

Bridle Joseph Alfred Pte. No. 5727935 7th Bn. between 20/05/40 and 21/05/40
Abbeville Communal Cemetery Extension
Plot 9. Row D. Grave 3.

Bruce Ernest Pte. No. 6402746 4th Bn. 28/05/40
Caestre Communal Cemetery
Plot 5. Row A. Grave 7.

Buckman Edward Pte. No. 6396521 2nd Bn. between 26/05/40 and 28/05/40
Hazebrouck Communal Cemetery
Plot 4. Row C. Grave 4.

Burns Thomas Victor Pte. No. 6400220 2nd Bn. between 24/05/40 and 04/06/1940
Dunkirk Memorial
Column 64

Buss Sidney George Pte. No. 6402080 4th Bn. 29/05/40
Lille Southern Cemetery
Plot 5. Row D. Grave 7.

Calthrop Hugh Ledward Pte. No. 5728172 7th Bn. 20/05/40
Abbeville Communal Cemetery Extension
Plot 9. Row G. Grave 4.

Card Wallace Syril C.Q.M.S. No. 6395628 7th Bn. 20/05/40
Abbeville Communal Cemetery Extension
Plot 9. Row E. Grave 13.

Cardwell Desmond Fitzroy 2/Lt. 78571 5th Bn. 27/05/40
Straveele Communal Cemetery
Grave 1.

Carpenter George Alfred Leslie Pte. No. 6401706 6th Bn. between 20/05/40 and 16/06/40
Abbeville Communal Cemetery Extension
Plot 9. Row G. Grave 12.

Carse William Pte. No. 6400488 4th Bn. 22/05/40
Outtersteene Communal Cemetery Extension, Bailleul
Plot 3. Row A. Grave 15.

Cassells James Stuart Mjr. M.C.,M.I.D. No. 13193 7th Bn. 21/05/40
Morvillers-St. Saturnin Churchyard

Charman Arthur Pte. No. 6397054 Unk/Bn. 07/06/40
Neufchatel-en-Bray Communal Cemetery
Grave ref: Mil. Plot, Row 1, Grave 10.

Chawner Charles Frederick Cpl. No. 5668383 5th Bn. 16/06/40
Bertenacre Military Cemetery, Fletre
Plot 2. Row G. Grave 12.

Chisham John Henry Pte. No. 5501259 5th Bn. 16/05/40
Meteren (Mont-des-Cats) Communal Cemetery
Grave 14.

Chittenden Alan Reginald No.278354 attd. 5th Bn. Wiltshire Regt. 05/08/44
St. Manvieu War Cemetery, Cheux
Grave ref: VIII. G. 16.

Clark Frederick John Pte. No. 5439409 7th Bn. 20/05/40
Dunkirk Memorial
Column 64

Clasen William Henry Pte. No. 6401787 5th Bn. 27/05/40
Longuenesse (St. Omer) Souvenir Cemetery
Plot 8. Row A. Grave 27.

Cleverly Reginald Sgt. No. 6396608 5th Bn. 16/05/40
Bertenacre Military Cemetery, Fletre
Plot 2. Row G. Grave 3.

Coleman Stanley Norman L/Cpl. No. 5439434 7th Bn. 20/05/40
Salouel Communal Cemetery
Row B. Grave 9.

Colling Charles Edward (Ted) Pte. No. 6401105 5th Bn. 27/05/40
Bertenacre Military Cemetery, Fletre
Plot 2. Row G. Grave 10.

Cooney Harold Pte. No. 6396777 2nd Bn. 18/05/40
Hazebrouck Communal Cemetery
Plot 4. Row C. Grave 2.

Cooper Patrick Henry Pte. No. 6399691 4th Bn. 26/05/40
Dunkirk Memorial
Column 64

Corbett-Ward John Pte. No. 6444679 4th Bn. 23/05/40
Outtersteene Communal Cemetery Extension, Bailleul
Plot 3. Row A. Grave 9.

Cornford Frederick John Pte. No. 6397482 2nd Bn. 28/05/40
Hazebrouck Communal Cemetery
Plot 4. Row B. Grave 29.

Court Arthur Ernest Pte. No. 6401459 5th Bn. 27/05/40
Bertenacre Military Cemetery, Fletre
Plot 2. Row G. Grave 16.
Cowell Alfred Graham Drmr. No. 6400087 2nd bn. 21/05/40
Dunkirk Memorial
Column 64

Cox Joseph Victor Pte. No. 5499040 2nd Bn.
Le Grand Hasard Military Cemetry, Morbeccque
Grave ref: Sp. Mem. 5. B. 14.

Crossman Clifford William Pte. No. 5622070 4th Bn. between 29/05/40 and 27/02/41
Lille Southern Cemetery
Plot 5. Row E. Grave 25.

Cummings John Moir Pte. No. 6401154 7th Bn. 21/05/40- 09/06/1940
Dunkirk Memorial
Column 64

Davies Thomas Henry Cpl. No. 5568581 2nd Bn. 29/05/40
Dunkirk Memorial
Column 64

Dawson Charles Henry Pte. No. 6403210 7th Bn. 20/05/40
Abbeville Communal Cemetery Extension
Plot 9. Row F. Grave 6.

Dengate Patrick Donald Pte. No. 6400849 5th Bn. 27/05/40
Bertenacre Military Cemetery, Fletre
Plot 2. Row G. Grave 2.

Denyer Albert William Pte. No. 6400186 4th Bn. 29/05/40
Lille Southern Cemetery
Plot 5. Row E. Grave 16.

Dodge Charles Henry L/Cpl. No. 6397926 7th Bn. 20/05/40
Dunkirk Memorial
Column 63

Downs Jack Pte. No. 5439181 7th Bn. 20/05/40
Salouel Communal Cemetery
Row E. Grave 6.

Duffy Andrew Thomas Pte. No. 5439182 7th Bn. 20/05/40
Salouel Communal Cemetery
Row D. Grave 2.

Eastwood Frederick Charles Pte. No. 6403152 7th Bn.   18/05/40
Dunkirk Memorial
Column 64

Edmonds Edward Harold Lt. No. 124147 7th Bn.   20/05/40
Marissel French National Cemetery
Grave 275

Edwards Francis John Pte. No.6400151 5th Bn. between 27/05/1940 and 05/01/1941
Bertenacre Military Cemetery, Fletre
Plot 2. Row G. Grave 3.

Elliott Sidney Charles Pte. No. 6088915 6th Bn.
Outtersteene Communal Cemetery Extension, Bailleul
Plot 3. Row A. Grave 17.

Ellis Frederick Charles Pte. No. 6401939 7th Bn.   20/05/40
Abbeville Communal Cemetery Extension
Plot 9. Row G. Grave 11.

Ellis Thomas Meadcalfe Pte. No. 6401487 4th Bn.   26/05/40
Dunkirk Memorial
Column 64

Fallon Reuben Pte. No. 5724055 7th Bn.   between 19/05/40 and 12/06/40
Dunkirk Memorial
Column 64

Fazan Gilbert Roy Lt. No. 129362 No.6 Commando 07/07/44
Ranville war Cemetery
Grave ref: IIIA. O. 3.

Fenn Sidney Arnold Harewood Pte. No. 6395624 2nd Bn. 22/05/40
Dunkirk Memorial
Column 64

Fisher Charles Percy Pte. No. 2nd Bn. 6399914 between 25/05/40 and 04/06/40
Le Grand Hasard Military Cemetry, Morbeccque
Grave ref: 5. B. 8.

Foley Daniel Patrick Pte. No. 5727966 7th Bn. 20/05/40
Dunkirk Memorial
Column 64

Franklin Maurice Harry Pte. No. 6402425 7th Bn. 18/05/40
Marissel French National Cemetery
Grave 222

Friend John Frederick Pte. No. 6402287 5th Bn. 16/05/40
Dunkirk Memorial
Column 64

Fuller Frederick Mark Pte. No. 6397322 7th Bn. 20/05/40
Abbeville Communal Cemetery Extension
Plot 9. Row D. Grave 11.

Fuller Thomas Frederick Pte. No. 6396360 2nd Bn. between 10/05/40 and 28/05/40
Hazebrouck Communal Cemetery
Plot 4. Row C. Grave 5.

Funnell Jack James Pte. No. 6401151 7th Bn. 20/05/40
Dunkirk Memorial
Column 64

Funnell William Albert Pte. No. 6398577 2nd Bn. 29/05/40
Hazebrouck Communal Cemetery
Plot 4. Row C. Grave 9.

Gascoigne John Pte. No. 5501830 5th Bn. 27/05/40
Bertenacre Military Cemetery, Fletre
Plot 2. Row F. Grave 2.

Gaskell Jack Pte. No. 6400280 2nd Bn. between 26/05/40 and 28/05/40
Hazebrouck Communal Cemetery
Plot 4. Row C. Grave 10.

Gibson James George Pte. No. 013558 7th Bn. 20/05/40
Salouel Communal Cemetery
Row A. Grave 5.

Giles William Aubrey Pte. No. 5439190 7th Bn. 20/05/40
Salouel Communal Cemetery
Row C. Grave 2.

Gillett John Charles Pte. No. 6397691 7th Bn. 20/05/40
Dunkirk Memorial
Column 64

Glover Lawrence Frederick Pte. No. 6402206 4th Bn. 28/05/40
Caestre Communal Cemetery
Plot 5. Row B. Grave 9.

Gurr Ronald William Pte. No. 6399675 5th Bn. 28/05/40
Pradelles Churchyard
Row C. Grave 1.

Hadler Norman Stanley Pte. No. 5622191 5th Bn. between 10/05/40 and 30/06/40
Dunkirk Memorial
Column 64

Harland Robert Harland Pte. No. 6401941 7th Bn. 20/05/40
Dunkirk Memorial
Column 64

Harris George Alfred Pte. No. 5438526 7th Bn. Between 21/05/40 and 09/06/40
Pont-de Metz Churchyard
Plot 4. Row A. Grave 8.

Hatch Frederick George Pte. No. 2034041 7th Bn. between 21/05/40 and 09/06/40
Pont-de-Metz Churchyard
Plot 4. Row A. Grave 14.

Haughton Frederick Charles Pte. No. 6403284 7th Bn. between 20/05/40 and 09/06/40
Abbeville Communal Cemetery Extension
Plot 9. Row E. Grave 5.

Hawe Robert Pte. No. 7011540 2nd Bn. between 22/05/40 and 31/05/40
Dunkirk Memorial
Column 64

Haycock Edward Pte. No. 5439460 7th Bn. 20/05/40
Salouel Communal Cemetery
Row E. Grave 1.

Heweth Edward Pte. No. 5437924 7th Bn. between 18/05/40 and 20/05/40
Salouel Communal Cemetery
Row E. Grave 7.

Hewitt William Matthew Pte. No. 2402301 5th Bn. 22/05/40
Bertenacre Military Cemetery, Fletre
Plot 2. Row F. Grave 7.

Hincks John Hawkeswood 2/Lt.. No. 79908 7th Bn. between 27/05/40 and 20/05/40
Caestre Communal Cemetery
Plot 5. Row B. Grave 3.

Hogg Frederick Walter Maurice Pte. No. 6402477 7th Bn. 20/05/40
Dunkirk Memorial
Column 64

Holder Frederick Thomas Cpl. No. 6396441 2nd Bn. between 24/05/40 and 26/05/40
Meteren (Mont-des-Cats) Communal Cemetery
Grave 18

Holford Hugh Funnell Pte. No. 6401865 2nd Bn. 24/05/40
Le Grand Hasard Military Cemetry, Morbeccque
Grave ref: 6. B. 7.

Hollyman Thomas William Pte. No. 6400122 7th Bn. 22/05/40
Dunkirk Memorial
Column 64

Hood John William Cpl. No. 6396447 2nd Bn. between 27/07/40 and 17/08/40
Dunkirk Town Cemetery
Plot 2 Row 1 Joint grave 13.

Hope John L/Cpl. No. 6395265 2nd Bn. 04/02/45
Dunkirk Memorial
Column 63

House Arthur Bennington Pte. No. 5501308 5th Bn. 29/05/40
Caestre Communal Cemetery
Plot 5. Row B. Grave 4.

Hudson Leslie Harold Cpl. No. 6395141 2nd Bn. 30/05/40
St. Pol War Cemetery
Row C. Grave 16.

Hull Robert William Pte. No. 6392308 5th Bn. 16/06/40
Bertenacre Military Cemetery, Fletre
Plot 2. Row G. Grave 6.

Hunter Sidney Albert Pte. No. 6711434 2nd Bn. 27/05/40
Le Grand Hasard Military Cemetry, Morbeccque
Grave ref: Sp. Mem. 5. B. 10.

Hyatt George William Pte. No. 6402385 7th Bn. 18/05/40
Pont-de-Metz Churchyard
Plot 4. Row A. Grave 32.

Jeffery William Ernest Pte. No. 5767248 7th Bn. 19/05/40
Abbeville Communal Cemetery Extension
Plot 9. Row F. Grave 10.

Johns Robert Owen Pte. No. 6400916 4th Bn. between 29/05/40 and 02/06/40
Dunkirk Memorial
Column 64

Jolley Norman Thomas Pte. No. 6400741 7th Bn. between 20/05/40 and 20/06/40
Abbeville Communal Cemetery Extension
Grave ref: Sp. Mem. Plot 9. Row F. Grave 8.

Jones Oliver Pte. No. 5727313 7th Bn. 20/05/40
Abbeville Communal Cemetery Extension
Plot 9. Row E. Grave 12.

Jutsum Frederick John Pte. No. 5727565 7th Bn. 23/06/40
Abbeville Communal Cemetery Extension
Plot 9. Row F. Grave 3.

Kay Ronald McDonald L/Cpl. No. 5727594 7th Bn. 20/05/40
Salouel Communal Cemetery
Row E. Grave 5.

Keeley Arthur Lt. No. 307954 attd. 7th Bn. S.L.I. 10/08/44
Tilly-sur-Seulles War Cemetery
Grave ref: V. E. 10.

Keens Edmund Harold Pte. No. 6403281 7th Bn. between 20/05/40 and 23/05/40
Abbeville Communal Cemetery Extension
Plot 9. Row E. Grave 14.

Kember Donald Frank Pte. No. 6402616 5th Bn. 26/05/40
Bertenacre Military Cemetery, Fletre
Plot 2. Row G. Grave 19.

Kendall Edward Frank Pte. No. 5670313 5th Bn. 16/06/40
Dunkirk Memorial
Column 64

Keyworth Eric Frank Pte. No. 6402484 7th Bn. 20/05/40
Abbeville Communal Cemetery Extension
Plot 9. Row F. Grave 9.

Kilgarry James Pte. No. 5438537 7th Bn. 20/05/40
Salouel Communal Cemetery
Row D. Grave 3.

Kill Edward George Pte. No. 6394918 2nd Bn. 27/05/40
Dunkirk Memorial
Column 64

Killner Walter Alfred Pte. No. 6398198 2nd Bn. 18/05/40
Dunkirk memorial
Column 64

King Clifford John Pte. No. 5438522 7th Bn. 20/05/40
Dunkirk Memorial
Column 64

King Frank Pte. No. 6402726 Unk/Bn. between 10/05/40 and 30/06/40
Neufchatel-en-Bray Communal Cemetery
Grave ref: Mil. Plot, Row 1, Grave 5.

King George Stanley Lt. No. 189368 attd. 5th Bn. D.C.L.I. 11/07/44
Banneville-la-Campagne War Cemetery
Grave ref: X. C. 20.

King Gordon James William Pte. No.5727503 7th Bn.   between 21/05/40 and 12/06/40
Dunkirk Memorial
Column 64

King Leonard Alfred Pte. No. 5438523 7th Bn. 20/05/40
Salouel Communal Cemetery
Row D. Grave 5.

Kingsbury George Edward Sgt. No. 5667680 5th Bn. 04/06/40
St. Pol War Cemetery
Row E. Grave 14.

Kingston Walter Grove Cpl. No. 6399435 2nd Bn. 19/06/40
Etaples Military Cemetery
Grave ref: 46. B. 1.

Kinmond Jeffery Thomas Pte. No. 6402173 Unk/Bn. 22/05/40
Dunkirk Memorial
Column 64

Lancashire John Pte. No. 5728147 7th Bn. 20/05/40
Abbeville Communal Cemetery Extension
Plot 9. Row F. Grave 16.

Langley Charles Edward Pte. No. 5727666 7th Bn. between 26/05/40 and 09/06/40
Abbeville Communal Cemetery Extension
Plot 9. Row E. 1.

Laybourne Jim Pte. No. 5437865 7th Bn. 20/05/40
Salouel Communal Cemetery
Row D. Grave 4.

Light Roy George Algernon Pte. No. 6401866 4th Bn. 28/05/40
Caestre Communal Cemetery
Plot 5. Row B. Grave 6.

Linfield Albert David John Pte. No. 6403197 7th Bn. 26/05/40
Abbeville Communal Cemetery Extension
Plot 9. Row D. Grave 16.

Littlejohn John Pte. No. 6711116 7th Bn.   20/05/40
Dunkirk Memorial
Column 64

Looker George Sidney Pte. No. 6402460 7th Bn.   21/05/40
Pont-de-Metz Churchyard
Plot 4. Row A. Grave 12.

Loomes Ernest Herbert Pte. No. 5727521 7th Bn.   between 17/05/40 and 09/06/40
Abbeville Communal Cemetery Extension
Plot 9. Row F. Grave 4.

Maidment Benjamin Alfred Pte. No. 787940 2nd Bn.   28/05/40
Hazebrouck Communal Cemetery
Plot 4. Row A. Grave 28.

Mann Cyril Frederick Pte. No. 6402137 4th Bn.   29/05/40
Dunkirk Memorial
Column 64

Mann Hector William Cpl. No. 6402137 7th Bn.   18/05/40
Abbeville Communal Cemetery Extension
Plot 9. Row B. Grave 10.

Marchant Thomas L/Cpl. No. 6394589 2nd Bn.   26/05/40
Le Grand Hasard Military Cemetry, Morbeccque
Grave ref: 5. B. 4.

Marsh James Alfred Pte. No. 6400442 4th Bn.   08/06/40
Ecques Churchyard
Grave 3

Marshall Eric D.C.E. Pte. No. 6403153 7th Bn.   20/05/40
Salouel Communal Cemetery
Row C. Grave 1.

Martin Horace George Pte. No. 6396813 30/05/40
Le Grand Hasard Military Cemetry, Morbeccque
Grave ref: 5. B. 15.

Martin James Ernest (Jim) Pte. No. 6401336 5th Bn.   26/05/40
Bertenacre Military Cemetery, Fletre
Plot 2. Row G. Grave 18.

Martin Leonard John L/Cpl. No. 6401577 7th Bn.
Abbeville Communal Cemetery Extension
Plot 9. Row D. Grave 13.

Masters Frederick Charles Pte. No. 6397347 2nd Bn.   29/05/40
Helfaut Churchyard
Grave 4

Mayhead Charles Pte. No. 6402466 between 14/05/40 and 12/06/40
Pont-de-Metz Churchyard
Plot 4. Row A. Grave 5.

Meaney Richard George Pte. No. 6402513 7th Bn.   09/06/40
Abbeville Communal Cemetery Extension
Plot 9. Row F. Grave 1.

Miller Peter Tavener Mjr. No. 39804 7th Bn.   20/05/40
Dunkirk memorial
Column 63

Moon Frank Pte. No. 6401284 7th Bn. between 20/05/40 and 09/06/40
Abbeville Communal Cemetery Extension
Plot 9. Row G. Grave 9.

Moore Percy John Pte. No. 3965228 7th Bn.   between 21/05/40 and 09/06/40
Dunkirk Memorial
Column 64

Moore William Richard Pte. No. 6397184 2nd Bn. 27/05/40
Le Grand Hasard Military Cemetry, Morbeccque
Grave ref: 5. A. 6.

Moreby Richard Frederick Cpl. No. 6401650 7th Bn. between 22/05/40 and 09/06/40
Pont-de-Metz Churchyard
Plot 4. Row A. Grave 3.

Morford Reginald Stanley L/Sgt. No. 6397603 7th Bn.
Abbeville Communal Cemetery Extension
Plot 9. Row G. Grave 2.

Morris John Edward Pte. No. 6401257 7th Bn. between 21/05/40 and 09/06/40
Abbeville Communal Cemetery Extension
Plot 9. Row G. Grave 5.

Morton Geoffrey Pte. No. 5439504 7th Bn. 20/05/40
Pont-de-Metz Churchyard
Plot 4. Row A. Grave 30.

Murphy Philip Julian No. 6401038 4th Bn. between 29/05/40 and 21/08/40
Dunkirk Town Cemetery
Plot 2 Row 1 Joint grave 14.

McKenna Peter Pte. No. 7011736 2nd Bn. 22/05/40
Dunkirk memorial
Column 64

McLean Gilbert Charles Pte. No. 5727349 7th Bn. 07/06/40
Abbeville Communal Cemetery Extension
Plot 9. Row E. Grave 16.

Niblett Percy Henry Pte. No. 5727680 7th Bn. 20/05/40
Pont-de-Metz Churchyard
Plot 4. Row A. Grave 26.

Nixon Charles Wallace L/Sgt. No. 6401580 7th Bn. 22/05/40
Dunkirk Memorial
Column 63

Overington Cyril Henry William Pte. No. 639950 2nd Bn. 22/05/40
Hazebrouck Communal Cemetery
Plot 4. Row A. Grave 12.

Page Frederic Pte. No. 6399564 4th Bn. 27/05/40
Caestre Communal Cemetery
Plot 5. Row A. Grave 1.

Page Frederick Pte. No. 6400215 2nd Bn. 28/05/40
Hazebrouck Communal Cemetery
Plot 4. Row C. Grave 8.

Page Leonard Robert Pte. No. 6402476 7th Bn. 20/05/40
Salouel Communal Cemetery
Row E. Grave 8.

Page William Alfred Pte. No. 5501285 5th Bn. 27/05/40
Bertenacre Military Cemetery, Fletre
Plot 2. Row F. Grave 3.

Page William Joseph Pte. No. 6399235 4th Bn. 27/05/40
Dunkirk Memorial
Column 64

Parlett Douglas Charles Pte. No. 6398930 5th Bn. 29/05/40
Bertenacre Military Cemetery, Fletre
Plot 2. Row G. Grave 22.

Parnham Thomas Pte. No. 4801660 4th Bn. 28/05/40
Caestre Communal Cemetery
Plot 5. Row A. Grave 8.

Patching Albert Ernest Pte. No. 6396879 2nd bn. 27/05/40
Calais Canadian War Cemetery, Leubringhen
Grave ref: 5. H. 5.

Pilbeam John Lawrence Phipps Pte. No. 6403250 7th Bn. 19/05/40
Abbeville Communal Cemetery Extension
Plot 9. Row F. Grave 14.

Pluckrose Kenneth George Pte. No. 5727380 7th Bn. 20/05/40
Abbeville Communal Cemetery Extension
Plot 9. Row E. Grave 11.

Porter Reginald Harold John Pte. No. 5439837 7th Bn. 20/05/40
Abbeville Communal Cemetery Extension
Plot 9. Row A. Grave 14.

Pritchard Edward Sgt. No. 4740695 7th Bn. 20/05/40
Salouel Communal Cemetery
Row D. Grave 1.

Rackham Howard Edward Sgt. No. 6395870 2nd Bn. 26/05/40
Le Grand Hasard Military Cemetry, Morbeccque
Grave ref: Sp. Mem. 5. B. 7.

Rainbow Samuel Frederick Pte. No. 6397797 2nd Bn. 27/05/40
Dunkirk Memorial
Column 63

Rancom Harry Bent Pte. No. 6393319 7th Bn. 20/05/40
Abbeville Communal Cemetery Extension
Plot 9. Row D. Grave 9.

Reason Jack Stuart Lt. No. 69980 4th Bn. 20/05/40
Dunkirk Memorial
Column 63

Regan William James Pte. No.5439364 7th Bn. 20/05/40
Pont-de-Metz Churchyard
Plot 4. Row A. Grave 9.

Reid Ronald Alexandria George Pte. No. 6403306 7th Bn. 21/05/40
Abbeville Communal Cemetery Extension
Plot 9. Row E. Grave 15.

Richards Eldred Pte. No. 5439965 7th Bn. 20/05/40
St. Server Cemetery Extension, Rouen
Block "S". Plot 4. Row N. Grave 10.

Ridley Robert Edgar Pte. No. 6399997 5th Bn. 27/05/40
Bertenacre Military Cemetery, Fletre
Plot 2. Row F. Grave 6.

Roberts Kenneth William Pte. No. 5727679 7th Bn. 17/05/40
Abbeville Communal Cemetery Extension
Plot 9. Row F. Grave 2.

Roberts Thomas Raymond Leslie Pte. No. 6402078 4th Bn. 28/05/40
Lille Southern Cemetery
Plot 5. Row D. Grave 1.

Roffey John Christopher Pte. No. 6402346 5th Bn. 22/05/40
Outtersteene Communal Cemetery Extension, Bailleul
Plot 3. Row B. Grave 32.

Rollings Clifford Albert Pte. No. 6396202 2nd Bn. 16/04/40
Dunkirk Memorial
Column 64

Ronald R. Pte. No. 6400094 9th Bn. Para. Regt. A.A.C. 06/06/44
Ranville War Cemetery
Grave ref: VA. D. 1.

Rucker Patrick William Capt. No. 108679 7th Bn. 20/05/40
Dunkirk memorial
Column 63

Rundle George Henry Pte. No. 5439946 7th Bn. 19/05/40
Dunkirk Memorial
Column 64

Sarfaty Douglas Jack Pte. No. 3965149 7th Bn. 14/05/40
Abbeville Communal Cemetery Extension
Plot 9. Row G. Grave 8.

Secretan Holford Cave 2/Lt. No. 75863 2nd Bn. 23/05/40
Dunkirk memorial
Column 63

Shard Ernest Ronald Pte. No. 5501313 5th Bn. 27/05/40
Bertenacre Military Cemetery, Fletre
Plot 2. Row G. Grave 9.

Shippam Frank Norman Capt. M.I.D. No. 180207 attd. 1/7th Middlesex Regt. 10/07/44
La Delivandre War Cemetery, Douvres
Grave ref: VII. A. 2.

Smith Frank Burton Pte. No. 6399784 5th Bn. 21/05/40
Dunkirk Memorial
Column 64

Smith William Alfred Pte. No. 6402754 5th Bn. 27/05/40
Strazeele Communal Cemetery
Grave 2

Soby Reginald Squire Pte. No.572718 7th Bn. 20/05/40
Abbeville Communal Cemetery Extension
Plot 9. Row D. Grave 15.

Southart Albert George Pte. No. 6402361 5th Bn. 30/05/40
Dunkirk Memorial
Column 64

Spouge Edward Stanley Pte. No. 5439998 7th Bn. 20/05/40
Pont-de-Metz Churchyard
Plot 4. Row A. Grave 31.

Steer James Harry Pte. No. 6597505 2nd Bn. 27/05/40
Le Grand Hasard Military Cemetry, Morbeccque
Grave ref: 5. B. 13.

Stevenson Ernest Leslie Pte. No. 6399820 2nd Bn. 10/05/40
Le Grand Hasard Military Cemetery, Morbeccque
Grave ref: 5. B. 11

Stredwick Harold Pte. No. 6403258 7th Bn. 20/05/40
Dunkirk memorial
Column 64

Stubbington Leslie Pte. No. 6402587 Unk/Bn. 07/06/40
Neufchatel-en-Bray Communal Cemetery
Grave ref: Mil. Plot, Row 1, Grave 9.

Symons Kenneth George Pte. No. 5439985 7th Bn. 21/05/40
Pont-de-Metz Churchyard
Plot 4. Row A. Grave 6.

Taylor Basil Edgar Pte. No. 6410789 9th Bn. Para. Regt. A.A.C. 07/06/44
Ranville War Cemetery
Grave ref: IA. L. 3.

Teague Idris Cpl. No. 5668586 5th Bn. 05/09/41
Dunkirk Memorial
Column 63

Teague John Alfred Cpl. No. 6398786 Unk/Bn. 07/06/40
Neufchatel-en-Bray Communal Cemetery
Grave ref: Mil. Plot, Row 1, Grave 13.

Thomas Arthur Elwyn Pte. No. 5728154 7th Bn. 20/05/40
Dunkirk Memorial
Column 64

Thomas James Charles Pte. No. 6395597 4th Bn. 27/05/40
Dunkirk Memorial
Column 64

Thomas Thomas Edward Pte. No. 5727421 7th Bn. 21/05/40
Dunkirk Memorial
Column 64

Thompson John Henry Pte. No. 6396723 Unk/Bn. 10/05/40
Caestre Communal Cemetery
Plot 5. Row B. Grave 2.

Thornton Desmond Brooking Lt. No. 153263 1st Bn. attd. 9th Bn. D.L.I. 15/06/44
Bayeux War Cemetery
Grave ref: XIV. J. 16.

Timmis Eric Pte. No. 5439491 7th Bn. 18/05/40
Salouel Communal Cemetery
Row E. Grave 2.

Toms Douglas Owen Pte. No. 5439757 7th Bn. 20/05/40
Salouel Communal Cemetery
Row D. Grave 8.

Townley Neville Thomas Pte. No. 5501312 5th Bn 22/05/40
Bertenacre Military Cemetery, Fletre
Plot 2. Row G. Grave 23.

Tucker Sidney David Pte. No.5439820 7th Bn. 20/05/40
Salouel Communal Cemetery
Row F. Grave 4.

Turner Alan Richard Eric Pte. No. 5728167 7th Bn. 21/05/40
St. Server Cemetery Extension, Rouen
Block "S". Plot 4. Row N. Grave 9.

Upperton Albert George Pte. No. 6402572 5th Bn. 22/05/40
Bertenacre Military Cemetery, Fletre
Plot 2. Row G. Grave 14.

Voysey Albert Pte. No. 5439357 7th Bn. 18/05/40
Abbeville Communal Cemetery Extension
Plot 9. Row G. Grave 3.

Wadey Harvey George Cpl. No. 6402186 7th Bn. 20/05/40
Dunkirk Memorial
Column 63

Walker Anthony Grahame Sgt. No. 6396551 2nd Bn. 29/05/40
Hazebrouck Communal Cemetery
Plot 4. Row C. Grave 13.

Walkley Percy Philip Pte. No.5501331 5th Bn. 26/05/40
Bertenacre Military Cemetry, Fletre
Plot 2. Row F. Grave 4.

Walters Henry Pte. No. 6398176 5th Bn. 16/06/40
Dunkirk Memorial
Column 64

Walton Hugh Shaw Pte. No. 5728149 7th Bn. 15/05/40
Dunkirk Memorial
Column 64

Waters Garnet Sgt. No. 5492922 4th Bn. 01/06/40
Lille Southern Cemetery
Plot 5. Row D. Grave 26.

Weeks Arthur Frank Pte. No. 5728133 7th Bn. 20/05/40
Dunkirk Memorial
Column 64

Weeks Frederick Ernest Pte. No. 6402497 7th Bn. 18/05/40
Abbeville Communal Cemetery Extension
Plot 9. Row B. Grave 3.

Wells George William Pte. No. 6402377 5th Bn. 27/05/40
Bertenacre Military Cemetry, Fletre
Plot 2. Row G. Grave 4.

West Harry Ernest Pte. No. 6402551 Unk/Bn.
Neufchatel-en-Bray Communal Cemetery
Grave ref: Mil. Plot, Row 1, Grave 12.

Westoby George Pte. No. 6399671 7th Bn. 20/05/40
Abbeville Communal Cemetery Extension
Plot 9. Row G. Grave 10.

Wheatley David Pte. No. 6402412 7th Bn.
Abbeville Communal Cemetery Extension
Plot 9. Row C. Grave 15.

White Alfred Pte. No. 6396823 2nd Bn. 28/05/40
Meteren (Mont-des-Cats) Communal Cemetery
Grave 19

Whitlock Denis Eric Pte. No. 5501343 5th Bn. 22/0/40
Bertenacre Military Cemetry, Fletre
Plot 2. Row C. Grave 20.

Wymark Frank Pte. No. 6402532 5th Bn. 26/05/40
Bertenacre Military Cemetry, Fletre
Plot 2. Row F. Grave 5.

Willett Ronald Wilfred Capt. No. 37451 2nd Bn. 28/05/40
Hazebrouck Communal Cemetery
Plot 4. Row C. Grave 3.

Williams Samuel Pte. No. 3449536 7th Bn. 18/05/40
Salouel Communal Cemetery
Row B. Grave 8.

Williamson Edward Pte. No. 6397817 2nd Bn. 27/05/40
Dunkirk Memorial
Column 64

Wilson William Herbert Pte. No. 5727642 7th Bn. 20/05/40
Dunkirk Memorial
Column 64

Wingfield Frederick Jack Pte. No. 6402233 Unk/Bn. 04/06/40
St. Pol War Cemetery
Row C. Grave 18.

Witchell Michael James Hensall L/Cpl. No. 6401679 5th Bn. 21/05/40
Dunkirk Memorial
Column 63

Woolgar John Charles Pte. No. 6402379 5th Bn. 16/06/40
Bertenacre Military Cemetry, Fletre
Plot 2. Row G. Grave 8.

Germany

Armond Victor L/Bmdr. No. 6103838 109 (7th Bn. The Royal Sussex Regt.) Lt. A.A. Regt. 25/11/45
Hamburg Cemetery
Grave ref: 3A. E. 11.

Backhouse David Lt. No. 360649 attd. 1st Bn. Worcestershire Regt. 30/08/46
Hanover War Cemetery
Grave ref: 14. G. 16.

Bally John Harold Capt. No. 92180 6th Bn. 25/04/45
Becklingen War Cemetery
Grave ref: 15. A. 5.

Brown Robert Macdonald Cpl. No.6398666 1st Bn. 21/06/44
Berlin 1939-1945 War Cemetery
Grave ref: 10. G. 15.

Burbidge Samuel Raymond Evelynn Richard Lt. No. 304907 attd. 1st (Airborne) Royal Ulster Rifles 31/03/45
Reichswald Forest Cemetery
Grave ref: 33. D. A.

Crabb James William Gnr. 6408292 357 Bty., 109 (7th Bn. The Royal Sussex Regt.) Lt. A.A. Regt. 28/02/45
Reichswald Forest Cemetery
Grave ref: 53.D.9.

Fletcher Leonard John Pre. No. 6397703 2nd Bn. 11/04/45
Durnbach War Cemetery
Joint Grave 3. B. 12-13.

Freeman Alfred George Sgt. No. 2060187 109 (7th Bn. The Royal Sussex Regt.) Lt. A.A. Regt. 11/07/45
Hamburg Cemetery
Grave ref: 2A. A. 15.

Goldsmith Fred Gnr. No. 6398630 109 (7th Bn. The Royal Sussex Regt.) Lt. A.A. Regt. 01/11/45
Hamburg Cemetery
Grave ref: 3A. J. 3.

Horner Thomas Pte. No. 6402389 7th Bn. 29/06/42
Berlin 1939-1945 War Cemetery
Grave ref: 11. G. 6.

Milne Stanley George Lt. No. 296425 Unk/Bn. 26/03/45
Reichswald Forest Cemetery
Grave ref: 58. G. 18.

Phillips William James Pte. No. 6394532 2nd Bn. 25/03/45
Berlin 1939-1945 War Cemetery
Grave ref: 11. D. 9.

Roach Frederick John L/Cpl. No. 6406757 10th Bn. Para. Regt. A.A.C. 24/01/45
Berlin 1939-1945 War Cemetery
Grave ref: 10. Z. 11.

Seagrave David Morley 2/Lt. No. 330210 attd. 4th Bn. Welch Regt. 13/02/45
Reichswald Forest Cemetery
Grave ref: 51. F. 4.

Stockley Alfred Thomas Gnr. No. 41313600 109 (7th Bn. The Royal Sussex Regt.) Lt. A.A. Regt. 20/05/45
Hamburg Cemetery
Grave ref: 3A. H. 12.

Udell Cecil John L/Bmdr. No. 6399993 109 (7th Bn. The Royal Sussex Regt.) Lt. A.A. Regt. 30/04/45
Hamburg Cemetery
Grave ref: 2A. E. 9.

Villiers-Tothill 2/Lt. No. 376528 attd. 1st Bn. Royal Fusiliers (City of London) 19/09/47
Munster Heath War Cemetery
Grave ref: 3. B. 25.

Vogel Egon (served as Villiers, Ernest Robin) Sgt. No. 6436356 No. 10 Commando 24/03/45
Reichswald Forest Cemetery
Grave ref: 62. B. 2.

Wheeler Sidney John Lt. No. 179805 attd. 5th Bn. D.C.L.I.
Rheinberg War Cemetery
Grave ref: 12. J. 15.

Whitwell Thomas Francis George Pte. No. 6396829 2nd Bn. 11/04/45
Berlin 1939-1945 War Cemetery
Grave ref: 10. H. 7.

Greece

Bartlett Henry Richard Pte. No. 6407813 1st Bn. 10/03/45
Phaleron War cemetery
Grave ref: 21. D. 5.

Burns Robert James Pte. No. 14284476 1st Bn. 26/02/45
Phaleron War Cemetery
Grave ref: 21. C. 19.

Clarke John William Pte. No. 3864127 1st Bn. 06/09/45
Phaleron War Cemetery
Grave ref: 21.D. 19.

Humphrey Bert Pte. No. 6402436 1st Bn. 27/07/41
Phaleron War cemetery
Grave ref: 15. B. 5.

Smith Michael Arnold 2/Lt. No. 143725 2nd Bn. 28/02/41
Athens Memorial
Face 6.

Tunstall Francis Barnard Pte. No. 6400012 1st Bn. 28/02/41
Athens Memorial
Face 6.

Wilson Ronald John Pte. No. 14549281 1st Bn. 30/05/45
Phaleron War Cemetery
Grave ref: 21. C. 20.

India

Allitt Harold Frederick Sgt. No. 6404518 9th Bn. 22/12/44
Gauhati War Cemetery
Grave ref: 3.F. 4.

Ayris Hugh Michael Capt. No. 366828 13/10/47
Delhi War Cemetery
Grave ref: 5. A. 12.

Ballard Victor Dennis Pte. No. 14635511 9th Bn. 28/05/44
Kirkee War Cemetery
Grave ref: 1. D. 17.

Bedwell Frederick George Thomas Sgt. No. 20026041 9th Bn. 01/01/46
Madras War Cemetery, Chennai
Grave ref: 1. L. 18

Beech James Frederick Pte. No. 14404860 No. 1 Commando 05/08/45
Kirkee War Cemetery
Grave ref: 9.G. 14.

Boxall Clarence William John Pte. No. 14547166 9th Bn. 12/10/44
Gauhati War Cemetery
Grave ref: 4. A. 20.

Bradford-Martin Mertyn Swainston Mjr. No. 328739 attd. 1st Bn. 9th Gurkha Rifles 20/09/47
Delhi War Cemetery
Grave ref: 3. C. 14.

Brooker John Pte. No. 6408102 attd. H.Q. XXXIII Indian Corps. 06/12/44
Imphal War Cemetery
Grave ref: 3. D. 22.

Brown Raymond John Pte. No. 14212755 9th Bn. 22/08/44
Digboi War Cemetery
Grave ref: 3. E. 1.

Budd Maurice Arthur Jack Mjr. M.C. No. 200854 9th Bn. 23/11/45
Gauhati War Cemetery
Grave ref: 3. E. 2.

Cole Alfred Peter Pte. No. 6412225 9th Bn. 11/08/44
Calcutta (Bhwonipore) Cemetery, Kolkata
Plot L. Grave 180.

Hiscock Frederick Pte. No. 14518902 9th Bn. 03/06/45
Imphal War Cemetery
Grave ref. 7.K. 10.

Martin Kenneth Richard Pte. No. 14204368 9th Bn. 25/11/44
Digboi War Cemetery
Grave ref: 3. L. 5.

Moore Charles Bertram Lt. No. 141631 attd. Indian Army Ordnance Corps. 30/07/43
Kirkee War Cemetery
Grave ref: 9. K. 12.

Nix Ronald Percy Pte. No. 5393346 9th Bn. 29/09/44
Kirkee War Cemetery
Grave ref: 1. K. 11.

Page John Edward Sgt. No. 6402928 9th Bn. 20/12/43
Kirkee War Cemetery
Grave ref: 10.F. 3.

Pickering John Francis Lt. No. 20772 attd. 13th Bn. The King's Regt. (Liverpool) 15/06/43
Kohima War Cemetery
Grave ref: 11. A. 24.

White Arthur William Pte. M.M. No. 6407586 9th Bn. 22/10/44
Digboi War Cemetery
Grave ref: 3. D. 5.

Winder Stanley William Pte. No. 6407658 9th Bn. 27/01/44
Kirkee War Cemetery
Grave ref: 10. F. 9.

Iran

Beames Herbert William L/Sgt. No. 5573624 2nd Bn. 13/08/43
Tehran War Cemetery
Grave ref: C. 6. 11.

Bensley Ernest Henry L/Cpl. No. 6406221 2nd Bn. 20/08/43
Tehran War Cemetery
Grave ref: 6. D. 4.

Clark Albert Pte. No. 5671564 2nd Bn. 13/08/43
Tehran War Cemetery
Grave ref: 6. C. 8.

Cotton William Thomas Pte. No.6471003 2nd Bn. 13/08/43
Tehran War Cemetery
Grave ref: 6. C. 9.

Moody Ernest James Pte. No. 5348984 2nd Bn. 13/08/43
Tehran War Cemetery
Grave ref: 6. C. 13.

Ripley Moses William Pte. No. 6404199 2nd Bn. 13/08/43
Tehran War Cemetery
Grave ref: 6. C. 12.

Shervill Herbert James Pte. No. 6411104 2nd Bn. 13/08/43
Tehran War Cemetery
Grave ref: 6. C. 10.

Iraq

Duke Sidney John Pte. No. 5501299 4/5th Bn. 21/1043
Baghdad (North Gate) War Cemetery
Grave ref: 23. F. 20.

Lee Ernest James L/Cpl. No. 5573640 2nd Bn. 18/08/43
Baghdad (North Gate) War Cemetery
Grave ref: 22. N. 9.

Rose Donald Henry (Don) L/Cpl. No. 6400756 2nd Bn. 05/12/43
Baghdad (North Gate) War Cemetery
Grave ref: 22. M. 18

Watkins William Frederick Cpl. No. 3961551 2nd Bn. 14/02/44
Basra War Cemetery
Grave ref: 7. U. 10.

Watson Peter de Lannoy Paxton Capt. No. 91910 2nd Bn. 30/10/43
Basra War Cemetery
Grave ref: 7. V. 3.

Ireland (Republic of)

Dunne Michael Pte. No. D/41669 Unk/Bn. 02/05/44
Glasnevin (or Prospect) Cemetery, Dublin
Screen Wall Panel 1

Eager John Pte. No. 6405010 8th Bn. 12/08/40
Dean's Grange Cemetery, Dublin
St. Fintan. Grave 3.

Israel & Palestine(including Gaza)

Elliott Gerald Pte. No. 6405180 4/5th Bn. 16/03/44
Khayat Beach War Cemetery
Grave ref: D. E. 19.

Stibbon Thomas Kitchener L/Sgt. No. 6406105 2nd Bn. 04/02/44
Khayat Beach War Cemetery
Grave ref: D. E. 3.

Italy

Akehurst James Harold Pte. No. 6404023 1st Bn. 19/02/44
Cassino War Cemetery
Grave ref: VII. E. 6.

Aldrich John Wilfred Lt. No. 256423 10th Bn. attd. 1st East Surrey's 23/12/44
Santerno Valley War Cemetery
Grave ref: II. D. 17

Alford Denis Pte. No. 5505230 1st Bn. 16/02/44
Cassino War Cemetery
Panel 7.

Allan Wilfred Claude Lt. No. 262140 1st Bn. 27/02/44
Minturno War Cemetery
Grave ref: VI. E. 24.

Andrews Ronald Frederick Pte. No. 5626363 1st Bn. 17/02/44
Cassino War Cemetery
Grave ref: XIV. K. 9.

Andrews Thomas Sidney Sgt. M.M. No. 6403616 1st Bn. 17/03/44
Cassino War Cemetery
Grave ref: III. E. 5.

Anger Wilfred John Pte. No. 6405891 1st Bn. 28/03/44
Cassino War Cemetery
Grave ref: XIV. F. 16.

Annis Henry Pte. No. 6404384 1st Bn. 21/01/44
Sangro River War Cemetery
Grave ref: V. B. 18.

Arnett Victor John Lt. No. 162508 attd. 1st Green Howards 19/10/43
Cassino War Cemetery
Grave ref: VIII. K. 21.

Ashworth Robert John Lt. No. 277983 attd. 1/7 Queen's Royal Regt. 10/10/43
Naples War Cemetery
Grave ref: III. R. 18

Atkinson Charles Ernest Pte. No. 4752164 1st Bn. 26/09/44
Coriana Ridge War Cemetery
Grave ref: XVII. B. 11

Backshell Ernest Arthur Pte. No. 6404905 1st Bn. 07/04/44
Coriano Ridge War Cemetery
Grave ref: XIV. H. 23.

Bacon Dennis L/Cpl. No. 14408851 1st Bn. 22/03/44
Cassino War Cemetery
Grave ref: XIV. K. 16.

Baldock Harold Pte. No.6412555 1st Bn. 06/06/44
Sangro River War cemetery
Grave ref: V. B. 10.

Bates Alfred John Pte. No. 6403570 4th Bn. 07/11/43
Milan War cemetery
Grave ref: II. B. 8.

Bauer John Ernest Pte. No. 6403626 1st Bn.
Catania War Cemetery, Sicily
Grave ref: IV. D. 43.

Bishop Leslie Reginald Pte. No. 1463447 1st Bn. 20/02/44
Cassino War Cemetery
Grave ref: XIV. K. 6.

Booker Ronald Frederick Pte. No. 6412013 1st Bn. 21/07/44
Arezzo War Cemetery
Grave ref: I. C. 30.

Brand David Halyburton Mjr. No.75258 1st Bn. 12/07/44
Arezzo War Cemetery
Grave ref: IV. D. 21.

Brown Earnest Charles Pte. No. 6411719 1st Bn. 12/07/44
Assisi War Cemetery
Grave ref: IX. G. 3.

Burridge Edward Douglas Pte. No. 6404056 1st Bn. 25/09/44
Coriano Ridge War Cemetery
Grave ref: XVII. C. 5.

Burtenshaw Albert Pte. No. 6403856 1st Bn. 07/03/44
Cassino War Cemetery
Grave ref: VII. K. 6.

Carpenter George Laurence Pte. No. 6401102 1st Bn. 17/02/44
Cassino War Memorial
Panel 7.

Chaplin Arthur James L/Cpl. No. 5573784 1st Bn. 14/02/44
Cassino War Cemetery
Grave ref: XIV. H. 10.

Clare Alfred George Pte. No. 6403794 1st Bn. 29/08/44
Gradara War Cemetery
Grave ref: II. B. 5.

Clements Wilfred Cecil Pte. No. 14222139 1st Bn. 12/07/44
Arezzo War Cemetery
Grave ref: IV. D. 14.

Crunden Sydney Thomas Pte. No. 6403929 1st Bn. 17/02/94
Cassino War Cemetery
Grave ref: XVIII. G. 9.

Cummings George L/Col. No. 6405825 1st Bn. 11/07/44
Arezzo War Cemetery
Grave ref: IV. D. 23.

Curran Joseph Thomas Pte. No. 10573684 1st Bn. 16/02/44
Cassino War Cemetery
Grave ref: XVIII. C. 4.

Curtis Percy Pte. No. 6402842 1st Bn. 17/05/44
Sangro River War Cemetery
Grave ref: V. B. 6.

Davis Leonard Arthur Lt. No. 251289 attd. 5th Hampshire's 29/01/44
Minturno War Cemetery
Grave ref: III. H. 1.

Dickson Murray James Angus Capt. No. 138855 1st Bn. 13/07/44
Arezzo War Cemetery
Grave ref: III. D. 14.

Diffey Robert Joseph Pte. No. 5726704 1st Bn. 08/11/45
Padua War Cemetery
Grave ref: II. B. 13.

Dillon Joseph Francis Pte. No. 6405924 10th Bn. Para. Regt. A.A.C. 14/07/43
Catania War Cemetery, Sicily
Joint Grave IV. C. 2-3.

Dudley Alfred George Pte. No. 6213637 1st Bn. 16/02/44
Cassino Memorial
Panel 7.

Durling Richard Joseph L/ Sgt. No. 6404956 1st Bn. 13/02/44
Cassino War Cemetery
Grave ref: VII. K. 3.

Ellis Christopher Frederick L/Cpl. No. 5436730 1st Bn. 26/09/44
Coriano Ridge War Cemetery
Grave ref: XVII. B. 4.

Evans Peter Rankin Lt. No. 112863 4th Bn. 18/09/44
Coriana Ridge War Cemetery
Grave ref: XI. B. 3.

Evins Percy Thomas Robert L/Cpl. No. 14406559 1st Bn. 12/07/44
Arezzo War Cemetery
Grave ref: IV. D. 15.

Excell Roy Oliver Lt. No. 284552 10th Bn. attd. 5th Buffs 03/02/44
Cassino Memorial
Panel 7.

Fade William Richard Pte. No. 14600170 1st Bn. 19/02/44
Cassino War Cemetery
Grave ref: XVIII. C. 5.

Fairbrother John William Pte. No. 6404140 4th Bn. 18/09/44
Caserto War Cemetery
Grave ref: IV. B. 14.

Fase Sidney Stanley Lt. No. 200268 1st Bn. 04/06/44
Sangro River War Cemetery
Grave ref: V. B. 19.

Fears Leonard Frank Pte. No. 6403429 1st Bn. 26/09/44
Coriana Ridge War Cemetery
Grave ref: XVII. B. 6.

Finch Cyril Frank Pte. No. 6408496 1st Bn. 02/03/44
Cassino War Cemetery
Grave ref: XIV. K. 21.

Fleetwood John Desmond Lt. No. 258276 attd. 5th Hampshire's 07/10/44
Assisi War Cemetery
Grave ref: II. D. 4.

Forster Ronald Arthur Victory Sgt. No. 6406158 1st Bn. 13/07/44
Arezzo War Cemetery
Grave ref: IV. D. 17.

Foster Albert Henry Pte. No. 6397659 1st Bn. 18/09/44
Ancona War Cemetery
Grave ref: IV. B. 17

Gardner James Albert Pte. No. 14380323 1st Bn. 23/02/44
Cassino War Cemetery
Grave ref: I. C. 5.

Gasson George Edward Pte. No. 6403491 1st Bn. 11/02/44
Cassino War Cemetery
Grave ref: VII. K. 7.

Gee-Williams Paul Lt. No. 284554 attd. Royal Warks. Regt. 01/02/44
Minturno War Cemetery
Grave ref: VIII. F. 4.

Goldsmith James William Pte. No. 6408722 1st Bn.
Cassino War Cemetery
Grave ref: VII. K. 2.

Goode Maurice Henry Pte. No. 5504864 1st Bn.
Cassino War Cemetery
Grave ref: XVIII. G. 1.

Goodwin William Kenneth Pte. No. 5626294 16/02/44
Cassino War Cemetery
Grave ref: XVIII. G. 16.

Gorringe Sydney Harold Cpl. No. 6404028 16/02/44
Cassino War Cemetery
Grave ref: XIX. J. 22.

Gould Leslie Ernest Pte. No. 6408235 09/09/44
Gradara War Cemetery
Grave ref: II. B. 41.

Greene Andrew Paxton Pte. No. 5347582
Coriana Ridge War Cemetery
Grave ref: VII. C. 2.

Gregory Dennis Philip Pte. No. 1439731 1st Bn. 25/09/44
Coriana Ridge War Cemetery
Grave ref: VII. B. 7.

Gregory James Pte. No. 6408365 1st Bn. 18/03/44
Cassino War Cemetery
Grave ref: III. D. 5.

Gregory Kevin Donald Sgt. No. 6397428 1st Bn. 26/09/44
Coriana Ridge War Cemetery
Grave ref. XVII. B. 12.

Gunn George Stanley Cpl. No. 6403868
Cassino War Cemetery
Grave ref: XIV. K. 2.

Hall Reginald Alfred Pte. No. 5573678 1st Bn. 21/01/44
Sangro River War Cemetery
Grave ref: V. B. 12.

Hammett Reginald William Sgt. No. 6406056 1st Bn. 20/03/44
Cassino War Cemetery
Grave ref: XIV. E. 13.

Handley John Miles L/Cpl. No. 6401888 1st Bn. 10/03/44
Cassino War Cemetery
Grave ref: VIII. G. 18.

Harland Edward Arthur Pte. No. 6406829 1st Bn. 16/02/44
Cassino War Cemetery
Grave ref: XVIII. G. 8.

Harmsworth William Arthur Pte. No. 5499564 5th Bn. 14/11/42
Bari War Cemetery
Grave ref: II. E. 5.

Harper Wilfred Pte. No. 5626329 1st Bn. 17/01/44
Sangro River War Cemetery
Grave ref: V. B. 13.

Harrison Reginald Stanley Pte. No. 5338643 1st Bn. 12/07/44
Arezzo War Cemetery
Grave ref: IV. D. 6.

Henry Alfred William Pte. No. 6405982 1st Bn. 18/02/44
Cassino War Cemetery
Grave ref: XIV. D. 17.

Hickey Thomas Richard Cpl. No. 6406435 1st Bn. 02/03/44
Cassino War Cemetery
Grave ref: XIV. K. 17.
Hill George Henry Pte. No.14405795 1st Bn. 21/02/44
Cassino War Cemetery
Grave ref: I. C. 17.

Holmes Charles George Pte. No. 14534767 1/6th Bn. 26/09/44
Coriano Ridge War Cemetery
Grave ref: XVII. C. 4.

Holzer John Albert Pte. No. 6407077 1st Bn. 16/02/44
Cassino War Cemetery
Grave ref: XVIII. G. 20.

Inches John William No. 14407273 1st Bn. 19/02/44
Cassino War Cemetery
Grave ref: XVIII. G. 4.

King Jack Anthony Pte. No. 6405398 1st Bn. 25/05/44
Sangro River War Cemetery
Grave ref. V. B. 8.

Knight Robert L/Cpl. No. 6402872 1st Bn. 26/09/44
Coriano Ridge War Cemetery
Grave ref: XVII. C. 1.

Le Grice Ernest Cpl. No. 6402987 1st Bn. 09/09/44
Gradara War Cemetery
Grave ref: II. B. 16.

Lee Peter Leslie John Pte. No. 14392229 1st Bn. 27/09/44
Ancona War Cemetery
Grave ref: IV. C. 13.

Levander Anthony James 2/Lt. No. 315392 attd. 2nd Bn. King's (Liverpool) Regt. 12/05/44
Cassino War Cemetery
Grave Ref: XIV. B. 20.

Lock Thomas John Pte. No. 6411466 1st Bn. 17/02/44
Cassino War Cemetery
Grave ref: XVIII. G. 10.

Lowe William Cpl. No. 4924276 4/5th Bn. 21/05/46
Udine War Cemetery
Grave Ref: I. D. 9.

Macefield James Edward Pte. No. 6411053 4th Bn. 17/02/44
Ancona War Cemetery
Grave ref: III. H. 11.

Manley Charles Sgt. No. 6404445 1st Bn. 16/02/44
Cassino War Cemetery
Grave ref: XVIII. G. 15.

Marchant Eric Pte. No. 6411900 1st Bn. 28/09/44
Coriano War Cemetery
Grave ref: XVII. B. 8.

Marsh Cecil Reginald Pte. No. 5670177 1st Bn. 01/03/44
Cassino War Cemetery
Grave ref: XIV. E. 12.

Martin Raymond Pte. No. 6405833 2nd Bn. Para. Regt. A.A.C. 12/09/43
Bari War Cemetery
Grave ref: II. A. 4.

May Victor Gilbert W.O.11 No. 6395476 No. 1st Bn. 02/03/44
Cassino War Cemetery
Grave ref: XIV. K. 23.

Meachen Arthur James Pte. No. 6401019 1st Bn. 15/11/44
Caserta War Cemetery
Grave ref: V. A. 2.

Mears William Pte. No. 13095091 1st Bn. 12/07/44
Arezzo War Cemetery
Grave ref: IV. D. 18.

Minns David George Pte. No. 14625437 1st Bn.   13/07/44
Assisi War Cemetery
Grave ref: X. H. 1.

Moore Albert George Robert Pte. No. 6406287 1st Bn. 16/02/44
Cassino War Cemetery
Grave ref: XVIII. G. 11.

Moore Ernest Charles Pte. No. 6406973 1st Bn. 26/05/44
Sangro River war Cemetery
Grave ref: V. B. 9.

Morgan Edward George Pte. No. 14630419 1st Bn. 01/10/44
Ancona War Cemetery
Grave ref: IV. B. 14.

Morris Wilfred Pte. No. 6397399 1st Bn. 26/09/44
Coriano Ridge War Cemetery
Grave ref: XVII. B. 5.

Mulholland John Patrick Christopher Pte. No. 6404185 4th Bn. 19/01/43
Ancona War Cemetery
Grave ref: II. K. 10.

Murduck Victor Percival L/Sgt. No.14891162 4/5th Bn. 24/04/46
Udine War Cemetery
Grave ref: I. A. 14.

Murray John L/Cpl. No. 6406288 1st Bn. 26/09/44
Coriano Ridge War Cemetery
Grave ref: XVII. B. 10.

Murray John Pte. No. 6400406 4th Bn. 02/12/44
Milan War Cemetery
Grave ref: IV. C. 8.

McDonald John Patrick Pte. No. 6411821 1st Bn. 29/02/44
Cassino War Cemetery
Grave ref: XVIII. A. 15.

North Victor George Pte. No. 6403906 1st Bn. 29/08/44
Gradara War Cemetery
Grave ref: II. B. 6.

Nugent Guy Patrick Douglas John Capt. No. 200859 1st Bn. 06/09/44
Gradara War Cemetery
Grave ref: II. B. 15.

O'Brien Timothy Pte. No. 5626370 1st Bn. 31/10/45
Padua War Cemetery
Grave ref: II. A. 13.

O'Keeffe Robert James L/Cpl. No. 6411504 1st Bn. 17/02/44
Cassino War Cemetery
Grave ref: Vii. C. 23.

Ovenden Harry Victor Pte. No. 14217066 1st Bn. 16/02/44
Cassino War Cemetery
Grave ref: XVIII. G. 21.

Pannett Joseph Pte. No. 6405077 1st Bn. 10/05/44
Sangro River War Cemetery
Grave ref: V. B. 17.

Parris Ronald Allen Sgt. No. 6397742 4th Bn. 10/05/45
Cassino War Cemetery
Panel 7.

Passenger Albert Robert Pte. No. 6396444 1st Bn. 30/08/44
Gradara War Cemetery
Grave ref: II. B. 7.

Payne William George L/Cpl. No. 5626433 20/02/44
Cassino War Cemetery
Grave ref: XVIII. C. &.

Peacock Ernest George M.M. L/Cpl. No. 6402589 1st Bn. 19/02/44
Cassino War Cemetery
Grave ref: XVIII. G. 2.

Peberdy William George Pte. No. 6411794 1st Bn. 26/09/44
Cassino Memorial
Panel 7.

Peel Dennis Frederick Charles 2/Lt. No. 293249 attd. 2/5th Bn. Queen's Royal Regt. 29/02/44
Beach Head War Cemetery, Anzio
Grave ref: VI.A. 1.

Phillips James Ernest Pte. No. 6404722 1st Bn. 12/07/44
Arezzo War Cemetery
Grave ref: IV. D. 20.

Pile Herbert Cecil L/Cpl. No. 6408458 1st Bn. 14/02/44
Cassino War Cemetery
Grave ref: XIX. D. 4.

Piper Robert William Pte. No. 14427795 1st Bn. 11/09/44
Coriano Ridge Cemetery
Grave ref: XVIII. J. 10.

Ranson Philip Cpl. No. 6400035 1st Bn. 25/02/44
Cassino War Cemetery
Grave ref: XIV. K. 14.

Relph Allan Geoffrey Lt. No. 253957 1st Bn. 10/02/4
Minturno War Cemetery
Grave ref: V. F. 25.

Ridgway James Richard Pte. No. 6412208 1st Bn. 13/07/44
Assisi War Cemetery
Grave ref: X. H. 12.

Roach Arthur Henry Pte. No. 6411757 1st Bn. 29/05/44
Coriano Ridge Cemetery
Grave ref: XVII. C. 3.

Roskilly William Francis Pte. No. 5573606 1st Bn. 17/02/44
Cassino War Cemetery
Grave ref: XIX. J. 21.

Rought Charles Herbert Pte. No. 14603502 1st Bn. 18/02/44
Cassino War Cemetery
Grave ref: XVIII. C. 6.

Sallis Charles Frederick Pte. No. 6403100 1st Bn. 16/02/44
Cassino War Cemetery
Grave ref: XVIII. G. 14.

Salmon Edward David Pte. No. 3970570 1st Bn. 25/05/44
Sangro River War Cemetery
Grave ref: V. B. 11.

Sampson Frederick Douglas Pte. No. 5626298 1st Bn. 11/07/44
Arezzo War Cemetery
Grave ref: IV. D. 22.

Sandells Samuel Pte. No. 6403366 1st Bn. 26/09/44
Coriano Ridge War Cemetery
Grave ref: XVII. C. 6.

Scoble Peaceful George Sydney Cpl. No. 5439304 1st Bn. 19/05/44
Sangro River War Cemetery
Grave ref: V. B. 14.

Sealy George Cecil Capt. No. 189369 attd. 3rd Bn. 15th Punjab Regt. 22/11/43
Sangro River War Cemetery
Grave ref: XI. B. 13.

Sharples John Lt. No. 198217 1st Bn. 09/09/43
Salerno War Cemetery
Grave ref: III. C. 25.

Sheridan John Pte. No. 6410875 1st Bn. 20/03/44
Cassino War Cemetery
Grave ref: XIV. E. 11.

Shooster Barnett Pte. No. 5439803 1st Bn. between 16/02/44 and 18/02/44
Cassino Memorial
Panel 7.

Sims Frederick Richard Pte. No. 6406310 1st Bn. 02/03/44
Cassino War Cemetery
Grave ref: XIV. K. 15.

Sinclair-Thomson Charles Gilroy Capt. No. 166033 1st Bn. 29/08/44
Montecchio War Cemetery
Grave ref: II. E. 16.

Smith Alan Pte. No. 6402634 Army Catering Corps. attd. 1st Bn. 23/03/44
Cassino War Cemetery
Grave ref: XIV. K. 22.

Southard James Richard L/Cpl. No. 6408016 1st Bn. 03/08/44
Arezzo War Cemetery
Grave ref: V. C. 26.

Southgate Edward Pte. No. 14338664 1st Bn. 02/03/44
Cassino War Cemetery
Grave ref: XIV. K. 13.

Stanford Harry Augustus L/Sgt. No. 6404314 1st Bn. 25/05/44
Sangro River War Cemetery
Grave ref: XI. B. 23.

Stepney Derek William Pte. No. 6410217 1st Bn. 20/03/44
Cassino War Cemetery
Grave ref: XIV. E. 7.

Stepney Herbert Pte. No.6404315 1st Bn. 06/09/44
Gradara War Cemetery
Grave ref: II. B. 13.

Stevens Cyril William James L/Cpl. No. 5626291 1st Bn. 30/09/44
Coriano Ridge War Cemetery
Grave ref: XVII. B. 9.

Stevens George William Pte. No. 6402752 1st Bn. 11/09/44
Gradara War Cemetery
Grave ref: II. B. 18.

Stubbington James Cpl. No. 6408201 1st Bn. 12/07/44
Arezzo War Cemetery
Grave ref: IV. D. 19.

Taylor Ernest Frank Pte. No. 6403948 1st Bn. 03/03/44
Cassino War Cemetery
Grave ref: XIV. K. 18.

Taylor Richard L/Cpl. No. 1st Bn. 6409463 26/05/44
Sangro River War Cemetery
Grave ref: XI. B. 22.

Templeman Thomas Christopher 2/Lt. No. 308554 attd. 1st Bn. K.S.L.I. 04/02/44
Cassino Memorial
Panel 7.

Thacker Bernard Ernest Pte. No. 6406876 1st Bn. 16/03/44
Cassino War Cemetery
Grave ref: VII. E. 3.

Thompson Robert Oliver Vere D.S.O. Lt-Col. No. 30951 attd. 1/6th East Surrey Regt. 07/06/44
Cemetery: Rome War Cemetery, Italy
Grave Ref: II. E. 16

Tipler Charles Frederick Sgt. No. 6404093 1st Bn. 29/02/44
Cassino War Cemetery
Grave ref: XVIII. A. 12.

Trigg Frederick Harry M.M. Pte. No. 6399046 1st Bn. 16/02/44
Cassino memorial
Panel 7.

Vale Charles Samuel L/Cpl. No. 6407010 1st Bn. 23/02/44
Cassino War Cemetery
Grave ref : XVIII. G. 7.

Venner Norman Pte. No. 6407004 1st Bn. 30/08/44
Montecchio War Cemetery
Grave ref: II. E. 5.

Vickery Peter George Lt. No. 268904 1st Bn. 28/09/44
Argenta War Cemetery
Grave ref: II. G. 13.

Vincent George Anthony Pte. No. 1457644 11st Bn. 20/02/44
Cassino War Cemetery
Grave ref: XVIII. G. 23.

Vine Arthur John Cpl. No. 6404087 1st Bn. 01/02/44
Caserta War Cemetery
Grave ref: VI. E. 8.

Vine John Douglas Lt. No. 300205 attd. 1st Bn. K.S.L.I. 13/03/44
Naples War Cemetery
Grave ref: II. N. 10.

Wallis William Pte. No. 641799 1st Bn. 20/03/44
Cassino War Cemetery
Grave ref: XIV. E. 14.

Walls Henry James Pte. No. 6403245 1st Bn. 10/09/44
Gradara War Cemetery
Grave ref: II.B. 17.

Ward Albert William Pte. No. 6408727 4th Bn. Para. Regt. A.A.C. 02/03/45
Rome War Cemetery
Grave ref: I. D. 49.

Watts William Thomas Pte. No. 6470610 1st Bn. 27/03/44
Cassino War Cemetery
Grave ref: XIV. F. 5.

Webster Maurice Ernest Pte. No. 5501258 1st Bn. 25/02/44
Cassino War Cemetery
Grave ref: VII. E. 2.

Weeks Lawrence William Capt. M.C. No. 155698 1st Bn. 22/02/44
Cassino War Cemetery
Grave ref: I. C. 3.

Welsh Leslie Cpl. No. 6401022 1st Bn. 20/04/44
Sangro River War Cemetery
Grave ref: XIV. C. 14.

West George Robert Frederick Lt. No. 258681 08/08/43
Catania War Cemetery
Grave ref: III. B. 50.

Wheeler Kenneth Frank Capt. No. 156507 1st Bn. 18/02/44
Cassino War Cemetery
Grave ref: XVIII. G. 3.

Whittington Norman Colin Pte. No. 6411800 1st Bn. 24/02/44
Cassino War Cemetery
Grave ref: I. C. 13.

Woodhams Thomas Henry Sgt. No. 6402702 1st Bn. 24/05/44
Sangro River War Cemetery
Grave ref: IX. B. 34.

Woods Bernard Pte. No. 6403568 5th Bn. 14/01/43
Caserta War Cemetery
Grave ref: VII. A. 7.

Wyatt Leonard Sidney Pte. No. 6923884 1st Bn. 28/02/44
Cassino Memorial
Panel 7.

Young Kenneth Lincoln Sgt. No. 5501327 1st Bn. 13/07/44
Arezzo War Cemetery
Grave ref. III. D. 13.

Korea

Philpott W. Pte. No. 19090813 1st Bn. attd. K.S.L.I. 01/05/52
Commemorated on the Commonwealth Memorial at the United Nations Memorial Cemetery, Pusan.

Maskell Alfred Henry No. 14184609 1st Bn. attd. The Buffs 31/01/53
Commemorated on the UN Wall of Remembrance, Pusan, Korea

Libya

Batchelor Charles Reuben Pte. No. 6399412 1st Bn. 09/01/43
Tripoli War Cemetery
Grave ref: 10. C. 13.

Cereley Wilfred Ernest Michael Capt. No. 138854 attd. 3rd Royal Bn. 12th F.F. Regiment 22/0/3/43
Tripoli War Cemetery
Grave ref: 5. A. 18

Chessell Thomas Charles Pte. No. 6406241 4th Bn. 28/11/42
Tripoli War Cemetery
Grave ref: 11. C. 24

Davis Cecil Pte. No. 6406149 1st Bn. 05/06/43
Tripoli War Cemetery
Grave ref: 5. C. 1.

Finch John Lennard Cpl. No. 6403959 1st Bn. 08/12/41
Knightsbridge War Cemetery, Acroma
Grave ref: 16. E. 19.

Hand Richard Thomas Guy Pte. No. 6399456 1st Bn. 29/01/42
Benghazi War Cemetery
Grave ref: 2. D. 31.

Lane Arthur James Pte. No. 6407932 1st Bn. 16/06/43
Tripoli War Cemetery
Grave ref: 11. G. 27.

Leppard Fred Pte. No. 6403060 1st Bn. 29/01/42
Benghazi War Cemetery
Grave ref: 2. D. 33.

Lucas Herbert Harold Pte. No. 5573768 1st Bn. 11/04/43
Tripoli War Cemetery
Grave ref: 6. E. 5.

Mayers William Patrick Lt. No. 138168 1st Bn. 29/01/42
Benghazi War Cemetery
Grave ref: 2. D. 30

Malaysia

Gray Douglas Ronald Pte. No. 6411881 9th Bn. 30/09/45
Taiping War Cemetery
Grave ref: 4. B. 15.

Harley Eric Pte. No. 14842337 9th Bn. 1501/46
Taiping War Cemetery
Grave ref: 4. B. 18.

Hiscocks Thomas John Richard Pte. M.I.D. No. 5576992 9th Bn. 01/11/45
Taiping War Cemetery
Grave ref: 3. B. 18.

Laker Peter John Pte. No. 14266811 9th Bn. 04/03/46
Taiping War Cemetery
Grave ref: 4. B. 17.

Myanmar (Burma)

Allen Frederick Richard Sgt. M.I.D. No. 5337445 9th Bn. 05/08/44
Taukkyan War Cemetery
Grave ref: 7. G. 4.

Beer Albert Edward Pte. No. 6410931 9th Bn. 16/02/45
Rangoon Memorial
Face 14.

Bell Leslie Albert L/Cpl. No. 6407599 9th Bn. 26/03/44
Taukkyan War Cemetery
Grave ref: 4. F. 11

Brewster Maurice Joseph Lt. No. 233262 9th Bn. 06/08/44
Taukkyan War Cemetery
Grave ref: 6. G. 18.

Bridle Alan Pte. No. 57344266 9th Bn. 17/01/45
Taukkyan War Cemetery
Grave ref: 27. F. 15.

Brierley John Pte. No.5350674 9th Bn. 03/02/45
Taukkyan War Cemetery
Grave ref: 27. F. 12.

Bright Frederick Albert Pte. No. 5350376 15/08/44
Taukkyan War Cemetery
Grave ref: 7. J. 15.

Bright William Pte. No. 5350377 05/08/44
Taukkyan War Cemetery
Grave ref: 7. B. 8.

Bristow Victor William Reginald L/Cpl. No. 6405048 9th Bn. 06/08/44
Taukkyan War Cemetery
Grave ref: 7. A. 21.

Britchford Leonard Arthur Pte. No. 14214195 9th Bn. 09/11/44
Taukkyan War Cemetery
Grave ref: 6. J. 3.

Brock Sidney Anthony Pte. No. 14511552 9th Bn. 05/08/44
Taukkyan War Cemetery
Grave ref: 7.B. 11.

Burdon Geoffrey Arthur Pte. No. 5341095 9th Bn. 11/03/44
Rangoon Memorial
Face 14.

Burman Frank Leonard Pte. No. 14391983 9th Bn. 26/03/44
Taukkyan War Cemetery
Grave ref: 11. D. 1.

Burnham Norman Frederick L/Cpl. M.I.D. No. 5958799 9th Bn. 29/01/45
Rangoon Memorial
Face 14.

Butler Godfrey James Pte. No. 6411661 9th Bn. 18/08/44
Taukkyan War Cemetery
Grave ref: 7. J. 10.

Caldwell John Pte. No. 14515556 9th Bn. 14/11/44
Taukkyan War Cemetery
Grave ref: 6.H. 22.

Chambers David James Sgt. No. 6404933 9th Bn. 22/05/45
Rangoon Memorial
Face 14.

Cherryman Laurence Edward W.O.1 No. 6394174 attd. Indian Army Corps. of Clerks 01/07/42
Rangoon Memorial
Face 88.

Coad Cyril Victor Sgt. No. 5728025 9th Bn. 09/11/44
Taukkyan War Cemetery
Grave ref: 7. A. 5.

Cockle Reginald Pte. No. 14203998 9th Bn. 24/01/45
Taukkyan War Cemetery
Grave ref: 27. F. 16.

Cosgrove Patrick Cpl. No. 5575609 9th Bn. 24/11/44
Taukkyan War Cemetery
Grave ref: 7. H. 17.

Crane Albert Edward Cpl. No. 6410964 9th Bn. 05/08/44
Taukkyan War Cemetery
Grave ref: 7. B. 9.

Crunden Frederick George L/Sgt. M.I.D. No. 6396611 9th Bn. 05/08/44
Taukkyan War Cemetery
Grave ref: 7. G. 5.

Dennis John Alan Sgt. No. 6406412 9th Bn. 06/09/44
Rangoon Memorial
Face 14.

Doherty Thomas Christopher Pte. No. 14432978 9th Bn. 17/02/45
Rangoon Memorial
Face 14.

Dudley Stanley Cyril Cpl. No. 6097124 9th Bn. 25/11/44
Taukkyan War Cemetery
Grave ref: 7.H. 20.

Dunford Percy Lt. No. 249228 9th Bn. 05/08/44
Taukkyan War Cemetery
Grave ref: 7. A. 11.

Duplock Richard George Pte. No. 6412038 9th Bn. 10/11/44
Taukkyan War Cemetery
Grave ref: 6. K. 17.

Dyer Stanley Cecil Pte. No. 6410976 9th Bn. 16/08/44
Rangoon Memorial
Face 14.

Edelsten Hubert Arthur Christopher Capt. M.C. No. 109220 attd. 4th Bn. 14th Punjab Regt. 05/04/44
Rangoon Memorial
Face 14.

Edwards Edward Thomas Pte. No. 14402492 9th Bn. 26/03/44
Taukkyan War Cemetery
Grave ref: 5. D. 6.

Edwards Frank George Cpl. No. 6412387 9th Bn. 25/02/45
Rangoon Memorial
Face 14.

Everson Arthur Frederick Sgt. M.I.D. No. 6408083 9th Bn. 06/08/44
Taukkyan War Cemetery
Grave ref: 7. A. 22.

Ferguson John William Sgt. No. 6407877 9th Bn. 16/11/44
Rangoon Memorial
Face 14.

Franklin John William Pte. No. 6410990 9th Bn. 23/11/44
Taukkyan War Cemetery
Grave ref: 6.H. 9.

George Ernest Charles L/Cpl. No. 5350829 9th Bn. 24/01/45
Rangoon memorial
Face 14.

Godley Herbert Oliver Cpl. No. 6401827 9th Bn. 14/11/44
Taukkyan War Cemetery
Grave ref: 7. A. 14.

Goldsmith Rupert Sgt. No. 6408123 9th Bn. 02/11/44
Taukkyan War Cemetery
Grave ref: 6. J. 19.

Green Alfred James Pte. No. 6098595 9th Bn. 10/11/44
Rangoon Memorial
Face 14.

Hammond William Allan Cpl. No. 14204190 9th Bn. 14/11/44
Taukkyan War Cemetery
Grave ref: 7. A. 15.

Hardy Albert Edward Albie L/Sgt. No. 6407619 9th Bn. 05/08/44
Taukkyan War Cemetery
Grave ref: 7. K. 8.

Honeywill John Pte. No. 6407078 9th Bn. 09/11/44
Taukkyan War Cemetery
Grave ref: 6.J. 16.

Jenner Stanley Harold Pte. No. 6412067 9th Bn. 27/03/44
Taukkyan War Cemetery
Grave ref: 5.H. 17.

Jones William Henry Pte. No. 5342602 9th Bn. 17/01/45
Taukkyan War Cemetery
Grave ref: 27. F. 14.

Kirkman Alfred Leslie Cpl. No. 6407929 9th Bn. 05/08/44
Taukkyan War Cemetery
Grave ref: 7.G. 6.

Lipscomb Charles Albert Pte. No. 6407506 9th Bn. 26/03/44
Taukkyan War Cemetery
Grave ref: 3. E. 10.

Luisignani Romualdo Pte. No. 14653844 9th Bn. 05/12/44
Taukkyan War Cemetery
Grave ref: 7. G. 13.

Marchant Albert James Pte. No. 14207030 9th Bn. 03/02/45
Taukkyan War Cemetery
Grave ref: 27.F. 13.

Mitchell John Sgt. No. 6146027 9th Bn. 09/11/44
Taukkyan War Cemetery
Grave ref: 6. J. 13.

Mitchell Samuel George Cpl. No. 6407518 9th Bn. 09/11/44
Taukkyan War Cemetery
Grave ref: 7. A. 2.

Morrison William Charles L/Sgt. No. 6407944 9th Bn. 26/03/44
Taukkyan War Cemetery
Grave ref: 11. D. 16.

Mould Gordon Frederick L/Cpl. No. 6404184 9th Bn. 05/01/45
Rangoon Memorial
Face 14.

McGrath Thomas Pte. No. 6411468 9th Bn. 12/11/44
Taukkyan War Cemetery
Grave ref: 7. B. 5.

Nolan Paul Victor John 2/lt. No. 330737 9th Bn. 19/11/44
Taukkyan War Cemetery
Grave ref: 6.K. 13.

Payne Harold Percy Sgt. No. 6407525
Taukkyan War Cemetery
Grave ref: 27. G. 4.

Payne William Eric Pte. No. 6407711 9th Bn. 01/11/44
Taukkyan War Cemetery
Grave ref: 7. B. 4.

Pierce Dennis George Frank Lt. No. 94074 9th Bn. 26/03/44
Taukkyan War Cemetery
Grave ref: 5. C. 9.

Petersen Harold David Pte. No. 6856634 9th Bn. 05/08/44
Taukkyan War Cemetery
Grave ref: 7. F.5.

Pickford Edward James Pte. No. 6412092 9th Bn. 05/08/44
Taukkyan War Cemetery
Grave ref: 7. B. 12.

Pinn Albert John Cpl. No. 6407779 9th Bn. 16/08/44
Rangoon memorial
Face 14.

Polkinhorn Frederick William Pte. No. 14392911 9th Bn. 05/08/44
Taukkyan War Cemetery
Grave ref: 7. A. 12.

Ponting George Pte. No. 5577317 9th Bn. 06/08/44
Taukkyan War Cemetery
Grave ref: 7.A. 19.

Rowland David Macdonald Lt. No. 207775 attd. 13th Bn. The King's Regt. (Liverpool) 30/04/43
Rangoon Memorial
Face 14.

Schul Pinkus Pte. No. 13117960 9th Bn. 06/02/45
Taukkyan War Cemetery
Grave ref: 27. G. 1.

Seager Richard Gleadowe Capt. No. 87927 seconded 1st Bn. 16th Punjab Regiment 13/11/43
Rangoon memorial
Face 14.

Selby Charles L/Sgt. M.I.D. No. 6407374 9th Bn. 06/08/44
Taukkyan War Cemetery
Grave ref: 7. A. 23.

Selkirk Neil Alexander Mjr. No. 72906 9th Bn. 24/03/44
Taukkyan War Cemetery
Grave ref: 4. E. 18.

Sharpe Dennis Frederick Gordon Pte. No. 5783396 9th Bn. 05/08/44
Taukkyan War Cemetery
Grave ref: 7. B. 10.

Shorey Jack Pte. No. 5350856 9th Bn. 27/02/45
Taukkyan War Cemetery
Grave ref: 27. G. 8.

Simmonds Frank Thomas Pte. No. 6408003 9th Bn. 26/03/44
Taukkyan War Cemetery
Grave ref: 11. C. 13.

Smith Albert Thomas Pte. No. 5784234 9th Bn. 05/08/44
Taukkyan War Cemetery
Grave ref: 7. A. 10.

Smith Arthur Edward L/Cpl. No. 6406491 9th Bn. 14/11/44
Taukkyan War Cemetery
Grave ref: 7. A. 13.

Smith John Wilfred Pte. No. 5341708 9th Bn. 15/08/44
Taukkyan War Cemetery
Grave ref: 7.K. 3.

Steadman Maurice John Sgt. M.I.D. No. 6404210 9th Bn. 32/11/44
Taukkyan War Cemetery
Grave ref: 6. J. 10.

Sternheim Chaim Pte. No. 13106915 9th Bn. 15/02/45
Rangoon Memorial
Face 14.

Stocks John Malcolm Patrick Capt. No. 186153 attd. 82nd Bn. W.A.R. Regt., R.W.A.F.F. 07/02/45
Rangoon memorial
Face 14.

Taylor Anthony Albert Frank Pte. No.6412614 9th Bn. 18/08/44
Taukkyan War Cemetery
Grave ref: 7.J. 17.

Thompson Warwick Mjr. No. 203808 attd. 4th Bn. 15th Punjab Regt. 30/07/45
Taukkyan War Cemetery
Grave ref: 20. H. 19.

Truby Raymond Pte. No. 7945302 9th Bn. 26/03/44
Taukkyan War Cemetery
Grave ref: 5. H. 1.

Vieth Frank L/Cpl. No. 5347370 9th Bn. 17/08/44
Taukkyan War Cemetery
Grave ref: 7.J. 7.

Ward George Pte. No. 101513 9th Bn. 21/10/44
Taukkyan War Cemetery
Grave ref: 7. J. 12.

Warren Alfred George L/Sgt. No. 6408048 9th Bn. 15/08/44
Taukkyan War Cemetery
Grave ref: 7.j. 21.

Webb Stanley Arthur Cpl. No. 5350778 9th Bn. 15/08/44
Taukkyan War Cemetery
Grave ref: 7. J. 13.

Wentworth John Merritt Pte. No. 6152359 9th Bn. 13/02/45
Taukkyan War Cemetery
Grave ref: 27. E. 14.

Whale William Walter Cpl. No. 5732732 9th Bn. 16/08/44
Taukkyan War Cemetery
Grave ref: 6. G. 17.

Whitehouse Gilbert Harry L/Cpl. No. 5125694 9th Bn. 06/08/44
Taukkyan War Cemetery
Grave ref: 7. A. 20.

Wyeth Douglas Ben Jeffery L/Cpl. M.I.D. No. 5351082 9th Bn. 22/11/44
Taukkyan War Cemetery
Grave ref: 7. H. 22.

Netherlands

Ashworth Charles Frederick Mjr. No. 156502 10th Bn. Para. Regt. A.A.C. between 20-21/09/44
Arnhem Oosterbeek War Cemetery
Grave ref: 5. D. 11

Beardmore Clement Maxton L/Cpl. No. 6410619 10th Bn. Para. Regt. A.A.C. 21/09/44
Arnhem Oosterbeek War Cemetery
Grave ref: 5. A. 14.

Clifford Edmund Norris Sgt. No. 6397640 10th Bn. Para. Regt. A.A.C. 20/09/44
Arnhem Oosterbeek War Cemetery
Grave ref: 5. C. 6.

Foxworthy Harry Victor James Gnr. No. 5622595 109 (7th Bn.Ryl Sussex Regt.) Lt. A.A. Regt. 19/12/44
Brunssum War Cemetery
Grave ref: VI. 323.

Garibaldi William L/Cpl. No. 6400067 M.I.D. 10th Bn. Para. A.A.C. 20/09/44
Arnhem Oosterbeek War Cemetery
Grave Ref: 5. D. 14.

Glazier John Charles Joseph Sgt. No. 6397198 10th Bn. Para. Regt. A.A.C. between 18-25/09/44 Groebeek Memorial
Panel 8.

Green Anthony Charles 2/Lt. No. 314915 attd. 13th Bn. Queen's Royal Regiment 27/09/44
Arnhem Oosterbeek War Cemetery
Grave ref: 14. B. 1.

Hide George Henry L/Cpl. No. 6396186 2nd Bn. 29/05/40
Bergen-op-Zoom War Cemetery
Grave ref: 12. C. 10.

Howard John Capt. No. 200853 "D" Coy 10th Bn. Para. Regt. A.A.C. 20/10/44
Groebeek Memorial
Panel 8.

Jenkins Joseph Pte. 6402977 10th Bn. Para. Regt. A.A.C. 03/02/43
Fayid War Cemetery
Grave ref: 5. A. 1.

Lowman Charles Frederick Sgt. No. 6403388 10th Bn. Para. Regt. A.A.C.
Groebeek Memorial
Panel 8.

Queripel Lionel Ernest Captain V.C. No. 108181 10th Bn. Para. Regt. A.A.C. 19/09/44
Arnhem Oosterbeek War Cemetery
Grave ref: 5. D. 8.

Rose William Frederick Pte. No. 6396746 10th Bn. Para. Regt. A.A.C. 19/09/44
Arnhem Oosterbeek War Cemetery
Grave ref: 5. C. 10.

Tarrant Edward John Lt. No. 189370 30th Bn. attd. 4th Bn. Royal Welsh Fusiliers 22/11/44
Swartbroeke Churchyard
Row 1 Grave 5

Weich Salo Cpl. No. 6436350 attd. No. 10 Commando 01/11/44
Bergen-op-Zoom War Cemetery
Grave ref: 5. C. 11.

White Frederick James L/Cpl. No. 6400954 10th Bn. Para. Regt. A.A.C. 23/09/44
Arnhem Oosterbeek War Cemetery
Grave ref: 27. A. 9.

(Known Royal Sussex Regiment by their Army Number. 90, 10th Bn. Para. Regt. A.A.C. lost their lives.)

Norway

Skelton John L/Cpl. No. 5668195 attd. No. 3 Commando 27/12/41
Trondheim (Stavne) Cemetery
Grave ref: A IV British H. 10.

Poland

Belam Leslie Allan Pte. No. 5727861 7th Bn. 19/02/41
Krakow Rakowicki Cemetery
Grave ref: 5. D. 6.

Clark Eric Albert W.O.111 No. 6630701 2nd Bn. 15/12/40
Malbork Commonwealth Cemetery
Grave ref: 9. A. 9.

Collins Sidney Pte. No. 6282522 4th Bn. 26/04/40
Krakow Rakowicki Cemetery
Grave ref: 2A. D. 4.

Dell Albert Leslie Pte. No. 5439307 7th Bn. 14/04/43
Krakow Rakowicki Cemetery
Grave ref: 3. C. 7.

Hart William Arthur Pte. No. 5727667 7th Bn. 29/10/42
Poznan Old Garrison Cemetery
Grave ref: 8. A. 3.

Kingsland Henry James Pte. No. 6401263 7th Bn. 10/09/42
Krakow Rakowicki Cemetery
Grave ref: 3. B. 7.

Napper Edward Phil Pte. No. 6400193 5th Bn. 26/05/42
Malbork Commonwealth Cemetery
Grave ref: 7. B. 9.

Parker John Frederick Henry Pte. No. 6402693 Unk/Bn. 26/08/44
Krakow Rakowicki Cemetery
Grave ref: 2.B. 1.

Smith Sidney Frank Pte. No. 6400395 5th Bn. 01/04/42
Krakow Rakowicki Cemetery
Grave ref: 4. D. 10.

Thompson Robert Pte. No. 6394883 2nd Bn. 20/09/41
Malbork Commonwealth Cemetery
Grave ref: 4. A. 1.

Webster Maurice Pte. No. 6399818 2nd Bn. 20/09/41
Malbork Commonwealth Cemetery
Grave ref: 7. A. 2.

South Africa

Matthews Stanley Pte. No. 6407698 9th Bn. 16/01/45
Johannesburg (West Park) Cemetery
Grave ref: Mil. Sec. Grave 289.

Verrall Albert Leonard Frank Cpl. No. 6398927 1st Bn. 06/07/42
Durban (Stellawood) Cemetery
Block F. Grave 238.

Sudan

Brown Frederick George Pte. No. 6403559 1st Bn. 04/05/41
Khartoum War Cemetery
Grave ref: 2. D. 22.

Carter George Pte. No. 6391987 1st Bn. 25/01/41
Khartoum War Cemetery
Grave ref: 7. A. 10.

Holman Wallace George Pte. No. 6404025 1st Bn. 17/04/41
Khartoum War Cemetery
Grave ref: 2. D. 14.

Seabourne John Sidney Pte. No. 6403916 1st Bn. 25/01/41
Khartoum Memorial
Panel 1

Tunisia

Apthorpe Denys Gerald Winton Capt. No. 105807 1st Bn. 20/04/43
Enfidaville War Cemetery
Grave ref: VII. C. 13.

Bennett Henry William L/Cpl. No. 6939843 1st Bn. 22/04/43
Enfidaville War Cemetery
Grave ref: IV. C. 8.

Bish Edward Victor L/Cpl. No. 6402426 06/04/43
Sfax War Cemetery
Grave ref: VII. E. 24.

Boarer Victor Pte. No. 6402685 1st Bn. 06/04/43
Sfax War Cemetery
Grave ref: VII. E. 23.

Carter Edward Sgt. No. 6402213 1st Bn. 19/03/43
Sfax War Cemetery
Grave ref: XIII. B. 4.

Clevett Charles Albert Pte. No. 6398858 1st Bn. 21/04/43
Enfidaville War Cemetery
Grave ref: VI. D. 6.

Conway Patrick Pte. No. 6409851 1st Bn. Para. Regt. A.A.C. 02/03/43
Massicault War Cemetery
Grave ref: III. N. 7.

Corbyn Robert Albert Pte. No. 6400926 1st Bn. 20/04/43
Enfidaville War Cemetery
Grave ref: VII. C. 12.

Cornford Charles John Cpl. No. 6398692 1st Bn. 28/04/43
Enfidaville War Cemetery
Grave ref: VII. C. 10.

Drudge Leonard William Pte. No. 130448271 1st Bn. 28/04/43
Enfidaville War Cemetery
Grave ref: IV. C. 10.

Fahey Pierre Maurice Pte. No. 6405124 1st Bn. 20/04/43
Enfidaville War Cemetery
Grave ref: VI. D. 8.

Gaylard Derrick William Capt. M.C. No. 99819 1st Bn. 06/04/53
Sfax War Cemetery
Grave ref: VII. E. 20.

Glue Frank William Sgt. No. 854456 1st Bn. 10/05/43
Massicault War Cemetery
Grave ref: I. C. 1.

Goldsmith Ernest Cpl. No. 6398887 1st Bn. 21/04/43
Enfidaville War Cemetery
Grave ref: VI. D. 12.

Gunningham William Henry Pte. No. 13048250 1st Bn. 06/04/43
Sfax War Cemetery
Grave ref: VII. E. 21.

Heasman Leslie Ernest Pte. No. 6403877 1st Bn. 28/04/43
Enfidaville War Cemetery
Grave ref: IV. C. 9.

Herbert Frederick Dennis Pte. No. 6402208 2nd Bn. Para. Regt. A.A.C. 14/12/42
Medjez-el-Bab Memorial
Face 35.

Hill William George L/Cpl. 6400928 3rd Bn. Para. Regt. A.A.C. 26/02/43
Medjez-el-Bab War Cemetery
Grave ref: 2. C. 17.

Lewis William Douglas 2/Lt. No. 253671 attd. 2/4th Hampshire Regt. 19/03/43
Medjez-el-Bab War Cemetery
Grave ref: 12. G. 2.

Lucas Albert John Pte. No. 6404081 1st Bn. 21/04/43
Enfidaville War Cemetery
Grave ref: VI. D. 9.

McCarthy Michael Pte. No. 6403167 2nd Bn. Para. Regt. A.A.C 29/03/43
Beja War Cemetery
Grave ref: 2. J. 2.

Millard John Wilfred Lt. No. 233263 1st Bn. 06/05/43
Massicault War Cemetery
Grave ref: III. J. 7.

Reese Charles Pte. No. 6399455 1st Bn. 06/04/43
Sfax War Cemetery
Grave ref: VII. E. 22.

Stenning George Franklin Sgt. No. 6398044 1st Bn. 30/04/43
Enfidaville War Cemetery
Grave ref: IV. E. 19.

Symonds Richard Norris Lt. No. 203446 1st Bn. 06/04/43
Sfax War Cemetery
Grave ref: VII. E. 19.

Thorn Leonard Sgt. No. 6397403 1st Bn. 19/03/43
Sfax War Cemetery
Grave ref: XIII. B. 3.

Thorpe Albert Edward Pte. No. 6408520 1st Bn. 07/05/43
Massicault War Cemetery
Grave ref: III. H. 17.

Traylor Robert George Pte. No. 6478441 1st Bn. 11/05/43
Enfidaville War Cemetery
Grave ref: VIII. F. 4.

Turner William Ronald Charles Pte. No. 5350601 1st Bn. 28/04/43
Enfidaville War Cemetery
Grave ref: VII. C. 9.

Wiggs James Henry Pte. No. 6408530 1st Bn. 06/04/43
Sfax War Cemetery
Grave ref: XIII. E. 14.

Woolven Ernest Lt. No. 237670 seconded 5th Bn. Northamptonshire Regt. 14/04/43
Medjez-el-Bab War Cemetery
Face 21

United Kingdom

Addy John Robert Pte. No.6400458 7th Bn. 14/06/41
Lydd Churchyard, Kent

Albon Ernest Arthur Pte. No. 6400425 Unk/Bn. 01/04/47
Littlehampton Cemetery
Sec. A. Gen. Grave 1019.

Allcorn Alfred Richard Charles Pte. No. 14336002 Unk/Bn. 26/06/44
Streatham Cemetery
Block 17. Grave 602.

Allistone Harry Lester Pte. No. D/14719 4th Bn. 12/06/40
Rottingdean (St. Margaret) Churchyard

Andrews Frederick George Sgt. No. 776757 6th Bn. 20/03/42
Uckfield Cemetry
Sec. N. Grave 1430.

Avis Arthur Frederick Pte. No. 6401084 2nd Bn. 14/01/41
Rye Cemetery
Sec. B.C. Grave 6283.

Ayshford Reginald Frederick Cpl. No. 5626359 6th Bn. 01/04/46
Torquay Cemetery and Extension, Devon
Sec. P. Grave 16108

Bareham Douglas Mortimer L/Cpl. No. 6398453 2nd Bn. 04/04/41
Exeter Higher Cemetery, Devon
Sec. Z.K. Grave 35.

Barker Henry Pte. No. 6400801 4th Bn. 04/10/44
Boldon Cemetery (South Tyneside and Wear)
Sec. 2. Grave 1327.

Barnard George Edward Sgt. No. 6402811 2nd Bn. Para. Regt. A.A.C. 17/04/45
Brighton (The Downs) Cemetery
Sec. R. Grave 212.

Barnes Thomas Alfred Pte. No. 6405591 70th Bn. 23/01/41
Pett (SS Mary and Peter) Churchyard

Barth George Bryan Officer Cadet No. 6436371 Unk/Bn. 29/06/44
Barmouth and Llanaber Joint Burial Ground, Barmouth, Wales
Row B. Grave 49.

Bartholomew Eric Albert Rudolph Pte. No. 6410093 70th Bn. 27/06/43
Bexhill Cemetery
Div. C. Sec. D. Row G. Grave 23.

Benwell Edward James Pte. No. 6203793 7th Bn. 17/10/40
Isleworth Cemetery, London
Block R. Class C.D. Grave 88.

Bickell Dennis Ray Pte. No. 5626293 Unk/Bn. 17/09/45
Plymouth (Efford) Cemetery
Sec. B. Cons. Grave 6802.

Bliss Raymond Dennis Pte. No. 6402922 4th Bn. 14/04/45
Dover (Charlton) Cemetery, Kent
Sec. 3. R. Grave 27.

Bonfield Alfred William Sgt. No. 6406030 10th Bn. 17/01/43
Edmonton Cemetery, Middlesex
Sec. N. Grave 1374

Booth Clifford George Pte. No. 6407665 Unk/Bn. 28/09/44
Lewes Cemetery
Sec. K. Grave 101.

Bowden John Gnr. No. 1554748 358 Bty., 109 (7th Bn. Royal Sussex Regt.) Lt. A.A. Regt. 01/03/43
Bingley Cemetery
Sec. B.B. Row 4 Grave 82.

Boxall Percy Wyndham Pte. No. 6402072 4th Bn. 18/08/40
Lodsworth (St. Peter) Churchyard

Bray Jack Pte. No. 6407602 Unk/Bn. 27/07/42
Liverpool (Walton Park) Cemetery, Lancashire
Plot M. Grave 15.

Briggs Edgar Wilkinson Pte. No. 6405486 27/11/42
Shipley (Nab Wood) Cemetery, Yorkshire
Sec. M. Grave 648.

Britton Reginald Arthur Pte. No. 14055350 Unk/Bn. 06/04/46
Lambeth Cemetery, London
Sec. B. 1. Cons. Grave 72.

Broomfield Thomas Martin Pte. No. D/41221 11th (H.D) Bn. 05/05/41
Uckfield Cemetery
Sec. R. Grave 2056.

Bruce Arthur Pte. No. D/33169 8th (H.D.) Bn. 18/08/40
Eastbourne (Langley) Cemetery
Sec. B. Grave 154.

Buckland Edward William Pte. No. 6402906 Unk/Bn. 30/01/40
Seaford Cemetery
Sec. W. Grave 1.

Bunce Paul Pte. No. 6409385 70th Bn. 15/08/41
Tottenham Cemetery, London
Gen. Sec. Grave 10372.

Burgess Simon Peter Pte. No. D/34367 Unk/Bn. 05/03/43
Henfield Cemetery
Sec. F. Grave 50.

Bush George Pte. No. 5949539 6th Bn. 14/08/45
Bacton (St. Andrew) Churchyard, Norfolk
Sec. G. Grave 7.

Butler Clarence Victor Leslie Pte. No. 6395465 4th Bn. 17/02/46
Chichester Cemetery
Square 158. Grave 6.

Butler Frederick John Sgt. No. 6393654 Unk/Bn. 10/01/45
Pett (SS Mary and Peter) Churchyard

Cannell George Frank L/Cpl. No. 5617050 2nd Bn. 15/01/41
Rye Cemetery
Sec. B.C. Grave 6284.

Carpenter Frederick Henry Pte. No. 6405814 70th Bn. 29/09/41
West Blatchington (St. Peter) Churchyard

Carroll John Joseph Pte. No. 6409403 70th Bn. 29/09/41
West Thorney (St. Nicholas) Churchyard
Plot1. Row C. Grave 5.

Carter James Robert Nelson L/Cpl. No. 7621512 No. 6th Bn. 25/04/41
Crowthorne (St. John the Baptist) Churchyard
South side Row 16. Grave 1.

Chainey Robert John Stewart Cpl. No. 6399229 7th Bn. 19/08/40
Hastings Cemetery, Hastings
Div. O. Sec. A. Grave 65.

Chatterley Edward William Pte. No. 6408666 Unk/Bn. 12/04/43
Acton Cemetery, London
Sec. M. Row W. Grave 88.

Childs George William Pte. No. 6407412 9th Bn. 09/12/41
Reading (Henley Road) Cemetery, Berkshire
Block 2. Grave 2961

Collins Arthur Walter W.O.1 No. 6394556 10th Bn. 19/05/43
Haywards Heath (Western Road) Cemetery
Plot B.G. Grave 25.

Cook Bertie Edwin Pte. No. 6402570 2nd Bn. 03/06/40
Chester (Overleigh) Cemetery, Cheshire
New Portion Joint grave 3842.

Cooper Ernest William Pte. No. 6405874 8th Bn. 07/12/43
Willesden New Cemetery, London
Screen Wall X. 475.

Damara John Pte. No. D/38869 8th (H.D.) Bn. 06/12/40
Brighton City (Bear Road) Cemetery
Sec. Z.G.L. Grave 34.

De la Chapelle Robin Xavier Alfred Vicomte Lt. No. 94950 2nd Bn. 26/04/41
Maidstone Cemetery, Kent
Plot C.C. 1. Grave 89.

Dell Patrick Sgt. No. 6397701 2nd Bn. 26/04/41
Maidstone Cemetery, Kent
Plot C.C. 1. Grave 32.

Dobson Harry Charles Pte. No. 6401675 7th Bn. 10/02/40
Seaford Cemetery
Sec. W. Grave 2.

Dobson William Pte. No. 1606328 Unk/Bn. 07/08/45
Walker (Christ Church) Cemetery, Newcastle-upon-Tyne
Sec. D.P. Grave 109.

Drewett Charles William L/Cpl. No. D/23545 11th Bn. 09/09/41
Shoreham-by-Sea Cemetery
Sec. B. Row 32. Grave 4. Extension.

Driver Walter Sgt. No. D/23543 8th (H.D.) Bn. 20/09/40
Newhaven Cemetery
Grave 529.

Etherton Sidney L/Cpl. No. 6397846 Unk/Bn. 26/07/45
Colchester Cemetery, Essex
Sec. B. Div. B. Grave 98.

Findley Eric George Albert L/Cpl. No. 6406049 50th Bn. 24/06/43
Leeds (Harehills) Cemetery, Yorkshire
Sec. G. Coll. Grave 115.

Finklestein Julius Pte. No. 13095019 30th Bn. 25/08/42
East Ham (Marlow Road) Jewish Cemetery, London
Block 1. Grave 412.

Firth Walter Pte. No. 4542775 Unk/Bn. 20/07/42
Calverley (St. Wilfred) Churchyard, Yorkshire
Grave 638.

Foot Reginald Daniel Charles Pte. No. 5622081 7th Bn. 18/06/41
Streatham Cemetery, London
Block 17. Grave 705.

Fowler Percy Ronald Pte. No. 6410293 70th Bn. 09/06/42
Brighton City (Bear Road) Cemetery
Sec. Z.G.N. Grave 48.

Frampton George Pte. No. D/7369 Unk/Bn. 03/01/42
Uckfield Cemetery
Sec. R. Grave 2057.

French William Joseph Pte. No. 6401645 5th Bn. 20/06/40
Uckfield Cemetery
Sec. K. Grave 1113.

Frew Alexander James C.Q.M.S. No. 6392462 Unk/Bn. 20/09/40
Brighton City (Bear Road) Cemetery
Sec. Z.G.L. Grave 32.

Gabbitas Peter Gerald Pte. No. 6408494 70th Bn. 27/01/41
Fairlight (St. Andrew) Churchyard
Grave 73.

Gardner James Pte. No. 64075306 8th Bn. 27/01/41
Manchester (Gorton) Cemetery, Lancashire
Sec. A. Grave 561.

Gent George Henry Pte. No. 6407889 9th Bn. 09/12/41
Moseley Cemetery, Surrey
Class C. Grave 1365.

Gibson D.P.T. W.O.11 No. 640210 Unk/Bn. 08/02/45
Brighton (Woodvale) Borough Crematorium
Panel 2.

Gordon John Edmund Lt. No. 5237 Unk/Bn. 02/08/42
Ferring (St. Andrew) Churchyard, Sussex

Goulborn Rodney Ryle L/Cpl. No. 6403496 2nd Bn. 21/03/42
Charing (Kent County) Crematorium

Green Arthur Pte. No. D/11277 8th Bn. 03/05/44
Walberton St. Mary) Churchyard

Hall James William Gnr. No. 11251179 109 (7th Bn. The Royal Sussex Regt.) Lt. A.A. Regt. 01/11/46
Sheffield (Burngreave) Cemetery
Sec. K.K. Gen. Grave 966.

Harrison Harry John Pte. No. 141790 1st Bn. 14/05/47
Hove New Cemetery
Block 1. Grave 44.

Harrison John Herbert Stellman Lt. No. 6239 8th Bn. 12/10/40
Brookwood 1939-945 Memorial, Surrey
Panel 11 Column 3.

Heather William Bernard L/Cpl. No. 6400817 Unk/Bn. 28/03/42
Brookwood 1939-945 Memorial, Surrey
Panel 11 Column 3.

Hedgler Frederick George Stephen Pte. No. 6400565 5th Bn. 10/06/40
Rye Cemetery
Grave 6247.

Hemingray Harold Cpl. No. 4805775 7th Bn. 24/11/40
Nottingham Southern Cemetery, Nottinghamshire
Sec. T. 25 Grave 64A.

Hills Leslie Herbert Pte. No. D/30669 8th (H,D.) Bn. 03/04/40
Ditchling (St. Margaret of Anitoch) Churchyard
Sec. B. Grave 40.

Hopkin Norman Pte. No. 6412583 10th Bn. 07/05/43
Portslade Cemetery
Sec. O.O Grave 8.

Jarrold George Albert Pte. No. D/21660 30th Bn. 09/05/42
Brighton (The Downs) Cemetery
Sp. Mem.

Jenner Edward William L/Cpl. No. 6393150 Unk/Bn. 15/02/40
Chichester Cemetery
Square 115. C. O.E. Plot Grave 1.

Jones Arthur Walter Pte. No. D/38489 8th Bn. 24/08/40
Portsmouth (Kingston) Cemetery, Hampshire
Plot C.W.D. Row 1. Grave 19.

Kemp Bertram Pte. No. 6400667 4th Bn. 22/12/42
Chichester Cemetery
Square 141. Grave 34.

Kenchington Charles J. Pte. No. 5573709 2nd Bn. 10/08/44
Salisbury (London Road) Cemetery, Wiltshire
Sec. H. Grave 581.

King Thomas Joseph Sgt. M.I.D. No. 2021962 1st Bn. 03/12/43
Brighton (Woodvale) Borough Crematorium
Panel 2.

Kirk Fred 2/Lt. No. 141218 8th (H.D.) Bn. 18/08/40
Kingston-Upon-Thames Cemetery, Surrey
Class C. (Cons.) Grave 6681.

Kirk Roy Pte. No. 14388153 Unk/Bn. 19/06/47
Enfield Crematorium, Hertfordshire
Panel 2.

Kirkby Samuel Alexander Holwell Colonel M.C. 4th Bn. 28/05/43
Alderbury (St. Mary) Churchyard, Wiltshire
P.S.C.

Kitchin Henry Pte. No. 6411440 4th Bn. between 08/06/42 and 09/06/42
Brookwood 1939-1945 Memorial, Surrey
Panel 11. Column 3.

Koley Frank Pte. No. D/13965 Unk/Bn. 29/01/42
Hastings Cemetery, Sussex
Div. O. Sec. A. Grave 81.

Lagden Henry George Pte. No. 6407931 9th Bn. 08/12/41
Felixstowe New Cemetery, Suffolk
Block B. Sec. L. Grave 21.

Lake Ronald Charles H. Pte. No. 6400403 6th Bn. 03/01/40
Littlehampton Cemetery
Sec. D. Grave 4227.

Lee William Walter Pte. No. 6396214 6th Bn 30/11/46
Worthing (Durrington) Cemetery
Sec. 2. Row A.6. Grave 22.

Legge-Wilkinson Aubrey Pte. No. D/21811 8th (H.D.) Bn. 07/12/39
Brookwood 1939-1945 Memorial, Surrey
Panel 11. Column 3.

Liley Frederick Albert Cpl. No. 6401251 4th Bn. 05/10/46
Horsham(Hills) Cemetery
Block H. Grave 522.

Linnington Frederick Pte. No. 3905076 10th Bn. 04/11/42
Tunbridge Wells Cemetery, Kent
Row C. Grave 1.

Lockey Roy John Pte. No. 5439339 6th Bn. 01/01/42
Liss (St. Mary) Churchyard, Hampshire

Lush Peter Sidney Pte. No. 6412507 Unk/Bn. 02/09/42
East Preston (St. Mary) Churchyard

Mace Douglas Herbert Pte. No. 640857 70th Bn. 29/09/41
Edmonton Cemetery, Middlesex
Sec. W. Grave 57.

Madle Patrick Driscoll Pte. No. 14807526 Unk/Bn. 26/10/44
Ticehurst (St. Mary) Churchyard

Malden Clifford Cecil Mjr-Gen. 25/03/41
Frant (St. Alban) Churchyard

Malthouse Frederick Pte. No. 6399934 7th Bn. 19/01/43
Rodmell (St. Peter) Churchyard

Manouch Thomas George Sgt. No. 6398426 6th Bn. 18/02/44
Chichester Cemetery
Square 115. C.O.E. Plot Grave 26

Martin Albert Edward Pte. No. 6408795 70th Bn. 23/11/40
Brookwood 1939-1945 Memorial, Surrey
Panel 11. Column 3.

Martin Stanley Sgt. No. 6405183 11th Bn. 21/05/41
Horsham (Hills) Cemetery
Block U. Grave 251.

Marlew Frederick Charles George Pte. No. 6399010 Unk/Bn. 14/10/41
Brookwood Military Cemetery, Surrey
Grave ref: 5. I. 4.

Maynard Hubert Arthur Frank Cpl. No.5501341 5th Bn. 30/05/40
Dover (St. James's) Cemetery, Kent
Row J. Grave 26.

Miles Douglas Cpl. No. 6399321 1st Bn. 01/01/47
Dover (Charlton) Cemetery, Kent
Sec. 2. V. Joint grave 5.

Murphy Michael Christopher Pte. No. 6404615 70th Bn. 27/01/41
Hastings Cemetery, Sussex
Div. O. Sec. A. Grave 75.

Neale Frederick John Pte. No. 6401337 5th Bn. 09/09/40
Coleman's Hatch (Holy Trinity) Churchyard

Norman Thomas Edward Capt. No. 121064 10th Bn. 26/08/41
Crawley (Snell Hatch) Burial Ground
Sec. C. Grave 159.

O'Hanlon James Patrick Pte. No. 5441841 7th Bn. between 18/08/40 and 19/08/40
Liverpool (Ford) Roman Catholic Cemetery
Screen Wall (Sec. S.V. Grave 3531.)

Ogg Edward Cumming Sgt. No. 6399704 4th Bn. 22/05/40
Thakeham (St. Mary) Churchyard

Paisley Edward Pte. No. 14450344 2nd Bn. 11/02/47
Brookwood Military Cemetery, Surrey
Grave ref: 34A. D. 7.

Payne Ernest Albert Pte. No. 6405984 22/11/44
Eltham Cemetery, Woolwich, London
Sec. A. Grave 721.

Philcox Edward Cecil Sgt. No. 6396167 4th Bn. 05/02/41
Horsham (Hills) Cemetery
Block T. Grave 147.

Pickhard-Cambridge Trenchard Duroure Capt. M.C. 98567 Unk/Bn. 22/09/40
Seaford Cemetery
Sec. W. Grave 4.

Pickering Ronald Sgt. No. 6402592 Unk/Bn. 28/07/45
East Chiltington Churchyard

Potter Arthur Charles Pte. No. 5573674 2nd Bn. 25/04/42
Market Lavington (The Assumption) Churchyard, Wiltshire
North Part

Pullinger Albert Charles Cpl. No. 6396820 10th Bn. 11/01/47
Rye Cemetery
Sec. B.C. Grave 6610.

Reed Digby George Pte. No. 6403937 Unk/Bn. 29/06/44
Fleet (All Saints) Churchyard, Hampshire

Reeves William George Pte. No. 6402797 6th Bn. 08/03/44
Storrington (St. Mary) Churchyard

Rice John Robert Sgt. No. 6396088 2nd Bn. 25/09/40
Goole Cemetery, Yorkshire
Sec. D. Plot 5. Grave 23.

Roberts John Sgt. No. 6393369 Unk/Bn. 12/01/42
Pulborough (St. Mary) Churchyard

Rogers Cuthbert Frank Graydon Capt. No. 62619 1st Bn. 31/01/42
Brookwood 1939-1945 Memorial, Surrey
Panel 11. Column 3.

Romyn Ronald Hoskins 2/Lt. No. 137321 9th Bn. 13/11/40
Oystermouth Cemetery, Swansea
Sec. N. Grave 15.

Rose Frederick W. W.O.1 No. 6394367 1st Bn. 17/09/47
Hither Green Cemetery, London
Sec. F.F. Grave 71.

Rowden Alfred Sydney Pte. No. 6406485 7th Bn. 04/11/44
City of London Cemetery and Crematorium Manor Park
Screen Wall. Square 241. Coll. Grave 1008102

Scrase Cyril Edward Lt. No. 199550 6th Bn. 02/01/45
Patcham (All Saints) Churchyard
In Extension

Shacketon Thomas George Lt. No. 226590 4th Bn. 12/12/47
Princes Risborough (St. Mary) Churchyard, Buckinghamshire
Row 5. Grave 3.

Shaw Joseph Pte. No. 6408778 70thBn. 29/09/41
Milton (SS Philip and James) Churchyard, Hampshire
Row 3. Grave 28.

Sheail Sidney Thomas John Pte. No. 6406195 10th Bn. 16/05/47
Petworth (Hampers Green) Cemetery
Grave A. 38.

Short William Percy Pte. No. 6397724 6th Bn. 17/09/47
Wandsworth (Earlsfield) Cemetery, London
Block 33. Grave 139.

Small Harry Pte. No. 6396530 2nd Bn. 05/11/40
Brookwood 1939-1945 Memorial, Surrey
Panel 11. Column 3.

Somerville George Pte. No. 6398442 2nd Bn. 30/05/40
Geldeston (St. Michael) Churchyard, Norfolk

Sopp Arthur James L/Cpl. No. 6396620 2nd Bn. 16/04/40
Bath (Haycombe) Cemetery
Plot 52. Sec. F. Row. V. Grave 269.

Spall Albert William Bmdr. No. 11251179 357 Bty. 109 (7th Bn. Ryl Sussex Regt.) Lt. A.A. Regt. 08/10/43
Collyweston Cemetery
Grave 77.

Sparkes A. Pte. No. 6400271 10th Bn. Para. Regt. A.A.C. 13/08/47
Brighton City (Bear Road) Cemetery
Sec. Z.F.U. Grave 52.

Spooner Percy Alfred Victor Pte. No. 6403289 Unk/Bn. 03/07/46
Eastbourne (Langley) Cemetery
Sec. A. Grave 176.

Stokes Arthur Pte. No. 5338661 6th Bn. 02/10/40
Ridge (St. Margaret) Churchyard, Hertfordshire
West of Tower near West Boundary.

Strickland George Pte. No. D/5064 4th Bn. 18/02/43
Worthing (Broadwater) Cemetery
Sec. A. 16. Row 7. Grave 26.

Tompsett Harry Sydney Pte. No. 6396541 2nd Bn. 10/06/40
Tunbridge Wells Cemetery, Kent
Row A. Grave 4.

Townsend Charles Frederick Pte. No. 6397881 2nd Bn. 09/09/41
Ballyscullion Parish Churchyard, Bellaghy N.I.

Treacher Donald Harold (Don) Pte. N. 6411613 Unk/Bn. 05/06/42
Hove New Cemetery
Block 3. Grave 940.

Tullett Arthur Roland Pte. No. 6405342 Unk/Bn. 28/05/43
Lancing (St. James the Less) Churchyard Extension
Plot T. Grave 142.

Tullett Thomas Arthur Pte. No. 6400977 1st Bn. 19/10/46
Burstow (St. Bartholomew) Churchyard, Horley, Surrey
Row 5. G4.

Tunbridge Herbert Cpl. No. 64055713 8th Bn.   10/08/41
Cowfold (St. Peter) Churchyard Extension
Plot 2. Row G. Grave 123.

Upton Ronald Sydney Pte. No. 6400922 6th Bn.   09/02/41
Cuckfield Cemetery
Plot 6. S.E. Grave 362.

Verrall Hugh Gerrard Washington L/Cpl. No. 6405435 70th Bn.   14/10/40
West Grinstead (St. George) Churchyard
Block D. Row I. Grave 11.

Verrall Walter Pte. No. D/1612 Unk/Bn. 12/12/41
Arundel Roman Catholic Cemetery
Grave 59 West.

Wall Henry Harold Pte. No. D/27246 8th (H.D.) Bn. 12/08/40
Uckfield Cemetery
Sec. K. Grave 1100.

Warner Henry George Pte. No. 6397777 2nd Bn. 07/06/46
Hounslow Cemetery
Plot D. Row E. Grave 6.

Whiting John Crowley Lt. No. 60015 8th (H.D.) Bn. 13/08/40
Southampton Crematorium
Panel 6.

Whitmarsh Edward Francis Pte. No. 6400853 5th Bn. 12/06/40
Ninfield (St. Mary) Churchyard Extension
Row B. Grave 27.

Wiilliams Arthur Robert Pte. No. 6407800 9th Bn. 04/01/41
Shaw Cemetery, Newbury
Grave 1915.

Willoughby Gordon Thomas Pte. No. 14582722 6th Bn. 18/12/43
Littlehampton Cemetery
Sec. D. Grave 4347.

Youngman Philip Owen Pte. No. 14623015 Unk/Bn. 05/11/43
Frant (St. Alban) Churchyard

Zackheim David Alfred 2/Lt. No. 242759 6th Bn. 04/02/43
Willesden Jewish Cemetery
Sec. G.X. Row 6. Grave 284

United States of America

Borrow George Henry Capt. M.C. No. 228394 Served with the "Chindits" 24/03/44
Arlington National Cemetery
Sec. 12 Coll. Grave 288

Yemen

Wildy Peter Capt. No. 186154 Unk/Bn. 04/03/44
Maala Cemetery
Grave ref: 101.

www.ingramcontent.com/pod-product-compliance
Lightning Source LLC
Chambersburg PA
CBHW080826010526
44111CB00016B/2615